The Literature of
AUTOBIOGRAPHICAL NARRATIVE

The Literature of AUTOBIOGRAPHICAL NARRATIVE

VOLUME 2

DIARIES AND LETTERS

THOMAS RIGGS, *editor*

ST. JAMES PRESS
A part of Gale, Cengage Learning

Detroit • New York • San Francisco • New Haven, Conn • Waterville, Maine • London

The Literature of Autobiographical Narrative
Thomas Riggs, Editor
Andrea Kovacs Henderson, Project Editor

Artwork and photographs for *The Literature of Autobiographical Narrative* covers were reproduced with the following kind permission.

Volume 1
For foreground painting "Chief Geronimo, 1899" by Elbridge Ayer Burbank. © Butler Institute of American Art, Youngstown, OH USA/Museum Purchase 1912/The Bridgeman Art Library.

For background image of a band of Apache Indian prisoners, 1886. The Art Archive/National Archives Washington DC.

Volume 2
For foreground portrait "Anne Frank, 1960" (coal with pastel on paper) by Ilya Glazunov (b. 1930). Private Collection/The Bridgeman Art Library.

For background image of 263 Prinsengracht in Amsterdam, the house where Anne Frank and her family spent two years in hiding during the German occupation of The Netherlands during World War II. The Art Archive/Culver Pictures.

Volume 3
For foreground "May the Whole Country from the Mountains to the Rivers be a Sea of Red, 1960" (colour litho). Private Collection/© The Chambers Gallery, London/The Bridgeman Art Library.

For background image of detail of Political Relief Sculpture in Tiananmen Square. © Brian A. Vikanders/CORBIS.

© 2013 Gale, Cengage Learning

ALL RIGHTS RESERVED. No part of this work covered by the copyright herein may be reproduced, transmitted, stored, or used in any form or by any means graphic, electronic, or mechanical, including but not limited to photocopying, recording, scanning, digitizing, taping, Web distribution, information networks, or information storage and retrieval systems, except as permitted under Section 107 or 108 of the 1976 United States Copyright Act, without the prior written permission of the publisher.

For product information and technology assistance, contact us at
Gale Customer Support, 1-800-877-4253.
For permission to use material from this text or product,
submit all requests online at **www.cengage.com/permissions.**
Further permissions questions can be emailed to
permissionrequest@cengage.com.

While every effort has been made to ensure the reliability of the information presented in this publication, Gale, a part of Cengage Learning, does not guarantee the accuracy of the data contained herein. Gale accepts no payment for listing; and inclusion in the publication of any organization, agency, institution, publication, service, or individual does not imply endorsement of the editors or publisher. Errors brought to the attention of the publisher and verified to the satisfaction of the publisher will be corrected in future editions.

Library of Congress Cataloging-in-Publication Data

The literature of autobiographical narrative / Thomas Riggs, editor.
   volumes cm
   Includes bibliographical references and indexes.
   ISBN 978-1-55862-870-0 (set : alk. paper) -- ISBN 978-1-55862-871-7 (vol. 1 : alk. paper) -- ISBN 978-1-55862-872-4 (vol. 2 : alk. paper) -- ISBN 978-1-55862-873-1 (vol. 3 : alk. paper)
   1. Autobiography. 2. Biography as a literary form. 3. Authors--Biography--History and criticism. 4. Literature--History and criticism. I. Riggs, Thomas, 1963-
   CT25.L58 2013
   920.02--dc23
                                                2013002574

Gale
27500 Drake Rd.
Farmington Hills, MI, 48331-3535

ISBN-13: 978-1-55862-870-0 (set)   ISBN-10: 1-55862-870-3 (set)
ISBN-13: 978-1-55862-871-7 (vol. 1)   ISBN-10: 1-55862-871-1 (vol. 1)
ISBN-13: 978-1-55862-872-4 (vol. 2)   ISBN-10: 1-55862-872-X (vol. 2)
ISBN-13: 978-1-55862-873-1 (vol. 3)   ISBN-10: 1-55862-873-8 (vol. 3)

This title will also be available as an e-book.
ISBN-13: 978-1-55862-881-6 ISBN-10: 1-55862-881-9
Contact your Gale, a part of Cengage Learning, sales representative for ordering information.

Printed in the United States of America
1 2 3 4 5 6 7 17 16 15 14 13

 Advisory Board

CHAIR

Richard Bradford
Research Professor of English and Senior Distinguished Research Fellow, University of Ulster, Ulster, Northern Ireland. Author of *A Brief Life of John Milton* (2013); *The Odd Couple: The Curious Friendship between Kingsley Amis and Philip Larkin* (2012); *Martin Amis: The Biography* (2011); *The Life of a Long-Distance Writer: The Authorized Biography of Alan Sillitoe* (2008); *First Boredom, Then Fear: The Life of Philip Larkin* (2005); and *Lucky Him: The Life of Kingsley Amis* (2001). Editor of *Life Writing: Essays on Autobiography, Biography and Literature* (2010).

ADVISORS

Lynn Abram
Professor of Gender History, University of Glasgow, Glasgow, Scotland. Author of *Oral History Theory* (2010); *Myth and Materiality in a Woman's World: Shetland 1800–2000* (2005); *The Making of Modern Woman: Europe, 1789–1918* (2002); and *The Orphan Country: Children of Scotland's Broken Homes from 1800 to the Present Day* (1998). Series editor of Manchester University Press Gender in History series (2003–).

Suzanne Bunkers
Professor of English, Minnesota State University, Mankato, Mankato, Minnesota. Author of *In Search of Susanna* (1996). Coauthor, with Frank W. Klein, of *Good Earth, Black Soil* (1981). Editor of *Diaries of Girls and Women: A Midwestern American Sampler* (2001); *A Pioneer Farm Girl: The Diary of Sarah Gillespie, 1877–1878* (2000); *"All Will Yet Be Well": The Diary of Sarah Gillespie Huftalen, 1873–1952* (1993); and *The Diary of Caroline Seabury, 1854–1863* (1991). Coeditor, with Cynthia Huff, of *Inscribing the Daily: Critical Essays on Women's Diaries* (1996).

Cynthia Huff
Professor of English, Illinois State University, Normal, Illinois. Editor of *Towards a Geography of Women's Life Writing and Imagined Communities* (2005). Coeditor, with Suzanne Bunkers, of *Inscribing the Daily: Critical Essays on Women's Diaries* (1996). Contributor to the journals *Biography* and *a/b: Auto/Biography Studies*. Editorial board member of *a/b*.

Geneva Cobb Moore
Professor of English, University of Wisconsin-Whitewater, Whitewater, Wisconsin. Contributor to *Inscribing the Daily: Critical Essays on Women's Diaries* (1996), edited by Suzanne Bunkers and Cynthia Huff; and to *The Oxford Companion to African American Literature,* edited by William L. Andrews, Frances Smith Foster, and Trudier Harris (1997). Contributor of essays on Africa, Zora Neale Hurston, Alice Walker, Harriet Jacobs, Toni Morrison, and Danzy Senna to journals including the *Southern Literary Journal,* the *Black Scholar,* and the *Western Journal of Black Studies.* Former Fulbright Scholar of American and African American Literature at the University of Ghana, West Africa. Recipient of grants and awards from the National Endowment for the Humanities and the Paul W. Mellon Foundation.

Harry Ross
Associate Professor of Secondary Education, National Louis University, Chicago, Illinois. Coauthor of *13 Steps to Teacher Empowerment: Taking a More Active Role in Your School Community* (2009). National presenter on life writing, multicultural literature, urban teacher preparation, and teacher collaboration and leadership. Lead scholar on a National Endowment for the Humanities grant to teach the life stories written by the 1930s Federal Writers' Project authors.

Amanda Rust
English and Theatre Librarian, Northeastern University, Boston, Massachusetts.

Sharon Cadman Seelig
Roe/Straut Professor in the Humanities, Smith College, Northampton, Massachusetts. Author of *Autobiography and Gender in Early Modern Literature: Reading Women's Lives, 1600–1680* (2006); *Generating Texts: The Progeny of Seventeenth-Century Prose* (1996); and *The Shadow of Eternity: Belief and Structure in Herbert, Vaughan, and Traherne* (1981). Editorial board member of *English Literary Renaissance.*

Eugene Stelzig
Distinguished Teaching Professor of English, State University of New York at Geneseo, Geneseo, New York. Author of *Henry Crabb Robinson in Germany: A Study in Nineteenth-Century Life Writing* (2010); *The Romantic Subject in Autobiography: Rousseau and Goethe* (2000); *Herman Hesse's Fictions of the Self: Autobiography and the Confessional Imagination* (1988); and *All Shades of Consciousness: Wordsworth's Poetry and the Self in Time* (1975). Contributor to journals in the areas of Romantic studies and autobiography studies. Editor of *Romantic Autobiography in England* (2009).

Editorial and Production Staff

Associate Publisher
Marc Cormier

Product Manager
Philip J. Virta

Project Editor
Andrea Kovacs Henderson

Editorial Support
Rebecca Parks

Editorial Assistance
Laura Avery, Lisa Kumar, Michelle Lee, Margaret Mazurkiewicz, Tracie Moy

Art Director
Kristine Julien

Composition and Imaging
Evi Seoud, John Watkins

Manufacturing
Wendy Blurton

Rights Acquisition and Management
Kimberly Potvin, Margaret Chamberlain-Gaston

Technical Support
Luann Brennan, Mike Weaver

Table of Contents

Introduction xiii
Editor's Note xvii
Contributors xix
Academic Reviewers xxi

Adversity and Resistance

The Cancer Journals by Audre Lorde 3

Child of the Dark: The Diary of Carolina Maria de Jesus by Carolina Maria de Jesus 6

De Profundis by Oscar Wilde 9

Detained: A Writer's Prison Diary by Ngũgĩ wa Thiong'o 12

Diaries of Beatrice Webb by Beatrice Webb 16

The Good Man of Nanking: The Diaries of John Rabe by John Rabe 19

An Interrupted Life: The Diaries of Etty Hillesum by Etty Hillesum 22

Journal of George Fox by George Fox 26

The Journals of Charlotte Forten Grimké by Charlotte Forten Grimké 29

Letter from the Birmingham Jail by Martin Luther King Jr. 32

Letter to Her Daughter by Lady Mary Wortley Montagu 35

Letter to His Son by Robert E. Lee 38

Letter to Maria Clemm by Edgar Allan Poe 41

Letter to the Reverend Samson Occom by Phillis Wheatley 44

Letters Home by Sylvia Plath 47

Letters Underway by 'Izzat Ghazzawi 50

Spandau: The Secret Diaries by Albert Speer 54

Historical Perspectives

Confessions of Lady Nijo by Lady Nijo 59

The Diaries of Lady Anne Clifford by Lady Anne Clifford 62

The Diary of John Evelyn by John Evelyn 65

The Diary of John Quincy Adams by John Quincy Adams 69

The Diary of Samuel Pepys by Samuel Pepys 72

Diary, Reminiscences and Correspondence of Henry Crabb Robinson, Barrister-at-Law by Henry Crabb Robinson 75

Jemima Condict: Her Book, Being a Transcript of the Diary of an Essex County Maid during the Revolutionary War by Jemima Condict 78

Journal des Goncourt: Mémoires de la vie littéraire by Jules de Goncourt and Edmond de Goncourt 81

The Last Diary of Tsaritsa Alexandra by Alexandra Feodorovna 84

"Letter to Her Daughter from the New White House" by Abigail Adams 87

Letters of a Woman Homesteader by Elinore Pruitt Stewart 91

The Letters of the Younger Pliny by Pliny the Younger 94

The Literary Remains of Edward VI by Edward VI 97

Selected Letters of Martha Gellhorn by Martha Gellhorn 101

A Young Palestinian's Diary, 1941–1945: The Life of Sāmī 'Amr by Sāmī 'Amr 104

Literary Lives

The Collected Letters of Mary Wollstonecraft by Mary Wollstonecraft 109

The Complete Notebooks of Henry James by Henry James 113

TABLE OF CONTENTS

Diaries, 1931–1949 by George Orwell **117**

The Diaries of Franz Kafka by Franz Kafka **120**

The Diary of Anaïs Nin by Anaïs Nin **123**

Estrangement, Being Some Fifty Extracts from a Diary Kept in 1909 by William Butler Yeats **126**

The Habit of Being: Letters of Flannery O'Connor by Flannery O'Connor **129**

Journal of Katherine Mansfield by Katherine Mansfield **133**

The Journals of Arnold Bennett, 1896–1928 by Arnold Bennett **136**

Journals of Ralph Waldo Emerson by Ralph Waldo Emerson **139**

Letters and Journals of Lord Byron, with Notices of His Life by George Gordon Noel Byron **143**

The Letters of John Keats, 1814–1821 by John Keats **146**

Letters to a Young Poet by Rainer Maria Rilke **149**

Notebooks by Tennessee Williams **152**

THEORIES

The Annals of Ballitore by Mary Leadbeater **157**

Collected Letters of a Renaissance Feminist by Laura Cereta **160**

The Extraordinary Work of Ordinary Writing: Annie Ray's Diary by Jennifer Sinor **163**

Journals of Søren Kierkegaard by Søren Kierkegaard **166**

Letters between Two by Lu Xun and Xu Guangping **170**

"Practice of the Private Journal" by Philippe Lejeune **174**

"Some Observations on Diaries, Self-Biography, and Self-Characters" by Isaac D'Israeli **177**

A Writer's Diary by Virginia Woolf **180**

A Writer's Notebook by W. Somerset Maugham **183**

TRAVEL AND EXPLORATION

As I Crossed a Bridge of Dreams by Lady Sarashina **189**

The Congo Diary by Joseph Conrad **192**

Journals of John Wesley by John Wesley **195**

A Journal of the First Voyage of Vasco da Gama, 1497–1499 **198**

Journal of the First Voyage to America by Christopher Columbus **201**

The Journals of Jonathan Carver and Related Documents, 1766–1770 by Jonathan Carver **205**

Leaves from the Journal of Our Life in the Highlands, from 1848 to 1861 by Queen Victoria **209**

Letters from an American Farmer by Michel-Guillaume Saint-Jean de Crèvecoeur **213**

The Letters of Lady Anne Barnard to Henry Dundas, from the Cape and Elsewhere by Anne Barnard **217**

Motorcycle Diaries by Ernesto "Che" Guevara **220**

Notebooks and *Letters* by Nathaniel Hawthorne **223**

The Pylgrymage of Sir Richard Guylforde by Richarde Guylforde **226**

The Travels of Dean Mahomet, a Native of Patna in Bengal, through Several Parts of India, While in the Service of the Honourable the East India Company Written by Himself, in a Series of Letters to a Friend by Dean Mahomet **229**

WAR EXPERIENCES

Among You Taking Notes: The Wartime Diary of Naomi Mitchison, 1939–1945 by Naomi Mitchison **235**

Army Life in a Black Regiment by Thomas Wentworth Higginson **238**

The Boer War Diary of Sol Plaatje: An African at Mafeking by Solomon Tshekisho Plaatje **241**

Brokenburn: The Journal of Kate Stone, 1861–1868 by Kate Stone **244**

Diaries, 1915–1918 by Siegfried Sassoon **247**

A Diary from Dixie by Mary Boykin Miller Chesnut **250**

The Diary of Anne Frank by Anne Frank **253**

The Diary of Sir Henry Slingsby by Sir Henry Slingsby **256**

A Diary without Dates by Enid Bagnold **259**

Journal, 1955–1962: Reflections on the French-Algerian War by Mouloud Feraoun **262**

Nella Last's War: The Second World War Diaries of Housewife, 49 by Nella Last **265**

A Pacifist's War: Diaries 1939–1945 by Frances Partridge **268**

Shadows on My Heart: The Civil War Diary of Lucy Rebecca Buck of Virginia by Lucy Buck **271**

Thura's Diary: A Young Girl's Life in War-Torn Baghdad by Thura Al-Windawi **275**

A Woman at War by Molly Moore **278**

A Woman in Berlin: Eight Weeks in the Conquered City: A Diary by Anonymous **281**

Work and Family Life

A Country Parson: James Woodforde's Diary, 1759–1802 by James Woodforde 287

The Diary of Lady Murasaki by Lady Murasaki Shikibu 290

Go Ask Alice by Anonymous 294

The Gossamer Years by Michitsuna No Haha 297

Grasmere Journals by Dorothy Wordsworth 300

I Will Bear Witness: A Diary of the Nazi Years, 1933–1945 by Victor Klemperer 303

The Journal of Marie Bashkirtseff by Marie Bashkirtseff 306

The Journal of Sir Walter Scott by Sir Walter Scott 309

Letters and Journals of Fanny Burney by Fanny Burney 312

Letters from Jefferson to His Daughter by Thomas Jefferson 316

London and the Life of Literature in Late Victorian England: The Diary of George Gissing, Novelist by George Gissing 320

The Love Letters of Dorothy Osborne to Sir William Temple, 1652–54 by Dorothy Osborne 324

London Journal, 1762–1763 by James Boswell 328

A Midwife's Tale: The Life of Martha Ballard, Based on Her Diary, 1785–1812 by Laurel Thatcher Ulrich 331

Records of a Girlhood by Fanny Kemble 335

Zlata's Diary: A Child's Life in Sarajevo by Zlata Filipovic 338

Subject Index 341

Author Index 451

Title Index 455

Introduction

An autobiographical narrative is an account by the teller of some aspect of his or her life. Yet beneath this overarching definition lie myriad variations upon a theme. For the modern reader the best-known manifestations of the genre are book-length memoirs or autobiographies. Their authors usually feel that they have something significant to say about their private experiences or that their role as witnesses to moments in history merits permanent record. Classic instances, covered in the *Autobiography and Memoir* volume of *The Literature of Autobiographical Narrative,* include Rosa Parks's *My Story* (1992). Parks propelled herself into fame in 1955 when she, an African American, refused to give up her bus seat to a white passenger. As a resident of Montgomery, Alabama, she was subject to the legally legitimatized system of segregation enforced in virtually all parts of the southern states of the United States. Her memoir covers that incident and also offers an account of her early life of subjection and injustice and provides readers with an insight into the growth of the civil rights movement, in which she became an activist.

Generically, Vladimir Nabokov's *Speak, Memory* (1951) belongs in the same category as Parks's book, but it is difficult to conceive of two more contrasting volumes. Nabokov is best known for *Lolita* (1955), a controversial novel narrated by a self-confessed pedophile who spends most of the book reflecting upon his obsession with the eponymous schoolgirl, but *Speak, Memory,* ostensibly at least, is not concerned with its author's career as a novelist. It covers the first four decades of his life, in which he witnessed some of the key transformative events in European history, notably, as a child, the Bolshevik Revolution (1917) in his native Russia. In this respect Nabokov and Parks might seem, as autobiographers, similarly motivated. Despite the significance of what they experienced, however, they differ radically in the telling of their stories. As an author, Parks is largely unobtrusive and transparent, allowing where possible the events of her life to bear witness to their political and emotional resonance. For Parks, memory and history are indistinguishable. Nabokov, on the other hand, writes about his life in much the same way that, as a novelist, he would describe the worlds of his inventions. At one point he tells of how the Russian Imperial Minister of War, Aleksey Kuropatkin, a friend of the Nabokov family, would amuse young Vladimir with a trick involving a match box; Nabokov then connects this anecdote with the story of Kuropatkin, now in disguise and on the run from the Bolsheviks, surreptitiously asking his father for a light. Nabokov does not alter the facts; rather, he believes that memory should be treated as a series of episodes that depend as much upon the impressions of their perceiver for significance as upon objective description.

Maya Angelou's autobiography *I Know Why the Caged Bird Sings* (1969) should, we might assume, have more in common with Parks's than Nabokov's book: it is the searingly honest story of her own experiences of racist violence and oppression in the American South. However, it is celebrated as much for its formal literary qualities as for its revelations. Angelou's manner of relating her shared history lends the latter a special degree of vividness and durability, and in this respect Angelou invites comparison with Nabokov. Like both, Tepilit Ole Scitoti, in *The World of a Maasai Warrior* (1986), wraps an emotionally charged autobiography—specifically its author's crossing of the boundary between precolonial African tribal existence and Western society—in a text that bears

INTRODUCTION

a close resemblance to what we expect of fiction: dialogue, historical narrative and myth are blended in a less than predictable manner.

Such variations in manner and theme reflect the richness and diversity of autobiography as a genre, in terms of both its informative, even educational, power and its strength as a literary form in its own right. How, then, should we classify Adolf Hitler's *Mein Kamf* (1925) in relation to the books so far mentioned? In order to qualify for inclusion and coverage in these volumes, a work must at least enlighten us as to the mindset of its author and the circumstances that led to its composition. The fact is that were it not for Hitler's hideous acts and legacy subsequent to the publication of *Mein Kamf* the book would have disappeared from the landscape of twentieth century history of writing. It is poorly written, its author is at time deranged in his avowed worship of the Aryan race, and its purely autobiographical passages are littered with stories that have since been proved to be exaggerations at best and often outright falsehoods. Its endurance as a "significant" autobiographical work has been ensured by events that no sane or decent person would have wished upon those affected by them. Here we come upon the uniqueness and importance of autobiographical narrative. Hitler's book might well be a compendium of half-truths and evil avocations, but it adds something to our knowledge of how a particularly foul individual came to power and wreaked havoc on the world. Like every work covered in these volumes, it carries a trace of our past and in particular the imprint of its author's involvement therein.

The second volume of *The Literature of Autobiographical Narrative* covers diaries and letters. The most obvious difference between these and autobiography is that while virtually all of the latter are addressed to a general readership, the former are works generally underpinned by a notion of confidentiality, privacy or intimacy. In this regard the diary is a particularly troubling genre. It is, by its nature, a record—often a day-to-day record—of its author's activities, some of them utterly mundane, that typically contains observations on the events and moods of his or her world. The motive or impulse behind the keeping of a diary remains a matter for speculation, but most would agree that it is a private endeavor with the author also its single reader (though intimate friends or family members have on occasions been allowed access to entries). We might, therefore, expect from such documents a different level of candor than is generally found in autobiographies intended for publication. It is not that authors of the latter deliberately set out to mislead—with the exception of figures such as Hitler—but rather that, even in unadorned acts of truth-telling such as Parks's *My Story*, there is a degree of performance. Honesty might be maintained but consideration is also given to the experience of the reader. Diaries, being designed for self-consumption, carry no such responsibilities.

Two of the best-known early-modern examples of the form are *The Diary of John Evelyn* (1818) and *The Diary of Samuel Pepys* (1825). Both are treated an invaluable insights into the events and mannerisms of mid-to-late seventeenth-century Britain. The period involved momentous occurrences, most notably the Civil War, the execution of Charles I, the establishment of the first modern European republic and the Restoration of the Monarchy. The printing press was more than a century old, and for the first time in history an abundance of documents, including government statements, manifestos, and declarations by individuals with an interest in the future of society, became available for later scrutiny by historians. Evelyn and Pepys provide an invaluable supplement to the largely impersonal evidence of print, taking us on a tour of their particular worlds, from what they wore and ate to their encounters with epoch-making events; Evelyn's account of the return of the monarch, Charles II, to London contains everything from the minutiae of the floral decorations to his own understated reflections on the significance of the day. Diaries bridge the divide between introspective impressionistic records of a time and a state of mind—so often lacking in works intended for publication—and a more objective conception of a historical milieu. Diaries and notebooks are immensely important too in our broader appreciation of how writers work. Even if in, for instance, Joseph Conrad's *Congo Diary* (1952), there is little direct reference to how his experience influenced his fiction, the implied connections are self-evident.

We should, however, deal cautiously with the commonplace assumption that the diary is always an impeccably candid record of its author's thoughts and impressions. That Evelyn's and Pepys's works did not go into print until over a century after they had been completed would seem to testify to both men's sense of them as private documents. Yet it is possible to imagine that Anne Frank, hiding from the Nazis, harbored a sense of duty to those who would later try to document the horrors of World War II. Even if, as she feared, she would not live to adulthood, perhaps she hoped that her words would survive as a record of a fate she shared with so many others. The same can be said of Victor Klemperer as he composed his *Diary of the Nazi Years* (1995). In a different context George Gissing, who was at the center of the thriving cultural and literary life of Victorian England, was surely not so naïve as to believe that his *Diary* would remain forever untouched and unpublished.

The letter involves a different level of candor in that, once the piece is dispatched, the recipient is trusted as its sole reader, but in this respect correspondence can be just as revealing as the private diary or notebook. Sylvia Plath's *Letters Home* (1975), mostly addressed to her mother, tells us more about her state of distress and her sense of vocation as a writer than anything primarily intended for publication.

The third volume of *The Literature of Autobiographical Narrative* covers oral histories, and the best introduction to this complex means of recording and preserving the past is Lynn Abrams's *Oral History Theory* (2010). Abrams examines the tendentious issues that surround the collecting of oral histories, principally the implicit tension between a voluntary spoken testimony and the role of the person who asks questions, edits, and coordinates this material: how much does the latter impose upon the former? One of the most famous nonacademic examples of the form is Ronald Blythe's *Akenfield: Portrait of an English Village* (1969), in which Blythe attempts to capture life in a fictionalized rural English community through a set of interviews with individuals such as farmworkers and blacksmiths who have known of little more than their immediate environment since the nineteenth century. Blythe's *Akenfield* is not a real village but a fictionalized composite based on interviews with residents of various villages. Although he does his best to remain in the background, Blythe's editorial approach has led critics to wonder to what extent the "Portrait" carries something of his influence.

Oral histories that are more rigorous than Blythe's in their maintenance of objectivity include Jeremy Seabrook's *Working-Class Childhood* (1982), in which Seabrook, as interviewer, refrains from any prompts and directions in his recordings of British working-class individuals during the late 1970s and early 1980s. As Lynn Abrams argues, however, it is virtually impossible to claim that an exercise in oral history can be a purely objective record, unaffected by the presence of the interviewer or coordinator. For example, Rhoda Lewin's *Witnesses to the Holocaust* (1991) is composed of her interviews with sixty survivors and liberators of the Nazi concentration camps. While Lewin scrupulously avoids leading her interviewees, the fact that they were all then residents of Minnesota suggests that their testimonies may have been skewed by a shared experience of the postwar years. Similarly, in Alison Baker's *Voices of Resistance: Oral Histories of Moroccan Women* (1998), women involved in the Moroccan independence movement speak freely of their personal lives, but this material is embedded in contextual information on Moroccan society, history, and politics and quotations from songs and poems, largely for the benefit of Western readers unfamiliar with the region. In this respect, then, Baker's choice and use of contextual material will in some way inevitably affect the reader's impression of the women themselves.

Esteban Montejo's *Autobiography of a Runaway Slave* (1993) originates from a series of interviews given by Montejo in 1963 to Miguel Barnet, who subsequently transcribed them as a book with the former as first-person narrator. Montejo, then aged 103, was thought to be the last surviving ex-slave on the island of Cuba; his testimony provided one final opportunity to record this period in Caribbean history. The book blurs the distinction between autobiography and oral history. One assumes that it is placed in the latter category because, without Barnet's act of recording the oral testimony, it would not exist, yet its potential status as a hybrid form makes it all the more intriguing. Once again questions arise about the concepts of fact and truth and the extent to which they are influenced by oral testimony and conventional notions of writing.

Oral history is the most complex of the three categories of autobiographical narrative and for this reason it is one of the most richly rewarding. For all of its variety, at its heart is the quintessential notion of a voice unsullied by the formalities and conventions of writing and print.

Only a few pieces covered in these three volumes predate the history of the printing press, notably St. Augustine's *Confessions* (397 CE) and Marcus Aurelius's *Meditations* (180 CE). Some, such as Marco Polo's *Travels* (c. 1300) and King Henry VI's *Literary Remains* (1549), found their way into print well within a century of their composition, but the vast majority of the pieces were either spoken, recorded, written or published during or after the seventeenth century. Autobiographical narrative, including oral history, will always owe something to the mechanism of print, including its recent electronic form, but its value as a means of understanding the human condition and permutations through ethnicity, region, history, and culture remains uncorrupted by this.

These three volumes will stand as an invaluable tool for researchers who wish to locate a starting point for a detailed scrutiny of a place, an event, or a state of mind. Their structure, including the subclassification of each of the three forms according to context and frame of reference, will assist greatly in its function as a basis for curriculum building. Each volume can serve numerous and often overlapping disciplinary roles. Writers' autobiographies, diaries, and notebooks offer invaluable insights into the relationship between private inspiration and the unfolding of literary history. Throughout, students of history, politics, and society will find testimonies to personal experience that underpin and illuminate a broader perception of our pasts and differences.

It is a unique enterprise, gathering seemingly disparate elements within a space to which all human beings will at some point commit themselves: speaking or writing to someone, even to ourselves, of our lives and experiences.

Richard Bradford

Editor's Note

The Literature of Autobiographical Narrative, a three-volume reference guide, provides critical introductions to 300 autobiographies, memoirs, diaries, letters, and oral histories. All the works are based on the lives of the authors, but a wide variety of interests and ambitions, from the personal and artistic to the historical and political, motivated writers to share their intimate and exceptional memories.

An early memoir covered in the guide is *The Travels of Marco Polo*, which recounts the journey of the Venetian explorer in the 1290s to the Far East and the court of Kublai Khan. In 1298, three years after returning from Asia, Marco Polo was captured in a battle against the Genoese. Over several months in prison, with the help of his cellmate, Rustichiello of Pisa, he wrote his travelogue, filled with exotic tales set in a faraway land, which fascinated his European audience. Other works discussed in the guide had more private goals. Edgar Allan Poe's "Letter to Maria Clemm," written to his Aunt Maria on August 29, 1835, declares his love for her thirteen-year-old daughter, Virginia, and offers financial assistance to them both. Kept from publication for more than a century by Poe's family, the letter—in particular the passionate desire Poe expresses for his young cousin (later his wife)—is fundamental to the modern understanding of Poe as a transgressor of moral boundaries. *Japanese War Brides in America* (1998), an oral history of nineteen Japanese women who married American soldiers during the post-World War II occupation of Japan, is an example of an autobiographical work for which the motivation to publish was less an author's desire for self-expression than an outsider's interest in another person's story.

The structure and content of *The Literature of Autobiographical Narrative* was planned with the help of the project's advisory board, chaired by Richard Bradford, Professor of English and Senior Distinguished Research Fellow, University of Ulster, Northern Ireland. His introduction explains some of the concerns behind the development of the guide and provides a brief overview of autobiographical genres.

ORGANIZATION

All entries share a common structure, providing consistent coverage of the works and a simple way of comparing basic elements of one text with another. Each entry has six parts: overview, historical and literary context, themes and style, critical discussion, sources, and further reading. Entries also have either an excerpt from the original text or a sidebar discussing a related topic, such as the life of the author.

The Literature of Autobiographical Narrative is divided into three volumes, each with 100 entries organized into subject-oriented sections. The sections in volume 1, *Autobiographies and Memoirs,* are Adversity and Resistance, Between Cultures, Coming of Age, Contemplation and Confession, Theories, and War Experiences. Among the works representing "adversity" is *The Story of My Life* (1903), by Helen Keller, who describes her experience being a blind and deaf child in late-nineteenth-century Alabama. Her efforts to express herself and become educated came at a time when many disabled children in the United States were considered a lost cause and institutionalized. Volume 2, *Diaries and Letters,* includes the sections Adversity and Resistance, Historical Perspectives, Literary Lives, Theories, Travel and Exploration, War Experiences, and Work and Family Life. Under "Historical Perspectives" is *Jemima Condict,* the diary of young New Jersey maid during the American Revolution who records thoughts about her family, community life, and newly independent country. The works discussed in volume 3, *Oral Histories,* stand apart from the books in the other volumes in their absence of a premeditated written structure. The volume is divided into the sections Adversity and Resistance, Communities, Culture and Tradition, Theories, War Experiences, Witnessing History, and Work and Family Life. Covered in the latter section is *Soviet Baby Boomers* (2012), in which sixty men and women from two elite Russian schools discuss their lives in the late twentieth century; a major theme of the book is remembering things from the past that state propaganda tried to conceal.

Among the criteria for selecting entry topics were the importance of the work in university and high school curricula, the genre, the region and country of the author and text, and the time period. Entries can be looked up in the author and title indexes, as well as in the subject index.

ACKNOWLEDGMENTS

Many people contributed time, effort, and ideas to *The Literature of Autobiographical Narrative.* At Gale, Philip Virta, manager of new products, developed the original plan for the book, and Andrea Henderson, senior editor, served as the in-house manager for the project. *The Literature of Autobiographical Narrative* owes its existence to their ideas and involvement.

We would like to express our appreciation to the advisors, who, in addition to creating the organization of *The Literature of Autobiographical Narrative* and choosing the entry topics, identified other scholars to work on the project and answered many questions, both big and small. We would also like to thank the contributors for their accessible essays, often on difficult topics, as well as the scholars who reviewed the text for accuracy and coverage.

I am grateful to Greta Gard, project editor, and Erin Brown, senior project editor, especially for their work with the advisors and on the entry list; Mary Beth Curran, associate editor, who oversaw the editing process; David Hayes, associate editor, whose many contributions included organizing the workflow; and Hannah Soukup, assistant editor, who identified and corresponded with the academic reviewers. Other important assistance came from Mariko Fujinaka, managing editor; Anne Healey, senior editor; and Janet Moredock and Lee Esbenshade, associate editors. The line editors were Cheryl Collins, Chuong-Dai Vo, Constance Israel, Donna Polydoros, Harrabeth Haidusek, Holli Fort, Jane Kupersmith, Jill Oldham, Joan Hibler, Kathy Wilson Peacock, Kerri Kennedy, Laura Gabler, Lisa Trow, Natalie Ruppert, Tony Craine, and Will Wagner.

Thomas Riggs

Contributors

David Aitchison
Aitchison is a PhD candidate in literary studies and a university instructor.

Greg Bach
Bach holds an MA in classics and is a freelance writer.

Katherine Barker
Barker has an MA in English literature.

Craig Barnes
Barnes holds an MFA in creative writing and has been a university instructor and a freelance writer.

Katherine Bishop
Bishop is a PhD student in English literature and has been a university instructor.

Allison Blecker
Blecker is a PhD candidate in Near Eastern languages.

Wesley Borucki
Borucki holds a PhD in American history and is a university professor.

Gerald Carpenter
Carpenter holds an MA in U.S. intellectual history and a PhD in early modern French history. He is a freelance writer.

Alex Covalciuc
Covalciuc is a PhD candidate in English literature. He has been a university instructor and a freelance writer.

Jenny Dale
Dale holds an MFA in creative writing and has been a university instructor.

Farnoosh Fathi
Fathi has a PhD in English literature and creative writing and has been a university instructor.

Jen Gann
Gann holds an MFA in creative writing and has been a university instructor.

Daisy Gard
Gard is a freelance writer with a background in English literature.

Greta Gard
Gard is a PhD candidate in English literature and has been a university instructor and a freelance writer.

Tina Gianoulis
Gianoulis is a freelance writer with a background in English literature.

Cynthia Giles
Giles holds an MA in English literature and a PhD in interdisciplinary humanities. She has been a university instructor and a freelance writer.

Kristen Gleason
Gleason holds an MFA in creative writing and has been a university instructor.

Nicole Grant
Grant holds an MA in English and has been a university instructor.

Quan Manh Ha
Ha holds a PhD in American literature and is a university professor.

Irene Hsiao
Hsiao has a PhD in literature and has been a university instructor.

Franklin Hyde
Hyde holds a PhD in English literature and is a university instructor.

Anna Ioanes
Ioanes is a PhD student in English language and literature and has been a university instructor.

Laura Johnson
Johnson holds a PhD in English and has been a university instructor.

Emily Jones
Jones holds an MFA in creative writing and has been a university instructor.

Alicia Kent
Kent holds a PhD in English literature and is a university professor.

Kristin King-Ries
King-Ries holds an MFA in creative writing and has been a university instructor.

Lise LaLonde
LaLonde holds MAs in English literature and translation and has been a university instructor.

Gregory Luther
Luther holds an MFA in creative writing and has been a university instructor and freelance writer.

Katie Macnamara
Macnamara holds a PhD in English literature and has been a university instructor.

Maggie Magno
Magno has an MA in education. She has been a high school English teacher and a freelance writer.

xix

CONTRIBUTORS

ABIGAIL MANN
Mann holds a PhD in English literature and is a university professor.

EMILY MANN
Mann has an MA in library and information science.

THEODORE MCDERMOTT
McDermott holds an MFA in creative writing and has been a university instructor and a freelance writer.

LISA MERTEL
Mertel holds an MA in library science and an MA in history.

RACHEL MINDELL
Mindell holds an MFA in creative writing and has been a freelance writer.

JIM MLADENOVIC
Mladenovic holds an MS in clinical psychology and is pursuing an MA in library science.

KATHRYN MOLINARO
Molinaro holds an MA in English literature and has been a university instructor and a freelance writer.

CAITIE MOORE
Moore holds an MFA in creative writing and has been a university instructor.

ROBIN MORRIS
Morris holds a PhD in English literature and has been a university instructor.

JANET MULLANE
Mullane is a freelance writer and has been a high school English teacher.

ELLIOTT NIBLOCK
Niblock holds an MTS in the philosophy of religion.

KATRINA OKO-ODOI
Oko-Odoi is a PhD candidate in Spanish language and literature and a university instructor.

JAMES OVERHOLTZER
Overholtzer holds an MA in English literature and has been a university instructor.

IOANA PATULEANU
Patuleanu holds a PhD in English literature and has been a university instructor.

EVELYN REYNOLDS
Reynolds is pursuing an MA in English literature and an MFA in creative writing and has been a freelance writer.

CHRIS ROUTLEDGE
Routledge holds a PhD in English literature and is a university lecturer and a freelance writer.

REBECCA RUSTIN
Rustin holds an MA in English literature and is a freelance writer.

ANTHONY RUZICKA
Ruzicka is pursuing an MFA in poetry and has worked as a university instructor.

CATHERINE E. SAUNDERS
Saunders holds a PhD in English literature and is a university professor.

CARINA SAXON
Saxon is a PhD candidate in English literature and has been a university instructor and a freelance editor.

JACOB SCHMITT
Schmitt holds an MA in English literature and has been a freelance writer.

NANCY SIMPSON-YOUNGER
Simpson-Younger is a PhD candidate in literary studies and a university instructor.

CLAIRE SKINNER
Skinner holds an MFA in creative writing and is a university instructor.

ROGER SMITH
Smith has an MA in media ecology and has been a university instructor and a freelance writer.

NICHOLAS SNEAD
Snead is a PhD candidate in French language and literature and has been a university instructor.

SARAH STOECKL
Stoeckl holds a PhD in English literature and is a university instructor and a freelance writer.

PAMELA TOLER
Toler has a PhD in history and is a freelance writer and former university instructor.

GRACE WAITMAN
Waitman is pursuing a PhD in educational psychology. She holds an MA in English literature and has been a university instructor.

ALLYNA WARD
Ward holds a PhD in English literature and is a university professor.

JENNA WILLIAMS
Williams holds an MFA in creative writing and has been a university instructor and a freelance writer.

Academic Reviewers

BARBARA ALLEN
Associate Professor of History, La Salle University, Philadelphia, Pennsylvania.

KHALED AL-MASRI
Assistant Professor of Arabic, Swarthmore College, Swarthmore, Pennsylvania.

HOLLY ARROW
Professor of Psychology, Institute of Cognitive and Decision Sciences, University of Oregon, Eugene.

STEPHEN BEHRENDT
George Holmes Distinguished Professor of English, University of Nebraska-Lincoln.

WILLIAM BELDING
Professorial Lecturer, School of International Service, American University, Washington, D.C.

AMY BELL
Associate Professor of History, Huron University College, London, Ontario, Canada.

ALAN L. BERGER
Raddock Family Eminent Scholar Chair in Holocaust Studies; Professor of Jewish Studies, English Department; Director, the Center for the Study of Values and Violence after Auschwitz, Florida Atlantic University, Boca Raton.

MOULAY-ALI BOUÂNANI
Professor of Africana Studies, Binghamton University-State University of New York, Vestal.

CLAIRE BOYLE
Lecturer in French, University of Edinburgh, United Kingdom.

MICHAEL BREEN
Associate Professor of History and Humanities, Reed College, Portland, Oregon.

GERRY CANAVAN
Assistant Professor of English, Marquette University, Milwaukee, Wisconsin.

NATHAN CLARKE
Assistant Professor of History, Minnesota State University Moorhead.

WILLIAM CLEMENTE
Professor of Literature, Peru State College, Peru, Nebraska.

MARC CONNER
Ballengee Professor of English, Washington and Lee University, Lexington, Virginia.

JANE CRAWFORD
Faculty, History and Political Science Department, Mount St. Mary's College, Los Angeles, California.

SONJA DARLINGTON
Professor of Education and Youth Studies, Beloit College, Beloit, Wisconsin.

GABRIELE DILLMANN
Associate Professor of German, Denison University, Granville, Ohio.

JEANNE DUBINO
Professor of English and Global Studies, Appalachian State University, Boone, North Carolina.

ELIZABETH DUQUETTE
Associate Professor of English, Gettysburg College, Gettysburg, Pennsylvania.

BREANNE FAHS
Associate Professor of Women and Gender Studies, Arizona State University West, Glendale.

DANINE FARQUHARSON
Associate Professor of English, Memorial University of Newfoundland, St. John's.

LUANNE FRANK
Associate Professor of English, University of Texas at Arlington.

GREGORY FRASER
Professor of English, University of West Georgia, Carrollton.

JAMES GIGANTINO
Assistant Professor of History, University of Arkansas at Fayetteville.

QUAN MANH HA
Assistant Professor of American Literature and Ethnic Studies, University of Montana, Missoula.

KEVIN J. HAYES
Professor of English, University of Central Oklahoma, Edmond.

RICHARD HIGGINS
Lecturer in English, Franklin College, Franklin, Indiana.

NELS HIGHBERG
Associate Professor and Chair of Rhetoric and Professional Writing Department, University of Hartford, West Hartford, Connecticut.

ACADEMIC REVIEWERS

WALTER HÖLBLING
Professor of American Studies, Karl-Franzens-Universität Graz, Austria.

FRANKLYN HYDE
Adjunct Professor of English, University of Manitoba, Winnipeg.

PETER IVERSON
Regents' Professor of History, Arizona State University, Tempe.

KELLY JEONG
Assistant Professor of Comparative Literature and Korean Studies, University of California, Riverside.

A. YEMISI JIMOH
Professor of African American Literature and Culture, University of Massachusetts Amherst.

JEFFREY W. JONES
Associate Professor of History, University of North Carolina at Greensboro.

ALICIA A. KENT
Associate Professor of English, University of Michigan-Flint.

CHRISTOPHER KNIGHT
Professor of English, University of Montana, Missoula.

LEAH KNIGHT
Associate Professor of Literature, Brock University, St. Catharines, Ontario.

MARY LARSON
President of Oral History Association; Head of Oklahoma Oral History Research Program, Oklahoma State University, Stillwater.

CHANA KAI LEE
Associate Professor of History and of the Institute for African American Studies, University of Georgia, Athens.

WEIJING LU
Associate Professor of History, University of California, San Diego, La Jolla.

CAROL MACKAY
Professor of English, University of Texas at Austin.

BRIDGET MARSHALL
Associate Professor and Associate Chair of English Department, University of Massachusetts Lowell.

MARIA DEL CARMEN MARTINEZ
Assistant Professor of English, University of Wisconsin-Parkside.

LUCINDA MCCRAY
Professor and Chair of History Department, Appalachian State University, Boone, North Carolina.

CAROL MCFREDERICK
Adjunct Instructor of English, Florida International University, Miami.

GORDON MCKINNEY
Professor Emeritus, Berea College, Berea, Kentucky.

LAURIE MERCIER
Professor of History, Washington State University, Vancouver.

DANIEL METRAUX
Professor of Asian Studies, Mary Baldwin College, Staunton, Virginia.

GENEVA COBB MOORE
Professor of English and Women's Studies, University of Wisconsin-Whitewater.

EARL MULDERINK
Professor of History, Southern Utah University, Cedar City.

SHAKIR MUSTAFA
Visiting Associate Professor of Arabic, Northeastern University, Boston, Massachusetts.

SEIWOONG OH
Professor and Chair of English Department, Rider University, Lawrenceville, New Jersey.

MICHEL PHARAND
Director of the Disraeli Project, Queen's University, Kingston, Ontario, Canada.

JANET POWERS
Professor Emerita of Interdisciplinary Studies and Women, Gender, and Sexuality Studies, Gettysburg College, Gettysburg, Pennsylvania.

JOHN R. REED
Distinguished Professor of English, Wayne State University, Detroit, Michigan.

PATRICIO RIZZO-VAST
Instructor of Spanish and Portuguese, Northeastern Illinois University, Chicago.

ASHRAF RUSHDY
Professor and Chair of African American Studies Program; Professor of English, Wesleyan University, Middletown, Connecticut.

ANDRE SIMIĆ
Professor of Anthropology, University of Southern California, Los Angeles.

CARL SMELLER
Associate Professor of English and Humanities, Texas Wesleyan University, Fort Worth.

MARY ZEISS STANGE
Professor of Women's Studies and Religion, Skidmore College, Saratoga Springs, New York.

REBECCA JANE STANTON
Assistant Professor of Russian, Barnard College, New York, New York.

RICHARD STOFFLE
Professor of Anthropology, University of Arizona, Tucson.

BILINDA STRAIGHT
Professor of Anthropology, Western Michigan University, Kalamazoo.

GWEN TARBOX
Associate Professor of English, Western Michigan University, Kalamazoo.

BARBARA TRUESDELL
Assistant Director of the Center for the Study of History and Memory, Indiana University, Bloomington.

CHUONG-DAI VO
Visiting Scholar, Foreign Language and Literatures, Massachusetts Institute of Technology, Cambridge.

ALLYNA E. WARD
Assistant Professor of English, Booth University College, Winnipeg, Manitoba.

RICHARD WEIKART
Professor of History, California State University-Stanislaus, Turlock.

ACADEMIC REVIEWERS

DOROTHY WILLS
Professor of Anthropology, California State Polytechnic University, Pomona.

MICHAEL WILSON
Associate Professor of English, University of Wisconsin-Milwaukee.

SIMONA WRIGHT
Professor and Director of Italian Program, The College of New Jersey, Ewing.

PRISCILLA YBARRA
Assistant Professor of English, University of North Texas, Denton.

GERALD ZAHAVI
Professor of History; Director of Documentary Studies Program, University at Albany-State University of New York.

PIERANTONIO ZANOTTI
Adjunct Professor of Japanese Language, Università Ca' Foscari Venezia, Italy.

Adversity and Resistance

The Cancer Journals by Audre Lorde	3
Child of the Dark: The Diary of Carolina Maria de Jesus by Carolina Maria de Jesus	6
De Profundis by Oscar Wilde	9
Detained: A Writer's Prison Diary by Ngũgĩ wa Thiong'o	12
Diaries of Beatrice Webb by Beatrice Webb	16
The Good Man of Nanking: The Diaries of John Rabe by John Rabe	19
An Interrupted Life: The Diaries of Etty Hillesum by Etty Hillesum	22
Journal of George Fox by George Fox	26
The Journals of Charlotte Forten Grimké by Charlotte Forten Grimké	29
Letter from the Birmingham Jail by Martin Luther King Jr.	32
Letter to Her Daughter by Lady Mary Wortley Montagu	35
Letter to His Son by Robert E. Lee	38
Letter to Maria Clemm by Edgar Allan Poe	41
Letter to the Reverend Samson Occom by Phillis Wheatley	44
Letters Home by Sylvia Plath	47
Letters Underway by 'Izzat Ghazzawi	50
Spandau: The Secret Diaries by Albert Speer	54

The Cancer Journals
Audre Lorde

OVERVIEW

The Cancer Journals (1980) by Audre Lorde chronicles the author's battle with breast cancer and has become a classic study on women and illness, mainly due to the way the author combines personal pain with political awareness of her disease and its ramifications. Divided into three chapters, *The Cancer Journals* alternates between essays, poetry, and journal entries that begin with Lorde's biopsy of a malignant tumor in 1977 and end eighteen months later, after her mastectomy. A slim volume, the book is composed of less than eighty pages of text. Although the author was already an established poet when she wrote *The Cancer Journals,* it was her first book of prose. The work deals with her fear and pain and includes a critique of what she calls Cancer, Inc. *The Cancer Journals* also further explores themes that appear in Lorde's other works, such as the power of resisting silence, opposing racism, embracing lesbianism, and dealing with perpetual outsider status.

Lorde wrote the final essay for the journals on August 29, 1980, and the first edition was on the shelves before the end of the same year. Academic interest in *The Cancer Journals* has remained high in the three decades since publication. Scholars have examined the use of symbolism in *The Cancer Journals* and have studied the book for insights into decoding the U.S. medical profession's use of militaristic language to describe disease. Recently a scholar investigated the work for evidence of Lorde's mischievous side—her playfulness with written language and her identification with the trickster tale of African legend. *The Cancer Journals* remains one of the definitive works on breast cancer and gender theory.

HISTORICAL AND LITERARY CONTEXT

The Cancer Journals was part of an emerging trend of outsider literature in the United States in the 1970s. In academia and elsewhere, those who were considered outsiders were rebelling against the silence demanded of them about difference of any kind. Feminists wrote about sexism, African Americans wrote about racism, and homosexuals were beginning to write about discrimination toward gays and lesbians. Initially liberating, the new outsider literature quickly developed its own set of unspoken rules. A black woman was supposed to choose between her race and her gender; she was supposed to identify as either a feminist or a black person, not both. What set Lorde apart from her peers was her refusal to fit into a narrow category at the expense of truncating a part of who she was, and for that she paid a high price. In the journals she writes, "I am defined as other in every group I am a part of." Lorde's work embraces and examines the pain and complexity of her multiple outsider statuses in order to turn the discourse on difference into "useful strengths for change." More than once in *The Cancer Journals* she expresses longing for a black lesbian breast cancer survivor role model, while acknowledging that there are none.

In her journal entries and essays, Lorde writes about encounters and conversations with other lesbian academics and writers, including her close friend, the highly regarded poet Adrienne Rich, whom Lorde met in the early 1970s. *The Cancer Journals* was the author's first major prose work and her first book on cancer. The disease became a theme she would revisit in later work, most notably in *A Burst of Light,* a collection of essays published in 1988, after she was diagnosed with liver cancer.

In addition to detailing her diagnosis, surgery, and recovery from breast cancer, Lorde rages against a society that encourages women to pretend that their mastectomies had not happened. She recounts a postoperative checkup at her surgeon's office in which the nurse, an otherwise supportive woman, chides Lorde for refusing to wear a prosthesis, a choice she believes hurts office morale. Lorde also refers to comments made by Mary Daly, a prominent white lesbian feminist and theologian, in her 1978 book titled *Gyn/Ecology: The Metaethics of Radical Feminism.* Lorde observes that there is much false spirituality "too cheaply bought" that saps rather than replenishes, such as Daly's metaphor of goddess worship. In her introduction to *The Cancer Journals,* Lorde writes, "The blood of black women sloshes from coast to coast and Daly says race is of no concern to women."

The Cancer Journals is especially notable for the connections the author makes between politics, the economy, and illness in the United States. Cancer, she writes, is a disease caused largely by environmental factors that are preventable. For example, Lorde argues that carcinogenic, fat-stored hormones in beef could be outlawed by the government through food inspection programs. She exposes the American Cancer Society's hypocrisy in placing greater emphasis on prosthetics and cosmetic surgery—both profitable—rather than

❖ *Key Facts*

Time Period:
Late 20th Century

Relevant Historical Events:
Lorde's battle with breast cancer; growth of outsider literature

Nationality:
American

Keywords:
breast cancer; mastectomy; feminism

ADVERSITY AND RESISTANCE

Audre Lorde giving a lecture in 1983 at the Atlantic Center for the Arts in New Smyrna Beach, Florida. © ROBERT ALEXANDER/ARCHIVE PHOTOS/GETTY IMAGES

on prevention or finding a cure. "Any serious information about the prevention or treatment of breast cancer, which might possibly threaten the vested interests of the American medical establishment, is difficult to find in this country."

THEMES AND STYLE

The Cancer Journals focuses on many of the same themes found in Lorde's poetry, including the strength of women loving women, the scourge of racism and exclusion of any kind, and the power of self-conscious living. She also addresses themes specific to breast cancer. However, the overarching theme of this book and of all Lorde's work is the idea that it is dangerous to ignore differences. "My silences had not protected me. Your silence will not protect you. But for every real word spoken, for every attempt I had ever made to speak those truths for which I am still seeking, I had made contact with other women while we examined the words to fit a world in which we all believed, bridging our differences." Ultimately, Lorde writes that difference must serve as a reason for celebration and growth. "The fact that we are here and that I speak now these words is an attempt to break that silence and bridge some of those differences between us, for it is not difference which immobilizes us, but silence. And there are so many silences to be broken."

Lorde used writing to get through the fear and pain of her illness. In a 1982 interview with Marge Piercy, Fran Moira, and Lorraine Sorrel for the magazine *Off Our Backs,* Lorde said that the book kept her alive. Writing it also helped her feel that at least her suffering would serve some greater purpose. She wrote essays about her cancer that incorporated journal entries; poems; and, in one instance, the content of a speech she delivered at an academic conference as a way to translate her understanding to others. "It only remained for me to give it voice, to share it for use, that the pain not be wasted." Characteristically, she rejected the traditional categories of the public and private when she wrote *The Cancer Journals,* choosing to use whatever material best suited her purpose, from the deeply personal entry "And, of course, I am afraid—you can hear it in my voice" to an article published in the *New York Times* about prosthetics fraud.

According to scholar Elizabeth Alexander in *American Literary History,* Lorde's work is notable for its personal honesty and its lack of pretentiousness. *The Cancer Journals* is no exception. Her forthright manner in the work is less present in her poetry, which is probably attributable to the seriousness of her illness. Unlike the journal entries, Lorde's poetry draws on allegory, myth, and symbolism and at times includes such fantastic creatures as the Black Unicorn. However, in the journal entries, Lorde pulls no punches. She writes in chapter 3, "I think I was fighting the devil of despair within myself for my own soul." The book is also notable for its fluctuation between moments of accusatory rage and openhearted generosity.

CRITICAL DISCUSSION

Sandwiched between the 1978 publication of her most highly acclaimed book of poetry, *The Black Unicorn,* and the 1982 publication of her only work of fiction, the novel *Zami*, *The Cancer Journals* did not initially receive as much scholarly attention as it might have otherwise. Feminists and cancer survivors alike celebrated *The Cancer Journals* as a triumph of truth-telling. It was also one of the first books written from the viewpoint of a lesbian of color. For these reasons, the book was the target of criticism from conservative political figures such as then-U.S. Senator Jessie Helms of North Carolina. Readership received a boost when the book won the American Library Association's Gay Caucus Book of the Year award in 1981.

Due to steadily growing interest in *The Cancer Journals* over the years, its publisher issued two later editions, one in 1992 and one in 2006. Each subsequent version has spawned additional rounds of academic writing as well as popular articles and web postings. The 2006 edition contains supplementary materials including photographs and tributes from a number of notable writers as well as friends and family, which were written after Lorde's death in 1992. *The Cancer Journals* continues to serve as a lifeline for people of all races and backgrounds—men as well as women—whose lives have been affected by breast cancer.

Recent scholarship has focused on the lamentable lack of progress in what scholar Robina Josephine Khalid calls "the narrative of breast cancer" in her 2008 article in *African American Review*. She observes that the medical establishment and the culture at large still have not acknowledged what Lorde recognized in 1978, primarily that women of color, especially poor women, are at a significantly higher risk of being diagnosed with and dying from breast cancer due to capitalism and the way research continues to be compromised by corporate interests.

AN OPEN LETTER TO MARY DALY

While writing *The Cancer Journals*, which contained a somewhat oblique criticism of Mary Daly's book *Gyn/Ecology* (1978), Lorde wrote a letter to Daly asking her to explain why she chose to leave out black legends and goddesses in her pantheon of female icons and why she chose to ignore black women's experiences, except as victims in the chapter on genital mutilation. Four months after Lorde sent the letter, Daly had not responded, and Lorde, feeling distressed and betrayed by someone she had thought of as an ally, wrote an open letter to Daly in the press. The letter was later printed as a pamphlet by Crossings Press in Berkeley in 1984. This letter has been taught in college courses as a primer on racism in some white feminist scholarship. The dispute attracted attention in academic circles and, to a lesser extent, in the press. In an interview in 1982, Lorde said she had never received an answer. Until her death, she maintained that Daly had never responded to her letter.

However, in 2003, while doing research for her book on Lorde, biographer Alexis De Veaux discovered a response letter from Daly in Lorde's files. It was dated four and a half months after Lorde sent the first, private letter. Though Daly supporters made much of this discovery and Daly herself included it when she explained her side of the story in 2006, there is little of substance in the letter, which is perhaps why Lorde never referred to it. Daly's very short response was more of a nonresponse. She wrote, "But of course to point out this restriction in the first passage is not really to answer your letter. You have made your point very strongly and you most definitely do have a point. I could speculate on how *Gyn/Ecology* would have been affected had we corresponded about this before the manuscript went to press, but it doesn't seem creativity-conducing to look backward. There is only now and the hope of breaking the barriers between us—of constantly expanding the vision."

BIBLIOGRAPHY

Sources

Alexander, Elizabeth. "Coming Out Blackened and Whole": Fragmentation and Reintegration in Audre Lorde's *Zami* and *The Cancer Journals*. *American Literary History* 6.4 (1994): 695–715. JSTOR. Web. 5 Dec. 2012.

Daly, Mary. *Gyn/Ecology: The Metaethics of Radical Feminism*. Boston: Beacon, 1978. Print.

Jain, S. Lochlan. "Cancer Butch." *Cultural Anthropology* 22.4 (2007): 501–38. JSTOR. Web. 5 Dec. 2012.

Khalid, Robina Josephine. "Demilitarizing Disease: Ambivalent Warfare and Audre Lorde's *The Cancer Journals*." *African American Review* 42.3–4 (2008): 697–714. JSTOR. Web. 5 Dec. 2012.

Lorde, Audre. *The Cancer Journals*. San Francisco: Spinsters, 1980. Print.

Provost, Kara. "Becoming Afrekete: The Trickster in the Work of Audre Lorde." *MELUS* 20.4 (1995): 45–59. JSTOR. Web. 5 Dec. 2012.

Rich, Adrienne. Interview with Audre Lorde. *Signs: Journal of Women in Culture and Society* 6.4 (1981): 713–36. JSTOR. Web. 5 Dec. 2012.

Further Reading

Brooks, Jerome. "Audre Lorde." *Black Women Writers (1950–1980)*. Ed. Mari Evans. New York: Doubleday, 1984. Print.

Cobb-Moore, Geneva. "Diaries and Journals." *The Oxford Companion to African American Literature*. Ed. William L. Andrews, et al. New York: Oxford University Press, 2001.

De Veaux, Alexis. *Warrior Poet: A Biography of Audre Lorde*. New York: W. W. Norton, 2004.

Keating, AnaLouise. *Women Reading Women Writing: Self-Invention in Paula Gunn Allen, Gloria Anzaldua, and Audre Lorde*. Philadelphia: Temple University Press, 1996.

Lorde, Audre. *I Am Your Sister: Collected and Unpublished Writing of Audre Lorde*. Ed. Rudolf Byrd, Johnetta Betsch Cole, and Beverly Guy-Sheftall. New York: Oxford University Press, 2009.

Lorde, Audre. *An Open Letter to Mary Daly*. Berkeley, Calif.: Crossing Press, 1984. 66–71. Print.

Walker, Alice. Introduction. *The Audre Lorde Compendium: Essays, Speeches & Journals*. London: Pandora, 1996. Print.

Kristin King-Ries

CHILD OF THE DARK
The Diary of Carolina Maria de Jesus
Carolina Maria de Jesus

❖ Key Facts

Time Period:
Mid-20th Century

Relevant Historical Events:
De Jesus's childhood in a Sao Paulo favela; increased social reform in Brazil

Nationality:
Brazilian

Keywords:
favela; poverty; hunger

OVERVIEW

Child of the Dark: The Diary of Carolina Maria de Jesus, a selection of the 1955–58 diary entries of Carolina Maria de Jesus, was first published serially in 1959 in the Brazilian newspaper *Diário da Noite* by the author's editor and agent, Audálio Dantas. The Portuguese-language compilation, *Quarto de despejo* ("Room of Garbage"), was published in 1960 and sold 90,000 copies in six months despite mixed reviews. An English-language version appeared in 1962, translated by David St. Clair. The diary exposes the truth about living in the Sao Paulo *favelas* (shantytowns) and tells of daily hunger, violence, sickness, and death while criticizing politicians for ignoring the conditions of the poor. Intelligent and perceptive, de Jesus reveals herself to be hopeful and tenacious in the face of her rather bleak reality.

The immediate success of her book allowed de Jesus to move out of the favela with her three children and into a small, brick house. As a black single mother, she was held to different standards than the literary elite, and she met with a near-constant judgment of her clothing and mannerisms, as well as her politics, which were characterized as too radical for polite society yet not communist enough for Brazil's radical left. Her editors failed to pay de Jesus according to the terms of her contract, and they pressured her to finance publication on her own for her subsequent fictional works, which did not sell well. She died in poverty of an acute asthma attack in 1977, and today her diary continues to be analyzed more by scholars in the United States than in Brazil.

HISTORICAL AND LITERARY CONTEXT

Child of the Dark was marketed as an anomaly for someone of de Jesus's status; that is, an uneducated female living in the favelas. When de Jesus moved from the interior state of Minas Gerais to Sao Paulo for work in the 1940s, she found herself in Canindé, one of seven favelas in the city. By then the favelas had 50,000 inhabitants, called *favelados*—mostly black migrant workers who had moved to urban centers when Brazil industrialized in the late 1800s. De Jesus built her shack in Canindé with wood she collected and carried alone, after becoming pregnant and losing, for the third time in a row, her job as a maid. As she relates in her diary, scavenging became her only source of income; she sold scraps of metal and paper to buy milk, bread, and shoes, and she occasionally shared the best places to find materials with other favelados in need.

Dantas, then twenty-four years old and writing for *Diário da Noite,* met de Jesus when he visited the favela in 1958 to report on the unveiling of a playground. He overheard her mentioning her book to the other favelados, threatening that she would write about them. When Dantas inquired about her book, de Jesus escorted him to her house and showed him the pages of her diaries and stories written on scraps of paper she had collected. He was intrigued by the frank and highly literate way in which de Jesus wrote about hunger and poverty in her diary entries. Brazil had entered a period of mild reforms, rendering an open critique of its class system more acceptable than in the past. However, while Dantas left intact some proper names (of prominent politicians and de Jesus's neighbors), he edited out what he deemed unpublishable, including the author's analysis of falling wages and bus fare hikes.

De Jesus learned the subtleties of class disparity and public policy not only through her lived experience of them but also through periodicals that she read at the newsstand. Poetic aspects of her text—musings on birdsong, or the color of the sky, for instance—may have been influenced by authors she was exposed to while working for the physician Euricledes Zerbini, but there is no evidence that she owned books herself until after she left the favela.

Often noted by the literary elite as a text that came out of an otherwise silent population, *Child of the Dark* focuses on critical social issues in a moderate tone that many readers found palatable. This style brought de Jesus brief fame, and it was subsequently emulated by other women. Maura Lopes Cançado, for instance, the author of *Hospicio é Deus* (1965), made an attempt to write from the margins, but she failed to achieve any measure of success. Due to the domestic issues addressed by de Jesus, scholars today regard the diary as one of the first feminist texts to emerge from Brazil.

The Rocinha slum in Rio de Janeiro, Brazil, celebrating Holy Week in 2012. The slums of Sao Paolo, Brazil, are the setting for Carolina Maria de Jesus's firsthand account *Child of the Dark*. © AP IMAGES/FELIPE DANA

THEMES AND STYLE

Child of the Dark records themes of poverty, violence, and motherhood, as well as the unrestrained racism and classism of the Brazilian elite. In the opening entry for June 15, 1955, de Jesus recounts the humiliation and disappointment she feels at not being able to buy her daughter shoes for her birthday, noting that she and her children "are slaves to the cost of living." Throughout her diary she refuses to accept as inevitable the poverty in which she and her children live. She observes of Sao Paulo that "the Governor's Palace is the living room. The mayor's office is the dining room and the city is the garden. The favela is the backyard where they throw the garbage." The filth of Canindé was among the things she could tolerate least.

De Jesus wrote in order to reflect on the world around her and to preserve her sanity. The more lyrical passages in *Child of the Dark* spring from her professed need to balance her hardship with optimism. Entries that recount negative experiences, such as being sick or making no money for her scraps, frequently end on a positive note. Typical of such entries is one in which she goes at dawn to collect water from the communal well. In it, she writes, "The sparrows have just begun their morning symphony. The birds must be happier than we are. Perhaps happiness and equality reigns among them." Her hope of eventually publishing her account gave her an imaginative release from her situation and was also a weapon she frequently wielded against her neighbors, whom she would often find beating her children when she returned from work.

The diction is straightforward and at times self-aware. It describes the conditions of the favelas as though to an audience unfamiliar with them. Though Dantas chose to edit out occasional repetitions in which de Jesus accused neighbors or relayed mundane details, he retained poetic descriptions such as "the sky is peppered with stars. I have the crazy desire to cut a piece of the sky to make a dress," which set the text apart from dry or depressing accounts of class systems. Nonetheless, when scholar Robert Levine visited de Jesus's daughter and examined the unedited manuscripts, as he writes in his essay "Different Carolinas," he discovered that "the editing muted her personality, which in reality was more feisty and angry than readers of her published diaries know."

CRITICAL DISCUSSION

Child of the Dark garnered positive reviews from the English-speaking press. Reviewer Madaline W. Nichols, in her 1963 review in the *Hispanic American Historical Review,* names it "a truly great book" that "brings vividly alive a woman of astounding courage." Richard M. Morse added in the *Annals of the American Academy of Political and Social Science* in 1964 that the power of the book was owed to its "raw, spontaneous cry from the normally inarticulate proletariat of Latin America." The press in Brazil was less generous, frequently diverting attention away from the diary to focus on de Jesus. Levine notes in his 1994 essay "The Cautionary Tale of Carolina Maria de Jesus" that the author posed some threat to the sociopolitical structure of Brazil and that "by emphasizing

CAROLINA MARIA DE JESUS: FALLEN "STAR"

Carolina Maria de Jesus's diary *Child of the Dark* was popular enough that she should have been able to live comfortably for the remainder of her life. It sold more copies than the works of Brazilian novelist Jorge Amado, a fact that scandalized the Brazilian literati. Robert Levine noted in 1994 that both her Brazilian publisher and the one in the United States failed to pay her all of the royalties she was due. According to Levine, "Carolina and her family should have received more than one hundred and fifty thousand dollars" from her United States contract alone, but "no evidence has been found that she received even a small portion of this amount."

The press in Brazil chastised de Jesus for how she spent her new money. Levine notes that one unnamed reporter commented that she went out "with mascara-painted eyelashes and high-heeled shoes, dressed in silk and elegant accessories from the best downtown shops." This class criticism was leveled at the author from all sides. In an article in *Criticism,* Eva Paulino Bueno writes that after de Jesus fell back into poverty, she told reporters that many of her old customers would not buy her metal and paper scraps, "because the buyers refused to do business with a 'star.'"

Carolina's eccentricities, the elitist press trivialized her importance and depoliticized her message."

Following the text's initial reception, scholarship focused on the identity construction of de Jesus via her published and unpublished manuscripts, as well as her portrayal by various international media. This emphasis on the author herself instead of on her text was the norm since at least 1967, when Levine notes that "newspapers across Brazil and around the world published a photograph of Carolina picking up waste paper in the streets of Sao Paulo." Levine quotes Brazilian journalist Neide Ricosti as writing in 1975 that "with mud-covered feet, badly dressed, and disheveled," de Jesus had fallen back into poverty. Levine asserts that "once again, Carolina was blamed in elitist and racist terms for what had happened to her." Contemporary scholars continue to examine racist, sexist, and classist reactions to the work.

Recent scholarship has focused on how and why *Child of the Dark* has been left out of academic core curriculum in the United States. Typical of such scholarship is Eva Paulino Bueno's 1999 article in *Criticism.* Bueno maintains that, in contrast to Rigoberta Menchu's seminal work, *I, Rigoberta Menchu: An Indian Woman in Guatemala* (1983), in which Menchu is said to be the voice of her community, de Jesus is viewed as anomalous and isolated. According to Bueno, "the denial of Black culture leads to the denial of the work by Black artists and intellectuals as representative of a culture." She argues that despite the political content of de Jesus's text, scholars still have not viewed her as an important activist, due in part to the fact that de Jesus was black, "never married, and had no other society but the one represented by her young, dependent children."

BIBLIOGRAPHY

Sources

Bueno, Eva Paulino. "Carolina Maria de Jesus in the Context of 'Testimonios': Race, Sexuality, and Exclusion." *Criticism* 41.2 (1999): 257–84. *JSTOR.* Web. 1 Dec. 2012.

De Jesus, Carolina Maria. *Child of the Dark: The Diary of Carolina Maria de Jesus.* Trans. David St. Clair. London: Penguin, 1963. Print.

Levine, Robert M. "The Cautionary Tale of Carolina Maria de Jesus." *Latin American Research Review* 29.1 (1994): 55–83. *JSTOR.* Web. 1 Dec. 2012.

———. "Different Carolinas." *Luso-Brazilian Review* 38.2 (2001): 61–73. *JSTOR.* Web. 1 Dec. 2012.

Morse, Richard M. Rev. of *Child of the Dark: The Diary of Carolina Maria de Jesus,* by Carolina Maria de Jesus. *Annals of the American Academy of Political and Social Science* 353 (1964): 176. *JSTOR.* Web. 1 Dec. 2012.

Nichols, Madaline W. Rev. of *Child of the Dark: The Diary of Carolina Maria de Jesus,* by Carolina Maria de Jesus. *Hispanic American Historical Review* 43.3 (1963): 448–50. *JSTOR.* Web. 1 Dec. 2012.

Further Reading

Arrington, Melvin S., Jr. "From the Garbage Dump to the Brick House: The Diaries of Carolina Maria de Jesus." *South Eastern Latin Americanist* 36.4 (1993): 1–12. *MLA International Bibliography.* Web. 1 Dec. 2012.

De Jesus, Carolina Maria. *Betita's Diary: The Childhood of Carolina Maria de Jesus.* Trans. Emanuelle Oliviera and Beth Joan Vinkler. Armonk, N.Y.: Sharpe, 1998. Print.

Feracho, Lesley. "Transgressive Acts: Race, Gender, and Class in the Poetry of Carolina Maria de Jesus and Miriam Alves." *Afro-Hispanic Review* 18.1 (1999): 38–45. *MLA International Bibliography.* Web. 1 Dec. 2012.

Meihy, José Carlos Sebe Bom, and Robert M. Levine. *The Life and Death of Carolina Maria de Jesus.* Albuquerque: New Mexico University Press, 1995. Print.

Nance, Kimberly A. "From Quarto de Despejo to a Little House: Domesticity as Personal and Political Testimony in the Diaries of Carolina Maria de Jesus." *PALARA: Publication of the Afro-Latin/American Research Association* 5 (2001): 42–48. *MLA International Bibliography.* Web. 1 Dec. 2012.

Platt, Kamala. "Race and Gender Representations in Clarice Lispector's 'A Menor Mulher do Mundo' and Carolina Maria de Jesus' Quarto de Despejo." *Afro-Hispanic Review* 11.1–3 (1992): 51–57. *MLA International Bibliography.* Web. 1 Dec. 2012.

Wasserman, Renata R. Mautner. *Central at the Margin: Five Brazilian Women Writers.* Lewisburg: Bucknell University Press, 2007. *MLA International Bibliography.* Web. 1 Dec. 2012.

Caitlin Moore

DE PROFUNDIS
Oscar Wilde

OVERVIEW

Composed by Oscar Wilde while he was in prison and published in 1905, five years after his death, *De Profundis* continues to be of interest to those exploring the legendary writer from both autobiographical and literary angles. One hundred years after its original publication, in 2005, editor Ian Small included the work in the second volume of *The Complete Work of Oscar Wilde*, titled *De Profundis; "Epistola: In carcere et vinculis."* Because *De Profundis* begins with an address and ends with a sign off, some critics call it a love letter. Others, however, consider it to be an essay. Regardless of its designation, *De Profundis* provides autobiographical insight into Wilde and explores the personal themes he wrestled with while in prison, including relationships, art, culture, suffering, and redemption.

When he was released from prison, Wilde gave the text to his literary executor, Robert Ross, and requested one copy for himself and another for Lord Alfred Douglas (to whom the work is addressed and with whom Wilde had a romantic relationship). When Ross first published it, he made sure no mention of Douglas's family remained. Later versions, some with additional materials (including mentions of Douglas's family), have appeared in other editions of Wilde's work. Current Wilde scholars and fans can read *De Profundis* to see a different side of the carefully controlled and cultured writer, a side originating from the depths of his incarceration.

HISTORICAL AND LITERARY CONTEXT

During Wilde's lifetime, homosexuality was illegal in England. Though he married Constance Lloyd and had two sons with her, he also had relationships with men. One such man was Douglas, whose father, the Marquess of Queensberry, vehemently opposed their relationship and sought to out Wilde's homosexuality by leaving a note in a club where Wilde often socialized. After Wilde attempted to sue the Marquess for libel, details about the writer's relationship with Douglas became clear, and Wilde soon found himself facing the trials that led to his conviction for gross indecency with other men and a two-year prison term (1895–97). Among other issues, the specific relationship between Wilde and Douglas—along with its consequences—is thoroughly explored in *De Profundis*.

The circumstances of Wilde's imprisonment dictated the writing and structure of *De Profundis*. Initially without writing utensils, Wilde implored prison officials to provide him with materials, and by the time he composed *De Profundis* in 1897, he was allotted a few writing pages per day. Though he was not allowed to send his letter to Douglas, he was able to take the letter with him when he was released from prison. The title *De Profundis* does not come from Wilde himself but rather from Ross, who named it such when he published it in 1905.

Because it was written while Wilde was incarcerated, *De Profundis* is different from his plays and novels. However, while this isolation accounts for stylistic aspects of the text, it did not prevent him from including a number of literary allusions, notably to Dante, Johann Wolfgang von Goethe, William Wordsworth, Victor Hugo, and Charles Baudelaire. In its explorations of Wilde's preoccupation with Douglas and the consequences of their relationship, *De Profundis* echoes the themes of obsession and sensual pleasure in Wilde's *The Picture of Dorian Gray* (1890). However, while sensual pleasure and physical beauty are revered in that novel, these themes are examined with much darker tones in *De Profundis*.

De Profundis is one of two final literary contributions Wilde made before his death in 1900. The other work published after his incarceration, *The Ballad of Reading Gaol* (1898), was not written but conceptualized while he was in prison. Included and reprinted in a number of letters and anthologies since its inception, *De Profundis* is of interest to contemporary readers tracking the effects of Wilde's imprisonment on his writing and on his soul.

THEMES AND STYLE

De Profundis explores the consequences of Wilde's relationship with Douglas and examines the notions of art, culture, suffering, and redemption. Before his trials and imprisonment, Wilde was at the height of his career, basking in the success of his play *The Importance of Being Earnest* (1895). *De Profundis* delves into these career highs and lows and their ties to his personal highs and lows. He writes, "I was a man who stood in symbolic relations to the art and culture of my age," then decides, "But I let myself be lured into long spells of senseless and sensual ease…. I became the spendthrift of my own genius, and to waste an eternal youth gave me a curious joy."

Key Facts

Time Period:
Late 19th Century

Relevant Historical Events:
Wilde's incarceration for his homosexuality

Nationality:
English

Keywords:
homosexuality; incarceration; love

De Profundis was written by Oscar Wilde to Lord Alfred Douglas while the former was in jail after being convicted of gross indecency. Shown here is a scene from *The Judas Kiss*, a play about the relationship between Wilde and Douglas. Liam Neeson, left, played Wilde, while Tom Hollander, right, played Douglas. © ROBBIE JACK/CORBIS

During his time in prison, Wilde composed *De Profundis* to communicate to Douglas, but he also imagined a larger audience (as evidenced by his later request for two copies of the letter). In a different letter composed to his friend More Adey in February 1987 and published in *The Complete Letters of Oscar Wilde* in 2000 (edited by Vyvyan B. Holland, Merlin Holland, and Rupert Hart-Davis), Wilde writes of his letter to Douglas: "It is the most important letter of my life, as it will deal ultimately with my future mental attitude toward life, with the way in which I desire to meet the world again, with the development of my character: with what I have lost, what I have learned, and what I hope to arrive at."

De Profundis vacillates between a direct, personal address to Douglas and a wider, more universal tone, which indicates the author's early thoughts of eventually publishing the letter. In a 2006 article for *English Literature in Transition 1880–1920,* Wilde scholars Ian Small and Josephine M. Guy note the letter's "most obvious literary shortcomings—its repetitions, rambling structure, frequent contradictions." In *Oscar Wilde* (1988), Richard Ellman finds that "*De Profundis* suffers from the adulteration of simplicity by eloquence, by an arrogance lurking in its humility and by its disjointed structure. But as a love letter it has all the consistency it needs." Though the purposes driving *De Profundis* may be dual or inconsistent, the continued examination of the letter demonstrates both its literary and autobiographical value to Wilde enthusiasts.

CRITICAL DISCUSSION

In the initial critical response to *De Profundis,* most critics praised it for its (at times) graceful writing style but characterized Wilde's overall stance as insincere. In his 1905 review for the *Times Literary Supplement,* E. V. Lucas wrote that the letter "contains some beautiful prose" but also maintained, "Even in prison, even at the end of everything he most valued, his artifice was too much for him; his poses were too insistent—had become too much a part of the man—to be abandoned."

More recent Wilde scholars have focused on the various views on and versions of *De Profundis.* Because of the circumstances surrounding the letter's original composition, much debate exists about the accuracy of the various versions. When Ross first published the letter, his edits produced a more polished version of Wilde's original text. In the *Collected Works of Oscar Wilde,* published between 1908 and 1922, Ross included more of the original material. He then gave the original letter to the British Museum in 1909, under the condition that it would not be revealed until 1960, when scholars found that it did differ from the previously published versions. The debate among scholars over the letter's different forms and perceived accuracy has extended its critical life.

Modern scholars also debate whether *De Profundis* should be viewed as a love letter or an essay. Unlike Wilde's other literary works, *De Profundis* has not been easy for critics to categorize. In "Oscar Wilde, *De Profundis,* and the Rhetoric of Agency," David Foster characterizes *De Profundis* as having "a precarious place in Oscar Wilde's canon" because "it does not fit neatly into any single genre; it does not resemble any of the other works that made Wilde famous; it is full of irritating inconsistencies and contradictions; and it seems ambiguously aimed at a wider audience than its inscription to Alfred Douglas suggests."

BIBLIOGRAPHY

Sources

Ellman, Richard. *Oscar Wilde*. New York: Vintage, 1988. Print.

Foster, David. "Oscar Wilde, *De Profundis,* and the Rhetoric of Agency." *Papers on Language & Literature* 37.1 (2001): 85. *Literature Resource Center.* Web. 19 Dec. 2012.

Guy, Josephine M., and Ian Small. "Reading *De Profundis.*" *English Literature in Transition 1880–1920*

49.2 (2006): 123+. *Literature Resource Center.* Web. 19 Dec. 2012.

Lucas, E. V. "'De Profundis.'" *Times Literary Supplement* [London] 24 Feb. 1905: 64+. *Times Literary Supplement Historical Archive.* Web. 19 Dec. 2012.

Wilde, Oscar. "De Profundis." *The Complete Letters of Oscar Wilde.* Ed. Rupert Hart-Davis, Vyvyan B. Holland, and Merlin Holland. New York: Henry Holt, 2000. 683–780. Print.

Further Reading

Godwin, Kelli M. "Oscar Wilde's *De Profundis*: A Narrative of Sexual Sin and Forgiveness." *Explicator* 67.1 (2008): 58+. *Literature Resource Center.* Web. 20 Dec. 2012.

Goodenough, Elizabeth. "Oscar Wilde, Victorian Fairy Tales, and the Meanings of Atonement." *Lion and the Unicorn* 23.3 (1999): 336–54. Rpt. in *Nineteenth-Century Literature Criticism.* Ed. Kathy D. Darrow. Vol. 212. Detroit: Gale, 2009. *Literature Resource Center.* Web. 20 Dec. 2012.

Losey, Jay. "The Aesthetics of Exile: Wilde Transforming Dante in *Intentions* and *De Profundis.*" *English Literature in Transition, 1880–1920* 36.4 (1993): 429–50. Rpt. in *Literature Resource Center.* Detroit: Gale, 2013. *Literature Resource Center.* Web. 20 Dec. 2012.

Marcovitch, Heather. "Oscar Wilde." *Nineteenth-Century British Dramatists.* Ed. Angela Courtney. Detroit: Gale, 2008. *Dictionary of Literary Biography.* Vol. 344. *Literature Resource Center.* Web. 20 Dec. 2012.

Maxson, Helen F. "Sincerity and the Subject in Wilde's *De Profundis.*" *Nineteenth-Century Prose* 25.2 (1998): 103+. *Literature Resource Center.* Web. 20 Dec. 2012.

McKenna, Neil. *The Secret Life of Oscar Wilde.* New York: Basic Books, 2005. Print.

Schmidgall, Gary. *The Stranger Wilde: Interpreting Oscar.* New York: Dutton, 1994.

Schulz, David. "Redressing Oscar: Performance and the Trials of Oscar Wilde." *TDR* 40.2 (1996): 37+. *Literature Resource Center.* Web. 20 Dec. 2012.

Wheatcroft, Geoffrey. "Not Green, Not Red, Not Pink: Oscar Wilde Cannot Be Simplified into an Irish Rebel, a Subversive Socialist, or a Gay Martyr." *Atlantic* May 2003: 125+. *Literature Resource Center.* Web. 20 Dec. 2012.

Wilde, Oscar. *The Complete Works of Oscar Wilde: De Profundis; "Epistola: In carcere et vinculis."* Ed. Ian Small. Vol. 2. Oxford: Oxford University Press, 2005. Print.

Jacob Schmitt

PRIMARY SOURCE

EXCERPT FROM *DE PROFUNDIS*

For us there is only one season, the season of sorrow. The very sun and moon seem taken from us. Outside, the day may be blue and gold, but the light that creeps down through the thickly-muffled glass of the small iron-barred window beneath which one sits is grey and niggard. It is always twilight in one's cell, as it is always twilight in one's heart. And in the sphere of thought, no less than in the sphere of time, motion is no more. The thing that you personally have long ago forgotten, or can easily forget, is happening to me now, and will happen to me again to-morrow. Remember this, and you will be able to understand a little of why I am writing, and in this manner writing….

A week later, I am transferred here. Three more months go over and my mother dies. No one knew how deeply I loved and honoured her. Her death was terrible to me; but I, once a lord of language, have no words in which to express my anguish and my shame. She and my father had bequeathed me a name they had made noble and honoured, not merely in literature, art, archaeology, and science, but in the public history of my own country, in its evolution as a nation. I had disgraced that name eternally. I had made it a low by-word among low people. I had dragged it through the very mire. I had given it to brutes that they might make it brutal, and to fools that they might turn it into a synonym for folly.

What I suffered then, and still suffer, is not for pen to write or paper to record. My wife, always kind and gentle to me, rather than that I should hear the news from indifferent lips, travelled, ill as she was, all the way from Genoa to England to break to me herself the tidings of so irreparable, so irremediable, a loss. Messages of sympathy reached me from all who had still affection for me. Even people who had not known me personally, hearing that a new sorrow had broken into my life, wrote to ask that some expression of their condolence should be conveyed to me….

Three months go over. The calendar of my daily conduct and labour that hangs on the outside of my cell door, with my name and sentence written upon it, tells me that it is May….

SOURCE: Wilde, Oscar. "De Profundis." *The Complete Letters of Oscar Wilde.* Ed. Rupert Hart-Davis, Vyvyan B. Holland, and Merlin Holland. New York: Henry Holt, 2000. 683–780.

Detained
A Writer's Prison Diary
Ngũgĩ wa Thiong'o

✦ Key Facts

Time Period:
Late 20th Century

Relevant Historical Events:
Mau Mau rebellion; formation of the Kenya African National Union; Ngũgĩ's imprisonment

Nationality:
Kenyan

Keywords:
incarceration; colonialism; independence

OVERVIEW

Detained: A Writer's Prison Diary, the record of Ngũgĩ wa Thiong'o's detainment without trial in Kenya's Kamĩtĩ Maximum Security Prison, was first published in 1981, three years after his release. The diary focuses on a period just shy of one year but draws on the events leading to Ngũgĩ's arrest and detainment as well as his experiences trying to reclaim his position at the University of Nairobi after his release. In addition to describing his fellow inmates and the guards at the prison, Ngũgĩ incorporates prominent figures in Kenya's history of colonialism and its struggle for independence. He also details his own struggles in Kenya with the vestiges of colonialism as a beneficiary of the colonial educational system and as an educator in a premier Kenyan university. Long before his detainment, he had changed his name from James Ngũgĩ to the more traditional Ngũgĩ wa Thiong'o and had influenced the University of Nairobi to rebrand the English Department. It became the Department of Literature and emphasizes African works. As he makes clear in this and other texts, Ngũgĩ feels Kenya's story is tied inextricably to his own.

Though he did try his hand at writing a diary while in prison, *Detained* was written primarily after Ngũgĩ's release. Instead, while in prison, he wrote the first modern Gikuyu-language novel, *Caitaani Mutharabaini* (*Devil on the Cross*; 1980). Because writing supplies were limited, Ngũgĩ wrote on toilet paper. Between his release and the publication of *Detained*, Ngũgĩ fought what he believed was his unfair and unlawful dismissal from his teaching position at the University of Nairobi, a topic he takes up at length in the appendix to *Detained*, which contains correspondence with university officials regarding his dismissal and the possibility of reinstatement.

HISTORICAL AND LITERARY CONTEXT

Following the Berlin Conference of 1885, Kenya was a protectorate and then a colony of the British Empire until it became independent in 1963. After World War II African soldiers who had fought to defend the British Empire returned to continued oppression at home. They joined with many of their dispossessed compatriots, including Ngũgĩ's brother, to form the Kenya Land and Freedom Army. They fought British rule through the Mau Mau rebellion (1952–56). Following Kenyan independence, Jomu Kenyatta founded the Kenya African National Union (KANU), for a time Kenya's only legal political party, and became the first Kenyan president in 1964. Vice President Daniel arap Moi succeeded Kenyatta after his death in 1978.

Though Ngũgĩ was told he was detained after police officers found contraband books in his possession, a document included in *Detained* shows that Moi had called for Ngũgĩ's detainment a day before the police searched his house. Ngũgĩ postulates that his 1977 Gikuyu-language play *Ngaahika Ndeenda* (*I Will Marry When I Want*) led to his detainment. Cowritten with Ngũgĩ wa Mirii and the local proletariats who acted in and produced the play, *I Will Marry When I Want* focuses on the daily injustices faced by the common people in post-independence Kenya and is considered very radical. Other people, such as journalist James Brooke, believe Ngũgĩ's 1977 novel *Petals of Blood*, which was very critical of postcolonial Kenya, was the impetus for his detainment. The diary and the novel Ngũgĩ wrote in prison serve as acts of resistance against those who would stop his pen.

Ngũgĩ cites many texts within *Detained* as important to his life and work. Chief among them are *The Man Died: The Prison Notes of Wole Soyinka* (1971) and *Ghana: The Autobiography of Kwame Nkrumah* (1957). He wrote that a line from Soyinka's autobiography, "the man dies in all who keep silent in tyranny," stayed with him always. Also formative to his own works were the writings of non-native residents of African countries, including Karen Blixen, Robert Ruark, and Elspeth Huxley, in whose works Ngũgĩ was reminded of the power of words to create "a ruling-class culture of fear." He strove to empower his countrymen through his works by using elements such as the Gikuyu language and satirical humor.

During his time in prison, Ngũgĩ's conviction that writing was a crucial act of resistance grew. With Kenyatta's death came a struggle for power that sparked the additional repression of cultural production and resistance. After writing against these new measures in *Barrel of a Pen: Resistance to Repression in Neo-Colonial Kenya* (1983), Ngũgĩ was labeled a public enemy in Kenya and had to seek exile. He took up

A Kenyan prison in 2009. Kenyan writer Ngũgĩ wa Thiong'o wrote *Detained: A Writer's Prison Diary* after his political imprisonment. © SIEGFRIED MODOLA/ALAMY

the theme of the power of language again in *Decolonising the Mind: The Politics of Language in African Literature* (1986), a text in which he argues that only by writing in African languages can an African writer create authentic African literature free of the crush of colonialism. *Detained* is now regarded as a key text in the struggle for democracy and true independence in Kenya and a turning point in Ngũgĩ's oeuvre.

THEMES AND STYLE

Detained is a testament to Ngũgĩ's rebellion against the state's attempts to silence, isolate, and quell his resistance to oppression by detaining him and effecting his termination from the University of Nairobi. It also is a treatise on the power of writing and solidarity, on the importance of fighting for one's ideals, and on standing up to tyranny. Nkrumah's method of hoarding toilet paper to write upon mirrors Ngũgĩ's own practice and that of the long list of his fellow prisoners who wrote or composed on toilet paper to, as Ngũgĩ puts it, "defy daily the intended detention of [our] mind[s]."

Ngũgĩ believes he was held by those wishing to "teach him a lesson in submission, silence and obedience," and *Detained*, along with the novel he wrote while in prison, is intended to show that he cannot be cowed by imprisonment. Ngũgĩ's diary is also representative of his larger interest in democracy and justice, which, he writes, "can only be achieved when the various interest groups voice their positions and fight for them." Though the book's subtitle is "A Writer's Prison Diary," Ngũgĩ makes no mention of writing a diary until the seventh chapter (of nine), and then calls it a failed experiment. Despite feeling compelled to write while imprisoned, he was inspired not by his daily life but by a one-inch-square piece of contraband newspaper, which prompted him to begin writing *Devil on the Cross*. Unlike most diaries, Ngũgĩ's fits no coherent temporal framework. It presents his experiences not as a day-to-day chronicle but as a reflection of events. His life is woven into his diary as part of a social and historical process rather than the life story of a solitary individual. *Detained* converges many voices, a practice Adele Holoch finds is typical of many of Ngũgĩ's later novels. Holoch argues in her 2012 dissertation that the practice draws attention away from a "controlling center" so that "a multiplicity of perspectives" can engage as authorities on an issue.

The diary is as much about the need to speak as it is about the need for Kenyan economic, educational, and linguistic autonomy. An example of the latter is that "yes" and "no" are set up as polarized choices in a "culture of fear and silence"; however, even in his writing Ngũgĩ refuses those restricted options. Instead of only providing the options "yes" and "no," he sets the Gikuyu words against the English—"yes, no. Ndio, La"—and thus provides more expressive options than previously presumed. Ngũgĩ uses other non-English words occasionally, such as *sjambok,* a type of whip commonly used in African colonies. Never translating these words, the author reminds the reader that English is not the only viable language and that other cultures cannot be wholly excised or written over.

ARRESTING A CHARACTER: THE WARRANT FOR MATAGARI

Returning to satire, a critical mode for which he is well known, in 1986 Ngũgĩ wa Thiong'o published his sixth book, *Matagari wa Njiruungi*. It was released in English as *Matagari* in 1989. Modeled on a Kikuyu folktale by the same name, *Matagari* is a platform in which Ngũgĩ criticizes corruption, the use of Christianity to further imperialism, and native collusions with foreign capitalists in post-independence Kenya. The Gikuyu title, *Matagari wa Njiruungi,* means "the patriot who has survived bullets" and implies that resisting tyranny despite adversity is more patriotic than escaping unscathed through silence.

That *Matagari* was first written in Gikuyu is important, as the language made it accessible to the common people. Writing about the work in *Literature of Africa* (2004), Douglas Killam reports that *Matagari* was "widely read aloud to illiterate people in Kenya" and that Ngũgĩ believed Gikuyu to be the "best medium to alert a generality of people to the degree to which they have been betrayed and are being exploited." The book so incensed Kenyan President Daniel arap Moi that he had a warrant written for the title character Matagari's arrest. Upon realizing *Matagari* was fictional and the character Matagari was therefore beyond his reach, Moi had the novel seized from bookshops and banned from Kenya. Moi also forbade the teaching of Ngũgĩ's works in schools.

CRITICAL DISCUSSION

Initial reactions to Ngũgĩ's diary were positive, but *Detained* has received less critical attention than many of his other works. The diary is primarily discussed in the context of Ngũgĩ's other works, his detainment, and his acts of resistance to oppression. In a 1982 review that covers three of his texts, Victoria Brittain writes in the *London Review of Books* that *Detained* is "a wonderful testimony to friendship" that "stands beside that other great African prison testimony," Soyinka's *The Man Died.*

Though scholars have shown more interest in Ngũgĩ's novels and other essays than in his prison diary, *Detained* is regarded as typical of the best of Ngũgĩ's oeuvre as he is set in the thick of the system he is writing against. Critics such as Simon Gikandi find the author at his best when in the midst of political turmoil. Ngũgĩ is considered a major force in postcolonial literature and political activism and has received seven honorary doctorates.

Detained is frequently discussed in conjunction with other African autobiographies and memoirs, leading Jane Wilkinson to argue in a 1983 piece that "perhaps the greatest value of *Detained* lies in the new dimension it offers in its presentation of a work in progress." Wilkinson calls the work "a clamorous refutation of Makouta M'Boukou's last statement, for in it the author *only* speaks of himself insofar as he is thereby 'necessarily speaking of others.'" Wilkinson highlights the centrality of the subtitle to *Detained*, emphasizing that "*Detained* is not Ngugi wa Thiongo's [sic] *Prison Diary* but *A Writer's Prison Diary:* Ngugi is presenting himself not as an individual but as a writer, the writer that he has always seen as an essential component of his society, engaged not only in 'explaining the world but in changing it.'" In her 1988 article in *Research in African Literatures,* Govind Sharma has a different opinion. Sharma likens *Detained* to a *consolatio* in the tradition of Boethius's *Consolation of Philosophy* (c. 524), finding that while the diary includes an analysis of Kenya's history, it is "primarily a human document" in which Ngũgĩ attempts to console, justify, and understand himself.

BIBLIOGRAPHY

Sources

Brittain, Victoria. "Kenya's Dissident." Rev. of *Devil on the Cross, Detained,* and *Writers in Politics,* by Ngũgĩ wa Thiong'o, and *Ake: The Years of Childhood,* by Wole Soyinka. *London Review of Books.* London Review of Books, 3 June 1982. Web. 12 Dec. 2012.

Brooke, James. "African Writers Note Hazards of the Trade." *New York Times* 9 Nov. 1985: 18. *ProQuest.* Web. 12 Dec. 2012.

Gikandi, Simon. "On Culture and the State: The Writings of Ngũgĩ wa Thiong'o." *Third World Quarterly* 11.1 (1989): 148–56. *JSTOR.* Web. 16 June 2010.

Gikandi, Simon. "Traveling Theory: Ngugi's Return to English." *Research in African Literatures* 31.2 (2000): 194–209. Print.

Holoch, Adele. "The Serious Work of Humor in Postcolonial Literature." Diss. University of Iowa, 2012. Print.

Killam, Douglas. "*Matagari* (1989)." *Literature of Africa.* Westport, Conn.: Greenwood, 2004. 94–97. Print.

Sharma, Govind. "Ngugi's *Detained* as a Modern *Consolatio.*" *Research in African Literatures* 19.4 (1988): 520–28. *JSTOR.* Web. 11 Dec. 2012.

Wilkinson, Jane. "A Writer's Prison Diary: Ngugi wa Thiong'o's *Detained.*" *Africa: Rivista Trimestrale di Studi e Documentazione Dell'Istituto Italiano per l'Africa e l'Oriente* 38.4 (1983): 613–23. *JSTOR.* Web. 9 Dec. 2012.

Further Reading

Cook, David, and Michael Okenimkpe. *Ngugi wa Thiong'o: An Exploration of His Writings.* London: Heinemann, 1983. Print.

Gikandi, Simon. *Ngũgĩ wa Thiong'o.* Cambridge, U.K.: Cambridge University Press, 2000. Print.

Lovesey, Oliver, ed. *Approaches to Teaching the Works of Ngũgĩ wa Thiong'o.* New York: Modern Language Association, 2012. Print.

Lovesey, Oliver. *Ngũgĩ wa Thiong'o.* New York: Twayne, 2000. Print.

Mills, Bronwyn. "Ngugi Wa Thiong'o: Exile and Resistance." *Frigate Zine.* 13 Nov. 2001, n.p. *Frigate.* Web. 25 Nov. 2012.

Nazareth, Peter. Critical Essays on *Ngũgĩ wa Thiong'o.* New York: Twayne, 2000. Print.

"Ngugi wa Thiong'o: Free Thoughts on Toilet Paper." *Index on Censorship* 10.3 (1981): 41–46. *Sage.* Web. 10 Dec. 2012.

Ogude, James. *Ngũgĩ's Novels and African History: Narrating the Nation.* London: Pluto, 1999. Print.

Olney, James. *Tell Me Africa: An Approach to African Literature.* Princeton, N.J.: Princeton University Press, 2003. Print.

Pozo, Michael. "An Interview with Ngugi Wa Thiong'o." *St. John's University Humanities Review* 2.2 (2004). *St. John's English Department.* Web. 3 Dec. 2012.

Williams, Patrick. *Ngũgĩ wa Thiong'o.* Manchester, U.K.: Manchester University Press, 1999. Print.

Katherine Bishop

Diaries of Beatrice Webb

Beatrice Webb

❖ *Key Facts*

Time Period:
Late 19th to Early 20th Century

Relevant Historical Events:
Development of the Labour Party; growth of Victorian-era reform movements

Nationality:
English

Keywords:
women's writing; socialism; poverty

OVERVIEW

The diaries of British social scientist and political reformer Beatrice Webb, written between 1873 and 1943, were edited by Margaret I. Cole and published in several volumes between 1952 and 1959. Another four-volume edition, edited by Norman and Jeanne MacKenzie, was published between 1982 and 1985. A seminal thinker in the fields of sociology and economics, Webb was also an active socialist and an important figure in the development of the Labour Party. Her diaries provide an incisive personal record of important figures and events in the political and intellectual life of Britain during the late nineteenth and early twentieth centuries and are a revealing portrait of a creative and ambitious woman.

Webb's diaries received critical praise both for their penetrating analysis and for their vivid portraits of influential figures in British society, such as Irish playwright George Bernard Shaw and English novelist Virginia Woolf. Published during a period of economic hardship in postwar Britain, Webb's diaries were viewed by some as a call to action for socially responsible economic development. In the decades following their publication, Webb's personal recollections of seventy years of British social history became both a resource and an inspiration to a wide variety of readers, including sociologists, economists, and feminists.

HISTORICAL AND LITERARY CONTEXT

England's Victorian era (1837–1901) was a period of both great prosperity and grinding poverty, along with rampant social injustice. The Industrial Revolution had transformed production but also led to enormous inequities in housing, education, and the treatment of workers. Under Queen Victoria, the British Empire expanded until it controlled almost a sixth of the world, while complex social and ethical issues fomented in its colonies and at home. By the mid-1800s a social reform movement arose in response to what many saw as an alarming rise in poverty and injustice among the working classes. Activists in this movement sought to increase access to the political and educational systems for the working and middle classes, to improve working conditions, and to institute a system of social welfare to protect the poor.

As calls for reform grew stronger, a group of British intellectuals and activists began to investigate solutions to their nation's social problems. In 1884 they formed an organization based on principles of socialism, democracy, and nonviolent political change, which they called the Fabian Society, named after a Roman general. The group included such thinkers as Shaw, Thomas Davidson, and the economist Sidney Webb, Beatrice's eventual husband. Angered by a Parliament that seemed oblivious to the issues of the poor and working class, the Fabians were instrumental in the 1906 formation of the Labour Party to represent the interests of working people in government. The Fabian Society's campaign against poverty is outlined in one of Webb's early, significant writings, the 1909 *Minority Report to the Commission of the Poor Law.*

The Romantic period, which reached its peak during the mid-nineteenth century, fostered the exploration of the individual's inner life and resulted in a surge of journals and autobiographies. Many of these focused on the lives of eminent men, such as John Stuart Mill's 1873 *Autobiography,* but a number of independent-minded women recorded their thoughts and experiences as well. The daughter of poet Samuel Taylor Coleridge told of her isolation and despair as a young mother in *Memoirs and Letters of Sara Coleridge* (1870). The lyrical writing in Dorothy Wordsworth, exhibited in *The Grasmere Journal* (1800–03), influenced the poetry of her famous brother William. In this atmosphere, a diary was a logical outlet for Webb's thoughts.

Both the 1952 and the 1982 editions of Webb's diaries were greeted with respect by critics fascinated by the social scientist's intimate reflections. The diaries not only gave readers background information about an important social movement but also provided a glimpse into the personal lives of literary and political figures and an articulate expression of the frustrations faced by a brilliant woman in a male-dominated society. Still studied as relevant historical, sociological, and feminist documents, Webb's diaries became available online in 2012 as part of the launch of the digital library of the London School of Economics and Political Science, the college that Webb and her husband helped establish with Shaw in 1895.

THEMES AND STYLE

As a Victorian woman, Webb was conflicted between her need for personal expression and her duty to society.

This struggle is apparent in descriptions of her youth, which she called a "quiet and perfectly lonely life" and her desperate "want of employment which makes life almost torture." She is torn between "a mischievous desire to achieve" and the quality she admires in a friend—a "gentle and loving contempt for any *special* work outside the ordinary sphere of a woman's life." She is "haunted by … the vulgar wish to write a novel" but fears such work "would begin in self-indulgence and end in a craving for popularity—for a day's fame!" Webb had higher ambitions, and her diaries give voice to her outrage over injustice, as when she describes the dishonesty of bankers in terms that ring true a century later: "They first make an appalling mess of their own business … and then by the most bare-faced dissimulation and political intrigue they throw out one Cabinet and put in their own nominees in order to recover the cost of their miscalculation by hook or crook from the community as a whole."

Webb kept her diary to "brood over the past and reflect on men and their affairs; I want to summarise my life and see what it all amounts to." A prolific writer of scholarly sociological tracts, she finds in her diaries a comfortable place to expose her desires, fears, and disappointments. Through her writing she comes to terms with her inner conflicts. In describing the painful end of a romantic relationship with British politician Joseph Chamberlain, she writes that she "cannot feel, or think, or see, without a desire to formulate; and then desire is not satisfied unless the formula is as complete as I can make it and expressive of the whole experience."

Unlike her sociological studies based on the scientific method, Webb's journal writing style is imaginative and descriptive, containing both introspection and lively gossip. She demonstrates a novelist's sense of character analysis, describing Labour Prime Minister Ramsay MacDonald as "a magnificent substitute for a leader" and saying of Shaw, her friend and colleague, that his "personality is a work of art, and grows more attractive with age—almost mythical!" Webb shows little interest in the supposedly feminine arenas of fashion and housekeeping, and even her early descriptions of Sidney Webb, who eventually became her husband and literary partner, are unromantic and incisive. "His tiny tadpole body, unhealthy skin, lack of manner, cockney pronunciation, poverty are all against him," she writes. "He has the conceit of a man who has raised himself out of the most insignificant surroundings into a position of power."

CRITICAL DISCUSSION

The first edition of Webb's diaries received solid praise from critics upon its publication in 1952. Some commended the journal's serious political analysis, including Mary Murphy of the *Annals of the American Academy of Political and Social Science,* who noted that "the Diaries have important implications for this generation of Laborites and Conservatives who are struggling to

MY APPRENTICESHIP: BIOGRAPHY OF AN ERA

Martha Beatrice Potter was born in 1858, the eighth of nine daughters of a wealthy Gloucester businessman. Undervalued in a family overburdened with girls and in a society that exalted masculinity, young Beatrice was largely self-educated and possessed an inquiring and perceptive intellect. While still a teenager, she began to keep a journal in which she examined her surroundings, her society, and her developing ideas.

Decades later, having established herself as a leader in a dynamic movement for social change and having married fellow reformist Sidney Webb, Beatrice began to edit her diaries into an autobiographical work describing her early life and career. The resulting book, *My Apprenticeship* (1926), delineates both her "creed," or personal moral and emotional development, and her "craft," or her work as an activist. With chapter headings such as "Character and Circumstance" and "Why I Became a Socialist" and subheadings such as "An Unhappy Childhood" and "Conflicting Aims: Home-keeping and Entertaining versus Self-Development," *My Apprenticeship* paints a nuanced portrait of a woman determined to explore and nurture her social conscience and of the end of the Victorian era itself. Though Webb omits much of her diaries' intimate personal revelations, the biography of her early life is a poignant and influential work.

revive the flagging British economy." Others, such as Edgar Rosen of *Books Abroad,* commented on "Webb's wonderful talent of portraying in a strikingly vivid manner some of the eminent figures of the era between 1912 and 1924." Even greater acclaim greeted the MacKenzies' more extensive edition of the diaries in the 1980s. Jane Marcus of the *New York Times* described Webb as "a diarist with the obvious gifts of a novelist," and Barbara Caine, reviewing the first volume for *Victorian Studies,* wrote that "the combination of fascinating social commentary with the frank and moving account of … [Webb's] struggle to establish an identity … and a place in the world make this volume of her diary quite compelling."

The journals have continued to be valued for their unique contribution to both the history of her times and the development of the modern sciences of sociology and economic theory in which she played so large a part. In 2001 the MacKenzies released an abridged edition of Webb's diaries, bringing her observations to an even wider audience. Webb also based a number of her other autobiographical writings on her diaries, including *My Apprenticeship* (1926), about her early political career, and *Our Partnership* (1948), which describes her working relationship with Sidney.

Scholars have found a wealth of material to study in Webb's personal chronicles. Writing for *English*

Historical Review, British historian Eric J. Hobsbawm described the 1952 edition as "one of the most impressive works of their kind in our literature," asserting that "the historian who wishes to understand the British labour movement will neglect Beatrice Webb at his or her peril." In 1982 Jane Lewis examined the diaries in feminist terms, concluding that "a sensitive rereading of the famous Diary can illuminate many of the tensions experienced by middle class Victorian women." Modern scholars continue to depend on Webb's diaries as an authoritative historical source. Angela K. Smith included excerpts from Webb's journal in *Women's Writing of the First World War: An Anthology* (2000), and Sylvia Nasar made extensive use of the diaries in profiling Webb for her 2011 study *Grand Pursuit: The Story of Economic Genius.*

BIBLIOGRAPHY

Sources

Caine, Barbara. "Beatrice Webb and Her Diary." Rev. of *The Diary of Beatrice Webb,* by Beatrice Webb. *Victorian Studies* 27.1 (1983): 81–89. *JSTOR.* Web. 15 Dec. 2012.

Hobsbawm, Eric J. Rev. of *Diaries, 1912–1924,* by Beatrice Webb. *English Historical Review* 68.267 (1953): 293–95. *JSTOR.* Web. 16 Dec. 2012.

Lewis, Jane. "Re-reading Beatrice Webb's Diary." *History Workshop* 16 (1983): 143–46. *JSTOR.* Web. 16 Dec. 2012.

Marcus, Jane. "A Work of Her Own." Rev. of *The Diary of Beatrice Webb,* by Beatrice Webb. *New York Times* 12 Dec 1982: BR9. *ProQuest Historical Newspapers.* Web. 12 Dec. 2012.

Murphy, Mary E. Rev. of *Diaries, 1912–1924,* by Beatrice Webb. *Annals of the American Academy of Political and Social Science* 285 (1953): 211–12. *JSTOR.* Web. 14 Dec. 2012.

Onslow, Barbara. "The Diaries of Beatrice Webb." *NWSA Journal* 15.3 (2003): 205–08. *Literature Resource Center.* Web. 12 Dec. 2012.

Rosen, Edgar R. Rev. of *Diaries, 1912–1924,* by Beatrice Webb. *Books Abroad* 29.2 (1955): 235. *JSTOR.* Web. 13 Dec. 2012.

Webb, Beatrice. *My Apprenticeship.* 1926. Cambridge, U.K.: Cambridge University Press, 1980. Print.

———. *Diaries.* London School of Economics Digital Library. Web. 3 Jan. 2013.

Further Reading

Nasar, Sylvia. "Miss Potter's Profession: Webb and the Housekeeping State." *Grand Pursuit: The Story of Economic Genius.* New York, Simon & Schuster, 2011. 91–139. Print.

Romano, Mary Ann. *Beatrice Webb (1858–1943): The Socialist with a Sociological Imagination.* Lewiston, N.Y.: Edwin Mellen, 1998. Print.

Seymour-Jones, Carole. *Beatrice Webb: A Life.* Chicago: I. R. Dee, 1992. Print.

Smith, Angela K. *Women's Writing of the First World War: An Anthology.* Manchester, U.K.: Manchester University Press, 2000. Print.

Tina Gianoulis

The Good Man of Nanking
The Diaries of John Rabe
John Rabe

OVERVIEW

First published in 1998, *The Good Man of Nanking: The Diaries of John Rabe* provides a historical account of the infamous 1937 massacre in Nanking, China, or "rape of Nanking," and also records the heroic efforts of Rabe (1883–1950), who protected some 250,000 Chinese citizens, including 650 on his own property. The diaries begin in September 1937, extensively chronicling the atrocities the German-born Rabe witnessed as Japanese soldiers looted, raped, and killed the Chinese who were not able to flee the city. It also recounts the author's impressions of the fall of Berlin and its Soviet occupation. *The Good Man of Nanking* is a crucial eyewitness account of a historic event that was, for many years, unrecognized.

Rabe wrote almost 1,200 pages recording the events that took place in Nanking during the six weeks following the Japanese invasion but was prevented of speaking of his experiences when he returned to Nazi Germany. His diaries remained obscure for many years, until a Chinese American author, Iris Chang, learned of Rabe's existence from Nanking citizens and sought out his granddaughter, who had the texts in her attic. They were edited by Erwin Wickert, a German scholar who served as an ambassador to China from 1976 to 1980 and also claimed to have discovered them. The diaries were immediately hailed as crucial to building the historical record, although controversy ensued over the accuracy of his estimates of the number of deaths and rapes that took place.

HISTORICAL AND LITERARY CONTEXT

Rabe worked for thirty years in Nanking as a businessman for the German company Siemens. At the time, many foreign businesses had an interest in capturing the rapidly modernizing Chinese market. Meanwhile, Japan was intent upon annexing China for its many natural resources. In 1937 Japan captured Shanghai and moved north to Nanking, China's capital city. While Siemens gave its employees permission to flee, Rabe chose to stay to try to protect his company's commercial interests and the people of the country where he had lived for so long.

Because Japan was an ally of Germany and Rabe was a Nazi Party member, he believed he would be able to prevent many atrocities: with the twenty-seven other Westerners who remained in the city, he formed the "Nanking Security Zone," a six-square-kilometer area for Chinese civilians in which some 250,000 people managed to gain sanctuary. Rabe also wrote and cabled the Chinese, Japanese, and German government to try to draw attention to the horrors he was witnessing. His diary includes copies of the many letters, telegrams, and reports he sent and is clearly meant to serve as a record. Indeed, Rabe wrote to Adolf Hitler himself, believing that if he knew of the atrocities taking place in Nanking, he would act to stop them.

While Rabe sought to save rather than exterminate, his diaries are quite similar to the obsessive records kept by the Nazis. The Nazis listed every detail about the inmates in their concentration camps; Rabe provides detailed accounts of the number of people shot or raped each day. In this way, his writing is quite different from the diaries and memoirs about World War I that were being published at the time, as these works focus on emotional reactions to the death and destruction witnessed. Rabe's writing also bears little resemblance to the diaries of contemporaneous Westerners living or traveling in China, which either highlight its mysteriousness or mourn its backwardness. In contrast, Rabe, though slightly condescending at times, portrays the Chinese as valued colleagues and neighbors.

When Rabe returned to Germany in 1938, he traveled around the country lecturing about and displaying pictures of the atrocities taking place in Nanking. He was arrested by the Gestapo and jailed for three days, after which he was forbidden to speak of Nanking. Rabe was forgotten until the revival of interest in Nanking in the late 1980s. Since then, his diaries have been seen as a valuable part of the historical record. Besides the publication of *The Good Man of Nanking*, several films have been made based on Rabe's experiences.

THEMES AND STYLE

The Good Man of Nanking is focused on recording the many outrages Rabe witnessed during the Nanking massacre, as well as his compassion for the people of China. He writes of his own horror at the atrocities

❖ Key Facts

Time Period:
Mid-20th Century

Relevant Historical Events:
Nanking Massacre; Second Sino-Japanese War

Nationality:
German

Keywords:
war; massacre; invasion

A statue in honor of John Rabe outside of his former residence in Nanjing, China. © CHRISTINE KLEIN/ALAMY

he saw: "You can't breathe for sheer revulsion when you keep finding the bodies of women with bamboo poles thrust up their vaginas." Additionally, he tries to explain his motivations for staying. In a conversation with a Japanese major who asks why he is remaining when so many others have fled, he says, "I have been living here in China for over thirty years." He continues:

> My kids and grandchildren were born here, and I am happy and successful here. I have always been treated well by the Chinese people, even during the war. If I had spent thirty years in Japan and were treated just as well by the Japanese people, you can be assured that, in a time of emergency, such as the situation China faces now, I would not leave the side of the people in Japan.

In a private letter from October 1942 that is excerpted in the foreword of *The Good Man of Nanking*, Rabe reveals his motives for keeping his diary, writing that "it is a record of facts, a diary, which was not written for the public but for my wife and the closest circle of my family." Initially Rabe compiled 2,000 pages of his own observations and public notices, newspaper clippings, letters, telegrams, and photographs, which he then edited into a 400-page document. In a 2001 review of *The Good Man of Nanking*, Xu Xin writes that "even if we accept the notion that he originally wrote for private reasons, he certainly had some purpose when he edited and assembled what he considered the most important entries from the original version of his diaries into two volumes…. Regardless of Rabe's intent, his diaries save the victims of the Nanking massacre from oblivion."

The most notable stylistic element of *The Good Man* is the unemotional way Rabe writes of the atrocities he witnessed. He frequently turns to understatement to make his points, as when he writes that "one might well believe the Japanese Army is made up of ex-convicts. Normal people do not behave this way." Even in discussing his "revulsion" at rapes, his focus is more on facts than emotion. For example, in one of the many reports he forwarded to the British embassy and included in his diary, he writes: "Case 16—A Chinese girl named Loh, who, with her mother and brother, was living in one of the Refugee Centers in the Refugee Zone, was shot through the head and killed by a Japanese soldier. The girl was 14 years old. The incident occurred near the Kuling Ssu, a noted temple on the border of the Refugee Zone."

CRITICAL DISCUSSION

Many of the initial reviews of *The Good Man of Nanking* emphasized the human-interest element of Rabe's story. Because he was a member of the Nazi party, Rabe was referred to as the "Oskar Schindler of China." Fara Warner wrote in a 1998 *Wall Street Journal* review that the entries in *The Good Man of Nanking* "reveal a simple man who is at best just a human driven by the duty he feels toward people with whom he has lived and worked for 30 years. That such acts of kindness could come from someone who himself subscribed to a hate-filled political ideology makes his case all the more strange and interesting."

There is little scholarly writing about *The Good Man of Nanking* specifically, but it has nevertheless become an important historical document. For almost half a century, the rape of Nanking was virtually ignored. Not only did Japanese history books gloss over the event, but it was also seldom discussed in China due to political concerns. *The Good Man of Nanking* was rediscovered when Chang was writing her work on the Nanking Massacre and is one of the few eyewitness sources in existence. Chang conveys a Japanese historian's claim that "the meaning of this report is significant in the sense that a German, whose country was allied with Japan, depicts the atrocity of Nanking objectively."

However, there continues to be scholarly dissent over what events actually took place in Nanking, as well as the actual death tolls. As Sheryl Wudunn writes in an article for the *New York Times Book Review*:

> One of the most intriguing aspects of these diaries is that while Rabe recounts tortures, rapes and mass murders by the Japanese, he appears not to have seen many of the atrocities that are commonly described by the Chinese themselves. There are no accounts of live burials, mass disembowelments, deaths by freezing or death by being eaten alive by dogs.

Wudunn adds that Rabe's estimate of the death toll was about 150,000 fewer than Chinese claims. Chang, however, writes that Rabe "never had time to conduct a systematic body count because his primary concern was to protect the thousands of Chinese refugees who sought shelter in the Nanking safety zone. Moreover, he left Nanking before the massacre was over."

BIBLIOGRAPHY

Sources

Chang, Iris. *The Rape of Nanking: The Forgotten Holocaust of World War II.* New York: Basic, 1997. Print.

Chang, Iris. Rev. of *The Rape of Nanking,* by John Rabe. *New York Times Book Review* Jan. 10 1999: 2. *Academic Search Complete.* Web. 5 Dec. 2012.

Rabe, John, and Erwin Wickert. *The Good Man of Nanking: The Diaries of John Rabe.* New York: A. A. Knopf, 1998. Print.

Warner, Fara. "Bookmarks." Rev. of *The Good Man of Nanking: The Diaries of John Rabe,* by John Rabe. *Wall Street Journal* 20 Nov. 1998: W6. *Academic Search Complete.* Web. 5 Dec. 2012.

Wudunn, Sheryl. "The Good Nazi." *New York Times Book Review* 13 Dec. 1999: 2. *Academic Search Complete.* Web. 5 Dec. 2012.

Xu Xin. Rev. of *The Good Man of Nanking: The Diaries of John Rabe,* by John Rabe. *Holocaust and Genocide Studies* 15 (2001): 331–34. Print.

Further Reading

Chen, David. "At the Rape of Nanking: A Nazi Who Saved Lives." *New York Times* 12 Dec. 1996: A3. *Academic Search Complete.* Web. 17 Dec. 2012.

Dai, Jinhua. "I Want to Be Human: A Story of China and the Human." *Social Text* 29.4 (2012): 129–50. *Academic Search Complete.* Web. 5 Dec. 2012.

"THE GOOD NAZI" AND CHINA

John Rabe used his Nazi Party membership to save countless Chinese citizens during the Nanking Massacre. Rabe wore his swastika armband as he walked the streets of the Nanking Security Zone to keep the attackers at bay. Various justifications have been offered for Rabe's membership in the Nazi Party, from expediency (he founded a school in Nanking in the 1930s and needed to be a party member in order to garner the permits) to fervent belief (the fact that Rabe wrote a letter to Adolf Hitler to try to save Nanking suggests that he did think the Nazi Party was fighting for equality and justice).

Rabe's Nazi membership cost him greatly after the war: he was arrested by both Soviet and British troops and later had to go through a process of "de-Nazification," which depleted his savings. Upon hearing this, the people of Nanking, who had not forgotten his efforts, immediately raised money that the mayor of Nanking took to Rabe. Nanking continued to send monthly food packets to him until the communist takeover of China.

French, Howard W. "Letter from China: China Hails a Good Nazi and Makes Japan Take Notice." *New York Times* 15 Mar. 2006: 4. *Newspaper Source Plus.* Web. 6 Dec. 2012.

Pye, Lucian W. Rev. of *The Good Man of Nanking: The Diaries of John Rabe,* by John Rabe. *Foreign Affairs* March/April 1999: 157. *Academic Search Complete.* Web. 5 Dec. 2012

Wing, Tek L. "At the Foot of Mufu Mountain." *Amerasia Journal* 32.3 (2006). Print.

Abigail Mann

An Interrupted Life
The Diaries of Etty Hillesum
Etty Hillesum

✦ Key Facts

Time Period:
Mid-20th Century

Relevant Historical Events:
Holocaust; World War II; Nazi occupation of the Netherlands

Nationality:
Dutch

Keywords:
Holocaust; ethics; persecution

OVERVIEW

First published in the United States in 1984, *An Interrupted Life: The Diaries of Etty Hillesum* covers Etty (Esther) Hillesum's life from 1941 to 1943 and is part of the rich body of Holocaust writing that continues to fascinate modern scholars. In the collection, Hillesum moves from focusing on romantic affairs to responding to the Holocaust. It records her developing identity—as a woman and as a Jew—and her maturing spirituality. Unlike some other Holocaust diaries, Hillesum's exhibits hopefulness, compassion, and emotional variety despite persecution and deprivation. Instead of hating or fleeing the Nazis, Hillesum proclaims a love for all humanity that derives from her desire to achieve fellowship with God.

Hillesum, a Jew, was living in Amsterdam when World War II began in 1939. She worked in Westerbork, a Nazi holding camp in northeastern Netherlands, and from there was deported to the extermination camp Auschwitz in southern Poland with her parents and older brother. Hillesum died in the gas chamber on November 30, 1943. Her diaries were first published in 1981 in the Netherlands. They were translated into English and published in the United Kingdom in 1983, with the first U.S. edition appearing in 1984. They are abridged in every version, though subsequent editions usually include Hillesum's letters. Since the book's initial publication, *An Interrupted Life* has received widespread attention from Holocaust scholars. The author's unusual response to the Nazis has garnered intense critical debate, with some scholars even refusing to classify her diary as a Holocaust narrative. It has become an integral part of the Holocaust canon, however, fascinating both academic writers and nonacademic readers.

HISTORICAL AND LITERARY CONTEXT

An Interrupted Life does more than respond to Jewish suffering in the Netherlands during Nazi occupation. It also embodies the value placed on the individual psyche that was prevalent in mid-twentieth-century Europe. Having earned a law degree and studied Slavonic languages and psychology at the University of Amsterdam, Hillesum was familiar with contemporary intellectual culture. Her writing incorporates introspective musings derived from psychologists such as Sigmund Freud. This interior stance becomes more complex when she tries to readjust this ethical framework to respond to Nazi cruelty.

During an age of psychological enlightenment, Hillesum tests the boundaries of traditional gender roles. Her diary frequently references her romantic affairs, particularly with Julius Spier, a German Jew who had been trained by Carl Jung as a psychotherapist. Though the Nazis invade and occupy the Netherlands in 1940, Hillesum rarely mentions them until their persecution becomes particularly cruel in 1942. Then she turns from romance to trying to fathom the proper moral and ethical response to persecution. Her letters from Westerbork to friends in Amsterdam reflect deep sympathy with Jews placed on the train to Auschwitz. Both her letters and diary end when Hillesum is deported in 1943.

Literature is an integral part of Hillesum's mental development. She frequently mentions the Bible, Russian novelist Fyodor Dostoyevsky, German-language poet Rainer Maria Rilke, and Christian thinker St. Augustine as she attempts to create meaning out of the chaos that surrounds her. Indeed, like the young Jewish girl Anne Frank, whose diary details daily life sometimes to the exclusion of external suffering (1942–44), Hillesum focuses more on burgeoning spirituality than on Nazi brutality. Her integration of Jewish and Christian theologies often baffles critics, as does her insistence on hopefulness and pity despite death's grim inevitability. In this sense, Hillesum is similar to contemporary Jewish diarist Hannah Senesh and French activist and writer Simone Weil, who both focus their works more on mystical spirituality than on fear or survival. Yet Hillesum is also relentlessly active, as her letters reveal, seeking persistently to make God's mercy a reality in Westerbork, where inhuman pain prevails.

An Interrupted Life is particularly exceptional for the unusual combination of interiority and exteriority under the pressure of persecution. As a result, like other spiritually minded World War II authors, including German philosopher Hannah Arendt and Protestant theologian Dietrich Bonhoeffer, Hillesum has a transcendent voice in Holocaust literature. As academic Marie Syrkin writes in a 1984 review of

An Interrupted Life, "Her dialogue with God, her religious transcendence, account for the great impression this diary made in Holland when it appeared in 1981. Affiliated neither with synagogue nor church, and not a mystic in the strict sense, Etty escapes categories." *An Interrupted Life* has not only been part of the ongoing academic dialogue about Holocaust writing, Jewishness, and female spirituality but has also been lauded in popular culture. Her inclusion in religious and special interest magazines, such as *U.S. Christian* and *Women's Health,* exemplifies this wider appeal.

THEMES AND STYLE

An Interrupted Life tackles themes that might appear ancillary to the Holocaust, such as femininity, philosophy, ethical dilemmas, and faith. At times Hillesum seems detached from Nazi persecution, even complicit with it: she was a cleric for the Nazi-organized Jewish Council at Westerbork. Yet her intellectual convictions only reinforce her desire to alleviate the terrors of the Holocaust: "I want to be sent to every one of the camps that lie scattered all over Europe.... I want to understand what is happening and share my knowledge with as many as I can possibly reach." She chooses to go to Westerbork to participate in the suffering there and endures overwork, anemia, and severe headaches. Though Hillesum's philosophizing may occasionally feel self-righteous, she constantly questions her ethical position. Staring covertly at the German guards, she rejects her earlier refusal to fear the Nazis: "I have never been so frightened of anything in my life.... I sank to my knees with the words that preside over human life: And God made man after His likeness. That passage spent a difficult morning with me."

The daughter of well-educated parents, Hillesum began writing to grow intellectually. She confesses that her ideas "may seem rather clumsily put, but I know what I mean." As persecution worsened, however, her goal became to be a witness to her life and times. As scholar Yasmine Ergas notes in her review of *An Interrupted Life,* Hillesum's writings "are not 'camp' stories.... Instead, they tell of the attempt to maintain or construct normalcy in a rapidly bestializing civil society." Hillesum's writing functions both as an index for her interior experience and as a memorial to her dying people. Though she did not explicitly write for publication, her desire to "[mark] well everything that happens in this world" has been realized with the posthumous popularity of her writing.

Hillesum's writing style balances between matter-of-factness and exalted, biblical language. In *An Interrupted Life* she never shies from detailing her thoughts. She opens her diary with "Here goes, then"

Wooden watchtower at former World War II concentration camp Westerbork, Drenthe, Netherlands, photographed in July 2011. In her diaries and letters, Etty Hillesum describes the horrors of life at Westerbork. © ALLARD SCHAGER/ALAMY

AN INTERRUPTED LIFE'S ARTISTIC REINCARNATIONS

Like Anne Frank's *Diary of a Young Girl,* Etty Hillesum's *An Interrupted Life* has been the catalyst for many creative adaptations. Hillesum has inspired poems by Irish language author Dolores Stewart and Israeli poet Tal Nitzan. In his 1991 article "Life Indestructible," Cyrus Cassells gives the longest poetic tribute to Hillesum. Addressing her directly, he says, "You've haunted me—/ I can't stop hearing your voice." Toward the end of his poem, he echoes scholars' attempts to apply Hillesum to the twenty-first-century world. For him this move is personal: "Today I went out into the sun, / With your injunction to *feel,* / To refuse every pill, every soporific." Throughout, Cassells quotes Hillesum's diary, breaking passages into short lines to integrate them into his poem.

In the twenty-first century, *An Interrupted Life* provided material for Susan Stein's one-woman play, *Etty,* which was nominated for an Amnesty International Freedom of Expression Award in 2009. Another play based on Hillesum's writing, *The Wrestling Patient,* by Kirk Lynn (in collaboration with Anne Gottlieb and Katie Pearl), was a National Endowment for the Arts finalist for Outstanding New American Play in 2008. Hillesum's life even inspired "The Thinking Heart: The Life and Loves of Etty Hillesum" by American poet Martin Steingesser, who set sections of her diary and letters to music.

and proceeds to discuss frankly her sexual experience. Later, she muses about her response to seeing "a beautiful, well-groomed, wholly feminine, albeit dull woman," who makes her "want to be … a desirable plaything for a man." Detailing every mental step, she concludes that this is "only a primitive instinct." As politics begin to impinge on her psychological scrutiny, her language becomes more spiritual. Though she is a Jew, she often uses Christian modes of expression. As she witnesses suffering and suffers herself, she reaches new spiritual heights. In elevated, sacramental language, her last entry conveys her compassion for all humans: "I have broken my body like bread and shared it out among men…. We should be willing to act as balm for all wounds."

CRITICAL DISCUSSION

Responses to *An Interrupted Life* at each publication were glowing. Syrkin's review mentions the "great impression this diary made in Holland" in 1981. When the U.S. edition appeared in 1984, reviewers were no less impressed. In a profile of the author in *Twentieth-Century Literary Criticism,* scholar Terrence Des Pres comments, "Holocaust documents are supposed to be artless and wounded, but the diaries of this young Dutch Jew are written with the interior richness and woven design of a Jamesian novel." Just as Hillesum uses adjectives such as "austere" and "fervent" to describe Augustine, one of her favorite authors, reviewers applied this language to her, giving her the pedigree of great confessional writers from Augustine to Weil.

Since the initial reviews, scholars have debated the relationship between *An Interrupted Life* and other Holocaust narratives. On the one hand, many critics—including Ergas in 1987, Rachel Brenner in 1997, and Doris Bergen in 1998—have contextualized Hillesum among female Holocaust authors, praising these women for their steadfast hope and humanity despite persecution. Hillesum has been included on syllabi for college classes about female spirituality and World War II history. In addition, many artists and general readers have sympathized with Hillesum as the embodiment of positive response to suffering, turning to her for inspirational quotes and creative impetus. On the other hand, Lawrence Langer and David Patterson, in books published in 1995 and 1999, respectively, dismissed her as a Holocaust writer since she does not depict the terrors of concentration camps.

Recent scholarship has plumbed Hillesum's spiritual pilgrimage, her awareness of how gender and race construct her identity, and her ethical concerns. Special emphasis has been placed on her spirituality, as demonstrated in books such as *Anne Frank and Etty Hillesum* (1998) by Denise de Costa and *Dark Night Spirituality* (1995) by Peter King. In a 2012 essay titled "'Heroism on an Empty Stomach': Weil and Hillesum on Love and Happiness amid the Holocaust," Christian ethics professor Timothy P. Jackson discusses these women's struggles to determine the balance between altruism and self-love. Jackson claims, "When allowed to correct one another, Weil and Hillesum show us … how Christian agapism can refuse both hatred and false security, even in an era of terrorism and torture." He thus uses Hillesum to model an ethical response to current events.

BIBLIOGRAPHY

Sources

Erspamer, Peter R. "Hillesum, Etty." *Reference Guide to Holocaust Literature.* Ed. Thomas Riggs. Detroit: St. James, 2002. 141–42. *Gale Virtual Reference Library.* Web. 5 Dec. 2012.

"Etty Hillesum (1914–1943)." *Twentieth-Century Literary Criticism.* Ed. Laurie Di Mauro. Vol. 49. Detroit: Gale Research, 1993. 170–90. *Literature Criticism Online.* Web. 3 Dec. 2012.

Hillesum, Etty. *An Interrupted Life and Letters from Westerbork.* Trans. Arnold J. Pomerans. New York: Holt, 1996. Print.

"The Holocaust and the Atomic Bomb: Fifty Years Later." *Contemporary Literary Criticism.* Ed. Brigham Narins. Vol. 91. Detroit: Gale Research, 1996. 331–82. *Literature Criticism Online.* Web. 3 Dec. 2012.

Jackson, Timothy P. "'Heroism on an Empty Stomach': Weil and Hillesum on Love and Happiness amid the Holocaust." *Journal of Religious Ethics* 40.1 (2012): 72–98. *JSTOR.* Web. 6 Dec. 2012.

Kamel, Rose. "Interrupted Lives, Inner Resources: The Diaries of Hannah Senesh and Etty Hillesum." *Women's Studies Quarterly* 17.3–4 (1989): 45–58. *JSTOR.* Web. 6 Dec. 2012.

Further Reading

Brenner, Rachel Feldhay. *Writing as Resistance: Four Women Confronting the Holocaust: Edith Stein, Simone Weil, Anne Frank and Etty Hillesum.* University Park: Pennsylvania State University Press, 1997. Print.

Cassells, Cyrus. "Life Indestructible." *Kenyon Review* 13.4 (1991): 32–39. *JSTOR.* Web. 5 Dec. 2012.

Coetsier, Meins G. S. "Etty Hillesum and the Flow of Presence: A Voegelinian Analysis." *Eric Voegelin Institute Series in Political Philosophy: Studies in Religion and Politics.* Columbia: University of Missouri Press, 2008. Print.

De Costa, Denise. *Anne Frank and Etty Hillesum: Inscribing Spirituality and Sexuality.* Trans. Mischa F. C. Hoynick and Robert E. Chesal. New Brunswick, N.J.: Rutgers University Press, 1998. Print.

King, Peter. *Dark Night Spirituality: Thomas Merton, Dietrich Bonhoeffer, Etty Hillesum: Contemplation and the New Paradigm.* London: SPCK, 1995. Print.

Langer, Lawrence L. *Admitting the Holocaust: Collected Essays.* New York: Oxford University Press, 1995. Print.

Leonard, Joan. "Teaching Introductory Feminist Spirituality: Tracing the Trajectory through Women Writers." *Journal of Feminist Studies in Religion* 6.2 (1990): 121–35. *JSTOR.* Web. 5 Dec. 2012.

Nitzan, Tal. "I Remember Etty Hillesum." *Bridges* 12.2 (2007): 65–66. *JSTOR.* Web. 6 Dec. 2012.

Patterson, David. *Along the Edge of Annihilation: The Collapse and Recovery of Life in the Holocaust Diary.* Seattle: University of Washington Press, 1999. Print.

Stewart, Dolores. "Etty Hillesum—Cín Lae 1943." *Comhar* 64.5 (2004): 11. *JSTOR.* Web. 6 Dec. 2012.

Evelyn Reynolds

Journal of George Fox

George Fox

❖ Key Facts

Time Period:
Mid-17th Century

Relevant Historical Events:
Founding of Quakerism; persecution and imprisonment of Fox

Nationality:
English

Keywords:
Quakerism; incarceration; persecution

OVERVIEW

Encompassing the whole of George Fox's life, from his childhood in the 1620s to his death in 1691, the *Journal* follows the founder of Quakerism as he withstands incarceration, melancholy, and political oppression. The first volume of the *Journal* was originally published in 1694 as part of a community effort by the Quaker Friends to memorialize their leader. After opening "testimonies" about Fox's character and life by his wife, Margaret; colonist William Penn; and editor Thomas Ellwood, the volume features his dictated autobiography, along with decades of letters and messages to community members. Through these collected documents, Fox emerges as a confident spiritual leader, asking his followers to turn to their own inward experiences of Christ's light in order to weather adversity.

For the early Friends, Fox's *Journal* became a written record of his beliefs, his practices, and historical developments. Originally conceived toward the end of his life, it is not a day-by-day account of events, written as they occurred, but instead a revised and edited version of remembered occurrences. As H. Larry Ingle points out in his profile of the author in the *Oxford Dictionary of National Biography,* the *Journal* glosses over some crucial figures in the development of Quakerism, including Jamaican minister Elizabeth Hooten and Fox's rival James Naylor. However, the *Journal* does present a vibrant portrait of Fox's inner life, such as his bouts of depression and the "openings" that allow him to experience God's truth. As such, the *Journal* stands as a record of one man's religious perseverance in the face of frequent imprisonments and governmental persecution.

HISTORICAL AND LITERARY CONTEXT

During the seventeenth century, religion and political turmoil were deeply interlinked. With the rise of Oliver Cromwell and his New Model Army, England fell under the leadership of a militant Protestant government, one that executed King Charles I in 1649. The country foundered, however, after Cromwell's death in 1658. In 1660, with the return of the monarchy in the person of Charles II, the ruling class began to embrace a more conservative style of religious practice. Religious thinkers were faced with a dilemma: should they persist in the more radical mold of Cromwell or turn again toward institutionalized Anglicanism?

As the leader of a religious movement that was even more radical than Cromwell's, Fox had to negotiate the changing political climate in his speeches and writings. Fox famously maintained that Friends would not take up arms in a conflict, but he disliked paying tithes to support institutionalized religion and took exception to the idea of any mandatory, nationalized church allegiance. These positions made him unpopular with both the Cromwellians and the returning Royalists, and they led to his arrest on at least nine occasions. During his time in jail, Fox focused on suffering patiently and productively: he wrote many letters to his followers (and jailers), forming the groundwork for his *Journal*.

While religious struggle was a daily, political fact of life in the seventeenth century, literary autobiographies began to feature the inward struggles of individual Christians, who wrestled with fear, doubt, despair, and feelings of inadequacy. The most famous of these autobiographies was John Bunyan's *Grace Abounding to the Chief of Sinners* (1666), but members of Fox's Society of Friends, such as William Caton, also wrote and published similar documents. Adhering to the movement's focus on plainness and introspection, Quaker spiritual autobiographies tended to feature simple prose that explored thoughts and feelings. Like Fox's *Journal,* these autobiographies highlight the mercy and ongoing intervention of God as a person progresses toward a state of perfection.

In addition to its focus on Fox's inner life, the *Journal* encapsulates both the geographical reach and the local practice of early Quakerism. Summarizing his extensive travels, including trips to Ireland, Europe, and North America, the *Journals* portray a vibrant, expanding community that organized itself with monthly "meetings." Absent leaders or Friends could send letters to be publicly read during these meetings, creating a sense of unity and common ground between far-flung groups. One example is Fox's own epistle "All Friends every where this is the Word of the Lord unto you All" (1683).

THEMES AND STYLE

Within the *Journal* itself, Fox offers a personal story about suffering patiently through adversity. Framing himself as an "instrument" of God, he tries to convince his readers that this chosen status is uncomfortable but productive. This path creates the grounds for faithful service and ultimate Christian perfection, even as it also exposes him to physical beatings, unkindness from "Christian" priests, and prolonged illnesses in jail. At stake for Fox in enduring these challenges is the development of an inward stillness that enables him to sense and learn from God. He hopes to instill a similar sense of quietness in his listeners and readers; he is "endeavouring to bring [his listeners] from Self-performances, Testifying and turning to the Light of Christ within them, and encouraging them to wait in Patience to feel the Power of it to stir in their Hearts, that their Knowledge and Worship of God might stand in the Power of an Endless Life."

Fox was motivated to capture moments of inward development or insight, which he calls "openings." Inspired by the spirit of God, these are revelations of divine truth, supplying Fox with information about his missionary outreach and his own relationship with God. By recording the insights from these openings in a published work, Fox implies that God is still revealing his truth to chosen humans, in a way that is just as authoritative as scriptural revelation. Moreover, he uses his *Journal* to share this authoritative truth with the Friends, who are all encouraged to look "inward" to access similar revelations. Politically, this was an extremely dangerous move because it gave individual Friends a great measure of religious authority: anyone could receive an opening from the spirit, regardless of rank, gender, or membership in an officially sanctioned church.

As a dictated work, the *Journal* reads in a simple and straightforward manner, illustrating ideal Quaker language. A "yea" is simply a "yea," and a "nay" is simply a "nay," without any embellishments, oaths, or caveats. Fox, however, does use a specific set of Quaker vocabulary to describe religious events. A conversion experience is the act of becoming "convinced," and non-Quaker churches are called "steeple-houses," highlighting their unnecessary adornment. The style of the work changes in the middle, as Hilary Hinds points out in her essay "'And the Lord's Power Was over All'": from a spiritual narrative of doubt and anxiety, the text emerges as a confident, outward-looking exploration after Fox embraces the idea that "Christ had died for all men … and had enlightened all." The *Journal* also contains epistolary extracts that feature an oral style characterized by repeated phrases (such as "the Seed") and many clauses in the same sentence.

CRITICAL DISCUSSION

The initial reaction to Fox's *Journal* was polarized and political. Writing in 1700, Edward Beckham called Fox's work and other Quaker documents explosively "blasphemous and seditious" and threatening to both religious and governmental officials. These types of strong reactions underscored the precarious legal position of the Friends, for example, they had only won the right to assemble for meetings in 1689, five years before the publication of the *Journal*. Orthodox Anglicans

Illustration depicting Quaker founder George Fox talking with women in a field. © NORTH WIND PICTURE ARCHIVES/ALAMY

also felt threatened by Fox's work, which accuses them of hypocrisy: "I was sensible, [these Christians] did not Possess, what they Professed."

In later years, the perspectives of Fox and the Quakers came to seem less threatening. For their refusal of violence and their willingness to stand up to authority, the Friends were awarded the Nobel Peace Prize in 1947. Building on these ideas, modern critics have investigated the way that Fox constructed a confident self in the face of political oppression. For example, Hinds argues that Fox derived inward strength from the idea of an indwelling Christ in a way that counteracted the spiritual anxiety experienced by his religious contemporaries (such as Bunyan). In "Roger Williams and George Fox," David Lovejoy explores a similar topic, asking where the idea of "arrogance" fits into the equation. As Lovejoy illustrates, Fox's *Journal* has supplied crucial information about the development of inward spirituality and personal affect within the context of the Interregnum and Restoration.

Recently, critics have also begun to explore the way that masculinity impacted the production and content of the *Journal*. In "Out of the Paths and Steps of Solid Men," Naomi Winter cites evidence of multiple "masculinities" in the text. Hinds continues the conversation by pointing out that Fox's masculine persona evolved over the course of his career, eventually becoming fully aligned with divine power through the notion of the internalized light. While this alignment made him confident and unafraid to speak to the authorities, it also set a precedent that exposed his followers to

GEORGE FOX AND THE MORALITY OF SPEECH

As a writer and a speaker, George Fox made his priorities very clear: anyone who carried a message from the Lord was welcome to share that message in public. When opponents began to question the existence of special women's meetings, in which female Friends could gather and speak messages to each other, Fox was quick to defend the practice. Just as Hebrew women like Miriam had shared God's word in the Bible, he argued, modern women deserved to experience the spirit and share their gleanings with an audience.

This stance played into one of Fox's principal beliefs: that anyone could become an instrument of the Lord, regardless of gender or birth rank. To emphasize this notion, he encouraged his followers to use only "thee" and "thou" as forms of address when speaking to each other, eliminating rank-conscious phrases such as "my lord" and creating a more equitable field for community conversation. Whether defending his position on women speaking in public or minimizing rank-based distinctions among Friends, Fox strove to cultivate an atmosphere of tolerance and equality surrounding the spoken word.

suffering. As Ingle observes, more than 1,600 Quakers were imprisoned for failure to attend a recognized church on Sundays, until James II pardoned them in 1686. Fox's legacy, then, becomes intertwined with a larger movement of civil disobedience, in which participants could look inward to find strength and solace.

BIBLIOGRAPHY

Sources

Beckham, Edward. "The Principles of the Quakers…" London: Brabazon Aylmer, 1700. *EEBO.* Web. 11 Dec. 2012.

Fox, George. "All Friends Every Where This Is the Word of the Lord unto You All." 1683. *EEBO.* Web. 10 Dec. 2012.

———. *A Journal of Historical Account of the Life, Travels, Sufferings, Christian Experiences and Labour of Love in the Work of the Ministry of That Ancient, Eminent and Faithful Servant of Jesus Christ, George Fox, Who departed This Life in Great Peace with the Lord, the 13th of the 11th Month, 1690.* Vol. 1. London: Thomas Northcott, 1694. Print.

Hinds, Hilary. "'And the Lord's Power Was over All': Calvinist Anxiety, Sacred Confidence, and George Fox's *Journal.*" *ELH* 75.4 (2008): 841–70. Print.

Ingle, H. Larry. "Fox, George, 1624–1691." *Oxford Dictionary of National Biography.* Oxford: Oxford University Press, 2004. Print.

Further Reading

Greaves, Richard L. "Shattered Expectations? George Fox, the Quakers, and the Restoration State, 1660–1685." *Albion* 24.2 (1992): 237–59. Print.

Hinds, Hilary, and Alison Findlay. "The *Journal* of George Fox: A Technology of Presence." *Quaker Studies* 12.1 (2007): 89–106. Print.

Ingle, H. Larry. *First among Friends: George Fox and the Creation of Quakerism.* Oxford: Oxford University Press, 1994. Print.

Knott, John R., Jr. "The Acts of George Fox: A Reading of the *Journal.*" *Prose Studies* 6.3 (1983): 215–38. Print.

Lovejoy, David S. "Roger Williams and George Fox: The Arrogance of Self-Righteousness." *New England Quarterly* 66.2 (1993): 199–225. Print.

Patuleanu, Ioana. "George Fox's *Journal* and the Practice of Self-Observation in Restoration England." *Restoration: Studies in English Literary Culture, 1660–1700* 32.2 (2008): 25–44. Print.

Winter, Naomi, "Out of the Paths and Steps of Solid Men: Masculinities in George Fox's *Journal.*" *Literature and Theology* 14.2 (2000): 145–59. Print.

Nancy Simpson-Younger

The Journals of Charlotte Forten Grimké

Charlotte Forten Grimké

OVERVIEW

The Journals of Charlotte Forten Grimké (1988), published by the Schomberg Library of Nineteenth-Century Black Women Writers, details Grimké's life as an African American writer, teacher, and abolitionist. The *Journals* contains all five volumes of her diaries, the first four of which span the period from 1854 to 1864, while the fifth was begun in 1885 and completed in 1892. In Grimké's text, she writes of her feelings of alienation from the upper class to which she belonged, as it was predominantly white. Grimké also notes feeling estranged from the uneducated African Americans whom she taught during the Civil War. Her unique insight into both of these worlds remains compelling to contemporary scholars.

A highly educated woman of color in antebellum Philadelphia, Grimké grew up in a community of intellectual abolitionists that included her grandfather James Forten, her father Richard Forten, journalist William Lloyd Garrison, poet John Greenleaf Whittier, and writer Harriet Martineau. As a teacher, Grimké participated in the Port Royal Experiment, a collaborative effort by the government and philanthropic organizations on the Sea Islands off the coast of South Carolina to educate African Americans there and prepare them for their lives as free blacks. Grimké's diaries detail these experiences, but, unlike her essays on race and her poems, they were not published in her lifetime. Decades after her death, Ray Allen Billington edited the first edition of her journals (1953), providing a partial view of Grimké's 700 pages of text. The more recent collection, edited by Brenda Stevenson, reveals Grimké's anxieties regarding racism in Philadelphia and her role as the first African American teacher for the Port Royal Experiment.

HISTORICAL AND LITERARY CONTEXT

A member of the Salem Female Anti-slavery Society, Grimké was conscious of current political events. She wrote passionately about Anthony Burns, an African American apprehended in Boston in 1854 under the Fugitive Slave Act of 1850. The law required fugitive slaves be returned to their masters even when they had crossed state lines. Grimké also noticed the plight of Native Americans, who lived in impoverished camps around the Northeast, though she did not take up their cause with the same fervor that she did abolition work.

In her journals, Grimké mentions meeting many key activists, including the renowned underground railroad organizer Harriet Tubman, with whom Grimké became acquainted in South Carolina. The abolitionist and founder of the publication *Liberator*, William Lloyd Garrison, was a family friend who influenced her development as an artist and thinker. Garrison was among the first to champion Grimké's work and published "Poem for Normal School Graduation" in 1856. While teaching in South Carolina, Grimké met Thomas Wentworth Higginson, leader of the first regiment of former slaves. Prior to his Civil War days, he had raised economic support for the abolitionist John Brown following the latter's failed raid on Harpers Ferry in 1859. Higginson invited Grimké to teach his soldiers in Florida, but, as she notes in her journals, this became impossible due to Union soldiers losing ground in the South.

The period during which Grimké's journals were composed is characterized by a proliferation of slave narratives, the interest in which may have delayed engagement with, and publication of, Grimké's text. Scholar Lisa Long, in her 1999 article in *Legacy*, writes that "Harriet Jacob's *Incidents in the Life of a Slave Girl* (1861) is in many ways more compelling than Forten's journals" for its incendiary critique of race relations. Grimké's *Journals,* while lacking the drama of a slave narrative, is notable for its resistance to racism within the elite contexts of the boarding school, intellectual society, and literary publications.

The passages in the journal assert Grimké's interest in a broad range of literature and the impact other authors had on her work. She was deeply moved by the poem "The Runaway Slave at Pilgrim's Point" by Elizabeth Barrett Browning and wrote of Browning's poems that "one cannot read them without feeling an increased love for the good and the beautiful." When Grimké was young her uncle read her passages from Frederick Douglass's speeches. She later met Douglass himself, an event that occasioned Grimké's essay "At the Home of Frederick Douglass," which was published in the 1890s.

THEMES AND STYLE

The Journals of Charlotte Forten Grimké touches on themes of racism, oppression, and the miseducation of former slaves, relaying how these issues shaped her

Key Facts

Time Period:
Mid- to Late 19th Century

Relevant Historical Events:
Growth of abolitionism; Civil War; emancipation of U.S. slaves

Nationality:
American

Keywords:
abolitionism; emancipation; women's writing

White teachers operating a school for liberated slaves during the Civil War. Charlotte Forten Grimke spent eighteen months teaching in a similar school in the Sea Islands of South Carolina. © BETTMANN/CORBIS

loneliness and anxiety. Often, she "found it almost impossible to concentrate," owing to her "troubled thoughts." Regarding the "trifle" of being ignored by her white schoolmates when she met them in public, Grimké writes "to those who experience them, these apparent trifles are most wearing and discouraging.… They reveal volumes of deceit and heartlessness and early teach a lesson of suspicion and distrust." However, she constantly strove to counter her reaction to such behavior, encouraging herself to "labor earnestly and faithfully to acquire knowledge, to break down the barriers of prejudice and oppression."

Grimké's intention for her diaries was that they be a record of her daily life and friendships that would "afford much pleasure in other years." She writes of receiving letters and her feelings regarding the sender, frequently notes what she read and a brief analysis of it, and often compares passages from the Bible or antislavery lectures to contemporary American life. In one entry, she writes of heaven as a place "where slavery and prejudice, sin and sorrow in every form, are unfelt and unknown." The Bible verse "Remember them that are in bonds as bound with them" prompted her to understand slavery as a reality that touched every sector of society.

Grimké's prose is lofty and poetic for even the most quotidian of her days. Recounting a visit to the ocean, she writes "liberty, glorious, boundless liberty reigned there supreme! How very grand were those immense rocks overhanging the sea!" Silvia Xavier argues in *Rhetoric Review* (2005) that the style of the journals was instrumental in shaping Grimké's published essays and poems. Xavier points to uses of "exclamation and apostrophe," which are typical of more public address. She writes that "Forten's diary, in which she is *rehearsing* an eloquence to debate the abolition of slavery, is an audience-directed text." Xavier considers political aspects of the text a "conscious appeal" that are likely directed at "white readers."

CRITICAL DISCUSSION

Critical reception of *The Journals of Charlotte Forten Grimké* has been positive and note the author's activist endeavors. Frances Gaither, in the *New York Times Book Review* in 1953, writes that Grimké "was afire to serve those others of her own race, who unlike herself, had been born to slavery," adding that the text makes "a valuable contribution to the most momentous chapter in American Negro history." Christine Ferrari, reviewing Brenda Stevenson's edition for the *Australasian Journal of American Studies* in 1993, argues that Grimké's "most interesting entries are those which … refer to Grimké's position as a teacher of contraband ex-slaves on St. Helena Island during the Civil War." Ferrari also notes Grimké's "class-bound ambivalence" when it comes to some of the black soldiers she encounters in the South; Grimké writes of one man: "he has such a good, honest face. It is pleasant to look at—although it is black."

Grimké interacted differently with those in the upper- and lower-class spheres and in white and African American spaces, and many scholars have noted her perspective as an important one. In *American Women Prose Writers: 1820–1870* (2001), Katharine Rodier traces Grimké's description of her experience teaching at Port Royal from her journal entries; through her letters in the *Liberator* as "Interesting Letter from Miss Charlotte L. Forten St. Helena Island, Beaufort, S. C. Nov. 27, 1862"; and finally to her essay "Life in the Sea Islands," published in the *Atlantic Monthly* (1864), which was Grimké's most significant publication in her lifetime. Brenda Stevenson argues in her introduction that Grimké may have internalized the racism around her and manifested this in her journals. However, her public works, such as her essay "One Phase of the Race Question" (*Commonwealth* 1885), are purged of this aspect.

Recent scholarship has focused on the role the journals played in the formation of Grimké's complex identity. Long writes that "Forten's trip to the South was clearly an effort to rediscover her racial identity, to work for and connect with her 'people,'" finding that Grimké was not as bound by her class identity as previous scholars have suggested. Similarly, Joanne M. Braxton, in her 1988 essay "Charlotte Forten and the Search for Public Voice," examines the journals as "a vehicle for the development of a black and female poetic identity, a place of restoration and self-healing."

CHARLOTTE FORTEN GRIMKÉ

Charlotte Forten Grimké is remarkable for her independence as a single African American woman and for her work as an educator and a writer. She remained single for much of her life, though she writes of her longing for companionship and of her close friendship with the married doctor, Seth Rogers. Chronically ill for many years with respiratory problems, Grimké became acquainted with Dr. Rogers because of his "water cure." In her journal she writes, "Dr. R did me a world of good.... To me he seems one of the best and noblest types of manhood I ever saw."

In 1878 she married Reverend Francis Grimké, nephew of the abolitionists Sarah and Angelina Grimké. The Reverend Grimké, the son of a slaveholder and an ex-slave who himself was born a slave, delivered rousing sermons concerning oppression and the path to racial equality. Following the death of their infant daughter, the Grimkés assumed custody of Francis Grimké's niece, Angelina Weld Grimké, who followed Charlotte in her calling as a poet and activist. During Reconstruction, the Grimkés continued their antiracism work and collaborated on their critical essays. Charlotte helped to found the National Association of Colored Women in 1896.

BIBLIOGRAPHY

Sources

Braxton, Joanne M. "Charlotte Forten Grimké and the Search for Public Voice." *The Private Self: Theory and Practice of Women's Autobiographical Writings*. Ed. Shari Benstock. Chapel Hill: University of North Carolina Press, 1988. 254–71. Rpt. in *Literature Resource Center*. Detroit: Gale, 2013. *Literature Resource Center*. Web. 20 Dec. 2012.

Ferrari, Christine. Rev. of *The Journals of Charlotte Forten Grimké*, by Charlotte Forten Grimké. *Australasian Journal of American Studies* 12.2 (1993): 67–69. *JSTOR*. Web. 19 Dec. 2012.

Gaither, Frances. "The Will to Serve." *New York Times Book Review* 12 Apr. 1953: 6. Rpt. in *Twentieth-Century Literary Criticism*. Ed. Dennis Poupard. Vol. 16. Detroit: Gale Research, 1985. *Literature Resource Center*. Web. 20 Dec. 2012.

Grimké, Charlotte Forten. *The Journals of Charlotte Forten Grimké*. Ed. Brenda Stevenson. New York: Oxford University Press, 1988. Print.

Long, Lisa A. "Charlotte Forten's Civil War Journals and the Quest for 'Genius, Beauty, and Deathless Fame.'" *Legacy: A Journal of American Women Writers* 16.1 (1999): 37–48. *JSTOR*. Web. 19 Dec. 2012.

Rodier, Katharine. "Charlotte L(ottie) Forten Grimké." *American Women Prose Writers: 1820–1870*. Ed. Amy E. Hudock and Katharine Rodier. Detroit: Gale Group, 2001. Rpt. in *Dictionary of Literary Biography*. Vol. 239. Detroit: Gale Group, 2001. *Literature Resource Center*. Web. 20 Dec. 2012.

Xavier, Silvia. "Engaging George Campbell's 'Sympathy' in the Rhetoric of Charlotte Forten and Ann Plato, African-American Women of the Antebellum North." *Rhetoric Review* 24.4 (2005): 438–56. *JSTOR*. Web. 20 Dec. 2012.

Further Reading

Cobb-Moore, Geneva. "When Meanings Meet: The Journals of Charlotte Forten Grimké." *Inscribing the Daily: Critical Essays on Women's Diaries*. Ed. Suzanne L. Bunkers and Cynthia A. Huff. Amherst: University of Massachusetts Press, 1996. 139–55. *MLA International Bibliography*. Web. 19 Dec. 2012.

Hoffman, Nancy. "'Inquiring after the Schoolmarm': Problems of Historical Research on Female Teachers." *Women's Studies Quarterly* 22.1–2 (1994):104–18. *JSTOR*. Web. 19 Dec. 2012.

Kelley, Mary. "Reading Women/Women Reading: The Making of Learned Women in Antebellum America." *Journal of American History* 83.2 (1996): 401–24. *JSTOR*. Web. 19 Dec. 2012.

Koch, Lisa M. "Bodies as Stage Props: Enacting Hysteria in the Diaries of Charlotte Forten Grimké and Alice James." *Legacy: A Journal of American Women Writers* 15.1 (1998): 59–64. *MLA International Bibliography*. Web. 19 Dec. 2012.

Peterson, Carla L. "Frances Harper, Charlotte Forten, and African-American Literary Reconstruction." *Challenging Boundaries: Gender and Periodization*. Ed. Joyce W. Warren and Margaret Dickie. Athens: University of Georgia Press, 2000. 39–61. *MLA International Bibliography*. Web. 19 Dec. 2012

Caitlin Moore

Letter from the Birmingham Jail
Martin Luther King Jr.

❖ **Key Facts**

Time Period:
Mid-20th Century

Relevant Historical Events:
Civil rights movement; incarceration of King; nonviolent Birmingham campaign

Nationality:
American

Keywords:
nonviolence; civil rights; racism

OVERVIEW

"Letter from the Birmingham Jail," first published in 1963, is one of Martin Luther King Jr.'s best-known writings and one of the most important historical documents of the civil rights movement in the United States. Written during the Birmingham campaign while King was jailed for breaking Alabama's laws prohibiting public demonstrations, the letter speaks out against the South's segregationist practices. It was King's public response to criticism from Alabama clergymen who believed his unlawful actions to end racial discrimination were ill conceived. The letter provides an eloquent delineation of King's nonviolent direct-action campaign as well a moving, detailed account of the dire conditions and circumstances that had made the Birmingham demonstrations a necessity and moral obligation for African Americans. "Letter from the Birmingham Jail" became a vehicle for King to address the spiritual malaise of America, as reflected in its segregationist mentality and unpardonable violence against its African American citizens. He brings the intimacy of direct address and a learned and impassioned style to the text, embodying the imprisoned state of the oppressed.

When King's letter was published, he was already a prominent figure in the civil rights movement. The clergymen to whom the letter is addressed found King's message to be hurtful and believed he had misunderstood them. Nevertheless, the letter was widely circulated through media outlets, gaining the attention and, soon, the appreciation of the public. The clergy witnessed mounting public tensions as a result of the letter, which impressed upon the nation's conscience, as well as King's former opponents, the need for social change. Today the letter is admired for its vision of equality and liberty for all Americans.

HISTORICAL AND LITERARY CONTEXT

In 1955, as the civil rights movement was gaining traction, King rose to prominence as a young Baptist pastor who organized a boycott of the Montgomery, Alabama, bus system. In 1960 and 1961 his efforts inspired thousands of students to conduct sit-ins and members of the Congress of Racial Equality to put their lives on the line in an effort to end segregation. King's letter was written in the midst of the Birmingham campaign, a massive nonviolent protest against the city's segregated infrastructures. By staging the protests during Easter, one of the busiest commercial holiday seasons, organizers hoped to coerce merchants into removing their segregationist practices to spur economic development. The campaign, headed by the Alabama Christian Movement for Human Rights and King's Southern Christian Leadership Conference, was only a week old when King was arrested. On the day of his arrest, eight white moderates, all clergymen from Birmingham, published a criticism of the campaign, "A Call for Unity," in the *Birmingham News*. Their statement objected to the unlawful protests, calling King's direct-action strategy "unwise and untimely." King was moved not only to defend his methods and vision to members of the clergy but also to bring attention to the Birmingham campaign, which he feared was losing momentum. His letter served as a broad indictment of the "gradualist" approach to racism favored by the clergy and adopted by white moderates and some in the black community.

Through his eloquent and passionate letter, King helped Americans understand the plight of African Americans and the ominous consequences of racism for all citizens. The Birmingham campaign wound up being a significant success, to which the letter certainly contributed. The U.S. Supreme Court ruled that Alabama's segregation laws were unconstitutional, and President John F. Kennedy publicly praised the protestors, calling for Congress to pass new civil rights legislation. King's relationship with Kennedy, as well as the Nobel Peace Prize he was awarded in 1964, further solidified his image as a respectable and powerful reformer.

As an argument for human rights—specifically, the right to practice civil disobedience of unjust laws—King's letter has many precedents. The works of ancient Greeks such as the philosopher Plato and the playwright Sophocles, American transcendentalist Ralph Waldo Emerson, and Indian pacifist Mohandas Gandhi all recognize the natural right to peacefully oppose laws contrary to the eternal law of God, and they profoundly influenced King's thinking.

The integrative rhetoric employed in King's letter, as well as in his famous 1963 speech "I Have a Dream," have informed the writings and methodologies of generations of human rights activists, thinkers, and politicians, including presidents Kennedy, Ronald

Reagan, and Barack Obama. The importance of his life's work is honored with a national holiday, which was signed into law by Reagan in 1986.

THEMES AND STYLE

The letter's main theme is a justification of civil disobedience and direct action against racism; violence toward African Americans; and the obstacles to freedom, equality, and fulfillment of the American dream. King lays bare what he describes as Birmingham's "ugly record of brutality" to show why direct action is necessary. He argues in favor of civil disobedience and explains that after "[you] have seen vicious mobs lynch your mothers and fathers at will and drown your sisters and brothers at whim," gradualism is not a viable solution. King also expounds upon his two major disappointments, the clergy and white moderates, whom he sees as turning a blind eye to the "disinherited children of God." As with the Birmingham campaign, he seeks "to create a situation so crisis-packed that it will inevitably open the door to negotiation." His letter is meant to explain the "hard, brutal facts" behind the Birmingham protests to his critics and to show that "one has a moral responsibility to disobey unjust laws."

King clearly considered an audience beyond the clergy. He believed that racism against blacks was a symptom of the entire nation's malaise, a sign that democracy in the United States had strayed from the social and political course laid out in the U.S. Constitution. In order to reach out to the entire nation—to the oppressors and oppressed alike—his tone is decidedly measured. Cognizant of the mindset of his opponents, he is careful not to adopt the pro-violence rhetoric of other active African American antisegregationist campaigns of the day.

King's letter is a prime example of high oratorical style. As scholar Richard Fulkerson notes in his 1979 essay in *Quarterly Journal of Speech,* King employs the ancient Greek conventions of argumentation, moving from proposition to division, confirmation, refutation, and peroration. The structure of the letter reveals a deft management of audience and style, as King appeals first to his white-moderate audience on its own Anglicized terms before shifting to more emotionally direct speech when addressing the African American community. He utilizes a variety of literary devices to make his case for the urgency of racial equality. His repetition of the phrase "when you have" as he lists racist acts of violence against African Americans has an incantatory effect. The letter's metaphorical language, such as the "stinging darts of segregation" and "clouds of inferiority," effectively evokes the suffering of African Americans. In expressing his disappointments and frustrations, King's tone is disapproving but ultimately benevolent. As James A. Colaiaco notes in *Phylon,* "Maintaining a conciliatory tone, King also insists that although he wept over the laxity of the church, his disappointment stems from deep love."

Civil rights activist Martin Luther King Jr. in Atlanta, Georgia, October 24, 1966, three years after he penned his "Letter from the Birmingham Jail."
© AP IMAGES

CRITICAL DISCUSSION

King's letter and his life in general have held significance for scholars from a wide variety of disciplines. The majority of early discussions referencing "Letter from the Birmingham Jail," such as Adam Roberts's 1968 article in *World Today,* were efforts to carry on King's legacy, commemorating his contributions to U.S. history. Early criticism also focused on how the letter reveals the methodology behind King's leadership.

Later, the letter was contextualized as a key document in the annals of American resistance. In religious and theological studies, it was viewed as a sermon, as evidence of the religious culture in the South; in literary circles, it was seen as a masterpiece of prison literature. Scholars of rhetoric and political history have examined the letter as an exemplar of American public address, while others have studied King's legacy and the appropriation of his thinking and style by later politicians and leaders. Denise M. Bostdorff and Steven R. Goldzwig, for example, argue in their 2005 article in *Presidential Studies Quarterly* that Reagan betrayed King's vision by appropriating King's thought for his own purposes.

Recent trends in scholarship include the application of literary and linguistic theories to unlock the letter's anthropological insights, as in Susan Tiefenbrun's "Semiotics and Martin Luther King's 'Letter from Birmingham Jail.'" The passing of time has delivered an element of clarity to the letter, which through King's fame and assassination became shrouded in myth and contradictory accounts of its origins and reception. Typical of this demystifying approach is Jonathan S. Bass's book-length study of the letter, *Blessed Are the Peacemakers.* Bass dedicates his text to offering a more complete and complex picture of the eight clergymen who received the letter and, after withdrawing from the public debate spurred by King's response, were never fully examined by journalists or scholars. Bass's insights shed light on the motivations behind King's letter and offer a richer understanding of the complicated moral

EYES ON THE PRIZE

Eyes on the Prize is an award-winning, fourteen-hour television series about the civil rights era in the United States. It premiered in 1987 and is widely considered the definitive documentary on the subject. Created and produced by Henry Hampton, one of the twentieth century's most influential documentary filmmakers, the series chronicles the history of the movement through the stories of its heroes, ordinary citizens whose courage led them to fight for freedom and equality. Through historical footage and contemporary interviews, *Eyes on the Prize* exhaustively depicts every milestone of the civil rights movement from 1954 to 1985.

Martin Luther King Jr. is featured in multiple episodes, including "No Easy Walk," which covers the years 1961 to 1963. King is shown to be the movement's most prominent leader, spearheading the mass demonstrations in Alabama and Washington DC that helped to result in President John F. Kennedy proposing the Civil Rights Act. The episode "Two Societies," covering events from 1965 to 1968, follows King's Southern Christian Leadership Conference in its efforts to stop segregated housing in Chicago. The episode shows King enacting his methods of nonviolent direct action in marches meant to bring about negotiations.

and cultural challenges characterizing this significant moment in U.S. history.

BIBLIOGRAPHY

Sources

Bass, Jonathan S. *Blessed Are the Peacemakers: Martin Luther King Jr., Eight White Religious Leaders, and the "Letter from Birmingham Jail."* Baton Rouge: Louisiana State University Press, 2002. Print.

Bostdorff, Denise M., and Steven R. Goldzwig. "History, Collective Memory, and the Appropriation of Martin Luther King, Jr.: Reagan's Rhetorical Legacy." *Presidential Studies Quarterly* 35.4 (2005): 661–90. Print.

Colaiaco, James A. "The American Dream Unfulfilled: Martin Luther King, Jr. and the 'Letter from Birmingham Jail.'" *Phylon* 45.1 (1984): 1–18. Print.

Fulkerson, Richard, "The Public Letter as a Rhetorical Form: Structure, Logic, and Style in King's 'Letter from Birmingham Jail.'" *Quarterly Journal of Speech* 65 (1979): 121–36. Print.

King, Martin Luther, Jr. "Letter from Birmingham Jail." *King Institute.* Web. 27 Dec. 2012.

Sturm, Douglas. "Crisis in the American Republic: The Legal and Political Significance of Martin Luther King's 'Letter from a Birmingham Jail.'" *Journal of Law and Religion* 2.2 (1984): 309–24. Print.

Further Reading

Branch, Taylor. *Parting the Waters: America in the King Years 1954–1963.* New York: Simon and Schuster, 1988. Print.

Carson, Clayborne, et al., eds. *The Eyes on the Prize Civil Rights Reader.* New York: Penguin, 1991. Print.

Carson, Clayborne. *In Struggle: SNCC and the Black Awakening of the 1960s.* Cambridge, Mass.: Harvard University Press, 1995. Print.

Carson, Clayborne, ed. *The Autobiography of Martin Luther King, Jr.* New York: Warner, 1998. Print.

King, Martin Luther, Jr. *Why We Can't Wait.* New York: Penguin, 2000. Print.

Tiefenbrun, Susan. "Semiotics and Martin Luther King's 'Letter from Birmingham Jail.'" *Cardozo Studies in Law and Literature* 4.2 (1992): 255–87. Print.

Washington, James M., ed. *A Testament of Hope: The Essential Writings and Speeches of Martin Luther King, Jr.* New York: HarperOne, 1990. Print.

Farnoosh Fathi

Letter to Her Daughter

Lady Mary Wortley Montagu

OVERVIEW

Written and sent in January 1753 but not published until 1803, Lady Mary Wortley Montagu's "Letter to Her Daughter" (the Countess of Bute) outlines an educational program for her young granddaughter, the twelve-year-old Lady Mary Stuart, alongside a series of shrewd reflections on the opportunities, or rather lack thereof, for women in the eighteenth century. While Montagu primarily focuses on the advantages of female education and the differences between the lives of her daughter and granddaughter, she also describes in passing some of the difficulties and regrets of her childhood and adult life. The letter is marked by cautionary words about marriage that are informed by Montagu's own joyless union to Edward Wortley Montagu.

With the exception of her *Turkish Embassy Letters* (written in the 1720s but not published until 1763), Montagu never intended her private correspondence to be published. In the early 1800s the publisher Richard Phillips acquired more than 200 letters written by Montagu, her husband, and their acquaintances. The Marquess of Bute (Montagu's grandson) consented to their publication, but in exchange certain letters were withheld that he felt were detrimental to the family's reputation. The appearance of the first collection of Montagu's works in 1803 met with some success, though it was incomplete and poorly edited. The leading reviewer of the age, Francis Jeffrey of the *Edinburgh Review,* noted that Montagu's letters to her daughter "abound[ed] in lively and judicious reflections." In particular, her thoughts on gender and education remain valuable for scholars interested in eighteenth-century culture.

HISTORICAL AND LITERARY CONTEXT

Montagu's "Letter to Her Daughter" was written at a time when women were afforded few, if any, educational and vocational opportunities, circumstances alluded to in Montagu's reference to the "fame which men have engrossed to themselves, and will not suffer us to share." Barred from the traditional mediums of knowledge (schools and universities), women were expected to "know how to use a needle" and draw. Self-assertive women such as Montagu, however, managed to acquire a thorough knowledge of traditionally masculine subjects through private tutors and home-schooling programs akin to the one Montagu recommends for her granddaughter. While aristocratic women such as Montagu and her daughter were groomed to be attractive to potential suitors, marriage was a course fraught with many "hazards" (namely unhappiness), as Montagu pessimistically asserts.

When Montagu penned her "Letter to Her Daughter" in 1753, she had been separated from her husband and living on the European continent, mostly in Gottolengo, Italy, for fourteen years. Ongoing bouts of illness beginning in 1747 had necessitated frequent visits to the therapeutic mineral waters of Lovere, Italy (on the western shore of Lake Iseo), where the letter was written. A letter writer for most of her life, she corresponded with, among other people, Pope, Congreve, and assorted counts and countesses. Her epistolary pastime assumed a new significance during her voluntary exile; letters became a way of maintaining a connection to England, where she finally returned in 1762, only to die shortly thereafter.

The eighteenth-century book market was saturated with both collections of letters, real and feigned, and letter-writing manuals. Such works undoubtedly influenced Montagu's own epistolary ventures, as did the posthumously published letters of the seventeenth-century French aristocrat Madame de Sévigné, who served as a model, source of entertainment, and imaginary literary adversary. The ideas about female education espoused in Montagu's "Letter to Her Daughter" owe their origins to earlier, proto-feminist works, such as Montagu's friend Mary Astell's *A Serious Proposal to the Ladies* (1694, 1697) and Bathsua Makin's *An Essay to Revive the Antient Education of Gentlewomen* (1673).

Because she was recognized as a model of epistolary excellence in the early decades of the nineteenth century, young women were, according to nineteenth-century essayist Walter Bagehot in "Lady Mary Wortley Montagu," "enjoined to form their style upon" Montagu's. While her status as an exemplar had declined by 1862, when Bagehot was obliged to "recommend the letters … as an instructive and profitable study," her letters remained "instructive" in a sense unintended by Bagehot. Indeed, throughout the nineteenth and twentieth centuries the letters were read as sources of information about both Montagu's "eccentric personal life" and the "customs" of eighteenth century life, according to Patricia Meyer Spacks in *The Cambridge History of English Literature, 1660–1780.* The "Letter

❖ **Key Facts**

Time Period:
Mid-18th Century

Relevant Historical Events:
Montagu's move to Italy; subjugation of women

Nationality:
English

Keywords:
women's writing; feminism; education

Lady Mary Wortley Montagu in a portrait painted by Jonathan Richardson. © SHEFFIELD GALLERIES AND MUSEUMS TRUST, UK/ MUSEUMS SHEFFIELD/THE BRIDGEMAN ART LIBRARY

to Her Daughter" in particular has increasingly been viewed as an early, candid indictment of eighteenth-century gender restrictions.

THEMES AND STYLE

The central theme of Montagu's "Letter to Her Daughter" is that Lady Bute should encourage and superintend her daughter's education in languages, English poetry, and other subjects. Such an education, Montagu writes, will make her "happy" in the "retirement to which she is destined" (Montagu's euphemistic description of a woman's confined life). The thematic concerns of Montagu's "Letter to Her Daughter" are informed by a keen awareness of the adversities confronting the eighteenth-century woman, in particular marriage. While Montagu suggests that education can make the disappointment of a woman's expectations more palatable, she also implies that it is a form of resistance, a way to make her granddaughter "happy in a virgin state." This "virgin state" is "safer than any marriage," and knowledge is a source of "amusement" that will either make her granddaughter's potentially lamentable "fate" more joyous or negate the need for such a course.

Montagu ostensibly wrote the "Letter to Her Daughter" to outline an educational program for her granddaughter. As she notes near the letter's conclusion, her "design" is "only to say what I think useful for the instruction of my granddaughter, which I have much at heart." Despite the apparent narrowness of her "design," Montagu nevertheless offers sundry critical remarks about marriage and female education in the eighteenth century, comments that imply her letter was also written with the purpose of decrying the "contempt" with which women were treated: "We are educated in the grossest ignorance, and no art omitted to stifle our natural reasons."

Like many other so-called eighteenth-century "familiar letters" written under the pervasive influence of letter-writing manuals, Montagu's "Letter to Her Daughter" employs a highly cultivated prose style that is alternately elaborate and pithy. Montagu's syntactical oscillations are matched by the presence of apparently conflicting claims. While she boldly champions a female education in traditionally masculine subjects such as Greek and Latin, she is also quick to defend the importance of traditionally female accomplishments and a conventionally feminine reserve: "The second caution … is to conceal whatever learning she attains … [because] the parade of it can only serve to draw on her … envy." Montagu's letter evinces what Cynthia Lowenthal describes in *Lady Mary Wortley Montagu and the Eighteenth Century Familiar Letter* as an "essentially subversive [rhetorical] strategy," one that "cloaks" the potentially scandalous in the "language of respectability."

CRITICAL DISCUSSION

The majority of Montagu's letters were not published until 1803, when James Dallaway edited the first complete edition of her works, in five volumes. In the memoir he appended to the edition, Dallaway remarks, "Her letters from this retreat [Lovere] breathe a truly philosophic spirit, and evince that her care of her daughter and her family was ever nearest to her heart." Francis Jeffrey of the *Edinburgh Review* echoed Dallaway's remarks in his review of the edition, noting that Montagu's letters to her daughter have "more heat and affection in them than any other of her Ladyship's productions." Dallaway's volumes were extremely popular; by 1817 they were in their sixth edition.

As the nineteenth century progressed, however, Montagu's literary reputation waned. In 1862 Bagehot lamented that most English readers barely even knew of her, a fact that made the letters newly interesting to him. Nevertheless, Montagu's works and letters were frequently republished, and she remained an object of praise, interest, and occasional derision for various Victorian and Edwardian literati, including Thomas Carlyle, James Henry Leigh Hunt, and Lytton Strachey. Montagu was always admired as one of the best letter writers of the eighteenth century, and scholars have begun to examine her correspondence with more than just an aesthetic lens.

Montagu's "Letter to Her Daughter" has benefited from the recent increase in scholarly attention paid to issues of gender and education in the eighteenth century. Critics such as Robert Halsband, editor of the standard edition of Montagu's letters, have frequently dilated on her feminist bent. In *Lady Mary Wortley Montagu and the Eighteenth Century Familiar Letter*, Cynthia Lowenthal remarks that Montagu championed the "equal power of the female mind." Critics such as Katharine Rogers, on the other hand, have been less generous about Montagu's proto-feminism, given the letter's apparent support of the restrictive gender roles feminism claims to subvert. (Montagu, for example, encourages needlework.) Thus, Rogers, in Lowenthal's description, argues that Montagu "undercuts her feminism by camouflaging her ideas in flippancy or apology."

BIBLIOGRAPHY

Sources

Bagehot, Walter. "Lady Mary Wortley Montagu." *Literary Essays*. Vol. 2. Ed. Norman St. John-Stevas. Cambridge, Mass.: Harvard University Press, 1965. 208–36. Print.

Grundy, Isobel. *Lady Mary Wortley Montagu*. New York: Oxford University Press, 1999. Print.

Halsband, Robert. "'Condemned to Petticoats': Lady Mary Wortley Montagu as Feminist and Writer." *The Dress of Words: Essays on Restoration and Eighteenth Century Literature in Honor of Richmond P. Bond*. Ed. Robert B. White Jr. Lawrence: University of Kansas Libraries, 1978. 35–52. Print.

Jeffrey, Francis. "Lady Mary Wortley Montagu." *Contributions to the Edinburgh Review*. Vol. 3. London: Longman, Brown Green, and Longmans, 1846. 556–71. *Google Books*. Web. 27 Dec. 2012.

Lowenthal, Cynthia. *Lady Mary Wortley Montagu and the Eighteenth Century Familiar Letter*. Athens: University of Georgia Press, 1994. Print.

Montagu, Lady Mary Wortley. *The Works of the Right Honourable Lady Mary Wortley Montagu*. 5 vols. Ed. James Dallaway. London: Richard Phillips, 1803. *Hathi Trust*. Web. 27 Dec. 2012.

———. *The Complete Letters of Lady Mary Wortley Montagu*. 3 vols. Ed. Robert Halsband. New York: Oxford University Press, 1965. Print.

Spacks, Patricia Meyer. "Personal Letters." *The Cambridge History of English Literature, 1660–1780*. Ed. John Richetti. New York: Cambridge University Press, 2005. 625–48. *Cambridge Histories Online*. Web. 27 Dec. 2012.

Further Reading

Bannet, Eve Tavor. *Empire of Letters: Letter Manuals and Transatlantic Correspondence, 1688–1820*. New York: Cambridge University Press, 2005. Print.

Bohls, Elizabeth. "Aesthetics and Orientalism in Lady Marty Wortley Montagu's Letters." *Studies in Eighteenth Century Culture* 23 (1994): 179–205. *Project MUSE*. Web. 27 Dec. 2012.

Grundy, Isobel. "Lady Mary Wortley Montagu and her Daughter:" *Women's Writing and the Circulation of Ideas: Manuscript Publication in England, 1550–1800*. Ed. George L. Justice and Nathan Tinker. New York: Cambridge University Press, 2002. 182–200. Print.

LADY MARY WORTLEY MONTAGU'S *TURKISH EMBASSY LETTERS*

In 1763, a year after her death, Lady Mary Wortley Montagu's *Turkish Embassy Letters* were published. The letters were written mostly between 1716 and 1718, when her husband was the British ambassador to Constantinople, but Montagu continued to work on the manuscript throughout her life. Although her superintendence of these letters suggests that she intended that they be published, Montagu's only explicit instructions to the Reverend Benjamin Sowden, to whom she gave the manuscript, were that they were "to be dispos'd of as he [thought] proper," according to Cynthia Lowenthal in *Lady Mary Wortley Montagu and the Eighteenth Century Familiar Letter*. Sowden, however, did not publish the letters; they were temporarily stolen from him, copied, and printed without his or Montagu's family's permission.

For many years Montagu's fame rested on this epistolary travelogue (a favorite form among eighteenth-century literary adventurers) and its survey of Ottoman culture. Writers as varied as Edward Gibbon, Samuel Johnson, Tobias Smollett, and Voltaire offered high praise. The contrasts Montagu draws between East and West, coupled with her dilation on the Turkish practice of inoculation (unknown in Britain at the time Montagu observed it), have ensured the work a place among scholars interested both in eighteenth-century orientalism and the history of medicine.

Halsband, Robert. "Lady Mary Wortley Montagu as Letter-Writer." *The Familiar Letter in the Eighteenth Century*. Ed. Howard Anderson, Philip B. Daghlian, and Irvin Ehrenpreis. Lawrence: University of Kansas Press, 1966. 49–70. Print.

How, James. *Epistolary Spaces: English Letter Writing from the Foundation of the Post Office to Richardson's Clarissa*. Aldershot, U.K.: Ashgate, 2003. Print.

Looser, Devoney. "Scolding Lady Mary Wortley Montagu: The Problematics of Sisterhood in Feminist Criticism." *Feminist Nightmares: Women at Odds: Feminism and the Problem of Sisterhood*. Ed. Susan Ostrov Weisser and Jennifer Fleischner. New York: New York University Press, 1994. 44–61. Print.

Montagu, Lady Mary Wortley. *Turkish Embassy Letters*. Ed. Malcolm Jack. London: Virago Press, 1994. Print.

Redford, Bruce. "Lady Mary Wortley Montagu: The Compass of the Senecan Style." *The Converse of the Pen: Acts of Intimacy in the Eighteenth-Century Familiar Letter*. Chicago: University of Chicago Press, 1986. 19–48. Print.

Alex Covalciuc

Letter to His Son

Robert E. Lee

❖ **Key Facts**

Time Period:
Mid-19th Century

Relevant Historical Events:
Southern secession; preparation for the American Civil War

Nationality:
American

Keywords:
civil war; militarism; loyalty

OVERVIEW

The renowned general Robert E. Lee wrote his "Letter to His Son" on January 23, 1861, on the eve of the Civil War. While portions appeared in print in 1874, the letter was not published in its entirety until 1961, when the *Virginia Magazine of History and Biography* published it under the title "Secession Is Nothing but Revolution." In only six paragraphs, Lee speaks kindly and instructively to his son about family finances, pondering investments in Virginia stock when the state seemed poised to secede from the Union. These concerns inspired Lee's bittersweet reflections on his northern and southern loyalties.

Though Lee, a native of Virginia, eventually rose to command the main army of the Confederacy and later all Confederate armies in early 1861, when he penned the "Letter to His Son," he was still a U.S. Army colonel. During the two preceding months, South Carolina, Mississippi, Louisiana, Florida, Alabama, Texas, and Georgia had seceded under the assumption that the new president, Abraham Lincoln, would outlaw slavery. Anticipating that Virginia too would soon secede and that secession would lead to war, Lee writes as one torn by his attachments to both the Union and Virginia. Critics lauded his writings, including the "Letter," collected in *Personal Reminiscences, Anecdotes and Letters of General Robert E. Lee* (1874) by J. William Jones. A reviewer for *Georgia Weekly Telegraph* (1875) describes Lee as "probably the purest, if not the most salient and illustrious character that ever figured upon the stage of life." The "Letter" continues to inform debates over Lee and the legacy of the South.

HISTORICAL AND LITERARY CONTEXT

Lincoln was elected president in November 1860, with few southern votes. The former lawyer was against the expansion of slavery into the western territories. In 1854 he opposed the Kansas-Nebraska Act because it would extend slavery into a region in which the practice had previously been prohibited by federal law. Similarly, in 1857 he spoke out against the U.S. Supreme Court's *Dred Scott* decision, which prohibited federal regulation of slavery in the territories and declared that individuals of African descent could not be U.S. citizens. Lee's "Letter" came at a moment when those states invested in slavery believed that Lincoln and his free-soiler opinions might pose a substantial threat to their ways of life and livelihood.

In 1857 Lee's father-in-law died, leaving a debt-ridden Virginia estate and slave plantation to Lee and his wife, Mary. Though Lee discusses the growing unrest between the North and the South, his "Letter to His Son" is primarily concerned with setting the estate in order. The purpose of the letter, in which he thanks his son, "Rooney," for having finally settled the accounts, was to urge caution in investing "surplus funds"—chiefly because Lee had planned on purchasing "Virga" (Virginia) state bonds but was now apprehensive that if Virginia seceded, its debts would rise and its bonds depreciate. In sum, he saw his family's prospects bound closely to the fate of the state and the nation.

While Lee's "Letter" is in many respects a unique document, it can be likened to *Shadows on My Heart: The Civil War Diary of Lucy Rebecca Buck of Virginia*, another work discussing attachments to and dissatisfaction with the South in the Civil War era. Also worth comparing is Thomas Jefferson's "Letter to His Daughter" (1783), as the work of a prominent leader writing with fatherly guidance to his child, though Jefferson's impatience with his daughter differs vastly from Lee's affection for his son.

Since the initial publication of the "Letter to His Son," Lee's ruminations on Virginia, the Union, and the possibility of civil war have been of continued interest to scholars. Indeed, his feeling for the Union and his reluctance to fight against Virginia were nothing less than instrumental in shaping the nation's history. Though Lee ultimately failed as a general—that is, in spite of several significant victories, he eventually surrendered his army to General Ulysses S. Grant at Appomattox Court House in April 1865—on account of his writings, Lee has been remembered as a patriotic southerner.

THEMES AND STYLE

Though relatively short (just under 1,300 words), the "Letter" touches on a number of themes that unite Lee's concerns for the care and well-being of both private and public spheres. On the home front, he thanks Rooney for "the pleasing account of your quiet & happy Xmas … & the christening of your boy," going on to ask, "what is the matter with my precious Chass? … Tell her I want to see her very much & love her more & more." This tender care shifts into practical territory as he tells Rooney, "I am glad you have settled up so promptly all the accounts of the Estate," at which point the theme of familial bonds leads to the subject of financial concerns and investments and in turn to a different kind of attachment, for not just the home but the homeland.

Lee works hard to validate his son in both personal and professional terms. He opens by commending Rooney on the christening of his son, insisting that "you must teach him then to love his Grand Papa, to bear with his failings & avoid his errors, to be to you as you have been to me, & he may then enjoy the love & confidence of his father which I feel for you, greater than which no son has ever possessed." Conscious of his own life and legacy, the elder Lee affirms his attachments to his family as it grows. The pleasure he shows in his son continues as he turns to the practicalities of settling accounts. Here, in the most involved paragraph of the letter, he asks Rooney to consolidate the financial records of the estate, a request that prompts Lee to think in broader terms of state economics and national politics.

The "Letter" ranges widely in sentiment, at one point intimate and affectionate (reaching out to his son), at another technical and practical (instructing Rooney on managing the estate) or critical and analytical (addressing political crisis). Lee is especially elegant when talking politics. He writes:

> As an American citizen, I take great pride in my country, her prosperity & institutions & would defend any State if her rights were invaded. But I can anticipate no greater calamity for the country than a dissolution of the Union. It would be an accumulation of all the evils we complain of, & I am willing to sacrifice every thing but honour for its preservation. I hope therefore that all Constitutional means will be exhausted, before there is a resort to force. Secession is nothing but revolution.

These lines are especially significant because Lee fought against the Union he otherwise loved.

CRITICAL DISCUSSION

Historians have taken interest in Lee since the mid-1860s, when such publications as *Life and Campaigns of General Robert E. Lee* (1866) by Dabney McCabe, *Lee and His Generals* (1867) by William Snow, and *Lee and His Lieutenants* (1867) by Edward Pollard first explored the general's military legacy. Interest continued following Lee's death in 1870. Jones, in *Personal Reminiscences,* was the first editor to publish the "Letter." Though early commentary does not single out the "Letter," a review in the *Georgia Weekly Telegraph* declares that the collection "supplie[d] a great want by revealing the inner life of the hero, his transcendent modesty, unaffected piety, great endurance and unexampled patriotism."

Lee has been hailed as a hero, a passionate defender of states' rights, a master military strategist, a scourge, a slaveholder, and a callous general who led thousands of troops to their slaughter. Understandably he continues to fascinate historians, who regularly extract and cite the thoughts expressed in his "Letter to His Son" in an effort to explore Lee's view of secession. What intrigues above all is his passion for the Union even as he anticipates seceding, prompting such scholars as Gamaliel Bradford to ask the fundamental question "Why, then, did Lee leave the Union?" Critics have long been interested in the ways in which Lee's private and domestic life informed his role as general.

Scholars rarely discuss the "Letter to His Son" in its own right; rather, as in the work of Michael Fellman, they treat it as a source for explicating that turning point when Lee began to transfer his official

Author and Confederate general Robert E. Lee, circa 1864–65. Portrait by Edward Caledon Bruce. © NATIONAL PORTRAIT GALLERY, SMITHSONIAN INSTITUTION/ART RESOURCE, NY

PRIMARY SOURCE

EXCERPT FROM "LETTER TO HIS SON"

I received Everett's *Life of Washington* which you sent me, and enjoyed its perusal. How his spirit would be grieved could he see the wreck of his mighty labors! I will not, however, permit myself to believe, until all ground of hope is gone, that the fruit of his noble deeds will be destroyed, and that his precious advice and virtuous example will so soon be forgotten by his countrymen. As far as I can judge by the papers, we are between a state of anarchy and civil war. May God avert both of these evils from us! I fear that mankind will not for years be sufficiently Christianized to bear the absence of restraint and force. I see that four states have declared themselves out of the Union; four more will apparently follow their example. Then, if the border states are brought into the gulf of revolution, one half of the country will be arrayed against the other. I must try and be patient and await the end, for I can do nothing to hasten or retard it.

The South, in my opinion, has been aggrieved by the acts of the North, as you say. I feel the aggression and am willing to take every proper step for redress. It is the principle I contend for, not individual or private benefit. As an American citizen, I take great pride in my country, her prosperity and institutions, and would defend any state if her rights were invaded. But I can anticipate no greater calamity for the country than a dissolution of the Union. It would be an accumulation of all the evils we complain of, and I am willing to sacrifice everything but honor for its preservation. I hope, therefore, that all constitutional means will be exhausted before there is a resort to force. Secession is nothing but revolution. The framers of our Constitution never exhausted so much labor, wisdom, and forbearance in its formation, and surrounded it with so many guards and securities, if it was intended to be broken by every member of the Confederacy at will. It was intended for "perpetual union," so expressed in the preamble, and for the establishment of a government, not a compact, which can only be dissolved by revolution or the consent of all the people in convention assembled. It is idle to talk of secession. Anarchy would have been established, and not a government, by Washington, Hamilton, Jefferson, Madison, and the other patriots of the Revolution.... Still, a Union that can only be maintained by swords and bayonets, and in which strife and civil war are to take the place of brotherly love and kindness, has no charm for me. I shall mourn for my country and for the welfare and progress of mankind. If the Union is dissolved, and the government disrupted, I shall return to my native state and share the miseries of my people; and, save in defense, will draw my sword on none.

SOURCE: Lee, Robert E. "Letter to His Son," 1861.

allegiances to the Confederacy. Most Lee scholarship has examined Lee's roles as soldier and as slaveholder. His private life has begun to garner renewed interest, particularly in the wake of the discovery in 2002 of two trunks of letters collected by his eldest daughter, Mary Custis Lee. In keeping with the "Letter to His Son," these "letters from after the Civil War," Kevin Vance in a *Washington Times* article reports, "reveal a man struggling with the consequences of the decisions he made in April 1861, when Virginia seceded to the Confederacy and Lee went with it," summing up the continued appeal of Lee's letters.

BIBLIOGRAPHY

Sources

Bradford, Gamaliel. *Lee the American.* Mineola, N.Y.: Dover, 2004. Print.

Fellman, Michael. *The Making of Robert E. Lee.* Baltimore: Johns Hopkins University Press, 2003. Print.

Jones, J. William. *Personal Reminiscences, Anecdotes, and Letters of Gen. Robert E. Lee.* New York: D. Appleton, 1874. *Google Books.* Web. 20 Dec. 2012.

Rev. of *Personal Reminiscences, Anecdotes, and Letters of General Robert E. Lee*, by J. William Jones. *Georgia Weekly Telegraph and Georgia Journal and Messenger* 12 Oct. 1875: 6. *EBSCOhost Newspaper Source Plus.* Web. 10 Dec. 2012.

Vance, Kevin. "Robert E. Lee's Private Side." *Washington Times* 21 June 2007. *EBSCOhost Newspaper Source Plus.* Web. 10 Dec. 2012.

Further Reading

Axelrod, Alan. *Generals South, Generals North: The Commanders of the Civil War Reconsidered.* Guilford, Conn.: Lyons/Globe Pequot, 2011. Print.

Carmichael, Peter S. "Truth Is Mighty and Will Eventually Prevail." *Southern Cultures* 17.3 (2011): 6–27. *Project MUSE.* Web. 10 Dec. 2012.

Friedmann, Greg. "Robert E. Lee, Slave Owner." *Washington Post* 7 May 2011. *EBSCOhost Newspaper Source Plus.* Web. 10 Dec. 2012.

Hewitt, Lawrence Lee, and Thomas E. Schott, eds. *Lee and His Generals: Essays in Honor of T. Harry Williams.* Knoxville: University of Tennessee Press, 2012. Print.

Horn, Stanley F., ed. *The Robert E. Lee Reader.* Whitefish, Mont.: Kessinger, 2005. Print.

David Aitchison

LETTER TO MARIA CLEMM
Edgar Allan Poe

OVERVIEW
On August 29, 1835, Edgar Allan Poe wrote an anguished letter to his aunt, Maria Clemm, declaring his love for her thirteen-year-old daughter, Virginia, and begging Maria to accept him as their financial provider—since they were then in dire financial straits—and to move from Baltimore, Maryland, to Richmond, Virginia, to be with him. The letter was written after Poe discovered that a cousin of his, Neilson Poe, had offered to become Virginia's guardian and provide for her education. Poe, realizing that the Clemms' acceptance of this offer would keep Virginia in Baltimore and hinder his relationship with her, urged Maria to reject Neilson's help. The letter stands as a key document of Poe's bizarre courtship of his much younger cousin, and its intense emotionality and preoccupation with financial woes provide insight into the travails and concerns that recurred throughout Poe's life.

Poe's letter to Maria remained unpublished until nearly a century after his death, partly because Neilson, according to a 1912 letter written by his daughter Amelia, would not allow it to appear in print. In the decades since it became available to scholars, it has become one of the most widely studied and scrutinized of Poe's letters, and it is highly valued for the insight it provides into Poe's tumultuous personal and professional life, as well as into his relationship with his aunt and his cousin (and eventual wife). It remains regularly cited in contemporary biographies of Poe, and it serves as an uncommonly intimate glimpse into both Poe's personal relationships and his psychological state in a condition of extreme distress.

HISTORICAL AND LITERARY CONTEXT
The letter reflects the historical singularity of Poe's professional and personal life, displaying aspects of both that were significantly out of step with American culture in the first half of the nineteenth century. Poe was the first major American author to attempt to earn a living solely through his writing, and his preoccupation with financial matters throughout the letter reflects the extreme difficulty he faced in pursuing this career path. Likewise, his unabashed declaration of love for his young cousin openly flouted contemporary standards of propriety, not on the grounds of incest—marriages between first cousins were accepted and fairly common at the time—but because thirteen was considered a scandalously young age for marriage. Precisely when (and if) their marriage was consummated remains a disputed issue within Poe scholarship.

Poe's letter was written relatively early in his literary career, nearly a decade before the publication of "The Raven" would bring him widespread fame if not financial success. At the time, he had recently moved from Baltimore to Richmond to join the editorial staff of the *Southern Literary Messenger,* hence his references in the letter to the salary he hoped to receive from Thomas Willis White, the magazine's founder. Poe was soon fired for criticizing how the magazine was run but was rehired after promising White he would behave, and he remained on the staff for more than a year afterward, writing numerous articles and contributing to the magazine's growing eminence within the literary world.

Poe's 1835 letter to Maria encapsulates many of the recurring themes of his lifelong correspondence. In their introduction to Poe's *Collected Letters,* Burton R. Pollin and Jeffrey A. Savoye identify his "search for a sanctuary in the face of unyielding difficulties" and his "emotional dependence on various women" as parts of "a series of leitmotifs" that emerges from a reading of Poe's letters. Both of these motifs can clearly be discerned in the letter to Maria, which also prefigures "the influence of Virginia Clemm Poe's lingering illness and ultimate death" that pervades many of the author's future letters, making the 1835 letter a sort of concentrated representative of much of Poe's epistolary life.

In the decades since it was written, the letter—one of Poe's least guarded—has become one of the single most widely cited documents in his voluminous correspondence. Though it is not principally concerned with literary matters, it has contributed significantly to his reputation as a tormented genius. Likewise, the disreputable nature of Poe's ardor for his cousin, as expressed in the letter, is fundamental to modern perceptions of Poe as a transgressor of moral boundaries, perceptions that have endured since the publication of a damning, libelous biographical sketch by Rufus W. Griswold, Poe's literary executor. The letter remains an important source for scholarly writing on Poe's life.

THEMES AND STYLE
Central to the letter is Poe's emphasis on the extraordinary emotional pain he has felt as a result of the Clemms' interest in accepting Neilson's offer. He begins

Key Facts

Time Period:
Mid-19th Century

Relevant Historical Events:
Poe's courtship of his young cousin; Poe's struggle to make a living as a writer

Nationality:
American

Keywords:
love; courtship; scandal

American author and poet Edgar Allan Poe. Maria Clemm was both Poe's aunt and mother-in-law. © LEBRECHT MUSIC AND ARTS PHOTO LIBRARY/ ALAMY

The letter is feverishly written and intemperate in tone, likely reflecting Poe's emotional state at the time he wrote it. The language is bleakly impassioned throughout, though also quite repetitive; Poe twice uses the phrase "God have mercy on me," and he repeatedly calls attention to both his personal alienation—"What have I *to live for?* Among strangers with *not one soul left to love me*"—and his loss of the will to live—"My last my last my only hold on life is cruelly torn away—I have no desire to live and *will not*"— in alarmingly extreme terms. This repetitive quality, along with a number of misspellings, grammatical errors, and other stylistic infelicities, are perhaps an indication of the impassioned speed with which Poe likely wrote the letter—it is among the most seemingly uncontrolled and nakedly emotional of Poe's writings.

CRITICAL DISCUSSION

It is not definitively known how Maria and Virginia reacted to Poe's entreaties, but his ultimate success in persuading them to move in with him suggests that the letter succeeded in its rhetorical goals. Shortly after its composition Poe visited the two in Baltimore (where he may have married Virginia in secret, though this is a matter of scholarly debate), and by October the Clemms had joined him in Richmond. The letter was received with great interest when it finally became widely available to Poe scholars; Arthur Hobson Quinn, in a biography published in 1941 (the same year the letter first appeared in print), asserted that "the letter reveals Poe's situation so completely that it becomes one of the most important documents in his biography."

Ever since it became publicly available, the letter has played a foundational role in Poe's subsequent legacy, particularly for its illumination of his relationship with his aunt and cousin. Quinn notes, "If it were not so necessary to correct the errors that have constantly been made with regard to Poe's feeling for Virginia, the publication of this letter might almost be deemed a violation of the privacy to which even a dead man is entitled." Likewise, James M. Hutchisson's 2005 biography asserts that the letter's "pleas for love and intimate attachment are essentially the same requests that Poe had made so many times of [his foster father] John Allan. Simply put, Poe needed unmitigated love and unqualified approval." This type of biographical analysis is typical of scholarly writing on the letter.

with an extravagant outburst of misery—"I am blinded with tears while writing thi[s] letter—I have no wish to live another hour"—and goes on to assert that his "thoughts are occupied with the supposition that both you & she will prefer to go with N. Poe. ...It is useless to disguise the truth that when Virginia goes with N. P. that I shall never behold her again—that is absolutely sure." Poe's feelings of loneliness and isolation are dwelled upon at length—"Pity me, my dear Aunty, pity me. I have no one now to fly to—I am among strangers, and my wretchedness is more than I can bear"— though he acknowledges the self-interest of his pleadings: "Can I, in honour & in truth say—Virginia! do not go!—do not go where you can be comfortable and perhaps happy—and on the other hand can I calmly resign my—life itself."

Poe's letter was written for the specific purpose of affirming his love for Virginia and persuading his two relatives to accept his own financial support rather than that of Neilson. To that end, much of the letter is devoted to demonstrating Poe's financial solvency— "White has engaged to make my salary $60 a month, and we could live in comparative comfort and happiness"—and he enclosed five dollars with his letter along with promises of more. Likewise, though the letter was ostensibly addressed to Maria, Poe's attempts to appeal to Virginia's affections are demonstrated when he urges Maria to "Ask Virginia. Leave it to her. Let me have, under her own hand, a letter, bidding me *good bye*—forever—and I [m]ay die—my heart will break— but I will say no more," as well as by a brief postscript addressing Virginia directly: "my darling little wifey, thi[nk w]ell before you break the heart of your cousin."

Critical discussion of the letter tends to cite it as support for various assertions about Poe's life. Pollin, writing in the *Mississippi Quarterly* in 1995, argues that Maria manipulated Poe into marrying Virginia in order to ensure her own financial security, asserting of the letter's inquiry, "If she goes with N. P. what are you to do, my own dear Aunty,? [*sic*]." Pollin continues, "That worrisome question is Maria's real concern." Other scholarship discusses the letter in terms of Poe's psychology, as in Julian Symons's 1978 monograph, which states that "it is clear that when he wrote of loving Virginia 'passionately devotedly' he did not

PRIMARY SOURCE

EXCERPT FROM *LETTER TO MARIA CLEMM*

My dearest Aunty,

I am blinded with tears while writing this letter—I have no wish to live another hour. Amid sorrow, and the deepest anxiety your letter reached—and you well know how little I am able to bear up under the pressure of grief. My bitterest enemy would pity me could he now read my heart. My last my last my only hold on life is cruelly torn away—I have no desire to live and *will not*. But let my duty be done. I love, *you know* I love Virginia passionately devotedly. I cannot express in words the fervent devotion I feel towards my dear little cousin—my own darling. But what can [I] say? Oh think for me for I am incapable of thinking. Al[l of my] thoughts are occupied with the supposition that both you & she will prefer to go with N. [Neilson] Poe. I do sincerely believe that your *comforts* will for the present be secured—I cannot speak as regards your peace—your happiness. You have both tender hearts—and you will always have the reflection that my agony is more than I can bear—that you have driven me to the grave—for love like mine can never be gotten over. It is useless to disguise the truth that when Virginia goes with N. P. that I shall never behold her again—that is absolutely sure. Pity me, my dear Aunty, pity me. I have no one now to fly to. I am among strangers, and my wretchedness is more than I can bear. It is useless to expect advice from me—what can I say? Can I, in honour & in truth say—Virginia! do not go!—do not go where you can be comfortable & perhaps happy—and on the other hand can I calmly resign my—life itself. If she had truly loved me would she not have rejected the offer with scorn? Oh God have mercy on me! If she goes with N. P. what are you to do, my own Aunty?

I had procured a sweet little house in a retired situation on Church Hill—newly done up and with a large garden and [ever]y convenience—at only $5 month. I have been dreaming every day & night since of the rapture I should feel in [havin]g my only friends—all I love on Earth with me there, [and] the pride I would take in making you both comfor[table] & in calling her my wife. But the dream is over [Oh G]od have mercy on me. What have I *to live for*? Among strangers with *not one soul to love me*.

[…]

The tone of your letter wounds me to the soul—Oh Aunty, aunty you loved me once—how can you be so cruel now? You speak of Virginia acquiring accomplishments, and entering into society—you speak in so *worldly* a tone. Are you sure she would be more happy. Do you think any one could love her more dearly than I? She will have far—very far better opportunities of entering into society here than with N. P. Every one here receives me with open arms.

Adieu my dear aunty. I *cannot advise you*. Ask Virginia. Leave it to her. Let me have, under her own hand, a letter, bidding me *good bye*—forever—and I may die—my heart will break—but I will say no more.

E A P.

SOURCE: Poe, Edgar Allan. "Letter to Maria Clemm. *Edgar Allan Poe: Letters and Documents.* In the Enoch Pratt Free Library, Scholars' Facsimiles & Reprints, 1941. Maryland's State Library Resource Center. All rights reserved. Used with permission. Unauthorized reproduction or use prohibited.

---

mean physical love. His anguish at the thought of losing her sprang partly from the breaking up of what he thought of as his family, partly from the loss of an ideal woman."

BIBLIOGRAPHY

Sources

Hutchisson, James M. *Poe.* Jackson: University of Mississippi Press, 2005. Print.

Poe, Edgar Allan. *The Collected Letters of Edgar Allan Poe.* 2 vols. Ed. John W. Ostrom, Burton R. Pollin, and Jeffrey A. Savoye. 3rd ed. Staten Island, N.Y.: Gordian, 2008. Print.

Pollin, Burton R. "Maria Clemm, Poe's Aunt: His Boon or His Bane?" *Mississippi Quarterly* 48.2 (1995): 211–24. *Academic OneFile.* Web. 12 Dec. 2012.

Quinn, Arthur Hobson. *Edgar Allan Poe: A Critical Biography.* 1941. Baltimore: Johns Hopkins University Press, 1998. Print.

Symons, Julian. *The Tell-Tale Heart: The Life and Works of Edgar Allan Poe.* New York: Harper, 1978. Print.

Further Reading

Coviello, Peter. "Poe in Love: Pedophilia, Morbidity, and the Logic of Slavery." *ELH* 70.3 (2003): 875–901. Print.

Hayes, Kevin J., ed. *The Cambridge Companion to Edgar Allan Poe.* Cambridge, U.K.: Cambridge University Press, 2002. Print.

Meyers, Jeffrey. *Edgar Allan Poe: His Life and Legacy.* New York: Charles Scribner's Sons, 1992. Print.

Poe, Edgar Allan. *Collected Works of Edgar Allan Poe.* 3 vols. Ed. Thomas Ollive Mabbott. Cambridge, Mass.: Belknap-Harvard University Press, 1969–78. Print.

Silverman, Kenneth. *Edgar A. Poe: Mournful and Never-Ending Remembrance.* New York: Harper, 1991. Print.

Thomas, Dwight R., and David K. Jackson. *The Poe Log: A Documentary Life of Edgar Allan Poe, 1809–1849.* Boston: Hall, 1987. Print.

Zimmerman, Brett. *Edgar Allan Poe: Rhetoric and Style.* Montreal: McGill-Queen's University Press, 2005. Print.

James Overholtzer

LETTER TO THE REVEREND SAMSON OCCOM

Phillis Wheatley

+ *Key Facts*

Time Period:
Mid-18th Century

Relevant Historical Events:
Wheatley's emancipation from slavery; birth of abolitionism

Nationality:
American

Keywords:
abolitionism; slavery; Christianity

OVERVIEW

Phillis Wheatley's letter to the Reverend Samson Occom, first published in the *Connecticut Gazette* on March 11, 1774, seeks to insert a reconsideration of slavery into the contemporary American conversation about liberty and human rights. Born in West Africa and kidnapped into slavery around the age of seven, the recently emancipated Wheatley had established a reputation as a poet and an exemplar of the intellectual potential of people of African descent. She had also, with the help of Susanna Wheatley, the mistress who raised and educated her, built a social and political network that included Occom, a Presbyterian minister born into the Mohegan tribe. The letter represents their joint effort to leverage Wheatley's fame to make a public statement denouncing slaveholding.

The epistolary form, with its ability to imply shared responsibility for the ideas expressed, seems to have emboldened Wheatley to pen one of her most direct statements of opposition to slavery. Because the letter uses sharp satirical language to expose the hypocrisy of Americans who criticize the British monarchy for depriving them of their God-given right to liberty while holding others in bondage, it suggests the presence of more subtle satire in earlier poetry by Wheatley. Some of these poems, when read as entirely earnest, imply that the poet acquiesced in the idea that slavery was a reasonable price to pay for exposure to Christianity. The letter's satirical approach suggests a need to reexamine these poems for a more sophisticated invocation of shared Christian values to condemn slaveholding.

HISTORICAL AND LITERARY CONTEXT

Wheatley's authorial practices were typical of her time and place. However, as the descriptions of her age, gender, and status appended to her published poems reveal, it was highly unusual for an enslaved female teenager, kidnapped from Africa barely a decade before, to participate in a literary culture that combined private circulation of manuscripts with publication in newspapers, broadsides, or books. Wheatley's writings, in addition to allowing her to participate in the private and public conversations of the day, served as evidence of the potential of people of African descent to engage on an equal basis in civic and cultural discourse.

Wheatley's reply to Occom was written as the publication of her 1773 volume of verse, *Poems on Various Subjects, Religious and Moral,* was consolidating and extending her reputation in England and New England and as conversations about oppression and liberty were reaching an intensity that would lead, two years later, to the American Revolution. While the letter to which Wheatley replied has been lost, and it is unclear who initiated publication of Wheatley's reply, the exchange appears to be a cooperative effort on the parts of the recently emancipated slave and the Native American minister to interject the rights of African Americans into contemporary political and cultural conversations about freedom.

In publishing her work, Wheatley joined a small but growing circle of eighteenth-century Afro-Atlantic writers. In the American colonies two apparently unrelated men with the last name of Hammon—Britton and Jupiter—had, starting in the 1760s, published writings including an autobiography, sermons, and poetry, including a 1778 poem by Jupiter Hammon celebrating Wheatley. In England the Countess of Huntingdon, who became Wheatley's patroness, had assisted with the 1772 publication of the autobiography of James Albert Ukawsaw Gronniosaw, a self-identified "African prince," and in 1789 would provide similar help to Olaudah Equiano, a former slave who became involved in abolishing the slave trade. Ignatius Sancho, whose collection of letters was published posthumously in 1782, was often cited alongside Wheatley as evidence of Africans' intelligence and literary ability.

The rapid and widespread reprinting of Wheatley's letter to Occom suggests that both its author and its subject interested Wheatley's contemporaries. Between March and May 1774 all or part of the letter appeared in at least eleven newspapers published in three New England colonies—Massachusetts, Connecticut, and Rhode Island—and in Nova Scotia. In October 1775 Wheatley openly embraced the cause of American independence from Britain—about which she and the Wheatley family had heretofore been circumspect—in the poem "To His Excellency General Washington." She sent the poem to Washington, and it was printed in spring 1776 in the *Virginia Gazette* and in Thomas Paine's *Pennsylvania Magazine or American Monthly Museum.*

THEMES AND STYLE

In her letter to Occom, Wheatley inserts Africa and people of African descent into a larger narrative of progress based on an opposition between humans' God-given desire for liberty and their temptation to oppress others. "The divine light," she writes, "is chasing away the thick Darkness which broods over the Land of Africa … reveal[ing] more and more clearly, the glorious dispensation of civil and religious liberty, which are so inseparably united, that there is little Enjoyment of one without the other." Comparing enslaved Africans to the enslaved Israelites in Exodus, she calls New England slaveholders—descendants of the Puritans accustomed to styling themselves modern Israelites—"our modern Egyptians," marking them as oppressors. She closes with a wish that "God grant deliverance" to modern captives "in his own Way and Time" and vanquish "those whose Avarice compels them to countenance and help forward the Calamities of their Fellow Creatures … not for their Hurt, but to convince them of the strange Absurdity of their Conduct whose Words and Actions are so diametrically opposite."

The epistolary form, in which Wheatley paraphrases and then builds on Occom's argument, allows her to make a particularly bold and direct statement of opposition to slavery. She opens by thanking Occom for his letter, saying that she is "greatly satisfied with [Occom's] Reasons respecting the Negroes" and that she "think[s] highly sensible what [Occom] offer[s] in Vindication of their natural Rights." The long sentence that follows makes it hard to judge exactly where the paraphrase of Occom's argument ends and the expression of Wheatley's own ideas begins, though the phrase "I will assert" toward the end signals that Wheatley is, by that point, expressing ideas she claims as her own. The result is, in effect, a joint public statement in which Occom and Wheatley each lend authority to their shared beliefs.

As the letter progresses, Wheatley's tone becomes increasingly sharp. The first indication that hypocrisy will be one of her major themes comes early in the letter, with the declaration that "those who invade" the "natural Rights" of "the Negroes … cannot be insensible" of progress in Africa and among people of African descent. The next barb comes with her description of slaveholders as "modern Egyptians" and her reminder that her voice can only be heard "by the[ir] leave"—presumably because they control avenues of publication. The closing of the letter is more satirical still, suggesting that it "does not require" the sort of erudition for which Wheatley was famous (and that many of her white contemporaries found improbable)—"the Penetration of a Philosopher"—to understand the contradiction inherent in joining "the cry for Liberty" while continuing to "exercise … oppressive Power over others."

CRITICAL DISCUSSION

The clearest available evidence of contemporary interest in Wheatley's letter lies in multiple newspaper editors' decisions to reprint it. Mukhtar Ali Isani argues in the *Journal of Negro History* that the "narrow … tenday … span of dates" over which the letter was initially republished "suggest[s] that the submission of the letter" to the newspapers "was the work of one hand," most likely Occom's. However, as Isani points out, "the limited space of the colonial newspaper gives significance even to the usual scanty notices of the time"; in this context the editors' individual decisions to republish a substantial if compact letter suggest genuine interest in Wheatley's ideas.

In the decades following the American Revolution, Wheatley's work was regularly cited in debates over slavery. Thomas Jefferson, in his *Notes on the State of Virginia,* dismissed Wheatley's poems as "below the dignity of criticism" while simultaneously implying doubt that Wheatley had written them. As David Waldstreicher argues in his article "The Wheatleyan Moment," Jefferson's "vituperative response to Wheatley" belies his dismissal of the poet, "suggest[ing] the threat that her poems and her public actions … posed for Jefferson." Abolitionists also invoked Wheatley; as Jennifer Rene Young recounts in *New Essays on Phillis Wheatley,* in 1832 the antislavery newspaper the *Liberator* reprinted "almost all of Wheatley's poems from the 1773 volume," even though most of them "did not have overt messages of abolition … probably … as evidence of African capabilities."

Recent critics cite Wheatley's letter to Occom as evidence of her active participation in literary and political networks and of her sophisticated adaptation of tone to audience and situation. For these critics the letter, particularly its biting conclusion, provides

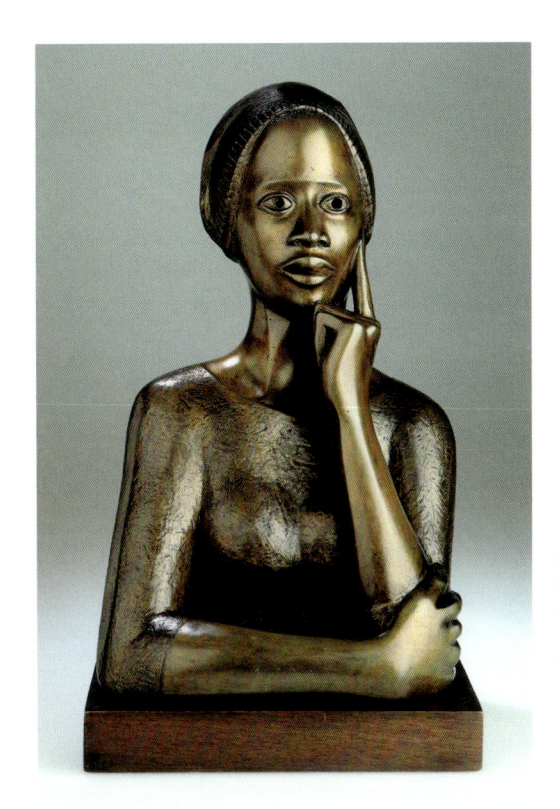

Bronze bust of Phillis Wheatley, the first African American woman to have her poetry published. Created by artist Elizabeth Catlett in 1973. © CINCINNATI ART MUSEUM/THE BRIDGEMAN ART LIBRARY

REVEREND SAMSON OCCOM

Phillis Wheatley's correspondent and collaborator, Samson Occom, was born into the Mohegan tribe in Connecticut in 1723. He converted to Christianity as a teenager and was ordained as a Presbyterian minister in 1759. In 1764 he joined evangelist George Whitefield on a preaching tour of New England and probably met Susanna Wheatley and Phillis Wheatley during a stop in Boston. In subsequent years he corresponded with both Susanna and Phillis and stayed frequently at the Wheatley home. Phillis's first known letter, written in 1765 or 1766 and now lost, was reportedly written to Occom while he was on a fund-raising tour in England.

While on this tour Occom made the acquaintance of the Countess of Huntingdon, who later served as dedicatee and sponsor of Wheatley's book of poems. Though his efforts to support the founding of a school for Indians ended in betrayal by missionary Eleazar Wheelock, who chose instead to found a school for white students that eventually became Dartmouth College, Occom remained an effective advocate for Native American rights. Like Wheatley he was skilled at using Christian rhetoric to support arguments for racial equality, an ability that is evident in, among other texts, his 1772 sermon delivered before the execution of fellow native Moses Paul.

a lens through which to view what Henry Louis Gates calls "the most reviled poem in African-American literature," Wheatley's "On Being Brought from Africa to America." This perspective allows the poem's closing lines, which urge "Christians" to "remember" that "*Negros,* black as *Cain,* / may be refin'd, and join th'angelic train," to be read, like the closing of the letter, as satirical. Rather than betraying "racial self-hatred," Vincent Carretta argues in *Phillis Wheatley: Biography of a Genius in Bondage,* the poem's ending illustrates Wheatley's "repeated appropriat[ion]" of "the values of Christianity to judge and find wanting hypocritical self-styled Christians of European descent."

BIBLIOGRAPHY

Sources

Carretta, Vincent. *Phillis Wheatley: Biography of a Genius in Bondage.* Athens: University of Georgia Press, 2011. Print.

Gates, Henry Louis. *The Trials of Phillis Wheatley.* New York: Basic, 2003. Print.

Isani, Mukhtar Ali. "The Contemporaneous Reception of Phillis Wheatley: Newspaper and Magazine Notices during the Years of Fame, 1765–1774." *Journal of Negro History* 85.4 (2000): 260–73. Web. *JSTOR.* 17 Dec. 2012.

Jefferson, Thomas. *Writings.* Ed. Merrill D. Peterson. New York: Library of America, 1984. Print.

Waldstreicher, David. "The Wheatleyan Moment." *Early American Studies* 9.3 (2011): 522–51. Web. *Project MUSE.* 18 Dec. 2012.

Wheatley, Phillis. *Complete Writings.* Ed. Vincent Carretta. New York: Penguin, 2001. Print.

Young, Jennifer Rene. "Marketing a Sable Muse: Phillis Wheatley and the Antebellum Press." Ed. John C. Shields and Eric D. Lamore. *New Essays on Phillis Wheatley.* Knoxville: University of Tennessee Press, 2011. 209–46. Print.

Further Reading

Brooks, Joanna. "Our Phillis, Ourselves." *American Literature* 82.1 (2010): 1–28. Web. *e-Duke.* 24 Dec. 2012.

Chiles, Katy L. "Becoming Colored in Occom and Wheatley's Early America." *PMLA* 123.5 (2008): 1398–417. *MLA Journals.* Web. 26 Dec. 2012.

Erkkila, Betsy. *Mixed Bloods and Other Crosses: Rethinking American Literature from the Revolution to the Culture Wars.* Philadelphia: University of Pennsylvania Press, 2004. Print.

Foster, Frances Smith. *Written by Herself: Literary Production by African American Women, 1746–1892.* Bloomington: Indiana University Press, 1992. Print.

Occom, Samson. *The Collected Writings of Samson Occom, Mohegan: Leadership and Literature in Eighteenth-Century Native America.* Ed. Joanna Brooks. New York: Oxford University Press, 2006. Print.

Robinson, William H., ed. *Critical Essays on Phillis Wheatley.* Boston: G. K. Hall, 1982. Print.

Shields, John C., and Eric D. Lamore, eds. *New Essays on Phillis Wheatley.* Knoxville: University of Tennessee Press, 2011. Print.

Wilcox, Kirstin. "The Body into Print: Marketing Phillis Wheatley." *American Literature* 71.1 (1999): 1–29. *JSTOR.* Web. 24 Dec. 2012.

Cathy Saunders

Letters Home
Sylvia Plath

OVERVIEW

First published in 1975, Sylvia Plath's *Letters Home* is a compilation of letters written by Plath in the period between her departure from home to attend Smith College in 1950 and her death by suicide in 1963. Edited by Plath's mother, Aurelia Schober Plath, the book consists mostly of letters addressed to Aurelia (along with a smaller quantity sent to Plath's brother Warren and her friend and benefactor, Olive Higgins Prouty). The letters address many aspects of the author's life, including her literary endeavors, her various youthful romances, her anxieties and occasional mental breakdowns, her marriage with and eventual separation from English poet Ted Hughes, and her relationship with her children. With a number of significant exceptions, the tone of the letters is generally cheerful and upbeat, giving the reader a markedly different perspective on the events of Plath's life than that of her published journals and semiautobiographical literary writings.

Letters Home appeared in the wake of a massive upswing in Plath's fame—fueled by the publication of several posthumous volumes of poetry as well as the long-awaited U.S edition of her novel *The Bell Jar* in 1971—and a corresponding interest in the details of her life. Despite this widespread interest, the book sold relatively poorly and received mixed reviews, with Aurelia's numerous editorial cuts to her daughter's letters a frequent target of criticism. The book is nevertheless an important and illuminating contribution to the study of Plath's life and work, and both the letters themselves and Aurelia's editing of them have been subject to copious scholarly analysis.

HISTORICAL AND LITERARY CONTEXT

Plath's letters reflect the relatively narrow range of cultural expectations for women that predominated during her lifetime. Notwithstanding a number of advances in women's rights throughout the twentieth century, American women were often still valued primarily in relation to their prescribed roles as mothers and homemakers. Despite Plath's literary success and her obvious concern for her own intellectual independence, the extreme importance her letters place on her marriage to Hughes and their young family demonstrates the extent to which she had internalized contemporary gender roles as a means of personal validation. This influence likely contributed to the psychologically devastating effects of the marriage's ultimate collapse.

Apart from a few gaps, the correspondence in *Letters Home* covers the entirety of Plath's life from September 1957 onward, making the book an enlightening (albeit one-sided) glimpse into Plath's development and participation in the American and British literary scenes of the twentieth century. The letters document Plath's education, first at Smith College (where the noted essayist and critic Alfred Kazin served as an important mentor figure) and then at Cambridge. They also detail her and Hughes's subsequent personal and professional interactions with literary figures such as Peter Davison, T. S. Eliot, W. S. Merwin, and Marianne Moore.

The publication of *Letters Home* was largely a response to the widespread public interest in (and mythologizing of) Plath's life that had built up in the years following her death and was partly intended to counteract the perceptions fostered by *The Bell Jar*. The mother of that novel's protagonist was widely believed to be an unflattering fictionalization of Plath's own mother. Indeed, Aurelia consented to the novel's U.S. publication only on the condition that Hughes, the inheritor of Plath's literary estate, allow her to release *Letters Home*, which was substantially pruned by both Aurelia and Hughes before publication. The warm mother-daughter relationship suggested by the published letters served as an apparent refutation (or at least a complication) of the animosity indicated by *The Bell Jar*, a novel whose influence Aurelia had grown to deeply resent.

In the decades since its publication, *Letters Home* contributed significantly to the public understanding of Plath's life, though it did not ultimately change the basic tenor of that understanding, which remained heavily influenced by *The Bell Jar* and the confessional poems assembled in the collection *Ariel*. The first of several posthumous volumes of Plath's personal writings, *Letters Home* was supplemented in 1982 by the release of an abridged version of her journals, which was far more commercially successful and contained bleak, bitter material that contrasted sharply with the relative cheerfulness of Aurelia's book. *Letters Home* continues to attract interest from scholars and enthusiasts of Plath's work, but its guardedly optimistic tone,

❖ *Key Facts*

Time Period:
Mid-20th Century

Relevant Historical Events:
Plath's sudden fame and the failure of her marriage to poet Ted Hughes

Nationality:
American

Keywords:
poetry; fame; women's writing

"that sometimes when all your chickens come home to roost at the same time, broken and bloody, it is a little discouraging."

The contents of *Letters Home* were ostensibly written in order to maintain communication with Plath's correspondents and keep them apprised of her life's events, but they also likely served both as a way for her to meditate on those events herself and as a means of presenting an idealized version of her life to others. Many of Plath's statements, especially those about her life with Hughes, may well have been written more for the author's benefit than that of the letter's recipient: "Oh, we have rousing battles every so often in which I come out with sprained thumbs and Ted with missing earlobes, but we feel so perfectly at one with our work and reactions to life and people that we make our own world to work in." Aurelia alludes to this function, saying Plath wrote the reassuring letters after the separation with Hughes "to reassure herself as well."

Though the letters vary widely in tone, the majority of them are bright and enthusiastic, bearing little obvious resemblance to the literary work for which Plath is most well known. Affirmations of delight or satisfaction are common, as when she notes, "Yesterday the proofs of my book *The Colossus* came in a paper binding. We are so excited. The book will look handsome, 88 pages long. The poems look so beautifully *final*." Likewise, though admissions of depression or adversity are fairly common, these tend to be accompanied by attempts to cast recent events in a positive light, as in a letter written the day after Christmas, several months after the separation with Hughes: "It is amazing how much my new hairdo and new clothes have done for my rather shattered morale. I had a lovely tea with the Frankforts."

CRITICAL DISCUSSION

Upon its initial publication in 1975, *Letters Home* met with unspectacular sales—particularly in relation to the commercial success of previous Plath books—and mixed reviews. Many critics expressed dismay at the extent to which Plath's letters had been bowdlerized throughout the editing process; Maureen Howard, writing in the *New York Times Book Review*, called attention to "the problem of deletions which reduce some of the letters to bits and pieces and suggests the mother's need to contain at last the daughter's life." This criticism was echoed by numerous other contemporary reviewers, who nonetheless acknowledged the insight into Plath's life offered by the publication of the letters, even in an expurgated form.

Since its release, *Letters Home* has substantially influenced Plath's legacy, though not always in ways intended by Aurelia. As with various other posthumous collections of Plath's writing, the book's editorial process has been subject to almost as much scrutiny as its actual content; Steven Gould Axelrod, in his 1990 study of Plath's life and work, notes,

Author Sylvia Plath in an undated photo. © EVERETT COLLECTION

coupled with the intrusiveness of Aurelia's editorial redactions, have made it one of the less popular volumes in Plath's bibliography.

THEMES AND STYLE

Central to *Letters Home* is a sense of Plath's overachieving nature and pride in her work, as well as her ongoing, intermittently successful attempts to prevent various setbacks from disastrously affecting her mental outlook. Much of the text consists of effusive reports on her academic or literary endeavors, as when she writes to Aurelia, "My mind seethes with ideas for stories; my novel preoccupies me; and I am spending this year daily doing a detailed notebook of Cambridge with sketches, trying to sell chapters as stories, then [will] finish the writing of it next summer." Her letters often convey a positive frame of mind—likely for her mother's benefit—even in the face of misfortune, but at times this gives way to unconcealed and somewhat intemperate dismay, as in a letter lamenting her rejection by a scholarship committee and noting

"The volume contains two overlapping but distinguishable dialogues: the one between mother and daughter preserved in the letters themselves and the one between editor-mother and author-daughter created by the volume's published form." Scholarly writing on *Letters Home* frequently addresses both of these dialogues, in addition to mining the book for straightforward biographical information.

Scholarship discussing *Letters Home* often focuses on the ramifications of Aurelia's editorship, as in Jacqueline Rose's 1991 study *The Haunting of Sylvia Plath:* "Going from the published to the unpublished letters, the impression is constantly of something one *already* knows—as if the published text was operating rather like the contents of a psychoanalytic setting, where what is presented to consciousness bears the most intimate relation to the unconscious thoughts it is most concerned to disguise." Other critics focus on the vagaries of the letters themselves, as in Wendy Whelan-Stewart's 2008 article in *Intertexts,* which discusses how, throughout the letters, Plath "performs for her audience (Mrs. Plath) the roles her mother wishes to see and manipulates her image so that, more often than not, she represents an ideal daughter, student, or wife."

SYLVIA PLATH'S JOURNALS

Although *Letters Home* met with a fairly tepid financial reception, Plath's journals attained instant success upon their publication. They initially appeared in 1982 in a severely redacted edition whose various omissions, done at the editorial behest of Ted Hughes, contributed significantly to the already-considerable animosity felt toward him by many admirers of Plath's work. This antipathy was not improved by Hughes's claim that he had burned a journal from Plath's final days. Before his death in 1998, Hughes unsealed two journals he had previously suppressed, and a largely complete version (minus the destroyed journal and one other that Hughes claimed had disappeared) was finally published in 2000.

The journals are far more raw and emotionally intense than Plath's letters. Much of the text consists of straightforward narration of events, but also present are profuse outpourings of emotion and lengthy philosophical ruminations. Unsurprisingly, Plath makes little effort in the journals to conceal the extent of her anxieties, making the journals a much more obvious testament to Plath's personal unhappiness than *Letters Home.* Her relationship with her mother—for whom she repeatedly declares her hatred at one point in the journal—likewise emerges as far more complex and troubled than the letters suggest.

BIBLIOGRAPHY

Sources

Axelrod, Steven Gould. *Sylvia Plath: The Wound and the Cure of Words.* Baltimore: Johns Hopkins University Press, 1990. Print.

Howard, Maureen. "The Girl Who Tried to Be Good." Rev. of *Letters Home,* by Sylvia Plath. *New York Times Book Review* 14 Dec. 1975: 1–2. *ProQuest Historical Newspapers: The New York Times (1851–2009).* Web. 19 Dec. 2012.

Plath, Sylvia. *Letters Home: Correspondence 1950–1963.* Ed. Aurelia Schober Plath. New York: Harper & Row, 1975. Print.

Rose, Jacqueline. *The Haunting of Sylvia Plath.* 1991. Cambridge, Mass.: Harvard University Press, 1992. Print.

Whelan-Stewart, Wendy. "Role-Playing the 'Feminine' in *Letters Home.*" *Intertexts* 12.1–2 (2008): 129–43. *Literary Reference Center.* Web. 19 Dec. 2012.

Further Reading

Alexander, Paul. *Rough Magic: A Biography of Sylvia Plath.* New York: Viking, 1991. Print.

Bayley, Sally, and Tracy Brain, eds. *Representing Sylvia Plath.* Cambridge, U.K.: Cambridge University Press, 2011. Print.

Brain, Tracy. *The Other Sylvia Plath.* Harlow, U.K.: Longman, 2001. Print.

Gill, Jo, ed. *The Cambridge Companion to Sylvia Plath.* Cambridge, U.K.: Cambridge University Press, 2006. Print.

Hughes, Ted. *Birthday Letters.* New York: Farrar, Straus and Giroux, 1998. Print.

Middlebrook, Diane. *Her Husband: Hughes and Plath—A Marriage.* New York: Viking, 2003. Print.

Plath, Sylvia. *The Bell Jar.* 1963. New York: Harper & Row, 1971. Print.

———. *The Collected Poems.* Ed. Ted Hughes. New York: Harper & Row, 1981. Print.

———. *The Unabridged Journals of Sylvia Plath, 1950–1962.* Ed. Karen V. Kukil. New York: Anchor, 2000. Print.

James Overholtzer

LETTERS UNDERWAY
'Izzat Ghazzawi

❖ **Key Facts**

Time Period:
Late 20th Century

Relevant Historical Events:
First Palestinian intifada; Ghazzawi's imprisonment; Israeli-Palestinian conflict

Nationality:
Palestinian

Keywords:
Israel; Palestine; imprisonment

OVERVIEW

'Izzat Ghazzawi's *Letters Underway* (1991) recounts the two years the author spent in prison, from 1988 to 1990, during the first Palestinian intifada (1987–93). It combines letters, poetry, reminiscences, and meditations in an effort to describe the continued suffering of the Palestinians nearly half a century after the 1948 creation of the state of Israel. Ghazzawi calls for the creation of an independent Palestinian state, but he condemns the use of violence and recognizes the loss that has occurred on both sides of the conflict. Confirming the principles and ideals that Ghazzawi devoted his life to promoting, *Letters Underway* seeks international acknowledgment of the Palestinian experience as a necessary prerequisite for peace, even as it anticipates its message's failure to reach its intended audience.

Although prison narratives are common in Arabic literature, and autobiographical accounts of internment in Egypt, Morocco, and Iraq have been well received and widely studied both in Arabic and in English, *Letters Underway* has failed to attract significant critical or scholarly attention. Following its translation into English in 1993, the book continued to be overshadowed by Ghazzawi's other publications and interest in his political role in the intifada and its aftermath. In 1994 *Letters Underway* was translated into Norwegian and was awarded the Stavanger International Prize for Freedom of Expression. Some scholars have expressed hope that the work may be utilized as a historical document for future studies on Israeli prisons. This approach, however, ignores the importance of the book's literary qualities and style, which allow it to escape the physical confines of the prison to address a variety of themes.

HISTORICAL AND LITERARY CONTEXT

A series of increasingly aggressive Israeli policies against the Palestinian population both within Israel and in the occupied territories led in 1987 to the outbreak of the first intifada, a popular Palestinian uprising that relied on civil disobedience as well as violence in its attempt to end the Israeli occupation of the Palestinian territories, halt attempts at annexation, and secure an independent Palestinian state. Ghazzawi, a professor at Birzeit University, a center of Palestinian political activity and consciousness during the intifada until it was temporarily shut down in 1988, was given a twenty-seven-month prison sentence for what were considered incendiary writings, as well as for his involvement in the secular nationalist Palestine Liberation Organization (PLO).

Ghazzawi published *Letters Underway* in 1991 following his release from prison. The intifada began to lose its momentum in the early 1990s, and its end is generally marked by the signing of the 1993 Oslo Accords by Israeli Prime Minister Yitzhak Rabin and PLO Chairman Yasser Arafat in Washington DC. That same year, Ghazzawi's sixteen-year-old son, Rami, was killed by Israeli troops as he attempted to aid a wounded classmate.

Letters Underway is part of a long and sizable Arabic tradition of prison narratives. Among the predecessors of Ghazzawi's text were Abdelrahman Munif's *East of the Mediterranean* (1972), a novel that addresses the experience of internment, and Mu'in Bisisu's *Palestinian Notebooks* (1978), which describes the Palestinian author's imprisonment in Egypt's Wahat prison camp. Ghazzawi had previously authored a collection of fictional short stories called *The Woman Prisoner* (1987), which center on the experience of imprisonment. In *Letters Underway*, Ghazzawi also locates himself within a broader corpus of activist literature written in both Hebrew and Arabic about the ongoing conflict, addressing Palestinian poet Mahmoud Darwish and Israeli poet Yair Hurvitz in his letters. Stylistically, the text's combination of poetry and prose, as well as its mixture of autobiography and fiction, is reminiscent of Darwish's *Memory for Forgetfulness* (1982).

Ghazzawi's simultaneous condemnation of Israeli and Palestinian aggression and support of dialogue in *Letters Underway* reveal a commitment to justice and abhorrence of violence that are reflected in his later activities and writings. When his son was killed, Ghazzawi was serving on the editorial board of a new Palestinian-Israeli magazine called the *Palestine-Israel Journal of Politics, Economics, and Culture* that sought to understand the underlying sources of the ongoing conflict. The magazine's first issue was dedicated to Rami. Ghazzawi later founded the Bereaved Family Forum with university professor Nurit Peled-Elhanan, whose thirteen-year-old daughter, Smadar, was killed by a Palestinian suicide bomber in 1997. Together they were awarded the European Parliament's Sakharov

Prize for Freedom of Thought in 2001 for their continued support of peace.

THEMES AND STYLE

In *Letters Underway*, Palestinian prisoners are described metaphorically as postal letters, providing testimony—through their experiences of torture, oppression, and dehumanization—to the reality of Israeli policies and to the obstacle these policies present to a lasting peace. Ghazzawi situates himself as a "postman for humanity," in the words of Turkish poet Nazim Hikmet, attempting to deliver messages that expose his and his fellow prisoners' suffering to Israelis and the international community, even while he tries to explain the necessity of nonviolence to fellow Palestinians. He attempts to communicate retroactively to his Israeli interrogator that "we [the Palestinians] don't want our state at your expense" and later addresses the new generation of Palestinians born under occupation who "have to understand that there are two states for two people; human values must be firmly implanted in them so that the internalized brutality does not become second nature. They have to understand that we can change these cellars and prisons into schools, that we must fear blood." By framing his text as a collection of letters, Ghazzawi indicates that *Letters Underway* only fulfills its function once its missives have been received by their intended recipients.

Ghazzawi wrote *Letters Underway* in an effort to raise Israeli and international consciousness of Palestinian suffering, believing that it was only through this recognition that a lasting peace could be achieved. He expresses the need to "rewrite history" to provide "a gauge for the accumulated years of subjugation and dispersal." In order to achieve this goal, he argues, Palestinian prisoners who have been denied justice must tell their stories to "[their] people, wives, children and friends," but they must also reach "another people who share [their] life": "Our song is predestined to convey two languages at once, lest we should lose our home forever." Despite Ghazzawi's urgency and determination, *Letters Underway* contains a self-awareness of the difficulty of the task he faces: "My letters are still underway, and may never be delivered." The premonition that his message would fail to reach its intended recipients is borne out by the almost complete lack of scholarly and critical attention received by the text.

Through the mixture of poetry and prose, including letters, memories, meditations, bits of dialogue, and accounts of other prisoners' experiences, Ghazzawi aspires to a universal poetic language that succeeds in widely communicating the message of Palestinian suffering where more straightforward linear narratives

West Bank of the Jordan River, 1982. Since World War II the ownership of this territory has been in dispute, being claimed by Jordan, Israel, and the Palestinian people who constitute about eighty percent of its population. A native of the West Bank, Palestinian writer 'Izzat Ghazzawi described the hardships he witnessed there and spent time in prison as punishment for his political activities. © ALAIN LE GARSMEUR/ CORBIS

THE FIRST INTIFADA (1987–93)

During the 1980s the Likud, a conservative political party that hoped to annex the occupied Palestinian territories, dominated Israeli politics. Under its leadership, the Israeli state pursued a series of policies aimed at subduing the Palestinian population in the occupied territories, confiscating land, holding Palestinians under administrative detention without charging them, raising taxes, increasing bureaucracy and security in the territories, and adopting a number of other practices designed to consolidate land claims.

Demonstrations began spontaneously on December 9, 1987, when four Palestinians were killed in a traffic accident involving an Israeli military vehicle. Violence escalated in the following days, and by January 1988 the Palestinian Unified National Leadership had arisen, adopting an administrative role to organize the uprising. The goal was an independent Palestinian state, and the first few years of the intifada were characterized by strikes, demonstrations, tax boycotts, and other acts of civil disobedience. Weapons were at first limited to stones and slingshots, although the use of guns became increasingly common as the struggle continued, and the first suicide bombings were carried out targeting Israelis. Palestinians who were identified as collaborators with Israel were relentlessly persecuted by their own communities. A large death toll and massive arrests gradually weakened the intifada's momentum, paving the way in 1993 for the Oslo Accords. More than a thousand Palestinians were killed by Israeli security forces between December 1987 and the signing of the Oslo Accords, and about a hundred Israelis were killed by Palestinians. It is estimated that between 35,000 and 40,000 Palestinians had been arrested by the end of 1990.

have failed. *Letters Underway* opens with eight poems by the author: seven "entrances" and one "exit." These are followed by a first chapter explaining that the poem "is not a way out," but "the dream of perfecting it to God's perfection may be the way out." By the end of the text, however, Ghazzawi concludes that while "the Messiah has said that people should be given just a hook, not fish ready caught," the unfinished poem "will always remain ineffective," seeming to indicate that the dream of perfection, the hook alone, will not succeed in communicating the necessary message. All the same, the variety of approaches adopted by the author—as well as the diversity of his addressees, who range from Israeli and Turkish poets to a Red Cross worker—suggest a hopefulness that he has granted his readers the tools they need to better understand "the tragedy of exile in the homeland, alienation in the homeland." On a personal level, the use of experimental poetic language represents a means of resistance in its ability to expand the limits of language, creating a free space that challenges the author's physical confinement within a cell and within the larger prison that the occupied territories had become.

CRITICAL DISCUSSION

When *Letters Underway* was first translated into English in 1993, it received little critical attention. In the preface to the 1996 English edition, 'Abd al-Karim Khashan compares Ghazzawi to other revolutionary poets and writers, such as Bisisu, Abu Firas al-Hamdani, Paul Eluard, and Louis Aragon, and notes the text's importance, writing, "Dear 'Izzat, if Tagore, Lorca, Ya'ir Horowitz, Nathem Hikmet and so many others died before your voice reached them through these letters, then your child and all the children with her will read these heartbeats with pride." However, no reviews of the text, positive or negative, were published in English in the years that followed.

In *Confronting the Occupation* (2004), Maya Rosenfeld identifies *Letters Underway* as "an invaluable resource" for information about "the internal organization of Palestinian political prisoners in Israeli jails." She argues that since there has been no scholarly work on the subject, accounts like *Letters Underway*, in combination with unpublished notes and explicit works of fiction such as Sami Kilani's *Three Minus One* (1990), provide necessary insight. Despite the possibilities opened up by this of line of inquiry, scholarly treatment of the text as a historical document has been limited.

Although some studies make note of *Letters Underway*, almost all of the small body of scholarship on Ghazzawi is concerned with his political activities. For example, Mary Elizabeth King, in *Quiet Revolution* (2007), lists *Letters Underway* in a short, footnoted biography but primarily focuses on Ghazzawi's role in drafting leaflets for the Unified National Leadership Command of the Uprising, which aimed to coordinate the various nationalist groups involved in the intifada.

BIBLIOGRAPHY

Sources

"Fatalities in the First Intifada." Table. *B'Tselem—The Israeli Information Center for Human Rights in the Occupied Territories.* B'Tselem, n.d. Web. 4 Dec. 2012.

Ghazzawi, 'Izzat. *Letters Underway.* Trans. Marieke Bosman. Birzeit, Palestine: Birzeit University Press, 1996. Print.

Khashan, 'Abd al-Karim. Preface. *Letters Underway.* Trans. Marieke Bosman. Birzeit, Palestine: Birzeit University Press, 1996. 9–12. Print.

King, Mary Elizabeth. *Quiet Revolution: The First Palestinian Intifada and Nonviolent Resistance.* New York: Nation, 2007. Print.

Nashif, Esmail. *Palestinian Political Prisoners: Identity and Community.* New York: Routledge, 2008. Print.

Rosenfeld, Maya. *Confronting the Occupation: Work, Education, and Political Activism of Palestinian Families in a Refugee Camp.* Stanford, Calif.: Stanford University Press, 2004. Print.

Further Reading

Carter, Jimmy. *Palestine: Peace Not Apartheid.* New York: Simon & Schuster, 2006. Print.

Darwish, Mahmoud. *Memory for Forgetfulness.* Trans. Ibrahim Muhawi. Berkeley: University of California Press, 1995. Print.

———. *Unfortunately, It Was Paradise.* Berkeley: University of California Press, 2003. Print.

El Saadawi, Nawal. *Memoirs from the Women's Prison.* London: Women's Press, 1986. Print.

Ghazzawi, 'Izzat. *Nebo Mountain.* Trans. 'Izzat Ghazzawi. Ed. Penny Johnson. Birzeit, Palestine: Birzeit University Press and the Palestinian Writers Union, 1996. Print.

Habiby, Emile. *The Secret Life of Saeed: The Pessoptimist.* Trans. Salma Khadra Jayyusi and Trevor Le Gassick. Brooklyn, N.Y.: Interlink, 2003. Print.

Lockman, Zachary, and Joel Beinin, eds. *Intifada: The Palestinian Uprising against Israeli Occupation.* Washington, DC: MERIP, 1989. Print.

Makdisi, Saree. *Palestine Inside Out: An Everyday Occupation.* New York: Norton, 2008. Print.

Pappe, Ilan. *The Ethnic Cleansing of Palestine.* Oxford: Oneworld, 2006. Print.

Ta'mari, Salah. "Journey into Hades: Diary of a Palestinian in an Israeli Prison." *Anthology of Modern Palestinian Literature.* Ed. Salma Khadra Jayyusi. New York: Columbia University Press, 1992. 705–11. Print.

Allison Blecker

Spandau
The Secret Diaries
Albert Speer

✢ Key Facts

Time Period:
Mid-20th Century

Relevant Historical Events:
Holocaust; World War II; Speer's imprisonment for war crimes

Nationality:
German

Keywords:
Holocaust; Nazism; incarceration

OVERVIEW

Spandau: The Secret Diaries (1975) is an account of the twenty years Albert Speer (1905–81) spent in Spandau prison in Berlin following his conviction for war crimes committed during his tenure as armaments minister for Nazi Germany during World War II. Written between October 1946 and September 1966 and smuggled out of prison, *Spandau* was published several years after Speer's autobiographical *Inside the Third Reich* (1969) and is often described as a more personal companion to Speer's first book. The entries describe daily life in prison and explore Speer's memories of his relationship with Hitler and others as he grapples with questions about his responsibility as a participant in the government that slaughtered millions of Jews and other innocent people.

Published three decades after the end of the war, *Spandau* was received as both an invaluable addition to the growing body of work about Nazi Germany and as a war criminal's attempt at self-justification, which should be regarded with skepticism. Speer, who is sometimes referred to as the "Nazi who said sorry," remains a controversial figure. While the debate about him will likely never be settled, *Spandau* endures both as an important historical document and as an affecting portrait of a complex individual caught up in a state-sanctioned atrocity.

HISTORICAL AND LITERARY CONTEXT

Speer, an architect by training, joined the Nazi party in 1931 and was instrumental in developing the distinctive look and feel of the large rallies that would characterize the public face of the Nazi regime. Promoted to inspector general of the Reich in 1937, he was responsible for designing and overseeing the construction of important Reich buildings, including the Chancellery and the Nuremberg Palace. In the early 1940s his office assumed responsibility for buildings in Berlin from which Jews had been evicted. A member of Hitler's inner circle, he was named minister of armaments in 1942 and was charged with overseeing production of military hardware and supervising the construction of roads and strategic installations—projects that were carried out mainly by slave labor. Speer fell out of favor with Hitler as Allied troops advanced and as Speer resisted carrying out Hitler's "scorched earth" policies regarding the destruction of factories and lands in Germany (Speer believed such infrastructure would be necessary for reconstruction following the war).

In 1946, twenty-two Nazi officials were tried in Nuremberg, Germany, for crimes committed during World War II. Twelve were sentenced to death. Speer, one of seven convicted and sentenced to prison, served twenty years. The sentence was carried out in Spandau, a large prison that was vacant except for the war criminals, who were kept in a state of isolation from the world and at least initially had no access to newspapers or other media. Because they were denied writing materials, the early notes and drafts for what would become *Spandau* were written on toilet paper, gum wrappers, and other scraps.

Spandau is part of the larger tradition of post–World War II writings about Nazi Germany and the much smaller body of work produced by former members of the Nazi state, including government officials, military officers, and civilians who served the interests of the Reich in various capacities. The prison writings of Rudolph Hoess and Wilhelm Keitel provide a notable counterpoint to Speer's diaries. Hoess, commander of Auschwitz, penned his memoir *My Soul* (1947), along with various essays on the workings of the camp, while awaiting execution for his crimes. Similarly, Keitel, war minister and commander of the armed forces, wrote his memoirs before being hanged at Nuremberg. The works, like Speer's, add to the historical record of Nazi Germany and the Holocaust. However, unlike Speer, who had a much longer time to write about and reflect upon his guilt, neither Hoess nor Keitel claimed responsibility for his participation.

A number of works were written in response to Speer's account of his culpability and subsequent punishment, seeking to assess the veracity of the self-portrait Speer paints in *Spandau* and *Inside the Third Reich*. Matthias Schmidt's *Albert Speer: The End of a Myth* (1984), among others, takes a skeptical view of *Spandau* and the claims Speer made about being ignorant of the extermination of Jews in the death camps. Serena Getty's *Albert Speer: His Battle with Truth,* perhaps the most famous work on Speer and his writing, is

Germany's Spandau Prison in 1971. Architect and political figure Albert Speer spent time in this prison for his participation in the Nazi regime. He chronicles his life and prison sentence in *Spandau: The Secret Diaries*. © AP IMAGES

less conclusive in its judgment of Speer. More recently, German historian Joachim Fest, who helped Speer edit *Spandau* for publication, examined Speer's diaries and life more generally in *Speer: The Final Verdict* (2003).

THEMES AND STYLE

At its root, *Spandau* is an exploration of physical and psychological imprisonment. Speer details the challenges he faces as part of daily life in prison. In an entry from October 17, 1946, he describes fighting "to keep my composure" while being forced to clean the floor over which his former comrades had been hanged. Many entries discuss the boredom and isolation he experiences as part of daily life, along with petty struggles between former Nazi officials now stripped of their power. He was generally disliked by his fellow prisoners, who felt that his assumption of responsibility during the trial constituted a betrayal of Hitler. In addition, he writes about the ways in which his participation in Hitler's government permanently defined his life and the lives of his family members. In the epilogue, Speer tells of recurring dreams of returning to Spandau and discovering that he was released by mistake, suggesting that he cannot escape his past.

In the book's preface, he calls his writing "one concentrated effort to survive" imprisonment and "to arrive at some sort of moral reckoning with what lay behind it all." His use of whatever scraps he could lay his hands on hints at an obsessive need to write. His efforts to preserve this writing and smuggle it out of Spandau suggest that he was also interested in creating a permanent record of his experience and a portrait of himself. "Diaries are usually the accompaniment of a lived life," he writes in the preface. "This one stands in place of a life."

Spandau is written in a reflective, analytic style, which affords Speer both distance from his memories and a position of authority from which to evaluate them. Descriptions of his present circumstances often lead to meditation on past events and their meaning. Speer writes about Hitler in great detail, recounting the Führer's personal habits in an attempt to explain the Nazi leader's influence. Speer contrasts conventional views of Hitler as "a dictator given to raging uncontrollably and biting the rug" with Hitler's "persuasiveness, his engaging characteristics, and even the Austrian charm he could trot out" to attract and keep otherwise rational and moral people, like Speer, in his orbit. Moreover, as *Spandau* progresses, and as Speer gains access to outside media, he often makes comparisons between the acts of Germany during World War II and the acts of other nations, such as Korea, during wartime.

THE NUREMBERG TRIALS

Following Adolf Hitler's defeat, the Allied forces tried captured Nazi officials before a series of multination tribunals in Nuremberg, Germany. Most significant was the Trial of the Major War Criminals, held before the International Military Tribunal between November 1945 and October 1946. Twenty-four high-ranking Nazis were indicted, although only twenty-two, including Albert Speer, appeared in person. Twelve of these defendants received death sentences, and ten were executed at Spandau, an event that is described in Speer's diaries. Seven others remained in custody with sentences ranging from ten years to life. Speer's diaries describe the relationship between the seven men who were incarcerated at Spandau, several of whom were extremely critical of Speer for his perceived disloyalty to Hitler.

The Nuremberg trials were decried by a number of officials, including chief justice of the U.S. Supreme Court Harlan Fiske Stone. Critics argued that the crimes with which the defendants were charged had not been defined before the charges were brought. Further, in some cases there were no clear lines separating the behavior of Allied forces in their treatment of prisoners, for example, and the behavior of Nazi criminals. Controversy surrounding the trials led to the formation of the International Law Commission, the United Nations body that develops and codifies international law, and a number of specific measures, for example, the Geneva Convention on the Laws and Customs of War (1949).

CRITICAL DISCUSSION

Following Speer's acclaimed *Inside the Third Reich,* interest was high in *Spandau.* Many critics lauded the book for its historical insight, and some, including Norbert Muhlen in a 1976 article in *America,* praised Speer's "day-to-day log of survival" as "a great human and psychological document." Other commentary, such as a 1975 review in *Kirkus Review,* cautioned that Speer's "self-presentation as an urbane professional betrayed by his emotional confidence in Hitler may lull some readers into forgetting his complicity in genocide." Ted Morgan, writing in the *Washington Post* in 1974, is critical of the book, saying it fails as a meditation on guilt insofar as that guilt is "first acknowledged and then shrugged off."

Speer's *Spandau,* in addition to providing important historical insight from inside the Third Reich, has provoked much conversation about the historical and personal conditions that permit intelligent, seemingly normal people to participate in genocide and other atrocities. The author's attempts to claim responsibility for his crimes raise questions about the nature of guilt and the personal and social implications of attempts at atonement. These questions remain relevant in the twenty-first century, even as scholars continue to debate the sincerity of Speer's motives and the nature of his character and its susceptibility to Hitler's influence.

Spandau is most often studied as part of a broader attempt to understand Speer and, more generally, Nazi Germany. Fest speculates about the contradiction between the man who initially viewed his role in the relocation of thousands of Jews and forced labor in the German war industry as primarily administrative, and the man who spent the rest of his life haunted by his involvement. Fest conjectures that by the early 1940s, Speer "had long been totally more or less absorbed by the world of official responsibilities and specific aims," a world that had become so insular "that no human appeal could penetrate."

BIBLIOGRAPHY

Sources

Fest, Joachim. *Speer: The Final Verdict.* New York: Harcourt, 2003. Print.

Morgan, Ted. "Lives in a Cell" Rev. of *Spandau: The Secret Diaries,* by Albert Speer. *Washington Post* 29 Feb. 1974. *ProQuest Historical Newspapers.* Web. 2 Jan. 2013.

Muhlen, Norbert. Rev. of *Spandau: The Secret Diaries,* by Albert Speer. *America* 8 May 1976. *EBSCOhost.* Web. 3 Jan. 2013.

Rev. of *Spandau: The Secret Diaries,* by Albert Speer. *Kirkus Review* 25 Feb. 1975. Web. 3 Jan. 2013.

Speer, Albert. *Spandau: The Secret Diaries.* Trans. Richard and Clara Winston. New York: Macmillan, 1976. Print.

Further Reading

Barbour, John D. *The Conscience of the Autobiographer: Ethical and Religious Dimensions of Autobiography.* New York: St. Martin's, 1992. Print.

Gilbert, G. M. *Nuremberg Diary.* New York: Farrar, Straus, 1947. Print.

King, Henry, and Bettina Elles. *The Two Worlds of Albert Speer: Reflections of a Nuremberg Prosecutor.* Lanham, Md.: University Press of America, 1997. Print.

Schmidt, Matthias. *Albert Speer: The End of a Myth.* New York: St. Martin's, 1984. Print.

Sereny, Gitta. *Albert Speer: His Battle with Truth.* London: Picador, 1996. Print.

Shirer, William. *The Rise and Fall of the Third Reich: A History of Nazi Germany.* New York: Simon & Schuster, 1981. Print.

Speer, Albert. *Inside the Third Reich.* New York: Simon & Schuster, 1970. Print.

Tooze, J. Adam. *The Wages of Destruction: The Making and Breaking of the Nazi Economy.* New York: Viking, 2007. Print.

Daisy Gard

HISTORICAL PERSPECTIVES

Confessions of Lady Nijo by Lady Nijo	59
The Diaries of Lady Anne Clifford by Lady Anne Clifford	62
The Diary of John Evelyn by John Evelyn	65
The Diary of John Quincy Adams by John Quincy Adams	69
The Diary of Samuel Pepys by Samuel Pepys	72
Diary, Reminiscences and Correspondence of Henry Crabb Robinson, Barrister-at-Law by Henry Crabb Robinson	75
Jemima Condict: Her Book, Being a Transcript of the Diary of an Essex County Maid during the Revolutionary War by Jemima Condict	78
Journal des Goncourt: Mémoires de la vie littéraire by Jules de Goncourt and Edmond de Goncourt	81
The Last Diary of Tsaritsa Alexandra by Alexandra Feodorovna	84
"Letter to Her Daughter from the New White House" by Abigail Adams	87
Letters of a Woman Homesteader by Elinore Pruitt Stewart	91
The Letters of the Younger Pliny by Pliny the Younger	94
The Literary Remains of Edward VI by Edward VI	97
Selected Letters of Martha Gellhorn by Martha Gellhorn	101
A Young Palestinian's Diary, 1941–1945: The Life of Sāmī 'Amr by Sāmī Amr	104

Confessions of Lady Nijo

Lady Nijo

OVERVIEW

Written in the fourteenth century, *Confessions of Lady Nijo* (originally titled *Towazugatari,* or "An Unasked-for Tale," in Japanese) documents thirty-six years (1271–1306) in the life of a woman in the powerful Fujiwara Nijo family. Nijo served at the imperial court, either as a wife or a concubine to the former emperor (her status has been debated by scholars), before becoming a Buddhist nun. The journal is divided into five books, the first three covering Nijo's experiences in the imperial court and the last two addressing her new life and travels as a Buddhist nun after she was expelled from the court in 1283.

Nijo sat down to write her memoirs around 1307, during a growing division in the imperial family between former emperor GoFukakusa and his brother Kameyama, whom she took as a lover while still in a relationship with GoFukakusa. *Confessions* was not widely distributed during Nijo's lifetime, most likely as a result of her frank portrayal of tensions in the imperial court, and the text was quickly forgotten. A Japanese scholar rediscovered the journal in 1940, and it was first published in Japan in 1950, with a complete and annotated edition printed in 1966. Karen Brazell's English translation and annotation of the journal was released in 1973. Since the publication of Brazell's edition, *Confessions* has received growing scholarly interest due to its candid representation of courtly life during the Kamakura period in Japan.

HISTORICAL AND LITERARY CONTEXT

The majority of *Confessions* covers the minute and scandalous details of the daily occurrences in the imperial court. Nijo served as an imperial concubine or wife during the Kamakura period (approximately 1185 to 1333), and it is likely that she played a central role in the growing divisions within the imperial family in the second half of the thirteenth century, since she betrayed the former emperor by sleeping with his brother. She did not live in the Kamakura court (now Tokyo) but rather in the Kyoto imperial court; the name "Nijo" is taken from the street in Kyoto on which her family lived. During her time at the palace, Nijo maintained relationships with several men at the same time, including a long-term relationship with a Buddhist high priest named Shoojo, with whom she had two children. She bore her master GoFukakusa one child, who died shortly after birth, and as a result the former emperor greatly resented her other children.

At the beginning of the period covered by *Confessions,* the Kamakura regime was dealing with Mongol invasions into Japan, the first in 1274 and another in 1281. The empire's resources were drained from years of battling against foreign invaders. Nijo does not mention the invasions (women were deemed unfit for discussing political and military affairs), but the details she gives of the imperial court during this time reflect the growing tensions within the imperial family, which would eventually lead to Nijo's expulsion from the court in 1283. At the same time, outside Kyoto, several Buddhist sects emphasizing compassion and piety, including Amidism and Zen, were gaining in influence. Nijo's decision to become a Buddhist nun of the Amidist sect reflects the value she placed on a compassionate god who offered salvation to all beings.

Like the imperial court literature of Nijo's time, *Confessions* is written in prose but incorporates much poetry. It follows in the tradition of *The Tale of Genji,* penned by Lady Murasaki Shikibu in the eleventh century, as well as earlier female autobiographical texts, such as *The Pillow Book,* written by lady-in-waiting Sei Shōnagon circa 1002. *The Tale of Genji,* in which Murasaki records details of the lives of high courtiers in the imperial palace, is now considered a classic Japanese text. As Haruo Shirane notes in *Envisioning the Tale of Genji: Media, Gender, and Cultural Production* (2008), Nijo's text draws heavily from *Genji,* and in *Confessions* Nijo actually describes an instance when a scene from *Genji* was reenacted in the court. *Genji,* which is based on Murasaki's personal experience as a lady-in-waiting in the court, reads more like a novel than a memoir or journal. She also wrote *The Murasaki Shikibu Diary,* which records her memories of life in the imperial palace.

Similar to Murasaki's texts centuries earlier, Nijo's memoir was not highly regarded during her lifetime, most likely due to her gender and the fact that her writing revealed the inner workings of the imperial court. As a result, it is difficult to identify any direct influence that *Confessions* had on the literary sphere for several centuries following its initial limited publication. Nijo's book has only become a well-known classical Japanese text in the last few decades, and today it is lauded for the unique and intimate glimpse it

✤ Key Facts

Time Period:
Late 13th to Early 14th Centuries

Relevant Historical Events:
Struggles of the Kamakura Court; Mongol invasions of Japan; rise of Buddhism

Nationality:
Japanese

Keywords:
Buddhism; women's writing; Japan

HISTORICAL PERSPECTIVES

Helen Anderson portraying Nijo in a 2002 London production of Caryl Churchill's play *Top Girls*. Nijo captured her extraordinary life in the renowned fourteenth-century Japanese work *Towazugatari*, known in English as *The Confessions of Lady Nijo*. © ELLIOTT FRANKS/ARENAPAL/TOPHAM/THE IMAGE WORKS

gives into Japanese courtier life. Passages from *Confessions* have even been incorporated into some Japanese school curriculum.

THEMES AND STYLE

Confessions is unique as a journal in that it provides modern-day readers with a glimpse into Japan's imperial past. Nijo describes her personal life in detail, including her numerous love affairs as well as the ceremonies and parties she attended while living in the palace. Her records of imperial life highlight the lingering importance of Heian culture from the time of Murasaki in the tenth and eleventh centuries, including the four main social ideals of the Heian court, which emphasized love, music, poetry, and wine. Nijo often quotes the poetry spoken by members of the court, including her protector and lover, the former emperor. In one instance, she recalls, "GoFukakusa returned to his own quarters before daybreak. 'The cherry blossom is beautiful to behold, but too easily broken,' he commented, and I had to agree." The entries in volumes four and five, following Nijo's consecration as a Buddhist nun, emphasize the values of compassion and piety.

As Brazell notes in her introduction to *Confessions*, Nijo wrote her memoirs primarily to revive the former literary prestige of her family. Thus, her composition of original poems throughout the text reflects an attention to the arts that was paramount in Japanese culture during her lifetime. She often recorded her emotions in poetry form, as when she expresses her grief at the death of her grandmother: "First autumn dew, now the rain / Of winter, chill and soaking / On sleeves already damp." Little is known of the resources Nijo employed when writing her memoirs—whether she had notes or recollections already jotted down—although it is clear that she did not write the text as a journal at the time of her experiences, but rather she composed *Confessions* later in life based on her memories. The text has a distinct oral quality in its reproduction of the language and atmosphere of the imperial court, which is captured in the dialogue and poetry Nijo recalls.

In the tradition of earlier Japanese memoirs written by women, Nijo's text adopts a melancholy tone—a tone, as Brazell notes, that was valued by her contemporaries as exemplary of a woman's sensitivity to the "transience of life." After learning of the passing of another former lover, Nijo reflects, "Life is more fleeting than a dream within a dream, I realized then…. Would I not have fewer worries now if we had parted forever that sad night?" At the same time, she delivers a candid and human portrayal of herself, incorporating humor into the text that serves to lighten the mood. "Suddenly I was struck with the comical thought that my plight resembled that of the person who wrote the poem 'When Love Pursues from All Sides.' How could I not be amused?" Nijo's ability to regard her own life with humor further humanizes her for the reader.

CRITICAL DISCUSSION

There is no available record of the initial response to *Confessions*. The work was forgotten for centuries, and it is only after its rediscovery in the twentieth century that contemporary scholars responded to the text. In her 1974 review of Brazell's English translation in the *Journal of Japanese Studies*, Marian Ury notes that the text "has a boldness that sets it off from other Japanese female memoirs," but Ury shies away from placing *Confessions* at the same level as *The Tale of Genji*, noting that Nijo's text "lacks the special nuances of ambivalence between Duty and Desire, between the inability to be quite honest with oneself about one's motives and the lurking knowledge of the sweetness of it all that to my mind is the special mark of the greatness of *The Tale of Genji*."

Confessions has garnered considerable public and scholarly interest for its representation of gender roles and sexual relations during the Kamakura period in

Japan. Scholars such as Saeko Kimura have used Nijo's memoir as a window into the complex gender relations of the period, providing modern-day readers with further insight into the life of an imperial concubine. In "Regenerating Narratives: *The Confessions of Lady Nijo* as a Story for Women's Salvation," Kimura writes, "Nijo's status and that of her family is important in terms of interpreting her sexuality as either productive or nonproductive within the power structure of GoFukakusa's court." Similarly, in *The Aesthetics of Discontent* (1991), Michael Mara examines Nijo's role in exposing the degradation of Japanese women in court and society, relating the author's perspective in *Confessions* to that of earlier works by Japanese authors, including *Genji* and *Ise Monogatari*, a ninth-century collection of medieval Japanese poems whose author is unknown.

Much of the scholarship on *Confessions* focuses on the debate of whether Nijo was a legitimate wife to GoFukakusa or just a favored imperial concubine. In "Coercive Sex in the Medieval Japanese Court: Lady Nijo's Memoir," Hitomi Tonomura interprets an early sexual encounter between Nijo and GoFukakusa as rape. Tonomura asserts that Nijo was not a formal wife of the former emperor, but that "Nijo discursively filled this absence by constructing her identity as a woman who was bound to him nonetheless through emotional ties made through the flesh." Other scholars are interested in Nijo's reason for writing her memoirs. In "A Book of One's Own," Barbara Ruch emphasizes Nijo's "vivid awareness and strong sense of the self" that motivates her desire for "posterity to remember and appreciate her."

JAPAN'S KAMAKURA PERIOD

The Kamakura period spanned the thirteenth and early fourteenth centuries, following the Heian period. The Kamakura shogunate was established by the first shogun, Minamoto no Yoritomo, in his hometown of Kamakura (modern-day Tokyo). The period is associated with the emergence of feudalism due to a transition to economies based on landholding, as well as the establishment of the warrior caste and the samurai. Despite Yoritomo's consolidation of power, a separate imperial court remained in Kyoto throughout his regime. Yoritomo lived until 1199, during which period he controlled large regions of Japan but not the entire nation.

The Kamakura Empire remained embroiled in warfare with the northern Fujiwara, a Japanese noble family that ruled the northern Tohoku region as if it were their own empire until 1189, when Yoritomo defeated them and secured the north for his empire. After his death, the Kamakura imperial family began to struggle for supremacy with members of the imperial court in Kyoto. These struggles were brought to an end by Kamakura's defeat of the Kyoto imperial army in the Jokyu disturbance of 1221.

Chinese influence was relatively strong during the Kamakura period, with the introduction of New Buddhism and Zen Buddhism around the twelfth century. Due to divisions within the imperial family, decreasing loyalty of lords, and financial crisis, the Kamakura Empire was overthrown in the early 1300s by emperor Go-Daigo, which led to civil war and definitively split the royal family into two rival factions.

BIBLIOGRAPHY

Sources

Brazell, Karen, ed. *The Confessions of Lady Nijo*. Garden City: Anchor, 1973. Print.

Kimura, Saeko. "Regenerating Narratives: *The Confessions of Lady Nijo* as a Story for Women's Salvation." *Review of Japanese Culture and Society* 19 (2007): 87–102. Print.

Ruch, Barbara. "A Book of One's Own." *Masterworks of Asian Literature in Comparative Perspective: A Guide for Teaching*. Ed. Barbara S. Miller. Armonk: Sharpe, 1994. 400–19. Print.

Shirane, Haruo. *Envisioning the Tale of Genji: Media, Gender, and Cultural Production*. New York: Columbia University Press, 2008. Print.

Tonomura, Hitomi. "Coercive Sex in the Medieval Japanese Court: Lady Nijo's Memoir." *Monumenta Nipponica* 61.3 (2006): 283–338. Print.

Ury, Marian. Rev. of *The Confessions of Lady Nijo*, ed. Karen Brazell. *Japanese Studies* 1.1 (1974): 173–79. Print.

Further Reading

Abbott, Elizabeth. "Eastern Concubines and Harems." *Mistresses: A History of the Other Woman*. London: Duckworth, 2010. Print.

Childs, Margaret H. "The Value of Vulnerability: Sexual Coercion and the Nature of Love in Japanese Court Literature." *Journal of Asian Studies* 58.4 (1999): 1059–79. Print.

Kahler, Karl. Rev. of *The Confessions of Lady Nijo*, ed. Karen Brazell. *Journal of the Association of Teachers of Japanese* 9.2–3 (1974): 81–84. Print.

Keene, Donald. "Diaries of the Kamakura Period." *Seeds in the Heart: Japanese Literature from Earliest Times to the Late Sixteenth Century*. New York: Henry Holt, 1993. 825–51. Print.

Richard, Kenneth L. Rev. of *The Confessions of Lady Nijo*, ed. Karen Brazell. *Pacific Affairs* 47.2 (1974): 241–42. Print.

Seidensticker, Edward. Rev. of *The Confessions of Lady Nijo*, ed. Karen Brazell. *Monumenta Nipponica* 29.2 (1974): 225–27. Print.

Katrina White

The Diaries of Lady Anne Clifford

Lady Anne Clifford

❖ Key Facts

Time Period:
17th Century

Relevant Historical Events:
English Civil War; accession of Charles II; Clifford's disinheritance

Nationality:
English

Keywords:
inheritance; early modern England; gender

OVERVIEW

The Diaries of Lady Anne Clifford, written from 1603 until 1676, chronicles the baroness's determined fight to win possession of the land she felt she should have inherited at the age of fifteen. The diaries cover four distinct periods in Lady Anne Clifford's life: 1603 (when she was a teenager at court), 1616–1619 (also known as the "Knole Diary," documenting her life a young married woman), 1650–1675 (when she was finally in possession of her hereditary lands in northern England and compiled a brief summary of each year's events in the "Kendal Diary"), and 1676 (detailing the last few months before her death). Only the 1676 diary survives from Clifford's lifetime; the others exist as copies from later centuries. Together these diary fragments present a vital resource for scholars, who have used them to investigate issues of local authority, gender, family history, land transfers, and legal proceedings in early modern England.

Clifford's diaries were originally produced in a community context alongside other writings. As a committed record keeper, she asked her staff to create three "Great Books" that would contain summaries of the family genealogy and history, as well as her own personal reminiscences. In turn, portions of these books and similar materials were copied by later scribes. More recently, segments of *The Diaries of Lady Anne Clifford* have been published individually, such as the "Knole Diary" in 1923 by Vita Sackville-West and a fuller edition in 1990 by D. J. H. Clifford. As of late 2012, scholars were preparing the first edition of the Great Books themselves for publication, enabling further research on Clifford's life and legacy.

HISTORICAL AND LITERARY CONTEXT

As a noblewoman growing up under the reigns of Elizabeth I and James I, Clifford's experienced firsthand the high drama of the court life of the Stuart monarchs, who ruled England between 1603 and 1714. Her 1603 diary, for example, tells of her family's participation in Queen Elizabeth's funeral rituals; later, she was welcomed at court by the first Stuart king, James, and his wife, Anne of Denmark. This upbringing exposed her to a range of gendered models of power that would influence her later in life. For example, King James portrayed himself as the father or husband of the nation, while Elizabeth I ruled as the powerful virgin queen. Anne of Denmark influenced events quietly, from behind the scenes. In Clifford's own life, as she fought for the inheritance that her father willed away from her, she deployed at least two powerful personae: a quiet but determined wifely persona and a more commanding "lady of the manor" version of herself.

The Diaries of Lady Anne Clifford participates in the religious tradition of keeping a diary to investigate God's interventions in daily life. By recording scriptural citations and explicitly thanking God for his providence during difficult moments, Clifford uses her writing as a devotional aid. Journaling also assisted her in keeping track of her possessions, lands, and family members—noting purchases, interactions with tenants and staff, and minute details about births and deaths. Moreover, by writing and dictating remembered snippets of information, Clifford created a culture of remembrance within her circle of Elizabethan and Jacobean writers, including Samuel Daniel (her former tutor), Edmund Spenser, Michel de Montaigne, and John Donne (who personally complimented her knowledge).

As a noblewoman writing in the seventeenth century, Clifford held two potentially contradictory positions: she was an aristocrat, capable of patronizing writers and encouraging literary production, and she was a woman, whose voice theoretically fell under her husband's authority. Like Lady Margaret Hoby, another early female diarist, Clifford needed to negotiate these dueling positions safely. She did so by portraying herself as a constant, virtuous noble figure, just as Lady Mary Wroth and Lady Margaret Cavendish did in their semiautobiographical fictions. As Clifford underscores throughout the diaries, she is working toward the reclamation of her hereditary lands—which fell into the hands of her uncle after her father's death. By chronicling both the pious pursuit and the eventual realization of this goal, she is able to paint herself as a dutiful family member who is simply seeking to claim her birthright.

Although Clifford's writing was not widely circulated until the twentieth century, her work as the overseer of her estates left a lasting imprint on the northern English countryside. As the diary recounts, the baroness carried out essential maintenance and restoration work on Brougham Castle, Skipton Castle, and many other local landmarks. From a religious perspective, *The Diaries of Lady Anne Clifford* was an example to many, as mentioned by Edward Rainbow in her funeral sermon: it shows how a close examination of daily life can lead to "serenity of conscience." Rainbow also points out that the diaries were expected to have historical ramifications for her own descendants: "From her great diligence her Posterity may find contentment in reading these abstracts of Occurrences in her own Life."

THEMES AND STYLE

From a modern standpoint, *The Diaries of Lady Anne Clifford* is a vital source of information about issues important to many historians, including land law, gender, family relationships, and even the balance of power within a kingdom. As Julie Crawford points out in her 2006 essay in *PMLA,* Clifford attempts to consolidate her inheritance by navigating overlapping feudal and absolutist systems of government—signaling that the Stuart monarchy and courtier system was not quite as dominant (or absolute) as many believed. Additionally, her writing portrays her relationships with two successive noble husbands—the Earl of Dorset and the Earl of Pembroke and Montgomery—whose profligacy, imperiousness, and comparative neglect of their families are undercurrents of the diaries. In 1617, for example, Clifford comments, "This night my Lord and I had a falling out about the Land"; similar statements are sprinkled throughout the early work.

For the most part, Clifford wrote her diaries retrospectively, noting political and personal events that were sometimes many years in the past. She also details God's intervention in her life; for example, thanking God for his aid after a confrontation with her husband and the king about her inheritance. Intended as a semipublic record, the diaries use a nonlinear structure to reflect a community ethos of remembrance: they mark anniversaries of births, illnesses, and deaths and use those occasions to reminisce about the past in a way that transmits knowledge to the future. In a 1676 entry, Clifford writes, "I remembered how this day was 59 years [since] my first and then only childe … did in the night fall desperately sick of her long Ague." The next day she records that she signed a letter to that child, now grown up and the Countess of Thanet. Using her writing as a method of remembering the past and celebrating the present, Clifford reflects on providential events even as she records them for the larger community.

Clifford's style is marked by its plainness and focus on action; meaning is often conveyed by an event. When her daughter Margaret puts on "the first velvet coat she ever had," this action signals the child's recovery from illness, as well as her maturation. Similarly, when the baroness records a death, she takes care to note the exact age of the person involved (down to the day or week) and the exact location where the event occurred (down to the specific room). This level of detail conveys important historical and genealogical messages: it preserves the significance of manor-house geography, for example, and links the figures from the past and present through common experiences in the same bedrooms and chambers. By recording events such as the deaths of noblemen that happened hundreds of miles away, Clifford and her family participate in the larger English community without being physically present. The diary serves to unite them with other mourners as it confirms and solidifies their noble identities.

CRITICAL DISCUSSION

In the seventeenth century, Clifford's writings were well known within a small coterie environment, which consisted mainly of family members, servants, and local community figures. Still, her relative withdrawal from court in later life meant that comparatively few people had access to her work, which was preserved in the Great Books. However, her legacy was entrenched in a number of ways. She erected monuments at her father's tomb, her tutor Daniel's tomb, and the last place where she saw her mother, and these monuments share some of the same genealogical and historical information that her diaries impart. In the collection *Anglorum Speculum* (1684), which lists notable English figures and their accomplishments, she is praised

Portrait of Anne Clifford painted by John Bracken in 1671. © TULLIE HOUSE MUSEUM & ART GALLERY, CARLISLE, CUMBRIA, UK/THE BRIDGEMAN ART LIBRARY

HISTORICAL PERSPECTIVES

"THE CHILD" AND "THE BUSINESS"

Throughout the "Knole Diary," Clifford chronicles two pressing topics in shorthand: First, she refers to her daughter, Margaret Sackville, as "the Child," and tracks her comings and goings. During the years of the diary, the Child is summoned to visit her father in London; she also suffers from recurrent fits of "Ague" and begins to wear whalebone corsets. Interlaced with these accounts of the Child's progress are comments on "the Business"—Clifford's ongoing quest to reclaim her territorial inheritance, which went to her uncle instead of her. As the diaries unfold, parallels emerge between the Child's movements and the inheritance quest. Both are governed by patriarchal systems, which Clifford must confront and negotiate. At the same time, the evolving circumstances of the Child and the Business enact and modify her identity as a genealogical inheritor of land who exists within a chain of interlinking historical figures. Without the Child or the Business, Clifford would be unable to consolidate her identity from a social or historical standpoint.

for building a hospital and working as a "benefactor to the public." In addition, when Clifford died in 1676, the bishop of Carlisle published his eighteen-point funeral sermon for her, sharing her personality and the ideas of her writing with a larger audience.

Clifford's work has been periodically revisited by scribal copyists but did not become a literary focal point until the twentieth century. Then, Virginia Woolf began to use Clifford's situation as inspiration for her 1928 novel *Orlando,* and Sackville-West released an edition of the "Knole Diary" in 1923. Eventually, after the upsurge in feminist criticism in the 1990s, a new generation of scholars began to discover Clifford's work and published articles examining her organizational practices and social identity. Mihoko Suzuki's 2009 anthology collects many of these articles, including Barbara Lewalski's work on Clifford's challenges to patriarchal models of authority and Mary Ellen Lamb's examination of the baroness's "split" identity as both a subordinate wife and an efficacious heiress.

More recently, scholars have become interested in the way that Clifford's body of work (from her writing to her architectural and manorial pursuits) shaped a community ethos. Writing for *ELH* in 2004, Aaron Kunin emphasizes that Clifford's writing and reading always took place in a community atmosphere, surrounded by servants, tutors, and family members; the diaries must therefore be read as evidence of community work and conversations. In *Autobiography and Gender in Early Modern Literature* (2006), Sharon Cadman Seelig argues that the diaries constitute Clifford's "deliberate construction of herself, subject to later revision, within a larger realm." Katherine O. Acheson has produced two scholarly editions of Clifford's work, enabling further exploration of these ideas. It is also worth noting that both Sackville-West and D. J. H. Clifford claim distant kinship ties with Clifford—hinting that a sense of lasting familial community still dominates the publication and reception of the diaries and their contents.

BIBLIOGRAPHY

Sources

Acheson, Katherine O. *The Diary of Anne Clifford, 1616–1619: A Critical Edition.* New York: Garland, 1995. Print.

Clifford, Lady Anne. *The Diaries of Lady Anne Clifford.* Ed. D. J. H. Clifford. London: Alan Sutton, 1990. Print.

Crawford, Julie. "The Case of Lady Anne Clifford; or, Did Women Have a Mixed Monarchy?" *PMLA* 121.5 (2006): 1682–89. Print.

Kunin, Aaron. "From the Desk of Anne Clifford." *ELH* 71.3 (2004): 587–608. Print.

Rainbow, Edward. "A Sermon Preached at the Funeral of the Right Honourable Anne Countess of Pembroke, Dorset and Montgomery." 1675. *EEBO.* Web. 2 Dec. 2012.

Seelig, Sharon Cadman. *Autobiography and Gender in Early Modern Literature: Reading Women's Lives, 1600–1680.* Cambridge: Cambridge University Press, 2006. Print.

Spence, Richard T. "Clifford, Anne, Countess of Pembroke, Dorset, and Montgomery (1590–1676)." *Oxford Dictionary of National Biography.* Web. 2 Dec 2012.

Further Reading

Malay, Jessica L. "Anne Clifford: Appropriating the Rhetoric of Queens to Become a Lady of the North." *The Rituals and Rhetoric of Queenship: Medieval to Early Modern.* Ed. Liz Oakley-Brown and Louise Wilkinson. Dublin: Four Courts, 2009. 157–70. Print.

Matchinske, Megan. "Serial Identity: History, Gender, and Form in the Diary Writing of Lady Anne Clifford." *Genre and Women's Life Writing in Early Modern England.* Ed. Michelle M. Dowd and Julie A. Eckerle. Farnham: Ashgate, 2007. 65–80. Print.

Myers, Anne M. "Construction Sites: The Architecture of Anne Clifford's Diaries." *ELH* 73.3 (2006): 581–600. Print.

Salzman, Paul. "Anne Clifford: Writing for Oneself, Writing for Others." *Parergon: Journal of the Australian and New Zealand Association for Medieval and Early Modern Studies* 27.1 (2010): 125–41. Print.

Suzuki, Mihoko, ed. *Anne Clifford and Lucy Hutchinson.* Farnham: Ashgate, 2009. Print.

Wiseman, Susan. "Knowing Her Place: Anne Clifford and the Politics of Retreat." *Textures of Renaissance Knowledge.* Ed. Philippa Berry and Margaret Tudeau-Clayton. Manchester: Manchester University Press, 2003. 199–221. Print.

Nancy Simpson-Younger

The Diary of John Evelyn

John Evelyn

OVERVIEW

The Diary of John Evelyn (1818), composed during the late seventeenth century (c. 1660–1665 and 1684–1706), is neither purely memoir nor strictly journal. It not only records the author's life from his birth in 1620 to just weeks before his death in 1706 but also offers an unusually protracted description of one of the most momentous periods in English history. The manuscript remained unpublished until librarian William Upcott discovered it at the Evelyn ancestral family home in 1813. The work makes brief references to major events in John Evelyn's family life (including the deaths of seven of his eight children). Often impersonal, the *Diary* combines daily minutiae with elaborate scenic narratives of major historical events. It exposes readers to a unique early-modern cultural atmosphere in which multitalented aristocratic virtuosos such as Evelyn naturally flourished.

Written during a period when diary keeping was on the rise in England, the work Evelyn had called his *Kalendarium Hortense or, The Gard'ners Almanac* was transcribed and edited by antiquarian William Bray. It became an instant sensation when it was published in two volumes along with Evelyn's correspondence in 1818. Although Bray's transcription contains a number of significant mistakes and omissions, it went through several editions in the nineteenth and early twentieth centuries before Esmond S. de Beer issued a new, more accurate version of the complete manuscript in 1955. The *Diary* remains indispensable to historians for its detailed depiction of several key decades of seventeenth-century life. However, it has long been valued less for presenting the pious Evelyn to a role-model-seeking Victorian readership than for introducing statesman Samuel Pepys's infamously impious diaries to an even more extensive and enthusiastic audience.

HISTORICAL AND LITERARY CONTEXT

Evelyn's *Diary* covers the period from the English Civil Wars (1642–1652) through the Commonwealth and the Protectorate (1653–1659) and from the Restoration (1660–1685) through the Glorious Revolution (1688) to the beginning of Queen Anne's reign (1702). It was popular for its descriptions of King Charles I's execution (1649), Oliver Cromwell's funeral procession (1658), and Charles II's sensational restoration (and scandalous reign); its eyewitness accounts of torture, surgeries performed without anesthetics, monstrous births, freak show attractions, and public executions; its detailed reporting of London's Great Plague (1664–1666), Great Fire (1666), and Great Frost (1683–1684); and its narratives of the author's encounters with such key historical figures as scientist Robert Boyle, architect Sir Christopher Wren, and doctor-scholar Sir Thomas Browne. Although Evelyn had been taking notes since he was about ten years old, he was not, according to de Beer, compelled to mold them into a proper set of memoirs until he was forty. He had gone abroad during the wars and until the Restoration was unsure of his public footing as a royalist Anglican in an era of Puritan republican power.

During his early career, he had labored mostly over translations, but by 1660 he had begun publishing original works, including *A Character of England* (1659), a description of England as told by a fictional foreign persona; *Fumifugium* (1661), a tract on London pollution dedicated to Charles II; and *Sculptura* (1662), a history of engraving. Once he was comfortably settled with his wife and growing family outside London and was prominently involved in the founding of the new scientifically oriented Royal Society, he took up the *Kalendarium* project with renewed purpose. After a bout of ill health beginning in 1665 and his semiretirement from public life, he returned to the project in 1682. By 1684 he had brought it up to date, and he continued to make entries once or twice a week during the ten-plus years thereafter.

During and after the Civil Wars, the practice of diary keeping became widespread in England as its population's literacy increased and individualism became more universally valued. In addition, dramatic events were inspiring everyday historicizing, and religious reformation had led devout Protestants of various denominations, now freed from the Catholic confessional, to experiment with more personal methods of spiritual self-evaluation. Diaries describing particular military campaigns also became more common, and travel diaries grew so abundant that the Royal Society issued directives for their composition in 1666. Evelyn's *Diary* indicates that he was inspired by his father to begin periodic note taking as a youth. During his early manhood, he encountered nearly twenty of the figures that bibliographer William Matthews lists as pre-1660 diary writers.

✧ **Key Facts**

Time Period:
Late 17th Century

Relevant Historical Events:
English Civil War; establishment of the Commonwealth and Protectorate; the Restoration; the Glorious Revolution

Nationality:
English

Keywords:
civil war; restoration; monarchy

HISTORICAL PERSPECTIVES

A portrait of John Evelyn by Robert Walker (1648). Evelyn was a writer, was active in government affairs, and helped found the scientific Royal Society. © PHILIP MOULD LTD, LONDON/THE BRIDGEMAN ART LIBRARY

The writings of Francis Bacon (1561–1626)—the first great English essayist and the father of the scientific method—were influential to Evelyn as a student at Oxford. Bacon's advice to young men to keep detailed diaries and to engage in empirical observation had a particular impact on the diligent Evelyn.

Evelyn's experiment in life writing was not widely read until the nineteenth century, when the modest memoir's appearance led to the publication of Pepys's more candid confessions in 1825 and helped spark a Victorian diary-publishing frenzy that reached its climax in 1860. Although this craze gradually abated, as Martin Hewitt points out in his essay "Diary, Autobiography and the Practice of Life History" in *Life Writing and Victorian Culture* (2006), it nevertheless transformed diaries into the salable commodities they continue to be today.

THEMES AND STYLE

Although Evelyn was a devout Anglican, he refrained from using his diary as a spiritual account, unlike many of his contemporaries. Nevertheless, the most consistent theme of his *Diary* is religion. He sees no need to explore an "inner self," instead expressing his faith in a largely routine fashion that both passively exemplifies and actively exalts loyalty above all else. He frequently paints pictures that celebrate religious or political fidelity, as in his descriptions of worship among royalist exiles in Paris during the Protectorate and of clandestine religious services in private London homes and chapels. He introduces such figures as Margaret Godolphin, the maid of honor to Queen Catherine, whom he praises as a "rare example of so much piety, & Virtue," even as she dutifully serves a "licentious Court" to which she, like Evelyn, chooses to remain faithful. At the same time, he fills his diary's pages with prayers that he may resist temptation and entreaties to God that his family may avoid danger, as well as expressions of thanks to his Maker for his continued preservation and notes about the sermons he devoutly listened to throughout his long life.

The ardent appeals to and appreciations of God that pervade the diary indicate that Evelyn was not only recording his observations as Baconian educational aids but also compiling them for the edification of his descendants. Although "there is no ground for supposing that Evelyn ever envisaged the publication of the Diary," writes de Beer in his introduction to the 1955 edition, there is reason to believe that he intended it to serve as a "family book"—much as the brief memoir *De Vita Propria* (published in the 1955 *Diary*), which was derived from pre-1644 *Kalendarium* material, and the volume *Memoires for My Grand-Son* (1926), which Evelyn drafted in 1704. His increasingly detailed reconstructions of sermons and frequent borrowings from newspapers, guidebooks, and topographical works suggest that he believed his chronicles might help guide his progeny on their religious, educational, and geographic journeys.

The tone of the diary is pious, and its language is simple, spare, and habitual. Its structure, however, is often uneven. Entries vary vastly in length, with some—as Virginia Woolf writes in a 1920 essay appearing in *The Essays of Virginia Woolf: 1925–1928* (1994)—composed like excerpts from a memoir and others "jotted down" like notes on "a calendar." One of the most striking examples of this apparent haphazardness suggests that Evelyn's method is not arbitrary at all: he spends several diary pages lamenting the loss of his virginal daughter Mary just a few entries before reporting the death of his daughter Elizabeth, whose elopement he disapproved of, in a few short lines. This disparity reveals the profound effect loyalty had on the structural choices he made in his memoir.

CRITICAL DISCUSSION

Upon its publication, Evelyn's *Diary* met with immediate and enormous success. Published near the end of the Romantic period and at the dawn of the Victorian era, it was typically evaluated as a primarily historical document (favorably, for instance, by Robert

Southey and less favorably by Thomas De Quincey) or as the portrait of an exemplary man (for example, by Sir Walter Scott) rather than as a specifically literary achievement. Jeanne K. Welcher points out in *John Evelyn* (1972), "For the first seventy-five years after its publication," the *Diary*'s commentators generally "reviewed only the man, not the book." According to Welcher, they either celebrated the exhibition of Evelyn's "intelligence, urbanity, ideas, virtue, learning, contribution to the arts, [and] amiability" or, less frequently, criticized the "solemnity," "complacency," and "loftiness" that distinguish him from Pepys.

In spite of these early reactions, the *Diary*'s most important legacy is literary. While it is impossible to say that the posthumously issued work directly influenced any nineteenth-century life writers (the twentieth-century novelist James Joyce, among others, appears to have mimicked Evelyn's style in the "Oxen of the Sun" episode in *Ulysses* [1922]), it is undeniable that the *Diary*'s publication and popularity opened the floodgates for a torrent of other such works. Largely because of this inundation, Hewitt argues, diaristic writing found its way not only into the popular fiction of such nineteenth-century masters as the Brontë sisters and Wilkie Collins but also into "many of the weighty 'Life and Letters' biographies so characteristic of Victorian letters." Although Woolf joins numerous fin de siècle and early twentieth-century reviewers in criticizing Evelyn for his self-importance, humorlessness, and coldness, she assesses his *Diary* in literary terms when she concedes that his way of "going on with the day's story circumstantially, bringing in people who will never be mentioned again, leading up to crises which never take place, [and] introducing Sir Thomas Browne but never letting him speak" constitutes "an artistic method" that "has its fascination."

Without turning away from questions of method, twenty-first-century scholarship has retrained its gaze on Evelyn's persona. However, these newer strands of criticism do not focus merely on Evelyn as he presents himself in his diary. In *John Evelyn: Living for Ingenuity* (2006), Gillian Darley studies how he expresses his varied interests and aims in the great number of other books he published during his lifetime. By contrast, Glynis Ridley and Jessica Munns discuss the rhetorical strategies he uses in approaching nature, God, and the king, and how they differ from those of other seventeenth-century thinkers.

BIBLIOGRAPHY

Sources

Evelyn, John. *The Diary of John Evelyn*. Ed. E. S. de Beer. 6 vols. Oxford: Oxford University Press, 1955. Print.

Hewitt, Martin. "Diary, Autobiography and the Practice of Life History." *Life Writing and Victorian Culture*. Ed. David Amigoni. Aldershot: Ashgate, 2006. 21–40. Print.

Matthews, William. *British Diaries: An Annotated Bibliography of British Diaries Written between 1442 and 1942*. Gloucester: Smith, 1967. Print.

Welcher, Jeanne K. *John Evelyn*. New York: Twayne, 1972. Print.

PRIMARY SOURCE

EXCERPT FROM *THE DIARY OF JOHN EVELYN*

10th October. I went by waggon, accompanied with a jovial commissary, to Dunkirk, the journey being made all on the sea-sands. On our arrival, we first viewed the court of guards, the works, the town-house, and the new church; the latter is very beautiful within; and another, wherein they showed us an excellent piece of *Our Saviour's bearing the Cross*. The harbour, in two channels, coming up to the town was choked with a multitude of prizes.

From hence, the next day, I marched three English miles towards the packet-boat, being a pretty frigate of six guns, which embarked us for England about three in the afternoon.

At our going off, the fort, against which our pinnace anchored, saluted my Lord Marshal with twelve great guns, which we answered with three. Not having the wind favourable, we anchored that night before Calais. About midnight, we weighed; and, at four in the morning, though not far from Dover, we could not make the pier till four that afternoon, the wind proving contrary and driving us westward: but at last we got on shore, October the 12th.

From Dover, I that night rode post to Canterbury. Here I visited the cathedral, then in great splendour; those famous windows being entire, since demolished by the fanatics. The next morning, by Sittingbourne, I came to Rochester, and thence to Gravesend, where a light-horse-man (as they call it) taking us in, we spent our tide as far as Greenwich. From hence, after we had a little refreshed ourselves at the College (for by reason of the contagion then in London we balked the inns), we came to London, landing at Arundel-stairs. Here I took leave of his lordship, and retired to my lodgings in the Middle Temple being about two in the morning, the 14th of October.

16th October. I went to see my brother at Wotton. On the 31st of that month (unfortunate for the Irish Rebellion which broke out on the 23rd), I was one and twenty years of age.

7th November. After receiving the Sacrament at Wotton church, I visited my Lord Marshal at Albury.

23rd. I returned to London; and, on the 25th, saw his Majesty ride through the City after his coming out of Scotland, and a Peace proclaimed, with great acclamations and joy of the giddy people.

15th December. I was elected one of the Comptrollers of the Middle Temple-revellers, as the fashion of the young students and gentlemen was, the Christmas being kept this year with great solemnity; but, being desirous to pass it in the country, I got leave to resign my staff of office, and went with my brother Richard to Wotton.

SOURCE: Evelyn, John. *The Diary of John Evelyn*. Volume 1, pp. 39–40. London: J.M. Dent & Sons, Ltd., 1950.

Willy, Margaret. *English Diarists: Evelyn & Pepys.* London: Longmans, 1963. Print.

Woolf, Virginia. "Rambling round Evelyn." *The Essays of Virginia Woolf: 1925–1928.* Ed. Andrew McNeillie. New York: Harcourt, 1994. 91–98. Print.

Further Reading

Barchas, Janine. "'The Celebrated Mr. Evelyn' of *Silva* in Burney and Austen." *Matters of Fact in Jane Austen: History, Location, and Celebrity.* Baltimore: Johns Hopkins University Press, 2012. 127–65. Print.

Darley, Gillian. *John Evelyn: Living for Ingenuity.* New Haven: Yale University Press, 2006. Print.

Evans, Joan. Introduction. *The Diary of John Evelyn.* Ed. Guy de la Bédoyère. Suffolk: Boydell Press, 1995. 5–18. Print.

Evelyn, John. *Sylva: A Discourse of Forest Trees & the Propagation of Timber.* Ed. John Nisbet. 2 vols. New York: Doubleday, 1908. Print.

———. *Memoires for My Grand-Son.* Ed. Geoffrey Keynes. London: Nonesuch, 1926. Print.

Harris, Frances. *Transformations of Love: The Friendship of John Evelyn and Margaret Godolphin.* New York: Oxford University Press, 2004. Print.

Harris, Frances, and Michael Hunter, eds. *John Evelyn and His Milieu.* London: British Library, 2003. Print.

Keynes, Geoffrey, ed. *John Evelyn: A Study in Bibliophily with a Bibliography of His Writings.* London: Clarendon, 1968. Print.

Munns, Jessica. "Accounting for Providence: Contemporary Descriptions of the Restoration of Charles II." *Recording and Reordering: Essays on Seventeenth- and Eighteenth-Century Diary and Journal.* Ed. Dan Doll and Jessica Munns. Lewisburg, Pa.: Bucknell University Press, 2006. 102–121. Print.

Ridley, Glynis. "Sacred and Secular Places: An Atlantic Divide." *Recording and Reordering: Essays on Seventeenth- and Eighteenth-Century Diary and Journal.* Ed. Dan Doll and Jessica Munns. Lewisburg, Pa.: Bucknell University Press, 2006. 22–42. Print.

Katie Macnamara

The Diary of John Quincy Adams

John Quincy Adams

OVERVIEW

John Quincy Adams's diaries were first published between 1874 and 1877 as a twelve-volume set edited by his son, Charles Francis Adams, and titled *Memoirs of John Quincy Adams, Comprising Portions of His Diary from 1795 to 1848*. The original diaries, which were begun in 1779 when John Quincy Adams was twelve years old, amount to almost seventeen thousand pages and constitute one of the most substantial firsthand accounts of America's early years as a republic. Speaking variously as student, lawyer, professor, diplomat, the U.S. secretary of state, the sixth president of the United States, and finally as a U.S. congressman, Adams ranges widely in his entries, writing with great insight and emotion about politics and culture at home and abroad.

As the son of women's rights advocate Abigail Adams and second president of the United States, John Adams, John Quincy grew up in an intellectual household that was both socially and politically well connected. While still in his teens, he served as his father's secretary during the signing of the 1783 Treaty of Paris, which ended the American Revolutionary War. The American struggle for independence from Great Britain and the ensuing territorial negotiations with the other remaining colonial powers, primarily France and Spain, provide the broad context for the content and scope of Adams's *Diary*. Though Adams anticipated that his diaries would eventually be published, it took his son a quarter of a century after his father's death to sift through and prepare what he termed the "superabundance" of papers. To this day, *The Diary of John Quincy Adams*, as it is more commonly known, remains a major text for historians of American independence and the expansion of the late eighteenth to the mid-nineteenth centuries.

HISTORICAL AND LITERARY CONTEXT

When the young Adams began his diary, the American Revolutionary War (1775–1783) was underway. Prior to the war, the colonies of North America had amassed an extensive number of grievances against the British parliament, with unjust taxation at the top of the list. Delegates from the colonies, including Adams's father, George Washington, and Patrick Henry, convened a Continental Congress to organize appeals to Parliament and King George III. Following fighting at the Massachusetts towns of Lexington and Concord between local militias and British troops, however, the British king declared the Continental Congress traitors, to which they responded in 1776 with the Declaration of Independence. In his diary, Adams gives his chief attention to the political life of the United States emerging in this period, with firsthand accounts of key figures and events.

In the years covered by the *Diary*, the country underwent incredible transformation, much of which Adams comments on directly. He records, for example, the discussions that surrounded the framing of the bill that allowed the 1803 purchase of the French territory of Louisiana. He similarly notes debates over slavery (including his own vocal contributions), which, though partially abolished by 1804 in the northern states, continued in the South throughout Adams's lifetime. He was also instrumental in negotiating the Treaty of Ghent, which ended the War of 1812 with Britain; the annexation of Spanish Florida in 1819; and the signing of the Oregon Treaty of 1846, which gave the United States control of the northwest.

Adams's diaries probably owe much to the influence of his mother and father, who were both prolific writers. Like his son, John Adams kept a diary, ultimately running to fifty-one volumes, in which he meditated on his private and public life. These and the thousand-plus letters he and Abigail exchanged would have had a significant presence in the Adams household. Together with *The Diary of John Quincy Adams*, these documents are now held in the Adams Family Papers collection at the Massachusetts Historical Society. Also comparable to the *Diary* as a political and historical document is Thomas Jefferson's *Autobiography* (1821), in which the third president of the United States reflects on personal circumstances and matters of state during the founding of the republic, such as his drafting of the Declaration of Independence. Notably, Jefferson makes regular reference to John Adams, just as both John and John Quincy record the presence of Jefferson in both private and public contexts.

Adams and his *Diary* continue to hold strong appeal for biographers and historians. Numerous new biographies have appeared in recent decades, many of which give more nuanced analyses of the private Adams in order to revise earlier, less sympathetic perspectives, which often cast him as a failed politician. While it may be hard to say if Adams's

❖ Key Facts

Time Period:
Late 18th to Mid-19th Centuries

Relevant Historical Events:
American Revolutionary War; Treaty of Paris, Adams's election to the U.S. presidency

Nationality:
American

Keywords:
presidency; politics; U.S. history

HISTORICAL PERSPECTIVES

John Quincy Adams, who served as U.S. president from 1825 to 1829. Portrait by George Peter Alexander Healy. © PRIVATE COLLECTION/ PETER NEWARK AMERICAN PICTURES/THE BRIDGEMAN ART LIBRARY

writings provided direct inspiration for other presidential memoirs, the politics and ethics informing the *Diary* are similar to those of the post-presidential autobiographies of later presidents, from Theodore Roosevelt to Ronald Reagan.

THEMES AND STYLE

Spanning almost seventy years, *The Diary of John Quincy Adams* is diverse in subjects and themes, though the account of his ongoing struggle with Congress over the institution of slavery is one of his most constant topics. For almost a decade he fought a "gag rule" preventing abolitionist petitions to be heard in the House of Representatives. When the rule was first passed in 1836, the House prohibited Adams from speaking against it. Six years later, the House considered a motion to censure Adams for persisting with "extreme petitions." As he wrote in 1842, his peers presented "a flaming preamble charging me in substance with subornation of perjury and high treason, and resolutions that the House might well expel me." The *Diary* does not contain an entry for the day in 1844 when the rule was finally defeated, though in later entries Adams reflects on what he called "the life-and-death struggle for the right of petition."

Though the *Diary* is oriented toward political life in the early republic, it was for Adams a very private medium, in which he vented feelings he otherwise had difficulty expressing. Indeed, commentators often remark how humorless and cool Adams appeared in public life. As Allan Nevins notes in his introduction to a 1928 edition of the *Diary*, "To his contemporaries he was a frigid and icy New Englander." Adams himself was aware of his disposition, recording how "stiff and dull" he often was in company. In his *Diary*, however, as Nevins puts it, "he was really of a hot and passionate nature, volcanic in his hates, intense in his loves, compact of fervent feelings, and sometimes wrought up to the most extreme emotional pitch. The emotionalism of the diary is indeed one of its most appealing qualities."

Adams lived a full and busy life as a statesman, much of which he documented in painstaking detail. While certain themes persist throughout the *Diary*, however, such as fighting the anti-abolitionists, they come peppered with relatively inconsequential accounts. A typical 1841 entry (in the Nevins edition) begins: "March 1st. I went to the Supreme Court, and concluded my argument in the case of the *Amistad* captives. I spoke about four hours, and then closed somewhat abruptly," only to go on and describe how he took letters to the post office; spoke with a colleague seeking a recommendation; revised a report on a speech he had given on a "Treasury Note bill"; returned to the Supreme Court to hear further claims in the *Amistad* trial; visited the House to hear bills under consideration; spoke with colleagues; and, finally, went to the clerk's office to further research the *Amistad* case.

CRITICAL DISCUSSION

The Diary of John Quincy Adams was originally published to mixed reviews, with critics acknowledging its profound historical value yet losing patience with Adams's love of mundane details. As one *New York Times* critic put it, "We heartily wish that the writer had given us more … contemporaneous portraits at the sacrifice of some of his record of dull daily routine." Another *Times* critic similarly noted that "it would be much better if in the coming volumes the editor would … limit his selections to passages of personal moment and significance, and to the record of public events of general and enduring interest." Meanwhile, journals such as the *International Review* claimed that "there is no other book in existence which gives so vivid, complete, and accurate a picture of public life in the United States, through the first half of this century."

Following its initial publication, the *Diary* remained constantly in print, reissued in one form or another in 1903, 1928, 1951, 1969, 1970, and 1981. More recently, the Massachusetts Historical Society scanned fifteen hundred pages from the fifty-one original handwritten volumes and made them available online as part of the Adams Family Papers—a much larger archive of papers, letters, and manuscripts pertaining to John and Abigail Adams and their descendants. As a significant part of this collection, the *Diary*—in which John Quincy records meetings with notables such as Alexander I of Russia, George III of England, Franklin, Jefferson, Alexis de Tocqueville, and Charles Dickens—remains a major and credible source for scholarship on the early United States.

Beyond editors' introductions to the various reprints of the *Diary*, scholars rarely, if ever, discuss Adams's diaries as literature. Rather, the work features—sometimes heavily—as a primary source for historians and biographers documenting the life of Adams and the early United States alike. For example, it informed discussions of the slavery debate, as in the work of William Lee Miller, and new perspectives on Adams, most notably in the work of Paul C. Nagel, Robert V. Remini, and Harlow Giles Unger, all of whom are keen to point out its historical importance. Nagel, for example, claims that "most scholars agree … that Adams's enormous diary is the most valuable historical and personal journal kept by any prominent American." Similarly, Unger states that the work "remains the most complete, personal, day-to-day record of events and life in the New World and Old, from the 1770s to the 1840s" and its author "one of the most courageous figures in the history of American government."

BIBLIOGRAPHY

Sources

Adams, Charles Francis, ed. *Memoirs of John Quincy Adams, Comprising Portions of His Diary from 1795 to 1848*. 12 vols. Philadelphia: J. B. Lippincott, 1874–77. Print.

Adams, John Quincy. *The Diary of John Quincy Adams, 1794–1845: American Political, Social and Intellectual Life from Washington to Polk*. Ed. Allan Nevins. New York: Longmans, Green, 1928. Print.

Miller, William Lee. *Arguing about Slavery: The Great Battle in the United States Congress*. New York: Knopf, 1997. Print.

"New Publications: Memoirs of John Quincy Adams, Comprising Portions." Rev. of *The Diary of John Quincy Adams*, by John Quincy Adams. *New York Times*. New York Times, 9 Jul. 1876. Web. 14 Dec. 2012.

"New Publications: The Adams Memoirs." Rev. of *The Diary of John Quincy Adams*, by John Quincy Adams. *New York Times*. New York Times, 12 Aug. 1875. Web. 14 Dec. 2012.

Remini, Robert V. *John Quincy Adams*. New York: Times Books, 2002. Print.

JOHN QUINCY ADAMS VERSUS "THE WORLD, THE FLESH, AND ALL THE DEVILS IN HELL"

In 1839 Portuguese slavers illegally captured a number of Africans in Sierra Leone and shipped them to Havana, Cuba. Here, the Africans were sold to two Spanish planters, who in turn shipped them to a Caribbean plantation. Onboard the Spanish schooner *La Amistad*, however, the Africans wrested control of the ship, killed the captain and the cook, and forced the planters to sail for Africa. But the navigator tricked them and headed for the East Coast of North America, where U.S. authorities captured the ship and imprisoned the Africans for murder. The murder charges were soon dismissed, but the case continued to be fought over salvage claims and property rights. When the trial went before the U.S. Supreme Court, John Quincy Adams defended the Africans and won their freedom.

In 1997 Steven Spielberg adapted the story for his movie *Amistad*, with Anthony Hopkins playing Adams in an ambivalent light, as an old man who must be persuaded to come around to helping the Africans. In reality, Adams was anything but ambivalent; as he wrote in *The Diary of John Quincy Adams*, "The world, the flesh, and all the devils in hell are arrayed against any man who now in this North American Union shall dare to join the standard of Almighty God to put down the African slave-trade; and … what can I do …? Yet my conscience presses me on."

Rev. of *Memoirs of John Quincy Adams*, by John Quincy Adams. *International Review* 4 (1877): 856. *ProQuest Historical Newspapers: American Periodicals*. Web. 17 Dec. 2012.

Unger, Harlow Giles. *John Quincy Adams*. Boston: Da Capo, 2012. Print.

Further Reading

Adams, Abigail Smith, John Adams, L. H. Butterfield, and Marc Friedlaender. *The Book of Abigail and John: Selected Letters of the Adams Family, 1762–1784*. Boston: Northeastern University Press, 2002. Print.

Allen, David Grayson, Robert J. Taylor, Marc Friedlaender, and Celeste Walker, eds. *Diary of John Quincy Adams*. 2 vols. Cambridge: Harvard University Press, 1981. Print.

"The Diaries of John Quincy Adams: A Digital Collection." The Adams Family Papers. *Massachusetts Historical Society*. Web. 6 Dec. 2012.

Holton, Woody. *Abigail Adams*. New York: Free Press, 2009. Print.

Nagel, Paul C. *John Quincy Adams: A Public Life, a Private Life*. New York: Knopf, 1997. Print.

Parsons, Lynn Hudson. *John Quincy Adams*. New York: Rowman and Littlefield, 1998. Print.

David Aitchison

The Diary of Samuel Pepys

Samuel Pepys

✥ Key Facts

Time Period:
Mid-17th Century

Relevant Historical Events:
Death of Cromwell; restoration of the British monarchy; Protestant Reformation

Nationality:
English

Keywords:
history; politics; Reformation

OVERVIEW

The Diary of Samuel Pepys, which records the thoughts and experiences of a British naval administrator during the historically significant years 1660 to 1669, was carefully preserved by its author but not published until 1825, when excerpts were first released. Various expanded editions of Samuel Pepys's diary appeared over the following decades, but the entire six-volume work did not see print until 1970–1983. Richly detailed, lively, and intimately revealing, the diary gives a vibrant portrait of its age, shining a personal light not only on such pivotal events as the Great Plague and the Great Fire of London but also on theater, marriage, cuisine, and other features of daily middle-class life in the seventeenth century.

Pepys's engaging journal lifts the veil on a tumultuous time in British history, and his unguarded revelations about his life, aspirations, and attitudes represent an innovative approach to autobiography. In the centuries since its first publication, the journal has been embraced enthusiastically by a wide variety of readers, including historians seeking insights into seventeenth-century life, linguists studying the development of the English language, and literary scholars analyzing the work as the forerunner of a new genre of personal writing.

HISTORICAL AND LITERARY CONTEXT

The first half of the seventeenth century was a time of political and religious turmoil in Britain. In the early 1500s Martin Luther had begun his struggle in Germany to reform corrupt practices in the Catholic Church, and Henry VIII had, for the more secular reason of wanting to divorce and remarry, cut ties with the Roman Catholic Church to form a separate Church of England. During the rule of Elizabeth I (1558–1603), a powerful sect of Protestants called Puritans argued that the Anglican Church retained too much of the ritual and idolatry of Catholicism, and by 1645 one of these Puritans, Oliver Cromwell, had seized power in a military coup. Four years later, King Charles I was executed, and in 1653 Cromwell declared himself Lord Protector of England, ushering in a period of harsh religious repression.

Pepys's diary begins at the dawn of a new era in British politics and culture. In 1658 Cromwell died suddenly, leaving no strong leader to replace him. Though his son Richard tried to retain power, the army revolted, and Parliament demanded the restoration of the monarchy. The coronation of King Charles II in 1660 not only led to a more powerful Church of England and Parliament but also introduced a period of renewed social activity. Britons, happy to be released from Puritanical restrictions, reveled in such forbidden pursuits as theater, music, dancing, and gambling.

Much Reformation-era literature in Britain was devoted to spiritual improvement, such as the *Primers* and *Homilies,* which offered instruction on morality and righteousness. However, some writers, including Pepys, foreshadowed a modern self-revelatory approach to writing. In France, Michel de Montaigne introduced an innovative style of personal reflection in his *Essais* (1580). Some English writers of the era kept journals that were later published; John Evelyn, Pepys's contemporary, offered a less personally revealing portrait of the times in his diaries, first published in 1818 under the title *Memoirs Illustrative of the Life and Writings of John Evelyn.* Portions of seventeenth-century scientist Robert Hooke's memoirs were published in 1935 as *The Diary of Robert Hooke, M.A. F.R.S. 1672–1680.*

Excerpts of Pepys's journals were first published during the height of the Romantic era and had great appeal for readers who valued emotionality and individual expression. With their detailed accounts of day-to-day life as well as cataclysmic events, the diaries became an important source of historical information about Restoration society. Pepys chronicled his life with precision, writing entries almost every day for eight and a half years, and the result is one of the most complete pictures available of the professional, domestic, and social life of the seventeenth-century British middle class.

THEMES AND STYLE

Though Pepys's work is a daily journal, it contains themes worthy of any novel. Self-improvement, a major concern of the Reformation, is an obsession with Pepys, who was raised with Puritan leanings. He repeatedly renounces alcohol ("Since my leaving drinking of wine, I do find myself much better and do mind my business better, and do spend less money, and less time in idle company") and womanizing ("I have used ... to make a bad use of my fancy with whatever woman I have a mind to, which I … shall endeavour to do so no more"). Common humanity is another of Pepys's preoccupations, and his cheerfully prosaic view of his own successes ("chance without merit brought me in, and … diligence only keeps me so") expands to include the nobility: "God forgive me, though I adore them with all the duty possible, yet the more a man considers and observes them, the less he finds of difference between them and other men."

There is evidence that Pepys intended his diary for posterity. Though he wrote his entries in shorthand and kept their existence secret during his lifetime, he did not destroy them; instead, he had the books meticulously bound and left with the rest of his library to his former school, Magdalene College. He begins his journal at age twenty-six, on January 1, 1660, with his characteristic combination of history and confession: "Blessed be God, at the end of the last year I was in very good health, without any sense of my old pain, but upon taking of cold…. The condition of the State was thus; viz. the Rump [Parliament], after being disturbed by my Lord Lambert, was lately returned to sit again." Pepys ends his diary on May 31, 1669. Fearful that he is losing his eyesight, he resolves only to record that which he can dictate to others, forgoing personal revelation, "and therefore resolve from this time forward to have it kept by my people in longhand, and must therefore be contented to set down no more than is fit for them and all the world to know."

Pepys employs an engaging writing style that showcases a lively curiosity. His personal focus gives immediacy to his narrative, as seen in his descriptions of his own experience of the Great Fire of London, which started on September 2, 1666. "All over the Thames, with one's face in the wind, you were almost burned with a shower of fire-drops…. I also did see a poor cat … with all the hair burned off its body and yet alive." Yet Pepys's buoyancy prevails, as, after mourning the city's losses, he goes "to Sir R. Ford's and there dined on an earthen platter; a fried breast of mutton; a great many of us, but very merry."

CRITICAL DISCUSSION

Pepys's personal perspective on history, coupled with his unstinting portrait of his own imperfections, made the book an instant favorite upon publication. Frequently quoted by delighted readers, it impressed scholars and critics such as Francis Jeffrey of the *Edinburgh Review*, who writes, "There is very little of it which does not help us to understand the character of his times and his contemporaries, better than we should ever have done without it." An 1881 *New York Times* review of a Pepys biography concurs, "The minute information Pepys gives us of manner and customs in his diary [is] … photographic."

Writing in 1886 author Robert Louis Stevenson describes Pepys as an "unparalleled figure in the annals of mankind" because of the way he infuses his personality into his portrait of an age. Indeed, Pepys's journals, partly because they seem to be an illicit peek into a private life, are unique as historical, sociological, and literary documents. Writing for *New Criterion* in 2003, Brooke Allen asserts, "Pepys's vivid insider's account of the political turmoil of the Restoration, as well as his famous eyewitness reports of public events and panics … have probably done more to shape our vision of Restoration London than the work of any other artist or writer of the period, including Marvell, Dryden, Milton, and the great court painter Lely."

Early, heavily censored versions of Pepys's diaries were followed by later editions more faithful to the author's original explicit text. Long a part of the canon of English literature, Pepys is still examined by scholars for his insights into his age. Claire Tomalin, a Pepys biographer, notes the continuing accuracy of his observations, particularly about marriage, calling the diary "as good an account of the married state as has ever been written, its struggles, its woes, its pleasures and its discontents. You might put the *Diary* into the hands of a Martian to explain the institution and its workings." Literary scholar Elihu Pearlman views Pepys's reserved and obsessive personality as key to the diary's success, writing, "Verve alone would have resulted in a marvelous life, but verve allied to secrecy and orderliness produced the marvelous diary."

Portrait of Samuel Pepys painted by John Hayls in 1666. © NATIONAL PORTRAIT GALLERY, LONDON, UK/THE BRIDGEMAN ART LIBRARY

WALLINGTON'S WORLD: A PURITAN ARTISAN IN SEVENTEENTH-CENTURY LONDON

While a number of sixteenth- and seventeenth-century diaries and memoirs have survived to provide future generations with a clearer picture of life during Britain's tumultuous Reformation and Restoration periods, most of these were written by members of the nobility, the clergy, or the upper middle class, who had both the education and the time for such record keeping. In 1985, however, Paul S. Seaver delved into the journals and notes of a London tradesman to produce a uniquely constructed autobiography of a working-class Puritan of the early 1600s.

Nehemiah Wallington, who lived from 1598 to 1658, followed his father into the wood-turning trade and was a staunch Puritan. Though he was neither rich nor successful in business, he monitored his spiritual rectitude with meticulous diligence, writing fifty volumes of notes and meditations during his lifetime. Seaver organized and edited Wallington's six surviving notebooks, along with thousands of pages of other notes and papers, to create a vibrant portrait of an ordinary urban workingman and devout nonconformist who found Oliver Cromwell's policies too tolerant. Though mainly religious in subject matter, Wallington's papers, like Samuel Pepys's diaries, give a vivid picture of the writer's family life, aspirations, and disappointments as he lives through the overthrow and restoration of the British monarchy.

BIBLIOGRAPHY

Sources

Allen, Brooke. "The Irrepressible Pepys." *New Criterion* 21.5 (2003): 14+. *Literature Resource Center.* Web. 27 Nov. 2012.

Jeffrey, Francis. "An Excerpt from a Review of *Memoirs of Samuel Pepys, Esq.*" *Edinburgh Review* 43.85 (1825): 23–54. Rpt. in *Literature Criticism from 1400 to 1800.* Ed. James E. Person Jr. Vol. 11. Detroit: Gale, 1990. *Literature Resource Center.* Web. 28 Nov. 2012.

Pearlman, Elihu. "Samuel Pepys." *British Prose Writers, 1660–1800: First Series.* Ed. Donald T. Siebert. Detroit: Gale, 1991. *Dictionary of Literary Biography.* Vol. 101. *Literature Resource Center.* Web. 27 Nov. 2012.

"Pepys and His World." Rev. of *Samuel Pepys and the World He Lived In,* by Henry B. Wheatley. *New York Times* 2 Jan. 1881: 4. *ProQuest Historical Newspapers.* Web. 28 Nov. 2012.

Poquette, Ryan D. "Critical Essay on *The Diary of Samuel Pepys.*" *Nonfiction Classics for Students: Presenting Analysis, Context, and Criticism on Nonfiction Works.* Ed. David M. Galens, Jennifer Smith, and Elizabeth Thomason. Vol. 4. Detroit: Gale, 2002. *Literature Resource Center.* Web. 27 Nov. 2012.

Stevenson, Robert Louis. "Samuel Pepys." *Essays, English and American, with Introductions, Notes and Illustrations.* New York: P. F. Collier & Son, c. 1910. *Fordham University.* Web. 28 Nov. 2012.

Tomalin, Claire. *Samuel Pepys: The Unequalled Self.* New York: Knopf, 2002. Print.

Further Reading

Coote, Stephen. *Samuel Pepys: A Life.* London: Hodder & Stoughton, 2000. Print.

Dawson, Mark S. "Histories and Texts: Refiguring the Diary of Samuel Pepys." *Historical Journal* 43. 2 (2000): 407–31. *JSTOR.* Web. 28 Nov. 2012.

De la Bédoyère, Guy, ed. *Particular Friends: The Correspondence of Samuel Pepys and John Evelyn.* Woodbridge, U.K.: Boydell, 2005. Print.

Kunin, Aaron. "Other Hands in Pepys's Diary." *Modern Language Quarterly* 65.2 (2004): 195+. *Literature Resource Center.* Web. 28 Nov. 2012.

Taylor, Ivan E. "A Puritan at the Theater." *Samuel Pepys: Updated Edition.* Boston: Twayne, 1989. 83–100. Rpt. in *Literature Criticism from 1400 to 1800.* Ed. Lawrence J. Trudeau. Vol. 58. Detroit: Gale, 2000. *Literature Resource Center.* Web. 28 Nov. 2012.

Tina Gianoulis

Diary, Reminiscences and Correspondence of Henry Crabb Robinson, Barrister-at-Law

Henry Crabb Robinson

OVERVIEW

Diary, Reminiscences and Correspondence of Henry Crabb Robinson, Barrister-at-Law—which addresses subjects such as literature, religion, and philosophy, arising from Henry Crabb Robinson's friendships with some of the greatest minds of his age—has remained of interest to scholars since the time of its earliest publication in 1869. Divided into three volumes that follow a chronological order, Robinson's diary entries, reminiscences, and correspondence make up sixteen hundred pages of text but amount to only one twenty-fifth of the extant entries. Later editions of Robinson's personal papers have appeared, but the definitive collection was the first, edited by Thomas Sadler. Presenting a wealth of information and insight into the daily lives and works of illustrious thinkers spanning several countries and two epochs, *Diary, Reminiscences and Correspondence* also chronicles Robinson's own remarkable life, that of a self-made, self-educated man who was an inveterate reader, the first foreign correspondent for the London *Times*, a barrister, a generous but candid critic, a skilled translator, an habitué of the theater, and a trusted and valued friend.

Robinson (1775–1867) did not publish his diary or letters during his lifetime. However, he appears to have anticipated their eventual publication, for he notes in his diary that he hopes his observations may be of some use to others. Macmillan in London made the first edition of these works available two years after Robinson's death, and other editions followed. Academic work on the personal writings began appearing in the 1920s and has remained steady. In particular, scholars of literary luminaries such as William Wordsworth and Charles Lamb have scoured Robinson's papers for information on their subjects.

HISTORICAL AND LITERARY CONTEXT

Robinson's personal papers reveal a singular man whose interests and attitudes were broader than those of most of his peers in the eighteenth and nineteenth centuries in England. However, they convey remarkably little about the man himself, as his focus remains external. Despite being born to a family of "as insignificant a class as can be imagined" in class-conscious England, Robinson managed to acquire a first-rate education and to meet and befriend members of the most illustrious circles of his day, not just in England but also in Germany, Italy and France. He adopted the gentleman's habit of keeping a diary, as was the social convention of the privileged classes in Victorian England. Robinson also followed the convention of maintaining regular correspondence with friends and acquaintances. His childhood was dominated by the debates on religion that were raging in England at the time, and his young adulthood coincided with widespread and acrimonious debates in England over the principles of liberty and republicanism that the French Revolution had made matters of vital importance.

Robinson corresponded with several notable figures, including the British writers Lamb, Wordsworth, and Samuel Taylor Coleridge; the abolitionist Thomas Clarkson; and the French novelist Madame de Staël. He also exchanged letters with his family and the families of his famous friends. Later in his life, his circle of acquaintances extended to American luminaries such as Ralph Waldo Emerson and the lawyer Daniel Webster. *Diary, Reminiscences and Correspondence* represents the bulk of Robinson's written work, though he did publish numerous newspaper articles as a foreign correspondent for the *Times* on the Napoleonic Wars, as well as critical reviews on a variety of subjects. His diary includes details about his travels abroad and his years as a student at the University of Jena in Germany.

Diary, Reminiscences and Correspondence responds to the works of poets, philosophers, theologians, and economists of the time. Examples from the hundreds include his opinions on Johann Wolfgang von Goethe's *Naturliche Tochter* and the works of Jeremy Bentham. When he was not engaged in conversation, Robinson took every opportunity to read, recording his observations and criticisms in his diary. His letters do not contain the rhetorical flourishes or vivid narrative styles of diarists such as Samuel Pepys. Rather, they more closely resemble the private papers of another contemporary, American writer Nathaniel Hawthorne, in their candid and unpretentious approach.

Notably, Robinson's letters and recollections reflect his deep, personal knowledge of public people and the influence he had on their work. He is known as an early informant about some of the leading writers of the Romantic period. For example, Madame de Stael asked him to assist her in translating and

❖ Key Facts

Time Period:
Early to Mid-19th Century

Relevant Historical Events:
Robinson's friendship with notable contemporary intellectuals; emergence of German Romanticism

Nationality:
English

Keywords:
intellectualism; Romanticism; republicanism

HISTORICAL PERSPECTIVES

1828 depiction of a Unitarian chapel in London. Solicitor, intellectual, and writer Henry Crabb Robinson was involved with the Unitarian movement in England. © PRINT COLLECTOR/HIP/ THE IMAGE WORKS

explaining the writings of Romantic German philosophers, knowledge that she then used in her book *De l'Allemagne* (1813).

THEMES AND STYLE

Though a wide range of interests are covered in *Diary, Reminiscences and Correspondence,* the primary emphasis is on theological certainty, friendship, and books. Scholars have written less about Robinson's abiding quest for theological certainty than the other two topics, but religion was an important part of his life. Not only did he discuss and read theology, but he also attended numerous services in churches of many sects. In one entry he writes, "I heard three sermons in one day." Despite a strict religious upbringing, he showed genuine curiosity and open-mindedness toward all doctrines. He publicly praised the gifts of infamous atheist novelist William Godwin, much to the horror of devout acquaintances, even though Robinson himself remained a Christian. He sought out others to talk about religion, such as Baron Hohenfels, a German bishop and "a very liberal and philosophic churchman" who "taught me much by the questions he was in the habit of putting to me." Robinson was initially drawn to the work of German philosophers because they were "poetic-metaphysical religionist."

Robinson used his diary and correspondence to record his responses to books, encounters with people, talks on religion, reactions to theatrical performances, and professional employments, but there is little of a truly personal nature in the papers. Though he had many friends, they knew little of him except that he was amiable, loyal, and candid. He simply wrote down everything he saw, heard, read, and experienced. His correspondence is similarly filled with descriptions of people, places, and books. Even his letters to his brother focus on information and anecdotes rather than private, personal emotions. Robinson makes no mention of feeling anything deeper than admiration or affection for others. According to his papers, he lived ninety-one years without once being in love.

All three volumes are written in the same naturalistic diction; there is no discernible difference between his daily diary entries and his letters to famous writers. Though Robinson published a number of articles and reviews, he concluded when he was thirty-six that he lacked the talent to be a literary writer and decided to give up trying. "It was the failure of my attempt to gain distinction by writing that made me willing to devote myself honestly to the law, and so saved me from the mortification that follows a *little* literary success," he writes. It seems that for decades, most scholars agreed with Robinson's self-assessment. In a 1928 article on Robinson's papers for the *Sewanee Review,* Charles Harrold wrote, "It can in no real sense of the term be called literature." However, recent scholarship has challenged that assumption.

CRITICAL DISCUSSION

Initial critical response to *Diary, Reminiscence and Correspondence* was largely positive. By the 1920s, however, scholars who had access to the tremendous mass of papers expressed concern. In a 1928 article, R. W. King referred to Sadler's edits as useful but drastic. A year later, D. G. Larg wrote in the *Review of English Studies* that Sadler had taken so many liberties with the original text that his edition "would nowadays bring him to the Old Bailey." Professor Edith Morley's selections from the diary, published in 1922, were thought to be truer to Robinson's work, though they covered less ground. Derek Hudson's 1968 abridged version of Morley's three volumes was deemed to have added nothing and subtracted too much. Perhaps daunted by the sheer volume of writing, scholars have bitten off only subsections of his work. For example, there are published volumes of his correspondence with the Wordsworth circle (671 letters).

Twentieth-century scholars mined Robinson's papers for information on Romantic and early Victorian authors. In the twenty-first century academics have focused on his time in Germany and his role in introducing German writers to England and English writers. They also have examined Robinson's study of continental writers outside of Germany, including the three volumes of his diary devoted to commentary on the Italian poets of the 1820 and 1830s.

Other recent scholarship has focused on Robinson as an autobiographer in his own right. Along with the usual articles on his papers in relation to his famous friends, scholars have begun to see Robinson himself as worthy of study, a man whose insights into social history, cross-cultural understanding, and the world of the theater are well worth reading. Eugene Stelzig observes in a 2005 article in *Biography* that Robinson "deserves to be considered an important 19th century autobiographer." Indeed, his intelligent sympathy, personal modesty, independence, and enlightened views continue to charm. In the 1994 novel *Possession* by esteemed British writer A. S. Byatt, Robinson appears as a minor character. Byatt creates fictional additions to Robinson's diary in which two of the main characters meet at one of his famous breakfast parties.

BIBLIOGRAPHY

Sources

Baker, John Milton. *Henry Crabb Robinson of Bury, Jena, "The Times" and Russell Square.* London: Allen and Unwin, 1937. Print.

Byatt, A. S. *Possession.* London: Chatto and Windus, 1990. Print.

Halmi, Nicholas. Rev. of *Essays on Kant, Schelling, and German Aesthetics,* by Henry Crabb Robinson. Ed. James Vigus. *Coleridge Bulletin* 39 (2012): 103–5. *LION.* Web. 13 Dec. 2012.

Harrold, Charles F. "A Spectator of a Life: Henry Crabb Robinson." *Sewanee Review* 36 (1928): 46–61. *LION.* Web. 13 Dec. 2012.

HENRY CRABB ROBINSON AND THE UNIVERSITY OF LONDON

Being the child of religious dissenters, Henry Crabb Robinson was not able to study at either of the ancient English universities, so he took an interest in the founding of the University of London (now called University College, London) in 1826 for students of all faiths and none. As he notes in his diary, he saw his contribution "as a sort of debt to the cause of civil and religious liberty." In February 1835 he was elected to the council of the university, in 1838 he became a member of the committee of management, and in 1842 he became vice president of the senate.

Robinson was an active member of the University of London community, attending meetings regularly and thus taking part in the appointment of professors and other important matters. It was thanks to the patient efforts of Robinson that the collection of the famous sculptor John Flaxman came to the university. A typical day's business in 1850 for the seventy-five-year-old Robinson would consist of his hosting a breakfast for professors, students, and literary friends before visiting friends at the Ladies College, tending to university business, and going to the library to read the *Times* and write letters.

Owens, Thomas. "A Wordsworth Manuscript and a Little-Known Literary Connection." *Notes & Queries* 58.1 (2011): 74–75. *LION.* Web. 13 Dec. 2012.

Robinson, Henry Crabb. *Diary, Reminiscences and Correspondence of Henry Crabb Robinson.* Ed. Thomas Sadler. Boston: Houghton Mifflin, 1869. *Google Books.* Web. 10 Dec. 2012.

Stelzig, Eugene. "A Cultural Tourist in Romantic Germany: Henry Crabb Robinson as a 19th Century Life Writer." *Biography* 28.4 (2005): 515–33. *JSTOR.* Web. 10 Dec. 2012.

Further Reading

Brewster, Glen. "'New Words' and 'New Ideas.' Henry Crabb Robinson as Cultural Tourist." *Prose Studies* 31.2 (2009): 141–50. *LION.* Web. 13 Dec. 2012.

Morley, Edith J. *The Life and Times of Henry Crabb Robinson.* London: Dent. 1935. Print.

———. *Henry Crabb Robinson on Books and Their Writers.* London: Dent, 1938. Print.

Stelzig, Eugene. *Henry Crabb Robinson in Germany.* Lewisburg, Pa.: Bucknell University Press, 2010. *LION.* Web. 13 Dec. 2012.

Wu, Duncan. "The Lamb Circle and the *Monthly Repository.*" *Romanticism* 12:2 (2006): 143–49. *LION.* Web. 13 Dec. 2012.

Kristin King-Ries

Jemima Condict
Her Book, Being a Transcript of the Diary of an Essex County Maid during the Revolutionary War
Jemima Condict

❖ **Key Facts**

Time Period:
Late 18th Century

Relevant Historical Events:
American Revolutionary War; achievement of American independence

Nationality:
American

Keywords:
women's writing; piety; domesticity

OVERVIEW

Published in 1930, *Jemima Condict: Her Book, Being a Transcript of the Diary of an Essex County Maid during the Revolutionary War* is, as the subtitle suggests, a diary kept by a young New Jersey woman between 1772 and 1779, as the United States rebelled against and broke free from British colonial control and established a new nation. Jemima Condict notes and opines on this grander historical context throughout her diary, but many of the entries are devoted to recording the minor events of her family and community life. A lifelong resident of rural Pleasantdale, New Jersey, Condict was born on August 24, 1754, and began her diary at the age of seventeen. The diary ends with her premature death in 1779. It documents her personal opinions, experiences, and aspirations, offering a rare glimpse into the developing consciousness of a young adult woman as the thirteen British colonies in America moved toward, fought for, and achieved independence.

Condict's diary was not published until 1930, a century and a half after her death. As a mere two hundred copies of that first public edition of the text were printed, it was not widely noticed, read, or reviewed. However, the diary came to greater attention in 1975, when it was generously excerpted in Elizabeth Evans's *Weathering the Storm: Women of the American Revolution* and became more widely read by critics and historians, who saw it as an important document of life in late-eighteenth-century America. Today *Jemima Condict* continues to attract scholarly attention for its insight into the social, religious, and familial milieu of Revolutionary War–era America.

HISTORICAL AND LITERARY CONTEXT

Condict's diary was written during the American transition from British colony to independent nation, a time when women were severely disenfranchised and religious piety and meekness were highly valued. A descendant of British settlers, Condict was born in 1754 and lived her entire, brief life in the mountains northwest of Newark, New Jersey. Like much of colonial America, the area was remote and rustic and ruled by tradition. Though education was difficult to attain, especially for women, Condict was able to receive occasional schooling between working on her parents' farm and performing housework. Her education focused primarily on the Bible and manners.

In her diary, Condict records the effect of disease, death, religion, and the Revolutionary War on herself, her family, and her community. Soon after she began writing, in 1773, a series of epidemics hit her mountain community. Dysentery, smallpox, and throat distemper spread through the area, killing and debilitating people and testing their religious convictions. Condict's piety was unshaken, despite the suffering, and it continued to inform her take on contemporary events. When the Revolutionary War broke out 1775, men from the area joined the war effort as part of the Continental army. The diary records her personal impressions of the war, as well as those of other members of her community, including her pastor. Condict's writing continues through her marriage and ends just before she died soon after giving birth to her only child, a son, in 1779.

Though women's writing from the American colonies is rare, *Jemima Condict* does exist within a larger tradition of autobiographical writing composed by women in the seventeenth and eighteenth centuries. *The Journal of Madam Knight* is one of the more prominent of these texts. Composed by Sarah Kemble Knight (1666–1727), the journal was written between 1704 and 1705 while its author traveled from Boston to New York, and it records her impressions of the northeastern colonies. Other journals, diaries, and letters by women from South Carolina, Vermont, and elsewhere in the colonies provide important precedents and context for Condict's diary. Together, these texts offer a patchwork account of the lives of American women before national independence.

Condict's diary was kept private until 1930 and, therefore, did not influence her contemporaries. That said, the notes she kept and the impressions she recorded were part of a much larger body of autobiographical writing by women about the American transition from colony to nation. These writings include the journal of Sally Wister (1761–1804), a Quaker from Philadelphia who recorded her experience during the Revolutionary War, when officers from the

Continental army quartered with her family. Also part of this body of work is the diary of Grace Growdon Galloway, also of Philadelphia, who documented her struggles to prevent her property from being confiscated as part of the penalty for her husband's loyalty to Britain during the war.

THEMES AND STYLE

The central theme of *Jemima Condict* is that religious piety allows one to endure despite the constancy of suffering and error. After beginning with epigraphs from Proverbs 14:34 ("Righteousness exalteth a nation but Sin is a Reproach to any People") and Isaiah 45:22 ("Look unto me and be ye Saved all the ends of the Earth for I am God there is None Else"), as well as a brief prayer, the diary's first entry records the death of Condict's nineteen-year-old cousin and prays that the "lord grant that this stroke of thy providence May be for my good. O that it might awaken me o that it might take a right efect upon me." As the diary proceeds, Condict records a litany of deaths and deprivations and seeks comfort in her faith in God's omnipotent justice.

Condict used her diary to record the mundane suffering of daily life and, therefore, redeem that suffering by placing it within the context of a heavenly plan. As she records local deaths and laments her moral failings, she documents the sermons of her pastor, Jedediah Chapman, and includes passages from the Bible. In so doing, she seeks to explain her experience through the prism of her religion. In an entry from 1774, for example, she laments her misery but takes solace in attributing her suffering to her own moral failings: "Oh I think this is a troublesome World for I a Poor Miserable Wicked Creature. find But little Comfort but tis because my mind is taken up in Vanity & I am a discontented Moral I am So Indeed."

Jemima Condict is notable for its sense of addressing an audience, despite having been written, seemingly, exclusively for private use. This sense that Condict is writing for a reader is implicit in her tallying of information about community life, especially in her long lists of deaths and her recording of sermons. However, it is also made explicit in her occasional address of the reader. On a Tuesday in 1774, she writes, "Well how is it with you my friends?" In 1779, shortly before her death, she addresses her sister: "My Dearest & Loving Sister, you & I have Lived many years together, But Now we must Part, which is a hard thing to me, O how Can I?" In these passages and others like them, Condict breaks from the confines of diaristic writing and demonstrates that the recording of her life served more than a private function—that her writing was also a means of connecting with her larger community.

CRITICAL DISCUSSION

Jemima Condict's first edition of only two hundred copies was not widely noticed. However, the publication did eventually draw the attention of scholars, who viewed the diary as offering a rare view of life in colonial and revolutionary America from a common woman's point of view. In order to bring the rare and limited text to a wider critical and popular audience, Evans included substantial excerpts from *Jemima Condict* in her book *Weathering the Storm*. Published in celebration of the country's bicentennial anniversary, *Weathering the Storm* was widely acclaimed when it first appeared, but the excerpts from *Jemima Condict* were deemed "dull" by the reviewer Mary McDougall Gordon in her analysis in *Pennsylvania History*.

Jemima Condict has provided historians and scholars a more complete account of life in mid- to late-eighteenth-century America. That account was dramatically altered in the late twentieth century, as scholarship in women's history and women's literature helped bring to light more and fuller accounts by women from American history. Many such texts had been ignored, bowdlerized, or injudiciously edited, but that changed, particularly in the 1970s and 1980s. As the scholar Joyce D. Goodfriend writes in *The Published Diaries and Letters of American Women*, these personal and autobiographical writings "convey the experiential dimension of history in ways that no other sources can." Today, *Jemima Condict* has attracted a small body of criticism that considers the book in relationship to American colonial history, the Revolutionary War, and the role women played in the nation's early years.

Condict's diary is valued by scholars for the view it offers of a woman struggling with her role in colonial and revolutionary America. As Goodfriend writes, "The inner turmoil that Jemima experienced during this period of her life was undoubtedly linked to the pressure she felt to marry, and her hesitation about taking this big step is reflected in her comments on marriage in general and on the choice of a mate." Critics have also remarked upon Condict's defiance in the face of

In her diary, Jemima Condict describes not only religious teachings and the lives of her family and community, but also such major events as the Revolutionary War and the Boston Tea Party, depicted here. © NORTH WIND PICTURE ARCHIVES/ALAMY

HISTORICAL PERSPECTIVES

MARGARET MORRIS: HER JOURNAL

Not far from Jemima Condict's home, in the town of Burlington, New Jersey, lived Margaret Hill Morris, a Quaker widow who worked as a medical practitioner to support her four children. Morris was born in 1737 outside Annapolis, Maryland, and was almost twenty years older than Condict when the Revolutionary War broke out in 1775. Throughout her life, Morris had documented the private joys and troubles she encountered. Like Condict, she was a pious Christian and looked to her faith for comfort when things were hard, as they often were. For example, when her husband and a daughter died in 1765, Morris wrote in her diary, "Thou, oh Lord has been seen good to try me many times with the loss of dear parents, children and friends; and at none of thy dispenses has my heart murmured or repined; I have constantly and daily endeavored to say, thy will be in me."

In a journal that spanned December 6, 1776, to June 14, 1777, Morris recorded the events of the Revolutionary War in far greater detail than Condict did. Her accounting of the war began on December 6, 1776, when British troops came within thirty-five miles of Burlington. On that day she writes that "my heart almost died within me" upon reports of the threat of violence. As the war continued, Morris witnessed and documented the pillaging, destruction, and violence that raged around her.

pressure to act according to expectations incumbent on women of her era. As Evans writes, "Despite pressures to conform, Jemima retained an individualistic, impulsive nature, and a sensitive compassion toward others."

BIBLIOGRAPHY

Sources

Condict, Jemima. *Jemima Condict: Her Book, Being a Transcript of the Diary of an Essex County Maid during the Revolutionary War.* Ed. Wilbur Macey Stone. Newark: Carteret Book Club, 1930. Print.

Evans, Elizabeth. *Weathering the Storm: Women of the American Revolution.* New York: Scribner, 1975. Print.

Goodfriend, Joyce D. *The Published Diaries and Letters of American Women: An Annotated Bibliography.* Boston: G. K. Hall, 1987. Print.

Gordon, Mary McDougall. Rev. of *Weathering the Storm: Women of the American Revolution,* by Elizabeth Evans. *Pennsylvania History* 43.4 (1976): 368–69. JSTOR. Web. 17 Dec. 2012.

Matthews, William. *American Diaries: An Annotated Bibliography of American Diaries Written Prior to the Year 1861.* Boston: J. S. Canner, 1959. Print.

Morris, Margaret. *Margaret Morris: Her Journal.* Philadelphia: G. S. MacManus, 1949. Print.

Further Reading

Berkin, Carol. *First Generations: Women in Colonial America.* New York: Hill and Wang, 1996. Print.

———. *Revolutionary Mothers: Women in the Struggle for America's Independence.* New York: Knopf, 2005. Print.

Buel, Joy Day. *The Way of Duty: A Woman and Her Family in Revolutionary America.* New York: Norton, 1984. Print.

Ellet, E. F. *Revolutionary Women in the War for American Independence: A One-Volume Revised Edition of Elizabeth Ellet's 1848 Landmark Series.* Westport: Praeger, 1998. Print.

Gundersen, Joan R. *To Be Useful to the World: Women in Revolutionary America, 1740–1790.* New York: Twayne, 1996. Print.

Kelley, Mary. *Learning to Stand and Speak: Women, Education, and Public Life in America's Republic.* Chapel Hill: University of North Carolina Press, 2008. Print.

Vietto, Angela. *Women and Authorship in Revolutionary America.* Burlington: Ashgate, 2005. Print.

Theodore McDermott

Journal des Goncourt
Mémoires de la vie littéraire

Jules de Goncourt, Edmond de Goncourt

OVERVIEW

Journal des Goncourt: Mémoires de la vie littéraire is an immense daily diary begun by Jules and Edmond de Goncourt in 1851 and continued by Edmond for twenty-six years after his younger brother's untimely death at the age of thirty-nine in 1870. Aristocrats, art connoisseurs, novelists, and experts on eighteenth-century history, the Goncourts inhabited the elite literary and social circles of Paris. They filled the pages of their journal with their aesthetic opinions and with frank and often lurid observations on the celebrities of the day, many of them friends and acquaintances who had achieved the literary fame they so desperately sought for themselves, among them Gustave Flaubert, Honoré de Balzac, Émile Zola, Théophile Gautier, Ernest Renan, and Charles Augustin Sainte-Beuve.

An expurgated version of the *Journal* was published in nine volumes from 1887 to 1896, the year of Edmond's death. Although Edmond had removed the most scandalous anecdotes, critics and literary friends alike denounced the Goncourts for their indiscretion. The full text of the *Journal* was not made public until a twenty-two-volume collection was published between 1956 and 1959. The work has since been reassessed as an indispensable account of literary intrigues and developments in French letters during the second half of the nineteenth century. The *Journal* is also a testament to one of the most remarkable literary partnerships in history. Describing themselves in the *Journal* as "one soul placed in two bodies," the Goncourts wrote as a single entity, collaborating so closely on this and their other writings that scholars have found it impossible to distinguish their individual contributions.

HISTORICAL AND LITERARY CONTEXT

Geoff Dyer notes in his 2007 foreword to *Pages from the Goncourt Journal*, "Among many other things the *Journal* is a vast archive of anxiety and thwarted ambition." The Goncourts claimed to have developed a new type of documentary fiction with a series of novels they published in the 1860s, all psychological case studies of neurotic and debauched types meant to accurately reflect the ugliness wrought by industrialization. They complain bitterly in the *Journal* of their reputation as dilettantes.

Obsessed with objets d'art and bibelots, the Goncourts believed that the truth of history resides in seemingly insignificant details and artifacts. In his 1962 introduction to the first edition of *Pages from the Goncourt Journal,* Robert Baldick observes that the Goncourts "were inspired by a new and fruitful concept of history, using the trivia of everyday life, from dinner menus to dress patterns, to create a vivid picture of the period under examination." The Goncourts, in fact, claim in the *Journal* that their own neuroses had made them hypersensitive, attuned to minutiae undetected by the average observer. "Sickness makes a man sensitive like a photographic plate," they declare. For the purpose of capturing the nuances of their heightened perceptions, the brothers developed their own highly impressionistic and mannered prose style, the *écriture artiste* (artistic writing).

The Goncourts intended to create an accurate history of contemporary French society in the *Journal*. The diary partakes of the emerging vogue for literary realism in its precise reportage, even though the Goncourts' objectivity is sometimes compromised by their malevolent attitudes toward more successful writers. The *Journal* is both an intensely personal account of their own lives and a highly public record containing detailed sketches of the appearance, behavior, and habits of some of the most famous people in Paris. In a 2011 essay for the *Australian Journal of French Studies,* critic Sonia Wilson observes a tension in the *Journal* between its aspirations to be a private diary on the one hand and its precise, "up-to-the-minute" reporting on the other, featuring verbatim records of conversations the Goncourts took part in or overheard, many of them occurring at the salon of Princess Mathilde, the cousin of Emperor Louis-Napoleon, and at the fashionable Magny restaurant in Paris. Wilson argues that the *Journal* reflects two new trends in French journalism of the time, the *journal intime,* or confessional memoir, and the literary interview.

The *écriture artiste,* which features invented vocabulary, contorted syntax, and layered imagery, has posed challenges to translators. Thus, only selections from the *Journal* have appeared in English. Several of these partial translations came out in response to the renewed interest in the work occasioned by the publication of the full text in the 1950s. Modern criticism of the *Journal*

Key Facts

Time Period:
Mid- to Late 19th Century

Relevant Historical Events:
Industrial Revolution; the Goncourt brothers' involvement in the elite Parisian social and literary scenes

Nationality:
French

Keywords:
literature; industrialization; neuroses

A poster by French artist Adrien Marie (1848–1891) depicting Parisians at the beach in 1887. The brothers Edmond and Jules de Goncourt chronicled Parisian society over a period of many years, depicting people from various walks of life. © ALFREDO DAGLI ORTI/ THE ART ARCHIVE AT ART RESOURCE

has focused on its value as a repository of nineteenth-century literary theory and as an insiders' perspective on the exclusive social and intellectual circles of Paris.

THEMES AND STYLE

The *Journal* both exemplifies and explains the Goncourts' theories of history and literary realism. The object of the *Journal,* as an entry dated May 22, 1865, explains, is "the study of living reality … life itself with its entrails warm and active, its guts palpitating." The brothers established a habit of daily transcription so as to preserve the immediacy of their experiences. They chronicle the habits and haunts of their friends and acquaintances with titillating frankness but also reveal their own sordid comings and goings and perversions of mind, writing at length about their hypochondria, their frazzled nerves, their suspicions of women and other writers, their drinking sprees and trips to brothels, and their excursions into the slums to collect data for their novels. Edmond describes Jules's slow and painful death from syphilis in excruciating detail. Politics is rarely discussed, except for Edmond's firsthand account of the overthrow of the government of Napoleon III and the fall of Paris in 1871 to the Prussian army.

The Goncourts began the *Journal* on December 2, 1851, the day they hoped to make a name for themselves with the publication of *En 18…*, their first novel. However, the novel's appearance coincided with Louis-Napoleon's coup d'état and went completely unnoticed amid the confusion that brought martial law to the streets of Paris. From this point forward, the *Journal* records the Goncourts' mounting literary frustrations and their much professed "thirst for approbation." The brothers protest their anonymity and the critical injustices they have suffered with repeated declarations of their superior talents. Their determination to achieve literary immortality ultimately took shape in Edmond's decision to provide in his will for the establishment of a literary academy in the Goncourts' name. Since 1903 the ten-member board of the Académie Goncourt has annually recognized the year's best work of fiction with the Prix Goncourt, now France's most prestigious literary award.

Much of the reason succeeding generations have found the *Journal* so readable and entertaining is its gossipy, often sniping tone. The diary is filled with anecdotes of indecorous behavior and mocking caricature. Hippolyte Taine, for example, appears as a "pot-bellied clergyman" with a "hypocritical gaze" and a wife "who looks like a diseased silkworm." Novelist Georges Sand is a "ghostly automaton," poet Algernon Charles Swinburne a "little man with a forked chin, a hydrocephalus forehead, and a narrow chest." Typical of the Goncourts' self-promotion, Zola is described at one point as an "admirer and pupil."

CRITICAL DISCUSSION

The publication of the first volume of the expurgated *Journal* in 1887 scandalized Paris's upper-crust society. Friends of the Goncourts complained that they had been betrayed, and reviewers were shocked by the unsavory subject matter. Henry James wrote in the *Fortnightly*

Review in 1888, "The Journal of MM. de Goncourt will have rendered at least the service of fortifying the blessed cause of occasional silence." By the time the seventh volume was published in 1894, Edmond Daudet deeply regretted having encouraged Edmond de Goncourt to make the *Journal* public. An entry from April 30, 1884, that appears in the seventh volume reports that Daudet lost his virginity during a week long stay at a brothel at the age of twelve. A review of the same volume in London's *Pall Mall Gazette* observed that Edmond de Goncourt had published the *Journal* to "terrorize his intimates."

The Goncourts' reputation as minor writers persisted until the publication of the complete *Journal* in the 1950s. Critics of the first part of the twentieth century had claimed that the *écriture artiste* was a gimmick and, worse, one that lent artificiality to the Goncourts' alleged "living reality." However, subsequent scholars have cited the Goncourts' novels as a major influence on Zola, the best-known representative of naturalism. Nonetheless, the *Journal* is widely judged the Goncourts' greatest achievement.

Baldick's concluding remarks in his 1960 study *The Goncourts* are representative of current opinion:

> It seems strange to us today that apparently neither Jules nor Edmond ever realized that it was their *Journal* which would prove their best defence against the oblivion which both dreaded…. The work combines realistic observation with fragmentary presentation, purple passages with starkly simple vignettes, serenely objective entries with paragraphs of unexampled malevolence or warm sympathy; it is of equal interest to the historian, the stylist and the student of human nature.

Twenty-first-century critics have praised the *Journal* as both a sourcebook of nineteenth-century literary history and a forerunner of the gossip column, modern in its preoccupation with celebrity and self-exposure.

BIBLIOGRAPHY

Sources

Baldick, Robert. *The Goncourts*. London: Bowes & Bowes, 1960. Print.

———. Introduction. *Pages from the Goncourt Journal*. By Edmond and Jules de Goncourt. Ed. and trans. Robert Baldick. London: Oxford University Press, 1962. xvii–xxvii. Print.

Dyer, Geoff. Foreword. *Pages from the Goncourt Journal*, By Edmond and Jules de Goncourt. Ed. and trans. Robert Baldick. New York: New York Review Books, 2007. ix–xvi. Print.

Goncourt, Edmond de, and Jules de Goncourt. *Journal: Mémoires de la vie littéraire*. 22 vols. Paris: Les Éditions de Minuet, 1956–59. Print.

———. *Pages from the Goncourt Journal*, Ed. and trans. Robert Baldick. London: Oxford University Press, 1962. Print.

AN INTIMATE LITERARY PARTNERSHIP

Edmond de Goncourt maintained the *Journal des Goncourt* and continued to write novels and art criticism for many years after the death of his brother, Jules. Still, critics rarely separate their careers because of how closely the two collaborated on developing their theories of art, history, and the novel. Robert Baldick notes in his introduction to *Pages from the Goncourt Journal*, "This astonishing partnership owed its cohesion and duration … not only to the brothers' affection and regard for each other but also to their fear, suspicions, and dislike of the outside world."

Among their many mutual fears was a profound mistrust of women. Lifelong bachelors, neither brother married—though they admit in the *Journal* to enjoying the company of courtesans and prostitutes and at one time shared the same mistress. The Goncourts were convinced that the presence of women in their lives on any constant basis would destroy their writing relationship. After learning that their housekeeper, Rose Malingre, had been stealing from them for years to finance a secret life of dissipation, the brothers wrote in their diary on October 26, 1862: "Suspicion of the entire female sex has entered into our minds for the rest of our lives."

James, Henry. Rev. of the *Journal* of the Brothers de Goncourt, by Edmond and Jules de Goncourt. *Fortnightly Review* 44.262 (1888): 501–20. Rpt. in *Henry James Literary Criticism: French Writers*. New York: Library of America, 1984. 404–28. Print.

"The New Academician." *Pall Mall Gazette* 5 June 1894. *19th Century British Library Newspapers*. Web. 16 Dec. 2012.

Wilson, Sonia. "Daily Writing and the Construction of the Author as Public Figure: The *Journal des Goncourt*." *Australian Journal of French Studies* 48.3 (2011): 282–97. *HighBeam Research*. Web. 17 Dec. 2012.

Further Reading

Billy, André. *The Goncourt Brothers*. Trans. Margaret Shaw. London: A. Deutsch, 1960. Print.

———. *Paris under Siege, 1870–71: From the Goncourt Journal*. Ed. and trans. George J. Becker. Ithaca: Cornell University Press, 1969. Print.

———. *Paris and the Arts, 1851–1896: From the Goncourt Journal*. Ed. and trans. George J. Becker and Edith Philips. Ithaca: Cornell University Press, 1971. Print.

———. *Germinie Lacerteux*. Trans. Leonard Tancock. Harmondsworth: Penguin Classics, 1984. Print.

Liston, Mairi. "'Le Spectacle de la rue': Edmond de Goncourt and the Siege of Paris." *Nineteenth-Century French Studies* 32.1–2 (2003): 50+. *Literature Resources from Gale*. Web. 14. Dec. 2012.

Schier, Donald. "The Talk of the Town." *Sewanee Review* 102.2 (1994): 321–25. *JSTOR*. Web. 14 Dec. 2012.

Janet Mullane

The Last Diary of Tsaritsa Alexandra

Alexandra Feodorovna

❖ *Key Facts*

Time Period:
Early 20th Century

Relevant Historical Events:
Bolshevik Revolution; Nicholas II's abdication of the Russian throne

Nationality:
Russian

Keywords:
monarchy; revolution; communism

OVERVIEW

The Last Diary of Tsaritsa Alexandra (1995) contains the complete text of Alexandra Feodorovna's final diary, written between January and July in 1918. The diary, which was made available to scholars after Russia opened its archives following the collapse of the Soviet Union in 1991, details the daily lives of the Romanov family living in captivity following Nicholas II's abdication of the throne and the Bolshevik Revolution of 1917. The final entry, dated July 16, was written hours before the family of six and other members of the household were executed in the basement of Ipatiev House in Ekaterinburg.

Following the executions, personal papers were seized by the Bolsheviks, eventually making their way to Soviet Archives, where they remained inaccessible until the fall of the Soviet Union. After the archives were opened in January 1992, a number of important documents were published as part of Yale University's Annals of Communism series. *The Last Diary of Tsaritsa Alexandra* was published to largely positive reviews. Generally studied as part of the historical record of a seminal period in Russian history, the diary is also notable as a record of the last days of one of the more controversial figures of the period.

HISTORICAL AND LITERARY CONTEXT

Born in Darmstadt, Germany, Alexandra, who was known to possess a reserved and at times austere disposition, was generally disliked by the aristocratic Russian society that felt her judgment, and she spent much of her time in relative seclusion, writing letters and keeping diaries in lieu of socializing beyond her small family circle. In addition, the empress, who had given birth to five children in the first ten years of her marriage, suffered from a variety of physical and possibly mental ailments. She was particularly anxious about the health of her youngest and sole male child, Alexei, who was a hemophiliac during a period when little could be done to treat the condition. Dwelling in the domestic world of Alexander Palace, Alexandra, though forced to act in her husband's stead as he commanded the Russian army fighting in World War I, was insulated from the worst of Russia's economic and political crisis and unaware of the degree to which the Romanov dynasty had become imperiled.

Following the February Revolution of 1917, Nicholas abdicated the throne and was, along with his family, confined by the Provisional Government to the family home in Tsarskoye Selo. In January 1918 Alexandra began her final diary in captivity, first in Tobolsk, Siberia, and later in Ekaterinburg in the Russian Urals, where the entire Romanov family was executed under the command of Yakov Yurovsky, who was in close contact with Vladimir Lenin's new Bolshevik government at the Kremlin. *The Last Diary* details the final six months of Alexandra's life, including the month-long separation of the czar and his wife from their children when the czar was forced to leave Tobolsk for Ekaterinburg without Alexei, who was too ill to travel.

In keeping with the dictates of her class, Alexandra wrote often, both diaries and letters. The letters she exchanged with Nicholas during the Great War, also an important account of the end of the Romanov dynasty, are stylistically divergent from *The Last Diary*, containing more effusive language and freer expressions of the empress's views. For example, Alexandra offers detailed political advice to Nicholas about maintaining a firm hand in the midst of Russia's turmoil, urging him to imagine the sort of situation their son would inherit.

Yale University's Annals of Communism series, of which *The Last Diary* is a part, is a selection of works produced by pairs of Western and Russian scholars using materials from the State Archive of the Russian Federation. The series attempts to provide a robust history of the Soviet Union, beginning with the end of the czarist period. Material published in *The Last Diary*, along with excerpts from Alexandra's earlier diaries and letters, serve as building blocks for assembling the broader picture of the era presented in *The Fall of the Romanovs: Political Dreams and Personal Struggles in a Time of Revolution* (1995) and other histories of the Romanovs.

THEMES AND STYLE

The entries in Alexandra's final diary focus on the routines of the household, listing the day's activities along with notes about the weather and the health of various family members, especially Alexei. Typical entries begin with two dates, corresponding to the Julian calendar, closely associated with Alexandra's beloved Orthodox Church, and to the Gregorian calendar, which was officially adopted by the government in February 1918. The entries also note the time the empress awoke, the times and places of meals, games of cards played, and books read.

Throughout her life, Alexandra used her diaries to record her everyday activities rather than to reflect deeply on events or express her emotions. Commentators have suggested that this recitation of normalcy was particularly important during the final six months of her life, when she was faced with unfamiliar surroundings, an uncertain future, and the continued ill health of her son. She did not express the emotional impact of the family's captivity, although her love for her children is evident, for example, in the way she refers to Alexei as "Baby." The diary's final entry mentions the sudden departure of the kitchen boy but does not attach any special significance to the event beyond wondering "if we shall ever see the boy again." The entry, which was written just a few hours before the family's execution, concludes with the mundane "played bezique with N. To bed at 10:30," a jotting made poignant by Alexandra's innocence of what was to come.

The bulk of *The Last Diary* is written in list like rather than narrative form, with unadorned prose, sentence fragments, and enough erratic punctuation and capitalization to suggest that the empress did not anticipate it being read by others or, alternately, thought it might be read by the soldiers guarding the family. Although mostly written in English, Russian, and German, the diary opens with an iteration of the Cyrillic Old Church Slavonic alphabet and also contains, intermixed with the daily entries, brief coded scribblings, which contain numbers and Greek letters. While contemporary scholars have regarded these coded phrases as private notations to herself, it has also been suggested that authorities who gained possession of the diary following the family's execution may have regarded it with suspicion because of these passages, combined with rumors that Alexandra was guilty of spying for Germany, or other anti-Bolshevik intrigue.

CRITICAL DISCUSSION
While considered by some scholars to be one of the lesser works found in the Russian archives, *The Last Diary* was published to generally positive reviews. Writing in London's *Sunday Times*, Norman Stone called the book "a marvelous description of the monarchy's last hours," adding, "The scholarship involved in explaining the references (and who is who) is also of a superlative order: even the numerical allusions are sometimes explained."

Alexandra remains a contested figure in Russian history, with historians disagreeing about her role in creating animosity toward the royal family, particularly in her dealings with the mystic Grigori Rasputin. Her correspondence with Nicholas perhaps does more to humanize the empress than does her diary, but *The Last Diary* is valuable as a detailed record of the final days of the dynasty that had ruled Russia for hundreds of years. Scholars have used the insights gleaned from the collapse of czarist rule to help illuminate events that would follow in the twentieth century. In an interview with Barbara Karkabi in the *Houston Chronicle*, Jonathan Brent, editorial director of the Yale University Press, describes the utility of the Russian archives in general: "This is not just Russian history. This is trying to understand the meaning of Sputnik, what that man meant when he said, 'We will bury you,' and really what the meaning of the history in the middle of our century was all about." Indeed, the diary's attraction for scholars has most often been in its ability to add to contemporary understanding of both Russian and world history in the twentieth century.

Little critical analysis has been undertaken on *The Last Diary* as a stand-alone text. Brent's prefatory

Tsaritsa Alexandra Feodorovna, wife of Nicholas II, the last emperor of the Russian Empire. © MARY EVANS/ JOHN MASSEY STEWART RUSSIAN COLLECTION/ EVERETT

GRIGORI RASPUTIN

Grigori Rasputin, who became a close confidant of Alexandra Feodorovna due to her perception that he possessed powers that could heal her son, remains a relatively inscrutable figure in Russian history. Born in Siberia around 1869, Rasputin entered the Verkhoture Monastery as a young man but left abruptly to marry. After settling down for a time and fathering three children, he embarked on a series of travels to the Middle East and elsewhere, earning a reputation as a wanderer and something of a healer and mystic.

Upon his return to Russia, he gained entry to the court by virtue of his reputation for curing difficult medical conditions. Rasputin seems to have had some success in treating Alexei, earning the devotion of the empress. However, various Russian officials were suspicious of Rasputin and used his association with the Romanovs to discredit their rule, implying that he negatively influenced the domestic policies Alexandra initiated while Nicholas was commanding troops in World War I. Rasputin was assassinated by anti-czarists in 1916 but not before damaging the reputation of Alexandra, which was already tenuous among the Russian people.

"The 1918 Diary of Tsaritsa Alexandra" to the work provides some critical content, arguing that in Alexandra's use of both Julian and Gregorian dates in her entries, "the diary records not only the empress's own day-to-day descent into the maelstrom of the revolution and the modern world, but principally her symbolic accommodation of the new, and her resistance to the destruction of a traditional order of thought, action and belief." Brent sees symbolic significance in her last days and her death, which "proved synonymous with the death of the old calendar itself."

BIBLIOGRAPHY

Sources

Brent, Jonathan. "The 1918 Diary of Tsaritsa Alexandra." *The Last Diary of Tsaritsa Alexandra.* Ed. Vladimir A. Kozlov and Vladimir M. Khrustalëv. New Haven: Yale University Press, 1997. Print.

Feodorovna, Alexandra. *The Last Diary of Tsaritsa Alexandra.* Ed. Vladimir A. Kozlov and Vladimir M. Khrustalëv. New Haven: Yale University Press, 1997. Print.

Karkabi, Barbara. "Shedding New Light on Old World; Access to Russian Archives Sparks Project." *Houston Chronicle* 12 May 1999. *LexisNexis Academic.* Web. 20 Dec. 2012.

Stone, Norman. "Death of an Empress." Rev. of *The Last Diary of Tsaritsa Alexandra,* by Alexandra Feodorovna. *Sunday Times* 12 Oct. 1997. *Academic OneFile.* Web. 19 Dec. 2012.

Further Reading

Bunin, Ivan Alekseevich. *Cursed Days: A Diary of Revolution.* Trans. Thomas Marullo. Chicago: Ivan R. Dee, 1998. Print.

Massie, Robert. *Nicholas and Alexandra.* New York: Atheneum, 1967. Print.

———. *The Romanovs: The Final Chapter.* New York: Ballantine, 1996. Print.

Nicholas, Emperor of Russia; Alexandra, Empress Consort of Nicholas II Emperor of Russia; and Joseph T. Fuhrmann. *The Complete Wartime Correspondence of Tsar Nicholas II and the Empress Alexandra: April 1914–March 1917.* Bridgeport: Greenwood, 1999. Print.

Rappaport, Helen. *The Last Days of the Romanovs: Tragedy at Ekaterinburg.* New York: St. Martin's, 2009. Print.

Steinberg, Mark, and Vladimir M. Khrustalëv. *The Fall of the Romanovs: Political Dreams and Personal Struggles in a Time of Revolution.* New Haven: Yale University Press, 1995. Print.

Daisy Gard

Letter to Her Daughter from the New White House
Abigail Adams

OVERVIEW
Written November 21, 1800, and published by her grandson Charles Francis Adams in 1840, Abigail Adams's letter to her daughter Abigail Adams Smith captures the First Lady's earliest impressions of the new capital of the United States and the mansion designed to be the home of the president. Adams's "Letter to Her Daughter from the New White House" is part of an extensive body of correspondence that was collected by Charles and published after his grandmother's death as *Letters of Mrs. Adams, the Wife of John Adams.* Lively and personal, Adams's sharp observations bring the history of the new nation to life. The November 21 letter to her daughter in particular exhibits the First Lady's humor and adventurous spirit as she describes the dauntingly rustic nature of her new home.

Though the writing of letters was a significant form of literary expression for eighteenth-century women, Adams expressed some horror during her lifetime at the idea that her personal correspondence might be read by a wider public. Upon their publication decades after her death, however, her perceptive observations illuminated an important historical era and revealed the humanity of its political icons. Charles's collection of his grandmother's letters became so popular that three additional editions were released within ten years of the first.

HISTORICAL AND LITERARY CONTEXT
The last decades of the 1700s were pivotal years in the creation of the United States. The Revolutionary War ended in 1783 with the Treaty of Paris being signed by Britain and the United States. Massachusetts statesman John Adams had spent the war years in Europe—mainly in France and Holland—working to build support for the rebellious colonists, but he returned in 1788 to take part in the formation of the new government. He had married Abigail Smith in 1764, but his legal and political work had separated the couple for many of the intervening years, resulting in a large body of correspondence between them. In 1789 John was elected vice president, serving two terms alongside President George Washington. With Washington declining to run for a third term, John ran a successful campaign and became president in 1797.

Though the first seats of governmental power were in New York City and Philadelphia, in 1790 the U.S. Congress gave permission for President Washington to choose a site for a new national capital on the banks of the Potomac River. The states of Maryland and Virginia ceded land for the site of the new city, chosen because of its intermediate location between the contending regions of the north and south. Washington hired French architect Pierre L'Enfant to design the new capital, but Congress had little money to fund the building of a new city and progress was slow. When John and Abigail Adams arrived to take possession of the new presidential residence in the fall of 1800, the city of Washington was little more than a scattered collection of buildings along a few muddy streets.

Before and during the creation of the United States, the earliest literature to appear was largely religious, such as the works of Puritan minister Cotton Mather (*Magnalia Christi Americana,* 1702), or political, such as *The Federalist,* written from 1787 to 1788

❖ **Key Facts**

Time Period:
Early 19th Century

Relevant Historical Events:
John Adams's election to the U.S. presidency; creation of Washington, D.C.; building of the White House

Nationality:
American

Keywords:
presidency; politics; Washington, D.C.

An engraving of Abigail Adams dated 1790. She was the wife of President John Adams and mother of President John Quincy Adams. © MONTAGE/GETTY IMAGES

HISTORICAL PERSPECTIVES

PRIMARY SOURCE

EXCERPT FROM "LETTER TO HER DAUGHTER FROM THE NEW WHITE HOUSE"

Washington, 21 November 1800

My Dear Child:

I arrived here on Sunday last, and without meeting with any accident worth noticing, except losing ourselves when we left Baltimore and going eight or nine miles on the Frederick road, by which means we were obliged to go the other eight through woods, where we wandered two hours without finding a guide or the path. Fortunately, a straggling black came up with us, and we engaged him as a guide to extricate us out of our difficulty; but woods are all you can see from Baltimore until you reach *the city,* which is only so in name. Here and there is a small cot, without a glass window, interspersed amongst the forests, through which you travel miles without seeing any human being. In the city there are buildings enough, if they were compact and finished, to accommodate Congress and those attached to it; but as they are, and scattered as they are, I see no great comfort for them. The river, which runs up to Alexandria, is in full view of my window, and I see the vessels as they pass and repass. The house is upon a grand and superb scale, requiring about thirty servants to attend and keep the apartments in proper order, and perform the ordinary business of the house and stables; an establishment very well proportioned to the President's salary. The lighting of the apartments, from the kitchen to parlors and chambers, is a tax indeed; and the fires we are obliged to keep to secure us from daily agues is another very cheering comfort. To assist us in this great castle, and render less attendance necessary, bells are wholly wanting, not one single one being hung through the whole house, and promises are all you can obtain. This is so great an inconvenience that I know not what to do, or how to do. The ladies from Georgetown and in the city have many of them visited me. Yesterday I returned fifteen visits—but such a place as Georgetown appears—why, our Milton is beautiful. But no comparisons—if they will put me up some bells and let me have wood enough to keep fires, I design to be pleased. I could content myself almost anywhere three months; but surrounded with forests, can you believe that wood is not to be had

by noted statesmen James Madison, Alexander Hamilton, and John Jay to defend the proposed U.S. Constitution. As early as 1732, Benjamin Franklin began the invention of an irreverent American literary "personality" in his popular *Poor Richard's Almanac.* The candid observations found in letters and diaries such as *The Private Journal of Aaron Burr,* written between 1808 and 1812 and published in 1838, were often more easily accepted from a distance of several decades, when readers' eagerness for personal detail did not conflict with author embarrassment.

The abundant correspondence between Adams and her family and friends was received enthusiastically by mid-nineteenth-century readers and critics who were delighted with her perceptive and intimate view of the formation of the United States. Entries such as the "Letter to Her Daughter from the New White House" were especially welcome, as they provided a wealth of personal detail that helped to paint a vivid portrait of the families that helped create the new nation. The insights in Adams's "Letter to Her Daughter" have been studied in historical curriculums into the twenty-first century.

THEMES AND STYLE

"Letter to Her Daughter" reflects archetypal national themes of conquest of the frontier and cheerful persistence in the face of adversity. The letter begins with the description of the writer's journey to Washington: "... [w]e wandered two hours without finding a guide, or the path," she writes, explaining that "woods are all you see from Baltimore until you reach *the city,* which is so only in name." Though fifty-six years old and fatigued from travel and the strain of family troubles, an optimistic pioneering spirit shows through Adams's words as she makes the best of the lack of amenities: "The fires we are obliged to keep to secure us from daily agues is another very cheering comfort." Each wry criticism is countered with determined buoyancy, such as "It is a beautiful spot, capable of every improvement, and the more I view it, the more I am delighted with it."

Though Adams's letter would ultimately belong to millions of readers separated from her by miles and centuries, it was originally intended as a personal communication with a beloved daughter. Undoubtedly a bit lonely and overwhelmed by her primitive new household, Adams confides her housewifely concerns about the vast unfinished house with neither adequate firewood nor bells to summon servants, concluding with typical brightness: "But no comparisons—if they will put me up some bells and let me have wood enough to keep fires, I design to be pleased." Never content to recount only her personal affairs, Adams finds space, even in the brief letter, to comment on her prominent neighbors ("I have been called down to a because people cannot be found to cut and cart it? Briesler entered into a contract with a man to supply him with wood. A small part, a few cords only, has he been able to get. Most of that was expended to dry the walls of the house before we came in, and yesterday the man told him it was impossible for him to procure it to be cut and carted. He has had recourse to coals; but we cannot get grates made and set. We have, indeed, come into a new country.

You must keep all this to yourself, and, when asked how I like it, say that I write you the situation is beautiful, which is true. The house is made habitable, but there is not a single apartment finished, and all withinside, except the plastering, has been done since Briesler came. We have not the least fence, yard, or other convenience, without, and the great unfinished audience-room I make a drying room of, to hang up the clothes in. The principal stairs are not up, and will not be this winter. Six chambers are made comfortable; two are occupied by the President and Mr. Shaw; two lower rooms, one for a common parlor, and one for a levee room. Upstairs there is the oval room, which is designed for the drawing room, and has the crimson furniture in it. It is a very handsome room now; but, when completed, it will be beautiful. If the twelve years, in which this place has been considered as the future seat of government, had been improved, as they would have been if in New England, very many of the present inconveniences would have been removed. It is a beautiful spot, capable of every improvement, and the more I view it, the more I am delighted with it.

Since I sat down to write, I have been called down to a servant from Mount Vernon [George Washington's home], with a billet [note] from Major Custis, and a haunch of venison, and a kind, congratulatory letter from Mrs. Lewis, upon my arrival in the city, with Mrs. Washington's love, inviting me to Mount Vernon, where, health permitting, I will go before I leave this place.

Affectionately, your mother

SOURCE: Adams, Abigail. *Letters of Mrs. Adams, the Wife of John Adams. With an Introductory Memoir by her Grandson, Charles Francis Adams.* Vols. I & II. Ed. Charles Francis Adams. Boston: C. C. Little and J. Brown, 1840.

---

servant from Mount Vernon, with a billet from Major Custis, and a haunch of venison.") and political activity ("The Senate is much behind-hand. No Congress has yet been made.").

The tone of Adams's letter to her daughter is relaxed, affectionate, and conversational, beginning "My Dear Child." Though there is no personal psychological revelation, she instead conveys a real sense of her surroundings with evocative descriptions, noting that "[h]ere and there is a small cot, without a glass window, interspersed among the forests, through which you travel miles without seeing any human being." Though she vividly details her inconveniences by commenting that "the great unfinished audience-room I make a drying room of, to hang up the clothes in," she invokes the privacy of the family, writing, "You must keep all this to yourself, and, when asked how I like it, say that I write you the situation is beautiful, which is true."

CRITICAL DISCUSSION

Though few early critics singled out Adams's "Letter to Her Daughter from the New White House," her correspondence was generally hailed as an important contribution to historical literature. When Charles collected, edited, and published his grandmother's letters in 1840, a *North American Review* article described the resulting volume in words that would remain accurate for decades: "As a picture of past times, as an exhibition of an extraordinary character, as a contribution to the public history of the country, it has great attraction and value." In an 1893 *Chicago Daily Tribune* article, Lillie Devereux Blake asserted the work's literary value, saying Adams's "letters remain as a lasting proof of the noble qualities of her mind and may serve in their diction as models of composition."

As the wife of the second president of the United States and mother of the sixth, Adams was remarkably well placed to give an insider's view of the birth of a nation. Not content to remain in a separate woman's world on the sidelines, she took part in history through the route available to her—letters to her husband, to other members of her family, and to her friends. Edith Gelles, a recognized authority on Adams's life and works, points out that the letters have enduring literary value in addition to their historic importance: "Unschooled though she was, Abigail's letters are still literature; they are read today because they are stylistically, tonally, and intellectually attractive." However, it is chiefly Adams's insider knowledge of the political development of the new republic that has continued to fascinate readers and scholars. "Letter to Her Daughter" remains a significant achievement a century and a half after it was written because of the human voice in which it captures a specific moment in the history of a growing nation.

In the ensuing decades, Adams's writing has gained in stature for its contribution to historical knowledge. In his 1988 article "The Limits of a Vicarious Life," historian Richard Alan Ryerson writes of Adams that "both in her success and in her failure, she produced perhaps the finest body of letters written by any American in the eighteenth century." In a 2002 study of White House history, Gelles explores the way in which Adams "used the metaphor of travel to describe the connection she experienced between duty and affection," a device evident in the difficult trip to Washington described in "Letter to Her Daughter." History professor Woody Holton's 2009 biography of Adams won a prestigious Bancroft Prize from New York's Columbia University for its analysis of the historic writer's sharp perception of the limitations placed upon her as an eighteenth-century woman. In his introduction to the work, Holton notes the value of the Adams correspondence: "A matchless trove of personal information—primarily letters—makes it possible to trace the evolution of her personality in astonishing detail."

BIBLIOGRAPHY

Sources

Adams, Abigail. *Letters of Mrs. Adams, the Wife of John Adams. With an Introductory Memoir by her Grandson, Charles Francis Adams.* Vols. I & II. Ed. Charles Francis Adams. Boston: C. C. Little and J. Brown, 1840. Print.

Blake, Lillie Devereux "Due to Their Wives: Eminence of Some Men Not Wholly Self-Attained." *Chicago Daily Tribune* 12 Feb. 1893: 35. *ProQuest Historical Newspapers.* Web. 7 Dec. 2012.

Gelles, Edith B. "More than a Wife." Rev. of *Abigail Adams,* by Phyllis Lee Levin. *Women's Review of Books* 5.5 (1988): 18–19. *JSTOR.* Web. 6 Dec. 2012.

———. *"First Thoughts": Life and Letters of Abigail Adams.* New York: Twayne, 1998. Print.

———. "Abigail Adams as First Lady." *The White House: Actors and Observers.* Ed. William Seale. Boston: Northeastern University Press, 2002. Print.

Holton, Woody. *Abigail Adams.* New York: Free Press, 2009. Print.

Rev. of *Letters of Mrs. Adams, the Wife of John Adams. With an Introductory Memoir by Her Grandson, Charles Francis Adams.* Ed. Charles Francis Adams. *North American Review* 51.109 (1840): 362–84. *JSTOR.* Web. 5 Dec. 2012.

Ryerson, Richard Alan. "The Limits of a Vicarious Life: Abigail Adams and Her Daughter." *Proceedings of the Massachusetts Historical Society* 3.100 (1988): 1–14. *JSTOR.* Web. 7 Dec. 2012.

Further Reading

Crane, Elaine Forman. "Political Dialogue and the Spring of Abigail's Discontent." *William and Mary Quarterly* 56 (1999): 745–74. *JSTOR.* Web. 7 Dec. 2012.

Hogan, Margaret A., and C. James Taylor, eds. *My Dearest Friend: Letters of Abigail and John Adams.* Cambridge: Belknap/Harvard University Press, 2007. Print.

Levin, Phyllis Lee. *Abigail Adams: A Biography.* New York: St. Martin's, 2002. Print.

Parry-Giles, Shawn J., and Diane M. Blair. "The Rise of the Rhetorical First Lady: Politics, Gender Ideology, and Women's Voice, 1789–2002." *Rhetoric & Public Affairs* 5.4 (2002): 565–99. *Project MUSE.* Web. 5 Dec. 2012.

Seale, William. *The White House: The History of an American Idea.* Washington, D.C.: American Institute of Architects, 1992. Print.

Withey, Lynne. *Dearest Friend: A Life of Abigail Adams.* New York: Touchstone, 2002. Print.

Tina Gianoulis

LETTERS OF A WOMAN HOMESTEADER
Elinore Pruitt Stewart

OVERVIEW
Elinore Pruitt Stewart's *Letters of a Woman Homesteader* was published in 1914 and contains twenty-six letters written by Stewart to Mrs. Juliet Coney, her former employer in Denver. The letters extend from Stewart's arrival in Burnt Fork, Wyoming, in 1909 with her two-year-old daughter, Jerrine, until 1913, by which time she also had a husband (Clyde Stewart) and two sons. In this collection, Stewart relates a variety of experiences in a lively and entertaining way, beginning with her acceptance of a housekeeping job on land adjacent to her desired claim and concluding with a letter bearing the chapter title "Success," having fruitfully labored to build up an abundant and thriving ranch.

Stewart's letters reached Ellery Sedgwick, then editor of the journal *Atlantic Monthly*, by way of Coney, and in October 1913 a dozen of them were printed in the journal. In 1914 Houghton Mifflin published *Letters of a Woman Homesteader*. Sedgwick commissioned another series from Stewart, which was also published by Houghton Mifflin—*Letters on an Elk Hunt*. According to Susanne K. George, author of *The Adventures of the Woman Homesteader* (1992), Stewart "spoke to the hearts of early-twentieth century Americans," advocating "the myths of the West as a Garden of Eden and of homesteading as a means to achieve the American Dream." Stewart was an important historical figure, both for what she symbolized and what she achieved.

HISTORICAL AND LITERARY CONTEXT
Ranching and homesteading in Sweetwater County, Wyoming (where Stewart lived), continued to develop through 1920. The area at the time of Stewart's letters was very much divided, both ethnically and in terms of urban and rural areas. According to John Mack Faragher in his 1998 review of Dee Garceau's *The Important Things of Life* in the *Journal of Family History*, ranching was "a very isolated way of life," and women "worked in the old ways, cooking over wood stoves, washing clothes with washboard and tub, hauling wood." Stewart's difficult childhood in Chickasaw Indian Territory, throughout which she experienced considerable poverty and, beginning at age eighteen, was responsible for seven siblings, prepared her for a life of tough labor. Single women like Stewart accounted for 5 to 15 percent of Western homesteaders prior to 1900, and nearly 20 percent in the early twentieth century. As Faragher also indicates, "homesteading was not something easily accomplished by lone individuals—whether men or women—but required the cooperative work of the whole family."

After a failed first marriage, Stewart moved to Denver in 1906 and worked her way up to a twenty-cent-an-hour laundry job while supporting her daughter and two sisters. In 1909 she responded to an ad seeking a housekeeper for a Wyoming rancher, which offered less pay but a powerful incentive, since she might also file a claim on the adjoining quarter section of land. She journeyed with her daughter via train and stagecoach and began writing to Coney, her former Denver employer, shortly upon arrival in Burnt Fork on April 18, 1909. Stewart had several correspondents during her homesteading days, but her letters to Coney have received the greatest acclaim. Although Stewart published two collections of letters and seven stories, according to George she was disappointed that her later writing did not reach a wider audience. Many of her works remained unpublished before her death in 1933.

Stewart was not the only woman homesteader during that period to record the experience for posterity. Ida Mary and Edith Ammonds filed on South Dakota land in 1907; their story (*Land of the Burnt Thigh*) was written by the latter and published in 1938. Cecilia Hennel Hendricks moved to northwestern Wyoming with her husband to purchase land and start a bee farm. She followed a spirit of adventure rather than necessity, and her letters from 1914 through 1931 were released in 1986.

Not only was *Letters of a Woman Homesteader* significant at the time of its release, but a reissue of the work by Houghton Mifflin in 1982 cemented the book's role in academia, particularly women's studies. According to scholar Melody Graulich, "the book became one of the classic feminist texts, frequently used in women's literature and history courses." Even prior to this, in 1979, the movie *Heartland* was released, based roughly on Stewart's first experiences in Wyoming (although it is interesting to note that the movie was actually filmed in Montana). Still, perhaps the most significant contribution to Stewart's letters was made by George, whose 1992 book, according to

❖ **Key Facts**

Time Period:
Early 20th Century

Relevant Historical Events:
Expansion to the American West; homesteading movement

Nationality:
American

Keywords:
women's writing; ranching; homesteading

Old farm in the Wyoming countryside, near Randolf, July 2006. Elinore Pruitt Stewart wrote *Letters of a Woman Homesteader* at her isolated ranch in Wyoming. © DAVID PERKINS/ALAMY

Graulich, "opened up the ambiguities and complexities of Stewart's life," in which contradictions between Stewart's stories and "the truth" can be observed.

THEMES AND STYLE

Letters of a Woman Homesteader focuses on the events and people that surrounded Stewart, arguing for the joys of homesteading. She refers to a colorful cast, whose way of talking she presents idiomatically in quotations, including her Scottish employer (whom she married after just eight weeks in Wyoming) and her friends Mrs. Lauderer, an old German rancher, and Mrs. O'Shaughnessy, with whom she traveled and threw marvelous, spontaneous events. Further, as she attests in her letters to Coney, "any woman who can stand her own company, can see the beauty of a sunset, loves growing things, and is willing to put in as much time at careful labor as she does over the wash tub will certainly succeed."

Different motivations have been suggested for Stewart's letter writing. Her pursuit of writing work in Colorado and the character-driven, storytelling nature of her letters seem to indicate she hoped for a wider readership than just Coney. According to Judith Long, who reviewed the 1982 reissue for the *Nation,* Stewart wrote "to amuse herself and to interest the folks back in the city." Further, according to a letter—published in George's book—that Stewart penned to Coney's daughter, "It was a pleasure to share adventures with [Mrs. Coney].... I used to try to shock her mildly and at the same time give her as nearly as I could a true picture of the West."

Stewart's letters are notable for their richly detailed descriptions of people, events, and places. She writes with equal enthusiasm about grand natural surroundings—"the silvery gold of the willows, the russet and bronze of the currants, and patches of cheerful green"—and simple meals, claiming, "you must be away out in Wyoming" with pork and beans "heated in a disreputable old frying-pan, served with coffee boiled in a battered old pan and drunk from a tomato-can," to discover the best breakfast possible. Stewart, though clearly passionate about homesteading, does also express certain humility, as she writes, "If you only knew how short I fall of my own hopes you would know I could *never* boast." As Graulich asserts, the "real appeal" of Stewart's writings "lies in her spunky, strong voice and in her story telling skills."

CRITICAL DISCUSSION

The appearance of Stewart's letters in *Atlantic Monthly* is indicative of the literary esteem they received, and the positive initial reaction to them is widely apparent elsewhere. A 1914 review in the *Dial* calls *Letters of a Woman Homesteader* "a hearty and wholesome book" that gives "promise of attaining no inconsiderable fame in the literary world." In 1915 the *Mississippi Valley Historical Review* published a review by William V. Pooley that called *Letters* "decidedly worthwhile," attesting "there is not a dull page in the book." The University of Nebraska Press reissued the book in 1961, and a review from that year in *Western Folklore* by Gordon W. Davidson backhandedly compliments it (considering Stewart's purported lack of education) for having been "written with a style, humor and acute observation that might easily be considered professional."

Although twentieth-century scholars have questioned, as Davidson did, the amount of editing Stewart's *Letters* received, as well as the authenticity of their content, the work is still regarded for its considerable significance, especially for women's writing. According to Faragher, *Letters of a Woman Homesteader* "sparked the emergence of an important minigenre of similar stories appearing in national publications" from 1910 through 1920 that were "paeans to an ethic of female individualism." In *Grit and Grace,* George argues further that Stewart was a significant example of American attitudes historically, such that "nearly one hundred years later, audiences are still drawn to the Woman Homesteader's ... alluring belief that health, happiness and the American Dream can still be realized."

Criticism of *Letters of a Woman Homesteader* since the 1970s has focused on the complications of the stories Stewart tells. How much of what she wrote was truthful? George asserts that "Stewart was never above rearranging facts to her advantage" and that some "tales appear to be based on true experiences that were creatively embellished or 'embroidered' to make a better story." George further claims that Stewart's "search for her own identity, her persona became her ... means of self-identification." With a bit less compassion, according to Faragher, Garceau attested that "we should read the woman homesteader literature ... much as we should read the stories of heroic cowboys: not as depictions of reality, but as metaphors for the life of freedom that many a woman hoped for but few actually achieved."

BIBLIOGRAPHY

Sources

Davidson, Gordon W. Rev. of *Letters of a Woman Homesteader*, by Elinore Pruitt Stewart. *Western Folklore* 22.1 (1963): 62–63. *JSTOR*. Web. 12 Dec. 2012.

Faragher, John Mack. Rev. of *The Important Things of Life: Women, Work, and Family in Sweetwater County, Wyoming, 1880–1929*, by Dee Garceau. *Journal of Family History* 23 (1998): 327–28. *Sage Journals*. Web. 20 Dec. 2012.

Faragher, John Mack, and Robert V. Hine. *Frontiers: A Short History of the American West*. New Haven: Yale University Press, 2007. Print.

George, Susanne K. *The Adventures of the Woman Homesteader: The Life and Letters of Elinore Pruitt Stewart*. Lincoln: University of Nebraska Press, 1992. Print.

———. "Elinore Pruitt Stewart: The Adventurous Woman Homesteader." *By Grit & Grace: Eleven Women Who Shaped the American West*. Ed. Glenda Riley and Richard W. Etulain. Golden: Fulcrum, 1997. Print.

Graulich, Melody. Rev. of *The Adventures of The Woman Homesteader: The Life and Letters of Elinore Pruitt Stewart*, by Susanne K. George. *Legacy* 11.2 (1994): 174–75. *JSTOR*. Web. 22 Dec. 2012.

"The Joys of Homesteading." *Dial; a Semi-monthly Journal of Literary Criticism, Discussion, and Information (1880–1929)* 1 July 1914: 21+. *American Periodicals*. Web. 27 Dec. 2012.

Pooley, William V. Rev. of *Letters of a Woman Homesteader*, by Elinore Pruitt Stewart. *Mississippi Valley Historical Review* 2.3 (1915): 451–52. *JSTOR*. Web. 20 Dec. 2012.

Stewart, Elinore Pruitt. *Letters of a Woman Homesteader*. Boston: Houghton Mifflin, 1914. Print.

Further Reading

Bakken, Gordon Morris, and Brenda Farrington. *The American West: Interactions, Intersections, and Injunctions (The Gendered West)*. New York: Garland, 2001. Print.

LIFE BEFORE HOMESTEADING

Elinore Pruitt Stewart was born on June 3, 1876, on territory belonging to the Chickasaw Nation in the town of White Bread Hill, Oklahoma. She lost her father early and, after her mother got remarried (to the brother of Stewart's father), was raised in extreme poverty with seven half-brothers and half-sisters and no shoes until the age of six. She taught herself to read and write, and her only opportunity to attend school ended abruptly when her teacher was dragged from the classroom and hanged for horse thievery. According to Susanne K. George in her essay in *By Grit & Grace* (1997), Stewart witnessed so much violence in her early life that she did not realize until the age of ten that someone could die without being shot. Stewart's mother passed away in 1893, and her stepfather died later that year.

In 1906 Stewart married Harry Cramer Rupert, a man twenty-two years her senior. Although she claimed to have been widowed, it has become clear she left Rupert after the birth of daughter Jerrine, and she risked losing custody if they were divorced. She moved to Colorado with two of her sisters and her daughter, with, as George has observed, "no job, no friends, no money and a family to feed and clothe." When her sisters left to seek better opportunities in California, Stewart was well prepared to attempt homesteading, thanks to a life of toiling at survival.

Bartley, Paula, and Cathy Loxton. *Plains Women: Women in the American West*. Cambridge: Cambridge University Press, 1991. Print.

Butruille, Susan G. *Women's Voices from the Western Frontier*. Boise: Tamarack, 1995. Print.

Long, Judith. "Book Notes." *Nation* 244.11 (1987): 371. *Points of View Reference Center*. Web. 23 Dec. 2012.

Merrill, Karen. Rev. of *The Adventures of the Woman Homesteader: The Life and Letters of Elinore Pruitt Stewart*, by Susanne K. George. *Montana: The Magazine of Western History* 44.1 (1994): 80–81. *JSTOR*. Web. 22 Dec. 2012.

Rachel Mindell

The Letters of the Younger Pliny

Pliny the Younger

✤ Key Facts

Time Period:
Early 2nd Century

Relevant Historical Events:
Persecution of early Christians; eruption of Mount Vesuvius

Nationality:
Roman

Keywords:
politics; society; religion

OVERVIEW

The Letters of the Younger Pliny (106–13 CE) by Pliny the Younger address more than one hundred people and deal with a wide variety of topics that reflect the social and political concerns of the Roman aristocracy at the turn of the first century CE. The first nine books hold 247 letters, while a tenth volume contains 121 official letters to and from the Roman emperor Trajan. Although the correspondence mainly covers the time span between 96 and 111 CE, Pliny recalls historic events such as the eruption of Mount Vesuvius that destroyed Pompeii in 79 CE. Many critics regard *The Letters* as one of the best sources of historical information on ancient Rome as well as a rare glimpse into a Roman's public and private life; thus, the work has been labeled an epistolary self-portrait.

Pliny wrote these as private letters, later revising and polishing the first nine books for publication (the tenth book was published posthumously). The initial reaction to *The Letters* is relatively unknown, though Pliny expresses satisfaction when he learns from a friend that his book was seen for sale in a bookshop in the remote city of Lugdunum (Lyon). *The Letters* received greater attention in the fourth century with the revival of the Silver Age Latin writers, and early Christians such as Tertullian, Jerome, and Eusebius were familiar with the work. More recently, *The Letters* has attracted a wide variety of scholarship that examines individual letters rather than the entire corpus: for example, many have focused on topics such as the persecution of the early Christians, the eruption of Mount Vesuvius, and Pliny's Laurentine villa.

HISTORICAL AND LITERARY CONTEXT

Pliny's letters are in keeping with the evolution of early letter writing. In *History Begins at Sumer* (1988), author Samuel Kramer theorizes that the Sumerians in Mesopotamia were the first letter writers, composing in cuneiform on clay tablets that bore official commands from the ruler. Greek letter writing differed greatly from the Sumerian tradition; most surviving Greek letters are long addresses by rhetoricians meant for publication. One example is Isocrates's *To Nicocles* (c. 372 BCE), in which the Greek orator addresses the prince and lays out his educational system. The famous *Seventh Letter* (c. 353 BCE) of Plato—an epistle that explicates the philosopher's time spent in Syracuse—was intended for public perusal. Demetrius composed a treatise on letter writing, *De Interpretatione,* in the third century BCE, in which he expounds that a letter should not be merely a technical treatise with an attached greeting and farewell.

Pliny the Younger used reed pens and papyrus in order to write letters concerning both public and private matters. In *The Letters,* he corresponds with several notable Romans, including historians Cornelius Tacitus and Suetonius Tranquillus, his uncle Pliny the Elder, and Emperor Trajan. In his monumental work *History of Rome* (1965), Max Cary observes that Pliny's era, though it followed a period of brutal conflict during the reign of Domitian, was one of "widespread goodwill" and "freedom from strain." Cary continues: "At a time when Rome was most powerful, its sense of pietas was also strongest." Pliny, for example, endowed a secondary school and founded a library in his native town of Comum. He had sufficient leisure time to compose letters from his luxurious summer villas, at times lamenting the loss of a grape harvest and the overflowing of the Tibur River.

Although letter writing varied in both style and intent from one writer to the next, epistolography was considered a distinct literary form. The Romans Cicero and Seneca published letters that subsequently had a tremendous influence over Pliny. Cicero's letters are relaxed in tone and written in colloquial language, lacking the literary concerns of his orations. These are private letters composed for family members, including his brother Quintus. In letter 9.2, Pliny himself writes with humble deference to Cicero's superior letter writing skills: "He was not only richly gifted, but was supplied with a wealth of varied and important topics to suit his abilities…. I might decide to send you a sort of pupil's exercise for a letter." Seneca's letters, like Pliny's, relate daily events, anecdotes, and advice.

Early Christian apologists and church fathers were influenced by and indebted to Pliny's *Letters*. Tertullian paraphrases letters 10.96 and 10.97 in his *Apologeticum,* and Jerome and Eusebius frequently quote them. Saints Cyprian, Ambrose, and Augustine—to name a few—composed letters to educate and admonish the spread-out Christian communities, thus establishing orthodoxy. Pliny's epistles were especially popular during the fourth-century pagan revival; for example, Symmachus—a Roman statesman—imitated Pliny by publishing ten books of correspondence, nine of which were personal and one of which was professional. More recently, scholars have produced up-to-date commentaries, translations, and critical works on *The Letters.*

THEMES AND STYLE

The only surviving ancient Roman document in which the author describes his daily routine, Pliny's letters cover a variety of themes and offer a rich historical perspective. *The Letters* reflect the way in which a senator thought and lived at the turn of the first century, with his concerns over, for example, a journey to an estate by carriage, the manumission of slaves, and leisurely pastimes such as hunting and fishing. In letter 2.8, Pliny addresses Caninius Rufus, "Are you reading, fishing or hunting or doing all three? You can do all together on the shores of Como.... I hanker after them as a sick man does for wine, baths, and cool springs ... but I see my work stretching out farther and farther every day." The most famous letter (6.20) describes the eruption of Mount Vesuvius: "I looked round: a dense black cloud was coming up behind us, spreading over the earth like a flood.... You could hear the shrieks of women, the wailing of infants, and the shouting of men."

Pliny's epistles offered an efficient way for a busy official to communicate with family, friends, and other public officials. Because of the personal and informal nature of Roman imperial administration (senators relied on friends and clients to carry out their duties), the letters also often served political purposes, including maintaining contacts and currying favor. In the opening letter (1.1), Pliny addresses Roman prefect Septicus Clarus: "You have often urged me to collect and publish any letters of mine which were composed with some care. I have now made a collection, not keeping to the original order as I was not writing a history, but taking them as they came to my hand." Because of the nonchronological order and the multifarious topics, many critics deny the autobiographical intention of the author, but the wealth of autobiographical information contained in *The Letters* is undeniable. In *Reading the Letters of Pliny the Younger* (2012), Roy Gibson and Ruth Morello suggest, for example, that letter 2.17—which describes in detail Pliny's Laurentine villa—serves as a "revelation of character" and that Pliny intended it as such.

Pliny composes his epistles in a natural style that brims with confidence; for example, "My love of liberal giving, long and deeply reasoned, has freed me from these besetting bonds of avarice." Although he was influenced by the writing of Cicero, he does not employ Cicero's stylistic trademark, the periodic sentence—a long and involved sentence in which the main clause is withheld until the end for emphasis. In *Fifty Letters of Pliny* (1967), A. N. Sherwin-White describes Pliny's sentence construction as "plain and logical.... The main sentence has the non-periodic word order with the verb and predicate thrust prominently forward." Each letter is confined to one theme, and Pliny often follows the rhetorical rules of his teacher Quintilian; for example, Pliny supports anecdotal letters with three examples. As a collected whole, *The Letters* has been described by some as mosaic or kaleidoscopic because of the nonchronological order and the vast number of short letters dealing with a variety of topics.

Renaissance statue of Pliny the Younger on the facade of the Cathedral of Saint Maria Maggiore in Como, northern Italy. © DEA PICTURE LIBRARY/ART RESOURCE, NY

CRITICAL DISCUSSION

The initial reaction to *The Letters,* like many ancient works, is relatively unknown, though the work appears to have enjoyed some success. At the turn of the first century, there was an increase in schools, libraries, and overall literacy, and the book trade was thriving. Cary explains that "books were obtainable at such moderate prices, that even poor men could keep a few favorite texts, and private libraries were to be found

HISTORICAL PERSPECTIVES

PLINY'S KINDNESS TO HIS SLAVES

In ancient Greece and Rome, slavery was considered part of the natural world; the morality of the institution was unquestioned. According to Aristotle, some people were inferior to others, slaves by their very nature. In some instances, freed slaves themselves became slave owners and traders. Epictetus was a slave turned Stoic philosopher, teaching students how to accept one's lot in life. Ancient slavery was peculiar in that virtually anyone at any time might be enslaved through warfare. Some slaves were highly skilled physicians and tutors or played important roles in imperial households, while others were worked to death on huge Sicilian estates.

In the ancient world, the moral question did not revolve around the slave trade's existence but rather the treatment of slaves. Both Seneca and Pliny were well known for their kindness to slaves. In *Reading the Letters of Pliny the Younger,* Roy Gibson and Ruth Morello briefly observe: "Egalitarian behavior is important to Pliny; the famous letters about his kindness to his slaves are just a little further along the same spectrum." In letter 3.14, Pliny condemns Larcius Macedo—a senator murdered by his slaves—as "a cruel and overbearing master, too ready to forget that his father had been a slave." In letter 8.16, he writes to his uncle Pliny the Elder, "I have been much distressed by illness amongst my servants…. I am always ready to grant my slaves their freedom." And in letter 5.19, Pliny confesses his deep "affection" for his freedman Zosimus and his willingness to provide funds to help restore his health.

even in provincial country villas." In letter 9.11, Pliny expresses his confident delight to Rosianus Geminus: "I didn't think there were any booksellers in Lugdunum, so I was all the more pleased to learn from your letter that my efforts are being sold. I'm glad they retain abroad the popularity they won in Rome, and I'm beginning to think my work must really be quite good when public opinion in such widely different places is agreed about it."

Pliny's epistles have provided a unique perspective of ancient Rome for nearly two millennia. However, in comparison with other classical works, *The Letters* has been relatively neglected. In *The Art of Pliny's Letters* (2008), Ilaria Marchesi explains: "Pliny's epistles have long suffered from a double critical misfortune. Their author was the practitioner of prose-epistolography, an understudied, because allegedly sub-literary, genre; and he was active during a traditionally devalued period, the disparagingly labeled Silver Age." Scholarly interest in Pliny's work has greatly increased since the 1960s, and the international conference "Re-imagining Pliny the Younger" in 2000 at the University of Manchester helped to produce vital critical works, particularly literary-historical monographs such as John Henderson's *Pliny's Statue* (2002).

Diverse scholarship reflects Pliny's wide-ranging topics. Gibson and Morello demonstrate how *The Letters* has attracted "prosopographers, social historians, political historians, legal historians, economic historians, architects, garden designers, archaeologists, and—of course—literary critics of all hues." The epistles, in particular, have shed light on social and political concerns at the turn of the first century. In *Roman Letters: History from a Personal Point of View* (1991), Finley Hooper and Matthew Schwartz discuss the implications of Pliny's charitable works and how there was a "shift in the official policy of the government towards the poor…. The government began to offer help for the destitute…. Pliny's own contribution, described in a letter to his friend Caninius Rufus, is evidence of the new interest in caring for less fortunate persons in the population."

BIBLIOGRAPHY

Sources

Cary, Max. *History of Rome.* New York: Macmillan, 1965. Print.

Gibson, Roy, and Ruth Morello. *Reading the Letters of Pliny the Younger: An Introduction.* Cambridge: Cambridge University Press, 2012. Print.

Hooper, Finley, and Matthew Schwartz. *Roman Letters: History from a Personal Point of View.* Detroit: Wayne State University Press, 1991. Print.

Marchesi, Ilaria. *The Art of Pliny's Letters.* Cambridge: Cambridge University Press, 2008. Print.

Pliny the Younger. *The Letters of the Younger Pliny.* Ed. and trans. Betty Radice. Baltimore: Penguin, 1963. Print.

Sherwin-White, A. N. *Fifty Letters of Pliny.* Oxford: Oxford University Press, 1967. Print.

Further Reading

Grieg, Clarence. *Pliny: A Selection of His Letters.* Cambridge: Cambridge University Press, 1978. Print.

Henderson, John. *Pliny's Statue: The Letters, Self-Portraiture & Classical Art.* Exeter: University of Exeter Press, 2002. Print.

Hoffer, Stanley. *The Anxieties of Pliny the Younger.* Atlanta: Scholars, 1999. Print.

Kramer, Samuel. *History Begins at Sumer.* Philadelphia: University of Pennsylvania Press, 1988. Print.

Morello, Ruth, and A. D. Morrison. *Ancient Letters.* Oxford: Oxford University Press, 2007. Print.

Sherwin-White, A. N. *The Letters of Pliny: A Historical and Social Commentary.* Oxford: Clarendon, 1985. Print.

Gregory Bach

The Literary Remains of Edward VI

Edward VI

OVERVIEW

The Literary Remains of Edward VI, including his letters, orations, journal, biblical extracts, and religious compositions, paint a valuable picture of the education of a boy-king during the 1540s and 1550s. Coming to the throne at the age of ten, Edward VI received exhaustive training in languages (including Latin, Greek, and French), and his literary production makes use of all of these skills. It also shows off his understanding of classical rhetoric, philosophy, and governmental theory, as well as his abiding interest in the Protestant religious cause. While each element of Edward's work survives as an individual manuscript (many of which are still housed in the British Library), the pieces were first collected together in the compiler John Gough Nichols's printed edition of 1857. Taken together, these manuscripts and school exercises illustrate the training and thoughts of a young Renaissance king in rich detail.

While Edward's life and works remain less studied than those of his stepsister, Elizabeth I, they offer a vibrant portrait of a religious young man and his development as a (future) monarch. Nichols points out that many of the pieces were printed by Horace Walpole (an eighteenth-century historian and politician) and that his own edition was printed for the Roxburghe Club of literary historians. The content of Edward's work has primarily interested scholars of the Reformation movement, who seek to understand England's transition from being a mostly Catholic country to crafting its own Anglican identity. Under the reign of Edward VI (and his two Lords Protector, both Protestant noblemen), England made decisive breaks with Catholic ritual and tradition, detaching itself further from the influence of the pope. Reflecting the ideas and educational methods that propelled this shift, Edward's papers help historians to examine the rhetoric and convictions of early Protestant governmental officials in England.

HISTORICAL AND LITERARY CONTEXT

As a prince growing up in sixteenth-century England, Edward VI was educated in the humanist tradition, with an emphasis on learning ancient ideas and applying them to current events. His curriculum, designed and supervised by John Cheke, involved sending letters in Latin to his relatives, composing speeches in Latin and Greek, and keeping track of important quotations in multiple languages—all school exercises that are preserved and published in *The Literary Remains*. On a practical level, this curriculum had two important outcomes. First, it prepared Edward to make impromptu speeches in Latin, the international language of diplomacy. Second, it taught the young prince about classical concepts of virtue, which he was to imitate in his personal conduct. According to John Foxe in *The Actes and Monuments* (1583), a massive volume of tales of Protestant martyrdom and heroism, Edward was overwhelmingly successful as a student, with a sharp memory and strong convictions.

As Henry VIII's only son, Edward VI grew up as a king in training, debating serious moral propositions such as "many people are bad people of their own free will." These debates, preserved in section two of *The Literary Remains,* were shaping the king into a particular type of ruler, focused, as Foxe records, on both compassion and justice. Edward was also surrounded by people with strong Protestant convictions. His stepmother, Queen Katherine Parr, was a devoted Protestant, as was his uncle the Duke of Somerset, who would later become Edward's first Lord Protector. Edward's journals were written while Somerset was jostling with his brother Thomas and other nobles for the power to control the throne during the king's youth. The journals reflect the period's focus on courtly events at home, as well as (ostensibly religious) wars abroad.

Edward's work always exists within a courtly and family context of Protestant humanist learning. For example, Queen Katherine Parr's *Lamentation of a Sinner,* influenced by the work of radical-leaning Protestant reformers such as Thomas Cranmer, Hugh Latimer, and William Tyndale, affirms and transmits the doctrine of faith-based salvation. Latimer himself became a court preacher during Edward's reign, writing vivid prose sermons that were subsequently published by John Day. Later in the century, after Edward's death, Day published *The Acts and Monuments;* Edward VI is described in Book Nine of this volume as a new Josias, beloved by his people and determined to rid them of the vestiges of idolatrous practice. Framed in this way, Edward becomes a royal enabler of Protestant literary tracts and sermons: his reign encouraged and cultivated a climate where writers such as Foxe and Latimer could thrive.

✥ Key Facts

Time Period:
Mid-16th Century

Relevant Historical Events:
Ascendance of Edward VI; Edward VI's classical education

Nationality:
English

Keywords:
education; royalty; classicism

King Edward VI of England, painted by Guillaume Scrots. © PHILIP MOULD LTD, LONDON/THE BRIDGEMAN ART LIBRARY

One of the most significant literary developments under Edward's reign was the development of the *Book of Common Prayer* (1549), put together by Cranmer. Setting out basic liturgical guidelines for the church service, including its prayers and its calendar, the book organized and standardized weekly rituals for the whole Church of England and remains in effect today. By creating an atmosphere that encouraged a reinvestigation of ritual practices, Edward's reign and writings set the tone for such works, leading Edward to be celebrated as a forward-thinking, pious figure by Protestants during subsequent eras of religious tension. For example, in 1682 he was called the "Captain of our Reformation" by the anonymous publisher of one of his antipapal tracts.

THEMES AND STYLE

Since *The Literary Remains* are partially a record of Edward's school exercises and partially a record of his personal experiences at court, they contain a range of themes and styles. While Edward is still young, his letters to figures such as the Duke of Somerset consist of simple Latin sentences, including greetings, acknowledgments of favors, and simple requests. As the prince grows, his prose structure and organization become more complicated, eventually falling into the scholarly Latin structure recommended by the humanist Desiderius Erasmus. Thematically, this evolving style is accompanied by a maturing zeal for church affairs, as Edward begins to make princely requests about matters of religion. Writing to his stepmother, for example, he asks that his stepsister Mary cease to pursue "foreign dances and merriments which do not become a most Christian princess." As he grows, this theme of serious Protestant commitment begins to become more and more apparent.

As Dale Hoak points out in his profile of Edward in *Oxford Dictionary of National Biography*, the "tone" of Edward's school exercises and journal entries "reveals nothing conclusive about [his] inner life"—but the materials themselves constitute an extremely rich source of information about religious education and the English court. When the twelve-year-old Edward was assigned to write an exercise in French called "Treatise against the Supremacy of the Pope," for example, the resulting document shows Edward's Protestant connections: he dedicated it to the Duke of Somerset, wrote it at the request of his Protestant French master Belmaine, and used traditional antipapist rhetoric, popular since Martin Luther's day (for example, calling the pope "our Antichrist"). By illustrating these connections, Edward's document outlines the transmission of Protestant ideas between subsequent generations. It also shows how the educational techniques of the Renaissance could re-entrench partisan feelings about religious truths.

Because Edward was writing as both a well-educated monarch and a minor, under the legal control of his Lord Protector, his literary productions are both circumspect and erudite. Whether he writes to his stepmother, half-sisters, or uncle, the language is carefully poised to reflect the complex power dynamics in the family, including his own pending kingship and current youthfulness. The result is a curious blend of gratitude (thanking Parr for her "loving kindness to me and my sister") and uneasy command (asking Mary to intervene with a delicate marriage situation, which Mary decorously refused to do). When Edward writes his own journal notes about current events, his prose is often "derivative," according to Hoak, simply reflecting the opinion of a courtier or a report about an issue. Still, Edward's journal and school exercises remain unique examples of a monarch's youthful training and perspectives, and they show his intellectual capacity to absorb information, as well as his fledgling attempts to negotiate the courtly hierarchy.

CRITICAL DISCUSSION

When Edward died at the age of sixteen, Protestants initially reacted by framing him as a devout hero figure, whose every deed and virtue had helped England to transcend its Catholic past. As Foxe reports, the academic Hieronymus Cardanus memorialized him as a rising star in the fields of language, science, and logic, saying, "Briefly, it might seem a miracle of nature, to behold the excellent wit and forwardness that appeared in him, being yet but a child." Bearing witness to his piety, Protestant scholars also printed copies of his deathbed prayer in 1553, which asks God to "defende this Realme from papistrye, and mayntayne thy true religion." At the same time, this printed sheet concludes with the ominous statement "God save the Quene"—reminding readers that Edward's Catholic half-sister Mary was now on the throne, threatening the Protestant cause. In 1560, after Mary's death and the accession of Protestant Elizabeth I, William Baldwin's *The Funerals of King Edward the Sixth* exhorted the English to repent from their sins, to prolong and preserve the lives of future Protestant monarchs.

During the next few centuries, Edward's work became a touchstone for political, religious, and historical commentators. In the mid-1600s, for example, the Anglican clergyman Peter Heylin condemned Edward's character, arguing that he was a weak king who could not control the overzealous courtiers surrounding him. This assessment was based on John Hayward's (inaccurate) representation of his reign and was linked to Hayward's attack on Henry VIII and his actions against Rome. In response, an anonymous supporter rallied to Edward's cause, decrying the "snarling censure" that Heylin produced and commending the king's devotion to Protestant religious ideals. In the nineteenth century, this exchange was recorded by Nichols, along with several other historical perspectives on Edward's reign. Nichols's exhaustive edition of Edward's works was produced for the Roxburghe Club, a group of forty book lovers who swap and print important volumes.

More recent critics, meanwhile, have also used the texts to ask how much control Edward really had over the events in his reign. Hoak argues that Edward was an apt student, absorbing everything presented to him at court but not yet personally controlling the government at the time of his death. At the same time, as both Hoak and Suzanne Westfall point out, Edward was clearly involved in the procedures of cultural self-promotion that characterized a Renaissance monarch. He participated in processions and dramatic performances called masques, and his portraits show his interest in appearing visually similar to his powerful father. While his papers never show a precise picture of his character or leadership status, Edward VI remains a compelling historical figure, whose intelligence and Protestant beliefs made his beliefs a rallying point for his supporters.

BIBLIOGRAPHY

Sources

Baldwin, William. *The Funerals of King Edward the Sixth*. London, 1560. *EEBO*. Web. 18 Dec. 2012.

SISTERS AND "SISTERS"

As a child, Edward VI shared humanist tutors such as Roger Ascham with his half-sister, Princess Elizabeth (who would become Queen Elizabeth I). He also knew and exchanged letters with his older half-sister, Princess Mary (who would become Queen Mary I). Living under the care and protection of Katherine Parr, though sometimes in separate households, Edward and Elizabeth came to embrace Protestant beliefs and policies—but Mary, the daughter of a Catholic queen with ancestral ties to Spain, remained firmly Catholic herself. Of Henry VIII's children, then, Edward (the first to reign) pulled the country into a radical Protestant position; Mary (the second), took England dramatically back toward Catholicism, executing radical Protestants and becoming known as "Bloody Mary." It was only with the accession of Elizabeth I that a relative compromise was reached, with the Church of England embracing a more moderate brand of Protestant practice.

However, anticipating trouble with his extreme Protestant reforms, Edward VI made a last-ditch effort to affect the order of succession before he died. Although he could not legally make a will, being too young, he demanded a document that would prefer Lady Jane Grey (a fellow Protestant, and Edward's spiritual "sister") above Princess Mary for the succession. While Queen Jane did rule very briefly, Mary was able to raise an army of supporters and defeat her claim—temporarily bringing Catholicism back to England, against Edward's wishes.

Edward VI. "The Prayer of Kynge Edwarde the Syxte." London: Richard Jugge, 1553. *EEBO*. Web. 8 Dec. 2012.

———. *Literary Remains of King Edward the Sixth: Edited from His Autograph Manuscripts, with Historical Notes, and a Biographical Memoir*. 2 vols. Ed. John Gough Nichols. London: Roxburghe Club, 1857. Print.

Foxe, John. *The Actes and Monuments*. London: John Day, 1583. *EEBO*. Web. 8 Dec. 2012.

Hoak, Dale. "Edward VI (1537–1553)." *Oxford Dictionary of National Biography*. Oxford: Oxford University Press, 2004. Web. 6 Dec. 2012.

King, John N. "Religious Writing." *The Cambridge Companion to English Literature, 1500–1600*. Ed. Arthur F. Kinney. Cambridge: Cambridge University Press, 1999. *Cambridge Collections Online*. Web. 8 Dec. 2012.

Further Reading

Booty, John E. "Communion and Commonweal: The Book of Common Prayer." *The Godly Kingdom of Tudor England: Great Books of the English Reformation*. Ed. Booty. Wilton, Conn.: Morehouse-Barlow, 1981. 139–216. Print.

Euler, Carrie. "Anabaptism and Anti-Anabaptism in the Early English Reformation: Defining Protestant Heresy and Orthodoxy during the Reign of Edward VI." *Heresy, Literature, and Politics in Early Modern*

English Culture. Ed. David Loewenstein and John Marshall. Cambridge: Cambridge University Press, 2006. 40–58. Print.

Johnston, Michael. "From Edward III to Edward VI: The Vision of Piers Plowman and Early Modern England." *Reformation* 11 (2006): 47–78. Print.

King, John N. "The Book-Trade under Edward VI and Mary I." *The Cambridge History of the Book in Britain, III: 1400–1557.* Ed. Lotte Hellinga and J. B. Trapp. Cambridge: Cambridge University Press, 1999. 164–78. Print.

Westfall, Suzanne: "The Boy Who Would Be King: Court Revels of King Edward VI, 1547–1553." *Comparative Drama* 35.3–4 (2001): 271–90. Print.

Nancy Simpson-Younger

Selected Letters of Martha Gellhorn

Martha Gellhorn

OVERVIEW

Selected Letters of Martha Gellhorn (2006), edited by Caroline Moorehead, contains portions of the writer's correspondence from her early adulthood in France in the 1930s through her death in London in 1998. Martha Gellhorn, who traveled extensively as a war correspondent, was an obsessive letter writer, often sending many per day to friends and family around the world. She was the third wife of Ernest Hemingway, and her letters provide a window into both Hemingway's artistic process and life. Furthermore, they chronicle many important events of the twentieth century, including World War II, as seen through the eyes of a sharp-eyed and sharp-tongued observer.

At the end of Gellhorn's life, she was persuaded by Howard Gotlieb of Boston University's Mugar Memorial Library to donate her papers under the stipulation that only a portion of the cache would be available until twenty-five years after her death. As the daughter of Gellhorn's friends and the sole biographer authorized by her estate, Moorehead was granted access to the correspondence, parts of which were published as the 2006 volume. The work received generally positive reviews, although some critics lamented not being able to read the full collection. Even in abridged form, the letters stand as a compelling portrait of a woman who broke ground for women covering wars.

HISTORICAL AND LITERARY CONTEXT

Gellhorn came of age during a time when letters were the standard form of communication when one was traveling. Her first destination, Paris, was the epicenter of literary innovation throughout the 1920s. The American expatriate community, which included such writers as F. Scott Fitzgerald, Hemingway, and Gertrude Stein, made the city a popular destination for young Americans interested in the literary life, and many began arriving in the Left Bank during this period.

Gellhorn had caught the travel bug during family trips to Europe. After dropping out of Bryn Mawr College at the age of twenty-one, she left the United States and would live much of her adult life abroad. As a war correspondent during the Spanish Civil War and World War II, Gellhorn spent weeks near the front lines and had few options other than letter writing for communicating with those back home. She made numerous friends throughout her travels, and as she rarely settled down for long in any one place, writing letters remained a vital means of staying connected to and intellectually engaged with her wide circle. Gellhorn corresponded with a number of notable figures of the twentieth century, including Eleanor Roosevelt, Charles Scribner, H. G. Wells, and Adlai Stevenson in addition to Hemingway, who would become her second husband.

Beyond detailing her own writing process, Gellhorn's letters provide insights into Hemingway's work on *For Whom the Bell Tolls* (1940), which she calls "a very, very fine book," and engage with the various works she read. An avid reader, she wrote to her friends about works ranging from nonfiction such as George Steer's *The Tree of Gernika: A Field Study of Modern War* (1938), which she describes to Roosevelt as "beautifully written and true," to poetry such as Elizabeth Bowen's *Look at All Those Roses* (1941) and classics by Henry James and Anthony Trollope, the latter of whom she listened to on audiotape at the end of her life when her eyesight was failing.

Some commentators have suggested that Gellhorn's letters, along with her war reporting, represent the best of her writing. Indeed, many of her works, which include a number of novels and short stories, fell out of print despite being well reviewed when they were initially published. The appearance of her letters sparked a renewed interest in her, prompting reprints of her novels, including *The Trouble I've Seen* (1936), her heralded series of novellas about the Great Depression.

THEMES AND STYLE

The centrality of her work and the desire to engage with people, politics, and public life dominate Gellhorn's letters. Particularly in the early years, the focus is on her travels, the articles and books she was writing, and her thoughts about turmoil around the world. Of her work, she writes, "I like working. In the end it is the only thing which does not bore or dismay me, or fill me with doubt. It is the only thing I know absolutely and irrevocably to be good in itself, no matter what the result." Gellhorn also writes of her personal relationships, although to a lesser extent in her surviving letters.

✣ Key Facts

Time Period:
Mid- to Late 20th Century

Relevant Historical Events:
Spanish Civil War; World War II; development of modernism

Nationality:
American

Keywords:
women's writing; war; journalism; modernism

American war correspondent, travel writer, and novelist Martha Gellhorn (1908–1998), photographed in 1990 by Steve Pyke. © STEVE PYKE/GETTY IMAGES

Gellhorn viewed her correspondence as conversations—in fact, she often writes in her letters, "I want to talk." In a 1974 letter to Betsy Drake, written as Gellhorn contemplated returning from Kenya to England, she says, "Your letters mean everything to me. It is not only that they carry messages of love but they are a voice, speaking. This is a dialogue; I am not always talking to myself anymore." By contrast, in a letter to Drake composed several months later, she describes the difficulty of working, especially when her writing is going poorly: "It eats away in the brain, a ceaseless conversation with oneself." For Gellhorn, writing letters seemed to be something of an antidote to the loneliness inherent in her work. At the same time, she often used her letters to process things she had witnessed, sometimes relating the same story to several people before including it later in a story or novel.

Gellhorn's conversational tone is often marked by self-deprecating humor and clever quips. In a letter to Bertrand de Jouvenel, for instance, about her own difficult character, she writes, "You'll have to think of me as oysters—you wouldn't want oysters everyday for breakfast?" She is also prone to using endearments such as "lamb," especially to her male friends and lovers. Her names for Hemingway—"Rabby" and "Dr. Warp Dimpy Gellhorn Bongie Hemmy"—are especially fanciful. At the same time, on the subjects of injustices in the "smeared odious world," Gellhorn's words are often angry. Although her letters clearly express a desire to entertain her friends, she is not afraid to be frank about her dissatisfactions.

CRITICAL DISCUSSION

Selected Letters of Martha Gellhorn garnered generally positive reviews when it was published, with critics noting both the interesting nature of Gellhorn's life and Moorehead's skill as an editor. Neal Ascherson of the *Nation* called the book "a masterpiece of biography." Byron Rogers, who reviewed it in the *Spectator*, was somewhat less positive, noting, "The Martha of the letters is not an entirely likeable human being. As you read on and on, page after page, you begin to realise that the recipients mostly had one thing in common: they were already famous, and thus might be of some use."

As Francine du Plessix Gray mentions in her review of the book in the *New York Times*, "This collection is equally notable because it chronicles a life tightly intermeshed with the pivotal events of the 20th century." While Gellhorn's important reporting on the Spanish Civil War and World War II, including the liberation of Dachau, are collected in *The Face of War* (1959), her letters provide a more complete account of war correspondence during the twentieth century, as well as its impact on the individual. Gellhorn is remarkable, too, as perhaps the most pioneering woman in the field. Because she disliked biography and never spoke at length to a biographer, her letters remain an important source of information about her life. Nevertheless, her letters have received little scholarly attention.

Scholars have, however, used Gellhorn's letters to elucidate elements of Hemingway's work, especially what he wrote during the period the two were involved. In an essay for *Modern Drama*, Lisa Jackson-Schebetta writes of Hemingway's treatment of the character Dorothy in his play *The Fifth Column* (1938): "It is possible that some of the insulting or demeaning passages concerning Dorothy were a kind of jest between Hemingway and Gellhorn." Jackson-Schebetta backs this up by noting that their correspondence "suggests that the two developed a rapport at least partially built on playful and incisive jibes about one another's habits, histories, and foibles."

BIBLIOGRAPHY

Sources

Ascherson, Neal. "The Foreign Correspondent." Rev. of *Selected Letters of Martha Gellhorn*, by Martha Gellhorn. *Nation* 8 Dec. 2003: 36–40. Print.

Gellhorn, Martha. *Selected Letters of Martha Gellhorn*. Ed. Caroline Moorehead. New York: Henry Holt, 2006. Print.

Gray, Francine du Plessix. "Woman of Letters." Rev. of *Selected Letters of Martha Gellhorn*. Ed. Caroline Moorehead. *New York Times*. New York Times, 27 Aug. 2006. Web. 10 Dec. 2012.

Jackson-Schebetta, Lisa. "Between the Language and Silence of War: Martha Gellhorn and the Female Characters of Hemingway's *The Fifth Column*." *Modern Drama* 53.1 (2010): 57–75. Print.

Rogers, Byron. "A Tendency to Collect Kings." Rev. of *Selected Letters of Martha Gellhorn*, by Martha Gellhorn. *Spectator* 15 July 2006. *Literature Resource Center*. Web. 10 Dec. 2012.

Further Reading

Gellhorn, Martha. *The Face of War*. New York: Simon and Schuster, 1959. Print.

———. *Travels with Myself and Another*. New York: Dodd, Mead, 1978. Print.

———. *The View from the Ground*. New York: Atlantic Monthly, 1988. Print.

Hemingway, Ernest. *Ernest Hemingway Selected Letters 1917–1961*. Ed. Carlos Baker. New York: Scribner, 1981. Print.

Moorehead, Caroline. *Gellhorn: A Twentieth Century Life*. New York: Henry Holt, 2003. Print.

Daisy Gard

MARTHA GELLHORN'S WAR REPORTING

Martha Gellhorn's war coverage has been evaluated as among the best of her generation. She covered the Spanish Civil War; World War II; Vietnam; and, in her eighties, the U.S. invasion of Panama. During World War II, when the U.S. military would not allow female reporters on the front lines, Gellhorn hid on a hospital ship so that she could write a firsthand account of D-day. This account, which appeared in *Collier's*, is considered among her finest and among the finest accounts of the invasion of Normandy. Gellhorn also covered the liberation of Dachau, an event that affected her profoundly, especially in her pro-Israeli position in later decades.

In a letter to Eleanor Roosevelt about the Spanish Civil War, Gellhorn ventures, "Perhaps because I try to be a writer, perhaps because I am a woman, I cannot avoid seeing history always in terms of people. And I see this disaster in terms of the plain soldiers I know." This ethos, along with her skill at placing her stories within a broader context of the political conflicts surrounding war, gave Gellhorn's reporting particular power.

A Young Palestinian's Diary, 1941–1945

The Life of Sāmī 'Amr

Sāmī 'Amr

❖ **Key Facts**

Time Period:
Mid-20th Century

Relevant Historical Events:
World War II; Arab Revolt; establishment of Israel

Nationality:
Palestinian

Keywords:
youth; colonialism; war

OVERVIEW

A Young Palestinian's Diary, 1941–1945: The Life of Sāmī 'Amr describes Sāmī 'Amr's daily struggles with women, his employers, and his family throughout his late teens and early twenties while providing insight into the historical and political realities of the British Mandate for Palestine during World War II (1939–1945). Although 'Amr's focus is generally personal, nearly every aspect of his life was affected by the British presence, increasing Jewish immigration to Palestine, and the war, and his diary contributes an important, underrepresented perspective to the historical record. The Arabic title of the diary, translated as *My Memoirs of This Life: The Battle of Life,* indicates the daily struggles that consume its pages.

'Amr's diary remained in his family for several decades and was not published until 2009, when it appeared in English. It has not yet been published in Arabic. Scholarship on *A Young Palestinian's Diary* has been limited to materials written by translator Kimberly Katz and sociologist Salim Tamari that introduce the English translation. Both scholars stress the text's historical importance. 'Amr's diary complicates historical narratives of pre-1948 Palestine that rely primarily on accounts written by scholars and intellectual and political leaders, largely neglecting less elite, and also less ideological and politically aware, perspectives.

HISTORICAL AND LITERARY CONTEXT

'Amr, born in 1924, was a teenager during the Arab Revolt (1936–1939), a popular uprising against British governance and Jewish immigration to Palestine. He wrote his diary during World War II, in the aftermath of the revolt, while Palestine was still under British control. The 1922 Mandate for Palestine legitimized the British presence in the region that had begun in 1917 and lasted until the 1948 establishment of the State of Israel.

During World War II the British armed forces offered opportunities for employment to a population no longer able to rely on a traditional agricultural economy. Although many Arab Palestinians opposed the British mandate, some viewed collaboration with the British as a necessary defense against the greater threat posed by Zionism. 'Amr's diary begins on April 30, 1941, following his graduation from the seventh grade at the age of seventeen. It describes his move from Hebron to Jerusalem and his employment as an errand boy at the British Navy, Army, and Air Force Institute, an organization charged with providing members of the British armed forces with recreational services and goods while stationed overseas. He was later promoted to clerk and then worked in the industrial sector as a welder. In addition to the many Arabs like 'Amr who held noncombat posts in the British colonial state, nine thousand Palestinians volunteered to serve in the British Army. 'Amr's brother, Sa'di, was among their ranks, and 'Amr devotes several pages in his diary to criticizing his brother's decision to enlist and then to bemoaning Sa'di's imprisonment after he was charged with being AWOL (absent without leave) during his deployment in Egypt.

A Young Palestinian's Diary can be located within a tradition of diary keeping in Palestine during the mandate period that encompasses the writings of Jews, British officials and soldiers, and other Palestinian Arabs. Jewish and British perspectives include Zionist leader Arthur Ruppin's *Arthur Ruppin: Memoirs, Diaries, Letters* (1971) and Palestinian police lieutenant Roger Courtney's *Palestine Policeman: An Account of Eighteen Dramatic Months in the Palestine Police Force during the Great Jew-Arab Troubles* (1939). A rich corpus of texts written in Arabic also exists, such as Palestinian Arab nationalist Khalil al-Sakakini's expansive diary, *Yawmiyyat Khalil al-Sakakini: Katha Ana Ya Dunya* (1955; The Diary of Khalil al-Sakakini: Such Am I, O World), and Palestinian oud player and composer Wasif Jawhariyyeh's memoirs, which cover the period between 1904 and 1968.

Notable for the nonelite perspective it presents of daily life in mandated Palestine, 'Amr's diary contributes an important voice to the historical record of Palestine. Al-Sakakini was an intellectual and writer, and other accounts, usually in the form of memoirs, were written by political and military leaders such as commander of the Arab Liberation Army Fawzi al-Qawuqji and Arab nationalist leader and politician Muhammad 'Izzat Darwaza. *A Young Palestinian's Diary* provides unique insight into the experiences of an ordinary young man impacted by contemporary political realities, although he was not directly involved in shaping them.

THEMES AND STYLE

A Young Palestinian's Diary focuses on the personal and quotidian, examining in particular 'Amr's encounters with women and his search for love as well as his anxiety over maintaining his moral purity. The text, however, also reveals a concern with broader social and political issues, such as the encounter between tradition and modernity, attachment to place and the Zionist threat to place-based Palestinian identity, and the plurality of contemporary Jerusalem. 'Amr stressed the necessity of abandoning tradition, most clearly embodied by the nomadic Bedouin, and embracing the new modernity taking shape in urban centers. In a letter to his brother-in-law, reproduced or perhaps drafted in his diary, 'Amr writes: "Yes! The world is progressing and will wipe out the old corrupt traditions, and what will remain from it, what is appropriate from it, is the triumphant city." Although 'Amr addresses Jewish immigration to Palestine only once, the lengthy entry on the subject views conflict as inevitable and expresses a passionate attachment to place, echoed in detailed descriptions of the land and especially Hebron elsewhere in the diary. 'Amr declares that the Zionist Jews "have forgotten that we will not leave our country to satisfy [their] aspirations and facilitate their comfort in Palestine while bearing the pain of exile and dispersion. In fact, we entered Palestine by the sword and would only leave it, God forbid, by the sword and would take our last breath trying to save it." At the same time, his accounts of daily life at his jobs, as well as his love for a Jewish girl named Tsipora, speak to a more comfortably diverse Jerusalem before the establishment of Israel and its subsequent fragmentation.

'Amr never explains his motivations for writing his diary, but it seems probable that he viewed it as a confidant with whom he could share his ideas, thoughts, and fears, especially while away from his home in Hebron. He confesses his loneliness on several occasions and addresses the diary as "my friend." When he is engaged to his cousin, Suhayla, he asks, "But, to whom shall I talk now, you, my friend, to whom I always poured out my complaints, or to you, Suhayla, you who have now become my main goal in this life and my companion when I am lonely?" The abrupt end to the diary, the last full entry bearing only the word *marriage* suggests that 'Amr no longer needed his diary once he had Suhayla. Although it is unlikely that he wrote with the goal of publication in mind, especially as he does not provide any personal or historical context to frame the text, he may have considered it later. Marginalia stressing the importance of clearly identifying his work as nonfiction suggests that he in time came to understand the broader value of his diary. Katz, who translated the diary into English, speculates that following the 1948 establishment of the State of Israel and Israel's 1967 occupation of the West Bank, including Hebron, 'Amr "reached the conclusion that one way to make a contribution to Palestinians' living memory was to make his voice heard, to add it to the historical record."

A Young Palestinian's Diary includes a number of entries, often very short, that describe recent events, but other characteristics question the book's categorization as a narrowly defined diary. 'Amr did not write regularly, and it seems that he may have at times recorded his thoughts elsewhere and later copied them into his diary. He also incorporates poetry, speeches, and political essays, as well as letters, which were either drafted in the diary and then rewritten for delivery to their intended recipients or written elsewhere and then recorded in the diary.

CRITICAL DISCUSSION

The critical and scholarly response to *A Young Palestinian's Diary* has been mostly positive, which is not surprising since it has received little attention outside of the introductory materials published with the English translation. In his foreword, Tamari notes the diary's historical importance, writing that "'Amr's mandate-era memoirs of his days working for the British in Palestine in the 1940s provide us with a rare intimate window into the world of thousands of Palestinians who flocked from their villages and provincial towns during the crucial years between the two great wars to seek employment opportunities and social advancement in the British Mandate capital of Jerusalem." In her introduction, Katz expands upon Tamari's praise, asserting that "['Amr's] diary makes a significant contribution to the history of Arabic self-literature, to Palestinian and Arab history, and to the history of the British Mandate in Palestine."

Both Tamari and Katz treat the diary as a historical document rather than a literary text, suggesting that later scholarship on *A Young Palestinian's Diary* will similarly focus on incorporating 'Amr's first-person

Jerusalem's Damascus Gate, photographed in about 1940. In *A Young Palestinian's Diary: 1941–1945*, Sāmī 'Amr describes his travels through his country, including Jerusalem. © NIDAY PICTURE LIBRARY/ALAMY

KHALIL AL-SAKAKINI: EDUCATIONAL REFORMER

While Sāmī 'Amr delivered a commoner's view in his writing, Khalil al-Sakakini wrote from an intellectual perspective. A Palestinian of Greek Orthodox origin, al-Sakakini was born in Jerusalem in 1878 during the Ottoman period. He was inspired by the Young Turk Revolution, which in 1908 had successfully restored the constitution and parliament suspended by Ottoman Sultan Abdul Hamid in 1876. In 1909 al-Sakakini founded the private, secular Dusturiyya (Constitutional) School, later called the Wataniyya School, in Jerusalem, creating an alternative to missionary and Ottoman education. He introduced new, progressive teaching methods with the goal of shaping a Palestinian intellectual elite. Classes were taught in Arabic rather than Turkish, and both corporeal punishment and grades were abolished. In 1910 al-Sakakini established *al-Dustur* newspaper, which was published by the private school.

Although not personally religious, al-Sakakini was a leader in the Greek Orthodox revolution, which sought to replace Greek church leadership with local Arab leadership. An Arab nationalist, he opposed Zionist immigration and the British mandate, opinions he expressed in his political writings. Al-Sakakini's diaries, spanning the years from 1908 to 1951 and first published in 1955, have been used extensively as a primary source by historians.

account into historical narratives often shaped by elite and non-Arab perspectives. The current lack of critical studies of the diary, however, makes it difficult to determine its long-term legacy.

The introductory materials to the English translation point to several possible areas for future inquiry by scholars. Tamari proposes a comparison between 'Amr's "fascination with colonial modernity" and that expressed by other contemporary Palestinian writers, such as al-Sakakini and educator Khalil Totah. Another route for comparative study is identified by Katz, who differentiates between the perspective expressed by 'Amr in his diary and that found in the interviews conducted by Nabil 'Alqam in his *Ahd al-Intidab al-Baritani fi al-Dhakirah al-Sha'biyah al-Filastiniyah* (2001; The British Mandate in the Memories of the Palestinian People). While 'Amr viewed Zionism as the biggest problem for Arab Palestinians during the last years of the mandate, later interviewees, looking back retrospectively, instead pointed to British colonialism. Katz suggests that "the contrast presents an opportunity to consider the difference between ['Amr's] writing in the moment, reacting to what he saw happening around him, and the interviewees' responses to questions about the subject at least forty years after the fact."

BIBLIOGRAPHY

Sources

Cleveland, William L. *A History of the Modern Middle East*. 3rd ed. Boulder: Westview, 2004. Print.

Katz, Kimberly. Introduction. "History and Historiography of the Diary." *A Young Palestinian's Diary, 1941–1945*. By Sāmī 'Amr. Trans. Katz. Austin: University of Texas Press, 2009. 1–68. Print.

Mattar, Philip. "Al-Sakakini, Khalil." *Encyclopedia of the Palestinians*. Ed. Philip Mattar. Rev. ed. New York: Facts On File, 2005. 436–37. Print.

Pappe, Ilan. *The Ethnic Cleansing of Palestine*. Oxford: Oneworld, 2006. Print.

Sa'di, Ahmad H., and Lila Abu-Lughod, eds. *Nakba: Palestine, 1948, and the Claims of Memory*. New York: Columbia University Press, 2007. Print.

Tamari, Salim. Foreword. "Away from [Dura] (or Life in the Margins)." *A Young Palestinian's Diary, 1941–1945*. By Sāmī 'Amr. Trans. Kimberly Katz. Austin: University of Texas Press, 2009. xi–xiv. Print.

Further Reading

Courtney, Roger. *Palestine Policeman: An Account of Eighteen Dramatic Months in the Palestine Police Force during the Great Jew-Arab Troubles*. London: Jenkins, 1939. Print.

Ruppin, Arthur. *Arthur Ruppin: Memoirs, Diaries, Letters*. Ed. Alex Bein. Trans. Karen Gershon. London: Weidenfeld and Nicolson, 1971. Print.

Sakakini, Khalil al-. "Such Am I, O World." *Anthology of Modern Palestinian Literature*. Ed. Salma Khadra Jayyusi. New York: Columbia University Press, 1992. 671–84. Print.

Swedenburg, Ted. *Memoirs of Revolt: The 1936–1939 Rebellion and the Palestinian National Past*. Minneapolis: University of Minnesota Press, 1995. Print.

Tamari, Salim. "Jerusalem's Ottoman Modernity: The Times and Lives of Wasif Jawhariyyeh." *Jerusalem Quarterly* 9 (2000): 5–27. Print.

Tamari, Salim, and Ihsan Turjman. *Year of the Locust: A Soldier's Diary and the Erasure of Palestine's Ottoman Past*. Berkeley: University of California Press, 2011. Print.

Tuqan, Fadwa. *A Mountainous Journey: An Autobiography*. Trans. Olive Kenny. London: Women's Press, 1990. Print.

Allison Blecker

Literary Lives

The Collected Letters of Mary Wollstonecraft by Mary Wollstonecraft	109
The Complete Notebooks of Henry James by Henry James	113
Diaries, 1931–1949 by George Orwell	117
The Diaries of Franz Kafka by Franz Kafka	120
The Diary of Anaïs Nin by Anaïs Nin	123
Estrangement, Being Some Fifty Extracts from a Diary Kept in 1909 by William Butler Yeats	126
The Habit of Being: Letters of Flannery O'Connor by Flannery O'Connor	129
Journal of Katherine Mansfield by Katherine Mansfield	133
The Journals of Arnold Bennett, 1896–1928 by Arnold Bennett	136
Journals of Ralph Waldo Emerson by Ralph Waldo Emerson	139
Letters and Journals of Lord Byron, with Notices of His Life by George Gordon Noel Byron	143
The Letters of John Keats, 1814–1821 by John Keats	146
Letters to a Young Poet by Rainer Maria Rilke	149
Notebooks by Tennessee Williams	152

The Collected Letters of Mary Wollstonecraft

Mary Wollstonecraft

OVERVIEW

Published in 2003 and edited by Janet Todd, *The Collected Letters of Mary Wollstonecraft* assembles all of early feminist writer Mary Wollstonecraft's (1759–1797) known extant letters, which encompass the bulk of her life. The collection begins in approximately 1773 with a series of letters she wrote as a teenager to her friend Jane Arden and ends in 1797 with several notes she left for her husband, William Godwin, shortly before the birth of daughter Mary Wollstonecraft Godwin (later Shelley) and the author's death due to complications from the delivery. The letters touch upon a wide variety of topics—including friendships and familial relationships, professional travails, various travels, and romantic affairs—and are generally concerned with conveying her emotional state, often featuring earnest discussions of her feelings. The letters provide an informative, often intimate glimpse at Wollstonecraft's subjective responses to the historical details of her life.

Todd's book was the second of two overlapping volumes of Wollstonecraft's collected letters, the first being an almost identically titled compilation edited by Ralph M. Wardle and published in 1979. (The 2003 book, in addition to containing a number of newly discovered letters, revises the dating of the correspondence and adds hundreds of explanatory annotations.) Regardless of edition, the letters have become an important element of Wollstonecraft scholarship. Although the letters seldom discuss her literary work or the social and philosophical issues that were often its focus, the insight they provide into her outlook sheds considerable light onto her development as an intellectual and a literary figure. They remain an important source for biographical scholarship.

HISTORICAL AND LITERARY CONTEXT

Wollstonecraft's letters reflect the intellectual climate of England during the Age of Enlightenment, a cultural movement that emphasized science, human reason, and skepticism toward tradition. These ideas played a significant role in the American and French revolutions, the latter of which was supported by many British intellectuals and frequently invoked in arguments about the need to reorganize British society along more equitable lines. Enlightenment ideas were also central to many arguments in favor of women's rights, which nonetheless remained severely circumscribed throughout the eighteenth century and beyond.

Wollstonecraft's correspondence documents her firsthand involvement with many of the historical realities she later addressed in her public writings. Letters written during her attempt to run a school for girls with her sisters and during her time in Ireland working as a governess for Lord and Lady Kingsborough likely prefigured her various literary statements about gender roles and the education of women. Likewise, the letters she wrote while staying in revolutionary France display her initial reaction to events she would later discuss at much greater length in print, though some of her most famous statements regarding the French Revolution actually predate her visit to the country. Meanwhile, her prominent involvement in British intellectual life is demonstrated by her exchanges with noteworthy figures such as Joel Barlow, Mary Hays, and William Godwin, her eventual husband.

Her epistolary style was in many ways atypical of eighteenth-century British writers. Todd, in her introduction to the collection, notes that contemporary letter-writing standards, as codified by the prominent rhetorician Hugh Blair, emphasized "the Augustan notion of correspondence as good conversation, sprightly, witty and seemingly natural, above all entertaining, with a constant eye to the recipient." In contrast, Wollstonecraft's letters, though deeply self-conscious, come across as effusive and uninhibited. They are also unusually internal in focus. Rather than discussing the outside world in any detail, the letters "reveal mostly her thoughts, sensations, and emotions. In many respects offending the canons of good letter-writing, she was rarely concise, graphic, direct, realistically detailed or detached."

Since Wollstonecraft's death, her letters—variously available in print or manuscript form before they were compiled into a single volume in 1979—have contributed significantly to her subsequent cultural legacy. They have served as an important source of information for biographers, starting with her husband, whose 1798 *Memoir* unintentionally ruined her posthumous reputation by disclosing aspects of her life widely regarded as scandalous—including her romantic affairs, illegitimate daughter, and suicide attempts. Since her scholarly

❖ *Key Facts*

Time Period:
Late 18th Century

Relevant Historical Events:
Enlightenment; birth of women's rights movement; French Revolution

Nationality:
English

Keywords:
women's writing; feminism; rationalism

LITERARY LIVES

The Young Schoolmistress, a painting by Jean-Baptiste-Siméon Chardin painted around 1735. Writer, educator, and feminist Mary Wollstonecraft promoted women's education and rights in the eighteenth century; her letters have been published as *The Collected Letters of Mary Wollstonecraft*. © NATIONAL GALLERY, LONDON/ART RESOURCE, NY

rehabilitation in the twentieth century, the letters have come to be regarded as an invaluable testament to the personal travails of a pioneering feminist ideologue, and they remain central to studies of both her life and the biographical elements of her work.

THEMES AND STYLE

Wollstonecraft's letters reflect many of the preoccupations of her literary and polemical writing, including a concern for the roles of women and an emphasis on rationality. She demonstrates her displeasure at the often frivolous nature of traditionally female pursuits during her time as a governess: "Confined to the society set of silly females, I have no social converse—and their boisterous spirits and unmeaning laughter exhausts me, not forgetting, hourly domestic bickering—The topics of matrimony and dress take their turns." She likewise urges her friend Hays to be wary of the possibly condescending literary praise of men and to allow her work to stand on its own: "let me remind you that when weakness claims indulgence it seems to justify the despotism of strength." This allegiance to impartial rationality can also be glimpsed in Wollstonecraft's assertion that her failed suicide attempt was "one of the calmest acts of reason"—not an atypical belief within eighteenth-century intellectual circles.

The act of letter writing served primarily as a means for Wollstonecraft to record and share her interior experiences. One of the most common motifs in her letters is the enumeration of her physical or mental ailments, as in a letter to friend George Blood in which she states, "I am sick of every thing under the sun—for verily every thing is grievous to me—all our pursuits are vain only the end which they bring us to is of consequence." For the most part the letters were outpourings of her constantly evolving thoughts rather than premeditated assertions. As Todd points out, "The letters themselves often formed a large part of the drama of her life. Wollstonecraft would begin to write in one state and end in another or write herself into dramatic misery." The letters were thus a more immediate type of literary self-expression than her other writings.

Her deeply personal approach to letter writing resulted in a raw, emotionally intense, unpolished prose style reflective of her tendency to think and write at the same time. In a letter to her lover Gilbert Imlay, the father of her first daughter, she laments his mistreatment of her: "I did not expect this blow from you. I have done my duty to you and my child; and if I am not to have any return of affection to reward me, I have the sad consolation of knowing that I deserved a better fate." She then castigates herself for straying from her intended topic: "You see how stupid I am, uttering declamation, when I simply meant to tell you, that I consider your requesting me to come to you, as merely dictated by honour." Her writing throughout the letters is seldom careful but often scrupulous.

CRITICAL DISCUSSION

The Collected Letters of Mary Wollstonecraft was warmly received upon its publication in 2003, mainly for the perspicacity of its annotations. Only eight previously unpublished letters had surfaced in the decades since Wardle's 1979 edition was published, so most of the new material in Todd's book consisted of nearly a thousand footnotes, which supplemented the letters with far more contextual information than the earlier volume had provided. These annotations were widely praised. Eleanor Ty, writing in *Eighteenth-Century Fiction* in 2005, declared them to be "thorough, well researched, and meticulous." Other reviewers echoed this sentiment and the book was hailed as a significant contribution to Wollstonecraft studies, notwithstanding its relative lack of new primary source material.

Wollstonecraft's letters have played a significant role in molding her posthumous reputation almost since her death. Godwin published some of them—including her love letters to Imlay—just a year later, thereby providing documentation, in Wollstonecraft's words, of what many perceived as her scandalous life. Her life remained a subject of great interest after her work entered the feminist canon, resulting in further—albeit more sympathetic—scrutiny of the letters. In Todd's 2000 biography of Wollstonecraft, *Mary Wollstonecraft: A Revolutionary Life,* which makes extensive use of the letters, she asserts, "I see her ideas as inextricably linked to her experience. She is at her best and most original when her writing interacts with her life." The insight her letters provide into this interaction has precipitated copious biographical scholarship.

Scholarly writing addressing the letters frequently incorporates them into discussions of the intersection between Wollstonecraft's life and her philosophical convictions. An important example is Barbara Taylor's *Mary Wollstonecraft and the Feminist Imagination* (2003), which contextualizes Wollstonecraft's radicalism within her historical circumstances. Taylor notes that "ripping her from her own intellectual world to claim her for ours has had the paradoxical effect of reducing her real intellectual significance." Likewise, Cynthia D. Richards, writing in *Tulsa Studies in Women's Literature* in 2006, makes ample use of Wollstonecraft's letters to Imlay in her discussion of the relationship between their problematic affair and Wollstonecraft's intellectual development. Richards argues, "What seems most disturbing about the affair—the discrepancy it points to between Wollstonecraft's words and her behavior—can instead emerge as 'poignantly harmonious' when viewed in the right context."

LETTERS WRITTEN DURING A SHORT RESIDENCE IN SWEDEN, NORWAY, AND DENMARK

In 1796 Mary Wollstonecraft published the last of her books to appear during her lifetime, *Letters Written during a Short Residence in Sweden, Norway, and Denmark,* an epistolary travelogue of her time in Scandinavia handling the business affairs of her lover Gilbert Imlay, to whom the twenty-five letters contained in the book were implicitly directed. However, she did not reproduce her personal correspondence with him: although she used those letters in composing *Short Residence,* the volume does not refer to Imlay by name or discuss the details of their relationship or her reasons for being in Scandinavia.

Instead the book consists mostly of lengthy meditations on philosophy, identity, and the effects of travel, as well as a great deal of commentary on society in general and Scandinavia in particular. The emotional vicissitudes of her relationship with Imlay are pervasive but obliquely presented, and the tone is far more sentimental than that of her previous, polemical works—though *Short Residence* is considerably more outward looking than the intense self-obsession of many of her private letters. The book was by far Wollstonecraft's most admired work during her lifetime, but it has since been surpassed in esteem by her more incendiary writings.

BIBLIOGRAPHY

Sources

Richards, Cynthia D. "Romancing the Sublime: Why Mary Wollstonecraft Fell in Love with That Cad, Gilbert Imlay." *Tulsa Studies in Women's Literature* 25.1 (2006): 71–91. *JSTOR.* Web. 26 Dec. 2012.

Taylor, Barbara. *Mary Wollstonecraft and the Feminist Imagination.* Cambridge: Cambridge University Press, 2003. Print.

Todd, Janet. *Mary Wollstonecraft: A Revolutionary Life.* New York: Columbia University Press, 2000. Print.

Ty, Eleanor. Rev. of *Mary Wollstonecraft and the Accent of the Feminine,* by Ashley Tauchert; *The Cambridge Companion to Mary Wollstonecraft,* ed. Claudia L. Johnson; and *The Collected Letters of Mary Wollstonecraft,* ed. Janet Todd. *Eighteenth-Century Fiction* 17.2 (2005): 294–98. *Academic Search Complete.* Web. 26 Dec. 2012.

Wollstonecraft, Mary. *The Collected Letters of Mary Wollstonecraft*. Ed. Janet Todd. New York: Columbia University Press, 2003. Print.

Further Reading

Barker-Benfield, G. J. "Mary Wollstonecraft: Eighteenth-Century Commonwealthwoman." *Journal of the History of Ideas* 50.1 (1989): 95–115. Print.

Franklin, Caroline. *Mary Wollstonecraft: A Literary Life*. Basingstoke: Palgrave Macmillan, 2004. Print.

Gordon, Lyndall. *Vindication: A Life of Mary Wollstonecraft*. New York: HarperCollins, 2005. Print.

Johnson, Claudia L., ed. *The Cambridge Companion to Mary Wollstonecraft*. Cambridge: Cambridge University Press, 2002. Print.

Kelly, Gary. *Revolutionary Feminism: The Mind and Career of Mary Wollstonecraft*. New York: St. Martin's, 1992. Print.

Pendersen, Joyce Senders. "Friendship in the Life and Work of Mary Wollstonecraft: The Making of a Liberal Feminist Tradition." *Literature & History* 17.1 (2008): 19–35. Print.

Waters, Mary A. "'The First of a New Genus': Mary Wollstonecraft as a Literary Critic and Mentor to Mary Hays." *Eighteenth-Century Studies* 37.3 (2004): 415–34. Print.

Wollstonecraft, Mary. *The Works of Mary Wollstonecraft*. 7 vols. Ed. Marilyn Butler and Janet Todd. New York: New York University Press, 1989. Print.

James Overholtzer

The Complete Notebooks of Henry James

Henry James

OVERVIEW

The Complete Notebooks of Henry James (1987), edited by Leon Edel and Lyall H. Powers, contains Henry James's personal journals and undeveloped manuscripts and remains a useful insight into the writing process of a canonical giant. Previously unpublished material includes the author's seven remaining "Pocket Diaries" (composed between 1909 and 1915), which detail financial transactions, addresses, and appointments; "The Deathbed Dictation" (1915); and an unfinished story, "Hugh Merrow." Most significant are the nine extant notebooks (1878–1911), primarily comprising nascent novels and novel ideas, sketches, and narrative outlines from which eighty future fictions would be fully fleshed.

The Edel and Powers edition expands on *The Notebooks of Henry James* (1947), edited by F. O. Matthiessen and Kenneth B. Murdock, with additional documents and corrections. Current scholarship prefers this earlier edition because of its extensive annotations. Despite the title, *Complete Notebooks* contains only the notebooks and diaries that survived James's determinedly destructive hand. Examination of these personal writings reveals a writing process by turns exacting, persistent, and even incantatory, making the work a fascinating glimpse into the mind of a literary master.

HISTORICAL AND LITERARY CONTEXT

Born in New York City but educated abroad, James belonged to a social class in which journaling was a matter of course; he and two of his siblings, William (the renowned psychologist and philosopher) and Alice, were all practiced, and eventually published, diarists. They were a family of abolitionists, and their ideal of a slave-free United States was put to the test during the Civil War (1861–1865), in which James's two younger brothers served. While James published fiction during this time, based on actual events, no notebooks of this period survive. In 1869, when James was twenty-six, his adored cousin Mary "Minny" Temple died of tuberculosis. Matthiessen and Murdock see her as the specter of passion that haunted him for the rest of his life, serving as a basis for his characters Isabel Archer (*The Portrait of a Lady*; 1881) and Milly Theale (*The Wings of the Dove*; 1902). Both represent American earnestness and self-determination. His prolific writing provided financial insurance in post–Civil War capitalist America. In 1881 James returned to the United States for a lengthy visit, primarily to commune with family, taking advantage of the abundant impressions that would make their way into *The Bostonians* (1886).

The *Notebooks* are remarkable for their devotion to observations of contemporary events and persons. Several notable literary luminaries, such as Edith Wharton, Émile Zola, Morton Fullerton, and Guy de Maupassant, appear in James's pages, with the latter occasionally serving as a muse ("Oh, spirit of Maupassant, come to my aid!"). Ralph Waldo Emerson, whose transcendentalism had spread across mid-nineteenth-century New England—and had influenced James's father—was also a friend to James, although James did not subscribe to transcendental philosophies. His reality-based *Notebooks* can be seen as an answer to Emerson's idealism.

In 1879 James wrote a monograph about Nathaniel Hawthorne, whose personal journals and letters (*Notebooks*, covering the years 1835–1859) were published posthumously in 1864. Although James considered Hawthorne a literary genius, he lamented his fellow diarist's quotidian subject matter and unresponsiveness to European and English culture. Like Hawthorne, James had both native New England sensibilities and European acculturations. James's *Notebooks*, in contrast to Hawthorne's, however, rhapsodize the expansiveness of erudition, enlightenment, and the experience of living abroad. In various ways his masterful novels *The Portrait of a Lady* (1881), *The Wings of the Dove* (1902), *The Ambassadors* (1903), and *The Golden Bowl* (1904) all address the allure of life on the Continent and in England and, by comparison, disdain what he saw as the culturally impoverished life of Americans. James moved effortlessly within Victorian and Edwardian circles, and his "American Journal I" is particularly resolute in asserting that his birthplace was no longer his home.

The *Notebooks* provide blueprints for his novels and references to characters, events, and places as they appear in the published works. Beyond serving as a repository for rough-draft material, the journals show James summoning a muse or arguing with himself about a particular detail, providing emotional connections of the kind he found missing in

Key Facts

Time Period:
Late 19th to Early 20th Centuries

Relevant Historical Events:
James's success as a writer and move from the United States to Europe

Nationality:
American

Keywords:
literature; creativity; identity

Portrait of Henry James by John Singer Sargent, 1913. Although an American by birth, James lived in Europe for much of his life and became a British citizen in 1915. © CORBIS

Hawthorne's personal papers. In the aftermath of the failure of his staged drama *Guy Domville* in 1895, for example, he writes, "I take up my old pen again—the pen of all my old unforgettable efforts and sacred struggles."

THEMES AND STYLE

Motifs of confidence, self-affirmation versus self-recrimination, and identity, everywhere in James's published fiction, likewise pervade his private notebooks. According to James, European authors could write as if the United States never existed, but the corollary did not hold true for American writers; however, he considered that "fifty years hence," this would no longer be true. Although he spent more of his time living and writing in Europe and England than in the United States, he could not completely rid himself of his American roots. Cambridge, Massachusetts, he wrote, "hangs there behind, like a pale, pathetic ghost … fixing me with tender, pleading eyes … holding up the silver mirror … that is like a sphere peopled with the old ghosts." While in the United States he reminisced about Europe, laying claim to the English identity that would not be officially conferred for another thirty-five years (he achieved citizenship the year before his death): "My work lies there—and with this vast new world, *je n'ai que faire*." He knew, though, that his work really lay between both worlds: "As I feared, the 'New England II' gives me a marked muchness of material to deal with, but the only way is to let it all come—that serves me well." The easy manner of Americans may have affronted his English sensibility, but those transatlantic annoyances added sinew to his realist fiction.

The constant, in the United States or abroad, was the note taking, the subjects and practice of which he remained ever confident: "No effort in this direction is vain, no confidence idle, no surrender but is victorious."

The resultant eighty publications confirm James's assertion that the purpose of the *Notebooks* was the development of his fiction. The task of journaling did not become routine for James until after he had received acclaim for such early works as the novel *Roderick Hudson* (1875) and the novella *Daisy Miller* (1878), although the cultivation of his novel *Confidence* (1878) can be charted from the first notebook entry of 1878 to its serialization in *Scribner's Monthly* the following year. As late as 1881, however, he lamented that he had "lost too much by losing, or rather by not having acquired, the note-taking habit." Thereafter, he approached his literary sketches with a singular focus: "Now that I am older … I ought to endeavor to keep, to a certain extent, a record of passing impressions." He was intent on keeping the *Notebooks* private, intentionally destroying them as he deemed necessary. While the precise number of irretrievable documents is unknown, James made implicit references to "French" and "Italian" notebooks, presumed lost, and explicitly mentioned a discarded "Project for the Wings of the Dove."

James's notes exalt his process ("*Causons, causons, mon bon*—oh celestial soothing, sanctifying process"), conveying the vitality he found lacking in Hawthorne. His privacy, then, suggests that he felt vulnerable in that vitality, that moment where overconfidence conjures insecurity that he wished unseen. The *Notebooks* give primacy to vision; the emphasis on showing rather than telling steadily increases: "I think I see it—must see it—as a young man—a young man who goes to see for the first time." Much has been said of his impressionistic writing style, but the effect of his detailed presentation aligns with the visual art of pointillism. The writing itself is replete with dashes and dotted with exclamation points. Mark Edelman Boren, one of several scholars to write about James as a visual artist, describes in his article "More than a Line" (1998) the numerous horizontal lines that scatter the original notebooks: "They delineate thoughts, break apart clauses, underscore ideas, and give emphasis. In short, they are … integral to the decoding of his thoughts."

CRITICAL DISCUSSION

James's *Notebooks* were published for the first time thirty years after his death. Scholars immediately applauded the 1947 Matthiessen and Murdock volume, praising the commentary and the care taken in indexing the material. Critic Newton Arvin, who reviewed the book in 1948 in the *New England Quarterly*, writes that it reveals both James's technical skill and the absence of grand ideas about how life should be lived; scenes of life as it is lived appear instead. Katherine Hoskins, reviewing the *Notebooks* in a 1948 edition of the *Hudson Review*, praises the editors' deciphering of the journals but criticizes the commentary as detrimental to the fluidity of the original text. A minority opinion in the field, she suggests that James wanted the notebooks published. The 1987 *Complete Notebooks* was recognized for its corrections of earlier errors, elucidation of names and places, and additional story notes. Nevertheless, current scholarly consensus prefers the earlier Matthiessen and Murdock edition, primarily because of its chronological fidelity and the running analysis and commentary after each entry. Edel and Powers abstain from annotating the stories, content to leave that to "the alert reader," and, according to James scholars, fail to improve on the index.

Because of the errors in the 1947 edition and the lack of critical commentary in the 1987 version, scholars have minimized the usefulness of both, and James's *Notebooks* do not enjoy the same attention as his novels and short stories. Interest in his personal life has seen a resurgence since the 1990s, however, and in the twenty-first century he has been the subject of three historical fictions, an eventuality that likely would have left the realist author unimpressed. In their *Critical Companion to Henry James* (2009), Eric Haralson and Kendall Johnson quote James as writing, "The only reason for the existence of a novel is that it does attempt to represent life."

Scholars continue to debate the authenticity of James's insistence on the privacy of his *Notebooks*. Raymond Thorberg examines French novelist Edmond About's *Germaine* (1857) alongside *Notebooks* and *The Wings of the Dove* to suggest that James may have borrowed more heavily from About's novel than his *Notebooks* indicate; if that proves to be the case, then the belief that James maintained full confidence in his pages is called into question. Scholars of nineteenth-century literature find a rich harvest in his working notes. Drawing parallels with Henry David Thoreau and Hawthorne, scholar Martha Banta's "'There Is Surely a Story in It'" (1988) calls for a more expansive study of the collection. She comments that where Hawthorne might note an artifact for a story, James presents the artifact and a story line. It is precisely because of his faithful representation of life in his private *Notebooks* that sociohistorical scholars have turned to him for studies of race, class, and gender in the nineteenth century.

BIBLIOGRAPHY

Sources

Arvin, Newton. Rev. of *The Notebooks of Henry James*, by Henry James, ed. F. O. Matthiessen and Kenneth B. Murdock. *New England Quarterly* 21.1–4 (1948): 110–11. *JSTOR*. Web. 23 Dec. 2012.

HENRY JAMES'S ROMANTIC LIFE

Henry James died a bachelor with no children, and exhaustive study suggests that he had no grand passionate romances with women. These facts have led some scholars to speculate about his sexuality, with conclusions varying between clearly homosexual and unquestionably asexual. His assiduousness in maintaining an observer's and a narrator's distance in his fictions accords with his claim to be "the loneliest of men."

Epistolary evidence of an ardent physical longing for a man, however, is collected in Rosella Mamoli Zorzi's 2004 *Beloved Boy: Letter to Hendrik C. Andersen 1899–1915*, which Sean O'Toole uses as a basis for his exploration of homosexuality in James's *The Spoils of Poynton* in the *Henry James Review* (2012). While several studies previous to Zorzi's had uncovered homoerotic tones or expressions in James's works, none had collected evidence with the same level of breadth and fervor. O'Toole quotes a letter from James to Andersen: "I feel, my dear boy, my arm around you; & I feel the pulsation, thereby, as it were, of our future & your admirable endowment." James maintained close friendships with several gay men, including Hugh Walpole, Howard Sturgis, and Morton Fullerton (who was bisexual). James's sexuality, a secret during his life, may be one reason that he was protective of his *Notebooks*.

Banta, Martha. "'There Is Surely a Story in It': James's *Notebooks* and the Working Artist." *Henry James Review* 9.3 (1988): 153–65. *JSTOR*. Web. 23 Dec. 2012.

Boren, Mark Edelman. "More than a Line: The Unmistakable Impression of Significance and the Dashes of Henry James." *Philological Quarterly* 77.3 (1998): 329–47. *JSTOR*. Web. 23 Dec. 2012.

Haralson, Eric, and Kendall Johnson, eds. *Critical Companion to Henry James: A Literary Reference to His Life and Work*. New York: Infobase, 2009. Print.

Hoskins, Katherine. Rev. of *The Notebooks of Henry James*, by Henry James, ed. F. O. Matthiessen and Kenneth B. Murdock. *Hudson Review* 1.1 (1948): 124–26. *JSTOR*. Web. 23 Dec. 2012.

James, Henry. *The Complete Notebooks of Henry James*. Ed. Leon Edel and Lyall H. Powers. New York: Oxford University Press, 1987. Print.

O'Toole, Sean. "Queer Properties: Passion and Possession in *The Spoils of Poynton*." *Henry James Review* 33.1 (2012): 30–52. *Project MUSE*. Web. 23 Dec. 2012.

Further Reading

Anesko, Michael. *Monopolizing the Master: Henry James and the Politics of Modern Literary Scholarship*. Stanford: Stanford University Press, 2012. Print.

Freedman, Jonathan, ed. *The Cambridge Companion to Henry James*. Cambridge: Cambridge University Press, 1998. Print.

Hannah, Daniel K. "The Private Life, the Public Stage: Henry James in Recent Fiction." *Journal of Modern Literature*. 30.3 (2007): 70–94. *JSTOR*. Web. 23 Dec. 2012.

James, Henry. *The Art of the Novel.* New York: Scribner. 1962. Print.

———. *The Notebooks of Henry James.* Ed. F. O. Matthiessen and Kenneth B. Murdock. New York: Oxford University Press, 1947. Print.

Powers, Lyall H. "On the Use of James's Notebooks." *A Companion to Henry James Studies.* Ed. Daniel Mark Fogel. Westport, Conn.: Greenwood, 1993. Print.

Rawlings, Peter, ed. *Critical Essays on Henry James.* Aldershot: Scolar, 1993. Critical Thought Ser. 5.

Richards, Bernard. Rev. of *The Complete Notebooks of Henry James,* by Henry James, ed. Leon Edel and Lyall H. Powers. *Review of English Studies* 39.156 (1998): 578–82. *JSTOR.* Web. 23 Dec. 2012.

Nicole Grant

DIARIES, 1931–1949
George Orwell

OVERVIEW

George Orwell is widely considered one of the most important English writers of the twentieth century, and his diaries are of considerable significance in understanding his life and work. The diaries were first published in 1998 as part of the twenty-volume *Complete Works of George Orwell,* edited by Peter Davison; then in a single volume (also edited by Davison) in 2009. The single volume, *Diaries, 1931–1949,* was rereleased in 2012 with an introduction by British American author and journalist Christopher Hitchens. Orwell was a lifelong diarist and note taker, and his diaries record his life in considerable detail, from his hop-picking days in Kent, England, in 1931 almost up to his death in 1950. The diaries take several forms. There are diaries of travel, recording trips to exotic places such as Marrakech as well as throughout England (where he researched *The Road to Wigan Pier,* his 1937 book about industrial northern England), and there are domestic diaries, from his time in Morocco as well as from the end of his life, on the island of Jura off the west coast of Scotland.

As the author of notable works including *Animal Farm* (1945) and *Nineteen Eighty-Four* (1949), Orwell's fame is such that it could hardly be enhanced by the publication of his diaries, sections of which include, famously, mundane details such as the number of eggs his chickens laid each day. However, while these details have led several critics to suggest the diaries are not for casual readers, their value lies in Orwell's observations on war and the culture of mid-twentieth-century Europe as well as the insight offered into his meticulous, practical approach to life.

HISTORICAL AND LITERARY CONTEXT

Orwell's diaries contain a curious mixture of domestic details, travelogue, and commentary on British life before, during, and after World War II. Britain had suffered economic difficulties since the end of World War I, and Orwell was keen to report on working-class life. Some of the diaries take the form of research for his published works. He slept rough with the London hop pickers before their seasonal journey to Kent, and he lived among the poor in Wigan to find out about "distressed" industrial northern England in 1936. A political writer who disliked imperialism of all kinds, Orwell was investigated by several secret service organizations. It is thought that at least two diaries were seized by police in Barcelona during the Spanish Civil War and are still believed to be held in the secret police state security archive in Moscow.

First published in 1998 as part of Orwell's *Complete Works, Diaries* then appeared as a single volume in the United Kingdom in 2009, perhaps reflecting a growing popular interest in his work in the twenty-first century. Written during the period 1931–1949, they represent the personal records and reflections of a writer closely associated with the struggle against fascism and communism in Europe and with working-class struggles at home. Observations recorded in the diaries—for example, on the "phony" media reports of Russian victories in World War II—informed his well-known views on censorship and government alteration of news stories.

In some ways Orwell's diaries are typical of diaries by other twentieth-century writers, such as Siegfried Sassoon, in that they contain personal notes alongside more "writerly" observations on current events, books, the arts, and other areas of intellectual life. They are unusual, however, in that they rarely mention his own books or his family, displaying instead an intense interest in current affairs and the implications of political events. The domestic diaries are still more unusual, containing little beyond the tiny details of household accounts and gardening. They may appear dull and irrelevant, but as Hitchens notes in his introduction to the 2012 edition of *Diaries,* a detail about rats in a 1939 entry might later have informed "one of the most arresting images of terror in all of his fiction." It is impossible to say how significant Orwell's experience of raising farm animals later turned out to be.

Through his many newspaper articles, radio broadcasts, and books—including *The Road to Wigan Pier, Animal Farm,* and *Nineteen Eighty-Four*—Orwell earned a reputation as perhaps the preeminent English political writer and journalist of the twentieth century. As Hitchens writes, Orwell's "need to *know* things" sets him apart from many other writers and made him a model for good investigative journalism. The diaries reveal the process by which he lived and experienced the subject matter of many of his published works.

THEMES AND STYLE

Because they were written in response to events taking place around him, Orwell's diary entries range widely across his interests and ideas. His social and political

❖ **Key Facts**

Time Period:
Mid-20th Century

Relevant Historical Events:
World War II; Orwell's success as a fiction writer

Nationality:
English

Keywords:
working-class life; war; politics

Joy Batchelor and John Halas's cover for an edition of George Orwell's novel *Animal Farm.* © HALAS & BATCHELOR COLLECTION LTD./THE BRIDGEMAN ART LIBRARY

concerns—championing working class causes and disparaging the idea that the Soviet Union should be viewed as a good alternative to Western capitalism—are supported with detailed observation. For example, in 1940 he records the proportion of newspaper advertising devoted to "useless luxuries," attacking popular culture and the "waste" of consumerism and noting that "so much of the good of modern life is actually evil that it is questionable whether on balance war does harm." The mundane domestic details of his life at home in Wallington, Hertfordshire, and at Barnhill, on Jura, offered a form of escape from this vision of a corrupted modern world.

The diaries were written with several different motivations: to record events as research for specific projects; to work through ideas that would later take shape in his books; and to keep an accurate record of his garden, the output of his hens, and the business of farming. The effect of this variety of purpose is that the diaries as a whole vary greatly in style and interest. For example, the domestic diary records, "*Smallholder* advises sowing broad beans now & planting shallots, so shall do so if I get time. 6 eggs." By contrast, in the second wartime diary Orwell comments, "German propaganda is inconsistent … deliberately so, with an utter unscrupulousness in offering everything to everybody." The overall picture given by the diaries is of a man engaging with important ideas while remaining focused on the details and practicalities of living.

The stylistic variety of the diaries equals that of their subject matter, ranging from extended, opinionated commentaries on current affairs to to-do lists and simple, factual records of the weather. Much of the material, as several critics have noted, is very dull. Hitchens points out that Orwell was living in a "culture of censorship and denial [that] also necessitated a coarsening of attitudes to language and truth" and that the diaries reflect his "declining to lie, even as far as possible to himself." An example of his polemical style comes in a response to an Italian radio report of food shortages in Britain: "You can go on and on telling lies, and the most palpable lies at that, and even if they are not actually believed, there is no strong revulsion either."

CRITICAL DISCUSSION

Although Orwell's diaries had been published before, as part of the *Complete Works,* their separate publication was received with much acclaim, both for Orwell and the volume's editor, Davison. Critics viewed the volume as an extended autobiography that reveals aspects of the author and his work hitherto unseen. Hitchens's introduction, which also appeared in modified form in *Vanity Fair,* advises, "Read with care, George Orwell's diaries, from the years 1931 to 1949, can greatly enrich our understanding of how Orwell transmuted the raw material of everyday existence into some of his best-known novels and polemics."

Orwell's thoughts on government, propaganda, and language are best known from his novels and essays, but the diaries provide autobiographical detail and further expression of his ideas, helping scholars to explore his work in general. They have proved invaluable as a resource to biographers such as Gordon Bowker, whose 2003 Orwell biography took advantage of the diaries as they appeared in *Complete Works.* The diaries themselves, as David Ulin in the *Los Angeles Times* observed, reveal a human dimension to Orwell that is less evident in his published work.

Davison's editorial work represents the most extensive scholarship on the diaries themselves and is impressive in its detail. A great deal of early Orwell scholarship focused on the writer's major works, in particular *Nineteen Eighty-Four,* or on his role as a "proletarian novelist" or "condition of England" novelist. Since the 1990s Orwell's reliability as an accurate and objective observer has become an important question for many critics, including Loraine Saunders. She quotes Davison's note on Orwell's "A Short Story" in the *Complete Works,* in which he identifies Orwell's "capacity for writing on the narrow edge that separates fact and fiction." Hitchens did most to popularize Orwell as an intellectual in the twenty-first century. In *Why Orwell Matters* he argues that "Orwell can be read as one of the founders of the discipline of post-colonialism."

BIBLIOGRAPHY

Sources

Bowker, Gordon. *George Orwell*. London: Little, Brown, 2003. Print.

Hitchens, Christopher. *Why Orwell Matters*. New York: Basic Books, 2002. Print.

Orwell, George. *Complete Works of George Orwell*. Ed. Peter Davison. 20 vols. London: Secker and Warburg, 1998. Print.

———. *Diaries, 1931–1949*. Ed. Peter Davison. 2009. New York: W. W. Norton, 2012. Print.

Saunders, Loraine. *The Unsung Artistry of George Orwell*. Abington: Ashgate, 2008. Print.

Ulin, David. "George Orwell's 'Diaries' Show Balance between Big and Small Vision." *Los Angeles Times*. Los Angeles Times, 13 Aug. 2012. Web. 21 Dec. 2012.

Further Reading

Davison, Peter. *George Orwell: A Literary Life*. London: Macmillan, 1998. Print.

Marks, Peter. "The Ideological Eye-Witness: An Examination of the Eye-Witness in Two Works by George Orwell." *Subjectivity and Literature from the Romantics to the Present Day*. Ed. Philip Shaw and Peter Stockwell. London: Pinter, 1991. 85–92. Print.

Orwell, George. *Burmese Days*. New York: Harper Brothers, 1934. Print.

———. *The Road to Wigan Pier*. London: Gollancz, 1937. Print.

———. *Animal Farm*. London: Secker and Warburg, 1945. Print.

———. *Nineteen Eighty-Four*. London: Secker and Warburg, 1949. Print.

Rodden, John. *The Cambridge Companion to George Orwell*. Cambridge: Cambridge University Press, 2007. *Cambridge Collections Online*. Cambridge University Press. Web. 18 Dec. 2012.

Taylor, D. J. *Orwell: The Life*. London: Chatto & Windus, 2003. Print.

BURMESE DAYS

George Orwell was born in India in 1903, when the country was still governed as part of the British Empire. He grew up in England and joined the Imperial Police Force in 1922, serving five years in colonial Burma (now Myanmar). His first novel, *Burmese Days,* is based on his observations of the workings of imperial power. The novel sets John Flory, a colonist timber merchant against the Burmese magistrate U Po Kyin. The magistrate takes bribes from all sides and then, for the sake of fairness, makes his decisions according to the law.

However, the novel is much more than an attack on corrupt officials. Orwell's dislike of colonialism and the shame he felt at being part of the mechanism of empire are clear in the debased and immoral behavior of the characters: their racism, their duplicity, and their greed. While the myth of the British Empire suggests that well-run institutions brought order to "chaotic" nations, what we learn from *Burmese Days* is that Orwell believes favoritism and violent racial discrimination debase both the colonists and the colonized.

Chris Routledge

The Diaries of Franz Kafka

Franz Kafka

Key Facts

Time Period:
Early 20th Century

Relevant Historical Events:
Increasing German nationalism; Kafka's experience as Jewish insurance agent and writer

Nationality:
Czech

Keywords:
alienation; Jewishness; literature

OVERVIEW

The Diaries of Franz Kafka, which include observations on the author's life and work, drafts of stories, and literary influences, cover the years 1910 to 1923 and were published in two volumes in 1948 and 1949. Culled from thirteen quarto notebooks by Franz Kafka's editor Max Brod, the material was initially published in English as *The Diaries of Franz Kafka (1910–1913)* and *The Diaries of Franz Kafka (1914–1923)*. An original German-language version was published in 1951 under the title *Franz Kafka: Tagebücher 1910–1923*. Other published versions of Kafka's diaries, such as scholarly publisher Kritische Ausgabe's *Tagebücher*, also include material from the quarto notebooks. It is unclear if Kafka himself ever considered his notebooks to be diaries in a strict sense, though they provide much insight into the themes central to his fiction, including alienation, the frustrations of daily of life, and self-loathing.

After Kafka died in 1924, Brod, the executor of his will, ignored the writer's request to burn his existing papers and instead began publishing them. Scholarship on the various versions of the diaries is extensive; literary critics have looked to them for information on Kafka's life and writing process. For instance, they have been perceived as a window into Kafka's creative routine, offering glimpses into the development of his characters and themes. Today, the *Diaries* continue to influence and interest scholars, writers, and fans.

HISTORICAL AND LITERARY CONTEXT

Many of Kafka's literary contemporaries kept diaries, and though Kafka's often stray from a conventional form and content, they do include daily observations and records of events that are the hallmarks of the diary as a literary form. First gaining popularity in the late Renaissance, diaries appeared with greater frequency in the early twentieth century, alongside increased interest in the burgeoning field of psychoanalysis as promoted by Sigmund Freud, which encouraged reflection and introspection of one's consciousness. Brod had encouraged Kafka to maintain and share his diaries, especially because personal diaries were becoming popular among members of the literary scene. In his diaries, Kafka mentions many writers who inspired him, including Russian novelist Leo Tolstoy and the late eighteenth-century German master Johann Wolfgang von Goethe, who both kept diaries.

Kafka's diaries detail his experience as a German-speaking, middle-class Jewish writer forced to make his living as an insurance agent—a job that he despised—in Prague, a city largely populated by Czech-speaking Christians that was also the site of increasing German nationalism. While Kafka's relationship to his Jewishness has been debated, his diaries do demonstrate his participation in a circle of German-speaking Jewish writers, including Brod, Oskar Baum, and Franz Werfel, as well as his interest in Zionism, Yiddish writers, and Jewish mysticism. He mentions that Eastern Jews are superior to those living in the West and sharply critiques social and intellectual life in Prague in general. Although Kafka was not overtly political, his diaries contains evidence of his disgust with bureaucracy and his fascination with certain anarchist writings, including texts by the Russian communist Peter Kropotkin; the Russian proto-socialist Alexander Herzen; and the founding father of anarchism, Mikhail Bakunin.

In addition to outlining Kafka's family and romantic relationships, the *Diaries* recount his literary musings. He praises Russian novelist Fyodor Dostoyevsky, criticizes Victorian stalwart Charles Dickens, and discusses Swedish playwright August Strindberg and Norwegian luminary Knut Hamsun. He notes similarities between his own ideas and those he has read in the letters of French novelist Gustave Flaubert and comments on Dostoyevsky's letter to his brother from prison and Goethe's diaries. Kafka's *Diaries* did not adhere to diaristic conventions; he often failed to date his entries, wrote them out of order, and sometimes included fiction. In its fragmented, atemporal style and inclusion of sketches, the *Diaries* are reminiscent of those of German modern painter Paul Klee.

The *Diaries* contain early drafts of the first chapter of *Amerika* (1927), early treatments of Kafka's novels *The Castle* (1926) and *The Trial* (1925), and segments of his short story "The Great Wall of China" (1931). Kafka is often extremely critical of his abilities as a writer, frequently noting the seeming futility of his task: "How time flies; another ten days and I have achieved nothing. It doesn't come off. A page now and then is successful, but I can't keep it up." He compares his own observations to those of Goethe, writing, "Read a little [of] Goethe's diaries. Distance already holds this life firm in tranquility, these diaries set fire to it." He also writes both in positive and negative terms of Brod and their friendship.

THEMES AND STYLE

Kafka's *Diaries* deal with many of the same themes as his fiction, including alienation, frustration, indignation, self-loathing, obstacles, and anxiety. He was ruled by feelings of illness and incapacity; he often describes the futility of undertaking any writing project, as when he states that "it is certain that everything I have conceived in advance, even when I was in a good mood, whether word for word or just casually, but in specific words, appears dry, wrong, inflexible, embarrassing to everybody around me, timid, but above all incomplete when I try to write it down at my desk." Additionally, Kafka records his struggles with illness, real and imagined, noting that "it is certain that a major obstacle to my progress is my physical condition. Nothing can be accomplished with such a body. I shall have to get used to its perpetual balking."

Kafka used his *Diaries* to record his observations on daily life and his relationships, as well as to generate ideas for his fiction. He did not follow a strict order; sometimes he began a diary on the last page only to stop halfway through and begin again from the other side. He did take care to date many—but not all—entries. And, while he included fiction and drawings, he did keep a somewhat consistent record of his daily impressions from 1910 to 1923 as an attempt to spark his creative impulses. Kafka also maintained travel diaries, and though his diaries were, for the most part, intended for private use, he shared some of them, including a portion he penned during a trip to the German city of Weimar, with others, most notably Brod. As Kafka wrote to Brod, "As you will see, I faked a little because it was not intended for me alone. I can't help that; at any rate, such faking is not in the least deliberate. Rather, it came from my inmost nature and I really ought to look down there with respect."

The text of the *Diaries* is stylistically similar to much of Kafka's fiction; it is by turns circuitous, surreal, and absurd. He often records his dreams and impressions and their startling imagery. He describes one "apparition" as a "blind or weak-sighted child [who] had both eyes covered by a pair of glasses, the left … was milky-grey and bulbous, the other receded and was covered by a lens … from this lens a little rod descended into the cheek, there disappeared into the pierced flesh and ended on the bone." In his postscript, Brod asserts that he assembled the text of the *Diaries* with the understanding that they were never intended for public view, eliminating "things that were too intimate, as well as scathing criticism of various people that Kafka certainly never intended for the public."

CRITICAL DISCUSSION

Early critics of Kafka's *Diaries* tended to view the text through the lens of his posthumously published novels. Brod published much of Kafka's fiction prior to the first section of the diaries in 1948, and the first volume was published in an English translation by Joseph Kresh. The second section of the diaries followed in 1949, in an English translation by Martin Greenberg and Hannah Arendt. Horace Gregory, writing in a *New York Times* review, noted that "the translation of the second volume of Kafka's *Diaries* is less at odds with the English language than the first, but neither volume is of the quality that has distinguished the fine translations of Kafka into English by Edwin and Willa Muir." In general, however, the critical response was positive, as exemplified by Paul Engle's review in the *Chicago Tribune:* "Above all, there is the same refusal to tell anything less than the entire truth, and most of all to tell the exact truth about himself."

Later scholars focused on comparing other translations of the diary to Brod's 1948 and 1949 translations and tracing the development of Kafka's novels through his daily writings. In particular, critics focused on the appearance in the *Diaries* of Joseph K., the protagonist of *The Trial,* which was written in 1914 and 1915 but remained unpublished until after Kafka's

Photograph from 1995 of a display at a Franz Kafka bookstore in Prague, Czech Republic. © BARRY LEWIS/CORBIS

THE UNPUBLISHED KAFKA

Beginning in late 1917 and ending in June 1919, Franz Kafka stopped keeping his diary in the quarto notebooks from which Max Brod compiled the text of *The Diaries of Franz Kafka*. Instead, he wrote in smaller, octavo-sized notebooks. In these he penned short fictions and literary fragments, which Brod chose not to include in the *Diaries* because he felt they were not "notations of a diary nature." Instead, they were published in English as *The Blue Octavo Notebooks* in 1981, though segments of the notebooks had appeared earlier in *Dearest Father, Stories and Other Writings* (1954).

These notebooks comprise only a fraction of Kafka's unpublished material, most of which has been the subject of legal dispute since Brod's death in 1968. Brod bequeathed Kafka's remaining papers to his secretary, Esther Hoffe. When Hoffe died in 2007, the legality of her will, in which she had left the Kafka material to her elderly daughters, was called into question by the National Library of Israel. In 2012 the Tel Aviv District Court ordered that the papers be turned over to the National Library, entitling the sisters to royalties from any future publication of said papers.

death. Other critics have noted the importance of the *Diaries* to the genre. American essayist Susan Sontag, as quoted by Jerome Maunsell in his essay in *Journal of Modern Literature*, spoke of Kafka as one of "the principal exemplars" of diary writing, noting that his diaries proved to be more of an influence on Sontag's writing than his fiction. Into the twenty-first century, Kafka's *Diaries* continue to be read as revelatory texts on the nature of his creative process and inner life.

More recent scholarship has focused on the *Diaries* as a key to deciphering Kafka's fiction and sexuality, as well as on their description of "minor literatures," as discussed in Gilles Deleuze and Félix Guattari's *Kafka: Toward a Minor Literature* (1986). Scholar Scott Spector, in his book *Prague Territories* (2000), discusses Kafka's diaries as evidence that he "stood at a philosophical moment apart from and yet fused to a lost past and an unresolved historical possibility," the tension of which he tried to resolve through language. Stanley Corngold, in his 2007 essay in *Daedalus*, suggests that Kafka's diary entries demonstrate how the writer offered "his verbal body in place of his actual, unavailable body … writing to erase the text of desire."

BIBLIOGRAPHY

Sources

Brod, Max. "Postscript." *The Diaries of Franz Kafka, 1910–1923*. Ed. Max Brod. Trans. Joseph Kresh, Martin Greenberg, and Hannah Arendt. New York: Schocken, 1964. 489–92. Print.

Corngold, Stanley. "Kafka and Sex." *Daedalus* 136.2 (2007): 79–87. *MIT Press Journals*. Web. 29 Nov. 2012.

Deleuze, Gilles, and Félix Guattari. *Kafka: Toward a Minor Literature*. Trans. Dana Polan. Minneapolis: University of Minnesota Press, 1986. Print.

Engle, Paul. "Kafka's Inner Self Revealed in His Diaries." Rev. of *The Diaries of Franz Kafka, 1914–1923*, by Franz Kafka. *Chicago Daily Tribune* 13 Feb. 1949: 4. *ProQuest Historical Newspapers*. Web. 29 Nov. 2012.

Gregory, Horace. "Kafka's Facts and Fables." Rev. of *The Diaries of Franz Kafka, 1914–1923*, by Franz Kafka. *New York Times* 10 Apr. 1949: 4. *ProQuest Historical Newspapers*. Web. 29 Nov. 2012.

Kafka, Franz. *The Diaries of Franz Kafka, 1910–1923*. Ed. Max Brod and Trans. Joseph Kresh, Martin Greenberg, and Hannah Arendt. New York: Schocken, 1964. Print.

———. *Letters to Friends, Family, and Editors*. Trans. Richard and Clara Winston. New York: Schocken, 1977. Print.

Maunsell, Jerome Boyd. "The Writer's Diary as Device: The Making of Susan Sontag in *Reborn: Early Diaries 1947–1963*." *Journal of Modern Literature* 35.1 (2011): 1–20. *JSTOR*. Web. 29 Nov. 2012.

Spector, Scott. *Prague Territories: National Conflict and Cultural Innovation in Franz Kafka's Fin de Siècle*. Berkeley: University of California Press, 2000. *ProQuest Ebrary*. Web. 29 Nov. 2012.

Further Reading

Bloom, Harold, ed. *Franz Kafka*. Philadelphia: Chelsea House, 2003. Print.

Corngold, Stanley, and Ruth V. Gross, eds. *Kafka for the Twenty-First Century*. New York: Camden House, 2011. Print.

Leavitt, June O. *The Mystical Life of Franz Kafka: Theosophy, Cabala, and the Modern Spiritual Revival*. New York: Oxford University Press, 2012. Print.

Robertson, Ritchie. *Kafka: A Very Short Introduction*. Oxford: Oxford University Press, 2004. Print.

Wilke, Sabine, ed. *From Kafka to Sebald: Modernism and Narrative Form*. New York: Continuum, 2012. Print.

Kristen Gleason

The Diary of Anaïs Nin
Anaïs Nin

OVERVIEW

The Diary of Anaïs Nin presents the evolution of an artistic female self in the twentieth century. The French-born author began her diaries at age eleven and kept them throughout her life. In 1966 she began publishing a series of six volumes, distilled from many more written texts, covering the years from 1931 to 1966. After her death, an additional four volumes detailing her early years were published. Following the death of her first husband, Hugh Parker Guiler, whose existence had been edited out of the first series, Anaïs Nin's literary executor published three new volumes that included explicit sexual material. All of the diaries contain vivid descriptions of the places and people Nin loved, as well as introspective musings on her journey as a woman and a writer.

Multilingual and tri-national, Nin initially wrote her journals in French but adopted English after a few years, coming of age as modernism dominated the artistic world. Her first publication was a study of writer D. H. Lawrence, whose frankly sexual novels had been subject to censorship. Moving to France in the 1930s, Nin found a place among the avant-garde but, upon returning to the United States, had difficulties achieving recognition until the first volume of her journals was published in 1966. *The Diary of Anaïs Nin* was praised for its poetic language and for its insight into the artist's struggle as a female. The early feminist movement embraced Nin as a liberating role model, but a more critical attitude prevailed upon the later release of her unexpurgated diaries.

HISTORICAL AND LITERARY CONTEXT

From her childhood through the 1930s, Nin lived in both New York and Paris, centers of modernist experimentation. Psychology was then a developing science, and Nin's psychoanalyst, Otto Rank, was an estranged disciple of Sigmund Freud. World War II raged during the years covered in her second and third volumes. Although she offers some description of politically active friends, she rejects Marxism, believing that psychology best explains humanity's ills.

Nin began journaling in 1914, when she sailed with her Cuban-born mother and brothers to the United States from a Europe about to erupt into war. The longing for connection and integration would contribute to her obsessive diary writing, which was in full force when the published diaries began in 1931. At that time, she was living in France amid a vibrant world of artists and writers. After Nin returned to the United States, during the war, she focused on trying to get her avant-garde writing published. The volumes take the reader to their moment of publication in 1966, when Nin finally achieves the fame she has craved. The public's interest in the diaries was piqued by her detailed depictions of her intimates: Rank, novelists Henry Miller and Lawrence Durrell, poet Robert Duncan, and other notable figures of the time.

The diaries establish Nin as part of the conversation of literary modernism. Against the backdrop of highly crafted, difficult works of literature, numerous writers of the period, including H.D. (Hilda Doolittle) and Dorothy Richardson, were publishing thinly disguised autobiographical fiction. One of the period's preeminent novelists, Virginia Woolf, wrote extensive diaries that began in 1915. Miller's 1934 novel, *Tropic of Cancer*—which was so sexually explicit that it was banned in the United States until 1964—combined autobiography and fiction. Some events from Nin's diary made their way into Miller's novels. Nin also provided financial support and editorial assistance for Miller's writing, and he is an important figure in her diary.

Nin's diaries were consequential even before they were published, because she shared them with writer friends, including Miller, who wrote an essay about them. Her friendship with Duncan in the 1940s inspired his use of a journal, contributing to his success as a poet. In 1966—the same year Nin's journals were first published—Jungian psychologist Ira Progoff developed a therapeutic use for journals. Although Nin felt his Intensive Journal Method was too restrictive for her, she endorsed it for others. The continuing fascination with self-exploration through writing can be seen in today's proliferation of web diaries and blogs and the passion for memoirs. The popularity of "mommy porn" such as *Fifty Shades of Grey* can also be considered descendants from Nin's unedited diaries and erotica writings.

THEMES AND STYLE

Nin's initial motivation for journaling was to connect with her abandoning, abusive father. Her diaries then became the site where she wrote herself into existence. She notes in 1931, "I am possessed by a fever

Key Facts

Time Period:
Mid-20th Century

Relevant Historical Events:
Development of modernism; development of feminism; World War II

Nationality:
American/French/Cuban

Keywords:
modernism; feminism; psychoanalysis

Anaïs Nin, whose journals and other writings were among the first published erotic literature by an American woman. © EVERETT COLLECTION INC/ALAMY

for knowledge, experience, creation…. But it is also true that when I write afterwards, I see much more, I understand better, I develop and enrich." She sought beauty and heightened experiences of love, becoming fascinated with others (mostly men, though Miller's wife, June, was also an obsession) and describing them in detail, including pages of reconstructed dialogue and lengthy letters. With and against other artists, she defined her own aesthetic, traced her artistic development, and presented herself as the nurturing mother of artists.

Nin's journal writing eventually "held [her] body and soul together, held together all of [her] many selves." Writing at night, by hand, carrying the current diary with her at all times, she wrote continuously for self-discovery and to create her place in modern literature. Publishing the work broadened her field of admirers, and Nin edited the text to further mythologize and romanticize herself. She includes letters that reflect her desired image, such as a note from Miller telling her that at a concert he "was dazzled by [her] beauty" because she looked like the "Infanta of Spain." The letter also quoted a friend amazed that such a beautiful woman could have written a book on Lawrence.

Such observations confirmed her protean personality: she wanted to prove herself on all battlefields.

Nin's published diaries were carefully shaped from the more than 15,000 handwritten (and possibly as many as 35,000) pages she had composed during her life. The inclusion of dialogue and letters helped create a sense of direction, of movement through relationships on the way to self-realization and recognition as an author. She writes, "The hero of this book may be the soul, but it is an odyssey from the inner to the outer world, and it is Henry [Miller] who is dispelling the fogs of shyness, of solitude, taking me through the streets, and keeping me in a café—until dawn." The mundane details of life are rarely included; the majority of the writing is full of poetic language and emotional intensity: "Ordinary life does not interest me. I seek only the high moments. I am in accord with the surrealists, searching for the marvelous."

CRITICAL DISCUSSION

References to Nin's diaries by those who had read them privately aroused curiosity, and the public embraced them when they were first published. The first and most enthusiastic report of the work appeared in a 1939 essay by Miller, who described the diary as "a mythological voyage towards the source and fountain head of life." For Miller, notebooks and diaries provided a more direct contact with personality than literary forms, though he goes on to admit that they only provide illusions of truth.

When the first series of diaries was published in the 1960s and 1970s, critics embraced them for their depiction of a passionate, artistic life. Some feminist critics thought that Nin's fluid writing style illustrated *écriture féminine* (French feminist Hélène Cixous's term for a writing style emerging from the female body). From the perspective of the 1990s, Lynette Felber writes in her essay for *Tulsa Studies in Women's Literature* that associating Nin's diaries with this feminine writing was "astute merchandising" but has since led to marginalization of her work. Critic and poet Katha Pollitt is representative of contemporary feminism, which rejects essentialism (and *écriture féminine*). Never a fan of Nin's "staggering self-absorption," Pollitt, in a review of *Incest,* a volume containing previously unpublished material from Nin's diaries, expresses anger at the revelation that Nin's stillbirth, which became the story "Birth," was really an abortion. Pollitt argues that sharing the truth at the time, when abortion was illegal, would have been brave and useful. The sexual relationship Nin describes having with her father when she is thirty is less of a concern to Pollitt, though most readers experience some shock at the revelation.

As literary interest in Nin fades, attention has arisen from another direction. In her study on Nin for *Personality and Individual Differences,* psychologist Angie Kehagia interprets the diaries to diagnose the author as suffering from histrionic personality disorder. Kehagia argues that this psychopathology shaped Nin's writing, and the diary "became her ultimate instrument of dissociation, through which she reconstructed her reality, shielded herself from painful memories of paternal abuse and rejection and created a self-image that enabled her to live with her intense insecurities and fears of abandonment."

BIBLIOGRAPHY

Sources

Felber, Lynette. "The Three Faces of June: Anaïs Nin's Appropriation of Feminine Writing." *Tulsa Studies in Women's Literature.* 14.2 (1995): 309–24. *Literature Criticism Online.* Web. 14 Dec. 2012.

Kehagia, Angie A. "Anaïs Nin: A Case Study of Personality Disorder and Creativity." *Personality and Individual Differences* 46 (2009) 800–08. *ProQuest Central.* Web. 12 Dec. 2012.

Miller, Henry. "Un Etre Etoilique." *Criterion* 1937. Rpt. in *Twentieth-Century Literary Criticism.* Vol. 224. Detroit: Gale Research, 2009. *Literature Criticism Online.* Web. 14 Dec. 2012.

Nin, Anaïs. *The Diary of Anaïs Nin, 1931–1934.* Ed. Gunther Stuhlmann. New York: Swallow, 1966. Print.

Pollitt, Katha. "Sins of the Nins." *New York Times.* New York Times, 22 Nov. 1992. Web. 13 Dec. 2012.

Further Reading

Bair, Deidre. *Anais Nin: A Biography.* New York: Putnam, 1995. Print.

Herron, Paul. *A Cafe in Space: The Anaïs Nin Literary Journal.* Vol. 9. Troy, Mich.: Sky Blue, 2012. Print.

Jason, Philip K. *Anaïs Nin and Her Critics.* Columbia, S.C.: Camden House, 1993. Print.

Nalbantian, Suzanne. *Aesthetic Autobiography: From Life to Art in Marcel Proust, James Joyce, Virginia Woolf and Anais Nin.* Basingstoke: Macmillan, 1994. Print.

Nin, Anaïs. *Delta of Venus: Erotica by Anaïs Nin.* New York: Harcourt, Brace, Jovanovich, 1969. Print.

———. *Henry & June: From the Unexpurgated Diary of Anaïs Nin.* San Diego: Harcourt, Brace, Jovanovich, 1986. Print.

———. *Incest: From "A Journal of Love."* New York: Harcourt, Brace, Jovanovich, 1992. Print.

Pineau, Elyse Lamm. "A Mirror of Her Own: Anaïs Nin's Autobiographical Performances." *Text and Performance Quarterly* 12.2 (1992): 97–112. Print.

Podnieks, Elizabeth. *Daily Modernism: The Literary Diaries of Virginia Woolf, Antonia White, Elizabeth Smart, and Anaïs Nin.* Montreal: McGill-Queen's University Press, 2000. Print.

Progoff, Ira. *At a Journal Workshop: Writing to Access the Power of the Unconscious and Evoke Creative Ability.* New York: Penguin/Putnam, 1975, 1992. Print.

Scholes, Robert. "The Monstrous Personal Chronicles of the Thirties." *Novel* 31.3 (1998): 414–29. *ProQuest Central.* Web. 12 Dec. 2012.

Tookey, Helen. *Anaïs Nin, Fictionality and Femininity: Playing a Thousand Roles.* Oxford: Oxford University Press, 2003. Print.

Robin Morris

PRIMARY SOURCE

EXCERPT FROM *DIARY OF ANAÏS NIN*

Am I, at bottom, that fervent little Spanish Catholic child who chastised herself for loving toys, who forbade herself the enjoyment of sweet foods, who practiced silence, who humiliated her pride, who adored symbols, statues, burning candles, incense, the caress of nuns, organ music, for whom Communion was a great event? I was so exalted by the idea of eating Jesus's flesh and drinking His blood that I couldn't swallow the host well, and I dreaded harming it. I visualized Christ descending into my heart so realistically (I was a realist then!) that I could see Him walking down the stairs and entering the room of my heart like a sacred Visitor. That state of this room was a subject of great preoccupation for me. I fancied that if I had not been good, this room would appear ugly in the eyes of Christ; I fancied He could see as soon as he entered whether it was clear, empty, luminous, or cluttered, dark, chaotic. At that age, nine, ten, eleven, I believe I approximated sainthood. And then, at sixteen, resentful of controls, disillusioned with a God who had not granted my prayers (the return of my father), who performed no miracles, who left me fatherless in a strange country, I rejected all Catholicism with exaggeration. Goodness, virtue, charity, submission, stifled me. I took up the words of [D. H.] Lawrence: "They stress only pain, sacrifice, suffering and death. They do not dwell enough on the resurrection, on joy and life in the present."

Today I feel my past like an unbearable weight, I feel that it interferes with my present life, that it must be the cause for this withdrawal, this closing of doors.

Until now, I had the feeling of being anew, with all the hopes and freshness and freedom which erases the past mysteries and restrictions. What has happened?

And what sorrow, and coldness. I feel as if I carried inscribed over me: my past killed me.

I am embalmed because a nun leaned over me, enveloped me in her veils, kissed me. The chill curse of Christianity. I do not confess any more, I have no remorse, yet am I doing penance for my enjoyments? Nobody knows what a magnificent prey I was for Christian legends, because of my compassion and my tenderness for human beings. Today it divides me from enjoyment in life.

SOURCE: Nin, Anaïs. *The Diary of Anaïs Nin, 1931–1934.* Orlando: Harcourt Inc., 1969 by the Anaïs Nin Trust. All rights reserved. Reproduced by permission.

Estrangement, Being Some Fifty Extracts from a Diary Kept in 1909

William Butler Yeats

Key Facts

Time Period:
Early 20th Century

Relevant Historical Events:
British rule of Ireland; Yeats's early success as a playwright

Nationality:
Irish

Keywords:
literature; creativity; playwriting

OVERVIEW

Estrangement, Being Some Fifty Extracts from a Diary Kept in 1909 is composed of fifty-five of poet William Butler Yeats's (1865–1939) earliest journal entries, collected and modified for publication in 1926, almost twenty years after they were written. Selected by the author from more than one hundred journal entries within the brief period (January 14–March 12, 1909), the nearly twenty-five pages offer glimpses into his early autobiographical writing. Although printed in several editions, *Estrangement* appears in its most definitive selection in *The Collected Works of W. B. Yeats, Volume III: Autobiographies* (1999), which uses slight variations of the 1932 proofs approved by the author and his wife, Georgie Hyde-Lees, and later edited by Yeats's trusted Macmillan editor, Thomas Mark. For *Estrangement,* Yeats selected journal entries written in 1909 that are largely disconnected meditations on biographical events from a period of transition. The journal entries include candid ruminations on wide-ranging subjects, from ideological alienation in Ireland to playwriting.

Cuala Press, a private press owned by Yeats's sister Elizabeth, published *Estrangement* in 1926, thirteen years before his death. This selection of journal entries followed the publication of his autobiographical works *Reveries over Childhood and Youth* (1914), *The Trembling of the Veil* (1922), and *The Bounty of Sweden* (1925). *The Death of Synge* and *Dramatis Personae: 1896–1902* (also collections of journal entries) followed *Estrangement* in 1928 and 1935, respectively. *Estrangement* continues to be the subject of some attention from Yeats scholars and biographers interested in his early autobiographical endeavors, though mostly as a comparison to his later autobiographies. On the whole, these entries have leveled off in critical attention, with the entirety of Yeats's autobiographical collection in sharper focus. However, they have endured as important textual artifacts of this period of his life.

HISTORICAL AND LITERARY CONTEXT

Born in Ireland, Yeats was an Anglo-Irish Protestant who lived in London for many of his formative years. In the late Victorian period in Europe, journal writing was a popular custom in well-educated households such as Yeats's. However, his engagement in the form of autobiography pushed against the Tennysonian Victorian literary principles that held that poets' personal lives should be private. The period of active political and religious tensions between the Protestant upper-class minority and the lower-class majority of Catholics in Ireland served as a constant source of meditation in his journals and in his poetry, plays, and essays. Although he grew up in an Anglo-Protestant family, he was inspired by Irish patriots and was tenaciously devoted to Irish folklore and legend.

In *Estrangement,* he describes and reflects on several interactions with notable literary and political figures in Ireland, including Ireland's chief secretary Augustine Birrell, Irish nationalist writer George Russell, and playwrights Lady Gregory and John Millington Synge. As he was writing these journal entries, he became highly involved in writing plays while managing Dublin's Abbey Theatre. Much of his journaling centers on Irish drama in Dublin and includes anecdotes about attending plays that he himself wrote and produced, often focused on resolute characters devoted to Irish nationalism.

Yeats records some anecdotes from his daily life in *Estrangement,* but the majority of the entries consist of reflections on literary and philosophical ideas about the state of Irish culture. *Estrangement* journal entries eschew many linear conventions of the time, but their occasional grounding in narrative provides some structural equilibrium for the selection. The traditional style of journaling in *Estrangement* gives way to autobiography that is more cohesive and composed in form. Poet Ezra Pound encouraged Yeats to explore the process of fictional autobiographical recording used by Irish writer James Joyce in *Portrait of the Artist as a Young Man* (1916). Joyce's autobiographical novel is more stylistically similar to Yeats's later autobiography, and both chronicle earlier periods in the writers' lives, including their childhood experiences.

Estrangement is particularly notable for the impact it had on Yeats's work, serving as a traditional form of memoir for the author to later depart from. He wrote many of the journal entries while he was composing some of his more linear dramas, such as *Cathleen Ni Houlihan* (1902), *Deirdre* (1907), and *The Unicorn from the Stars* (1908), during a time when plot-driven narratives were exalted. He went on to write autobiography with a much more unified experiential and modern sensibility. Written after—though published before—*Estrangement*, Yeats's *Reveries over Childhood and Youth* is cited by many critics as an example of a departure from traditional autobiographic journal style, providing more-disjointed, though more aesthetically polished, views of his childhood.

THEMES AND STYLE

Estrangement focuses on themes that were relevant to this period in his life and writing career, including his growing distaste for the thoughtless rhetoric of Irish nationalism, tension between "philosophical idea" and "spiritual experience," and romantic love. He repeatedly expresses his struggle with the existence of an ideology blindly accepted by a majority of Irish citizens. He reflects on frequent exchanges with people who had "every thought made in some manufactory and with the mark upon it of its wholesale origins—thoughts never really thought out in their current form in any individual mind." Much of his ruminations linger on spirituality set against ignorant acceptance of religion. At the time, he was also managing his ultimately disheartening relationship with his longtime love interest, Irish nationalist playwright Maud Gonne. Although he does not directly address ongoing or past romantic relationships, he often revisits the theme of love, including a passage that consists entirely of a quote from his father explaining that a man does not love a woman because he admires her but because "he likes the way she has of scratching her head."

Less linear than traditional journals of the Victorian period, Yeats's journal entries document his state of mind and reflect on the nature of art and theology rather than record the events of everyday life. The entry that introduces the collection announces his intentions for the journal: "To keep these notes natural and useful to me I must keep one note from leading on to another, that I may not surrender myself to literature. Every note must be a casual thought, then it will be my life." He uses this opening to guide his journal writing and adheres to its meditative contract. While he never identifies an audience other than himself, his involvement in selecting and publishing the material suggests consideration of readership, at least in the editing process.

The *Estrangement* journal selection develops tightly rendered philosophical thought through a candid, conversational tone. Often the entries begin anecdotally, referring to a meeting with a fellow writer or public figure in Dublin, for instance, before delving further into an analysis of the conversation or even a single comment. Following his guiding opening statement, the entries consist of disparate notes that range from circuitous thoughts on tragedy and comedy to short aphoristic entries ("Nobody running at full speed has either head or heart"). His language also fluctuates from richly poetic ("The soul of Ireland has become a vapor and her body a stone") to highly abstract philosophical meanderings.

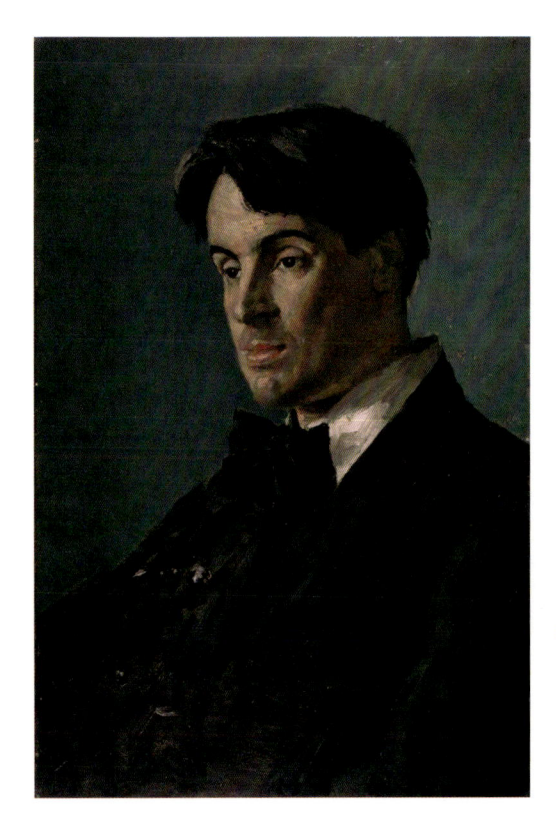

Portrait of William Butler Yeats painted by Augustus Edwin John in 1907. © MANCHESTER ART GALLERY, UK/THE BRIDGEMAN ART LIBRARY

CRITICAL DISCUSSION

The majority of critical responses to Yeats's autobiographical work focus on the collection as a whole or on individual works that were more fully realized, such as *Reveries over Childhood and Youth* and *The Trembling of the Veil*. Little critical attention was paid to the brief diary entries contained in *Estrangement* upon its publication. In a vein typical of scholarship at the time, a 1927 review in *Overland Monthly and Out West Magazine* remarks, "While the autobiographies do not necessarily remain a cemented document of vivid importance to the age, they are finely chiseled examples of a life and people many remember, daintily misted at times with the dull polish of excellent fiction."

When addressing *Estrangement* as part of Yeats's collection of memoirs, twentieth-century critics often remark on the selection's amorphous and aphoristic style. The journal selections contained in *Estrangement* are often grouped by critics and reviewers with the selection published two years later, *The Death of Synge*. Yeats compiled both sections of *Autobiographies* from a similar diary, and the selections share not only temporal proximity but stylistic compatibility as well. There is some debate among scholars as to the merits of *The Autobiography of William Butler Yeats* (1938),

THE ABBEY THEATRE

The Abbey Theatre was founded in the latter part of 1904 upon the insistence of W. B. Yeats and Lady Gregory, and with the financial support of Annie Horniman, a native of Manchester who stood firmly against Irish nationalism. The presence of the Abbey Theatre allowed, for the first time, the emergence of serious Irish drama. Horniman would eventually disassociate with the theater as it came to house productions by some of the most prominent Irish nationalist playwrights of the time, including George Russell (who wrote under the pseudonym AE), Edward Martyn, and a young George Bernard Shaw. Many of those involved in the Abbey Theatre were members of the recently founded Irish National Theatre Society, which consisted of groups of talented amateur Irish actors assembled by brothers Willie and Frank Fay.

In 1907 John Millington Synge's production of *The Playboy of the Western World,* a play that was deemed as disparaging of the virtue of Irish womanhood, caused a near riot in the Abbey Theatre, with viewers still tender from Synge's comparable offense in *In the Shadow of the Glen* (1903). Yeats held a debate on the value of artistic freedom at the theater shortly after, which led to similar eruptions. Later known as the National Theatre of Ireland, the venue saw fewer monumental works after its early productive and tumultuous years.

which excludes the *Estrangement* selection and other less highly regarded essays, versus *Autobiographies* (1999). Scholars in favor of the former find the polished selectivity of the shorter version more literary and authoritative, while scholars in favor of the latter point to the more formless inclusions as Yeats's argument for contrasting modes of self-expression and disunity.

Current critical analysis often casts *Estrangement* as malformed half-thoughts on art that consistently lean toward aphorism. Most consider this selection of journals only narrowly autobiographical and less complete than much of the rest of *Autobiographies*. Some critics focus on the allegorical and inventive aspects of Yeats's autobiographical writing, as David Herman (1995) does in the *British Journal of Aesthetics,* arguing that one of the purposes of Yeats's autobiography is "to make us re-evaluate the possibilities and limits of strategies for creating a self." Regardless, critics recognize the importance of the period of Yeats's life documented in *Estrangement,* in which he was, as Daniel O'Hara (1977) puts it in *Boundary 2,* "in the midst of a crisis of bitter disappointment and growing alienation." There continues to be a great deal of scholarship on *Autobiographies* as a whole and lasting interest in the life of this monumental poet.

BIBLIOGRAPHY

Sources

"Autobiography of William Butler Yeats." *Overland Monthly and Out West Magazine* June 1927: 183. *American Periodicals.* Web. 13 Dec. 2012.

Brown, Terence. *The Life of W. B. Yeats.* Oxford: Blackwell, 1999. Print.

Herman, David. "Autobiography, Allegory, and the Construction of Self." *British Journal of Aesthetics* 35.4 (1995): 351–60. *Literature Resource Center.* Web. 11 Dec. 2012.

O'Hara, Daniel. "The Irony of Tradition and W. B. Yeats's Autobiography: An Essay in Dialectical Hermeneutics." *Boundary 2* 5.3 (1977): 679–710. Print.

Yeats, W. B. "Estrangement: Extracts from a Diary Kept in 1909." *The Collected Works of W. B. Yeats, Volume III: Autobiographies.* Ed. Douglas N. Archibald and William H. O'Donnell. New York: Macmillan, 1999. 339–66. Print

Further Reading

Alexander, Neal. "Dialogues of Self and Soul: The Autobiographies of W. B. Yeats and R. S. Thomas." *Almanac: A Yearbook of Welsh Writing in English* 12 (2007): 1–31. Print.

Bruś, Teresa. "Louis MacNeice and W. B. Yeats Autobiographically." *The Playful Air of Light(ness) in Irish Literature and Culture.* Newcastle upon Tyne: Cambridge Scholars, 2011. 141–50. Print.

Fletcher, Ian. "Rhythm and Pattern in Autobiographies." *An Honoured Guest: New Essays on W. B. Yeats.* London: Arnold, 1965. 165–89. Print.

Greaves, Richard. *Transition, Reception and Modernism in W. B. Yeats.* Basingstoke: Palgrave Macmillan, 2001. Print.

Johnston, Dillon. "The Perpetual Self of Yeats's Autobiographies." *Éire-Ireland* 9.4 (1974): 69–85. Print.

Olney, James. "The Uses of Comedy and Irony in *Autobiographies* and *Autobiography.*" *Yeats: An Annual of Critical and Textual Studies* 2 (1984): 195–208. Print.

Peterson, Robert C. "Yeats the Autobiographer: Dialogue of Self and Soul." *English Literature in Transition, 1880–1920* 26.2 (1983): 143–44. Print.

Tony Ruzicka

The Habit of Being
Letters of Flannery O'Connor
Flannery O'Connor

OVERVIEW

Published posthumously in 1979, *The Habit of Being: Letters of Flannery O'Connor* is a lengthy compilation of letters written by Flannery O'Connor throughout her life. Selected and edited by her friend Sally Fitzgerald, the correspondence included in the volume spans the entirety of O'Connor's professional life as a writer, beginning in 1948 with a letter she wrote to her future literary agent while staying at the Yaddo artists' colony and continuing through 1964, the year of her death. Her correspondence to friends, colleagues, and professional acquaintances touches upon a wide variety of subjects, including the author's literary work, her life on her mother's farm in rural Georgia, and her deeply held Catholic convictions. The letters—one of her most important means of keeping in touch with the outside world following her confinement at home after she was stricken with lupus—shed considerable light on O'Connor's life and work, as well as on her own feelings about both.

Although a small amount of O'Connor's correspondence had previously appeared in print, the appearance of *The Habit of Being* was a watershed moment within her posthumous bibliography, unearthing hundreds of previously unseen documents. The book was received with great interest among devotees and scholars of her work, and the intimacy, warmth, and playfulness the author exhibits in many of the letters did much to dispel the widespread public perception of her as reclusive and bad-tempered. O'Connor's frequent statements about her own work in her correspondence has led to the book's frequent citation in critical analysis of her fiction, and the collection contributed significantly to her subsequent literary legacy.

HISTORICAL AND LITERARY CONTEXT

The letters assembled in *The Habit of Being* reflect O'Connor's mid-twentieth-century milieu in the southern United States, though her own viewpoint is frequently shown to be at odds with her surroundings. The pervasive influence of Christianity on the ontological character of the rural South is observable in O'Connor's consistent preoccupation with religious issues throughout the letters, though her deeply held orthodox Catholicism stood in sharp contrast to the prevailing Protestant religious climate. Likewise, the escalating racial tensions of the era often come out in O'Connor's remarks, especially in some of her playfully antagonistic correspondence with her friend Maryat Lee, who was much more liberal and more of an activist on the subject of civil rights than the relatively conservative O'Connor. Fitzgerald omitted many of these letters, however, and only alludes to them in her editorial comments.

O'Connor's letters document her correspondence with many significant figures in the U.S. literary world. Included are many letters to longtime friends, such as the celebrated translator and poet Robert Fitzgerald (then the husband of Sally) and the poet Robert Lowell, whom O'Connor befriended at the Yaddo artists' colony. Also present is the author's correspondence with notable literary figures with whom she became acquainted as her own work gained renown, including authors Elizabeth Bishop and Walker Percy.

Many of the letters in *The Habit of Being* are situated within the larger literary conversation of the mid-twentieth-century United States. O'Connor frequently references the literature—both classic and contemporary—that she has been reading or thinking about, commenting on authors as varied as Wyndham Lewis, Ayn Rand, and Vladimir Nabokov; these remarks stand as a counterpart to the numerous book reviews (collected in the 1983 volume *The Presence of Grace*) O'Connor wrote for Catholic diocesan newspapers. The letters are also a manifestation of the author's direct participation in a tradition of literary mentorship: many either respond to or solicit writing advice from other authors—particularly Caroline Gordon—or else proffer O'Connor's own advice to other writers.

In the years since its publication, *The Habit of Being* has attracted particular interest for the insight it gives into the author's thoughts on her fiction, especially in light of the relative scarcity of public statements by O'Connor on her own work. Despite her frequent reluctance to provide readers with interpretations of her stories, as well as her belief that literature should be considered independently of its author, her letters nonetheless contain

❖ *Key Facts*

Time Period:
Mid-20th Century

Relevant Historical Events:
O'Connor's success as a writer, battle with lupus, and confinement at home

Nationality:
American

Keywords:
lupus; Catholicism; literature

LITERARY LIVES

Andalusia Farm in Milledgeville, Georgia, April 25, 2007. Flannery O'Connor moved to the farm upon being diagnosed with lupus in 1951, writing some of her best works while in residence. © ZUMA WIRE SERVICE/ALAMY

numerous comments in which she discloses her literary intentions, as when she says of "A Good Man Is Hard to Find" that "the story is a duel of sorts between the Grandmother and her superficial beliefs and the Misfit's more profoundly felt involvement with Christ's action which set the world off balance for him." These remarks remain widely consulted and cited in contemporary analysis of O'Connor's fiction.

THEMES AND STYLE

A principal theme of *The Habit of Being* is the extent to which her literary endeavors were informed by her Catholic faith. O'Connor considered her Catholicism to be an indispensable element of her writing, asserting in one letter that "I write the way I do because and only because I am a Catholic. I feel that if I were not a Catholic, I would have no reason to write, no reason to see, no reason ever to feel horrified or even to enjoy anything." She refers to noteworthy Catholic writers such as Graham Greene and François Mauriac at least as often as she refers to the southern authors with whom she is more often compared, and her letters frequently express annoyance at her readers' failure to grasp the Catholic underpinnings of her work: "Many of my ardent admirers would be roundly shocked and disturbed if they realized that everything I believe is thoroughly moral, thoroughly Catholic, and that it is these beliefs that give my work its chief characteristics."

The letters collected in *The Habit of Being* were written for a wide variety of purposes, from straightforward professional communication to friendly correspondence. Many reveal details of O'Connor's publishing travails, as when she writes to her agent, "I presume [Rinehart editor John] Selby says either that Rinehart will not take the novel as it will be if left to my fiendish care … or that Rinehart would like to rescue it at this point and train it into a conventional novel." Most of the letters are more socially motivated, however, representing an indispensable aspect of O'Connor's social life after her ability to travel was curtailed by her illness. The importance of letters as a method of meaningful communication for the author is demonstrated by her eager response to a letter from Elizabeth Hester (referred to as "A" by Fitzgerald to protect her identity), with whom O'Connor would later have lengthy exchanges about religious matters: "You were very kind to write me and the measure of my appreciation must be to ask you to write me again. I would like to know who this is who understands my stories."

The tone of the letters is generally casual and upbeat. They are frequently unconcerned with political correctness, occasionally supercilious, and often mordantly humorous. Exchanges with friends tend to be warm and polite, though they are also frank and peppered with wry remarks, as when she comments on Hester's reaction to her fame: "If the fact that I am a 'celebrity' makes you feel silly, what dear girl do you think it makes me feel? It's a comic distinction shared with Roy Rogers's horse and Miss Watermelon of 1955. In a great many ways it makes things difficult, for the only friends you can have are old friends or new ones who are willing to ignore it. I am very thankful that you are willing to ignore it." Other remarks are less sanguine, particularly those referring to people she believes have grossly misinterpreted her work, but are often still touched with humor.

CRITICAL DISCUSSION

The Habit of Being was generally well reviewed upon its publication in 1979, with critics praising its wit and intellectual acumen, along with the insight it provided into the life of its author. Richard Gilman, writing in the *New York Times Book Review,* asserted that "to compare her with the great letter writers in our language may seem presumptuous … but Byron, Keats, Lawrence, Wilde and Joyce come irresistibly to mind: correspondence that gleams with consciousness." Gilman, like many other reviewers, went on to laud the book as a window into the author's mind, stating that the letters "are dispatches from a life and serve to construe it to those out of earshot. She never gives the impression of writing anything 'strategic,' or, indeed, of presenting herself as anything more or less than she was."

In the decades since its initial appearance, *The Habit of Being* has contributed significantly to public knowledge about O'Connor's life and helped to consolidate her literary legacy, despite a growing awareness of the limitations imposed by Fitzgerald's occasionally sanitizing editing work. Jean W. Cash observes in her 2002 biography of O'Connor that "it was not … until … *The Habit of Being* appeared in 1979 that the full range of O'Connor's personal sense of humor became apparent. Readers of her fiction alone might label O'Connor a dour religious fanatic whose only pleasure evolved from her treatment of spiritual themes." Much remained undisclosed due to Fitzgerald's various omissions, however. Cash and other scholars have made ample and revelatory use of letters omitted by Fitzgerald and made available in the years after the publication of *The Habit of Being,* but the book nonetheless remains a standard reference.

Much recent scholarship on *The Habit of Being* has focused on the vagaries of Fitzgerald's editing of the material. Gretchen Dobrott Bernard, writing in *Atlantis* in 2004, comments on O'Connor's epistolary relationships with Hester and Lee, observing of the latter correspondence that "by omitting many of these friends' exchanges from *The Habit of Being,* Fitzgerald achieved two things: an unbalanced representation of O'Connor, and the consequent awakening of scholars' curiosity as to why she might have made this choice." Robert McGill's 2004 article in *Southern Literary Journal* likewise scrutinizes Fitzgerald's decisions in the course of an analysis of the book as a sort of makeshift autobiography: "The sum effect of such an epistolary collection's abridgements and editing is to reify a chaotic and disparate range of communications into a single, homogeneous text under the auspices of a single authorial Name."

MYSTERY AND MANNERS: OCCASIONAL PROSE

The Habit of Being was the second of three posthumously published volumes of Flannery O'Connor's work that were edited by her longtime friend Sally Fitzgerald. The first of these books, 1969's *Mystery and Manners* (coedited with Robert Fitzgerald), brings together an assortment of nonfiction essays O'Connor left behind, some of them previously unpublished and many of them originating as typescripts for lectures she delivered on various occasions. The book stands as an important resource for O'Connor's only public writings (apart from her book reviews, of which only a brief sampling is included) on the nature of literature and the process of writing, as well as for her only public written remarks about her own life and work.

Most of the essays in *Mystery and Manners* are concerned with literary matters, focusing variously on Catholic writing, regional writing, and literary pedagogy, as well as more generally on the function and creation of fiction. Also present but much less plentiful are a number of statements addressing O'Connor's own writing. Least typical of the collection is "The King of the Birds," an account of the author's experiences raising peacocks, which is notable for being perhaps the only piece of writing about her own life that she intended for publication, though it discusses peacocks far more than it does O'Connor herself.

BIBLIOGRAPHY

Sources

Bernard, Gretchen Dobrott. "Flannery O'Connor's Written Correspondence: An Inside Glimpse at the Forging of Art and Persona." *Atlantis* 26.2 (2004): 25–33. *JSTOR.* Web. 5 Dec. 2012.

Cash, Jean W. *Flannery O'Connor: A Life.* Knoxville: University of Tennessee Press, 2002. Print.

Gilman, Richard. "A Life of Letters." Rev. of *The Habit of Being,* by Flannery O'Connor. *New York Times Book Review* 18 Mar. 1979: 1+. *ProQuest Historical Newspapers: New York Times (1851–2009).* Web. 5 Dec. 2012.

McGill, Robert. "The Life You Write May Be Your Own: Epistolary Autobiography and the Reluctant Resurrection of Flannery O'Connor." *Southern Literary Journal* 36.2 (2004): 31–46. *Academic Search Complete.* Web. 5 Dec. 2012.

O'Connor, Flannery. *The Habit of Being: Letters of Flannery O'Connor.* Ed. Sally Fitzgerald. New York: Farrar, Straus & Giroux, 1979. Print.

Further Reading

Ficken, Carl. "Theology in Flannery O'Connor's *The Habit of Being.*" *Christianity and Literature* 30.2 (1981): 51–63. Print.

Gooch, Brad. *Flannery: A Life of Flannery O'Connor.* New York: Little, Brown, 2009. Print.

Gordon, Sarah. "Maryat and Julian and the 'Not So Bloodless Revolution.'" *Flannery O'Connor Bulletin* 21 (1992): 25–36. Print.

Nichols, Loxley F. "Flannery O'Connor's 'Intellectual Vaudeville': Masks of Mother and Daughter." *Studies in the Literary Imagination* 20.2 (1987): 15–29. Print.

O'Connor, Flannery. *Mystery and Manners: Occasional Prose.* Ed. Sally and Robert Fitzgerald. New York: Farrar, Straus & Giroux, 1969. Print.

———. *The Presence of Grace and Other Book Reviews.* Comp. Leo J. Zuber. Ed. Carter W. Martin. Athens: University of Georgia Press, 1983. Print.

———. *Collected Works.* Ed. Sally Fitzgerald. New York: Library of America, 1988. Print.

Robillard, Douglas, ed. *The Critical Response to Flannery O'Connor.* Westport: Praeger, 2004. Print.

Wood, Ralph C. *Flannery O'Connor and the Christ-Haunted South.* Grand Rapids, Mich.: William B. Eerdmans, 2004. Print.

James Overholtzer

Journal of Katherine Mansfield
Katherine Mansfield

OVERVIEW

Journal of Katherine Mansfield spans the New Zealand writer's later years, from 1914 to 1922, and quickly became a best seller upon its publication in 1927. Although structured as a journal, the book actually brings together Katherine Mansfield's dispersed writings from numerous notebooks and loose scraps of paper, presenting them in chronological order in a way that resembles diary entries. The journal covers the years when Mansfield suffered most from tuberculosis, chronicling her declining health while also reflecting on the process of writing. In addition, she writes about relationships with friends and lovers, her childhood growing up in New Zealand, and the great loss she suffered when her younger brother died. Mansfield's journal eloquently and hauntingly brings the writer's final life chapter to a close.

Mansfield never intended for the materials included in the journal to be published—hence, the very personal, intimate nature of some of the entries. However, her husband and editor, John Middleton Murry, compiled her writings into *Journal of Katherine Mansfield,* publishing it four years after her death in 1923 at age thirty-four. The journal earned her more critical acclaim and fame than she ever received during her lifetime and contributed to an idealized image of Mansfield. Due to his censorship of many of his wife's entries, many scholars have criticized Murry's role in editing and publishing the journal as misleading and manipulative. A scholarly edition of Mansfield's papers was published in 1997 by Margaret Scott, *The Katherine Mansfield Notebooks,* and is now the preferred source for scholars studying Mansfield's papers.

HISTORICAL AND LITERARY CONTEXT

Mansfield's journal, along with the rest of her work, is part of an era in English literature associated with the Bloomsbury group that included writers such as Virginia Woolf, T. S. Eliot, and James Joyce. However, Mansfield was a New Zealand writer, and this set her apart from her London contemporaries, situating her on the fringes of a higher-class intellectual society that saw her as a "colonial." While journal writing was a common pastime for many women in the late nineteenth and early twentieth centuries, Mansfield's diary entries do not follow traditional journal-writing conventions. *Journal of Katherine Mansfield* coincides with World War I, and certain aspects of her writing reflect the chaos and fear of that period in Europe, especially when the war hit close to home with the death of her brother Leslie.

During the period covered in her journal, Mansfield traveled almost constantly, living in London; Paris; Cornwall, England; the Swiss Alps; and the French and Italian Riviera for no more than a few months at a time. This lifestyle was a result of both her poor financial situation and her failing health, which required Mansfield to spend the winter in a milder climate. She was usually accompanied by her companion and occasional lover Ida Baker, referred to in the journal as "L.M.," and sometimes Murry. The writer's declining health and attempts at seeking treatment in 1918 were hindered by the close of the war, contributing further to her illness.

Mansfield's journal is intellectual in nature, and it reflects frequently on the writing of other literary figures of her time. Passages address writers such as Charles Dickens; Jane Austen; Fyodor Dostoyevsky; William Shakespeare; and, most importantly, Anton Chekhov, "whom she revered, loved and used as a model," according to Hermione Lee in her 2006 review of *Journal of Katherine Mansfield* in the *Guardian.* Mansfield shared a passion for the beauty of creating and enjoying art with the Bloomsbury circle, specifically the act of writing. Unlike *The Diary of Virginia Woolf,* in which the author lists the mundane events of her life, Mansfield's journal presents a series of reflections on life and writing.

Journal of Katherine Mansfield is unique in its critical reflection on her own work. In one passage, she writes, "I'm not at all sure about that story ['At the Bay']. It seems to me a little 'wispy'—not what it might have been. 'The G[arden] P[arty]' is better. But that is not good enough, either." Many of Mansfield's contemporaries were impacted by her work, most notably Woolf and Elizabeth Bowen, whose narratives, including the novel *The Death of the Heart* (1938), reflect the same observational descriptions and perceptions of light and atmosphere. American writer Dorothy Parker also admired Mansfield, and some her short stories, such as "Big Blonde" (1929), exhibit a finely tuned conciseness and unsentimental tone that are reminiscent of Mansfield's style.

❖ **Key Facts**

Time Period:
Early 20th Century

Relevant Historical Events:
Mansfield's battle with tuberculosis and involvement with the Bloomsbury group

Nationality:
New Zealander

Keywords:
literature; creativity; illness

Katherine Mansfield, photographed in 1914. © UNIVERSAL HISTORY ARCHIVE/UIG/THE BRIDGEMAN ART LIBRARY

Mansfield employs a candid and morose tone in her journal, which is reflective of the suffering she endured from chronic illness. For example, she writes of "bounding" back into bed one morning, observing, "The bound made me cough—I spat it—it tasted strange—it was bright red blood. Since then I've gone on spitting each time I cough a little more. Oh yes, of course I am frightened." Although Murry attempted to place the entries into chronological order, the structure is fragmented and lacks cohesion since the material is drawn from numerous sources. In a 2000 essay published in the *Journal of New Zealand Literature,* Mansfield scholar Anna Jackson remarks that "the focus is more than usually on the moment. There are no references from one entry to another." Jackson adds, "In fact it is not quite accurate to call them 'entries' since few of them were 'entered' into any sort of ongoing text."

CRITICAL DISCUSSION

Journal of Katherine Mansfield was received warmly by critics, garnering more attention than much of her fiction did during her lifetime. Murry went on to publish the *Scrapbook of Katherine Mansfield* in 1940, and then he combined *Journal* and *Scrapbook* into what he called the "definitive edition" of Mansfield's journal, which was published in 1954. In her 1927 review of the journal, Parker found beauty in the anguish expressed by Mansfield, remarking that it was "the saddest book I have ever read. Here, set down in exquisite fragments, is the record of six lonely and tormented years, the life's-end of a desperately ill woman."

Scholarship in the late twentieth century turned primarily to comparisons between the original 1927 *Journal of Katherine Mansfield* and the papers from which the book was drawn. These papers became accessible to the public in 1958 at the Alexander Turnbull Library in Wellington, New Zealand. In his 1974 article in *Twentieth Century Literature,* Philip Waldron notes the many differences between *Journal of Katherine Mansfield* and Mansfield's original papers, including "the omission or toning down of material which would reflect Katherine Mansfield's tetchy, even bitchy personality or her less conventional sexual proclivities; arbitrary dating and arrangement of passages." Today's scholars completely discount Murry's 1927 version of the journal and instead regard Scott's *The Katherine Mansfield Notebooks* as the reliable academic source on Mansfield's papers.

Current scholarship continues to focus on the publication history of Mansfield's notebooks. In *Katherine Mansfield* (2004), Andrew Bennett laments "the perhaps rather falsified, romanticized image of Mansfield presented in the decades after her death by Murry, whose publication of edited, revised, and selected versions of letters and notebooks included countless editorial decisions that often seem to have more to do with his own somewhat idealistic, even mystical notion of Art and Literature than with hers." Other scholars are interested in the notion of the

THEMES AND STYLE

Journal of Katherine Mansfield addresses a broad range of themes, including her childhood in New Zealand, her turbulent relationship with writing, and the loneliness and pain of her illness. She lived a rather tormented life in her later years, worrying that something would be left unfinished upon her death. Of her story "The Daughters of the Late Colonel" (1922), she writes, "I wrote as fast as possible for fear of dying before the story was sent." Mansfield's entries are often foreboding and express an intense feeling of loneliness, as when she notes, "I seem to spend half of my life arriving at strange hotels … waiting for the shadows to come out of the corners and spin their slow, slow web."

Mansfield's journal is unique in that she never intended its personal, scattered writings to be published, much less compiled into a single "journal." She had specifically requested that Murry "tear up and burn as much as possible," as Lee notes in her review. The fact that Mansfield was only writing for herself explains the candid and intimate nature of the editing. Murry's heavy-handed censoring and editing was aimed at preserving a respectable image of his late wife. More recent scholars of her papers, including Ian Gordon and Scott, have noted that Murry excluded the majority of Mansfield's more scandalous pieces.

"diary" or "journal" as a genre and whether Mansfield's notebooks fit into that category. Jackson, for example, writes, "The passages were written at different times, in different books, and are different lengths depending in part on where they were written and how much space was allotted them. Katherine Mansfield did not 'keep a diary.' Can she then have written one?"

BIBLIOGRAPHY

Sources

Bennett, Andrew. *Katherine Mansfield*. Devon: Northcote House, 2004. Print.

Gordon, Ian. "The Editing of Katherine Mansfield's *Journal* and *Scrapbook*." *Landfall* 13.1 (1959): 62–69. Print.

Jackson, Anna. "The 'Notebooks,' 'Journal,' and Papers of Katherine Mansfield: Is Any of This Her Diary?" *Journal of New Zealand Literature* 18–19 (2000–01): 83–99. Print.

Lee, Hermione. Rev. of *Journal of Katherine Mansfield*, by Katherine Mansfield. *Guardian*. The Guardian, 1 Dec. 2006. Web. 1 Dec. 2012.

Mansfield, Katherine. *Journal of Katherine Mansfield*. Ed. J. Middleton Murry. New York: Knopf, 1927. Print.

Parker, Dorothy. "The Private Papers of the Dead." Rev. of *Journal of Katherine Mansfield*, by Katherine Mansfield. *The Portable Dorothy Parker*. New York: Penguin Books, 1976. 451–52. Print.

Waldron, Philip. "Katherine Mansfield's Journal." *Twentieth Century Literature* 20.1 (1974): 11–18. Print.

Whitridge, Arnold. "Katherine Mansfield." *Sewanee Review* 48.2 (1940): 256–72. Print.

Further Reading

Alpers, Antony. *The Life of Katherine Mansfield*. New York: Viking, 1980. Print.

Cox, Sidney. "The Fastidiousness of Katherine Mansfield." *Sewanee Review* 39.2 (1931): 158–69. Print.

Kimber, Gerri. *Katherine Mansfield: The View from France*. New York: Peter Lang, 2008. Print.

Kleine, Don W. "An Eden for Insiders: Katherine Mansfield's New Zealand." *College English* 27.3 (1965): 201–9. Print.

Meyers, Jeffrey. *Katherine Mansfield: A Biography*. New York: New Directions, 1980. Print.

Moran, Patricia L. *Word of Mouth: Body Language in Katherine Mansfield and Virginia Woolf*. Charlottesville: University Press of Virginia, 1996. Print.

Smith, Angela. *Katherine Mansfield: A Literary Life*. New York: Palgrave, 2000. Print.

Tomalin, Claire. *Katherine Mansfield: A Secret Life*. New York: Knopf/Random House, 1988. Print.

THE LIFE OF KATHERINE MANSFIELD

Kathleen Mansfield Beauchamp, a well-known modernist writer whose pen name was Katherine Mansfield, was born in Wellington, New Zealand, in 1888. She grew up in a rural New Zealand town, receiving little early education at the village school. Despite her lack of early education, she began writing at a young age. Mansfield was sent to England at the age of thirteen to continue her education at Queen's College, Harley Street, where she edited the college magazine and was exposed to prominent writers of the time, including Oscar Wilde.

Mansfield was forced to return to New Zealand after college, but finding herself extremely unhappy in the rural environment, she persuaded her parents to allow her to return to London. She spent her remaining years in Europe, traveling between England, France, and other neighboring countries and publishing short stories regularly in a variety of periodicals. In 1911 Mansfield was reunited with her younger brother Leslie, who would become an officer in the British army during World War I. His death in 1915 affected Mansfield deeply. She was married twice, first to George Bowden and later to John Middleton Murry, who played a central role in her literary career. After suffering from tuberculosis for several years, Mansfield died in 1923 at just thirty-four. Her best-known works include *The Garden Party: And Other Stories* (1922), *Bliss: And Other Stories* (1923), and *Journal of Katherine Mansfield* (1927).

Katrina White

The Journals of Arnold Bennett, 1896–1928

Arnold Bennett

Key Facts

Time Period:
Late 19th to Early 20th Centuries

Relevant Historical Events:
Bennett's success as a writer; Industrial Revolution

Nationality:
English

Keywords:
literature; modernity; industrialization

OVERVIEW

The Journals of Arnold Bennett, 1896–1928 was published in three volumes in 1932 and 1933. The Edwardian novelist, playwright, critic, editor, and all-round man of letters Arnold Bennett (1867–1931) began keeping a regular journal in 1896, the year he started *Anna of the Five Towns,* one of his most admired "serious" novels. He continued keeping it, with his customary scrupulousness, until his death. The journal is mainly a chronicle of the daily life of an ambitious and successful writer—filled with luncheons, journeys, meetings, hotels, and the like. Although he is continually watching and appraising himself in their pages, the journals are neither intimate nor confessional in tone. Volume I, which covers the period from 1896 to 1910, contains a detailed, detached chronicle of his life and opinions between the time he began to write his first important novel and when he published the first volume of the famous *Clayhanger* trilogy of novels (in which the eponymous main character is closely modeled on Bennett himself).

Bennett was of a generation of British novelists who took a detailed, realistic, socially defined approach to the novel and who wrote of the middle and/or working classes. Others in this group included John Galsworthy (1867–1933), H. G. Wells (1866–1946), W. Somerset Maugham (1874–1965), and the American writer Theodore Dreiser (1871–1945). They all considered themselves "moderns" and were much concerned with the problems of modernity, even though the seeds of their oblivion (as modernists, at any rate) were even then being sown by the likes of Virginia Woolf, Katherine Mansfield, Marcel Proust, and James Joyce. In his role as a critic, Bennett had already noted and approved of the work of D. H. Lawrence (1885–1930), who examined situations, characters, and narratives that bore more than a passing resemblance to those treated by Bennett—except that instead of Bennett's obsessive attention to physical detail, Lawrence applied a marked degree of psychological insight, powered by a furious emotional intensity—and so came up with a very different kind of novel, though still realistic.

HISTORICAL AND LITERARY CONTEXT

The Industrial Revolution began in England in the latter half of the eighteenth century. Bennett was native to the Midlands, where he grew up in a loose federation of towns—which he later immortalized in his fiction as the "Five Towns" (though, in fact, there were six)—and which have since grown together as Stoke-on-Trent, in Staffordshire, about thirty miles northwest of Birmingham. The business of the region was ceramics, and the collected towns were known as "the Potteries." The skies over the Potteries were usually dark with the smoke from the massive kilns. Bennett's father had begun his working life as a master potter and went through several changes of career until, aged thirty-four, he qualified as a solicitor. Bennett had passed his exams for a Cambridge scholarship, but his father wanted him as a clerk in his office, so he never went to university. He said to a friend, "I'm going to get out of this." Yet, as Graham Greene observed, a writer's youth is his capital, and all of Bennett's most successful serious works are set in the Potteries.

Bennett began his journals in the same year that he became assistant editor of the periodical *Woman* (appropriately so, as he was to become known for the sympathetic and insightful portraits of women in his novels). He had moved to London in 1889, but the only job he could get at first was that of lawyer's clerk. Two years after joining *Woman,* with the publication of his heavily autobiographical first novel, *A Man from the North,* Bennett was made editor of *Woman.* He was determined to make a living from his writing from then on. Bennett became remarkably prolific, publishing serious and light novels, plays, self-help books such as *Journalism for Women* and *Self-Efficiency,* war propaganda, and reams of journalism, and he still found time to commit more than a million words to the pages of his journals. By 1910, when the first volume of *The Journals of Arnold Bennett* closes, he had published his two masterpieces, *Anna of the Five Towns* and *The Old Wives' Tale,* and had been living and writing in Paris for eight years.

The Elementary Education Act of 1870 had initiated the mandate for education for all children between ages five and twelve in England and Wales. Apart from other benefits, the exponential rise in literacy led to an unpredented expansion of the reading public, and this new market naturally led to a similar expansion of subject matter. The new readers from the industrial Midlands or rural Wessex wanted stories that spoke to their condition. Thomas Hardy gave up architecture and began to publish his (often grimly) realistic novels set in his native Dorset during the 1870s. Bennett later came to admire Hardy's novels a great deal, but the author whose work inspired him the most was Eden Phillpotts (1862–1960), whose eighteen novels and two volumes of short stories set in Dartmoor became Bennett's models for novels with regional settings.

The Journals of Arnold Bennett, like all Bennett's published work, suffered an eclipse of public attention in the decades after his death. Scholars seeking information and anecdotes on Bennett found a good deal of gossip in his journals, but none is of a scandalous nature. The friendships he made—with Wells, Galsworthy, Frank Harris, George Bernard Shaw, and many others—were not friendships of convenience. Indeed, the journals show that Bennett's public and private personae were integrated.

THEMES AND STYLE

The two recurring themes in *The Journals of Arnold Bennett*—his incessant self-scrutiny and his voracious curiosity about the world and everything in it—are also the main themes of his fiction. His self-appraisals are neither preening nor scolding, even when he is admitting to something most people would prefer to conceal. He was, for instance, in a serious railway accident in 1909 that left him ruffled but undamaged. After he had "soothed" an old woman in his compartment, he put on his hat and climbed out of the car. "I had no desire of any sort to help." As for his compulsive, omnivorous observing of life, examples abound. He was certainly not above name dropping, either: "Dinner last night at Maurice Ravel's. He played us extracts from the proofs of his new ballet, *Daphnis et Chloe,* and I was much pleased."

Like so much of Bennett's life, his motives for keeping the journals are all in plain sight: he wanted to organize and keep track of his crowded social life, his progress in his writing projects, and his insights as they came to him. He was especially scrupulous in recording word counts, reviews, contracts, and logistical problems. Working on the second book of the *Clayhanger* trilogy, he writes, "I got as far as the death of Mrs. Lessways in *Hilda Lessways* on Sunday afternoon, and sent off the stuff as a specimen to [literary agent J. B.] Pinker yesterday. 33,000 words." After noting his satisfaction with Ravel's new ballet, he writes, "On Monday and yesterday I wrote one complete chapter each day of *Hilda Lessways,* 5,000 words in all."

Stylistically, Bennett rarely adopts in the diaries the tone of levity and man-of-the-world archness used in his lighter stories such as *The Grand Babylon Hotel* or *Buried Alive.* The descriptions are precise and detailed rather than vivid. His judgments of people or works of art are quick and facile, though they generally hold up. His theoretical pronouncements about his craft sometimes sound oracular: "Essential characteristic of the really great novelist: a Christ-like, all-embracing compassion."

A nineteenth-century watercolor portrait of Arnold Bennett. © PRIVATE COLLECTION/ THE BRIDGEMAN ART LIBRARY

CRITICAL DISCUSSION

The initial publication of *The Journals of Arnold Bennett,* just a year after the author's death, gave critics an opportunity to sum up his entire oeuvre. Writing in the *Virginia Quarterly Review* in 1932, Edward Wagenknecht concludes, "Probably he was as great an artist as a man can be without religion, and the measure of his greatness is to be found in his straining against the limitations he so needlessly imposed upon himself." However, H. L. Mencken, writing in 1919 about Bennett's novels, had already sounded the theme about Bennett's work that would be developed by one critic or another for the next seventy years:

> [The novels] are magnificent as representation, they bristle with charming detail, they radiate the humors of an acute and extraordinary man, they are entertainment of the best sort—but there is seldom anything in them of that clear, well-aimed and solid effect which one associates with the novel as work of art.

This is the same complaint made by Woolf in her famous essay, "Mr. Bennett and Mrs. Brown" (1924), in which she states that Bennett's characters have only outsides, no insides at all. In the same year, J. B. Priestley, though he spent most of his essay being funny at Bennett's expense, observed that Bennett "has taken ugly places in ugly epochs and by dint of rare understanding and noble labour has transformed their chronicles into art."

The mostly positive reviews of the journals when they were published in 1932 and 1933 did not halt Bennett's posthumous neglect. A novelist such as John O'Hara, while clearly writing with Bennett's detail and detachment, might never have considered the debt owed. In literary circles, Bennett's name simply did

MR. BENNETT AND MODERNISM

Unfortunately, much of the contemporary discussion of Arnold Bennett still relies upon the terms set by Virginia Woolf in her essay "Mr. Bennett and Mrs. Brown" (1924), which places Woolf and her friends on the side of "Modernism," and the "Edwardians" Bennett and H. G. Wells on the side of conservative "traditionalists." There was something real at the core of the debate, a disagreement about the purpose of the novel form and about the best way to create convincing characters. It is an endless, irresolvable comparison of apples and oranges. But the question of who invents the more believable characters—the kind that live for the reader and make the reader care how their story turns out—is an important topic.

Bennett began the debate, inadvertently, with a 1923 review of Woolf's novel *Jacob's Room*. He praised its originality and the beauty of her prose but found that her "characters do not vitally survive in the mind." This led, the following year, to Woolf's memorable essay "Mr. Bennett and Mrs. Brown," in which she says of his characters in the novel *Hilda Lessways*: "But we cannot hear her mother's voice, or Hilda's voice; we can only hear Mr. Bennett's voice telling us facts about rents and freeholds and copyholds and fines…. He is trying to make us imagine for him; he is trying to hypnotise us into the belief that, because he has made a house, there must be a person living there." Bennett was too gentle-spirited to be a good debater, and he suffered lifelong from a terrible stammer. Woolf's bons mots carried the day and are carrying it still. Yet Bennett, despite his avoidance of violence, sensationalism, and pornography, wrote stories that a great many people wanted to read, and he became rich writing them.

not come up. The American and British film industries, however, have never forgotten Bennett: more than twenty motion pictures and television series have been based upon his novels and stories.

Bennett's reputation began its long journey back from the shadows with the 1963 publication of James Hepburn's *The Art of Arnold Bennett*, followed in 1966 by Hepburn's edition of Bennett's *Letters*. The 1978 memoir *Arnold Bennett: A Last Word*, by Bennett's friend Frank Swinnerton, also put the author's name back in circulation. Yet when the influential English critic John Carey wrote about him with sympathetic approval in his 1993 book *The Intellectuals and the Masses*, Bennett's reputation improved significantly in scholarly and critical circles. Most would now agree with Anita Miller that "a consensus seems to be growing, despite the mass of negative comment which grew during Bennett's last years and for three decades or so after his death, that he was in fact a great novelist, and that ignorance of his work impoverishes the body of English literature."

BIBLIOGRAPHY

Sources

"Arnold Bennett." *Contemporary Authors Online*. Detroit: Gale, 2007. *Gale Biography in Context*. Web. 10 Nov. 2012.

Bennett, Arnold. *The Journals of Arnold Bennett, 1896–1928*. 3 vols. Ed. Newman Flower. London: Cassell, 1932–33. Print.

Mencken, H. L. "Arnold Bennett." *Prejudices*. New York: Knopf, 1919. 36–51. Rpt. in *Twentieth-Century Literary Criticism*. Ed. Dennis Poupard. Vol. 20. Detroit: Gale Research, 1992. *Literature Resource Center*. Web. 28 Dec. 2012.

Miller, Anita. "(Enoch) Arnold Bennett." *British Novelists, 1890–1929: Traditionalists*. Ed. Thomas F. Staley. Detroit: Gale Research, 1984. *Dictionary of Literary Biography* Vol. 34. *Literature Resource Center*. Web. 1 Jan. 2013.

Priestley, J. B. "Mr. Arnold Bennett." *Figures in Modern Literature*. London: Lane, 1924. 3–30. Rpt. in *Twentieth-Century Literary Criticism*. Vol. 197. Detroit: Gale, 2008. *Literature Resource Center*. Web. 28 Dec. 2012.

Woolf, Virginia. "Mr. Bennett and Mrs. Brown." London: Hogarth, 1924. Print.

Young, Kenneth. "(Enoch) Arnold Bennett." *British Writers*. Ed. Ian Scott-Kilvert. Vol. 6. New York: Scribner, 1979. *Scribner Writers Series*. Web. 19 Dec. 2012.

Further Reading

Bennett, Arnold. *Letters of Arnold Bennett*. 4 vols. Ed. James Hepburn. London: Oxford University Press, 1966–1986. Print.

Carey, John. *The Intellectuals and the Masses: Pride and Prejudice among the Literary Intelligentsia, 1880–1939*. New York: St. Martin's, 1993. Print.

Howe, Irving. "Mr. Bennett and Mrs. Woolf: Late Justice for One of Modernism's Victims." *New Republic* 4 June 1990: 26. *Academic OneFile*. Web. 29 Dec. 2012.

Jones, Jason B. "Revisiting 'Mr. Bennett': Pleasure, Aversion, and the Social in *The Old Wives' Tale* and *Riceyman Steps*." *English Literature in Transition 1880–1920* 46.1 (2003): 29. *Academic OneFile*. Web. 1 Jan. 2013.

Lesser, Wendy. "Who's Afraid of Arnold Bennett?" *New York Times Book Review* 28 Sept. 1997. *Academic OneFile*. Web. 2 Jan. 2013.

Pound, Reginald. *Arnold Bennett: A Biography*. London: Heinemann, 1952. Print.

Swinnerton, Frank. *Arnold Bennett: A Last Word*. London: Hamish Hamilton, 1978. Print.

Wagenknecht, Edward. "Arnold Bennett." *Virginia Quarterly Review*. Virginia Quarterly Review, Autumn 1932. Web. 2 Jan. 2013.

Gerald Carpenter

Journals of Ralph Waldo Emerson

Ralph Waldo Emerson

OVERVIEW

Published first in ten volumes from 1904 to 1914, the *Journals of Ralph Waldo Emerson* contain a record of Ralph Waldo Emerson's intellectual and philosophical development from age sixteen (1820), before he entered Harvard Divinity School, to age seventy-four (1877), five years before his death and well after he had made a name for himself as one of the most prominent American thinkers of his age. Emerson produced in his lifetime a number of influential speeches and essays that helped shape his country's national character. His soul-searching journals contain the seeds of his most powerful thoughts as well as a number of revealing insights that have refined readers' understanding of his life and works and his relationships with almost every major literary figure of the era.

Emerson's journals, which he would refer to throughout his life as his "Savings Bank," include numerous published and unpublished poems and letters, early drafts of speeches and essays, character sketches, brief and witty observations on life in the United States during the country's formative years, and touching personal reminiscences on the many joys and heartbreaks he experienced. Though Emerson is often criticized for his oblique and convoluted writing style, as in "Nature" (1836), "The American Scholar" (1837), and "The Over-Soul" (1841), the publication of his journals altered the way such works were perceived by providing penetrating glimpses into the experiences and influences that occasioned them. Though the journals have not been the subject of intense academic study, scholars agree with Harold Bloom's 1984 assessment that "Emerson's journals are his authentic work."

HISTORICAL AND LITERARY CONTEXT

The first entry in Emerson's journal is dated January 25, 1820, when he was a sixteen-year-old junior at Harvard College. He aptly titled his journal at the time "Wide World," reflecting not only his voracious reading habits and rapidly broadening intellect but also a pervasive feeling of limitless potential brought about by rampant expansionism. In the early 1800s, explorers including Meriwether Lewis, William Clark, and John Jacob Astor probed the country's western boundary, sparking a massive movement of people from the eastern states to the western territories from 1820 to 1860. Writing in his journal on December 21, 1822, Emerson states, "There is everything in America's favour, to one who puts faith in those proverbial prophecies of the Westward progress of the Car of Empire," implicitly linking the expansion of the United States to the classical notion of *translatio*, or the westward progress of civilization. Like most Americans at the time, the young Emerson was enthralled with the idea of the United States as a place where "new Romes are growing," and he spent the rest of his life trying to define and shape a national character worthy of such comparisons.

Because Emerson's journals cover such an expanse of time, they contain not only records of his own personal maturation but also of the national growth that occurred in the nineteenth century. He comments on technological developments such as the emergence of the daguerreotype—the first commercially viable form of photography, popular in the 1840s—and the discovery of ether, as well as the social movements that he supported, including abolitionism and women's suffrage, and the major sociopolitical events of his day, such as the financial Panic of 1837, the Mexican-American War (1846–1848), and the Civil War (1861–1865). Alongside such events of broad national concern are reminiscences of the personal events that shaped his life, among them his enrollment at Harvard Divinity School; the deaths of his brothers Edward and Charles, his first wife, and his protégé, philosopher and naturalist Henry David Thoreau; his abandonment of the ministry and eventual disillusionment with organized Christianity; his numerous travels in Europe; his meetings with President Abraham Lincoln during the Civil War; his marriage to his second wife, Lydia, and the birth and tragic death of their son; his involvement with the influential publications the *Dial* and the *Atlantic Monthly*; and the gradual weakening of his intellectual and linguistic faculties toward the end of his life.

The journals show Emerson's interest in the writings and daily lives of a number of influential New England authors and thinkers, including his friends and neighbors Ellery Channing, Margaret Fuller, Nathaniel Hawthorne, Caroline Sturgis, and Thoreau. But most significantly they reveal a deep engagement with the works of his philosophical forebear, Thomas Carlyle, whom he met while traveling in England and

✤ **Key Facts**

Time Period:
Mid-19th Century

Relevant Historical Events:
Western expansion; Mexican-American War; Civil War

Nationality:
American

Keywords:
empire; intellectualism; politics; transcendentalism

LITERARY LIVES

Essayist and poet Ralph Waldo Emerson. © NORTH WIND PICTURE ARCHIVES/ ALAMY

with whom he maintained a correspondence throughout his life. In a revealing passage from June 1847, one that perhaps pinpoints the source of critical consternation with Emerson's writing, he writes of Carlyle's writing that "one is more struck with the rhetoric than with the matter. He has a manly superiority rather than intellectuality, & so makes good hard hits all the time." Also contained in the journals from 1847, written during and immediately after Emerson's second of three tours of Europe, are written sketches of a number of leading literary figures whom he met on his way, including Thomas De Quincey, Charles Dickens, and Alfred Tennyson.

In the eighteenth and nineteenth centuries it was common for writers and intellectuals to keep a written record of their studies and the evolution of their thought. Often known as "commonplace books," such works were sometimes published and served as study guides for young scholars. One of the most well-known commonplace books that Emerson was familiar with was written by seventeenth-century philosopher John Locke, whom Lawrence Alan Rosenwald calls Emerson's "diaristic authority" in *Emerson and the Art of the Diary* (1988), though he goes on to note that Emerson's inclusion of more personal and emotional details in his journals can be seen as a "rebellion against the model he begins with." Emerson and his New England circle all kept journals, though in most cases such works were not intended for publication. Emerson reportedly encouraged Thoreau to start a journal (which was published posthumously in 1906), and, like Emerson, a number of Thoreau's most popular published works, including *A Week on the Concord and Merrimack Rivers* (1849) and *Walden* (1854), are drawn directly from the experiences and observations recorded in his diary.

THEMES AND STYLE

Emerson's journals cover such a range of subject matter and expanse of time that it is nearly impossible to identify a single theme or feature that characterizes the entire work. His focus in his journals generally evolves along with that of his published works: The early journals show his admiration for and indebtedness to major literary figures such as William Shakespeare and John Milton; the journals of the 1830s and 1840s show him finding his own voice and developing what would become the major tenets of the transcendentalist movement, such as the importance of self-reliance, the unity of God and nature, and the significance of one's intuition as a spiritual and moral guide; and the later journals reveal his growing concern with incorporating such principles into civic life, so that the country might emerge from the Civil War as the true home of liberty and justice in the world. Throughout the journal's numerous volumes, though, Emerson's faith in literature and language as a powerful transformational force is apparent. Leading Emerson critic Joel Porte, writing in *Emerson in His Journals,* sums up the relationship between language and national progress in Emerson's thought by noting that "Emerson had long believed that America was a poem only waiting for the right meters."

When Emerson began writing his journal, he committed his writing to "all the various purposes and utility real or imaginary which are usually comprehended under the comprehensive title *Common Place book*" and noted his "serious expectation of burning this book," but as he left Harvard and embarked on a career as a public figure and man of letters, his entries became less studious and reverential in tone and more poetic, searching, and conscious of a potential public interest in his private thoughts. An entry from December 1827, for example, in which he describes meeting his first wife, contains a parenthetical aside directed at readers of his diary: "(I ought to apprise the reader that I am a bachelor and to the best of my belief have never been in love.)" Though Emerson's first major publication, the essay "Nature," would not be published until 1836, the journals contain the words "my readers" as far back as 1824, when he was just twenty-one years old.

The tone of the journals is consistent with Emerson's published works, relying largely upon elevated, quasi-religious language, as exemplified by a passage from May 14, 1838: "Our thought is the income of God. I taste therefore of eternity & pronounce of eternal law now & not hereafter. Space & time are but forms of thought. I proceed from God now & ever shall so proceed. Death is but an appearance." Much of Emerson's reputation as a quiet, reclusive, and oftentimes cranky individual who held the human soul in far greater esteem than the living, breathing person that housed it is confirmed in the journals, such as in his 1833 comments on meeting Samuel Taylor Coleridge, William Wordsworth, and other prominent British writers: "To be sure not one of them is a mind of the very first class," he writes, going so far as to call them "deficient" in their lack of "insight into religious truth." However, as Arthur M. Cory points out in his essay "Humor in Emerson's *Journals*" the journals also reveal Emerson's lighter side, which is largely absent from his published essays: "The many amusing quotations in the *Journals* show clearly that Emerson had a sense of humor. In his youth this took the form of the pretentiously mock-serious; as he grew older he mellowed and became more genial, and his humor took on richness and warmth."

CRITICAL DISCUSSION
Since their initial publication, Emerson's journals have sustained scholarly and popular interest and have been republished in a number of forms. After the ten-volume Houghton Mifflin edition of 1904–1914, the journals were subsequently released in condensed form as a Book of the Month Club selection in 1926, as a comprehensive sixteen-volume annotated version published by Harvard University Press from 1960 to 1982, again in condensed form in 1982, as a three-volume selected set by the University of Missouri Press from 1990 to 1994, and as a Library of America two-volume set in 2010. Writing in 1917, John Burroughs proclaims, "They will find him in his Journals the same spur and challenge that they found him in his Essays so long ago. He sets one's mental currents going, and whether we go his way or not matters little to him, so that we only go somewhere."

Despite their popularity among Emerson enthusiasts and scholars, the journals were not the subject of any major studies until Rosenwald's *Emerson and the Art of the Diary*. Perhaps because of the sheer volume of the journals themselves, or because Emerson's more famous essays are viewed as condensed and refined presentations of the same thoughts contained in the journals, scholars have largely avoided making critical commentary on the journals themselves. Robert D. Richardson, in the biography *Emerson: The Mind on Fire* (1995), summarizes this notion of the essays as superior versions of the content in the journals, writing, "each essay would represent the best of the journal comments, which were themselves the best of each day and its thought and reading."

The scholars that have made Emerson's journals their primary focus have often treated the journals as literary works themselves. For example, Evelyn B. Greenberger, in her 1974 essay in *American Transcendental Quarterly*, identifies a number of recurring symbols in the journals and connects them to certain characteristics of Emerson's psychology that she gleans from the journals and a number of biographies. Others, such as Len Gougeon in *Emerson & Eros: The Making of a Cultural Hero* (2007), contrast journal entries from various eras in Emerson's life as evidence of his "dramatic personal transformation." Because Emerson produced some of the most influential and widely read essays in American literary history, his journals seem destined to remain an afterthought. But for those readers who are interested in the intellectual processes and personal experiences that brought Emerson to produce such vital essays and speeches, there is no greater or more reliable source of information than the author's own records in his journal.

BIBLIOGRAPHY
Sources
Bloom, Harold. "Mr. America." *New York Review of Books* 22 Nov. 1984: 19–20. Print.

Burroughs, John. "A Glance into Emerson's Journals." *Art World* 3.2 (1917): 105–8. *JSTOR*. Web. 22 Dec. 2012.

Cory, Arthur M. "Humor in Emerson's *Journals*." *University of Texas Studies in English* 34 (1955): 114–24. Print.

Emerson, Ralph Waldo. *The Journals and Miscellaneous Notebooks of Ralph Waldo Emerson*. Ed. William H. Gillman, et al. 16 vols. Cambridge: Belknap, 1960–82. Print.

Emerson, Ralph Waldo, and Joel Porte. *Emerson in His Journals*. Cambridge: Belknap, 1982. Print.

Gougeon, Len. *Emerson & Eros: The Making of a Cultural Hero*. Albany: State University of New York Press, 2007. Print.

Greenberger, Evelyn B. "The Phoenix on the Wall: Consciousness in Emerson's Early and Late Journals." *American Transcendental Quarterly: A Journal of New England Writers* 21 (1974): 45–56. Print.

Richardson, Robert D. *Emerson: The Mind on Fire*. Berkeley: University of California Press, 1995. Print.

Rosenwald, Lawrence. *Emerson and the Art of the Diary*. New York: Oxford University Press, 1988. Print.

Further Reading

Buell, Lawrence. *Emerson.* Cambridge: Belknap, 2003. Print.

Habich, Robert D. *Building Their Own Waldos: Emerson's First Biographers and the Politics of Life-Writing in the Gilded Age.* Iowa City: University of Iowa Press, 2011. Print.

Lysaker, John T. *Emerson and Self-Culture.* Bloomington: Indiana University Press, 2008.

McMillin, T. S. *Our Preposterous Use of Literature: Emerson and the Nature of Reading.* Urbana: University of Illinois Press, 2000. Print.

Meehan, Sean R. *Mediating American Autobiography: Photography in Emerson, Thoreau, Douglass, and Whitman.* Columbia: University of Missouri Press, 2008. Print.

Jacob Schmitt

Letters and Journals of Lord Byron, with Notices of His Life

George Gordon Noel Byron

OVERVIEW

An 1830 anthology edited by Thomas Moore, *Letters and Journals of Lord Byron, with Notices of His Life* contains 561 of the famous English Romantic poet's letters and a number of his diaries, with inserted commentary to provide narrative linkage. The collected letters and diary entries, comprising two volumes and some fifteen hundred pages of text, create a dynamic portrait of George Gordon Noel Byron, a man who had been a public scandal for years before his death in 1824 when he was thirty-six years old. Moore's collection of the poet's personal writings, censored to remove the most socially inappropriate content, works to complicate Byron's libertine image, showing all the multifarious facets of the poet's thought.

During his lifetime Byron was already regarded as a foremost figure in the emerging Romanticist school of poetry. Romanticism, which eschewed the mechanistic view of the universe underlying much eighteenth-century poetry, focused on the poet's emotions and experiences, often, as in the early Romantic works of William Wordsworth and Samuel Taylor Coleridge, in response to encounters with the beauty and vitality of nature. Byron's own poetic works deviated somewhat from these themes, instead exploring imaginative narratives, dramatic scenes, and illicit passions. Enthusiastically received, Moore's collection was among the first to publish the poet's private writings, making a major contribution to the "Byromania" that has continued from the early nineteenth century to the present day.

HISTORICAL AND LITERARY CONTEXT

The descendant of a Scottish noble family, Byron was in many ways the archetypal Romantic hero: brooding, melancholic, with a reputation for immorality and wildness. His lover Lady Caroline Lamb memorably described him as "mad—bad—and dangerous to know." He had many extramarital affairs, including one with his half-sister Augusta Leigh, and as a result fathered a number of illegitimate children. Like many other poets of the Romantic school, including Percy Bysshe Shelley and Leigh Hunt, Byron was politically radical; his death was caused by a fever caught while fighting for Greek independence from Turkey.

Byron had given his memoirs to his friend Moore, who, short of money, sold them to Byron's publisher, John Murray. Murray burned the memoirs weeks after Byron's death in the belief that their publication would tarnish the poet's posthumous reputation. Moore asserted that most of the destroyed manuscript's content could still be found in the letters and diaries that remained undamaged; the contents of his eventual volume presumably reflect Byron's own autobiographical stylings.

Byron was the subject of no less than thirty-eight biographies published between 1801 and 1838. Nineteenth-century texts on his life range from heavily fictionalized accounts, such as the anonymous 1824 *Narrative of Lord Byron's Voyage to Corsica and Sardinia* and John Mitford's salacious *The Private Life of Lord Byron: Comprising His Amours with Ladies of Various Rank and Fame* (1836), to the more factual biographies that followed Moore's, such as those written by John Trelawney (1858) and Harriet Beecher Stowe (1870). The "life and letters" form used by Moore typifies the Victorian approach to biography; similarly styled biographies of the period include John Lockhart's *Life of Sir Walter Scott* (1837–1838), Elizabeth Gaskell's *Life of Charlotte Brontë* (1857), and G. O. Trevelyan's *Life and Letters of Lord Macaulay* (1876), interspersing lengthy and discursive excerpts of personal writing with connective narration. These biographies are also similar in their concern with social morality, sometimes censoring the less acceptable episodes in the lives of their subjects.

It is difficult to underestimate Byron's impact as a literary and cultural figure; among those inspired by his life and work are Aleksandr Pushkin, Pyotr Ilyich Tchaikovsky, and J. M. W. Turner. Although Moore is less well known in his own right, his biographical labor of love over *Letters and Journals of Lord Byron* is still seen as notable and praiseworthy and remains a key resource for students of Byron's life and works.

THEMES AND STYLE

Byron's correspondence forms a heterogeneous mass, albeit with a number of thematic throughlines: philosophies of poetry, descriptions of his literary milieu, addresses to his lovers. The extraordinary range of

❖ *Key Facts*

Time Period:
Early 19th Century

Relevant Historical Events:
Growth of Romanticism; Byron's death while fighting in Greece

Nationality:
English

Keywords:
poetry; Romanticism; scandal

Portrait of author Lord Byron by Théodore Géricault. © IMAGNO/GETTY IMAGES

topics and styles present in the collected works speaks to the complexity of Byron's thought and experience, defying his stereotyped and often oversimplified public image. His various writings employ multiple styles and personae, and sometimes the ideas put forth in them contradict others written elsewhere; by his own admission Byron tended to write "in great haste— … you have it hot & hot—just as it comes," as he explained in an 1815 letter to Hunt.

In his preface Moore comments on the "degree of attraction and interest" present in the materials compiled in *Letters and Journals of Lord Byron,* adding that, in the case of Byron, "in whom the literary and the personal character were so closely interwoven, that to have left his works without the instructive commentary which his Life and Correspondence afford, would have been equally an injustice both to himself and to the world." However, the mixture of the personal and the literary that Moore identifies as the greatest value of Byron's private writings also proved one of the more difficult factors to deal with in the editing of the work; Moore omitted text that referenced the more scandalous aspects of the poet's life, such as his homosexual tendencies and his incestuous affairs, in addition to making structural changes in some of the letters and removing references to people still living at the time of the work's publication.

Unlike previous publications of Moore's, *Letters and Journals of Lord Byron* uses a light editorial touch, largely allowing the poet to speak for himself. Byron's prose is less moody than much of his poetry, exhibiting sarcastic humor as well as considered philosophy. In his book *Byron, Sully, and the Power of Portraiture,* John Clubbe argues that "the letters often read like dramatic monologues. Although they are remarkably free of pose, Byron assumes with each correspondent a slightly different persona or mask." The variety and changefulness of Byron's prose confounds attempts to simplify his complex life and character, revealing the diversity of thought within a single fecund mind.

CRITICAL DISCUSSION

Positive initial reviews of *Letters and Journals of Lord Byron* focused on the balance and fairness of Moore's presentation of Byron's life. Thomas Macaulay's 1831 review claimed that the volume "deserves to be classed among the best specimens of English prose which our age has produced," while John Gibson Lockhart's review in the same year opined that Byron would "henceforth hold a place in the very first ranks of English letter-writers." Negative reviews were largely focused on what was perceived as the immoral content of Byron's letters, although there was also some disagreement as to whether Moore's portrait was completely true to life.

Despite Thomas Carlyle's injunction in *Sartor Resartus* (1836) to "close thy Byron," the poet has remained a potent figure in literary and cultural imagination. As Andrew Elfenbein notes in his *Byron and the Victorians* (1995), Byron's biography formed a key part of overarching Victorian cultural narratives, with the poet representing the wild youth that was seen as maturing in the mid-century. The archive of Byron's writings has remained in constant study since their publications, with contemporary scholarship often using biographical details to piece together the fraught relationship between his poetry and his cultural and historical moment.

While Moore's work remained the definitive resource on Byron's life for many decades, recent biographical research has supplemented his partial and sometimes-bowdlerized collection of Byron's personal writings. Leslie A. Marchand's thirteen-volume *Byron's Letters and Journals,* published between 1973 and 1982, forms one of the most impressive enlargements on Moore, with some 2,900 letters, left unexpurgated whenever possible. William Clair (1989) examines Moore's life of Byron against the historical record unearthed by other biographers, concluding that while it distorted the truth less than many other works, it still very much shapes a narrative out of the raw material of Byron's writings, one that portrays Moore himself in a much more flattering light. Post-1990s criticism is often concerned with Byron's celebrity and the resulting narrativization of his life in Victorian popular culture; examples of this critical strain include the work of Elfenbein and Clubbe.

BIBLIOGRAPHY

Sources

Clair, William. "The Byron Journal." *Byron Journal* 17 (1989): 50–56. Rpt. in *Nineteenth-Century Literature Criticism.* Ed. Thomas J. Schoenberg and Lawrence J. Trudeau. Vol. 110. Detroit: Gale, 2002. *Literature Resource Center.* Web. 6 Dec. 2012.

Clubbe, John. *Byron, Sully, and the Power of Portraiture.* Hampshire: Ashgate, 2005. Print.

Elfenbein, Andrew. *Byron and the Victorians.* Cambridge: Cambridge University Press, 1995. Print.

Lockhart, John Gibson. "Moore's Life of Byron." Rev. of *Letters and Journals of Lord Byron, with Notices of His Life,* by Thomas Moore. *Quarterly Review* Jan. 1831: 168–226. Print.

Macaulay, Thomas Babington. "Moore's Life of Lord Byron." Rev. of *Letters and Journals of Lord Byron, with Notices of His Life,* by Thomas Moore. *Edinburgh Review* June 1831: 544–72. Print.

Marchand, Leslie A. *Byron's Letters and Journals: The Complete and Unexpurgated Text of All the Letters Available in Manuscript and the Full Printed Version of All the Others.* Cambridge: Harvard University Press, 1973–82. Print.

Moore, Thomas. *Letters and Journals of Lord Byron, with Notices of His Life.* London: John Murray, 1830. Print.

Further Reading

Atkinson, Juliette. *Victorian Biography Reconsidered: A Study of Nineteenth-Century "Hidden" Lives.* Oxford: Oxford University Press, 2010. Print.

Clubbe, John, and Ernest J. Lovell Jr. *English Romanticism: The Grounds of Belief.* De Kalb: Northern Illinois University Press, 1983. Print.

Diakonova, Nina. "Byron's Prose and Byron's Poetry." *Studies in English Literature, 1500–1900* 16.4 (1976): 547–61. Print.

FICTIONAL BYRONS

Lord Byron's dramatic life has a proven lure for subsequent authors. This is demonstrated by the dozens of works of fiction, cinema, and theater that feature him as a character. Byron's lover Lady Caroline Lamb and his acquaintance Mary Shelley included thinly veiled versions of him in their respective novels *Glenarvon* (1816) and *The Last Man* (1826). Twentieth-century pop culture representations of Byron in his own person include appearances on episodes of *Highlander, Blackadder,* and *Star Trek.* The friendship between Byron and the Shelleys, particularly the time they spent together in Switzerland in 1816, has proven particularly fertile ground for filmmakers; the moment was depicted in *Gothic* (1986), *Haunted Summer* (1988), and the Spanish *Remando al viento* (1988). Attesting to the draw of Byron's biography on even the contemporary imagination, Tom Stoppard's 1993 play *Arcadia,* hailed by some critics as one of the finest plays in the English language, centers on questions of Byron's life and history.

Whether creators reinterpret Byron as a vampire, as in the novels of Tom Holland, or as the prime minister of an alternate England, as in the steampunk fiction of William Gibson and Bruce Sterling, Byron remains a compelling and much-talked-of figure in the Western cultural imagination.

Feldman, Paula R. "Mary Shelley and the Genesis of Moore's *Life* of Byron." *Studies in English Literature* 20 (1980): 611–20. Print.

Lovell, Ernest J. *His Very Self and Voice: Collected Conversations of Lord Byron.* New York: Macmillan, 1954. Print.

Mole, Tom. *Byron's Romantic Celebrity.* Basingstoke: Palgrave, 2007. Print.

North, Julian. *The Domestication of Genius: Biography and the Romantic Poet.* New York: Oxford University Press, 2009. Print.

Carina Saxon

The Letters of John Keats, 1814–1821

John Keats

Key Facts

Time Period:
Early 19th Century

Relevant Historical Events:
Growth of Romanticism; Keats's success as a poet

Nationality:
English

Keywords:
literature; sexuality; Romanticism

OVERVIEW

The Letters of John Keats, 1814–1821 provide insight into the intellectual and spiritual development of one of England's greatest Romantic poets, as well as an account of the political, social, and artistic life of London in the early nineteenth century. The letters are often considered among the most important to be written by an English poet. Divided into a two-volume set, they cover John Keats's entire poetic career, which spanned roughly the last eight years of his life. By presenting aspects of the author's personal development, as well as the details of his artistic milieu, the letters serve to illuminate Keats's poetic work and his times, with their emphasis on spiritual and literary growth, the relationship between art and politics, the idea of "negative-capability," and the nature of love and sexuality.

Keats did not publish any of his letters during his lifetime. They were first collected more than twenty years after his death in *Life, Letters, and Literary Remains* (1848). (The scholarly standard edition, *The Letters of John Keats, 1814–1821,* was not published until 1958.) Keats's poetry—and as a result, his letters—would eventually receive the serious critical attention they deserve, but for much of the nineteenth century scholars failed to recognize the importance of his works. Indeed, many of his contemporaries, as well as the English poets who immediately followed him, attacked the letters for what was deemed to be vulgarity. Scholars now recognize that the letters form an invaluable bridge between the literary work and the personal life of a major English poet.

HISTORICAL AND LITERARY CONTEXT

In the years preceding the writing of the letters, England witnessed an increase in literacy that led to a concomitant increase in correspondence. According to Andrés Rodríguez in *Book of the Heart* (1993), "By the early nineteenth century people wrote letters normally as we talk on the telephone, and for much the same reason." Keats was raised in a solidly middle-class family, one that, writes Jon Mee in his 2002 introduction to *Selected Letters,* "struggled to maintain and improve their precarious social standing," a theme often reflected in the letters. In addition, Keats's youth coincided with the massive social transformations that occurred during England's period of industrialization, an era that influenced the notion of "progress" found frequently in Keats's letters.

In the letters, Keats corresponded with several notable figures in London's literary milieu, including Leigh Hunt, the editor of the *Examiner,* a liberal newspaper that blended politics and commentary on the arts. He also maintained a correspondence with the artist Benjamin Haydon, as well as fellow poets John Hamilton Reynolds and Percy Bysshe Shelley, who influenced the primacy that Keats gives to sensuality in his prose. Although many of the letters are also addressed to audiences outside of these artistic circles, they too frequently attest to Keats's attempt to make a name for himself in the world of literary London.

In addition to detailing the development of Keats's intellect and soul, his letters evoke a number of historical literary figures. In an 1818 letter to Reynolds, Keats expresses his own aesthetic preferences, arguing that the "cold and artificial compositions" of Alexander Pope should be replaced with earlier examples of Geoffrey Chaucer, Edmund Spenser, John Milton, and William Shakespeare. Among contemporary poets, William Wordsworth had a significant influence, although Keats disagreed with what he perceived to be his excessively solemn Christian religiosity. Keats's letters differ from those of many of his famous epistolary predecessors, such as Thomas Gray and Horace Walpole, in that they are written in a more natural style rather than a polished and impersonal one.

The Letters of John Keats are notable because he formulated his poetics through their composition. Mee argues that Keats "seems to put ideas forward so as to explore and test them out in the letters." The lack of formal constraint in his epistolary writing allowed for a freedom of expression that was more rigorously formalized in his poetry. His letters are often read alongside his poetry, as the thoughts and explorations in the former serve to better illuminate understanding of the latter. Scholars have also studied the letters in order to trace the influence on Keats of writers within his literary milieu. In addition to his correspondences with certain contemporary poets, the letters detail Keats's thoughts about and reactions to other thinkers and writers of his time, such as William Hazlitt, Wordsworth, and Lord Byron.

THEMES AND STYLE

A central thrust of *The Letters of John Keats* is the process of his poetic development, but the letters also address themes of love, politics, and religion. In perhaps his most famous correspondence, written on December 21, 1871, to his brother George, Keats describes the quality par excellence of a great poet, the "one which Shakespeare possessed so enormously—I mean *Negative Capability,* that is when man is capable of being in uncertainties, Mysteries, doubts, without any irritable reaching after fact & reason." Although the term *negative capability* occurs only once in the letters, it is their most studied phrase, one that, according to the scholar Li Ou in *Keats and Negative Capability* (2009), bespeaks Keats's "belief that great poetry is marked by its allowance for a full-scale human experience that is too copious and diverse to be reduced to a neatly unified or conceptualized system." Along with passages that address his thoughts on poetry, the letters evince Keats's engagement with liberal politics and his religious sense of the "untrodden region" of the mind.

Keats's letters are, first and foremost, personal communications to friends, colleagues, and family members, but, as Susan Wolfson writes in "Keats the Letter-Writer," their composition offered the poet the opportunity to enact "processes of the mind … wherein the mind's various actions and attitudes can be framed as performances to be studied for their plays of error or energy." While this is certainly the main reason why he wrote the letters, they also exhibit numerous second-order motivations that vary depending upon the intended audience. His correspondence with a publisher, for example, with its emphasis on business issues, differs significantly from the passionate love letters Keats sent to his fiancée Fanny Brawne during the final years of his life.

The letters are also remarkable for the breadth of stylistic variation. As Mee notes, Keats often "puts on different kinds of identity…. With Reynolds he is often playful and punning…. With Bailey he strives to present himself as serious minded and philosophically inclined…. To the attentive Woodhouse, axioms are delivered to someone who he knows regards him seriously as a poet." In a letter to Brawne, he begins simply, almost plaintively, "Your Letter to me at Bedhampton hurt me very much." Such candor shows a turn away from the rhetorical flourishes that typified much eighteenth-century correspondence in favor of a more intimate, conversational tone.

CRITICAL DISCUSSION

The initial scholarly response to *The Letters of John Keats* was overshadowed by the critical attention given to his poetry. In the years immediately following his death, there was some limited critical analysis, but it was, for the most part, negative. As Rodriguez observes, "the detractors were many and the language of vituperation incredibly cruel." He goes on to list numerous English poets who attacked the letters, including Algernon Swinburne, Matthew Arnold, and Coventry Patmore. Gerard Manley Hopkins, however, praised Keats's letters, saying that he saw in them "an interest in higher thing, and of powerful and active thoughts."

John Keats, Romantic poet. Although Keats's work was not critically well received during his life, his reputation grew after his death and he eventually became one of the best loved of English poets. © GL ARCHIVE/ALAMY

Twentieth-century scholars and poets came to recognize the letters as significant literary achievements in their own right. In his 1933 essay "Shelley and Keats," T. S. Eliot states that the letters were "models of correspondence" and "certainly the most notable and most import ever written by any English poet." The poet W. H. Auden expressed similar sentiment when praising the letters as Shakespearean and speaking of the day when they might be more read than the poems themselves. Although that day has not quite come to pass, Keats's reputation as a letter writer does rival his stature as a poet, and *The Letters of John Keats* have attracted significant scholarly interest in the twenty-first century.

The literature surrounding the letters is considerable, with almost all Keats scholars devoting at least some time to them and their influence on his poetry. Much contemporary scholarship has focused on the way the letters help to define Keats's poetics. According to Wolfson, there are two distinct poetics in Keats's oeuvre, that of the poems and that of the correspondence. Rodríguez argues against this, writing that the letters, the poems, and Keats's life contain "a remarkable wholeness that is everywhere evident in all he did." A considerable amount of scholarship has also focused on Keats's idea of negative capability. Ou seeks to define the term and trace the influence of Shakespeare's *King Lear* on its inception.

BIBLIOGRAPHY

Sources

Eliot, T. S. "Shelley and Keats." *The Use of Poetry and the Use of Criticism.* London: Faber and Faber, 1933. Print.

PRIMARY SOURCE

EXCERPT FROM *THE LETTERS OF JOHN KEATS, 1814–1821*

To Fanny Brawne, 1 March(?) 1820

My dearest Fanny,

The power of your benediction is of not so weak a nature as to pass from the ring in four-and twenty hours—it is like a sacred Chalice once consecrated and ever consecrate. I shall kiss your name and mine where your Lips have been—Lips! why should a poor prisoner as I am talk about such things. Thank God, though I hold them the dearest pleasures in the universe, I have a consolation independent of them in the certainty of your affection. I could write a song in the style of Tom Moore's Pathetic about Memory if that would be any relief to me—No it would not. I will be as obstinate as a Robin, I will not sing in a cage—Health is my expected heaven and you are the Houri—this word I believe is both singular and plural—if only plural, never mind—you are a thousand of them.

Ever yours affectionately

my dearest—

J.K.

To Fanny Brawne, March(?) 1820

My dearest Fanny, I slept well last night and am no worse this morning for it. Day by day if I am not deceived I get a more unrestrain'd use of my Chest. The nearer a racer gets to the Goal the more his anxiety becomes so I lingering upon the borders of health feel my impatience increase. Perhaps on your account I have imagined my illness more serious than it is: how horrid was the chance of slipping into the ground instead of into your arms—the difference is amazing Love—Death must come at last; Man must die, as Shallow says; but before that is my fate I feign would try what more pleasures than you have given so sweet a creature as you can give. Let me have another opportunity of years before me and I will not die without being remember'd. Take care of yourself dear that we may both be well in the Summer. I do not at all fatigue myself with writing, having merely to put a line or two here and there, a Task which would worry a stout state of the body and mind, but which just suits me as I can do no more.

Your affectionate

J.K.—

To Fanny Brawne, March(?) 1820

My dearest Fanny,

Though I shall see you in so short a time I cannot forbear sending you a few lines. You say I did not give you yesterday a minute account of my health. To-day I have left off the Medicine which I took to keep the pulse down and I find I can do very well without it, which is a very favourable sign, as it shows there is no inflammation remaining. You think I may be wearied at night you say: it is my best time; I am at my best about eight o'clock. I received a Note from Mr. Proctor today. He says he cannot pay me a visit this weather as he is fearful of an inflammation in the Chest. What a horrid climate this is? or what careless inhabitants it has? You are one of them. My dear girl do not make a joke of it: do not expose yourself to the cold. There's the Thrush again—I can't afford it—he'll run me up a pretty Bill for Music—besides he ought to know I deal at Clementi's. How can you bear so long an imprisonment at Hampstead? I shall always remember it with all the gusto that a monopolizing carle should. I could build an Altar to you for it.

Your affectionate

J.K.

SOURCE: Keats, John. *Letters of John Keats to Fanny Brawne: Written in the Years of MDCCCXI and MDCCCXX*. New York: G. Broughton and B. Dunham, 1901.

Hopkins, Gerard Manley. *Further Letters of Gerard Manley Hopkins*. Ed. Claude Coller Abbott. London: Oxford University Press, 1956. Print.

Keats, John. *Selected Letters*. Ed. Robert Gittings. Oxford: Oxford University Press, 2002. Print.

Kuron, Ann Marie. "An Approach to Keats through His Letters." Diss. Kean University, 1965. *ProQuest*. Web. 28 Nov. 2012.

Mee, Jon. Introduction. *Selected Letters*. Ed. Robert Gittings. Oxford: Oxford University Press, 2002. Print.

Ou, Li. *Keats and Negative Capability*. New York: Continuum International, 2009. Print.

Rodríguez, Andrés. *Book of the Heart: The Poetics, Letters, and Life of John Keats*. New York: Lindisfarne, 1993. Print.

White, R. S. *John Keats: A Literary Life*. London: Palgrave Macmillan, 2010. Print.

Wolfson, Susan J. "Keats the Letter-Writer: Epistolary Poetics." *Romanticism Past and Present* 6.2 (1982): 43–61. Print.

Further Reading

Bloom, Harold. *The Odes of Keats*. New York: Chelsea House, 1987. Print.

Gittings, Robert. *The Living Year: 21 September 1818 to 21 September 1819*. Bloomington: Heinemann, 1954. Print.

Keats, John. *Endymion*. Cambridge: ProQuest, 1992. Print.

———. *Complete Poems of John Keats*. New York: Modern Library, 1994. Print.

Rollins, Hyder Edward. *Keats' Reputation in America to 1848*. Cambridge: Harvard University Press, 1946. Print.

Greg Luther

Letters to a Young Poet

Rainer Maria Rilke

OVERVIEW

First published in English in 1934, eight years after the author's death, *Letters to a Young Poet,* by Austrian poet Rainer Maria Rilke (1875–1926), contains ten letters written between 1903 and 1908 to officer and journalist Franz Xaver Kappus. One of the most renowned German-language poets, Rilke was also an active writer of letters, and this particular collection remains extremely popular. The correspondence spans a significant time in the author's life during which he published several works, lived throughout Europe, and apprenticed under the sculptor Auguste Rodin. Kappus first wrote to Rilke in 1902 to ask his opinion on some writing after discovering the poet had attended Kappus's military academy in Wiener-Neustadt. Rilke's generous and insightful responses examine, among other topics, art, life, God, and love.

Letters to a Young Poet was initially published in German in 1931 by Rilke's daughter Ruth and his son-in-law in compliance with the author's will. The English translation by M. D. Herter Norton was issued three years later and rereleased in 1954. Other translations came after, but the original, with the possible exception of the Stephen Mitchell edition from 2001, remains the most widely referenced. *Letters to a Young Poet* was well received by critics, as evidenced by a *New York Times* review from December 23, 1934, by Peter Monro Jack, which calls the book "a delight" and "a charming evocation of Rilke's personality, with a sense of grave wisdom in the finely written lines."

HISTORICAL AND LITERARY CONTEXT

The impetus for the correspondence featured in *Letters to a Young Poet* can be traced to Parson Horacek, who witnessed Kappus reading a collection of Rilke's poems. The poet had once been Kappus's student at the military academy. However, Kappus felt his job at the military academy ran counter to his poetic instincts. Rilke, meanwhile, considered his time in the military academy to be a low point of his life, and he wrote in a letter to his former lover Lou Andreas-Salomé in July 1903 that he found Paris, where he was living upon receiving his first letter from Kappus, to be a similar experience in that "a great fearful astonishment" and "terror assailed" him. He was thus superbly conditioned to express compassion for an artistic impulse coming from an environment as disciplined as a military academy.

According to Wolfgang Leppmann in *Rilke: A Life* (1984), the spring of 1903 marked a period of "exhaustion and dejection that bedeviled" the poet. He was poor and "homeless," relying on the kindness of acquaintances to accommodate himself throughout Europe. Rilke moved between France, Italy, Germany, and Sweden during the period when he wrote the letters to Kappus. According to William H. Gass in *Reading Rilke: Reflections on the Problems of Translation* (1999), he led a life of "loneliness, of brooding, self-absorption … because all the hours most of us spend making a living … Rilke had on his hands. Hence all those letters, of course."

Rilke was an avid and meticulous writer of letters. Over the course of his fifty-one years, he is credited with penning more than seven thousand. He was known to rewrite an entire page to correct one phrase and to recopy letters for his own records. In his letters to Kappus, Rilke writes that his greatest influences were the Bible, Danish writer Jens Peter Jacobsen, and Rodin. According to Annemarie S. Kidder in her translation of Rilke's *Letters on God and Letters to a Young Woman* (2012), other recipients of the poet's letters included "friends and family, novelists and poets, painters and sculptors, literary critics and publishers, and those who upon the reading his work had contacted the poet."

Kidder calls *Letters to a Young Poet* Rilke's "best known collection today." The book remains popular, according to Leppmann, because "from Rilke's responses one could easily compile a whole inventory of the views he held at the time." Although Rilke established a sterling reputation for himself as a poet, he reminds Kappus in Letter 8 that his "life has much difficulty and sadness and remains far behind yours." Indeed, as he writes in Letter 3, he could not even afford copies of his own books. During their correspondence, Rilke published five works, including *The Book of Hours* (1905) and *New Poems* (1907).

THEMES AND STYLE

Rilke's *Letters to a Young Poet* focuses on many of the same themes he examines in his poetry, including isolation, intimacy, nature, theology, and artistic duty. Perhaps his most consistent argument centers on the necessity of solitude and self-reflection for a writer. In Letter 1 he writes, "There is only one single way.

❖ Key Facts

Time Period:
Early 20th Century

Relevant Historical Events:
Rilke's success as a writer and frequent moves around Europe

Nationality:
German

Keywords:
poetry; advice; aesthetics

Poet Rainer Maria Rilke photographed circa 1910, a few years after he wrote the letters collected in *Letters to a Young Poet.*
© INTERFOTO/ALAMY

Go into yourself." In Letter 6 he adds, "The necessary thing is after all but this: solitude, great inner solitude." He implores Kappus in Letter 7 to convene with nature, in which one is offered such rich poetic material and an important example of holding "to what is difficult" in one's life rather than resisting it. He considers love, relationships, and sex to be among these difficulties, though they are also sources of great joy.

The ten letters function much as Rilke's other works do in that they are marked by contradictions. According to H. F. Peters in *Rainer Maria Rilke: Masks and the Man,* Rilke was both magnetically drawn to embrace life but was quite hostile toward it. Peters writes, "The intensity of feeling for these contradictory emotions causes great inner tension in Rilke's work. It oscillates between total rejection and total acceptance of life, between negation and affirmation, lament and praise." This paradox leads to his focus on "the difficult" that one might transcend, which, Peters contends, "occurs in his letters as a guide to life for those who ask his advice." It also allows him to boldly state opinions while affirming his deep humility and gratitude.

Given that Rilke never carried on a personal relationship with Kappus, the language of the letters indicates a remarkable generosity, often addressed to "dear Mr. Kappus." The poetic artistry of their content is substantial, as is the depth with which Rilke attends to his addressee's art, personal concerns, and philosophical queries. In Letter 7, for example, Rilke recopies the sonnet that Kappus had penned. According to W. W. Norton in the introduction to *Letters of Rainer Maria Rilke, 1892–1910,* "Many of the letters in Rilke's extraordinary correspondence have an artistic validity of their own and are to be enjoyed for themselves."

CRITICAL DISCUSSION

Letters to a Young Poet was initially overshadowed by Rilke's poetry and prose, though it garnered positive reviews, adding to his reputation as a writer. Peters makes laudatory references to Rilke's letters to Kappus and also clearly establishes the poet's influence throughout the United States and Europe through quotes from Paul Valéry (who calls him "fascinating" and "mysterious") and W. H. Auden, quoted in a 1939 review in the *New Republic* as arguing, "Rilke's most immediate and obvious influence has been on diction and imagery."

Letters to a Young Poet has served as a model for many books in recent years. Beginning in 2001, Basic Books issued thirteen volumes as part of its Art of Mentoring series, including *Letters to a Young Contrarian* by Christopher Hitchens and *Letters to a Young Gymnast* by Nadia Comaneci. Similar titles have emerged from other publishers, including *Letters to a Young Teacher* by Jonathon Kozol and *Letters to a Young Novelist* by Mario Vargas Llosa. In 2006 poets Dana Teen Lomax and Jennifer Firestone began the Letters to Poets project, a response to the fact that none of Kappus's letters to Rilke was ever printed. Their series includes correspondence (some via e-mail) between both emerging and established poet pairs.

The legend of Rilke has not gone unquestioned. In a review of Gass's highly regarded *Reading Rilke,* poetry scholar and native German speaker Marjorie Perloff criticizes "the cult-like worship of a poet by later poets who can barely read the poetry." The major translators of Rilke, including Gass, Galway Kinnell, and Edward Snow, are not bilingual, she points out. Further, she argues, the high drama of passages from *Letters to a Young Poet,* such as when Kappus is asked whether he "would have to die" if denied writing, furthers the "cult" that includes American and English poets of considerable fame (Robert Bly and Louise Gluck, for example) who live at a time when art's value has been "commodified."

BIBLIOGRAPHY

Sources

Gass, William H. *Reading Rilke: Reflections on the Problems of Translation.* New York: Knopf, 1999. Print.

Jack, Peter Monro. "Rainer Rilke's Personal Philosophy." *New York Times* 23 Dec. 1934. *ProQuest Historical Newspapers.* Web. 20 Dec. 2012.

Kidder, Annemarie S. Introduction. *Letters on God and Letters to a Young Woman.* Trans. Annemarie S. Kidder. Evanston, Ill.: Northwestern University Press, 2012. Print.

Leppmann, Wolfgang. *Rilke: A Life.* Trans. Russell M. Stockman. New York: Fromm International, 1984. Print.

Norton, W. W. Introduction. *Letters of Rainer Maria Rilke, 1892–1910.* Trans. Jane Bannard Greene and M. D. Herter Norton. New York: Norton, 1945. Print.

Perloff, Marjorie. "Reading Gass Reading Rilke." *Parnassus: Poetry in Review* 25.1–2 (2001): 486. *Academic Search Elite.* Web. 22 Dec. 2012.

Peters, H. F. *Rainer Maria Rilke: Masks and the Man.* Seattle: University of Washington, 1960. Print.

Rilke, Rainer Maria, and Franz Xaver Kappus. *Letters to a Young Poet.* Trans. M. D. Herter Norton. New York: Norton, 1954. Print.

Further Reading

Gordon, Ken. "What about Franz?" *Poets & Writers* Nov.–Dec. 2006. Poets & Writers. Web. 23 Dec. 2012.

"Rainer Maria Rilke." *The Poetry Foundation.* The Poetry Foundation, n.d. Web. 21 Dec. 2012.

Rilke, Rainer Maria. *Letters of Rainer Maria Rilke, 1892–1910.* Trans. Jane Bannard Greene and M. D. Herter Norton. New York: Norton, 1945. Print.

Rilke, Rainer Maria. *Letters on God and Letters to a Young Woman.* Trans. Annemarie S. Kidder. Evanston, Ill. Northwestern University Press, 2012. Print.

Rose, William, and G. Craig Houston, eds. *Rainer Maria Rilke: Aspects of His Mind and Poetry.* London: Sidgwick & Jackson, 1938. Print.

Rachel Mindell

RAINER MARIA RILKE AND LOU ANDREAS-SALOMÉ

At the time he was writing to Franz Xaver Kappus, Rainer Maria Rilke also nurtured several other correspondences, including one with his wife Clara Westoff and another with his former lover Lou Andreas-Salomé. Rilke met Salomé, the daughter of a Russian general, in 1897 in Munich. She was fifteen years his senior and at the time was married to Friedrich Andreas. An intellectual and writer, she is considered to have had a major influence on Rilke's life and work. Rilke traveled with her and her husband throughout Germany, Italy, and most significantly Russia, where he met important writers, including Leo Tolstoy. Although Salomé and Rilke were lovers for only a brief time, the length of their passionate written relationship was notable.

More than twenty-five years of their correspondence was released in a 2006 collection, *Rainer Maria Rilke and Lou Andreas-Salomé: The Correspondence,* translated by Edward Snow and Michael Winkler, and again in 2008 as *Rilke and Andreas-Salomé: A Love Story in Letters.* Salomé has been considered a sort of muse to important men of her time, including Sigmund Freud and Friedrich Nietzsche. She purportedly rejected the latter's proposal of marriage when she was twenty-one. According to William H. Gass in *Reading Rilke: Reflections on the Problems of Translation,* Salomé was Rilke's "match."

Notebooks
Tennessee Williams

Key Facts

Time Period:
Mid- to Late 20th Century

Relevant Historical Events:
Williams's success as a writer; World War II; House Un-American Activities Committee (HUAC)

Nationality:
American

Keywords:
literature; homosexuality; alcoholism

OVERVIEW

Tennessee Williams's *Notebooks* (1936–1981), published in 2006, reveals the playwright's most intimate thoughts and impressions and provides insight into his published plays, poems, and short stories. The earliest entries chart Williams's progress from penniless aspiring writer in St. Louis to globe-trotting postwar celebrity to cultural outcast, all while revealing a man intensely focused on his immediate environment. He was particularly close to his sister, who was institutionalized for schizophrenia, and to his grandfather, an Episcopalian minister. Although the earliest entries date from 1936 and the latest from 1981, *Notebooks* contains no entries between October 1958 and March 1979. The work tracks the smallest variations in Williams's own moods, his numerous but mostly minor health issues, the complexities of the homosexual world he was part of, and his intense relationship to his work. As in his plays and stories, alcohol abuse, self-doubt, fear of hospitalization, and the fragility of the human mind feature prominently, as do the difficulties of love relationships.

Born in 1911, Williams had already fallen from grace in the eyes of many critics by the time he published his *Memoirs* in 1975. Critics were shocked and offended by his unapologetic descriptions of his life as a gay man. Williams explained the reason for his bluntness at the time by stating that "I thought I'd be dead when it came out." In contrast, *Notebooks* shows a far more sensitive side of Williams, navigating his tumultuous relationships as best he could and exploring his lifelong anxiety that made even basic social interactions a strain. For scholars of Williams, *Notebooks* provides valuable context for his literary works.

HISTORICAL AND LITERARY CONTEXT

Notebooks is mostly apolitical and unconcerned with world events, even though it begins during the Great Depression and spans World War II and subsequent eras. Also glossed over is the controversy surrounding the legendary director Elia Kazan, who, after directing the film version of Williams's play *A Streetcar Named Desire,* revealed names of suspected communists in the theater community to the House Un-American Activities Committee (HUAC) in 1952. Later, Kazan directed the 1956 film *Baby Doll,* for which Williams adapted the script from his one-act play *27 Wagons Full of Cotton.* The play concerns two rival cotton gin owners, one of whom attempts to seduce the other's teenage virgin bride as retaliation for past transgressions. Although it received critical acclaim, *Baby Doll* was condemned by the archbishop of New York City and the Catholic-led Legion of Decency. Despite this controversy, Williams briefly converted to Catholicism in 1969, the same year his brother—himself a convert to Catholicism—signed Williams into a hospital to treat his drug addiction.

Williams's journals show his preoccupation with and his desire to be counted among the important literary figures of his time. For example, he describes a dream in 1936 that features Josephine Johnson, winner of the 1935 Pulitzer Prize for fiction. As he is increasingly successful, particularly after the 1944 premiere of the play *The Glass Menagerie,* Williams chronicles his travels and his relationships with such writers as Truman Capote, Gore Vidal, and Jean-Paul Sartre; noted arts patron Peggy Guggenheim; and other famous figures of arts and letters. After a 1979 party in London at which Princess Margaret called him "a dirty old man," Williams counters in his journal that he is merely "an angry old man." Most of *Notebooks* covers Williams's more productive and successful years, although his creative output remained steady until his death in 1983.

Throughout his journals Williams speaks of writers he admires—William Faulkner, Ernest Hemingway, D. H. Lawrence, Rainer Maria Rilke, Hart Crane, Katherine Anne Porter—as well as those he disdains, such as Graham Greene and Eugene O'Neill. Of Christopher Isherwood's 1954 novel *The World in the Evening,* Williams comments that it is "disappointing, doesn't seem to be anything deeply personal or creative, but still has passages that are good prose." British playwright and actor Noël Coward, who Williams met in Rome in 1952 ("Find him good company. He praises my work!"), published his own *Diaries,* which were coedited by his companion Graham Payn, posthumously, in 2000. Even more star-studded than Williams's, they recount time spent in some of the same European locales Williams frequented but are far less anxiety-ridden.

Williams laments in a 1943 entry that his journals, "despite their attempt at merciless candor … perhaps really distort unfavorably for I seem inclined to note only the seedier things," and he rarely expresses confidence in his work: "I am not sure *Cat [on a Hot Tin Roof]* is a truly good play, still it's a bit uncanny that I was able to make it as good as it is," he writes in 1955. When it comes to Williams's reputation, *Notebooks* bears witness to what Vidal wrote in his foreword to Williams's *Memoirs*: "You've had too much bad personal exposure for anything to help you much anymore."

THEMES AND STYLE

Notebooks is marked, as are Williams's plays, poems, and stories, by preoccupations with beauty, longing for a sense of safety among fellow human beings, drugs and alcohol, and the baffling intricacies of romance. Family is also a major element, as Williams maintained close bonds with his grandfather and his sister Rose. *Notebooks* also contains many of Williams's sketches and paintings. In spite of his extensive socializing, he often seems lonely, such as in his description of a day on the Amalfi Coast: "A gentle sadness, 'heimwehr' [German for 'homesickness'] or something of the sort, came over me as I tried to take a nap before dinner and a corn on my little toe ached." Waiting for Frank Merlo, his longtime partner, to join him in Rome, Williams writes: "There's a glass of liquor and 2 capsules by the bed but I wish, I would prefer, to avoid them—Feel dreadfully alone."

The diaries that became *Notebooks* served as "someplace else," to paraphrase Williams's description of religion, as "a form of art: it is another 'something else': another exercise for the mysterious new perceptions which are beginning to slowly emerge from the human consciousness." They afforded a safe place for him to air his consciousness, no matter how ignoble its contents. In his *Memoirs*, Williams writes about an episode that took place when he was sixteen, on a trip to Europe with his grandfather: "Abruptly, it occurred to me that the process of thought was a terrifyingly complex mystery of human life." The journals, perhaps, were a means of containing that terrifying process. Williams sometimes revisited old entries, making notes beside them, not with a view toward eventual publication but rather, as editor Margaret Bradham Thornton observes, to commune with his former self. However, he did envision their possible compilation and publication. Thornton quotes Williams in her introduction: "I want very much to get all these journals together and publish them intact. I think they should eventually be published that way with footnotes by their author, since they may have some usefulness as a history of an individual's fight for survival, emotional travail."

Williams's writing style in *Notebooks* varies depending on the topic. "I was tired of being treated like a stupid, unsatisfactory whore by a bad-tempered pimp," Williams writes of one of his and Merlo's "periodic cathartic discussions" in 1953. Describing his ever-present anxiety in 1944, he says that his "mind is clear although sorrowful and prescient of sorrow to come—if not catastrophe.... Am I altogether selfish? How does one find out—weigh his decency?" In 1979 Williams wonders about the demise of his career: "Did I die by my own hand or was I destroyed slowly and brutally by a conspiratorial group?" Writing in the *Sewanee Review* in 2008, A. Banerjee observes that "Williams recognized that he was 'two' selves, one that was acutely sensitive to life's disappointments and the other that was determined to carry on."

Author Tennessee Williams in 1981, the year of his death. His *Notebooks* includes works from 1936 to 1981. © NATHAN BENN/ALAMY

CRITICAL DISCUSSION

Initial critical responses to *Notebooks* were mixed. From an academic perspective, Susan Savage Lee, writing in 2008 for *Rocky Mountain Review*, applauded Thornton's edition, which provides a full page of notes for every page of the journal, along with many photographs. Lee considers *Notebooks* to be "far more thorough" than similar literary endeavors, including *The Journals of Sylvia Plath* and *Henry James' Letters*. Banerjee notes the "painstaking meticulousness" of Thornton's research and the possibility that Williams's "inability to write as he wanted to led to permanent melancholia." In *Theatre History Studies*, reviewer Joan Wylie Hall writes, "*Notebooks* is indeed 'a writer's journal.'" Writing for the *Telegraph* in 2007, however, Philip Hensher "gets the impression that [Williams] wasn't really that interested in writing," calling his comments on other writers "polite book-club murmurs." Hensher concludes that "most of all, though, the notebooks are a running account of the various men Williams had sex with."

In her 2008 essay for *Theatre History Studies*, Thornton explained her process in compiling and editing *Notebooks*. She is slightly less generous to Williams in the essay than in her introduction and footnotes to the book. One of her most surprising assertions is that his "wretched whining was just a form of indulgence.... Williams inhabited moods and dispositions to better understand their range."

The disdain expressed by early reviewers may be the reason for the limited scholarly interest in *Notebooks*. Writing for the *Observer* in 2007, Peter Conrad mocks everything from "the battalions of male hookers that troop through his rented bedrooms"

CAMINO REAL

Tennessee Williams wrote an experimental play, *Camino Real,* that ran for less than two months in New York in 1953. *New York Times* critic Walter Kerr worried that Williams was "heading toward the cerebral" and urged the playwright against it. "What makes you an artist of the first rank is your intuitive gift for penetrating reality," Kerr wrote. "An intuitive artist starts with the recognizable surface of things and burrows *in*. Don't swap this for the conscious, rational process of the analyst."

The play is set in the plaza of "a tropical port that bears a confusing, but somehow harmonious, resemblance to such widely scattered ports as Tangiers, Havana, Vera Cruz, Casablanca, Shanghai, New Orleans," Williams wrote in his prologue. The characters include Casanova; Don Quixote; and his squire, Sancho Panza. One scene has Lord Byron mourning the drowning death of his friend the poet Percy Bysshe Shelley, whose body is burned on shore. In Williams's version, Byron has Shelley's friend Edward John Trelawny, who arranged the unconventional funeral, pluck Byron's heart out of his corpse as it burns on the funeral pyre "as a baker reaches quickly into an oven!" In spite of its nonlinear structure; strange mixture of fable, myth, and history; and initial critical failure, *Camino Real* survived. A March 2012 production mounted in Chicago prompted one critic to declare Williams "a poet of the universal soul."

to the "editor's notes, which take up half of this unwieldy volume." Simon Callow, writing in the *Guardian,* disagrees: "The revelation of Margaret Bradham Thornton's stupendous, superbly annotated edition of Williams's *Notebooks* is that nothing ever poured out of him. Everything, from the beginning, was squeezed out with agonizing difficulty." However, culture critic Stephen Emms, also writing in the *Guardian,* sees a valuable cautionary tale in the "stark warning they offer the unpublished writer about the lack of peace that success—or rather, the attempts at its sustainment—can bring."

BIBLIOGRAPHY

Sources

Banerjee, A. "The Travails of Tennessee Williams." Rev. of *Notebooks,* by Tennessee Williams. *Sewanee Review* 116.2 (2008): 326–31. *Project MUSE.* Web. 17 Dec. 2012.

Callow, Simon. "The Long Way Down." Rev. of *Notebooks,* by Tennessee Williams. *Guardian.* Guardian News and Media, 17 Feb. 2007. Web. 24 Dec. 2012.

Conrad, Peter. "Oh Look, It's All about Me." Rev. of *Notebooks,* by Tennessee Williams. *Observer.* Guardian News and Media, 18 Feb. 2007. Web. 24 Dec. 2012.

Emms, Stephen. "The Strange Allure of Tennessee Williams's *Notebooks.*" *Guardian.* Guardian News and Media, 25 Mar. 2011. Web. 24 Dec. 2012.

Hall, Joan Wylie. Rev. of *Notebooks,* by Tennessee Williams. *Theatre History Studies* 28 (2008): 168–70. *Project MUSE.* Web. 24 Dec. 2012.

Hensher, Philip. Rev. of *Notebooks,* by Tennessee Williams. *Telegraph.* Telegraph Media Group, 25 Feb. 2007. Web. 10 Jan. 2013.

Jones, Chris. "Bieito's 'Camino Real' Puts the Spotlight on Tennessee Williams." *Chicago Tribune.* Chicago Tribune, 12 Mar. 2012. Web. 10 Jan. 2013.

Kerr, Walter. Private Letter to Williams Dated 13 April 1953. *Tennessee Williams. Dictionary of Literary Biography, Documentary Series: An Illustrated Chronicle.* Vol. 4. Ed. Margaret Van Antwerp and Sally Johns. Detroit: Gale Research, 1984. Print.

Lee, Susan Savage. Rev. of *Notebooks,* by Tennessee Williams. *Rocky Mountain Review* 53 (2008). *Rocky Mountain Modern Language Association.* Web. 10 Jan. 2013.

Pike, Rosamund. "Put Some South in Yer Mouth." *Guardian.* Guardian News and Media, 11 Oct. 2006. Web. 21 Dec. 2012.

Rader, Dotson. "Tennessee Williams, the Art of Theater No. 5." Interview with Tennessee Williams. *Paris Review* 81 (1981). Print.

Thornton, Margaret Bradham. "Between the Lines: Editing the Notebooks of Tennessee Williams." *Theatre History Studies* 28 (2008): 7–15. *Project MUSE.* Web. 24 Dec. 2012.

Williams, Tennessee. *Notebooks.* Margaret Bradham Thornton, ed. New Haven: Yale University Press, 2006. Print.

Further Reading

Bloom, Harold. *Tennessee Williams.* New York: Chelsea House, 1987. Print.

Coward, Noel. *The Noel Coward Diaries.* Boston: Da Capo, 2000. Print.

Meek, Michele. "Marriage, Adultery, and Desire: A Subversive Subtext in *Baby Doll.*" *Tennessee Williams Annual Review.* Tennessee Williams Annual Review, 2011. Web. 10 Jan. 2013.

Murphy, Brenda, ed. *Tennessee Williams.* Pasadena: Salem, 2011. Print.

St. Just, Maria. *Five O' Clock Angel.* New York: Knopf, 1990. Print.

Shaland, Irene. Rev. of *The Glass Menagerie,* by Tennessee Williams. *Theatre Journal* 42.1 (1990): 121–23. *JSTOR.* Web. 10 Jan. 2013.

Vineberg, Steve. Rev. of *A Streetcar Named Desire,* by Tennessee Williams. *Theatre Journal* 39.2 (1987): 235–36. *JSTOR.* Web. 10 Jan. 2013.

Williams, Tennessee. *Memoirs.* New York: New Directions, 2006. Print.

Rebecca Rustin

Theories

The Annals of Ballitore by Mary Leadbeater	157
Collected Letters of a Renaissance Feminist by Laura Cereta	160
The Extraordinary Work of Ordinary Writing: Annie Ray's Diary by Jennifer Sinor	163
Journals of Søren Kierkegaard by Søren Kierkegaard	166
Letters between Two by Lu Xun and Xu Guangping	170
"Practice of the Private Journal" by Philippe Lejeune	174
"Some Observations on Diaries, Self-Biography, and Self-Characters" by Isaac D'Israeli	177
A Writer's Diary by Virginia Woolf	180
A Writer's Notebook by W. Somerset Maugham	183

The Annals of Ballitore
Mary Leadbeater

OVERVIEW

The Annals of Ballitore, which was published as part of *The Leadbeater Papers* (1862), documents the life of Mary Leadbeater from 1766 to 1818. Leadbeater compiled the *Annals* from selected entries in her unpublished journals, fulfilling her desire to share her life story while also maintaining a degree of privacy in keeping with her Quaker ideals. The text, which is divided into chapters representing years, includes details about historical events, most notably the Irish Rebellion of 1798. Leadbeater also affectionately describes her family and fellow townsfolk, in the process sharing details of village life in eighteenth-century Ireland.

While Leadbeater published a number of works during her lifetime, the *Annals* did not appear until some forty years after her death. Little is known about the book's immediate reception, although it has been noted more generally that Quaker works, which were allied with neither Protestants nor Catholics on religious issues, may be of more interest to contemporary scholars than they were in popular discourses of their day. The *Annals* was regarded with interest by scholars when it was reprinted in 1986 and again in 2008. Notable for its wealth of details about lives that were not given wide consideration in literature, the text is also of interest to students of autobiography and Irish political history.

HISTORICAL AND LITERARY CONTEXT

Mary Shackleton Leadbeater was born in 1758 Ballitore, County Kildare, Ireland, a village founded by Quakers. Her grandfather, Abraham Shackleton, had emigrated from Yorkshire to start a Quaker school there in 1726; one of his pupils was the famed Irish statesman and philosopher Edmund Burke, who Mary became well acquainted with. Her father, Richard Shackleton, served as schoolmaster after Abraham. Founded as the Religious Society of Friends in 1647, Quakerism took a more equitable view of the role of women than was common in the broader Irish society of the day. Eighteenth-century Quaker girls tended to be educated more liberally than their Catholic and non-Quaker Protestant counterparts, and Quaker women were permitted to preach and to publish religious pamphlets. Leadbeater was educated at her father's school and was encouraged to express her ideas in writing. She began keeping a diary when she was eleven years old and continued until her death in 1826. After she married William Leadbeater in 1791, she became the village postmistress.

Two years before her death, Leadbeater drew on her diaries to compile *The Annals of Ballitore,* which chronicle life in her home village. The work exhibits the sharp-eyed observations of a woman who was immersed in her community and alive to its details. Ballitore was touched by significant historical events during Leadbeater's lifetime, most notably the three-month Irish Rebellion of 1798, in which early republicans led a rebellion against British rule. During the upheaval Ballitore was occupied by British yeomanry (militia), as well as by the Suffolk Fencibles and the Ancient Britons (British troops), all of whom disrupted village life, carrying out reprisals, looting, burning homes, and in some cases beating and murdering villagers. Leadbeater was forced to flee with her family to nearby Carlow, returning to rebuild after the unrest had died down. She devotes a significant section of *Annals* to the horrifying events. The forty-five volumes she produced in total are archived at the National Library of Ireland, Dublin.

During her lifetime Leadbeater published a number of poems as well as instructional tracts, including *Cottage Dialogues among the Irish Peasantry* (1811) and a companion piece, *The Landlord's Friend* (1813). *Cottage Dialogues* includes an introduction by novelist Maria Edgeworth, whose own writing was similarly concerned with both capturing the Irish spirit and with providing practical and moral instruction to her readers. *The Landlord's Friend* was followed by another instructive, *Tales for Cottagers* (1814), which Leadbeater coauthored with her stepmother, Elizabeth Shackleton; and *The Cottage Diaries* (1822), which provides biographical sketches of Leadbeater's Ballitore neighbors. Leadbeater's interest in documenting village life and in sharing her reflections on right living (the latter firmly rooted in her Quakerism), evident in these earlier works, is also prominent in the *Annals.*

The Annals of Ballitore was not printed until 1862, decades after Leadbeater's death, and details of the publication are sketchy. Most accounts cite her niece Betsy Leadbeater, working in conjunction with Quaker publisher Richard Davis Webb, as responsible

❖ **Key Facts**

Time Period:
Late 18th to Early 19th Centuries

Relevant Historical Events:
Irish Rebellion of 1798; persecution of Quakers

Nationality:
Irish

Keywords:
Quakerism; women's writing; religion

THEORIES

United Irishmen in Training, a print by English artist James Gillray depicting a British imagining of the Irish Rebellion of 1798. During this uprising Mary Leadbeater witnessed British troops brutalizing the residents of her hometown, including one soldier who almost killed her. © EILEEN TWEEDY/ THE ART ARCHIVE AT ART RESOURCE, NY

for the project, although Leadbeater's daughter Lydia may also have been involved. Volume 1 of the resulting two-volume *Leadbeater Papers* comprises the *Annals* along with a brief biographical sketch, "Mary Leadbeater: A Memoir," penned by Betsy. Volume 2 includes Leadbeater's correspondence with writers such as Burke and the poet George Crabbe, another documenter of ordinary life. The *Papers* have provided further material for scholars of these eminent men and their circle.

THEMES AND STYLE

The Annals of Ballitore focuses on the life of her village, documenting both everyday happenings and historically significant events as the latter impacted Ballitore and its inhabitants. The work opens with a section of "preliminary remarks," which characterize the village as "this lovely spot, where nature assisted by art gave us the most perfect gratification." After introducing the village, Leadbeater describes her grandfather's house and invites the reader to walk with her through the streets as she remarks on the details she has known since childhood. The remainder of the text is divided into sections by year, detailing births, marriages, illnesses, and deaths, as well as providing accounts of the people with whom Leadbeater was acquainted. Her involvement with the Society of Friends is also present in the *Annals*, although her discussions of the Quakers, and of her own beliefs, are generally circumspect.

Early in the *Annals*, Leadbeater writes of feeling, with regard to her children and grandchildren, the desire "to trace for their amusement and my own, those scenes indifferent to other eyes, which have passed before mine not unnoticed." Scholars and others believe that her decision to publish an edited version of her diaries, rather than publish them in their entirety, may be attributable to her adherence to Quaker notions of modesty and humility. Indeed, she writes, "My abilities are limited; my sphere is limited also." By excising self-reflection from the chronicle of her life, she could fulfill her ambition to record her experiences for posterity while remaining true to her ideals.

The tone of the *Annals* is personal—despite the lack of extensive self-revelation—and affectionately evocative of the eighteenth-century Irish voices of Leadbeater's neighbors. She writes of her home smilingly as "the sweetest spot of the world." She is angry and heartsick as she describes the pillage of Ballitore during the Irish Rebellion of 1798. At the same time, she expresses admiration for the villagers, the "houseless wretches" who in spite of having their homes reduced to "blackened ruins … expressed thankfulness that their lives were spared." Her reproduction of the idioms of the day—for instance, such phrases as "we'll be out in a shot"—help to establish a sense of time and place for future students of Irish history.

CRITICAL DISCUSSION

There is little record of critical response to *The Annals of Ballitore* when it was published as part of the *Leadbeater Papers* in 1866. It was not reprinted again for more than one hundred years, which suggests that it was not widely read. When it was republished in 1986, the *Annals* drew a positive response. In his review of the reprint, Leo Daly calls the work an "astonishing chronicle … of this unique woman and her community." An edition published in 2008 brought additional praise, including a highly laudatory review from Lucille Redmond in *Books Ireland* (2009), which reflects a continuing interest in Leadbeater and the vanished society in which she lived.

The Annals of Ballitore is notable for providing what scholar Barbara Hughes calls, in her 2010 book *Between Literature and History*, "a rare record of the poorly documented Irish villager." In addition to offering valuable details about the events of 1798, the *Annals* describes village customs, such as the mock burial and resurrection of a newborn infant to cancel out what was thought to be an unlucky birth date. Leadbeater's use of such anecdotes to construct an Irish identity, as well as her own self-portrait, has provided a trend in recent critical scholarship.

Leadbeater's text has been investigated as both autobiography and political history. Hughes examines the manner in which, by publishing an amended version of her diaries, Leadbeater effectively "depict[s] idealized familial relationships" rather than the "more complex" picture that emerges through study of her private papers. In "Nation or Neighbourhood? Mary Leadbeater's Public and Private Writing" (2005), Kevin O'Néill analyzes Leadbeater's construction of "the neighbourhood" as a "theater of practical reform" that offers "a constructive alternative identity to those offered by either a vanquished Irish republicanism or the new triumphant United Kingdom loyalism/nationalism that served as orthodoxy in the post-Rebellion era."

BIBLIOGRAPHY

Sources

Daly, Leo. "Speaking of '98." Rev. of *The Annals of Ballitore*, by Mary Leadbeater. *Books Ireland* 110 (1987): 6–7. *JSTOR*. Web. 14 Jan. 2013.

Hughes, Barbara. *Between Literature and History: The Diaries and Memoirs of Mary Leadbeater and Dorothea Herbert*. Bern: Lang, 2010. Print.

THE IRISH REBELLION OF 1798

The success of the French and American revolutions inspired early Irish republicans to form, in 1791, the Society of United Irishmen. Under the leadership of Theobald Wolfe Tone, the group sought to unite Protestants and Catholics in seeking parliamentary reform and, ultimately, an end to British rule in Ireland. Suspicious of the group's ties with the French government, the British government passed the Insurrection Act in 1796, allowing the government broad powers over districts it deemed unstable, and worked to suppress republican publications.

The rebellion initially broke out in counties around Dublin, including Mary Leadbeater's home county, Kildare. Although fighting in this area was put down quickly, it erupted again after reports of republican success in other regions. Both rebel forces and loyalist troops were responsible for death and destruction in Ireland's villages, and after the fighting was extinguished, contrary to the aims of the Society of United Irishmen, sectarian resentments were high. Following the three-month rebellion, the Irish parliament was disbanded, and writing that did not conform to the official government version of events was suppressed. Several centuries later the events of 1798 continue to be a subject of interest and argument.

Leadbeater, Mary. *The Leadbeater Papers*. London: Bell, 1862. *Google Books*. Web. 12 Jan. 2013.

O'Neill, Kevin. "Nation or Neighbourhood? Mary Leadbeater's Public and Private Writing." *These Fissured Isles: Ireland, Scotland and the Making of Modern Britain 1798–1848*. Ed. Terry Brotherstone, Anna Clark, and Kevin Whelan. Edinburgh: Donald, 2005. Print.

Redmond, Lucille. "Memories of '98." Rev. of *The Annals of Ballitore*, by Mary Leadbeater; ed. Mario Corrigan, Michael Kavanagh, and Karel Kiely. *Books Ireland* 313 (2009): 138–39. *JSTOR*. Web. 14 Jan. 2013.

Further Reading

Coolahan, Marie-Louise. *Women, Writing, and Language in Early Modern Ireland*. Oxford: Oxford University Press, 2010. Print.

Donovan, Josephine. *European Local-Color Literature: National Tales, Dorfgeschichten, Romans Champêtres*. London: Continuum, 2010. Print.

Leadbeater, Mary. *Cottage Dialogues among the Irish Peasantry: With Notes and a Preface*. London: Johnson, 1811. *Google Books*. Web. 14 Jan. 2013.

Livesy, James. *Civil Society and Empire: Ireland and Scotland in the Eighteenth-Century Atlantic World*. New Haven: Yale University Press, 2009. Print.

Ryan, Salvador, and Brendan Leahy, eds. *Treasures of Irish Christianity: People and Places, Images and Texts*. Dublin: Veritas, 2012. Print.

Caitlin Moore

COLLECTED LETTERS OF A RENAISSANCE FEMINIST
Laura Cereta

❖ Key Facts

Time Period:
Late 15th Century

Relevant Historical Events:
Renaissance; birth of feminism

Nationality:
Italian

Keywords:
women's writing; intellectualism; humanism

OVERVIEW

Laura Cereta's *Collected Letters of a Renaissance Feminist* is a modern edition of the author's *Epistulae familiares,* which circulated in manuscript form between 1488 and 1492. During Cereta's lifetime (1469–1499) these letters found a wide readership of Italian scholars in Brescia, Verona, and Venice, although they were not formally published until the seventeenth century, when they were edited by her first biographer, Giacomo Filippo Tomasini, in Padua. He published the collection, eighty-two Latin letters with a variety of humanist and antihumanist themes, in 1640. Although Cereta, like the male writers of the era, was interested in finding patronage, her works differ from her male contemporaries in that instead of focusing on demonstrating prowess in Latin composition, her letters concentrate on her relationships and are addressed to her friends and family, including other women. Her themes include common humanist topics, personal relationships, and the importance of women's education and participation in society.

Though highly regarded by a number of influential Italian scholars whom she counted as friends, Cereta was initially received in a spirit of hostility because of her gender. She was even accused of plagiarism by one male scholar who believed her Latin and her knowledge of astronomy were too accomplished to be the true work of a woman. She defended herself admirably against such charges, using the fundamentals of Renaissance humanism to uphold her position as a female intellectual and, according to Sarah Gwyneth Ross in *The Birth of Feminism* (2009), "[holding] her own as a writer in displaying the depth and breadth of her erudition."

HISTORICAL AND LITERARY CONTEXT

Cereta's letters are important in the history of the *querelle de femmes,* or the debate about women, a genre initiated by Christine de Pisan (1363–1430) in early modern Europe. As was the norm in most upper-class families in fifteenth-century Italy, Cereta (the descendant of a prominent Brescia family) was sent to a convent in order to learn basic reading and writing skills as well as the rudiments of Latin. At age eleven she returned home, where she continued to pursue her interests in Latin, Greek, mathematics, philosophy, and astronomy. *Collected Letters of a Renaissance Feminist* reveal the importance of these studies to her development as a writer and her interest in a variety of subjects. However, according to Ross, Cereta departed from the norm in using "her father-sponsored education in the service of feminism."

Cereta corresponded with several important Italian scholars, priests, and potential patrons in Brescia and Chiari, including Lodovico Cendrata, Giovanni Olivieri, and Tommaso da Milano. In addition, she wrote a number of letters to Cardinal Ascanio Maria Sforza (the younger son of the Duke of Milan) in search of patronage. Cereta also developed friendships with important women of Brescia, including Nazaria Olympica and Cassandra Fedele, cited as the most celebrated female scholar in Italy during the late fifteenth century. Cereta's letters address a number of significant events and are directed to some of these notable figures of the cultural movement known as the Italian Quattrocento.

Cereta was part of a new generation of female humanist writers in Italy who found their model in de Pisan Women of Cereta's class had the unique experience of being the first generation to be granted a humanist education outside of the household; as Diana Robin points out in her introduction to *Collected Letters,* "These women … were the first female writers in Italy to mobilize their talents to advance their own interests rather than those of their families." Such women were constantly defending their place in the literary arena against the hegemonic view of male dominance. Cereta's letters showcase some of the difficulties women writers of the era had to confront in their engagement with the dictates of a patriarchal society that banned them from speaking in public and argued against women's cultural emancipation. These attitudes stemmed from the belief that women should be chaste and that chastity was equivalent to silence.

Cereta's letters offer a significant contribution to the accepted wisdom regarding the place of women in Renaissance Europe. In response to accusations that she did not compose her own letters, she writes, "The source of [Eusebio's] accusation, lambent and furtive, remains unclear to me. Never has my muse concealed herself in a cave. My abilities are obvious to everyone, and the speculation that has surfaced about me, late and unseasonably, serves only to increase not my fear but my diligence." Cereta's seventeenth-century editor, Tomasini (who had also published the works of Fedele), made details about Cereta's life and works available in print for the first time. His edition includes a detailed biography alongside her letters and a discussion of their reception.

THEMES AND STYLE

In *Women's Writing in Italy 1400–1650* (2008), Virginia Cox claims that "Cereta's epistolary is generally acknowledged as … most original and distinctive, notable especially for its foregrounding of domestic and family contexts and its broad and thematic and tonal range." More specifically, in the more autobiographical of her letters, Cereta particularly focuses on topics important to fifteenth-century women, such as friendship, community, women's education, and her own *ingenium*—that is, natural talent or genius. In a letter to her friend Olympica she writes a detailed account of her early childhood, praising her first teacher: "I was entrusted to a woman highly esteemed both for her counsel and sanctity, whose learning, habits, and discipline I, who was to be educated, intently absorbed." In the autobiographical details of her letters, and in the one to Olympica in particular, Cereta emphasizes the importance of educated women to her intellectual development. The letters also reveal her close connection to God and religious matters. In some of the letters she turns her attention from secular matters to the sacred and acknowledges her call to service: "I blamelessly devoted myself to obedience and I was always ready … to go to the aid of those who called me."

Like other humanist writers of the period, Cereta attempted to use her collection of letters in order to attract a patron to sponsor her writing. The collection she circulated during her lifetime begins and ends with letters to Sforza, an influential, wealthy, and well-known patron of the arts in Renaissance Italy. The letters to Sforza, written in 1488, offer insight into the position of fifteenth-century women writers and her own unique position as both a widow and an intellectual. Unlike other humanists, who argued that highly educated women were extraordinary rather than common, she defends her accomplishments and shows that she had worked hard: "Through my own intelligence and natural talents, I was able to acquire the beginnings of an education."

Cereta's letters are noteworthy for their repeated emphasis on the role of women in the cultural, intellectual, and religious life of Renaissance Italy. In one particularly caustic letter addressed to Paolo Zane, the bishop of Brescia, she points out his poor maintenance of the city's cathedral: "Look at how our church, which is half in ruins, languishes under a crumbling roof." She draws attention to gender distinctions of the period by calling herself, "an unlearned girl" who is stepping outside of accepted cultural norms to criticize the church. She sarcastically contrasts the bishop's learnedness ("most learned in all law") with that of her own feminine self and asks him to "decide either what [she] should think" or explain to her what she should "unlearn."

CRITICAL DISCUSSION

One of the first pieces of writing Cereta publicly exhibited was a lamentation on the death of a donkey. In a letter to Sforza she comments that it was premature to publish this work that had brought harsh criticism from a group of learned men: "Stimulated by a desire for fame, I was drawn into a prodigious error in the course of my writing. Namely, the first thing I wrote was a funeral oration composed to be read over the corpse of a donkey." Her response to her male attackers was a series of letters in which she carefully demonstrates her intellectual abilities. She defends herself admirably in a number of letters, including one to Sforza in which she explains her purpose in sharing her letters with the public: "For a long time I bore all these attacks patiently in order that no one would be able to accuse me of writing about the consolation of philosophy while I indulged the whims of an unstable mind." She goes on to say that the criticism

A fifteenth-century illustration by Mariano Taccola showing a woman at a well. During that same century, writer Laura Cereta advocated women's rights and education and talked about her daily life in a number of letters, published as *Collected Letters of a Renaissance Feminist*. © WOMAN DRAWING WATER FROM A WELL, ILLUSTRATION FROM "DE MACHINIS" (PEN AND INK AND W/C ON PAPER), MARIANO DI JACOPO (DETTO IL TACCOLA) (1382–C.1453) (AFTER)/ BIBLIOTECA MARCIANA, VENICE, ITALY/GIRAUDON/ THE BRIDGEMAN ART LIBRARY

THEORIES

CHRISTINE DE PISAN'S *THE BOOK OF THE CITY OF LADIES*

One goal of humanist writer Christine de Pisan (1363–1430) was to disprove the claims of earlier male authors who identified women as inherently more sinful than men. In *The Book of the City of Ladies,* she says that while people are prone to sin, women are no more prone to do so than men. In the introduction she claims that three celestial "Ladies" appeared to her and criticized her for reading past authors as truth. The Ladies, later identified as Reason, Rectitude, and Justice, tell Christine to reevaluate her sources and to seek the truth behind the text. They encourage her to think critically about the past and use evidence to assess reality.

Specifically, the Ladies draw her attention to the historical women she had read about—all intelligent, highly accomplished philosophers and equally competent governors of their household and, sometimes, of the state. The Ladies are careful to specify that although men and women are equal, they have each been designed to serve God in different ways and this is why there is a gender division in society. However, they also point out to Christine pertinent examples of women who governed their household and the state once their husbands passed away or were rendered incompetent.

of her writings propelled her to prove her worth through the pen, "thus a stern excellence of mind taught me to disdain those slanderers." In other letters she defends her learning and abilities against her male critics and accuses them of dishonesty and arrogance. Despite the numerous attacks, it is clear that Cereta was well respected by the people of Brescia. Upon her death the city granted her a public funeral and continued to honor her memory.

Her letters circulated throughout Italy during her lifetime, but not until they were published in the seventeenth century did they gain wider recognition in Europe. By the mid-seventeenth century she had gained some recognition in England, as evidenced by Thomas Heywood's mention of her in his *General History of Women,* published in 1657. Heywood calls her a "brave Venetian Lady" and one of the remarkable women who had excelled in the arts and sciences.

Today *Collected Letters of a Renaissance Feminist* is appreciated and valued for the insight it offers into the way women viewed their position in early modern society. The letters are also important because they reveal how women engaged in the discussions about their participation in society and challenged the traditional models of gender identity in humanist Europe. Prudence Allen includes Cereta in her study of women in humanist reform, *The Concept of Woman* (2006), noting in particular those letters that offer a theory of gender. For example, Cereta writes, "Nature has granted to all enough of her bounty; she opens to all the gates of choice, and through these gates, reason sends legates to the will." Allen notes, "When the content of her writing is evaluated, it becomes clear that Laura Cereta truly entered into a reform of the concept of woman in an even more personal manner than her predecessors."

BIBLIOGRAPHY

Sources

Allen, Prudence. *The Concept of Woman: The Early Humanist Reformation, 1250–1500, Part 2.* Grand Rapids, Mich.: Eerdmans, 2006. Print.

Cereta, Laura. *Collected Letters of a Renaissance Feminist.* Ed. Diana Robin. Chicago: University of Chicago Press, 1997. Print.

———. *Laurae Ceretae Brixiensis feminae clarissimae epistolae iam primum e MS in lucem productae.* Ed. Giacomo Filippo Tomasini. Padua, 1640. Print.

Cox, Virginia. *Women's Writing in Italy 1400–1650.* Baltimore: Johns Hopkins University Press, 2008. Print.

Robin, Diana. Introduction. *Collected Letters of a Renaissance Feminist.* By Laura Cereta. Chicago: University of Chicago Press, 1997. 3–19. Print.

Ross, Sarah Gwyneth. *The Birth of Feminism: Woman as Intellect in Renaissance Italy and England.* Cambridge: Harvard University Press, 2009. Print.

Further Reading

Benson, Pamela Joseph, and Victoria Kirkham, eds. *Strong Voices, Weak History: Early Women Writers and Canons in England, France, and Italy.* Ann Arbor: University of Michigan Press, 2005. Print.

Gill, Amyrose McCue. "Fraught Relations in the Letters of Laura Cereta: Marriage, Friendship, and Humanist Epistolarity." *Renaissance Quarterly* 62.4 (2009): 1098–1129. Print.

Jansen, Sharon L. *Debating Women, Politics, and Power in Early Modern Europe.* New York: Palgrave Macmillan, 2008. Print.

King, Margaret L., and Albert Rabil, eds. *Her Immaculate Hand: Selected Works by and about the Women Humanists of Quattrocento Italy.* Binghamton: Center for Medieval and Early Renaissance Studies, 1983. Print.

Labalme, Patricia A., ed. *Beyond Their Sex: Learned Women of the European Past.* New York: Columbia University Press, 1980. Print.

Rabil, Albert. *Laura Cereta, Quattrocento Humanist.* Binghamton: Center for Medieval and Early Renaissance Studies, 1981. Print.

Smarr, Janet Levarie. *Joining the Conversation. Dialogues by Renaissance Women.* Ann Arbor: University of Michigan Press, 2005. Print.

Allyna Ward

THE EXTRAORDINARY WORK OF ORDINARY WRITING

Annie Ray's Diary

Jennifer Sinor

OVERVIEW

The Extraordinary Work of Ordinary Writing: Annie Ray's Diary (2002), by Annie Ray's great-great-great-niece Jennifer Sinor, contains excerpts of Ray's diary (1881–1885) detailing her life as a settler in the Dakota Territory tending animals, making food, and caring for her homestead. The entries are interspersed with Sinor's theory and own diary entries. Sinor examines her aunt's diary as an example of ordinary writing, or daily work that Sinor believes "forces both writer and reader into the immediate present." Though Ray's diary records little more than her routine days on the plains, Sinor argues that it is precisely the "boring" and "private" aspects of the text that make it essential to the field of feminist diarist scholarship.

Excerpts of the diary have accompanied Sinor's theory since 1998, when she delivered her paper "Waiting for the Words of Annie Ray" at the 49th Conference on College Composition and Communication, though she claims she initially attempted to construct a dramatic narrative out of Ray's work by including only the longer, more emotional entries. *The Extraordinary Work of Ordinary Writing*, in contrast, provides substantial excerpts from 1881 and 1882 between Sinor's chapters of close readings, analysis of Ray's writing choices, and overview of the history of the diurnal form.

HISTORICAL AND LITERARY CONTEXT

Ray's settler life with her husband, Charles, was made possible by the Land Ordinance of 1785, which divided the frontier into "six-hundred-and-forty-acre sections without pause for natural boundaries or previous claims made by Native Peoples." Her life on the plains was predicated on another piece of legislation as well: due to the Homestead Act of 1862, as Peter Mortensen notes in his 2004 review of the diary, "more than 270 million acres of public land were parceled out to private citizens before the act's repeal in 1976." Ray's journal entries focus less on government policies that enabled her to claim land with her spouse than on the relative hardships she faced while there, including inclement weather and bouts of depression.

Ray's diary is typical of someone with little formal education living on the frontier. Her entries are informed by her sparse social outlets and her lack of experience in domesticating land. She creates order in her life by writing in her logbook nearly every day. Sinor suggests that just as large, empty tracts of land did not exist for white settlers "until the Land Ordinance maps their existence," it is equally true that "empty spaces in the diary do not exist until the diurnal form defines" them.

In Sinor's introduction to the text, she contrasts Ray's diary with others that are more typically anthologized and "tend toward the literary," providing as examples the diaries of Anaïs Nin, Virginia Woolf, and Charlotte Forten Grimké. In the *Western Historical Quarterly* (2004), Liahna Armstrong compares Sinor's text with *Moving Out: A Nebraska Woman's Life* (2002) by Polly Spence, which was edited by her son Karl Spence Richardson and which similarly recounts the "diurnal dullness and piquant earthiness" present in *The Extraordinary Work of Ordinary Writing*.

Just as Ray's work is distinguished from more literary diarists, Sinor's scholarship lies in opposition to theory that privileges such texts. She notes that the diaries of Nin, Woolf, and Grimké are framed as stories, or as texts "with a beginning, middle, and end," and worries about what happens to the "diurnal qualities" of the journals in such readings. Sinor argues that if a woman chooses to keep a diary, it should be read as such, no matter how mundane, for "the inscription of nothing is as complicated a rhetorical act as the fabrication of something."

THEMES AND STYLE

The themes in Ray's diary focus on traditional "women's work" such as cleaning, sewing, baking, and women's health. The passages convey Ray's anxiety about urinary tract infections; infertility; and, to a lesser extent, her husband's infidelity. Her entry on January 18, 1881, reflects a typical passage: "This is a beautiful warm day. Oh! That my life was beautiful, warm and sunny too. It is such heartaching as this which makes people grow old before their time." Sinor's assertion is

❖ *Key Facts*

Time Period:
Late 19th Century

Relevant Historical Events:
American western expansion; homesteading movement

Nationality:
American

Keywords:
homesteading; settlement; women's writing

President Abraham Lincoln signed the Homestead Act of 1862 into law. This law allowed Annie Ray and her husband to claim land in the Dakota Territory. © WORLD HISTORY ARCHIVE/ALAMY

that these daily details have been deemed disposable by scholars and society alike, effectively erasing much of women's history in the United States. What is also lost, she argues, is the reason behind more emotional passages such as "I am suffering from great mental depression" and "I feel just like flying to pieces," both also recorded in 1881.

Sinor employs Ray's diary to reclaim women's private spaces, which were often experienced as fragmented and unstable. By analyzing the minutia of her aunt's text, including Ray's use of the margins and her self-censorship, Sinor validates the ordinary and reframes how historical diaries are read. She also argues that it is the ordinary work that shapes our perception of the extraordinary, noting, "When we view a picture, our eye pays attention to the colors, to the forms. We don't typically see the ways in which the white space, the ordinary, defines these figures, causes them to appear through negation."

The Extraordinary Work of Ordinary Writing is straightforward and rarely lyrical. Ray writes of her husband, who traveled as a blacksmith: "It is 65 days since Charley went away." She writes equally openly of her loneliness: "I wish I had a near neighbor to associate with." Sinor notes that in Ray's diary, as in many typical diurnal texts, "ideas trail off, halt, or pile up" and do not cohere to create a "seamless text." In addition, Sinor believes that direct passages like these turn "our attention away from what the writing does (whether it is coherent, valuable, literary, readable) and toward what the writer is doing." In light of Ray's stunted educational background, the harsh winters she endures, and her adulterous husband, her careful self-editing strikes Sinor as "vigorous and complicated work," which she attempts to expose through meticulous deconstruction.

CRITICAL DISCUSSION

The Extraordinary Work of Ordinary Writing has received little negative criticism since its appearance. Critical interest has centered on Sinor's question of how to accept the ordinary in diurnal texts and around the unique form of her aunt's diary. Armstrong writes that the work "transcends easy categorization. It interweaves Sinor's own memories of childhood and the shaping of her female and writerly identities … incorporating incisive analysis of life-writing as genre and ordinariness as an experiential condition." She goes on to praise Sinor's "exceptional skill at probing the lyricism of commonplace particulars."

Sinor argues that diarist scholarship has tended toward feminists resurrecting texts to reclaim the space that was historically kept from women, namely spaces of autobiography and literature. Mortensen supports her view, claiming that "either ordinary writing is made over into something it isn't, or it is made to vanish altogether." Scholarship has favorably viewed Sinor's insistence that there be a shift to acknowledging the spaces that women inhabited rather than those they were denied. Mortensen echoes Sinor's hope that the "the diurnal form … be prized for its unique power to parse space and time into meaningful units that exist independent of narrative."

Sinor initially "edited Annie's diary into a narrative of loss, crafting scant entries into dramas of infidelity and barrenness," as she writes in her introduction, and feels that she "moved … readers with the tale," but most scholars have remained more impressed with her insight into the legibility of ordinariness, what she refers to as "the act of writing *in* the days rather than *of* the days." In her review of the work for *Great Plains Quarterly*, scholar Julie Nichols notes Sinor's ability to demonstrate that the "value" of the ordinary texts "lies in their ordering of self within a life." Nichols also calls attention to the "inter-chapter" longer passages of Ray's unbroken text, which were absent from earlier iterations of Sinor's theoretical engagements with the diary, and underlines how important it is that the reader "experience the accumulation of her days."

BIBLIOGRAPHY

Sources

Armstrong, Liahna. Rev. of *The Extraordinary Work of Ordinary Writing: Annie Ray's Diary,* by Jennifer Sinor. *Western Historical Quarterly* 35.3 (2004): 384–86. *JSTOR.* Web. 2 Jan. 2013.

Mortensen, Peter. Rev. of *The Extraordinary Work of Ordinary Writing: Annie Ray's Diary,* by Jennifer Sinor. *College Composition and Communication* 55.4 (2004): 771–73. *JSTOR.* Web. 2 Jan. 2013.

Nichols, Julie. Rev. of *The Extraordinary Work of Ordinary Writing: Annie Ray's Diary,* by Jennifer Sinor. *Great Plains Quarterly* (2004): 297. digitalcommons.unl.edu. Web. 2 Jan. 2013.

Sinor, Jennifer. *The Extraordinary Work of Ordinary Writing: Annie Ray's Diary.* Iowa City: University of Iowa Press, 2002. Print.

———. "Reading the Ordinary Diary." *Rhetoric Review* 21.2 (2002): 123–49. *JSTOR.* Web. 2 Jan. 2013.

Further Reading

Logan, Lisa M. Rev. of *The Extraordinary Work of Ordinary Writing: Annie Ray's Diary*, by Jennifer Sinor. *Biography* 27.3 (2004): 620–22. Print.

Sinor, Jennifer. "Making Ordinary Writing: One Woman's Diary." *Dissertation Abstracts International, Section A: The Humanities and Social Sciences* 61.7 (2001): 2963–64. *MLA International Bibliography.* Web. 3 Jan. 2013.

———. "Inscribing Ordinary Trauma in the Diary of a Military Child." *Biography: An Interdisciplinary Quarterly* 26.3 (2003): 405–27. *MLA International Bibliography.* Web. 3 Jan. 2013.

———. "The Life Writing of a Military Child." *Arms and the Self: War, the Military, and Autobiographical Writing.* Ed. Alex Vernon. Kent, Ohio: Kent State University Press, 2005. 236–56. *MLA International Bibliography.* Web. 3 Jan. 2013.

———. "When a Syllabus Is Not Your Own." *Chronicle of Higher Education* 54.48 (2008). *MLA International Bibliography.* Web. 3 Jan. 2013.

Caitlin Moore

REPEALING THE HOMESTEAD ACT OF 1862

Annie Ray was one of many white settlers who saw the land "as undifferentiated, unrecognizable, and unorganized into anything other than emptiness," as Jennifer Sinor notes in her 2002 article "Reading the Ordinary Diary." Sinor includes Ray's drawing of her land claim in the article, which portrays a modest house; a well; a tethered donkey; some poultry; and a fence, with a steam train in the background. Part of Ray's anxiety in her diary stems from her inability to tame her land. Like many settlers, she found her plot was too small and arid to farm effectively.

Arid land was not the only problem with the Homestead Act, however. As Peter Mortensen notes in his 2004 review of Sinor's text, the act "famously ... encouraged the widespread Euramerican settlement of the western states and territories, but in so doing, it accelerated the infamous expropriation of land from native peoples and intensified federal initiatives that hastened their relocation, confinement, and genocide." When the act was repealed in 1976, it was not to repair damage done to native culture but rather to allocate the remaining "unclaimed" western land to federal reserves.

Journals of Søren Kierkegaard

Søren Kierkegaard

Key Facts

Time Period:
Mid-19th Century

Relevant Historical Events:
Denmark's golden age; Kierkegaard's development as a philosopher

Nationality:
Danish

Keywords:
philosophy; melancholy; salvation

OVERVIEW

The journals of Søren Kierkegaard, an influential figure in both philosophy and theology, began to be published fourteen years after his death, in 1869, and provide valuable insights into his deeply interconnected life and ideas. The first English edition in 1938 was a mere single volume, though multivolume editions have followed. The journals contain some of the expected personal information, such as Kierkegaard's agony over a broken engagement, descriptions of his melancholy, his difficult relations with his father, and his sense of himself as a writer. More importantly, these life experiences are subject to extensive interrogation, since the individual human existence is, by his reckoning, central in the quest each person must make for salvation.

After Danish military defeats in the early nineteenth century, the small Scandinavian kingdom's national identity was weak; intellectually, German thinkers such as Johann Wolfgang von Goethe and Georg Wilhelm Friedrich Hegel predominated. Kierkegaard began keeping a diary while studying at the University of Copenhagen and also began publishing philosophical works under his own name and pseudonymously, opposing Hegelian idealism and criticizing the state church. Kierkegaard was scorned by much of the Danish intelligentsia during his lifetime; after his death, many scholars saw the publication of his journals as an opportunity to untangle the persona he had created. Other contemporaries saw the publication as a violation of privacy. Today, scholars of philosophy and religion find the personal material and notes useful in understanding Kierkegaard's sense of the individual's eternal significance.

HISTORICAL AND LITERARY CONTEXT

Kierkegaard studied theology at the University of Copenhagen during Denmark's golden age, a period of artistic energy and a religious awakening that often rankled the state church. He began to break with the "Goetheo-Hegelian" world of rationalism and humanism and to believe that passion is the key to knowledge that can only be communicated indirectly. His intense analysis of his own states of feeling owes much to Goethe's fictional young Werther, whose letters describing his painful passion struggle against the limitations of language to express subjectivity. Also lurking in the background of Kierkegaard's notebooks is the Christian tradition of spiritual autobiography begun by St. Augustine and revived during the Protestant Reformation.

Kierkegaard began keeping a journal when he was a twenty-one-year-old student in 1834 and continued writing in it extensively until his death. When his father, who believed he would outlive his children as punishment for some sin, died in 1838, Kierkegaard had to rethink his understanding of his adored father's life and his own destiny. He worked out these philosophical and religious problems in his diaries, allowing readers insight into their development. He also vents his anger at the contemporary literary scene and important figures such as N. F. S. Grundtvig, who shared many of Kierkegaard's hopes for revitalizing the church but approached the issue from a different viewpoint.

Kierkegaard's practice of maintaining a journal was not unusual for the time. His contemporary, Hans Christian Andersen, whose first novel Kierkegaard scathingly reviewed, was another avid diary keeper; Andersen, however, wrote more directly of sexual desires than did Kierkegaard. The Protestant Reformation's view of the individual's role in salvation encouraged people to keep records of their spiritual development, though a more simple style than Kierkegaard's was suggested. Kierkegaard found a contemporary practice of diary keeping useful: pages were creased vertically into columns. His inner column contained initial observations, while the outer column was for later reflections on the incidents.

The complicated publication history of Kierkegaard's diaries has been an impediment for scholars. The first editor to work with the material followed typical practices of the day by cutting, pasting, and annotating the original texts, and some pages have been lost. In English, the most reliable translation, a six-volume series issued between 1967 and 1978, is more complete, but it is still only a selection, organized topically and not chronologically. To rectify these problems, the Danish National Research Foundation set up a center in 1995 to produce the definitive, Danish-language *Søren Kierkegaards Skrifter* (*Søren Kierkegaard's Writings*). As of late 2012, the series' fifty-five volumes, which contain journals, notebooks, and loose papers, are being translated into English by the Princeton University Press.

THEMES AND STYLE

Kierkegaard's notebooks served as sketchpads for self-examination, upon which he built philosophical and religious theories that depended on inward reflection rather than objective knowledge. After realizing that he would not predecease his father, as family mythology had led him to believe, he had to reconsider his ideas about his destiny. However, the melancholy of his upbringing had formed him, so that, as he writes, "my suffering and anguish made me inventive in delving for the Truth which, in turn, might benefit others." In his journals he explores whether he would do this by being a minister or a writer. He chose writing. For Kierkegaard, the inward sphere took precedence over reason, which had been valorized by rationalism and humanism.

Though Kierkegaard's motivation for keeping the diaries was to further understand himself, he wondered about his "great reluctance to commit various observations to paper" and decided to write more frequently and impressionistically in the hope that no significant idea would be lost. Only occasionally does he recount daily events; instead, he offers aphorisms to tantalize the future readers he knew his notebooks would attract, writing that "after my death no one will find among my papers a single explanation as to what really filled my life." He self-edited his journals, removing pages and crossing out passages. He writes that he wanted to "remove the secret note that explains everything," a note that probably does not exist, the secret being that the truth of a life is elusive and requires literary imagination.

Kierkegaard's writing is often witty, sometimes impassioned, and always erudite. He wrote in different notebooks during the same period, filling them front to back and then, on the reverse of the pages, back to front. Since editors later cut and pasted and lost pages, the original structure is hard to determine. He kept notes on lectures, wrote travel descriptions, and vented his disgust at contemporary thinkers. His tone becomes literarily contemplative at times, as when he observes that "the sea sounded its song with deep but quiet solemnity … and the birds sang their vespers." On this particular walking tour, he entered a peasant's cottage. Before describing the inhabitants, he writes, "We will now have a little look at them," a narrative style more like that of a contemporary short-story writer than a typical diarist. Kierkegaard also includes satirical dramatizations, such as a conversation between Socrates and Hegel.

CRITICAL DISCUSSION

When the first volume of Kierkegaard's diaries appeared in 1869, Danish reviewers reacted unfavorably to what they saw as a violation of privacy. By the time the remaining volumes were published in 1881, critics had grasped their usefulness. Translations into

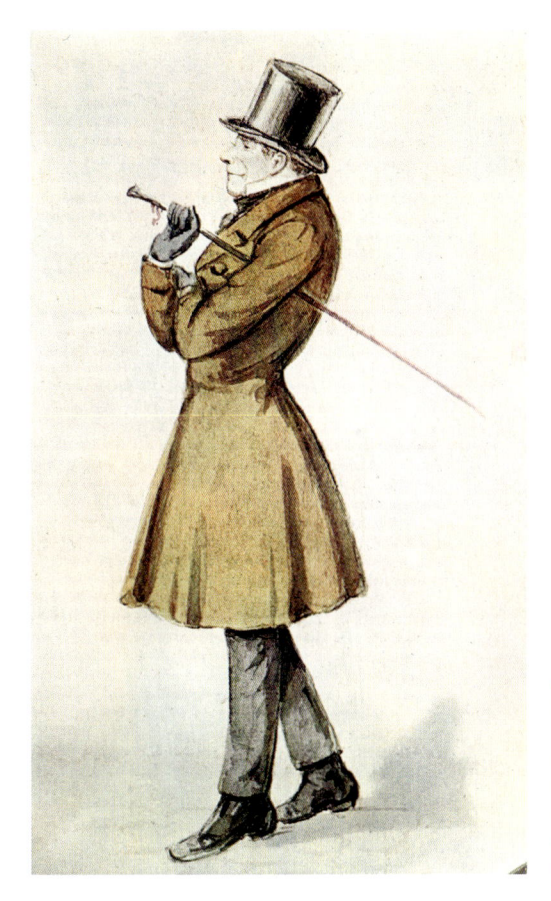

Peter Klæstrup's portrait of nineteenth-century Danish philosopher Søren Kierkegaard. © PRIVATE COLLECTION/ARCHIVES CHARMET/THE BRIDGEMAN ART LIBRARY

German were published in the early part of the twentieth century, which shook the German intellectual world, according to philosopher Karl Jaspers. Jaspers notes in his essay "The Importance of Kierkegaard" that "before the first World War he became an event…. Dialectical theology and all shades of existentialism have relied heavily on Kierkegaard." In response to the English edition of 1940, John Short found material relevant to the question of whether pacifism was in keeping with, as he puts it in "The Journals of Søren Kierkegaard," Kierkegaard's "teleological suspension of the ethical."

Kierkegaard has been an important figure for many schools of philosophy and religion. Jean-Paul Sartre and the existentialists saw him as their founder, Karl Barth embraced his views on his way toward neo-orthodox Christianity, and the deconstructionist thought of Jacques Derrida leaned heavily on Kierkegaard. John D. Caputo, a scholar of the relationship between postmodern thought and religion, observes that postmodernists claim Kierkegaard as their progenitor; Kierkegaard's rejection of objective truth resonates with this sensibility.

In using the journals and papers to construct his biography of Kierkegaard in 2000 (translated to English, 2005), Joakim Garff found that the pseudonymous personae in his published writings were as reliable, if not more so, in revealing the "true" Kierkegaard than

THEORIES

PRIMARY SOURCE

EXCERPT FROM *THE DIARY OF SØREN KIERKEGAARD*

LIFE MOOD

1.

1836.

I have just returned from a party of which I was the life and soul; witty banter flowed from my lips, everyone laughed and admired me—but I came away, indeed that dash should be as long as the radii of the earth's orbit——————wanting to shoot myself.

2.

1836.

Death and Damnation, I can dissociate from everything else but my own self; I can't even forget myself when I am asleep.

3.

An ambulant musician played the minuet from Don Giovanni on some kind of reed-pipe (I couldn't see what it was as he was in the next courtyard), and the druggist was pounding medicine with his pestle, and the maid was scouring in the yard*, etc., and they noticed nothing and maybe the piper didn't either, and I felt such well-being.

June 10, 1836.

† and the groom curried his horse and beat off the curry-comb against the curb, and from another part of town came the distant cry of a shrimp vender.

4.

1837.

There are many people who arrive at the result of their lives like schoolboys; they cheat their teacher by copying the answer from the key in the arithmetic-book, without bothering to do the sums themselves.

January 17, 1837.

5.

1837.

The path we all must take—across the Bridge of Sighs into eternity.

6.

1837.

It is those petty teasings that embitter life so much. I will gladly struggle on in the face of a gale, my veins almost bursting; but a wind that blows a speck of dust into my eyes can vex me to such an extent that I stamp my foot.

---

the image created in the journals. His complex persona continues to be interrogated: in an essay for *Philosophy and Social Criticism,* Joseph Westfall uses the journals to understand how Kierkegaard's *The Point of View for My Work as an Author* (published in the 1850s) "brings authorship to the fore as a philosophical issue and … despite the fact that the book was clearly written by Søren Kierkegaard—the book's author cannot be identified." A recent study of Kierkegaard and Socrates completes its investigation by utilizing Kierkegaard's late journal entries. Just as twentieth-century philosophers applied Kierkegaard's ethics to their responses to war, contemporary ethicist Mark Coeckelbergh, writing in *Science and Engineering Ethics,* employs "Kierkegaardian notions of tragedy and moral responsibility in order to account for experiences of the tragic in technological action."

BIBLIOGRAPHY

Sources

Coeckelbergh, Mark. "Moral Responsibility, Technology, and Experiences of the Tragic: From Kierkegaard to Offshore Engineering." *Science and Engineering Ethics* 18.1 (2012): 35–48. Print.

Jaspers, Karl. "The Importance of Kierkegaard." *Modern Critical Views: Søren Kierkegaard.* Ed. Harold Bloom. New York: Chelsea House, 1989. Print.

Kierkegaard, Søren. *Kierkegaard's Journals and Notebooks.* Ed. Niels Jørgen Cappelørn, et al. Princeton: Princeton University Press, 2007–13. Print.

Kirmmse, Bruce H. "Introduction to the English Language Edition." *Kierkegaard's Journals and Notebooks.* Ed. Niels Jørgen Cappelørn, et al. Princeton: Princeton University Press, 2007–13. *Princeton University Press.* Web. 2 Dec. 2012.

Short, John. "The Journals of Søren Kierkegaard." *Theology* 41.36 (1940). *Sagepub.* Web. 18 Oct. 2012.

Westfall, Joseph. "Who Is the Author of *The Point of View*? Issues of Authorship in the Posthumous Kierkegaard." *Philosophy and Social Criticism,* 38.6 (2012): 569–89. *Sagepub.* Web. 2 Dec. 2012.

Further Reading

Caputo, John D. *How to Read Kierkegaard.* New York: Norton, 2007.

Garff, Joakim. *Søren Kierkegaard: A Biography.* Trans. Bruce H. Kirmmse. Princeton: Princeton University Press, 2005. Print.

These petty teasings are as if a man wanted to engage in a great work, a great enterprise on which his own life and the lives of many others depended—and then a gadfly settled on his nose.

7.

1837.

One thought chases the next; no sooner have I thought it and am about to write it down than a new one comes along—hold it, grasp it—Madness—Insanity!

8.

1837.

Altogether I hate these pseudo-scholars—how often at a party have I not deliberately sat down by some elderly spinster-lady who feeds on repeating family news, and with the utmost gravity listened to her chatter.

9.

1837.

I prefer talking with old persons of the female sex who peddle family gossip; next, with the insane—and last, with very sensible people.

10.

1837.

I can't bother to do anything whatsoever; I can't bother to walk—the effort is too great; I can't bother to lie down, for either I would lie too long, and I can't bother to do that, or I would get up at once, and I can't bother to do that either—I can't bother to go horseback-riding—the exercise is too strenuous for my apathy; all I can bother to do is ride in a carriage, comfortably, and, while being evenly rocked, let a multitude of objects glide past me, lingering over each lovely bit of scenery only to savor my languor—my thoughts and notions are as sterile as a eunuch's heat—in vain I seek something that might enliven me—not even the pithy language of the Middle Ages can overcome the void that pervades my being. Now I realize in truth what is meant by the saying about Christ's words, that they are life and spirit—in brief: I can't bother to write what I have just written, and I can't bother to blot it out.

SOURCE: Kierkegaard, Søren. *The Diary of Søren Kierkegaard*. Ed. Peter P. Rohde. New York: Philosophical Library, Carol Publishing Group, 1993. Reprinted by permission of Philosophical Library, Inc. All rights reserved.

Howland, Jacob. *Kierkegaard and Socrates: A Study in Philosophy and Faith.* New York: Cambridge University Press, 2006. Print.

Schlaeger, Jürgen, "Self-Exploration in Early Modern English Diaries." *Marginal Voices, Marginal Forms: Diaries in European Literature and History.* Amsterdam: Rodopi, 1999. *Google Books*. Web. 20 Oct. 2012.

Shain, Ralph. "Situating Derrida: Between Kierkegaard and Hegel." *Philosophy Today* (2000): 388–403. *ProQuest Central*. Web. 2 Dec. 2012.

Stack, George J. "The Inward Journey: *Kierkegaard's Journals and Papers*." *Philosophy Today* 23.2 (1979). *ProQuest*. Web. 18 Oct. 2012.

Robin Morris

Letters between Two

Lu Xun, Xu Guangping

✦ Key Facts

Time Period:
Early 20th Century

Relevant Historical Events:
Chinese Revolution of 1911–1912; rise of the Chinese Communist Party

Nationality:
Chinese

Keywords:
revolution; love; communism

OVERVIEW

Letters between Two (1933) comprises a correspondence between Lu Xun (1881–1936), a celebrated poet, fiction writer, essayist, translator, and critic, and one of his students, Xu Guangping (1898–1968), a fiery political radical. The work served as a public declaration of the couple's love, and despite his being already married, it established her as his wife in the eyes of society. When scholars studied the original letters, they discovered that Lu had heavily edited them for publication. Critics presume that he did so in order to streamline and clarify his political evolution over his lifetime, as well as to legitimize the pair's unorthodox relationship. The publication was also likely motivated by the couple's need for the money the book would generate.

Letters between Two appeared in the midst of decades of political unrest in China. Although he was originally dubious about the role of politics in art and of art in politics, Lu eventually embraced the need for revolutionary literature and made his views public in many of his writings. He edited the letters with an eye to this legacy. The book met with a popular success that guaranteed Xu financial and social status after Lu's death. By revising the story of Lu's political development, Mao Zedong and the Communist Party were able to claim Lu as an ideal modern Chinese writer, and he remains among the best-known Chinese authors of the twentieth century.

HISTORICAL AND LITERARY CONTEXT

The nationalist Chinese Revolution of 1911–1912 overthrew the Qin dynasty and established the Republic of China. Sun Yat-sen briefly led a provisional coalition national assembly, but corruption, governmental weakness in the face of the military, and violent control by ruling warlords led to decades of lingering unrest. It was in this atmosphere that Lu became an established writer. The Chinese Communist Party, founded in 1921, originally worked with the nationalists to defeat the warlords and form a stronger centralized government but later became a target of nationalist brutality. A nationalist during the revolution, Lu subsequently began moving to the left in his politics. In 1925 he met Xu, an iconoclast agitating for the right of students to engage in political movements. As a young girl, she had talked her father into leaving her feet unbound, and she rejected an arranged marriage so vehemently that her brother finally reneged on the contract after their father's death. Her family encouraged her education.

As a college student Xu became enamored with Lu and began corresponding with him. Her first letter to him is a brash epistle requesting Lu's opinion on student engagement in politics. In his response he teasingly addresses her as "elder brother" and recommends restraint. Their initial relationship was based on ideological intercourse, but they eventually became lovers. Some even credit her influence for his heightened political consciousness. Although he had communist sympathies, he never joined the Communist Party and had an ambivalent relationship with it. As was customary, Lu had participated in an arranged marriage from his youth. The upheaval of the period may have enabled the love affair between him and Xu to exist. Although the two maintained the appearance of propriety for a time, they eventually lived together openly. Xu gave up her own literary aspirations and worked as Lu's secretary in addition to caring for their sickly son.

When the couple decided to publish their letters in 1933, they seized on a vogue for books focused on correspondence between famous literary couples. They knew that both the popularity of the genre and Lu's fame would help the book sell well. Arguably, it also aligned with a vibrant sentimental tradition in early-twentieth-century China, despite Lu's evident disdain for sensational, sentimental fiction. His edited version of their letters suggests that their relationship was as much a meeting of the minds as a merging of the hearts. Nevertheless, in the charged political climate in which the letters appeared, and because of their commitment to their affair despite social and familial obstacle, their relationship seemed highly romantic to a public eager for idealism.

Xu outlived Lu by more than thirty years, and as his recognized partner, she devoted considerable energy to sustaining his legacy. Shortly after his death she collaborated with friends on a compilation of his collected works and was a catalyst for subsequent publications and reprints as well. She was motivated both by admiration for his work and by financial necessity. Because of Lu's prominence, his solo writings and life story overshadowed Xu's achievements as an activist, and she and *Letters between Two* have received little acknowledgement from scholars. Nevertheless, as a portrait of a liaison between two revolutionary intellectuals and of the developing political thought of a revered author, *Letters between Two* provides insight into Chinese literature and political history, as well as the limitations enforced on women of the time.

THEMES AND STYLE

Among the prevailing themes throughout *Letters between Two* are the couple's shared interest in politics and their desire for privacy. Xu often appears as the more radical of the two, goading Lu into greater activism, rejecting his assessment of "feminine" writing, and complaining about the shallowness of her fellow female students. Lu takes on the persona of self-possessed older teacher, using his impassioned protégée as a sounding board for his ideas. For example, he takes activists to task for the imprecision of their endeavors: "All idealists, it seems to me, either hark back to the 'past' or find hope in the 'future,' but on the question of the 'present' all of them hand in blank papers, because no-one can prescribe a remedy." Besides portraying a relationship between two fervently political people, the letters also depict Lu as an evolved political thinker in the midst of cultural revolution. His literary fame, which grew during the 1920s and 1930s, brought him public scrutiny, and his existing marriage and the difference between his age and Xu's encouraged speculative gossip. Their letters often show their desire for a life together, free from the world's prying eyes and judgment. Scholar Bonnie S. McDougall writes in *Love-Letters and Privacy in Modern China* (2002) that the book also "shows them in pursuit of their individual privacy: he did not discuss his wife or his estranged brother with her; she did not tell him about [an] early love affair. Writing and reading the letters reinforced the bond between them, creating their own world of intimacy."

Lu and Xu may have agreed on the motivations and goals for publishing their correspondence, but he altered her letters in his editing more than his own, and it remains unclear how involved she was in this process. As published, the letters represent the couple as political and intellectual soulmates rather than reckless lovers caught up in a swirl of passion. This depiction served to strengthen the image of Xu as Lu's true wife in the minds of the public, a status she both needed and desired. Simultaneously, making their relationship appear rational and founded on intellectualism furthered Lu's presumed intention of rewriting his history to make his political perspective appear more coherent. The multilevel functions of *Letters between Two* emphasize the way that life writers construct a portrait of self for a particular audience or, in the case of *Letters between Two*, the original audience of one—the beloved—and the secondary audience of the public.

In his preface Lu openly states that *Letters between Two* breaks with the style conventions of published correspondence: "There is no passion for 'Life' or 'Death!,' nor fine words such as 'Flowers!' or 'Moon!' We did not study the 'essence of epistolary art' or 'rules of correspondence' for our diction but let our words flow from our pens, ignoring rules of grammar…. If the book must be praised for having a special quality then I'm afraid it will have to be on account of being ordinary." The letters are so restrained that some readers complained that they were not love letters. The pair often discusses politics, art, or logistics. They call each other by nicknames that bend gender and age standards as if to emphasize their intellectual equality. Further, Lu's edits jettisoned many of their more sentimental endearments and statements and obfuscated the details of their early relationship. The distance thus achieved helped preserve some amount of privacy, controlling readers' access to and interpretations of their lives. At the same time, the letters could be read

Lu Xun, shown here in a 1930 photograph, is often considered one of the greatest modern writers in China. © BETTMANN/CORBIS

THEORIES

MORE THAN ROMANCE: BEATRICE AND SIDNEY WEBB

Across the globe from Lu and Xu, yet part of the same era, was another couple whose shared political ideals imbued their personal relationship with depth and endurance. When British social activists Beatrice Potter and Sidney Webb met in 1890, she was the intellectually perceptive daughter of a wealthy family, determined to combat poverty and injustice, and he was an educational reformer and a leading member of the socialist Fabian Society. Though not drawn to each other in a traditionally romantic sense, the two became close friends working toward their common ideals, and they married in 1892. The couple shared a supportive and productive relationship until Potter's death in 1943. They left many concrete expressions of their collaboration, including publications such as *The History of Trade Unionism* (1894) and the prestigious London School of Economics and Political Science, which they helped found in 1895.

Potter was a prolific diarist, and together the Webbs were inexhaustible correspondents. Therefore, an abundant record of their relationship exists, written in their own words. In 1948 Barbara Drake and Margaret I. Cole edited and released posthumously the work *Our Partnership*, a collection of excerpts from Potter's journals describing the importance of her working relationship with Sidney. In 1978 Norman Mackenzie released three volumes of *The Letters of Sidney and Beatrice Webb*, which recorded not only an affectionate alliance between equals but also the development of important British social movements.

as highlighting the restraint and equality celebrated by Chinese communism.

CRITICAL DISCUSSION

Letters between Two was met with popular acclaim. Lu's literary standing and the book's tale of romance and iconoclasm ensured a broad audience. After Lu's death in 1936, the Communist Party embraced and touted him as a foundational revolutionary writer and Chinese intellectual, mythologizing his life in a way that supported their ideology. Kirk A. Denton's biography of Lu (2002) on the *Modern Chinese Literature and Culture Resource Center*'s website details the Communist Party narrative, in which Lu developed from a conservative into an iconoclast and finally a leftist revolutionary. Although he had indeed followed this trajectory to a certain extent, his process and his end point were more nuanced and disordered than the party's rendering. Ironically, his edits of *Letters between Two* can be read as having laid the groundwork for the party's self-serving simplification.

Critics have contested the Communist Party's depiction of Lu's political legacy; for example, Leo Ou-Fan Lee contends in "Literature on the Eve of Revolution" (1976) that, at times, "Lu Xun felt profoundly alienated from political power" because "the Chinese state was utterly incapable of meeting the increasingly radical demands of Chinese society." Lu's literary legacy is the subject of further scholarship. Ming Dong Gu and Shumei Shi read him as a participant in Chinese modernism; Lee also describes the influence on Lu of Western writers, particularly the Russian writers he studied and loved in his later years, including Nikolay Gogol and Leon Trotsky. Because of the primacy placed on Lu's other works in Chinese and Marxist literary history, *Letters between Two* fell into obscurity and little attention was paid to it or to Xu—particularly in English. More recently, cultural and feminist critics such as McDougall have examined *Letters between Two* for clues about life during the complicated revolutionary years of the early twentieth century in China and for insight into Xu, a fascinating figure in her own right.

The move to reconsider Xu in relationship to Lu and their shared work that was initiated within Chinese studies in the 1980s and 1990s spread as scholars became more interested in women's lives, cultural history, and the nature of autobiography. In English, McDougall has been the most prominent defender of *Letters between Two*, translating the book and producing a scholarly monograph on it and its authors. She argues that the letters do not represent Xu at all accurately. Instead, the book's "special quality lies in the extent and nature of its editing, which give it the status of a semi-fictional work comparable to the semi-autobiographic epistolary fiction of its time." The expansion of scholarship on China in the United States and Britain in recent years may bring further analysis of the work.

BIBLIOGRAPHY

Sources

Denton, Kirk A. "Lu Xun Biography." *Modern Chinese Literature and Culture (MCLC) Resource Center.* Ohio State University, 2002. Web. 28 Dec. 2012.

Gu, Ming Dong. "Lu Xun and Modernism/Postmodernism." *Modern Language Quarterly* 69.1 (2008): 29–44. *Ebscohost.* Web. 7 Jan. 2013.

Lee, Leo Ou-Fan. "Literature on the Eve of Revolution: Reflections of Lu Xun's Leftist Years, 1927–1936." *Modern China* 2.3 (1976): 277–326. *JSTOR.* Web. 19 Aug. 2012.

Lu Xun and Xu Guangping. *Letters between Two.* Trans. Bonnie S. McDougall. Beijing: Foreign Language, 2000. Print.

McDougall, Bonnie S. *Love-Letters and Privacy in Modern China: The Intimate Lives of Lu Xun and Xu Guangping.* Oxford: Oxford University Press, 2002. Print.

Shi, Shumei. *The Lure of the Modern: Writing Modernism in Semicolonial China, 1917–1937.* Berkeley: University of California Press, 2001. Print.

Further Reading

Danzker, Jo-Anne Birnie, Ken Lum, and Zheng Shengtian, eds. *Shanghai Modern, 1919–1945.* Ostfildern-Ruit, Germany: Hatje Cantz, 2004. Print.

Davies, Gloria. *Lu Xun's Revolution: Writing in a Time of Violence.* Cambridge: Harvard University Press, 2013. Print.

Denton, Kirk A. "Lu Xun Biography: Relations with Xu Guangping." *Modern Chinese Literature and Culture (MCLC) Resource Center.* Ohio State University, 2002. Web. 8 Oct. 2012.

Lee, Haiyan. "All the Feelings That Are Fit to Print: The Community of Sentiment and the Literary Public Sphere in China, 1900–1918." *Modern China* 27 (2001): 291–327. *Sage Publications.* Web. 8 Oct. 2012.

Lee, Leo Ou-Fan, ed. *Lu Xun and His Legacy.* Berkeley: University of California Press, 1985. Print.

Lu Xun. *Silent China: Selected Writing of Lu Xun.* Ed. and trans. Gladys Yang. Oxford: Oxford University Press, 1973. Print.

Pollard, David. *The True Story of Lu Xun.* Hong Kong: Chinese University Press, 2002. Print.

Tambling, Jeremy. *Madmen and Other Survivors: Reading Lu Xun's Fiction.* Hong Kong: Hong Kong University Press, 2007. Print.

Sarah Stoeckl

Practice of the Private Journal
Philippe Lejeune

✥ Key Facts

Time Period:
Late 20th Century

Relevant Historical Events:
Lejeune's turn from studying literature to diaries

Nationality:
French

Keywords:
theory; criticism; personal narrative

OVERVIEW

Philippe Lejeune's essay-cum-diary "Tenir un journal" was first published in the French journal *Poetique* in September 1997. In 1999 an English version titled "The Practice of the Private Journal" was published as a chapter in the book *Marginal Voices, Marginal Forms: Diaries in European Literature and History* edited by Rachel Langford and Russell West. In 2009 the essay became the introduction to the Lejeune anthology *On Diary*, edited by Jeremy D. Popkin and Julie Rak. The text is at once a theoretical essay, an impromptu treatise on methodology, and a journalistic record of, according to Langford and West, "the many directions which his research into private diaries has taken up to the present time." Like everything Lejeune has published, the essay was immediately absorbed into his unique canon of works on the personal narrative.

Through works such as *L'autobiographie en France* (1971) and *Moi aussi* (1986), Lejeune founded the study of autobiography as a scholarly discipline. By steady exertion of his genial and attractive personality, he helped gain acceptance for the discipline throughout the Western world, inspiring many disciples. By coining such paradigms as "the autobiographical pact"—in which the autobiographer promises to be honest and the reader promises to believe the writer—Lejeune provided a framework for new perspectives on the genre. Between 1986 and 1998, over the course of more than thirty publications of various length and focus, he performed a similar service for the long-maligned diary. In "The Practice of the Private Journal," he sums up the research of the past twelve years and offers some tentative conclusions.

HISTORICAL AND LITERARY CONTEXT

Although diaries and journals have been kept for millennia, until recently most were valued solely as a primary source for historical research. Most diarists did not aim to publish their diaries. Because privacy was a defining characteristic of the genre, the great virtue of the diary was that others would not read it. The fame of such diarists as the Duc de Saint-Simon (1675–1755) and Samuel Pepys (1633–1703) was entirely posthumous: neither Saint-Simon nor Pepys was published until the early nineteenth century. In the eighteenth century, the diary or journal enjoyed modest popularity as a format for fictional narratives—for instance, Daniel Defoe's *Journal of the Plague Year*—though the epistolary form was much more popular. In the nineteenth century multivolume editions of the diaries and letters of eminent personages became a staple of publishing houses. The diary form continued to be a useful and convenient form for fiction, as in Nikolay Gogol's *Diary of a Madman* (1835) and the Grossmith brothers' *The Diary of a Nobody* (1888–89).

Lejeune's work on autobiography inevitably concentrated his studies on the personal narratives of literary types. For a long time he continued to support the notion that literary criticism ought to confine itself to the work of those who had adopted the profession of letters. Ultimately, however, he found this too restrictive, and he began to tire of writers and literary culture as subjects. When he turned to the study of diaries, he began with the published diaries of writers. Soon, however, he discovered that what he really wanted to study was "the reasons why, and the ways in which, so many 'ordinary' people who are not writers keep a diary." He had kept a diary as a young man—"from the age of fifteen, for a good ten years"—but gave it up as he grew older. He writes that after his *Moi aussi* (Me too) was published in 1986, "I found myself one day, pen in hand, paper before me, writing a date at the top of the page and starting to narrate; my journal began to follow its course once again like a river welling up after a long underground trajectory. Since then I have hardly stopped writing."

Thanks largely to his efforts, the intellectual situation in which "The Practice of the Private Journal" appeared was much different from the one into which *L'autobiographie en France* entered in 1971. The self-narrated life was now accepted—though not by all—as a legitimate subject of academic or scholarly inquiry. The essay did not bring as dramatic a change as some of his earlier works had, mainly because of the pioneering nature of his early works. Also, many of the theoretical structures built by his older contemporaries had decayed, and their ideological rigidity now inspired irritation rather than fear. Lejeune's relaxed, nondoctrinaire approach made the intellectual workplace an environment more conducive to research and less prone to destructive arguments.

The full influence of "The Practice of the Private Journal" has not yet been realized. Lejeune's work on autobiography has already opened new fields of study, and the study of diaries has been further bolstered by the publication of his *On Diary*. In the twenty-first century, he has continued to study electronic diaries and blogs as new forms of public and private journaling.

THEMES AND STYLE

The main themes of Lejeune's "The Practice of a Private Journal" are the story of his elevation of the diary to the status of a scholarly discipline and his return to diary writing after abandoning it, almost in shame, when he was twenty-five. He composes the essay as a narrative that follows his winding, uneven road back to journaling. As a chronicle of the maturation of a scholarly discipline, "The Practice of a Private Journal" resembles Sigmund Freud's *The Origin and Development of Psychoanalysis* (1910).

Lejeune's motives for composing this journal-essay are to report on his research in the form of a journal rather than a monograph. Eschewing scholarly dogma, he demonstrates amazing fluency and compels the reader's attention. His motives are purely scientific, demonstrating his desire to follow his curiosity wherever it leads. He writes, "I started, to be absolutely candid, without knowing quite where I was headed, and the rest followed step by step."

His style is both idiosyncratic and accessible. The affable, easy flow of his prose is spiked with technical language—"it is simply a matter of honesty to contextualize, at least briefly, my own situation as a diarist"—and unexpected similes—"references to the publications will punctuate my narrative like the beads of a rosary." He is charming and even self-deprecating—"My mother was an English teacher, as is my older sister, who often serves as my translator. She regularly sighs, 'You are so difficult to translate!' and on days when she can no longer take it, she says, 'You are a bad writer!'" He even calls his "adolescent journal … badly written, indeed, utterly *un*written: I considered it rubbish. I wanted to move on in my writing style, to become presentable in public."

CRITICAL DISCUSSION

The reception of a new publication by Lejeune, at least in the English-speaking world, is generally enthusiastic and admiring. Reviewing *On Diary* for the *Romanic Review* in 2010, Lorry Perry states that "generosity and willingness to revise his first impressions [are] qualities … utterly characteristic of Lejeune's scholarship throughout the book." In *Biography* (2001), Roland A. Champagne finds Lejeune ever ready to take on new media and to derive useful insight from them: "Lejeune observes … that the computer intrudes like an arrogant cat, making us negotiate anew the stakes for inscribing the self." Reviewing *On Diary* for *Canadian Literature* in 2011, Laurie McNeill finds Lejeune "a remarkably productive and influential scholar."

Lejeune's legacy relies on his cumulative body of work rather than on any one work in particular.

Jeremy Popkin, in the introduction to *On Diary* (2009), writes that the author's most enduring contribution is as an explorer: "Lejeune cannot resist the lure of territories that have not been mapped, where rumor says the game is plentiful, and no rules have been imposed." Popkin's coeditor, Julie Rak, writes, "Listening to Philippe Lejeune unfold the mysteries of diary writing … was a defining experience for me as a scholar of autobiography and life writing."

For such an important writer, Lejeune is surprisingly uncontroversial. No school of scholarship has yet emerged to debunk his theories. Neither is there a unified school of thought among his followers. Most Lejeune scholars have pursued unique lines of inquiry based on a specific remark or discovery of Lejeune's that has inspired their research. Perhaps because of this breadth of scholarship deriving from Lejeune's work, the author continues to elude major scholarly scrutiny.

In "Practice of the Private Journal," Philippe Lejeune discusses his investigation into the reasons ordinary people keep diaries.
© PATRICK LANE/SOMOS IMAGES/CORBIS

BIBLIOGRAPHY

Sources

Champagne, Roland A. "Nanterre: Le centre de recherches interdisciplinaires sur les textes modernes de l'universite de Paris X, 2000." *Biography* 24.3 (2001): 595–98. *Literature Resource Center.* Web. 29 Dec. 2012.

Langford, Rachel, and Russell West, eds. *Marginal Voices, Marginal Forms: Diaries in European Literature and History.* Amsterdam: Rodopi, 1999. Print.

Lejeune, Philippe. "How Do Diaries End?" *Biography* 24.1 (2001): 99–112. *Literature Resource Center.* Web. 29 Dec. 2012.

———. "The Practice of the Private Journal." *On Diary.* Ed. Jeremy D. Popkin and Julie Rak. Trans. Katherine Durnin. Honolulu: University of Hawaii Press, 2009. Print.

McNeill, Laurie. "Rethinking the Diary." Rev. of *On Diary*, by Philippe Lejeune; ed. Jeremy D. Popkin and Julie Rak; trans. Katherine Durnin. *Canadian Literature.* Canadian Literature, 8 Dec. 2011. Web. 31 Dec. 2012.

ON METHOD

Philippe Lejeune devotes a considerable portion of "The Practice of the Private Journal" to the development of a suitable methodology for studying diaries. He outlines two main approaches. One, the most obvious, is to read the diaries. However, according to Lejeune, this method forces the scholar to focus on published texts, causing the phenomenon of "sampling." He explains, "Publishing privileges texts by writers or prominent personalities" and also leads to "transformations" in the form of "rewording or cuts." In addition, publishing diaries suggests that they are artifacts, whereas Lejeune believes that "the private diary is a *practice* … a way of life."

The other approach to studying diaries is to "question the writers of diaries themselves, without reading their journals." According to this method, Lejeune writes, he need not treat diaries as literature: "We need to leave the domain of the printed book." But this method, too, has drawbacks, and he admits that he alternates between the two approaches. Although his manner may seem daffy, he is a highly practical scholar. He writes, "My researches resemble those Russian dolls where each element emerges from the one preceding it."

Perry, Lorry. Rev. of *On Diary*, by Philippe Lejeune; ed. Jeremy D. Popkin and Julie Rak; trans. Katherine Durnin. *Romanic Review* 101.3 (2010): 585–87. *Literature Resource Center*. Web. 6 Jan. 2013.

Further Reading

Benjamin, Walter. *Illuminations*. Ed. Hannah Arendt. New York: Schocken, 1969. Print.

Lejeune, Philippe. "Calicot." *Biography* 26.3 (2003): 444–47. *General OneFile*. Web. 25 Oct. 2012.

Maunsell, Jerome Boyd. "The Writer's Diary as Device: The Making of Susan Sontag in *Reborn: Early Diaries 1947–1963.*" *Journal of Modern Literature* 35.1 (2011): 1–20. *General OneFile*. Web. 1 Jan. 2013.

McNeill, Laurie. "Teaching an Old Genre New Tricks: The Diary on the Internet." *Biography* 26.1 (2003): 24–47. *Literature Resource Center*. Web. 7 Jan. 2013.

Popkin, Jeremy D. "Coordinated Lives: Between Autobiography and Scholarship." *Biography* 24.4 (2001): 781–805. *General OneFile*. Web. 25 Oct. 2012.

Gerald Carpenter

Some Observations on Diaries, Self-Biography, and Self-Characters

Isaac D'Israeli

OVERVIEW

The essay "Some Observations on Diaries, Self-Biography, and Self-Characters" by Isaac D'Israeli (1766–1848) was published in London in the omnibus volume *Miscellanies; or, Literary Recreation* (1796). (Presumably it had appeared singly sometime earlier, as a journal article.) "Some Observations" was among the first essays in English to take a general, quasi-theoretical approach to the self-composed personal narrative. A contemporary of Jeremy Bentham (founder of utilitarianism) and James Mill (father of the philosopher John Stuart Mill), D'Israeli stresses the diary's utility to scholars and critics as a means of better understanding the minds and characters of their subjects. Despite the title, however, the main subject of the essay is not the keeping of a diary but the writing of a biography.

As the English middle class expanded throughout the eighteenth century, so did the English reading public. Readers were more interested in novels and the chatty essays of such periodicals as the *Spectator* and the *Tattler* than they were in deeper works of philosophy and religion. In 1791 D'Israeli had published, anonymously, the first volume of his *Curiosities of Literature,* an entertaining collections of essays, anecdotes, and excerpts that caught the fancy of this new reading public and sold well enough to support the publication of five more volumes of the work. Somewhat different in content and organization, *Miscellanies* was aimed at the same public and also sold quite well.

HISTORICAL AND LITERARY CONTEXT

D'Israeli's career represents the confluence of several historical developments in European, particularly English, culture. One development was the liberation of the Jews from their medieval sequestration in the ghettos and their eventual involvement with the rest of European society. (It was not complete, of course. To get a college education D'Israeli had to go to the University of Leiden in Holland because Oxford and Cambridge admitted only members of the Church of England. Also, if D'Israeli had not had his sons baptized as Christians, his son Benjamin could never have entered Parliament, let alone become prime minister.) Other developments included a growing middle-class reading public; the emergence of histories and biographies based on primary sources; the rise of "book culture" (with private collections and libraries, antiquarians, and bibliophiles); and the Enlightenment itself, with its signature publication the *Encyclopedia,* which sought to make all knowledge available to whoever wanted it.

The publication of *Miscellanies,* which included "Some Observations on Diaries," came less than a year after the death of James Boswell, whose *Life of Dr. Samuel Johnson* (1791) remains universally acknowledged as the premier biography in English. France was halfway between the fall of the Bastille and Napoleon Bonaparte's crowning himself emperor. The Romantic movement was under way, and all across Europe Romantic egotists were starting to keep daily records of their self-absorption, to project themselves backward as figures in an imaginary past. Although many people kept diaries and journals in the eighteenth century, it was in the Romantic nineteenth century that such records were published on a regular basis.

D'Israeli's antiquarianism was not Romantic in origin but stands in direct descent from the torrential outpourings of such men as Hugo Grotius (1583–1645) and Robert Burton (1577–1640), whose large volumes are bursting with undigested quotations held together by minimal original prose. D'Israeli was much more sophisticated and genteel, with a much surer grasp of public tastes and his readers' abilities to absorb information in quotation marks. Burton and Grotius use quotations for the authority their antiquity bestows upon them; D'Israeli uses quotations in the modern way, as texts for analysis—he seeks not the authority of the past, only points of interest to pass on to his readers.

The influence of D'Israeli on his immediate posterity is complex. His long career became a footnote to that of his remarkable son, who was nevertheless a dutiful child, overseeing the editing his father's collected works and writing an informative introduction. The essay on diaries proved to be prophetic, suggesting that a flood of autobiographical writing was on the horizon, but it cannot be said to have provoked that flood or even to have encouraged it. D'Israeli's works continue to be read and republished because of his graceful and conversational style, his passionate

❖ **Key Facts**

Time Period:
Late 18th Century

Relevant Historical Events:
Expansion of the middle class; growth of literacy; Romantic period

Nationality:
English

Keywords:
Romanticism; biography; personality

Illustration depicting Joseph Smith, the Mormon prophet, reading the Bible as a youth. In his autobiography Smith depicted himself as a religious and mystical boy. In "Some Observations on Diaries, Self-Biography, and Self-Characters," Isaac D'Israeli comments on the place autobiographies have in the world of writing. © 7 CONTINENTS HISTORY/EVERETT COLLECTION

and communicable devotion to the literary life, and his uncanny instinct for a good story. The *Jewish Encyclopedia* (1906) notes that "these works contain a large amount of interesting matter, not always very reliable, on the lives of authors, and have formed a fund of anecdotage from which succeeding writers have drawn copiously." "Some Observations on Diaries" historically has not been distinguished as being of a different quality or relevance from the rest of D'Israeli's considerable output.

THEMES AND STYLE

The main theme of "Some Observations" is the emergence of the literary biography as a taste and the use of private diaries and journals as keys to unlock what was, at the time, called the "character"—a combination of the modern notion of the individual "personality" and older ideas of moral definition—of the biographical subject. D'Israeli believed that the biographer had to get inside the head of his or her subject, insofar as was possible. He declares:

> It has now become the labour of criticism to compose the life of an author; and no writer can now successfully accomplish his Biographic attempts, unless he comes with a portion of that genius, the history of whose mind he records; he must possess a flexibility of taste, which, like the cameleon, takes the colour of that object on which it rests.

In D'Israeli's view, the quickest route to such insights was through the diaries and journals of the subject.

D'Israeli approaches readers not as the writer of a diary or a journal but as an observer of the journal writing of others. Of that kind of self-report, he says, "There are two species of minor Biography [that is, self-written but not a formal autobiography or memoir] which may be discriminated; detailing our own life, and portraying our own character." D'Israeli stresses the uniqueness of the individual and the profit to be had from considering that uniqueness:

> Our souls, like our faces, bear the general resemblance of the species, but retain the particular form which is peculiar to the individual. He who studies his own mind, and has the industry to note down the fluctuations of his opinions, the fallacies of his passions, and the vacillations of his resolutions, will form a journal to himself peculiarly interesting, and probably, not undeserving the meditations of others.

D'Israeli's style, in this essay as in everything in his oeuvre, is simple and direct. He never talks down to his readers or uses elaborate words and phrases for humor. There are peculiarities of syntax—some shaped by the usage of his time and others by the particulars of his life and personality—that arise from his having developed his manner through reading rather than through conversation. "Simplicity of language and thought," he asserts, "are sweet and natural graces, which every Self-biographer should study." D'Israeli also makes telling psychological observations, usually as asides, that only modern readers' ignorance of the examples he uses prevents their perfectly grasping his point. He writes, "He who can, without reserve or hesitation, form such a journal, may be safely pronounced an honest man. Few great men, and no villain, can pursue, with any regularity, a series of their actions; not for want of patience, but of courage." D'Israeli wonders whether such men as Robert Clive, the ruthless conqueror of India, or Oliver Cromwell, who sanctioned the execution of Charles I and slaughtered thousands to subdue Ireland, could have composed a diary. "Neither of these men," D'Israeli argues, "could suffer solitude and darkness; at the scattered thoughts of casual reflection they started; what would they have done, had memory marshaled their crimes, and arranged them in the terrors of chronology?"

CRITICAL DISCUSSION

Contemporary critics reviewed D'Israeli's books, although the writings belonged to a species of literary entertainment for which reviews were usually deemed irrelevant. If the works were mentioned in passing, the tone was likely to be patronizing. An assessment published in *Tait's Edinburgh Magazine* in 1841 is typical: "Of the greater part of the topics which he has discussed, that numerous and important division of society, the *Reading Public,* as distinguished from the learned and the studious, would, save for him have known nothing, and cared nothing." A review of *Amenities of Literature* in the *Eclectic Review* that same year proclaims D'Israeli "the first writer who endeavoured to allure the general reader from the beaten path of popular history, and every day literature," into the realms of the bibliophile or the antiquary. Not all critics approved, however. Writing in the *British Critic* in 1793, an anonymous reviewer made some of the same objections to D'Israeli's books of miscellanies and curiosities that later writers would make about condensed versions of books: "It may be feared lest minds accustomed to them should reject severer diet…. Should the taste for them grow into *a rage*, it will be an alarming symptom for literature."

D'Israeli's most lasting legacy is as a popularizer and composer of digests. He gave his middle-class readers a taste for what might be called "antiquarianism-lite," lasting well into the twentieth century. On the writing of diaries and journals, D'Israeli stands more like a prophet than a professor. Future journals and biographies, which abounded in the nineteenth century, were not composed under his instruction, though they uncannily bear out his "Observations." Too often they became either tedious literal chronicles from which all self-criticism is banished or propaganda: "If [the diarist] is solicitous of charming and dazzling, he is not writing his life, but pourtraying the ideal adventurer of a romance." It may be said, however, that insofar as he promoted the reading of diaries and journals, D'Israeli had considerable impact on the history of taste.

Most modern scholars take a positive view of D'Israeli. Ina Ferris, in her essay "Antiquarian Authorship: D'Israeli's Miscellany of Literary Curiosity and the Question of Secondary Genres" (2006), observes that "D'Israeli's commitment to literary culture makes him part of the wider movement in the late eighteenth century to valorize literature as the new repository of public and national virtue," adding that he always sought "to promote a model of reading as active engagement rather than passive reception or absorption." In "Reading Romantic Autobiography" (2001), James Treadwell credits D'Israeli, in the "Observations" essay, with discovering autobiography as an "art" rather than a form. Treadwell goes further, suggesting that D'Israeli's discovery means that "the particular 'art' of life-writing … lies in its representation of a person as a private being rather than an historical agent."

BIBLIOGRAPHY

Sources

Disraeli, Benjamin. "On the Life and Writings of Mr. Disraeli. By His Son." *Curiosities of Literature; Edited, with Memoir and Notes, by His Son, the Earl of Beaconsfield.* By Isaac D'Israeli. eBooks @ Adelaide. University of Adelaide, 2012. Web. 1 Dec. 2012.

"D'Israeli, Isaac." *Jewish Encyclopedia.* New York: Funk and Wagnalls, 1901–06. *JewishEncyclopedia.com.* Web. 3 Dec. 2012.

D'Israeli, Isaac. *Miscellanies; or, Literary Recreations.* London: T. Cadell and W. Davies, 1796. *Google Books.* Web. 2 Dec. 2012.

ISAAC D'ISRAELI: FORWARD-LOOKING ANTIQUARIAN

In many ways Isaac D'Israeli fits the stereotype of the antiquarian. His own loving son, Benjamin, Lord Beaconsfield, described him as "a man who really passed his life in his library." Nevertheless, D'Israeli seems to have had a quite modern attitude about his Jewish ethnicity, attaching himself to the Bevis Marks Synagogue as a social rite but with little or no religious conviction. In 1813 the synagogue elected D'Israeli warden. He declined by letter, which was ignored. When he did not show up at meetings, he was fined forty pounds. A heated exchange of letters ensued, concluding with one from D'Israeli, cited in the *Jewish Encyclopedia,* in which he resigned from the synagogue and, by inference, the Jewish people: "I am under the painful necessity of wishing that my name be erased from the list of your members of Yehedim." His sons were baptized as Christians, but D'Israeli did not convert.

D'Israeli was not himself a Romantic, though he was of the great Romantic generation of Ludwig van Beethoven and Johann von Goethe, William Wordsworth and Germaine de Staël. He was, perhaps as a by-product of his literary interests, a romantic enabler, unleashing a tide of Romantic egotism. He was also quite literally a Romantic enabler in the spectacular career of his son, first as a novelist and then as a politician.

Ferris, Ina. "Antiquarian Authorship: D'Israeli's Miscellany of Literary Curiosity and the Question of Secondary Genres." *Studies in Romanticism* 45.4 (2006): 523–42. *JSTOR.* Web. 4 Dec. 2012.

Rev. of *Amenities of Literature*, by Isaac D'Israeli. *Eclectic Review* 10 (1841): 431–51. *Google Books.* Web. 15 Jan. 2013.

———. *Tait's Edinburgh Magazine* 8 (1841): 638–48. *Google Books.* Web. 15 Jan. 2013.

Rev. of *Curiosities of Literature: Volume the Second*, by Isaac D'Israeli. *British Critic* 1 (1793): 324–29. *Google Books.* Web. 15 Jan. 2013.

Treadwell, James. "Reading Romantic Autobiography." *Nineteenth-Century Prose* 28.2 (2001): 1–27. *Academic OneFile.* Web. 5 Dec. 2012.

Further Reading

Colclough, Stephen. "Recovering the Reader: Commonplace Books and Diaries as Sources of Reading Experience." *Publishing History* 44 (1998): 5–37. Print.

Ferris, Ina. "The 'Character' of James the First and Antiquarian Secret History." *Wordsworth Circle* 37.2 (2006): 73–76. *General OneFile.* Web. 4 Dec. 2012.

Keen, Paul. *The Crisis in Literature in the 1790s: Print Culture and the Public Sphere.* Cambridge: Cambridge University Press, 1999. Print.

Siskin, Clifford. *The Work of Writing: Literature and Social Change in Britain 1700–1830.* Baltimore: Johns Hopkins University Press, 1998. Print.

Gerald Carpenter

A Writer's Diary
Virginia Woolf

❖ **Key Facts**

Time Period:
Mid-20th Century

Relevant Historical Events:
Woolf's success as a writer; formation of the Bloomsbury group; growth of modernism

Nationality:
English

Keywords:
modernism; literature; creativity

OVERVIEW

Virginia Woolf's *A Writer's Diary*, edited by Woolf's husband, Leonard, and published posthumously in 1953, is a highly selective assemblage of extracts from her diary, containing entries written from 1918 to 1941, the year of Woolf's death. Redacted and occasionally censored from twenty-six volumes of text, the book focuses specifically on material pertaining to Woolf's literary career, reproducing, according to Leonard's preface, "practically everything which referred to her own writing," along with a number of writing exercises; comments on the books she was reading; and a few passages unrelated to literature that "give the reader an idea of the direct impact upon her mind of scenes and persons, i.e. of the raw material of her art." A unique document of Woolf's recorded thoughts on the composition, publication, and reception of her literary works, *A Writer's Diary* offers a sustained glimpse at her creative process throughout the duration of her career.

Published at a time when public opinion on Woolf's literary stature was relatively ambivalent, *A Writer's Diary* was well received, helping to galvanize interest in her writing and strengthen her eminence within canons of modern literature. The book—the first publication of Woolf's personal diary in any form—attracted considerable scholarly interest and played a significant role in the shaping of popular conceptions of her life and personality. In more recent decades *A Writer's Diary* has in many ways been superseded by the appearance of both Woolf's full, unexpurgated diary (published in five volumes from 1977 to 1984) and a less narrowly focused abridged version (published in 1990 under the title *A Moment's Liberty*), but its particular emphasis on Woolf's life as a writer has made it enduringly appealing to readers specifically concerned with how she wrote the literature for which she is famous.

HISTORICAL AND LITERARY CONTEXT

Woolf's various statements throughout *A Writer's Diary* reflect the modernist preoccupations of England's social and intellectual milieu during the first half of the twentieth century. During this period, the intelligentsia of English society (and elsewhere) was characterized by the increasing sense that the philosophical and religious certainties of prior epochs in Western civilization—in particular, faith in God and human reason—were no longer relevant to the fragmentary modern world, whose social landscape had been utterly transformed by scientific breakthroughs and industrialization. The extreme bloodshed of World War I, fought with unprecedented technological advances that made the tremendously high body count seem even more mechanistically obscene than in past wars, added to the sense of an irrevocable rupture from the past, contributing to the perceived need—in literature and elsewhere—to devise new ways of addressing the modern world.

Before and during the composition of *A Writer's Diary*, Woolf was a prominent member of the Bloomsbury group, a loose, informal coterie of primarily upper-middle-class British artists and intellectuals who lived in the general vicinity of Bloomsbury, London. Woolf's diary provides a literary record of many of her interactions with other members of the group, including the influential economist John Maynard Keynes and the celebrated novelist E. M. Forster. The book likewise documents Woolf's dealings with multiple prominent British figures from outside the group, such as T. S. Eliot, Katherine Mansfield, and Thomas Hardy.

A Writer's Diary contains numerous reactions from Woolf to the literature—both older and contemporary—that she happened to be reading at the time, and the book as a whole places her and her work firmly within the literary milieu of English modernism. The diary contains Woolf's oft-quoted assessment of James Joyce's seminal modernist novel *Ulysses* (1922) as the work of "a queasy undergraduate scratching his pimples," as well as an indication of perplexity at Eliot's admiration for the book. Given *A Writer's Diary*'s status as a book specifically devoted to documenting Woolf's writing process, the book's closest formal antecedent is perhaps André Gide's *Log-book of the Coiners* (1926), though the latter work was deliberately written as a document of literary composition, whereas Woolf's book exists only as such because Leonard carved it out of a much more diffuse preexisting text.

The publication of *A Writer's Diary* helped to renew interest in Woolf's life and work, and in the two decades following its appearance it was heavily mined for the light it shed on her life as a writer. This interest intensified during the scholarly rediscovery of her work precipitated by the advent of feminist literary criticism in the late 1960s and early 1970s. Today scholarly attention on the book has largely died out, the publication of the uncut diary having supplanted the truncated 1953 version as a source of information. However, *A Writer's Diary* remains in print, a fact that testifies to its enduring interest among more casual Woolf enthusiasts and aspiring writers drawn to the book's literary focus.

THEMES AND STYLE

Central to *A Writer's Diary* is the message that a pattern of psychological strain and exhilaration exists within the process of literary creation. As Woolf documents the events surrounding the composition of each of her books, the diary soon emerges as a series of recurring cycles. She repeatedly sketches out a book's initial inspiration and conception, as when she muses on what would eventually become the novel *Orlando:* "it might be a way of writing the memoirs of one's own times during people's lifetimes. It might be a most amusing book. The question is how to do it. Vita [Sackville-West, Woolf's friend] should be Orlando, a young nobleman." She likewise discusses the vagaries of the writing process—"I begin to see what I had in my mind; and want to begin cutting out masses of irrelevance and clearing, sharpening and making good phrases shine"—and discusses her thoughts on how her books are received—"I was floating rather lazily on praise, when [reviewer J. C.] Squire barked in the *Observer,* but even as I sat reading him … I felt the rock of self esteem untouched in me."

The excerpts that make up *A Writer's Diary* are where Woolf recorded her thoughts and meditations on the various aspects of her craft. The diary entries contain occasional references to possible future publication, with Woolf suggesting at one point that she might use them as the basis for a memoir and elsewhere indicating that if she dies, Leonard "should make up a book from them, I think, and then burn the body." However, the organization and narrative shape of *A Writer's Diary* have little to do with Woolf's original intent when she composed its raw material. The published book instead serves as a vehicle for Leonard's avowed project of "[throwing] light upon Virginia Woolf's intentions, objects, and methods as a writer" in order to demonstrate that she was "a serious artist and all her books are serious works of art. The diaries at least show the extraordinary energy, persistence, and concentration with which she devoted herself to the art of writing."

A Writer's Diary is written in a relatively straightforward, conversational style that reflects Woolf's literary mentality without attempting to emulate the meticulously crafted sentences of her fiction. Her fondness for precise details, striking imagery, and evocative similes are much in evidence, as when she says of Hardy that "he puts his head down like some old pouter pigeon. He has a very long head; and quizzical

Virginia Woolf, English novelist and essayist.
© LEBRECHT MUSIC AND ARTS PHOTO LIBRARY/ALAMY

bright eyes, for in talk they grow bright." Meanwhile, the tone of the diary reflects Woolf's frequently fluctuating emotional state. The text is sometimes elated—in response to Leonard's praise of *The Waves,* Woolf writes, "but Lord! What a relief! I stumped off in the rain to make a little round to Rat Farm in jubilation"—and just as frequently depressive—"I must write off my dejected rambling misery—having just read over the 30,000 words of *Flush* and come to the conclusion that they won't do. Oh what a waste—what a bore!"

CRITICAL DISCUSSION

A Writer's Diary was well received upon its initial publication, garnering considerable praise for the glimpse it offered into Woolf's mind and the light it shed on her work. Elizabeth Bowen, writing in the *New York Times Book Review,* approved of the book's focus on Woolf's writing, asserting that "'A Writer's Diary,' as it reaches us, never shifts from its focus: it is internal. Its continuity is not merely *a* continuity; it *is* Virginia Woolf. Here we have what she was and what she was for. In a genius writer, is being ever separated from purpose?" Years later, with the publication of the complete diary, the emergence of a more fully rounded (and uncensored) portrait of Woolf would greatly vitiate the early assumption that *A Writer's Diary* was a full and accurate representation of the writer's consciousness.

A Writer's Diary made substantial and lasting contributions to Woolf's iconic cultural status, though not always positively. Anne Olivier Bell, who edited

MOMENTS OF BEING

A Writer's Diary was only one of a large number of books collecting Virginia Woolf's writings that appeared in the years after her death. Another noteworthy posthumous volume was *Moments of Being,* which appeared in 1976 under the editorship of Jeanne Schulkind and collected the entirety of Woolf's explicitly autobiographical writing—five previously unpublished essays Woolf left behind in various stages of revision. The book's contents shed valuable light on both the events of Woolf's life and how she later came to regard those events, as well as illuminating the extent to which her fiction drew upon her own experiences.

The essays span the length of Woolf's writing career: she began the first piece, a childhood memoir titled "Reminiscences," eight years prior to the publication of her first novel, while she ceased work on the last piece—"A Sketch of the Past," which covers many of the same events from a vastly different perspective—only four months prior to her death. The other three essays were written in the early 1920s ("22 Hyde Park Gate" and "Old Bloomsbury") and the late 1930s ("Am I a Snob?") and are products of the Memoir Club, a close-knit group of friends who congregated periodically to read frank memoirs to each other.

the unexpurgated five-volume version of Woolf's diary, noted in 2002 that "Leonard's publication of *A Writer's Diary* set off a revival of interest in Virginia Woolf, who had rather sunk to the bottom in public esteem after her death," but also observed that "its publication probably did a good deal to create or reinforce the popular journalistic image of Virginia Woolf, the moody, arrogant, and malicious Queen of Bloomsbury."

There is not a great deal of recent scholarship specifically focusing on *A Writer's Diary,* but an exception is Kate Briggs's 2011 article in *Textual Practice,* which evaluates the nature of Leonard's editorial intentions. Briggs compares the book to Gide's similar volume and discusses the work in relation to the tradition of "genetic criticism," which attempts to reconstruct the process by which a literary work was written through the analysis of manuscripts and other primary documents. Meanwhile, the diary entries collected in *A Writer's Diary*—though not the book itself—remain widely cited within Woolf studies; Julia Briggs's 2005 biography *Virginia Woolf: An Inner Life* (which, like Woolf's text, is primarily concerned with Woolf's life as a writer) makes particularly extensive use of them.

BIBLIOGRAPHY

Sources

Bell, Anne Olivier. "Editing Virginia Woolf's Diary." *Editing Virginia Woolf: Interpreting the Modernist Text.* Ed. James M. Haule and J. H. Stape. Basingstoke: Palgrave, 2002. 11–24. Print.

Bowen, Elizabeth. "The Principle of Her Art Was Joy." Rev. of *A Writer's Diary,* by Virginia Woolf. *New York Times Book Review.* New York Times, 21 Feb. 1954. Web. 28 Nov. 2012.

Briggs, Julia. *Virginia Woolf: An Inner Life.* Orlando: Harcourt, 2005. Print.

Briggs, Kate. "The Making of *A Writer's Diary: Being Extracts from the Diary of Virginia Woolf.*" *Textual Practice* 25.6 (2011): 1033–50. *Taylor and Francis Online.* Web. 28 Nov. 2012.

Woolf, Virginia. *A Writer's Diary: Being Extracts from the Diary of Virginia Woolf.* Ed. Leonard Woolf. New York: Harcourt Brace Jovanovich, 1954. Print.

Further Reading

Gide, André. *Log-book of the Coiners.* Trans. Justin O'Brien. London: Cassell, 1952. Print.

Lee, Hermione. *Virginia Woolf.* London: Chatto and Windus, 1996. Print.

Podnieks, Elizabeth. *Daily Modernism: The Literary Diaries of Virginia Woolf, Antonia White, Elizabeth Smart, and Anaïs Nin.* Montreal: McGill-Queen's University Press, 2000. Print.

Sellers, Susan. "Virginia Woolf's Diaries and Letters." *The Cambridge Companion to Virginia Woolf.* Ed. Sue Roe and Susan Sellers. Cambridge: Cambridge University Press, 2000. 109–26. Print.

Woolf, Virginia. *The Diary of Virginia Woolf.* 5 vols. Ed. Anne Olivier Bell. New York: Harcourt Brace Jovanovich, 1977–84. Print.

———. *Moments of Being.* Ed. Jeanne Schulkind. 2nd ed. San Diego: Harcourt Brace Jovanovich, 1985. Print.

———. *A Passionate Apprentice: The Early Journals 1897–1909.* Ed. Mitchell A. Leaska. San Diego: Harcourt Brace Jovanovich, 1990. Print.

———. *The Virginia Woolf Reader.* Ed. Mitchell A. Leaska. San Diego: Harcourt Brace Jovanovich, 1984. Print.

James Overholtzer

A Writer's Notebook

W. Somerset Maugham

OVERVIEW

W. Somerset Maugham's *A Writer's Notebook* (1949) contains a variety of notes written by the prolific author, including character and scene sketches, travel descriptions, and reflections about his life and life in general. The entries are divided into short sections of varying lengths; the earliest entry was written in 1892, when Maugham was eighteen, the latest in 1944, when the author was seventy. In 1949 Maugham penned the final postscript, including commentary on his previous conclusion (written in 1944). The notes total 365 pages and showcase Maugham's keen observational eye, tendency toward brutal honesty, and evolution as a writer.

Eleven years before the publication of *A Writer's Notebook*, Maugham published *The Summing Up*, which he describes as an effort to create "a coherent picture" of his "feelings and opinions." In contrast to this self-proclaimed more autobiographical work, *A Writer's Notebook* is offered (by Maugham) as an insight into the creative process. More than half a century after its original publication, Vintage Classics deemed the material worth revisiting and reprinted *A Writer's Notebook* with the original preface in 2001, issuing an additional reprint in 2009. Though seemingly outspoken and honest as a person and in his notebooks, Maugham kept certain areas of his life quite private and was not alive when some of these private aspects became public. For this reason, Maugham fans and enthusiasts comb *A Writer's Notebook* for possible clues about both Maugham the writer and Maugham the man.

HISTORICAL AND LITERARY CONTEXT

Maugham came of age during a time when homosexuality was illegal in England and many other countries. Influenced by the 1895 Oscar Wilde indecency trial, Maugham, who had relationships with both men and women, avoided homosexual themes throughout his career and included no direct references to homosexuality in his notes. Despite this, he dedicated *A Writer's Notebook* to Frederick Gerald Haxton, whom he calls a friend but was in fact his longtime lover.

Having wanted to become a writer since age fifteen, Maugham kept notebooks throughout his rich life, including the five years he spent as a medical student in London (1892–1897), during his service in both world wars, and while he traveled around the globe. In the preface to *A Writer's Notebook*, Maugham claims his notes are devoid of his celebrity friends. To the contrary, the notebooks do mention a number of notables, including Charlie Chaplin and H. G. Wells. *A Writer's Notebook* also contains detailed descriptions of Maugham's travels, including the time he spent in Russia as a spy in 1917.

In the opening to *A Writer's Notebook*, Maugham declares *The Journal of Jules Renard* (1925) a direct influence on his decision to publish his notes. Though dismissive of Jules Renard as a writer, he maintains that Renard's journals are a useful tool. In the notes themselves, Maugham reflects upon other writers' work, particularly the nineteenth-century literature published by the generation prior to his. The notes include thoughts on the works of Fyodor Dostoyevsky, Guy de Maupassant, and Ivan Turgenev, among others, with occasional addenda and apologies from the older Maugham regarding the opinions of his younger self.

Maugham's notebooks serve as a road map to his literary development. When Maugham began writing in the 1890s, Wilde and other writers were arguing that literature should strive for elevation and be practiced in the style of Walter Pater, who left a legacy of complicated, ornate sentences when he died in 1894. As a young writer, Maugham took Wilde's urging to heart and attempted to write in a style resembling Pater's. *A Writer's Notebook* contains some of these attempts, including imagery fashioned from flowery descriptions of jewels at the British Museum. In an accompanying note, Maugham explains that he went to the British Museum and described what he saw with a passage from Wilde's *Salomé* (1894) in mind. When Maugham reflects on his work overall, he writes simply, "I have had my say and I am well pleased to let others occupy my small place in the world of letters." Subsequent reprints of *A Writer's Notebook* and *The Journal of Jules Renard* (in 2009 and 2008, respectively) show that contemporary writers and readers can still find guidance and intrigue within these texts.

THEMES AND STYLE

A Writer's Notebook explores many of the same themes as his novels, short stories, and plays, including religion, relationships, and human disconnect and frailty.

❖ **Key Facts**

Time Period:
Late 19th to Mid-20th Centuries

Relevant Historical Events:
Maugham's success as a writer; World War I; World War II; Maugham's world travels

Nationality:
English

Keywords:
literature; creativity; travel

THEORIES

A portrait of W. Somerset Maugham, English novelist, playwright, and short-story writer, by Charles Alexandre Picard Ledoux. © SIMON CARTER GALLERY, WOODBRIDGE, SUFFOLK, UK/THE BRIDGEMAN ART LIBRARY

As a result of a disrupted and traumatic childhood—he was orphaned by age ten—Maugham developed a stammer and a lifelong shyness. These afflictions morphed into what biographers have noted was a tendency to ridicule others before he himself could be ridiculed. The notes, however, do not reveal many instances of self-doubt and instead mainly chronicle Maugham's views of people and places from the outside, echoing the sharp observation and unwavering honesty his literary works are known for. In a note composed the day after he turned seventy, Maugham attributes his willingness to deliver uncompromising truths to his age: "I no longer mind what people think of me. They can take me or leave me."

Maugham used his notebooks to gather material for his work and to record his reflections on art, literature, society, and religion. His early notes contain scraps of dialogue intended for plays (though not as many as were present in the originals), while his later ones chronicle his travels and explore his thoughts about the people, places, and notions he encounters. During a visit to Russia, for example, he writes both about the ordinary people he meets (such as a mostly absent Russian teacher) and the work of Dostoyevsky (whose grave Maugham visited). It is not clear, especially in earlier entries, that Maugham ever thought they would be published. Though he states that the notes are presented as is, he did select, condense, and comment on them, the effect of which produces a very particular portrait. Later in his life Maugham destroyed many of his papers, as well as the notes not included in *A Writer's Notebook*.

For the most part, Maugham's signature straightforward and realistic diction pervades the notes. The exceptions to this style are the entries in which he experiments with imitating writers more effuse and flowery than himself, including Wilde and Pater, such as this one in 1901: "In the sun the wet leaves glistened like emeralds, meretricious stones which might fitly deck the pompous depravity of a royal courtesan." This 1922 passage is more representative of the notes' overall style and of Maugham's increased confidence in his (by then) established straightforwardness: "The sky was grey, and against the greyness hung black fantastic clouds, and the high sun, breaking through the greyness, touched their summits with silver."

CRITICAL DISCUSSION

The initial critical reaction to *A Writer's Notebook* was mixed. Writing in the *American Mercury*, Charles Angoff praises Maugham's "powers of acute observation" and finds that "his artistic antennae are always up and extremely sensitive" but ultimately declares him a failure, claiming that the writer sometimes "seems not to belong to the human race." By contrast, William Rose Benét of the *Saturday Review* concludes that the notebooks are "a rich fruit-cake of good reading, tart and mellow, not to be assessed from a bit nibbled here or there!"

In the last part of the twentieth century, critical interest in Maugham's overall work was revived. While most critics tend to reserve only a comment or two for the existence of *A Writer's Notebook*, in *Somerset Maugham* (1982), Anthony Curtis uses the notebooks to trace Maugham's development as a writer. He concludes that the notes reflect the author's literary techniques: "Little escaped his clear-sighted vision. He was always looking for those tell-tale details that give the game away." According to Curtis, the notebooks display the evolution of Maugham's style and show that he "worked assiduously to fashion the lucid, easy manner that suited him best." While the depiction of Maugham's literary development in *A Writer's Notebook* continues to influence young writers, most current critics, with a few exceptions, have not given the notebooks much attention.

Contemporary Maugham coverage, including Selina Hastings's *The Secret Lives of Somerset Maugham* (2010), has focused on the secretive aspects of the writer's life while granting *A Writer's Notebook* little mention. The most recent critical pieces citing the work use it as a supplement to discuss Maugham's other writing, as in Nikky-Guninder Kaur Singh's 1995 article in the *Durham University Journal* about Maugham's novel *The Razor's Edge*, in which she notes that *A Writer's Notebook* "offers a sobering picture of cross-cultural understanding." In a discussion of Maugham's overall work in the *New Criterion*, Joseph Epstein argues that the sentiments in *A Writer's Notebook* are reflected "subtly, dramatically" in his work and, therefore, Maugham "shall always be a writer for readers who care for more than writing alone."

BIBLIOGRAPHY

Sources

Angoff, Charles. "W. Somerset Maugham." Rev. of *A Writer's Notebook*, by W. Somerset Maugham. *American Mercury* Jan. 1950: 111–16. Print.

Benét, William Rose. "Maughamana, 1892–1949." Rev. of *A Writer's Notebook*, by W. Somerset Maugham. *Saturday Review* 22 Oct. 1949: 16. Print.

Curtis, Anthony. "Untitled." *Somerset Maugham*. Windsor: Profile, 1982. Rpt. in *Twentieth-Century Literary Criticism*. Vol. 208. Detroit: Gale, 2009. *Literature Resource Center*. Web. 11 Dec. 2012.

Epstein, Joseph. "Is It All Right to Read Somerset Maugham?" *New Criterion* 4.3 (1985): 1–13. Rpt. in *Short Story Criticism*. Ed. Thomas Votteler. Vol. 8. Detroit: Gale Research, 1991. *Literature Resource Center*. Web. 11 Dec. 2012.

Maugham, W. Somerset. *The Summing Up*. Garden City: Doubleday, 1938. Print.

FAMILY TIES: MAUGHAM'S NEPHEW ROBIN

As his uncle W. Somerset Maugham had as a young man, Robin Maugham aspired to be a writer. Unlike his uncle (and according to Somerset himself), however, Robin did not possess natural storytelling abilities. Despite Somerset's harsh assessment of his literary aspirations, Robin became infatuated with his uncle's way of life at his estate, Villa Mauresque, and spent a considerable amount of time there.

In addition to literary counsel, Robin sought advice from Somerset about how to cope with his homosexuality. Somerset, who was deeply affected by the Oscar Wilde trial, urged Robin both to inwardly accept himself and to outwardly conceal that self. In spite of this caution, Robin did not immediately turn down the publisher who contacted him with an offer to write about his famous uncle. Instead, Robin told Somerset he could not financially afford to refuse the offer. In the same spirit that Somerset censored *A Writer's Notebook,* he paid his nephew the equivalent of the publisher's advance and asked him to promise to keep his private life private. But after Somerset's death in 1965, Robin broke his promise, speaking about his uncle to the press and eventually publishing four books about him: *Somerset and All the Maughams* (1966), *Escape from the Shadows* (1972), *The Search for Nirvana* (1975), and *Conversations with Willie* (1978).

———. *A Writer's Notebook*. Garden City: Doubleday, 1949. Print.

Singh, Nikky-Guninder Kaur. "Crossing the Razor's Edge: Somerset Maugham and Hindu Philosophy." *Durham University Journal* 87.2 (1995): 329–42. Rpt. In *Novels for Students*. Ed. Sara Constantakis. Vol. 23. Detroit: Gale, 2006. *Literature Resource Center*. Web. 13 Dec. 2012.

Further Reading

Connon, Bryan. *Somerset Maugham and the Maugham Dynasty*. London: Sinclair-Stevenson, 1997. Print.

Hastings, Selina. *The Secret Lives of Somerset Maugham*. New York: Random House, 2010. Print.

Maugham, W. Somerset. *The Skeptical Romancer: Selected Travel Writing*. Ed. Pico Iyer. New York: Vintage, 2009. Print.

Meyers, Jeffrey. *Somerset Maugham: A Life*. New York: Vintage, 2005. Print.

Raphael, Frederic. "The Alien Maugham." *PN Review* 20.5 (1994): 19–23. Rpt. in *Twentieth-Century Literary Criticism*. Vol. 208. Detroit: Gale, 2009. *Literature Resource Center*. Web. 13 Dec. 2012.

Shakespeare, Nicholas. Introduction. *Collected Stories*. By W. Somerset Maugham. New York: Random House, 2004. Print.

Willy, Margaret. "W. Somerset Maugham: Overview." *Reference Guide to English Literature*. Ed. D. L. Kirkpatrick. 2nd ed. Chicago: St. James, 1991. *Literature Resource Center*. Web. 4 Dec. 2012.

Jen Gann

Travel and Exploration

As I Crossed a Bridge of Dreams by Lady Sarashina	189
The Congo Diary by Joseph Conrad	192
Journals of John Wesley by John Wesley	195
A Journal of the First Voyage of Vasco da Gama, 1497–1499	198
Journal of the First Voyage to America by Christopher Columbus	201
The Journals of Jonathan Carver and Related Documents, 1766–1770 by Jonathan Carver	205
Leaves from the Journal of Our Life in the Highlands, from 1848 to 1861 by Queen Victoria	209
Letters from an American Farmer by Michel-Guillaume Saint-Jean de Crèvecoeur	213
The Letters of Lady Anne Barnard to Henry Dundas, from the Cape and Elsewhere by Anne Barnard	217
Motorcycle Diaries by Ernesto "Che" Guevara	220
Notebooks and *Letters* by Nathaniel Hawthorne	223
The Pylgrymage of Sir Richard Guylforde by Richarde Guylforde	226
The Travels of Dean Mahomet, a Native of Patna in Bengal, through Several Parts of India, While in the Service of the Honourable the East India Company Written by Himself, in a Series of Letters to a Friend by Dean Mahomet	229

As I Crossed a Bridge of Dreams

Lady Sarashina

Key Facts

Time Period:
Early 11th Century

Relevant Historical Events:
The "rule of taste"; peace and prosperity of the Heian period

Nationality:
Japanese

Keywords:
women's writing; Buddhism; Shinto

OVERVIEW

As I Crossed a Bridge of Dreams (c. 1059) is the journal of a Japanese woman known only as Takasue's daughter (also called Lady Sarashina by some scholars) that chronicles her life in the later part of the Heian period (794–1185). The work is also referred to as *Sarashina Nikki* (*Sarashina Diary*). Sarashina was a member of a social class relegated to relatively menial positions in the Heian imperial court. Her father (Takasue) and husband served as mid-level functionaries in unfashionable provinces, and Sarashina herself acted as lady-in-waiting to an infant princess. The Heian period was a time of heightened cultural activity, and Sarashina's poems, sprinkled liberally throughout the text, allude to other famous authors of the era. There are poems and anecdotes about places and things seen on pilgrimages to shrines and temples near the capital, Heian-kyō (now Kyōto), and descriptions of dreams involving symbols, spirits, and gods. Sarashina's perspective is that of a tender soul to whom nature and the Shinto and Buddhist gods believed to govern the universe are sometimes more real to her than anything else, including her husband and children.

The original version of *As I Crossed a Bridge of Dreams* was lost, and the oldest extant version is a handwritten copy by Japanese poet Fujiwara Teika (first mentioned in his diary, *Meigetsuki*), pages of which were, at some point, undone and rebound in the wrong order. In 1924 Tamai Kōsuke, a Japanese expert on the Heian period, recognized the mistake and arranged the text in its current form. Along with other examples of writing by women of the Heian period—such as Michitsuna no Haha's *Kagerō Nikki* (c. 974), translated in 1955 as *The Gossamer Years* (1955); Sei Shōnagon's journal *The Pillow Book* (c. 1002); and Murasaki Shikibu's novel *The Tale of Genji* (early eleventh century)—*As I Crossed a Bridge of Dreams* is a mainstay of Japanese literature.

HISTORICAL AND LITERARY CONTEXT

As I Crossed a Bridge of Dreams affords a peek into a culturally fruitful moment in Japanese history, with refinement and civilization emanating from the imperial court at Heian-kyō, established there in 794. During the Nara period (710–784) the capital was fixed, for the first time, at Heijō-kyō (now Nara), but before that it had shifted with every new emperor. During the sixth century Japan came under the influence of China, adopting Buddhism, elements of the Chinese language, new systems of weights and measures, and other innovations. Both Nara and Heian-kyō were modeled on China's capital, the ancient city of Chang'an (now Xi'an), according to a grid pattern consisting of square blocks. Heijō-kyō became a major Buddhist center; some scholars think the imperial capital was moved to Heian-kyō to separate the emperor from influential Buddhist priests. Sarashina's ancestor, Sugawara no Michizane (Tenjin) (845–903), a poet and favorite of the emperor, was pushed out of his position at the imperial court in 901 by a jealous member of the influential Fujiwara clan. Her father lamented the bad karma that relegated him to a mid-level provincial governorship.

Sarashina's work covers the years between 1020 and 1058, a time of peace and prosperity in the capital. The phrase "rule of taste," coined by historian George Sansom, describes the social dynamic at play in eleventh-century Heian-kyō. The imperial court, with the emperor at its center, cultivated a society in which people communicated via poetry as a matter of course. Aesthetic refinements of dress and elaborate ceremonies were sources of collective pride and enjoyment. Modest Sarashina, with her lifelong love of tales, had difficulty finding a place in the world, and her journal mentions nothing in the way of concern for fashion.

As I Crossed a Bridge of Dreams is part of an outcropping of diary writing by women that arose during the Heian period, composed in vernacular Japanese (*wabun*), which is distinct from the Sino-Japanese (*kambun*) favored by male scholars. Her maternal aunt, the author of *The Gossamer Years,* had died by the time Sarashina was born, leaving behind a tortured account of an unhappy marriage. *The Pillow Book* takes a more detached approach, commenting on aspects of court life and the subtle hierarchies of society in an almost Austenesque manner. Also leaving behind a diary (c. 1007) was noted royal mistress Izumi Shikibu (974–1034). She was one of the Thirty-Six Poetry Immortals who composed Japan's best existing *waka,* poems of thirty-six syllables, as selected by poet, scholar, and politician Fujiwara no Kintō. However, the most important work from the period is

TRAVEL AND EXPLORATION

Murasaki-shikibu, the famous learned Woman in the Age of the Hei-an.

A depiction of Murasaki Shikibu, a lady of the Japanese court who wrote *The Tale of Genji* in the early eleventh century. The story inspired Sarashina as she wrote her own memoirs and lyrical poems soon afterward, during the Heian period in Japan. © THE ART ARCHIVE AT ART RESOURCE, NY

daughter of a provincial governor, she moved multiple times before the family arrived at the capital. Taking up a role at the palace, she found herself "so used to staying with my old-fashioned parents at home, gazing hour after hour at the Autumn moon or the Spring blossoms, that when I arrived at Court I was in a sort of daze." As for piety, Sarashina criticizes herself: "Though I made occasional pilgrimages to temples, I could never bring myself to pray sincerely for what most people want…. The height of my aspirations was that a man of noble birth … someone like Shining Genji in … [Murasaki's] Tale, would visit me just once a year in the mountain village where he would have hidden me like Lady Ukifune."

Sarashina used her diary to record the many changes she had to accommodate over the course of her life. The short poems, composed by her and others, evoke those changes, as well as the beauty of the natural world. When a friend visiting Sarashina in the eastern hills leaves, she (the friend, according to most interpretations) sends a regretful poem (in Edwin A. Cranston's 1972 version): "Behind the mountain crest / The outline of the setting sun / Sank and was gone—/ And still in loneliness of heart / My gaze was drawn across the sky." Traveling through a sparsely populated section of the western hills, she notices a field of flowers: "Here they grow in the mountain depths / Far from any dwelling place, / And no one ever comes to view their blooms." Sarashina likely envisioned others reading her diary, writing, "Anyone reading this account of visits to one temple after another might well imagine I was forever going on pilgrimages."

As I Crossed a Bridge of Dreams is notable for its elegiac style and its sense of unfulfilled yearning. As the diary opens, the young Sarashina is living far from the capital, "beyond the end of the Great East Road." Her dreams are full of portent and surprisingly specific: "One night I dreamt that a handsome priest appeared before me in a yellow surplice and ordered me to learn the fifth volume of the Lotus Sutra as soon as possible." Sarashina's diary has more poems than *The Pillow Book* and, notes Amy Lowell in her 1920 introduction to *Diaries of Court Ladies of Old Japan*, covers a much longer period than do Murasaki's and Izumi's.

The Tale of Genji, which scholars have also called the world's first novel. It is an extravagant psychological story about dashing princes, beloved but socially marginalized beauties, and doomed romance.

Whether Sarashina composed other works is uncertain. In a colophon attached to the Teika manuscript, she is credited with authoring several works of fiction, including two that survive: *Hamamatsu Chūnagon Monogatari* and *Yowa no Nezame* (*The Tale of Nezame*). While the former bears a marked preoccupation with dreams, scholars have been unable to confirm Sarashina's authorship.

THEMES AND STYLE

Sarashina's diary is replete with religious influences, dreams, problems related to home and belonging, and the sadness of parting with loved ones. As the

CRITICAL DISCUSSION

Until the mistakes in the order of Sarashina's pages were corrected, the diary, though respected as a piece of history, did not enjoy much of a reputation. Eighteenth-century classical expert Motoori Norinaga, quoted in translator Ivan Morris's introduction to a 1971 version, said the "book is nothing but a vague, rambling account of her life." An 1890 anthology also got the page order wrong, and 1920 translators Annie Shepley Omori and Kochi Doi write that "there exist a few manuscript copies, and three or four publications.… Some of them are confused and unreadably incoherent." After Tamai Kōsuke corrected

190   THE LITERATURE OF AUTOBIOGRAPHICAL NARRATIVE ❖ VOLUME 2 ❖ Diaries and Letters

seven major errors in 1924, the 1931 editor Miyata Waichirō hailed the occasion, writing, "What a blessed event it was for the world of scholarship."

Twentieth-century scholars carried on the work of placing *As I Crossed a Bridge of Dreams* in the context of the literary fluency of the Heian period. Scholar Donald Keene observes in his 1989 anthology *Travelers of a Hundred Ages* that "only in Japan did the diary acquire a status as a literary genre comparable in importance to novels, essays, and other branches of literature." Sarashina remains less known than other women writers of her time, but *World Literature Today* reviewer W. H. Archer, writing in 1979, compares her diary favorably to that of Murasaki, of whom he observes, "A bold thought never crosses her mind," while Sarashina's "pages, pervaded with a romantic melancholy, are punctuated generously with many tanka (short poems) which reveal her sensitive nature."

Scholarly interest in *As I Crossed a Bridge of Dreams* continues, as the work touches on many aspects of Heian aristocratic society, including religious practices, the emerging role of culture in daily life, and gender roles. John R. Wallace, writing in his 2005 book *Objects of Discourse: Memoirs by Women of Heian Japan,* sees Sarashina as playing "three prominent objects of desire against one another: tales, capital, and Buddhism. While each embraces a specific set of meanings, the narrative is unresolved because these elements perpetually substitute for each other." In her 1999 book *Fictions of Femininity,* Edith Sarra writes that she does not observe an act of escapism in Sarashina's gleeful consumption of stories but rather a desire for self-determination and independence, a means by "which, if only through the agency of reading as interpretation, she might understand herself as a central figure within her own world."

BIBLIOGRAPHY

Sources

Ambros, Barbara. "Liminal Journeys: Pilgrimages of Noblewomen in Mid-Heian Japan." *Japanese Journal of Religious Studies* 24.3–4 (1997): 301–45. *JSTOR.* Web. 13 Dec. 2012.

Archer, W. H. Rev. of *Journal,* by Murasaki-Shikibu; René Sieffert; *Le Journal de Sarashina,* by Sarashina; René Sieffert. *World Literature Today* 53.4 (1979): 748. *JSTOR.* Web. 13 Dec. 2012.

Cranston, Edwin A. Rev. of *As I Crossed a Bridge of Dreams,* by Lady Sarashina. Trans. Ivan Morris. *Monumenta Nipponica* 27.4 (1972): 435–54. Print.

Diaries of Court Ladies of Old Japan. Trans. Annie Shepley Omori and Kochi Doi. Boston: Houghton Mifflin, 1920. *Digital Library.* University of Pennsylvania. Web. 12 Dec. 2012.

Keene, Donald. *Travelers of a Hundred Ages.* New York: Henry Holt, 1989. Print.

HEAVENLY BODIES

Though Japan is known as the land of the rising sun, the moon figures prominently in poems of the Heian era. An early example of the *nikki* genre is a diary written by a man in a woman's voice, which uses, as women did, the vernacular Japanese instead of *kambun,* the scholarly Chinese. Ki Tsurayuki (c. 870–945), governor of an island province, included the following *waka* (poem) in what is known as the *Tosa Nikki* (c. 935): "When I gaze over / The blue fields of the sea, / I wonder if the moon / Is the one that rose above / Misaka Mountain in Kasuga?" Expressing a similar sentiment, Sarashina decides in *As I Crossed a Bridge of Dreams* that the moon is, in fact, constant: "Even as I wander on my journey / It always stays above me in the sky—/ This moon at dawn, / This moon I gazed on in the Capital."

In Sarashina's initial encounter with Sukemichi, the nobleman with whom she falls in love but never quite connects, poetry ensues: "The hazy Springtime moon—/ That is the one I love, / When light green sky and fragrant blooms / Are all alike enwrapped in mist." Lonely and living in the Eastern Hills, Sarashina sighs, "If only I could share this moon / With one whose feelings are like mine—/ This moon that lights the mountain village in the Autumn dawn!"

Miyake, Lynne K. Rev. of *Objects of Discourse: Memoirs of Women of Heian Japan,* by John R. Wallace. *Japanese Language and Literature* 41.1 (2007). *JSTOR.* Web. 13 Dec. 2012.

Sansom, George. *A History of Japan to 1334.* Stanford: Stanford University Press, 1958. Print.

Sarashina (Daughter of Takasue). *As I Crossed a Bridge of Dreams.* Trans. Ivan Morris. New York: Dial, 1971. Print.

Sarra, Edith. *Fictions of Femininity: Literary Inventions of Gender in Japanese Court Women's Memoirs.* Stanford: Stanford University Press, 1999. Print.

Further Reading

Chambers, Anthony Hood. *The Secret Window: Ideal Worlds in Tanizaki's Fiction.* Cambridge: Harvard University Press, University Asia Center, 1994. *Google Books.* Web. 11 Dec. 2012.

D'Etcheverry, Charo B. *Love after* The Tale of Genji: *Rewriting the World of the Shining Prince.* Cambridge: Harvard University Press, University Asia Center, 2007. Print.

Karan, Pradyumna. *Japan in the 21st Century: Environment, Economy, and Society.* Lexington: University Press of Kentucky, 2010. *Google Books.* Web. 9 Dec. 2012.

Morris, Ivan. *The World of the Shining Prince: Court Life in Ancient Japan.* London: Oxford University Press, 1964. Print.

Murasaki Shikibu. *The Tale of Genji.* Trans. Arthur Waley. Garden City: Doubleday Anchor, 1955. Print.

Sei Shōnagon. *The Pillow Book.* Trans. Meredith McKinney. London: Penguin Classics, 2006. Print.

Rebecca Rustin

THE CONGO DIARY

Joseph Conrad

❖ **Key Facts**

Time Period:
Late 19th Century

Relevant Historical Events:
Belgian colonization of the Congo; Leopold II's brutal rule of the Congo; Conrad's trip to the Congo

Nationality:
Polish/English

Keywords:
colonialism; exploitation; alienation; Congo

OVERVIEW

First composed in 1890 but not published until 1926, *The Congo Diary* provides a spare account of Joseph Conrad's observations during an overland journey into the Congo Free State, a large Belgian colony in central Africa. Spanning from June 13 to August 1, 1890, *The Congo Diary* offers an autobiographical and impressionistic account of Conrad's experience packing ivory as part of a colonial enterprise that seemed increasingly absurd and immoral as he became more deeply involved in it. The short, fragmented text records the development of themes that Conrad would develop in later fiction, such as the short story "An Outpost of Progress" (1896) and the landmark novella *Heart of Darkness* (1899). Today, scholars view *The Congo Diary* as a significant work in the development of one of English literature's most important writers.

Conrad wrote *The Congo Diary* in the midst of a career at sea, while he was beginning to write fiction. Born Józef Teodor Konrad Korzeniowski in Ukraine to Polish parents in 1857, Conrad did not begin writing in English until the mid-1880s, while working as an officer aboard commercial English ships. Despite his late start, *The Congo Diary* provides evidence of the speed with which he grasped and mastered the English language. That mastery was first revealed to the public in 1895, when Conrad's first novel, *Almayer's Folly*, appeared in England. Over the course of the rest of his life, which ended in 1924, he continued to draw from the experience of alienation, exploitation, adventure, and disenchantment that he recorded in *The Congo Diary*.

HISTORICAL AND LITERARY CONTEXT

Conrad composed *The Congo Diary* as he was beginning to turn away from a career at sea and toward a life writing fiction. He was born to Polish parents and grew up during the Russian occupation of Poland. His father was a poet and an advocate for Polish independence, but both his parents were dead by the time Conrad was twelve. After performing poorly in school, he joined the French merchant navy and began a life of adventure and wanderlust at sea that would last some twenty years. After being barred from working as a sailor on French ships in 1878, he spent the next sixteen years sailing on British vessels and learning his third language, English. In 1889, two years after becoming a British subject, Conrad began *Almayer's Folly*, which he wrote in English and which drew from his experience as a sailor in the East Indies. During the journey recorded in *The Congo Diary*, he continued work on the book that would begin his long second career as an English novelist.

When Conrad wrote *The Congo Diary* in 1890, the present-day countries of the Republic of the Congo and the Democratic Republic of the Congo were known officially as L'État Independent du Congo. Though this translates as the "Congo Free State," the area was anything but free. Explored and exploited by European colonizers since the early nineteenth century, the Congo had become the property of Leopold II of Belgium in 1884, when European powers were dividing control of Africa among themselves. Leopold's rule of the Congo, which lasted until his death in 1908, was infamous for its brutality and callousness. Conrad's decision to go to a place known for the spectacular cruelty of its colonizers—and to participate in its exploitation—can be attributed to a practical need for employment, a chance to captain a vessel, and fascination with exploration in general and Africa in particular that can be traced to his childhood. The violence, injustice, amorality, and absurdity that he discovered there and recorded in his diary horrified him and compelled him to leave as soon as possible.

Though *The Congo Diary* was written in conditions of isolation and deprivation, Conrad's concern with morality, empire, and alienation can be traced to his early love of Polish Romantic literature. *Konrad Wallenrod* and *Forefathers' Eve* by the Polish poet Adam Mickiewicz were particularly influential in forming Conrad's notion that, according to Zdzisław Najder in *Conrad's Polish Background* (1964), "the moral problems of an individual were posed in terms of the social results of his actions." Throughout *The Congo Diary*, Conrad observes the fraught relationship between individual morality and social conditions in Africa. Writers such as Rudyard Kipling, who were documenting and exploring the realities and implications of European colonialism, also informed Conrad.

The Congo Diary proved enormously influential on the fiction Conrad wrote over the course of his career. This influence is most evident in his novella *Heart of Darkness*. Though not begun until more than a decade after he left Africa, *Heart of Darkness* offers a fictional account of a protagonist, Charles Marlow, who travels to the Congo and has experiences that closely mirror those recorded by Conrad in *The Congo Diary*. Not only does Marlow make much of the same journey as the author did from Matadi to Stanley Pool and then up the river aboard a steamer, but Marlow also experiences the disenchantment, alienation, and horror that Conrad recorded in his diary. Though *Heart of Darkness* shows the most apparent similarity to *The Congo Diary*, Conrad's fictional oeuvre bears the imprint of his African journey of 1890.

THEMES AND STYLE

The Congo Diary explores, in fragmented and impressionistic prose, many of the themes Conrad took up more fully in his later fiction, including morality, death, doubt, absurdity, and alienation. Conrad's pessimism about the project he is about to embark upon is evident from the diary's first entry, in which he writes, "Feel considerably in doubt about the future. Think just now that my life amongst the people (white) around here cannot be very comfortable." In the next entry, he refers to his job of "packing ivory in casks" as "Idiotic employment." Later, he sees a dead African and writes, "Shot? Horrid smell." Throughout the diary, Conrad's implication in, and disgust with, the cruel and oppressive colonial project emerges. The result is a text that, though slight, is rich with Conrad's sense of confusion and despair as he experiences the ennui and bewilderment of being a low-level laborer in the Belgian Congo.

Conrad used his diary to record his observations during a 230-mile trek from the Congolese seaport of Matadi to Stanley Pool (Pool Malebo), where the Congo River widens and becomes navigable. There, he was to take command of a river steamship owned by the Société Anonyme Belge pour le Commerce du Haut-Congo. Conrad came to Africa both to fulfill a boyhood dream of seeing the continent and out of desperation to find work during a period when available employment aboard ships was contracting. His diaries reflect this divided sense of purpose. Though motivated by his desire to catalog his adventures in a new land, the diaries quickly become a record of his disenchantment with his presence in the Congo. Composed while Conrad was sick, lonely, tired, and uncomfortable, *The Congo Diary* illustrates his growing ability both to document the extremes of the human experience and to vividly describe the state of a changing world.

Stylistically, *The Congo Diary* is notable for its terse and evocative descriptions. Throughout the text, Conrad offhandedly remarks on the horrible sights he sees during his trek through the Congo. In his entry for July 29, for example, he writes, "On the road today passed a skeleton tied-up to a post. Also a white man's grave—No name. Heap of stones in the form of a cross." This vivid and resonant set of fragmented images offers a compact description of the omnipresent and indiscriminate sense of death that pervades Conrad's diary. Elsewhere, he describes an albino: "Horrid chalky white with pink blotches. Red eyes. Red hair. Features very negroid and ugly." In this way, he demonstrates both his alienation from and his judgment of a world he has entered but cannot comprehend.

Nineteenth-century illustration featuring animals at the Congo River. Seaman and writer Joseph Conrad records his 1890 experiences along the river in *The Congo Diary*; these experiences would inform his famous novel *Heart of Darkness*. © NORTH WIND PICTURE ARCHIVES/THE IMAGE WORKS

CRITICAL DISCUSSION

The Congo Diary first appeared in 1926, thirty-six years after it was written and two years after Conrad's death. It was simultaneously published in the *Yale Review* in the United States and in *Blue Peter* in Britain and soon after was included in *Last Essays*, which gathered Conrad's uncollected and occasional nonfiction pieces. According to the introduction included in the 2010 edition of *Last Essays*, "Reaction to the publication of the fragmentary 'Congo Diary,' given wide circulation for the first time was mixed." For example, Will Cuppy, a humorist and detective story writer, was

TRAVEL AND EXPLORATION

THE "UP-RIVER BOOK"

During his time in the Congo, Joseph Conrad composed two notebooks. The first of these, *The Congo Diary*, recorded Conrad's journey from Matadi to Stanley Pool. The second took up Conrad's experience voyaging and working on a steamship that traveled up the Congo River. Not published until 1972—and then in Polish translation—this second notebook is known today as the "Up-river Book." In it, Conrad records information about the river and its navigation. He notes geographical features, as well as the growing infrastructure of the colonial enterprise. In notes, sketches, and charts, he describes channels, sandbars, islands, and bends, as well as factories, plantations, missions, and government outposts.

Less impressionistic and humane than *The Congo Diary*, the "Up-river Book" is factual, descriptive, and detailed. It offers instructions for navigating the river: "Proceeding cautiously must feel your way in 12 to 8 feet of water. The shore on the port side is the north Bank of the river." Though not as immediately compelling as the content of "The Congo Diary," these notes offer a glimpse into the professional life that Conrad led for some twenty years before turning to fiction: that of a seaman. These notes show that Conrad expected to remain on the Congo and captain ships of the colonial enterprise. That the "Up-river Book" breaks off midway through the journey to Stanley Falls is indicative of Conrad's growing disenchantment not only with Africa but also with his life at sea.

dismissive, while the critics in *Bookman* and the *Times* argued that the diary offered an important glimpse of the real-life origins of *Heart of Darkness* as well as Conrad's other fiction.

Since its initial publication, Conrad's diary, which was originally published in an abridged and edited form, has been restored and reprinted by scholars. Recent editions include the sketches, marginalia, and idiosyncratic punctuation of the original document, offering readers a more complete and accurate depiction of Conrad's text. This complete version offers an unparalleled glimpse into Conrad's growing disenchantment with the colonial enterprise, which he had taken part in as a European seaman for nearly twenty years at the time of the diary's composition. For the most part, scholars have studied the text to understand how the events, impressions, and writing style recorded in *The Congo Diary* proved formative on the novels and stories Conrad wrote later in his life.

Conrad's diary is most often considered in terms of its relationship to *Heart of Darkness*. Of *The Congo Diary*, the editors of *Last Essays* write, "Perhaps nowhere in Conrad is the interrelationship of personal experience and literature more intriguing than in the role that his Congo experience played in shaping 'An Outpost of Progress' (1896) and *Heart of Darkness* (1899), the two works he acknowledges as having brought of the 'centre of Africa.'" Citing such texts as Norman Sherry's *Conrad's Western World*, the critic Allan H. Simmons notes that "scholarship has long established the degree to which the novella [*Heart of Darkness*] is haunted by its biographical origins and historical facts." But the experience recorded in *The Congo Diary* had an impact beyond the bounds of Conrad's literary output. As Simmons writes, "African exploration and exploitation clearly fired Conrad's, yielding fictions that are shaped by and helped to shape their era's debates about colonialism."

BIBLIOGRAPHY

Sources

Conrad, Joseph. *Last Essays*. New York: Cambridge University Press, 2010. Print.

Najder, Zdzisław. *Conrad's Polish Background: Letters to and from Polish Friends*. Trans. Halina Carroll. London: Oxford University Press, 1964. Print.

Orr, Leonard, and Billy Thompson, eds. *A Joseph Conrad Companion*. Westport: Greenwood, 1999. Print.

Simmons, Allan H., ed. *Joseph Conrad in Context*. New York: Cambridge University Press, 2009. Print.

Further Reading

Bloom, Harold. *Joseph Conrad's Heart of Darkness*. New York: Chelsea House, 2008. Print.

De Lange, Attie, and Gail Fincham, eds. *Conrad in Africa: New Essays on "Heart of Darkness."* New York: Columbia University Press, 2002. Print.

Fincham, Gail, and Myrtle Hooper, eds. *Under Postcolonial Eyes: Joseph Conrad after Empire*. Rondebosch: University of Cape Town Press, 1996. Print.

Finston, Irving L., and Harry White. "Who Put Kurtz on the Congo?" *Conradiana* 42.1–2 (2011): 81+. *Academic OneFile*. Web. 11 Dec. 2012.

Hamner, Robert D. *Joseph Conrad: Third World Perspectives*. Washington, D.C.: Three Continents, 1990. Print.

Karl, Frederick R. *Joseph Conrad: The Three Lives—A Biography*. London: Faber and Faber, 1979. Print.

Knowles, Owen, and Gene M. Moore. *Oxford Reader's Companion to Conrad*. Oxford: Oxford University Press, 2000. Print.

Stape, J. H. *The Several Lives of Joseph Conrad*. London: Heinemann, 2007. Print.

Theodore McDermott

Journals of John Wesley

John Wesley

OVERVIEW

The Reverend John Wesley (1703–1791), an ordained priest in the Church of England, diligently kept a diary from age twenty-two until his death at eighty-eight. He began publishing portions of the diary as early as 1739. In his journals he records the details of his spiritual progress, his travels, and his experiences preaching the Gospel throughout Great Britain, Ireland, and the British colony of Georgia in North America. Even when describing his private turmoil, such as the attack on his character while serving in Georgia, he avoids divulging personal or emotional details. Instead he interprets the events of his life strictly in religious terms, detailing the philosophical origins of the Methodist Church, which he helped found in the mid-eighteenth century.

England had become more religiously tolerant under the Protestant Stuarts. The war between the Catholics and Puritans had ended, and dissenters, such as Quakers, were permitted to preach. Wesley, following his father and grandfather, studied at the University of Oxford, where he became an active participant in his brother Charles's Holy Club, which met to encourage members to serious devotion. However, the club's members were subject to mockery for their methodical way of organizing their lives (from which the name Methodism was derived). As Wesley began to publish portions of his journals, his writings became part of the struggle to save souls and guide them toward sanctification. Scholars continue to study the journals for their account of the origins of the Methodist Church and its members' work to improve conditions for the working class in eighteenth-century England.

HISTORICAL AND LITERARY CONTEXT

After the Restoration, Puritanism was in retreat and the Church of England was in disarray. Some priests grew wealthy while others could not support themselves. Six thousand parishes were without clergy. Wesley's father, one of the impoverished clergymen, served three months in Lincoln Castle, a debtors' prison, when Wesley was two. Shortly after that, the rectory where they lived burned and Wesley was barely rescued, a memory he would forever recall as proof that his life had been saved for a purpose.

Wesley was inspired to keep a diary upon the recommendation of Bishop Jeremy Taylor in Taylor's *Rule and Exercises of Holy Living and Dying* (1650–1651), which Wesley read in 1725. The first journals that Wesley published were from 1735, the year of his voyage to Georgia to preach "to the heathen" whom he believed were more "fit to receive the gospel" than the civilized. The voyage was a logical extension of the work he had begun in Oxford ministering to the poor and imprisoned. Upon his return to England, he crossed the countryside on foot and on horseback to preach. The journals record these journeys in great detail, praising God for the preacher's survival of difficult sea crossings and other perilous situations.

Letters, travel writing, and biography became popular in eighteenth-century England. Wesley's uncle by marriage, John Dunton, a bookseller, published *John Dunton's Letters from New-England (1686)* and *Teague Land, or, A Merry Ramble to the Wild Irish* (1698) about his life and travels. Two other works of life writing defined the period: *The Life of Samuel Johnson,* written by Wesley's friend James Boswell in 1791, and the publication of letters by Horace Walpole, Earl of Orford and son of England's first prime minister, in 1778. Walpole's published letters provided a lively picture of ruling-class society and a sharp contrast to Wesley's concern for the "glad tidings of salvation."

Wesley's journals inspired the practice of journal keeping as a spiritual discipline. His younger brother, Charles, a hymn writer and Wesley's partner in ministry, took up journaling, as did other followers. Today the Methodist Church still promotes maintaining a private journal for spiritual growth. A 2005 scholarly edition of Wesley's later journals, according to Robert Webster in a 2005 review for *Conversations in Religion & Theology,* is in keeping with the fact that "Contemporary Wesleyan and Methodist scholarship is convinced that John Wesley and the movement of renewal that he founded and sustained in eighteenth-century Britain, is a viable text for postmodern consciousness too."

THEMES AND STYLE

Wesley saw God at work in all things and believed that God had ordained him to preach the Gospel, not merely from his own pulpit but as a peripatetic preacher traveling throughout England, Wales, Scotland, and Ireland. A typical entry in Wesley's journal reads, "We rode [by horseback] to Glammis, about

❖ **Key Facts**

Time Period:
Mid-18th Century

Relevant Historical Events:
Restoration of the English monarchy; formation of Methodist movement

Nationality:
English

Keywords:
Methodism; religion; missionary travel

A portrait of John Wesley by William Hamilton. © WORLD HISTORY ARCHIVE/ALAMY

sixty-four measured miles; and on *Saturday,* 9, about sixty-six more, to Edinburgh. I was tired: However, I would not disappoint the congregation; and God gave me strength according to my day." He offers some commentary on his surroundings, such as his appreciation of Edinburgh "with the stately castle upon a craggy rock on the west," which he finds "inexpressibly fine"—though he complains about the "filth" that fills the streets. Thus, the world and its inhabitants, for Wesley, are in need of perfecting.

Wesley's personal diaries begin after his ordination to the deaconate in 1725 and continue until the end of his life. The entries that appear in the various published versions of his journals focus on revealing that "the hand of God is on every person and thing." The first volume of his published journals begins with his voyage to America, which he explains was undertaken "to save our souls; to live wholly to the glory of God." Although the journals were meant primarily to instruct, Wesley also used them to explain his side of various disputes. One such scandal occurred in Georgia, where he fell in love but, hesitating to marry, lost out to another suitor. After he refused communion to the newlyweds, he was sued and fined. Echoing the Bible, he writes that he "shook off the dust of my feet, and left Georgia," sailing back to England.

Wesley kept his personal diary to record his progress toward holiness. Many of the entries were written in code, allowing him to efficiently make repetitive entries and to maintain privacy. By 1734 he switched to what he called the "exacter" diary, which used a column format to indicate the activities for each hour alongside his self-examination. However, he abandoned this complex scheme and returned to a paragraph style, which grew shorter again in his later years and was characterized by its precision and detail. The published journals contain accounts of healings and conversions, letters sent and received, titles of sermons, and the weather.

CRITICAL DISCUSSION

Wesley published the first volume of his journals in 1739. He continued to publish extracts of his diaries throughout his lifetime, using them as a vehicle for responding to the public. In 1744 the Reverend Thomas Church wrote Wesley a lengthy letter reproving him for his association with the Moravians, a group of Protestants he had mentioned in his journals. In an introduction to *The Journal of John Wesley* (1906), F. W. McDonald recalls that *Lloyd's Evening Post* noted in 1772 that the journals were more entertaining than expected "as they are intermixed with such occasional reflections on men and manners, on polite literature, and even on polite places." Other writers used portions of the journal in satirical attacks against Wesley.

Nineteenth-century reaction to Wesley and his journals continued to run the gamut from admiration to contempt. Poet laureate Robert Southey emphasizes in *The Life of John Wesley* (1820) the hysterics often exhibited by those attending Wesley's preaching and questions Wesley's sanity, an interpretation that stirred controversy. Another poet, Edward FitzGerald, best known for his translation of the *Rubaiyat,* wrote in amazement at the contrasting picture of the world presented in Wesley's journals and in Walpole's letters, praising Wesley's "pure, unaffected, and undying English." Victorian Thomas Carlyle also extolled the journals' writing. However, little serious study was made of the journals in the nineteenth century except for the purpose of biography; interest in them remained confined to Methodists.

In the twentieth century, scholars began to investigate Wesley's approaches to psychology, medicine, and the role of women in his life and ministry. The debate as to whether Wesley and his Methodism were a repressive, bourgeois force or an inclusive one continues into the twenty-first century. Scholars such as Vicki Tolar Burton have situated Wesley's encouragement of reading and writing within current considerations of eighteenth-century literacy practices, arguing that his Sunday schools promoted the rights of individuals from all classes and genders. In 2003 a six-volume scholarly edition of Wesley's journals and diaries was completed, and for the first time his earliest private diaries were published. Contemporary theologians continue to embrace Wesley's preference for the poor and the powerless, and his use of scripture has been seen as more nuanced than that of his contemporaries.

BIBLIOGRAPHY
Sources

Dunton, John. *John Dunton's Letters from New-England.* Boston: Perry, 1867. Web. 27 Dec. 2012.

FitzGerald, Edward. *Letters and Literary Remains of Edward FitzGerald.* Vol. 2. Ed. W. Aldis Wright. New York: Macmillan, 1902. Print.

McDonald, F. W. Introduction. *The Journal of John Wesley.* Vol. 1. London: Dent, 1906. ix–xiii. Print.

Webster, Robert. "Formulating Renewal: Emerging Trends in Wesleyan Studies." *Conversations in Religion & Theology* 3.2 (2005): 204–16. *ProQuest.* Web. 26 Dec. 2012.

Wesley, John. *The Journal of John Wesley: A Selection.* Ed. Elisabeth Jay. Oxford: Oxford University Press, 1987. Print.

Wood, A. Skevington. "Wesley as a Writer." *John Wesley: Contemporary Perspectives.* Ed. John Stacey. London: Epworth, 1988. 190–201. Web. *Literature Criticism Online.* 12 Dec. 2012.

Further Reading

Burton, Vicki Tolar. *Spiritual Literacy in John Wesley's Methodism: Reading, Writing, and Speaking to Believe.* Waco: Baylor University Press, 2008. Print.

Gregory, Jeremy. "John Wesley: Tercentenary Essays: Proceedings of a Conference Held at the University of Manchester, June 2003." *Bulletin of the John Rylands University Library of Manchester* 85.2–3 (2003): 3–431. Print.

———. "Religion in the Age of Enlightenment: Putting John Wesley in Context." *Religion in the Age of Enlightenment* 2 (2010): 19–54. Print.

Heitzenrater, Richard P. *The Elusive Mr. Wesley.* 2nd ed. Nashville: Abingdon, 2003. Print.

Wesley, Charles. *The Manuscript Journal of the Reverend Charles Wesley, M.A.* Ed. S. T. Kimbrough Jr. and Kenneth G. C. Newport. Nashville: Kingswood, 2007.

EVANGELICAL REVIVAL: THE GREAT AWAKENING

The year John Wesley began his diary coincides with the start of the Great Awakening, a period of evangelical preaching that led to a multitude of conversions in Germany, Great Britain, and America. Operating alongside Enlightenment thinking, Evangelical preaching emphasized a personal experience of faith often accompanied by emotional and physical outpourings. The Moravian Church in Germany began the movement after Nikolaus Ludwig von Zinzendorf established a model Christian community on his property. The church's missionaries encountered Wesley aboard the ship that took him to America. He was so struck by their faith, which allowed them to keep calm amid the stormy seas, that he later traveled to Germany to meet with them. Despite his debt to them, Wesley later distanced himself from their teachings, which leaned toward quietism.

In the American colonies, Connecticut-born Jonathan Edwards preached fiery sermons and started a revival in western Massachusetts. Another member of Wesley's Holy Club from Oxford, George Whitefield, who traveled widely throughout the colonies, preached thousands of sermons. He had begun his open-air preaching in England, and Wesley, reluctantly at first, adopted the outdoor format, preaching to between seven thousand and nine thousand listeners at a time. The Methodist Church and the Evangelical Church are the products of this movement.

Wesley, John. *The Works of John Wesley: Journals and Diaries.* Ed. W. Reginald Ward and Richard P. Heitzenrater. Vols. 18–24. Nashville: Abingdon, 2003. Print.

Robin Morris

A Journal of the First Voyage of Vasco da Gama, 1497–1499

Author Unknown

Key Facts

Time Period:
Late 15th Century

Relevant Historical Events:
Da Gama's first voyage to India; birth of Portuguese colonial power

Nationality:
Portuguese

Keywords:
exploration; colonialism; trade

OVERVIEW

A Journal of the First Voyage of Vasco da Gama, 1497–1499 is a sailor's logbook published in Portuguese in 1838 (translated into English in 1898) that provides the only remaining firsthand record of Vasco da Gama's pioneering voyage from Portugal around the Cape of Good Hope and to India, a voyage that marked the beginning of Portugal's sixteenth-century prominence in global trade and exploration. Although the author is officially anonymous, many historians attribute the work to Álvaro Velho, a sailor on the expedition. Although da Gama was rumored to have kept (and even distributed) his own definitive journal of the expedition, no such document has been uncovered. As a result, in spite of the author's anonymity, *A Journal of the First Voyage of Vasco da Gama* is seen as providing a documentary glimpse into the life and historic journey of the renowned explorer.

The Hakluyt Society, founded in England in 1846 to publish early accounts of exploration, published the journal in English in 1898 with an introduction that provides the most detailed context available for the work. The introduction defends the significance of da Gama's voyage, describes the original manuscript of the journal, speculates on the identity of the author, and offers notes to the text. An 1898 review in *Scottish Geographical Magazine* commends the editor for his addition of relevant contextual information in appendixes containing maps and charts, as well as historical letters and documents. *A Journal of the First Voyage of Vasco da Gama* remains the authoritative work on da Gama's voyage and an enduring source of Portuguese pride.

HISTORICAL AND LITERARY CONTEXT

Prior to da Gama's voyage, trade and cultural interaction between Europe and Asia were dominated by Eastern incursions into the West, a pattern essentially ruptured and then reversed, G. V. Scammell argues in his 2000 essay in *Modern Asian Studies,* with da Gama's arrival in India. Scammell notes that da Gama left Portugal "inspired by expectations of great wealth tempered by strange dreams of freeing Jerusalem from the infidel and extending the bounds of Christendom." In search of spices and looking to convert others to Christianity, he followed established trade routes wherever possible and traced Bartolomeu Dias's 1488 journey around the Cape of Good Hope. He also inherited a legacy of Portuguese navigation and exploration begun by Prince Henry the Navigator's advances into West Africa in the early 1400s.

The rise to the throne of John II in 1481 renewed Portuguese interest in geography and exploration, which had died down since the time of Henry the Navigator, who oversaw Portuguese exploration of the African coast that laid the groundwork for the eventual discovery of North America. John and his successors wished to solidify Portugal's economic position by breaking the Venetian monopoly on the Asian spice trade. Venetian merchants had negotiated a relationship with Arab spice traders during the Middle Ages that made Venice the major distributor of Asian spices to Europe. With the Ottoman Empire's 1453 overthrow of Constantinople, overland trade routes from East to West (already compromised by their danger) were essentially closed, leaving Venice with an effective monopoly and the opportunity to charge high tariffs. The Portuguese monarchy saw the discovery of a sea route to India as the best way to break this monopoly. Accordingly, John's successor, Manuel I, hired da Gama to lead the expedition and document his findings. The expectation that the voyage would be documented likely explains the existence of *A Journal of the First Voyage of Vasco da Gama* and provides a set of formal conventions that the author followed.

A Journal of the First Voyage of Vasco da Gama has generic precedent in other journals of exploration and literary precedent in popular works of the time. *The Travels of Marco Polo* (c. 1300) was widely circulated among educated fourteenth-century Europeans and was in turn likely influenced by narratives of Christian pilgrimage that circulated at the time; similarly, *The Travels of Sir John Mandeville* (c. 1356) was a popular account of the travels of a (likely fictitious) Englishman through North Africa and the Middle East. Still, chronicles such as *A Journal of the First Voyage of Vasco da Gama* differ from pilgrimage narratives in that they have a more external, naturalistic (rather than internal, spiritual) angle. The "pilgrimage" of these later writings is less one of the individual seeking religious enlightenment than of the early-modern geographer studying and describing foreign locales or the royal agent establishing legal claims to territory or trade rights.

A Journal of the First Voyage of Vasco da Gama is one of the earliest written works of the age of discovery, and as such it can be seen as setting precedents more than following them, even though it was not published in its entirety until 1838. Still, the period between 1500 and 1800 saw an explosion of popularity of narratives of exploration, which also became more widely available thanks to the printing press. Such works met a public not only receptive to tales of foreign lands but hungry for them. The foundation of the Hakluyt Society, which published the English version of *A Journal of the First Voyage of Vasco da Gama,* attests to the popularity of the genre. Named for Elizabethan historian Richard Hakluyt the Younger, who collected and edited narratives of British overseas exploration, the Hakluyt Society was formed to expand the study of geography from contemporary to historical texts. The fact that *A Journal of the First Voyage of Vasco da Gama* was republished as recently as 2010 suggests its enduring interest value.

THEMES AND STYLE

A major theme of *A Journal of the First Voyage of Vasco da Gama* is the interaction between the Portuguese sailors and the African and Asian "natives" they encountered, which they describe in a seemingly scientific manner. Although it draws analogies between the places and cultures the expedition encounters and Portuguese culture (by comparing the landscape, the animals, and the foods), the journal, as explained by Manuela Mourão in her 2011 piece for the *Journal for Early Modern Cultural Studies,* emphasizes difference—particularly in skin tone, language, and customs. The author of the journal reveals "a patronizing attitude toward the different black cultures they encounter," claims Mourão. "They trade objects they deem worthless for ivory; the chronicler registers surprise at the beautiful music the Africans play…. The crew use cannons just as a show of force, and the fright and confusion of the natives is described in a deprecating tone." Thus the account reinforces the notion of supremacy of "whiter" peoples and imposes a hierarchical distinction between the Portuguese sailors and the people they meet.

The author of the journal most likely began the project as part of the commission from King Manuel I. The work is more ship's log than narrative planned for publication, suggesting that his motivation was simply to keep a record of the events of the journey. Accordingly, the diary moves through the day-by-day procedures, recording events and the Portuguese reaction to them, wind directions, distances traveled, and geographic features.

A Journal of the First Voyage of Vasco da Gama begins July 8, 1497, with the group's departure from Lisbon en route to the Canary Islands. Structured by chronological entries, its general tone is objective narration with minimal interpretation. It proceeds through the activities and observations of the crew, with emphasis on their interactions with native people. By Christmas, they pass the farthest point Dias had reached previously. They reach Calicut the following May and spend several months traveling in search of spices. The author's observations of the Indians reveal the theme of ethnocentrism in the work: he describes a group of Indians as "covetous and ignorant," and the crew famously mistakes a Buddhist temple for a Christian church. They return to Portugal in spite of advice against it because of the weather patterns. After spending a much longer time crossing the Indian Ocean than they had spent on the voyage out, they descend the east coast of Africa and round the Cape of Good Hope, at which point the journal abruptly ends in April 1499. Scholars speculate that the voyage reached Portugal in August or September.

CRITICAL DISCUSSION

After the journal's initial translation into and publication in English—before critiques of imperialism and condemnation of racism—most reviews of the work were positive. British newspapers praised the Hakluyt Society, the editor and translator (Ernest Ravenstein), and the work itself for its authoritative firsthand presentation of da Gama's leadership. Critical scholarship on the work that is truly critical did not begin until the twentieth century.

More recently *A Journal of the First Voyage of Vasco da Gama* has been seen as recording an iconic moment in the formation of Portuguese national identity.

Vasco da Gama, Portuguese explorer.
© LOOK AND LEARN/THE BRIDGEMAN ART LIBRARY

TRAVEL AND EXPLORATION

DA GAMA DAY

As G. V. Scammell notes in a 2000 essay in *Modern Asian Studies,* Vasco da Gama's voyage was "roughly eleven times as long as that of [Christopher] Columbus," his opening of a sea route to Asia was similarly consequential for his sponsoring country, his goals of Christianization and wealth were just as lofty, and his brutal treatment of the peoples he encountered was just as extreme. Yet Columbus has a day named for him and serves as the subject of elementary school rhymes while da Gama's global influence is widely commemorated only in Portugal and parts of India. Why?

Scammell argues that the major difference between the two expeditions is in their level of precedence. While Columbus sailed in a direction that was essentially unexplored, da Gama followed established trade routes and the guidance of Dias's earlier voyage to the tip of Africa. Furthermore, while Columbus initiated a pattern of colonization that would overrun and depopulate a previously unknown landmass, da Gama's voyage led to an invigoration of mostly established trade routes and an expansion of interaction between civilizations long aware of each other's existence. Thus their interaction was neither so radical nor so devastating as the interaction of the Spaniards with New World peoples.

According to Francisco Domingues in *Portuguese Studies,* da Gama's expedition recalls a golden age that the Portuguese have held up as a "mirror … to reflect [the country's] past as well as the future." The downside to this construction of a national identity is that the Portuguese have defined themselves against the people with whom they came into contact. Thus the same people who have looked to da Gama as a locus of national pride have also fostered the kind of distancing evident in the patronizing attitude of the journal's author. Mourão argues that this sense of Western superiority "led, in part, to the development of the concept of race." Admittedly, the development of racism came much later, but the sense of cultural and religious superiority evident in texts such as *A Journal of the First Voyage of Vasco da Gama* can be seen as laying the groundwork for the later emergence of race as a category.

The most prominent trend in criticism of the journal concerns the interaction of cultures. As Scammell notes, da Gama's voyage initiated "a quickening flow of European goods, money, peoples, manufactures, ideas and armed strength eastwards. In return, the East initially provided luxuries, then people and primary products, a handsome measure of imperial loot, ideas more rarely and now the whole range of manufactures." These economic relations led Adam Smith to proclaim in *An Inquiry into the Nature and Causes of the Wealth of Nations* (1776), "The discovery of America and that of a passage to the East Indies by the Cape of Good Hope are the two greatest and most important events recorded in the history of mankind." This suggests the significance of the journal as the only firsthand account of one of the two most formative events in human history. However, another trend in scholarship contests the importance of the voyage. Writing in *History Today* in 1997, Felipe Fernández-Armesto insists that the expedition had little immediate effect on local trade routes, that European sovereignty remained confined to small areas, and that the European merchants who followed da Gama were not radically different from "their ancient and medieval predecessors." Thus, he insists, da Gama biographers have relied on "a legend" of him that is largely untrue.

BIBLIOGRAPHY

Sources

Anonymous. *A Journal of the First Voyage of Vasco da Gama, 1497–1499.* Ed. and trans. Ernest George Ravenstein. Cambridge: Cambridge University Press, 2010. Print.

Domingues, Francisco Contente. "Vasco da Gama's Voyage: Myths and Realities in Maritime History." *Portuguese Studies* 19 (2003): 1–8. *EBSCO Academic Search.* Web. 15 Dec. 2012.

Fernández-Armesto, Felipe. "Times & Tides." *History Today* Dec. 1997: 7–10. *EBSCO Academic Search.* Web. 15 Dec. 2012.

Mourão, Manuela. "Whitewash: Nationhood, Empire, and the Formation of Portuguese Racial Identity." *Journal for Early Modern Cultural Studies* 11.1 (2011): 90–124. *Project MUSE.* Web. 15 Dec. 2012.

Rev. of *A Journal of the First Voyage of Vasco da Gama, 1497–1499,* by Anonymous. *Scottish Geographical Magazine,* 1 Sept. 1898: 491. *ProQuest.* Web. 20 Dec. 2012.

Scammell, G. V. "After da Gama: Europe and Asia since 1498." *Modern Asian Studies* 34.3 (2000): 513–43. *JSTOR.* Web. 15 Dec. 2012.

Smith, Adam. *An Inquiry into the Nature and Causes of the Wealth of Nations.* Vol. 2. New York: J. M. Dent and Sons, 1914. *Google Books.* Web. 14 Jan. 2013.

Further Reading

Cliff, Nigel. *Holy War: How Vasco da Gama's Epic Voyages Turned the Tide in a Centuries-Old Clash of Civilizations.* New York: Harper, 2011. Print.

Coates, Timothy J. "The Early Modern Portuguese Empire: A Commentary on Recent Studies." *Sixteenth Century Journal* 37.1 (2006): 83–90. *EBSCO Academic Search.* Web. 24 Dec. 2012.

Hair, P. E. H. "Before Vasco da Gama." *Bulletin of Spanish Studies* 79.1 (2002): 54–65. *EBSCO Academic Search.* Web. 24 Dec. 2012.

Seiber, R. Timothy. "Remembering Vasco da Gama: Contested Histories and the Cultural Politics of Contemporary Nation-Building in Lisbon, Portugal." *Identities* 8.4 (2001): 549–87. *EBSCO Academic Search.* Web. 24 Dec. 2012.

Subrahmanyam, Sanjay. *The Career and Legend of Vasco da Gama.* Cambridge: Cambridge University Press, 1997. Print.

Laura Johnson

Journal of the First Voyage to America
Christopher Columbus

OVERVIEW

Journal of the First Voyage to America is Bartolomé de Las Casas's reconstruction of Christopher Columbus's travel diary of his 1492 voyage to the West Indies. The *Journal* accounts how Columbus set sail from Spain in August 1492 in search of India, arrived instead at the West Indies, and returned to Spain the following spring. Las Casas assembled but did not publish the text of the *Journal* in 1531 from a copy of Columbus's original Spanish-language diary. Instead, it was published in Spanish in 1825 by Martín Fernández de Navarrete and in English two years later as *Personal Narrative of the First Voyage of Columbus*. Initially a willing participant in the Spanish conquests of the New World, Las Casas later openly condemned colonial Spain for its brutal treatment of America's indigenes. Thus, the *Journal*'s account of Columbus crossing the Atlantic, mistaking America for Asia, and his encounters with the native people there comes filtered through a highly critical lens.

Columbus presented one of two records of his voyage to King Ferdinand and Queen Isabella of Castille; the other was lost at sea. By the time Las Casas took an interest in the surviving journal, it too had disappeared, though he had access to a copy that had been commissioned by Isabella. In time, both this copy and Las Casas's reworking were lost; it was not until 1790 that the latter surfaced. Since then there has been increasing disagreement as to the true meaning of Columbus's legacy. Was he the hero who discovered the New World, or the villain who paved the way for brutal European colonialism? Either way, Las Casas's text, perhaps the earliest critical reflection on the European discovery of the Americas, remains a singular document.

HISTORICAL AND LITERARY CONTEXT

Columbus was determined to sail westward from Europe and arrive in Asia to prove the then-uncommon belief that the world was round. He initially appealed to both the Portuguese and Spanish crowns for funding and was rejected by both. He made a second request to Spain, with influential courtiers to back him, and Isabella eventually decided to fund the voyage. Their agreement, known as the Capitulations of Santa Fé, granted Columbus the office of viceroy and governor over all territories acquired on the voyage, one-tenth of all riches appropriated, and the title of "Admiral of the Ocean Sea."

The day-by-day record of the voyage began when Columbus set sail from the port of Saltes in southwestern Spain on Friday, August 3, 1492, and concluded with his return to the same port on Friday, March 15, 1493. In his prefatory remarks, he makes it clear that the point of the journal is to prove he has "discharge[d] the orders given" him by the Catholic monarchs. That is, the *Journal* had the professional purpose of not only documenting routes, discoveries, and acquisitions as he ventured westward across the Atlantic but also justifying the Castilian crown's trust and investment in him.

By the late 1500s Spanish law required ships' captains to keep journals, but in Columbus's time a journal was neither required nor common. As a travelogue detailing the experiences of the traveler and the places visited, the *Journal* belongs in the same tradition as *The Travels of Marco Polo* (1298), in which Rustichello da Pisa collected stories told by Polo of his journey through the Middle East to China and beyond. Also comparable are the journals of two Portuguese explorers: *A Journal of the First Voyage of Vasco da Gama, 1497–1499*, about the man who discovered the first direct ocean route from Portugal to India, and Antonio Pigafetta's *Journal of Magellan's Voyage,* which documented Ferdinand Magellan's voyage around the world from 1519 to 1522.

Whatever Columbus's intentions for his travel diary, the *Journal* is channeled through Las Casas, who achieved notoriety when he published *A Short Account of the Destruction of the Indies,* itself a literary "epitome" of his monumental *History of the Indies* begun in 1527 and completed in 1561. Las Casas's aim in both was to break the spell of New World accounts, beginning with Columbus's, that glossed over Spain's tortuous intrusion into the Americas. Though Columbus's arrival has been celebrated in the Americas for centuries, recent critics of colonialism have been more likely to read the *Journal* in the spirit of Las Casas, lamenting rather than celebrating the way Columbus approached and acted upon the New World.

THEMES AND STYLE

The main theme of the *Journal* is the quest for "gold and spices" cast as a holy colonialism: while "the object and sum of the present undertaking has been

✣ Key Facts

Time Period:
Late 15th Century

Relevant Historical Events:
Columbus's discovery of the New World; Spanish conquest in the Americas

Nationality:
Spanish

Keywords:
discovery; exploration; colonialism

TRAVEL AND EXPLORATION

Illustration by Theodor de Bry depicting Christopher Columbus being greeted by the native Taíno people upon his arrival in 1492 at the island of Hispaniola (the western part of which is now Haiti). Color engraving from Americae Tertia Pars IV, 1594. © BPK, BERLIN/ART RESOURCE, NY

the increase and glory of the Christian religion," according to a 1924 English translation of the book, Las Casas records Columbus saying, "Should I meet with gold or spices in great quantity, I shall remain till I collect as much as possible, and for this purpose I am proceeding solely in quest of them." The gold and spices never materialized, however, and the Native Americans—who, Columbus suggests, "would be good servants; and … would very readily become Christians"—habitually flee in terror wherever he sets foot. Even so, optimism prevails as Columbus persists in the belief that all these new territories "will, in my opinion, offer a vast trade to Europe, and especially to Spain, to which they must all necessarily be subject."

It is difficult to know whether Columbus is insensitive or Las Casas overly sensitive to the full implications of Spanish colonialism. In the early 1500s, Las Casas himself had been a willing participant in the typically bloody conquests; he even defended the *encomienda,* the legal system by which the Spanish enslaved Native Americans. But in the following decades he was struck by the injustice of the conquests and became a fierce advocate of native rights, writing to expose the devastating effects of the expeditions inaugurated by Columbus's first voyage. In both the passages he summarizes and those he claims to quote directly from the copy of Columbus's original manuscript, he reveals Columbus as an unlikely emissary for Christianity. He is, after all, in the habit of deceiving and manipulating the native people and his own crew alike. He lies to his men about how far they have sailed and leads the natives to believe he and his men are "honest people," even as he scoffs at how easily they are pacified with glass beads.

As a travelogue, the *Journal* is plain, unassuming, and even monotonous, concentrating mostly on details of navigation such as distances traveled, speeds attained, and directions followed. For example, a typical entry reads: "Most of the day calm, afterwards a little wind. Steered their course day and night, sailing less than thirteen leagues. In the morning found such abundance of weeds that the ocean seemed to be covered with them; they came from the west.... Saw a whale, an indication of land, as they always keep near the coast." Weeds, pelicans, water, air, and whales are studied only to the extent they signify the land Columbus desires to reach. In this sense, much of what is recounted in the *Journal* is rarely appreciated for its own sake but rather used to maintain optimism and hope that land—and later gold and fame—lie ahead.

CRITICAL DISCUSSION

Issued in various editions and languages over the last two centuries, Columbus's journal has had a complex publication history. While modern editions also draw on the work of Columbus's son Ferdinand, who summarized the voyage in his own 1571 biography of his father, Las Casas's manuscript remains the primary (and earliest extant) source. Because of his heavy criticism of the Spanish Empire, Las Casas was a controversial figure in Spain both during and after his lifetime; yet, when his text was discovered in 1790, his potential reinterpretation of the events was typically overlooked in people's eagerness to read the story of Columbus. American reviewers in particular were excited to hear accounts of the first European encounters on the continent. The numerous editions since then have interested scholars and popular audiences alike, but present-day readers, educated in multiculturalism and postcolonialism, have grown increasingly skeptical of Columbus's legacy.

For many years Columbus's voyages have taken center stage in U.S. grade-school curricula, which have tended to overlook Las Casas's criticisms. With the emergence of identity politics following the struggle for civil rights and the rise of multiculturalism in popular culture and academia, however, it has become difficult to ignore the racial, ethnic, and nationalist violence of Columbus's intrusion. Not surprisingly, much scholarship in recent decades has exploded the myth of the explorer, primarily by reminding readers, as Estelle Irizarry does in her 1993 essay in *Computers and the Humanities*, of the *Journal*'s second author. Las Casas's authorship, Irizarry notes, is a "detail, so essential to appraising Columbus as a writer," which "has not been sufficiently appreciated by Columbus scholars."

While there is no shortage of scholarship on Columbus, academics do not often discuss the journal as a subject in its own right. When they do, they typically treat it as a problematic document. For J. M. Cohen, writing in his introduction to *The Four Voyages: Being His Own Log-Book, Letters and Dispatches with Connecting Narratives* (1992), the culprit is Las Casas, at whose hands the document "suffers ... from the too frequent introduction of [his] favourite theme, the ill-treatment of the natives." While it is now common to acknowledge that the manuscript is riddled with errors that cast doubt on its accuracy, scholars such as David Henige insist that this is a question of not just authorship but also textual transmission; hence his critique in the 1991 book *In Search of Columbus: The Sources for the First Voyage* of "the cavalier attitude that modern editors of the diario have taken, as if the source that they thought important enough to edit was not important enough to present as itself." In 1991 Oliver Dunn and James E. Kelley Jr. returned to the original sources to produce a new transcription, translation, and concordance in the hope of dispensing with increasing deviations across the various editions. In spite of errors, distortions, and disagreements, however, as Laurence Bergreen reminds us in *Columbus: The Four Voyages, 1492–1504* (2012), the *Journal* "remains the best guide to both [Columbus's] deeds and deceptions."

LA NAVIDAD: THE FIRST EUROPEAN SETTLEMENT

In August 1492 Christopher Columbus set sail in search of Asia with three ships: the *Santa María*, captained by Columbus himself; *La Niña*; and *La Pinta*. Thirty-three days later, he reached the islands of what are now the Bahamas, Cuba, and the Dominican Republic/Haiti. In the early hours of December 25, the *Santa María* was sailing along the coast of Haiti, with only a boy at the helm. "Having taken no rest for two days and a night past," Columbus and his crew had gone to sleep early. The ship ran aground and was wrecked. When, with the help of Native Americans, Columbus's men had salvaged the ship's goods, Columbus took control of *La Niña* and set sail, leaving the crew of the wrecked ship to strip its timbers and use them to build a fort on the island, part of a settlement he called La Navidad (Christmas). He intended his men to gather all the gold presumed to be on the island. When he returned nine months later on his second voyage, Columbus found his men slain and what had been the first European settlement in the New World destroyed.

BIBLIOGRAPHY

Sources

Bergreen, Laurence. *Columbus: The Four Voyages, 1492–1504*. New York: Penguin, 2012. Print.

Cohen, J. M. Introduction. *The Four Voyages: Being His Own Log-Book, Letters and Dispatches with Connecting Narratives*. New York: Penguin, 1992. Print.

Columbus, Christopher. *Journal of the First Voyage to America*. Freeport: Books for Libraries, 1924. Print.

Dunn, Oliver Charles, and James E. Kelley Jr. "Editors' Introduction." *The Diario of Christopher Columbus's First Voyage to America, 1492–1493*. Norman: University of Oklahoma Press, 1991. Print.

Henige, David. *In Search of Columbus: The Sources for the First Voyage.* Tucson: University of Arizona Press, 1991. Print.

Irizarry, Estelle. "The Two Authors of Columbus' 'Diary.'" *Computers and the Humanities* 27.2 (1993): 85–92. Print.

Further Reading

Childs, Wendy R. "1492–1494: Columbus and the Discovery of America." *Economic History Review* 48.4 (1995): 754–68. Print.

Howarth, William. "Putting Columbus in His Place." *Southwest Review* 77.2–3 (1992): 153–65. *EBSCOhost Academic Search Premier.* Web. 14 Dec. 2012.

Mann, Charles C. *1493: Uncovering the New World Columbus Created.* New York: Vintage, 2012. Print.

McKee, Alexander. *A World Too Vast: The Four Voyages of Columbus.* London: Souvenir, 1990. Print.

Olson, Julius E., and Edward G. Bourne, eds. *The Northmen, Columbus and Cabot, 985–1503.* New York: Scribner, 1906. Print.

Provost, Foster. *Columbus: An Annotated Guide to the Study on His Life and Writings, 1750–1988.* Detroit: Omnigraphics, 1991. Print.

David Aitchison

THE JOURNALS OF JONATHAN CARVER AND RELATED DOCUMENTS, 1766–1770

Jonathan Carver

OVERVIEW

The Journals of Jonathan Carver and Related Documents, 1766–1770, edited by John Parker and published in 1976, made available for the first time the original journals kept by the explorer Jonathan Carver as he traveled in the late 1760s from Boston to Fort Michilimackinac (in what is now Mackinaw City, Michigan) and on to the upper Mississippi River. As a supplement Parker also includes James Stanley Goddard's journal of the same journey. Goddard, along with Carver and Captain James Tute, undertook the expedition planned by the adventurer Robert Rogers. The chief documents in the work are Carver's manuscript and survey journals, used as the basis for his book *Travels through the Interior Parts of North America in the Years 1766, 1767, and 1768* (1778), which made him both famous as an early explorer of the West and notorious as a suspected plagiarist.

The purpose of Rogers's expedition was twofold: to advertise the fur-trading outpost of Fort Michilimackinac to the upper Mississippi's native peoples as a potential trading post and to scout out a possible water route for a passage to China. Carver's task was to map the journey and to document regional resources, native communities, trading posts, and evidence of Spanish and French colonial activities. Carver's manuscript, which also includes drawings of native artifacts (such as tent, pipe, and weapons), was originally intended for a government audience. When the expedition fell through, he tried to recover his unpaid expenses by selling his records publicly—a task that took three further revisions and ten more years to accomplish.

HISTORICAL AND LITERARY CONTEXT

Following the French and Indian War, also called the Seven Years' War (1754–1763)—in which the British in America fought with the French and their native allies, primarily over territorial disputes—the British took over lands east of the Mississippi formerly held by the French. The colonial powers in this period were especially interested in searching for trade routes to the Pacific and in regulating a fur trade heavily dependent on native efforts. Under the French, agents had gone to native villages to exchange commodities for furs; under the British, natives were expected to travel to trading posts. Rogers, who had just taken command of Fort Michilimackinac and who was waiting for official approval for an expedition to seek a northwest passage, expected Carver to encourage natives to trade at the fort.

Carver experienced mixed fortunes during this period. He had served eight years in the Massachusetts Bay militia, guarding the western frontier from French and native incursions. When he was discharged in 1763, he did not receive the pension he had hoped for. Deciding to capitalize on his skills as a frontiersman, Carver hoped to find employment mapping uncharted territories and eventually offered his services to Rogers. When the expedition fell through—partly because Carver and Tute mismanaged Rogers's funds in giving too generously in their gifts to the natives—Carver was again left without income or employment. To make money, therefore, he tried to publish his journals.

Carver's journals resemble travel narratives such as *A New Discovery of a Vast Country in America* (1698) by Louis Hennepin, *New Voyages to North-America* (1703) by Baron de Lahontan, and *Journal of a Voyage to North-America* (1761) by Pierre-François-Xavier de Charlevoix, all of which he acknowledges in his *Travels*. More problematically, when critics in the 1780s began to cast aspersions on Carver's achievements, they accused him of plagiarizing the works of these very authors. Thus, as a travel document with a history of controversy over its authorship and authenticity, Carver's text is also comparable to the *Journal of the First Voyage to America,* Bartolomé de Las Casas's reconstruction of Christopher Columbus's 1492–1493 diary.

Because certain observations and details in Carver's accounts were lifted from earlier travel narratives (not by Carver but by his publisher, Parker claims), detractors as early as 1789 began to cast doubts on whether he had actually made the journey. Nevertheless, later travelers continued to rely on Carver's book to navigate the same territories. There was, however, a tendency to follow his route without acknowledging him as the source, suggesting that his name lent a certain incredulity to data otherwise of sound practical value. Since the original publication of the work, critics and scholars have treated Carver mostly with

✧ Key Facts

Time Period:
Mid-18th Century

Relevant Historical Events:
French and Indian War; Carver's western exploration

Nationality:
American

Keywords:
exploration; Native Americans; fur trade

TRAVEL AND EXPLORATION

In a contemporary reenactment, soldiers stand by the fort entrance at Colonial Michilimackinac (a reconstruction of the original village and fort) in Michigan. Jonathan Carver set out from the fort in the spring of 1766 to find a western water route to the Pacific Ocean. © KEN HACKETT/ALAMY

skepticism, leaving him to be recuperated periodically by such academics as Parker, who insist that the journals are authentic.

THEMES AND STYLE

Carver is interested in westward expansion, a theme developed in his preoccupations with the routes of the fur trade, potential settlements, and competing colonial interests. Throughout the text he emphasizes documenting terrain for commercial and territorial purposes. For example, on Green Bay he reflects the following:

> This vast tract of country now in great part under the dominion of our sovereign, capable of subsisting inconceivable numbers of inhabitants, abounding in variety of soils, climates, and natural productions, must afford many articles of commerce…. It has long been talkd that a very respectable province might [be] erected in the neighbourhood of Detroit of which this might be the capital.

This interest in appropriating the country is reflected in Carver's extensive accounts of the natives, made explicit in his record of the Naudowessie (Dakota Sioux) council, who "thanked me for the visit I had made them and wishd I would encourage the English to come among them and trade and settle near them." Carver aims to appease settlers' fears of tribal peoples, who in this period were typically viewed as savages.

As edited by Parker, the journals collate the work of all four versions of Carver's manuscript: Parker takes the first draft as the primary text, into which he inserts elaborations from the later drafts, adding annotations in the margins. Carver's motivations for writing seemed to have changed with his revisions. His earliest entries feature stark descriptions of the route ("August 15, 1766. Arrived at Saganaum Bay. This bay is about 90 mile deep; across the chops is about 24 mile"), the environment ("The land about Michillimackinac for some miles has a sandy, dry, barren soil"), and local customs ("The Naudowessee in their manner of goverment differ in some respects from the other nations of Indians and may more properly be calld a common wealth"). In later drafts Carver is more elaborate, as in the opening pages, in which he prefaces the blunt report of his departure from Boston with the story of military discharge and his intent to serve his country as a draftsman.

Apart from an extended account of the Naudowessie, the structure mainly follows the day-by-day account of Carver's journey: from Boston to Fort Michilimackinac, westward by canoe to the Mississippi, and up the Saint-Pierre River (now the Minnesota River), to winter with the Naudowessie before turning around for Michilimackinac. Carver's tone is generally neutral, and his style ranges from plain to lofty. For example, his account of two Naudowessie hunters who misinterpret his reluctance to lend his damaged canoe is matter of fact: "one of them in a great passion ran to my canoe and with his hatchet gave it several strokes which greatly damaged it. I was instantly informed of what the Indian was about and ran with a stick designing to chastize him." Here and throughout Carver strives for an air of objectivity, resisting a too-personal narrative.

CRITICAL DISCUSSION

Reviewers missed (or ignored) Parker's edition of the journals, though his introduction is typically cited as the definitive text on Carver's manuscript. *Travels*, as Parker notes, "was a success." Although a 1778 review of *Travels* for *Critical Review* calls Carver "a judicious and faithful observer," by the next decade critics suspected plagiarism. Since then Carver has fallen in and out of favor. In "The Travels of Jonathan Carver" (1906), for example, Edward Bourne outlines a case against Carver for plagiarism, yet in *Travelers and Travel Liars, 1660–1800* (1962), Percy Adams describes Carver as the "most notorious" of "travel liars." Carver's reputation recuperated somewhat following Norman Gelb's 1993 edition of *Travels*, which was hailed by Keith Mason in a review for *History* (1994) as "an intriguing, if ephemeral, historical curiosity" and as "a forgotten classic" by the reviewer for the *Times Literary Supplement* (1994).

Parker published Carver's journals to intervene critically in the debate over the importance and authenticity of *Travels*. The task was to show that the early manuscripts all consist of work original to Carver, a fact that Parker attempts to corroborate by including Goddard's journal, which converges with Carver's at strategic points in documenting the route and nature of the expedition. Additionally, Parker reveals that the allegedly plagiarized passages were inserted in the late stages of preparing the manuscript for publication, claiming that such passages were inserted not by Carver but by his editor, Alexander Bicknell. Despite Parker's efforts, however, some scholars remain unsympathetic to Carver, claiming that he was aware of and therefore responsible for the plagiarism.

While the journals have not been discussed as a work in their own right, modern scholars have looked to Carver's writings to put pressure on cultural, national, and literary boundaries. Janet Giltrow, for example, in "Westering Narratives of Jonathan Carver, Alexander Henry, and Daniel Harmon," uses the journals to "look to a time before national boundaries crystallized political and cultural divergence, and discover a shared, rather than divided, literary heritage." In his essay "On the Borders of the Adventure Novel: Narratives of 18th-Century Travel in Indian Territory," Robert Sayre reads Carver's text "as a kind of 'adventure' literature that, although in principle nonfictional, is closely related to the fictional genre of the adventure novel." Keith Widder, in his essay in *Michigan Historical Review*, looks not to Carver's text but to his map, revealing the expedition's role in reviving the fur trade with Native Americans as part of Rogers's plans to make a colony of Michilimackinac. Carver's depictions of the natives are also often challenged—in the work of Daniel Williams, for instance—as are his records of flora, fauna, and terrain.

BIBLIOGRAPHY

Sources

Adams, Percy G. *Travelers and Travel Liars, 1660–1800*. Berkeley: University of California Press, 1962. Print.

Bourne, Edward. "The Travels of Jonathan Carver." *American Historical Review* 11.2 (1906): 287–302. JSTOR. Web. 3 Jan. 2013.

Carver, Jonathan. *The Journals of Jonathan Carver and Related Documents, 1766–1770*. Ed. John Parker. St. Paul: Minnesota Historical Society, 1976. Print.

Giltrow, Janet. "Westering Narratives of Jonathan Carver, Alexander Henry, and Daniel Harmon." *Essays on Canadian Writing* 22 (1981): 27–41. EBSCOhost. Web. 3 Jan. 2013.

Mason, Keith. Rev. of *Travels through America, 1766–1768: An Eighteenth-Century Explorer's Account of Uncharted America*, ed. Norman Gelb. *History* 79.257 (1994): 440–41. EBSCOhost. Web. 3 Jan. 2013.

CARVER DESTITUTE: AN UNEXPECTED INFLUENCE

Though his writings eventually secured him fame, Jonathan Carver died destitute in London in January 1780. His physician, Dr. John Coakley Lettsom, came to the aid of Carver's English widow and in March of that year took out an advertisement in the *Gentlemen's Magazine:* "We are sorry to inform our readers that we are well assured Capt. Carver died absolutely and strictly starved, leaving a wife and two small children, for whom Dr. Letsome, with his wonted humanity, interests himself, and has disposed of many copies of his *Travels.*" In this same issue Lettsom published a letter titled "Hints for Establishing a Society for Promoting Useful Literature," proposing a fund to support impoverished writers, along with their widows and orphans. Lettsom's exact scheme did not take off but was recognized as an influence on the Literary Fund established by the Reverend David Williams in 1790. Lettsom celebrates this fund in his collection of essays *Hints Designed to Promote Beneficence, Temperance, and Medical Science* (1816). Now known as the Royal Literary Fund, this benevolent institution continues to support "professional published authors in financial difficulties," having helped such writers as Samuel Taylor Coleridge, Joseph Conrad, James Joyce, and D. H. Lawrence.

Parker, John. Introduction. *The Journals of Jonathan Carver and Related Documents, 1766–1770*, by Jonathan Carver. St. Paul: Minnesota Historical Society, 1976. 1–56. Print.

Rev. of *Travels through the Interior Parts of North America, in the Years 1766, 1767, and 1768*, by Jonathan Carver. *Critical Review* 46 (1778): 441–50. *Google Books*. Web. 3 Jan. 2013.

Sayre, Robert. "On the Borders of the Adventure Novel: Narratives of 18th-Century Travel in Indian Territory." *E-rea Revue Électronique d'Études sur le Monde Anglophone* 3.1 (2005). E-rea. Web. 3 Jan. 2013.

"Westward, Look!" Rev. of *Travels through America, 1766–1768: An Eighteenth-Century Explorer's Account of Uncharted America*, ed. Norman Gelb. *Times Literary Supplement* 10 June 1994: 26. *News International Associated Services*. Web. 3 Jan. 2013.

Widder, Keith R. "The 1767 Maps of Robert Rogers and Jonathan Carver: A Proposal for the Establishment of the Colony of Michilimackinac." *Michigan Historical Review* 30.2 (2004): 35–75. ProQuest. Web. 3 Jan. 2013.

Williams, Daniel E. "Until They Are Contaminated by Their More Refined Neighbors: The Images of the Native American in Carver's *Travels through the Interior* and Its Influence on the Euro-American Imagination." *Indians and Europe: An Interdisciplinary Collection*. Ed. Christian F. Feest. Lincoln: University of Nebraska Press, 1987. 195–214. Print.

Further Reading

Aarstad, Rich, and Jennie Stapp. "Travel and Exploration Narratives in the Montana Historical Society Collection." *Montana: The Magazine of Western History* 55.3 (2005): 63–65. ProQuest. Web. 3 Jan. 2013.

Carver, Jonathan. *Travels through America, 1766–1768: An Eighteenth-Century Explorer's Account of Uncharted America.* Ed. Norman Gelb. New York: Wiley, 1993. Print.

Greenfield, Bruce. "Creating the Distance of Print: The Memoir of Peter Pond, Fur Trader." *Early American Literature* 37.3 (2002): 415–38. *ProQuest.* Web. 3 Jan. 2013.

Macleod, David I., ed. *Mapping in Michigan and the Great Lakes Region.* East Lansing: Michigan State University Press, 2007. Print.

Medeiros, Patricia M. "Three Travelers: Carver, Bartram, and Woolman." *American Literature, 1764–1789: The Revolutionary Years.* Ed. Everett Emerson. Madison: University of Wisconsin Press, 1977. Print.

Pallante, Martha. "The Trek West: Early Travel Narratives and Perceptions of the Frontier." *Michigan Historical Review* 21.1 (1995): 83–99. *JSTOR.* Web. 3 Jan. 2013.

David Aitchison

Leaves from the Journal of Our Life in the Highlands, from 1848 to 1861

Queen Victoria

OVERVIEW

Queen Victoria's *Leaves from the Journal of Our Life in the Highlands, from 1848 to 1861,* published in 1868, chronicles the life of the royal family at its vacation home in Scotland and served as a memorial to Victoria's beloved husband, Albert. Victoria (1819–1901) recorded in both writing and sketches the daily excursions, family meals, and interactions with the Highlanders, who treated the royal family respectfully but with far less awe than they encountered in their everyday lives. *Leaves* allowed readers a peek at the daily life of the ruler of the world's largest empire and helped to solidify the image of middle-class domesticity Victoria sought to portray throughout her reign.

Leaves was first published privately in 1867 and then publicly in 1868. It was an immediate success, selling more than eighty thousand copies in three months, not only in Great Britain but also in the United States, where it was even more popular. It was translated into languages as diverse as Hindustani and Turkish. In recent years, critical interest in *Leaves* has decreased because it is clear that Victoria, a widow ruling in a patriarchal society, was highly selective as to what she chose to reveal about her private life, but the work has remained an important source for biographers as well as those interested in decisions she made about how she portrayed herself.

HISTORICAL AND LITERARY CONTEXT

Victoria's first visit to Scotland was in 1842. In the early nineteenth century, the Scottish Highlands were romanticized as a place of wild but heroic people and landscapes. Sir Walter Scott's novels were key to creating this portrayal, and the first novel Victoria read was Scott's *The Bride of Lammermoor.* Her journals contain frequent references to Scott and present a similar emphasis on the "wildness" of the Highlands and the nobility and frank, honest manners of the people who lived there.

Victoria's husband, Albert, died in 1861 after twenty years of devoted marriage. She entered into a period of deep mourning, which would last for virtually the rest of her life. *Leaves* served as a memorial to her husband and their family life together. Victoria, Albert, and their nine children had traveled to Scotland almost every year for an annual vacation; Albert purchased the castle at Balmoral in 1852 (and replaced it with the building that stands today), and the family was able to live relatively simply there, engaging in outdoor activities such as walks and hunting. Victoria described her time in the Highlands as some of the happiest in her life, and she excerpted her many, many pages written about their lives there (it is estimated that she averaged twenty-five hundred words of writing per day) into a single volume.

Although *Leaves* did pay homage to the romance of the Highlands originated by writers such as Scott, on the whole it fit into a growing Victorian emphasis on domesticity and the gentry, or upper middle class, rather than the aristocracy. Whereas many eighteenth-century novels highlighted the experiences of the very rich and frequently chronicled dramatic events, Victorian novels centered on less exalted characters who focused on family, work, and everyday activities. The emphasis on the picnics and excursions in *Leaves* helped, as Laurie Langbauer writes in her 2000 essay in *Victorian Afterlife,* to institute "a kind of state domesticity"; that is, a display of ways in which the royal family was similar to, rather than separate from, a common middle-class family. Indeed, keeping a journal had become a very popular pastime for the middle class.

Leaves sold extremely well during Victoria's lifetime, although some members of her family, particularly her eldest son, were uncomfortable with what they saw as indiscrete information about personal details. This was intensified with the publication of a second volume, *More Leaves from a Journal of a Life in the Highlands,* in 1884. Particularly worrisome were the many details in both journals of her relationship with John Brown, her guide and horseman in the Highlands, who is mentioned extensively in both diaries and whose relationship with the queen was a political scandal.

THEMES AND STYLE

The primary focus of *Leaves* is on describing the sights of the Highlands in enthusiastic, romantic terms and chronicling the family's adventures while exploring the landscape. Victoria, herself an avid painter

✣ Key Facts

Time Period:
Mid-19th Century

Relevant Historical Events:
Death of Victoria's husband, Albert; Victoria's visit to the Scottish Highlands

Nationality:
English

Keywords:
monarchy; women's writing; wildness

TRAVEL AND EXPLORATION

Queen Victoria, depicted three years after the publication of the second volume of *Leaves from the Journal of Our Life in the Highlands*.
© UNIVERSAL HISTORY ARCHIVE/GETTY IMAGES

(many of her sketches are included in *Leaves*), frequently describes images as "a picture." She seems to almost frame her observations, writing, for instance, "Immediately near the house the scenery is very wild, which is most enjoyable…. These Scotch streams, full of stones, and clear as glass, are most beautiful; the peeps between the trees, the depth of the shadows, the mossy stones, mixed with slate, etc., which cover the banks, are lovely." She also describes the enjoyment of her family on big occasions, such as when her oldest daughter becomes engaged, and in small, such as Albert's pleasure in hunting (at which he was notoriously bad). After Albert missed a stag while shooting, she writes, "We then rode on without getting off again, Albert talking so gaily with Grant. Upon which Brown observed to me in simple Highland phrases, 'It's very pleasant to walk with a person who is always "content."'"

Like many of her subjects, Victoria kept her diary scrupulously, chronicling the smallest details of her life. Although she declined to publish the majority of her journal writing and even left instructions that her youngest daughter, Princess Beatrice, copy out her diaries after her death and expunge private or controversial moments, she wanted to create a public monument to her life with Albert. The dedication of *Leaves* reads, "To the dear memory of him who made the life of the writer bright and happy, these simple records are lovingly and gratefully inscribed."

In *Queen Victoria: A Biographical Companion* (2003), Helen Rappaport writes of *Leaves* that "what made it so engaging was its candor and the engaging spontaneity of the queen's thought, despite her grammatical lapses." Certainly the journals are marked by wordy, complex sentences and gushing effusions about both the countryside and her beloved Albert; in a description of a carriage ride on the Balmoral estate, Victoria writes, "Oh! what can equal the beauties of nature! What enjoyment there is in them! Albert enjoys it so much; he is in ecstasies here." There are also moments in which genuine pleasure comes through, as when she describes an expedition when they traveled incognito so that people did not know the queen was passing through. She reports that "they never suspected that it could be ourselves!"

CRITICAL DISCUSSION

It is no surprise that the queen's journal would be heaped with approval; *Leaves* received, Rappaport writes, "excessive if not outlandish praise," such as one review that stated "if the Queen had been destined to write in lieu of ruling, she must have left a great mark on the literature of the country." Although novelist Margaret Oliphant, in her review of *Leaves,* joined in this praise, after Victoria's death she was less diplomatic, writing that the queen was "no student of style, nor does she ever, we imagine, ponder and wait for the best word." This assessment was nowhere near as harsh as that of Victoria's own son, Edward, who termed the journals "twaddle."

Praise for *Leaves,* and Victoria as a writer, did not end with her death. In his introduction to an edited selection of her work, Christopher Hibbert wrote in 1985 that "surely no monarch in the history of the world wrote as much, and few wrote so well, as Queen Victoria." Even those who might not admire Victoria's writing recognized the historical value of *Leaves*. A contemporary reviewer quoted in *Queen Victoria: A Biographical Companion* notes that "our descendants will have the great figures of the historical portrait set before them with a minuteness of description, a completeness of detail," and this has held true: the many biographies of Victoria all draw upon *Leaves* as a source that gives access into her inner thoughts.

Writing for *Victorian Literature and Culture* in 2001, Alison Booth adds that "in her own day, Victoria was associated with the triumph of women writers in her age"; examining female authorship and self-construction has been the primary critical

PRIMARY SOURCE

EXCERPT FROM *LEAVES FROM THE JOURNAL OF OUR LIFE IN THE HIGHLAND*

Visits to the Old Women

Saturday, September 26, 1857

Albert went out with Alfred for the day, and I walked out with the two girls and Lady Churchill, stopped at the shop and made some purchases for poor people and others; drove a little way, got out and walked up the hill to *Balnacroft*, Mrs. P. Farquharson's, and she walke'd round with us to some of the cottages to show me where the poor people lived, and to tell them who I was. Before we went into any we met an old woman, who, Mrs. Farquharson said, was very poor, eighty-eight years old, and mother to the former distiller. I gave her a warm petticoat, and the tears rolled down her old cheeks, and she shook my hands, and prayed God to bless me: it was very touching.

I went into a small cabin of old Kitty Kear's, who is eighty-six years old—quite erect, and who welcomed us with a great air of dignity. She sat down and spun. I gave her, also, a warm petticoat; she said, "May the Lord ever attend ye and yours, here and hereafter; and may the Lord be a guide to ye, and keep ye from all harm." She was quite surprised at Vicky's height; great interest is taken in her. We went on to a cottage (formerly Jean Gordon's), to visit old widow Symons, who is "past fourscore," with a nice rosy face, but was bent quite double; she was most friendly, shaking hands with us all, asking which was I, and repeating many kind blessings: "May the Lord attend ye with mirth and with joy; may He ever be with ye in this world, and when ye leave it." To Vicky, when told she was going to be married, she said, "May the Lord be a guide to ye in your future, and may every happiness attend ye." She was very talkative; and when I said I hoped to see her again, she expressed an expectation that "she should be called any day," and so did Kitty Kear.*

We went into three other cottages: to Mrs. Symons's (daughter-in-law to the old widow living next door), who had an "unwell boy"; then across a little burn to another old woman's; and afterwards peeped into Blair the fiddler's. We drove back, and got out again to visit old Mrs. Grant (Grant's mother), who is so tidy and clean, and to whom I gave a dress and handkerchief, and she said, "You're too kind to me, you're over kind to me, ye give me more every year, and I get older every year." After talking some time with her, she said, "I am happy to see ye looking so nice." She had tears in her eyes, and speaking of Vicky's going, said, "I'm very sorry, and I think she is sorry hersel'"; and, having said she feared she would not see her (the Princess) again, said: "I am very sorry I said that, but I meant no harm; I always say just what I think, not what is fut" (fit). Dear old lady; she is such a pleasant person.

Really the affection of these good people, who are so hearty and so happy to see you, taking interest in everything, is very touching and gratifying.

*She died in Jan. 1865.

SOURCE: Queen Victoria. *Leaves from the Journal of Our Life in the Highlands, from 1848 to 1861: To Which Are Prefixed and Added Extracts from the Same Journal Giving an Account of Earlier Visits to Scotland, and Tours in England and Ireland, and Yachting Excursions.* London: Smith, Elder, and Co., 1868.

---

use of *Leaves* in recent years. Although perhaps every female writer of the Victorian age faced a struggle for self-definition, Victoria faced a double challenge in both finding a place for a female authorial voice and not alienating those she ruled. Margaret Homans's 1998 study, for instance, reads *Leaves* as a strategic creation in which Victoria "pretends not to be the queen" so as to solidify her authority over a primarily middle-class populace; as Langbauer writes, the emphasis on the "personal and domestic," as in *Leaves,* "was a carefully orchestrated political move, the strategy of a female sovereign to rule indirectly by manipulating the cultural vocabulary of a woman's role current at the time."

BIBLIOGRAPHY

Sources

Booth, Alison. "Millennial Victoria." *Victorian Literature and Culture* September 2001: 159–70. *MLA International Bibliography.* Web. 11 Dec. 2012.

Homans, Margaret. *Royal Representations: Queen Victoria and British Culture, 1837–1876.* Chicago: University of Chicago Press, 1998. Print.

Langbauer, Laurie. "Queen Victoria and Me." *Victorian Afterlife: Postmodern Culture Rewrites the Nineteenth Century.* Ed. John Kucich and Dianne Sadoff. Minneapolis: University of Minnesota Press: 2000, 211–33. Print.

Rappaport, Helen. *Queen Victoria: A Biographical Companion.* Santa Barbara: ABC-CLIO, 2003. Print.

Victoria, Queen of Great Britain, and David Duff. *Queen Victoria's Highland Journals.* Exeter: Webb and Bower, 1980. Print.

Victoria, Queen of Great Britain, and Christopher Hibbert. *Queen Victoria in Her Letters and Journals: A Selection.* New York: Viking, 1985. Print.

Further Reading

Homans, Margaret. "'To the Queen's Private Apartments': Royal Family Portraiture and the Construction of Victoria's Sovereign Obedience." *Victorian Studies* Autumn 1993: 1–41. Print.

Homans, Margaret, and Adrienne Munich, eds. *Remaking Queen Victoria.* Cambridge: Cambridge University Press, 1997. Print.

Houston, Gail Turley. *Royalties: The Queen and Victorian Writers.* Charlottesville: University of Virginia Press, 1999. Print.

Huff, Cynthia. "Private Domains: Queen Victoria and Women's Diaries." *A/B: Auto/Biography Studies* Fall 1988: 46–52. *MLA International Bibliography.* Web. 11 Dec. 2012.

Munich, Adrienne. *Queen Victoria's Secrets.* New York: Columbia University Press, 1996.

Thompson, Dorothy. *Queen Victoria: The Woman, the Monarchy, and the People.* New York: Pantheon, 1990. Print.

Warner, Marina. *Queen Victoria's Sketchbook.* London: Macmillan, 1979. Print.

Abigail Mann

Letters from an American Farmer

Michel-Guillaume Saint-Jean de Crèvecoeur

OVERVIEW

Penned by Franco-American Michel-Guillaume Saint-Jean de Crèvecoeur, *Letters from an American Farmer* (1782) is a collection of twelve sketches describing life in the purportedly Edenic American colonies. Ostensibly written to an English friend by native Pennsylvanian James Hector St. John, the fictional narrative is so well crafted that many historians and critics have mistaken the work for an autobiography. Farmer James describes to his friend the endless opportunities available for immigrants in America and also extols the pleasures of farming. Crèvecoeur's most famous essay poses the question, "What is an American?" Although *Letters from an American Farmer* presents an idyllic vision of America, it also depicts the struggle to hold on to that vision in the face of conflict and hardship. In the final chapter, Crèvecoeur reports the coming of the American Revolution, which threatens to destroy his bucolic idyll.

Upon publication, *Letters from an American Farmer* enjoyed only moderate fame in the United States. However, it became an instant success in Europe, warranting several reprintings and translations into French, Dutch, and German. The work, widely read for nearly fifty years, provided Europeans with their primary impressions of the American colonies. Celebrated in Parisian salons and at the court of Versailles, it paved the way for Crèvecoeur to become the French consul to New York, New Jersey, and Connecticut. Although written by a native-born Frenchman and initially published in London, the work is considered an American classic.

HISTORICAL AND LITERARY CONTEXT

Crèvecoeur, born in Caen, France, in 1735, came from a Norman family belonging to minor nobility. He received a classical education at the Jesuit College de Mont. In 1755, as a soldier in the French colonial army, Crèvecoeur sailed to New France in North America and distinguished himself as an artillery officer in the French and Indian War. After being discharged in 1759, he explored the Atlantic seaboard and present-day St. Louis, Chicago, and Detroit. In *Liberalism, Puritanism and the Colonial Mind,* Vernon Parrington writes, "Perhaps no other man before the Revolution was so intimately acquainted with the French and English colonies as a whole, with their near background of frontier and the great wilderness beyond, as this French American." In 1765 he became a citizen of New York under the name J. Hector St. John and settled on a 250-acre farm in Orange County, New York, following his 1769 marriage to Mehetable Tippett.

The seven years following his wedding, during which he dedicated himself to farming and family, were the happiest of Crèvecoeur's life. In the introduction to a 1981 edition of *Letters from an American Farmer,* Albert E. Stone describes this "temporary Eden" thusly: "Children and livestock, buildings, fields, meadows, and woodlands waxed and were molded by hard work into a harmonious agrarian whole." Encouraged by his friend William Seton, Crèvecoeur began to record his impressions of agrarian life. However, his bliss was destroyed by the onset of the American Revolution in 1776. Crèvecoeur sailed to England in 1780, and the next year he sold the manuscript of *Letters from an American Farmer* to the firm of Davies and Davis in London. When the book was published, Crèvecoeur was living in France.

Before Crèvecoeur's book appeared, many types of literature had been written in the colonies, notably Benjamin Franklin's *Autobiography.* In *Studies in Classic American Literature,* D. H. Lawrence notes, "Franklin is the real practical prototype of the American. Crèvecoeur is the emotional.… We tend to forget the emotional heritage of Hector St. John de Crèvecoeur." *Letters from an American Farmer* is often compared to *The Journal of John Woolman* (1774). Woolman was a Quaker preacher and an abolitionist in the colonies.

While living in Paris, Crèvecoeur began working on an expanded version of *Letters from an American Farmer,* which was published in French in 1784 as *Lettres d'un cultivateur Americain.* In 1783 he returned to New York as an official representative of Louis XVI. As consul, Crèvecoeur served as a political and cultural liaison between France and the United States, promoted trade across the Atlantic, and corresponded with historically significant figures such as Franklin and Thomas Jefferson. According to Stone, Jefferson's private secretary, William Short, wrote the following about Crèvecoeur: "There is nobody who understands more perfectly the interests of the two countries, as they relate to each other, and none more zealous to promote them mutually."

✢ Key Facts

Time Period:
Mid-18th Century

Relevant Historical Events:
French and Indian War; American Revolution; Crèvecoeur's imprisonment

Nationality:
French/American

Keywords:
agrarianism; revolution; immigration

George Washington's first speech to the Indians. Michel-Guillaume Saint-Jean de Crèvecoeur expressed his feelings about the coming Revolutionary War and his desire to go and live among the Indians in *Letters from an American Farmer.* © PRIVATE COLLECTION/LOOK AND LEARN/THE BRIDGEMAN ART LIBRARY

THEMES AND STYLE

Central to *Letters from an American Farmer* is Crèvecoeur's love of peace and belief in a paradisiacal America. Through Farmer James, he states, "Here individuals of all nations are melted away into a new race of men, whose labours and posterity will one day cause great changes in the world." The first three epistles "tell the history of the American farmer and the peacefulness that have characterized life in America in comparison to Europe's long history of poverty and strife," according to John Harmon McElroy in *American Writers of the Early Republic.* Despite battles that raged in New England between colonial and British forces, Crèvecoeur attempts to present a picture of a peaceful America. As Stone writes, "The conflict between belief and experience provides the drama and the emotional tension that every reader feels building in the later chapters…. It is a tension the author does not or cannot resolve."

Although Crèvecoeur ostensibly wrote *Letters from an American Farmer* in order to record his blissful impression of American life, the work also criticizes Europeans for remaining entrenched in antiquated traditions. To prove his point, James presents the case of an impoverished Scotsman who increases his meager assets twentyfold when transplanted to America. Describing the Scotsman's change as a "sort of resurrection" and a "great metamorphosis," James contends that because Americans act on "new principles," they "entertain new ideas and form new opinions." He continues, "From involuntary idleness, servile dependence, penury, and useless labour has passed to toils of a very different nature, rewarded by ample subsistence."

While Everett Emerson, writing in *Benét's Reader's Encyclopedia of American Literature,* describes Crèvecoeur's style as "disarmingly unpretentious," Stone calls it "deliberately but deceptively self-mocking, a manner slyly satiric of the European reader before whom the untutored colonial pretends to prostrate himself." The "Introductory Letter" exemplifies this "slyly satiric" tone:

> My wife (and I never do anything without consulting her) laughs and tells me that you cannot be in earnest. "What!" says she: "James, would'st thee pretend to send epistles to a great European man who hath lived abundance of time in that big house called Cambridge, where, they say, that worldly learning is so abundant that people get it only by breathing the air of the place? Would'st not thee be ashamed to write unto a man who has never in his life done a single day's work?"

As Stone puts it, by using the naive Farmer James as a mouthpiece, Crèvecoeur "sets up the kind of ironic interplay between naive actor and knowing narrator that is … characteristic of many American novels and autobiographies."

CRITICAL DISCUSSION

In *American Nature Writers,* Michael P. Branch defines *Letters from an American Farmer* as "the first book to imaginatively construct the American experience in nature according to a fully Romantic sensibility." With its skillful blend of art and nature to present a veritable utopia, the work was embraced by the European readers of the Romantic era. However, in America it was not as warmly received, possibly because of its criticism of the American Revolution. After its initial publication, it was not republished in the United States until 1904. Consequently, American critics were late in recognizing Crèvecoeur's significant contribution to the nation's literature.

With the arrival of a more rationalistic age in Europe in the 1830s and 1840s, Crèvecoeur's writing receded into the background, overshadowed by, for example, Alexis de Tocqueville's detached cultural analysis and Charles Dickens's social critiques. Suddenly, Crèvecoeur's *Letters from an American Farmer* seemed old-fashioned and naive. Writes Stone, "The eclipse lasted until the turn of the twentieth century, when Americans recovered their colonial past along with its architecture, the paintings of John Singleton Copley … and the writings of Jefferson." Since

PRIMARY SOURCE

EXCERPT FROM *LETTERS FROM AN AMERICAN FARMER*

In this great American asylum, the poor of Europe have by some means met together, and in consequence of various causes; to what purpose should they ask one another what countrymen they are? Alas, two thirds of them had no country. Can a wretch who wanders about, who works and starves, whose life is a continual scene of sore affliction or pinching penury; can that man call England or any other kingdom his country? A country that had no bread for him, whose fields procured him no harvest, who met with nothing but the frowns of the rich, the severity of the laws, with jails and punishments; who owned not a single foot of the extensive surface of this planet? No! urged by a variety of motives, here they came.

. . .

What attachment can a poor European emigrant have for a country where he had nothing? The knowledge of the language, the love of a few kindred as poor as himself, were the only cords that tied him: his country is now that which gives him land, bread, protection, and consequence: *Ubi panis ibi patria,* is the motto of all emigrants. What then is the American, this new man? He is either an European, or the descendant of an European, hence that strange mixture of blood, which you will find in no other country. I could point out to you a family whose grandfather was an Englishman, whose wife was Dutch, whose son married a French woman, and whose present four sons have now four wives of different nations. *He* is an American, who leaving behind him all his ancient prejudices and manners, receives new ones from the new mode of life he has embraced, the new government he obeys, and the new rank he holds. He becomes an American by being received in the broad lap of our great *Alma Mater.* Here individuals of all nations are melted into a new race of men, whose labours and posterity will one day cause great changes in the world. Americans are the western pilgrims, who are carrying along with them that great mass of arts, sciences, vigour, and industry which began long since in the east; they will finish the great circle. The Americans were once scattered all over Europe; here they are incorporated into one of the finest systems of population which has ever appeared, and which will hereafter become distinct by the power of the different climates they inhabit.

The American ought therefore to love this country much better than that wherein either he or his forefathers were born. Here the rewards of his industry follow with equal steps the progress of his labour; his labour is founded on the basis of nature, *self-interest;* can it want a stronger allurement? Wives and children, who before in vain demanded of him a morsel of bread, now, fat and frolicsome, gladly help their father to clear those fields whence exuberant crops are to arise to feed and to clothe them all; without any part being claimed, either by a despotic prince, a rich abbot, or a mighty lord. Here religion demands but little of *him;* a small voluntary salary to the minister, and gratitude to God; can he refuse these? The American is a new man, who acts upon new principles; he must therefore entertain new ideas, and form new opinions. From involuntary idleness, servile dependence, penury, and useless labour, he has passed to toils of a very different nature, rewarded by ample subsistence.—This is an American.

SOURCE: Crèvecoeur, Michel-Guillaume Saint-Jean de. *Letters from an American Farmer.* London: Printed for Thomas Davies, 1782.

---

then, Americans have read Crèvecoeur with increasing interest, regularly finding something new and relevant in *Letters from an American Farmer.* Branch suggests that Crèvecoeur's book prefigures the agrarian ideology present in Jefferson's *Notes on the State of Virginia* (1785) and the romanticized wilderness in Henry David Thoreau's *Walden Pond* (1854), Herman Melville's tales of the South Pacific, and William Faulkner's *Big Woods* (1955).

Crèvecoeur is now recognized as a significant contributor to early American literature. In *American Literature 1764–1789*, A. W. Plumstead calls him "the first in our literature to find this dramatic voice in an imaginative work of power." In "The American Farmer's Letters, with a Checklist of the Different Editions," Howard C. Rice argues that "one of the merits of Crèvecoeur is to have seen, at a moment when most of his fellow Americans had neither the time nor inclination for literature, the artistic possibilities in certain truly American themes which later became matter for accomplished works of art." McElroy recognizes *Letters from an American Farmer* as "a classic representation of American faith in the possibility of renewal." At the same time, he criticizes modern commentators for focusing "attention only on Crèvecoeur's praise of America" in the initial part of the work because this emphasis has "affected appreciation of the artistic wholeness of his masterpiece, a wholeness that comes close making it the first American novel."

BIBLIOGRAPHY

Sources

Branch, Michael P. "Early Romantic Natural History Literature." *American Nature Writers.* Vol. 2. Ed. John Elder. New York: Scribner, 1996. *Scribner Writers Series.* Web. 29 Nov. 2012.

Crèvecoeur, Michel-Guillaume Saint-Jean de. *Letters from an American Farmer and Sketches of Eighteenth-Century America.* New York: Penguin, 1981.

Emerson, Everett. "Crèvecoeur, St. John de (1735–1813)." *Benét's Reader's Encyclopedia of American Literature.* Vol. 1. Ed. George B. Perkins, Barbara Perkins, and Philip Leininger. New York: HarperCollins, 1991. 229. *Literature Resource Center.* Web. 29 Nov. 2012.

Lawrence, D. H. *The Symbolic Meaning: The Uncollected Versions of Studies in Classic American Literature.* Ed. A. Arnold. Arundel: Centaur, 1962. 53–70. Print.

McElroy, John Harmon. "Michel Guillaume Jean de Crèvecoeur." *American Writers of the Early Republic.* Ed. Emory Elliott. Detroit: Gale Research, 1985. *Dictionary of Literary Biography.* Vol. 37. *Literature Resource Center.* Web. 29 Nov. 2012.

Parrington, Vernon. *Liberalism, Puritanism and the Colonial Mind: Main Currents in American Thought.* New York: Harcourt, Brace, 1927. Print.

Plumstead, A. W. "Hector St. John de Crèvecoeur." *American Literature 1764–1789: The Revolutionary Years.* Ed. Everett Emerson. Madison: University of Wisconsin Press, 1977. 213–31. Print.

Rice, Howard C. "The American Farmer's Letters, with a Checklist of the Different Editions." *Colophon* 18 (1933). Print.

Stone, Albert E. Introduction. *Letters from an American Farmer and Sketches of Eighteenth-Century America,* by Michel-Guillaume Saint-Jean de Crèvecoeur. New York: Penguin, 1981.

Further Reading

Allen, Gay Wilson, and Roger Asselineau. *St. John de Crèvecoeur: The Life of an American Farmer.* New York: Viking, 1987. Print.

Chevignard, Bernard. "St. John de Crèvecoeur in the Looking Glass: *Letters from an American Farmer* and the Making of a Man of Letters." *Early American Literature* 19 (1984). Print.

Davidson, Cathy N. *Revolution and the World: The Rise of the Novel in America.* Oxford: Oxford University Press, 1986.

Emerson, Everett. "Hector St. John de Crèvecoeur and the Promise of America." *Forms and Functions of History in American Literature.* Ed. Winfried Fluck, Jürgen Peper, and Willi Paul Adams. Berlin: E. Schmidt, 1981. Print.

Grabo, Norman S. "Crèvecoeur's American: Beginning the World Anew." *William and Mary Quarterly* 48 (1991). Print.

Hansen, Chadwick. "Michel Guillaume Jean de Crèvecoeur." *American Writers: A Collection of Literary Biographies, Supplement 1.* Vol. 1. Ed. Leonard Unger. New York: Scribner, 1979. *Scribner Writers Series.* Web. 29 Nov. 2012.

Hanson, Victor Davis. *The Land Was Everything: Letters from an American Farmer.* New York: Free Press, 2000. Print.

Kehler, Joel R. "Crèvecoeur's Farmer James: A Reappraisal." *Essays in Literature* 3.2 (1976): 206–13. Rpt. in *Nineteenth-Century Literature Criticism.* Vol. 105. Ed. Edna Hedblad. Detroit: Gale Group, 2002. *Literature Resource Center.* Web. 29 Nov. 2012.

Takahashi, Tsutomu. "The Myth of the Land and Crèvecoeur's Vision of Self in Letters from an American Farmer." *Studies in English Language and Literature* 40 (1990). Print.

Maggie Magno

The Letters of Lady Anne Barnard to Henry Dundas, from the Cape and Elsewhere

Anne Barnard

OVERVIEW

The Letters of Lady Anne Barnard to Henry Dundas, from the Cape and Elsewhere (1793–1803) offers a glimpse into the politics of the British Empire during the French Revolution and the rise of Napoleon Bonaparte. Out of the thirty-four surviving letters that Anne Barnard (1750–1825), the wife of a politician, addressed to Henry Dundas, who was at the time the secretary of state for war and the colonies, thirteen were sent from England and Ireland and twenty-one from the Cape of Good Hope. The letters from the Cape (1797–1802) are of particular importance as Dundas had asked Barnard to keep a journal during her stay in Africa. The letters explore themes of patriotism, slavery, and life in a multicultural colony.

Barnard's letters, most of which were preserved at Melville Castle, Midlothian, until 1926, were not published during her lifetime. Some of the letters were first published in 1901 by British author William Henry Wilkins (1861–1905) under the title *South Africa a Century Ago*. A revised and more complete edition was published by A. M. Lewin Robinson in 1973. Robinson also included a letter-journal that Barnard wrote for her sisters, *Journal of a Tour into the Interior*. While the tone of Barnard's letters to her old friend Dundas is conversational, her reports go beyond the themes of ordinary travel accounts: her sketches of the landscapes and people she encountered and the everyday life and events that took place during her stay in Africa (as well as in Ireland) are written with a conscious effort to provide details that might prove significant to a politician.

HISTORICAL AND LITERARY CONTEXT

Barnard was an extremely prolific correspondent in a century in which letter writing flourished in Britain. The "familiar letter" was a term that applied not only to the sphere of private correspondence or to the written exchange between literary figures but also to the correspondence found at the heart of business life and government. While the British admitted that the polite art of letter writing had been invented in France, French politeness was nonetheless considered to be hypocritical. Thus, the eighteenth century saw the rise of the letter-writing manual, which aimed to teach Britons how to craft letters that showed a natural form of politeness. Barnard's correspondence shows erudition but no unwanted artificiality. Her original observations are complemented by valuable sketches and watercolors, which she enclosed in her letters.

In the 1770s and 1780s, Barnard had met and entertained many of the leading intellectuals, writers, and politicians of the day. She had played hostess to British philosopher and statesman Edmund Burke and Anglo-Irish playwright Richard Brinsley Sheridan, as well as to the future prime minister William Pitt the Younger and to two of the future secretaries of war and colonies, Dundas and William Windham. During her stay at the Cape, Barnard corresponded not only with Dundas but also with British army commander and future prime minister Arthur Wellesley and with Windham in a style that is urbane, informed, and determined to demonstrate a judicious understanding of political situations both at the Cape and at home.

In eighteenth-century Britain, letters were highly desirable objects: they not only circulated in manuscript, thus routinely finding an audience beyond the intended addressee, but also were much sought after on the print market, especially if their authors were literary or political figures. Poet Alexander Pope, for instance, wrote his letters with publication in mind, and many other writers, from Mary Wortley Montagu to Samuel Johnson, wrote with posterity, if not immediate publication, in mind. Toward the end of the century, Pope's style was considered artificial and avoided by Barnard's contemporaries, such as Anna Seward and Frances Burney (who wrote from France, unable to return to Britain during the war), as well as by Barnard herself.

While Barnard was determined to maintain a high profile in politics and in literary salons, she recoiled from the publicity of authorship. In 1771 she composed a ballad, "Auld Robin Gray," that became famous, but she only admitted authorship of this work in a letter to Sir Walter Scott almost four decades later. While her letters, journals written to her family, and private diaries were not written with publication in mind, they were designed to play their part in the politics of the day. As such they offer a valuable panoramic view of colonial life in South Africa soon

❖ Key Facts

Time Period:
Late 18th to Early 19th Centuries

Relevant Historical Events:
French Revolution; expansion of the British Empire; rise of Napoleon

Nationality:
English

Keywords:
patriotism; slavery; colonialism; women's writing

Letter writer Anne Barnard, circa 1775. © HULTON ARCHIVE/GETTY IMAGES

after the British won the colony from the Dutch. Since eighteenth-century letter writers aimed to please their correspondents—in order to make reading and defraying the letter worth the recipient's while—Barnard's writings are full of highly entertaining detail. She is oftentimes an anthropologist, ethnographer, botanist, fiery politician, and humorous observer of character—all in one letter.

THEMES AND STYLE

Barnard's letters evince patriotism mixed with gratitude for the patronage that Dundas had offered to her husband. Patriotism offers Barnard an opportunity to articulate herself as a coherent British female subject in a multicultural world. Having ascended to the top of Table Mountain, the highest peak in the region and the most difficult to climb, she reports how she sang the national hymn: "God save great George our King, roard I, & my troop," She writes, "I wishd great George our King to have stood beside me at the moment, & to have thrown his eye over his new possessions." The same spirit of patriotism is at work when she writes about mutiny on British ships off the coast at a time when the sailors were believed to have been influenced by the example of French revolutionaries. She mixes patriotism with diplomacy especially in her treatment of the Dutch. She insists that unlike Britons, the Dutch had been unjust rulers, pointing out that they had forbidden industry and cultivation of the land, keeping the natives, especially the Khoi-Khoi (Hottentots) in poverty and idleness: "Hotentot Holland we found totally uninhabited by Hotentots, they poor things having been driven up the country by their avaricious masters."

Barnard's correspondence reveals the ingrained habit of maintaining a proper social intercourse typical of the time and of her social class. Since Dundas had asked her to send a log of her observations, she prefaces some of her political observations with conventional claims of being unequal to the task, although her modesty is mixed with anxiety at the prospect of making inaccurate or impolitic observations: "it would seem almost *conceited folly* in me to describe things as they appear around me, or still more to give my miserable *female notions* on any thing, was it not … that your friendship for me will contrive a general apology for every thing silly or erroneous."

Her letters demonstrate the conversational tone that marks eighteenth-century letter writing. She often refers to her writing as "chit chat." Throughout the eighteenth century, female correspondents were known to be rather loose spellers, to use plenty of dashes in their writing, and to mingle French words in their letters—and Barnard is no exception. There is a marked difference in style between the letters addressed to Dundas and the journal she writes for her sisters. Even if Barnard views Dundas as a friend and an equal, she was at the time indebted to him because he had provided her husband's position at the Cape. Since Dundas had asked her to be an "intelligent politician," the letters manifest eagerness to show both gratitude and competence in her observations. The journal of a trip inland, which she wrote for her sisters, however, shows the brilliance, freedom, and ease of a self-assured traveler and confident writer.

CRITICAL DISCUSSION

Since Barnard forbade publication of her journals and memoirs, literary scholars and historians have for the most part focused on her ballad "Auld Robin Gray." It would be difficult to ascertain whether or not her letters from the Cape helped Dundas form decisions with regard to British policy in Africa. Nevertheless, it is through the medium of the familiar letter that Barnard managed to obtain a position at the Cape for her husband. With this in mind, it can be assumed that her letters played a role in helping Dundas get a better understanding of the political situation at the Cape.

The end of World War II brought Barnard's writings from the Cape to public notice with the publication in 1948 of Madeleine Masson's monograph *Lady Anne Barnard: The Court and Colonial Service under George III and the Regency*. Masson's book discusses Barnard's corpus of writings at a time when the British Empire was in the process of dismantling and fresh questions about race were emerging. Since the 1990s, Barnard's writings have been read from a feminist and postcolonial perspective. In a 1992 essay for *English in Africa*, South African scholar Margaret Lenta argues that Barnard's Cape journals and diaries "always give the reader the sense that their author was a confident woman" rather than a passive and compliant subject.

Lenta offers useful information on the distinction between Barnard's understanding of the political situation in the Cape and what she prudently chooses to reveal in her letters to Dundas.

Her political views have received the greatest amount of attention in the twenty-first century. David Johnson's essay in *Irish and Postcolonial Writing: History, Theory, Practice* (2002) explores Barnard's nationalism in the context of Britain's expansion of colonial rule during the French Revolution. In *Imagining the Cape Colony: History, Literature, and the South African Nation* (2012), Johnson offers an astute reading of Barnard's political views by setting her writings in the context of Scottish Enlightenment philosophers' discourses on political economy and sentiment, as she "extends [Adam] Smith's discourse of sentiment to the Khoisan and Cape slaves."

BIBLIOGRAPHY
Sources
Barnard, Lady Anne Lindsay. *The Letters of Lady Anne Barnard to Henry Dundas, from the Cape and Elsewhere, 1793–1803, Together with Her Journal of a Tour into the Interior and Certain Other Letters*. Ed. A. M. Lewin Robinson. Cape Town: Balkema, 1973. Print.

Johnson, David. "Talking about Revolution: Lady Anne Barnard in France, Ireland, and the Cape Colony." *Irish and Postcolonial Writing: History, Theory, Practice*. Ed. Glenn Hooper and Colin Graham. Houndsmills: Palgrave Macmillan, 2002. Print.

———. *Imagining the Cape Colony: History, Literature, and the South African Nation*. Edinburgh: Edinburgh University Press, 2012. Print.

Lenta, Margaret. "Degrees of Freedom: Lady Anne Barnard's Cape Diaries." *English in Africa* 19.2 (1992): 55–68. Web. 8 Jan. 2013.

Further Reading
Bannet, Eve Tavor. *Empire of Letters: Letter Manuals and Transatlantic Correspondence, 1688–1820*. New York: Cambridge University Press, 2005. Print.

Brant, Clare. *Eighteenth-Century Letters and British Culture*. Houndsmills: Palgrave Macmillan, 2006. Print.

Driver, Dorothy. "Lady Anne Barnard's Cape Journals and the Concept of Self-Othering." *Pretexts: Studies in Writing and Culture* 5.1–2 (1995): 46–65. Web. 21 Dec. 2012.

Lenta, Margaret. "The Shape of a Woman's Life: Lady Anne Barnard's Memoir." *Literator* 14.2 (1993): 101–15. Web. 21 Dec. 2012.

———. Introduction. *Paradise, the Castle and the Vineyard: Lady Anne Barnard's Cape Diaries*. Johannesburg: Witts University Press, 2006. Print.

Masson, Madeleine. *Lady Anne Barnard: The Court and Colonial Service under George III and the Regency*. London: Allen, 1948. Print.

Redford, Bruce. *The Converse of the Pen: Acts of Intimacy in the Eighteenth-Century Familiar Letter*. Chicago: University of Chicago Press, 1986. Print.

Ioana Patuleanu

Motorcycle Diaries
Ernesto "Che" Guevara

✣ Key Facts

Time Period:
Mid-20th Century

Relevant Historical Events:
Spanish Civil War; Argentine coup of 1943; rise of Marxism

Nationality:
Argentine

Keywords:
politics; travel; Marxism

OVERVIEW

Ernesto "Che" Guevara's *Motorcycle Diaries*, which recounts Guevara's 1951 motorcycle journey through Latin America, provides an early portrait of one of the twentieth century's most important political figures. The diaries begin in December 1951, as Guevara, a twenty-three-year-old medical student from a well-to-do family, sets off from Buenos Aires with his friend and traveling companion Alberto Granado. The diaries trace the pair's seven-month journey through Argentina, Chile, Peru, Colombia, and Venezuela, where the two travelers parted ways in July 1952. Guevara traveled on to Miami before returning to Argentina. The diaries provide detailed accounts of Guevara's first experiences with social injustice and severe illness in Latin America. The diaries explore the awakening of Guevara's radical political conscience and his development into an iconic figure.

Despite writing and releasing other works, Guevara did not publish any of his journals during his lifetime. They were first released in 1993, in transcribed form, by Guevara's Personal Archive in Havana (now called the Che Guevara Studies Center of Havana, Cuba). There has been a limited amount of scholarly inquiry into the diaries, as the events, while formative and entertaining, are eclipsed by his later participation in the Cuban Revolution and in other communist revolutions in Africa and Latin America. *The Motorcycle Diaries*, however, continue to fascinate both scholars and amateurs interested in the personal life, the political and ethical development, and the myth of the famous revolutionary.

HISTORICAL AND LITERARY CONTEXT

Although it occurred on another continent, the Spanish Civil War, which lasted from 1936 to 1939, exerted a powerful influence on the young Guevara. As John Lee Anderson notes in his biography, "It was probably the first political event to impinge significantly on Ernesto Guevara's consciousness." Guevara's family staunchly defended the liberal Spanish Republicans. On the domestic, Argentine front, the coup of 1943 led, ultimately, to Juan Domingo Peron's rise to power in 1946. Anderson notes that in "observing Peron, Ernesto could see at work a political master who more often than not showed he could manipulate the magic keys to political success: knowing the mood of the people, knowing who his real friends and enemies were—and knowing when to act."

The diaries were initially composed in the midst of Guevara and Granado's motorcycle journey through Latin America, but they were later revised by Guevara. Publication, however, arrived late—posthumously, in fact—in 1993. In his 2004 article in the *New York Times*, Larry Rohter suggests that the publication of the book was "long-suppressed" in Cuba. In a published response, the international publisher of *The Motorcycle Diaries*, David Deutschmann, writes, "Having been personally involved in this and similar Che Guevara book projects in Cuba for more than 20 years, I can testify that there is no conspiracy to prohibit the publication in Cuba of this or any other book by Che Guevara."

The Motorcycle Diaries draws on a long tradition of travel literature, but Guevara's case differs in that first and foremost he is recognized as an iconic, revolutionary figure and only secondarily as a writer or an explorer. The same can be argued of diaries of figures such as Theodore Roosevelt, whose *Through the Brazilian Wilderness* (1914) recounts the politician's Brazilian travels with his son Kermit. But Guevara was influenced by a range of philosophical and psychological works. Anderson notes that "he consulted Benito Mussolini on Fascism, Josef Stalin on Marxism ... [Émile] Zola for a highly critical definition of Christianity, and Jack London for a Marxist description of social class."

The Motorcycle Diaries is most notable for its depiction of the development of Guevara's political consciousness. As Cintio Vitier writes in his introduction to the diaries, Guevara "felt helpless as a doctor and was approaching the awakening of conscience that would trigger his other, definitive vocation." The diaries gained renewed and broader cultural impact in 2004 when Walter Salles adapted *The Motorcycle Diaries* for the screen. The film went on to receive numerous awards, including an Academy Award given to the writer, José Rivera, for Best Adapted Screenplay.

THEMES AND STYLE

While the text primarily focuses on the travails of Guevara and Granado, a political and social ethos soon emerges in the diaries, which emphasize Guevara's reactions to the plight of the poor and sick, the social injustices of a capitalist system, and the concept of a united Pan-America—all of which would continue to captivate Guevara in his later writings and revolutionary activities. In an oft-recounted passage, Guevara tells of meeting a married couple, communist workers, who had been persecuted and jobless because of their political beliefs. "The couple, numb with cold, in the desert night, huddling against each other in the desert night, were a living representation of the proletariat in any part of the world." Such sympathetic portraits of the underprivileged suggest a developing deep political and social consciousness.

Guevara used his diaries to record both the difficulties and the pleasures of an arduous journey, as well as his internal reactions to the experiences of travel. The diaries recount his journey, his conversations with locals, and his experiences working as a doctor in a leper colony in the Peruvian Amazon. *The Motorcycle Diaries* was originally composed as a travelogue, primarily for private use, but Guevara later revised and edited it into a more narrative form. As such the book occupies a kind of cross-genre space between unexpurgated diaries and autobiographical memoir. Guevara makes note of his revisions, arguing that they are a product of his personal change and development: "The person who wrote these notes passed away the moment his feet touched Argentine soil again. The person who reorganizes and polishes them, me, is no longer, at least I am not the person once was. All this wandering around … has changed me more than I thought."

Stylistically *The Motorcycle Diaries* is notable for the polished, literary prose that Guevara crafted through the process of revision. He often utilizes metaphoric language: "The road snakes between the low foothills that sound the beginning of the great cordillera of the Andes." The diaries also exhibit sure-footed descriptions of the natural world: "The huge figure of a stag dashed like a quick breath across the stream and his body, silvered by the light of the rising moon, disappeared into the undergrowth. This tremor of nature cut straight to our hearts." While such descriptive passages are fundamental to the text, Guevara does not rely on them solely; the text moves fluidly from portrait to thought to narrative.

CRITICAL DISCUSSION

Initial response to Guevara's *Motorcycle Diaries* was mixed. In the *Antioch Review,* Adan Quan writes that, in *The Motorcycle Diaries,* "we see the glimmerings of the future Che who was to become an icon for the revolutionary aspirations of the Third World," but he also describes the prose as "somewhat stilted" and claims that the social injustices that are "occasionally noted" are viewed through a "rather passive optic." In a more dismissive review, in *New Statesman & Society,* Amanda Hopkinson writes that "there are fewer traces of Che's evolution as a revolutionary than of his vestigial racism and sexism." Such varying opinions about the book echo the reception of a politically polarizing figure such as Guevara.

While *The Motorcycle Diaries* has become a celebrated text that chronicles the early travels and political and social development of Guevara, its legacy pales in comparison to his later revolutionary achievements. His participation in the successful communist revolution in Cuba in 1959 stands as Guevara's most significant achievement, one that sparked a legacy of leftist political radicalization in Latin America. He also became an icon, often found on posters, flags, and T-shirts of the worldwide 1960s countercultural movement. The diaries play the role of a foundational story, or a bildungsroman, within Guevara's broader political and social legacy. The scholarship on Guevara reflects this trend, with the majority of it emphasizing his political achievements as opposed to his personal journals.

Scholarly inquiry regarding *The Motorcycle Diaries* has been relatively limited, but a small body of criticism has focused on how the diaries "de-trivialize"

A banner depicting communist revolutionary Che Guevara, who helped Fidel Castro rise to power in Cuba in 1959. In 1967, while attempting to instigate a Marxist uprising in Bolivia, he was captured and executed. Long after his death he has remained a heroic icon to followers in Latin America. © ROBERT JOHN/ ALAMY

THE CUBAN REVOLUTION

Though the revolution to overthrow the repressive regime of the Cuban dictator Fulgencia Batista began with an attack on the Moncada Barracks in 1953, Ernesto "Che" Guevara's involvement in the revolution did not begin until much later. In December 1956, Fidel Castro, Guevara, and eighty-two others aboard the ship *Granma* landed on Playa las Coloradas in southeastern Cuba. The rebels quickly made their way to the Sierra Maestra, but their numbers were soon decimated by Batista's forces. The remaining rebel soldiers—by some estimates, only twenty of them—reorganized in the mountains, waging guerrilla warfare and winning the support of the peasants in the east. In 1958 the Batista regime launched an offensive against Castro's rebels, but the offensive ultimately failed.

By August 1958 the Castro-led rebels launched a counteroffensive. Guevara, along with Jaime Vega and Camilo Cienfuegos, led rebel groups westward. In late December 1958 the rebel units, headed by Guevara and others, captured the city of Santa Clara. On January 1, 1959, fearing capture or defeat, Batista fled the country. On the following day the army laid down their weapons, and Castro's forces, including the units led by Guevara, took the city of Havana.

the otherwise empty social iconography and oversaturated marketing of Guevara's revolutionary narrative. In a 1997 essay Christopher Hitchens details the cult of personality around Guevara, arguing that "much of the attraction of the cult has to do with the grace of an early romantic death." Hitchens also argues that, if read as a piece of "magical realism," *The Motorcycle Diaries* is "another way of describing, and incidentally of de-trivializing, the legacy of Guevara." In her essay in *Confluencia*, Fernanda Bueno argues that Guevara is viewed through a mythical lens and "that the 'Real Che' is as unrecoverable as all legendary myths." The reader's approach to texts about Guevara, such as *The Motorcycle Diaries*, "necessarily passes through its prior textualization, its narrativization in the political unconscious."

BIBLIOGRAPHY

Sources

Anderson, John Lee. *Che: A Revolutionary Life*. New York: Grove, 1997. Print.

Bueno, Fernanda. "*Motorcycle Diaries:* The Myth of Che Guevara in the 21st Century." *Confluencia* 23.1 (2007): 107–14. Print.

Deutschmann, David. "Che Guevara's Diaries: Letter to the Editor." *New York Times*. New York Times, 2 June 2004. Web. 27 Dec. 2012.

Guevara, Ernesto. *The Motorcycle Diaries*. Melbourne: Ocean, 2003. Print.

Hitchens, Christopher. "Goodbye to All That." *New York Review of Books*. NYREV, 17 July 1997. Web. 21 Dec. 2012.

Hopkinson, Amanda. Rev. of *The Motorcycle Diaries*, by Ernesto Guevara. *New Statesman & Society* 8.357 (1995): 39. Print.

Quan, Adan. Rev. of *The Motorcycle Diaries: A Journey around South America*, by Ernesto Guevara. *Antioch Review* 54.2 (1996): 246–47. Print.

Rohter, Larry. "Letters from the Americas; Che Today? More Easy Rider than Revolutionary." *New York Times*. New York Times, 26 May 2004. Web. 27 Dec. 2012.

Vitier, Cintio. Introduction. *The Motorcycle Diaries*. By Ernesto Guevara. Melbourne: Ocean, 2003. 15–30. Print.

Further Reading

Granado, Alberto, and Lucia Alvarez de Toledo. *Traveling with Che: The Making of a Revolutionary*. New York: Harper, 2009. Print.

Luther, Eric, and Ted Henken. *Che Guevara*. Indianapolis: Alpha Books, 2001. Print.

Symmes, Patrick. *Chasing Che: A Motorcycle Journey in Search of the Guevara Legend*. New York: Vintage Books, 2000. *Google Books*. Web. 21 Dec. 2012. Print.

Whitehead, Laurence. Rev. of *The Motorcycle Diaries: A Journey around South America*, by Ernesto Che Guevara. *London Review of Books* 17.21 (1995): 21. Print.

Greg Luther

Notebooks and Letters
Nathaniel Hawthorne

OVERVIEW

The *Notebooks* and *Letters* of Nathaniel Hawthorne (1804–1864), which address a wide variety of subjects in Hawthorne's life and contain source material for his fiction and essays, have remained a subject of scholarly interest into the twenty-first century. Divided into *The American Notebooks* (four volumes, 1835–1852), *The English Notebooks* (seven volumes, 1853–1857), and *The French and Italian Notebooks* (six volumes, 1858–1859), Hawthorne's journals comprise more than two thousand pages of text. His more than one thousand extant letters have been presented in a variety of editions, with a definitive complete edition appearing in *The Centenary Edition of the Works of Nathaniel Hawthorne* (1989). Presenting aspects of the author's character that do not appear in his other writings, the *Notebooks* and *Letters* also explore prominent themes in Hawthorne's more famous works, such as sin, isolation, and self-loathing.

Hawthorne did not publish any material from his notebooks or letters during his lifetime; his wife, Sophia Peabody Hawthorne, made the first editions of these works available with her own significant editorial changes in 1868. (The first complete scholarly editions based off Hawthorne's original manuscripts did not appear until 1932.) Scholarship on these personal writings has grown as literary scholars and Hawthorne biographers have used the *Notebooks* and *Letters* to gain insight into the author's private life. For example, critical assessment of the *Notebooks* and *Letters* has challenged Hawthorne's historical reputation as an isolated and emotionally distant individual. Scholars have also used the collected writings to explore Hawthorne's development of settings, characters, and themes in his fiction and essays. Today the *Notebooks* and *Letters* continue to fascinate Hawthorne scholars and enthusiasts seeking a broader understanding of the man and his work.

HISTORICAL AND LITERARY CONTEXT

Hawthorne's *Notebooks* and *Letters* are in keeping with the intellectual and social conventions of his native early nineteenth-century New England. As a college-educated member of the middle class, Hawthorne was encouraged by social convention to maintain correspondence with his peers through letters. Personal journal keeping also was popular among the American middle class during the early modern Victorian era. In addition, Hawthorne's youth coincided with a period of greater interest in individual psychology and interiority in Western society, a theme reflected in both his fiction and in the *Notebooks* and *Letters* through his fixation on his mental state. In the *Notebooks,* he makes frequent reference to the influence of his Puritan New England ancestors, an association that both challenged and inspired him throughout his literary career.

In his letters, Hawthorne corresponded with several notable New England historical and literary figures, including his Bowdoin College classmates, the U.S. president Franklin Pierce, poet and educator Henry Wadsworth Longfellow, and naval officer Horatio Bridge. He also exchanged correspondence with such American authors as Ralph Waldo Emerson, Henry David Thoreau, Louisa May Alcott, and Herman Melville. The *Notebooks* constitute the bulk of Hawthorne's literary output after 1852 and include extensive details about his travels, including his tenure as the U.S. consul in Liverpool from 1853 to 1857. However, near the end of his life, his notebook work was disrupted by the outbreak of the U.S. Civil War in 1861.

In addition to detailing his private life, Hawthorne's *Notebooks* respond to the works of other literary figures of the time. His *English Notebooks,* which contain material contributed for the essay collection *Our Old Home* (1863), include criticisms of Frances Trollope's travel book *Domestic Manners of the Americans* (1832) and Charles Dickens's travelogue *American Notes* (1842). In spite of popular convention, his letters did not emulate the elaborate style of eighteenth-century epistolary novels and lacked the rhetorical flourish of some of his literary contemporaries' professional correspondence, of which Emerson's letters serve as a useful example. Instead, Hawthorne's letters, in their often simple and direct style, more closely resemble those of his close friend Longfellow.

Hawthorne's letters are especially notable for the author's literary criticism of his own works. In one letter, he refers to his best-known work, *The Scarlet Letter* (1850), as "positively a h—ll fired story into which I found it almost impossible to throw any cheering light." In another letter, he notes that *The House of the Seven Gables* (1851) was a better novel than *The Scarlet Letter* but worries that the former and one of his

❖ *Key Facts*

Time Period:
Early 19th Century

Relevant Historical Events:
Hawthorne's correspondence with notable figures; the author's notes for future works

Nationality:
American

Keywords:
literature; journaling; letter writing

NATHANIEL HAWTHORNE'S LOST NOTEBOOK

In 1976 author Barbara S. Mouffe discovered Nathaniel Hawthorne's original "lost notebook" in a long neglected cupboard in her attic. The cupboard had been in her family's possession for more than a century and contained possessions of her great-grandfather William James Reynolds, an early nineteenth-century Salem bookseller and publisher who shared mutual friends with Hawthorne. After investigating her family history, Mouffe concluded that the notebook was most likely given to her great-grandmother Harriet Reynolds by a friend of the Hawthorne family who might have had a quarrel over money with Hawthorne's wife, Sophia.

The lost notebook is notable for containing differing versions of some famous quotes from Hawthorne's published *Notebooks*, including a variation of Hawthorne's exuberant entry written after his first major work, *Twice-Told Tales* (1837, 1842), found publication. Referring to his writing room, he writes, "In this dismal *and squalid* chamber FAME was won!" (Before publication, Sophia Hawthorne had excised "and squalid" from the text.) Notably, when Mouffe discovered the lost notebook, she happened to be living on Hawthorn Avenue in Boulder, Colorado.

later novels, *The Marble Faun* (1860), "do not make their appeal to the popular mind." He also writes, "If I were to meet with such books as mine, by another writer, I don't believe I should be able to get through them." Many scholars have studied Hawthorne's and Melville's extensive correspondence during the summer of 1850 (the year Hawthorne published *The Scarlet Letter* and the year before Melville published his best known work, *Moby Dick*) for signs of literary influence.

THEMES AND STYLE

Hawthorne's *Notebooks* and *Letters* focus on many of the same themes as his fiction and essays, including isolation, sin, self-loathing, love, and the influence of the past. Hawthorne had a reputation among his contemporaries as a painfully shy man, and his *Notebooks* record his fears of isolation and his limited social interactions in detail. Nevertheless, the original notebook manuscripts—those not revised by Sophia after his death—suggest he moved in a wider social circle than originally believed. His *Notebooks* include telling passages about the nature of sin's influence on personal relations, such as one line imagining "the life of a woman, who, by the old colony law, was condemned always to wear the letter A, sewed on her garment, in token of her having committed adultery." His letters include numerous references to self-doubt ("I am heartily tired of myself") and are notable for their expressions of affection, including one letter to his then fiancée Sophia in which he writes, "My dear Sophie, your letters are no small portion of my spiritual food, and help to keep my soul alive, when otherwise it might languish unto death."

Hawthorne used his *Notebooks* to record both the mundane occurrences of daily life and more abstract meditations on art and society. His *English* and *French and Italian Notebooks* include numerous records of travel, visits to churches, museums, and cultural monuments, and conversations with American and English expatriates, constituting the most extensive journalistic undertaking of his literary career. His personal letters also focus on discussions of art and expressions of love and are often directed toward family and close friends in Massachusetts and England. He also exchanged numerous professional letters with his publishers William D. Ticknor and James T. Fields. Although the original notebook manuscripts show frequent signs of editing and copying from earlier versions of the text, Hawthorne never indicated he wished them to be published. He even directed his correspondence partners to destroy his letters several times throughout his life, especially his youthful letters, and recorded burning "great heaps of letters" in one notebook.

Both the *Notebooks* and the *Letters* are notable for the use of naturalistic diction, which is not present in Hawthorne's fiction and essays. Word choices such as "speechifying," "boozy," "queer," and "pigged in" indicate that Hawthorne's personal writing may not have been intended for public reading. This most likely influenced Sophia's decision to heavily edit the original *Notebooks* and *Letters* for what she deemed objectionable content. In her editorial notes, she emphasizes that "throughout his journals it will be seen that Hawthorne is entertaining, and not asserting, opinions and ideas. He questions, doubts, and reflects with his pen, and, as it were, instructs himself." She also claims to have made only minor changes to the original text. However, Hawthorne scholar Joel Myerson notes in his 2002 work *The Selected Letters of Nathaniel Hawthorne* that Hawthorne's original word choices indicate he viewed letter writing as an extension of conversation rather than as a performative exercise.

CRITICAL DISCUSSION

Initial critical response to Hawthorne's *Notebooks* and *Letters* was overshadowed by ongoing popular and scholarly interest in his fiction and essays. Sophia provided several letters for publication in the *Atlantic Monthly* in 1868 and published *Passages from the American Notebooks* (1868) and *Passages from the English Notebooks* (1870), all with significant editorial changes. Hawthorne's son, Julian, also used the *Letters* to publish a biography of his father in 1884. However, upon Julian's death in 1903, the *Notebooks* passed to literary agent Stephen H. Wakeman, who sold them in 1909 to the J. P. Morgan Library, where numerous Hawthorne scholars have since used them. The letters were first published in book form in *The Love Letters of Nathaniel Hawthorne* (1909), a publication dismissed by critics as adding little to Hawthorne scholarship. Critical reaction was also negligible for the subsequent publications *Letters of Hawthorne to William D. Ticknor, 1851–1864* (1910) and *Hawthorne and His Publisher* (1913).

Twentieth-century and twenty-first century scholars have focused on comparing Hawthorne's original manuscripts to Sophia's revisions, with Randall Stewart arguing in the 1932 edition of *The American Notebooks* that Sophia's revisions represent an attempt to obscure her husband's "rustic impropriety" in order to add "literary elegance" to the *Notebooks* and to remove negative references to Hawthorne's literary contemporaries such as Emerson and Thoreau. Other scholars have focused on Hawthorne's adaptation of material from the *Notebooks* in his fiction and essays such as *The Blithedale Romance* (1852; drawn from notebook material collected at Brook Farm in 1841), *The Marble Faun* (drawn from notebook material in *The French and Italian Notebooks*), and other works such as *The Old Manse* (1846) and *Browne's Folly* (1860).

Recent scholarship has focused on the discovery of the original manuscript of Hawthorne's so-called lost notebook in 1978 and on the evolving scholarly picture of Hawthorne's personal life. Regarding the lost notebook—which includes a large amount of previously undiscovered material that Hawthorne wrote between 1835 and 1841 and which Sophia excised from her original publication—Hawthorne scholar Hyatt Waggoner notes in the introduction to *Hawthorne's Lost Notebook, 1835–1841* (1978) that Hawthorne was at that point in his literary development "very clearly not a 'thinker'" and was "not concerned with the current of thought in his day or with conceptual, philosophic, or theological problems of any sort." Rather, Waggoner asserts, Hawthorne was interested "in the 'real world' outside himself, in the workings of the human psyche under stress, the 'deeper psychology,' and in curious facts, especially if they suggested what he once called 'the moral picturesque.'" Regarding Hawthorne's letters, Myerson in *The Selected Letters of Nathaniel Hawthorne* (2002) writes that Hawthorne's correspondence "allows readers both to confirm and to dispel the common … views of Hawthorne as the dour Calvinistic author of gloomy Puritan tales and as the painfully awkward man in public."

BIBLIOGRAPHY

Sources

Hawthorne, Nathaniel. *The American Notebooks*. Ed. Claude M. Simpson. 1835–52. Columbus: Ohio State University Press, 1972. Print.

———. *The English Notebooks*. Ed. Thomas Woodson. 1853–57. Columbus: Ohio State University Press, 1997. Print.

———. *The French and Italian Notebooks*. Ed. Thomas Woodson. 1858–59. Columbus: Ohio State University Press, 1980. Print.

———. *The Selected Letters of Nathaniel Hawthorne*. Ed. Joel Myerson. Columbus: Ohio State University Press, 2002. Print.

Mouffe, Barbara S. Preface. *Hawthorne's Lost Notebook, 1835–1841*. University Park: Pennsylvania State University Press, 1978. 3–20. Print.

Stewart, Randall. Introduction. *The American Notebooks*. New Haven: Yale University Press, 1932. xiii–xcvi. Print.

Waggoner, Hyatt H. Introduction. *Hawthorne's Lost Notebook, 1835–1841*. University Park: Pennsylvania State University Press, 1978. 21–28. Print.

Further Reading

Argersinger, Jana L., and Leland S. Person, eds. *Hawthorne and Melville: Writing a Relationship*. Athens: University of Georgia Press, 2008. Print.

Bell, Millicent, ed. *Hawthorne and the Real: Bicentennial Essays*. Columbus: Ohio State University Press, 2005. Print.

Fuller, Randall, and Robert Milder, eds. *The Business of Reflection: Hawthorne in His Notebooks*. Columbus: Ohio State University Press, 2009. Print.

Hawthorne, Nathaniel. *The Centenary Edition of the Works of Nathaniel Hawthorne*. 23 vols. Ed. William Charvat et al. Columbus: Ohio State University Press, 1962–94. Print.

———. *The Portable Hawthorne*. Ed. William C. Spengemann. New York: Penguin, 2005. Print.

Millington, Richard H., ed. *The Cambridge Companion to Nathaniel Hawthorne*. Cambridge: Cambridge University Press, 2004. Print.

Reynolds, Larry J., ed. *A Historical Guide to Nathaniel Hawthorne*. Oxford: Oxford University Press, 2001. Print.

Wineapple, Brenda. *Hawthorne: A Life*. New York: Knopf, 2003. Print.

Craig Barnes

THE PYLGRYMAGE OF SIR RICHARDE GUYLFORDE

Richarde Guylforde

❖ **Key Facts**

Time Period:
Early 16th Century

Relevant Historical Events:
Guylforde's pilgrimage to Jerusalem

Nationality:
English

Keywords:
religion; pilgrimage; travel

OVERVIEW

The Pylgrymage of Sir Richarde Guylforde, first published in 1511, contains an account of Sir Richarde Guylforde's journey to Jerusalem in 1506, as recorded by his chaplain. The chaplain's name has not been preserved, and the narrative itself has largely been forgotten. *Pylgrymage* covers the final months of Guylforde's life, from leaving England in April 1506 to his death in Jerusalem in September 1506. His party was one of the last to go on pilgrimage to Jerusalem before mercantile interests became the predominant reason for Europeans to travel to the Near East. Although parts of *Pylgrymage* may have been copied from other early modern travel manuals, it illustrates the difficulties inherent in expeditions during this period—sickness, hunger, hostility from Muslims, and bad weather—as well as pilgrims' awe as they visited churches, abbeys, and the Holy Land.

Pylgrymage does not seem to have been particularly popular following its publication, and just one extant copy remains. The only subsequent printing is Sir Henry Ellis's 1851 edition, published for Oxford's Camden Society. Part of the reason for this lack of impact may have been Guylforde's status: though he was an important member of King Henry VII's court, he was forced to retire because of debt and financial aberrances that involved the king's money, and his pilgrimage may have been his way of escaping the resulting poverty and shame. Because of the obscurity attendant on these factors, *Pylgrymage* has received little attention from modern scholars.

HISTORICAL AND LITERARY CONTEXT

As early as the ninth century, Europeans were traveling to Jerusalem and its environs because of the area's attachment to Jesus Christ, the apostles, and saints. When relics of Christian saints were discovered, they were often moved to a church, which then became a possible destination for pilgrims hoping to grow in their faith, display their spiritual devotion, and advance their status in heaven after they died. On these trips pilgrims often traversed Europe, especially Italy, and wrote accounts that include descriptions of the broader Mediterranean. These stories often consist of orderly lists of shrines, foreign customs, ports of call, and bad weather encountered on arduous voyages. *Pylgrymage* maintains this pattern by describing churches the travelers saw on their leisurely journey to Jerusalem, sites in Jerusalem, and storms they endured on their trip home.

In *Pylgrymage* the chaplain makes little mention of the journey's historical context. On many levels this silence emphasizes the cultural tensions that overshadow the work. Though it was written almost two centuries after the fall of Acre to Muslims in 1291, *Pylgrymage* describes European-Muslim hostility enduring beyond the Crusades, such as the party's day-and-night stay in a cave, which almost certainly led to Guylforde's illness and death.

Pylgrymage is one of the last in a long line of journals by pilgrims to the Holy Land. Most notably, Margery Kempe had visited Jerusalem less than a hundred years before and recorded the journey as part of *The Book of Margery Kempe* (1436–1438); however, her account is far more personal, centering on her unusual spiritual experiences and the reactions of her companions to her strange behavior. *Pylgrymage,* on the other hand, preserves the impersonal, less interior tone of narratives such as William Wey's (1458), which is a guidebook that lists itineraries, prices, and even basic Greek words needed for English pilgrims.

Despite its important place at the end of a period of pilgrimage writing, *Pylgrymage* had very little influence after its 1511 publication. Written on the eve of the Protestant Reformation, it depended on an atmosphere of Catholic devotion that was about to be shattered by Henry VIII's break from the Catholic Church in 1533 and the subsequent disruption of cultural acceptance of Catholic practices such as pilgrimage and the veneration of saints. In this sense *Pylgrymage* emblematizes the carrying of medieval faith into the early modern English world. However, even after such groundbreaking religious change, narratives such as *Pylgrymage* remained an essential part of the cultural milieu of sixteenth-century England; William Shakespeare, for example, likely depended on such accounts for material to describe the Mediterranean geographies of some of his plays, including *Two Gentlemen of Verona* and *The Winter's Tale.*

THEMES AND STYLE

Pylgrymage treats many themes common to pilgrimage narratives from medieval and early modern England, particularly needs for hospitality, awe at religious sites, and bewilderment at foreign customs. The chaplain pays special attention to the hospitality the group is shown by Guylforde's Italian relatives, the Pallavicinos, who "stuffed us with vitaylle [vittles], brede, and wyne." Before they reach the Near East, the pilgrims make an extensive tour of Italy's holy sites, visiting St. Anne's grave, among others. At the feast of St. Anthony they arrive in Padua and stay with an order of Grey Friars. Here, the chaplain recounts "a solempne processyon, where at were borne many relyques, and the noumbre of doctoures ... was grete excedyngly. In the sayde processyon we vysyted there [were] many seyntes and relyques [saints and relics], as seynt Luke and seynt Mathye."

However, the chaplain's motive for writing was not simply to record the group's itinerary. He also describes the intense devotion practiced by his group, a common motif in pilgrimage diaries. While they are in Jerusalem, after they have witnessed another religious parade, he writes that "euery man yaue hym selfe [gave himself] to prayer and contemplacion, ... vysynge [visiting] the holy places aforesayde after theyr deuocyon [devotion] durynge the hole nyght." For these travelers the trip is not merely a sightseeing venture but also an opportunity for spiritual meditation and devotion. The chaplain ties each site to the biblical narrative that gives it importance, such as the altar that was built on the spot where Christ's crucifiers cast lots for his clothing. In this way the account of a private venture becomes a devotional narrative with which English readers familiar with scripture could sympathize.

In its style *Pylgrymage* often feels like a dry recitation of facts. It bears very little mark of individual personality, either of that of Guylforde, who dies before the second half of the narrative, or that of the chaplain, who writes in the first-person plural. Furthermore, the chaplain frequently reuses the phrases "Item next" as he logs landmarks or "From thens" to indicate the group's progression during a day's expedition. Even Guylforde's death is treated almost impersonally: "Sonday at nyght, aboute .j or .ij [1 or 2] of the cloke at after mydnyght, my M. syr Ric. Guylford, whom God assoyle, diceased." Immediately after a sentence describing Guylforde's burial, the chaplain continues: "The same afternoone we went to Bethanye ... & sawe ye graue [grave] or monument in the whiche Lazarus lay .iiij. [4] dayes dede ... whome our Sauyour Criste raysed from dethe to lyfe." Here, perhaps, are glimmers both of personal grieving for the chaplain's master and of hope in the Christian doctrine of resurrection despite the diary's overall impersonality.

CRITICAL DISCUSSION

Little attention was paid to *Pylgrymage* after its initial printing by Richard Pynson in London. In his article "English Travel Books about the Arab near East in the Eighteenth Century," Mohamad Ali Hachicho notes that much of the book may have been "a literal translation from [Bernhard von] Breidenbach's famous *Peregrinationes in Montem Zion*." Such copying was common in early modern England since travel authors such as John Mandeville—and literary writers such as Shakespeare—often borrowed significant portions of their texts from other sources. In fact, Sir Richard Torkington, who went to the Near East in 1517, appears to have borrowed much of *Pylgrymage*'s accounts of wonders for his own travel journal.

Because of its obscurity, *Pylgrymage* did not make an impact of its own in the centuries following its first publication. Essentially, the genre of pilgrimage journal ceased with this account. As Hachicho writes:

> With Guildford and his party ends the chain of pilgrims who had no other interest or motive but to behold the heritage of Jesus Christ, and secure in Heaven the sweetness of Paradise and eternal life. These pilgrims took their long and risky route to the Near East, with no other motive in mind but the purely religious, and no other destination but the Holy Sepulchre.

Instead, many English travelers began to interact with the Near East on one theme: wealth. Trade blossomed in the mid-sixteenth century, ushering in a new era of international commerce.

Painting of a street in Jerusalem, the Holy Land, which is the destination in *The Pylgrymage of Sir Richarde Guylforde*. © LOOK AND LEARN/THE BRIDGEMAN ART LIBRARY

SIR RICHARDE GUYLFORDE'S LIFE

The son of Sir John Guylforde of Rolvenden, Sir Richarde Guylforde married Anne Pympe before 1479. This connected him with the Beauforts, with whom he participated in a conspiracy to revolt against Richard III and place Henry Tudor, later Henry VII, on England's throne. When the revolt failed, Guylforde fled England to join Henry in exile and, in 1485, was part of Henry's landing party. After the successful Battle of Bosworth Field, Guylforde's labors on Henry VII's behalf were rewarded. He spent most of his life as Master of Arms and Ordnance, managed estates in Surrey and Sussex, and used his shipbuilding and engineering expertise in the king's service on campaigns in Cornwall and France.

Despite his power, Guylforde was hounded by debt as early as 1485 and was forced to sell some of his properties. He seems to have embezzled funds from the Crown and was eventually imprisoned in the Fleet in 1505. Thus, his pardon from Henry VII in April 1506 was probably granted only pending his retirement from royal service. Under these circumstances, his pilgrimage is remarkable because voyages to Jerusalem were exorbitantly expensive. Nevertheless, the journey may have been an honorable way for Guylforde to lessen the burden of personal and public shame that had eclipsed his career.

Even after its publication as part of the Camden Society's effort to reprint obscure early modern books, *Pylgrymage* made little impact on modern scholarship. In 1917 M. P. Tilley used the diary to trace Italian geography in Shakespeare's *Two Gentlemen of Verona*; Terence Spencer in 1952 used it similarly in a discussion of the location of Shakespeare's Delos. The most recent extensive coverage of *Pylgrymage* is Hachicho's 1964 catalog of English books focused on travel to the Near East. Yet as a result of its role as a marker of the end of a religious and cultural era, *Pylgrymage* offers an opportunity for the study of the development of the diary as a genre and of English–Near Eastern relations.

BIBLIOGRAPHY

Sources

Cunningham, Sean. "Guildford, Sir Richard (*c.* 1450–1506)." *Oxford Dictionary of National Biography.* Oxford: Oxford University Press, 2004. *Oxford Dictionary of National Biography.* Web. 29 Nov. 2012.

Hachicho, Mohamad Ali. "English Travel Books about the Arab Near East in the Eighteenth Century." *Die Welt des Islams,* New Series 9.1/4 (1964): 1–206. *JSTOR.* Web. 28 Nov. 2012.

Ives, E. W. "Henry VIII (1491–1547)." *Oxford Dictionary of National Biography.* Oxford: Oxford University Press, 2004. *Oxford Dictionary of National Biography.* Web. 29 Nov. 2012.

The Pylgrymage of Sir Richard Guylforde. Ed. Sir Henry Ellis. London: Camden Society, 1851. *EEBO.* Web. 28 Nov. 2012.

Spencer, Terence. "Shakespeare's Isle of Delphos." *Modern Language Review* 47.2 (1952): 199–202. *JSTOR.* Web. 29 Nov. 2012.

Tilley, M. P. "Shakespeare and Italian Geography." *Journal of English and Germanic Philology,* 16.3 (1917): 454–55. *JSTOR.* Web. 29 Nov. 2012.

Further Reading

Beazley, C. R. "Torkington, Richard (*fl.* 1511–1518)." Rev. Andrew A. Chibi. *Oxford Dictionary of National Biography.* Oxford: Oxford University Press, 2004. Web. 29 Nov. 2012.

Cunningham, Sean. "Pole, Edmund de la, eighth earl of Suffolk (1472?–1513)." *Oxford Dictionary of National Biography.* Oxford: Oxford University Press, 2004. *Oxford Dictionary of National Biography.* Web. 29 Nov. 2012.

Dockray, Keith. "Guildford, Sir Henry (1489–1532)." *Oxford Dictionary of National Biography.* Oxford: Oxford University Press, 2004. *Oxford Dictionary of National Biography.* Web. 29 Nov. 2012.

Ford, L. L. "Vaux, Nicholas, first Baron Vaux (*c.* 1460–1523)." *Oxford Dictionary of National Biography.* Oxford: Oxford University Press, 2004. *Oxford Dictionary of National Biography.* Web. 29 Nov. 2012.

Gunn, S. J. "Henry VII (1457–1509)." *Oxford Dictionary of National Biography.* Oxford: Oxford University Press, 2004. *Oxford Dictionary of National Biography.* Web. 29 Nov. 2012.

The Pylgrymage of Sir Richard Guylforde. London: R. Pynson, 1511. *EEBO.* Web. 29 Nov. 2012.

Stopford, J. "Some Approaches to the Archaeology of Christian Pilgrimage." *World Archaeology* 26.1 (June 1994): 57–72. *JSTOR.* Web. 29 Nov. 2012.

Torkington, Richard. *Ye Oldest Diarie of Englysshe Travell … The Pilgrimage of Sir Richard Torkyngton.* Ed. W. J. Loftie. London: Field and Tuer, Ye Leadenhalle, 1884. Print.

Evelyn Reynolds

The Travels of Dean Mahomet, a Native of Patna in Bengal, through Several Parts of India, While in the Service of the Honourable the East India Company Written by Himself, in a Series of Letters to a Friend

Dean Mahomet

OVERVIEW

Published in 1794, the improbably named *The Travels of Dean Mahomet, a Native of Patna in Bengal, through Several Parts of India, While in the Service of the Honourable the East India Company Written by Himself, in a Series of Letters to a Friend* is the first book written in English by a native of the Indian subcontinent. The work covers the years between Dean Mahomet joining the East India Company Army in 1769 and his immigration to Ireland in 1784. As the title states, the book is in the form of a series of letters (composed long after the experiences chronicled) that describe what the author saw and heard on his military marches through India.

When Mahomet resigned his East India Company commission and moved to Ireland in 1784, England had just lost its most important colony in the Western Hemisphere—now called the United States—and was on the brink of confirming its acquisition of a vast new colony in southern Asia—India. While many Americans of English descent had returned to England by this time, very few Indians had settled in the homeland of their new masters. Mahomet was one of the first. His long career in the British Isles—in Ireland, in London, and in Brighton—and his many remarkable successes (including his book) suggest that racial prejudice had not yet had time or occasion to organize itself.

HISTORICAL AND LITERARY CONTEXT

Although India did not officially become a British colony until 1858, the Battle of Plassey in 1757 made India part of the British Empire. Before that the Mogul Empire controlled and stabilized North India for almost 200 years. Through a series of negotiations over several decades, however, the British East India Company became the de facto ruling authority of India in 1757—two years before Mahomet was born. Mahomet's family was Muslim, as were many rulers of smaller states. His father died in the service of the East India Company; Mahomet then attached himself to the East India Company military when he was about eleven.

In 1793 Mahomet put an advertisement in papers, inviting subscriptions to a book he wanted to write about his travels in India. While the work described his time in the military, he had resigned his commission years earlier. As a child, Mahomet had acquired a patron, Captain Godfrey Evan Baker, an Anglo-Irish Protestant officer, who raised Mahomet as one of his family—not a common arrangement, but by no means unprecedented. When Baker resigned his commission in 1782, Mahomet also resigned and went to Ireland with him. Under Baker's sponsorship, Mahomet began to attend school. In 1786 he met and married a fellow student, Jane Daly, a woman from a prominent Protestant family. (Mahomet had, by then, converted to Protestant Christianity.) In the same year Baker died, and his brother, William Massing Baker, took over the patronage.

Travel writing became a popular and common genre at the end of the 1700s; the British public was increasingly interested in travel narratives about the empire's acquired lands. *The Travels of Dean Mahomet* was one of the best of the genre. Of course, the British had a long-established appetite for travel writing—dating back at least to Richard Hakluyt's *Divers Voyages Touching the Discoverie of America* (1582) and *The Principal Navigations, Voiages, Traffiques and Discoueries of the English Nation* (1589–1600). The epistolary form was popular for both fiction and travelers' tales. Mahomet clearly consulted other notable travel books—among them, Jemima Kindersley's *Letters from the Island of Teneriffe … and the East Indies* (1777) and John Henry Grose's *Voyage to the East Indies* (1766). At times Mahomet uses these sources to the point of what would now be deemed plagiarism.

Mahomet's travel book was widely read, but no literary career followed. The work did, however, establish him as a distinct and interesting personality.

❖ *Key Facts*

Time Period:
Late 18th Century

Relevant Historical Events:
British colonization of India; growth of the East India Company

Nationality:
Bengali

Keywords:
colonialism; racism; Bengal

TRAVEL AND EXPLORATION

Dean Mahomet was affiliated with the British East India Company's army starting in the late eighteenth century. This image, from 1781, shows the Mogul of Hindostan reviewing this army's troops. © NORTH WIND PICTURE ARCHIVES/AP IMAGES

Despite Mahomet's years living in the British Isles, he did not present himself as assimilated. He remained an Indian, an exotic outsider. (It is interesting to note that many racial prejudices against people of color from the Empire would later develop; Mahomet, however, predates these biases.) His impact on British culture lay not only in the book but also in his other work—starting the first restaurant in England that featured Indian cuisine, for example. Notable is how Mahomet's achievements all involve bringing India to Britain.

THEMES AND STYLE

The main themes of *The Travels of Dean Mahomet* are the richness of Indian culture, the glory of the Indian past—especially Muslim India—and (though only by implication) the chaos of the Indian present. Although he loves and takes pride in his native land, he is not a patriot in the modern, anti-imperial sense of the word. His point of view is that of a soldier in a conquering/occupying army, and when he says "we" he means the members of that army, native and European. Nominally a Muslim, Mahomet describes that religion as if it were something he had nothing to do with, yet some bias may be detected when he says: "The Mahometans are, in general, a very healthful people: refraining from the use of strong liquors, and accustomed to a temperate diet, they have but few diseases." The autobiographical elements—even his father's death—chiefly serve as vehicles for his travelogue, not for self-revelation.

Mahomet's primary motive for writing his *Travels* was to launch himself—not as a literary man, but as a purveyor of Indian culture to the Irish and English in the British Isles. To "Dear Sir," his composite—presumably Anglo-Irish—correspondent, he says that his aim is "to be made acquainted with the early part of my Life, and the History of my Travels." Such explicit autobiographical aims notwithstanding, Mahomet seems mainly out to promote India: "The people of India, in general, are peculiarly favoured by Providence in the possession of all that can cheer the mind and allure the eye…. The traveller beholds with admiration the face of this delightful country." The difference is that instead of bringing tourists to India, Mahomet brings India to the tourists.

The letters that constitute *The Travels of Dean Mahomet* are structured to give a guided tour of India, with Mahomet as the Anglophone native guide, and his language and tone throughout—unctuous and compulsively informative—foreshadow precisely the chatter of such guides when, in the late-nineteenth and early-twentieth centuries, travel became "tourism." Even when narrating the most harrowing, tragic, or exciting incidents, Mahomet's tone is detached, and he is always ready to turn away from event itself and switch focus. For example, after a fierce battle against forces led by a man named Maboub, Mahomet notes, "A few of our Seapoys were killed; and the gallant Captain Gravely, no less distinguished for his prowess in the field, than his conduct in private life, received an ill fated wound, of which he died." Mahomet then goes on, in the next paragraph, with his travelogue: "Lecknow, the town, to which Maboub was sent, is a place of considerable trade…. The inhabitants are opulent and industrious."

CRITICAL DISCUSSION

The initial reception of *The Travels of Dean Mahomet* was positive and favorable. Because the book appeared to be merely a travel narrative, it passed below the radar of whatever critical establishment existed. After it had its vogue, the work passed into obscurity. Then, in 1997, the book was reborn in an edition edited by, and with a lengthy introduction from, Michael Fisher. Typical of the modern reaction is that of Francine Prose, writing in the *New York Times Book Review:* "His descriptions—of holy men and dancing girls, battles and weddings, unconventional snakebite cures and the nurturing kindness of elephants—are charming, but the facts of his biography, summarized in an introduction by the historian Michael H. Fisher, seem even more exotic." Not everyone was as pleased with Fisher, however. The *Spectator*'s William Dalrymple, for instance, says that "even Professor Fisher's plodding academese cannot quite take the bloom off this amazing man."

Despite its widespread popularity, Mahomet's travel book had little long-term impact, either on travel writing or on the careers of Indian writers working in English. Mahomet's impact on British society at large, on the other hand, was lasting. After moving to London, he worked in a "vapor bath"; there he introduced the Indian treatment, *champi* (shampooing), or therapeutic massage. In 1810 he then opened the first British restaurant to feature Indian cuisine. These two innovations had infinitely more impact than his book.

The two predominant trends in scholarship about *The Travels of Dean Mahomet*—since its republication in 1997—can be labeled "West" and "non-West." The reaction in the West is largely positive but concentrates on Fisher's apparatus: "[Fisher]," says Stephen Dale, writing in the *Historian,* "does a good job of putting things into context, and explaining the background and political significance behind the acts of a single individual." The non-Westerners are more concerned with Mahomet, and their feelings are mixed. Mona Narain, writing for *Studies in English Literature,* thinks Mahomet "performs the balancing act of the marginalized insider, both in India and in Britain, writing and working to familiarize alien identity and culture for the consumption of the British public." In "A Closer Look at Dean Mahomet (1759–1850)," Amardeep Singh detects an underlying dishonesty in Mahomet's writing. After quoting a passage of Mahomet describing a nawab's procession, Singh says, "As I'm looking over this language, it doesn't seem exactly 'neutral' or merely appreciative. It actually seems to ply the language of exoticism to excess. Is that really what Dean Mahomet thought as he watched the Nawab's procession, or is this simply an attempt to create a certain aura of mystery and power for his English readers?"

AMAR SINGH'S DIARY

In 1898, more than a century after *The Travels of Dean Mahomet* first appeared, a twenty-year-old Indian named Amar Singh began to record his own experience as a subject of—and participant in—Britain's ongoing rule of India. Nearly every day for the next forty-four years, Singh documented the events of his life, events that were closely bound with the historical progression of colonial India at the turn of the twentieth century. Serving as a military officer in various locations, ranging from China to Europe to Afghanistan, Singh documented his experience navigating between Indian and British culture, much as Dean Mahomet had before him.

Singh produced some eighty-nine volumes of diary during his adult life. Though unpublished during his lifetime, his writing was the subject of intense scholarly scrutiny beginning in the early 1970s. The result was two published volumes of Singh's diaries: *Reversing the Gaze: Amar Singh's Diary: A Colonial Subject's Narrative of Imperial India* (2002) and *Between Two Worlds: A Rajput Officer in the Indian Army, 1905–1921* (2005). Together, these texts trace Singh's progression from his privileged youth as a noble member of the Rajput clan to his service in the Indian military under British commanders. Like Mahomet's diary, Singh's account offers a revealing and personal perspective on the history of colonial India.

BIBLIOGRAPHY

Sources

Dale, Stephen F. Rev. of *The Travels of Dean Mahomet,* by Dean Mahomet. *Historian* 61.4 (1999): 934. *General OneFile.* Web. 20 Nov. 2012.

Mahomet, Dean. *The Travels of Dean Mahomet: An Eighteenth-Century Journey through India.* Ed. Michael Fisher. Berkeley: University of California Press, 1997. *UC Press E-Books Collection, 1982–2004.* Web. 20 Nov. 2012.

Narain, Mona. "Dean Mahomet's Travels, Border Crossings, and the Narrative of Alterity." *Studies in English Literature, 1500–1900* 49.3 (2009): 693+. *General OneFile.* Web. 21 Nov. 2012.

Prose, Francine. "Travel." *New York Times Book Review* 7 Dec. 1997. *General OneFile.* Web. 21 Nov. 2012.

Singh, Amardeep. "A Closer Look at Dean Mahomet (1759–1850)." *Amardeep Singh.* Lehigh University, 6 Sept. 2006. Web. 20 Nov. 2012.

Further Reading

Abu-Lughod, Ibrahim. *The Arab Rediscovery of Europe.* Princeton: Princeton University Press, 1963. Print.

Fisher, Michael H. *Politics of the British Annexation of India.* Delhi: Oxford University Press, 1993. Print.

"Owner of First Curry House in Britain." *Times* (London) 30 July 2003: 10. *Academic OneFile.* Web. 22 Nov. 2012.

Sattin, Anthony. "The Original Spice Boy; Biography." *Sunday Times* (London) 28 Sept. 1997: 10. *Academic OneFile.* Web. 22 Nov. 2012.

Sutherland, Lucy S. *The East India Company in Eighteenth Century Politics.* Oxford: Oxford University Press, 1952. Print.

Gerald Carpenter

War Experiences

Among You Taking Notes: The Wartime Diary of Naomi Mitchison, 1939–1945   235
   by Naomi Mitchison

Army Life in a Black Regiment by Thomas Wentworth Higginson   238

The Boer War Diary of Sol Plaatje: An African at Mafeking   241
   by Solomon Tshekisho Plaatje

Brokenburn: The Journal of Kate Stone, 1861–1868 by Kate Stone   244

Diaries, 1915–1918 by Siegfried Sassoon   247

A Diary from Dixie by Mary Boykin Miller Chesnut   250

The Diary of Anne Frank by Anne Frank   253

The Diary of Sir Henry Slingsby by Sir Henry Slingsby   256

A Diary without Dates by Enid Bagnold   259

Journal, 1955–1962: Reflections on the French-Algerian War   262
   by Mouloud Feraoun

Nella Last's War: The Second World War Diaries of Housewife, 49 by Nella Last   265

A Pacifist's War: Diaries 1939–1945 by Frances Partridge   268

Shadows on My Heart: The Civil War Diary of Lucy Rebecca Buck of Virginia   271
   by Lucy Buck

Thura's Diary: A Young Girl's Life in War-Torn Baghdad by Thura Al-Windawi   275

A Woman at War by Molly Moore   278

A Woman in Berlin: Eight Weeks in the Conquered City: A Diary by Anonymous   281

Among You Taking Notes
The Wartime Diary of Naomi Mitchison, 1939–1945
Naomi Mitchison

OVERVIEW

Among You Taking Notes: The Wartime Diary of Naomi Mitchison, 1939–1945, published in 1985, chronicles the Scottish activist and author's life during World War II, interspersing her view of the multinational struggle with observations about the people directly around her. Mitchison's prolific literary career began in 1923, when she was twenty-six years old, and she went on to publish more than ninety works in a wide range of genres, from historical novels to science fiction. Her wartime diary was preserved by the Mass Observation Project, which was designed to record daily life in Britain through personal journals, before being published.

Mitchison's diary writing provides a specific, unflinchingly, and detailed rendering of life on the home front during World War II. In particular, it offers insights into the impact of the war on feminist and socialist concerns. Although the Mass Observation Project has since been criticized by scholars for methodological sloppiness, class bias, and a general disregard for privacy, its collected testimonials have proved to be invaluable to historians of wartime Britain. As for Mitchison, her novels, diaries, and memoirs are recognized as a significant part of literary, Scottish, and feminist histories.

HISTORICAL AND LITERARY CONTEXT

The Mass Observation Project was started in 1937 in reaction to the 1936 abdication of King Edward VIII, who gave up the British throne in order to marry the American divorcée Wallis Simpson. Believing that the press reports on the public's reaction to this event were inaccurate, anthropologist Thomas Harrison, poet Charles Madge, and documentary filmmaker Humphrey Jennings began a project to create "an anthropology of ourselves/our own people." In August 1939 Mass Observation began collecting diaries from members of the general public at its London offices in an attempt to document wartime life for the British government. Mitchison's diary was among those collected.

Mitchison, a left-leaning member of an old Scottish family, records in her diary that she "felt sick" about the September 1939 declaration of England's entry into World War II. She had been politically active prior to the outbreak of hostilities, working for her husband's 1931 election campaign and, in 1932, visiting the Soviet Union on behalf of the socialist Fabian Society. She herself had run for Parliament as a Labour Party candidate in 1935. In addition to her socialist politics, Mitchison held fairly radical views on feminist issues such as contraception, sexual activity, and eugenics. During the war she spent the majority of her time on the family estate of Carradale, physically distant from the conflict, although she opened her home to both refugees and evacuees. She concludes the diary project with this pessimistic remark: "Well here is the end of the war, and the end of this diary … all older and tired."

Among You Taking Notes is part of a body of autobiographical writing produced by women during World War II. Other prominent texts in this tradition include the diaries of Nella Last; Vera Brittain; Anne Garnett; Clara Milburn; and Hermione, Countess of Ranfurly, each of whom open up a gendered perspective on violence, politics, and wartime life. Mitchison's diary is unique within the genre, however, due to the literary attention it attracted because of her career as a novelist.

The interplay between life and writing was a subject of particular interest for Mitchison, who published both fiction and memoir over the course of her long life. *Among You Taking Notes* offers a portrait of the English wartime literary scene, mentioning meetings with Stevie Smith, E. M. Forster, Cyril Connolly, Edith Summerskill, Nye Bevan, and Jennie Lee, as well as featuring correspondence with Leonard Woolf, Virginia Woolf's husband. Her diary can be seen as laying the autobiographical groundwork for her memoirs, *Small Talk: Memories of an Edwardian Childhood* (1973), *All Change Here: Girlhood and Marriage* (1975), and *You May Well Ask: A Memoir, 1920–1940* (1979).

THEMES AND STYLE

The themes of *Among You Taking Notes* include reflections on politics, family, education, marital sexuality, writing, and literature. The diary also includes a harrowing account of her emotional state in the aftermath of the death of her seventh child, Clemency, in 1940. Mitchison examines the impact of gender and class

❖ Key Facts

Time Period:
Late 20th Century

Relevant Historical Events:
World War II; impact of gender and class on the home front

Nationality:
Scottish

Keywords:
war; socialism; feminism

In this 1989 photograph, playwright Lord Willis, author Naomi Mitchison, and poet Sir Stephen Spender display a reprint of the "Black Book" originally compiled by the Gestapo in 1940. The book included the three writers in a "most wanted" list of people who were to be arrested immediately if the Nazis succeeded in conquering Great Britain. © UK HISTORY/ALAMY

on home-front happenings, describing her frustration with the attitudes of the "kitchen-proud" women around her. She chronicles her feelings of isolation and removal from the war-torn world as she struggles against restrictive gender and behavioral norms. During the bombing of London, she writes that "one feels one should be there." Overall, her diary reveals her angst about the passive role that circumstances forced her to play during the conflict. She explicitly links family life, geopolitical conflict, and creative processes: Clemency would have provided "an excuse to be out of the war, out of destruction, still on the side of creation; now that's over."

In her 1985 foreword to *Among You Taking Notes,* Mitchison lays out her motivation for the project: to create "a picture of how one family and friends lived during this period of history." In a September 1939 entry, she states a secondary purpose, declaring, "I shall write my diary and keep sane." Later entries show that she did not always succeed on that front. For example, she writes, "I have my human moments of wanting to talk about myself—instead of just putting it into this diary." Mitchison, however, also records feelings of positive accomplishment with regard to the project: "I felt … it was worth doing for itself, not just because it was a kind of thing to hold on to." *Among You Taking Notes* does not reproduce the entirety of Mitchison's diary, which contains more than a million words. As she writes in the 1985 foreword, "Who is going to read all that? Not me."

Mitchison's style is direct, bold, and confessional. She is explicit in her writing about sexuality, to a degree that would have been considered improper for a woman of her position: "I'm 44 and should know what I'm doing by now. I can think clearly and unresentfully of my lovers in the past, certainly of their naked bodies." Mitchison assumes that her reader will follow her drift, and she writes with little exposition. For example, she mentions more than 250 people over the course of her diaries, frequently only giving their first names. Her sentences are often disjointed or fragmentary as she records her thoughts with immediacy that transcends the bounds of strict grammar. Ideas often follow one another in quick succession, briefly summarized and juxtaposed with personal and political concerns.

CRITICAL DISCUSSION
Mitchison's diaries were not published until 1985, when a revival of critical interest in her life and work additionally led to the republication of a number of her novels. Editor Dorothy Sheridan played a key role in readying them for publication; she had been continuously involved with the Mass Observation archives since 1974. Early reviews celebrated the addition of Mitchison's diaries to the store of information about her life and creative processes. While Donald Smith's 1987 review in the *Scottish Historical Review* questions the usefulness of *Among You Taking Notes* as a viable historical resource, he concludes that what the work "lacks in elegant recall is more than made up for by raw emotional impact."

Mitchison's position as a scion of a creative and active family, her place in British literary traditions, and her clearly articulated radical political consciousness have come together to render *Among You Taking Notes* a significant archive for research on women during the war and wartime life in general. As Sandra M. Gilbert and Susan Gubar suggest in their book *No Man's Land: The Place of the Woman Writer in the Twentieth Century,* the coming of World War II on the heels of World War I created widespread responses of cynicism and despair among women, leading to renewed female antiwar activism and writing. In the realm of women's wartime voices, Mitchison's diary offers self-aware and insightful analyses of the connection between gender and war.

Among You Taking Notes is often read alongside other Mass Observation diaries, such as Karen Meschia's "Naomi the Poet and Nella the Housewife: Finding a Space to Write From," which has a working-class bent and stands in contrast to the upper-class Mitchison's writing, or Brian Street and David Bloom's *Writing Ourselves: Mass Observation and Literacy Practices* (2000), which examines the social implications of a government program encouraging private citizens to write reports on each other. Other scholarship positions the diary alongside Mitchison's fiction—or more broadly, women's wartime writing—as in Penny Summerfield's *Reconstructing Women's Wartime Lives* (1998) or Gill Plain's *Women's Fiction of the Second World War. Gender, Power and Resistance* (1996).

BIBLIOGRAPHY

Sources

Gilbert, Sandra M., and Susan Gubar. *No Man's Land: The Place of the Woman Writer in the Twentieth Century.* Vol. 3. New York: Binghamton, 1994.

Madge, Charles. "Anthropology at Home." *New Statesman* 2 Jan. 1937. Print.

Meschia, Karen. "Naomi the Poet and Nella the Housewife: Finding a Space to Write From." *Miranda.* Miranda, 13 Jul. 2010. Web. 22 Dec. 2012.

Sheridan, Dorothy, ed. *Among You Taking Notes. The Wartime Diary of Naomi Mitchison, 1939–1945.* London: Victor Gollancz, 1985. Print.

Smith, Donald. Rev. of *Among You Taking Notes: The Wartime Diary of Naomi Mitchison,* by Naomi Mitchison. *Scottish Historical Review* Oct. 1987: 235–36. Print.

NAOMI MITCHISON'S IMAGINATIVE REACH

Although Naomi Mitchison's creative works span a variety of genres, her oeuvre is connected by her imaginative dramatic reaches, either in the direction of early Roman history or toward the experience of life on other continents and even outer space. While Mitchison's early works *The Conquered* (1923) and *Cloud Cuckoo Land* (1925) are both set before the sixth century BCE, dealing with Julius Caesar's Gallic Wars and the ancient Greek Peloponnesian War, respectively, her 1962 novel *Memoirs of a Spacewoman* is considered to be one of the first major works in the tradition of feminist science fiction.

Her 1931 novel *The Corn King and the Spring Queen,* regarded by many as her finest work, combines historical fiction with fantasy in its juxtaposition of three different cultures. During the 1960s Mitchison visited and was adopted into the Botswanan Bakgatla tribe, and many of her later writings reflect the impact of this cross-cultural connection, particularly *Sunrise Tomorrow: A Story of Botswana* (1973) and *A Life for Africa: The Story of Bram Fischer* (1973), which seek to bring an understanding of African life to Western readers.

Further Reading

Benson, Jill. *Naomi Mitchison. A Biography.* London: Pandora, 1992. Print.

Higonnet, Margaret R., et al., eds. *Behind the Lines: Gender and the Two World Wars.* New Haven, Conn.: Yale University Press, 1987. Print.

Middelboe, Penelope, et al. *We Shall Never Surrender: Wartime Diaries 1939–1945.* New York: Pan, 2012. Print.

Schofield, Mary-Anne. "Underground Lives. Women's Personal Narratives. 1939–1945." *Literature and Exile.* Ed. David Bevan. Atlanta: Rodopi BV, 1990. 121–48. Print.

Street, Brian, and David Bloom. *Writing Ourselves: Mass-Observation and Literacy Practices.* Cresskill, N.Y.: Hampton, 2000. Print.

Summerfield, Penny. *Reconstructing Women's Wartime Lives.* Manchester, U.K.: Manchester University Press, 1998. Print.

Carina Saxon

Army Life in a Black Regiment

Thomas Wentworth Higginson

Key Facts

Time Period:
Mid-19th Century

Relevant Historical Events:
Civil War; Reconstruction; growth of the abolition movement

Nationality:
American

Keywords:
war; race; abolition

OVERVIEW

Composed by Thomas Wentworth Higginson (1823–1911), *Army Life in a Black Regiment,* published in 1869, recounts the author's experiences as the colonel of one of the first African American Civil War regiments, the First Carolina Volunteers. Assembled in part from sketches Higginson published in the *Atlantic Monthly* between 1864 and 1867 and drawing on a journal the author kept during the war, *Army Life* is essentially chronological. However, unlike many memoirists, Higginson, a white man, focuses less on himself and his experiences than on his observations of those around him, particularly the character of his black soldiers, in order to make an argument for African Americans' readiness for full citizenship.

Although *Army Life* recounts events during the Civil War, it was written during Reconstruction (1863–77), the post–Civil War period when Americans were negotiating how, and to what extent, former slaves would be absorbed into the body politic. Higginson's recollections of his soldiers' relatively quick transformation from former slaves to disciplined fighting men served as evidence that former slaves were ready for full citizenship. Today *Army Life* remains a valuable record of the role of African American soldiers in the Civil War and racial ideas held by the white officers who led black regiments.

HISTORICAL AND LITERARY CONTEXT

Higginson's leadership of an African American regiment was the product of two decades of activism. Born in Cambridge, Massachusetts, and educated at Harvard University and Harvard University Divinity School, Higginson lost his first pulpit in Newburyport due to his controversial antislavery stance. In the years that followed, he took an active part in the Underground Railroad and in 1856 led a party of settlers to Kansas, where the abolitionist struggle took violent form—though he did not participate in the violence. He also supported abolitionist John Brown's 1859 raid on the federal arsenal at Harpers Ferry. In accepting the colonelship of the First South Carolina Volunteers—who were drawn from recently freed slaves on the Sea Islands, located off the coast of South Carolina, and from slaves who had fled the South—Higginson felt he was fulfilling Brown's dream of leading a group of black men who would fight for their freedom.

The sketches that formed the nucleus of *Army Life* appeared in the mid-1860s, approximately the middle of the Reconstruction period, when the Fifteenth Amendment to the Constitution, which guaranteed black men the right to vote, was being debated and ratified. In this context, Higginson's recollections of former slaves' bravery, their willingness to fight for their own and others' freedom, and their general good conduct provided evidence that African Americans were deserving of and ready for full citizenship.

Army Life was among the first accounts of African American soldiers' contributions to the Civil War, although it had literary predecessors. William Wells Brown, a former slave and abolitionist author, published *The Negro in the American Rebellion: His Heroism and His Fidelity* in 1867. In 1861 Higginson published a series of sketches in the *Atlantic Monthly* on historic slave rebellions and their leaders, including Denmark Vesey and Nat Turner. Interest in northerners' work with residents of the Sea Islands was also fed by a pair of sketches published in 1864 in the *Atlantic Monthly* by Charlotte Forten, a free black from Massachusetts who was teaching former slaves on the Sea Islands. Like Higginson, Forten kept a journal during her time in the South.

Despite the timeliness of its publication, *Army Life* did not have any immediate appreciable effect on the American conversation about race. Higginson soon turned his activist energies to new causes, including women's rights, and devoted more of his time to literary work, including a complicated mentoring relationship with poet Emily Dickinson. It was not until the 1960s, when the civil rights movement generated renewed curiosity about African American history and prompted a reexamination of authors such as Higginson, that *Army Life* again attracted substantial public interest.

THEMES AND STYLE

Army Life alternates between two main themes: African Americans' success as soldiers and the soldiers' role as representatives of their race. While Higginson's military anecdotes and observations support the text's explicit argument for racial equality, his tendency to see his men as a racially defined group with particular, often

Come and Join Us Brothers, a nineteenth-century poster urging African Americans to volunteer for the Union Army in the Civil War. Abolitionist Thomas Wentworth Higginson led African Americans in that war and later wrote *Army Life in a Black Regiment*. © PETER NEWARK AMERICAN PICTURES/THE BRIDGEMAN ART LIBRARY

childlike characteristics sometimes undermines that argument. Nevertheless, his occasionally patriarchal view of the men under his command is clearly distinguishable from that of slaveholders, who also figured themselves as patriarchs of large families. Whereas slaveholders viewed their property as permanent children, unable to take charge of their own lives, Higginson sees military service as an opportunity for former slaves to gain skills they will use in freedom. "The increased self-respect of army life," he writes in the conclusion of *Army Life*, "fitted them to do the duties of civil life."

While parts of *Army Life* are presented as excerpts from Higginson's diary, the book is clearly designed to tell the story of the First Carolina Volunteers in a way that entertains an audience and reflects well on Higginson, his men, and the majority of his fellow officers. Higginson makes a literary and historical argument for his use of diary excerpts. "There is nothing like a diary for freshness—at least so I think," he declares in chapter 1, explaining that during his first months with the regiment, he had kept "a fragmentary journal, to send home, recording the many off or novel aspects of the new experience." A professional author, he no doubt saw his time in the South as an opportunity for gathering material and participating in a cause he supported.

The structure of *Army Life* follows the rhythm of regimental life, with chapters recounting expeditions ("Up the St. Mary's," "Up the St. John's," "Up the Edisto") or life in camp. Some of the chapters set in camp—especially "The Baby of the Regiment" and "Negro Spirituals"—allow Higginson to reflect at greater length on particular aspects of his experience. "The Baby of the Regiment," which serves mostly as a charming interlude that underlines some of the more pleasant aspects of southern life, also implicitly refutes the idea that black men are uncouth or dangerous by emphasizing the safety and comfort with which a white baby girl and her mother live among the black troops. "Negro Spirituals" gives Higginson the opportunity to follow the example of Scottish author Sir Walter Scott in recording an oral tradition, while also commenting on African American religion.

CRITICAL DISCUSSION

Initial reaction to *Army Life* was mixed. Scholar Tilden Edelstein records that Theodore Tilton, a longtime radical abolitionist, praised the book in the *Independent* but wished it had appeared in time to play a more significant role in political debates during Reconstruction. William Dean Howells, writing for the *Atlantic Monthly* in 1869, suggests that Americans were tired

THE FIRST SOUTH CAROLINA VOLUNTEERS

Although less well known than the Massachusetts Fifty-Fourth, the regiment depicted in the movie *Glory*, the first South Carolina Volunteers played a vital role in African American military history. Higginson's men were recruited from runaway slaves and from former slaves on the Sea Islands. Captured by Union troops early in the war, the area hosted several experiments in readying former slaves for full citizenship. Ultimately, Sea Islanders' aspirations to own the land they had long worked were disappointed when the federal government sold it or gave it to others, including northern investors.

When Higginson assumed command of his regiment in late 1862, he and his men were pioneers: President Abraham Lincoln had not yet authorized widespread recruiting of African American soldiers in either the South or the North. In the early days of the war, Higginson's soldiers played multiple roles, as fighters, exemplars of African Americans' capacities, and recruiters of fellow former slaves. While the regiment spent much of the war on picket duty, participating in only a few battles, it served as early proof that black men could be disciplined soldiers and could participate in other aspects of the fight for equality, including protests against unequal pay for black soldiers.

of thinking about "a race with which" they had been "occupied a long time" but calls Higginson's work "excellent and charming literature."

Taken as literature, *Army Life* can be seen as the beginning of a turn toward realism in the literary depiction of war. As R. D. Madison argues in its 1997 edition, "*Army Life in a Black Regiment* drew American Romanticism across the war years and into Reconstruction, into a time when William De Forest was demythologizing the war in *Miss Ravenel's Conversion* (1867), considered the first novel of American realism." The American realist movement would eventually include such luminary authors as Mark Twain, Ambrose Bierce, Stephen Crane, and Howells. As Edelstein notes in *Strange Enthusiasm: A Life of Thomas Wentworth Higginson* (1968), Higginson believed there was sufficient remaining interest in *Army Life* to publish a revised edition in 1900, with a dedication acknowledging that the "ultimate civil equality" for which he and his men had fought was yet to be realized.

As a historical document, Higginson's book began to draw renewed interest in the 1960s, with three reprint editions appearing between 1960 and 1962. According to Edelstein, "none of these editions emphasize the disparity in context, content, and form between Higginson's manuscript journals and *Army Life*," a subject that has occupied later historians and literary critics interested in Higginson's rhetorical choices. As Andre Fleche relates in an essay for *Civil War History* in 2005, critics of the late twentieth century also turned their attention to Higginson's approach to race, accusing *Army Life* of "giving in to what George Fredrickson has termed 'benign racialism' at best, and blatant paternalism and condescension at worst." More recently, critics including Fleche have pointed to Higginson's role in helping to create and perpetuate a memory of the Civil War that included—at least during the lives of white veterans—recollection of and respect for the contributions of black soldiers.

BIBLIOGRAPHY

Sources

Edelstein, Tilden G. *Strange Enthusiasm: A Life of Thomas Wentworth Higginson*. New Haven, Conn.: Yale University Press, 1968. Print.

Fleche, Andre M. "'Shoulder to Shoulder as Comrades Tried': Black and White Union Veterans and Civil War Memory." *Civil War History* 51.2 (2005): 175–201. *Project MUSE*. Web. 18 Dec. 2012.

Higginson, Thomas Wentworth. *Army Life in a Black Regiment and Other Writings*. Ed. R. D. Madison. New York: Penguin, 1997. Print.

Howells, William Dean. "Reviews and Literary Notices: Higginson's *Army Life in a Black Regiment*." *Atlantic Monthly* 24.145 (1869): 643–44. *Cornell University Library Making of America Collection*. Web. 28 Dec. 2012.

Further Reading

Brown, William Wells. *The Negro in the American Rebellion: His Heroism and His Fidelity*. Boston: Lee and Shepard, 1867. *Google Books*. Web. 28 Dec. 2012.

Foner, Eric. *Reconstruction: America's Unfinished Revolution, 1863–1877*. New York: Harper & Row, 1988. Print.

Grimke, Charlotte Forten. *The Journals of Charlotte Forten Grimke*. New York: Oxford University Press, 1988. Print.

Higginson, Thomas Wentworth. *The Complete Civil War Journal and Selected Letters of Thomas Wentworth Higginson*. Ed. Christopher Looby. Chicago: University of Chicago Press, 2000. Print.

———. *The Magnificent Activist: The Writings of Thomas Wentworth Higginson, 1823–1911*. Ed. Howard N. Meyer. Boston: Da Capo, 2000. Print.

Kytle, Ethan J. "From Body Reform to Reforming the Body Politic: Transcendentalism and the Militant Antislavery Career of Thomas Wentworth Higginson." *American Nineteenth Century History* 8.3 (2007): 325–50. *Academic Search Complete*. Web. 18 Dec. 2012.

Poole, W. Scott. "Memory and the Abolitionist Heritage: Thomas Wentworth Higginson and the Uncertain Meaning of the Civil War." *Civil War History* 51.2 (2005): 202–17. *Project MUSE*. Web. 27 Dec. 2012.

Cathy Saunders

The Boer War Diary of Sol Plaatje
An African at Mafeking
Solomon Tshekisho Plaatje

OVERVIEW

Written by black South African journalist, author, and political leader Solomon Tshekisho Plaatje, *The Boer War Diary of Sol Plaatje: An African at Mafeking* (1973) is a personal account of the great siege of Mafeking of 1899–1900. This firsthand report of an important battle in the Anglo-Boer War of 1899–1902 (also known as the South African War, or the Second Boer War) is notable as an early example of a major text written by a black South African in English. Plaatje's work provides a unique perspective of the siege and addresses several blind spots in standard histories of the battle.

The text, which takes the form of a private diary, was published approximately forty years after Plaatje's death. (Its existence was unknown until the original manuscript was discovered by Plaatje's grandson and gifted to anthropologist John Comaroff for part of his doctoral research.) As an early text in Plaatje's writing career, *Boer War Diary* can be taken as a precursor to Plaatje's other major texts *Mhudi* (1913) and *Native Life in South Africa* (1914) both in style and theme. Although usually overlooked in favor of those works, *Boer War Diary* remains a significant text in contemporary studies of South African history and culture.

HISTORICAL AND LITERARY CONTEXT

Plaatje's diaries are an important historical document of the Second Boer War, a defining moment of South African history that led to the unification of South Africa as a dominion of the British Empire in 1910. Among the principal causes of the war was the clash between British imperial ambition and Afrikaner nationalism in the independent states of the Orange Free State and Transvaal. The Afrikaners, or Boers, were colonists principally of Dutch descent, notorious for their independent spirit and, later, their leading role in the implementation of the racist policy of apartheid. Tensions were increased by the discovery of gold in 1886 in the Witwatersrand region (in Afrikaner territory and the basis of the city of Johannesburg).

At the outbreak of the war on October 11, 1899, the town of Mafeking was almost instantly besieged by Boer troops, whereupon the inhabitants were subjected to shortages of food and water. The successful defense of the town became a celebrated event in British imperial history. Plaatje was a firsthand witness to these events as a loyalist to the British defense of the city and was, according to Neil Parsons in his introduction to *Native Life in South Africa,* "one of the key players in the great siege as a magistrate's interpreter." In fact, Plaatje was responsible for collecting and translating the reports of a group of black African spies.

The Boer War Diary can be profitably read in conjunction with other firsthand accounts of the siege, including *The Siege of Mafeking* (1900) by J. Angus Hamilton of the *London Times;* the collected reports of special correspondent Filson Young of the *Manchester Guardian,* titled *The Relief of Mafeking* (1900); and the published diaries of Major F. D. Baillie and Trooper William Robertson Fuller. Plaatje's text also provides a point of comparison to famous texts by other participants in the war, including *The Great Boer War* (1900) by Arthur Conan Doyle (who volunteered as a doctor in the conflict) and *The Boer War* (1900) by Winston Churchill (a young army officer and newspaper correspondent).

Although *The Boer War Diary* remains somewhat obscure, Plaatje's subsequent influence on the political and cultural history of South Africa is incalculable. Along with Pixley ka Isaka Seme and John Dube, Plaatje established the South African Native National Congress in 1912, an organization that became the principal opposition group to apartheid, the African National Congress. Plaatje's text is an interesting point of comparison to *Mhudi* (1913), the first novel written in English by a black South African, and *Native Life in South Africa* (1914), an account of the effects of the Native Land Act of 1913 and the foundational work for black protest literature in South Africa.

THEMES AND STYLE

The Boer War Diary shows evidence of the great hope that the British Empire inspired in Plaatje, a man shaped foremost by his mission education and his belief that loyalty to the relatively liberal British would provide a better dispensation for the blacks of South Africa. Evidently, writes Elleke Boehmer in *Empire, the National, and the Postcolonial 1890–1920,* "the youthful Plaatje interpreted the war, and Mafeking's part in it, as a defence of the Cape/imperial principles he

❖ **Key Facts**

Time Period:
Late 19th to Early 20th Century

Relevant Historical Events:
Anglo-Boer War; growth of Afrikaner nationalism

Nationality:
South African

Keywords:
race; war; colonialism

Spion Kop, 1900, a chromolithograph by Neuman depicting the 1900 Battle of Spion Kop during the Boer War. South African writer, interpreter, and politician Solomon Tshekisho Plaatje chronicles the war in *The Boer War Diary of Sol T. Plaatje: An African at Mafeking.* © AFRICANA MUSEUM, JOHANNESBURG, SOUTH AFRICA/THE BRIDGEMAN ART LIBRARY

held so dear." (Plaatje later lost his faith in the British when the power of the country was effectively ceded to Afrikaner nationalist interests after the unification of South Africa in 1910.)

Plaatje apparently never intended *The Boer War Diary* to be published; his diary was meant as a strictly personal space to record the details of the siege and also explore his own relationship with British imperialism and how this represented the relationship of the British to the native population of Southern Africa more generally. The work shows Plaatje's characteristically exacting mind. His daily entries, for example, almost all contain a careful numeration of the shells fired from "Au Sanna" (the ninety-four-pound Creusot siege-gun used by the Boers in the bombardment of the town). Yet the entries also show the easy tone of Plaatje's other works. In *A History of South African Literature*, Christopher Heywood characterizes Plaatje's description of the "progress of the shells … [as being] as though they were engaged in an athletic contest."

Plaatje's works, including *Boer War Diary*, exemplify African authors' endeavors to fuse multiple traditions in their works, most notably the English literary and African oral conventions. Boehmer has identified Plaatje's *Native Life in South Africa*, for example, as having the style of a "layered verbal collage … [a] function of [Plaatje's] mission education combined with a powerful oral heritage." The combination of these features is certainly prefigured in *The Boer War Diary*. Heywood notes that Plaatje's work centers on the transposition of the specifically African oral tradition into prose work in English, citing the diary's similarity to Isaac Schapera's *Praise Poems of Tswana Chiefs* (1965) in its "ornate, condensed, and enigmatic style."

CRITICAL DISCUSSION

The impact of *The Boer War Diary* since its conception has been hampered considerably, of course, by the fact that its author did not intend for it to be published and by its disappearance for more than seventy years. Critical attention was scarce following the text's initial publication in 1973 and remained so for a subsequent edition published in 1990. However, scholar Jane Starfield suggests that some attention was given to the diary as part of the centennial anniversary of the Anglo-Boer War and the publication of a centennial edition of the text.

Peter Midgley, however, asserts in *Sol Plaatje: An Introduction* that "as [a] diarist, novelist, pamphleteer, translator, linguist, journalist, musician, politician and social critic, Sol Plaatje's impact on South African society is significant. His work is of interest to both literary and social historians as he is the only black South African to have kept an account of the Anglo-Boer War." Laura Chrisman further claims in *Postcolonial Contraventions* that Plaatje's "diary of the events [at Mafeking] is a valuable historical document, unique in its presentation of an African perspective."

As mentioned above, since its restoration to Plaatje's diffuse canon in 1973, the text has elicited little critical attention when taken in comparison to Plaatje's novel *Mhudi* and his classic travelogue *Native Life in South Africa.* Instead, the work appears critically as either a point of comparison to these later texts or as a curiosity related specifically to the siege at Mafeking. More broadly, Plaatje is of interest to postcolonial critics as a figure of cross-cultural indeterminacy. For instance, Boehmer discusses Plaatje's identity as a British colonial subject "caught up in all the contradictory *agon* of being 'civilized' and articulate by Western standards, but from a colonial point of view never quite adequately so because of his Africaness."

BIBLIOGRAPHY

Sources

Boehmer, Elleke. *Empire, the National, and the Postcolonial 1890–1920: Resistance in Interaction.* Oxford: Oxford University Press, 2003. Print.

Chrisman, Laura. *Postcolonial Contraventions: Cultural Readings of Race, Imperialism, and Transnationalism.* Manchester, U.K.: Manchester University Press, 2003. Print.

Comaroff, John. "Introduction." *Mafeking Diary: A Black Man's View of a White Man's War,* by Solomon Tshekisho Plaatje. Cambridge, U.K.: Meridor, 1990. 5–13. Print.

Heywood, Christopher. *A History of South African Literature.* Cambridge, U.K.: Cambridge University Press, 2004. Print.

Midgley, Peter. *Sol Plaatje: An Introduction.* Grahamstown: National English Literary Museum, 1997. Print.

Parsons, Neil. "Introduction." *Native Life in South Africa, before and since the European War and the Boer Rebellion,* by Solomon Tshekisho Plaatje. New Haven, Conn.: Yale University Press, 1993. 2–5. Print.

Plaatje, Solomon Tshekisho. *Mafeking Diary: A Black Man's View of a White Man's War.* Cambridge, U.K.: Meridor, 1990. Print.

Further Reading

Plaatje, Solomon Tshekisho. *Native Life in South Africa, Before and since the European War and the Boer Rebellion.* New Haven, Conn.: Yale University Press, 1993. Print.

THE SIEGE OF MAFEKING

The siege of Mafeking—lasting 217 days, from October 13, 1899, to May 17, 1990—was the most famous battle of the Anglo-Boer War of 1899–1902. At the outbreak of the war, the town was overrun by Boer troops that isolated the populace, which subsequently endured extreme hunger. In *The Boer War Diary of Sol Plaatje: An African at Mafeking,* for example, Solomon Tshekisho Plaatje tells of a local Zambesi digging up the corpses of unlicensed dogs for food.

The siege was eventually lifted when British and Australian reinforcements turned the tide of the conflict. The successful and unexpected defense of the city became a celebrated moment in British imperial history and was popularly characterized by accounts of the daring deeds of Robert Baden-Powell and his men. Though the Anglo-Boer War would continue for about two more years, the Boer failure to capture the towns of Kimberley, Ladysmith, and Mafeking while having a numerical advantage over the British eventually proved a decisive moment in the conflict.

———. *Sol Plaatje: Selected Writings.* Ed. Brian Willan. Athens: Ohio University Press, 1996. Print.

———. *Mhudi.* Ed. Stephen Gray. London: Penguin, 2005. Print.

Rall, Maureen. *Peaceable Warrior: The Life and Times of Sol T. Plaatje.* Kimberly, South Africa: Sol Plaatje Educational Trust, 2003. Print.

Starfield, Jane. "Rethinking Sol Plaatje's *Mafeking Diary.*" Rev. of *The Mafeking Diary of Sol Plaatje,* by Solomon Tshekisho Plaatje. *Journal of Southern Africa Studies* 27.4 (2001): 856–63. Print.

Van Wyk, Chris. *Sol Plaatje.* Kelvin, South Africa: Awareness, 2003. Print.

Willan, Brian. *Sol Plaatje: South African Nationalist, 1876–1932.* Los Angeles: University of California Press, 1984. Print.

Franklyn Hyde

BROKENBURN
The Journal of Kate Stone, 1861–1868
Kate Stone

Key Facts

Time Period:
Mid-19th Century

Relevant Historical Events:
Civil War; establishment of the Confederacy; Union victory

Nationality:
American

Keywords:
war; women's writing; rebellion

OVERVIEW

An American Civil War diary written by a young woman of the Louisiana planter class, *Brokenburn: The Journal of Kate Stone, 1861–1868* provides a firsthand account of civilian life in the Confederacy. Stone maintained the journal regularly from the start of the war to its close, making her first entry in May 1861, when her older brother, William, left to join the fighting, and her last entry in November 1865, when she and her family returned to their cotton plantation, Brokenburn, in Madison Parish, Louisiana, after having spent more than two years in exile in Texas. Stone added summary sections in 1867 and 1868 describing the family's efforts to rebuild the property, which had been devastated by neglect and the ravages of Yankee soldiers and former slaves. In 1900, seven years before her death, Stone recopied the diary on ledger sheets and attached a retrospective preface to the manuscript, which she then placed in the care of her daughter, Amy J. Holmes, who in turn allowed Texas educator and folklorist John Q. Anderson to publish in 1955.

Upon its first appearance, Stone's journal was praised as a vivid account of conditions and attitudes on the home front in the trans-Mississippi region of the Confederacy, an area west of the Mississippi River that included Missouri, Arkansas, Texas, and portions of Louisiana often neglected in histories of the Civil War South. The work has since been reevaluated from the perspectives of the civil rights and women's movements and within the context of a growing body of literature devoted to the social history of the Civil War.

HISTORICAL AND LITERARY CONTEXT

Before the start of the Civil War, Stone enjoyed the typical life of a wealthy white southerner who resided on a large cotton plantation. Her mother had purchased Brokenburn following her husband's death in 1855 and had managed to amass a fortune that included 1,260 acres of land and 150 slaves. The oldest of seven children, Stone had been educated by a private tutor and was looking forward to a full social life that included parties, courtship, and a European tour in 1862. She was twenty years old in April 1861 when the Confederate artillery bombarded the Union-occupied Fort Sumter in the harbor of Charleston, South Carolina, bringing the long-standing divisions between the northern and southern states on the issue of slavery to civil war.

Brokenburn details the increasingly difficult life of Stone's family, neighbors, and friends as the fortunes of the Confederacy declined. Life remained relatively unchanged at Brokenburn for the first year of the war, though most able-bodied men had departed for the front. As the war dragged on, food and other commodities became scarce, and news reached Brokenburn that Stone's younger brother, Walter, had died in the fighting and her uncle, Ashburn, had succumbed to yellow fever while with the army near Vicksburg, Mississippi. By early 1863, when the area around Brokenburn had become strategic to Union General Ulysses S. Grant's plan to divide the Confederacy along the Mississippi River, Stone and her family were forced to flee their property.

Hundreds of diaries were kept during the Civil War by men on the battlefields as well as by women confined to the home front who were fully aware of the momentousness of the times in which they lived. Many of these journals were published in the years immediately following the war. Dozens of women's diaries, however, were not made public until late in the twentieth century when the effects of the women's liberation movement intruded on Civil War scholarship and demanded that women's contributions be recognized. *Brokenburn* benefited from this flood of interest in women's experience of the Civil War and was reissued in 1972 and again in 1995 by the Louisiana State University Press as part of their Library of Southern Civilization series.

On March 17, 1955, almost 10,000 people gathered in Tallulah, Louisiana, to celebrate the initial publication of *Brokenburn* with a parade and a ceremonial presentation of the first copy of the book to Stone's daughter. Enthusiastic reviews of the work praised it as a worthy successor to the journals of the most famous female diarists of the Confederacy, South Carolinian Mary Boykin Chesnut and fellow Louisianian Sarah Morgan. These and the writings of many other female diarists of the period have now been reassessed as part of the new scholarly focus on the Civil War as a social and cultural phenomenon distinct from its significance as a military and political event.

Houma, a plantation in Louisiana. Living in a similar home during the Civil War, Kate Stone led a privileged existence until the Union Army entered the region. Under increasing duress, the Stone family fled to Texas, arriving as penniless refugees. © JAMES RANDKLEV/GETTY IMAGES

THEMES AND STYLE

Brokenburn describes the hardships endured by Stone and her family as the Civil War encroaches upon their privileged existence. The earliest entries, written when the war seemed remote, describe life as it had always been; there are accounts of crop management, social activities, church services, and household chores. As Grant's armies begin their assault on the Mississippi River, however, the Stone family endures depredation and abuse. Yankee scavengers roam throughout northern Louisiana, stealing dwindling food supplies, threatening to burn plantations, and encouraging slaves to revolt. In one of the most highly praised portions of the journal, Stone describes her family's harrowing flight through the Louisiana bayous to Texas to escape the invading Union armies. The second half of the journal is largely devoted to the Stones' life as refugees in Texas. Stone registers disgust with the primitive housing conditions on the frontier and the boorish manners of the Texans, who greatly resent the influx of refugees from Arkansas, Louisiana, and Missouri. Yet she gradually comes to terms with her new life of deprivation. She makes some friends, occupies her time sewing uniforms for the soldiers, and meets the man she will marry, Confederate Officer Henry Bry Holmes.

Stone was an ardent southern patriot, and her journal is throughout a defense of the Confederacy and the plantation lifestyle. She expresses resentment at being confined to the home front and channels her enthusiasm for the Confederate cause in the pages of her journal. She writes on June 10, 1861, "Oh! to see and be in it all. I hate weary days of inaction. But what can women do but wait and suffer?" In her retrospective preface, she consigns the journal to posterity: "How I wish I could write well so that this old life could live in the imagination of my children." Despite Stone's nostalgia for the Old South, her attitude toward slavery is ambivalent. Unlike many members of her class, she does not express surprise that once-loyal slaves would choose to run away when given the opportunity. But she nonetheless blames the Yankees for exacerbating the slaves' hostility toward their former owners; she notes on September 5, 1864, after freed slaves have entered military service for the North, that "the Paternal Government at Washington has done all in its power to incite a general insurrection throughout the South, in the hopes of thus getting rid of the women and children in one grand holocaust."

Reviewers characterize Stone's prose as unpretentious, often chatty, and strikingly vivid in its descriptions. They rarely fail to remark upon the fluctuations in the tone of the journal, as Stone's initial optimism and confidence in a swift Confederate victory give way to desperation and increasing contempt for the North. For example, Otis A. Singletary noted in his July 1956 review for the *Southwestern Historical Quarterly* that "because of the intensity of her devotion, [Stone] was an excellent emotional barometer, sensitively recording the various mental stages ranging from the fierce joy of the revolutionists to the brooding despair of the vanquished." Stone's entries for the spring of 1865 are especially bitter and vindictive. Hearing of General Robert E. Lee's surrender, she despairs, "*Conquered, Submission, Subjugation* are words

A SOUTHERN PATRIOT

Stone lost two younger brothers and an uncle in the Civil War. Her older brother, William, survived the fighting to return home and oversee the rehabilitation of Brokenburn plantation. Flooding, an infestation of cotton worm, and high labor costs led to the loss of Brokenburn within a few years after the war. William then moved the family to another plantation in Yazoo County, Mississippi. When the house there was destroyed by fire, along with the five hundred dollars William had saved for Kate's trousseau, the family once again moved. Kate married Henry Bry Holmes in 1869, and the couple migrated back to Madison Parish, Louisiana, where they built a house in Tallulah. Only two of their four children survived to adulthood.

In an essay on Stone in *Louisiana Women* (2009), Mary Farmer-Kaiser notes that emancipation and the Confederate defeat forced women of the planter class to construct new identities. She writes of Stone, "Beyond the Victorian roles of dutiful wife and devoted mother, Kate also came to embrace a new civic role for herself." Stone was the founder of the Madison Infantry Chapter of the United Daughters of the Confederacy and worked to have a granite monument in honor of the fallen Confederate soldiers of Madison County erected on the grounds of the courthouse in Tallulah. The monument was dedicated in 1890.

that burn into my heart…. [We] will be slaves, yes slaves, of the Yankee Government. The degradation seems more than we can bear." Learning of the assassination of President Abraham Lincoln, she unleashes more venom: "All honor to J. Wilkes Booth who has rid the world of a tyrant and made himself famous for generations."

CRITICAL DISCUSSION

When *Brokenburn* first appeared in 1955, it was widely admired as an important contribution to the little-documented refugee experience in the western states of the Confederacy. The eminent literary critic Edmund Wilson included a discussion of Stone's diary, along with those of Chesnut and Dawson, in his 1962 *Patriotic Gore: Studies in the Literature of the American Civil War*, and Mary Elizabeth Massey quoted liberally from Stone's journal in her 1964 *Refugee Life in the Confederacy*.

The focus of later criticism of *Brokenburn* has shifted from that of these early assessments, which generally place *Brokenburn* within the context of military campaigns and Confederate partisanship. As Sarah Woodfolk Wiggins noted in her June 1973 review of *Brokenburn* for the *Journal of American History*, "The first edition of the diary was praised for its description of refugee life in the trans-Mississippi Confederacy. Historical perspectives have shifted since 1955, and this second edition will be valued as an important commentary on slaves, overseers, and women in the Confederacy."

In her introduction to the 1995 edition of *Brokenburn*, Drew Gilpin Faust extolled *Brokenburn* for its challenge to ideals of Victorian domesticity that had dominated in the antebellum South. She writes:

> Kate Stone was a young woman in her own right, with her own set of experiences; she was not simply a window into the impact of military maneuvers or a mouthpiece for the politicians of her class. The Civil War Kate Stone recorded in her diary offers an invaluable portrait of the Confederate home front, of the world of women war created, of war's challenges to accustomed privileges of race and class as well as assumptions and delineations of gender…. For Stone, as for hundreds of other Confederate women, diary keeping would provide a means of participation in the war, a way of resisting the marginalization they felt because of their exclusion as females from "the tented field."

BIBLIOGRAPHY

Sources

Farmer-Kaiser, Mary. "Sarah Katherine (Kate) Stone." *Louisiana Women: Their Lives and Times*. Ed. Janet Allured and Judith F. Gentry. Athens: University of Georgia Press, 2009. 73–93. Print.

Faust, Drew Gilpin. Introduction. *The Journal of Kate Stone, 1861–1868*. By Kate Stone. Ed. John Q. Anderson. Baton Rouge: Louisiana State University Press, 1995. xxix–xl. Print.

Singletary, Otis A. Rev. of *Brokenburn: The Journal of Kate Stone, 1861–1868*, by Kate Stone. *Southwestern Historical Quarterly* 60.1 (1956): 183–85. JSTOR. Web. 22 Dec. 2012.

Stone, Kate. *Brokenburn: The Journal of Kate Stone, 1861–1868*. Ed. John Q. Anderson. Baton Rouge: Louisiana State University Press, 1995. Print.

Wiggins, Sarah Woodfolk. Rev. of *Brokenburn: The Journal of Kate Stone, 1861–1868*, by Kate Stone. *Journal of American History* 60.1 (1973): 137–38. JSTOR. Web. 20 Dec. 2012.

Further Reading

Anderson, John Q. Introduction. *Brokenburn: The Journal of Kate Stone, 1861–1868*. By Kate Stone. Ed. John Q. Anderson. Baton Rouge: Louisiana State University Press, 1995. xvii–xxviii. Print.

Chesnut, Mary Boykin. *Mary Chesnut's Diary*. New York: Penguin, 2011. Print.

Dawson, Sarah. *The Diary of a Southern Woman*. Ed. Charles East. New York: Touchstone, 1992. Print.

Juncker, Clara. "Confederate Languagescapes: Kate Stone's Brokenburn." *Southern Quarterly* 34.4 (1996): 37–42. MLA International Bibliography. Web. 19 Dec. 2012.

Massey, Mary Elizabeth. *Refugee Life in the Confederacy*. Baton Rouge: Louisiana State University Press, 1964. Print.

Wilson, Edmund. "Three Confederate Ladies: Kate Stone, Sarah Morgan, Mary Chesnut." *Patriotic Gore: Studies in the Literature of the American Civil War*. New York: Norton, 1994. 258–98. Print.

Janet Mullane

DIARIES, 1915–1918
Siegfried Sassoon

OVERVIEW

First published in 1983, Englishman Siegfried Sassoon's *Diaries, 1915–1918,* in which he chronicles his experiences in the trenches of the World War I battlefields, is among the most notable published diaries from the period. In addition to being one of the best-known poets of World War I, Sassoon was a hero who earned the Military Cross for "conspicuous gallantry." However, his view of the war contrasted with the heroic popular image of the soldier fighting for his country, as reflected in his diary entry from February 22, 1917: "For the soldier is no longer a noble figure; he is merely a writhing insect among this ghastly folly of destruction."

Sassoon's diaries were mostly written on the battlefields of northern France and in military hospitals, camps, and barracks. The three volumes were published in the early 1980s, edited by Rupert Hart-Davis. The 1915–18 volume includes Sassoon's period in the hospital in 1917, his refusal to go back to the battlefield, his treatment for "shell shock" (now known as combat stress reaction), and his subsequent return to combat, only to be wounded again in July 1918. The work underpins the sentiment of his antiwar poetry. He relates the deaths of David Thomas, with whom he was in love, and describes horrific scenes yet somehow also manages to read Thomas Hardy and publish a book of poetry. Today, the diary provides scholars with a way to better understand both his life and poetry.

HISTORICAL AND LITERARY CONTEXT

Although the diaries were not written specifically for publication, they contextualize Sassoon's developing poetic voice and his changing attitude to the war. The patriotic zeal that gripped England when World War I began prompted Sassoon to enlist not long before his twenty-eighth birthday in 1914. By 1917, however, the bitter realities of trench warfare had dissolved this optimism. Yet despite a growing pacifist movement, which included such public figures as the philosopher Bertrand Russell, Sassoon was appalled by the lack of awareness in England of the suffering of the troops. His diary entry from June 15, 1917, contains his statement against the war and was read to the British Parliament on July 30, 1917. It declares that the war "upon which I entered as a war of defence and liberation, has now become a war of aggression and conquest."

Discussing Sassoon's published works, such as the fictionalized *Memoirs of a Fox-Hunting Man* (1928) and *Sherston's Progress* (1936), Rupert Hart-Davis points out in his introduction to the 1915–18 volume that "close examination of these [earlier] books with the diaries shows that they are faithful records of his experiences." Sassoon also wrote three volumes of more conventional autobiography, but the directness of the diaries gives his experiences a raw and personal edge, such as when he describes the war as a conspiracy and explains that it is "bad form" for soldiers to tell the truth about it. In addition, the diaries contain poems that were never published in his lifetime as well as drafts of his better-known verse.

The historical context of the diaries can be seen in the works of near-contemporaries such as Enid Bagnold and Vera Brittain and the poetry of Wilfred Owen, who was also an Englishman and World War I soldier. During the late 1970s and early 1980s, writings about the war, including Brittain's memoir *Testament of Youth*

✥ Key Facts

Time Period:
Early 20th Century

Relevant Historical Events:
World War I; Sassoon's service in the British military

Nationality:
English

Keywords:
war; poetry; trauma

Author Siegfried Sassoon in 1915, the first year covered in his diaries.
© GEORGE C BERESFORD/GETTY IMAGES

SIEGFRIED SASSOON: "MAD JACK"

Siegfried Sassoon grew up in the privileged world of the landed gentry in Cheshire, England, and later Kent, England. He enjoyed outdoor sports such as fox hunting and point-to-point racing. Just before World War I was declared, when he was twenty-seven, he volunteered for the military and became known as a fierce, gallant officer who was admired by his men but whose bravery bordered on reckless.

In April 1916 Sassoon was grieving for David Thomas, a young officer who had traveled with him to France and with whom he was in love. Perhaps because of this grief, he undertook an almost suicidal task, going alone into no-man's-land to bring back the wounded and dying. He was awarded the Military Cross for valor and became known as "Mad Jack." He contracted gastroenteritis in July of that year and was sent home to England, where he became convinced that the war was being fought for reasons of imperialist expansion rather than defense. He made a public statement condemning the war but was saved from imprisonment by the poet Robert Graves, who persuaded the authorities to treat him for "shell shock." Though Sassoon returned to battle in 1918, he continued to hold his antiwar views, as evidenced by his best-known poem, "Counter-Attack."

(1933), began to find a new audience. In response to this growing interest, an anthology of women's poetry from the period, *Scars upon My Heart,* was published in 1981.

Sassoon's 1915–18 volume has continued to reverberate. His time at Craiglockhart hospital in 1917 for treatment of shell shock, his role in publishing the poetry of Owen, and his open opposition to the war are the basis for Pat Barker's best-selling 1991 novel *Regeneration.* The novel explores Sassoon's attitude toward the war, his relationship with psychiatrist W. H. R. Rivers, his friendship with Owen, and his homosexuality.

THEMES AND STYLE

The diaries contain poetry and descriptive vignettes such as "In the Ward" (April 23 and 24, 1917) that make it a writer's notebook, one in which he tries out ideas and styles, as much as a conventional journal. A striking feature is his detachment from the horror of the trenches, a disregard for danger that earned him the nickname "Mad Jack." However, he is also poetic, writing, "The stillness of the pine-trees is queer.... They seem to be standing quite still, waiting for the war to end." Though some of his entries have a political bent, they are delivered in personal and emotional ways, such as when he writes, "The ruling classes do all the talking. And their words convince no one but the crowds who are their dupes."

Sassoon returned to his diaries often, treating them as a personal record of the period. Of notable interest is the summer of 1917, after Sassoon had come out publicly against the war and was declared mentally unfit. The months that followed, in which he tried to be reinstated to active service while continuing to speak out against the conflict, are missing from his diary but are illuminated by letters to his friends. In a November 1917 letter to Robert Graves, he writes, "I was passed General Service.... The Board asked if I had changed my views on the war, and I said I hadn't, which seemed to cause surprise." Hart-Davis's volume attempts to show how Sassoon battled with his loyalty to fellow soldiers and his belief that the war was wrong.

The varied style of the diary demonstrates Sassoon's extraordinary facility with description and mood. John Stallworthy, reviewing the 1920–22 volume in the *Times Literary Supplement,* describes Sassoon as "an eighteenth-century gentleman, a connoisseur for all the arts, with a special taste and talent for verse satire, set down in the wrong century." His prose captures the battlefield's terrible beauty, the "massed stillness, and smoky silhouettes," the "shattered tower that might have been a huge tree." It is also self-reflective, as when Sassoon writes, "If I'm alive in 1926 I'll be a better poet at last."

CRITICAL DISCUSSION

Upon its publication, Sassoon's *Diaries* was welcomed by scholars who wanted to use it to fill in gaps in his biography and enhance their understanding of his other work. In an article in the *Times Literary Supplement* in April 1983, Dominic Hibberd notes that Sassoon "often reminds himself in the diaries to look for beauty," finding that references to the diaries can "reinforce" the origins of the published poems. Hibberd laments the missing part of the work, covering the time at Craiglockhart, because of what it might have told us about Owen's and Sassoon's treatment by Rivers. He concludes that the volume "could have been more thorough" but that the diaries "add to Sassoon's stature."

Although he kept writing after the war and died just a few days short of his eighty-first birthday in 1967, Sassoon is generally remembered as a poet of World War I. His protests on behalf of the ordinary soldier helped to secure his reputation in the popular mind. Though his work has been considered primarily in the context of war, it has also been examined more recently on the basis of his homosexuality and his Jewishness. However, Sassoon himself was aware of the uncertainties inherent in memoirs and wrote to Dame Felicitas Corrigan, who assembled a "poetic record" of his life, to say, "My real biography is my poetry."

Although there is very little critical writing on the 1915–18 volume itself, it has assisted in a wider understanding of Sassoon's life and work. For example, the diaries make it possible to appreciate more clearly Sassoon's relationship with his school friend and fellow soldier Gordon Harbord, including his grief following Harbord's death and how the poem "Together" emerged from it. Hibberd describes the volume as a "record of Sassoon's war experiences to set beside the memoirs of 'George Sherston' and the poems." Indirectly the diary has informed Sassoon scholarship in general since publication, including such biographies as Jean Moorcroft Wilson's two-volume *Siegfried Sassoon: The Making of a War Poet* (1998, 2004) and books such as Daniel Hipp's *The Poetry of Shell Shock* (2005).

BIBLIOGRAPHY

Sources

Corrigan, Felicitas. *Siegfried Sassoon: Poet's Pilgrimage*. London: Gollancz, 1973. Print.

Hibberd, Dominic. "A Pilgrim in Flanders." *Times Literary Supplement* [London] 22 Apr. 1983: 395. *Times Literary Supplement Historical Archive*. Web. 14 Dec. 2012.

Hipp, Daniel. *The Poetry of Shell Shock: Wartime Trauma and Healing in Wilfred Owen, Ivor Gurney and Siegfried Sassoon*. Jefferson, N.C.: McFarland, 2005. Print.

Moorcroft Wilson, J. *Siegfried Sassoon: The Making of a War Poet*. London: Duckworth, 1998. Print.

Stallworthy, Jon. "The Divided Hero." *Times Literary Supplement* [London] 9 July 1982: 733. *Times Literary Supplement Historical Archive*. Web. 14 Dec. 2012.

Sternlicht, Sanford. *Siegfried Sassoon*. New York: Twayne, 1993. *Twayne's English Authors Series 500*. The Twayne Authors Series. Web. 14 Dec. 2012.

Further Reading

Allen, Brooke. "Rediscovering Sassoon." *New Criterion* 24.3 (2005): 15+. *General OneFile*. Web. 10 Dec. 2012.

Campbell, Patrick. *Siegfried Sassoon: A Study of the War Poetry*. Jefferson, N.C.: McFarland, 1998. Print.

Egremont, M. *Siegfried Sassoon: A Biography*. London: Picador, 2005. Print.

Giddings, Robert. *The War Poets*. New York: Orion, 1988. Print.

Lloyd, Christopher. Rev. of *Siegfried Sassoon Diaries 1915–1918*, by Siegfried Sassoon. *Review of English Studies* 35.138 (1984): 263. Print.

Quinn, Patrick J. *The Great War and the Missing Muse: The Early Writings of Robert Graves and Siegfried Sassoon*. Selinsgrove, Penn.: Susquehanna University Press, 1994. Print.

Chris Routledge

A Diary from Dixie
Mary Boykin Miller Chesnut

Key Facts

Time Period:
Mid-19th Century

Relevant Historical Events:
American Civil War; election of Abraham Lincoln; the Confederacy's defeat

Nationality:
American

Keywords:
war; women's writing; slavery

OVERVIEW

First published in 1905, *A Diary from Dixie* consists of edited excerpts from the Civil War diaries of Mary Boykin Miller Chesnut, a member of a prominent southern family highly placed in the Confederacy. Chesnut understood the historic importance of the events she experienced, and she wrote her diary with the intention of creating an intimate record of the times. She spent the last years of her life reworking her copious journals for publication but died before their completion, leaving the task to her literary heir Isabella Martin, who—along with Myrta Lockett Avary—published a severely edited version in 1905. While retaining Chesnut's lively, often ironic, voice, Martin and Avary removed much of her challenging social commentary in order to present a more positive view of the Confederacy.

Appearing fifty years after the end of the divisive Civil War, Chesnut's inside view of the conflict was received with interest. Before its publication in book form, excerpts of the diary were serialized in the popular *Saturday Evening Post*, giving it a wide readership. The book version that soon followed generated enthusiasm, even in the midst of a glut of Civil War memoirs. A longer version of *A Diary from Dixie*, edited by Ben Ames Williams, was released in 1961. Historian Comer Vann Woodward published a more extensive edition, *Mary Chesnut's Civil War,* in 1981. Woodward then collaborated with Chesnut biographer Elisabeth Muhlenfeld to produce *The Private Mary Chesnut: The Unpublished Civil War Diaries* in 1984. Though sometimes criticized for the limitations of the author's perspective, Chesnut's writings continue to fascinate historians.

HISTORICAL AND LITERARY CONTEXT

Slavery had caused division in the United States since colonial times. The South's vast agricultural lands and appropriate climate for cash crops such as tobacco made the use of slave labor profitable, while in the North an economy based on trade and industry attracted waves of immigrants. Economic measures such as the Tariff of 1828, which protected the industrial North with a tax on imported goods but penalized southerners who then had to pay more for those products, exacerbated regional hostilities. By 1850 slavery had been abolished in the North, while slaves made up more than half the population in some southern states, and there was heated debate over extending the legality of slavery into new territories and states.

Most northerners dated the beginning of the Civil War from April 1861 when Confederate forces captured South Carolina's Fort Sumter; for many in the South, however, the war began in November 1860 when Abraham Lincoln, candidate of the antislavery Republican Party, was elected president. The following month, South Carolina—Chesnut's home state—seceded from the Union. By May 1861 eleven southern states had joined South Carolina in forming the Confederate States of America. *A Diary from Dixie* begins when Chesnut hears the news of Lincoln's election. She determines at that moment, "From to-day forward I will tell the story in my own way."

In describing her life and her male-dominated society from the point of view of a woman, Chesnut's diary has much in common with the outsider view of popular slave narratives, such as Harriet Jacobs's *Incidents in the Life of a Slave Girl* (1861) and Lucy Delaney's *From the Darkness Cometh the Light, or, Struggles for Freedom* (c. 1890). Most white southern writing following the Civil War was confined to military accounts, such as *Destruction and Reconstruction: Personal Experiences of the Late War* (1879) by Richard Taylor and *War Reminiscences and Stuart Cavalry Campaigns* (1887) by John Singleton Mosby, as well as thinly veiled mythology intended to glorify the "lost cause" of the old South, such as *Marse Chan: A Tale of Old Virginia* (1884) by Thomas Nelson Page.

A Diary from Dixie has piqued the interest of historians since its publication. Chesnut's narrative provided a unique perspective on the war, both as an insider who socialized with leading figures of the Confederacy (such as Jefferson and Varina Davis) and as a female outsider to the power structures of society. Williams's 1961 expanded edition, still titled *A Diary from Dixie,* is almost twice as long as the original and includes more of Chesnut's mordant societal criticism. Woodward's 1981 *Mary Chesnut's Civil War* and Woodward and Muhlenfeld's 1984 *The Private Mary Chesnut* include even more of the original journals along with Chesnut's own revisions, and these works are generally considered the most authoritative renditions of the author's intent.

THEMES AND STYLE

Chesnut's diary is, in all of the published versions, a deeply personal history of the war. "My father was a South Carolina nullifier ..., so I was of necessity a rebel born," she says in her first entry. Descriptions of her fears and the hardships of war are interspersed with an inside view of Confederate society. Especially in *Mary Chesnut's Civil War,* she also gives a vivid picture of women in wartime, forced to stand powerless in the face of destruction of their way of life. In April 1861, after the attack on Fort Sumter, she wrote, "Oh, if I could put some of my restless spirit into these discreet, cautious, lazy men." About slavery, the central issue of the war, Chesnut exhibits a slave owner's ambivalence, saying in March 1861, "God forgive us, but ours is a *monstrous* system," and in November 1861, "Slavery has to go, of course. All that has been gained by it goes to the North and to negroes. The slave owners when they are good men and women are the martyrs."

Chesnut's diaries, as she wrote them, spanned numerous notebooks; as the war progressed and supplies became scarce, she used scraps of paper and leaves torn from other books. When she feared she might be captured, she burned a number of journals: "In Stoneman's raid I burned my journal proper.... The guns did sound very near. And when Mr. C rode up and told me if Mrs. Davis left Richmond I must go with her, I confess I lost my head." These sections Chesnut reconstructed from memory after the war, producing more than 900 pages of written matter. She was not only a diarist but also a writer with ambitious plans for her work. In the decades after the war, she revised and rewrote her journal, transforming it into a unique genre. As G. Thomas Couser said in the 1989 study *Altered Egos,* "What Chesnut produced in the 1880s is perhaps best described as a novelized chronicle in diary format."

Much of the power of Chesnut's narrative lies in her distinctive voice. She describes the events swirling around her with directness, sincerity, and a wry humor that reveals underlying courage. In May 1864 she writes, "If I was a *man* I would not doze & drink & drivel here until the fight is over in Virginia.... These people make me weary of humanity.... Stopped by an obstacle that would not deter a chicken." Even her own literary efforts are the target of her ironic wit: "I think this journal will be disadvantageous for me, for I spend my time now like a spider spinning my own entrails."

CRITICAL DISCUSSION

Even before publication, Chesnut's diaries earned admiration. Elisabeth Muhlenfeld's 1981 biography of Chesnut quotes an 1885 letter in which Varina Davis, wife of the former president of the Confederacy, writes, "I think your diaries would sell better than any Confederate history of a grave character." A 1905 *New York Times* review by William E. Dodd commends the Martin/Avary version of *A Diary from Dixie,* saying, "In tone and character this new war book is admirable," though he is patronizing about its female point of view: "There is no general scheme or plan or even purpose except to record the talk of the time." In a 1949 *Times* review of Williams's reworking of the diary, Betty Smith has a similar tone: "This intimate record of the Civil War as set down by a witty South Carolina belle is more enthralling than many a fat, romantic Civil War novel. We are all petty eavesdroppers.... Well, read Mrs. Chesnut's journal and eavesdrop to your heart's content."

Biographer Muhlenfeld calls Chesnut's diary "an important literary portrait of the Confederacy." The various diary versions appeal to many readers, from the casual admirer of historical fiction to the serious analyst. The 1905 version offers insights into Confederate society and the postwar southern literature glorifying the Old South, while the 1981 edition illustrates the author's work in defining a new genre that encompasses both the immediacy of personal narrative and the dramatic momentum of a novel. At the same time, the role of the work as a historical source must be emphasized: it is key for scholars in talking about the Civil War era.

Perhaps the greatest evidence of the enduring legacy of Chesnut's work is the way historians have continued to examine and republish it. To create *Mary Chesnut's Civil War,* historian Woodward collected and edited the author's original journals, corrections, and additions to create the most accurate depiction of the author's original intent. Nonetheless, Kenneth Lynn, reviewing the version for the *New York Times,* claims Woodward's work exposed Chesnut's diary as a "fabrication." Later scholars have viewed Chesnut's blend of recollection and invention with more respect.

Illustration of Confederate president Jefferson Davis and others dancing on a flag of the United States, 1862. In *A Diary from Dixie,* Mary Boykin Chesnut, whose husband worked with Davis, describes life in the American South during the Civil War. © NORTH WIND PICTURE ARCHIVES/ALAMY

EMMA SPAULDING BRYANT: RECONSTRUCTION THROUGH A NORTHERN WOMAN'S EYES

The stories of many ordinary citizens who lived through the tumultuous years of the Civil War and its aftermath remain hidden in undiscovered letters and diaries. In 2004, following decades of compilation, historian Ruth Douglas Currie published excerpts from the journals and letters of Emma Bryant, a northerner who lived in Georgia during the Reconstruction period that followed the war. The resulting work, *Emma Spaulding Bryant: Civil War Bride, Carpetbagger's Wife, Ardent Feminist, Letters and Diaries, 1860–1900*, offers a unique view of the postwar period.

Emma Frances Spaulding was a mathematics teacher in Maine in 1864 when she married John Emory Bryant, a Union soldier. Following the war, she accompanied her husband when he traveled south to join the Freedman's Bureau and begin the work to create political, economic, and social structures that would include and empower newly freed black citizens. Like Mary Chesnut's writing, Bryant's diaries and letters create an intimate portrait of a pivotal era from a feminine point of view. Isolated and despised by many southern whites as a woman, an interloper, and a "carpetbagger," Bryant developed a strong sense of justice. Her writing reveals her as a profound thinker with progressive ideas about racial justice and the role of women.

In 2007's *Textual Cultures* Augusta Rohrbach asserts, "Chesnut's genius was in preserving the generic form of the diary and thus invisibly working a narrative trajectory into the story.… She can, in other words, eschew plot in favor of story by positing the book as a diary."

BIBLIOGRAPHY

Sources

Chesnut, Mary. *Mary Chesnut's Civil War*. Ed. C. Vann Woodward. New Haven, Conn.: Yale University Press, 1981. Print.

Couser, G. Thomas. "Mary Boykin Chesnut: Secession, Confederacy, Reconstruction." *Altered Egos*. New York: Oxford University Press, 1989. 156–88. *Literature Resource Center*. Web. 10 Dec. 2012.

Dodd, William E. "A Chronicle of Southern Life by the Wife of a Confederate Statesman and Soldier." Rev. of *Diary from Dixie*, by Mary Boykin Miller Chesnut. *New York Times*. New York Times, 22 Apr. 1905. Web. 12 Dec. 2012.

Lynn, Kenneth S. "The Masterpiece That Became a Hoax." Rev. of *Mary Chesnut's Civil War*, by Mary Chesnut. *New York Times* 26 Apr. 1981: A9. *ProQuest Historical Newspapers: The New York Times (1851–2009)*. Web. 12 Dec. 2012.

Muhlenfeld, Elisabeth. *Mary Boykin Chesnut: A Biography*. Baton Rouge: Louisiana University Press, 1981. Print.

Rohrbach, Augusta. "The Diary May Be from Dixie but the Editor Is Not: Mary Chesnut and Southern Print History." *Textual Cultures* 2.1 (2007): 101+. *Literature Resource Center*. Web. 10 Dec. 2012.

Smith, Betty. "Vivacious Lady: Confederate Style." Rev. of *Diary from Dixie*, by Mary Boykin Chesnut. *New York Times* 30 Oct. 1949: BR18. Print.

Further Reading

Bryant, Emma Frances Spaulding. *Emma Spaulding Bryant: Civil War Bride, Carpetbagger's Wife, Ardent Feminist, Letters and Diaries, 1860–1900*. Ed. Ruth Douglas Currie. New York: Fordham University Press, 2004. Print.

Chesnut, Mary Boykin Miller. *Diary from Dixie*. Ed. Isabella Martin and Myrta Lockett Avary. New York: Appleton, 1905. Print.

Chesnut, Mary Boykin. *Diary from Dixie*. Ed. Ben Ames Williams. Boston: Houghton Mifflin, 1949.

Chesnut, Mary Boykin Miller. *The Private Mary Chesnut: The Unpublished Civil War Diaries*. Ed. Elisabeth Muhlenfeld and C. Vann Woodward. New York: Oxford University Press, 1984.

Flynn, James. "Mary Chesnut's Reconstruction: The Literary Imagination of a Diarist." *Kentucky Philological Association Bulletin* (1983): 63–72. Print.

Stern, Julia A. *Mary Chesnut's Civil War Epic*. Chicago: University of Chicago Press, 2010. Print.

Tina Gianoulis

THE DIARY OF ANNE FRANK
Anne Frank

OVERVIEW

The Diary of Anne Frank (also published as *Anne Frank: The Diary of a Young Girl*) was written between 1942 and 1944 by a young Jewish girl hiding from the Nazis in German-occupied Holland. The diary begins on June 12, 1942, twenty-eight days before she entered hiding, and ends on August 1, 1944, a few days before she and her family were arrested. Three versions of the diary exist: one that Frank started in 1942 (at age thirteen) for personal use (known as version A); a second, self-redacted version begun in 1944 (version B) after she heard on Dutch radio that letters and diaries of ordinary citizens might be collected after the war; and a third version (version C) pieced together after the end of the war by Frank's father, Otto, who published the diary after Anne and the rest of the family perished in Nazi concentration camps. By 1986 the book had sold sixteen million copies internationally. It continues to hold scholarly interest in the twenty-first century.

When Frank's diary was published in 1947, Otto was the only member of the family still alive. After Nazis discovered the Franks' hiding place in 1944, Anne and her sister, Margot, were shipped to the Bergen-Belsen concentration camp, and their parents ended up at Auschwitz-Birkenau. Bergen-Belsen was rife with poor sanitation, overcrowding, and disease, including typhus, which killed both sisters. As the world reacted with horror in the years after the war, when the truth about the concentration camps emerged, Anne's diary was received with a great deal of sympathy.

HISTORICAL AND LITERARY CONTEXT

According to the United States Holocaust Memorial Museum, keeping diaries was a common practice among "children of assimilated Jewish parents from Germany, Austria, or the Czech lands" who left their homes in hopes of escaping Nazi persecution. The Franks were among the 34,000 German Jews who sought refuge in Holland after the Nuremberg Laws were enacted in 1935, criminalizing sexual relations between Jews and gentiles, decreeing that Jewish children could only attend Jewish schools, making it illegal for Jews to own businesses, and otherwise limiting the freedoms of Jews. In 1942, amid mounting pressure from the Nazis, Hermine (Miep) Santrouschitz helped hide the Franks in a building owned by the company she and Otto worked for, in a space they called "the secret annex." Santrouschitz and others ensured that the Franks, along with a dentist separated from his gentile wife and another family of three, maintained their connection with the outside world, bringing them newspapers, books, and magazines and helping Anne and Margot take correspondence courses.

Among the surviving diaries of European Jews living at the time of the Holocaust is the journal of Etty Hillesum, published in 1981. In the diary she describes her internment at the Westerbork detention camp before she boarded a train for Auschwitz, where she died. Miriam Wattenberg, whose family made it safely from Poland to the United States thanks to her mother's American citizenship, published a diary under the pseudonym Mary Berg, which she began in 1939 and which covered her family's time living in the Warsaw ghetto. Published in February 1945, Wattenberg's diary is one of the earliest published firsthand accounts of the atrocities committed by the Nazis. Jewish student David Koker's diary, *At the Edge of the Abyss: A Concentration Camp Diary, 1943–1944,* was translated from Dutch into English in 2012.

Otto's edition of his daughter's diary was published in Holland as *Het Achterhuis* (*The Secret Annex*) in June 1947 to warm critical reception. Subsequent translations into French (1950), English (1952), and German (1955) also proved successful. In the 1950s, *New York Times* reviewer Meyer Levin called for the book to be made into a play and a film. Although he insisted on writing it himself and pressured Otto to award him the contract, Otto and the project's backers rejected the script. Instead a script by Albert Hackett and Frances Goodrich was used for the stage and screen versions. American playwright Wendy Kesselman later gave the play new life in a 1997 adaptation.

THEMES AND STYLE

The Diary of Anne Frank often focuses on the author's thoughts about being stuck between childhood and young adulthood. Entries appear almost daily and include, at times, transcribed poems and letters, photographs, a group of notes addressed to fictional characters from Dutch literature, and other digressions from prose. Along the way, she makes sharp and often funny observations about the world around her. She is at her best when observing human behavior, including her own. An early, pre-secret annex entry describes "one of

Key Facts

Time Period:
Mid-20th Century

Relevant Historical Events:
World War II; German occupation of Holland; Holocaust

Nationality:
Dutch

Keywords:
Holocaust; persecution; Nazism

Various copies of *Anne Frank's Diary of a Young Girl*, which has been published in some 60 languages. © ANNE FRANK FONDS/ANNE FRANK HOUSE/GETTY IMAGES

my slightly melancholy days while I sat chin in hand, feeling too bored and limp to even make up my mind whether to go out, or stay at home." She observes of her family, "Daddy's the only one who understands me occasionally, but generally he sides with Mummy and Margot." She also voices complex thoughts typical of a teenage girl: "I know that I am far from being as I ought to be; will I ever be?"

At first, she considered the diary a substitute for the kind of friend she felt was missing from her life. An early entry reads, "Dear diary, I hope no one will ever read you except my dear sweet husband." She often addresses her entries to "Kitty," imagined as "the girl next door," with "a wine-red velvet frock for Sundays and a cotton one for every day; she has pale-blond hair with tiny braids, and clear blue eyes." Frank began version B of the diary after hearing a Dutch MP on the radio saying that wartime diaries and letters should be collected. In anticipation of submitting her diary, she reworked and added to some of her earlier entries. "No one will grasp what I'm talking about if I begin my letters to Kitty just out of the blue," she writes, proceeding to tell "the story of my life, much as I don't like to."

The language and style of versions B and C are more formal and self-conscious than version A. Some changes are minor, such as version A's "I ask myself whether one would have trouble in the long run, whomever one shared a house with" appearing in version B as "I continually ask myself whether one would have trouble in the long run, whomever one shared a house with." Others are more noticeable, such as a particularly wistful address to Kitty in version A that was omitted in version B's description of the items the annex inmates longed for from outside.

CRITICAL DISCUSSION

Initial critical response to Frank's diary was colored by the emerging discovery of Nazi atrocities committed against Jews, homosexuals, gypsies, and others. *The Diary of Anne Frank* was welcomed as a ray of light in the darkness that followed the war. After the success of the book's first Dutch edition in 1947, Otto commented, "If she had been here, Anne would have been so proud." In a June 1952 preface to the first American printing, former first lady Eleanor Roosevelt calls the diary "one of the wisest and most moving commentaries on war and its impact on human beings that I have ever read."

The Diary of Anne Frank has become a mainstay of school curricula throughout the Western world. Writing for the *English Journal* in 1968, teacher Elizabeth A. Mapes recommends both the book and play for junior high school students: "By the time that they are thirteen or fourteen, most students are already sharing Anne's inner turmoil about sex and parents and are beginning to be interested in moral questions, such as, in Anne's case, those raised by the Nazi persecutions." However, some critics have complained of whitewashing in both the print and film versions. Twelve years after the 1986 critical edition was published, five omitted pages surfaced, three of which, write Hyman A. Enzer and Sandra Solotaroff-Enzer, editors of *Anne Frank: Reflections on her Life and Legacy* (2000), "contain Anne's observation that Otto lacked passion for his wife, Edith." Scholars continue to investigate the implications of the different versions, the circumstances surrounding the Franks' capture, and how Anne and Margot fared in the concentration camps before they died.

Recent scholarship has envisioned the diary as presenting an alternate universe to the one in which it was written. In a 1994 article for *Utopian Studies*, Barbara Chiarello sees the diary as describing a utopia: "Anne's diary not only lists her experiences, it provides a blueprint on how to live … Anne's humor—part of her coping arsenal—takes the sting (and boredom) out of the didactic nature inherent in many utopian works," such as George Orwell's *1984* (1949). Gene A. Plunka writes in *South Central Review* in 2009 that Holocaust survivor Nelly Sachs's *Eli: A Mystery Play of the Sufferings of Israel* (1943) and *The Diary of Anne Frank* "transcend the Holocaust by universalizing the experience," turning it into "a momentary phase of history in which evil temporarily triumphed over good."

BIBLIOGRAPHY

Sources

Chiarello, Barbara. "The Utopian Space of a Nightmare: The Diary of Anne Frank." *Utopian Studies* 5.1 (1994): 128–40. *JSTOR*. Web. 8 Jan. 2013.

Enzer, Hyman A., and Sandra Solotaroff-Enzer, eds. *Anne Frank: Reflections on Her Life and Legacy*. Urbana and Chicago: University of Illinois Press, 2000. Print.

Frank, Anne. *The Diary of Anne Frank: The Critical Edition*. Ed. David Barnouw and Gerrold van der Stroom. Trans. Arnold J. Pomerans and B. M. Mooyaart-Doubleday. New York: Viking, 1986. Print.

Mapes, Elizabeth A. "Drama for Junior High School: The Diary of Anne Frank." *English Journal* 57.9 (1968): 1307–11. *JSTOR*. Web. 8 Jan. 2013.

Plunka, Gene A. "Transcending the Holocaust: Nelly Sachs's *Eli* and the Stage Version of *The Diary of Anne Frank*." *South Central Review* 26.3 (2009). *Project MUSE*. Web. 8 Jan. 2013.

United States Holocaust Memorial Museum. "Children's Diaries during the Holocaust." *Holocaust Encyclopedia*. United States Holocaust Memorial Museum, n.d. Web. 2 Jan. 2013.

Further Reading

Berg, Mary. *The Diary of Mary Berg: Growing Up in the Warsaw Ghetto*. London: Oneworld, 2006. Print.

Englander, Nathan. *What We Talk about When We Talk about Anne Frank*. New York: Random House, 2012. Print.

Graver, Lawrence. *An Obsession with Anne Frank: Meyer Levin and the Diary*. Berkeley: University of California Press, 1995. Print.

ANNE FRANK'S LEGACY

A museum dedicated to Anne Frank now occupies the space where she hid with her family. Attracting more than a million visitors in 2012, the museum also maintains the letters of Otto Frank. The museum reports that as of 2013, 263 schools in fourteen countries are named for Frank, with the mandate that "A school bearing the name of Anne Frank obliges itself to stand up for freedom, justice, tolerance and human dignity and to resolutely turn against any form of aggression, discrimination, racism, political extremism and excessive nationalism."

Twenty-first century writers have kept Frank alive in readers' imaginations. Poet Wallis Wilde-Menozzi's 2002 poem "Nearing Anne Frank" features a character recalling her childhood internment in Auschwitz, where one night "another child put a comforting hand, / numbered and half-dead, / on her tiny shoulder. The older girl / whispered rain-filled stories to her" (the older girl is Frank). Poet Mike White's 2004 "Anne Frank, Postscript" conveys the young writer's sense of wonder even when faced with disaster: "I caught my death / in the winter of the year, / when the fresh snow was falling / I caught it, amazed, / on the ready tip of my tongue." By contrast, Shalom Auslander's novel *Hope: A Tragedy* (2012) paints an absurdist tale of Frank as an embittered old woman living in the attic of a farmhouse in rural New York.

Hillesum, Etty. *The Letters and Diaries of Etty Hillesum 1941–1943*. Ed. Klaas A. D. Smelik. Trans. Arnold J. Pomerans. Grand Rapids, Mich.: Eerdmans, 1986. Print.

Jacobson, Sid, and Ernie Colón. *Anne Frank: The Anne Frank House Authorized Graphic Biography*. New York: Farrar, Straus and Giroux, 2010. Print.

Kirshenblatt-Gimblett, Barbara, and Jeffrey Shandler, eds. *Anne Frank Unbound: Media, Imagination, Memory*. Bloomington: Indiana University Press, 2012. Print.

Koker, David. *At the Edge of the Abyss: A Concentration Camp Diary, 1943–1944*. Ed. Robert Jan van Pelt. Trans. Michiel Horn and John Irons. Evanston, Ill.: Northwestern University Press, 2012. Print.

Melnick, Ralph. *The Stolen Legacy of Anne Frank: Meyer Levin, Lillian Hellman, and the Staging of the* Diary. New Haven, Conn.: Yale University Press, 1997. Print.

White, Mike. "Anne Frank, Postscript." *Iowa Review* 34.3 (2004–05): 174. *JSTOR*. Web. 2 Jan. 2013.

Wilde-Menozzi, Wallis. "Nearing Anne Frank." *AGNI* 56 (2002): 422–24. *JSTOR*. Web. 2 Jan. 2013.

Rebecca Rustin

The Diary of Sir Henry Slingsby

Sir Henry Slingsby

❖ **Key Facts**

Time Period:
Mid-17th Century

Relevant Historical Events:
English Civil War; rising power of the English parliament; decline of the monarchy

Nationality:
English

Keywords:
war; monarchism; royalism

OVERVIEW

Written between 1638 and 1648 (with a brief hiatus due to wartime obligations), *The Diary of Sir Henry Slingsby* gives an account of the English Civil War from the perspective of a country gentleman. Unflinchingly loyal to King Charles I and to the Church of England, Slingsby records his experiences in battle and on the home front as the Royalist side gradually loses ground. Although the original manuscript of the diary is lost, a handwritten copy of the original is held at Scriven, England, and a full version of this copy was edited and published by Daniel Parsons in 1836. As a whole, Slingsby's diary explains the religious and philosophical positions of a Royalist northern gentleman as he experiences grief and loss without changing loyalties.

Although Parsons's 1836 edition remains the only printed version of the diary, Slingsby's letter to his sons ("A Father's Legacy") was printed in 1658, and accounts of his legal trial and behavior on the gallows were also published that year. Although these documents have been relatively neglected by scholars, they contribute to a fuller understanding of the Civil War and its aftermath. When Slingsby describes his opinions on religious matters in the diary, writes parting advice to his sons on the eve of his execution, and acts in a quiet but dignified manner as he is put to death, he provides a useful case study of one landowner's unwavering commitment to the king's cause.

HISTORICAL AND LITERARY CONTEXT

The Diary of Sir Henry Slingsby is firmly situated within its historical context. During the 1630s and 1640s, the British Parliament was growing increasingly concerned about the amount of money that King Charles was spending on his ongoing war with Scotland and how exactly he was justifying his schemes for raising revenue. Slingsby had a front-row seat for the debates that took place in both of the Parliaments of 1640. He watched as more liberal parliamentarians, affiliated with Oliver Cromwell, began to ask why Parliament did not have more authority and why the conservative Church of England was still official and powerful.

As a record of the decade from 1638 to 1648, Slingsby's diary covers the rising power of Parliament and the diminishing power of the king. Although he sat in Parliament himself and disagreed with some of the new religious practices (such as bowing toward the altar), Slingsby remained loyal to both the king and the Church of England. The diary records his decision to vote for only some of the bills supporting the parliamentary cause, and Slingsby even argued on behalf of the king's proposed monetary compromise, taking up an unpopular position. Ultimately, Slingsby became a soldier on the king's behalf, raising and leading troops of volunteers after war finally broke out between the monarch and the parliamentary faction.

Although the military and political sides of his work are grounded in the immediate Civil War context, *The Diary of Sir Henry Slingsby* is also heavily influenced by the writing of the French essayist Michel de Montaigne. A witty skeptic, Montaigne wrote about his life and thoughts in the context of the French Wars of Religion (which took place about sixty years before Slingsby began his diary). In his article "Vernacular Humanism in the Sixteenth Century," writer Warren Boutcher suggests that Slingsby's engagement with Montaigne's unique style makes him similar to a group of Elizabethan humanist scholars and writers, including Edward Wotton, Samuel Daniel, and John Florio (who translated Montaigne's work into English).

Although the diary provides information about the war, Slingsby's estate, and family matters, it was the published letter "A Father's Legacy" (1658) that had more lasting historical ramifications. Written just before Slingsby was executed by the victorious parliamentarians, the letter is similar to the earlier text *Eikon Basilike* (1649)—a record of the king's own last days, with appended instructions to his children. When the parliamentarians were overthrown in 1660 and Charles II came to power, sentimental Royalist documents such as "A Father's Legacy" helped to establish the emotional groundwork upon which the new monarchy could build its authority, praising the constancy and heroic sufferings of those who died for its cause.

THEMES AND STYLE

The main themes of *The Diary of Sir Henry Slingsby* are constancy in the face of change and the need to keep supporting those who represent the established order. Slingsby merges the two themes by expressly praising the constancy of his monarch in 1645: "I do wonder at the admirable temper of the King, whose constancy was such that no perils never so unavoidable could move him to astonishment, but that still he set the

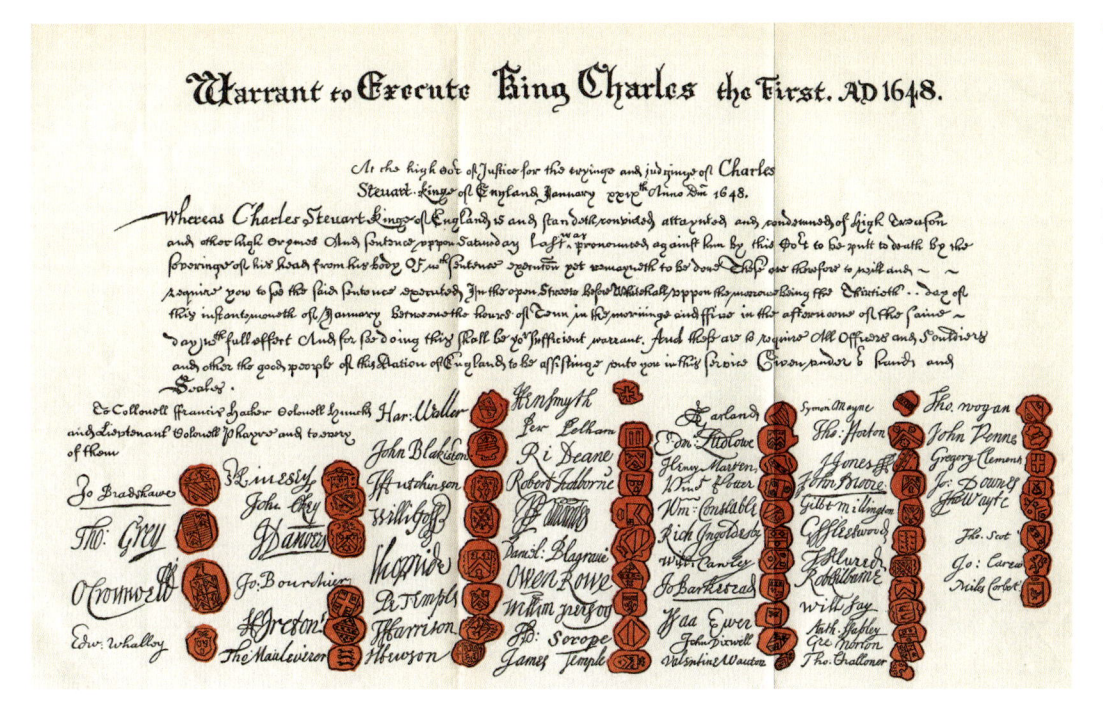

The High Court of Parliament's 1648 execution warrant for former king Charles I. Sir Henry Slingsby was loyal to the king but was executed himself in 1658.
© INTERFOTO/ALAMY

same face and settl'd countenance upon what adverse fortune soever befell him." Fighting for the existence of the royal and ecclesiastical hierarchies, Slingsby also emphasizes the need for subordinates to remain loyal and willingly subject to authority. He strongly criticizes the parliamentarians for trying to alter traditional hierarchical patterns in the church as well as the state: "You [Parliamentarians, now in power] turn'd Schismaticks and departed from that faith wherein you were baptized[;] we make not the Quarrel, it is you."

At the same time, Slingsby explicitly frames his diary as a personal work meant for personal consumption. Following Montaigne's advice, he uses the book for recording "such accidents as befall me[—] not that I make my study of it, but rather a recreation at vacant times, without observing any time, method, or order in my wrighting, or rather scribbling." The serious thoughts that he expresses in his diary, however, also find a more public form of expression in "A Father's Legacy." There, Slingsby emphasizes his religious hopes for his family, advising them to concentrate on God and not worldly things and to serve their social superiors. Slingsby also signals that he wants the "Legacy" to become publicly available, since it defends his honor after the parliamentarians accused him of treason during his trial: "The crime wherewith I stood charged, was Treason; which my Conscience dictated to me, bare the Cognizance of Loyalty. To which Principles, as I was nursed in, so I mean to death to continue a constant professor of it."

Though he was educated at Cambridge, Slingsby never considered himself a good public speaker or writer and referred to his work self-deprecatingly as "scribbling." He did pride himself on his honest virtues, though, and used his writing as a tool to investigate them, as well as to record neighborhood events and wartime news. His style is modeled after Montaigne's, relying on Latin quotations; frequent aphorisms; and a congenial, rambling sentence structure. Slingsby also peppered his work with anecdotes and quirky character portrayals, painting pictures of his servants or his nervous but pious wife during times of peace. During wartime, his extended but plain sentences relate the grim details of the action in an approachable, heartfelt way: "The countreys of the North were much wasted, and the armys could not long lye one against the other, but starve. Their horses dy'd and their men weary of such hard duty being in Winter frost and Snow, would not endure longer but began to run away."

CRITICAL DISCUSSION

Although *The Diary of Sir Henry Slingsby* was not printed until the nineteenth century, contemporaries read and reacted to Slingsby's letter "A Father's Legacy" beginning in 1658 (the year of his execution). Royalist sympathizers added his name to lists of suffering loyal subjects, explaining that Parliament had sold his estate out from under him and that he may even have become a closet Catholic in his last years (though this is disputed). Slingsby's final words were also recorded in the Royalist collection "England's Black Tribunal" (1660), preserving them alongside the words of Charles I and other fallen noblemen. In 1797 and 1806 flawed versions of quotations from the diary began to appear in collections of anecdotes. These were the most widely circulated versions of the work until Parsons's edition came out in 1836.

ENTRAPMENT, TREASON, AND RELIGION

After finishing his diary in 1649 (the year after the king's execution), Sir Henry Slingsby became active in the movement to restore Charles II to the throne. Although Slingsby was eventually jailed, he continued to try to win supporters for the monarch. Unfortunately, the jailers whom he approached had been instructed to "trapan" (entrap) Slingsby: they were working for the new government and led Slingsby on until they had enough evidence to convict him of treason. Interestingly, in their different accounts of the affair, both Slingsby and the government emphasize God's intervention on their behalf. An anonymous government writer claims that "if it had not been the Lord who was on our side, when men [like Slingsby] plotted and contrived our ruine, we had been destroyed." Slingsby, meanwhile, writes in "A Father's Legacy" that his time in prison had been a time of God's "powerful Sprit act[ing] upon [his] poor Soul." He further learned that endurance is key and that only "weak-hearted souldier[s] faint under the conduct of such a Commander, who patiently died for our sins, and victoriously rose for our justification."

Although both sides could make religious claims, however, even some on the side of the government felt sorry for Slingsby. The republican General Ludlow commented that "in the opinion of many men [Slingsby] had very hard measure.... He was a declared Enemy, and therefore by the Laws of War free to make any such Attempt."

In his work, Parsons frames Slingsby as an unmitigated moral hero, and he reads the diary as a conduit into Slingsby's inspiring character: "the whole narrative cannot fail to impress the reader with the conviction, that the writer was a sincerely religious man, and that whatever he did was from very pure and conscientious motives." Parsons also explains that Slingsby's noble principles resulted in no small measure from his noble blood. Although this character-emphasizing perspective is no longer in fashion, only one or two pieces of recent scholarship on Slingsby's work are available to counter this portrayal or to offer an alternative viewpoint. This lack of recent, extended attention to *The Diary of Sir Henry Slingsby* or to "A Father's Legacy" creates a promising opportunity for future investigations of loyalism in the North.

In his entry on Slingsby in the *Oxford Dictionary of National Biography* (2004), David Scott writes a paragraph on the diary, pointing out that it "is a valuable source for the civil war in northern England, and provides a revealing insight into the mind of an interesting, if not exactly typical, seventeenth-century country gentleman." Although this is true, more scholarship could expand these conclusions. For example, critics could investigate more deeply the way that the diary nuances or alters the concept of Royalist "patient fortitude" proposed by Raymond Anselment or the way that "A Father's Legacy" interacts productively with *Eikon Basilike* to produce intertextual meaning. In doing so, scholars could begin to reexamine the literary contributions of Sir Henry Slingsby's work as documents that open a window onto the Civil War in northern England.

BIBLIOGRAPHY

Sources

Boutcher, Warren. "Vernacular Humanism in the Sixteenth Century." *The Cambridge Companion to Renaissance Humanism*. Ed. Jill Kraye. Cambridge, U.K.: Cambridge University Press, 1996. *Cambridge Collections Online*. 13 Dec. 2012. Web.

A Brief Relation of the Proceedings of the High Court of Justice against Sir Henry Slingsby and Doctor John Hewet. London: John Andrews, 1658. *EEBO*. 11 Dec. 2012. Web.

A Father's Legacy. Sir Henry Slingsbey's Instructions to His Sonnes. London: J. Grismond, 1658. *EEBO*. 11 Dec. 2012. Web.

Scott, David. "Slingsby, Sir Henry, First Baronet (1602–1658)." *Oxford Dictionary of National Biography*. Oxford: Oxford University Press, 2004. 12 Dec. 2012. Web.

Slingsby, Sir Henry. *The Diary of Sir Henry Slingsby*. Ed. Daniel Parsons. Oxford: J. Vincent, 1836. Print.

Further Reading

Anselment, Raymond. *Loyalist Resolve: Patient Fortitude in the English Civil War*. Newark: University of Delaware Press, 1988. Print.

Eikon Basilike, with Selections from Eikonoklastes. Ed. Jim Daems and Holly Faith Nelson. London: Broadview: 2005.

Groot, Jerome de. *Royalist Identities*. New York: Palgrave Macmillan, 2004. Print.

Major, Philip, ed. *Literatures of Exile in the English Revolution and Its Aftermath, 1640–1690*. Surrey, U.K.: Ashgate, 2010. Print.

Sharpe, Kevin, and Peter Lake, eds. *Culture and Politics in Early Stuart England*. Stanford, Calif.: Stanford University Press, 1993. Print.

Smith, Geoffrey Ridsdill. *Without Touch of Dishonour. The Life and Death of Sir Henry Slingsby 1602–1658*. Kineton, U.K.: Roundwood, 1968.

Nancy Simpson-Younger

A Diary without Dates
Enid Bagnold

OVERVIEW
A Diary without Dates (1918) by Enid Bagnold (1889–1981) recounts the author's service as a hospital volunteer with the Voluntary Aid Detachment (VAD) in England during World War I. Bagnold is unremittingly honest and at times poetic, revealing her contempt for the seemingly cold hospital "gods"—the doctors and nurses—as well as her unflagging sympathy for the patients she tends to. Born into privilege, she is hyperaware of the class structures underpinning the hospital setting. She is also cognizant of the freedoms she enjoys as a volunteer nurse—the same freedoms once denied to her as an upper-class woman.

Her first publication, *A Diary without Dates* was particularly popular in the United States in 1935, the year of its first American printing. The same year, *National Velvet,* Bagnold's most well-known novel, was published. Readers appreciated how the author spoke out strongly against the dehumanization of war. Today Bagnold's *Diary* is largely read as one of the first published nurse's diaries of World War I, as the author's earliest work, and as a precursor to her war novel, *The Happy Foreigner,* the barely fictionalized account of her work as an ambulance driver in France.

HISTORICAL AND LITERARY CONTEXT
World War I, which began on July 28, 1914, and lasted until November 11, 1918, was known primarily as the Great War and the World War until World War II began in 1939. The predominantly European war drew most of the continent's powers into combat. During the conflict, many British women found themselves, like Bagnold, for the first time taking active roles outside the home, especially as private residences became convalescent homes. Bagnold, a New Woman discontented with staid traditionalism, was relieved to be able to serve as a nurse, calling marriage a "desperate remedy" to ills such as fading charms and boredom.

In her diary, Bagnold discusses working as a volunteer nurse in the officers' and soldiers' wards during World War I, touching very little on her life outside the hospital. She neither reflects on the past nor muses much on the future and has little to say of the present beyond the events surrounding her duties. She alludes to a forbidden romance with a patient in the vaguest terms. Her desires to blend in with her surroundings for the first time in her life and to be one in a crowd appear to have influenced the writing of her diary, making it more of an impressionistic text than a historical reference replete with valuable documentary evidence for historians. She writes primarily of her run-ins with the official hospital staff, of whom she names very few, and of her interactions with her patients, several of whom she names. It is these relationships, not her personal life or self, that she highlights in the diary.

Bagnold was one of the first to publish an account of her war experiences, releasing her *Diary* before the end of the conflict, when she was twenty-nine. As a result, she was released from her position at the unnamed hospital (later discovered to be the Royal Herbert Hospital in Woolwich) after the diary's publication. Another British woman famous for her war diary, Vera Brittain, published *Testament of Youth: An Autobiographical Study of the Years 1900–1925* (1933). Mary Borden, an American, set her war experiences in sketches, short stories, and poems in *The Forbidden Zone* (1929). Author Agatha Christie, who writes of VAD nurses in novels such as *The Mysterious Affair at Styles* (1920), also served as a volunteer nurse. VAD nurses are featured in other popular interwar works such as Ernest Hemingway's *The Sun Also Rises* (1926) and *A Farewell to Arms* (1929).

After being dismissed from the hospital upon the publication of her diary, Bagnold turned to driving an ambulance in France for the remainder of the war. She recalls these experiences in the novel *The Happy Foreigner* (1920). The forthright and unconventional approach to life she takes in *A Diary without Dates* resounds in her later fictional and nonfictional works, such as her books for a younger audience, among them *National Velvet* (1935), and plays such as *The Chalk Garden* (1955).

THEMES AND STYLE
A Diary without Dates catalogs Bagnold's experiences as a volunteer nurse confronting gender roles, class divisions, and the importance of maintaining empathy in difficult conditions. Known as a New Woman, or a woman who steps outside the bounds of proscribed social roles, Bagnold reveals her struggles against socially sanctioned rules as she expresses affection for patients, contempt for the coldness of the nurses and the disrespect with which they treat patients (referred

✤ Key Facts

Time Period:
Early 20th Century

Relevant Historical Events:
World War I

Nationality:
English

Keywords:
women's writing; war; nursing

Artist William Hatherell's 1915 design for a poster depicting a World War I nurse with a child and a wounded soldier. In A Diary without Dates, *Enid Bagnold describes her years as a VAD nurse during the war.* © IMPERIAL WAR MUSEUM/THE ART ARCHIVE AT ART RESOURCE, NY

blend into her surroundings. She begins her diary with a meditation on how being part of a disciplined institution "gives one more liberty than is possible among three or four observant friends." Later she writes, "[S]o long as I conform absolutely, not a soul will glance at my thoughts—few at my face. I have only to be silent and conform, and I might be in so far a land that even the eye of God had lost me."

A Diary without Dates jumps from topic to topic in a style similar to stream of consciousness. The entries range from several sentences to a single word followed by ellipses: "Measles…" In a 2004 essay for *College Literature,* Carol Acton, arguing that women were not supposed to admit to seeing certain things, even in wartime literature, writes that in the diary "ellipses become the unseen text; they imply a place and time when the men do not look like men—the image that is obscured by the surface sense of order and control." Acton finds that Bagnold uses tools such as ellipses to help her reveal trauma without directly showing it, thus circumventing proscriptions against graphic imagery in women's writing.

CRITICAL DISCUSSION

Aside from the hospital administration's reaction, the reception of Bagnold's diary was positive. In her 1969 autobiography, Bagnold writes, "I was sacked from the hospital by the Matron in the first half-hour of my Day. The *Daily Mail* had a Leader on it and I sprang into a tiny fame." However, she writes, the article "wasn't totally an explosion of praise about me. There had been a scandal in a hospital … and as they were exposing it my book illustrated it well." H. G. Wells's review of the diary is representative of the notes of other reviewers. In her autobiography, Bagnold reports that Wells stated in *The Dream* (1924), "[A]ll the official war histories sleep the eternal sleep in the vaults of the great libraries, but probably you have all read one or two such human books as Enid Bagnold's 'Diary without Dates.'" In characteristic modesty she deflects the praise, commenting, "I hope the compliment wasn't the greater because he already knew me."

In the wake of *National Velvet*'s success in 1935, *A Diary without Dates* enjoyed a resurgence in Britain and was printed in the United States. In a 1935 *New York Times Book Review* article, Edith Walton praises the diary for its "sharpness of observation and its delicate humor" and calls the hospital's reasons for dismissing Bagnold "incomprehensible." Walton writes, "[I]t is true that her book … shows a certain hostility to the sisters who were Miss Bagnold's superiors, but otherwise it could only have been offensive in that it was too clear-headed and realistic to please contemporary patriots." In 1935 an anonymous writer for the *Los Angeles Times* seconds the notion that the diary is inoffensive, calling it "an outstanding piece of prose rather than of propaganda against war." Thus, Bagnold is primarily remembered for her

to as "boys," to her annoyance), and her conflicted relationship to the war. She is grateful for the liberty she finds in nursing but saddened that her freedom comes only with the great suffering of her patients.

Many women of the era kept diaries because they did not have access to other creative and emotional outlets. However, many of these documents were published long after they were written—and not always by the writer. *A Diary without Dates* was published before the war's end and with the consent of the writer. Many entries, such as those in which Bagnold calls a new volunteer "stupid" and "ugly," reflect badly on the author, indicating that the diary may not have been written with public consumption in mind. Like many women who kept diaries in times of war, Bagnold wrote to create order in the chaos around her. However, the formless structure of her diary and the lack of dates and spatial references suggest a sense of lost control. Writing also allowed her an outlet for her displeasure with the management of the hospital and a place to confide her "exhilaration of liberty," born of being able to observations and style rather than for her criticism of the hospital system.

Bagnold's diary has figured prominently in recent studies of women's voices in World War I writing, such as Acton's article in *College Literature* (2004), in which she parses "the relationship between concealing and rewriting the image of the injured body and the cultural constraints influencing public representation of injury." Acton examines "the gendered question of authenticity that connects 'seeing' with 'knowing' in wartime." Angela Smith in *Women's Writing of the First World War: An Anthology* (2000) writes, "[T]he generic tone of the narrative does more to illustrate the atmosphere of the hospital and cause the reader to empathise with the wounded who are forced to inhabit it," capturing the experiences of those who experienced the war for future generations. Smith writes, "[T]he influence of modernism is clear in her style, which conveys these sentiments effectively, giving us, the future readers, a picture postcard of the war itself."

BIBLIOGRAPHY

Sources

Acton, Carol. "Diverting the Gaze: The Unseen Text in Women's War Writing." *College Literature* 31.2 (2004): 53–79. *Project MUSE.* Web. 17 Dec. 2012.

Bagnold, Enid. *A Diary without Dates.* London: Heinemann, 1918. *Internet Archive.* Web. 5 Dec. 2012.

———. *Enid Bagnold's Autobiography (From 1889).* London: Heinemann, 1969. *Open Library.* Web. 21 Dec. 2012.

"A Nurse Remembers." *Los Angeles Times.* Los Angeles Times, 24 Nov. 1935. Web. 21 Dec. 2012.

Sebba, Anne. *Battling for News: The Rise of the Woman Reporter.* London: Hodder, 1994. Print.

Smith, Angela, ed. *Women's Writing of the First World War: An Anthology.* Manchester, U.K.: Manchester University Press, 2000. Print.

Thornton, Michael. "Edith Bagnold: The Fascinating First Lady of a Gilded Dynasty." *London Telegraph.* The Telegraph, 27 Apr. 2012. Web. 20 Dec. 2012.

Walton, Edith. "The Wartime Diary of Enid Bagnold." Rev. of *A Diary without Dates,* by Enid Bagnold. *New York Times Book Review.* New York Times, 24 Nov. 1935. Web. 13 Dec. 2012.

LADY JONES, UNTAMED MAVERICK

Enid Bagnold was once moderately infamous for taking for her first lover the much older publisher and pornographer Frank Harris, who she wrote "made sin seem glorious." She eventually married Sir Roderick Jones, the chairman of Reuters, and became Lady Jones, a well-known society hostess. She is the great-grandmother of Samantha Cameron, wife of British prime minister David Cameron.

Bagnold's third novel, *National Velvet,* made her a household name (she always wrote under her maiden name). The book has not been out of print since its first edition in 1935, and a film adaptation starring a twelve-year-old Elizabeth Taylor was released in 1944. She was also an avid playwright, although only *The Chalk Garden* became a hit because, according to Michael Thornton, writing for the *London Telegraph* in 2012, Irene Mayer Selznick, the Broadway producer, "by the brutal imposition of her own will over Enid's, forced the writer to be 'plainer'" and to clarify her scenes. Thornton reports that Bagnold clashed with all the directors, producers, and actors who worked on her plays, except for Katharine Hepburn. In fact, after the opening night of *The Chinese Prime Minister* in 1962, Joseph Anthony, the play's Broadway director, sent Bagnold "a white china rosebud inscribed to 'a monster.'" She died in 1981 at age ninety-one.

Further Reading

Bagnold, Enid. *The Happy Foreigner.* New York: Century, 1920. Print.

Friedman, Lenemaja. *Enid Bagnold.* Boston: Twayne, 1986. Print.

Higgonnet, Margaret R., ed. *Lines of Fire: Women Writers of World War I.* New York: Plume, 1999. Print.

———. *Nurses at the Front: Writing the Wounds of the Great War.* Boston: Northeastern University Press, 2001. Print.

Sebba, Anne. *Enid Bagnold: The Authorized Biography.* New York: Thames, 1979. Print.

Tylee, Claire. *The Great War and Women's Consciousness: Images of Militarism and Womanhood in Women's Writings, 1914–64.* Iowa City: University of Iowa Press, 1990. Print.

Katherine Bishop

Journal, 1955–1962
Reflections on the French-Algerian War
Mouloud Feraoun

Key Facts

Time Period:
Mid-20th Century

Relevant Historical Events:
Algerian War of Independence; French colonization of Algeria

Nationality:
Algerian

Keywords:
colonialism; revolution; war

OVERVIEW

Journal, 1955–1962: Reflections on the French-Algerian War, by the French-educated Algerian writer and teacher Mouloud Feraoun, offers a candid and personal view of the Algerian War of Independence. The journal was published in September 1962, just months after Feraoun was murdered by the Organisation de l'Armee Secrete, a fascist organization of French military leaders, in March 1962. The war ended days after Feraoun's death. *Journal* combines anecdotes about Feraoun and his family's daily lives with news reports, Algerians' reactions to the conflict, and Feraoun's own frustrations and fears. The honest and straightforward writing provides a nuanced view of wartime and gives insight into the complex identity of those who live in a colonized country.

Feraoun intended to publish the journals, which he kept hidden in his students' notebooks because anticolonialist writing was strictly forbidden in Algeria. Feraoun's friend Emmanuel Robles edited the collection, which was translated from French into English in 2000. In his 1962 introduction, Robles describes Feraoun's courage in writing his diaries and the importance of the information Feraoun recorded. *Journal* has been read as a complement to Frantz Fanon's theoretical writing about the Algerian War, in which Fanon uses Algeria as a model for colonized people around the world. Feraoun also proved perceptive in his predictions of the problems an independent Algeria would face, forebodings that came true in the 1990s with fighting between the Algerian government and Islamic rebel groups.

HISTORICAL AND LITERARY CONTEXT

Algeria, a primarily Muslim country in North Africa, was colonized by the French in 1830. Algerians began fighting for their independence from France in November 1954, led by the National Liberation Front (FLN). The war remains notorious for its extreme violence on both sides of the conflict. Disgruntled French military leaders formed the extremist Organisation de l'Armee Secrete, which terrorized the country and attempted to assassinate Charles de Gaulle, president of France's Fifth Republic. The war ended in March 1962, when de Gaulle negotiated Algerian independence with the FLN.

Feraoun began his journal on November 1, 1955, the one-year anniversary of the beginning of the Algerian War. A teacher and writer best known for the 1950 novel *Le Fils du pauvre* (*The Poor Man's Son*) about a boy who grows up in the Kabylie mountains and advances himself through education, Feraoun was far from a revolutionary. Writing his diaries was a way to privately record the occurrences of the conflict. He also documents his debates and friendships with other writers, including Robles and Albert Camus. Feraoun did not edit the journals, which distinguishes them from works of fiction or theory.

Many Algerian writers, including Mouloud Mammeri, admitted that they were unable to write during the Algerian War because of restrictions and the conflict's mental toll. In 1958 *La Dernière impression,* by Malek Haddad, was published in Paris. It was the first novel that focused on the Algerian War. Si Abderrahmane Arab has studied French-language Algerian novels that, though not explicitly about the war, deal with themes of independence and nationalism. These novels include Mohammed Dib's trilogy (1952, 1954, and 1957) and Kateb Yacine's *Nedjma* (1956). Fanon, a psychiatrist born in the Caribbean country of Martinique and perhaps the best-known writer on the Algerian War, used the war to advance his ideas of violence as a "cleansing force" necessary to overcome the history of colonization.

Feraoun's *Journal* is important because of the breadth of information recorded, as well as the work's prescience. The book offers historical insight and is a valuable tool for postcolonial scholars to think about the transition from colonialism. Feraoun also foresaw the difficulties an independent Algeria would face. On January 12, 1957, he wrote, "Poor mountain people, poor students, poor young men, your enemies of tomorrow will be worse than those of yesterday." His predictions proved tragically accurate in the 1990s, when groups like the Armed Islamic Group of Algeria killed civilians in their attempt to overthrow the government, and the country spent the decade in what is sometimes called the Second Algerian War.

THEMES AND STYLE

Journal, 1955–1962 focuses on identity, a topic intensified by the war. Feraoun was French-educated, but as a native Algerian he did not have the same rights as French citizens, including his friends Camus and Robles. The cruelties committed by the French army during the war brought even greater attention to the inequalities between the colonized and the colonizer. Feraoun frequently grapples with his identity, asking rhetorically, "When I say that I am French, I give myself a label that each French person refuses me.... Can somebody tell me what I am!" (February 1, 1956). Feraoun movingly reveals the complexity of civil war and the feeling of being divided between two warring nations. Even though Feraoun supported Algerian independence, he maintained a nostalgia and appreciation for France, writing that on July 12, 1959, "when Algeria becomes independent and can hold her head high, I hope that she remembers France and all that she owes her."

Feraoun intended to publish his journals as a candid testimony of his experiences during the French-Algerian war. He could not know, though, that they would only become public posthumously. He explained in 1961 that his reason for writing is "simple": "It is appropriate that my journal supplement what has already been written about the Algerian war ... consider it one more document in an extremely poignant dossier." Although he took months-long breaks from his journals when he became overwhelmed by the tedium of the war, Feraoun wanted to use the project "to stand before the world and shout out the suffering and misfortune that have stalked me" (August 17, 1961). The journal format allowed Feraoun to relay stories from the news, record everyday occurrences in the lives of his friends and family, make observations, and express his own frustrations and opinions. *Journal* encompasses six and a half years of Feraoun's life, revealing changes in his feelings and offering a nuanced and honest portrayal of living through a conflict.

The bitter tone and unedited format of *Journal, 1955–1962* intimately reveal the complexity and emotional toll of war. Feraoun's tone remains despairing through much of *Journal*, a sharp contrast to the hopefulness of his *Le Fils du pauvre*. In his journals, Feraoun feels angry and "profoundly tired" (November 27, 1960) and writes that his "faith in man has been shaken" (August 17, 1961). Feraoun admits, looking back on older, unedited entries, that he is "frightened by my candor, my audacity, my cruelty, and, at times, my blind spots and prejudice" (August 17, 1961).

CRITICAL DISCUSSION

Journal, 1955–1962 was generally recognized for its depth of feeling and ability to provide details not reported elsewhere. In his introduction to the work, Robles writes that Feraoun's entries display the "anger and heartbreak that he used to express" in their meetings and letters. Seven years after it was published, Ernest Jackson of the University of Hawaii mentioned *Journal* in his review of *Jours de Kabylie*, a collection of Feraoun's essays. He declared *Journal* "a moving account of the war in Algeria." A 1971 article by Eric Sellin calls it "the most authentic literary statement" of the Algerian War and points out that Feraoun's willingness to confess his fears and doubts "in the midst of the slaughter took great courage." According to James Le Sueur, Feraoun's *Journal* was not as enthusiastically greeted by leftist intellectuals, who sided more strongly with the Marxist politics of Fanon's *The Wretched of the Earth*, published the year before.

Most often viewed as an affecting history of the Algerian War, *Journal* is also relevant in the wake of the Second Algerian War. In 2001 Phillip Naylor called it "a deeply personal memoir rather than a broad sweep of the war's events." In his 2002 review for *Research in African Literatures,* Irwin Wall writes that "as witness ... Feraoun's insights are most valuable." Although Feraoun was sometimes labeled an "assimilationist," scholars have pointed to *Journal* to show that he, while nostalgic for aspects of France's rule in Algeria, was, as Debra Kelly writes in her essay in *Autobiography and Independence* (2005), "fully aware of the legacy of colonialism ... and he is lucid in his analysis of French-Algerian relations."

Recent scholarship has focused on Feraoun's presentation of the colonized individual's identity during wartime and during the transition into independence. Kelly explains that Feraoun represents otherness and gives a "clear statement of the types of identity crisis provoked in the educated, colonised subject...."

A street sign in France commemorates the date of the end of the Algerian War. © URBAN IMAGES/ALAMY

THE POOR MAN'S AUTHOR

Mouloud Feraoun's best-known work of fiction is *Le Fils du pauvre* (*The Poor Man's Son*), published in 1950. The book is closely based on Feraoun's own background of growing up in poverty in the Kabylie Mountains in the north of Algeria. The protagonist, like Feraoun, is a Berber who receives an education within the French-colonized school system and becomes a schoolteacher.

Le Fils du pauvre is one of the first, if not the first, French-written works by a native North African. Though greeted warmly by French critics when it was published, the book was later criticized as too pro-colonialism because of its positive portrayal of Algerian life under French rule. Debra Kelly, however, asserts that the book is radical because it gives identities to poor Berbers. The farmers in the book are treated as individuals, and the novel provides a voice to those who had not appeared in French literature previously. Feraoun's attention to individual Algerians in *Le Fils du pauvre* foreshadows the way he would give voice to many ordinary Algerians in *Journal, 1955–1962*.

Feraoun is aware of inhabiting a space 'in between' two cultures, two histories, two value systems that are now in conflict with each other." Le Sueur encourages reading *Journal* as a complement to Fanon's texts because "we are able to use the *Journal* to compare the utopian revolutionary violence to the everyday, lived, ethical anxieties of a nation in the process of forming."

BIBLIOGRAPHY

Sources

"The Algerian War." *A Historical Companion to Postcolonial Literatures: Continental Europe and Its Empires.* Edinburgh: Edinburgh University Press, 2008. *Credo Reference.* 3 Mar. 2010. Web. 1 Jan. 2013.

Arab, Si Abderrahmane. "The National Liberation War in the French Language Novel of Algeria." *Bulletin (British Society for Middle Eastern Studies)* 17.1 (1990): 33–46. *JSTOR.* Web. 4 Jan. 2013.

Feraoun, Mouloud. *Journal, 1955–1962: Reflections on the French-Algerian War.* Ed. James D. Le Sueur. Trans. Mary Ellen Wolf and Claude Fouillade. Lincoln: University of Nebraska Press, 2000. Print.

Jackson, Ernest. "*Jours de Kabylie* by Mouloud Feraoun." *Books Abroad* 43.2 (1969): 303. *JSTOR.* Web. 4 Jan. 2013.

Kelly, Debra. "Mouloud Feraoun: Life Story, Life-Writing, History." *Autobiography and Independence: Selfhood and Creativity in North African Postcolonial Writing in French.* Liverpool: Liverpool University Press, 2005. 53–130. *Ebrary.* Web. 2 Jan. 2013.

Naylor, Phillip. Rev. of *Journal, 1955–1962: Reflections on the French-Algerian War*, by Mouloud Feraoun. *Journal of Military History* 65.1 (2001): 257–58. *JSTOR.* Web. 1 Jan. 2013.

Sellin, Eric. "Nationalism in World Literature: Irony, Sham, or in Earnest? Nationalism and the Development of Neo-African Literatures." *Books Abroad* 45.2 (1971): 199–207. *JSTOR.* Web. 4 Jan. 2013.

Wall, Irwin. Rev. of *Journal, 1955–1962: Reflections on the French-Algerian War,* by Mouloud Feraoun. *Research in African Literatures* 33.1 (2002): 195–97. *JSTOR.* Web. 1 Jan. 2013.

Further Reading

Ahmad, Fawzia. *A Study of Land and Milieu in the Works of Algerian-born Writers Albert Camus, Mouloud Feraoun, and Mohammed Dib.* Lewiston, N.Y.: Edwin Mellen, 2005. Print.

Camus, Albert. *The Stranger.* Trans. Matthew Ward. New York: Vintage International, 1989. Print.

Dib, Mohammed. *La Grande Maison: Roman.* Paris: Editions du Seuil, 1996. Print.

Fanon, Frantz. *The Wretched of the Earth.* New York: Grove, 1965. Print.

———. *A Dying Colonialism.* Trans. Haakon Chevalier. Harmondsworth, U.K.: Penguin, 1970. Print.

Feraoun, Mouloud. *The Poor Man's Son: Menrad, Kabyle Schoolteacher.* Trans. Lucy R. McNair. Charlottesville: University of Virginia Press, 2005. Print.

Le Sueur, James D. *Uncivil War: Intellectuals and Identity Politics during the Decolonization of Algeria.* Philadelphia: University of Pennsylvania Press, 2001. Print.

———. *Algeria since 1989: Between Terror and Democracy.* Halifax, NS: Fernwood, 2010. Print.

Kateb, Yacine. *Nedjma.* Trans. Richard Howard. Charlottesville: University of Virginia Press, 1991. Print.

Kathryn Molinaro

Nella Last's War
The Second World War Diaries of Housewife, 49
Nella Last

OVERVIEW

Nella Last's War: The Second World War Diaries of Housewife, 49 (1939–45) tracks the experiences of a woman in wartime Britain. First published in 1981, the diary was written as part of the Mass Observation Archive, a sociological research initiative funded by private individuals to gather information on the lives of ordinary British people. Nella Last (1889–1968) lived in the Cumbrian coastal town of Barrow, a German target during the war. A middle-class wife and mother of two who worked for the Women's Voluntary Service during the war, she had an intuitive grasp of storytelling. Her gossipy, entertaining style, combined with her enthusiastic willingness to bear witness to the political events of her time, make her diary a pleasurable read and a useful document of an important period in history.

Last and her husband, William, died within months of each other in 1968. In 1981 a selection of her wartime entries were published as *Nella Last's War: A Mother's Diary, 1939–1945*. One of the couple's two sons, Clifford, wrote the afterword to the 2006 edition. A television adaptation, *Housewife, 49,* followed that same year and was well received in Britain. In 2008 selected entries of Last's diaries from after the war were compiled into *Nella Last's Peace: The Post-War Diaries of Housewife, 49*. Because Last's writing is open to many interpretations and reveals the author's complex identity, scholars of British culture and history, autobiography, and feminist theory continue to admire the diaries.

HISTORICAL AND LITERARY CONTEXT

The collected entries of *Nella Last's War* represent an attempt to embody the ideal wartime matron. Last's preoccupation with and enactment of propriety constitute one of the most compelling aspects of her persona. Among the nearly five hundred mostly middle-class volunteers who wrote for the Mass Observation National Panel of Diarists from 1939 to 1967, Last speaks of her well-kept house with reverence. She capitalizes it as "HOME" when writing about her husband or sons, exhibiting their defiance against German attacks. Her diary also shows the comfort she takes in rendering her experience into words; she often seems to relish the chance to confide in a friend, albeit an imaginary one.

Her first entry, written the evening of Neville Chamberlain's 1939 announcement of war, begins, "Well, we know the worst." She later expresses approval of Britain's next prime minister, Winston Churchill, whose face she compares to that of "a bulldog living in our street who has done more to drive out unwanted dogs and cats than … all the complaints of householders." She mentions Adolf Hitler only occasionally; in one jarring passage, she admires his gassing of the mentally ill as a sort of mercy killing. However, when her son, Arthur, calls Jews "parasitic," Last disagrees. Nevertheless, in passages not included in the published edition, she occasionally displays a sense of ethnic superiority, describing a feud with a Women's Voluntary Service colleague whom she characterizes as "having a bit of the tar-brush in her" (the woman had an East Indian grandmother).

Although Last rarely mentions other writers, preferring movies and the radio, she nevertheless participates in a literary tradition. Invocations of astrology and descriptions of nature follow recognizable literary aesthetics. Her diary is often compared to the 1942 film *Mrs. Miniver,* the story of a middle-class British family living through the first few months of World War II, stoically withstanding the bombs and other hardships. In a similar vein, Clara Milburn, who lived in Coventry—an area heavily bombed by the Germans during the war—kept diaries of her wartime experiences, which were published in 1979 as *Mrs. Milburn's Diary: An Englishwoman's Reflections 1939–45*.

After the war ended, Last carried on with her diaries, most of which are preserved in the Mass Observation Archive. Some of her postwar diaries were published as *Nella Last's Peace* (2008), which editors Patricia and Robert Malcolmson note represent "a little less than a tenth of her original handwritten diary." In addition to Last's writing, the Mass Observation Archive maintains contributions from young men studying at Cambridge, women from social classes higher—though rarely lower—than Last's, and sundry other members of mostly left-wing British society. Despite the project's goals, historian Sandra Koa Wing points out in her 2007 book *Mass-Observation: Britain in the Second World War,* the group of writers "could never be a 'representative' sample of the British population, nor could it hope to paint a complete historical picture."

Key Facts

Time Period:
Mid-20th Century

Relevant Historical Events:
World War II; the German bombardment of Britain; Last's service in the Women's Voluntary Service

Nationality:
English

Keywords:
women's writing; war; bombardment

British poster urging women to join the workforce during World War II. English diarist Nella Last's account of her experiences during the war was published in 1981 as *Nella Last's War*. © LORDPRICE COLLECTION/ ALAMY

THEMES AND STYLE

Last's diary is infused with a sense of urgency. In the face of war she must define who she is, the nature of her relationships, her interactions with the community, and what she loves best about her home. She credits keeping the diary with causing a shift in her personality: "I'd never have spoken so plainly until now," she writes, patriotically refusing to look after the home of a neighbor who decamps to the countryside to avoid German attacks. She is surprised by the depth of her own emotions: "The dinner-time post brought a bidding to a funeral, and it was a bit of a shock. It was a boy Cliff played with." Faced with the prospect of death, she also reflects on her own mortality. She hopes to survive the war and attain a peaceful old age: "I would be quite content to end my days as my Gran did, with her garden and chickens."

Last knew what she wrote would be read by Mass Observation researchers and possibly included in one of their two thousand reports and twenty-five books published between 1937 and 1950. Although that knowledge may have colored her words, she expresses genuine pleasure in reading and writing. She particularly enjoys the freedom to turn on the light whenever she pleases to "have a read" or write letters. On a trip to the country, she thinks of her "wish to be cremated, of how I'd like my ashes to be strewn across the lake and to be a part of it—but it would so distress my husband." She goes on to imagine what sort of life she would want if she were reincarnated: "I think I'd like to be a man and have the freedom to go to the far ends of the earth … and be clever enough to write about it."

The diary is notable for its uncanny rendering of a voice with a distinctive quality that rings true and familiar. In her first entry, she writes, "I'm a self-reliant person, but today I've longed for a close woman friend—for the first time in my life." Although the first part of the sentence employs a declarative, conversational style that marks her gender, class, identification with ingrained British values such as personal independence, and even marital status, the latter part shows the individual behind the facade. An entry from Easter Monday 1941 begins, "Last night a noise like the crack of Doom sounded." Her ear for diction, finely attuned to the particularities of the English language as spoken in her part of the world, and her appreciation for subtle iterations of pettiness, sarcasm, and kindness create a sturdy prose that is sustained throughout her entries.

CRITICAL DISCUSSION

Jeremy Mulford of Falling Wall Press published the first edition of Last's diaries in 1981. The volume enjoyed a warm reception among general readers and was also welcomed by historians, anthropologists, sociologists, and other scholars. After the success of the television adaptation, a new edition was issued in 2006 with Mulford's consultation. His interest was primarily aesthetic, as he remarks in the 2006 edition: "When I first read parts of Nella Last's Diary, I thought it should be left virtually unchanged for publication." Philip Ziegler, Mass Observation's original publisher, remarks in his foreword to 2007's *Mass-Observation: Britain in the Second World War* that the human capacity for dwelling on catastrophe is limited. He suggests that the Mass Observation diaries "show that, as is so often the case in moments of great crisis, people were more concerned with the trivia of survival than with world-shaking events."

Subsequent interpretations of Last's writing have focused on elements ranging from her marital frustrations and denial of her son Clifford's probable homosexuality to her participation in a bygone, idealized era of British citizenship. The television adaptation took numerous liberties with Last's text, changing the names of her neighbors and extrapolating a higher degree of marital discord than Last's text describes. In the 2010 book *Nine Wartime Lives,* historiographer James Hinton questions the cherished notion of a "wartime unity" in which British society was at its patriotic best.

Scholars, including Hinton, continue to weigh the significance of Last's diary in terms of women's participation in activities outside the home during wartime. In a 2008 essay for Edinburgh Working Papers in Sociology, Andrea Salter considers Last's diary in terms of the sociological concept of indexicality, which defines how the situations people live in affect the way they use language. She calls diary writing an act that "denotes a nexus of mind, self and society at a particular time." Anthropologist Wing, discussing diarists' motivations in *Our Longest Days: A People's History of the Second World War* (2008), writes, "Mass Observation became a confidante, or witness of sorts, during terrifying air raids, at times of frustration with the war and with life in general, and when there was a need to express grief and distress over the absence or loss of loved ones."

MASS OBSERVATION: AN EXPERIMENT

With the goal of creating "a social anthropology of ourselves," the Mass Observation National Panel of Diarists tracked a range of phenomena, including dirty jokes and how they spread, what kind of hats people wore when seeing a movie, what proportion of men at a given sporting event wore beards, and what people kept in china cabinets and on mantels. The idea was that such ephemera, when combined, might offer a useful image of society and its overall tendencies.

In the 1970s, once the University of Sussex had rescued the Mass Observation Archive from a London basement, the diaries were made available to the public. Published editions of the diaries have proven very popular in Britain. Whether or not Britain was at its best during the war—pulling together as a society to make it through the worst of times—is difficult to ascertain. However, the interest and affection with which Mass Observation volunteers approached British society, and the openness with which the program received whatever volunteers were willing to share, offer fascinating insight into an important historical period.

BIBLIOGRAPHY

Sources

Hinton, James. *Nine Wartime Lives: Mass Observation and the Making of the Modern Self.* Oxford: Oxford University Press, 2010. Print.

Last, Nella. *Nella Last's War: The Second World War Diaries of Housewife, 49.* Eds. Richard Broad and Suzie Fleming. London: Profile Books, 2006. Print.

———. *Nella Last's Peace: The Post-War Diaries of Housewife, 49.* Eds. Patricia and Robert Malcolmson. London: Profile Books, 2008. Print.

Salter, Andrea. "Engaging with 'The Present'? Nella Last's Mass-Observation Diary." *Edinburgh Working Papers in Sociology* 26. Jan. 2008. Web. 30 Dec. 2012.

Wing, Sandra Koa, ed. *Mass-Observation: Britain in the Second World War.* London: Folio Society, 2007. Print.

———. *Our Longest Days: A People's History of the Second World War by the Writers of Mass Observation.* London: Profile Books, 2008. Print.

Further Reading

Calder, Angus. *The People's War: Britain 1939–1945.* New York: Pantheon, 1969. Print.

Dimmack, Max. *Clifford Last.* Melbourne: Hawthorn, 1972. Print.

Heimann, Judith. *The Most Offending Soul Alive: Tom Harrisson and His Remarkable Life.* Honolulu: University of Hawaii Press, 1998. *Google Books.* Web. 30 Dec. 2012.

Hinton, James. "Voluntarism and the Welfare/Warfare State: Women's Voluntary Services in the 1940s." *Twentieth Century British History* 9.2 (1998): 274–305. *Oxford Journals.* Web. 30 Dec. 2012.

———. *Women, Social Leadership and the Second World War: Continuities of Class.* New York: Oxford University Press, 2002. Print.

Malcolmson, Robert W., and Olivia Cockett, eds. *Love and War in London: A Woman's Diary 1939–1942.* Waterloo, ON: Wilfrid Laurier Press, 2005. Print.

Milburn, Clara Emily. *Mrs. Milburn's Diary: An Englishwoman's Day-to-Day Reflections, 1939–45.* Ed. Peter Donnelly. New York: Little, Brown, 1979. Print.

Mitchison, Naomi. *Among You Taking Notes: The Wartime Diaries of Naomi Mitchison 1939–1945.* London: Gollancz, 1985. Print.

Salter, Andrea. "Filling the Silences? Mass Observation's Wartime Diaries, Interpretive Work and Indexicality." *Life Writing* 7.1 (2010): 53–65. Web. 31 Dec. 2012.

Sheridan, Dorothy. "Ambivalent Memories: Women and the 1939–45 War in Britain." *Oral History* 18.1 (1990): 32–40. *JSTOR.* Web. 30 Dec. 2012.

Rebecca Rustin

A Pacifist's War
Diaries 1939–1945
Frances Partridge

❖ Key Facts

Time Period:
Mid-20th Century

Relevant Historical Events:
World War II; formation of the Bloomsbury group; German bombing of England

Nationality:
English

Keywords:
pacifism; literature; war

OVERVIEW

Frances Partridge's *A Pacifist's War: Diaries 1939–1945*, published in 1978, provides an insider's perspective of the daily travails of Partridge and her family and friends—some of them well-known members of the Bloomsbury Group—in England during World War II. The diaries begin as "1940 crept its way in, in a dense cold mist," and end on May 10, 1945, as the long-awaited end of the war brought about relief mixed with exhaustion. Partridge and her husband, Ralph, were conscientious objectors, and their Wiltshire home, Ham Spray, was treated as a refuge by friends suffering the effects of German attacks on England. In her diaries, Partridge holds her friends' experiences dear, quoting them often, though she considers consciousness and thinking to be most precious. She laments the war not only for its destructive brutality but also for its interruption and oppression of conscious reflection.

Partridge waited nearly twenty years after the death of her husband to publish *A Pacifist's War*, the first volume of her diaries. Five other volumes would follow. The diaries were well received for providing insight into the activities of the Bloomsbury Group, whose illustrious members were English artists and intellectuals including writers Virginia Woolf and Lytton Strachey. Named after the Bloomsbury section of London where they would meet, the group became notorious for its members' unconventional lifestyles and open attitudes toward sex. Today *A Pacifist's War* continues to provide an invaluable source of insight into the complex relationships that characterized wartime Bloomsbury.

HISTORICAL AND LITERARY CONTEXT

Partridge's writing style reflects the intellectual concerns and sensibilities of England during the early twentieth century. Born into a family acquainted with Bloomsbury members, Partridge was educated at Cambridge, where she studied English and the moral sciences, including logic and philosophy. She engaged in letter writing and journaling, which were commonplace among intellectuals of the period, including Woolf, Strachey, and others. Partridge and other Bloomsbury members often reflected individual psychology and human relationships as discussed by Sigmund Freud, whose papers were first published in English by Leonard and Virginia Woolf's Hogarth Press in 1924. Philosopher G. E. Moore also influenced Bloomsbury, and Partridge lived (and wrote) by his assertion in *Principia Ethica* (1903) that friendship and appreciation of beauty were "intrinsic goods."

A Pacifist's War features appearances by many noted intellectuals, including Oxford English professor David Cecil; Russian translator Constance Garnett; former *New Statesman* editor Desmond MacCarthy with his wife, Molly; and wartime *New Statesman* editor Raymond Mortimer. Another visitor to Ham Spray was Angelica Bell—the illegitimate daughter of artists Vanessa Bell (Woolf's sister) and Duncan Grant, whose work adorned Ham Spray's walls. Psychoanalysts Alix and James Strachey (the latter was Lytton's younger brother) also visited. The diary entries recount their perceptions and experiences of the group as the war waged on, such as the April 3, 1941, entry, which tells of Woolf's suicide on March 28. Partridge quotes art critic Clive Bell: "She was in for another of those long agonizing breakdowns.... The prospect—two years insanity, then to wake up to the sort of world two years of war will have made, was such that I can't feel sure that she was unwise."

Interspersed with Partridge's personal reminiscences are references to the literary works she engaged with, though they were seldom from her own time. La Marquise du Deffand's memoirs of seventeenth- and eighteenth-century France provided a view of war sympathetic to Partridge's. Gustave Flaubert's *Letters* inspired Partridge to marvel, "How his reactions remind me of ours!" Whereas Woolf's diaries reveal an intellect stirred by everything from a walk by the river to Adolf Hitler's maniacal rantings, Partridge's are primarily concerned with the perspectives of family and friends, to which she sparingly adds her own impressions.

The publication of *A Pacifist's War* late in Partridge's life earned her a measure of celebrity as one of the last surviving members of the Bloomsbury Group. Encouraged by the success of the first volume, she published the rest of her diaries and other titles including a biography of author Julia Strachey. In 2000 Partridge was named a Commander of the Order of the British Empire for her contributions to literature.

Shadows on My Heart
The Civil War Diary of Lucy Rebecca Buck of Virginia
Lucy Buck

OVERVIEW

Beginning on Christmas Day, 1861, and ending abruptly after the South's surrender in 1865, *Shadows on My Heart: The Civil War Diary of Lucy Rebecca Buck of Virginia* retells a young southern woman's experiences during the Civil War, addressing her inner feelings, recounting the banalities of domestic life, and relating her extended family's losses. It is likely that Buck began her diary sooner than 1861, but earlier manuscripts have been lost. Not written for posterity, *Shadows on My Heart* only became public in the last fifty years. In her 1997 edition of the work, editor Elizabeth Baer relies on two earlier versions of Buck's diary and additional historical artifacts.

First transcribed, abridged, and privately published by Captain Neville Buck in 1940, the diary, of which about seventy copies were made, was originally distributed to family members and archives. Initially, the family had hoped to interest a publisher such as the University of North Carolina Press or Wilfred Funk. However, Baer reports that in 1945 the family sent the transcribed diary to Major Thomas Suter, who had promised a large printing that was never realized; the original transcription was never recovered. A second edition, again edited by a member of the Buck family, was published under the title *Sad Earth, Sweet Heaven* in 1973 and was rereleased in 1992 by Buck Publishing. The second edition featured some of the previously excised entries, additional annotations on the Civil War, and a map of the Royal Front area.

HISTORICAL AND LITERARY CONTEXT

Though writer Daniel Aaron and others have somewhat misleadingly dubbed the Civil War an "unwritten war" because of the paucity of literary "masterpieces" produced during the time period, many letters, poems, short stories, essays, novels, and diaries arose from the conflict. As Baer notes, it was quite common for women such as Lucy Buck to keep diaries during the Civil War and then to leave off writing them at the close of the conflict. Many women across the country, such as Buck's acquaintance Sue Richardson, began and kept diaries at this time. Indeed, Baer looked to a few such artifacts to fill in gaps left by a five-month hiatus in Buck's narrative. Though few southern women at the time were writing works to be published, diaries and letters were a common outlet for their feelings and served to distance them from their daily trials.

Composed in multiple volumes, Buck's diary was written in old ledgers and on an assortment of paper. Some of the sheets were "cross-hatched" with text written in two directions, and Baer notes that Buck's handwriting also became smaller as paper became scarcer. All of these factors suggest that, despite material challenges, Buck was determined to continue writing. It appears several of the volumes were bound after Buck wrote them, as the binding obscures a number of words. Further, a few pages of the original diary were tipped into each of the seventy volumes produced in the 1940 edition. Thus, some of the passages that Captain Neville Buck excised were forever lost when the volumes were distributed.

Buck was not alone in her writing. Drew Gilpin Faust mentions at least 200 related documents in *Mothers of Invention: Women of the Slaveholding South in the American Civil War* (1996). Some of the most well-known examples of published Civil War diaries written by women include Buck's Shenandoah Valley neighbor Cornelia Peake McDonald's *A Diary with Reminiscences of the War and Refugee Life in the Shenandoah Valley, 1860–1865, Mary Chesnut's Civil War,* and *The Civil War Diary of Sarah Morgan.* Moreover, in the four-year span of her diary, Buck, an avid reader, mentions more than thirty titles, including popular works by Sir Walter Scott; historical essays by figures such as Benjamin Franklin; poetry by Alfred, Lord Tennyson; and the Bible.

After a hiatus of eight years, Buck commenced keeping a consistent diary, chronicling her life until her death in 1918. That her Civil War diary has been published in three separate editions within half a century of one another and is often quoted in studies of southern women's war experiences is an indication that individual perceptions and voices are gaining importance among historians and scholars of Civil War and American culture.

THEMES AND STYLE

Shadows on My Heart is a remarkably diverse work, especially as so much of her life was a set routine. Though her loyalties are always wholeheartedly secessionist, her

Key Facts

Time Period:
Mid-19th Century

Relevant Historical Events:
American Civil War

Nationality:
American

Keywords:
civil war; domesticity; women's writing

WAR EXPERIENCES

Many Civil War battles took place near diarist Lucy Buck's home in the Shenandoah Valley, including the 1862 Battle of Opequon, pictured here. © CULVER PICTURES/ THE ART ARCHIVE AT ART RESOURCE, NY

retelling of hosting Confederate and Union soldiers covers a variety of events, characterizations, and emotional reactions. Firmly a patriot of the Confederacy, Buck repeatedly states without intended irony that she refuses to be enslaved and oppressed by the Union; in nearly the same breath she calls the self-liberation of her enslaved "servants" ungrateful.

Any explicit explanation of Buck's motives for writing the work may have been lost along with the earlier volumes of her diary. Relying as she did on letters for contact with her two brothers during the war, her hopes to receive or to send mail were frequently disappointed due to paper shortages, an unreliable system, and the frequent destruction of mail bags by the Union army. Therefore, Buck's diaries also served as an outlet for her drive to communicate, even if only with herself. Moreover, Baer suggests that Buck used her diary as a mode of self-reflection that allowed her to develop beyond the constraining ideologies of idealized southern womanhood and to distance herself from the strains of life during the war.

A well-educated young woman, Buck frequently lapses into poetic reveries, seemingly as moved by her romantic style as by the events surrounding her. The opening entry, on Christmas Day, is an example of her "high style." She writes, "I think of how many hands that have wreathed the bowl and twined the holly last year are now mouldering in the dust. The bright locks that were then crowned with roses, now dabbled with gore and covered with the turf of the battlefield." At other times, her prose records events more stiffly and prosaically, as in a brief entry rife with sentence fragments and abbreviations: "Ma has concluded to go with Mrs. Van M to Harper's Ferry tomorrow. Busy making preparations…. Very tired and sleepy tonight." This admixture of styles indicates, as Baer argues, that *Shadows on My Heart* was a private document, written for her own edification and amusement rather than for future posterity. There are no apostrophes to a "Gentle Reader" or to any reader in general. In fact, there is at times a complete lack of context explaining events, and thus the narrative is frequently jarring. This lack of details indicates further that the diary was not intended for mass circulation and publication.

CRITICAL DISCUSSION

Shadows on My Heart remained unpublished until 1940, more than twenty years after her death and nearly sixty years after she began it. That the Buck family had difficulties interesting publishers in the text and even took to printing it themselves twice suggests that there was little attention paid to the diary until Baer reissued it, a supposition supported by the lack of critical articles or reviews on the diary. Baer's introductory and concluding remarks remain the most detailed critical reactions to Buck's diary, though scholars such as Drew Gilpin Faust use quotes such as "[w]e shall never any of us be the same as we have been" from the diary to underscore points related to the changes wrought by the war upon southern life and womanhood.

Buck's diary has won her and her home a place in records of mid-nineteenth-century southern womanhood, alongside Belle Boyd, an acquaintance of Buck's who worked as a Confederate spy, and "Captain" Sally Tompkins, who ran Robertson Hospital in Richmond, Virginia. Additionally, Buck's experiences have been immortalized in at least one painting. After being approached by the current resident of Buck's home Bel Air to include the structure in a painting, Mort Künstler read *Sad Earth, Sweet Heaven*, the second version of Buck's diary, and was inspired by Buck and her sister's reception of General Robert E. Lee and their acquisition of his autograph. He eventually produced "The Autograph Seekers of Bel Air" in 2009.

Though there are no critical studies of Buck's diary or life, several reviews list *Shadows on My Heart* as an important Civil War artifact and suggest it as a suitable text for the classroom. Michelle Krowl finds Baer's edition the best of the three available but wishes Baer had included a map of the Royal Front area such as the one in *Sad Earth, Sweet Heaven*. Marli Weiner likewise finds Baer's edition excellent but takes issue with her decision to abridge sections of the diary she deemed "extraneous" or "repetitive." Leah Berkowitz disagrees with Baer's supposition that the war caused Buck to revise her self-impression and to question the place of women in society, finding no textual evidence to support Baer's claims and declaring *Shadows* "far less dramatic than Mary Chesnut's, Sarah Morgan Dawson's, or the overlooked Belle Edmondson," particularly in terms of "how the war caused southern women to reevaluate their self-image." Berkowitz concludes, "It is hard to understand why this rather tedious journal has been published three times." However, Baer suggests that it is, in part, the elements of tedium that worked their way into the diary alongside amusements, work, and strife that make *Shadows on My Heart* a candid snapshot of life for a woman whose life was affected, but not devastated, by the war.

BELLE BOYD, "SIREN OF THE SHENANDOAH"

Lucy Buck lists the spy Belle Boyd among her acquaintances and refers to her daring occasionally in passing. In her most famous exploit, Boyd risked her life to report the Union Army's movements to General Stonewall Jackson. Buck reports, "[Boyd] wished some information conveyed to the army.... She went herself to a most exposed point, where the bullets fell like hail stones around her riddling her dress. I know not what truth there is in the rumor."

Later, Buck privileges her own culinary achievements over Boyd's spying, indicating her indifference to her acquaintance: "Tis said Belle Boyd is in town tonight. What next? My biscuits were pronounced faultless tonight." This ambivalence might stem from having caught Boyd flirting with a Yankee, or as she puts it, "appear[ing] upon such familiar terms with those whom we most dreaded"—behavior Buck could not condone. Little did she know flirtation was Boyd's main strategy for acquiring information to aid the Confederate cause.

BIBLIOGRAPHY

Sources

Aaron, Daniel. *The Unwritten War: American Writers and the Civil War*. Madison: University of Wisconsin Press, 1987. Print.

Baer, Elizabeth, ed. *Shadows on My Heart: The Civil War Diary of Lucy Rebecca Buck of Virginia*. Athens: University of Georgia Press, 1997. Print.

Berkowitz, Leah. Rev. of *Shadows on My Heart: The Civil War Diaries of Lucy Rebecca Buck of Virginia*, by Lucy Rebecca Buck. *H-Net*. Web. 02 Dec. 2012.

Buck, William Pettus, ed. *Sad Earth, Sweet Heaven: The Diary of Lucy Rebecca Buck*. Birmingham, Ala.: Cornerstone, 1973. Print.

Faust, Drew Gilpin. *Mothers of Invention: Women of the Slaveholding South in the American Civil War*. Chapel Hill: University of North Carolina Press, 1996. Print.

Groh, Mary Lou. "Maria 'Belle' Boyd." *Civil War*. Civil War Trust. n.d. Web. 03 Dec. 2012.

Krowl, Michelle A. Rev. of *Shadows on My Heart: The Civil War Diary of Lucy Rebecca Buck of Virginia*, by Lucy Rebecca Buck. *Virginia Magazine of History and Biography* 105.4 (1997): 481–82. JSTOR. Web. 01 Dec. 2012.

Robertson, Mary D. Rev. of *Shadows on My Heart: The Civil War Diary of Lucy Rebecca Buck of Virginia*, by Lucy Rebecca Buck. *Southern Voices from the Past: Women's Letters, Diaries, and Writings Series*, ed. Elizabeth R. Baer. *Georgia Historical Quarterly* 82.1 (1998): 203–04. JSTOR. Web. 02 Dec. 2012.

Weiner, Marli F. Rev. of *Tokens of Affection: The Letters of a Planter's Daughter in the Old South*, by Maria Brian. Ed. Carol Bleser; *The Diary of Dolly Lunt Burge, 1848–1879*, ed. Christine Jacobson Carter; and *Shadows on My Heart: The Civil War Diary of Lucy Rebecca Buck of Virginia*, ed. Elizabeth R. Baer. *Journal of American History* 86.1 (1999): 237–39. JSTOR. Web. 01 Dec. 2012.

Further Reading

Boyd, Belle. *Belle Boyd in Camp and Prison*. London: Saunders,1865. *Documenting the American South*. Web. 03 Dec. 2012.

Chesnut, Mary Boykin. *Mary Chesnut's Civil War*. Ed. C. Vann Woodward. New Haven, Conn.: Yale University Press, 1981. Print.

Dawson, Sarah Morgan. *The Civil War Diary of Sarah Morgan*. Ed. Charles East. Athens: University of Georgia Press, 1991. Print.

Forbush, Bradley M. "To Front Royal and Back." *13th Mass*. 13thMass.org, 2009. Web. 03 Dec. 2012.

McDonald, Cornelia Peake. *A Woman's Civil War: A Diary with Reminiscences of the War from March 1862*. Ed.

Minrose C. Gwin. Madison: University of Wisconsin Press, 1992. Print.

Roberts, Giselle. "Buck, Lucy Rebecca (1842–1918)." *Women in the American Civil War.* Ed. Lisa Tendrich Frank. Vol. 2. Santa Barbara, Calif.: ABC Clio, 2008. 145–46. Print.

Sullivan, Walter. *The War the Women Lived: Female Voices from the Confederate South.* Nashville: J. S. Sanders, 2005. Print.

Katherine Bishop

THURA'S DIARY
A Young Girl's Life in War-Torn Baghdad
Thura Al-Windawi

OVERVIEW

Thura's Diary: A Young Girl's Life in War-Torn Baghdad (2004) begins on March 15, 2003, days before the onset of the U.S.-led bombing of Iraq, and captures the first few months of the invasion from the perspective of nineteen-year-old Iraqi Thura Al-Windawi. Her last dated entry is June 4, 2003, her twentieth birthday. The published text includes an afterword discussing her subsequent admission to the University of Pennsylvania. A postscript dated December 14, 2003, follows and reflects on the capture of Saddam Hussein by U.S. troops the previous day. Writing in Arabic, Al-Windawi recorded her observations and thoughts in a notebook with the hope that they might one day help outsiders, especially Americans, understand the suffering of the Iraqi people. Although some entries cover multiple days, her in-the-moment impressions provide unique insight into the life of an ordinary Iraqi during this pivotal period.

Al-Windawi's text was a forerunner of the corpus of first-person accounts of the war by Iraqi women that appeared in English in subsequent years. Excerpts of Al-Windawi's diary were published in English as early as April 2003 and were well received. Although her diary continued to attract praise following its full-length publication, it was also the object of criticism. Some detractors faulted the author for her distant tone and failure to provide sufficient details, while others felt that the work's value was undermined by the discovery that her father was a high-ranking member of the Baath party. Nevertheless, in 2005 *Thura's Diary* won a Christopher Award, which is granted to stories that demonstrate courage in the face of adversity. Today scholarship on *Thura's Diary* focuses on the text as a teaching tool.

HISTORICAL AND LITERARY CONTEXT

Hussein became president of Iraq in 1979, and the United States backed him and the ruling secular, socialist Baath party through the 1980s. Prior to his reign, Iraq's educational system and infrastructure had improved, as had women's access to education, professional opportunities, and legal rights. But these advances stalled during his presidency, which was marked by horrendous human rights abuses, including torture, mass arrests, and the use of chemical weapons, as the regime attempted to suppress opposition. Following the 1991 Gulf War, U.S. support for Hussein and the Baath party waned.

In the aftermath of the 2001 al-Qa'ida terrorist attacks on the United States, U.S. president George W. Bush's war on terror led to the March 2003 invasion of Iraq. The United States accused Iraq of possessing weapons of mass destruction, using the human rights abuses committed by Hussein and the Baath party to further justify direct military intervention. Three days after Al-Windawi began writing her diary, Bush issued an ultimatum to Hussein and his sons: if they did not leave Iraq within forty-eight hours, they would face military action. On March 20, 2003, after Hussein and his sons failed to comply, the U.S.-led bombing of Iraq began. Bush reassured the people of Iraq that any attack would not target them, and he guaranteed that foreign intervention and the removal of Hussein would bring freedom and prosperity. However, as Al-Windawi records, civilian casualties were high, infrastructure was destroyed, crime and sectarian violence increased, and women suffered loss of mobility and greater oppression.

Thura's Diary bears many similarities to other accounts of war by young female diarists such as Anne Frank, who wrote about her experiences in the Netherlands during World War II, and Zlata Filipovic, who described life in Sarajevo during the war in Bosnia-Herzegovina. Al-Windawi's text also fits into a body of first-person activist narratives by Iraqi women published in English with the common goal of raising Western awareness about Iraqi experiences of war and occupation. These include *IraqiGirl: Diary of a Teenage Girl in Iraq* (2009), which describes life in Mosul from 2004 to 2007, and *Baghdad Burning: Girl Blog from Iraq* (2005) and *Baghdad Burning II: More Girl Blog from Iraq* (2006) by Riverbend, who began writing in August 2003 at the age of twenty-five.

Al-Windawi and her diary received considerable media attention even before the full work's publication. Excerpts appeared in the *Times of London* in April 2003, and Al-Windawi was interviewed by both the BBC and CBS in the subsequent months. With the help of her media contacts and the support of the

❖ *Key Facts*

Time Period:
Early 21st Century

Relevant Historical Events:
U.S. invasion of Iraq in 2003; American capture of Saddam Hussein

Nationality:
Iraqi

Keywords:
war; invasion; bombardment

Thura's Diary discusses the author's life just before and during the beginning of the Iraq War, including the 2003 "shock and awe" attack. Here, a government building in Baghdad burns during this attack. © AP IMAGES/JEROME DELAY

dean of admissions at the University of Pennsylvania, she was already a freshman at that school by the time she wrote the postscript in December 2003.

THEMES AND STYLE

Although Al-Windawi describes the key historical events of the invasion, the text is primarily concerned with capturing the everyday experience of the war. The pages of her diary reveal the simultaneous fear and boredom that characterized her experience. She worries about her family's safety as well as her future, especially since she is not sure if she will be able to return to college. She asks herself, "[W]hat do the years ahead hold in store for me?" At the same time, the house must be dusted and prepared to receive guests, even if there is no electricity or running water. She explains, "Baghdad may have fallen, but life goes on." The early days of the military campaign are full of terror. She writes on March 19, 2003, "This is the hardest day of my life…. We are like the *Titanic* going down, drowning in the ocean."

Al-Windawi kept her diary with the goal of sharing it with a Western audience and raising awareness about the suffering of the Iraqi people. She explains, "All I wanted was for my voice to reach out to the world, so that maybe people will understand what's going on here and what the Iraqi people are going through—even if I'm not an expert." Describing the fall of Baghdad on April 9, 2003, she pleads for empathy by comparing it to September 11, 2001, when the United States was attacked: "And just like the Americans will never forget that day, no Iraqi will ever forget 9 April, either." Her compassion is seemingly boundless. She expresses sympathy for American and British soldiers and their families and even for Hussein after his sons are killed: "I guess Saddam, too, came to understand what it means to lose a son."

The language of *Thura's Diary* is calm and detached, even as it describes the chaos of the war, perhaps because the author was consciously writing for an audience. Her account of the death of a childhood friend, Fahad, does not reveal the emotion that must have accompanied it: "We see Fahad as a martyr because he was a peaceful person who died while trying to help others." Her political and ideological beliefs are complex and often seem contradictory. Following the invasion, she condemns the loss of her personal freedom as she is forced to wear a head scarf to protect herself from the ire of religious extremists. Yet she also censures the U.S. army for allowing women to serve in its ranks. Her attitude toward Hussein is equally complex. Following his arrest, she writes, "A part of me felt sad … but not because Saddam was gone. I think it was just because we were used to seeing him like a lion. We were used to being afraid. But now, the lion is gone. I hope the fear will go away too."

CRITICAL DISCUSSION

Initial responses to Al-Windawi's writings were overwhelmingly positive, and her diary was widely excerpted. However, following the text's publication, some critics characterized her writing as uneven, attributing it to her age. In a 2004 article in the *Capital Times*, Karyn Saemann asserts, "Depending on the day, [Al-Windawi's] analysis of unfolding events is hauntingly poignant, spotty or nonexistent." Other critics have questioned the legitimacy of Al-Windawi's positioning as an "ordinary" Iraqi given her father's high-ranking involvement in the Baath party. Christopher Silvester notes in a 2004 *Independent* article, "Thura's father, Mouayad Al-Windawi, was … none other than the head of information and training at Saddam's notorious internal security organisation … with the rank of general."

During the War in Iraq and the early years of the occupation, *Thura's Diary* was recognized as an important addition to the historical record. Writing in *Booklist* in 2004, John Green predicted, "Although [*Thura's Diary*] discusses events already several months old, this will remain relevant for a long time, both because it illuminates the complex relationship between the U.S. and the average young Iraqi and because it lays bare the brutal nature of war." With this in mind, it is perhaps to be expected that recent discussion of the text has centered primarily on its pedagogical value.

Scholarship on *Thura's Diary* has focused on the text as a teaching tool in elementary, middle school, and high school classrooms. For example, in a 2006 article for *Journal of Adolescent & Adult Literacy*, Thomas W. Bean and Helen J. Harper seek to provide a "critical framework for use and adaptation in organizing class discussion in the study of young adult literature." They argue that *Thura's Diary*, "as well as a host of young adult novels set in sites of war, conflict, and civil unrest, offers teachers and students a powerful resource for the critical discussion of global and national politics."

BIBLIOGRAPHY

Sources

Al-Windawi, Thura. *Thura's Diary: A Young Girl's Life in War-Torn Baghdad*. New York: Viking, 2004. Print.

Bean, Thomas W., and Helen J. Harper. "Exploring Notions of Freedom in and through Young Adult Literature." *Journal of Adolescent & Adult Literacy* 50.2 (2006): 96–104. Print.

Green, John. Rev. of *Thura's Diary: My Life in Wartime Iraq*, by Thura Al-Windawi. *Booklist* 100.18 (2004): 1613. Print.

Saemann, Karyn. "Baghdad Teen Reveals Mixed Emotions." Rev. of *Thura's Diary: My Life in Wartime Iraq*, by Thura Al-Windawi. *Capital Times* 20 Aug. 2004: 11A. Print.

Silvester, Christopher, ed. "The Diary." *Independent on Sunday* 18 Apr. 2004: 26. Print.

"Tanya of Leningrad Died in 1943." *New York Times*. 24 May 1972: 3. *ProQuest Historical Newspapers*. Web. 2 Feb. 2013.

Further Reading

Antoon, Sinan, dir. *About Baghdad*. InCounter Productions, 2004. Film.

Blasim, Hassan. *The Madman of Freedom Square*. Manchester, U.K.: Comma, 2009. Print.

IraqiGirl. *IraqiGirl: Diary of a Teenage Girl in Iraq*. Trans. Elizabeth Wrigley-Field. Chicago: Haymarket, 2009. Print.

Riverbend. *Baghdad Burning: Girl Blog from Iraq*. New York: Feminist Press, 2005. Print.

Riverbend. *Baghdad Burning II: More Girl Blog from Iraq*. New York: Feminist Press, 2006. Print.

THE ENDURING LEGACY OF TANYA SAVICHEVA

Generations of readers have been moved by chronicles of the damage inflicted by war on the hopes and dreams of youth. Works such as Anne Frank's *Diary of a Young Girl* and *Thura's Diary* recount the horrors of war in deeply personal narratives that have received wide publication and critical notice. Eleven-year-old Tanya Savicheva of Leningrad in the Soviet Union was another young diarist whose writing had a deep impact, although it was never published and consisted of only seven 1-line entries.

A contemporary of Anne Frank, Savicheva was eleven when the war came to Leningrad in the form of a German blockade beginning in September 1941. Tanya worked with her family and neighbors digging defensive trenches, but the siege was inexorable. Soon the city was starving and, with the onset of winter, freezing as well. As she watched helplessly while her family grew weaker, Tanya made her record, a simple listing of the deaths of each member of her family. The last entry reads, "The Savichevs are dead. All are dead. Only Tanya is left." Tanya was finally evacuated from Leningrad. She died in 1943, but her poignant journal was presented at the Nuremburg trials during the late 1940s as evidence of Nazi war crimes and remains on display in the St. Petersburg History Museum.

Tripp, Charles. *A History of Iraq*. 2nd ed. Cambridge, U.K.: Cambridge University Press, 2002. Print.

Allison Blecker

A Woman at War
Molly Moore

Key Facts

Time Period:
Late 20th Century

Relevant Historical Events:
Persian Gulf War; Iraqi occupation of Kuwait

Nationality:
American

Keywords:
war; occupation; journalism; women's writing

OVERVIEW

A Woman at War, published in 1993 by Molly Moore, combines a blow-by-blow overview of the Gulf War in 1991 with the author's experience covering that war from the battlefield. Moore, a defense correspondent for the *Washington Post,* had a special vantage point for viewing the war's final days in Kuwait. She had accepted an invitation to shadow Lieutenant General Walter E. Boomer, the commanding general of U.S. Marine forces during Operation Desert Storm. The Gulf War was notable for the tight restrictions the military imposed on the news media, especially during the 100-hour ground war of February 24–28. Moore's is one of the most descriptive narrative accounts of that conflict. The numerous anecdotes conveying the unusual experience of a female civilian in a combat zone lend the book an additional layer of interest.

Upon its publication, *A Woman at War* was recognized for its detailed coverage of the intense ground battle with Iraqi forces occupying Kuwait—details to which few reporters had access and which Moore herself was unable to publish while the battle raged. Her text exemplifies the qualities of wartime coverage provided by an "embedded" journalist (one stationed with a military unit). Embedding effectively makes the reporter part of a military unit, and the unit is then responsible for the journalist's safety. Critics of the practice contend that it compromises journalistic objectivity and enables military officials to manage and control war coverage. The U.S. military widely expanded this practice during its second war against Iraq, beginning in 2003.

HISTORICAL AND LITERARY CONTEXT

The invasion of Kuwait on August 2, 1990, by Iraqi forces under President Saddam Hussein sparked the first major international crisis following the disintegration of the Soviet Union. Iraqi troops soon massed on Kuwait's southern border and threatened to advance into Saudi Arabia. The United Nations quickly imposed economic sanctions on Iraq and authorized a naval blockade, while U.S. President George H. W. Bush assembled a diplomatic and military coalition to force an Iraqi withdrawal. As war grew imminent, U.S. leaders grasped that one benefit of a smashing military victory would be that it would help restore morale to the armed forces nearly two decades after their ignominious defeat in Vietnam.

Two weeks after the invasion of Kuwait, Moore traveled from Washington to Saudi Arabia in the entourage of Secretary of Defense Dick Cheney. She elected to stay in the region as the United States and Arab nations prepared for war. Once Desert Storm got under way on the night of January 16, Moore and other reporters covered the air war from the Saudi city of Dhahran, mostly traveling in pools under tight military control. General Boomer invited Moore, along with five other journalists, to spend several days at the marine command post as the U.S. ground attack commenced. Only Moore accepted the invitation, and she thus witnessed the four days of intense combat up close, even spending nights in the commanding general's tent.

Working as a female war correspondent places Moore in select company. Some of her distinguished predecessors include Marguerite Higgins, Martha Gellhorn, and Dorothy Thompson, who wrote during World War II, and Gloria Emerson, who memorably covered the Vietnam War for the *New York Times.* The Gulf crisis provided career opportunities to journalists such as Christiane Amanpour of the CNN television network and Moore's colleague at the *Post,* Caryle Murphy, who won a 1991 Pulitzer Prize for her Gulf War reporting.

In *A Woman at War,* however, Moore goes beyond the conventions of daily journalism to write about her own experiences in the desert and her difficulties in negotiating the male-dominated cultures of the Middle East and the military. The resulting work sensitively conveys the lived experience of frontline combat from the viewpoints of both armed participants and civilian observers.

THEMES AND STYLE

The book expresses its theme of war as a human experience by portraying events largely through the eyes of a small group of people, including herself, General Boomer, and Lieutenant William Delaney, who commanded a marine tank platoon on the front lines in Kuwait. The author portrays many moments of danger and fear. She opens the book with a tense scene from the second night of the ground war, in which she accompanies Boomer's staff in a Chevrolet Blazer along a narrow desert lane through a minefield in pitch darkness. The vignette exemplifies the confusion and menace of life on the battlefield. It becomes clear that frustration, especially with the difficulties of communication and erratically functioning equipment, goes along with even the most successful missions.

Moore wrote *A Woman at War* in large part because communications failures kept her from delivering more than two of her articles in time for publication while the brief campaign on the ground was underway. The overall media coverage of the Gulf conflict, and particularly of this crucial phase of the fighting, was inadequate and incomplete, in the author's view. The book appears in the loose format of a reconstructed diary but is closer in substance to a work of journalism. Using information from interviews, letters, and other documents, the author intersperses scenes from the viewpoints of Boomer, Delaney, and other military personnel.

Apart from its opening chapter, the book is structured chronologically, interweaving events experienced by Moore and reported events such as Boomer's conversations with General Norman Schwarzkopf, the overall coalition commander during Desert Storm. The first half of the book chronicles the lead-up to the war and the five weeks of aerial bombing; the second half, "Boomer's War," concentrates on the days from February 23 to 28. Moore writes in a discursive style. Detailed descriptions of strategic and military matters give way to frank anecdotal accounts of activities such as eating MREs (meals ready to eat—or, as one soldier jokes, "meals rejected by Ethiopians") and donning suspect gas masks during air raids: "If I could smell the stench of tomatoes on the floor and the spoiled chicken parts on the counter above me, I figured chemical particles would have no trouble penetrating my pathetic mask." Moore emphasizes what she and her companions feared: that the Iraqis outnumbered the coalition forces and could attack Saudi Arabia before the coalition was fully mobilized and that Hussein might employ his arsenal of chemical weapons. As the narrative unfolds, such anxieties are gradually swept aside by the magnitude and relative ease of the coalition's triumph. Speaking of Hussein, Boomer tells Moore, "His heart just isn't in this fight."

CRITICAL DISCUSSION

Initial response to *A Woman at War* was generally favorable. At the time of its release, no comparably detailed firsthand account of the combat in Kuwait had appeared in print. A review in *Publishers Weekly* concluded, "Moore's book contains some of the finest war reporting of the past half-century." In *Editor & Publisher,* Hiley Ward predicted that the book's reportage "will have lingering historical value." However, some reviewers noted limitations in the development of underlying themes in the book. Writing in *Library Journal,* for example, John Yurechko found that Moore's assessment of the complicated relations between the press and the military "deserves more deliberate study than the angry afterthought at the end of this book." In a *Los Angeles Times* review, Jonathan Kirsch concluded that because of the performance of women on and off the battlefield in the gulf, "*A Woman at War*—with its insistent emphasis on a woman's perspective—is already something of an antique."

Moore's book, to a greater degree than her news coverage, has found a place in the lineage of war reportage in general and in particular of war literature by women. At least one published anthology of women's war writing contains an excerpt from *A Woman at War.* A lengthy study of female war reportage, printed in the *American Journalism Review* in 1994, placed Moore's work alongside that of correspondents covering the war in Bosnia. In the journal *Foreign Affairs,* neoconservative defense analyst Eliot Cohen assessed Moore's book as informative but complained that it "exhibits modern journalists' fascination with exploring their emotions at the expense of portraying unfolding events."

A woman soldier in the U.S. Army demonstrates a light machine gun in Saudi Arabia during the Gulf War. © MIRRORPIX/COURTESY EVERETT COLLECTION

DICKEY CHAPELLE

As Molly Moore's narrative attests, journalists who cover warfare from the front lines face real personal danger. Decades before Moore went into battle, Dickey Chapelle, a pioneer in many aspects of war journalism, became the first female American reporter to be killed while on assignment—as well as the first war correspondent killed in Vietnam. Born Georgette Meyer in 1919, she assumed the surname Chapelle when she married and later officially changed her first name to Dickey, after military hero Admiral Richard Byrd. One of the first women to study engineering at the Massachusetts Institute of Technology, Chapelle was drawn to piloting airplanes and to photojournalism. She began her career as a war correspondent during World War II and continued covering conflicts around the globe for more than two decades.

In 1962 Chapelle published her autobiography, *What's a Woman Doing Here?: A Reporter's Report on Herself*. In a straightforward, personable style she describes her career, from covering the World War II battles of Iwo Jima and Okinawa to being one of the first American journalists to interview Fidel Castro during the Cuban Revolution. Although she continually faced the book's title question, Chapelle's courage and unaffected good humor won the respect of many of the military personnel with whom she worked. She was killed in 1965 while on patrol with U.S. soldiers in Vietnam.

A Woman at War is also notable from the vantage point of media criticism. Cohen, for example, notes that the hospitality Boomer extended to Moore was part of a successful effort by the marines during the Gulf War to outflank the other branches of the armed services in media relations. Moore's work also offers an extensive illustration of the pros and cons of embedded journalism. In response to complaints by media organizations over restricted pool coverage and news blackouts during the Gulf War, the Pentagon undertook an extensive program to embed journalists within frontline units when U.S. forces returned to Iraq in March 2003. Pentagon public affairs officials and media executives may well have looked to Moore's book for guidance ahead of the invasion of Iraq.

BIBLIOGRAPHY

Sources

Chapelle, Dickey. *What's a Woman Doing Here?: A Reporter's Report on Herself*. New York: Morrow, 1962. Print.

Cohen, Eliot A. "Tales of the Desert: Searching for Context for the Persian Gulf War." *Foreign Affairs* May–June 1994: 141–48. *General OneFile*. Web. 20 Dec. 2012.

Kirsch, Jonathan. "'A Woman at War' in the Persian Gulf: Diary of a Correspondent." *Los Angeles Times*. Los Angeles Times, 16 June 1993. Web. 18 Dec. 2012.

Moore, Molly. *A Woman at War: Storming Kuwait with the U.S. Marines*. New York: Charles Scribner's Sons, 1993. Print.

Rev. of *A Woman at War*, by Molly Moore. *Publishers Weekly*. Publishers Weekly, May 31, 1993. Web. 20 Dec. 2012.

Ward, Hiley. Rev. of *A Woman at War*, by Molly Moore. *Editor & Publisher* 31 July 1993: 21. *General OneFile*. Web. 20 Dec. 2012.

Yurechko, John. Rev. of *A Woman at War*, by Molly Moore. *Library Journal* 15 May 1993: 85. *General OneFile*. Web. 20 Dec. 2012.

Further Reading

Ewing, Robin Galloway. "Women Reporting War: The History and Evolution of the Woman War Correspondent." MA thesis, University of Texas at Austin, 2005. *robinewing.com*. Web. 20 Dec. 2012.

Katovsky, Bill, and Timothy Carlson, eds. *Embedded: The Media at War in Iraq*. Guilford, Conn.: Lyons, 2003. Print.

Kellner, Douglas. *The Persian Gulf TV War*. Boulder, Colo.: Westview, 1992. Print.

Ricchiardi, Sherry. "Women on War." *American Journalism Review*. American Journalism Review, Mar. 1994. Web. 18 Dec. 2012.

Schwarzkopf, H. Norman. *It Doesn't Take a Hero*. New York: Random House, 1993. Print.

Sheldon, Sayre P. *Her War Story: Twentieth-Century Women Write about War*. Carbondale: Southern Illinois University Press, 1999. Print.

Smith, Hedrick, ed. *The Media and the Gulf War: The Press and Democracy in Wartime*. Santa Ana, Calif.: Seven Locks, 1992. Print.

Roger Smith

A Woman in Berlin
Eight Weeks in the Conquered City: A Diary

Anonymous

OVERVIEW

A Woman in Berlin: Eight Weeks in the Conquered City: A Diary (1954) is an anonymously composed diary of a woman struggling to survive rape, violence, and hunger in Berlin after its fall to the Soviet Union in 1945. The diary, which was composed by a thirty-four-year-old journalist, begins on April 20, 1945, several days after the Red Army began the bombardment that would liberate Berlin. The entries continue for a little more than two months, until June 22, 1945. The diary's depiction of war-torn Berlin reveals the author's talent for closely observed detail; its unflinching narration of rape attests to her strength and will to survive.

The anonymous diary was first published in the United States in an incomplete English translation dated 1954. It was initially printed in Germany in 1959 but was not reissued until after the author's death in June 2001. A controversy arose in 2003 when, against the wishes of the diarist and publisher, German editor Jens Bisky identified the author as Marta Hillers, a journalist who had written for numerous German newspapers and magazines; however, the executor of the diarist's estate has refused to confirm Bisky's claim. Regardless of the diarist's identity, *A Woman in Berlin* continues to fascinate World War II enthusiasts as well as historians seeking a deeper understanding of life in the days immediately following the fall of Nazi Germany.

HISTORICAL AND LITERARY CONTEXT

A Woman in Berlin was written in a city under siege by the Soviet Red Army. In 1942 the German armed forces, the Wehrmacht, advanced eastward into Russia but were turned back during the Battle of Stalingrad, which ended in February 1943. The battle was a turning point in the war, and by April 1945 the Red Army had begun its bombardment of Berlin. The city contained some two million residents at the time, the vast majority of whom were women and children, yet Adolf Hitler rejected any possibility of evacuating. In his introduction to the diary, historian Anthony Beevor claims that in the case of Berlin, "Hitler appears to have imitated [Joseph] Stalin's refusal to allow the evacuation of civilians from Stalingrad in order to force his troops to defend the city more bravely." The Germans surrendered the city on May 2, 1945; the war in Europe had ended by May 8.

The diary spans just more than two months, a period that witnessed the city's bombardment, brief street fighting, Hitler's suicide, the fall of the Nazi regime, and the subsequent Soviet occupation. Rumors of rapes and murders had reached the city far in advance of the front. By April 27 the soldiers had reached the diarist's street. As the Red Army took control of the city, thousands of residents were raped by the Soviet soldiers. The two leading Berlin hospitals estimated that there were 95,000 to 130,000 rape victims in Berlin in 1945. The anonymous diarist was among the many who were raped, and her writing served as a therapeutic tool in the face of such savagery.

Critics who do not believe in the authenticity of the diary often compare it to other works that are believed to have been fabricated, such as *Hitler Diaries* (1983) or *Last Letters from Stalingrad* (1950), both of which were presented as narratives of personal experience in World War II. Despite such claims, the majority of critics believe in the veracity of *A Woman in Berlin*, which, despite significant differences of age, ethnicity, and nationality, shares traits of other authentic personal narratives of suffering that emerged from World War II, most notably Anne Frank's *The Diary of a Young Girl* (1947).

A Woman in Berlin is especially notable because it is a clear-eyed first-person account of the atrocities suffered by German women during the Soviet occupation of Berlin. Along with its importance as a historical document, the text has received broad critical praise since its reissuance in 2003. The diary has also inspired a critically acclaimed German film of the same name, directed by Max Färberböck.

THEMES AND STYLE

A Woman in Berlin focuses on the theme of survival in war, particularly the survival of women who endure brutal sexual violence at the hands of the "liberating" Soviets. Not only does the author detail the gang rape that she suffers as the Soviets conquer the city, but she also explains how, like many women in Soviet-occupied Berlin, she offered herself to a high-ranking officer in exchange for his protection. The diarist narrates her own self-loathing: "I don't want to touch myself, can barely look at my body," as well as the gallows humor that helps her—and others like her—survive.

Key Facts

Time Period:
Mid-20th Century

Relevant Historical Events:
World War II; Soviet occupation of Berlin; fall of the Third Reich

Nationality:
German

Keywords:
rape; occupation; women's writing

This Soviet propaganda poster from 1945 states that "Our Only Target Is Berlin." The autobiography *Woman in Berlin* describes the effect of this Soviet focus on Berliners as the city fell. © RIA NOVOSTI/ALAMY

Although primarily about sexual violence, the diary also details the societal disintegration and breakdown of order that occurred after the fall of the Nazi regime.

The anonymous author of *A Woman in Berlin* composed the diary for its therapeutic benefits. She makes this explicit, claiming that she is simply trying to "get all this confusion out of my head and heart." Elsewhere she writes, "It does me good, takes my mind off things." The diary was not written for posterity. As Joseph Kanon writes in his 2005 *New York Times* review of the book, it was "scribbled in a notebook and on odd pieces of paper." The author considers showing the diary to her fiancé, "if he comes back," but beyond this she holds no literary aspirations. Even after publication she sought no fame for the work, despite its literary merits; she refused to publish an updated edition during her life, and she remains anonymous even after her death.

Stylistically, the diary is notable for its open and detailed narration, as well as its laconic sense of humor. Regarding the diary's style, Kanon writes, "The book is graphic and unflinching, but what makes it so remarkable is its determination to see beyond the acts themselves." The author does not indulge in sentiment, and she avoids self-pity in order to present a clear-eyed observation of violence and rape. The author uses dry gallows humor but she recognizes how such humor—in her own writing and in the comments of other victims—is a tactic for survival in the face of horrible brutality. "Slowly but surely," she writes, "We're starting to view all the raping with a sense of humor."

CRITICAL DISCUSSION

The initial response to *A Woman in Berlin* was quiet but decidedly negative. In the foreword to the 2006 English translation of the book, Hans Magnus Enzensberger explains its early critical reception: "German readers were obviously not ready to face some uncomfortable truths, and the book was met with either hostility or silence. One of the few critics who reviewed it complained of the author's 'shameless immorality.'" Following the negative response, the diary all but disappeared. However, essayist Jody Raphael, in her 2006 piece "Silencing Reports of Sexual Assault: The Controversy over *A Woman in Berlin*," notes that "photocopies did circulate in Berlin among students and feminists in the late 1960s."

Following the reissue of the diary in 2003 and its subsequent English translation, the work climbed to the top of the German best-seller list as it became recognized not only as a compelling and harrowing read but also as an essential personal documentation of postwar Berlin. The resurgence in interest, however, was not without its controversy. Some critics have challenged the authenticity of the work, claiming that it was significantly altered by Kurt Marek, the initial editor of the diary. In a 2005 letter to the *New York Times*, Christoph Gottesmann claims that "there was no serious investigation of the authenticity of the handwritten notes." In a response, Beevor notes that "the original notes and typescript were subject to close examination by a well-known diary expert … and declared authentic."

Along with a discussion of the authenticity of the diary, recent scholarship has utilized the text as a document for studying the psychology of sexual violence in warfare. In his introduction to the diary, Beevor argues that mass rapes in Germany in 1945 were not used as a tactic in the war, noting, "No document from the Soviet archives indicates anything of the sort." In his 2006 essay in *Violence against Women*, J. W. Messerschmidt counters Beevor's claims: "Although no document yet exists declaring rape a formal war strategy in Berlin, mass rape served effectively as an unofficial masculine maneuver to frighten and intimidate the Berlin civilian population into complying with the wishes and demands of its Soviet occupiers."

BIBLIOGRAPHY

Sources

Anonymous. *A Woman in Berlin: Eight Weeks in the Conquered City: A Diary*. Trans. Phillip Boehm. New York: Picador, 2006. Print.

Beevor, Anthony. Introduction. *A Woman in Berlin: Eight Weeks in the Conquered City: A Diary*, by Anonymous. New York: Picador, 2006. Print.

Beevor, Anthony. "A Woman in Berlin" [Letter to the editor]. *New York Times*. New York Times Book Review, 25 Sept. 2005. Web. 19 Dec. 2012.

Enzensberger, Hans Magnus. Foreword. *A Woman in Berlin: Eight Weeks in the Conquered City: A Diary*, by Anonymous. New York: Picador, 2006. Print.

Gottesmann, Christoph. "A Woman in Berlin" [Letter to the editor]. *New York Times*. New York Times Book Review, 11 Sept. 2005. Web. 19 Dec. 2012.

Harder, Luke. "Row over Naming of Rape Author." *Observer*. Guardian News and Media, 4 Oct. 2003. Web. 19 Dec. 2012.

Kanon, Joseph. Rev. of *A Woman in Berlin: Eight Weeks in the Conquered City: A Diary*, by Anonymous. *New York Times*. New York Times, 17 Aug. 2005. Web. 19 Dec. 2012.

Messerschmidt, J. W. "The Forgotten Victims of World War II—Masculinities and Rape in Berlin, 1945." *Violence against Women* 12.7 (2006): 706–12. Print.

Raphael, Jody. "Silencing Reports of Sexual Assault: The Controversy over *A Woman in Berlin*." *Violence against Women* 12.7 (2006): 693–99. Thousand Oaks, Calif.: Sage. Web. 19 Dec. 2012.

Further Reading

Annan, G. Rev. of *A Woman in Berlin: Eight Weeks in the Conquered City: A Diary*, by Anonymous. *New York Review of Books* 52.15 (2005): 17–19. Print.

Bell, J. Rev. of *Anonyma: A Woman in Berlin*, by Max Färberböck. *Sight and Sound* 20.3 (2010): 96. Print.

Bletzer, K. V. "A Voice for Every Woman and the Travesties of War." *Violence against Women* 12.7 (2006): 700–05. Print.

Redmann, J. "*A Woman in Berlin*: Diary as History or Fiction of the Self?" *Colloquia Germanica* 41.3 (2008): 193–210. Print.

Greg Luther

RAPE AND WORLD WAR II

While *A Woman in Berlin* provides an unflinching portrait of the atrocities visited upon German women by Red Army soldiers during the Soviet occupation of Berlin, it is only one chapter in the history of sexual violence in World War II. In *Against Our Will: Men, Women and Rape* (1975), Susan Brownmiller addresses the topic of rape in many of its social contexts. She begins with a study of the mass psychology of rape but also addresses issues such as the myth of the heroic rapist and the practice of rape as an exertion of institutionalized power, as in the cases of prison and police rape. The most pertinent chapter to students of *A Woman in Berlin* is her discussion of rape during war.

In her book, Brownmiller details the mass rape of Jewish women, as well as women of other ethnicities, by Nazi soldiers as they advanced eastward into the Soviet Union. Many Russian women were also kidnapped and enslaved in prostitution; they were forced to serve in brothels for German officers. Brownmiller argues that in response to these atrocities, the Red Army exacted revenge through the mass rape of German women as they fought westward toward Berlin.

Work and Family Life

A Country Parson: James Woodforde's Diary, 1759–1802 by James Woodforde	287
The Diary of Lady Murasaki by Lady Murasaki Shikibu	290
Go Ask Alice by Anonymous	294
The Gossamer Years by Michitsuna No Haha	297
Grasmere Journals by Dorothy Wordsworth	300
I Will Bear Witness: A Diary of the Nazi Years, 1933–1945 by Victor Klemperer	303
The Journal of Marie Bashkirtseff by Marie Bashkirtseff	306
The Journal of Sir Walter Scott by Sir Walter Scott	309
Letters and Journals of Fanny Burney by Fanny Burney	312
Letters from Jefferson to His Daughter by Thomas Jefferson	316
London and the Life of Literature in Late Victorian England: The Diary of George Gissing, Novelist by George Gissing	320
The Love Letters of Dorothy Osborne to Sir William Temple, 1652–54 by Dorothy Osborne	324
London Journal, 1762–1763 by James Boswell	328
A Midwife's Tale: The Life of Martha Ballard, Based on Her Diary, 1785–1812 by Laurel Thatcher Ulrich	331
Records of a Girlhood by Fanny Kemble	335
Zlata's Diary: A Child's Life in Sarajevo by Zlata Filipovic	338

A Country Parson
James Woodforde's Diary, 1759–1802
James Woodforde

OVERVIEW

First published between 1924 and 1931, *A Country Parson: James Woodforde's Diary, 1759–1802*, chronicles forty-three years of James Woodforde's life as an Anglican clergyman in England in the late eighteenth century. His meticulous, transparent style permeates the diary as he describes everyday matters in minute detail: meals, servants' comings and goings, purchases, and interactions with members of his household and parish. Woodforde's laissez-faire attitude toward religious duties, his love of creature comforts, and his opinions about his neighbors provide a glimpse into the mentality of an average member of British society before the advent of modernity. Being ordinary does not necessarily doom a writer to obscurity, as the diary demonstrates. It provides scholars with abundant data about middle-class life before England's agricultural reform and the Industrial Revolution.

A Country Parson was published more than a century after the author's death. Shortly after World War I, a distant descendant of Woodforde (a doctor from Hertfordshire) invited Oxford University Press editor John Beresford to peruse the notebooks. Beresford edited them as a five-volume abridged edition, and Oxford University Press published them. A one-volume, abridged edition appeared in 1985. In its entirety, the diary occupies seventeen volumes, and its only complete edition was published by the Parson Woodforde Society, with the last volume printed in 2007. The original edition was received with great public acclaim, garnering praise from famous writers including Virginia Woolf and Siegfried Sassoon. Today, however, interest in Woodforde's diary has waned, although cultural historians of the late eighteenth century still treasure the complex portrait it gives of one man and his now-vanished cultural milieu.

HISTORICAL AND LITERARY CONTEXT

A Country Parson demonstrates the provincial mindset of late-eighteenth-century rural England. Like many middle-class young men at the time, Woodforde's career options were limited to army, university, or church—a situation famously captured by Jane Austen's novels. Following in his father's footsteps, Woodforde chose the church. His worldview is much like that satirized by Austen in her portraits of clergymen: religious complacency; lack of concern about social ills; love of comfort; devotion to social hierarchy, particularly the aristocracy; and fascination with material goods. Yet Woodforde also has considerable compassion for other suffering creatures, a deep appreciation for natural beauty, and a sensitivity to the foibles of others.

A Country Parson portrays the everyday events of its author's adult life. It begins on July 21, 1759, when Woodforde became a scholar at Oxford. The opening portion of the diary, from 1759 to 1763, depicts student activity in one of England's greatest academic institutions. In 1763 Woodforde returned to Somerset, his family's parish, where he worked as his father's curate for ten years. When his father died in 1771 and Woodforde did not inherit his father's parish, he lost the affection of the woman he hoped to marry and returned to Oxford as subwarden of Oriel College. In 1773 he became a rector at Weston Longville, Norfolk, where he remained for the rest of his life. He did not experience the spiritual revival that John Wesley's preaching ignited in 1739, but he did take an active interest in some political events, such as the peace treaty signed between Great Britain and the American colonies on January 25, 1783.

Containing meticulous records about money, servants, food, and medicine, Woodforde's diary is in some ways more similar to household account books kept by medieval aristocrats than to the intellectual narratives of other British diarists. Unlike the earlier diarist John Evelyn, Woodforde hardly used his classical education, and he read little. Furthermore, because of his provincial lifestyle, he did not know famous literary or political figures—associations that give James Boswell's diary (1762–95) its prestige and modern popularity. He is more similar to Francis Kilvert (1793–1863), an Anglican clergyman in northern England who chronicled gentrified rural life. However, instead of Kilvert's poetic musings about the countryside, Woodforde reports on activities in simple, conversational language.

A Country Parson is especially important for its unvarnished depiction of everyday work and family life. Despite its unpretentious style, it captured the attention of readers after its first publication and

❖ **Key Facts**

Time Period:
Late 18th to Early 19th Century

Relevant Historical Events:
Woodforde's matriculation at Oxford; Woodforde's work as a rector

Nationality:
English

Keywords:
Anglicanism; faith; the middle class

The pulpit at St. Margaret, a church in Hales, Norfolk, England. James Woodforde served as a member of the clergy in Norfolk in the eighteenth century. His diary has been published as *A Country Parson*. © JIM LAWS/ALAMY

has subsequently been useful for scholars of English material history. In one of its most recent abridged editions, the diary is accompanied by sketches, photographs, paintings, and other visual representations of Woodforde's world. For many readers, this captures the diary's chief value: its ability to make the quiet, complacent world of agricultural Georgian England come alive.

THEMES AND STYLE

A Country Parson focuses on Woodforde's quotidian concerns. On January 9, 1785, for example, he details a dream in which a corpse chased him, which he sees as a portent of his maid's sister's approaching death from consumption. A few days later he notes, "Mr. Custance at Church but not Mrs. Custance," demonstrating his perennial concern with the local gentry. He describes trips to Bath and London, as well as dinner parties and card games with local socialites. He often records dishes served at meals. In one of many such entries, he writes, "We had for Dinner, a Neck of Mutton boiled and Capers and a rost Shoulder of Pork alias mock Goose and a nice plumb Pudding." However, loneliness also pervades Woodforde's diary: "I was very dull and low this Evening." Thus his diary concerns itself with small joys and worries—the pathos of everyday life.

As Ronald Blythe notes in his introduction to the 1985 edition, "The world can only guess at James Woodforde's motive for not letting his very solid life vanish into thin air, although it certainly wasn't vanity." Woolf introduces her essay on Woodforde by attempting to fathom his motives, positing that perhaps he desired "intimacy," a sense of sympathy from a second self. He details everything, from purchases of mahogany tables to compensation paid his private rat-catcher—yet with matter-of-fact language that hints at no motives for this painstaking catalog of daily work. He loves lists: lists of dinner parties, of card games, of expenditures, and of food. Nevertheless, implicit in this attention to detail is his sense of prosperity, as enjoying such luxuries was a way for the middle class to exhibit status. For Woodforde, writing was perhaps another marker of the prosperous life, a leisurely way of conversing with his own psyche and reminding himself of the stability he enjoyed.

In contrast to Boswell's Latinate diction and Kilvert's sentimental ramblings, Woodforde uses plain language to chronicle his activities and emotions. Though he seldom transcribes conversations (a hallmark of Boswell's diary), he uses conversational rhythms. He often gives thumbnail portraits of people. On one occasion he visits a neighboring village and meets three young women, describing them in the diary as "very reserved and not handsome," "very agreeable and pretty," and "very still and coarse." Occasionally these portraits contain glimmers of humor, as when Jigg, Woodforde's greyhound, gets into the cellar and eats meat meant for a meal with visitors, which causes "Sister Pounsett and Nancy" to be "mortally vexed at it." Despite his role as clergyman, he seldom references God or spirituality aside from occasional comments in times of sickness or distress: "Pray God Almighty comfort her—and with patience wait the Almighty's Will."

CRITICAL DISCUSSION

After publication of its first volume in 1924, *A Country Parson* received acclaim from reviewers in newspapers and academic journals. On April 10, 1924, the *Times Literary Supplement* commented, "This diary is not only attractive from the human standpoint, but historically it is of the greatest possible interest, as presenting a complete and rare view of village life in the second half of the eighteenth century." Likewise, the *Scottish Historical Review* in July 1924 called the diary "delightful," describing Woodforde as a "good-natured scholarly gentleman." Similarly positive remarks welcomed the subsequent volumes.

Writers were particularly interested in Woodforde's diary. In her *Second Common Reader* Virginia Woolf explored her experience of reading Woodforde. She reveled in his unchanging, archetypal image of a rural world, writing, "It is the great towns that are ravaged with anarchy and confusion. But the river Wensum still flows … , and Parson Woodforde takes his greyhounds out a-coursing." Siegfried Sassoon also reviewed Woodforde in letters to Max Beerbohm, calling the diary "a tranquil pool of joy, and I love every inch of all the duck-weed on it." Since these responses, though, *A Country Parson* has left few cultural ripples, except as a guide to eighteenth-century food. In a 2007 review of *Ralph Ayres' Cookery Book*, Bee Wilson mentions Woodforde's account of a meal and concludes, "There is something Enid Blyton-ish in such feasting." According to Blythe, the emphasis on meals "is so disproportionate to that placed on anything else that Woodforde has acquired a reputation for gluttony."

Woodforde's diary has received little recent critical attention except by scholars of English cultural history. Margot Finn compares four British diarists in her 2000 study "Men's Things: Masculine Possession in the Consumer Revolution." In 2009 Janet E. Mullin examines Woodforde in a discussion of card games in the eighteenth century, and Celia A. Easton uses Woodforde's account of parish life in her 2010 exploration of Jane Austen. Aside from this cultural-historical approach, however, *A Country Parson* has not been analyzed either for its literary qualities or for its psychological portrait of one man and his world.

BIBLIOGRAPHY

Sources

Le Quesne, A. L. "Kilvert, (Robert) Francis (1840–1879)." *Oxford Dictionary of National Biography*. Oxford: Oxford University Press, 2004. Web. 11 Dec. 2012.

"Oxford University Press." *Times Literary Supplement* 10 Apr. 1924: 219. *Times Literary Supplement Historical Archive*. Web. 11 Dec. 2012.

Rev. of *The Diary of a Country Parson, the Reverend James Woodforde, 1758–1781*, ed. John Beresford. *Scottish Historical Review* 21.84 (1924): 313–14. *JSTOR*. Web. 11 Dec. 2012.

Turnbull, Gordon. "Boswell, James (1740–1795)." *Oxford Dictionary of National Biography*. Oxford: Oxford University Press, 2004. Web. 11 Dec. 2012.

Wilson, Bee. "Potted Dons." *Times Literary Supplement* 30 June 2006: 4. *Times Literary Supplement Historical Archive*. Web. 11 Dec. 2012.

Woodforde, James. *A Country Parson: James Woodforde's Diary 1759–1802*. Oxford: Oxford University Press, 1985. Print.

Woolf, Virginia. *The Common Reader: Second Series*. London: Hogarth, 1932. Print.

JAMES WOODFORDE'S HOUSEHOLD: PEOPLE, PETS, AND PESTS

Since Woodforde never married, his niece, Anna Maria Woodforde (Nancy), lived with him at Weston as a housekeeper and companion. Woodforde's household included five servants who cooked, cleaned, and maintained his horses. He was their banker, giving them 5 percent interest on their annual savings. He occasionally hired other people, including "Cobb of Mattishall a Rat-Catcher," whom he paid "to kill all my Rats … and likewise to kill all my Mice."

Woodforde kept greyhounds, cats, a spaniel, and two horses. Typical of his attention to detail is an entry about the spaniel Mab, who "was hung this Morn' she being very old and almost blind. I had her hanged out of Charity." Woodforde acted as doctor and veterinarian not only for his household but also for his parishioners, and his diary records many common eighteenth-century maladies as well as their medical treatments. When one of his cats broke a rib, he used a penknife to perform surgery on her, noting that "she was much better after, the incision was half an inch." Horrific as this solution may seem, it demonstrates the pain-filled world in which Woodforde lived. For Woodforde burying infants and marveling at the colorful spread of a peacock's tail coexist in entries only days apart.

Further Reading

Chambers, Douglas D. C. "Evelyn, John (1620–1706)." *Oxford Dictionary of National Biography*. Oxford: Oxford University Press, 2004. Web. 11 Dec. 2012.

Easton, Celia A. "'The Probability of Some Negligence': Avoiding the Horror of the Absent Clergyman." *Persuasions: The Jane Austen Journal* 32 (2010): 154+. *General OneFile*. Web. 11 Dec. 2012.

Finn, Margot. "Men's Things: Masculine Possession in the Consumer Revolution." *Social History* 25.2 (2000): 133–55. *JSTOR*. Web. 11 Dec. 2012.

Gregory, Jeremy. *Restoration, Reformation and Reform, 1660–1828*. Oxford: Oxford University Press, 2000. Print.

Jacob, W. M. *The Clerical Profession in the Long Eighteenth Century, 1680–1840*. Oxford: Oxford University Press, 2007. Print.

Mullin, Janet E. "'We Had Carding': Hospitable Card Play and Polite Domestic Sociability Among the Middling Sort in Eighteenth-Century England." *Journal of Social History* 42.4 (2009): 989–1001. *General OneFile*. Web. 11 Dec. 2012.

Siegfried, Sassoon. *Letters to Max Beerbohm with a Few Answers*. Ed. Rupert Hart-Davis. London: Faber and Faber, 1986. Print.

Winstanley, R. L. "Woodforde, James (1740–1803)." *Oxford Dictionary of National Biography*. Oxford: Oxford University Press, 2004. Web. 11 Dec. 2012.

Evelyn Reynolds

The Diary of Lady Murasaki

Lady Murasaki Shikibu

Key Facts

Time Period:
Early 11th Century

Relevant Historical Events:
Creation of political stability in Japan; Murasaki's involvement in the court of Empress Shōshi

Nationality:
Japanese

Keywords:
Buddhism; poetry; women's writing

OVERVIEW

Murasaki Shikibu Nikki (*The Diary of Lady Murasaki*) is a fusion of fragmented anecdotes from Lady Murasaki Shikibu's time in the court of Empress Shōshi (Akiko) between 1008 and 1010. The memoirs consist of a narrative surrounding the birth of Emperor Ichijō and Empress Shōshi's first son, followed by observations on the imperial court as well as poetry and personal reflections. The diary has had two significant English translations in the twentieth century: a 1920 translation by Annie Shepley Omori and Kochi Doi and Richard Bowring's 1980s translation. The latter version inspired debate concerning the extent of Murasaki's critical tone toward others in the imperial court following her great literary success with her novel *The Tale of Genji*. Themes in the diary include Buddhism's importance in classical Japan, poetry's centrality in court culture, and the significance of women writers during the Heian period.

Murasaki left little autobiographical writing; aside from *The Diary of Lady Murasaki,* only a collection of autobiographical poems—what Bowring called "Poetic Memoirs" when he published them with her *nikki,* or diary—appeared around 1014. The author's real name remains unknown; Murasaki Shikibu is a nickname from the time derived from the character Murasaki in *The Tale of Genji* and the term for an administrator, which her father was. In a 1982 review, scholar Aileen Gatten even posits that Murasaki may not have written the whole nikki. Yet, because she was already an established writer who did not need to boost her reputation at court, her work is regarded as a fearless critique of prominent individuals—including Minister of the Left Fujiwara no Michinaga, Empress Shōshi's father. The work also helped establish Japanese kana characters (the preferred writing of women at the time, while male scholars at court generally wrote in Chinese) as the national written language.

HISTORICAL AND LITERARY CONTEXT

The Diary of Lady Murasaki's very appearance is emblematic of a long period of stability in which women gained a prominent voice in Japan. Kyoto was the capital of Japan between 794 and 1185; it was also known as Heian-kyō ("capital of peace")— hence the name "Heian period." It was a time before shoguns, daimyo, and samurai defined a more feudal era. Emperors' several wives vied to invite the most learned ladies to their entourages. In an effort to ensure the Fujiwara family's continued prominence, Michinaga married his daughter Shōshi to Emperor Ichijō and two other daughters to the emperors who followed. Murasaki, herself from a minor Fujiwara branch, came to serve Empress Shōshi in 1006, five years after her husband's death. In doing so she simultaneously was addressing her grief, concerns about her status, and new surroundings amid courtiers and rival ladies-in-waiting.

The diary that resulted from Murasaki's time at court is a mixture of personal reflections, in which she expresses a desire to lead a religious life, and her impressions of both unnamed and influential courtiers, including Emperor Ichijō and Empress Shōshi; Michinaga and his wife Minamoto no Rinshi; and other prominent writers, such as Izumi Shikibu (no relation) and Sei Shōnagon. Gatten believes that Murasaki intended for her nikki to be widely read, while Bowring and other scholars have suggested that it was meant for her daughter, who was born in 1000.

The Diary of Lady Murasaki is one of several memoirs recorded by Heian-era women. In 974 a woman known as Michitsuna No Haha (Mother of Michitsuna) composed *Kagerō Nikki* (*The Gossamer Years),* which describes her relationship with a prince and her lonely pilgrimages and pursuit of a religious life as the prince gradually abandons her and their son. Sei Shōnagon, a rival of Murasaki who was in Ichijō's first wife's retinue, wrote a collection of observations at court titled *Makura Shōshi (The Pillow Book).* In the early eleventh century, another of Murasaki's rivals, Izumi Shikibu, wrote and circulated her nikki, which detailed an affair between a woman and a prince fueled with romantic poetry; its autobiographical nature has been questioned because it is written in the third person. At least part of Murasaki's *Tale of Genji* predates her nikki in the same decade; as she discusses male improprieties, Buddhist spirituality, and her worries about the passing of beauty in her diary, so the amorous Prince Genji hesitates in a sort of spiritual awe before one of his lovers, faces exile for going too far an affair, and dies with no descendants to match his brilliance.

At least one other nikki of the Heian period follows Murasaki's, showing the endurance of the genre. In *Sarashina Diary,* which appeared around 1059, a

THE DIARY OF LADY MURASAKI

A twelfth-century drawing by Fujiwara Takayoshi illustrating a scene from the novel The *Tale of Genji*, by Murasaki Shikibu. © AISA/TOKUGAWA REIMEIKAI FOUNDATION, TOKYO, JAPAN/THE BRIDGEMAN ART LIBRARY

woman only known as the daughter of administrator Sugawara no Takasue goes to the imperial court from one of the provinces in her teens. She recounts her loneliness after enduring the deaths of her nurse, sister, and husband, events that make her want to pursue a religious life. Murasaki's diary, like the others, contains many observations in both prose and poetry; *Lady Murasaki Shu* is a collection of her best poems that was compiled (likely by Murasaki herself) in the mid-1010s. If, as some scholars believe, parts of *The Tale of Genji* were written later (the writer of *Sarashina Diary* comments about receiving a full version of it), then *The Diary of Lady Murasaki* was a forerunner to much of her later poetry.

THEMES AND STYLE

Overriding themes of *The Diary of Lady Murasaki* are the importance of court ceremony; the importance of Buddhism, poetry, and fashion in court culture; and women's status. Writing about the birth of the prince, for example, Murasaki describes the ceremony of bathing the child. Priests were part of the birth and bathing ceremonies, and during the labor several priests were present whose "prayers would reach to the Buddhas of the three worlds." Later, during the preparations for the emperor's arrival after the birth, Murasaki muses how Buddhism attracts her: "I wish I could be more adaptable and live more gaily in the present world—had I not an extraordinary sorrow—but whenever I hear delightful or interesting things my yearning for a religious life grows stronger." As Bowring relates, other court ladies critique Murasaki's attempt to find solace in Buddhist sutras, citing the taboo over women reading and writing Chinese: "What kind of lady is it who reads Chinese books?" they whisper. Murasaki's father laments as she learns Chinese: "Just my luck," he says. "What a pity she was not born a man!"

Because other women were often rivals and men often made unwanted advances, Murasaki's loneliness at court is palpable, especially as she experiences a widow's grief. Thinking about her old home, she writes, "Those in whose eyes I had wished to be of some consequence undoubtedly thought of me now as no more than a common lady-in-waiting who would treat their letters with scant respect.… There were others who no longer came to see me.… Indeed everything, however slight, conspired to make me feel as if I had entered a different world." Aside from the empress and Lady Dainagon, the author finds no true confidants, and her written criticisms of others are many times harsh. She observes as Minister of the Left Michinaga early in the narrative takes the liberty of peeking at her over a screen; later he is described as prone to drunkenness and embarrassing to other ladies. Much later in the narrative, Sei Shōnagon is described as "imperfect" and "in spite of herself will lose control."

EVIL SPIRITS IN LADY MURASAKI'S WORKS

The Diary of Lady Murasaki contains several references in its first part to precautions taken to ward off evil spirits from Empress Shōshi and her son before and after his birth. Belief in evil spirits was so pervasive, despite the promise of tranquility sought through Buddhism, that it is a motif throughout Murasaki's writings—including *The Tale of Genji* and her "Poetic Memoirs." In *Genji* Murasaki's "Shining Prince" is married to Aoi but has mistresses in Lady Rokujō; and Yūgao. Rokujō becomes so jealous that her spirit leaves her body, and Yūgao and Aoi die after spirit possession. Rokujō also dies.

This vignette from Murasaki's poetry collection, translated by Susan Klein, also refers to spirits:

Someone had drawn on a scroll the unpleasant form of a woman possessed by an evil spirit. Behind the possessed woman, a priest was restraining the husband's former wife, who had appeared as a demon. The husband was trying to subdue the evil spirit by reading a sutra.

Upon seeing the illustrated scroll, I wrote:

In his anguish

he has blamed it on his dead wife.

But is it not

the demon in his own heart?

The diary contains language that reflects Murasaki's great sensitivity to detail and propriety according to one's rank and station at court. She has a great eye for fashion and shows a deep appreciation of nature. She describes the dress of ladies around court who wear beautiful "brocaded *karaginu*" (short garments with long sleeves) and "brocaded *uchigi*" (longer robes) "trimmed with three or five folds." Breaches of etiquette draw her criticism with varying degrees of subtlety. While her critiques can be scathing, she comments on the bearers of the emperor's palanquin: "Even in the highest society there are grades of courtesy, but these men were too humble." Her language boosts the royal family: the empress "wore a look of extreme purity," and the emperor is described as "brightness" personified. Thus, Murasaki appears to be writing in order to check improper behavior at court, make herself appear morally superior in her position, and express her indignation within the limited means of expression available to a woman at the time.

CRITICAL DISCUSSION

While *The Tale of Genji* made Murasaki famous, evidence of how her diary was received at that time is unclear. Although she was critical of some individuals in the capital, she remained in Kyoto in Shōshi's service until 1011, and all accounts of her life concur that she was untouched by scandal. She apparently stayed in Shōshi's service for a few years longer when the empress retired to the countryside outside Kyoto following Ichijō's death in 1011. Murasaki and her nikki were sufficiently regarded in Japanese literary history. *Emaki,* or painted picture scrolls of anecdotes from the diary, were produced during the thirteenth century.

Twentieth-century English-speaking scholars have shown increasing interest over the values the various nikki reflect. In the first English translation of *The Diary of Lady Murasaki,* which appeared in *Diaries of Court Ladies of Old Japan* (1920), Amy Lowell notes in the introduction the need to "gain a sort of perspective for them [the ladies] and their time." Omori and Doi acknowledge that the translations of poetry in the nikki "presented problems of great difficulty" due to word plays and attempted double meanings evident in many examples of the Heian-era Japanese-language genre of poetry known as *waka,* and thus Bowring published a new translation of Murasaki's diary and poetry in the early 1980s. His translation of the nikki was reprinted in 1996.

Since Bowring's translation, critics have debated whether he ascribed too much hostility toward others in Murasaki's criticisms of the court. For example, when Rinshi, Michinaga's first wife, gives Murasaki a gift of chrysanthemum leaves, which were thought to preserve youth, she writes a poem from which Bowring translates the last two lines: "I restore it to the owner / To work its wonders." Bowring characterizes it as a "vicious reply," as if the older woman is lacking in youth. However, Gatten sees no malice in the lines, stating they could be translated in a kinder spirit: "I shall let the flowers' owner / Have the immortality they bring." In a 1983 review Marian Ury takes issue with Bowring's translation as well as his view that Murasaki's reaction suggests there was a romantic relationship between her and Michinaga. More recently, scholars have focused on what the nikki reveals about gender relations in the Heian period. In a 2000 piece for *Positions: East Asia Cultures Critique,* Tomiko Yoda explains how female Heian writers popularized kana writing, though prohibitions of them learning Chinese writing have been overstated. Male scholars fluent in Chinese wrote in a female voice to use kana as well. In *At the House of the Gathered Leaves* (2004), Joshua Mostow writes that the diaries of the period generally were political, as authors such as Murasaki criticized powerful males and massaged their egos by writing about their romantic—and implicitly their political—prowess.

BIBLIOGRAPHY

Sources

Bowring, Richard, trans. *Murasaki Shikibu: Her Diary and Poetic Memoirs.* Princeton, N.J.: Princeton University Press, 1985. Print.

———. *The Diary of Lady Murasaki.* New York: Penguin, 1996. Print.

Gatten, Aileen. "Murasaki's Literary Roots." Rev. of *Murasaki Shikibu: Her Diary and Poetic Memoirs,* trans. by Richard Bowring. *Journal of the Association of Teachers of Japanese* 17.2 (1982): 173–91. Print.

Mostow, Joshua S. *At the House of the Gathered Leaves: Short Biographical and Autobiographical Narratives from Japanese Court Literature.* Honolulu: University of Hawaii Press, 2004. Print.

Omori, Annie Shepley, and Kochi Doi. *Diaries of Court Ladies of Old Japan.* Boston: Houghton Mifflin, 1920. Print.

Seidensticker, Edward. Rev. of *Murasaki Shikibu: Her Diary and Poetic Memoirs,* trans. by Richard Bowring. *Journal of Japanese Studies* 9.2 (1983): 335–40. Print.

Ury, Marian. "The Real Murasaki." Rev. of *Murasaki Shikibu: Her Diary and Poetic Memoirs,* trans. by Richard Bowring. *Monumenta Nipponica* 38.2 (1983): 175–89. Print.

Wallace, John R. "Tarrying with the Negative: Aesthetic Vision in Murasaki and Mishima." *Monumenta Nipponica* 52.2 (1997): 181–99. Print.

Yoda, Tomiko. "Literary History against the National Frame, or Gender and the Emergence of Heian Kana Writing." *Positions: East Asia Cultures Critique* 8.2 (2000): 465–97. Print.

Further Reading

Bowring, Richard. *Murasaki Shikibu: The Tale of Genji.* Cambridge, U.K.: Cambridge University Press, 2004. Print.

Keene, Donald. *Seeds in the Heart: Japanese Literature from Earliest Times to the Late Sixteenth Century.* New York: Columbia University Press, 1999. Print.

Mulhern, Chieko Irie. *Japanese Women Writers: A Bio-critical Sourcebook.* Westport, Conn.: Greenwood, 1994. Print.

Sarra, Edith. *Fictions of Femininity: Literary Inventions of Gender in Japanese Court Women's Memoirs.* Palo Alto, Calif.: Stanford University Press, 1999. Print.

Tyler, Royall. "'I Am I': Genji and Murasaki." *Monumenta Nipponica* 54.4 (1999): 435–80. Print.

Wallace, John R. *Objects of Discourse: Memoirs by Women of Heian Japan.* Ann Arbor: Center for Japanese Studies, University of Michigan, 2005. Print.

Wesley Borucki

GO ASK ALICE

Anonymous

Key Facts

Time Period:
Mid-20th Century

Relevant Historical Events:
Rise of the drug culture; "war on drugs"; Controlled Substances Act

Nationality:
American

Keywords:
drugs; addiction; recovery

OVERVIEW

Go Ask Alice (1971) is a fictionalized diary allegedly written by an anonymous teenage girl that discusses her drug addiction and the tragic effects of that addiction. The book was instantly popular and controversial for its ability to approach sex and drugs in a way that teenagers could understand, and it quickly generated a legacy for being a didactic work about drugs from the accessible voice of an average teenager. Despite the controversy surrounding the book, *Go Ask Alice* was instrumental in facilitating intergenerational communication about the dangers associated with sex and drugs, topics that the anonymous narrator of *Go Ask Alice* felt she could not broach with her parents.

The book was released at the height of the drug culture of the 1960s. Published anonymously, the text was believed to be authentic and quickly became a best seller. It was adapted into a television movie in 1973 and has been translated into sixteen languages. In 1978, however, the book's reputation was questioned when another book dealing with adolescents and drugs, titled *Voices: The Stories of Four Troubled Teenagers as Told in Personal Interviews to Beatrice Sparks,* was published by Times Books with the boldly printed statement: "from Beatrice Sparks, the author who brought you *Go Ask Alice.*" Further scholarship revealed Sparks's questionable qualifications for working with troubled youth and her religious bias in creating a story about a girl who rejects her Christian values for the dangerous world of sex and drugs. This led scholars to label her later books as propaganda and disregard them in literary discussions. Despite the controversy surrounding the revelation of *Go Ask Alice* as a work of fiction, it was one of the ten best-selling books of the 1970s, selling millions of copies during that decade.

HISTORICAL AND LITERARY CONTEXT

The drug culture and its consequences for teenagers in the 1960s were both taboo and titillating subjects for adults and adolescents alike. A combination of factors caused the number of drug users in the United States to increase rapidly as the baby boomers reached their teenage years, including advancements in travel and technology that made illegal drugs more accessible, the influence of the Vietnam War and addicted soldiers returning home, and the adolescent desire to rebel against authority. Between 1960 and 1967 the number of teenage arrests for drug-related charges was 800 percent higher than in the previous decade. When President Richard Nixon took office in 1969, he launched a "war on drugs" that included passage of the Controlled Substances Act of 1970, which defined and classified various illegal substances. Despite the government's involvement, however, teen drug use continued to rise.

The actual details surrounding the composition of *Go Ask Alice* are vague, with many scholars doubting Sparks's claim that the protagonist was an actual person who sought her advice. The author claims she was contacted by a young girl she calls "Alice" who was struggling with addiction and had heard Sparks present at a conference for troubled youth. Seeking help, Alice supposedly gave Sparks copies of two diaries and several scraps of paper that would form the basis of *Go Ask Alice,* and the two of them became friends as Sparks tried to help Alice and her family. After Alice's death from an overdose, which Sparks later claimed in an interview with Alleen Pace Nilsen was accidental, she decided to edit the diaries, adding relevant material from other addicts she knew, to produce a book that would serve as a warning to young readers about the dangers of substance abuse and addiction.

Books on the consequences of addiction were only beginning to be conceived when *Go Ask Alice* was published, and the topic was still largely avoided because it was thought to be inappropriate for adolescents. The publication of a book dealing directly with drugs and sex from a teenage perspective, therefore, was considered quite revolutionary and controversial. Sparks had previously published religious material through her church, but *Go Ask Alice* was her first major publication and proved to be the catalyst that began her literary career.

The success of *Go Ask Alice* inspired Sparks to continue writing books from the perspective of adolescents about other troubling issues, including *Jay's Journal* (1979), about youth involvement in occult practices; *It Happened to Nancy* (1994), about the dangers of adolescent sexual relations and the transmission of AIDS; and *Annie's Baby, The Diary of Anonymous, a Pregnant Teenager* (1998), about rape and teenage pregnancy. None of her subsequent books enjoyed the success of *Go Ask Alice,* and scholarship about Sparks is minimal, largely due to the questionable authenticity of her books and their didactic religious morals.

THEMES AND STYLE

The main theme of *Go Ask Alice* is that drugs and the culture associated with drugs are accessible to children of all ages and that clearer communication between parents and children is necessary in order to keep kids off drugs. The narrator, "Alice," is a bright teenager from a typical family. She writes that she comes from a loving home, but her communication problems with her mother often leave her feeling as though she has nowhere to turn. She frequently mentions the availability of drugs in relation to legal substances that are less accessible: "Lots of kids never try booze, not only because it's their parents' thing, but because it's a lot harder to get than pot" and "I bet the pill is harder to get than drugs—which shows you how screwed up this world really is." In addition to using illegal drugs, Alice also peddles them to young children: "The high school kids are one thing and even the junior high, but today I sold ten stamps of LSD to a little kid at the grade school who was not even nine years old, I'm sure."

Sparks told Nilsen that she published *Go Ask Alice* as a tool to communicate with teenagers from a perspective they could understand. Drugs were largely not discussed at the time, and the literature that did exist was not applicable to young people wanting to rebel. Alice states, "All the things I've heard about LSD were obviously written by uninformed, ignorant people like my parents who obviously don't know what they're talking about." By using the voice of Alice, Sparks could get her message across without revealing her status as an "ignorant" adult meddling in the affairs of teenagers. The chronological layout expected of the diary entries and the narrative voice that allows the entries to appear private demonstrate that Sparks constructed *Go Ask Alice* to appear as a private internal dialogue while at the same time intending it to raise public awareness.

The text is styled to show the progression of Alice's drug use, from her first unintentional incident to her dependence and eventual overdose. The voice at the beginning of the book is innocent and naive but otherwise polite, and it demonstrates Alice's broad vocabulary, with such elaborate passages as: "Dear precious Diary, I am baptizing you with my tears. I know we have to leave and that one day I will even have to leave my father and mother's home and go into a home of my own." As the diary and Alice's addiction progress, her diction becomes less eloquent and she begins to swear and use vulgar language to describe the situations she finds herself in: "Another day, another blow job. The fuzz has clamped down till the town is mother dry. If I don't give Big Ass a blow he'll cut off my supply." When Alice stops using drugs and returns home, her diction improves, but when she finds herself using again her vocabulary and grammar quickly degrade to vulgarities and "street talk."

A still from the 1973 TV movie adaptation of *Go Ask Alice*, starring Andy Griffith and Jamie Smith Jackson. © EVERETT COLLECTION

CRITICAL DISCUSSION

Initially thought to be the authentic diary of a deceased addict, *Go Ask Alice* received positive reviews for its frank discussion of drug culture and the dangers of peer pressure facing teenagers. Typical of such acclaim is John Conner's 1973 review in which he calls *Go Ask Alice* "the most exciting book about adolescent involvement in the drug scene published this past year" and claims that reading it is a "sobering experience." Nilsen notes in "The House That Alice Built" (1979) that the book is "more or less exempt from the regular kind of literary criticism since it was supposedly the diary of a deceased young girl."

The book's social legacy is attributed to its narrative voice and the accessibility of that voice to an adolescent audience. Lina Goldberg in "Curiouser and Curiouser" (2002) claims, "One of the reasons the didactic tone was accepted by teenagers was they believed it to be a true story coming from one of their peers." However, the subject matter of the book and its frank language generated controversy among educators and parents over whether or not it was appropriate for young adults, its target audience. Goldberg notes that *Go Ask Alice* was "assigned as required reading by some schools" and was "banned" by others "for discussing such racy topics as sex and drugs," making it "one of the most-often challenged books in the country" in the 1970s.

Trends in scholarship changed in 1978 with the revelation of Sparks as the author and the exposed fabrication of much of the book. Scholars began to target Sparks and question the authenticity of her other

BETTER THAN THE TRUTH: *A MILLION LITTLE PIECES*

Other diarists have followed Beatrice Sparks's example in creating false autobiographical narrative. One notable example became a public scandal in 2005 when James Frey's best-selling memoir *A Million Little Pieces* was exposed as a fraud. Frey's gritty book is the redemption story of a misfit Ohio adolescent who develops serious drug and alcohol addictions. His deep anger and extreme substance abuse lead him into an increasingly violent and self-destructive life and finally into rehab. Writing in a starkly graphic stream-of-consciousness style, Frey describes his life of inebriated binges, rages, and arrests with self-revealing frankness.

Frey approached publishers with *A Million Little Pieces*, first characterizing the work as a novel. However, it was accepted for publication only after he reworked it as a memoir. After its publication in 2005, television host Oprah Winfrey gave Frey's memoir a boost when she selected it for her book club. In January 2006 allegations surfaced that Frey had exaggerated or fabricated many of the most sensational parts of his memoir, such as a three-month jail term that had in reality only lasted a few hours. After repeated denials, Frey finally admitted to having fictionalized many pivotal details, but he insisted that the spirit of the book remained true to his life story. Many readers expressed outrage over the deception—most famously Winfrey, who gave him a public dressing-down on her show that made headlines across the country.

works that were also allegedly based on the lives of real adolescents. Typical of this type of criticism is Lauren Adams's "*Go Ask Alice:* A Second Look" (1998), which says, "much of the book's merit was derived from its status as a 'real diary.'" And because the narrative, previously thought to be authentic, is actually fictitious, Adams asks, "If it's not all Alice talking, does it deserve to be judged differently?"

BIBLIOGRAPHY

Sources

Adams, Lauren. "*Go Ask Alice:* A Second Look." *Horn Book Magazine* 74.5 (1998): 587–92. Rpt. in *Children's Literature Review.* Ed. Tom Burns. Vol. 139. Detroit: Gale, 2009. *Literature Resource Center.* Web. 12 Dec. 2012.

Anon. *Go Ask Alice.* Ed. Beatrice Sparks. New York: Simon and Schuster, 1971. Print.

Conner, John W. Rev. of *Go Ask Alice*, by Anon. *English Journal* 62.1 (1973): 146–47. *JSTOR.* Web. 12 Dec. 2012.

Frey, James. *A Million Little Pieces.* New York: Doubleday, 2003. Print.

Goldberg, Lina. "'Curiouser and Curiouser': Fact, Fiction, and the Anonymous Author of *Go Ask Alice.*" linagoldberg.com. 2002. Web. 12 Dec. 2012.

Nilsen, Alleen Pace. "The House That Alice Built." *School Library Journal* 26.2 (1979): 109–12. Rpt. in *Children's Literature Review.* Ed. Tom Burns. Vol. 139. Detroit: Gale, 2009. *Literature Resource Center.* Web. 14 Dec. 2012.

Further Reading

"Explanation of: 'Go Ask Alice' by Beatrice Sparks." *LitFinder Contemporary Collection.* Detroit: Gale, 2010. *LitFinder for Schools.* Web. 14 Dec. 2012.

"Go Ask Alice." *American Decades Primary Sources.* Ed. Cynthia Rose. Vol. 8: 1970–79. Detroit: Gale, 2004. 361–65. *Gale Biography in Context.* Web. 14 Dec. 2012.

Jonnes, Jill. *Hep-Cats, Narcs, and Pipe Dreams: A History of America's Romance with Illegal Drugs.* New York: Scribner, 1996. Print.

Sparks, Beatrice. *Voices: The Stories of Four Troubled Teenagers as Told in Personal Interviews to Beatrice Sparks.* New York: Times Books, 1978. Print.

———. *Jay's Journal.* New York: Times Books, 1979. Print.

———. *It Happened to Nancy.* New York: Avon, 1994. Print.

———. *Annie's Baby: The Diary of Anonymous, a Pregnant Teenager.* New York: Avon, 1998. Print.

Katherine Barker

The Gossamer Years
Michitsuna No Haha

OVERVIEW

The Gossamer Years (1955) is an English translation by Edward Seidensticker of *Kagerō Nikki*, the diary of a Japanese noblewoman that covers the years 954–74—including her courtship with, marriage to, and estrangement from a husband one level above her in the ruling Fujiwara clan of the Heian period (794–1185). Her husband became regent in 986 and chancellor in 989, the year before he died. The author's name is not recorded—she is known as Michitsuna No Haha, or "Mother of Michitsuna"—and her dates can only be approximated (c. 936–95). The diary is notable for its realistic account of upper-class life in the period and for the startling candor with which the author reveals her emotional disturbances, her resentments, and her disillusionments.

No contemporary manuscript survives of *Kagerō Nikki*; the earliest text dates from the seventeenth century. Several critical texts have appeared in Japan, rendering the work into modern Japanese. Seidensticker made the first complete English translation in 1952; it was published as *The Gossamer Years* in 1955. He released a second edition, considerably revised and with an expanded and useful introduction, in 1964. In 1997 a more literal and arguably more gender-appropriate translation was produced by scholar Sonja Arntzen of the University of Toronto and published as *The Kagero Diary*. Both versions have been widely read for the insights they provide into aristocratic life of the Heian period and the position of women in that era of Japanese history.

HISTORICAL AND LITERARY CONTEXT

The Heian period takes its name from Japan's capital city, Heian-kyō, which is now known as Kyōto. It is considered the third and final era of classical Japanese history. There is no useful correlation between periods of European American history and those of Japanese history. Both societies had notions of class and nobility, but they did not share a universal definition of these concepts. Similarly, marriage in Japan during this period—at least at the upper levels of society—was a shadowy, transitory matter, not at all the sacramental relationship of a European couple. There was a hereditary emperor of Japan at this time, and he was legally absolute in his authority, but the country was run by members of the Fujiwara clan—to which Mother of Michitsuna and her husband belonged—including regents, chancellors, and provincial governors. Japanese society was severely isolated; the only outside cultural influences came sporadically from China.

The time period covered by *The Gossamer Years* was particularly turbulent politically, though, with one exception: current events of the high government make no appearance in the journal. The sole exception was when Minamoto Takaaki, a high official, was charged in 969 with conspiring to have his son-in-law, Prince Tamehira, made crown prince. Takaaki was found guilty and exiled to Kyushu. If Takaaki had succeeded—if indeed he was really plotting—it would have been a serious blow to the Fujiwara clan, but for some reason Mother of Michitsuna sided with Takaaki, and her journal has a fairly detailed account of the episode.

The Heian period was a particularly productive time in Japanese literature. The prevalence of women authors and poets (Mother of Michitsuna was apparently a well-known poet) does not quite square with the anonymity of many of the best women writers. Seidensticker notes that the author of *The Gossamer Years* was a member of a class that included other well-known women writers: The author of this diary was the aunt of the author of the *Sarashina Nikki* (*The Sarashina Diary*). One of her sisters was married to a great-uncle of Murasaki Shikbu, author of *Genji Monogatari* (*The Tale of Genji*), and one of her brothers was married to a sister of Sei Shōnagon, author of *Makura Shōshi* (*The Pillow Book*).

Those who have most closely studied the writings of the author's successors have concluded that her diary was read fairly widely by the writers of subsequent eras. The book's impact and influence may be deduced from Seidensticker's remark that "[*The Gossamer Years*] is the first attempt in Japanese literature, or in any case the first surviving attempt, to capture on paper, without evasion or idealization, the elements of a real social situation." The book did not exactly usher in an era of naturalistic writing in Japan, but it certainly pointed the way.

THEMES AND STYLE

The overarching themes of *The Gossamer Years* are disillusionment and loneliness. Though the author is skeptical during her courtship and finds her future husband's suit "inappropriate," once they are married she thinks

Key Facts

Time Period:
Mid-10th Century

Relevant Historical Events:
Peace and prosperity of the Heian period; author's involvement with the Fujiwara clan

Nationality:
Japanese

Keywords:
women's writing; domesticity; politics

Main Hall of the Byodoin Temple in Kyoto, Japan, built during the Heian period in 1053. © AISA/EVERETT COLLECTION

he will live with her, or she with him. Her hopes are soon dashed, however: "Toying with my writing box one morning just after he had left, I came upon a note obviously intended for another woman. My chagrin was infinite, and I felt that I must at least let him know I had seen the thing. 'Might it be a bill of divorcement,' I wrote, 'this note that I see for another?'" Her husband has other wives and many mistresses, and ultimately he stops visiting—and declares his heir to be not the writer's son, Michitsuna, but his son by another wife. The author seems unable to initiate action, either by going to see him or by writing the first poem of any exchange, but whether this is by law or convention or simply by choice is never made clear. Sometimes months pass between his visits, but for the reader, it is just the next paragraph, as if nothing worth mentioning happened in between. The book is not a story of her life overall but only of her relationship with "the Prince."

For all her apparent candor, the author is surprisingly unforthcoming about any fact of her existence save her husband's visits—and she is cryptic about her motives in writing the journal. She touches on them obliquely in her first paragraph in *The Gossamer Years,* which, unlike the rest of the book, is written in the third person: "Perhaps, she said to herself, even the story of her own dreary life, set down in a journal, might be of interest; and it might also answer a question: had that life been one befitting a well born lady? But they must all be recounted, events of long ago, events of but yesterday. She was by no means certain that she could bring them to order." The same passage is translated quite differently by Arntzen: "… she thinks perhaps if she were to make a record of a life like her own, being really nobody, it might actually be novel, and could even serve to answer, should anyone ask, what is it like, the life of a woman married to a highly placed man, yet the events of the months and years gone by are vague; places where I have just left it at that are indeed many." Seidensticker suggests that "the diary is in a sense her protest against the marriage system of the time, and her exposition of the thesis that all men are beasts."

Written in the form of a journal, Book I and half of Book II are probably, according to Seidensticker, not diary entries at all, but memoirs written long after the fact. Even in the second half of Book II and all of Book III, though the entries are more detailed, there is little to be learned about family life—still less about work life—but only about the author's relationship with her husband and how she feels about it. The dialogue is unusual too. Except for the occasional, and usually sarcastic, comment from her mother or her "women," most of the conversations between the author and her husband take the form of one-sentence poems, either sent back and forth by messenger or exchanged by hand in each other's presence. It is as if the two of them have lost the power of speech.

CRITICAL DISCUSSION

Since *Kagerō Nikki* was not formally published until many centuries after it was written and was only circulated in handwritten copies and possibly read aloud in company, the question of its immediate reception is a matter for speculation only. Seidensticker notes that the book "was known in the late Heian and Kamakura (1185–333) periods and is mentioned in the early Kamakura journal of Fujiwara Teika," so, presumably, the work found favor with a consistent readership, albeit one of indeterminate size and composition.

The legacy of *Kagerō Nikki* is most productively assessed in conjunction with the other female-authored books of the Heian period by Lady Murasaki, Lady Sarashina, Sei Shōnagon, and others. The unusual liberties exercised by women—in the upper classes, at least—during this era did not lead directly to gender equality in Japan. In fact, women in that country had to suffer another thousand years of servitude before they began to make the first tentative steps to equality. But those steps coincide with the rediscovery of the diary and other texts of Heian female authors.

Outside of Asia, scholarly approaches to the work have tended to focus not on its literary merits but its historical context, its place at the beginning of the tradition of "diaries of literary merit." Writing in the *Cultural History of Reading*, Samaya L. S. Chanthaphavong notes, "Journals have helped to shape the historical understanding of the cultural and sociopolitical make-up of traditional Japanese society by offering an intimate glimpse into the past that is often overlooked by conventional cultural readings." On questions of theoretical relevance, Edith Sarra notes in *The Princeton Encyclopedia of Poetry and Poetics* that "the complexity of the *Kagerō Nikki*'s prose and its apparent influence on poetic diaries by later aristocratic wives and ladies-in-waiting suggest the development of a differently configured set of motives, forms, and implied readers in the 11th century." Sarra also raises the possibility that Mother of Michitsuna, having read and dismissed the popular romantic fictions of the day, decided to try her hand at writing one herself. In a 1997 review of Arntzen's translation, Brantislav Slantchev praises the author's courage and honesty: "In many ways [*The Kagero Diary*] has not been surpassed by any … in subtlety of expression, stark honesty of emotion, and the author's changing attitudes toward her own existence."

SCENES FROM A HEIAN MARRIAGE

One of the most difficult contexts to grasp for the modern Western reader of *The Gossamer Years* is the nature of the author's marriage to the prince. It was obviously much less formally binding, legally and financially, than modern marriage. The woman did not have to be a virgin when the arrangements were finalized. Marriage was "matrilocal": the husband was expected to move in with the wife's family and use his father-in-law for political clout. Though polygamy was forbidden, there was no limit to the number of concubines a man could take, and the concubines became de facto wives. Descent was completely patrilineal, and a concubine's children could inherit if the man decreed. Some liberties accrued to the woman in this time, but as Edward Seidensticker observes, "the uncertainty of a badly articulated system of polygamy must have been intense."

Mother of Michitsuna's marriage has some features that are unusual, though probably not unique. Husband and wife are of the same clan, but the prince has married beneath himself. Her father is a provincial governor; her husband stands near the top in the seat of power for the entire country. Being so highly placed, the prince is able to spread himself far and wide among the available women. For all her supposed sophistication, the author is naïve enough to expect her husband for "thirty days and thirty nights every month." Divorce during this time was even more casual—the husband simply stopped coming by. "One day," the author writes, after sixteen years of marriage, "as I sat looking out at the rain, knowing that today there was less chance than usual of seeing him, my thoughts turned to the past. The fault was not mine, there was something wanting in him. It had seemed once that wind and rain could not keep him away."

Slantchev, Brantislav. Rev. of *The Kagero Diary*, by Michitsuna No Haha. Ann Arbor: Center for Japanese Studies, University of Michigan, 1997. *Götterdämmerung*. Web. 6 Dec. 2012.

Further Reading

Childs, Margaret H. "The Value of Vulnerability: Sexual Coercion and the Nature of Love in Japanese Court Literature." *Journal of Asian Studies* 58.4 (1999): 1059–80. Print.

Kornicki, Peter. *The Book in Japan: A Cultural History from the Beginnings to the Nineteenth Century*. Honolulu: University of Hawaii Press, 2000. Print.

McKinney, Meredith. "'Pillow Book' Talk: Meredith McKinney Reflects on Translating a Japanese Classic." *Meanjin* 64.4 (2005): 54+. *General OneFile*. Web. 14 Dec. 2012.

Morton, W. Scott, and J. Kenneth Olenik. *Japan, Its History and Culture*. New York: McGraw-Hill, 2005. Print.

Murasaki Shikibu. *The Tale of Genji: A Novel in Six Parts*. Trans. Arthur Waley. Rutland, Vt.: Charles E. Tuttle, 1993. Print.

Gerald Carpenter

BIBLIOGRAPHY

Sources

Chanthaphavong, Samaya L. S. "Japan." *Cultural History of Reading. Vol. 1: World Literature*. Ed. Gabrielle Watling. Westport, Conn.: Greenwood, 2008. 325–39. *Gale Virtual Reference Library*. Web. 15 Dec. 2012.

Michitsuna No Haha. *The Kagero Diary*. Trans. Sonja Arntzen. Ann Arbor: Center for Japanese Studies, University of Michigan, 1997. Print.

———. *The Gossamer Years*. Trans. Edward Seidensticker. Boston: Tuttle, 2001. Print.

Nickerson, Peter. "The Meaning of Matrilocality: Kinship, Property, and Politics in Mid-Heian." *Monumenta Nipponica* 48.4 (1993): 429–67. Print.

Sarra, Edith. "Japanese Poetic Diaries." *The Princeton Encyclopedia of Poetry and Poetics*. 4th ed. Ed. Roland Greene and Stephen Cushman. Princeton, N.J.: Princeton University Press, 2012. 756–57. *Gale Virtual Reference Library*. Web. 10 Dec. 2012.

Grasmere Journals
Dorothy Wordsworth

❖ **Key Facts**

Time Period:
Early 19th Century

Relevant Historical Events:
Rise of "natural philosophy"; growth of Romanticism; increasing economic disparity as a result of industrialization

Nationality:
English

Keywords:
women's writing; Romanticism; nature

OVERVIEW

Dorothy Wordsworth's *Grasmere Journals* (1800–1803)—a set of four notebooks written while she lived with her brother, the poet William Wordsworth, at Grasmere, a village in the English Lake District—are remarkable for their detailed descriptions of nature. She began writing the journals in order to come to terms with her brother's temporary absence. Written specifically for him, they contain keen observations of nature and individuals set within the framework of everyday life. The journals dwell on the theme of nature as a flourishing entity separate from the observer. Since Wordsworth (1771–1855) had been brought up by relatives (her mother died when she was six years old), the journals also reflect her lifelong preoccupation with home and with coping with the loss of loved ones.

Although she composed journals, letters, poems, and short stories, she likely did not wish to publish them—at least not under her own name. In an 1810 letter she claims that she "should detest the idea of setting myself up as an Author." William Angus Knight published the *Grasmere Journals* in 1897, decades after her death. Scholars of William Wordsworth have found in the *Grasmere Journals* a rich source of information on one of his most creative periods. The journals have also attracted a great deal of attention for their literary merit, especially for the fascinating attention to detail they exhibit in their descriptions of nature and for the striking choices the author made as to what to include and what to leave unwritten.

HISTORICAL AND LITERARY CONTEXT

Wordsworth wrote during a time when diary and journal keeping were widespread among the educated. In *The Poetry of the Earth,* E. D. H. Johnson dubs late eighteenth and early nineteenth century the golden age of British nature writing. Wordsworth's interest in nature was constantly stimulated by the long walks she took with her brother and by the intellectual energy of the conversations she had with him and poet Samuel Taylor Coleridge, who often visited. At the same time, this golden age was inspired by a climate of unabated interest in so-called natural philosophy. Diarists who had read nature journals—such as those of the reverend Gilbert White, who wrote in great detail about his surroundings, or the popular scientific works of Swedish scientist Carl Linnaeus, known as the father of taxonomy—acquired the habit of recording the minutia of natural life with the greatest accuracy.

Wordsworth began the *Grasmere Journals* on May 14, 1800, while William was away from Dove Cottage, the home they shared, in order to propose marriage to Mary Hutchinson. The journal ends with William's marriage, which Wordsworth reports in her last entry on January 16, 1803. Although she began keeping the journals to cope with loneliness, they quickly becomes a lens through which the reader sees not only the Wordsworths' domestic life and their long walks through nature but also "an alteration in the times," including the effects of enclosures, technological advancements, and massive changes in the distribution of property. These shifts led Wordsworth to note in her journal that soon there would be "only two ranks of people, the very rich & the very poor." The journal records interactions with dozens of impoverished people, many of whom knocked on her door in order to beg, and the emergence of new homes for the wealthy.

Recording the details of one's natural surroundings in a fastidiously accurate and literary manner was an active preoccupation for women at the end of the eighteenth century. It was associated with larger projects of improving both self and society. Famous journalists such as Sarah Trimmer and Priscilla Wakefield wrote about nature in order to contribute to the education of children. Linnaeus's work found favor with poets such as Charlotte Smith, whose poems were part of the Wordsworths' reading regimen at Dove Cottage.

Scholars of William Wordsworth argue that he referred to his sister's journal for no less than thirty-five poems. The *Grasmere Journals* contain a description of the daffodils on which his famous "I Wandered Lonely as A Cloud" (1807) is based, as well as records of the ways in which he used her notes to write "Resolution and Independence" in 1802 and his poems centered on beggars. Coleridge also benefited from Dorothy's notes: in particular, his poem "Christabel" (1816) is linked to her journal notes.

THEMES AND STYLE

Wordsworth's journal weaves the themes of love and fear of loss within a discourse on the majesty of nature and the life-affirming pleasures of domesticity. When she writes that "after dinner we made a pillow of my shoulder, I read to him & my Beloved slept," she knows that her brother will soon be married and that she will no longer enjoy his undivided attention. "We were deep in Silence and Love, a blessed hour," she writes in another entry, noting the fleetingness and fragility of what she considers the happiest time of her life.

In the first entry, she admits that she started the journal to compensate for her brother's absence: "because I will not quarrel with myself" and "because I shall give Wm Pleasure by it when he comes home again." Because one of her goals is to provide William with material for his poems, many readers find the journals to be an overly objective study of nature rather than an inward-looking autobiographical endeavor. At the same time, the journals detail the more mundane aspects of her life including her time spent baking, starching, mending and ironing linen, gardening, and nailing beds, as well as her headaches and need to lie down when she feels "unwell."

Although her renderings of nature are objective, she adopts a sentimental tone similar to that of eighteenth-century novels—including her favorite, Samuel Richardson's *Clarissa* (1748)—when she records major life events such as her brother's trip to propose to his future wife or his wedding day. This style is particularly evident in her portrait of herself in her first entry: "I sate a long time upon a stone at the margin of the lake, & after a flood of tears my heart was easier. The lake looked to me I knew not why dull and melancholy, the weltering on the shores seemed a heavy sound." While famous for original poetic images—"[t]he moonshine like herrings in the water"—Wordsworth is often remembered for the accuracy of her nature descriptions.

CRITICAL DISCUSSION

An initial critical response to Wordsworth's writings is offered in her brother Christopher's *Memoirs of William Wordsworth* (1851), which features selections from the writings of both brothers and includes pages from the *Grasmere Journals*. Christopher, who points out the great role that Wordsworth played in the composition of William's most famous poems and the substantial amount of writing she contributed to his *Guide to the Lakes* (1822), was a great admirer of her journals because, as he writes, they are "full of vivid descriptions and natural beauty."

Twentieth-century scholars also came to recognize Wordsworth for her work's merit. Nonetheless, as Patricia Comitini observes in a 2003 essay in the *European Romantic Review,* "Whether characterizing her as a domestic subject, novice writer or helpmate, scholarship has focused primarily on her failure to realize herself, develop her talent, or establish her own home." Indeed, Susan M. Levin argues in *Dorothy Wordsworth and Romanticism* (2009) that her writing "is characterized by refusal: refusal to generalize, refusal to move out of a limited range of vision, refusal to speculate … refusal to undertake the act of writing."

Reflecting a trend that started in the twenty-first century, Comitini presents a picture of Wordsworth as a "half poet," by her own choice. Her "vocation," argues Comitini, was philanthropy and social amelioration, and "her feelings, duties, and beliefs all correspond to what she thinks is her special feminine capacity to rationalize, sympathize, and normalize the social sphere she supervises," a sphere that "extends beyond the Wordsworths' circle to include townspeople, servants, and beggars." Comitini adds that Wordsworth "clearly perceives authorship, and the notoriety it brings, to be a display of vulgar productivity, complicit with motivations of profit." Mary Ellen Bellanca, writing in *Daybooks of Discovery: Nature Diaries in Britain, 1770–1870* (2007), also sees Wordsworth as a successful contributor to "her culture's dialogue about nature and landscape with no less zest and savvy than writers with more public ambitions, such as Charlotte Smith, Mary Roberts, John Leonard Knapp, or the many other authors of popular natural histories and nature journals." Her writings, Bellanca contends, "reached her readers by means of William's poetic reputation and in contexts ancillary to it. But reach readers they certainly did."

Dove Cottage in the village of Grasmere, England. Dorothy Wordsworth lived in the house with her brother, the poet William Wordsworth. © DAVID LYONS/ALAMY

WILLIAM WORDSWORTH'S AUTOBIOGRAPHICAL MASTERPIECE

One of the best-known works of British Romanticism, *The Prelude* (1850) is a poetic autobiography authored by Dorothy Wordsworth's brother William. Although William's fame as a poet earned him the position of poet laureate of England, his masterpiece went unpublished until after his death. It traces his idealized childhood in the Lake District, his time at Cambridge, and his travels to the continent, where he witnessed the tumult of the French Revolution. He chronicles the loss of his youthful idealism following the escalating violence in France, his ensuing struggle with depression, and the peace that he found in nature and the ameliorative powers of his bond with Dorothy. Throughout, he emphasizes a handful of what he calls "spots of time," strong and enduring memories that have the power to stir sentiment and alleviate the burdens of a troubled mind.

The Prelude occupied much of William's adult life. He began writing the poem in 1798, completing an early version in 1799, while Europe was still reeling from the French Revolutionary Wars. A much-expanded version of the poem was completed in 1805. He continued to revise the text throughout the remainder of his life. The final version was published three months after his death in 1850, its title chosen by his widow.

BIBLIOGRAPHY

Sources

Bellanca, Mary Ellen. *Daybooks of Discovery: Nature Diaries in Britain, 1770–1870*. Charlottesville: University of Virginia Press, 2007. Print.

Comitini, Patricia. "More Than Half a Poet: Vocational Philanthropy and Dorothy Wordsworth's *Grasmere Journals*." *European Romantic Review* 14 (2003): 307–22. Web. 2 Jan. 2013.

Johnson, E. D. H., ed. *The Poetry of the Earth: A Collection of English Nature Writings*. New York: Atheneun, 1966. Print.

Levin, Susan M. *Dorothy Wordsworth and Romanticism*. London: McFarland, 2009. Print.

Wordsworth, Christopher. *Memoirs of William Wordsworth*. Boston: Ticknor, Reed, and Fields, 1851. Print.

Wordsworth, Dorothy. *The Grasmere Journals*. Ed. Pamela Woof. Oxford: Clarendon, 1991. Print.

Further Reading

Cervelli, Kenneth R. *Dorothy Wordsworth's Ecology*. New York: Routledge, 2007. Print.

Gunn, Elizabeth. *A Passion for the Particular: Dorothy Wordsworth: A Portrait*. London: Gollancz, 1981. Print.

Heinzelman Kurt. "The Cult of Domesticity: Dorothy and William at Grasmere." *Romanticism and Feminism*. Ed. Anne K. Mellor. Bloomington: Indiana University Press, 1988. 52–78. Print.

Lokke, Kari. "'My Heart Dissolved in What I Saw': Displacement of the Autobiographical Self in Dorothy Wordsworth and Gertrude Stein." *Romantic Autobiography in England*. Ed. Eugene Stelzig. Farnham: Ashgate, 2009. 15–30. Print.

Newlyn, Lucy. "Dorothy Wordsworth's Experimental Style." *Essays in Criticism* 57.4 (2007): 325–49. Web. 2 Jan. 2013.

Page, Judith W. "Dorothy Wordsworth's 'Gratitude to Insensate Things': Gardening in the *Grasmere Journals*." *Wordsworth Circle* 39.1–2 (2008): 19–23. Web. 2 Jan. 2013.

Smith, Kenneth Edward. *Dorothy Wordsworth and the Profession of Authorship: A Critical Commentary on Her Letters, Journals, Life Writing, and Poetry*. New York: Mellen, 2011. Print.

Stewart, Suzanne. "'The Eye It Cannot Choose but See': Dorothy Wordsworth, John Constable, and the *Plein-Air* Sketch." *English Studies* 92.4 (2011): 405–31. Web. 2 Jan. 2013.

Wallace, Anne D. "Home at Grasmere Again: Revising the Family in Dove Cottage." *Literary Couplings: Writing Couples, Collaborators, and the Construction of Authorship*. Ed. Judith Thompson. Madison: University of Wisconsin Press, 2006. 100–23. Print.

Wilson, Frances. *The Ballad of Dorothy Wordsworth*. London: Faber and Faber, 2008. Print.

Nancy Simpson-Younger

I Will Bear Witness
A Diary of the Nazi Years, 1933–1945
Victor Klemperer

OVERVIEW

I Will Bear Witness: A Diary of the Nazi Years, 1933–1945 is Jewish professor Victor Klemperer's diary of daily life in Germany leading up to and during World War II. First published in German in 1995, it is one of the most significant and thorough records of the rise of Nazism and the attempted annihilation of the Jews. The 1,000-page English version of the diary, selected from more than 5,000 pages of Klemperer's writing, was divided into two volumes: *1933–1941* (published in 1998) and *1942–1945* (published in 2000). Offering an eyewitness view of the Nazi era in Dresden from the point of view of a Jewish intellectual, the diary explores Klemperer's frustrations with the political situation in Germany, his disbelief at the rise of Nazism, and his eventual terror of the Nazi party's murderous anti-Semitism.

Following Klemperer's death in 1960, a former student discovered his diaries in the Dresden State Library and, believing in their historical import, began to transcribe them. Berlin publisher Aufbau Verlag published the work in 1995 to resounding popular success (the diaries sold 125,000 copies in the first year) and later sold the English-language publishing rights to Random House for a record-setting $550,000. Following the worldwide publication of the diaries, scholarship and critical interest in them increased, as the text presents an honest and unflinching portrait of the Jewish-German experience during the Nazi era. Today *I Will Bear Witness* is considered one of the most important Jewish Holocaust diaries.

HISTORICAL AND LITERARY CONTEXT

That Klemperer kept a diary was not unusual; he was an academic, accustomed to expressing himself in writing. In addition, many people, especially members of the Jewish intelligentsia who were being censored and silenced in the 1930s and 1940s, had reason to chronicle their experiences in private diaries. As Klemperer saw his teaching position revoked and his opportunities for academic publication vanish under the Nazi regime, his diary became an ever more important outlet for his grievances, fears, and otherwise stifled intellectual expression. Klemperer, a philologist, remains a scholar in his diary, documenting the Nazis' subversion of the German language to propagandistic purpose. He painstakingly documents the gradual limiting of his rights as a Jew married to a gentile and the accompanying restrictions on his personal and professional life, the effects of which would shape his development as an academic and a citizen of Germany in the years following the war.

The selection of Klemperer's writings published in *I Will Bear Witness* detail his experience living as a Jewish man in Germany in the years during which the Nazis came to power and attempted to exterminate the Jews. Klemperer describes a number of notable historical moments, including the Nazis' assumption of power in 1933; the November 1938 pogrom; the forced relocation of many Jews to ghettos or "Jews' houses"; the gradual restriction of Jewish rights, including the mandate to wear the identifying yellow star; and the eventual deportation of many Jews to concentration camps. Klemperer, as the husband of a gentile woman and a veteran of World War I, saw his rights disappear at a slower pace; however, on February 13, 1945, he, too, was facing deportation to a concentration camp when the Allied Forces bombed Dresden. The resulting confusion allowed Klemperer and his wife, Eva, to flee to safety in American-occupied southern Bavaria. *I Will Bear Witness* ends in June 1945, when Klemperer and Eva were able to return to their home in Dölzschen, Germany.

In addition to describing historical events in Germany, *I Will Bear Witness* provides unique insight into the day-to-day Jewish-German experience under the Third Reich. Other Holocaust diaries describing the Jewish experience during World War II include *Anne Frank's The Diary of a Young Girl* (1947), *The Warsaw Diary of Adam Czerniaków* (1979), and *Notes from the Warsaw Ghetto: The Journal of Emmanuel Ringelblum* (2006). Klemperer's diary is unique in that it describes the Jewish experience within Germany, whereas the above-mentioned Holocaust diaries were written by Jews living in hiding (Frank) or in ghettos in Holland (Czerniaków) or Poland (Ringelblum). As a Jewish Holocaust diarist, Klemperer is also notable for having survived World War II.

I Will Bear Witness is distinguished by Klemperer's scholarly observations on patriotism, the average German's reaction to Nazism, the Nazi vocabulary, and

❖ Key Facts

Time Period:
Mid-20th Century

Relevant Historical Events:
World War II; Holocaust; rise of Nazism

Nationality:
German

Keywords:
war; holocaust; Judaism

WORK AND FAMILY LIFE

Actor Gerd Rigaur played author Victor Klemperer in *Gehen-Bleiben*, a 2007 play that features readings from Klemperer's diary. © AP IMAGES/STEPHAN TRIERENBERG

Nazi propaganda. Though he was not able to publish, or, eventually, to teach at all, Klemperer continued to work on his academic writing during the war. Throughout *I Will Bear Witness*, he describes working on a book-length treatise on Romanticism. The diary also examines the manner in which Nazis used language; in 1947 Klemperer would publish a book on this subject, *Lingua Tertii Imperii* (*LTI*). During this time he also began work on *Curriculum Vitae* (1996), a memoir of his earlier life. Finally, a third volume of Klemperer's diary, *The Lesser Evil: The Diaries of Victor Klemperer, 1945–1959*, was published in 2003. Although he was not considered a highly important scholar during his lifetime, Klemperer and his writings gained a wider appreciation in the years following his death.

THEMES AND STYLE

I Will Bear Witness focuses on themes central to Jewish life in Germany under Nazi rule, including struggle, fear, and disbelief. Klemperer reacts with increasing incredulity as the Nazis come to and maintain power: "The masses let themselves be talked into believing everything. If for three months all the newspapers are forced to write that there was no World War, then the masses will believe that it really did not happen." He also spends considerable time writing about the gradual restriction of his freedoms and his mounting fear of what's to come. In 1933, he writes about his fear of the Nazi party: "It openly threatens to proceed against the German Jews—if the mischief making by 'World Jewry' does not stop. Meanwhile there is no bloodshed in this country, but oppression, oppression, oppression. No one breathes freely anymore, no free word, neither printed nor spoken."

Klemperer kept a detailed record of his daily doings in his diary, but he also used it as a space for scholarship and reflection on his role as a Jewish citizen of Germany. While he may not have intended his diaries for publication, he certainly used his daily journal as a testing ground for musings on linguistics, Romanticism, patriotism, and his situation as a Jew during the Third Reich, all of which would appear in slightly different form in Klemperer's subsequent publications. Significantly, he viewed his diary as a record, writing, "I shall go on writing. That is my heroism. I will bear witness, precise witness!" The diary also contains more private examinations of his life with his wife, their hypochondriacal tendencies, and their love of the cinema. Klemperer felt that it was his duty to "observe, study, record everything that happens—tomorrow it'll look different, tomorrow it will feel differently. Seize it as it happens and feels."

I Will Bear Witness is remarkable for its detail; use of metaphor; and precise, scholarly language. As a writer and scholar, Klemperer had a facility with language, as evidenced here: "For the moment I am still safe. But as someone on the gallows, who has the rope around his neck, is safe. At any moment a new 'law' can kick away the steps on which I'm standing and then I'm hanging." In a preface to *I Will Bear Witness*, Martin Chalmers discusses the particular qualities of Klemperer's language: "His words and responses have a rare immediacy…. [He] displayed a disarming honesty and directness." Chalmers also notes the fact that Klemperer seems not to have censored himself in order to appear more noble; the resulting text is a complex, contradictory, and candid view of life under Nazi rule.

CRITICAL DISCUSSION

When *I Will Bear Witness* was published in Germany in 1995, the initial critical response was largely positive. Published posthumously by then-minor Berlin publisher Aufbau Verlag, it achieved considerable commercial success, resulting in a radio adaptation; an abridged version; and, in 1998 and 2000, an English-language version published in two volumes. Of particular interest to German readers was Klemperer's knowledge of the death camps, which he mentions in his diaries as early as March 1942. Israeli journalist Amos Elon notes that following the diary's publication, prominent German literary critic Marcel Reich-Ranicki "announced on television that no one would ever again be entitled to claim he or she 'did not know'" of the existence of the death camps. Author Peter Gay, reviewing the first volume of the diary published in English, calls Klemperer "one of the greatest diarists—perhaps the greatest—in the German language."

Contemporary scholars have focused on Klemperer's depiction of "ordinary" Germans, his thoughts on German nationalism, and his use of and thoughts on language. Shortly after its German-language publication, *I Will Bear Witness* was discussed in the context of the debate surrounding Daniel Goldhagen's book *Hitler's Willing Executioners* (1996), which postulates that Germans had taken part in the mass extermination of the Jews as a result of an "eliminationist anti-Semitism" that was part of German national identity. American critic Katie Trumpener argues that Klemperer's diary offers evidence contradicting Goldhagen's claim by describing "a staggeringly large number of personally witnessed incidents of resistance" by sympathetic Germans. Other scholars have noted Klemperer's adaptation of portions of his diaries for inclusion in his books *LTI* and *Curriculum Vitae*.

Recent scholarship has focused on his use of language. While Klemperer meticulously documented the ways in which the Nazis used language to gain power, scholar Wolfgang Mieder observes that Klemperer himself "intentionally used popular proverbs and proverbial expressions to add power to his observations and statements. The proverbial language he shows us is a two-edged sword, as it serves both perpetrators and victims of the Third Reich alike…. The proverbial wealth of the Diaries 1933–1945 is a sign of their linguistic and factual authenticity." Critics have also noted the irony of the diary's commentary on Nazi Germany given Klemperer's decision to live in East Germany late in life. Critic John Wesley Young asserts that *I Will Bear Witness* "provokes questions about [Klemperer's] understanding of another form of totalitarian discourse, the Soviet, as well as his vocal support for the Communist dictatorship that succeeded Hitler's in eastern Germany."

EVA KLEMPERER

Eva Klemperer (née Schlemmer) was a musicologist when she married Victor Klemperer in 1906, to the dismay of both their families. A German-Protestant and concert pianist, Eva shared Victor's love of cinema and intellectual discussion. It was largely due to her "Aryan" heritage that Victor was temporarily able to avoid the harshest persecutions meted out by the Nazi regime. Following the couple's 1945 expulsion from their home in Dölzschen, Eva remained with Victor and supported him though she endured difficult conditions; during a Gestapo search of the Klemperers' home following their relocation to the "Jews' houses," Eva was beaten and called a "Jew's whore."

In his diaries, Victor notes Eva's growing unhappiness leading up to and during the war, as well as her hypochondria. She is often described as feeling poorly or needing to rest, though following the end of the war her spirits seem to rise as she and Victor are able to return to their home in Dölzschen. On June 23, 1945, Victor writes: "To just once eat well again, to drink well, to drive well, to go to the seaside, to sit comfortably in the cinema…. No 20 year-old can be half as hungry for life…. And with all of that it makes me happy, that E. is working on HER HOUSE, on HER garden and is coming to life again."

BIBLIOGRAPHY

Sources

Elon, Amos. "The Jew Who Fought to Stay German." Rev. of *The Diary of Victor Klemperer,* by Victor Klemperer. *New York Times*. New York Times, 24 Mar. 1996. Web. 20 Dec. 2012.

Gay, Peter. "Inside the Third Reich." Rev. of *I Will Bear Witness: A Diary of the Nazi Years, 1933–1941,* by Victor Klemperer. *New York Times*. New York Times, 22 Nov. 1998. Web. 20 Dec. 2012.

Klemperer, Victor. *I Will Bear Witness: A Diary of the Nazi Years, 1933–1941*. Trans. Martin Chalmers. New York: Random House, 1998. Print.

———. *I Will Bear Witness: A Diary of the Nazi Years, 1942–1945*. Trans. Martin Chalmers. New York: Random House, 2000. Print.

Mieder, Wolfgang. "The 2000 Archer Taylor Memorial Lecture: 'In lingua veritas' Proverbial Rhetoric in Victor Klemperer's Diaries of the Nazi Years (1933–1945)." *Western Folklore* 59.1 (2000): 1–31. *JSTOR*. Web. 12 Dec. 2012.

Trumpener, Katie. "Diary of a Tightrope Walker: Victor Klemperer and His Posterity." *Modernism/modernity* 7.3 (2000): 487–507. *Project MUSE*. Web. 12 Dec. 2012.

Young, John Wesley. "From LTI to LQI: Victor Klemperer on Totalitarian Language." *German Studies Review* 28.1 (2005): 45–64. *JSTOR*. Web. 12 Dec. 2012.

Further Reading

Aschheim, Steven E. *Scholem, Arendt, Klemperer: Intimate Chronicles in Turbulent Times*. Bloomington: Indiana University Press, 2001. Print.

Cole, Tim. *Traces of the Holocaust: Journeying in and out of the Ghettos*. New York: Continuum, 2011. Print.

Czerniaków, Adam. *Prelude to Doom: The Warsaw Diary of Adam Czerniaków*. Ed. Raul Hilberg, Stanislaw Staron, and Josef Kermisz. Chicago: Ivan R. Dee, 1999. Print.

Klemperer, Victor. *The Language of the Third Reich: LTI, Lingua Tertii Imperii: A Philologist's Notebook*. Trans. Martin Brady. London: Athlone, 2000. Print.

———. *The Lesser Evil: The Diaries of Victor Klemperer, 1945–1959*. Trans. Martin Chalmers. London: Weidenfeld & Nicolson, 2003. Print.

Kristen Gleason

The Journal of Marie Bashkirtseff
Marie Bashkirtseff

✢ Key Facts

Time Period:
Mid-19th Century

Relevant Historical Events:
Growth of feminism; Bashkirtseff's immigration to France; rise of French cultural decadence

Nationality:
Ukrainian

Keywords:
feminism; women's writing; creativity

OVERVIEW

The Journal of Marie Bashkirtseff, translated from its original Ukrainian version (1887) into two English volumes (1890)—*I Am the Most Interesting Book of All (Vol. 1)* and *Lust for Glory (Vol. 2)*—addresses the events of an adolescent Russian socialite while she was living in France in the late nineteenth century. Bashkirtseff's journal was only the second diary written by a woman to be published in France, and it is unique in the candid, humorous, and often self-centered tone employed by the young author. The diary covers Bashkirtseff's life from the age of fourteen to her untimely death in 1884, addressing social visits and events, fleeting romances, the author's radical views on gender equality, and the battle with tuberculosis that ended her life. It reveals much about the daily life of an upper-class immigrant family in turn-of-the-century France.

None of Bashkirtseff's diaries or letters appeared during her lifetime, but her mother published the first version of the journal after her daughter's death, following Bashkirtseff's wishes to remain alive in posterity through her writing. (A complete scholarly edition of *The Journal of Marie Bashkirtseff*, based on the original notebooks, did not appear until the mid-1990s.) Upon its initial publication, the work quickly became popular in France, partially because it differed greatly from earlier diaries published by European women. It continues to capture the attention of the public and academics alike.

HISTORICAL AND LITERARY CONTEXT

Bashkirtseff settled in Nice, France, in 1871 with her mother after leaving Russia because of her parents' separation. The fourteen-year-old socialite found herself in the midst of the vibrant cultural scene of fin-de-siècle France, characterized by, among other things, a fascination with escapism, sophistication, and extreme aestheticism. All of this is captured in Bashkirtseff's journal. Relatively sheltered from politics and war, the social unrest, and the political scandals of the period, the precocious, unabashed Bashkirtseff thrived in France's culture of decadence as it moved toward modernity.

Bashkirtseff's creative aspirations led her to become acquainted with some of the well-known artists of the time, including Louise Breslau of Switzerland, with whom she studied at Académie Julian, and French painter Jules Bastien-Lepage, who became her close friend and mentor. Bashkirtseff was greatly influenced by the naturalist techniques in Bastien-Lepage's work, and she tried to capture these forms in her own paintings. Her journal entries amount to a revealing portrayal of the French bourgeoisie and also depict her growing feminist involvement in the 1880s, when she wrote articles for the feminist newspaper *La Citoyenne* under the penname Pauline Orell and called for the right of women to vote and changes to conservative French legislation.

By keeping a journal, Bashkirtseff followed in the footsteps of high-society European women since the Victorian era. She credited her writing style to the influence of French authors Edmond de Goncourt, Guy de Maupassant, and Émile Zola. However, the flamboyant tone of Bashkirtseff's entries differentiate them from those of other well-known diarists, such as the solitary and pious Eugénie de Guérin, whose journals were published in 1862. Indeed, Bashkirtseff's journal seems to have more in common with *Memoirs of the Princess Daschkaw* (1840), written by Ekaterina Dashkova, the trusted confidante of Catherine the Great. Much like Dashkova, Bashkirtseff reveals the limitations placed on elite-class women.

Bashkirtseff's style influenced an entire generation of female writers who followed in her footsteps, including Katherine Mansfield, Anaïs Nin, and Mary MacLane. Feminist scholars in the United States and Europe took up her text during the 1980s as an example of early feminist values. Bashkirtseff's writing was limited to her journaling and correspondence, as she dedicated her artistic skills to painting in the later years of her life. However, an additional collection of the author's writing, *The Last Confessions of Marie Bashkirtseff and Her Correspondence with Guy De Maupassant*, was published in 1901. It presents further material written by Bashkirtseff, including her extensive correspondence with the French author for many years, throughout which she curiously maintained her anonymity.

THEMES AND STYLE

Much of Bashkirtseff's extensive journal is, at once, a reflection on her identity as a woman and an account of French bourgeois life at the turn of the nineteenth century. The majority of her entries address her active social life, recalling encounters with men she admires and recording her attire and appearance in minute detail. On August 10, 1875, she writes: "The landau came, and we went to all these places that work to make me beautiful: a yellow-white dress … and an Italian straw hat all covered with white feathers." Love is constantly on her mind, and she often thinks about marriage. For example, she writes of a suitor, "A devil blowing in my ear that he does not love me seriously. I mean, he dares to speak to me of love but does not want to get married."

Bashkirtseff began to write her journal at a young age, recording the whimsical dreams and aspirations of a young aristocratic girl, as well as the details of her social outings and events. Her entries are clearly composed as private thoughts and often serve to air her frustrations. At one point, she offers, "Well, it made me feel much better to write all this! I feel calmer." However, as she became increasingly ill from tuberculosis in the last years of her life, Bashkirtseff saw that her desire for celebrity may not be realized during her lifetime, and she used her journal as an opportunity to make her name known in posterity. In the preface to her journal, which she penned in May 1884, the last year of her life, she writes, "If I don't die young, I hope to become a great artist. If I do, I want my journal to be published. It cannot fail to be interesting. Does my anticipation of its being read spoil or destroy the merit of such a book? Not at all."

Bashkirtseff employs a sentimental, impassioned tone that reveals the constant flux and intensity of her emotions. She often conveys her indignation at the actions of men through melodramatic words such as "scoundrel" and "vagabond." Yet the author's writing style also indicates her high level of education, as she utilizes a diction that is quite sophisticated for a person of her age. Describing an outing to a cave, she recalls, "The horse martyrized me, and I was delighted to arrive"; later she explains that "the impassable passages are marvels where one hangs on with all four paws, closed in on both sides," and describes the underground river as "narrow, swift, black, and slippery." She often writes with a certain lyricism that is complemented by the poetry she sometimes incorporates into her entries.

CRITICAL DISCUSSION

Upon its publication, *The Journal of Marie Bashkirtseff* met with great success. In her review of *Personal Effects: Reading the Journal of Marie Bashkirtseff*, Valerie Raoul notes that it "provoked such intense interest and loyalty among a wide range of readers" throughout Europe and the United States. Among the publications that embraced the book was *Nineteenth Century*, whose reviewer, W. E. Gladstone, recognized the tragic humanity in Bashkirtseff's portrayal of her defiant struggle with the illness that would end her life: "The workings of this abnormally uplifted and yet profoundly harrowed soul … supply an object-lesson in human nature, and tell us things new and strange about its widest and wildest contrasts."

The Journal of Marie Bashkirtseff continued to be popular among young men and women through the 1930s, inspiring plays, novels, and a film based on Bashkirtseff's life. Nevertheless, after the actual journal was donated to the Bibliothèque Nationale in Paris upon the death of Bashkirtseff's mother in 1920, it became clear that she had omitted material that she had deemed unsuitable or feared would tarnish the family's reputation. This discovery led many people to question the apparent truthfulness that had originally attracted them to the book. In the mid-1990s two complete scholarly editions of *The Journal of Marie Bashkirtseff* emerged, published by Cercle des Amis de Marie Bashkirtseff and L'Age d'Homme, respectively. Much scholarship has focused on the implications of the initial version's misleading nature and on the journal's complex publication history since then.

Recent scholarship, including work by Sonia Wilson and Peter Collister, reflects an interest in the intertextual relationship between Bashkirtseff's diary and the narrative of French novelist Edmond de Goncourt. In her 2001 essay in *French Studies*, Wilson examines the intertextual dialogue between *The Journal of Marie Bashkirtseff* and Goncourt's novels

A painting by the artist Marie Bashkirtseff titled *The Meeting*. It is mentioned in her journal. © IVY CLOSE IMAGES/ALAMY

THE MOST INTERESTING WOMAN OF ALL: MARIE BASHKIRTSEFF

Artist and writer Maria Constantinova Bashkirtseff was born in Poltava, Russia (Ukraine), on November 12, 1858, to a family of Russian nobility. After leaving Russia with her mother at the age of seven, they settled in Nice, France, where she spent her adolescence traveling often throughout Western Europe with her family. Bashkirtseff was educated privately, learning to write four languages and read Greek and Latin. She studied in Italy to become a singer, but her voice failed her, a sign of her delicate health. By 1874 she had started showing signs of tuberculosis. Her dream of being a singer shattered, she moved to Paris in 1877 to study painting at Académie Julian, one of the few schools of the period that accepted female students.

By 1880 Bashkirtseff had started to receive recognition for her painting. That same year she became involved in the feminist movement, contributing articles to a local feminist newspaper. As her success as an artist grew, Bashkirtseff also became involved in the Parisian fashion scene. However, by 1882 her illness worsened considerably, and she was nearly deaf by the following year. Bashkirtseff passed away in Paris on October 31, 1884, at the age of twenty-five.

La Faustine and *Cherie*, writing, "Bashkirtseff's setting up of a 'before' and 'after' scenario hints that her diary text can be read precisely in terms of the loss-of-innocence narrative for which Goncourt professes such a predilection." Other scholars of the diary genre, such as Nadia Clare Smith, have explored the influence of Bashkirtseff's journal on later female diarists. Smith notes in her 2010 piece in *Eire-Ireland* that "by the late nineteenth century Marie Bashkirtseff made it more acceptable for a young woman to be rebellious, self-focused, and emotional, rather than meek and self-effacing, in her diary."

BIBLIOGRAPHY

Sources

Barrés, Maurice. "La légende d'une cosmopolite." *Huit jours chez Monsieur Renan. Très stations de psychothérapie.* Paris: Emile-Paul, 1913.125–63. Print.

Bashkirtseff, Marie. *The Journal of Marie Bashkirtseff, Volume II (Lust for Glory).* Trans. Mathilde Blind. Paris: Cassell, 1890. Print.

———. *I Am the Most Interesting Book of All: The Diary of Marie Bashkirtseff, Vol. I.* Trans. Phyllis Kernberger and Katherine Kernberger. San Francisco: Chronicle, 1997. Print.

Collister, Peter. "Marie Bashkirtseff in Fiction: Edmond de Goncourt and Mrs. Humphry Ward." *Modern Philology* 82.1 (1984): 53–69. Print.

Raoul, Valerie. Rev. of *Personal Effects: Reading the Journal of Marie Bashkirtseff*, by Sonia Wilson. *Biography* 34.2 (2011): 343–46. Print.

Smith, Nadia Clare. "'A Good Quaker and a Bad Sinn Feiner': Identity Formation in Rosamond Jacob's Diary." *Eire-Ireland* 45.3–4 (2010): 124–46. Print.

Wilson, Sonia. "Making an Exhibition of Oneself in Public: The Preface to Marie Bashkirtseff's *Journal Intime*." *French Studies* 55.4 (2001): 485–97. Print.

Further Reading

Bashkirtseff, Marie. *The Further Memoirs of Marie Bashkirtseff, Together with a Correspondence between Marie Bashkirtseff and Guy De Maupassant.* London: Grant Richard, 1901. Print.

Creston, Dormer. *Fountains of Youth: The Life of Marie Bashkirtseff.* London: Thornton Butterworth, 1938. Print.

Molloy, Sylvia. "Voice Snatching: 'De Sobremesa,' Hysteria and the Impersonation of Marie Bashkirtseff." *Latin American Literary Review* 25.50 (1997): 11–29. Print.

Ruthchild, Rochelle Goldberg. "On the Edge of Emancipation." Rev. of *I Am the Most Interesting Book of All: The Diary of Marie Bashkirtseff*, by Marie Bashkirtseff. *Women's Review of Books* 15.2 (1997): 20–21. Print.

Wilson, Sonia. "Reading the Preface to Marie Bashkirtseff's 'Journal' through Rousseau's 'Confessions.'" *French Review* 80.1 (2006): 140–56. Print.

Zimmerman, Enid. "The Mirror of Marie Bashkirtseff: Reflections about the Education of Women Art Students in the Nineteenth Century." *Studies in Art Education* 30.3 (1989): 164–75. Print.

Katrina White

The Journal of Sir Walter Scott

Sir Walter Scott

OVERVIEW

The Journal of Sir Walter Scott, published posthumously in 1890, documents day-to-day events in its author's life from November 1825 to September 1832. Scott began writing his journal at age fifty-four, at the height of his international fame and fortune. It covers the last seven years of his life. During the first year of the journal Scott's wife died, and he lost his entire fortune. He responded to adversity with resiliency. Even while suffering from sickness, pain, and depression, Scott attempted to do what he considered honorable: pay off his debts by composing numerous books with an intense industry. In just more than five years he earned the staggering sum of 50,000 pounds from his writings to pay his creditors. *The Journal of Sir Walter Scott,* more than any other work by Scott, reveals the writer's perseverance, generosity, sincerity, and common sense.

The diaries of Samuel Pepys and Lord Byron inspired and influenced Scott. Internal evidence indicates that Scott intended his journal for publication, just as his son-in-law John Gibson Lockhart contended. Lockhart first published lengthy extracts from Scott's journal in his *Memoirs of the Life of Sir Walter Scott* (1837–38) with the help of his wife, Sophia, Scott's daughter. Scott's journal, as a work in its own right, was first published in 1890 by David Douglas, with the text established by professor Hume Brown. The public received it with tremendous enthusiasm. *The Journal of Sir Walter Scott* is considered by many to be the finest diary in the English language because of its candidness and the author's ability to overcome life's hardships. Scholars have used Scott's journal to gain insights into his daily life in Edinburgh society and in the country at Abbotsford.

HISTORICAL AND LITERARY CONTEXT

The French Revolution (1789–99) had divided political opinion in Great Britain, and this schism intensified when Great Britain went to war with France in 1793. Liberal Whigs and reformers in Scotland viewed the French Revolution as an opportunity for political reform; for example, the Society of the Friends of the People formed in 1792 and demanded greater enfranchisement. Most conservative Tories and landowners such as Scott opposed reform. In 1797 the British government allowed the formation of militia groups in Scotland because of the threat of a French invasion. Scott was instrumental in raising the Royal Edinburgh Volunteer Light Dragoons to protect his homeland from invasion, acting as quartermaster. Many of his novels, such as *Waverley* (1814), and his journal deal with the subject of societal change and the author's major concern over the preservation of Scottish traditions.

Scott began his journal on November 20, 1825. The financial crisis in Great Britain led to the fall of Scott's publishers, Archibald Constable & Coy, in 1826 along with the firm James Ballantyne & Coy, in which Scott was a partner. Scott's total indebtedness amounted to 126,838 pounds, and he decided to sign a trust deed for his creditors. This allowed him continued use of his library and furniture at Abbotsford so that he could write. He told friends who offered him money: "No! this right hand shall work it all off." Between 1825 and 1832—the period of the journal—Scott spent most of his free time writing in Edinburgh and at Abbotsford, despite his poor health.

Scott recognized the popularity of autobiographical works during his time. He begins his *Memoirs* (1808) with the following observation: "The present age has discovered a desire, or rather a rage, for literary anecdote and private history that may be well permitted to alarm one who has engaged in a certain degree the attention of the public." Scott composed numerous autobiographical writings, including *Memoirs,* his journal, travel diaries, and letters. His journal begins by acknowledging Byron's influence: "I have bethought me on seeing lately some volumes of Byron's notes that he probably hit upon the right way of keeping such a memorandum-book by throwing aside all pretense of regularity and order and marking down events just as they occurred to recollection." Scott was also inspired by Pepys's *Diary,* which he wrote favorably about in the *Quarterly Review.*

The Journal of Sir Walter Scott greatly influenced Lockhart, who incorporated lengthy excerpts from Scott's journal into his famous *Memoirs of the Life of Sir Walter Scott,* published five years after Scott's death. Lockhart's work has been considered a masterpiece comparable to Boswell's *Life of Samuel Johnson.* Scott's extant journal was published in 1890, but his popularity waned in the twentieth century. In his essay "Scott and the Really Great Tradition," Richard Waswo

❖ Key Facts

Time Period:
Mid-19th Century

Relevant Historical Events:
Scott's wife's death, fall from fortune, and productivity as a writer

Nationality:
Scottish

Keywords:
debt; literature; Scotland

Sir Walter Scott, who was inspired to write his own journal after reading journals written by Samuel Pepys and Lord Byron. © GL ARCHIVE/ALAMY

claims that "never before or since in Western culture has a writer been such a power in his own day and so negligible to posterity." Some critics condemn Scott's novels as second rate and as mere entertainments, but the admiration of his journal has increased through time, and it is frequently used by scholars to better understand the fascinating life of Scott.

THEMES AND STYLE

Scott writes about day-to-day events in his journal, informing the reader about Scottish mores of the nineteenth century. For example, he describes dinner parties, political conversations, breakfast with his printer and publisher James Ballantyne, and his painstaking efforts on the nine-volume work *Napoleon*. The foremost theme is Scott's economic downfall and his industrious response to it. He writes, "My cash affairs stand thus" and then charts out his debts. He tersely complains: "again a day of hard work," "worked seriously all morning," and "all this day occupied with cammomile poultices and pen and ink." Scott details his insomnia, poor health, and depression: "I cannot say I have been happy for the feeling of increasing weakness in my lame leg is a great offset—I walk now with pain and difficulty at all times and it sinks my soul to think how soon I may be altogether a disabled cripple. I am tedious to my friends." But for the most part Scott remains pleasant and generous, giving money to friends in need and taking joy in reading.

Scott begins his journal by declaring his motivation for writing it: "I have all my life regretted that I did not keep a regular [journal]. I have myself lost recollection of much that was interesting and I have deprived my family and the public of some curious information by not carrying this resolution into effect." Scott also wrote the journal in order to help pay off his debt. In his will he explicitly specifies what his executors should do with the money earned from his journal. Because he intended this work for publication, Scott is candid about himself but reticent concerning others. In the introduction to the journal, W. E. K. Anderson states that Scott "is much franker—and ruder—in his correspondence than in his *Journal*" and with the publication of the journal "he had no wish to cause embarrassment to the people he wrote about or to his own family."

The Journal of Sir Walter Scott is typical of an uncorrected daily entry book, "throwing aside all pretence to regularity and order and marking down events just as they occurd to recollection. I will try this plan," the author pens. Scott desires to be true to the journal form by not altering anything he composed. His voice is unpretentious and stoic in outlook when facing life's burdens. He is candid and sincere, and he writes, "I have refrained as much as human frailty will permit from all satirical composition." The difficulty of reading Scott's handwriting increases as the journal progresses, and editors have highlighted various informal peculiarities. At times he omits parts of words, such as "irritabi" for "irritability" and "bein" for "being." Frequently misspelled words abound, such as "freind," "untill," and "wellcome." Scott crosses out words, and his dates are not always reliable.

CRITICAL DISCUSSION

Early criticism of *The Journal of Sir Walter Scott* is scarcely existent. After his death in 1832 and before the extant publication of the journal in 1890, Lockhart had incorporated lengthy excerpts from his journals into *Memoirs of the Life of Sir Walter Scott*. Lockhart's work was largely not reviewed, and the lengthy seven volumes had very limited sales potential. In the work Lockhart immortalized Scott, transforming his life into a classic tragedy. After reading *Memoirs of the Life of Sir Walter Scott*, Thomas Carlyle highly praised Scott, and in 1859 Samuel Smiles composed his popular manual *Self-Help*, in which he used Scott as an example of virtue and hard work. The first extant edition of Scott's journal was published posthumously by David Douglas more than fifty years after Lockhart's work. One reviewer, according to David Masson in

Edinburgh Sketches and Memories (2011), commended Scott's incredible strength and industry.

Because many twentieth-century critics considered Scott's novels as mere works of entertainment, some focused instead on his autobiographical writings. Rather than perpetuating the hero worship of Scott by taking Lockhart's text at face value, scholars attempted to understand his life by means of reestablishing the original text of Scott's journal. In the "Textual Introduction" of *Scott on Himself*, David Hewitt writes that Anderson provides a fine introduction and annotation, "but his text is unsatisfactory." Hewitt continues, "At the period of the *Journal*, Scott's hand is immensely difficult and no editor could ever claim to have transcribed accurately what Scott wrote." Hewitt states that Anderson should have worked from the manuscript rather than a photostat for purposes of accuracy and that his "editorial principles were inconsistent."

Recent scholars have used *The Journal of Sir Walter Scott* to better understand Scott's life; thus many fine biographies, such as John Sutherland's *The Life of Walter Scott*, have been written that refute Lockhart's idealization. Other scholars have focused on Scott's journal and its relationship with memory. In *Literary Memory*, Catherine Jones writes:

> His purpose in the journal is to "piece" the past together through the acts of the mind ... to counteract his sense of disintegration attendant upon the [economic] crash, the death of lady Scott, his failing health, and the [political] reform ascendancy. The act of recollection affirms identity, as Scott selects from his memories to present an ordered account of disordering experience.

In *Afterlives of Walter Scott*, Anne Rigney demonstrates how Scott's works, including his journal, offer new perspectives on the interplay between modernization and memory-making.

BIBLIOGRAPHY

Sources

Anderson, W. E. K. "The *Journal*." *Scott Bicentenary Essays*. Ed. Alan Bell. New York: Harper & Row, 1973. Print.

Carlyle, Thomas. *Critical and Miscellaneous Essays*. 7 vols. London: Chapman and Hall, 1872. Print.

Hewitt, David, ed. *Scott on Himself*. Edinburgh: Scottish Academic, 1981. Print.

Jones, Catherine. *Literary Memory*. Lewisburg, Penn.: Bucknell University Press, 2003. Print.

Masson, David. *Edinburgh Sketches and Memories*. London: British Library—Historical Print Editions, 2011. Print.

Rigney, Anne. *The Afterlives of Walter Scott: Memory on the Move*. Oxford: Oxford University Press, 2012. Print.

SHERIFF OF SELKIRKSHIRE, CLERK OF THE SESSION, AND LAIRD OF ABBOTSFORD

Sir Walter Scott held two legal offices for more than twenty years. As sheriff of Selkirkshire he had administrative and magisterial duties such as superintending elections to Parliament and conducting investigations in cases of assault. Scott was also a principal clerk to the Court of Sessions, which allowed him to appoint a deputy when absent from his sheriffdom. As clerk of the session, Scott was in charge of paperwork connected with a case, and he made certain that legal procedures were followed correctly. Scott also paraphrased the judge's decision in a decree.

With these paid legal positions, various inheritances, the publication of poems, and dividends from his publishing partnership with Ballantyne, Scott was wealthy enough to buy the estate thirty miles from Edinburgh called Clarty Hole, or "dirty puddle," on July 1, 1811. He paid 4,000 guineas for it—a very high price because of the Napoleonic Wars. Scott renamed it Abbotsford and, in jest, called himself "Laird of Abbotsford." The property had neither trees nor major buildings. It was a tabula rasa—a blank slate for Scott's creative interest in Scottish landscape and architecture. He and his family moved there in May 1812, leaving behind the clamor of modern Edinburgh and returning to the countryside of their ancestors. He greatly expanded the estate and incorporated into the interior sentimental artifacts from Scotland's past. At Abbotsford Scott began to write and publish prose. He finished Abbotsford in 1825, just before his economic downfall.

Scott, Walter. *The Journal of Sir Walter Scott*. Ed. W. E. K. Anderson. Oxford: Clarendon, 1972. Print.

Waswo, Richard. "Scott and the Really Great Tradition." *Scott and His Influence*. Ed. J. H. Alexander and David Hewitt. Aberdeen: Association for Scottish Literary Studies, 1983. Print.

Further Reading

Brown, Iain, ed. *Abbotsford and Sir Walter Scott: The Image and the Influence*. Edinburgh: Society of Antiquaries of Scotland, 2003. Print.

Herman, Arthur. *How the Scots Invented the Modern World*. New York: Crown, 2001. Print.

McCracken-Flesher, Caroline. *Possible Scotlands: Walter Scott and the Story of Tomorrow*. Oxford: Oxford University Press, 2005. Print.

Oliver, Neil. *A History of Scotland*. London: Phoenix, 2010. Print.

Quayle, Eric. *The Ruin of Sir Walter Scott*. London: Rupert Hart-Davis, 1968. Print.

Sutherland, John. *The Life of Walter Scott*. Cambridge, U.K.: Blackwell, 1995. Print.

Greg Luther

Letters and Journals of Fanny Burney

Fanny Burney

✥ **Key Facts**

Time Period:
Early to Mid-19th Century

Relevant Historical Events:
Burney's success as a novelist; Battle of Waterloo

Nationality:
English

Keywords:
women's writing; domesticity; politics

OVERVIEW

The letters and journals of Fanny Burney (1768–1840)—which have been published in many editions, starting with the seven-volume *Diary and Letters of Madame D'Arblay* (1842–46)—capture the essence of various events in her life, including her thoughts on the four novels she published. From age fifteen, Burney kept detailed journals (referred to in some editions as "diaries") and corresponded frequently with family and friends. In addition to showcasing the same sharp powers of social observation evident in her fiction, the letters and journals reveal Burney's conflicted feelings about the fitness of women for novel writing and her frustrations over her thwarted ambitions to produce a successful drama for the stage.

Burney spent the last years of her life preparing her substantial volume of papers for probable publication, and these writings did not appear in print until after her death. Both popular and critically acclaimed when first published, the *Diary and Letters of Madame D'Arblay* established Burney's reputation as a diarist, which superseded her renown as a novelist until feminist critics rediscovered her fiction in the late twentieth century. Continuing interest in Burney's accounts of the eighteenth and early nineteenth centuries, and in her descriptions of important historical events such as the Battle of Waterloo, has led to a number of new scholarly editions in recent years.

HISTORICAL AND LITERARY CONTEXT

Burney's journals and letters reflect her upbringing in a household that was unusual for the respectable classes of eighteen-century England. Her father, Charles Burney, a talented musician, was cultured and well travelled, corresponding with a number of esteemed thinkers of the day, including Jean-Jacques Rousseau. While Burney's early years were spent in the countryside of Norfolk, her family moved to London in 1760 and settled on Poland Street in the bohemian area of Soho. The elder Burney entertained a number of musicians, artists, and writers. In a more typical upper-middle-class home of the period, particularly one with young women, such visitors would not have been welcomed. Charles, though traditional enough to initially object to the notion of his daughter writing and publishing novels, exposed Fanny to the variety of people and ideas that helped shape her literary ambitions.

Much of Burney's early correspondence was directed to her sister Susanna and to family friend Samuel Crisp, an author living in retirement at Chessington, Surrey. The subject matter includes quotidian events from the family's social life and humorous treatments of the foibles of people in the Burneys' circle. Likewise, her early journals contain details of daily life and much self-reflection, especially regarding her conflicted feelings on writing, given the social and parental proscriptions against it. As Burney grew into adulthood—publishing novels, spending time in the employ of King George III's court, and living for a number of years with her husband in France—the scope of her writing broadened to include public figures and historical events.

Burney's correspondence is very much in keeping with the grand style of the epistolary novels popular at the time, and indeed, her first published novel, *Evelina* (1778), is in that form. While her own letters and journals remained private during her lifetime, she was responsible for assembling her father's papers for publication after his death and was criticized for the resulting three-volume work, *The Memoirs of Dr. Burney* (1832), on the grounds that she had deliberately edited out incidents that painted her father and family in a less than flattering light.

Burney is often cited as one of the founders of the novel of manners, which was perfected by Jane Austen in works such as *Pride and Prejudice* (1813). While her fiction figures most prominently in such discussions, the descriptions of people and events in the many volumes of her diaries may have also inspired a number of subsequent writers. Most famously, some scholars have suggested that William Thackeray used Burney's account of her time in Brussels during the Battle of Waterloo in the development of chapters 28–32 of his most famous novel, *Vanity Fair* (1847–48).

THEMES AND STYLE

Burney's journals and letters detail the thoughts of a woman who, while longing for literary success, was concerned with propriety and with defining her work in a socially acceptable manner. For example, upon discovering that her name had been printed in a pamphlet in connection with the novel *Evelina,* which had been published anonymously, Burney wrote to Samuel

Portrait of author Frances "Fanny" Burney, painted by her relative Edward Francis Burney in 1784 or 1785. © DEAGOSTINI/GETTY IMAGES

Crisp, saying, "I would a thousand times rather forfeit my character as a writer, than risk ridicule or censure as a female." At the same time, Burney was pleased by praise and by the positive reviews of her work by male writers of the day, often recounting them in both her journal and letters. Writing of a discussion of *Evelina,* for example, she reports writer Samuel Johnson telling the antiquarian scholar Michael Lort that "there were things and Characters in it *more* than worthy of [Henry] Fielding."

The tension between Burney's passion for writing and her desire to conform to social norms of femininity recurs throughout her journals and letters. Scholars have suggested that her personal writings may have been a means of relieving this tension. Moreover, Burney, who was known to have carefully managed her family's image in publishing her father's memoirs, would have been sensible enough to provide an account of her justification for writing novels that reflected her sensibilities about the proper role of women. While some contemporary scholars have called Burney an early feminist, biographer Claire Harman contends that she deliberately distanced herself from more radical images of womanhood, such as

FANNY BURNEY'S *EVELINA*

Fanny Burney's first novel, *Evelina*, was published anonymously in 1778. It is something of a sequel to *The History of Caroline Evelyn*, a manuscript Burney had written in her teens but reportedly burned in a fit of guilt, as writing novels was not considered an appropriate pursuit for young women. *Evelina* follows the adventures of a young woman of aristocratic but obscure parentage as she learns to navigate London society and to catch a husband. Published in three volumes, the epistolary novel unfolds through a series of letters between Evelina and various friends and family members.

In his essay "Signing Evelina: Female Self-inscription in the Discourse of Letters Evelina," Samuel Choi compares Evelina's quest to establish her parentage, and a place in a society that refuses to recognize illegitimate children, to Burney's own struggles as a young female author seeking entry into the male-oriented literary world. Choi writes, "The clever narrative ironically describes, in letters, the history of men using social and cultural conventions to insinuate themselves into the life of a young woman, as the very story insinuates itself into the male-dominated realm of history by manipulating the formal and literary conventions of the 'republic of letters.'"

those presented by Mary Wollstonecraft in *A Vindication of the Rights of Women* (1792).

While Burney's journals and letters were written over a lifetime and vary in both tone and subject matter, they exhibit an almost journalistic level of detail, also a characteristic of her fiction. Critics have observed that the main stylistic difference between her fiction and her personal writings lies in the degree to which she expresses emotion in the journals and letters. Discussing Burney's style in her essay "Madame D'Arblay," Gamaliel Bradford notes that "she was a writer from her childhood to her death. Her experiences constituted 'copy,' first and foremost." In their introduction to a 2001 edition of *Journals and Letters*, Peter Sabor and Lars Troide also note the "confessional" nature of the work.

CRITICAL DISCUSSION

Diary and Letters of Madame D'Arblay, the first volume of which appeared in 1842, was a critical and popular success. Thomas Macauley, writing in the *Edinburgh Review*, praised the book as being written "in true woman's English, clear, natural, and lively." It has been speculated that Macauley wrote his positive review as, at least in part, a response to his rival John Croker's scathing attack on the diaries, which was published in the *Quarterly Review*. Croker described the first three volumes as "nearly the most worthless we have ever waded through," criticizing "the diffuseness—the pomposity—the prolixity—the false colouring—the factitious details—and, above all, the personal affectation and vanity of the author." While Croker's assessment of the *Diary and Letters* remains well known, it was not the predominant view of the time.

Since the initial publication of the seven-volume *Diary and Letters of Madame D'Arblay*, a number of versions of Burney's personal writings and correspondence have appeared. Notably, Joyce Hemlow and Troide completed a seventeen-volume edition that includes five volumes of *The Early Journals and Letters of Fanny Burney* (1988–2012) and twelve volumes of her later writing, *The Journals and Letters of Fanny Burney (Madame D'Arblay), 1791–1840* (1972–84). *The Court Journals and Letters of Frances Burney* has extended the modern editing of Burney's surviving journals and letters; as of 2012, three of the proposed six volumes had been published. In addition to including previously unpublished documents, these modern editions have attempted to restore much of the material that Burney herself redacted.

Burney's letters and journals have been treated by scholars as an important historical record of the period in which she lived. In an essay on the author, Margret Anne Doody calls her "a first-rate describer of people, manners, pastimes, and affairs of the eighteenth and early nineteenth centuries." Meanwhile, Burney's biographers have looked to the writings to settle questions about her views on the place of women in society. Claire Harmon, for instance, confirms Burney's aversion to the radical feminist formulations of the day, pointing to the absence of any reference to *A Vindication of the Rights of Women* in the journals as evidence.

BIBLIOGRAPHY

Sources

Bradford, Gamaliel. "Madame D'Arblay." *North American Review* 199.698 (1914): 108–19. Rpt. in *Nineteenth-Century Literature Criticism*. Ed. Laurie Lanzen Harris and Jay Parini. Vol. 12. Detroit: Gale Research, 1986. *Literature Resource Center*. Web. 4 Dec. 2012.

Burney, Frances. *Diary and Letters of Madame D'Arblay, Volume 1*. London: Henry Colburn, 1842.

Choi, Samuel. "Signing Evelina: Female Self-inscription in the Discourse of Letters." *Studies in the Novel* 31.3 (1999): 259. *Literature Resource Center*. Web. 4 Dec. 2012.

Croker, John Wilson. "Madame D'Arblay's 'Diary and Letters'." *Quarterly Review* 70.139 (1842): 243–87. Rpt. in *Nineteenth-Century Literature Criticism*. Ed. Laurie Lanzen Harris and Jay Parini. Vol. 12. Detroit: Gale Research, 1986. *Literature Resource Center*. Web. 4 Dec. 2012.

Doody, Margaret Anne. "Fanny Burney." *British Writers: Supplement 3*. Ed. George Stade. New York: Charles Scribner's Sons, 1996. *Scribner Writers Series*. Web. 4 Dec. 2012.

Harman, Claire. *Fanny Burney: A Biography*. New York: Alfred A. Knopf, 2001. Print.

Sabor, Peter, and Lars Troide. Introduction. *Journals and Letters.* By Frances Burney. London: Penguin, 2001. xiii–xxii. Print.

Further Reading

Adelstein, Michael E. "Chapter 10: Exciting Adventures and Disappointing Memoirs." *Fanny Burney.* New York: Twayne, 1968. *The Twayne Authors Series.* Web. 4 Dec. 2012.

Doody, Margaret Anne. *Frances Burney: The Life in the Works.* New Brunswick, N.J.: Rutgers University Press, 1988. Print.

Epstein, Julia. *The Iron Pen: Frances Burney and the Politics of Women's Writing.* Madison: University of Wisconsin Press, 1989. Print.

Johnson, Claudia. *Equivocal Beings: Politics, Gender, and Sentimentality in the 1790s—Wollstonecraft, Radcliffe, Burney, Austen.* Chicago: University of Chicago Press, 1995. Print.

Simons, Judy. *Diaries and Journals of Literary Women from Fanny Burney to Virginia Woolf.* Iowa City: University of Iowa Press, 1990. Print.

Daisy Gard

Letters from Jefferson to His Daughter

Thomas Jefferson

❖ **Key Facts**

Time Period:
Late 18th Century

Relevant Historical Events:
Enlightenment; achievement of American independence; death of Jefferson's wife

Nationality:
American

Keywords:
parenthood; education; advice

OVERVIEW

Thomas Jefferson's three letters to his eleven-year-old daughter Martha, written in 1783 and published in 1966, illuminated the Founding Father's philosophy of parenting and fatherhood. The first letter, dated November 28, is the most widely reproduced of the three and expresses Jefferson's desire for his eldest daughter to be successful in her studies and to write him regularly, describing her academic progress. Martha, also known as Patsy, does not appear to follow her father's desires, and a second letter, dated December 11, questions her ability to access the post office. The final letter, dated December 22, demonstrates Jefferson's disappointment in his daughter for not fulfilling her obligations. Jefferson's letters to his daughter represent a de facto style of autobiography—an uncensored look at his daily life that is at once more banal and more immediate than his formal autobiography, which was published in 1821.

Jefferson's interest in his daughter's education is aligned with the ideas about a women's place in elite society at the time. Women in the eighteenth century were expected to be dutiful wives and mothers, but they were not expected to understand business or politics. Their education was geared toward the care and maintenance of the home and childrearing, along with cultivating the necessary skills to attract a husband. Martha, under the advisement of her father, received this sort of education during her childhood and proved to be an excellent student. She was Jefferson's only child to survive past the age of twenty-five and served as the First Lady during her father's presidency. Together, Jefferson's letters to his daughter provide an intimate glimpse into the family life of one of America's founding statesmen.

HISTORICAL AND LITERARY CONTEXT

The eighteenth century saw the flowering of the Enlightenment in Western Europe, when the ideas about universal rights and freedoms gained traction alongside new ideas about national government. These ideas influenced the American and French Revolutions, whereby the United States gained independence from British rule and the French overthrew their monarchy. Jefferson was a key player in the development of the universal human rights philosophies, both in the United States and in France. His political career as a member of the Continental Congress, an overseas diplomat, a governor of Virginia, and the president of the United States was instrumental in shaping the new country's ideology about freedom and independence. He was still a man of his era, however, and despite his philosophies of universal human rights, he owned slaves and believed in the subordinate position of women in the household.

In September 1782, Jefferson's wife died during childbirth, leaving him responsible for their three surviving children: Martha, Mary, and Lucy. He entrusted the care of his daughters to close friends and family; Martha was sent to the household of Mrs. Thomas Hopkinson, the mother of Jefferson's friend Francis Hopkinson, in Philadelphia, while the younger children joined their maternal aunt, Elizabeth Eppes, in Virginia. Jefferson remained integral to their lives, however, through his letters. The November letter to Martha was written in Annapolis, where Jefferson had traveled for a Confederation Congress meeting. In this letter, Jefferson outlines a schedule for her studies and requests that she write to him on a weekly basis. When Martha fails to follow this schedule, Jefferson pens two subsequent letters in December of the same year, expressing his disappointment in her lack of communication. The strict tone of these letters is indicative of Jefferson's intentions for Martha to become the educated executor of his estate and eventual heir to his Virginia plantation, Monticello.

In the eighteenth century letter writing was an important part of everyday life for educated people who were separated from their loved ones. Thus, letters are a valuable primary source about all matters of history, from the political to the personal. Prominent individuals usually collected their letters for posterity, and in this practice Jefferson joined his colleagues John Adams, whose letters to his wife, Abigail, are renowned for their incisive portrait not only of a strong and loving relationship but also of the philosophy that provided the democratic foundation of the new nation. The James Madison Papers are a similar oeuvre of the time, as are George Washington's papers, which run to several dozen published volumes.

Jefferson's letters to Martha, however, provide a rare glimpse into fatherhood in which his persona of statesman and politician is discarded in favor of the less illustrious role of parent. This unguarded moment stands in contrast to Jefferson's more well-known works, A Summary View of the Rights of British America (1774) and the Declaration of Independence. After Martha's lack of response to her father's letters, Jefferson took her education into his own hands and brought her with him to France in 1784, where she stayed until the end of his term as a U.S. diplomat in 1789. There she learned French, studied music and classic literature, and often corresponded with her father via letters when he traveled to the south of the country, leaving her in Paris to continue her studies.

THEMES AND STYLE

The main theme of Jefferson's letter to Martha is his concern over her daily lesson schedule. He outlines a strict agenda for such activities as practicing music, dancing, drawing, and reading. In addition, Jefferson requests regular letters from her, updating him about her progress. "I expect you will write me by every post," he tells her, "Inform me what books you read, what tunes you learn, and enclose me your best copy of every lesson in drawing." In addition, Jefferson advises his daughter to write to her aunts and to be respectful to Mrs. Hopkinson. The second letter reflects Jefferson's confusion as to why Martha is not following his wishes: "I am afraid that you may not have been sent to the post office and therefore that my letter may be lying there." The third letter expresses Jefferson's disappointment: "I hoped before this to have received letters from you regularly and weekly by the post, and also to have had a letter to forward from you to one of your aunts as I desired in my letter of Nov. 28th."

Jefferson's purpose in writing the letters was his concern about Martha's well-being. His letters are informal and express both his love for his daughter and his desire for her to succeed. He laments having to leave his daughter in the care of another family: "The conviction that you would be more improved in the situation I have placed you than if still with me, has solaced me on my parting with you, which my love for you had rendered a difficult thing." When she does not respond to his requests, however, he sternly reprimands her in his third letter. "I am afraid you do not comply with my desires expressed in that letter," he says, concluding that he "shall be very much mortified and disappointed if you become inattentive to my wishes and particularly to the directions of that letter which I meant for your principal guide." The informal style reflects Jefferson's intentions to keep the letters private.

The style of the letters is stern but caring, and Jefferson demonstrates that although he expects his wishes to be followed, he is ultimately concerned for his daughter's benefit. He uses straightforward language, largely devoid of stylistic flair. His diction reflects his intended audience—an eleven-year-old girl. He places great expectations on her success: "I have placed my happiness on seeing you good and accomplished, and no distress which this world can now bring on me could equal that of your disappointing my hopes." Although Jefferson expects obedience and respect, his overall concern is for Martha's well-being.

CRITICAL DISCUSSION

Jefferson's letters to Martha were not published until long after his death. Editions of his *Farm Book* (1953) and *Garden Book* generated public interest in Jefferson's private life, and the publication of his family letters, including the letters to young Martha, provided yet another glimpse into his personal life. Edwin Morris Bates, in the introduction to *The Family Letters of Thomas Jefferson* (1966), summarizes the early response to Jefferson's private correspondence to Martha by stating that "the nature of his approach, didactic and moralistic as it may seem to us, did but prove he was a dedicated father, seriously concerned over rearing his daughters."

The letter of November 1783 is the most reproduced of the three he wrote to his daughter, and it marks the beginning of a long written correspondence between them. The subsequent letters Jefferson wrote while traveling in France now provide scholars with an idea about the relationship between parents and

Thomas Jefferson, third president of the United States, painted by Thomas Sully circa 1860.
© CHICAGO HISTORY MUSEUM, USA/THE BRIDGEMAN ART LIBRARY

PRIMARY SOURCE

EXCERPT FROM *LETTERS FROM JEFFERSON TO HIS DAUGHTER*

Loving advice to a motherless daughter

The conviction that you [Martha] would be more improved in the situation I have placed you than if still with me, has solaced me on my parting with you, which my love for you has rendered a difficult thing. The acquirements which I hope you will make under the tutors I have provided for you will render you more worthy of my love; and if they cannot increase it, they will prevent its diminution. Consider the good lady who has taken you under her roof … as your mother, as the only person to whom, since the loss with which Heaven has pleased to afflict you, you can now look up; and that her displeasure or disapprobation, on any occasion, will be an immense misfortune, which, should you be so unhappy as to incur by any unguarded act, think no concession too much to regain her good-will.

With respect to the distribution of your time, the following is what I should approve:

From 8 to 10, practice music.

From 10 to 1, dance one day and draw another.

From 1 to 2, draw on the day you dance, and write a letter next day.

From 3 to 4, read French.

From 4 to 5, exercise yourself in music.

From 5 till bedtime, read English, write, etc.…

I expect you will write me by every post. Inform me what books you read, what tunes you learn, and enclose me your best copy of every lesson in drawing.… Take care that you never spell a word wrong. Always before you write a word consider how it is spelt, and, if you do not remember it, turn to a dictionary. It produces great praise to a lady to spell well.

I have placed my happiness on seeing you good and accomplished, and no distress this world can now bring on me would equal that of your disappointing my hopes. If you love me, then strive to be good under every situation and to all living creatures, and to acquire those accomplishments which I have put in your power, and which will go far towards insuring you the warmest love of your affectionate father.

SOURCE: Jefferson, Thomas. "Letters to Martha Jefferson" *The Family Letters of Thomas Jefferson.* November 28, 1783.

---

children during this period, particularly the communication between a politically active father concerning the proper education of his daughter. Carol Sue Humphrey, in the introduction to *Raising Children* (2011), exemplifies this interest: "Whether a country is at peace or involved in a war, parents hope that their children can gain the sort of education they need for the future."

What little scholarship exists concerning the letters notes the difference in the expectations of education for girls between the eighteenth century and the present, and how Jefferson, for all his philosophical work on the universal rights of man, followed the gender stereotypes of his time by assuming that a girl's education need not include science, philosophy, or politics. As a writer in *Notable American Women* (1971) observes, "Although [Jefferson] had no advanced ideas about women, he took great interest in the education of his daughters." Another scholarship trend notes the universal nature of parental concern for the well-being of children. The website *EyeWitness to History* states that "Jefferson's letters reveal that the trials and tribulations of parenthood remain a constant through the passage of time."

BIBLIOGRAPHY

Sources

Betts, Edwin Morris. Introduction. *The Family Letters of Thomas Jefferson.* Ed. Edwin Morris Betts and James Adam Bear Jr. Columbia: University of Missouri Press, 1966. 3–14. Print.

Humphrey, Carol Sue. "Raising Children: Letters between Thomas Jefferson and His Daughter Martha (1783, 1787)." *Voices of Revolutionary America: Contemporary Accounts of Daily Life.* Ed. Carol Sue Humphrey. Santa Barbara, Calif.: Greenwood, 2011. 129–30. Print.

Jefferson, Thomas. Letters to Martha Jefferson: Nov. 28, Dec. 11, and Dec. 22. 1783. *The Family Letters of Thomas Jefferson.* Ed. Edwin Morris Betts and James Adam Bear Jr. Columbia: University of Missouri Press, 1966. 19–22. Print.

"Randolph, Martha Jefferson (Sept. 27, 1772–Oct. 10, 1836)." *Notable American Women: 1607–1950.* Cambridge, Mass.: Harvard University Press, 1971. *Credo Reference.* Web. 17 Dec. 2012.

"Thomas Jefferson's Advice to His Eleven-Year-Old Daughter, 1783." *Eye Witness to History.* Ibis Communications, 2007. Web. 17 Dec. 2012.

Further Reading

Betts, Edwin Morris, ed. *Thomas Jefferson's Farm Book with Commentary and Relevant Extracts from other Writings.* Memoirs of the American Philosophical Society Held at Philadelphia for Promoting Useful Knowledge 35. Princeton, N.J.: Princeton University Press, 1953. Print.

Betts, Edwin Morris, and Peter J. Hatch, eds. *Thomas Jefferson's Garden Book: 1766–1824, with Relevant Extracts from His Other Writings.* Charlottesville: University of Virginia Press, 2011. Print.

Cremin, Lawrence. *American Education: The Colonial Experience, 1607–1783.* New York: Harper & Row, 1970. Print.

Jefferson, Thomas. *A Summary View of the Rights of British America. Set Forth in Some Resolutions Intended for the Inspection of the Present Delegates of the People of Virginia. Now in Convention. By a Native, and*

Member of the House of Burgesses. Williamsburg, Virg.: Clementina Rind, 1774. *Eighteenth Century Collections Online.* Web. 17 Dec. 2012.

Kierner, Cynthia A. *Martha Jefferson Randolph, Daughter of Monticello: Her Life and Times.* Chapel Hill: University of North Carolina Press, 2012. Print.

Kukla, Jon. *Mr. Jefferson's Women.* New York: Knopf, 2007. Print.

"Thomas Jefferson." *Encyclopedia of World Biography.* Detroit: Gale, 1998. *Gale Biography in Context.* Web. 17 Dec. 2012.

Wayson, Billy L. *Martha Jefferson Randolph: The Education of a Republican Daughter and Plantation Mistress.* Dissertation, University of Virginia, 2008. Print.

Katherine Barker

London and the Life of Literature in Late Victorian England

The Diary of George Gissing, Novelist

George Gissing

❖ **Key Facts**

Time Period:
Late 19th to Early 20th Century

Relevant Historical Events:
Gissing's struggle to make a living as a writer and endure a difficult marriage; increase in British literacy rates; Victorianism

Nationality:
English

Keywords:
literature; Victorianism; marriage

OVERVIEW

London and the Life of Literature in Late Victorian England: The Diary of George Gissing, Novelist (1887–1902) offers an unparalleled glimpse into the author's struggles to write, to make a living from his fiction, and to weather a bitterly difficult marriage. Although voluminous and thorough, Gissing's diary is composed primarily of terse factual entries that rarely plumb psychological depths. A prolific novelist who produced some twenty-two books during his career, Gissing (1857–1903) is perhaps best known for *New Grub Street* (1891), a semiautobiographical novel about the British literary world of the 1880s. Although his journals were not published until 1978, the diary he kept between 1887 and 1902 offers insight into the literary process and personal tribulations of one of the Victorian era's most significant and fascinating writers.

When *London and the Life* first appeared, it was welcomed for providing access to a wealth of material that had existed only in manuscript form. The diaries were seen as not only offering a personal perspective on Gissing's life and works but also helping to expand historical knowledge of life during the Victorian period. Nearly a third of the text details the author's time spent traveling in Greece and Italy. Elsewhere, Gissing documents conversations with such important figures as writers H. G. Wells and George Meredith. Throughout, he records his almost unceasing literary productivity, which was imperative to his ability to support his family. Today, *London and the Life* is considered a vital document for scholars of Gissing's fiction and literary life in the later decades of the Victorian period.

HISTORICAL AND LITERARY CONTEXT

The monetary struggles that Gissing chronicles in his diaries can be traced to changes in literature and in literacy rates in Great Britain during the nineteenth century. Well into the century, the availability of literature for the masses was limited by low literacy levels among the working poor and a lack of affordable reading material. Although some "unstamped" publications flourished, the taxes on mainstream newspapers placed them out of the reach of the poor. With the repeal of these taxes in 1855, inexpensive periodicals aimed at working-class readers began to flourish. Literacy rates were buoyed by the Elementary Education Act of 1870, which, though not uniformly enforced, mandated education for children between the ages of five and twelve. The decades leading up to the events described in Gissing's diary saw the ascendancy of the Victorian novel and the celebrity of novelists including Charles Dickens, Anthony Trollope, and George Eliot. It also saw the proliferation of cheap and, to Gissing, lowbrow reading material. As his diary makes clear, he saw the booming literary marketplace as an unjust arena in which quality work went unrewarded while hastily produced texts succeeded.

Gissing's diaries describe in detail the process of writing, publication, and literary advertisement; they also offer a window into other aspects of Victorian culture. In his introduction to *London and the Life*, editor Pierre Coustillas asserts that "seen against the background of the late Victorian period, [the diary] stands by itself—a mirror of late Victorian life." Gissing chronicles the details of everyday life, recording a trip to see a Gilbert and Sullivan production, his travels through Italy using a Murray guidebook, and the popular street foods of the day. He also notes widespread poverty, the prevalence of the pawnbroker, and unnecessary deaths from privation and want.

Diary writing was a common pastime for educated men and women of the Victorian period. Coustillas suggests, however, that the breadth and detail of Gissing's text is somewhat unusual given that "very few novelists have ever had the taste or staying power to keep a diary." Although the journals and diaries of other prominent Victorian writers have been published, few are as focused on the struggles of literary production as Gissing's. In its emphasis on the often-mechanical nature of writing for a living, Gissing's diary has much in common with Trollope's 1883 autobiography, which similarly records the mundane details of his writing life.

Published seventy-five years after its author's death, Gissing's diary has had a lasting impact on scholarship on the author's life and work and the period in which he lived. Recording his choices of reading material and reading habits, Gissing offers valuable commentary on the lives and works of such prominent Victorian writers as Dickens, Thomas Carlyle, Charles Darwin, and Thomas Hardy. Although Gissing's novels have largely fallen out of fashion, his diary is nonetheless valued for its unique perspective on late Victorian authorship.

THEMES AND STYLE

Although Gissing's diary focuses equally on the minutiae of daily life and the author's emotions, the text is thematically dominated by discussions of the challenges of authorship in the late Victorian era. Gissing repeatedly notes the injustices of the literary marketplace with its preference for quick production. Following the success of *New Grub Street,* which brought him fame but not financial security, he complains, "I cannot buy books, I cannot subscribe to a library; I can just afford the necessary food from day to day; and have to toil in fear of finishing my money before another book is ready." This refrain is echoed throughout the book, as he describes the pressures of rapid production: "a horrible anguish of clockwork thought."

Although his diary was published posthumously, Gissing was known as a diarist during his lifetime. Coustillas records the interest that Gissing's diary provoked among members of his circle, who wondered whether and how they were portrayed in it. Despite such curiosity, Gissing kept the entries to himself, and his diary is not believed to have been read by any of his intimates until after his death. Despite his desire to keep his private life from public view, he was well aware that his fame as a novelist meant that his diary would eventually be made public. Indeed, Coustillas suggests that Gissing "conceived his diary to be a document for the scholars of generations yet unborn who would study his life and works," and "he regarded his journal as an object which would testify in his favour, and against his time of which he was by his own estimation, a victim."

Stylistically, many of the entries are notable for their brevity and for the absence of any literary pretense. Such brevity becomes increasingly pronounced in the final years of the diary, with many entries comprising fewer than five words. On October 13, 1898, for example, he records only "Dull. Walk and talk."

View of Kensington High Street, 1898, by Walker. The street is located in central Kensington, a district in western London. © EILEEN TWEEDY/ THE ART ARCHIVE AT ART RESOURCE, NY

GEORGE GISSING'S *NEW GRUB STREET*

In 1891, in the midst of writing the diary that would become *London and the Life of Literature in Late Victorian England,* George Gissing published the most enduring of his more than twenty works of fiction, *New Grub Street*. A clearly autobiographical novel, *New Grub Street* repurposes material from Gissing's diary in its bleak portrayal of the literary world of late nineteenth-century London. At the book's center is Edwin Reardon, a character who closely resembles the author. Reardon is a writer whose lofty artistic ambition is hampered by the imperative to achieve financial success, which his unsympathetic wife, Amy, refuses to let him forget.

Reardon's literary—and later romantic—rival is a reviewer and journalist named Jasper Milvain, whose attitude toward writing is practical and unromantic. As he plainly declares, "Literature nowadays is a trade. Putting aside men of genius, who may succeed by mere cosmic force, your successful man of letters is your skillful tradesman. He thinks first and foremost of the markets; when one kind of goods begins to go off slackly, he is ready with something new and appetizing." As Milvain rises to success, Reardon falls into obscurity, is left by his wife, and finally dies. In the end, Milvain marries the widowed Amy, and Gissing's bleak message is made clear: commercialization trumps artistic ambition.

At times, however, his writing is emotional, such as when he writes of his first wife, Marianne Helen, who died in dire poverty following their separation. Following his visit to the place of her death, he describes coming home to a "wretched night" and reaching the conclusion that "my life henceforth had a firmer purpose. Henceforth I [will] never cease to bear testimony against the accursed social order that brings about things of this kind."

CRITICAL DISCUSSION

When Gissing's diary was first published in full in 1978 as *London and the Life,* it received mixed reviews. Many scholars hailed the text for offering new insight. In a 1980 review in *Victorian Studies,* Jacob Korg writes, "Gissing's diary contains an enormous stock of biographical and literary facts, but it is also valuable as a document of the Victorian period, for it offers intimate reflections of three aspects of life of the time: the profession of authorship, the experience of travel, and the frustrations of a bitterly unhappy marriage." Others, however, were critical of the text. John Halperin, in a 1981 review in the *Yearbook of English Studies,* criticizes the volume for its lack of "discrimination and selectivity," writing that "much of it is very dull."

Publication of Gissing's complete diary from 1887 to 1902 occurred following a growth in scholarly interest in Gissing's work, and its appearance helped spur further scholarship. Between 1961 and 1978, more than thirty new editions of Gissing's fiction and nonfiction were published, along with seven volumes of his letters and other private papers. During that period, he was also the subject of some sixteen critical and biographical books. As a result, he came to be considered, along with Dickens and Hardy, a preeminent Victorian novelist. Thus, *London and the Life* helped to cement his reputation while also expanding knowledge about the relationship between his personal and professional lives.

Critics and scholars have mined Gissing's diary for information about the author's writing process and about the Victorian world in which he lived. In *The Character of Credit: Personal Debt in English Culture, 1740–1914* (2003), Margot Finn uses *London and the Life* to draw inferences about the economic and social situation in late nineteenth-century London. Of Gissing's response to learning that his wife had pawned clothes and her wedding ring to pay off debts, Finn writes, "The sense of shame suffered by husbands of the middling classes when their wives were forced to resort to the pawnshop emerges clearly from George Gissing's diary." Commentators have also noted the effect the diary's publication had on readers of Gissing's fiction. As George Packer writes in a 1991 piece for the *New York Times,* "The wilderness of diary entries turns out to be a stamp of authenticity, the key to whatever greatness Gissing has."

BIBLIOGRAPHY

Sources

Finn, Margot. *The Character of Credit: Personal Debt in English Culture, 1740–1914.* Cambridge, U.K.: Cambridge University Press, 2003. Web. 3 Jan. 2013.

Gissing, George. *London and the Life of Literature in Late Victorian England: The Diary of George Gissing, Novelist.* Ed. Pierre Coustillas. Lewisburg, Penn.: Bucknell University Press, 1978. Print.

Halperin, John. Rev. of *London and the Life of Literature in Late Victorian England: The Diary of George Gissing, Novelist,* by George Gissing. *Yearbook of English Studies* 11 (1981): 339–40. *JSTOR.* Web. 3 Jan. 2013.

Korg, Jacob. *George Gissing: A Critical Biography.* Seattle: University of Washington Press, 1963. Print.

———. Rev. of *London and the Life of Literature in Late Victorian England: The Diary of George Gissing, Novelist,* by George Gissing, and *The Alien Art: A Critical Study of George Gissing's Novels,* by Michael Collie. *Victorian Studies* 24.1 (1980): 130–31. *JSTOR.* Web. 3 Jan. 2013.

Packer, George. "The Struggle Writer: Gissing Had It Right." *New York Times.* New York Times, 13 Oct. 1991. Web. 3 Jan. 2013.

Further Reading

Altick, Richard D. *Victorian People and Ideas: A Companion for the Modern Reader of Victorian Literature.* New York: Norton, 1973. Print.

Born, Daniel. *The Birth of Liberal Guilt in the English Novel: Dickens to H. G. Wells*. Chapel Hill: University of North Carolina Press, 1995. Web. 3 Jan. 2013.

Coustillas. Pierre. *The Heroic Life of George Gissing*. 3 vols. London: Pickering and Chatto, 2011–12. Print.

Devine, Christine. *Class in Turn-of-the-Century Novels of Gissing, James, Hardy, and Wells*. Aldershot, U.K.: Ashgate, 2005. Web. 3 Jan. 2013.

Donnelly, Mabel Collins. *George Gissing, Grave Comedian*. Cambridge, Mass.: Harvard University Press, 1954. Print.

Gissing, George. *The Collected Letters of George Gissing*. 9 vols. Eds. Paul E. Mattheisen, Arthur C. Young, and Pierre Coustillas. Athens: Ohio University Press, 1990–96. Print.

———. *Selections Autobiographical and Imaginative from the Works of George Gissing, with Biographical and Critical Notes by His Son*. London: Cape, 1929. Print.

Halperin, John. *Gissing: A Life in Books*. New York: Oxford University Press, 1982. Print.

Phillips, Lawrence Alfred. *A Mighty Mass of Brick and Smoke: Victorian and Edwardian Representations of London*. New York: Rodopi, 2007. Web. 3 Jan. 2013.

Tindall, Gillian. *The Born Exile: George Gissing*. New York: Harcourt Brace Jovanovich, 1974. Print.

Jane Berard

The Love Letters of Dorothy Osborne to Sir William Temple, 1652–54

Dorothy Osborne

❖ Key Facts

Time Period:
Mid-17th Century

Relevant Historical Events:
British Civl War; Osborne's separation from William Temple before their marriage

Nationality:
English

Keywords:
love; romance; early modern period

OVERVIEW

Dorothy Osborne (1627–95) wrote her private letters to her eventual husband, Sir William Temple, between 1652 and 1654 during part of their courtship; the missives—which were not published until the 1800s—shed light on women's experiences during this tumultuous time in British history. Moreover, the letters show Osborne to be a savvy, capable writer who carefully crafted her prose to fit the genre and to engage her singular audience. Between their intimate nature and Osborne's skill, the letters give insight into how a thoughtful woman navigated the complicated social waters of her time.

Temple kept his wife's letters stored in a cabinet (only two remain of his to her), and the letters became a precious family heirloom. In 1836 excerpts of the letters were included as an appendix to a biography of Temple. Victorian critics and readers became enamored of Osborne's literary charm and skill; in 1888 Edward Abbott Parry edited a complete edition of her letters in a work titled *The Love Letters of Dorothy Osborne to Sir William Temple, 1652–54*. To many critics, Osborne seemed an ideal, ladylike counterpart to more flamboyant figures such as Aphra Behn and Margaret Cavendish. However, feminist critics, beginning with Virginia Woolf, have painted a more complicated portrait of Osborne. Politics aside, her work holds value both for its rhetorical sophistication and its addition to a very limited field of early modern women writers.

HISTORICAL AND LITERARY CONTEXT

Osborne grew up during the British Civil War, and her family suffered for their loyalty to the Crown. She met Temple on a trip to the Isle of Wight. At the time, Charles I was imprisoned there. When Osborne's brother publicly scrawled an anti-parliamentarian message, the whole party accompanying him was arrested. Osborne claimed responsibility, correctly assuming that as a woman she would be excused. Legend has it that Temple was already drawn to Osborne, and her quick thinking cemented his affection. However, both families were relying on their offspring to make wealthy marriages and opposed the engagement.

Osborne and Temple were nevertheless determined to marry and wrote to each other frequently. Osborne used the letters to create a certain persona—a witty and loving but also intelligent and thoughtful woman. Once the couple received permission to marry, their life together had ups and downs. Of their nine children, seven died in infancy; their beloved daughter, Diana, then died of smallpox at age fourteen, and their son, John, committed suicide as an adult after botching a political intrigue. Despite the tragedies, Temple built a successful career as a diplomat. He worked to bring about the Triple Alliance (1668) among Sweden, Holland, and England, and he brokered the marriage between William of Orange and Princess Mary. There is little verifiable knowledge about Osborne's perspective during these years. On one hand, she may have delighted in the life of a diplomat's wife; on the other, she had expressed her desire for privacy and a quiet life.

Osborne's letters are significant in part because so few women wrote during this period. As Woolf contends, "Had she been born in 1827, Dorothy Osborne would have written novels; had she been born in 1527, she would never have written at all. But she was born in 1627, and at that date though writing books was ridiculous for a woman there was nothing unseemly in writing a letter." Even though Osborne was limited in her choice of genre, the gentlewoman was a writer of caliber. As such, her work aligns with that of other women whose writing was celebrated only after their deaths, such as Dorothy Wordsworth's diaries or Charlotte Perkins Gilman's fiction and essays.

Osborne's letters have been praised for their rhetorical mastery, but she has also been offset against her peers—most notably Cavendish, who published her own writings and enjoyed being a public figure. Osborne claimed of Cavendish, "There are many soberer People in Bedlam." Victorian critics used this statement to praise Osborne's ladylike demeanor, while modern critics have sometimes disliked her for that same conservatism. However, the letters still provide modern readers with an unparalleled glimpse into how one woman handled the patriarchal strictures of her time.

THEMES AND STYLE

Discussions of relationships are a recurring theme in Osborne's letters. This theme makes sense in the letters of a woman to her fiancé, but it also gives Osborne an opportunity to voice what she wants in her marriage. She expresses concerns about maintaining happiness in marriage, proposing that couples live in the same house a year before marrying: "If in all that time they never disagreed they should then bee permitted to marry if they pleasd, but how few would doe it then." Not that she was pessimistic about her own relationship. She asks, "Can there bee a more Romance Story then ours would make if the conclusion should prove happy?" In the end, the letters gave Osborne a venue to express her ideas and dreams about marriage.

Osborne wrote to maintain contact with her fiancé during their long engagement. She reports on her daily life, her thoughts and feelings, and the local gossip. She thus wooed through her writing, creating a vivid version of herself. In addition to expressing her ideas of marriage, her literary re-creation of her life entertained her lover and sustained his interest. She wrote of her pleasure when Temple praised her writing: "If there were anything in my letter that pleased you I am extremely glad on't [on it], 'twas all due to you, and made it but an equal return for the satisfaction yours gave me." She wrote for an audience of one—the man she chose because she envisioned a better life with him than any other.

One of Osborne's key stylistic choices was a sarcastic, teasing tone. She reported on her other suitors, highlighting her desirability but also showing her faithfulness. She encourages Temple's jealousy by telling him of rivals but then reasserts her loyalty through her rejection of others. In another instance, she responds to Temple's question of the ideal qualities in a partner. She answers in the negative with what she does not want. For example, "He must not be so much a country gentleman as to understand nothing but hawks and dogs, and be fonder of either than of his wife." Further, "He must not be a town gallant neither … that makes court to all the women he sees, thinks they believe him, and laughs and is laughed at equally." By implication, Temple fits these requirements. Moreover, by describing her ideals through the negative, Osborne can praise her fiancé's good qualities while not pinning down any requirement he may see lacking in himself or their relationship. Thus, her playful reportage does double duty as being entertaining and building a connection between them.

CRITICAL DISCUSSION

Osborne's letters remained unviewed outside her family for two centuries. Selected ones were published in 1836 in her husband's biography—as an appendix that shed light on a great man. This glimpse into the world of Lady Temple fascinated nineteenth-century readers, and a heavily edited volume of her letters came out in 1888. Parry, her editor, claimed, "We may all visit her and hear her voice, even in the very tones in which she spoke to her lover." Victorian critics painted her as the epitome of British femininity. However, in 1932 Woolf presented a more nuanced picture, bemoaning Osborne's marriage because it meant she stopped writing: "Married to Temple, she wrote to him no longer. The letters almost immediately cease. The whole world that Dorothy had brought into existence is extinguished."

In one sense, the public perception of Osborne's letters has always been political. If the Victorians embraced her as an idealized lady, modern critics lamented her conservatism. Because so few women wrote during the period, each one's work seems representative of women's perspectives and experiences generally. Readers project their own biases onto the text. As with all intellectual work, the hope is that each interpretation captures an aspect of the author's intention, legacy, and experiences.

Certain scholars offer nuanced interpretations. In a 2007 essay for *Women's Writing*, Sasha Roberts argues that women in the early modern period used a mastery of literary form to exhibit their intelligence. In Osborne's case, this applies not only to the epistolary form but also her allusions to various literary touchstones. Sara Crangle, also writing for *Women's Writing*, contends that Osborne shows her awareness

William II and Queen Mary II of England, in a painting by Sir James Thornhill. Dorothy Osborne was central to the marriage negotiations between William and Mary because of her friendship with both. © JAMES BRITTAIN/THE BRIDGEMAN ART LIBRARY

PRIMARY SOURCE

EXCERPT FROM *LETTERS FROM DOROTHY OSBORNE TO SIR WILLIAM TEMPLE*

(Undated. Assumed date Sunday, March 6, 1653)

SIR,—Your last letter came like a pardon to one upon the block. I have given over the hopes on't, having received my letters by the other carrier, who uses always to be last. The loss put me hugely out of order, and you would both have pitied and laughed at me if you could have seen how woodenly I entertained the widow, who came hither the day before, and surprised me very much. Not being able to say anything, I got her to cards, and there with a great deal of patience lost my money to her—or rather I gave it as my ransom. In the midst of our play, in comes my blessed boy with your letter, and, in earnest, I was not able to disguise the joy it gave me, though one was by that is not much your friend, and took notice of a blush that for my life I could not keep back. I put up the letter in my pocket, and made what haste I could to lose the money I had left, that I might take occasion to go fetch some more; but I did not make such haste back again, I can assure you. I took time enough to have coined myself some money if I had had the art on't, and left my brother enough to make all his addresses to her if he were so disposed. I know not whether he was pleased or not, but I am sure I was.

You make so reasonable demands that 'tis not fit you should be denied. You ask my thoughts but at one hour; you will think me bountiful, I hope, when I shall tell you that I know no hour when you have them not. No, in earnest, my very dreams are yours, and I have got such a habit of thinking of you that any other thought intrudes and grows uneasy to me.

of the letter as both a private and public expression: "She placates her family, and stays as close to propriety as possible. But most importantly, she writes—secretly and persistently—to a lover of her own choosing." In *An Audience of One* (2005), Carrie Hintz discusses Osborne's limited circumstances: "The letters were Osborne's means of controlling the courtship, using the safe and informal space of the letters to experiment with ideas and stances." Together, these critics have added much to the understanding of Osborne's letters as literature in general and as life-writing in particular.

BIBLIOGRAPHY

Sources

Crangle, Sara. "Epistolarity, Audience, Selfhood: *The Letters of Dorothy Osborne to William Temple*." *Women's Writing* 12.3 (2005): 433–51. Print.

Hintz, Carrie. *An Audience of One: Dorothy Osborne's Letters to Sir William Temple, 1652–1654*. Toronto: University of Toronto Press, 2005. Print.

Osborne Temple, Dorothy. *Letters from Dorothy Osborne to Sir William Temple, 1652–1654*. Ed. Edward Abbott Parry. London: J. M. Dent and Sons, 1888. *University of Pennsylvania Digital Library*. Web. 5 Nov. 2012.

Roberts, Sasha. "Women's Literary Capital in Early Modern England: Formal Composition and Rhetorical Display in Manuscript and Print." *Women's Writing* 14.2 (2007): 246–69. *Taylor and Francis*. Web. 8 Oct. 2012.

Woolf, Virginia. "Dorothy Osborne's 'Letters.'" *The Common Reader, Second Series*. Adelaide, Australia: University of Adelaide Library, 2012. PDF file. 30 Oct. 2012.

Further Reading

Behn, Aphra. *Oroonoko, The Rover, and Other Works*. New York: Penguin Classics, 1993. Print.

I drink your health every morning in a drench that would poison a horse I believe, and 'tis the only way I have to persuade myself to take it. 'Tis the infusion of steel, and makes me so horribly sick, that every day at ten o'clock I am making my will and taking leave of all my friends. You will believe you are not forgot then. They tell me I must take this ugly drink a fortnight, and then begin another as bad; but unless you say so too, I do not think I shall. 'Tis worse than dying by the half.

[…]

My brother is gone to wait upon the widow homewards—she that was born to persecute you and I, I think. She has so tired me with being here but two days, that I do not think I shall accept of the offer she made me of living with her in case my father dies before I have disposed of myself. Yet we are very great [friends,] and for my comfort she says she will come again about the latter end of June and stay longer with me. My aunt is still in town, kept by her business, which I am afraid will not go well, they do so delay it; and my precious uncle does so visit her, and is so kind, that without doubt some mischief will follow. Do you know his son, my cousin Harry? 'Tis a handsome youth, and well-natured, but such a goose; and he has bred him so strangely, that he needs all his ten thousand pound a year. I would fain have him marry my Lady Diana, she was his mistress when he was a boy. He had more wit then than he has now, I think, and I have less wit than he, sure, for spending my paper upon him when I have so little.

SOURCE: Osborne Temple, Dorothy. *Letters from Dorothy Osborne to Sir William Temple, 1652–1654*. Ed. Edward Abbott Parry. London: J. M. Dent and Sons, 1888.

Cavendish, Margaret. *New Blazing World and Other Writings*. Ed. Sylvia Boiwerbank and Sara Mendelson. Peterborough, ON: Broadview, 2000. Print.

Dunn, Jane. *Read My Heart: A Love Story in England's Age of Revolution*. New York: Knopf, 2008. Print.

Hackett, Helen. *Women and Romance Fiction in the English Renaissance*. Cambridge, U.K.: Cambridge University Press, 2000. Print.

Ottway, Sheila. "Dorothy Osborne's Love Letters: Novelistic Glimmerings and the Ovidian Self." *Prose Studies* 19.2 (1996): 149–60. Print.

Salzman, Paul. *Reading Early Modern Women's Writing*. New York: Oxford University Press, 2007. Print.

Wilcox, Helen. "'Free and Easy as Ones Discourse'?: Genre and Self-Expression in the Poems and Letters of Early Modern Englishwomen." *Genre and Women's Life Writing in Early Modern England*. Ed. Michelle M. Dowd and Julie A. Eckerle. Burlington, Vt.: Ashgate, 2007. 15–32. Print.

Sarah Stoeckl

London Journal, 1762–1763

James Boswell

Key Facts

Time Period:
Mid-18th Century

Relevant Historical Events:
Formation of the United Kingdom; British victory in the Seven Years' War; growth of the British Empire

Nationality:
Scottish

Keywords:
chronicle; reflection

OVERVIEW

Not published until 1950, *London Journal, 1762–1763* by Scottish writer James Boswell (1740–95) recounts the year the young lawyer left Scotland and joined the intelligentsia of London society. The journal marks the beginning of Boswell's lifelong fascination with biography and memoir, two forms of writing he practiced enthusiastically until his death. The three major works he published during his lifetime—*Account of Corsica* (1768), *The Journal of a Tour to the Hebrides* (1785), and *Life of Samuel Johnson* (1791)—all drew heavily upon his journal. These documents, along with his copious notebooks and private papers, were dispersed after his death and did not come to light until the 1920s and 1930s, at which time they were bought up by an American collector who donated them to Yale University. *London Journal* was the first of these papers to appear in print.

London Journal became something of a best seller, notable for Boswell's candid pursuit of sexual encounters and other physical pleasures, and started a boom in Boswell scholarship that continues to this day. Prior to 1950 the author was known almost solely as the biographer of writer and raconteur Samuel Johnson (1709–84) and was thought to have done little more than write down everything Johnson said. The term "boswell" had come to mean a faithful, colorless chronicler of greatness. However, once Boswell's journals and correspondence were published, critical opinion changed. Critics came to understand that Boswell had much more to say than Johnson did and that his *Life of Samuel Johnson* is not proto oral history but, in fact, a great work of biography.

HISTORICAL AND LITERARY CONTEXT

In 1762 King George III had just begun his sixty-year reign in Great Britain, which had been established in 1707 with the political union of England and Scotland. Boswell, along with many other Scots, was devoted to the exiled House of Stuart that had ruled his homeland before the 1707 union. Skirmishes and rebellions proved that many Scots and Englishmen were less than comfortable with the new union, a feeling that followed Boswell to London. When he arrived in the capital, anti-Scot feeling was rife, because the prime minister, Lord Bute, was a Scot who had replaced the very popular William Pitt the Elder. Lord Bute was perceived as favoring Scots in his administration.

Boswell came to London seeking a commission in a fashionable regiment of royal household guards. Britain's expansion was nearly complete; the Seven Years' War with France ended with Great Britain in possession of all of Canada, the Ohio Valley, the West Indies, and the Philippines. In 1757 the British gained control of Bengal, the most populous state in India, and by 1764 England controlled the entire subcontinent. But Boswell was not seeking a commission in order to participate in empire building; he was only interested in the social prestige that a commission in an elite regiment would entail. As Frederick Pottle observes in his introduction to *London Journal,* "[Boswell] was quite frank in admitting that he had no stomach for fighting in Germany or America or anywhere else."

At the same time, Scotland was instrumental in Great Britain's intellectual domination over much of Europe through its contributions to the Enlightenment. Philosopher David Hume, the economist Adam Smith, the novelist Tobias Smollett, and the poet Robert Burns—all Scots—left an indelible mark on eighteenth-century English literature, which was flowering anew in the works of the poet Alexander Pope; the novelists Henry Fielding, Samuel Richardson, and Laurence Sterne; and the historian Edward Gibbon. There was, moreover, a flourishing scene of literary and cultural journalism in London at the time, with the success of the periodicals of Addison and Steele—the *Spectator,* the *Tattler,* etc.—leading the way. Boswell enthusiastically pursued joining this rarified social circle. In keeping a journal, he was unknowingly following a distinguished tradition of British diarists; however, the journals of his great predecessors such as John Evelyn (1620–1706) and Samuel Pepys (1633–1703) were not published until the nineteenth century.

Though his journal remained unpublished during his lifetime, his career, on the other hand, had enormous impact on popular culture, being that he was the first known celebrity interviewer. As *London Journal* makes clear, he saw his life's work as attaching himself to famous people and writing down what they said. Before he met Johnson, he was already collecting stories about him. "I like to mark every anecdote," he states, in his entry for December 17, 1762, "of men of so much genius and literature." When he traveled abroad, he met and talked with such luminaries as French Enlightenment writer Voltaire and French philosopher Jean-Jacques Rousseau.

THEMES AND STYLE

Boswell's theme in *London Journal* is his own progress through the world. He takes a detached, critical view of his own actions and is surprisingly nonjudgmental of others. People are not good or evil in Boswell's estimation, only interesting or tiresome. He is also a sharp observer of the effect he has on other people. After a meeting with Lord Eglington, who is sponsoring his request for an army commission, he writes that "he imagined me much in the style that I was three years ago: raw, curious, volatile, credulous. He knew little the experience I had got and the notions and the composure that I had obtained by reflection." But Lord Eglington brings him up short, telling him that he is only a little wiser than before because he was formerly so ignorant. Boswell admits that "there was some justice in what he said."

Boswell's motivation as a diarist was to make his journal into a primary source for his public writing. He also sought to live by the frugal plan he had set out for himself—living within his means, cultivating useful people, attending church regularly, and so on. Self-improvement was a primary motive. He says little about becoming a professional writer, except the occasional aside about some piece of ephemeral journalism for which he had just been paid. His official line was that he was seeking a commission in the army; failing that, he would take up the profession of law, as his father wished (and which he ultimately did).

The style of *London Journal* is easy, gossipy, and anecdotal: "I dined at … Col. Gould's. He is a most amiable man. I like him much for his great degree of indolence. He loves to lie abed dearly, and gently grumbles at the thoughts of undergoing the fatigues of dressing." Yet at the same time, Boswell can be highly self-conscious and technical. He debates the proper method of recording anecdotes and is always trying to describe people in as few words as possible. He did not write every day; sometimes he skipped a whole week and then caught up on events in one entry. This has the effect of making his daily life seem more coherent and organized than it perhaps really was.

CRITICAL DISCUSSION

Before the 1950 publication of *London Journal*, Boswell's reputation as a writer rested on his *Life of Samuel Johnson*, which many critics consider the greatest biography ever written. However, many of those same critics scarcely gave a nod to Boswell's skill in writing it. Thomas Babington Macaulay, in a retrospective review of the *Life of Samuel Johnson*, published in 1831, wrote that "Homer is not more decidedly the first of heroic poets. Shakespeare is not more decidedly the first of dramatists, Demosthenes is not more decidedly the first of orators, than Boswell is the first of biographers. He has no second. He has distanced all his competitors so decidedly that it is not worth while to place them." Yet, notes Macaulay, "of the talents which ordinarily raise men to eminence as writers, Boswell had absolutely none. There is not in all his books a single remark of his own on literature, politics, religion, or society, which is not either commonplace or absurd…. Of [his] observations we do not remember one which is above the intellectual capacity of a boy of fifteen."

After *London Journal* was published, Boswell studies became a viable academic pursuit, with his journals and letters yielding a rich harvest for literary and social historians. G. Scott-Moncrieff, writing in the *New Catholic Encyclopedia* (Boswell converted to Catholicism in 1757), encapsulates this new attitude by writing that "Boswell was an eccentric and remarkable character, often vehemently attacked for his sycophancy, his conceit, and his immorality… . Shrewd judgment and conscientious art underlie the deceptive ease of his narration. His writing is full of humor and captures unique pictures of life in Scotland and London in the 18th century." The broader influence of *London Journal* is found in the increased interest in the journal or diary as a literary form.

The scholarly interest in Boswell today, however, is mainly in his role as a source, not as an artist. Some have even questioned the worth of his masterpiece, *Life of Samuel Johnson*. Charles Hinnant mentions "the skepticism [of] many readers … —why be concerned with a work that is not really a biography at all, they

A 1765 portrait of James Boswell by George Willison. © SCOTTISH NATIONAL PORTRAIT GALLERY, EDINBURGH, SCOTLAND/THE BRIDGEMAN ART LIBRARY

THE BOSWELL PAPERS

By the time he died, James Boswell was in low standing with the other members of his strait-laced Presbyterian family on account of his wide-ranging friendships, his loose lifestyle, his compulsive womanizing, and his Catholicism. In his last years, as Christopher Morley says in his preface to *London Journal,* "he was already a legend of impropriety, which death transmuted to the skeleton in the family closet." The family was scandalized by what little they could bear to read of Boswell's private papers, and they would have destroyed them all if he had not appointed three of his friends as his literary executors. One of these executors, Edmond Malone, understanding that the family would never allow the papers to be published, managed to get most of the manuscripts into other estates in Scotland and Ireland for safekeeping.

Thus dispersed, the papers disappeared from the public realm. They rested in private vaults, cupboards, and closets until the 1920s, when a scholar visiting an Irish estate, looking for documents that might prove the existence of a large store of Boswell papers, uncovered samples of what looked to be a much larger collection. Another, even bigger cache was discovered in the early 1930s by a scholar searching for material on an unrelated topic. Other major finds followed. All were bought by an American collector, Lieutenant Colonel Ralph Hayward Isham, who turned them over to Yale University. At Yale, the papers were edited and published, under the series title "The Private Papers of James Boswell," between 1950 and 1989.

claim, but only a loose assemblage of materials hastily cobbled together? Why be interested in a life that pays little attention to its subject's poetry and moral essays, literary criticism, political thought, or religious convictions?" Most, however, echo Donna T. Andrew, who wrote in the *Canadian Journal of History* that "Boswell was one of the earliest eighteenth-century chroniclers to present his inner doubts and fears, as well as ambitions and self-evaluations, warts-and-all, to a critical public…. Boswell's genius lies in his ability to produce conversation in which one could hear the nuances and tones of individual character, to make the talk itself as exciting and compelling as any action or mystery-solving."

BIBLIOGRAPHY

Sources

Andrew, Donna T. "The Journals of James Boswell: 1762–1795." *Canadian Journal of History* 28.3 (1993): 587+. *General OneFile.* Web. 20 Dec. 2012.

Bering, Henrik. "The Ultimate Literary Portrait." *Policy Review* 149 (2008): 61+. *General OneFile.* Web. 21 Dec. 2012.

Boswell, James. *London Journal, 1762–1763.* Ed. Frederick A. Pottle. New York: McGraw-Hill, 1950. Print.

Brooks, A. Russell. *James Boswell.* New York: Twayne, 1971. 17–21. *Twayne's English Authors Series* 122. *Gale Virtual Reference Library.* Web. 10 Nov. 2012.

Hinnant, Charles H. "Bruce Redford. Designing the Life of Johnson." *Biography* 26.2 (2003): 319+. *General OneFile.* Web. 25 Dec. 2012.

Macaulay, Thomas Babington. "Boswell's 'Life of Johnson'." *DISCovering Authors.* Detroit: Gale, 2003. *Discover Collection.* Web. 24 Dec. 2012.

Scott-Moncrieff, G. "Boswell, James." *New Catholic Encyclopedia.* 2nd ed. Vol. 2. Detroit: Gale, 2003. 558–59. *Gale Virtual Reference Library.* Web. 22 Dec. 2012.

Further Reading

Boswell, James. *The Life of Samuel Johnson LL.D.* (1791). London: Oxford University Press, 1953. Print.

———. *The Journal of a Tour to the Hebrides.* London: J. M. Dent, 1958. Print.

Elkin, Stanley. *Boswell.* New York: Random House, 1964. Print

Gavin, Michael. "James Boswell and the Uses of Criticism." *Studies in English Literature, 1500–1900* 50.3 (2010): 665+. *General OneFile.* Web. 21 Dec. 2012.

Jackson, H. J. "An Important Annotated Boswell." *Review of English Studies* 49.193 (1998): 9+. *General OneFile.* Web. 21 Dec. 2012.

Zaretsky, Robert. "A Sentimental Education." *History Today* 61.4 (2011): 49+. *General OneFile.* Web. 23 Dec. 2012.

Gerald Carpenter

A Midwife's Tale
The Life of Martha Ballard, Based on Her Diary, 1785–1812
Laurel Thatcher Ulrich

OVERVIEW

Penned by U.S. historian Laurel Thatcher Ulrich and published in 1990, *A Midwife's Tale: The Life of Martha Ballard, Based on Her Diary, 1785–1812* recounts the life of an American midwife and mother of nine in Hallowell, Maine, during the years immediately following the American Revolution. In addition to public records and the diaries of other Hallowell residents, Ulrich's main source is Ballard's own diary, in which for more than twenty-seven years the midwife faithfully recorded her daily duties as both a housewife and a healer. Written in a dry, stoic manner, Ballard's brief daily entries offer glimpses into the network of relationships and activities occurring in the newly settled town and reveal the complex lives of eighteenth-century women. Ulrich argues that Ballard's diary is a crucial instrument for truly understanding the critical socioeconomic role women played in post-revolutionary America.

Although Ballard's diary was long dismissed by historians and feminists as the mundane recounting of one woman's domestic chores, Ulrich's insight into and interpretation of the text has rescued it from obscurity and has shown it to be an invaluable resource for the study of early American culture. *A Midwife's Tale* has been extremely well received and was adapted into a documentary by writer-producer Laurie Kahn-Levitt that was broadcast by PBS in 1998. Writing for the *Washington Post,* Florence King observed, "Bringing Martha Ballard's diary to light was an ingenious idea on Laurel Thatcher Ulrich's part, a venture into bona fide women's studies that is expertly executed and endlessly interesting." *A Midwife's Tale* won numerous awards, the most notable being the 1991 Pulitzer Prize for History.

HISTORICAL AND LITERARY CONTEXT

Ballard's diary begins two years after the end of the American Revolution and continues through the federalist era. These were pivotal historical periods as well as a time of transition in the North American medical community, as traditional midwifery was gradually being replaced by medical obstetrics. In urban areas doctors began attending births more often, using forceps to accelerate delivery and opiates to alleviate pain. Affluent urban women, who assumed doctors and their technology meant quicker and safer deliveries, began to employ midwives and their natural medicine less often. Although Ballard witnessed the growing influence of male physicians, midwifery persisted in Hallowell and other isolated rural communities until the end of the nineteenth century. In one entry, Ballard dryly criticizes the incompetence of one male physician: "Dr. Page … gave my patient 20 drops of Laudanum which put [Mrs. Sewall] into such a stupor her pains (which were regular & promising) in a manner stopt till near night when she pukt."

As one of Hallowell's premier midwives and healers, Ballard used her diary as a means of keeping track of the deliveries she attended, the herbal remedies and medical assistance she provided to the local townspeople, and the payments she received for the work she performed. The diary reveals that Ballard was not only responsible for delivering 816 babies in twenty-seven years but that she was also a dedicated mother, wife, healer, pharmacist, gardener, cloth maker, and "keeper of vital records." In fact, Hallowell's male physician, Dr. Daniel Cony, consulted Ballard's records for the town birth and death statistics.

After Ballard died in 1812, the diary was passed down to the midwife's female descendants, eventually being inherited in 1884 by Mary Hobart—a practicing physician. Parts of Ballard's diary were reprinted in Charles Elventon Nash's book *The History of Augusta: First Settlement and Early Days as a Town, Including the Diary of Mrs. Martha Moore Ballard (1785–1812),* which was printed in 1904 but was not officially published until 1961. Hobart donated the diary manuscript to the Maine State Library in 1930. In *American Women Writers to 1820,* Gail K. Smith claims that Ballard's diary is "of inestimable value as one of only a handful of surviving personal writings by American women of the late eighteenth century." In 1992 Ballard's diary was published in its entirety by Picton Press as the Maine Genealogical Society's *Special Publication No. 10.*

In addition to *A Midwife's Tale,* Ulrich has written several books that chronicle early American life. In *Good Wives: Image and Reality in the Lives of Women in*

❖ *Key Facts*

Time Period:
Late 18th to Early 19th Century

Relevant Historical Events:
American Revolutionary War; achievement of American independence

Nationality:
American

Keywords:
women's writing; feminism; midwifery

WORK AND FAMILY LIFE

In *Midwife's Tale*, Martha Ballard describes her work as a midwife and healer in detail. This woodcut from the nineteenth century depicts a midwife showing a new father his child after he learns that his wife has died in childbirth. Ballard shares information about similar difficult situations in her book. © NORTH WIND PICTURE ARCHIVES/AP IMAGES

Northern New England, 1650–1750 (1982) she demonstrates that colonial women played key roles in the economic and social structures of eighteenth-century life. As she did in *A Midwife's Tale,* Ulrich relied on court records, probate inventories, personal documents, and diaries from the colonial period to illustrate the multifaceted and demanding lives of women. Since *A Midwife's Tale* was published, two other historical texts about early American women have been written: *The Way of Duty: A Woman and Her Family in Revolutionary America* by Richard and Joy Day Buel and *Earthbound and Heavenbent: Elizabeth Porter Phelps and Life at Forty Acres (1747–1817)* by Elizabeth Pendergast Carlisle. Just as Ulrich used Ballard's diaries, Carlisle's text draws upon Phelps's modest diary in order to reconstruct the pioneer woman's life.

THEMES AND STYLE

A Midwife's Tale demonstrates the important roles women played in the medical, social, and economic realms of early America. Although male physicians are mentioned more often than midwives in town and regional records, midwives officiated at the vast majority of deliveries during Ballard's lifetime in Hallowell. Whereas Dr. Cony performed approximately ten deliveries a year, Ballard averaged nearly forty. In addition to delivering babies, Ballard was an accomplished healer who was frequently called upon to concoct herbal remedies, dress wounds, and treat the sick. Ulrich argues that "women contributed significantly to the economy in all kinds of ways" and that midwives were often paid in goods such as teakettles, lumber credits, or turkeys. Ballard's entries also reveal busy days of knitting, planting, spinning cloth, and bartering with other townsfolk for goods and services. As both a midwife and housewife, Ballard significantly contributed to her household's economy as well as the greater Hallowell economy.

A Midwife's Tale blends Ballard's voice with Ulrich's historical perspective. In each chapter, Ulrich presents excerpts from one month of Ballard's life and expounds upon the entries, dissecting the descriptions provided and filling in the details that Ballard left out. In this way, Ulrich not only fleshes out Ballard's life story but also presents a clear picture of Hallowell society and early American culture. Yet with all of Ulrich's added detail, she was careful to preserve Ballard's voice, making only minor punctuation and spelling corrections to the excerpts. For example, Ballard's fatigue is almost palpable in the following passage: "I Laid myself on the bed in the bedroom and was not able to rise from ther…. How many times I have been necasatated to rest my self on the bed I am not able to say."

The format of Ballard's diary imitates the style of an almanac: ruled margins, numbers for days of the week, and a "dominical letter" for Sundays. Eighteenth-century men often used the blank pages of an almanac to record the weather, discuss their gardens, and keep track of their social visits, just as Ballard did. The midwife's diary also resembles a daybook—a common form of everyday recordkeeping that typically recounted daily expenses, income, family events, and work performed. Although Ballard's entries are quite brief, she always managed to record the weather, her location, and the people with whom she interacted that day. She also recorded every delivery she attended and whether or not she was paid for her services. Ulrich describes Ballard's terse, factual tone as a "plain, matter-of-fact, and in the end unforgettable voice."

CRITICAL DISCUSSION

Ulrich explains that the "few historians who have known about [Ballard's] diary have not quite known what to do with it." James W. North quotes a few passages from the diary in his *History of Augusta* (1870), but he dismisses most of the entries as "brief and with some exceptions not of general interest." Similarly, Nash included an abridgement of the journal in his *History of Augusta* but claimed much of it was "trivial and unimportant … being but a repetition of what has been recited many times." Ulrich notes that in the 1970s the diary even failed to impress the feminist author of a text on historical midwifery, who wrote, "Like many diaries of farm women, it is filled with trivia about domestic chores and pastimes."

The diary lay dormant in the Augusta, Maine, public library until Ulrich brought its significance to light. As stated in the *Encyclopedia of Feminist Literature,* Ulrich's "purposeful, energetic" writing retrieves "from androcentric national history the invisible heroines." Using Ballard's life as proof, Ulrich argues that women played a much bigger role in early American society than is visible in contemporary public records, literature, and male diaries. If not for the diary, Ballard's life would have been a series of dates: her birth, marriage, the births of her children, the deaths of her three daughters, and her own death. Ulrich contends, "Without the diary we would know nothing of her life after the last of her children was born, nothing of the 816 deliveries she performed between 1785 and 1812. We would not even be certain she had been a midwife."

Several critics praised *A Midwife's Tale* for its medical, social, economic, and historical insight into early American life. In the *New York Times Book Review,* Carl N. Degler calls Ulrich "a truly talented historian" who "unravels out of those hard knots of recorded fact the fascinating life of a community that in its complexity is at once so foreign, and yet so similar, to our own." Ulrich's rich text is brimming with information about contemporary medical procedures, herbal remedies, and long-forgotten facts about life in the young republic. In *Journal of American History,* Carol F. Karlsen states, "Medical historians will especially appreciate the identification of the wide variety of medicinal ingredients mentioned in the diary and Ulrich's painstaking analyses of their uses."

MARTHA MOORE BALLARD— A BIOGRAPHICAL SKETCH

Martha Moore was born to Dorothy and Elijah Moore in Oxford, Massachusetts, in 1735. A member of a relatively well-educated family, Martha married Ephraim Ballard in 1754. By 1769 the couple had six children, three of whom died that same year during a diphtheria epidemic that ravaged Oxford. After the birth of two more children, Ephraim leased Fort Halifax and its surrounding lands in Winslow, Maine, in 1775; however, his family remained in Oxford. After the property was confiscated by the Revolutionary army, Ephraim moved his wife and five surviving children to Hallowell in 1777, where he managed a gristmill and sawmill. The family remained in Hallowell (part of which would eventually become Augusta) for the rest of their lives.

By the time Martha began recording her diary on January 1, 1785, she was already a skilled healer. In addition to delivering babies, she was a knowledgeable herbalist and knew how to treat many kinds of wounds and illnesses. Although Martha declares that she first officiated at a birth in July 1778, she probably assisted other midwives in previous deliveries as a sort of training period. Because Martha was one of the few older female citizens of Hallowell and had experience, her midwifery skills were in much demand and her practice grew quickly. After nearly three decades of delivering babies and healing the sick, Martha's health began to decline. She recorded her final diary entry on May 17, 1812.

BIBLIOGRAPHY

Sources

Degler, Carl N. "The Hidden Life of New England." *New York Times Book Review* 4 Mar. 1990. Print.

Karlsen, Carol F. Rev. of *A Midwife's Tale: The Life of Martha Ballard, Based on Her Diary, 1785–1812,* by Laurel Thatcher Ulrich. *Journal of American History* Mar. 1991: 1339–40. Print.

King, Florence. "The Midwife's History." *Washington Post* 5 Mar. 1990: D3. Print.

"Laurel Thatcher Ulrich." *Contemporary Authors Online.* Detroit: Gale, 2008. *Literature Resource Center.* Web. 27 Dec. 2012.

Nash, Charles Elventon. *The History of Augusta: First Settlements and Early Days as a Town, Including the Diary of Mrs. Martha Moore Ballard (1785–1812).* Augusta, Ga.: Charles E. Nash & Son, 1904. Print.

North, James W. *The History of Augusta.* Augusta, Ga.: Clamp & North, 1870. Print.

Smith, Gail K. "Martha Moore Ballard." *American Women Prose Writers to 1820*. Ed. Carla Mulford, et al. Detroit: Gale Research, 1999. *Dictionary of Literary Biography* 200. *Literature Resource Center*. Web. 18 Dec. 2012.

Snodgrass, Mary Ellen. "Ulrich, Laurel Thatcher (1938–)." *Encyclopedia of Feminist Literature*. New York: Facts On File, 2006. Print.

Ulrich, Laurel Thatcher. *A Midwife's Tale: The Life of Martha Ballard, Based on Her Diary, 1785–1812*. New York: Alfred A. Knopf, 1990. Print.

Further Reading

Bloom, Lynn Z. "Auto/Bio/History: Modern Midwifery." *Autobiography and Questions of Gender*. Ed. Shirley Neuman. London: Cass, 1991. 12–24. Print.

Cohen, Patricia Cline. "Dialogue." *Journal of Women's History* 14.3 (2002): 140–47. *Project MUSE*. Web. 4 Jan. 2013.

Larkin, Jack. *The Reshaping of Everyday Life: 1790–1840*. New York: Harper & Row, 1988. Print.

Mullaney, Marie Marmo. Rev. of *A Midwife's Tale: The Life of Martha Ballard, Based on Her Diary, 1785–1812*, by Laurel Thatcher Ulrich. *Library Journal* 15 Mar. 1990: 102. Print.

Stuttaford, Genevieve. Rev. of *A Midwife's Tale: The Life of Martha Ballard, Based on Her Diary, 1785–1812*, by Laurel Thatcher Ulrich. *Publishers Weekly* 26 Jan. 1990: 409. *Literature Resource Center*. Web. 4 Jan. 2013.

Trueheart, Charles. "The Arts of the Pulitzer Winners: Laurel Ulrich, Giving Birth to History." *Washington Post* 10 Apr. 1991: B1, B11. Print.

Ulrich, Laurel Thatcher. "Martha Moore Ballard and the Medical Challenge to Midwifery." *Sickness & Health in America: Readings in the History of Medicine and Public Health*. Ed. Judith Walzer Leavitt and Ronald L. Numbers. Madison: University of Wisconsin Press, 1997. Print.

Wilson, Philip K. *Childbirth: Changing Ideas and Practices in Britain and America 1600 to the Present*. New York: Garland, 1996. Print.

Wyatt, Neal. "Birth Pangs: Mothers of the American Revolution." *Library Journal* 15 June 2008: 105. *Literature Resource Center*. Web. 4 Jan. 2013.

Maggie Magno

Records of a Girlhood

Fanny Kemble

OVERVIEW

Published in 1878, *Records of a Girlhood,* by British actress Fanny Kemble (1809–93), covers Kemble's youth and her years performing on stage until her 1834 marriage to Pierce Mease Butler, a wealthy plantation owner. Kemble was well known as an actress, diarist, and writer of memoirs. Her earlier *Journal of a Residence on a Georgian Plantation* (1863), which chronicles the abuses to slaves she witnessed on her husband's plantation, was already popular with northern abolitionists and British readers. Although *Records of a Girlhood* presents some of the author's first impressions concerning American attitudes toward slavery, its main focus is on her rise to fame as an actress on the London stage, her discomfort with juggling femininity and public performance, and her ideas about acting.

In 1875 she published a series of articles in the *Atlantic* titled "An Old Woman's Gossip." A publisher offered her a contract for the rights to these articles, and she expanded them with journal entries and personal reminiscences into the four-hundred-page *Records of a Girlhood.* Initial reaction to the work was primarily positive, with critics extolling Kemble's personal charms and intelligence. In recent years, critical attention has focused on her writings about abolition and her travels in America; however, *Records of a Girlhood* continues to be valued as a source of information about early nineteenth-century acting and celebrity, and how women navigated the professional world.

HISTORICAL AND LITERARY CONTEXT

Kemble was born in London to a prominent theatrical family. In 1832 her father, actor Charles Kemble, decided to take her on a tour of the United States, and she saw a great deal of the country at a key period in its development. In 1834 she married an American man and moved with him to Georgia, where he owned one of the state's largest plantations. She subsequently wrote numerous letters about her disgust with the system of slavery. These letters were circulated among abolitionists and were published in 1863. She separated from her husband in 1845.

Many of Kemble's life experiences—such as her career as an actress, her travels, and her divorce—were considered socially suspect in the nineteenth century, when the idea of the "angel in the house," or the restrained, domestic woman who lived only to attend to her husband and her family, reigned supreme. Nevertheless, she traveled in exalted social circles. She interacted with novelists Sir Walter Scott and William Thackeray, poets Lord Byron and Alfred Tennyson, painter Sir Frederic Leighton, presidents Andrew Jackson and John Quincy Adams, and prominent abolitionists. Many of these individuals are discussed in *Records of a Girlhood.*

Although the autobiography was a tremendously popular form in Victorian England, the majority of autobiographies were authored by males. Female-penned autobiographies were relatively rare: writers Charlotte Tonna and Harriet Martineau published their works in 1841 and 1877, respectively. Their autobiographies, like Kemble's, offer judgments of the social and artistic events of the day and record the author's professional successes while offering protestations of modesty and reluctance to relinquish privacy. Anna Jameson's 1832 analysis of women in William Shakespeare is another example of successful female writing, and Kemble directly references her friendship with Jameson in *Records of a Girlhood.* Jameson began as a travel writer, as did Martineau. The form was a way that early nineteenth-century women could record their ideas about various social issues. Kemble's *Journal of a Residence in America* (1835) is dedicated to her travels, whereas *Journal of a Residence on a Georgian Plantation* adds political analysis. *Records of a Girlhood* combines elements of each.

By the end of the nineteenth century, female autobiographies were increasingly common and frequently recorded professional, as well as personal, development. Explorer Mary Kingsley's *Travels in West Africa* (1897) and writer Margaret Oliphant's *Autobiography* (1899) both focus on work in a manner similar to Kemble's *Records of a Girlhood,* as do the autobiographies of late nineteenth-century actress Ellen Terry. Kemble also had a surprising literary influence due to her friendship with author Henry James, who was both a personal friend and an avid reader of *Records of a Girlhood.* He used several of Kemble's experiences as plots in his own novels.

THEMES AND STYLE

Records of a Girlhood is notable for Kemble's struggles to define herself vocationally and personally. Her personal story concludes "happily" with her 1834 marriage, an

❖ Key Facts

Time Period:
Early 19th Century

Relevant Historical Events:
Kemble's immigration to the United States and success as a stage actress

Nationality:
English

Keywords:
women's writing; acting; celebrity

Fanny Kemble Butler, British actress and popular author whose writings included poetry, plays, and works about the theater. Portrait painted by Henry Inman. © BROOKLYN MUSEUM OF ART, NEW YORK, USA/GIFT OF CHARLES A. SCHIEREN/THE BRIDGEMAN ART LIBRARY

ironic ending because by the time the work was published, she had been separated from her husband for more than thirty years. This irony echoes the discomfort she displays with traditionally feminine roles; she did not think she was "fit to marry" because of her dislike for "matter of fact cares and duties." She displays equal ambivalence toward her career as an actress, exhibiting distaste for "the violence done … to womanly dignity and decorum in thus becoming the gaze of every eye and theme of every tongue." This protestation of feminine modesty may mask deeper dissatisfaction. She adds, "[T]he finest actor is but a good translator of another man's work; he does somebody else's thought into action, but he creates nothing." Comments such as this mark her interest in being a creator rather than an interpreter, a role that she enacts in *Records of a Girlhood* both through her discussions of the theory behind her performances and the act of writing itself.

She authored three diaries prior to *Records of a Girlhood: Journal of a Residence in America* (1835); *A Year of Consolation* (1847), a story of her travels in Italy; and *Journal of a Residence on a Georgian Plantation* (1863). She begins *Records of a Girlhood* with a direct description of the impetus for its publication.

"A few years ago," she writes, "I received from a friend to whom they had been addressed a collection of my own letters … [A]s the public appetite for gossip appears to be insatiable, and is not unlikely some time or other to be gratified at my expense, I have thought that my own gossip about myself may be as acceptable to it as gossip about me written by another." *Records of a Girlhood* can be seen as a preemptive strike against an increasingly celebrity-driven culture. At first glance, the format—which presents letters interspersed with Kemble's memories—seems to give direct access to her interior life in a unmediated manner. However, Kemble herself selected and arranged the letters, and through her narration, she guides the reader's understanding and interpretation of her work.

Indeed, *Records of a Girlhood* is a very deliberate textual performance of the character of Fanny Kemble, who had been displaying herself on stage and in writing for almost fifty years before the publication of these girlhood memoirs. She firmly instructs readers about how to "gossip" about her. In *Kemble: A Performed Life* (2007), Deidre David terms her a "supreme commander of the operation," suggesting that her ability to shape readers' perceptions "afforded her yet one more brilliant opportunity to perform before the public on her own terms."

CRITICAL DISCUSSION

The most famous contemporary critic of *Records of a Girlhood* was James, Kemble's close personal friend, who in his review of the diary praises Kemble for being both an observer and participant in the social and cultural world of the British and American intelligentsia. The text also served as a rehabilitation of sorts for Kemble's writing in the United States: whereas *Journals* contains unfavorable impressions about the country, and *Residence* is frankly critical of slavery, *Records of a Girlhood* is, according to A. R. McDonough in an 1879 article in *North American Review*, "spirited, sunny, and confidential."

For much of the twentieth century, *Records of a Girlhood* received relatively little attention. Although it had value to historians of theater, it was most popular as a source for biographers of Kemble, of whom there were many. Additionally, at least two novels and one 1996 television production have been based upon her life (primarily her time in Georgia). In the late 1970s, growing interest in Victorian autobiography, and specifically female autobiography, meant that renewed attention was focused on Kemble. In *The Private Lives of Victorian Women: Autobiography in Nineteenth-Century England* (1989), Valerie Sanders suggests that Kemble's work offers insight into the search for vocation within a culture with rigid gender, class, and race expectations. Kemble justifies her own professional drive as a battle between propriety (because no lady ought to work, especially in a way that put her in the public eye), genius (evidenced by her passion and love of drama), and necessity.

Recent critical approaches have continued to focus on how Kemble, as Mark Arkin writes in his 2010 article for *New Criterion*, "control[led] her own image while capitalizing on the public's fascination with the details of her glamorous life." Critics have also focused on the way in which *Records of a Girlhood* suggests how Kemble's control allowed her to comment obliquely upon issues important to her. In a 2005 article for *Restoration and 18th Century Theatre Research*, Carolyn Burroughs suggests that Kemble outlines a female theory of acting as opposed to simply reporting the experiences of a female actress of the time. Meanwhile, Alison Booth's 1995 essay for *Victorian Studies* examines Kemble's construction and examination of race in *Records of a Girlhood* as well as in *Journal of a Residence on a Georgian Plantation*, particularly in her discussion of Shakespeare's *The Tempest*.

BIBLIOGRAPHY

Sources

Arkin, Marc M. "The Many Roles of Fanny Kemble." *New Criterion* 29.3 (2010): 17–21. *Academic Search Complete*. Web. 30 Nov. 2012.

Burroughs, Catherine. "'If the Informing Spirit Be Mine': Frances Anne Kemble and Theory in Rehearsal." *Restoration and 18th Century Theatre Research* 20.1–2 (2005): 28–33. *MLA International Bibliography*. Web. 30 Nov. 2012.

David, Deirdre. *Kemble: A Performed Life*. Philadelphia: University of Pennsylvania, 2007. Print.

Kemble, Fanny. *Records of a Girlhood*. New York: Holt, 1879. Print.

McDonough, A. R. "Recent Miscellaneous Literature." Rev. of *Origin, Progress, and Destiny of the English Language and Literature*, by John Adam Weisse; *John Lothrop Motley*, by Oliver Wendell Holmes; *Demonology and Devil-Lore*, by Moncure Conway; *Records of a Girlhood*, by Fanny Kemble; and *History of American Literature*, by Moses Coit Tyler. *North American Review* 128.269 (1879): 438–45. Print.

Sanders, Valerie. *The Private Lives of Victorian Women: Autobiography in Nineteenth-Century England*. New York: St. Martin's, 1989. Print.

Further Reading

Armstrong, Margaret. *Fanny Kemble: A Passionate Victorian*. New York: Macmillan, 1938. Print.

Booth, Alison. "From Miranda to Prospero: The Works of Fanny Kemble." *Victorian Studies* 38.2 (1995): 227. *Academic Search Complete*. Web. 30 Nov. 2012.

FANNY KEMBLE'S SOLO CAREER

Although Fanny Kemble is generally listed as an actress, she valued poetry and writing over acting. In addition to her popular memoirs, she published several plays. Her career on stage was relatively short: she debuted as Juliet in 1829 (having studied the role for three weeks before going on stage) and spent three years on stage in London and two touring the United States before marrying Pierce Butler and retiring. When the two divorced in 1847, however, she returned to the stage to support herself.

She experienced moderate success returning to the roles she had played in her youth, but she found her greatest success as a monologist. She would perform all the roles in one of Shakespeare's plays in two hours, doing different voices and abridging as necessary. Her career as a monologist might be seen as a bridge between writing and acting, which she complained was always about interpreting another's work rather than creating one's own. In her memoirs as in her performances of Shakespeare, she decided which parts of existing texts—be they Shakespeare's plays or her own letters—to present and how to present them.

Dickerson, Vanessa D. *Dark Victorians*. Urbana: University of Illinois Press, 2008. Print.

Heilburn, Carolyn. *Writing a Woman's Life*. New York: Ballantine, 1988. Print.

Jenkins, Rebecca. *Fanny Kemble: A Reluctant Celebrity*. New York: Simon & Schuster, 2005. Print.

Johnson, Claudia. *American Actress: Perspective on the Nineteenth Century*. Chicago: Nelson-Hall, 1984. Print.

Kemble, Fanny. *Journal of a Residence on a Georgian Plantation in 1838–1839*. New York: Harper, 1863. Print.

Kemble, Fanny, and Catherine Clinton. *Fanny Kemble's Journals*. Cambridge, Mass.: Harvard University Press, 2000. Print.

Peterson, Linda H. *Victorian Autobiography: The Tradition of Self-Interpretation*. New Haven, Conn.: Yale University Press, 1986. Print.

Smith, Sidonie. *A Poetics of Women's Autobiography: Marginality and the Fictions of Self-Representation*. Bloomington: Indiana University Press, 1987. Print.

Abigail Mann

Zlata's Diary
A Child's Life in Sarajevo
Zlata Filipovic

Key Facts

Time Period:
Late 20th Century

Relevant Historical Events:
Bosnian War

Nationality:
Bosnian

Keywords:
war; ethnicity; siege

OVERVIEW

Zlata's Diary: A Child's Life in Sarajevo (1994) is Zlata Filipovic's firsthand account of the dangers and hardships her family faced during the Bosnian War. Beginning in September 1991 when she was eleven and concluding in October 1993, Filipovic's story chronicles her struggle to survive wartime adversity, including food-supply shortages, cramped quarters, regular bombing and gunfire, and the untimely deaths of friends and family. As a girl of mixed heritage, she attempts to understand the ethnic conflict: "Among my girlfriends, among our friends, in our family, there are Serbs and Croats and Muslims. It's a mixed group and I never knew who was a Serb, a Croat or a Muslim. Now politics has started meddling around…. It wants to separate them."

Zlata's Diary was an instant best seller in France, thus sparking a bidding war among U.S. publishing houses. Filipovic's journal was also successful in the United States, though the media's frequent comparison of Filipovic to Anne Frank incited a controversy among critics. The teenage Filipovic was interviewed by television networks and newspapers the world over. ABC News named her the "Person of the Week," but in an ironic twist, Filipovic could not view the program due to a lack of electricity, as she writes in her diary: "Just as I can't see myself on TV tonight, so the rest of the world probably can't see the darkness I'm looking at. We're at two ends of the world." *Zlata's Diary* has since been translated into more than a dozen languages.

HISTORICAL AND LITERARY CONTEXT

On December 3, 1980, in Sarajevo, Bosnia, Filipovic was born to Malik and Alica Filipovic, a lawyer and biochemist, respectively. As the only child of prosperous parents, she enjoyed music lessons, tennis, parties, and American entertainment such as MTV. However, her carefree childhood was forever altered in the spring of 1992 with the dawn of the Bosnian War. This territorial conflict resulted from multiethnic discord between Serbs (Eastern Orthodox), Croats (Roman Catholics), and Bosniaks (Muslims). The Bosnian Serbs began their violent siege of Sarajevo in April, roughly seven months after Filipovic began her diary. By the end of April, Filipovic's friends began to flee the city. When shelling and gunfire reached Filipovic's neighborhood, the family hid in the "ugly, dark, smelly" cellar and listened to the "pounding shells, the shooting, the thundering noise overhead."

In October 1992 Filipovic heard that the United Nations Children's Fund (UNICEF) was searching for a child's diary to publish. Addressing her diary as a beloved friend, she wrote, "And so I copied part of you into another notebook and you went to the City Assembly to be looked at. And I've just heard that you're going to be published! You're coming out for the UNICEF Week! SUPER!" In the ensuing year, Filipovic wrote her private thoughts for an audience. UNICEF's Croat edition of *Zlata's Diary* found its way to Robert Laffont, a French publisher who pressured authorities into evacuating Filipovic and her family to Paris. There, the text was published in French under the title *Journal de Zlata* in 1993.

As stated in her foreword to *The Freedom Writers Diary*, Filipovic began writing her journal "before the war in Bosnia because I wanted to have a place to record my childhood and create something that I could look back on and laugh, cry and reminisce." She was inspired by the diaries of Frank, the adolescent Jewish girl who maintained a journal while hiding from the Nazis during World War II, and Adrian Mole, a fictional character created by Sue Townsend who realistically and humorously expresses the inner life of a teenage boy. Although Filipovic wanted her diary "to be funny, like Adrian Mole," it is most often compared to Frank's journal.

When Filipovic escaped Sarajevo, she felt "a responsibility to talk, to tell the story, the truth." Writing in 1994 in (Chicago) *Tribune Books,* Bettina Drew assessed the social, historical, and literary importance of *Zlata's Diary* thusly: "Filipovic kept a continuous record of life under siege … [and] hopes to use her new fame to help the seventy thousand children still in Sarajevo. In this regard, and as a historical document, her diary has indisputable meaning and value." In 2006 Filipovic and her coeditor, Melanie Challenger, collected diary entries from young people around the world who had endured war and published them as *Stolen Voices: Young People's War Diaries, from World War I to Iraq.*

Zlata Filipovic testifies on March 10, 1994, in Washington D.C., before the congressional Helsinki Commission. In 1993 the United Nations helped Zlata and her family escape Sarajevo. © AP IMAGES/ PATSY LYNCH

THEMES AND STYLE

Central to Filipovic's diary is the role the war played in interrupting her childhood. After the electricity was cut, the television went dark, and the stove ceased to work, a housebound Filipovic lived "in misery." She writes she was a "schoolgirl without a school," a "child without birds, without nature, without fruit, without chocolate or sweets, with just a little powdered milk." The diary reflects Filipovic's growing depression about the seemingly endless war: "Gone will be my childhood, gone my youth, gone my life. And I'll die and this war still won't be over." With terror raging throughout her city of birth, Filipovic wonders about the senseless violence, writing, "Today a shell fell on the park in front of my house.... A lot of people were hurt ... AND NINA IS DEAD. A piece of shrapnel lodged in her brain and she died ... an innocent eleven-year-old little girl—the victim of a stupid war. I feel sad. I cry and wonder why."

Filipovic's book is meant to be the "diary of an ordinary girl," notes Drew. When she began writing her journal, she did not intend for it to be published, nor did she imagine it would become a war diary. She later stated in the introduction to *The Freedom Writers Diary*, "Some of my older girlfriends had their own diaries.... I was absolutely certain that writing a diary was the right thing to do." When Filipovic's friends abandoned the city, she grew desperate for companionship. As stated in Geraldine Baum's *Los Angeles Times*' article, Filipovic "needed friends. My real ones were leaving or I couldn't see or talk to them." Remembering that Frank had named her diary "Kitty," Filipovic decided to call her diary "Mimmy." She began writing as if she were truly addressing a friend and frequently ended entries with "Love, Zlata."

Stylistically, *Zlata's Diary* is notable for its innocent and uninhibited tone. "The only calculation or self-consciousness here is of a familiar, winning sort: the self-dramatizing of little girls telling all to their diaries. The utter ordinariness of Miss Filipovic's sensibility is what makes her book touching.... She's Everygirl in a war zone," comments Francine Prose in the *New York Times Book Review*. In the *Los Angeles Times Book Review*, Jack Miles notes the poignancy of viewing the war through a child's eyes, writing that "the voice heard here, impotently and angrily repeating the word *stupid* is the recognizable voice of a little girl pushed past her limit and about to burst into tears."

CRITICAL DISCUSSION

By March 1994 *Zlata's Diary* was a best seller in France and had been published in twelve countries. In addition, the movie rights to the book had been purchased. Upon its publication in the United States, *Publishers Weekly* described it as a "vivid, sensitive diary" that "sounds an urgent and compelling appeal for peace." In *Booklist* Donna Seaman declared that Filipovic writes "with a precision and vision beyond her years" and "brings Sarajevo home as no news report can."

At age thirteen, Filipovic became the unlikely spokesperson for the tragedy occurring in Bosnia. She sincerely wanted her book to increase public awareness

THE FREEDOM WRITERS DIARY

In the early 1990s, twenty-three-year-old Erin Gruwell was a first-year English teacher at Wilson High School, an "at-risk" public institution in Long Beach, California. Gruwell was assigned to the ninth-graders no other teacher wanted: a bickering, resistant, multicultural collection of immigrants, products of abusive homes, the learning disabled, and gang-affiliated malcontents. Gruwell was determined to make a difference and looked for creative avenues to reach the students, going so far as to abandon the standard curriculum.

When Gruwell learned the students had never heard of the Holocaust, she found her in-road to teaching them about tolerance. Using *Anne Frank: The Diary of a Young Girl* and *Zlata's Diary*, Gruwell created a new curriculum that hit home with many of the students who had come from war-torn countries, witnessed gang wars, or were victims of intolerance. Gruwell's students began keeping their own journals, in which they wrote about their daily hardships, past suffering, and hopes for the future. Excerpts from these writings were published in 1999 under the title *The Freedom Writers Diary: How a Group of Extraordinary Teens Used Writing to Change Themselves and the World around Them*. In March 1996 Zlata Filipovic and her family were invited to meet Gruwell's students. In her foreword to *The Freedom Writers Diary*, Filipovic writes, "My diary partially inspired the Freedom Writers.... I hope this book will inspire people to write their own diaries, stories, poems, books, to fight prejudice."

of the war and draw attention to the innocent people still trapped there. Prose reported that the French publishers donated part of the book's profits to war relief and hoped the American publisher would do the same "to help all the Bosnian 'Anne Franks' whose stories still lack happy endings." The Bosnian War finally ended in December 1995, but not before it had claimed more than 100,000 lives, rendered half the city homeless, and divided an ethnically mixed nation into "mono-ethnic enclaves," according to Harriet Alexander in the *Telegraph*.

Zlata's Diary caused much controversy among U.S. critics who questioned the comparison between Filipovic and Frank. Some of these critics argued Filipovic's writing is inferior to Frank's, while others felt the comparison dishonored Frank's memory. After all, Filipovic and her family were able to escape war after two years while Frank was separated from her family and died in a concentration camp. Drew argues that Frank was a particularly gifted writer who "had time, in her attic hideout from the Nazis, to write at length in studied observation ... her story made more poignant by the tragic circumstances of her death. Zlata Filipovic, living under fire, lacked the physical environment for reflection and was not motivated by a driving literary ambition or ability." Meanwhile, Davic Rieff's *New Republic* article "Zlata's Diary: A Child's Life in Sarajevo" examines the authenticity of the U.S. version of *Zlata's Diary*. He claims there is "material in the book that sits oddly with Zlata's customary childish tone" and cites several differences between the Croat and English versions, saying, "Again and again, Zlata's references to various political events are nowhere to be found in the original edition of her diaries."

BIBLIOGRAPHY

Sources

Alexander, Harriet. "Zlata Filipovic." *Telegraph*. Telegraph Media Group, 7 Apr. 2012. Web. 17 Dec. 2012.

Baum, Geraldine. "Dreams of Peace." *Los Angeles Times* 15 Mar. 1994. Print.

Drew, Bettina. "Nothing Here Is Normal." *Tribune Books* 13 Mar. 1994. Print.

Filipovic, Zlata. Foreword. *The Freedom Writers Diary*, by Erin Gruwell. New York: Random House, 1999. Print.

———. Preface. *Zlata's Diary: A Child's Life in Wartime Sarajevo: Revised Edition*. New York: Penguin, 2006. Print.

Miles, Jack. "Will the Shelling Never Stop: A Bosnian Girl Bears Witness." *Los Angeles Times Book Review* 27 Feb. 1994: 1, 15. Print.

Prose, Francine. "A Little Girl's War." *New York Times Book Review* 6 Mar. 1994. *General OneFile*. Web. 8 Dec. 2012.

Rev. of *Zlata's Diary: A Child's Life in Sarajevo*, by Zlata Filipovic. *Publishers Weekly* 21 Feb. 1994: 245. *Literature Resource Center*. Web. 8 Dec. 2012.

Rieff, Davic. Rev. of *Zlata's Diary: A Child's Life in Sarajevo*, by Zlata Filipovic. *New Republic* 28 Mar. 1994: 31+ *General OneFile*. Web. 8 Dec. 2012.

Seaman, Donna. Rev. of *Zlata's Diary: A Child's Life in Sarajevo*, by Zlata Filipovic. *Booklist* 1 Mar. 1994: 1138. *Literature Resource Center*. Web. 8 Dec. 2012.

Further Reading

"Author Collects Stories of Young Voices in Wartime." *Talk of the Nation* 1 Feb. 2007. *Literature Resource Center*. Web. 8 Dec. 2012.

Bellafante, Ginia. "Are You There, NBC? It's Me. Zlata." *Time* 21 Mar. 1994: 24. Print.

Filipovic, Zlata. Foreword. *Milosevic: The People's Tyrant*. London: I. B. Tauris, 2004. Print.

Filipovic, Zlata, and Melanie Challenger. *Stolen Voices: Young People's War Diaries, from World War I to Iraq*. New York: Random House, 2006. Print.

Lehmann-Haupt, Christopher. "Another Diary of a Young Girl." *New York Times* 28 Feb. 1994: C15. Print.

Vasilakis, Nancy. Rev. of *Zlata's Diary: A Child's Life in Sarajevo*, by Zlata Filipovic. *Horn Book Magazine* Sept.–Oct. 1994: 605. *Literature Resource Center*. Web. 8 Dec. 2012.

Viorst, Judith. "Girl in the Crossfire." *Washington Post Book World* 20 Mar. 1994: 2. Print.

"Zlata Filipovic." *Contemporary Authors Online*. Detroit: Gale, 2003. *Literature Resource Center*. Web. 8 Dec. 2012.

Maggie Magno

Subject Index

Italic page numbers indicate illustrations. **Bold** page numbers and titles refer to main articles.

A

AAC. *See* Army Air Corps
Aaron, Daniel, **2**:271
Abandoned Baobab, The (Bugul), **1:61–64**
Abandonment, Bugul (Ken) on experience of, **1**:61–62
a/b: Auto/Biography Studies (journal), **1**:246
Abbey, Edward, *Desert Solitaire*, **1**:234
Abbey Theatre (Dublin), **2**:126, 128
Abbott, Lyman, **1**:52
Abdel-Fattah, Randa, *Does My Head Look Big in This?*, **1**:41–42
Abdo, Diya M., **3**:49
Abdul Hamid (Ottoman sultan), **2**:106
"Able-bodied," social construction of concept, **1**:8
Abolition, of slavery
    in Britain and British colonies, **1**:34, 81, 111, **3**:23
    in Cuba, **3**:7
    in U.S., **1**:33, 50
Abolitionist movement
    Adams (John Quincy) in, **2**:70
    in Britain, **1**:81–83, 111, **3**:23
    Douglass (Frederick) in, **1**:33
    Equiano (Olaudah) in, **1**:81–83
    Grimké (Charlotte Forten) in, **2**:29
    Higginson (Thomas Wentworth) in, **2**:238
    Jacobs (Harriet A.) in, **1**:142
    James (Henry) in, **2**:113
    Kemble (Fanny) in, **2**:335
    origins and rise of, **1**:142
    Prince (Mary) in, **3**:23, 25
    Ruete's (Emily) critique of, **1**:92
    "tragic mulatto" tradition in literature of, **1**:72
    in U.S. South vs. North, **1**:33
    Wheatley (Phillis) invoked in, **2**:45
Abootalebi, Ali R., **3**:220
Aboriginal Land Rights Act of 1976 (Australia), **3**:334
Aborigines, Australian
    Unaipon (David) on life as, **1**:149–151
    women, oral histories of, **3**:334–336
Aborigines' Friends' Association (AFA), **1**:149, 150, 151
Aborigines' Progressive Association, **1**:150
Abortion, in *A Mountainous Journey* (Tuqan), **1**:226, 227
About, Edmund, *Germaine*, **2**:115
Abouzeid, Leila, **3**:49
Abraham, Peter, **3**:251
Abraham Lincoln: A History (Nicolay and Hay), **3**:261–262
Abraham Lincoln: A Life (Burlingame), **3**:264
Abraham Lincoln: Complete Works (Nicolay and Hay), **3**:262

Abrams, Lynn
    A History of Everyday Life in Twentieth Century Scotland, **3**:173, 175
    Myth and Materiality in a Woman's World, **3**:175
    Oral History Theory, **3:173–175**, 179, 181, 285
    on *Women and Families* (Roberts), **3**:146
Abrash, Barbara, **3**:340
Abudi, Dalya, **1**:227
Abu Ghraib prison (Iraq), **3**:231
Account of Corsica (Boswell), **2**:328
Acculturation, in U.S., **1**:15–17. *See also* Assimilation
Accuracy. *See* Truth
Acebey, David, **3**:322
Achebe, Chinua, **1**:214
Acheson, Katherine O., **2**:64
Acker, Kathy, **1**:249
Acting career, of Kemble (Fanny), **2**:335–337
Actions, in identity, Rousseau (Jean-Jacques) on, **1**:200, 201
Acton, Carol, **2**:260, 261
Acts and Monuments, The (Day), **2**:97
Acts of Conscience (Taylor), **3**:227
Adamovich, Ales, **3**:282, 285
Adams, Abigail, **2:87**
    Adams's (John) correspondence with, **2**:316
    family of, **1**:133, **2**:69
    Letters of Mrs. Adams, **2**:87, 89
    "Letter to Her Daughter from the New White House," **2:87–90**

341

SUBJECT INDEX

Adams, Ansel, **3:**102
Adams, Charles Francis, **1:**132, **2:**69, 87, 89
Adams, Henry
   The Education of Henry Adams, **1:**15, **132–134**, 180
   Mont-Saint-Michel and Chartres, **1:**132
Adams, John, **1:**132, **2:**69, 87, 316
Adams, John Quincy, **2:**70
   The Diary of John Quincy Adams, **2:69–71**
   family of, **1:**132, *133*
   Kemble's (Fanny) friendship with, **2:**335
Adams, Judith Porter, *Peacework*, **3:268–271**
Adams, Lauren, **2:**296
Adams, Marian, **1:**133
Adams, Percy, **2:**206
Adams, Timothy, **1:**124
Adams, Timothy Dow, **1:**165
Adler, Nanci, **3:**19
Adolescents
   as audience for *Go Ask Alice* (anonymous), **2:294–296**
   as audience for *Red Scarf Girl* (Jiang), **1:**161, 162
   drug use by, **2:294–296**
Adopted Territory (Kim), **1:102–103**
Adoption
   interracial/intercultural, **1:102–104**
   tradition of memoirs of, **1:**102
Adventures of Huckleberry Finn (Twain), **1:**146, 147–148
Advice
   in *The Autobiography of Ben Franklin* (Franklin), **1:**179
   in *Letters to a Young Poet* (Rilke), **2:**149–150
   in *Walden* (Thoreau), **1:**234
Aesthetics, Ruskin's (John) writings on, **1:**264
AFA. *See* Aborigines' Friends' Association
Afejuku, Tony, **3:**253
Affirmative action, in U.S.
   establishment and purpose of, **1:**15

Rodriguez's (Richard) critique of, **1:**15, 16
   state bans on, **3:**20
Afghanistan
   Ahmedi (Farah) on life in, **1:**40–42
   Soviet war in, **1:**40, **3:**233
   Taliban in, rise of, **1:**40
   U.S. war in, **1:**42, **3:**207, 233
AFL. *See* American Federation of Labor
Africa. *See also specific countries*
   autobiographical tradition of, **1:**64
   borders in, establishment of, **1:**114
   colonial (*See* Africa, colonialism in)
   feminist autobiographies from, **1:**64
   Haley's (Alex) travels in, **1:**262
   idealization of, by Laye (Camara), **1:**130
   négritude movement in, **1:**61
   non–Africans' collaboration with authors of, **1:**64
   oral traditions of, **1:**64, **2:**242
   trauma literature of, **1:**313–314
   trickster stories of, **2:**3
Africa, colonialism in. *See also specific countries*
   Bugul (Ken) on legacy of, **1:**61–64
   cultural impacts of, **3:**141
   end of, **1:**3, 61
   in interior of continent, **3:**37
   Lessing (Doris) on experience of, **1:**167–169
   Nigerian Civil War and, **1:**215
   origins of, **1:**61, **3:**141, 251
Africa, Thomas W., **1:**221
African, The (Courlander), **1:**262
African American(s)
   citizenship for, **1:**50, **2:**38, 238
   in Civil War regiments, **2:**238–240, *239*
   communism among, **1:**3–5
   discrimination against (*See* Civil rights movement; Racism)
   family life of, **1:**273–275
   folklore of, **1:**9
   genealogy of, **1:**261–263
   in Great Depression, **3:**99
   Great Migration of, **1:**50, 52, 84, 273, **3:**99

   in interracial relationships, **1:**72–74
   Islam among, **1:**186–188
   lynchings of, **1:**18, 50
   masking tradition of, **1:**144
   in Reconstruction era, **1:**50
   as slaves (*See* Slave(s))
   in theater, rise of, **1:**273
   in Vietnam War, **3:**199–201
   voting rights for, **1:**50, **2:**238
   women (*See* African American women)
   in World War II, **3:**248–250
African American autobiographical writing. *See also* Slave narratives; *specific works and writers*
   by Angelou (Maya), **1:**18–20
   by Du Bois (W. E. B.), **1:**3–5
   by Grimké (Charlotte Forten), **2:**29–31
   by Haley (Alex), **1:**261–263
   by Hansberry (Lorraine), **1:**273–275
   by hooks (bell), **1:**249–251
   by Hurston (Zora Neale), **1:**9–11
   by King (Martin Luther, Jr.), **2:**32–34
   by Lorde (Audre), **2:**3–5
   by Malcolm X, **1:**186–188
   by McBride (James), **1:**72–74
   by McKay (Claude), **1:**84–86
   by Obama (Barack), **1:**78–80
   by Parks (Rosa), **1:**37–39
   as staple of African American literature, **1:**37
   tradition of, **3:**23–24
   by Wheatley (Phillis), **2:**44–46
   by Wright (Richard), **1:**122–124
African American identity. *See also* Multicultural and multiracial identities
   vs. feminist identity, of women, **2:**3
   Haley (Alex) on, **1:**261–263
   Obama (Barack) on, **1:**78–80
African American oral histories
   of civil rights movement, **3:**44–46, 99–101
   of Coe Ridge colony, **3:**90–92
   of Detroit, **3:**99–101

of higher education at white colleges, **3:**20–22

of Tuskegee Airmen, **3:**248–250

of Vietnam War veterans, **3:**199–201

African American Review (journal), **1:**250, **2:**5

African American women

Angelou (Maya) on lives of, **1:**18–19

in feminism, **1:**249, 250, **2:**3, 5

feminist vs. black identity of, **2:**3

hooks (bell) on lives of, **1:**249–250

as slaves, Jacobs (Harriet A.) on lives of, **1:**34, 35

African National Congress (ANC)

AIDS epidemic and, **3:**272, 274

establishment of, **2:**241

Luthuli (Albert) in, **1:**24, 25

Mandela (Nelson) in, **1:**27, 28, 29, **3:**242

Plaatje (Solomon Tshekisho) in, **2:**241

Africans in America (television miniseries), **3:**45

African Studies (journal), **3:**243

African Studies Review (journal), **3:**259

Africa Remembered (Curtin), **3:**141

Africa Today (journal), **1:**25, 115, **3:**142, 252

Afrikaners, **1:**27, **2:**241, **3:**242

Afro-American Studies (journal), **1:**187

Age (journal), **1:**48

Agenda (journal), **1:**39

Age of Illusion, The (Blythe), **3:**61

Agnew, Christopher S., **3:**126

Agosín, Marjorie

Always from Somewhere Else, **1:**75

A Cross and a Star, **1:**75–77, 99

Uncertain Travelers, **1:**75

Agrarian ideology, **2:**215

Agrarian reform movement, in Mexico, **3:**302–304

Agrarista movement, **3:**302–304

Agriculture, in England, oral histories of life in, **3:**59–61, 63–65

AHA Foundation, **1:**209

Ahimsa, **1:**243, 244

Ahmedi, Farah, *The Story of My Life,* **1:40–42,** *41*

Ahn Doo-hee, **1:**322

AIDS

emergence of, **3:**85

in South Africa, **1:**29, **3:**272–274

in U.S., **3:**85

AIDS Doctors (Oppenheimer and Bayer), **3:**272, 273, 274

Aiken, Katharine, **3:**339

AIM. *See* American Indian Movement

Ain't I a Woman (hooks), **1:**250

Airline industry, arbitration in, **3:**154

Ai Weiwei, **3:**301

Akazawa, Dennis, **3:**85

Akenfield: Portrait of an English Village (Blythe), **3:59–62**

Akharbach, Latifa, *Femmes et Politique,* **3:**47

Akhtar, Aasim Sajjad, **3:**178

Akiga's Story (East), **3:**141

Akiyama, Itsu, **3:**81

Alabama, Montgomery bus boycott in, **1:**20, 37, 38, 39, **2:**32, **3:**44, 45

Alan Paton Prize, for *Country of My Skull* (Krog), **3:**243

Albert (prince consort), **2:**209, 210

Alberti, Rafael, **1:**222

Alcatraz Island (San Francisco), AIM occupation of, **1:**54

Alcohol

in Appalachia, **3:**90, 91

in Idaho, **3:**95

Alcott, Amos Bronson, **1:**235

Alcott, Louisa May, **2:**223

Alexander, Elizabeth, **2:**4

Alexander, Harriet, **2:**340

Alexander, John, **1:**150, 151

Alexander, Margaret Walker, *Jubilee,* **1:**262

Alexander II (tsar of Russia), **1:**193, 195

Alexander the Great, **1:**105, 218

Alexandra Feodorovna, *The Last Diary of Tsaritsa Alexandra,* **2:84–86,** *85*

Alexievich, Svetlana

Boys in Zinc, **3:**285

Voices from Chernobyl, **3:**265, **282–286**

Alexis, Phil, **3:**108

Alexius Comnenus, **1:**285

Alger, Derek, **1:**297

Algeria

Amrouche (Fadhma Aïth Mansour) on life in, **1:**93–95

Feraoun (Mouloud) on life in, **2:**262–264

French colonial rule of, **1:**93–94, **2:**262–264

postcolonial, challenges facing, **2:**262

War of Independence in, **1:**93, **2:**262–264, *263*

Algerian War of Independence (1954–1962), **1:**93, **2:**262–264, *263*

Ali, Muhammad, **3:**44

Alienation

of Agosín (Marjorie), **1:**75

of American workers, **3:**343

of Amrouche (Fadhma Aïth Mansour), **1:**93–94

of Bugul (Ken), **1:**61–62

of Conrad (Joseph), **2:**192, 193

of Kim (Elizabeth), **1:**103

of Laye (Camara), **1:**128, 129

of Obama (Barack), **1:**78

of Ruete (Emily), **1:**90

of Santiago (Esmeralda), **1:**108–110

Alien Land Law of 1913 (California), **3:**195

ALIS. *See* Association du Locked-in Syndrome

All Change Here (Mitchison), **2:**235

Allen, Brooke, **2:**73

Allen, Harley, **3:**159

Allen, Hope Emily, **1:**191

Allen, Prudence, **2:**162

Allen, Roger, **1:**137

Allen, William Sheridan, *The Nazi Seizure of Power,* **3:**245

Allende, Isabel, **1:**76

Paula, **1:**222

Allende, Salvador, **1:**222, *223*

All God's Dangers (Rosengarten), **3:**73, 179

Allison, A. Lynn, **3:**290

Allison, Fred H., **3:**211

SUBJECT INDEX

Almayer's Folly (Conrad), **2:**192
Almost a Woman (Santiago), **1:**108, 109
Along Freedom Road (Cecelski), **3:**21
Along This Way (Johnson), **1:**13, 84, 122
Alonso, Harriet Hyman, **3:**270
'Alqam, Nabil, **2:**106
Alta California, oral histories of, **3:**114–116, *115*
Alter, Robert, **1:**272
Alternative Service Program, **3:**229
Alvarez, Julia, *How the Garcia Girls Lost Their Accents,* **1:**108
Alvarez-Borland, Isabel, **1:**297
Always a People (Kohn and Montell), **3:**107–109, 325
Always from Somewhere Else (Agosín), **1:**75
Al-Windawi, Mouayad, **2:**276
Al-Windawi, Thura, *Thura's Diary,* **2:**275–277
Amado, Jorge, **2:**8
Amador, José María, **3:**114–116
Amalric, Mathieu, **1:**7
Amanpour, Christiane, **2:**278
Ambrose, **1:**196, 197
Amerasian Immigration Act of 1982 (U.S.), **1:**170
America (journal), **2:**56, **3:**46, 309
America, Columbus's (Christopher) discovery of, **2:**201–203
American Anthropologist (journal), **3:**81, 142, 168, 320, 324
American Anti-Slavery Society, **1:**33, 142
American Arbitration Association, **3:**154
American autobiographical writing. *See also* African American(s); Asian American(s); Native American(s); *specific works and writers*
    by Adams (Abigail), **2:**87–90
    by Adams (Henry), **1:**132–134
    by Adams (John Quincy), **2:**69–71
    by Bechdel (Alison), **1:**139–141
    by Buck (Lucy), **2:**271–273
    by Carver (Jonathan), **2:**205–207
    by Chesnut (Mary Boykin Miller), **2:**250–252

    by Condict (Jemima), **2:**78–80
    by Conroy (Frank), **1:**164–166
    by Crèvecoeur (Michel-Guillaume Saint-Jean de), **2:**213–215
    by Dillard (Annie), **1:**279–281
    by Emerson (Ralph Waldo), **2:**139–141
    by Franklin (Benjamin), **1:**179–182
    by Gellhorn (Martha), **2:**101–103
    by Hawthorne (Nathaniel), **2:**223–225
    by Higginson (Thomas Wentworth), **2:**238–240
    by Houston (James D.), **1:**299–301
    by James (Henry), **2:**113–115
    by Jefferson (Thomas), **2:**316–318
    by Keller (Helen), **1:**43–46
    by Lee (Robert E.), **2:**38–40
    by McCarthy (Mary), **1:**258–260
    by McCourt (Frank), **1:**119–121
    by Medina (Pablo), **1:**296–298
    by Moore (Molly), **2:**278–280
    by Nabokov (Vladimir), **1:**270–272
    by Nin (Anaïs), **2:**123–125
    by O'Connor (Flannery), **2:**129–131
    by Olney (James), **1:**246–248
    by Plath (Sylvia), **2:**47–49
    by Poe (Edgar Allan), **2:**41–43
    by Rodriguez (Richard), **1:**15–17
    by Rowlandson (Mary), **1:**325–328
    by Santiago (Esmeralda), **1:**108–110
    by Sinor (Jennifer), **2:**163–165
    by Stanton (Elizabeth Cady), **1:**12–14
    by Stein (Gertrude), **1:**332–334
    by Stewart (Elinore Pruitt), **2:**91–93
    by Stone (Kate), **2:**244–246
    by Styron (William), **1:**204–206
    by Thoreau (Henry David), **1:**233–236
    by Twain (Mark), **1:**146–148
    by Ulrich (Laurel Thatcher), **2:**331–333

    by Wiesel (Elie), **1:**318–320
    by Williams (Tennessee), **2:**152–154
    by Wolff (Tobias), **1:**47–49
American Book Award
    for *Lakota Woman* (Brave Bird), **1:**23
    for *Sophie's Choice* (Styron), **1:**204
    for *The Unknown Internment* (Fox), **3:**225
American Cancer Society, **2:**3–4
American Childhood, An (Dillard), **1:**279
American Civil War (1861–1865)
    African American soldiers in, **2:**238–240, *239*
    Buck (Lucy) on life in South during, **2:**271–273
    Chesnut (Mary Boykin Miller) on life in South during, **2:**250–252
    conscientious objectors in, **3:**223
    diaries kept during, **2:**244, 271
    Douglass (Frederick) in, **1:**33
    Lee (Robert E.) in, **2:**38, 39–40
    Lincoln (Abraham) in, **3:**261
    slavery as issue in, **1:**50, **2:**38, 250
    start of, **2:**250, **3:**261
    Stone (Kate) on life in South during, **2:**244–246
American Dream
    Franklin (Benjamin) and, **1:**180
    Hispanic Americans' pursuit of, **3:**121, 122
    homesteading and, **2:**91
    Siv (Sichan) on, **1:**306, 307, 308
American Dreams (Terkel), **3:**300
American Ethnologist (journal), **3:**142
American Experience, The (television show), **3:**45
American Federation of Labor (AFL), **3:**328
American Historical Review (journal)
    on *Doña María's Story* (James), **3:**75
    on *The First Agraristas* (Craig), **3:**303
    on *Freedom Flyers* (Moye), **3:**249
    on *Hooligans or Rebels?* (Humphries), **3:**311

on *Survivors* (Miller and Miller), **3:**42

on *The Voice of the Past* (Thompson), **3:**188

on *Women in the Chinese Enlightenment* (Wang), **3:**148

American Indian Movement (AIM)
   Brave Bird (Mary) in, **1:**21–23
   FBI in conflicts with, **1:**96
   occupation of Alcatraz by, **1:**54
   occupation of Wounded Knee by, **1:**21, 22–23, 96
   origins of, **1:**21, 54
   Peltier (Leonard) in, **1:**96–98

American Indians. *See* Native American(s)

American Journal of Sociology, **3:**342

American Leaders in Nursing (Safeir), **3:**170

American Literary History (journal), **1:**173, **2:**4

American literature
   disability studies on, **1:**8
   realism in, rise of, **2:**240

American Mercury (journal), **2:**184

American Music (journal), **3:**133

American Notes (Dickens), **1:**43, 146, **2:**223

American oral histories. *See also* African American oral histories; Native American oral histories
   of anarchists, **3:**3–5
   of Appalachians, **3:**66–69, 86–89, 90–92
   of coal miners, **3:**66–69, 96–98, 337–339
   of colonial Californians, **3:**114–116
   of draft resisters, **3:**221–223
   of gay Asian Americans, **3:**83–85
   on Great Depression, **3:**161–163
   of Hispanic Americans, **3:**121–123, 131–133
   of Idaho homesteaders, **3:**93–95
   of Iraq War veterans, **3:**231–233
   of Italian Americans, **3:**224–226
   of IWW members, **3:**328–330
   of Japanese American internees, **3:**80–81, 102–104, 195–198
   of Japanese immigrants, first-generation, **3:**80–82
   of Japanese war brides, **3:**127–130, *128*
   of Jewish Americans, **3:**118–120
   of labor arbitrators, **3:**153–155
   of Lincoln (Abraham), **3:**261–264
   of Los Alamos residents, **3:**239–241
   of Mexican Americans, **3:**131–134
   of nuns, **3:**308–310
   of Nuremberg trial participants, **3:**293–295
   origins of field, **3:**186
   of Owens Valley residents, **3:**102–104
   recognition of value of, **3:**20, 90
   of teachers, **3:**77–79
   of Tuskegee Airmen, **3:**248–250
   on Vietnam War, **3:**199–201, 209–211, 221–223, 275–277
   on war on poverty, **3:**254–256
   of women coal miners, **3:**337–339
   of women immigrants, **3:**305–307, *306*
   of women peace activists, **3:**268–271
   on workers' experiences, **3:**343–345
   on World War II, **3:**202–204, 212–214, 224–226, 248–250

American Prospect (magazine), **1:**209

American Quarterly, **1:**71

American Revolutionary War (1775–1783)
   Adams (John Quincy) on, **2:**69
   autobiographies of era of, **1:**179–180
   Condict (Jemima) on life during, **2:**78–80
   conscientious objectors in, **3:**223
   Crèvecoeur (Michel-Guillaume Saint-Jean de) on, **2:**213, 214
   end of, **2:**69
   Franklin (Benjamin) on, **1:**179
   socioeconomic role of women after, **2:**331–332
   start of, **2:**69
   Wheatley's (Phillis) views on, **2:**44, 45

American Scholar (journal), **1:**280

"American Scholar, The" (Emerson), **1:**180

American Slave, The (Rawick), **1:**35

American Slavery as It Is (Weld), **1:**33, 142

American Sociological Review (journal), **3:**320

American Spectator (magazine), **1:**307

American Splendor (Pekar), **1:**139, **3:**330

American Studies (journal), **1:**35

American Theater (journal), **3:**213

American Transcendental Quarterly, **2:**141

American Woman Suffrage Association, **1:**12

American women. *See also* African American women
   as coal miners, oral histories of, **3:**337–339
   colonial, autobiographical writing by, **2:**78–79
   education of, in eighteenth century, **2:**316–318
   gender roles of, eighteenth-century, **2:**316
   gender roles of, twentieth-century, **2:**47
   as immigrants, oral histories of, **3:**305–307
   Mexican American, oral histories of, **3:**131–133
   as nuns, oral histories of, **3:**308–310
   after Revolutionary War, socioeconomic role of, **2:**331–332
   as teachers, oral histories of, **3:**77–79
   in women's rights movement, **1:**12–14, **2:**47

Americas (journal), **3:**116

America's Invisible Gulags (Fox), **3:**226

AmeriCorps, **3:**254

Amerika (Kafka), **2:**120

Améry, Jean, **1:**318

Amidist Buddhism, **2:**59

Amistad (film), **2:**71

Amistad case, **2:**70, 71

SUBJECT INDEX

Amman, John, *Black Man's Grave*, **1:**312
Ammonds, Edith, **2:**91
Ammonds, Ida Mary, **2:**91
Among You Taking Notes (Mitchison), **2:235–237**
'Amr, Sa'di, **2:**104
'Amr, Sāmī, *A Young Palestinian's Diary*, **2:104–106**
Amritsar (India), massacre of 1919 in, **1:**242, 289
Amrouche, Fadhma Aïth Mansour, *My Life Story*, **1:93–95**
Amrouche, Jean, **1:**93, 94, 95
Amrouche, Taos (Mary-Louise), **1:**94
　Jacinthe Noir, **1:**93
　in *My Life Story* (Amrouche), **1:**93, 94, 95
Analytical Review (journal), **1:**82
Anarchism, in U.S., **3:**3–5
Anarchist Voices (Avrich), **3:3–6**
ANC. *See* African National Congress
An Ch'ang-ho, **1:**324
Andersen, Hans Christian, **2:**166
Andersen, Hendrik C., **2:**115
Anderson, Helen, **2:60**
Anderson, John Lee, **2:**220
Anderson, John Q., **2:**244
Anderson, Nan, **3:**92
Anderson, Stuart, **3:**170, 171
Anderson, Thomas P., **3:**207
Anderson, W. E. K., **2:**310, 311
And Justice for All (Tateishi), **3:195–198**, 224
Andonian, Aram, *The Memoirs of Naim Bey*, **3:**40
Andreas, Friedrich, **2:**151
Andreas-Salomé, Lou, **2:**149, 151
Andrew, Donna T., **2:**330
Angela's Ashes (McCourt), **1:119–121**
Angelico, Fra, **1:**197
Angelou, Maya, **1:**19
　I Know Why the Caged Bird Sings, **1:18–20**, 249
　"On the Pulse of the Morning," **1:**20
　A Song Flung Up to Heaven, **1:**18
　in tradition of Prince (Mary), **3:**24
　Wolff (Tobias) compared to, **1:**47

Anglia (journal), **1:**121
Anglicanism
　Book of Common Prayer in, **2:**98
　Edward VI in, **2:**97–99
　in English Civil War, **2:**26, 72, 256
　establishment of, **2:**72
　Methodism's rise and, **2:**195
　vs. Puritanism, **2:**26, 27
　rise of, **2:**97–98
　in slavery, **3:**23
　Wesley (John) in, **2:**195–196
　Woodforde (James) as clergyman in, **2:**287–289, *288*
Anglo–Boer War (1899–1902), **2:**241–243, *242*
Anglo–German Agreement (1890), **1:**114
Anglo-Iranian Oil Company, **3:**218
Anglorum Speculum, **2:**63–64
Angoff, Charles, **2:**184–185
Animal Farm (Orwell), **2:**117, *118*
Anisfield-Wolf Book Award
　for *The Autobiography of Malcolm X* (Malcolm X), **1:**186
　for *The Color of Water* (McBride), **1:**73
　for *Dust Tracks on a Road* (Hurston), **1:**9
　for *Maasai* (Beckwith and Saitoti), **1:**114
Aniwaya, Anigia Gltodi, **3:**326
Anna Karenina (Tolstoy), **1:**193
Annals of Ballitore, The (Leadbeater), **2:157–159**
Annals of the American Academy of Political and Social Science, **1:**291, **2:**7, 17, **3:**252
Anna of the Five Towns (Bennett), **2:**136
Anne Frank: The Diary of a Young Girl (Frank). *See Diary of Anne Frank, The* (Frank)
Anne of Denmark, **2:**62
Annie's Baby (Sparks), **2:**294
An Phoblacht (newspaper), **3:**316
Ansary, Tamim, **1:**40
Anselment, Raymond, **2:**258

Antelope's Strategy, The (Hatzfeld), **3:**258
Anthony, Joseph, **2:**261
Anthony, Susan B., **1:**12, 13
Anthropology
　in Africa, rise of, **3:**37
　Hurston's (Zora Neale) work in, **1:**9, 11
　Underhill's (Ruth) success in, **1:**70
　The Worlds of a Maasai Warrior (Saitoti) in, **1:**115
Antiautobiography
　Autobiography: Essays Theoretical and Critical (Olney) on, **1:**246, 247
　Roland Barthes (Barthes) as, **1:**268–269
Anticolonialism
　of Gandhi (Mohandas), **1:**242–244, 289
　of Nehru (Jawaharlal), **1:**289–291
Anti-Confucianism, **3:**124, 126
Antimiscegenation laws, U.S., **1:**72
Antioch Review (journal), **1:**124, **2:**221
Antiquarianism, **2:**177, 179
Antiretroviral therapy (ART), **3:**272, 273, 274
Anti-Semitism. *See also* Holocaust
　in Chile, Agosín (Marjorie) on, **1:**75
　in Germany, of Hitler (Adolf), **1:**31–32
　in Germany, Stein (Gertrude) on, **1:**333
　in Great Depression, **3:**118
Antiwar views. *See also* Pacifism; Peace activists
　of Sassoon (Siegfried), **2:**247, 248
　in *Strange Ground* (Maurer), **3:**275
　during Vietnam War, **3:**221, 222, 275, 277
Antoon, Sinan, **1:**255, 257
Antwerp (Belgium), Cavendish's (Margaret) exile in, **1:**229
ANZAC. *See* Australian and New Zealand Army Corp
"ANZAC Memories" (Thomson), **3:**177, 178
Anzaldúa, Gloria, *Borderlands/The Fontera*, **1:**56

Apache, Geronimo on, **1:**302–304
Apartheid, South African
    AIDS epidemic and, **3:**272
    end of, **1:**25, **3:**242
    establishment of, **1:**24, 27, **3:**242
    Luthuli (Albert) on, **1:**24–26
    Mandela (Nelson) on, **1:**27–29
    Truth and Reconciliation Commission on, **3:**242–244
Apess, William, *A Son of the Forest,* **1:**56, **3:**318
A/PLG. *See* Asian Pacific Lesbians and Gays
Apologia Pro Vita Sua (Newman), **1:**65
Appalachian Journal, **3:**92
Appalachian oral histories
    of African Americans of Coe Ridge, **3:**90–92
    of coal miners, **3:**66–69, 86, 87, *87, 91,* 96–98
    on culture, **3:**86–89
Appalachian Oral History Project, **3:**86–88
Appalachian stereotypes, **3:**68, 86, 96
Applegate, Wash, **3:**95
Apted, Michael, **3:**53
Aptheker, Herbert, **1:**3, 4
Apuleius of Madaura, *The Golden Ass,* **1:**198
Aquash, Mi'kmaq Anna Mae, **1:**98
Arab, Si Abderrahmane, **2:**262
Arab(s), racial profiling of, **3:**195, 197
Arabic autobiographical writing. *See also specific works and writers*
    by Al-Windawi (Thura), **2:**275–277
    by 'Amr (Sāmī), **2:**104–106
    by Darwish (Mahmoud), **1:**255–257
    by Ghazzawi ('Izzat), **2:**50–52
    by Hussein (Taha), **1:**135–137
    by Ruete (Emily), **1:**90–92
    tradition of, **1:**135–136, 137, 285, **2:**50
    by Tuqan (Fadwa), **1:**225–227
    by Usāmah ibn Munqidh, **1:**285–288
    by women, rise of, **1:**225–226

Arab–Israeli War (1967), **1:**225
Arab Revolt (1936–1939), **1:**227, **2:**104
Arab slavery, **1:**90, 92
Arab Studies Journal, **1:**287
Arab-Syrian Gentleman and Warrior in the Period of the Crusades, An (Usamah), **1:285–288**
Arafat, Yasser, **2:**50
Aragon, Louis, **2:**52
Arbitration, labor
    vs. mediation, **3:**155
    oral histories on development of, **3:**153–155
Arcadia (Stoppard), **2:**145
Archambault, Paul, **1:**183, 184
Archdiocese of Guatemala, **1:**99
Archer, W. H., **2:**191
Arctic (journal), **3:**139
Arctic Dreams (Lopez), **1:**279
Arden, Jane, **2:**109
ARENA. *See* National Republican Alliance
Arendt, Hannah, **2:**22, 121
Arethas of Caesarea, **1:**220
Are You My Mother? (Bechdel), **1:**140, 141
Argentina
    coup of 1943 in, **2:**220, **3:**73
    Guevara (Ernesto "Che") in, **2:**220–222
    Jews in, **1:**75
    labor movement in, oral histories of, **3:**73–75
    Peronism in, **3:**73–75
Arias, Arturo, **3:**165
Ariel (Plath), **2:**47
Aristocracy
    Chinese, **3:**124, 125
    French, **2:**306–307
    Japanese, **2:**297
Aristotle, **2:**96
Arizona
    coal mining in, **3:**11, 292
    Mexican American women in, oral histories of, **3:**131–133
    Navajo–Hopi land dispute in, oral histories of, **3:**10–12

Arizona Quarterly, **1:**281, **3:**201
Arkansas, Angelou (Maya) on life in, **1:**18
Arkansas Historical Quarterly, **3:**197
Arkin, Mark, **2:**337
Armed Forces & Society (journal), **3:**207
Armenian genocide, oral histories of, **3:**40–42, *41*
Armitage, Susan, **3:**191–192
Armstrong, Liahna, **2:**163, 164
Army Air Corps (AAC), U.S., Tuskegee Airmen in, **3:**248–250
Army Life in a Black Regiment (Higginson), **2:238–240**
Arnett, Edward, **3:**229
Arnold, Matthew, **1:**181, **2:**147
Arntzen, Sonja, **2:**297, 298, 299
Arranged marriage
    in China, **1:**153, 154, 338, 339, **2:**170
    in Montenegro, **3:**136, 137
ART. *See* Antiretroviral therapy
Art, of Bashkirtseff (Marie), **2:**306, *307,* 308
Art criticism, by Ruskin (John), **1:**264, 265
Arthur, Chester, **3:**10
Arthur, Emry, **3:**159
Arthur Ruppin (Ruppin), **2:**104
Arvin, Newton, **2:**114–115
Asa-Asa, Louis, **3:**24
Ascham, Roger, **2:**99
Ascherson, Neal, **2:**102
Ashkenazic Jews, **3:**118, 119
Ashmore, Susan Youngblood, *Carry It On,* **3:**254
Ashton, Susanna, **1:**52
Asia, Polo's (Marco) travels in, **1:**105–107. *See also* Southeast Asia; *specific countries*
Asian Affairs (journal), **1:**307
Asian American(s). *See also* Japanese American(s)
    gay, oral histories of, **3:**83–85, *84*
    racism against, **1:**103, 171
    stereotypes of, **1:**173, 174

SUBJECT INDEX

Asian American autobiographical writing. *See also specific works and writers*
    by Hayslip (Le Ly), **1**:335–337
    by Houston (Jeanne Wakatsuki), **1**:299–301
    by Kim (Elizabeth), **1**:102–104
    by Kingston (Maxine Hong), **1**:173–175
    by Min (Anchee), **1**:158–160
    by Nguyen (Kien), **1**:170–172
    by Siv (Sichan), **1**:306–308
    by Uchida (Yoshiko), **1**:309–311

Asian Pacific Lesbians and Gays (A/PLG), **3**:83, 84, 85

Asian Review of Books, **3**:16

Asian Studies Review (journal), **3**:148

As I Crossed a Bridge of Dreams (Sarashina), **2:189–191**, 290–291

Asisara, Lorenzo, **3**:114–116

Ask the Fellows Who Cut the Hay (Evans), **3:**59, **63–65**

Asleson, David, *Up the Swiftwater*, **3**:93

Assassination
    of Kennedy (John F.), **3**:254
    of Kim Ku, **1**:322
    of King (Martin Luther, Jr.), **1**:20
    of Lincoln (Abraham), **2**:246, **3**:261
    of Malcolm X, **1**:186, 188

Assimilation, in Australia, of Aborigines, **1**:149, 151, **3**:334

Assimilation, in U.S.
    of Japanese war brides, **3**:127
    of Native Americans, **3**:109
    oral histories of, **3**:305–307
    of refugees, **1**:307
    Rodriguez (Richard) on experience of, **1**:15–17
    Santiago (Esmeralda) on experience of, **1**:108

Association du Locked-in Syndrome (ALIS), **1**:7

Astell, Mary, *A Serious Proposal to the Ladies*, **2**:35

"As-told-to" accounts, of Native Americans, **1**:56

Atheism, of Darwin (Charles), **1**:65–67

Atlanta Compromise Address (Washington), **1**:50

Atlantic (magazine), **2**:335, **3**:61

Atlantic Monthly (magazine)
    Army Life in a Black Regiment (Higginson) in, **2**:238, 239–240
    Hawthorne's (Nathaniel) letters in, **2**:224
    Letters of a Woman Homesteader (Stewart) in, **2**:91, 92
    "Life in the Sea Islands" (Grimké) in, **2**:31
    Life on the Mississippi (Twain) in, **1**:146, 147
    on *The Story of My Life* (Keller), **1**:44

Atlantis (journal), **2**:131

Atom Boy (Osamu), **1**:293

Atomic weapons. *See* Nuclear weapons

At the Edge of the Abyss (Koker), **2**:253

"At the Home of Frederick Douglass" (Grimké), **2**:29

Audacity of Hope, The (Obama), **1**:78, 80

Auden, W. H., **1**:125, 276, **2**:147, 150

Audience
    adolescent, of *Go Ask Alice* (anonymous), **2**:294
    adolescent, of *Red Scarf Girl* (Jiang), **1**:161, 162
    authors' pact with, Lejeune (Philippe) on, **1**:239–240, **2**:174
    construction of memoirs to appeal to, **1**:164
    of *De Profundis* (Wilde), **2**:10
    European, of *Letters from an American Farmer* (Crèvecoeur), **2**:213, 214
    European, of *The Autobiography of Ben Franklin* (Franklin), **1**:181
    of letters, **2**:217
    white (*See* White audience)
    of *The Woman Warrior* (Kingston), **1**:174, 175

Audio adaptations, of *Dreams from My Father* (Obama), **1**:80

Augustine (saint), **1:197**
    City of God, **1**:198
    Confessions, **1**:183, 193, **196–199**, 201
    Dialogues, **1**:186

An Interrupted Life (Hillesum) on, **2**:22, 24
    Malcolm X compared to, **1**:186, 188
    Olney (James) on, **1**:248
    Retractions, **1**:196, 198
    Soliloquies, **1**:196
    Teresa of Ávila influenced by, **1**:211

Augustus (Roman emperor), **1**:218, 220

"Auld Robin Gray" (Barnard), **2**:217, 218

Auschwitz and After (Delbo), **3**:34

Auschwitz concentration camp, **1**:318–320, **2**:22, **3:35**, 51

Ausgabe, Kritische, **2**:120

Auslander, Shalom, **2**:255

Aus Meinem Leben (Goethe). *See Truth and Fiction Relating to My Life* (Goethe)

Austen, Jane, **2**:133, 287, 289, 312

Auster, Paul, *The Invention of Loneliness*, **1**:279

Austin, Kelly, **1**:223

Australasian Journal of American Studies, **2**:30

Australia
    Aborigines of, **1**:149–151, **3**:334–336
    British colonial rule of, **1**:149
    Unaipon (David) on life in, **1**:149–151
    Vietnamese refugees in, **1**:337
    Warlpiri people of, oral histories of, **3**:334–336
    in World War I, **3**:177

Australian and New Zealand Army Corp (ANZAC), **3**:177

Australian Journal of French Studies, **2**:81

Australian Journal of International Affairs, **3**:207

Austria
    Jewish immigration to China from, **3**:14–16
    Satrapi (Marjane) in, **1**:155, 156

Authenticity. *See also* Truth
    of *Black Boy* (Wright), **1**:124

of *Memories of a Catholic Girlhood* (McCarthy), **1**:260
of *The Sovereignty and Goodness of God* (Rowlandson), **1**:326
of *A Woman in Berlin* (anonymous), **2**:282
Author(s)
   autobiography's relationship to, Barthes (Roland) on, **1**:267–268
   in pact with audience, Lejeune (Philippe) on, **1**:239–240, **2**:174
Authority, shared, in oral histories, **3**:179–181, 190
Authorship
   of *Chona* (Chona and Underhill), **1**:69
   of *Go Ask Alice* (anonymous), **2**:294
   of *Incidents in the Life of a Slave Girl* (Jacobs), **1**:144
   of *Journal of the First Voyage to America* (Columbus), **2**:201, 203
   of *Left Handed, Son of Old Man Hat* (Dyk), **3**:318, 319, 320
   meaning of, Barthes (Roland) on, **1**:267–269
   of *Mein Kampf* (Hitler), **1**:30, 32
   of oral histories, **3**:179
   of slave narratives, **1**:82–83
Autobiographical Pact, The (Lejeune), **1**:239–241
Autobiographical studies
   Barthes (Roland) in, **1**:267–269
   D'Israeli (Isaac) in, **2**:177–179
   Lejeune (Philippe) in, **1**:239–240, **2**:174–175
   Olney (James) in, **1**:246–248
   origins and rise of, **1**:239–240, 246–248, **2**:174
Autobiography. *See also specific types and works*
   author's relationship to, Barthes (Roland) on, **1**:267–268
   definition of, **1**:239
   literary criticism as form of, **1**:247
   vs. memoir, **1**:248, 279
   origins and rise of, **1**:239, 246
   rules for genre of, **1**:239, 246
Autobiography (Mill), **2**:16
Autobiography (Oliphant), **2**:335

Autobiography (Thornton), **1**:230
Autobiography, 1743–1790 (Jefferson), **1**:179, **2**:69
Autobiography, An, or The Story of My Experiments with Truth (Gandhi), **1**:24, 242–245
Autobiography, An, with Musings on Recent Events in India (Nehru), **1**:289–292
Autobiography and Postmodernism (journal), **1**:167
Autobiography: Essays Theoretical and Critical (Olney), **1**:246–248, *247*
Autobiography in France (Lejeune), **1**:239, **2**:174
Autobiography of a Chinese Woman (Chao), **1**:338
Autobiography of Alice B. Toklas, The (Stein), **1**:332, 334
Autobiography of an Unknown Indian (Chaudhuri), **3**:251, 253
Autobiography of a Papago Woman, The (Underhill), **3**:318
Autobiography of a Runaway Slave (Barnet and Montejo). *See Biography of a Runaway Slave* (Barnet and Montejo)
Autobiography of a Schizophrenic Girl, The (Sechehaye), **1**:164
Autobiography of a Slave, The (Manzano), **3**:7
Autobiography of Ben Franklin, The (Franklin), **1**:179–182, **2**:213
Autobiography of Benjamin Rush (Rush), **1**:179–180
Autobiography of Charles Darwin, The (Darwin), **1**:65–68
Autobiography of Giambattista Vico, The (Vico), **1**:183–185
Autobiography of H.I.H. Soraya, The (Esfandiary), **3**:218
Autobiography of Malcolm X, The (Malcolm X), **1**:78, 186–188, **3**:44
Autobiography of W. E. B. Du Bois, The (Du Bois), **1**:3–5, *18*
Autobiography of William Butler Yeats, The (Yeats), **2**:127–128
Autoethnography
   Dust Tracks on a Road (Hurston) as, **1**:11
   Memoirs of an Arabian Princess from Zanzibar (Ruete) as, **1**:91

The Way to Rainy Mountain (Momaday) as, **1**:55
Automobile industry
   automation of, **3**:343
   in Detroit, **3**:99, 100, 101
Auyero, Javier, *Contentious Lives*, **3**:268
Avant-garde memoirs
   Bone Black (hooks) as, **1**:249
   The Diary of Anaïs Nin (Nin) as, **2**:123
   Stop-Time (Conroy) as, **1**:164
Avary, Myrta Lockett, **2**:250, 251
Aventure ambiguë, L' (Kane), **1**:61
Avery, Genevieve, **3**:94
Avery, Oral, **3**:94
Aviation, U.S.
   naval, oral histories of, **3**:202–204
   Tuskegee Airmen in, oral histories of, **3**:248–250
Avrich, Karen, **3**:3
Avrich, Paul
   Anarchist Voices, **3**:3–6
   Sasha and Emma, **3**:3
Awards, book. *See also* Nobel prizes
   for *Abraham Lincoln: A Life* (Burlingame), **3**:264
   for *Akenfield* (Blythe), **3**:59
   for *Angela's Ashes* (McCourt), **1**:120
   for *The Audacity of Hope* (Obama), **1**:80
   for *The Autobiography of Malcolm X* (Malcolm X), **1**:186
   for *The Barracks Thief* (Wolff), **1**:47
   for *The Cancer Journals* (Lorde), **2**:5
   for *The Color of Water* (McBride), **1**:73
   for *The Confessions of Nat Turner* (Styron), **1**:204
   for *Country of My Skull* (Krog), **3**:243
   for *The Dark Child* (Laye), **1**:128
   for *Dreams from My Father* (Obama), **1**:80
   for *Dust Tracks on a Road* (Hurston), **1**:9
   for *The Education of Henry Adams* (Adams), **1**:132, 134

SUBJECT INDEX

Awards, book, *continued*
    for *"The Good War"* (Terkel), **3:**161, 212, 234, 279, 343
    for *House Made of Dawn* (Momaday), **1:**54
    for *The Invisible Thread* (Uchida), **1:**309–310
    for *Lakota Woman* (Brave Bird), **1:**23
    for *Letters Underway* (Ghazzawi), **2:**50
    for *A Long Way Gone* (Beah), **1:**313
    for *Maasai* (Beckwith and Saitoti), **1:**114
    for *Memory and Narrative* (Olney), **1:**248
    for *An Oral History of Abraham Lincoln* (Burlingame), **3:**261
    for *The Order Has Been Carried Out* (Portelli), **3:**265, 267
    for *Pilgrim at Tinker Creek* (Dillard), **1:**279
    for *Red Scarf Girl* (Jiang), **1:**161
    for *Riwan ou le chemin de sable* (Bugul), **1:**64
    for *Roots* (Haley), **1:**261
    for *Sophie's Choice* (Styron), **1:**204
    for *Thura's Diary* (Al-Windawi), **2:**275
    for *The Unknown Internment* (Fox), **3:**225
    for *Voices from Chernobyl* (Alexievich), **3:**282
    for *Wild Swans* (Chang), **1:**159
    for *The Woman Warrior* (Kingston), **1:**173
Axelrod, Steven Gould, **2:**48–49
Axford, Roger W., *Too Long Been Silent,* **3:**196
Ayres, Lew, **3:**228
Ayyam, al- (Hussein). *See Egyptian Childhood, An* (Hussein)
Ayyam al-'Arab, **1:**137
Azuma, Eiichiro, **3:**82

B

B., David, *Epileptic,* **1:**155
Baath party (Iraq), **2:**275, 276

Baba of Karo (Smith), **3:**141
Baby boomers
    drug use by, **2:**294
    Mexican American, **3:**133
    Soviet, oral histories of, **3:**331–333
    in workforce, **3:**343
Baby Doll (film), **2:**152
Back Bay Banner (periodical), **1:**274
Back in the World (Wolff), **1:**47
Bacon, Francis, **2:**66
Badenhausen, Richard, **1:**331
Baden-Powell, Robert, **2:**243
Bad War, The (Willenson), **3:**275
Baer, Allison, **1:**41–42
Baer, Elizabeth, **2:**271, 272, 273
Baer, Elizabeth R., **3:**36
Baez, Joan, **3:**159
Bagehot, Walter, **2:**35, 36
Baggett, Paul, "Caught between Homes," **1:**113
Baghdad (Iraq)
    in Iraq War, **2:**275–276, **3:**231
    Jewish immigration to China from, **3:**16
Baghdad Burning (Riverbend), **2:**275
Baghdad Burning II (Riverbend), **2:**275
Bagnold, Enid
    Brittain (Vera) compared to, **1:**329, **2:**259
    The Chalk Garden, **2:**259, 261
    The Chinese Prime Minister, **2:**261
    A Diary without Dates, **1:**329, **2:**259–261
    The Happy Foreigner, **2:**259
    National Velvet, **2:**259, 260, 261
    Sassoon (Siegfried) compared to, **2:**247
Bahr, Howard, *The Navajo as Seen by the Franciscans,* **3:**290
Bailer, Kermit G., **3:**100
Bailey, Kevin, **3:**187
Bailey, Peter J., **1:**48
Baillie, F. D., **2:**241
Bai Wei, *Tragic Life,* **1:**338
Baker, Alison, *Voices of Resistance,* **3:**47–49
Baker, Donald M., **3:**256
Baker, Felicity, **1:**202

Baker, Godfrey Evan, **2:**229
Baker, Ida, **2:**133
Baker, James T., **3:**162
Baker, Mark, *Nam,* **3:**199, 209, 210, 221, 231
Baker, Simon, **1:**126
Baker, William Massing, **2:**229
Bakgatla tribe, **2:**237
Bakhtiar, Shapour, **3:**220
Bakunin, Mikhail, **2:**120
Balaban, John, **3:**222
Balch, J. S., **1:**85
Baldick, Robert, **2:**81, 83
Baldwin, James
    Go Tell It on the Mountain, **1:**167, 261
    Notes of a Native Son, **1:**79–80
    on *To Be Young, Gifted and Black* (Hansberry), **1:**274
    Wright's (Richard) influence on, **1:**122, 124
Baldwin, Roger, **3:**329
Baldwin, William, **2:**99
Balkan Wars (1912–1913), **3:**135, 293, 294
Ball, Dewi Ioan, *Fighting Words,* **1:**97
Ballad of Reading Gaol, The (Wilde), **2:**9
Ballantyne, James, **2:**310
Ballard, Ephraim, **2:**333
Ballard, George, **1:**231
Ballard, Martha, **2:**331–333
Ballard, Molly, **3:**92
Ballent, Anahi, **3:**75
Ballet, inspired by Unaipon (David), **1:**149
Bampfield, Joseph, **1:**315, 316
Bancroft, Hubert H., **3:**114, 116
Banerjee, A., **2:**153
Bangarra Dance Theatre, **3:**335
Bangladesh, establishment of, **1:**87
Banjo (McKay), **1:**86
Banks, Ann, *First Person America,* **3:**161
Banks, Dennis, **1:**23
Banta, Martha, **2:**115
Bánzer, Hugo, **3:**322
Baobab fou, Le (Bugul). *See Abandoned Baobab, The* (Bugul)
Barbalet, Margaret, **3:**313

Barber, Denise, **3**:345
Barberini, Francesco, **1**:220
Barefoot Gen (Nakazawa), **1:293–295**
Barker, Eileen, **3**:41
Barker, Pat, **2**:248
Barlow, Joel, **2**:109
Barlow, Nora, **1**:67
Barmé, Geremie, **3**:288
Barnard, Anne, **2:218**
    "Auld Robin Gray," **2**:217, 218
    Journal of a Tour into the Interior, **2**:217, 218
    The Letters of Lady Anne Barnard to Henry Dundas, **2:217–219**
Barnes, Djuna, **1**:333
Barnes, Steven A., **3**:19
Barnet, Miguel, *Biography of a Runaway Slave,* **3:7, 7–9**
Barnouw, Dagmar, **1**:248
Barracks Thief, The (Wolff), **1**:47
Barre, Mohamed Siad, **1**:207
Barrel of a Pen (Ngũgĩ), **2**:12
Barrett, S. M., *Geronimo: His Own Story,* **1:302–305**
Barrio Boy (Galarza), **1**:15
Barrios de Chungara, Domitila
    Here Too, Domitila, **3**:322
    Let Me Speak!, **3**:74, 114–115, **322–324**
Barry, Tom, *Guerilla Days in Ireland,* **3**:27
Barth, Karl, **2**:167
Barthes, Roland, **1:268**
    "The Death of the Author," **1**:267, 269
    Michelet par lui-même, **1**:267
    Roland Barthes, **1**:249, **267–269**
Bartlett, Rosamund, **1**:194, 195
Bashkirtseff, Marie
    The Journal of Marie Bashkirtseff, **2:306–308**
    The Last Confessions of Marie Bashkirtseff, **2**:306
    paintings of, **2**:306, *307*, 308
Baskin, John, *New Burlington,* **3**:86
Basler, Roy Prentice, *Collected Works of Abraham Lincoln,* **3**:262
Bass, Jonathan S., **2**:33–34
Bastien-Lepage, Jules, **2**:306

Bataille, Gretchen, **1**:23
Batchelor, Joy, **2:118**
Bates, Carl Murray, **3**:344
Bates, Edwin Morris, **2**:317
Batista, Ernesto, **2**:222
Batista, Fulgencio, **1**:296, *297*
Battlefields (television series), **3**:236
Battle of Valle Giula, The (Portelli), **3**:97, 157
Bauby, Jean-Dominique, *The Diving Bell and the Butterfly,* **1:6–8**
Baum, Geraldine, **2**:339
Baum, Oskar, **2**:120
Baum, Willa, **3**:188
Bauman, Janine, **3**:51
Baumel, Judith, *Double Jeopardy,* **3**:35
Baumgartner, Barbara, **3**:24–25
Bautista, Paul, **3**:85
Bawer, Bruce, **1**:280
Bayer, Ronald
    AIDS Doctors, **3**:272, 273, 274
    Shattered Dreams?, **3:272–274**
Beagle, H.M.S., **1**:65, 66
Beah, Ishmael, *A Long Way Gone,* **1:312–314,** *313*
Beamon, Mike, **3**:211
Bean, Thomas W., **2**:276
Bearden, Russell, **3**:197
Beatrice (princess), **2**:210
Beatty-Medina, Charles, *Contested Territories,* **3**:326
Beauchamp, Kathleen Mansfield. *See* Mansfield, Katherine
Beauchamp, Leslie, **2**:133, 135
Beaudry, Catherine, **1**:202
Bechdel, Alison
    Are You My Mother?, **1**:140, 141
    Dykes to Watch Out For, **1**:139, 141
    Fun Home, **1:139–141,** *140*
Bechdel, Bruce, **1**:139, 140
Bechdel test, **1**:141
Becker, Marshall Joseph, **3**:109
Beckham, Edward, **2**:27
Beckwith, Carol, *Maasai,* **1**:114
Becoming Madame Mao (Min), **1**:159
Bede, **3**:186
Bedoukian, Kerop, *The Urchin,* **3**:40
Beebe, Rose Marie

    The History of Alta California, **3**:115
    Testimonios, **3**:116
Beer and Revolution (Goyens), **3**:5
Beerbohm, Max, **1**:253, **2**:289
Beer brewing, in English villages, **3**:64
Beer Hall Putsch (1923), **1**:30
Beevor, Anthony, **2**:281, 282
Begging to Be Black (Krog), **3**:242
Begin, Menachem, **1**:225
Behar, Ruth
    on *Songs My Mother Sang to Me* (Preciado Martin), **3**:133
    Traveling Heavy, **1**:297
Behind the Burqa (Yasgur), **1**:40
Behind the Scenes (Keckley), **1**:52
Behn, Aphra, **1**:315, **2**:324
Beier, Lucinda McCray, *For Their Own Good,* **3**:144–145
Beik, Mildred Allen, **3**:67, 68, 95
Beineix, Jacques, **1**:6, 7
Bcirne, Paul, **1**:324
Belarus
    censorship in, **3**:282–284
    Chernobyl nuclear disaster and, **3**:282–284
Belgium
    Bugul's (Ken) experience as African in, **1**:61–62
    Cavendish's (Margaret) exile in, **1**:229
    Congo as colony of, **2**:192–194
    Rwanda as colony of, **3**:257
    women miners in, **3**:337
Bell, Angelica, **2**:268
Bell, Anne Olivier, **2**:181–182
Bell, Clive, **2**:268
Bell, Ian, **1**:202
Bell, Vanessa, **2**:268
Bellanca, Mary Ellen, **2**:301
Belles Lettres (journal), **1**:280
Bell Jar, The (Plath), **2**:47
Bells of Nagasaki, The (Nagai), **1**:293
Beloved Land (Preciado Martin), **3**:131
Beltrán, Alberto, **3**:167
Benally, Malcolm D., *Bitter Water,* **3:10–13**
Benderman, Kevin, **3**:229

Benét, William Rose, **2:**185
Bengal
    British colonial rule of, **2:**328, **3:**253
    Mahomet (Dean) in, **2:**229–231
    religious riots of 1946 in, **1:**244
Bengali Girls Don't (Sherman), **1:**312
Bennett, Andrew, **2:**134
Bennett, Arnold, **2:137**
    Anna of the Five Towns, **2:**136
    Clayhanger trilogy, **2:**136, 137
    Hilda Lessways, **2:**138
    The Journals of Arnold Bennett, **2:136–138**
    Letters of Arnold Bennett, **2:**138
    A Man from the North, **2:**136
    The Old Wives' Tale, **2:**136
    Woolf (Virginia) on novels of, **2:**137, 138
Bennett, James, **3:**311–312, 313
Bennett, John, *Uqalurait*, **3:**107, **138–140**
Bennett, W. C., **3:**320
Bennett, Yvonne, **1:**331
Bentham, Jeremy, **2:**177
Benyon, Hew, **3:**54
Berber Academy, **1:**93
Berber culture
    in Morocco, **3:**47
    preservation of, **1:**93–95
Berber Dahir, **3:**47
Beresford, John, **2:**287
Bergen, Doris, **2:**24
Bergen-Belsen concentration camp, **2:**253, **3:**51
Bergin, Thomas Goddard, **1:**183, 184, 185
Bergreen, Laurence, **2:**203
Berisso (Argentina), oral history of life in, **3:**73–75
Berkeljon, Sara, **1:**207
Berkowitz, Leah, **2:**273
Berlin (Germany)
    Soviet occupation of, **2:**281–282
    Spandau prison in, **2:**54–56, 55
Berlin, Isaiah, **1:**185
Berlin Wall, fall of, **3:**247
Berman, Marshall, **3:**344–345

Bermuda, oral histories of slavery in, **3:**23, 23–25
Bernard, Gretchen Dobrott, **2:**131
Berne, Suzanne, **1:**280
Bernstein, Gail Eiseman, **3:**119
Bernstein, Irving, **3:**154
Berridge, Virginia, **3:**170, 171
Bertaux, Daniel, *Living through the Soviet System*, **3:**331
Bertraux-Wiame, Isabelle, **3:**188
Best, Nicholas, *Five Days That Shocked the World*, **3:**235
Beston, John, **1:**150–151
Beti, Mongo, **1:**130
Betts, Paul, **3:**247
Between Management and Labor (Friedman), **3:153–156,** 157
Bevan, Nye, **2:**235
Beverley, John, **3:**74
Beyond Manzanar (Houston), **1:**299
Bhabha, Homi, **1:**87
BIA. *See* Bureau of Indian Affairs
Biafran War, **1:**312
Biblical references
    in *Confessions* (Augustine), **1:**196
    in *An Interrupted Life* (Hillesum), **2:**22
    in *Jemima Condict* (Condict), **2:**79
    in *The Sovereignty and Goodness of God* (Rowlandson), **1:**326
    in *The Story of My Life* (Keller), **1:**44
Bicknell, Alexander, **2:**207
Biddle, Francis, **3:**224
Biel, Steven, **3:**4, 5
Bierce, Ambrose, **2:**240
Bigelow, John, **1:**179, 181
Biggs, Henry, **3:**99
Big Sea, The (Hughes), **1:**84, 122
Big Woods (Faulkner), **2:**215
Bilbo, Theodore, **1:**123
Bildungsroman, **1:**30, **2:**221
Bilingual education, in U.S., **1:**15–17
Bilingual Education Act of 1968 (U.S.), **1:**17
Billington, Ray Allen, **2:**29
Bingham, Caleb, *The Columbian Orator*, **1:**33–34
Binoche, Juliette, **3:**242

Biographies, origins and rise of, **2:**177, 178
Biography (journal), **1:**205, 290, **2:**77, 175, **3:**73, 233
Biography of a Runaway Slave (Barnet and Montejo), **3:7–9**
Biomythography, *Zami* (Lorde) as, **1:**9, 39, 249
Bioy Casares, Adolfo, *Rest for Travelers*, **1:**223
Biracial individuals. *See* Multiracial individuals
Bird, Stewart, *Solidarity Forever*, **3:328–330**
Bird by Bird (Lamott), **1:**280
Birley, Anthony, **1:**220
Birmingham News (newspaper), **2:**32
Birrell, Augustine, **2:**126
Bishop, Elizabeth, **2:**129
Bisisu, Mu'in, **2:**52
    Palestinian Notebooks, **2:**50
Bisky, Jens, **2:**281
Bismarck, Otto von, **1:**90
Bitsui, Roman, **3:**12
Bitter Water (Benally), **3:10–13**
Black (color), hooks (bell) on meanings of, **1:**250
Black Americans. *See* African American(s)
Black Bolshevik (Haywood), **1:**4
Black Boy (Wright), **1:122–124**
Black Chronicle, The (Hampton), **3:**44
Black Collegian (journal), **1:**250
Black Cuban, Black American (Grillo), **1:**296
Black Elk, Benjamin, **3:**110
Black Elk, Nicolas, *Black Elk Speaks*, **1:**21, 56, 302, **3:110–113,** *111*, 318
Black Elk Speaks (Black Elk and Neihardt), **1:**21, 56, 302, **3:110–113,** 318
Blackest Page in Modern History, The (Gibbons), **3:**40
Black Flame trilogy (Du Bois), **1:**5
Blackgoat, Roberta, **3:**292
Black Hawk, **1:**302
Black Hawk War (1832), **1:**302
"Black History, Oral History, and Genealogy" (Haley), **3:**186

Black identity. *See* African American identity

Black Man's Grave (Stewart and Amman), **1**:312

Black Mesa (Arizona)
    coal mining on, **3**:10, 292
    Navajo–Hopi land dispute in, oral histories of, **3**:10–12

Black Muslims, **1**:186, 188

Black nationalism
    of Du Bois (W. E. B.), **1**:4
    of Malcolm X, **1**:78
    Obama's (Barack) rejection of, **1**:78, 79

Black Panthers, **3**:200

Black Power movement, **1**:21

Blacks at Harvard (Sollors et al.), **3**:21

Black Unicorn, The (Lorde), **2**:4

Blackwood's Edinburgh Magazine, **3**:25

Blackwood's Magazine, **1**:316

Black Words, White Page (Shoemaker), **1**:150, 151

Black Worker in the Deep South (Hudson), **1**:3

Blaeser, Kimberly, **1**:56

Blair, Dorothy S., **1**:93, 94, 95

Blair, Hugh, **2**:109

Blair, Walter, **1**:148

Blake, Debra J., **3**:132, 133

Blake, Lillie Devereux, **2**:89

Blalock, Lucy Sadie Parks, **3**:108

Blaxhall (England), oral histories of life in, **3**:63–65

Blayney, Michael, **1**:262

Blessed by Thunder (Fernández Barrios), **1**:296

Blight, David W., **3**:266–267

Blindness
    of Hussein (Taha), **1**:135, 136, 137
    Keller (Helen) on experience of, **1**:43–46

Blithedale Romance, The (Hawthorne), **2**:225

Blixen, Karen, **2**:12

Blood, George, **2**:110

Blood Diamond (film), **1**:312

Blood Meridian (McCarthy), **1**:304

Blood of Spain (Fraser), **3**:176

Bloods: An Oral History of the Vietnam War by Black Veterans (Terry), **3**:199–201
    Everything We Had (Santoli) vs., **3**:210
    Strange Ground (Maurer) vs., **3**:275
    The Strength Not to Fight (Tollefson) vs., **3**:221
    Tears before the Rain (Engelmann) vs., **3**:279, 280
    What Was Asked of Us (Wood) vs., **3**:231, 232

Bloody Harlan (Taylor), **3**:96

Bloom, David, **2**:237

Bloom, Harold, **2**:139

Bloomsbury group, **2**:133, 180, 268–269

Blue, Martha
    Indian Trader, **3**:290, 291
    The Witch Purge of 1878, **3**:290–292

Blue Genes (Lukas), **1**:204–205

Blue Octavo Notebooks, The (Kafka), **2**:122

Blue Peter (periodical), **2**:193

Bluest Eye, The (Morrison), **1**:19, 175

Bluett, Thomas, *Some Memories of the Life of Job,* **3**:141

Blumenfeld, Yorick, **3**:61

Blunden, Edmund, *Undertones of War,* **1**:329

Blythe, Ronald
    The Age of Illusion, **3**:61
    Akenfield, **3**:59–62
    on *A Country Parson* (Woodforde), **2**:288, 289
    A Treasonable Growth, **3**:61
    The View in Winter, **3**:60

Boarding schools
    experimental, Conroy (Frank) on, **1**:164
    Native Americans at, **3**:109, 318

Boas, Franz, **1**:9, 11

Boat people, Vietnamese, **3**:280

Boccaccio, Giovanni, *Decameron,* **1**:229

Body(ies)
    able, social construction of, **1**:8
    of black women, **1**:18
    in identity, Rousseau (Jean-Jacques) on, **1**:200, 201
    meatiness of, Suleri (Sara) on, **1**:89

Body and Soul (Conroy), **1**:166

"Body Talk" (Spitzack), **3**:190

Boehmer, Elleke, **2**:241–242, 243

Boer War, Second. *See* Anglo–Boer War

Boer War, The (Churchill), **2**:241

Boer War Diary of Sol Plaatje, The (Plaatje), **2**:241–243

Boethius, *Consolation of Philosophy,* **2**:14

Bogart, Barbara Allen, *From Memory to History,* **3**:90

Boggs, Grace Lee, **3**:101

Boggs, James, **3**:99

Bohannon, Horace Augustus, **3**:249

Bohr, Niels, **3**:239

Bolívar, Antonio, **3**:169

Bolivia, oral histories of working-class women in, **3**:322–324, *323*

Bolshevik Revolution (1917), **2**:84, **3**:331

Bolshevism, **1**:270, 271

BOMB (magazine), **1**:48

Bone Black (hooks), **1**:249–251

Bonhoeffer, Dietrich, **2**:22

BookBrowse, **1**:159

Booklist (magazine)
    on *Freedom Flyers* (Moye), **3**:249
    on *Habits of Change* (Rogers), **3**:309
    on *Into the Jet Age* (Wooldridge), **3**:203
    on *Between Management and Labor* (Friedman), **3**:155
    on *Prison Writings* (Peltier), **1**:97
    on *Red Scarf Girl* (Jiang), **1**:162
    on *Ten Thousand Sorrows* (Kim), **1**:104
    on *Thura's Diary* (Al-Windawi), **2**:276
    on *Untold Tales, Unsung Heroes* (Moon), **3**:100
    on "*We Have Just Begun to Not Fight*" (Frazer and O'Sullivan), **3**:229
    on *Zlata's Diary* (Filipovic), **2**:339

Bookman (journal), **2:**194
Book of Common Prayer, **2:**98
Book of Margery Kempe, The (Kempe), **1:189–192,** 211, **2:**226
Book of Memories, The (Shua), **1:**75
Book of My Mother (Cohen), **1:**99
Book of the City of Ladies, The (Christine), **2:**162
Books Abroad (magazine), **2:**17
Books & Culture (journal), **3:**68
Books Ireland (journal), **2:**159, **3:**316
Boomer, Walter E., **2:**278–279, 280
Boorman, John, **3:**68, 242
Booth, Alison, **2:**210–211, 337
Booth, John Wilkes, **3:**261
Bootlegging. *See* Moonshine
Bootstrap, Operation, **1:**108
Borden, Mary, *The Forbidden Zone,* **2:**259
Borderlands literature, *When I Was Puerto Rican* (Santiago) as, **1:**109
Borderlands/The Fontera (Anzaldúa), **1:**56
Bordin, Guy, **3:**139–140
Boren, Mark Edelman, **2:**114
Borges, Jorge Luis, **1:**224
Bornat, Joanna
  on *Daring Hearts* (Brighton Ourstory), **3:**72
  Oral History, Health and Welfare, **3:170–172**
Born on the Fourth of July (Kovic), **1:**335, **3:**209
Borowski, Tadeusz, **1:**318
Bosnia, Filipovic (Zlata) on life in, **2:**338–340
Bosnian War (1992–1995), **2:**338–339
Bosnik, Anton, **3:**235
Bosque Redondo Reservation, **3:**10, 290, *291*
Bostdorff, Denise M., **2:**33
Bostock, Lisa, **3:**171
Boston College, **3:**29
Boston Globe (newspaper), **1:**16, 72
Bostonians, The (James), **2:**113
Boston Irish Reporter, **3:**29
Boston Tea Party, **2:**79
Bostridge, Mark, **1:**330, **2:**269

Boswell, James, **2:329**
  Account of Corsica, **2:**328
  The Journal of a Tour to the Hebrides, **2:**328
  Life of Samuel Johnson, **2:**177, 195, 309, 328, 329–330
  London Journal, **2:328–330**
  Woodforde (James) compared to, **2:**287, 288
Bosworth, Johnny, **3:**344
Botswana, Mitchison's (Naomi) visits to, **2:**237
Bottrall, Margaret, **1:**316
Bouhaddou, Saadia, **3:**48
Boundary 2 (journal), **2:**128
Bourgeacq, Jacques, **1:**128
Bourne, Edward, **2:**206
Boutcher, Warren, **2:**256
Bow, Leslie, **1:**337
Bowden, George, **2:**135
Bowe, John, *Gig,* **3:**343, 345
Bowe, Marisa, *Gig,* **3:**343, 345
Bowen, Elizabeth, **2:**101, 181
  The Death of the Heart, **2:**133
Bowker, Gordon, **2:**118
Bowring, Richard, **2:**290, 291, 292
Boyd, Belle, **2:**273
Boyer, Paul, *By the Bomb's Early Light,* **3:**239
Boyle, Kevin, **3:**101
Boyle, Robert, **2:**65
Boyle, Tony, **3:**98
Boy scouts, **1:**47, 48
Boys in Zinc (Alexievich), **3:**285
Boys' Life (magazine), **1:**47
Boys Will Be Boys (Suleri), **1:**88
Boyyd, Nan Alamilla, **3:**85
Bracken, John, **2:63**
Bradbury, Malcolm, **1:**280
Bradford, Clare, **1:**41
Bradford, Gamaliel, **2:**39, 314
Bradley, David, *Dissent,* **1:**80
Bradley, Ed, **3:**200
Bradley, William A., **1:**86
Bradstreet, Anne, **1:**315
Bragg, Melvyn, *Speak for England,* **3:**144
Brahms, Johannes, **1:**206

Brainwashing, in Cultural Revolution, **1:**161, 162
Branch, Michael P., **2:**214, 215
Braudel, Fernand, **3:**159
Brave Bird, Mary
  Lakota Woman, **1:21–23**
  Ohitika Woman, **1:**21, 23
Bravman, Bill, **3:**142
Brawne, Fanny, **2:**147
Braxton, Joanne, **1:**19
Braxton, Joanne M., **2:**31
Bray, William, **2:**65
Brazell, Karen, **2:**59, 60
Brazil
  de Jesus (Carolina Maria) on experience of poverty in, **2:**6–8
  Jews in, **1:**75
Breast cancer, Lorde's (Audre) battle with, **2:**3–5
Brée, Germaine, **1:**246, 247
Breen, Joe, **1:120**
Breidenbach, Bernhard von, *Peregrinationes in Montem Zion,* **2:**227
Brennan, William J., Jr., **3:**294
Brenner, Rachel, **2:**24
Brent, Jonathan, **2:**85–86
Breslau, Louise, **2:**306
Bressler, Leo A., **1:**235
Brewsie and Willie (Stein), **1:**333
Brewton, Vince, **1:**35
Breytenbach, Breyten, **3:**242
Brezhnev, Leonid, **3:**331
Bride of Lammermoor, The (Scott), **2:**209
Bridge, Horatio, **2:**223
Bridgman, Laura, **1:**43
Brief History of the War with the Indians in New England, A (Mather), **1:**325
Briggs, Anthony, **1:**195
Briggs, Asa, **3:**64
Briggs, Julia, **2:**182
Briggs, Kate, **2:**182
Briggsoth, Jean L., *Never in Anger,* **3:**138
Brighton (England), oral histories of gay life in, **3:**70–72, *71*
Brighton Gay Switchboard, **3:**72

Brighton Ourstory, *Daring Hearts,* **3:**70–72

Brigido-Corachán, Anna, **1:**56

Brill de Ramirez, Susan B., **3:**320

Brink, André, **1:**27, **3:**242

Brinker, William, **3:**277

Brinkman, Antoinette, **1:**103

Brinnin, John Malcolm, **1:**332–333

Brinson, Betsy, **3:**159, 266

Brissman, Barry, **1:**338, 339

Brissman, Lily Chia, **1:**338, 339

Bristol (England), oral histories of working-class youth in, **3:**311–313, *312*

Britain. *See also* England; Ireland; Scotland; Wales

 abolitionist movement in, **1:**81–83, 111, **3:**23

 abolition of slavery in, **1:**34, 81, 111, **3:**23

 African Britons in, **1:**81–82

 censorship of Irish history in, **3:**27, 28, 29

 class in (*See* Social class)

 education in, **2:**136, 320, **3:**311–313

 empire of (*See* British Empire)

 establishment of Great Britain (1707), **2:**328

 Franklin (Benjamin) in, **1:**179

 Great Depression in, **3:**53

 health-care industry of, **3:**170–172

 homosexuality in, ban on, **2:**9, 183, **3:**70

 industrialization of, **2:**16, 146, 300, **3:**59, 63

 Iranian relations with, **3:**218

 Irish Rebellion (1798) against, **2:**157, *158,* 159

 in Israel's establishment, **1:**225

 letter writing in, **2:**146, 217

 literacy in, rise of, **2:**136, 146, 320

 lost generation of, **1:**329

 Mahomet's (Dean) influence on culture of, **2:**230, 231

 Mass Observation Project in, **2:**235, 236, 237, 265, 266, 267

 nature writing in, golden age of, **2:**300

 Palestine under, **2:**104–106, **3:**14

 racism in, **2:**230

 religion in (*See* British religion)

 slave trade in, **1:**34, 81, 111

 social history of, Webb (Beatrice) on, **2:**16–18

 travel narratives in, popularity of, **2:**229

 Victorian (*See* Victorian era)

 wars of (*See specific wars*)

 women's rights movement in, **1:**329, 331, **2:**109

British Critic (journal), **2:**179

British Empire

 abolition of slavery in, **1:**34, 81, 111, **3:**23

 African countries in, **1:**167

 Australia in, **1:**149

 Egypt in, **1:**135

 during French Revolution, **2:**217, 218, 219

 India in (*See* India, British)

 Jamaica in, **1:**111

 Kenya in, **2:**12, **3:**141–143

 Nigeria in, **1:**214

 racism against people of color from, **2:**230

 Seven Years' War in expansion of, **2:**328

 South Africa in, **2:**217–219, 241–243

 Victorian era expansion of, **2:**16

 Zimbabwe (Rhodesia) in, **1:**167, **3:**251–253

British Journal of Aesthetics, **2:**128

British Journal of Education Studies, **3:**313

British Mandate for Palestine, **2:**104–106

British Medical Journal, **1:**6, 7–8

British monarchy. *See also* English Civil War; *specific rulers*

 in Renaissance, **2:**97–99

 Slingsby (Henry) on loyalty to, **2:**256–258

British Museum, **2:**183

British oral histories. *See also* English oral histories; Irish oral histories

 on health-care industry, **3:**170–172

 origins of field, **3:**186

 recognition of value of, **3:**64

 on World War II, **3:**234–236

British Petroleum, **3:**218

British religion. *See also* Anglicanism

 Catholicism, decline of, **2:**97, 99, 226

 Christianity, arrival of, **1:**189

 Great Awakening in, **2:**197

 Methodism, **2:**195–196

 Puritanism, **2:**72, 74

 Quakerism, **2:**26–28, 157–159

British women. *See* English women

Brittain, Vera, **1:**330

 Bagnold (Enid) compared to, **1:**329, **2:**259

 Mitchison (Naomi) compared to, **2:**235

 Sassoon (Siegfried) compared to, **2:**247

 Testament of Experience, **1:**330

 Testament of Friendship, **1:**330, 331

 Testament of Youth, **1:**329–331, **2:**247–248, 259, 269, **3:**176

Brittain, Victoria, **2:**14

Brod, Max, **2:**120, 121, 122

Brokenburn (Stone), **2:**244–246

Brooke, James, **2:**12

Brook Farm (utopian community), **1:**14, 235

Brookfield strike of 1970s, **3:**96

Brooklyn Historical Society, **3:**180

Brooks, Max, **3:**212

Brooks, Pam, **1:**39

Brooks, Van Wyck, **1:**134

Brothers: Black Soldiers in the Nam (Goff et al.), **3:**199

Broussard, Allen, **3:**21

Brown, C. G., **3:**173

Brown, Hume, **2:**309

Brown, James W., *Long Journey Home,* **3:**107, **325–327**

Brown, Jennifer S. H., **3:**109

Brown, John (abolitionist), **1:**33, **2:**29, 238

Brown, John (servant), **2:**209

Brown, Joseph Epes, **3:**111
Brown, Patricia, **3:**338
Brown, William Wells
    Clotel, **1:**72
    Narrative, **1:**50
    The Negro in the American Rebellion, **2:**238
Browne, Janet, **1:**66, 67
Browne, Thomas, **2:**65, 67
Browning, Elizabeth Barrett, **2:**29
Browning, Orville H., **3:**263–264
Browning, Robert, **1:**264, 265
Brownmiller, Susan, **2:**283
Brown v. Board of Education, **1:**122, 249, **3:**44
Bruce, Edward Caledon, **2:**39
Bruce, Gary, *The Firm,* **3:245–247**
Bruckheimer, Jerry, **3:**345
Brugge, David M.
    The Navajo-Hopi Land Dispute, **3:**10
    "The Navajo Witch Purge of 1878," **3:**290
Bruner, Charlotte H., *Unwinding Threads,* **1:**94
Bruss, Elizabeth W., **1:**246
Bry, Theodor de, **2:202**
Bryant, Emma Spaulding, **2:**252
Bryant, Harold, **3:**201
Bryant, John Emory, **2:**252
Brydges, Samuel Egerton, **1:**231
Bryson, David, **3:**65
Buch, H. C., *Sansibar Blues,* **1:**92
Buchanan, John, **3:**177–178
Buchenwald concentration camp, **3:**51
Buck, Lucy
    Sad Earth, Sweet Heaven, **2:**271, 273
    Shadows on My Heart, **2:**38, **271–274**
Buck, Neville, **2:**271
Buck, Pearl S., *The Good Earth,* **1:**159
Budberg, Moura, **1:**254
Buddhism, in Japan
    Murasaki Shikibu on, **2:**290, 291
    Nijo (Lady) as nun in, **2:**59, 60
    rise of, **2:**59, 61, 189
Buel, Joy Day, **2:**332

Buel, Richard, **2:**332
Buell, Lawrence, **1:**236
Bueno, Eva Paulino, **2:**8
Bueno, Fernanda, **2:**222
Buergenthal, Thomas, *A Lucky Child,* **1:**312
Buff, Truman, **3:**103
Buggery Act of 1533 (England), **3:**70
Bugul, Ken, **1:62**
    The Abandoned Baobab, **1:61–64**
    Cendres et braises, **1:**61
    Riwan ou le chemin de sable, **1:**61, 64
Buhari, Muhammadu, **1:**216
Buhle, Paul, **3:**159, 181, 330
Bui Tin, **3:**280
Bulletin of the School of Oriental Studies, **1:**137, 287
Bundeson, Lynne, **1:**336
Bunin, Ivan, **1:**270
Bunyan, John, *Grace Abounding to the Chief of Sinners,* **2:**26
Burawoy, Michael, **3:**342
Burde, Edgar, **1:**147
Bureau of Indian Affairs (BIA), U.S., **1:**69
Burgos-Debray, Elisabeth, **3:**114, 164, 165, 322
Burgunder, Rose, **1:**206
Burke, Bonaventure, **3:**310
Burke, Edmund, **1:**88, **2:**157, 158, 217
Burke, Peter, **1:**185
Burkett, B. G., **3:**201, 211
Burlingame, Michael
    Abraham Lincoln: A Life, **3:**264
    An Oral History of Abraham Lincoln, **3:261–264**
Burma, British colonial rule of, **2:**119
Burmese Days (Orwell), **2:**119
Burnett, Richard, **3:**159
Burney, Charles, **2:**312
Burney, Edward Francis, **2:**313
Burney, Fanny, **2:**313
    Diary and Letters of Madame D'Arblay, **2:**312, 314
    Evelina, **2:**312–313, 314
    Letters and Journals of Fanny Burney, **2:312–315**

    The Memoirs of Dr. Burney, **2:**312, 313
    Pope (Alexander) and, **2:**217
Burns, Anthony, **2:**29
Burns, Harry, **3:**95
Burns, Patrick, **3:**241
Burns, Robert, **2:**328
Burqas, **1:**40
Burr, Aaron, *The Private Journal of Aaron Burr,* **2:**88
Burr, Anna Robeson, **1:**246
Burroughs, Carolyn, **2:**337
Burroughs, John, **2:**141
Burson, Harold, **3:**294
Burst of Light, A (Lorde), **2:**3
Burton, Robert, **2:**177
Burton, Vicki Tolar, **2:**196
Buruma, Ian, *Murder in Amsterdam,* **1:**209
Bush, George H. W., **1:**300, **2:**278
Bush, George W., **1:**306, **2:**275
Bush, Laura, **1:**41
BusinessWeek (magazine), **3:**277
Butcher, Tim, *Chasing the Devil,* **1:**312
Bute, Lord, **2:**328
Butler, Dino, **1:**96
Butler, George E., **1:**206
Butler, Pierce Mease, **2:**335, 337
Butler, Samuel, **1:**218–219
Butor, Michel, **1:240**
Byatt, A. S., **1:**168
    Possession, **2:**77
Bykaw, Vasily, **3:**282
Byodoin Temple (Kyoto), **2:**298
Byrd, Jim, **3:**87
Byrd, Richard, **2:**280
Byron, George Gordon Noel, **2:**144
    Camino Real (Williams) on, **2:**154
    The Journal of Sir Walter Scott (Scott) on, **2:**309
    Kemble's (Fanny) friendship with, **2:**335
    Letters and Journals of Lord Byron, **2:143–145,** 309
    The Letters of John Keats (Keats) on, **2:**146
By the Bomb's Early Light (Boyer), **3:**239

C

Cadle, Tillman, **3:**158
Cady, Daniel, **1:**13
Caesar, Julius, **1:**218, 220
Caillouet, Ruth R., **1:**40–41, 42
Cain, William E., **1:**4–5
Caine, Barbara, **2:**17
Cairnie, Julie, **1:**169
Caldas (destroyer), **3:**183, 185
California
    affirmative action in, **3:**20
    African Americans in higher education in, **3:**20
    colonial, oral histories of, **3:**114–116
    gay Asian Americans in, oral histories of, **3:**83–85
    Gold Rush in, **3:**114
    immigrant land ownership in, restrictions on, **3:**195
    Italian American relocation in, **3:**224
    Japanese American internment in, **1:**299–301, **3:**102–104, 197
    missions of, **3:**114–116
    Owens Valley region of, oral histories of, **3:**102–104
    statehood for, **3:**114
California History (journal), **3:**225
California State University at Fullerton, Japanese American Oral History Project at, **3:**80, 102, 195
Californios
    definition of, **3:**114
    oral histories of, **3:**114–116
Californio Voices (Savage), **3:**114–117, 121
Calked Boots and Other Northwest Writings (Russell), **3:**93
Call, M. S., **1:**32
Callaloo (journal), **1:**5, 251, **3:**24
Callow, Simon, **2:**154
Calvino, Italo, *Invisible Cities*, **1:**105
Cambodia, under Khmer Rouge, Siv (Sichan) on life in, **1:**306–308
Cambodian Americans, Siv (Sichan) on experience of, **1:**306–308
Camden Society, **2:**226, 228

Cameron, David, **2:**261
Cameron, Samantha, **2:**261
Camino Real (Williams), **2:**154
Camp and Community (Garrett and Larson), **3:**102, 103–104
Campbell, John Angus, **1:**67
Campesinos, **3:**302–303
Camus, Albert
    Feraoun's (Mouloud) friendship with, **2:**262
    The Myth of Sisyphus, **1:**204
    Styron (William) influenced by, **1:**204, 205
    Wright's (Richard) friendship with, **1:**124
Canada
    oral histories of Inuits in, **3:**138–140, *139*
    U.S. draft evasion in, **3:**221
Canadian Book Review Annual, **3:**140
Canadian Journal of History, **2:**330, **3:**29
Canadian Literature (journal), **1:**103, **2:**175
Canadian Review of American Studies (journal), **1:**157
Cancer, Lorde's (Audre) battle with, **2:**3–5
Cancer Journals, The (Lorde), **2:**3–5
Cancian, Frank, **3:**168
Candor. *See also* Truth
    in *The Long Walk to Freedom* (Mandela), **1:**29
Caninius Rufus, **2:**95, 96
Canterbury Tales (Chaucer), **1:**191, 229
Canto general (Neruda), **1:**223
Cape of Good Hope, **2:**198, 199, 217, 218
Capitalism
    IWW's opposition to, **3:**328, 329
    working class in, **3:**53
Capital punishment. *See* Execution
Capital Times (newspaper), **2:**276
Capitulations of Santa Fé, **2:**201
Capote, Truman, **2:**152
Captivity narratives, **1:**81, 325–326
Caputo, John D., **2:**167
Caputo, Philip, *A Rumor of War*, **3:**209
Carboni, Sante, **3:**158

Cardanus, Hieronymus, **2:**98–99
Cárdenas, Lázaro, **3:**302, 303, *303*, 304
Carey, John, **2:**138
Caribbean autobiographical writing
    by McKay (Claude), **1:**84–86
    by Medina (Pablo), **1:**296–298
    by Santiago (Esmeralda), **1:**108–110
    by Seacole (Mary), **1:**111–113
Carlisle, Elizabeth Pendergast, **2:**332
Carlo Tresca (Pernicone), **3:**5
Carlson, Timothy, *Embedded*, **3:**276
Carlyle, Thomas, **2:**139–140, 144, 196, 310, 321
Carmelite religious order, **1:**211, 212
Carmody, Deidre, **1:**262
Carnegie, Andrew, **1:**52
Carranza, Venustiano, **3:**167
Carrera, Elena, **1:**213
Carretta, Vincent, **1:**82, 83, **2:**46
Carrier Warfare in the Pacific (Wooldridge), **3:**202–204
Carril, Delia del, **1:**223
Carrington, Dora, **2:**269
Carry It On (Ashmore), **3:**254
Carter, Jimmy, **1:**311, **3:**221
Carter, John, **1:**18
Carter, Ross S., *Those Devils in Baggy Pants*, **3:**212
Carter, Steven, **1:**274
Cartesian rationalism, **1:**183, 184
Carver, Jonathan
    The Journals of Jonathan Carver and Related Documents, **2:**205–208
    Travels through the Interior Parts of North America, **2:**205
Cary, Max, **1:**218, **2:**94, 95–96
Casada, James, **3:**252
Casaubon, Méric, **1:**220
Casey-Leininger, Charles F., **3:**100
Cash, Jean W., **2:**131
Caspar, C., **1:**31, 32
Cassius Dio, *Historia Romana*, **1:**220
Cast a Cold Eye (McCarthy), **1:**258
Castellanos, Miguel, **3:**206
Castle, The (Kafka), **2:**120
Castro, Fidel, **1:**296, 298, **2:**222, 280

Cat(s)
- in *A Country Parson* (Woodforde), **2:**289
- Lessing (Doris) on, **1:**169

Catherine of Siena (saint), **1:**189

Catholicism. *See also* Christian autobiographical writing
- Augustine in, **1:**196–198
- Boswell's (James) conversion to, **2:**329
- Counter-Reformation in, **1:**211
- in England, decline of, **2:**97, 99, 226
- in Ireland, **1:**119–120
- of McCarthy (Mary), **1:**259
- of Mexican American women, **3:**132
- nuns in, oral histories of, **3:**308–310
- of O'Connor (Flannery), **2:**129, 130
- Teresa of Ávila in, **1:**211–213
- Vatican II in, **3:**308, 309
- Williams's (Tennessee) conversion to, **2:**152

Catlett, Elizabeth, **2:45**
Catliln, George, **1:**330
Caton, William, **2:**26
Caton-Jones, Michael, **1:**47, 49
Catt, Carrie Chapman, **1:**12
Caucasia (Senna), **1:**72, 74
Caudill, Harry, *Night Comes to the Cumberlands*, **3:**66
"Caught between Homes" (Baggett), **1:**113
Caught in a Tornado (Ross), **3:**287
Cavell, Stanley, **1:**236
Cavendish, Margaret, **1:230**
- Clifford (Anne) compared to, **2:**62
- *A Description of the New World*, **1:**231
- *Nature's Pictures Drawn by Fancy's Pencil to the Life*, **1:**229, 231
- Osborne (Dorothy) compared to, **2:**324
- *A True Relation of My Birth, Breeding, and Life*, **1:229–232**

Cavendish, William, **1:**229
Cavett, Dick, **1:**260

CCP. *See* Chinese Communist Party
CDC. *See* Centers for Disease Control and Prevention
Cecelski, David, *Along Freedom Road*, **3:**21
Cecil, David, **2:**268
Cefkin, J. Leo, **3:**252
Cellini, Benvenuto, **1:**239
Cendrata, Lodovico, **2:**160
Cendres et braises (Bugul), **1:**61
Censorship
- in Belarus, **3:**282–284
- in Britain, **3:**27, 28, 29
- in China, **3:**287, 301
- in Kenya, **2:**14
- in Mexico, **3:**31, 32
- in Russia, **1:**193, 194
- in U.S., **1:**20, **2:**123, **3:**201

Centenary Edition of the Works of Nathaniel Hawthorne, The (Hawthorne), **2:**223
Centers for Disease Control and Prevention (CDC), U.S., **3:**85
Central Intelligence Agency (CIA), U.S., **1:**298, **3:**164
Century Magazine, **3:**261
CEP. *See* Coal Employment Project
Cereta, Laura, *Collected Letters of a Renaissance Feminist*, **2:160–162**
Cerro Gordo (California), **3:103**
Cervantes, Lorna Dee, **3:**133
Cervetto, Joe, **3:**225
Césaire, Aimé, **1:**61
Cha, Theresa Hak Kyung, *Dictee*, **1:**102
Chadwick, Owen, **1:**239
Chai, May-Lee, **1:**307–308
Chalk Garden, The (Bagnold), **2:**259, 261
Challener, Daniel D., **1:**48
Challenger, Melanie, **2:**338
Chalmers, Martin, **2:**304
Chamberlain, John, **1:**32
Chamberlain, Joseph, **2:**17
Chamberlain, Mary
- *Fenwomen*, **3:**61
- on *Women's Words* (Gluck and Patai), **3:**191

Chamberlain, Neville, **2:**265

Chamberlain, Samuel, *My Confessions*, **1:**304
Chamosa, Oscar, **3:**74, 75
Champagne, Roland, **1:**268, **2:**175
Chamula (Mexico), oral histories of indigenous people of, **3:**167–169
Chander, Manu, **1:**256, 257
Chandler, Sally, **3:**188
Chang, Gordon, **3:**81
Chang, Iris, **2:**19, 20
Chang, Jung, *Wild Swans*, **1:**158–159
Change of Tongue, A (Krog), **3:**242
Channing, Ellery, **2:**139
Chanthaphavong, Samaya L. S., **2:**299
Chao, Buwei Yang, *Autobiography of a Chinese Woman*, **1:**338
Chapelle, Dickey, *What's a Woman Doing Here?*, **2:**280
Chaplin, Charlie, **2:**183
Chaplin, Ralph, **3:**329
Chapman, James, **3:**234, 236
Chapman, Jedediah, **2:**79
Chapman, Maria Weston, *The Liberty Bell*, **1:**142
Character of England, A (Evelyn), **2:**65
Chardin, Jean-Baptiste-Siméon, **2:110**
Charles I (king of England)
- *Eikon Basilike*, **2:**256, 258
- in English Civil War, **1:**315, 317, **2:**26, 65, 72, 178, 256, 257, *257*

Charles II (king of England), **1:316**
- Evelyn (John) and, **2:**65
- Halkett (Anne), **1:**315, 316
- restoration of, **1:**315, **2:**26, 65, 72, 256, 258

Charlevoix, Pierre-François-Xavier de, *Journal of a Voyage to North-America*, **2:**205
Chasing the Devil (Butcher), **1:**312
Chatterjee, Partha, **1:**291
Chaucer, Geoffrey
- *Canterbury Tales*, **1:**191, 229
- *The Letters of John Keats* (Keats) on, **2:**146

Chaudhuri, Nirad C., *Autobiography of an Unknown Indian*, **3:**251, 253
Chavez, Cesar, **3:**133
Che: A Graphic Biography (Buhle and Rodriguez), **3:**330

Cheke, John, **2:**97
Chekhov, Anton, **1:**47, **2:**133
Chekisty (Dziak), **3:**245
Chen, Joan, **1:**158
Chen, Paul, **3:**84
Cheney, Anne, **1:**274, 275
Cheney, Dick, **2:**278
Cheng, Nien, **1:**159
Cheng Yu-hsiu (Madame Wei), **1:**153
    A Girl from China, **1:**152, 154
    My Revolutionary Years, **1:152–154**
Cherie (Goncourt), **2:**308
Chernobyl nuclear disaster (1986), **3:**282–285, *283*
Chertkov, Vladimir, **1:**195
Chesnut, Mary Boykin Miller
    A Diary from Dixie, **2:250–252**
    Mary Chesnut's Civil War, **2:**250, 251, 271
    The Private Mary Chesnut, **2:**250
    Stone (Kate) compared to, **2:**244, 246
Chew, Daglish, **3:**243
Chiang Kai-sheck, **1:**338
Chiapas (Mexico), oral histories of indigenous people of, **3:**167–169, *168*
Chiarello, Barbara, **2:**255
Chicago (Illinois)
    Hansberry (Lorraine) on life in, **1:**273, 275
    Haymarket Riot in, **3:**4
    race riots in, **3:**45
    Wright's (Richard) move to, **1:**122
Chicago Daily Tribune (newspaper), **2:**89
Chicago Renaissance, **1:**273
Chicago Sun-Times (newspaper), **1:**40, 41
Chicago Tribune (newspaper), **1:**23, 40, 41, **2:**121
Chicana women, oral histories of, **3:**131–133, *132*
Chicano, use of term, **3:**133
Chicano movement, **3:**133
Chicano studies, rise of, **3:**131–133
Chicken with Plums (Satrapi), **1:**155–156
Chigwedere, P., **3:**274
Child, Lydia Maria, **1:**142, 144

Childhood
    in Arabic autobiographies, **1:**135, 136
    idealization of, **1:**128
    treatment of, in memoirs, **1:**47
    during wartime, memoirs of, **1:**312–314
Child in the House, The (Pater), **1:**276
Child of the Dark (de Jesus), **2:6–8,** **3:**164, 322
Children
    of British working class, **3:**53–54, *54*, 311–313, *312*
    as casualties of Holocaust, **3:**36
    Cuban, immigration of, **1:**298
    interracial adoption of, **1:**102–104
    of Los Alamos, oral histories of, **3:**239–241
    as soldiers in Sierra Leone, **1:**312–314
Children of Los Alamos (Mason), **3:239–241**
Children of Sanchez (Lewis), **3:**31
Children's of Cambodia's Killing Fields (Pran), **1:**306
Childress, Lee, **3:**209
Child's Christmas in Wales, A (Thomas), **1:125–127**
Chile
    Agosín (Marjorie) on experience of Jews in, **1:**75–77
    autobiographical tradition of, **1:**222
    German immigration to, **1:**75, 77
    mass disappearances in, **1:**75
    military coup of 1973 in, **1:**222
    Neruda (Pablo) on life in, **1:**222–224
Chimurenga (Liberation) War, First (1896–1897), **3:**251
Chimurenga (Liberation) War, Second, **3:**251
Chin, Frank, **1:**175
China. *See also* Chinese autobiographical writing; Chinese oral histories
    arranged marriage in, **1:**153, 154, 338, 339, **2:**170
    censorship in, **3:**287, 301
    Confucianism in, **3:**124–126

    Cultural Revolution in (*See* Cultural Revolution)
    Du Bois (W. E. B.) and, **1:**3, 4
    dynastic rule of, end of, **3:**124, 126, 147
    establishment of republic, **2:**170, **3:**124, 126, 147, 299
    feminism in, rise of, **3:**147–149
    folklore of, **1:**173, 174
    foot binding in, **1:**338, **3:**147, 289
    Gandhi's (Mohandas) influence on protests in, **1:**242
    gender roles in, **1:**153, 158, 160, 338, **3:**147–149
    Great Leap Forward in, **3:**287, 299, 300
    Japanese invasion of (1931), **3:**215
    Japanese relations with, **1:**340, **3:**149
    Japan influenced by, in Heian period, **2:**189
    Jewish refugees in, oral histories of, **3:**14–16
    Kingston (Maxine Hong) on culture of, **1:**173–175
    Korean Provisional Government in, **1:**322, 324
    Long March in, **1:**338
    May Fourth Movement in, **1:**338, **3:**126, 147–149
    Nanking Massacre in, **1:**340, **2:**19–21
    Northern Expedition in, **1:**338
    Polo's (Marco) travels in, **1:**105, 106, 107
    Rabe (John) in, **2:**19–21
    Revolution of 1911–1912 in, **2:**170
    in Sino–Japanese Wars, **1:**322, 339, 340
    women of (*See* Chinese women)
    during World War II, **1:**152, 153, **3:**14–16
China Candid (Sang), **3:**299–300
China Daily News (newspaper), **3:**299
China Journal, **1:**339, **3:**149, 301
China Men (Kingston), **1:**173
China Remembers (Zhang and McLeod), **3:**301
Chinchilla, Norma, **3:**323

Chinese American(s)
    Kingston (Maxine Hong) on experience of, **1:**173–175
    Min (Anchee) on experience of, **1:**158–160
    stereotypes of, **1:**173, 174
Chinese autobiographical writing. *See also specific works and writers*
    by Cheng Yu-hsiu (Madame Wei), **1:**152–154
    expatriate, tradition of, **1:**158–159
    by Jiang (Ji-li), **1:**161–163
    by Lu Xun and Xu Guangping, **2:**170–172
    by Min (Anchee), **1:**158–160
    by women, rise of, **1:**152–153, 159, 338
    by Xie Bingying, **1:**338–340
Chinese Civil War (1927–1950), **3:**126
Chinese Communist Party (CCP). *See also* Cultural Revolution
    censorship by, **3:**301
    Cheng Yu-hsiu on, **1:**152
    Jiang (Ji-li) on, **1:**161, 162
    in liberation of women, **3:**147, 148
    Lu Xun and, **2:**170, 172
    oppression under, **1:**338
    origins and rise of, **2:**170, **3:**287
Chinese language
    Japanese writers' use of, **2:**290, 292
    in *The Woman Warrior* (Kingston), **1:**173, 174
Chinese Lives (Zhang and Sang), **3:**288, **299–301**
Chinese Missionaries Oral History Collection (Peake and Rosenbaum), **3:**299
Chinese oral histories
    on Cultural Revolution, **3:**287–289, 299–300
    of descendants of Confucius, **3:**124–126
    government influence on, **3:**301
    on life in late twentieth century, **3:**299–301, *300*
    of women in May Fourth Movement, **3:**147–149
Chinese Oral History Project (Columbia University), **3:**299
Chinese Prime Minister, The (Bagnold), **2:**261

Chinese Revolution (1911–1912), **2:**170
Chinese women
    in arranged marriages, **1:**153, 154, 338, 339, **2:**170
    autobiographies by, rise of, **1:**152–153, 159, 338
    feminism among, rise of, **3:**147–149
    foot binding of, **1:**338, **3:**147, 289
    gender roles of, **1:**153, 158, 160, 338, **3:**147–149
    in May Fourth Movement, oral histories of, **3:**147–149
    in military, **1:**338–340
    stereotypes of, **1:**173, **3:**147
    traditional treatment of, **3:**147
    in World War II, Cheng Yu-hsiu on, **1:**152–154
    Xie Bingying of lives of, **1:**338–340
Chineworth, Mary Alice, **3:**309
Ch'ing, Ai, **1:**222
Chinweizu, **1:**115
Chiricahua Apache, Geronimo on, **1:**302–304
Chisholm, Anne, **2:**269
Chittister, Joan, **3:**308
Choi, Samuel, **2:**314
Choi, Young Back, **1:**323
Choice (journal), **3:**19, 249, 255, 326, 332
Chona (Chona and Underhill), **1:69–71**
Chona, Maria, *Chona*, **1:**69–71
Chrisman, Laura, **2:**242
Christian autobiographical writing. *See also specific works and writers*
    by Augustine, **1:**196–198
    by Fox (George), **2:**26–28
    by Guylforde (Richarde), **2:**226–228
    by Kempe (Margery), **1:**189–191
    by Kierkegaard (Søren), **2:**166
    by Rowlandson (Mary), **1:**325–328
    by Teresa of Ávila, **1:**211–213
    by Tolstoy (Leo), **1:**193–195
    tradition of, **2:**166
    by Wesley (John), **2:**195–197

Christian Gauss Award, for *Memory and Narrative* (Olney), **1:**248
Christian Herald (periodical), **3:**110
Christianity. *See also specific denominations*
    in Crusades, **1:**285–288
    early history of, **1:**196
    in England, arrival of, **1:**189
    fundamentalist, **1:**102, 103
    Great Awakening in, **1:**179, **2:**197
    hostility between Islam and, after Crusades, **2:**226
    Kim Ku influenced by, **1:**322
    The Letters of the Younger Pliny (Pliny) in, **2:**94
    Marcus Aurelius on, **1:**220
    pilgrimages to Jerusalem in, **2:**226–228
    Protestant Reformation in, **1:**211
    slavery and, **1:**34, 144, **2:**44, 46
    Wells's (H. G.) rejection of, **1:**252–253
Christianity, conversion to
    by Africans, **1:**64
    by Australian Aborigines, **1:**149, 151
    by Equiano (Olaudah), **1:**82
    by Native Americans, **1:**56, **2:**46, **3:**114, 115
Christie, Agatha, **2:**259
Christine de Pisan, **2:**160, 162
    The Book of the City of Ladies, **2:**162
Christmas, Thomas (Dylan) on, **1:**125–126, *126*
Christopher, Neil, *Ilagiinniq*, **3:**138
Christopher Award, for *Thura's Diary* (Al-Windawi), **2:**275
Chronology, lack of. *See* Nonchronological order
Church, Thomas, **2:**196
Churches, origins of abolitionist movement in, **1:**142
Churchill, Caryl, *Top Girls*, **2:60**
Churchill, Ward, *Struggle for the Land*, **3:**10
Churchill, Winston
    The Boer War, **2:**241
    Nella Last's War (Last) on, **2:**265

Church of England. *See* Anglicanism
Church of the Brethren, **3:**223, 227
Chute, Hillary, **1:**157
CIA. *See* Central Intelligence Agency
Ciberletras (journal), **1:**77
Cicero, Marcus Tullius, **2:**94, 95
   Hortensius, **1:**196, 198
Cichy, Rose M., **3:**35
Cienfuegos, Camilo, **2:**222
Cimarróns, **3:**7
Circumcision
   female, Hirsi Ali (Ayaan) on, **1:**207
   male, Perera (Victor) on, **1:**99, 100
Cisneros, Sandra, *The House on Mango Street,* **1:**108
Citizen 13660 (Okubo), **1:**299
Citizenship, Australian, for Aborigines, **1:**149
Citizenship, U.S.
   for African Americans, **1:**50, **2:**38, 238
   for Japanese immigrants, **1:**309
   for Puerto Ricans, **1:**108
Citoyenne, La (newspaper), **2:**306
City College (New York City), **1:**249, 251
City of God (Augustine), **1:**198
Civil disobedience
   in India, by Gandhi (Mohandas), **1:**242, **2:**32
   in Palestinian intifada, first, **2:**50
   in U.S. civil rights movement, **2:**32–33, **3:**101
Civilian Public Service (CPS), U.S., **3:**227–229
Civilians
   in Iraq War, **2:**275, **3:**231, 232
   in Vietnam War, **1:**335–337
   in World War II, **1:**332–333, **3:**235
"Civilized" mind, theories of, **3:**37
Civil Liberties Act of 1988 (U.S.), **1:**311, **3:**197
Civil rights
   for African Americans (*See* Civil rights movement)
   for gays and lesbians, **3:**70, 72, 83–84

   for Native Americans, **1:**21, **3:**291, 292
   in Reconstruction era, **1:**50
Civil Rights Act of 1964 (U.S.), **1:**20, **3:**339
Civil rights movement, U.S.
   Angelou (Maya) in, **1:**18, 20
   civil disobedience in, **2:**32–33, **3:**101
   debate over approach to, **1:**186
   in Detroit, **3:**99–101
   disability studies and, **1:**8
   Du Bois (W. E. B.) in, **1:**3–4
   Gandhi's (Mohandas) influence on, **1:**242
   gradualist approach to, **2:**32–33
   Hansberry (Lorraine) in, **1:**273–275
   Jewish support for, **3:**118
   King (Martin Luther, Jr.) in, **2:**32–34
   Malcolm X in, **1:**186
   Montgomery bus boycott in, **1:**20, 37, 38, 39, **2:**32, **3:**44, 45
   oral histories of, **3:**44–46, 99–101
   origins and development of, **3:**44
   Parks (Rosa) in, **1:**37–39, **3:**101
   SCLC in, **1:**18, 20
   Vietnam War and, **3:**199, 200
   war on poverty and, **3:**254, 256
Civil war(s). *See specific countries*
Civil War Diary of Sarah Morgan, The (Morgan), **2:**271
Civil War History (journal), **2:**240, **3:**261
Cixous, Hélène, **1:**250, **2:**124
Clair, William, **2:**144
Clarissa (Richardson), **2:**301
Clark, Gillian, **1:**197, 198
Clark, John Pepper, **1:**214
Clark, Mary Higgins, **1:**40
Clarkson, Thomas, **1:**81, 83, **2:**75
Clary-Lemon, Jennifer, **3:**175
Clasby, Nancy, **1:**188
Class. *See* Social class
Classic Slave Narratives, The (Gates), **1:**82, 83
Clayhanger trilogy (Bennett), **2:**136, 137

Clayton, Frances, **1:**39
Clemens, Samuel Langhorne. *See* Twain, Mark
Clemm, Maria, **2:**41–43
Clifford, Anne, **2:**63
   The Diaries of Lady Anne Clifford, **2:**62–64
   "Knole Diary," **2:**62, 64
Clifford, D. J. H., **2:**62, 64
Clifford, Geraldine Jončich, **3:**77
Clifford, James O., **3:**224
Cline, David, **3:**97, 98
Clinton, Bill, **1:**20, 219, **3:**166, 221
Clio (journal), **1:**272
Clive, Robert, **2:**178
Clodfelter, Mark, **3:**279
Clotel (Brown), **1:**72
Cloud Cuckoo Land (Mitchison), **2:**237
Clubbe, John, **2:**144, 145
Clybourne Park (Norris), **1:**273
Coal Employment Project (CEP), **3:**337, 339
Coal Hollow (Light and Light), **3:**66–69
Coal Miners' Wives (Giesen), **3:**337
Coal mining
   in Arizona, on Native American lands, **3:**10, *11,* 292
   in Kentucky, oral histories of, **3:**86–87, 96–98, *97,* 157
   in Ukraine, oral histories of, **3:**340–342
   in West Virginia, oral histories of, **3:**66–69, *67,* 91
   women in, oral histories of, **3:**337–339, *338*
Coburn, Carol, **3:**309
Codrescu, Andrei, **1:**167
Coe, Calvin, **3:**92
Coe, Joe, **3:**92
Coe, John, **3:**90
Coe, Little John, **3:**92
Coe, Samuel S., **3:**90
Coeckelbergh, Mark, **2:**168
Coe Ridge (Kentucky), oral histories of life in, **3:**90–92
Coetzee, J. M., **1:**27
Coeur d'Alene (Idaho), oral histories of life in, **3:**93, 95

SUBJECT INDEX

Coffee, **1:**257
Coffield, Frank, **3:**313
Cohen, Albert, *Book of My Mother,* **1:**99
Cohen, Eliot, **2:**279, 280
Cohen, Jacob, **3:**103
Cohen, J. M., **2:**203
Cohen, Joshua, **1:**255–256
Cohen, Lucy, **3:**122
Colaiaco, James A., **2:**33
Colby, Clara, **1:**12
Colby, William, **3:**279
Cold War
    Du Bois (W. E. B.) and, **1:**3
    Salvadoran Civil War in, **3:**205
    Soviet oral histories of, **3:**331–333
    in *This Boy's Life* (Wolff), **1:**47
    women's peace movement during, **3:**268
Cole, Lori E., **3:**191
Cole, Margaret I., **2:**16, 172
Coleman, Emily Holmes, **1:**127
Coler, Jack, **1:**96
Coleridge, Samuel Taylor
    Byron (George Gordon Noel) compared to, **2:**143
    Journals of Ralph Waldo Emerson (Emerson) on, **2:**141
    Literary Fund and, **2:**207
    The Rime of the Ancient Mariner, **3:**183
    Robinson (Henry Crabb) and, **2:**75
    Wordsworth (Dorothy) influenced by, **2:**300
Coleridge, Sara, *Memoirs and Letters of Sara Coleridge,* **2:**16
Collected Letters (Poe), **2:**41
Collected Letters of a Renaissance Feminist (Cereta), **2:**160–162
Collected Letters of Mary Wollstonecraft, The (Wollstonecraft), **2:**109–112
Collected Works of Abraham Lincoln (Basler), **3:**262
Collected Works of W. B. Yeats, The (Yeats), **2:**126, 128
Collective bargaining, arbitration in, **3:**153
Collective living, Stanton (Elizabeth Cady) on, **1:**14

Collective narratives, of Native Americans, **1:**54
Collective novels, **3:**282, 285
College Literature (journal), **1:**98, 141, 160, **2:**260, 261
Colleges, white, African Americans at, **3:**20–22
Collier's (magazine), **2:**103
Collingwood, Luke, **1:**83
Collins, Anne, *Divine Songs and Meditacions,* **1:**229
Collins, Michael, **3:**27
Collister, Peter, **2:**307
Colombia
    coup of 1953 in, **3:**183, 185
    oral history of shipwrecked sailor from, **3:**183–185, *184*
Colonialism. *See also* Africa, colonialism in; *specific countries*
    Fanon (Frantz) on violent resistance to, **1:**244, **2:**262
    Gandhi's (Mohandas) nonviolent resistance to, **1:**242–244
    Las Casas's (Bartolomé de) critique of, **2:**201, 202, 203
    Orwell's (George) critique of, **2:**119
Color
    hooks (bell) on meanings of, **1:**250
    Nabokov's (Vladimir) perception of, **1:**272
Colorado River, **1:**69
Color-graphemic synesthesia, **1:**272
Color of Water, The (McBride), **1:**72–74
Color Purple, The (Walker), **1:**18, 175
Columbian Orator, The (Bingham), **1:**33–34
Columbia University
    Chinese Oral History Project, **3:**299
    Maurer (Harry) at, **3:**277
    Obama (Barack) at, **1:**78
Columbus, Christopher, **2:**202
    Gama (Vasco da) compared to, **2:**200
    Journal of the First Voyage to America, **2:**201–204, 205
    in Puerto Rico, **1:**108
Columbus, Ferdinand, **2:**203

Comaneci, Nadia, *Letters to a Young Gymnast,* **2:**150
Comaroff, John, **2:**241
Comerford, Linda Brill, **1:**162
Comerford, Maire, **3:**29
Comics
    autobiographical, **1:**139–140, 155–157
    gay- and lesbian-themed, **1:**139, 141
    Japanese, **1:**293–294
    on labor movement, **3:**330
Coming-of-age
    in *Angela's Ashes* (McCourt), **1:**119–121
    in *Black Boy* (Wright), **1:**122–124
    in *Bone Black* (hooks), **1:**249
    in *A Child's Christmas in Wales* (Thomas), **1:**125–127
    in *Chona* (Chona and Underhill), **1:**69
    in *The Dark Child* (Laye), **1:**128
    in *Dust Tracks on a Road* (Hurston), **1:**9
    in *The Education of Henry Adams* (Adams), **1:**132–134
    in *An Egyptian Childhood* (Hussein), **1:**136
    in *Fun Home* (Bechdel), **1:**139
    in *Incidents in the Life of a Slave Girl* (Jacobs), **1:**144
    in *Left Handed, Son of Old Man Hat* (Dyk), **3:**318, 319
    in *Life on the Mississippi* (Twain), **1:**146
    in *My Life Story* (Unaipon), **1:**149–151
    in *My Revolutionary Years* (Cheng), **1:**152–154
    in *Under My Skin* (Lessing), **1:**167–169
    in *Persepolis* (Satrapi), **1:**155–157
    in *Red Azalea* (Min), **1:**158–160
    in *Red Scarf Girl* (Jiang), **1:**161–163
    in *Stop-Time* (Conroy), **1:**164, 165
    in *The Unwanted* (Nguyen), **1:**170–172
    in *The Woman Warrior* (Kingston), **1:**174, 175

Coming of Age in Mississippi (Moody), **1:**37
Comitini, Patricia, **2:**301
Committee for Effecting Abolition of the Slave Trade, **1:**81
Committee for Peasant Unity, **3:**166
Commonplace books, **2:**140
Communication Studies (journal), **1:**14
Communism
    in Cambodia, under Khmer Rouge, **1:**306
    in Cuba, establishment of, **1:**296
    Du Bois's (W. E. B.) support for, **1:**3–5
    in East Germany, oppression under, **3:**245–246
    in India, Nehru's (Jawaharlal) advocacy for, **1:**289
    McKay's (Claude) support for, **1:**84, 85
    in Russia, establishment of, **1:**270
    U.S. containment policy on, **3:**205
    in Vietnam, postwar, **1:**170, 171
Communist Party, Chilean, **1:**222
Communist Party, Chinese. *See* Chinese Communist Party
Communist Party, East German, **3:**245
Communist Party, South African, **1:**27
Communist Party, U.S., **1:**3, 4, 122, 123
Community, sense of, among gay Asian Americans, **3:**83–85
Comparatist (journal), **1:**223
Comparative Literature Studies (journal), **1:**277
Comparative Studies of Society and History (journal), **3:**96
Complete Notebooks of Henry James, The (James), **2:**113–116
Complete Works of George Orwell (Orwell), **2:**117, 118
Computers and the Humanities (journal), **2:**203
Conan Doyle, Arthur
    The Great Boer War, **2:**241
    Partridge (Frances) and, **2:**269
Concentration camps. *See* Holocaust concentration camps
Conclusive Evidence (Nabokov). *See Speak, Memory* (Nabokov)

Concubines, in Japan, **2:**299
Condict, Jemima, *Jemima Condict,* **2:**78–80
Coney, Juliet, **2:**91, 92
Confederacy. *See* American Civil War
Confession, A (Tolstoy), **1:**193–195, 270
Confessions (Augustine), **1:**196–199
    The Autobiography of Giambattista Vico (Vico) vs., **1:**183
    The Autobiography of Malcolm X (Malcolm X) vs., **1:**186
    Confessions (Rousseau) influenced by, **1:**197, 201
    A Confession (Tolstoy) vs., **1:**193
    as first autobiography, **1:**196
    Teresa of Ávila influenced by, **1:**211
Confessions (Rousseau), **1:**193, 197, **200–203,** 276
Confessions of Lady Nijō (Nijō), **2:**59–61
Confessions of Nat Turner, The (Styron), **1:**204, 206
Confidence (James), **2:**114
Confieso que he vivido (Neruda). *See Memoirs* (Neruda)
Conflict Quarterly, **3:**277
Confluencia (journal), **1:**109
Confucianism, **3:**124–126
    gender roles in, **3:**147
    Kim Ku influenced by, **1:**322
    Kong Decheng on, **3:**124–126
    movements against, **3:**124, 126
    rituals of, **3:**124, 125
Confucius, **3:**125
    descendants of, **3:**124–126
Congo
    Belgian colonial rule of, **2:**192–194, *193*
    Conrad's (Joseph) travels in, **2:**192–194
Congo Diary, The (Conrad), **2:**192–194
Congress, Continental, **2:**69
Congress, U.S.
    gag rule on slavery in, **2:**70
    House Un-American Activities Committee of, **2:**152

    and water resources on reservations, **1:**69
Congress of Racial Equality, **2:**32
Congress Party (India), **1:**242, 289, 290, 291
Connally, John B., **3:**202, 203
Connecticut Gazette (newspaper), **2:**44
Conner, John, **2:**295
Conner, Valerie Jean, *The National War Labor Board,* **3:**153–154
Connolly, Cyril, **2:**235
Conquered, The (Mitchison), **2:**237
Conquest, Robert, **3:**19
Conrad, Joseph
    Almayer's Folly, **2:**192
    The Congo Diary, **2:**192–194
    Dogs Bark, **1:**166
    Heart of Darkness, **2:**192–193, 194
    Last Essays, **2:**193, 194
    Literary Fund and, **2:**207
    "An Outpost of Progress," **2:**192, 194
    "Up-river Book," **2:**194
Conrad, Peter, **2:**153–154
Conroy, Frank, **1:**165
    Body and Soul, **1:**166
    Stop-Time, **1:164–166,** 270
Conscientious objectors (COs)
    in Vietnam War, **3:**221–223, *222*
    in World War II, **2:**268–269, **3:**223, 227–229
Conscientious Objectors and the Second World War (Eller), **3:**227
Consciousness
    double, Obama (Barack) on, **1:**79
    in locked-in syndrome, **1:**6
    racial, Du Bois (W. E. B.) in advancement of, **1:**4
Consolation of Philosophy (Boethius), **2:**14
Constantine (Roman emperor), **1:**196
Constitution, Mexican, **3:**302
Constitutional amendments, U.S.
    Fifteenth, **1:**50, **2:**238
    Fourteenth, **1:**50
    Nineteenth, **1:**13
    Thirteenth, **1:**50

Consumerism, rise of, before Great Depression, **3:**161
Containment policy, U.S., **3:**205
Conteh-Morgan, John D., **1:**129, 130
Contemporary Irish Traditional Narrative (Harvey), **3:**315
Contemporary Jewish Record (magazine), **1:**333
Contemporary Literary Criticism (journal), **1:**159
Contemporary Literature (journal), **1:**47, 48, 49
Contemporary Sociology (journal), **3:**303
Contentious Lives (Auyero), **3:**268
Contested Territories (Beatty-Medina and Rinehart), **3:**326
Continental Congress, **2:**69
Controlled Substances Act of 1970 (U.S.), **2:**294
Conversation in Religion & Theology (journal), **2:**195
Conversations with Myself (Mandela), **1:**27–28
Cony, Daniel, **2:**331, 332
Cook, E. T., **1:**265
Cook, Haruko Taya, *Japan at War*, **3:215–217**
Cook, Theodore F., *Japan at War*, **3:215–217**
Cooper, Ilene, **1:**162
Cooper, James Fenimore, *Last of the Mohicans,* **1:**56
Cooper, Laura, **3:**155
Coox, Alvin, **3:**216
Copenhagen (Frayn), **3:**239
Corcoran, Patrick, **1:**62
Corngold, Stanley, **2:**122
Corn King and the Spring Queen, The (Mitchison), **2:**237
Cornwell, Jocelyn, *Hard-Earned Lives,* **3:**170
Corr, Edwin G., **3:**205, 206
Correspondence. *See* Letter(s)
Corrigan, Felicitas, **2:**248
Corrigan, Philip, **3:**54
Corsini, Lorenzo, **1:**185
Cortizas, Nancy, **3:**122
Cory, Arthur M., **2:**141
COs. *See* Conscientious objectors

Costa, Richard, **1:**253
Costantino, Manuela, **1:**157
Cotnoir, Daniel, **3:**232
Cottage Dialogues among the Irish Peasantry (Leadbeater), **2:**157
Cottage Diaries, The (Leadbeater), **2:**157
Cottegnies, Line, **1:**231
Cottrell, Robert, **3:**229
Coulson, Robert, *Family Mediation,* **3:**154
Counterinsurgency, in Salvadoran Civil War, **3:**205, 206
Counter-Reformation, **1:**211
Count of Monte Christo, The (Dumas), **1:**6
Country of My Skull (Krog), **3:242–244**
Country Parson, A (Woodforde), **2:287–289**
Country Voices (Masumoto), **3:**224
Couple of Blaguards, A (McCourt), **1:**119
Courlander, Harold, *The African,* **1:**262
Courtney, Roger, *Palestinian Policeman,* **2:**104
Courts. *See* Judicial system; Supreme Court
Couser, G. Thomas, **2:**251
Coustillas, Pierre, **2:**320, 321
Coverdale, Linda, **3:**259
Coward, Noël, *The Noël Coward Diaries,* **2:**152
Cox, James M., **1:**246, 247
Cox, Virginia, **2:**161
CPS. *See* Civilian Public Service
Crabbe, George, **2:**158
Craig, Ann L.
  The First Agraristas, **3:**167, **302–304**
  Popular Movements and Political Change in Mexico, **3:**302
  Transforming State-Society Relations in Mexico, **3:**302
Crane, Hart, **2:**152
Crane, Stephen, **2:**240
Crangle, Sara, **2:**325–326
Cranmer, Thomas, **2:**97, 98
Cranston, Edwin A., **2:**190

Crapanzano, Vincent, *Tuhami,* **3:**47
Crashing Thunder (Radin), **3:**318
Crawford, Julie, **2:**63
Crawford, Miki Ward, *Japanese War Brides in America,* **3:127–130**
Creation stories
  Apache, **1:**302
  Kiowa, **1:**54, 55
Creswell, John, **1:**280–281
Crèvecoeur, Michel-Guillaume Saint-Jean de, *Letters from an American Farmer,* **2:213–216**
Crick, Francis, **3:**37
Crimean War (1853–1856), **1:**111–113
Criminal activity. *See* Hate crimes; War crimes
Crisis (journal), **1:**4
Crisp, Samuel, **2:**312–313
Critical Review (newspaper), **2:**206
Criticism. *See* Literary criticism
Criticism (journal), **1:**188, 260, **2:**8
Critique (journal), **1:**165, 166
Critofari, Rita, **1:**40
Croker, John, **2:**314
Cromwell, Oliver, **1:**315, **2:**26, 65, 72, 178, 256
Cross and a Star, A (Agosín), **1:75–77,** 99
Cross and the Pear Tree, The (Perera), **1:**99
Cross-cultural adoption, Kim (Elizabeth) on, **1:**102–104
Cross-cultural autobiographies
  The Abandoned Baobab (Bugul), **1:**61–64
  Chona (Chona and Underhill), **1:**69–71
  The Color of Water (McBride), **1:**72–74
  A Cross and a Star (Agosín), **1:**75–77
  The Dark Child (Laye), **1:**128–130
  Dreams from My Father (Obama), **1:**78–80
  Infidel (Hirsi Ali), **1:**207–209
  The Interesting Narrative of the Life of Olaudah Equiano (Equiano), **1:**81–83
  A Long Way from Home (McKay), **1:**84–86

Meatless Days (Suleri), **1**:87–89

Memoirs of an Arabian Princess from Zanzibar (Ruete), **1**:90–92

My Life Story (Amrouche), **1**:93–95

Prison Writings (Peltier), **1**:96–97

Rites: A Guatemalan Boyhood (Perera), **1**:99–101

Ten Thousand Sorrows (Kim), **1**:102–104

The Travels of Marco Polo (Polo), **1**:105–107

When I Was Puerto Rican (Santiago), **1**:108–110

The Woman Warrior (Kingston), **1**:173–175

The Wonderful Adventures of Mrs. Seacole (Seacole), **1**:111–113

The Worlds of a Maasai Warrior (Saitoti), **1**:114–116

Cross-cultural families. *See* Multicultural families

Cross-cultural identity. *See* Multicultural and multiracial identities

Crothers, A. Glenn, **3**:192

Crow, Liz, **1**:45

Crow Dog, Leonard, **1**:21

Crow Dog, Mary. *See* Brave Bird, Mary

Crowell, Sandra, *Up the Swiftwater*, **3**:93

Crowley, Stephen, **3**:341

Cruikshank, Julie, *Life Lived Like a Story*, **3**:320

Crusade in Europe (television show), **3**:234

Crusades, **1**:285–288, **2**:226

Cruse, Howard, *Stuck Rubber Baby*, **1**:139

Cruzeiro Internacional, O (magazine), **1**:222

Cry, the Beloved Country (Paton), **1**:27

Cuba
  immigration to U.S. from, **1**:296–298
  Medina (Pablo) on life in, **1**:296–297
  Motorcycle Diaries (Guevara) in, **2**:220
  Revolution in (*See* Cuban Revolution)
  runaway slaves in, oral histories of, **3**:7–9
  War of Independence in, **3**:7

Cuban American(s)
  autobiographical tradition of, **1**:296–297
  Medina (Pablo) on life as, **1**:296–298

Cuban identity, **1**:296–297

Cuban Revolution, **1**:296
  Chapelle's (Dickey) reporting on, **2**:280
  end of, **2**:222
  Guevara (Ernesto "Che") in, **2**:220, 221, 222

Cuban War of Independence (1895–1898), **3**:7

Cubilié, Anne, **3**:35

Cugoana, Ottobah, *Thoughts and Sentiments on the Evil and Wicked Traffic of the Slavery and Commerce of the Human Species*, **1**:81

Culman, Ernest, **3**:15

Cultural identity. *See also* Multicultural and multiracial identities
  of Korean American adoptees, **1**:102–103

Cultural Revolution (1966–1976)
  Cheng Yu-hsiu on, **1**:153
  Confucianism's rebirth after, **3**:124
  Jiang (Ji-li) on, **1**:161–162
  Kong Demao in, **3**:124–125
  Min (Anchee) on, **1**:158–160
  oral histories of, **3**:287–289, 299–300
  policies of, **3**:287, 299
  start of, **3**:287

Cultural studies, rise of, **1**:15

Cultural transmission, by Native Americans, **3**:107–109, 325–326

Culture. *See* Popular culture; *specific cultures*

Cumming, L. M., **1**:316

Cunningham, Valentine, **3**:59–60

Cuppy, Will, **2**:193–194

Curiosities of Literature (D'Israeli), **2**:177

Curious Journey (film), **3**:27, 28

Curious Journey (Griffith and O'Grady). *See Ireland's Unfinished Revolution* (Griffith and O'Grady)

Curnutt, Kirk, **1**:333

Curriculum Vitae (Klemperer), **2**:304, 305

Currie, Ruth Douglas, **2**:252

Curtin, Philip D., *Africa Remembered*, **3**:141

Curtis, Anthony, **2**:185

Custer, George, **3**:110

Custer Died for Our Sins (Deloria), **1**:54

Custis, Lemuel R., **3**:250

Cvetkovich, Ann, **1**:141

Cyprès, Jean-Philippe, *Women of Coal*, **3**:337

Czechoslovakia
  Kafka (Franz) on life in, **2**:120–122
  Prague Spring in, **3**:33

D

Daedalus (journal), **2**:122

Dahlgren, Dorothy, *In All the West No Place Like This*, **3**:93

Daily Arkansas Gazette (newspaper), **1**:147

Daily Show, The (television show), **1**:312

Daisy Miller (James), **1**:133, **2**:114

Daklugie, Asa, **1**:302

Dakota Territory, homesteaders in, **2**:163–164

Dalai Lama, **1**:96

Dale, Gareth, **3**:247

Dale, Stephen, **2**:231

Dalfiume, Richard M., *Desegregation of the U.S. Armed Forces*, **3**:248

Dallaire, Roméo, *Shake Hands with the Devil*, **3**:258

Dallaway, James, **2**:36

Dalrymple, William, **2**:231

Daly, Jane, **2**:229

Daly, Leo, **2**:159

Daly, Mary, *Gyn/Ecology*, **2**:3, 5

Dana, Richard Henry, *Two Years before the Mast*, **1**:234

SUBJECT INDEX

Dancing, by teachers, ban on, **3**:78
Daniel, Samuel, **2**:62, 63, 256
Daniels, Roger, **3**:225–226
Danish autobiographical writing, by Kierkegaard (Søren), **2**:166–169
Danish national identity, **2**:166
Dantas, Audálio, **2**:6, 7
Dardis, Kimiko, **3**:128
Daring Hearts (Brighton Ourstory), **3**:70–72
Dark Child, The (Laye), **1**:128–131
Darkness Visible (Styron), **1**:204–206
Darkwater (Du Bois), **1**:3
Darley, Gillian, **2**:67
Darry, Walt, **3**:95
Darwaza, Muhammad 'Izzat, **2**:104
Darwin, Charles, **1**:66
    The Autobiography of Charles Darwin, **1**:65–68
    The Descent of Man, **1**:65
    Journal and Remarks 1832–1835, **1**:65
    London and the Life (Gissing) on, **2**:321
    On the Origin of Species, **1**:65
Darwin, Emma, **1**:65
Darwish, Mahmoud, **1**:256
    In the Presence of Absence, **1**:255–257
    Journal of an Ordinary Grief, **1**:255
    Letters Underway (Ghazzawi) on, **2**:50
    Memory for Forgetfulness, **1**:255, 257, **2**:50
Das, Kamala, *My Life,* **1**:87
Dash, G. A., *Oral History Project,* **3**:153
Dashkova, Ekaterina, *Memoirs of the Princess Daschkaw,* **2**:306
Daudet, Edmond, **2**:83
Daugherty, Rae, **3**:108
Daughter of Isis, A (Saadawi), **1**:226
Daughters of the Shtetl (Glenn), **3**:305
David, Deidre, **2**:336
Davidson, Gordon W., **2**:92
Davidson, Thomas, **2**:16
Davies, Andrew, **3**:311, 313
Davies, Catherine, **3**:73, 75
Davies, David J., **3**:289

Davin, Delia, **3**:299
Davis, Angela, *Modern Motherhood,* **3**:145
Davis, Ann Marie, **3**:128–129
Davis, Jefferson, **2**:250, *251*
Davis, Margaret H., **1**:327
Davis, Philip, **3**:318, 320
Davis, Rocío G., **1**:172, 311
Davis, Rodney O., *Herndon's Informants,* **3**:264
Davis, Susan Schaefer, **3**:48
Davis, Thulani, **1**:250
Davis, Varina, **2**:250, 251
Davison, Peter, **2**:117, 118–119
Dawes Act of 1887 (U.S.), **3**:107
Dawkins, Richard, **1**:209
Dawn (Wiesel), **1**:319
Dawson, Sarah Morgan, **2**:244, 246
Day (Wiesel), **1**:319
Day, John, *The Acts and Monuments,* **2**:97
Dayal, Samir, **1**:88–89
Daybooks, **2**:333
Days of Decision (Gioglio), **3**:221
Deacon, Florence, **3**:309
Deaf-blindness, **1**:43–46
Dean, Bradley P., **1**:235
Death
    in *The Congo Diary* (Conrad), **2**:193
    in *In the Presence of Absence* (Darwish), **1**:255–257
Death of Luigi Trastulli and Other Stories, The (Portelli), **3**:96, 157–160
Death of Synge, The (Yeats), **2**:126, 127
"Death of the Author, The" (Barthes), **1**:267, 269
Death of the Heart, The (Bowen), **2**:133
Death penalty. *See* Execution
Death threats
    against Hirsi Ali (Ayaan), **1**:207
    against Rushdie (Salman), **1**:155
De Beer, Esmond S., **2**:65, 66
DeBlasio, Donna M., **3**:97
Decameron (Boccaccio), **1**:229
Declaration of Sentiments, The, **1**:12
Decolonising the Mind (Ngũgĩ), **2**:13

De Costa, Denise, **2**:24
Deering, Dorothy, **3**:345
Deffand, La Marquise du, **2**:268
Defoe, Daniel, **1**:92
    Journal of the Plague Year, **2**:174
    Robinson Crusoe, **3**:183
De Forest, William, *Miss Ravenel's Conversion,* **2**:240
Degen, Bill, **3**:94
Degler, Carl N., **2**:333
De Interpretatione (Demetrius), **2**:94
De Jesus, Carolina Maria, *Child of the Dark,* **2**:6–8, **3**:164, 322
De Klerk, Frederik Willem, **1**:27
Delaney, Lucy, *From the Darkness Cometh the Light,* **2**:250
Delaney, William, **2**:278, 279
Delaware Indians, oral histories of, **3**:107–109
Delaware Tribe in a Cherokee Nation (Obermeyer), **3**:326
Delbo, Charlotte, *Auschwitz and After,* **3**:34
Deleuze, Gilles, **2**:122
Del Giudice, Luisa, **3**:267
Deliverance (film), **3**:68
Deliverance (silent film), **1**:44
Dell'antichissima sapienza italica (Vico), **1**:183
Deloria, Vine, Jr., **3**:111
    Custer Died for Our Sins, **1**:54
Delta Airlines, **3**:154
Demetrius, *De Interpretatione,* **2**:94
Democracy, Du Bois (W. E. B.) on, **1**:4, 5
Democratic National Convention of 2004, **1**:78
Denetdale, Jennifer Nez, **3**:10, 12, 291
Deng Xiaoping, **3**:299
Denial
    as final phase of genocide, **3**:42
    of HIV-AIDS link, **3**:274
    of Holocaust, **3**:50
De Niro, Robert, **1**:47, 49
Denmark
    Kierkegaard (Søren) in, **2**:166–169
    national identity of, **2**:166
Denton, Kirk A., **2**:172

Depression (economic). *See* Great Depression

Depression (mood)

    Lincoln's (Abraham) struggle with, **3:**263

    rise of memoirs of, **1:**204–205

    Styron (William) on battle with, **1:**204–205

De Profundis (Wilde), **2:**9–11

De Quincey, Thomas, **2:**67, 140

Dernière impression, La (Haddad), **2:**262

Derounian-Stodola, Kathryn Zabelle, **1:**326, 327

Derrida, Jacques, **2:**167

Desai, Anita, *In Custody,* **1:**87

Descartes, René, *Discourse on the Method,* **1:**183, 184

Descent of Man, The (Darwin), **1:**65

Description of the New World, A (Cavendish), **1:**231

Desegregation of the U.S. Armed Forces (Dalfiume), **3:**248

Desert Exile (Uchida), **1:**309

Desert Solitaire (Abbey), **1:**234

Desert Storm, Operation. *See* Gulf War

Desmond, Adrian, **1:**67

Des Pres, Terrence, **2:**24

Destruction and Reconstruction (Taylor), **2:**250

Detained (Ngũgĩ), **1:**215, **2:**12–15

De Tilène au Plateau (Diallo), **1:**64

Detroit (Michigan)

    civil rights movement in, oral histories of, **3:**99–101

    migration of African Americans to, **3:**99

    race riots in, **3:**99, 100, *100,* 101

Detroit Lives (Mast), **3:**99

Detroit Summer, **3:**101

Detroit Urban League, **3:**99, 101

Detroit WestSiders, **3:**99

Deutschmann, David, **2:**220

De Valera, Eamon, **3:**27

De Veaux, Alexis, **2:**5

Dever, Carolyn, **1:**67

Devil on the Cross (Ngũgĩ), **2:**12, 13

Devil That Danced on the Water, The (Forna), **1:**312

DeVore, Irven, **3:**37

DeVoto, Bernard, **1:**148

DeWitt, John L., **3:**224

Dial (magazine), **1:**52, 233, **2:**92

Diallo, Bakary, *Force-Bonté,* **1:**61

Diallo, Nafissatou, *De Tilène au Plateau,* **1:**64

Dialogue and Armed Conflict (Roett and Smyth), **3:**205

Dialogues (Augustine), **1:**186

Dialogues (Rousseau), **1:**200

Diamonds, of Sierra Leone, **1:**312

Diaoyu/Senkaku (islands), **1:**340

Diaries. *See also specific works and writers*

    of American Civil War, **2:**244, 271

    British, in Mass Observation Project, **2:**235, 237

    D'Israeli (Isaac) on study of, **2:**177–179

    fictional, **2:**174

    Lejeune (Philippe) on study of, **2:**174–176

    posthumous publication of, **2:**174

    privacy as defining characteristic of, **2:**174

    rise in popularity of, **2:**65, 66, 120, 174, 177

    as source for biographies, **2:**177, 178

Diaries, 1915–1918 (Sassoon), **2:**247–249

Diaries, 1931–1949 (Orwell), **2:**117–119

Diaries of Beatrice Webb (Webb), **2:**16–18

Diaries of Franz Kafka, The (Kafka), **2:**120–122

Diaries of Lady Anne Clifford, The (Clifford), **2:**62–64

Diário da Noite (newspaper), **2:**6

Diary, Reminiscences and Correspondence of Henry Crabb Robinson (Robinson), **2:**75–77

Diary and Letters of Madame D'Arblay (Burney), **2:**312, 314

Diary from Dixie, A (Chesnut), **2:**250–252

Diary of a Madman (Gogol), **2:**174

Diary of Anaïs Nin, The (Nin), **2:**123–125

Diary of Anne Frank, The (Frank), **2:**253–255, *254*

    An Interrupted Life (Hillesum) vs., **2:**22

    Night (Wiesel) vs., **1:**320

    Red Scarf Girl (Jiang) inspired by, **1:**161

    Thura's Diary (Al-Windawi) vs., **2:**275, 277

    A Woman in Berlin (anonymous) vs., **2:**281

    A Woman Soldier's Own Story (Xie) vs., **1:**340

    Zlata's Diary (Filipovic) vs., **2:**338, 339, 340

Diary of a Nobody, The (Grossmith and Grossmith), **2:**174

Diary of John Evelyn, The (Evelyn), **2:**65–68, 72, 328

Diary of John Quincy Adams, The (Adams), **2:**69–71

Diary of Khalil al-Sakakini, The (Sakakini), **2:**104, 106

Diary of Lady Murasaki, The (Murasaki), **2:**59, 290–293

Diary of Robert Hooke, The (Hooke), **2:**72

Diary of Samuel Pepys, The (Pepys), **2:**72–74

    The Diary of John Evelyn (Evelyn) vs., **2:**65, 66, 72

    posthumous publication of, **2:**174, 328

    Scott (Walter) influenced by, **2:**309

Diary of Sir Henry Slingsby, The (Slingsby), **2:**256–258

Diary of Virginia Woolf, The (Woolf), **2:**133, 163, 180–182

Diary without Dates, A (Bagnold), **1:**329, **2:**259–261

Diary with Reminiscences of the War and Refugee Life in the Shenandoah Valley, A (McDonald), **2:**271

Dias, Bartolomeu, **2:**198, 199, 200

Díaz, Porfirio, **3:**167, 302, 303

Dib, Mohammed, **2:**262

DiCaprio, Leonardo, **1:**47, 49

Dickens, Charles
   American Notes, **1:**43, 146, **2:**223
   Crèvecoeur (Michel-Guillaume Saint-Jean de) and, **2:**214
   The Diaries of Franz Kafka (Kafka) on, **2:**120
   Emerson (Ralph Waldo) and, **2:**140
   Goethe's (Johann Wolfgang von) influence on, **1:**276
   Journal of Katherine Mansfield (Mansfield) on, **2:**133
   London and the Life (Gissing) on, **2:**321
Dickey, Roland, **1:**56
Dickinson, Emily, **2:**238
Dictators, Latin American right-wing, rise of, **3:**185
Dictee (Cha), **1:**102
Didion, Joan, *Slouching towards Bethlehem*, **1:**88
Diet, of Gandhi (Mohandas), **1:**243. See also Food
Dieterich-Ward, Allen, **3:**96, 98
Dietrich, Marlene, **3:**295
Different Voices (Rittner and Roth), **3:**34
Dillard, Annie, **1:**280
   An American Childhood, **1:**279
   Living by Fiction, **1:**279
   Pilgrim at Tinker Creek, **1:**279
   Teaching a Stone to Talk, **1:**279
   The Writing Life, **1:**168, **279–281**
Dillard, Ernest, **3:**99–100
Diné. See Navajo
Di Porcía, Gian Artico, **1:**183, 184
Direct action, in civil rights movement, **2:**32–34
Dirrane, Bridget, **3:**316
Dirty Realism movement, **1:**48
Disabilities, people with
   Bauby (Jean-Dominique) on experience of, **1:**6–8
   education of, **1:**43, 44–45
   Keller (Helen) on experience of, **1:**43–46
   social construction of "able body" and, **1:**8
Disability & Society (journal), **1:**45

Disability literature, *The Diving Bell and the Butterfly* (Bauby) as, **1:**8
Disability studies, **1:**8, 41
Disability Studies Quarterly, **1:**41
"Disabled" (Owen), **1:**8
Disappearances, mass
   in Chile, **1:**75
   in Guatemala, **1:**99
Discourse on the Method (Descartes), **1:**183, 184
Discovery of India, The (Nehru), **1:**290, 291
Disease. *See specific diseases*
Dispatches (Herr), **1:**259, **3:**209
D'Israeli, Benjamin, **2:**177, 179
D'Israeli, Isaac
   Curiosities of Literature, **2:**177
   Miscellanies, **2:**177
   "Some Observations on Diaries, Self-Biography, and Self-Characters," **2:**177–179
Dissent (Bradley), **1:**80
DiStasi, Lawrence, *Una Storia Segreta*, **3:**224
Diurnal texts, **2:**163, 164
Divers Voyages Touching the Discoverie of America (Hakluyt), **2:**229
Divine Songs and Meditacions (Collins), **1:**229
Divine visions, of Teresa of Ávila, **1:**211, 212
Divine will, Usāmah ibn Munqidh on, **1:**285, 286
Diving Bell and the Butterfly, The (Bauby), **1:6–8**
Diving Bell and the Butterfly, The (film), **1:**6, 7
Division Street (Terkel), **3:**161, 299, 343
Divorce, in Heian period of Japan, **2:**299
Djebar, Assia, **1:**93
   Women of Algiers in Their Apartment, **1:**207
Do, Anh, *The Happiest Refugee*, **1:**337
Dobe region (Africa), oral histories of !Kung people of, **3:**37–38
Documentary films. *See also specific films*

   on Ballard (Martha), **2:**331
   on Delaware Indians, **3:**325
   on Holocaust, **3:**50, 52
   on Irish independence movement, **3:**27, 28
   on IWW, **3:**328
   on Navajo-Hopi land dispute, **3:**10, 11, 12
   on Peltier (Leonard), **1:**96
   on Saitoti (Tepilit Ole), **1:**114
   on Ukrainian coal miners, **3:**340
   on World War II, **3:**234
Documentary prose, in *Voices from Chernobyl* (Alexievich), **3:**282, 285
Dodd, Thomas J., **3:**294
Dodd, William E., **2:**251
Does My Head Look Big in This? (Abdel-Fattah), **1:**41–42
Dogs, in *A Country Parson* (Woodforde), **2:**288, 289
Dogs Bark (Conrad), **1:**166
Doi, Kochi, **2:**190, 290, 292
Doing Oral History (Ritchie), **3:**186, 294, 345
Doing Time for Peace (Riegle), **3:**229
Domesticity
   Stanton (Elizabeth Cady) on, **1:**13, 14
   Wordsworth (Dorothy) on, **2:**300, 301
Domestic Manners of the Americans (Trollope), **2:**223
Domestic violence
   in Islam, Hirsi Ali (Ayaan) on, **1:**207–209
   Malcolm X on experience of, **1:**187
   Wolff (Tobias) on experience of, **1:**47–49
Domingo, Jesús, **3:**169
Domingues, Francisco, **2:**200
Donald, David Herbert, **3:**263
Doña María's Story (James), **3:73–76**
Donbass region (Ukraine), oral histories of miners in, **3:**340–342
Donne, John, **2:**62
Donovan, Frances R., *The Schoolma'am*, **3:**77
Doody, Margret Anne, **2:**314

Doolittle, Hilda. *See* H.D.
Door, The (film), **3:**284
Dore, Elizabeth, **3:**75
Dorfman, Ariel, *Heading South, Looking North,* **1:**75
Doris Duke Indian Oral History Project, **3:**290
Doss, Helen, *The Family Nobody Wanted,* **1:**102
Dostoyevsky, Fyodor, **2:**22, 120, 133, 183, 184
Double consciousness, Obama (Barack) on, **1:**79
Double Jeopardy (Baumel), **3:**35
Dougherty, Jack, **3:**22
Dougherty, Jane Elizabeth, **1:**263
Douglas, Alfred, **2:**9–10
Douglas, David, **2:**309, 310
Douglass, Frederick, **1:**34. *See also Narrative of the Life of Frederick Douglass* (Douglass)
    Grimké (Charlotte Forten) influenced by, **2:**29
    Life and Times of Frederick Douglass, **1:**34
    My Bondage and My Freedom, **1:**34
    "Self-Made Men," **1:**180
    "What, to the Slave, Is the Fourth of July?," **1:**79
Dove Cottage (Grasmere), **2:**300, *301*
Down Came the Rain (Shields), **1:**204
Downing, Taylor, **3:**235, 236
Down These Mean Streets (Thomas), **1:**109
Draft, U.S. military, **3:**221–223
Drake, Barbara, **2:**172
Drake, Betsy, **2:**102
Dreaming of Sheep in Navajo Country (Weisiger), **3:**10
Dream of Africa, A (Laye), **1:**129
Dreams from My Father (Obama), **1:78–80**
Dreams of Trespass (Mernissi), **1:**226, 227
Dred Scott decision, **2:**38
Dreiser, Theodore, **1:**273, **2:**136
    Harlan Miners Speak, **3:**96
Drew, Bettina, **2:**338, 339, 340
Drinnon, Richard, **3:**320

Drugs
    adolescent use of, *Go Ask Alice* (anonymous) on, **2:**294–296
    in culture of 1960s, **2:**294
    U.S. war on, **2:**294
    Williams's (Tennessee) struggle with addiction to, **2:**152
Drummond, Henry, **1:**150
Dryden, John, **1:**90
D'Souza, Dinesh, **3:**166
Dube, John, **2:**241
Duberman, Martin, **1:**4
Dublin (Ireland)
    Abbey Theatre of, **2:**126, 128
    oral histories of life in, **3:**315, 317
Dublin Pub Life and Lore (Kearns), **3:**315, 317
Dublin Voices (Kearns), **3:**315
Du Bois, W. E. B., **1:**4
    The Autobiography of W. E. B. Du Bois, **1:3–5,** 18
    on *Black Boy* (Wright), **1:**123
    Black Flame trilogy, **1:**5
    Darkwater, **1:**3
    Dusk of Dawn, **1:**3, 4
    on *Home to Harlem* (McKay), **1:**84
    The Souls of Black Folk, **1:**4, 51
    The Study of the Negro Problem, **1:**50
    on *Up from Slavery* (Washington), **1:**51, 52
    and Washington (Booker T.), debate between, **1:**186
Dudley, David L., **1:**4
Duesberg, Peter, **3:**274
Duffey, Carolyn, **1:**93, 94
Dumas, Alexandre, *The Count of Monte Christo,* **1:**6
Dumm, Gary, *Students for a Democratic Society,* **3:**330
Dunbar, Paul Laurence, "Sympathy," **1:**50
Duncan, Isadora, **1:**85
Duncan, Patti, **1:**159
Duncan, Robert, **2:**123
Dundas, Henry, **2:**217–219
Dunham, Ann, **1:**78
Dunham, Janice, **1:**97

Dunmore, Helen, **1:**195
Dunn, Oliver, **2:**203
Dunnaway, Jen, **3:**201
Dunton, John, **2:**195
Duong Thu Huong, *Paradise of the Blind,* **1:**335
Duong Van Minh, **3:**280
Durham University Journal, **2:**185
Durrell, Lawrence, **2:**123
Duryea, Lyman C., **3:**206
Dusk of Dawn (Du Bois), **1:**3, 4
Dustan, Hannah, **1:**326, 328
Duston, Troy, **3:**20
Dust Tracks on a Road (Hurston), **1:9–11,** 18, 122
Dutch autobiographical writing
    by Hillesum (Etty), **2:**22–24
    by Hirsi Ali (Ayaan), **1:**207–209
Dyer, Geoff, **2:**81
Dyer, Reginald, **1:**289
Dyk, Ruth, **3:**319
Dyk, Walter, *Left Handed, Son of Old Man Hat,* **3:318–321**
Dykes to Watch Out For (Bechdel), **1:**139, 141
Dylan, Bob, **3:**159
Dziak, John, *Chekisty,* **3:**245

E

Eaglestone, Robert, **1:**313–314
Eakin, Paul John, **1:**188, 246
Early American Literature (journal), **1:**327
Earthquakes
    in China, **3:**301
    in Iran, **3:**220
East, Rupert, *Akiga's Story,* **3:**141
East Anglia (England), oral histories of village life in, **3:**59–61, *60*
Eastern California Museum (ECM), **3:**102
Easter Uprising of 1916 (Ireland), **3:**27, *28,* 315
East Germany, oral histories of Stasi in, **3:**245–247
East India Company, **2:**229–231
East of the Mediterranean (Munif), **2:**50

Easton, Celia A., **2:**289
East West Exchange, **1:**163
Eberstadt, Fernanda, **1:**156–157
Ecce Homo (Nietzsche), **1:**183
Echeverría, Luis, **3:**32
Eclectic Review (journal), **2:**178–179
ECM. *See* Eastern California Museum
Eco-criticism, **1:**279
Economic disparity
    industrialization in rise of, **2:**300
    among Native Americans, **3:**290
    in oral histories, **3:**190
Economic opportunity, for blacks in Reconstruction era, **1:**50
Economic Opportunity Act of 1964 (U.S.), **3:**254, *255*
Economic problems. *See* Finances, personal
Economic racism, **1:**4
Economics, of cancer, **2:**3–4, 5
Economist, The (weekly), **1:**126, **3:**300–301
Economy
    Britain, working class in, **3:**53
    Chinese, as socialist market, **1:**158
    German, after World War I, **1:**30, **3:**234
    Mexican, indigenous people in, **3:**168
Economy, U.S. *See also* Great Depression
    prosperity in, before Great Depression, **3:**161
    slavery in, **1:**33
    women in post-revolutionary, **2:**331–332
    after World War II, **3:**343
Écriture artiste, **2:**81, 83
Écriture feminine, **1:**250, **2:**124
Edel, Leon, **2:**113, 115
Edele, Mark, **3:**332
Edelstein, Tilden, **2:**239, 240
Edgeworth, Maria, **2:**157
Edinburgh Review (journal), **2:**35, 36, 73, 314
Editor & Publisher (magazine), **2:**279

Education
    Arab, poetry in, **1:**287
    in Britain, **2:**136, 320, **3:**311–313
    of children with disabilities, **1:**43, 44–45
    French, in Algeria, **1:**93, 94, **2:**262–263
    Islamic, in Egypt, **1:**135
    self-, Franklin (Benjamin) on, **1:**179, 180
    of women (*See* Education, of women)
Education, in U.S.
    Adams's (Henry) critique of, **1:**132–134
    affirmative action in, **1:**15
    of African Americans, at white colleges, **3:**20–22
    of African Americans, in Reconstruction, **1:**51
    anarchists' critique of, **3:**5
    bilingual, **1:**15–17
    at experimental boarding schools, **1:**164
    of Native Americans, at boarding schools, **3:**109, 318
    oral histories of teachers in, **3:**77–79
    racial quotas in, **3:**20
    Rodriguez (Richard) on, **1:**15–16
    school desegregation in, **1:**122, 249, **3:**44
    secondary, as compulsory, **3:**343
    of slaves, in preparation for emancipation, **2:**29–31, *30*
Education, of women
    in eighteenth-century Europe, **2:**35–36
    in eighteenth-century U.S., **2:**316–318
    in fifteenth-century Europe, **2:**160–161
    in Morocco, **3:**49
Education Act of 1870 (Britain), **3:**311
Educational Studies (journal), **3:**78
Education of Henry Adams, The (Adams), **1:**15, **132–134**, 180
Edwardian Childhoods (Thompson), **3:**312

Edwardians, The (Thompson), **3:**176, 186, 311
Edwards, Beatrice, *Places of Origin,* **3:**205
Edwards, Jonathan, **2:**197
Edwards, Louise, **3:**148–149
Edwards, Matilda, **3:**263
Edwards, Reginald, **3:**201
Edward VI (king of England), *The Literary Remains of Edward VI,* **2:97–100**, *98*
Edward VII (king of Great Britain), **2:**210
Edward VIII (king of Great Britain), **2:**235
Egan, Susanna, **1:**248
Eggers, Dave, *Voice of Witness,* **3:**161
Eglington, Lord, **2:**329
Egocentrism, Soyinka (Wole) accused of, **1:**216
Egotism, Romantic, **2:**177, 179
Egypt
    autobiographical tradition of, **1:**136
    British colonial rule of, **1:**135
    Hussein (Taha) on life in, **1:**135–137
    independence of (1922), **1:**135
    Islamic education in, **1:**135
    Revolution of 1919 in, **1:**135
    Revolution of 1952 in, **1:**135
    Usāmah ibn Munqidh on history of, **1:**285
Egyptian Childhood, An (Hussein), **1:135–138**
Eickelcamp, Ute, **3:**334
Eighteen Poems (Thomas), **1:**125
Eighteenth-Century Studies (journal), **1:**327
8 mars (journal), **3:**47
Eighty Years and More, Reminiscences 1815–1897 (Stanton), **1:12–14**
Eikon Basilike (Charles I), **2:**256, 258
Einstein, Albert, **3:**239
Eire, Carlos, *Waiting for Snow in Havana,* **1:**296–297
Eire-Ireland (journal), **2:**308
Ejército Zapatista de Liberación Nacional (EZLN), **3:**304

Ejido (land collective), **3:**302–304

Elaine Massacre (1919), **1:**18

Elementary Education Act of 1870 (Britain), **2:**136, 320

Elena, Eduardo, **3:**75

El Fassi, Malika, **3:**48

Elfenbein, Andrew, **2:**144, 145

ELH (journal), **2:**64

Eli (Sachs), **2:**255

Eliach, Yaffa, **3:**34
    Holocaust Oral History Manual, **3:**35

Eliot, T. S., **2:**147, 180

Elizabeth Cady Stanton as Revealed in Her Letters, Diary and Reminiscences (Stanton and Stanton), **1:**13

Elizabeth I (queen of England), **2:**62, 72, 99

Elle (magazine), **1:**6

Eller, Cynthia, *Conscientious Objectors and the Second World War*, **3:**227

Ellipses, Bagnold's (Enid) use of, **2:**260

Ellis, Henry, **2:**226

Ellis, Russ, **3:**21, 22

Ellison, Ralph, **1:**122, 124

Ellman, Richard, **2:**10

Ellwood, Thomas, **2:**26

Elman, Richard, **1:**100

Elon, Amos, **2:**304

El Salvador, oral histories of civil war in, **3:**205–208, *206*

El Salvador at War (Manwaring and Prisk), **3:205–208**

El Salvador: Testament of Terror (Fish and Sganga), **3:**206

Eltis, David, **1:**263

Eluard, Paul, **2:**52

Éluard, Paul, **1:**222

Emancipation Act of 1834 (Britain), **1:**111

Emancipation Proclamation of 1863 (U.S.), **1:**50, **3:**261

Embedded journalism, **2:**278–280

Embedded: The Media at War in Iraq (Katovsky and Carlson), **3:**276

Embroideries (Satrapi), **1:**155

Emergence of a UAW Local, The (Friedlander), **3:**153

Emerson, Everett, **2:**214

Emerson, Gloria, **2:**278

Emerson, Ralph Waldo, **2:140**
    "The American Scholar," **1:**180
    Dillard (Annie) influenced by, **1:**279
    Hawthorne (Nathaniel) and, **2:**139, 223
    James's (Henry) friendship with, **2:**113
    Journals of Ralph Waldo Emerson, **2:139–142**
    "Nature," **2:**141
    Robinson's (Henry Crabb) friendship with, **2:**75
    "Self-Reliance," **1:**180
    Thoreau (Henry David) and, **1:**233, **2:**139, 140

Emigration. *See* Immigration

Emms, Stephen, **2:**154

Emotions
    of Christmas, Thomas (Dylan) on, **1:**125–126
    in *The Diary of John Quincy Adams* (Adams), **2:**70
    in "Letter to Maria Clemm" (Poe), **2:**41–43
    in Stoicism, **1:**218

Empathy, in feminist oral history, **3:**190

Enahoro, Peter, **1:**215–216

Encomienda system, **2:**202, **3:**302

En 18 (Goncourt and Goncourt), **2:**82

Enemies among Us (Schmitz), **3:**224

"Enemy aliens," U.S. treatment of, **3:**224

Enfance (Sarraute), **1:**268

Enfant Noir, L' (Laye). *See Dark Child, The* (Laye)

Engel, Jeff, **3:**232

Engelmann, Larry, *Tears before the Rain*, **3:**210, 265, **279–281**

Engendering the Chinese Revolution (Gilmartin), **3:**147

Enger, Leif, **1:**281
    Peace Like a River, **1:**281

England. *See also* Britain; English autobiographical writing; English oral histories
    agriculture in, **3:**59–61, 63–65
    Bloomsbury group in, **2:**133, 180, 268–269
    Catholicism in, decline of, **2:**97, 99, 226
    Christianity in, arrival of, **1:**189
    homosexuality in, **3:**70–72
    Irish conquest by, **3:**315
    Lessing's (Doris) move to, **1:**167
    Mansfield's (Katherine) travels in, **2:**133, 135
    Victorian (*See* Victorian era)
    women of (*See* English women)

Engle, Paul, **2:**121

English, Kathy, **3:**233

English autobiographical writing. *See also specific works and writers*
    by Bagnold (Enid), **2:**259–261
    by Barnard (Anne), **2:**217–219
    by Bennett (Arnold), **2:**136–138
    by Brittain (Vera), **1:**329–331
    by Burney (Fanny), **2:**312–314
    by Byron (George Gordon Noel), **2:**143–145
    by Cavendish (Margaret), **1:**229–231
    by Clifford (Anne), **2:**62–64
    by Conrad (Joseph), **2:**192–194
    by Darwin (Charles), **1:**65–67
    by D'Israeli (Isaac), **2:**177–179
    by Edward VI, **2:**97–99
    by Equiano (Olaudah), **1:**81–83
    by Evelyn (John), **2:**65–67
    by Fox (George), **2:**26–28
    by Gissing (George), **2:**320–322
    by Guylforde (Richarde), **2:**226–228
    by Halkett (Anne), **1:**315–317
    by Keats (John), **2:**146–148
    by Kemble (Fanny), **2:**335–337
    by Kempe (Margery), **1:**189–191
    by Last (Nella), **2:**265–267
    by Lessing (Doris), **1:**167–169
    by Maugham (W. Somerset), **2:**183–185
    by Montagu (Mary Wortley), **2:**35–37
    by Orwell (George), **2:**117–119
    by Partridge (Frances), **2:**268–270

English autobiographical writing, *continued*
- by Pepys (Samuel), **2:**72–74
- by Robinson (Henry Crabb), **2:**75–77
- in Romantic era, surge of, **2:**16
- by Ruskin (John), **1:**264–266
- by Sassoon (Siegfried), **2:**247–249
- by Slingsby (Henry), **2:**256–258
- by Victoria, **2:**209–211
- in Victorian era, traits of, **1:**65, 67
- by Webb (Beatrice), **2:**16–18
- by Wells (H. G.), **1:**252–254
- by Wesley (John), **2:**195–197
- by Wilde (Oscar), **2:**9–11
- by Wollstonecraft (Mary), **2:**109–111
- by Woodforde (James), **2:**287–289
- by Woolf (Virginia), **2:**180–182
- by Wordsworth (Dorothy), **2:**300–302

English Civil War (1642–1651)
- Anglicanism in, **2:**26, 72, 256
- Cavendish (Margaret) on life during, **1:**229, 231
- Evelyn (John) on life during, **2:**65
- Halkett (Anne) on life during, **1:**315–317
- Osborne (Dorothy) on life during, **2:**324
- Slingsby (Henry) in, **2:**256–258

English Historical Review (journal), **2:**17–18, **3:**313

English in Africa (journal), **2:**218

English Journal, **1:**16, 42, 253, **2:**254, **3:**345

English language
- *The Book of Margery Kempe* (Kempe) as first autobiography in, **1:**189
- in Puerto Rico, **1:**109
- in U.S. education, **1:**15, 16, 17

English Literature in Transition (journal), **2:**10

English oral histories
- of gays and lesbians, **3:**70–72
- of village life, **3:**59–61, 63–65
- of working-class women, **3:**144–146
- of working-class youth, **3:**311–313, *312*

English Studies in Canada (journal), **1:**169

English women
- eighteenth-century, Montagu (Mary Wortley) on opportunities for, **2:**35
- land inheritance by, Clifford (Anne) on, **2:**62–63, 64
- medieval, Kempe (Margery) on, **1:**189–191
- seventeenth-century, Clifford (Anne) on, **2:**62–64
- Victorian, Webb (Beatrice) on, **2:**16–18
- in workforce, entry of, **2:**266, **3:**145
- working-class, oral histories of, **3:**144–146
- in World War I, **1:**329–331, **2:**259

"Enigma of Arrival, The" (Paquet), **1:**112–113

Enlightenment
- Goethe (Johann Wolfgang von) in, **1:**276
- Jefferson (Thomas) in, **2:**316
- Scottish contributions to, **2:**328
- Wollstonecraft (Mary) in, **2:**109

Enneads (Plotinus), **1:**196

Enright, Pat, **3:**159

Entrepreneurs, Hispanic American, oral histories of, **3:**121–123

Entrepreneurs in Cultural Context (Greenfield), **3:**121

Environmental costs, of coal mining, **3:**66, 67, 86

Environmental factors, in cancer, **2:**3

Enzensberger, Hans Magnus, **2:**282

Enzer, Hyman A., **2:**254

Epictetus, **2:**96

Epileptic (David B.), **1:**155

Epistulae familiares (Cereta). *See Collected Letters of a Renaissance Feminist* (Cereta)

Eppes, Elizabeth, **2:**316

Epstein, Joseph, **2:**185

Equal Accommodations Act of 1938 (Michigan), **3:**99

Equality. *See* Gender equality; Racial equality; Social equality

Equal Pay Act of 1963 (U.S.), **3:**339

Equiano, Olaudah, **1:**82
- *The Interesting Narrative of the Life of Olaudah Equiano,* **1:**34, **81–83**, 142, **3:**23
- Wheatley (Phillis) compared to, **1:**81, **2:**44

Erasmus, Desiderius, **1:**196, **2:**98

Erbaugh, Mary S., **3:**301

Erdoes, Erich, **1:**23

Erdoes, Richard, **1:**21, 23

Ergas, Yasmine, **2:**23, 24

Escalante Fontaneda, Hernando de, **1:**325

Esfandiary, Soraya, *The Autobiography of H.I.H. Soraya,* **3:**218

Eskew, Glenn T., **3:**249–250

Eskimo, The (Weyer), **3:**138

Espada, Martin, **1:**109

Espectador, El (newspaper), **3:**183, 184, 185

Espionage, by Maugham (W. Somerset), **2:**183

Essais (Montaigne), **2:**72

Essay on the Principles of Population (Malthus), **1:**65

Essay to Revive the Antient Education of Gentlewomen, An (Makin), **2:**35

Essex (England), oral histories of working-class youth in, **3:**311–313, *312*

Estrangement (Yeats), **2:126–128**

Ethnic discrimination. *See* Anti-Semitism; Racism

Ethnic identity, assimilation and
- oral histories of, **3:**305
- Rodriguez (Richard) on, **1:**15–17
- Santiago (Esmeralda) on, **1:**108

Ethnicity, in *Dust Tracks on a Road* (Hurston), **1:**11

Ethnographic autobiography, Native American, **1:**69–70

Ethnography
- in *Doña María's Story* (James), **3:**73
- in *Juan the Chamula* (Pozas), **3:**167, 168
- in *Nisa* (Shostak), **3:**37–38

Ethnology (journal), **1:**115

Etter-Lewis, Gwendolyn, **3:**191
- *My Soul Is My Own,* **3:**21

Europe. *See also specific countries*
   The Autobiography of Ben Franklin (Franklin) in, **1**:181
   Bugul's (Ken) experience as African in, **1**:61–62
   colonies of (*See* Colonialism)
   gender roles in, eighteenth-century, **2**:35–37
   gender roles in, Renaissance, **2**:160–162
   instability in interwar period of, **1**:329
   James's (Henry) time in, **2**:113, 114
   Letters from an American Farmer (Crèvecoeur) in, **2**:213, 214
   querelle de femmes in early modern, **2**:160
   Ruete's (Emily) experience as African in, **1**:90–92
   student movements of 1968 in, **3**:33
   travel narratives of, **1**:90–91
   women of, vs. Muslim women, **1**:90
European Journal of American Studies, **1**:78
European Parliament, **3**:292
European Romantic Review (journal), **2**:301
Eusebius, **2**:94
Eustics, Ida Elrod, **1:10**
Evans, Elizabeth, **2**:78, 79, 80
Evans, George Ewart, *Ask the Fellows Who Cut the Hay,* **3**:59, **63–65**
Evans, Larry, **3**:340, 342
Evelina (Burney), **2**:312–313, 314
Evelyn, John, **2:66**
   Boswell (James) compared to, **2**:328
   A Character of England, **2**:65
   The Diary of John Evelyn, **2:65–68**, 72, 328
   Fumifugium, **2**:65
   Pepys (Samuel) compared to, **2**:65, 66, 72
   Sculptura, **2**:65
   Woodforde (James) compared to, **2**:287
Evelyn, Mary, **1**:229

Everybody's Autobiography (Stein), **1**:332
Everything We Had (Santoli), **3**:199, 201, **209–211**, 231, 275, 279
Evil spirits, *The Diary of Lady Murasaki* (Murasaki) on, **2**:292
Evolution, **1**:65–67
Ewen, Elizabeth, *Immigrant Women in the Land of Dollars,* **3**:305
Examiner (newspaper), **2**:146
Execution
   of Alexandra Feodorovna, **2**:84
   of Charles I, **2**:26, 65, 72, 178, 256, 257, *257*
   of Nazi war criminals, **2**:56
   of Slingsby (Henry), **2**:256, 257
Executive Order 8802, U.S., **3**:44, 248
Executive Order 9066, U.S., **1**:299, 311, **3**:104, 195, 224
Executive Order 9981, U.S., **3**:199, 249
Executive Order 11246, U.S., **3**:339
Exile
   Cavendish (Margaret) in, **1**:229
   Cubans in, **1**:296–297
   Darwish (Mahmoud) in, **1**:255
   Iranians in, **3**:218
   Jews in, **1**:75
   Laye (Camara) in, **1**:130
   Luthuli (Albert) in, **1**:24
   Nabokov (Vladimir) in, **1**:270
   Soyinka (Wole) in, **1**:214
Exiled Memories (Medina), **1:296–298**
Existentialism, Wiesel (Elie) influenced by, **1**:318
Exodus to Shanghai (Hochstadt), **3:14–16**
Experiment in Autobiography, An (Wells), **1:252–254**
Exploration, global
   by Columbus (Christopher), **2**:201–203
   by Gama (Vasco da), **2**:198–200
   tradition of narratives of, **2**:198–199
Exploration, of U.S. West, by Carver (Jonathan), **2**:205–207. *See also* Westward expansion
Expression, freedom of
   in China, **3**:301

   in South Africa, **1**:29
   in Soviet Union, **3**:333
Extraordinary Work of Ordinary Writing, The (Sinor), **2:163–165**
Extrapolation (journal), **1**:253
Extremist Islam. *See* Fundamentalist Islam
Eyes on the Prize (television series), **2**:34, **3**:44, 45, 46
Eyewitnesses at Nuremberg (Gaskin), **3**:293
EZLN. *See* Ejército Zapatista de Liberación Nacional

F

Fabian Society, **2**:16, 172, 235
Face of War, The (Gellhorn), **2**:102
Faces in a Mirror (Pahlavi), **3**:218
Fachinger, Petra, **1**:17
Faderman, Lillian, *Gay L.A.,* **3**:83–84
Fadiman, Jeffrey A.
   The Moment of Conquest, **3**:141
   An Oral History of Tribal Warfare, **3**:141
   South Africa's "Black" Market, **3**:142
   When We Began, There Were Witchmen, **3:141–143**
Faery, Rebecca Blevins, **1**:325–326
Faith. *See* Religious faith
Falk, Stanley, **3**:216
Fallen Leaves (Nguyen), **1**:335
Falling Leaves (Yen Mah), **1**:159
Fall of the Shah (Hoveyda), **3**:218
Familiar letters, **2**:217
Family(ies)
   African American, Hansberry's (Lorraine) depiction of, **1**:273–275
   Chinese, Cheng Yu-hsiu on, **1**:153
   dysfunctional, of Bechdel (Alison), **1**:139–140
   English working-class, oral histories of, **3**:144–146
   instability in, Wolff (Tobias) on, **1**:47–49
   multicultural (*See* Multicultural families)

SUBJECT INDEX

Family Letters of Thomas Jefferson, The (Jefferson), **2:**317
Family Mediation (Coulson), **3:**154
Family Nobody Wanted, The (Doss), **1:**102
Famine
   in China, **3:**287, 299, 300
   in Ireland, **3:**27, 315
   in Ukraine, **3:**19
Fano, Claudio, **3:**266
Fanon, Frantz
   Feraoun (Mouloud) compared to, **2:**262, 263, 264
   Gandhi (Mohandas) compared to, **1:**244
   The Wretched of the Earth, **1:**207, **2:**263
Fanshawe, Ann, *Memoirs,* **1:**229–230, 315, 316, 317
Fanshawe, Richard, **1:**317
Farabundo Marti National Liberation Front (FMLN), **3:**205
Faragher, John Mack, **2:**91, 92
Farah, Nurrudin, *Sweet and Sour Milk,* **1:**207
Färberböck, Max, **2:**281
Fard, W. D., **1:**188
Far Eastern Economic Review (journal), **3:**288
Farewell to Arms, A (Hemingway), **2:**259
Farewell to Manzanar (Houston and Houston), **1:299–301,** 309
Farmanfarmian, Abolbashar, **3:**220
Farmer, James, *Lay Bare the Heart,* **3:**44
Farmer-Kaiser, Mary, **2:**246
Farming. *See* Agriculture
Farming the Home Place (Matsumoto), **3:**80
Farral, Fred, **3:**177
Farrison, Edward, **1:**11
Fassin, Didier, *When Bodies Remember,* **3:**272
Fast Horse, Lizzy, **1:**22
Father's Law, A (Wright), **1:**124
"Father's Legacy, A" (Slingsby), **2:**256, 257, 258
Fatwa, against Rushdie (Salman), **1:**155

Faulkner, William, **1:**123, **2:**152
   Big Woods, **2:**215
Faunce, William, **1:**220
Fausel, Nettie, **3:**103
Faust, Drew Gilpin, **2:**246, 271, 272
Faustine, La (Goncourt), **2:**308
Favelas (shantytowns), **2:**6–8, *7*
Fay, Frank, **2:**128
Fay, Willie, **2:**128
Fayer, Steve, *Voices of Freedom,* **3:44–46**
FBI. *See* Federal Bureau of Investigation
FDR. *See* Revolutionary Democratic Front
February Revolution (1917), **2:**84
Fedele, Cassandra, **2:**160
Federal Bureau of Investigation (FBI), **1:**96–98, **3:**224
Federal Writers' Project (FWP), **3:**22, 86, 161, 173, 179
Feinesser, Bronislawa, **3:**35
Feinman, Ilene, **3:**270
Felber, Lynette, **2:**124
Fellman, Michael, **2:**39
Fellows, Jay, **1:**266
Female circumcision, Hirsi Ali (Ayaan) on, **1:**207
Female Peronist Party (Argentina), **3:**75
Feminine writing style, vs. masculine writing style, **1:**250
Feminism
   black perspective in, need for, **1:**249, 250, **2:**3, 5
   in China, rise of, **3:**147–149
   in field of history, **3:**176, 177
   in field of oral history, **3:**190–192
   first-wave, **3:**268
   global rise of, **3:**37
   and interest in women's autobiographies, **1:**37
   in peace movement, **3:**268
   second-wave, **3:**268
   of *Walden* (Thoreau), **1:**236
   during World War II, Mitchison (Naomi) on, **2:**235–236
Feminist autobiographical writing
   The Abandoned Baobab (Bugul) as, **1:**64
   Bone Black (hooks) as, **1:**249–250

   Child of the Dark (de Jesus) as, **2:**6
   Collected Letters of a Renaissance Feminist (Cereta) as, **2:**160–162
   The Collected Letters of Mary Wollstonecraft (Wollstonecraft) as, **2:**109–111
   Diaries of Beatrice Webb (Webb) as, **2:**16, 18
   The Diaries of Lady Anne Clifford (Clifford) as, **2:**64
   The Diary of Anaïs Nin (Nin) as, **2:**124
   The Journal of Marie Bashkirtseff (Bashkirtseff) as, **2:**306
   Let Me Speak! (Viezzer and Barrios de Chungara) as, **3:**322–323
   Letters and Journals of Fanny Burney (Burney) as, **2:**313–314
   Letters of a Woman Homesteader (Stewart) as, **2:**91
   The Letters of Lady Anne Barnard to Henry Dundas (Barnard) as, **2:**218
   "Letter to Her Daughter" (Montagu) as, **2:**35–37
   Meatless Days (Suleri) as, **1:**88–89
   A Mountainous Journey (Tuqan) as, **1:**225, 227
   tradition of, **1:**249
   Women in the Mines (Moore) as, **3:**337, 338
Feminist science fiction, **2:**237
Feminist Studies (journal), **1:**113
Femme d'Afrique (Kéita), **1:**64
Femmes et Politique (Akharbach and Rerhaye), **3:**47
Feng Jicai
   Let One Hundred Flowers Bloom, **1:**161
   Ten Years of Madness, **3:**287
   The Three-Inch Golden Lotus, **3:**289
   Voices from the Whirlwind, **3:287–289,** 301
Fenwomen (Chamberlain), **3:**61
Feraoun, Mouloud
   Journal, 1955–1962, **2:262–264**
   The Poor Man's Son, **2:**262, 263, 264
Ferdinand (king of Spain), **2:**201
Ferman, Claudia, **3:**166

Fermi, Enrico, **3:**239

Fernández-Armesto, Felipe, **2:**200

Fernández Barrios, Flor, *Blessed by Thunder,* **1:**296

Ferrari, Christine, **2:**30

Ferrie, Pauline, **3:**29

Ferris, Ina, **2:**179

Ferris, Jean Leon Gerome, **1:180**

Fest, Joachim, **2:**55, 56

Feudalism, in China, **3:**124

Fiction
    in collective novels, **3:**282, 285
    in *An Egyptian Childhood* (Hussein), **1:**136
    in *Go Ask Alice* (anonymous), **2:**294
    in novels of manners, **2:**312
    science, **1:**231, **2:**237
    in *Stop-Time* (Conroy), **1:**164, 165
    transcendental, **1:**281
    in *Truth and Fiction Relating to My Life* (Goethe), **1:**276

Fictional diaries, **2:**174

Fielding, Henry, **2:**328

Fields, James T., **2:**224

Fierce Attachments (Gornick), **1:**279

Fifteenth Amendment, **1:**50, **2:**238

Fifth Column, The (Hemingway), **2:**102

Fighting Words (Ball and Porter), **1:**97

Filipovic, Alica, **2:**338

Filipovic, Malik, **2:**338

Filipovic, Zlata, *Zlata's Diary,* **2:**275, **338–340,** *339*

Filippelli, Ronald L., **3:**329

Film adaptations. *See also* Documentary films; *specific films*
    of *Akenfield* (Blythe), **3:**59
    of *Angela's Ashes* (McCourt), **1:**120, *120*
    of *The Autobiography of Malcolm X* (Malcolm X), **1:**186
    of *Country of My Skull* (Krog), **3:**242
    of *The Diary of Anne Frank* (Frank), **2:**253, 254
    of *The Diving Bell and the Butterfly* (Bauby), **1:**6, 7, *7*
    of *An Egyptian Childhood* (Hussein), **1:**137

    of *Farewell to Manzanar* (Houston and Houston), **1:**299
    of *Geronimo* (Geronimo and Barrett), **1:**304
    of *The Good Man of Nanking* (Rabe), **2:**19
    of *Letters of a Woman Homesteader* (Stewart), **2:**91
    of *Motorcycle Diaries* (Guevara), **2:**220
    of *National Velvet* (Bagnold), **2:**261
    of *Native Son* (Wright), **1:**124
    of *Persepolis* (Satrapi), **1:**156, 157
    of *The Story of My Life* (Keller), **1:**44
    of *This Boy's Life* (Wolff), **1:**47, 49
    of *When Heaven and Earth Changed Places* (Hayslip), **1:**335, 336
    of Williams's (Tennessee) plays, **2:**152
    of *A Woman in Berlin* (anonymous), **2:**281

Finances, personal
    Poe's (Edgar Allan) preoccupation with, **2:**41–42
    Scott's (Walter) trouble with, **2:**309, 310

Finley, C. Stephen, **1:**265–266

Finn, Margot, **2:**289, 322

Finnegans Wake (Joyce), **1:**185

Firestone, Jennifer, **2:**150

Firestone, Shulamith, **3:**37

Firm, The (Bruce), **3:245–247**

First Agraristas, The (Craig), **3:167, 302–304**

First Household under Heaven, The (Meng), **3:**125

First Nations people. *See* Native American(s)

First Person America (Banks), **3:**161

First South Carolina Volunteers, **2:**238–240

First They Killed My Father (Ung), **1:**306

First Well, The (Jabra), **1:**136

Fisch, Max Harold, **1:**183, 184, 185

Fish, Joe, *El Salvador,* **3:**206

Fishburne, Laurence, **3:**249

Fishel, John T., *Uncomfortable Wars Revisited,* **3:**207

Fisher, Michael H., **2:**231

Fish in the Water, A (Vargas Llosa), **1:**168

Fishkin, Shelley Fisher, **1:**173

Fiss, Harry, **3:**295

FitzGerald, Edward, **2:**196

Fitzgerald, F. Scott, **1:**140
    The Great Gatsby, **1:**47

Fitzgerald, Robert, **2:**129, 131

Fitzgerald, Sally, **2:**129, 131

Fitzpatrick, David, *Politics and Irish Life,* **3:**27

Five Days That Shocked the World (Best), **3:**235

Flanagan, John Richard, **1:**154

Flaubert, Gustave, **2:**120, 268
    Letters, **2:**268
    Sentimental Education, **1:**128

Flaxman, John, **2:**77

Flcche, Andre, **2:**240

Fleishmann, Ulrich, **3:**8

Flenley, Paul, **3:**341–342

FLN. *See* National Liberation Front

Floating nation, Puerto Rico as, **1:**108

Florida, U.S. annexation of, **2:**69

Florio, John, **2:**256

Flu pandemic of 1918, **1:**258

Flynn, Sarah, **3:**44

FMLN. *See* Farabundo Marti National Liberation Front

Folklore
    African American, **1:**9
    Chinese, **1:**173, 174

Folk music, **3:**96, 157, 159

Follain, John, **1:**40

Fones-Wolf, Ken, **3:**97–98

Food
    in *A Country Parson* (Woodforde), **2:**288, 289
    diet of Gandhi (Mohandas), **1:**243
    in *Meatless Days* (Suleri), **1:**87, 88–89
    in *When I Was Puerto Rican* (Santiago), **1:**109

Foot, John, **3:**267

Foot binding, **1:**338, **3:**147, 289

SUBJECT INDEX

Forbes, Andrew, **3:**102
Forbes, Shannon, **1:**121
Forbidden Zone, The (Borden), **2:**259
Force-Bonté (Diallo), **1:**61
Forced labor
    in China, **1:**158
    in Soviet Union (*See* Gulag system)
Ford, Gerald, **1:**311, **3:**221
Ford, Henry
    The International Jew, **1:**30, 32
    My Life and Work, **1:**30
Forefathers' Eve (Mickiewicz), **2:**192
Foreign Affairs (journal), **2:**279, **3:**246, 332
Forgiveness, in Truth and Reconciliation Commission, **3:**243, 244
Forna, Aminatta, *The Devil That Danced on the Water,* **1:**312
Forrester, Michael, *Tsuchino,* **3:**127–128
Fors Clavigera (Ruskin), **1:**264
Forster, E. M., **2:**180, 235
Forten, James, **2:**29
Forten, Richard, **2:**29
For Their Own Good (Beier), **3:**144–145
For Those Who Come After (Krupat), **1:**71
Fortnightly Review (magazine), **2:**82–83
For Whom the Bell Tolls (Hemingway), **2:**101
Fosse Ardeatine massacre (1944), oral histories of, **3:**265–267, *266*
Fossey, Diane, **3:**37
Foster, David, **2:**10
Foster, David William, **1:**17
Foster, Ollie, **3:**100
Foundation Act of 1934 (Britain), **1:**149
Fourie, Pieter, *The Politics of AIDS Denialism,* **3:**272
Fourteen Points (Wilson), **3:**29
Fourteenth Amendment, **1:**50
Fox, George, *Journal of George Fox,* **2:**26–28, *27*
Fox, Margaret, **2:**26
Fox, Stephen
    America's Invisible Gulags, **3:**226
    UnCivil Liberties, **3:**226

The Unknown Internment, **3:**215, **224–226**
Foxe, John, **2:**97, 98–99
Foy, Harriet D., **1:**10
France. *See also* French autobiographical writing
    Algeria as colony of, **1:**93–94, **2:**262–264
    Bashkirtseff (Marie) as immigrant in, **2:**306–308
    cultural decadence of, **2:**306–307
    Franklin (Benjamin) as ambassador to, **1:**179, *180*
    in French and Indian War, **2:**205
    Guinea as colony of, **1:**128, 129, 130
    Indochina as colony of, **3:**279
    Jefferson (Thomas) as diplomat in, **2:**316, 317–318
    Laye's (Camara) education in, **1:**128–129
    letter writing in, **2:**217
    literary critical theories of, **1:**239
    locked-in syndrome in literature of, **1:**6
    Morocco as protectorate of, **3:**47
    Nin's (Anaïs) life in, **2:**123
    Revolution in (*See* French Revolution)
    Senegal as colony of, **1:**61
    student movements of 1968 in, **3:**33
    Vietnam under, **1:**335, **3:**279
    Wollstonecraft's (Mary) travels in, **2:**109
    women's rights movement in, **2:**306
    in World War II, German occupation of, **1:**332–334
    Wright's (Richard) move to, **1:**124
France, Peter, **2:**201
Francis, Charles E., *The Tuskegee Airmen,* **3:**212
Francophone literature
    of Algeria, **2:**262, 264
    of Senegal, **1:**61
Frank, Anne, *The Diary of Anne Frank,* **2:253–255,** *254*
    An Interrupted Life (Hillesum) vs., **2:**22

Night (Wiesel) vs., **1:**320
Red Scarf Girl (Jiang) inspired by, **1:**161
Thura's Diary (Al-Windawi) vs., **2:**275, 277
A Woman in Berlin (anonymous) vs., **2:**281
A Woman Soldier's Own Story (Xie) vs., **1:**340
Zlata's Diary (Filipovic) vs., **2:**338, 339, 340
Frank, Dana, **3:**338
Frank, Leslie, *Witnesses to Nuremberg,* **3:293–295**
Frank, Margot, **2:**253, 255
Frank, Otto, **2:**253, 254, 255
Franklin, Aretha, **1:**274–275
Franklin, Benjamin, **1:180**
    The Autobiography of Ben Franklin, **1:179–182,** **2:**213
    Poor Richard's Almanac, **2:**88
    Shadows on My Heart (Buck) on, **2:**271
Franklin, Ruth, **1:**320
Franklin, USS, **3:203**
Franklin, William, **1:**179
Franklin, William Temple, **1:**179
Franks, in Crusades, **1:**285–288
Franz Sternbalds Wanderungen (Tieck), **1:**276
Fraser, Roland, *Blood of Spain,* **3:**176
Frasher, Burton, **3:**102
Frayn, Michael, *Copenhagen,* **3:**239
Frazer, Heather T., *"We Have Just Begun to Not Fight",* **3:227–230**
Frederick II (king of Prussia), **1:**276
Frederick the Great, "Le Stoïcien," **1:**218
Frediani, Alex, **3:**225
Fredrickson, George, **2:**240
Freedom
    of expression (*See* Expression)
    Mandela's (Nelson) conception of, **1:**28
    mental, in locked-in syndrome, **1:**6–7
    moral imperative of, Soyinka (Wole) on, **1:**215
    value of, Jacobs (Harriet A.) on, **1:**143–145

Freedom (newspaper), **1:**273
Freedom Charter of 1955 (South Africa), **1:**24, 25
Freedom Flyers (Moye), **3:**99, **248–250**
Freedom Writers Diary, The (Gruwell), **2:**338, 339, 340
Freeman, James M., **3:**279
Freemont boarding school, **1:**164
Free schools, **3:**5
Free will, Augustine on, **1:**196, 198
French Americans, **2:**213–215
French and Indian War (1754–1763), **2:**205, 213
French autobiographical writing. *See also specific works and writers*
    by Barthes (Roland), **1:**267–269
    by Bauby (Jean-Dominique), **1:**6–8
    by Goncourt (Edmond de and Jules de), **2:**81–83
    by Lejeune (Philippe), **1:**239–240, **2:**174–176
    by Rousseau (Jean-Jacques), **1:**200–202
French education, in Algeria, **1:**93, 94, **2:**262–263
French Review (journal), **1:**128
French Revolution (1789–1799)
    Armenian nationalists influenced by, **3:**40
    British Empire during, Barnard (Anne) on, **2:**217, 218, 219
    British views on, **2:**309
    Enlightenment ideas in, **2:**109
    Goethe (Johann Wolfgang von) and, **1:**276
    U.S. anarchists influenced by, **3:**3
French Studies (journal), **2:**307
Frere, Bartie, **1:**91
Freud, Sigmund
    Andreas-Salomé (Lou) and, **2:**151
    on Augustine, **1:**197
    Barthes's (Roland) use of ideas of, **1:**267
    Bloomsbury group's discussions of, **2:**268
    and Darwin's (Charles) motivations, **1:**67
    and diaries, rise of, **2:**120
    The Origin and Development of Psychoanalysis, **2:**175
Frey, James, *A Million Little Pieces,* **1:**313, **2:**296
Friedan, Betty, **3:**37
Friedlander, Peter, **3:**174
    The Emergence of a UAW Local, **3:**153
Friedman, Clara, *Between Management and Labor,* **3:153–156,** 157
Frisbie, Charlotte, **3:**12
Frisch, Michael
    in field of oral history, **3:**173, 174
    on *Hard Times* (Terkel), **3:**162
    "Oral History and the Digital Revolution," **3:**181
    Portraits in Steel, **3:**181
    A Shared Authority, **3:**173, **179–182,** 190, 192
Fritz, Germaine, **3:**309
From Baghdad to Brooklyn (Marshall), **3:**120
From Behind the Veil (Stepto), **1:**35
From Memory to History (Montell and Bogart), **3:**90
Frommer, Harvey
    Growing Up Jewish in America, **3:118–120**
    It Happened in Brooklyn, **3:**118
Frommer, Myrna Katz
    Growing Up Jewish in America, **3:118–120**
    It Happened in Brooklyn, **3:**118
From Rhodesia to Zimbabwe (Vambe), **3:**251
From the Darkness Cometh the Light (Delaney), **2:**250
Fronto, Marcus Cornelius, **1:**220
Fruitlands (utopian community), **1:**235
Fry, Amelia, **3:**188
Frye, Northrop, **1:**276
Fuchs, Esther, *Women and the Holocaust,* **3:**35
Fugitive Slave Act of 1850 (U.S.), **2:**29
Fugitive slaves
    in abolitionist movement, **1:**142
    oral histories of, **3:**7–9
    return of, **2:**29
Fujii, Lee Ann, **3:**259
Fujiwara no Kintō, **2:**189
Fujiwara no Michinaga, **2:**290, 292
Fujiwara Takayoshi, **2:291**
Fujiwara Teika, **2:**189
Fulbrook, Mary, **3:**246
Fulkerson, Richard, **2:**33
Fuller, Margaret, **2:**139
Fuller, William Robertson, **2:**241
Fullerton, Morton, **2:**113, 115
Fulton, William, **3:**276
Fumifugium (Evelyn), **2:**65
Fundamentalist Christianity, **1:**102, 103
Fundamentalist Islam, **1:**156, 208
Fun Home (Bechdel), **1:139–141**
Fur, Gunlög Maria, *A Nation of Women,* **3:**326
Furey, Hester, **3:**329
Fürst, Juliane, **3:**332
Furuseth, Owen, **3:**123
Fussell, Paul, **3:**61
FWP. *See* Federal Writers' Project

G

Gaelic League, **3:**27
Gaitán Ayala, Jorge Eliécer, **3:**185
Gaither, Frances, **2:**30
Galarza, Ernesto, *Barrio Boy,* **1:**15
Galaty, John, **1:**114, 115, **3:**142
Galbraith, John Kenneth, **3:**255
Galloway, Grace Growdon, **2:**79
Galsworthy, John, **2:**136
Galvin, John, **3:**206
Gama, Vasco da, *A Journal of the First Voyage of Vasco da Gama,* **2:198–200,** *199,* 201
Gandhi, Mohandas, **1:**243
    An Autobiography, **1:**24, **242–245**
    civil disobedience by, **1:**242, **2:**32
    conscientious objectors influenced by, **3:**228
    Hind Swaraj, **1:**289
    Luthuli (Albert) influenced by, **1:**24
    Nehru's (Jawaharlal) relationship with, **1:**289–290, 291

Gandhi, Rajiv, **1:290**
Gangs, British youth, **3**:311–313
Gao, Anhua, *To the Edge of the Sky,* **1**:159
Gao Xingjian, **1**:159
GAP. *See* Gruppi di Azione Patriottica
Garceau, Dee, **2**:91, 92–93
García Lorca, Federico, **1**:222
García Márquez, Gabriel, *The Story of a Shipwrecked Sailor,* **3:183–185**
Gardiner, Samuel Rawson, **1**:316
Garff, Joakim, **2**:167–168
Garland, Anne Witte, *Women Activists,* **3**:268
Garland, Judy, **3**:295
Garnett, Anne, **2**:235
Garnett, Constance, **2**:268
Garrett, Daniel, **1**:256, 257
Garrett, Jessie, *Camp and Community,* **3**:102, 103–104
Garrison, William Lloyd, **1**:33, **2**:29
Garvey, Marcus, **1**:52, 84, 186, 187
Gary Convention of 1972, **3**:45
Gaskell, Elizabeth, **2**:143
Gaskin, Hilary, *Eyewitnesses at Nuremberg,* **3**:293
Gass, William H., **2**:149, 150
Gataker, Thomas, **1**:220
Gates, Henry Louis, Jr.
    The Classic Slave Narratives, **1**:82, 83
    In Search of Our Roots, **1**:263
    "Remembrance of Things Pakistani," **1**:88
    on Wheatley (Phillis), **2**:46
Gatten, Aileen, **2**:290, 292
Gatti, Tom, **1**:141
Gaulle, Charles de, **2**:262
Gay, Peter, **2**:304
Gay Caucus Book of the Year award, for *The Cancer Journals* (Lorde), **2**:5
Gay L.A. (Faderman and Timmons), **3**:83–84
Gay Liberation Front, **3**:72
Gay men. *See* Homosexuality
Gay rights movement, rise of
    in Britain, **3**:70, 72
    in U.S., **3**:83–84

Gay subculture, of Harlem Renaissance, **1**:84
Gay themes
    in comics, **1**:139, 141
    in *Hunger of Memory* (Rodriguez), **1**:17
Geertz, Clifford, **3**:74
Gehen-Bleiben (play), **2:304**
Geiger, H. Jack, **1**:73
Gelb, Norman, **2**:206
Gelles, Edith, **2**:89, 90
Gellhorn, Martha, **2:102**
    The Face of War, **2**:102
    Moore (Molly) and, **2**:278
    Selected Letters of Martha Gellhorn, **2:101–103**
    The Trouble I've Seen, **2**:101
Gellhorn, Walter, **3**:154, 155
Gender, in writing styles, **1**:250
Gender & History (journal), **3**:175
Gender discrimination, in coal mining, **3**:337, 339
Gender equality
    in Heian period of Japan, lack of, **2**:299
    Stanton (Elizabeth Cady) on, **1**:12, 13
Gender roles
    in Britain, **3**:144–146
    in China, **1**:153, 158, 160, 338, **3**:147–149
    in Europe, eighteenth-century, **2**:35–37
    in Europe, Renaissance, **2**:160–162
    in Iran, **1**:155
    in Ireland, **2**:157
    in Japan, **2**:60–61
    in Kenya, **3**:143
    in Montenegro, **3**:135, 136, 137
    in U.S., eighteenth-century, **2**:316
    in U.S., twentieth-century, **2**:47
    in World War I, **1**:331
Gender studies
    Red Azalea (Min) in, **1**:158, 160
    The Sovereignty and Goodness of God (Rowlandson) in, **1**:327
Genealogy, of Haley (Alex), **1**:261–263

General Allotment Act of 1887 (U.S.), **3**:107
General Magazine and Impartial Review, **1**:82
General Motors, **3**:343
Geneva Convention on the Laws and Custom of War (1949), **2**:56
Genghis Khan, **1**:105, 107
Genocide
    Armenian, **3**:40–42, *41*
    in Cambodia, **1**:306
    denial as final stage of, **3**:42
    in Guatemala, **3**:164
    in Nazi Germany (*See* Holocaust)
    in Rwanda, **1**:312, **3**:257–259, 293, 294
    in Ukraine, **3**:19
Genre (journal), **1**:248
"Gentlemen's Agreement" of 1907, **3**:80
Georgakas, Dan, *Solidarity Forever,* **3:328–330**
George, Keller, **3**:109
George, Susanne K., **2**:91–92, 93
George III (king of England), **2**:69, 328
Georgia, colonial, Wesley's (John) mission to, **2**:195, 196
Georgia Historical Quarterly, **1**:38
Georgia Review (journal), **1**:109
Georgia Weekly Telegraph (newspaper), **2**:38, 39
Gerardi, Juan, **1**:99
Géricault, Théodore, **2:144**
Gerlin, Valeria Mikhailovna, **3**:18
Germaine (About), **2**:115
German Americans, relocation in World War II, **3**:224, 226
German autobiographical writing. *See also specific works and writers*
    by Goethe (Johann Wolfgang von), **1**:276–278
    by Hitler (Adolf), **1**:30–32
    by Klemperer (Victor), **2**:303–305
    by Rabe (John), **2**:19–21
    by Rilke (Rainer Maria), **2**:149–151
    by Speer (Albert), **2**:54–56

German language, Nazi use of, **2:**303, 304, 305
German Romanticism, **2:**76
Germany. *See also* German autobiographical writing
　bildungsroman genre in, **1:**30
　economy of, **1:**30
　emigration to Chile from, **1:**75, 77
　Great Awakening in, **2:**197
　Künstler-Roman genre in, **1:**276
　nationalism in, **1:**30–32, 329, **2:**120, **3:**234
　Nazi (*See* Nazi Germany)
　reunification of, **3:**247
　Robinson's (Henry Crabb) travels in, **2:**75, 77
　Ruete's (Emily) move from Zanzibar to, **1:**90
　Stasi in, oral histories of, **3:**245–247
　student movements of 1968 in, **3:**33
　wars of (*See specific wars*)
Germany, Kent B., **3:**254
Geronimo (film), **1:**304
Geronimo, *Geronimo: His Own Story,* **1:**302–305, *303*
Geronimo: An American Legend (film), **1:**304
Geronimo: His Own Story (Geronimo and Barrett), **1:**302–305
Gerovitch, Slava, **3:**333
Gesner, Andreas, **1:**220
Gessen, Keith, **3:**282, 285
Getty, Serena, **2:**54–55
Gevisser, Mark, **3:**243
Gewen, Barry, **3:**213
Ghana (Nkrumah), **1:**290, **2:**12, 13
Ghana, Du Bois (W. E. B.) and, **1:**3, 4
Gharagozlou, Mary, **3:**220
Ghazzawi, 'Izzat
　Letters Underway, **2:**50–53
　The Woman Prisoner, **2:**50
Ghazzawi, Rami, **2:**50
Gheith, Jehanne M., *Gulag Voices,* **3:**17–19, 331
Ghent, Treaty of, **2:**69
Ghost Dance, **3:**110

Ghost masks, Chinese, **1:**174
Gibb, H. A. R., **1:**137, 287
Gibbon, Edward, **1:**198, **2:**37, 328
Gibbons, Herbert Adams, *The Blackest Page in Modern History,* **3:**40
Gibson, Marion, **1:**337
Gibson, Roy, **2:**95, 96
Gibson, William (playwright), **1:**43–44
Gibson, William Ford (novelist), **2:**145
Gide, André, **1:**278
　Log-book of the Coiners, **2:**180, 182
Giesen, Carol A. B., *Coal Miners' Wives,* **3:**337
Gig (Bowe and Bowe), **3:**343, 345
Gigliozzi, Liana, **3:**266
Gikandi, Simon, **2:**14
Gikuyu language, **2:**12, 13, 14
Gilbert, Sandra M., **2:**237
Gillette, Michael L., *Launching the War on Poverty,* **3:**254–256
Gillray, James, **2:**158
Gilman, Charlotte Perkins, **1:**14, **2:**324
Gilman, Richard, **2:**131
Gilmartin, Christina, **3:**149
Gilmartin, Elizabeth Kelley, *Engendering the Chinese Revolution,* **3:**147
Giltrow, Janet, **2:**207
Ginther, Ronald Debs, **3:**162
Gioglio, Gerald P., *Days of Decision,* **3:**221
Girl from China, A (Cheng), **1:**152, 154
Girl in the Tangerine Scarf, The (Kahf), **1:**41–42
Girl Rebel (Xie), **1:**338
Girl with the White Flag, The (Higa), **1:**153
Gissing, George
　London and the Life of Literature in Late Victorian England, **2:**320–323
　New Grub Street, **2:**320, 321, 322
Gittins, Diana, **3:**313
Gladiator (film), **1:**219
Gladstone, W. E., **2:**307
Glasgow, Jacqueline N., **1:**41–42, 311
Glasnost, **3:**282, 331, 333
Glass Menagerie, The (Williams), **2:**152

Glazier, Jack, **3:**141
Glenarvon (Lamb), **2:**145
Glendinning, Victoria, **1:**205
Glenn, Susan A., *Daughters of the Shtetl,* **3:**305
Glenny, William H., **3:**294
Globe & Mail (newspaper), **3:**119–120, 301
GLQ: A Journal of Lesbian and Gay Studies, **3:**72
Gluck, Sherna Berger
　Rosie the Riveter Revisited, **3:**224
　Women's Words, **3:**190–192
Go Ask Alice (anonymous), **2:**294–296
God, will of, Usāmah ibn Munqidh on, **1:**285, 286
Go-Daigo (Japanese emperor), **2:**61
Goddard, James Stanley, **2:**205, 207
God of Small Things, The (Roy), **1:**87
Godolphin, Margaret, **2:**66
Godwin, William, **2:**76, 109, 111
　Memoir, **2:**109
Goethe, Johann Wolfgang von, **1:**277
　Kafka (Franz) influenced by, **2:**120
　Kierkegaard's (Søren) critique of, **2:**166
　The Sorrows of Young Werther, **1:**276, 277, 339, **2:**166
　Styron (William) compared to, **1:**206
　Truth and Fiction Relating to My Life, **1:**276–278
　Wilhelm Meister's Apprenticeship, **1:**30
Goff, Stanley, *Brothers,* **3:**199
GoFukakusa (Japanese emperor), **2:**59, 60, 61
Gogh, Theo van, **1:**207, 209
Gogol, Nikolay, **2:**172
　Diary of a Madman, **2:**174
Going after Cacciato (O'Brien), **1:**335
Golb, Joel, **1:**32
Goldberg, Lina, **2:**295
Golden Ass, The (Apuleius), **1:**198
Goldenberg, Myrna, **3:**36
Golden Bones (Siv), **1:**306–308
Golden Book of the Emperor Marcus Aurelius (Guevara), **1:**218

SUBJECT INDEX

Goldensohn, Leon, *The Nuremberg Interviews,* **3:**293
Goldhagen, Daniel, **2:**304–305
Goldman, Emma, *Living My Life,* **3:**3
Gold Rush, California, **3:**114
Goldzwig, Steven R., **2:**33
Gomaa, Sally, **1:**144
Gomez, Iris, *Try to Remember,* **1:**108
Gómez, Laureano, **3:**183, 185
Gomez, Maximo, **3:**7
Goncourt, Edmond de
    Bashkirtseff (Marie) influenced by, **2:**306, 307–308
    Cherie, **2:**308
    En 18, **2:**82
    La Faustine, **2:**308
    Journal des Goncourt, **2:**81–83
Goncourt, Jules de
    En 18, **2:**82
    Journal des Goncourt, **2:**81–83
Gonne, Maud, **2:**127
Goodall, Jane, **3:**37
Goodbye to All That (Graves), **1:**329
Good Earth, The (Buck), **1:**159
Goodell, Stephen, **3:**254
Goodfriend, Joyce D., **2:**79
Good Housekeeping (magazine), **1:**154
"Good Man Is Hard to Find, A" (O'Connor), **2:**130
Good Man of Nanking, The (Rabe), **2:**19–21
Good Morning America (television show), **1:**40, 41
Goodrich, Chris, **1:**29, **3:**222
Goodrich, Frances, **2:**253
"Good War, The" (Terkel), **3:**212–214
    Bloods (Terry) vs., **3:**199
    Carrier Warfare in the Pacific (Wooldridge) vs., **3:**202
    Pulitzer Prize won by, **3:**161, 212, 234, 279, 343
    in rise of oral history, **3:**279
    The World at War (Holmes) vs., **3:**234
Goodwin, Jason, **1:**107
Good Wives (Ulrich), **2:**331–332
Goolagong, Evonne, **1:**149
Gorbachev, Mikhail, **3:**17, 282, 331, 333

Gordimer, Nadine, **1:**27
Gordon, Andrew, **3:**216
Gordon, Ann D., **1:**13
Gordon, Caroline, **2:**129
Gordon, Eleanor, **3:**175
Gordon, Ian, **2:**134
Gordon, Mary McDougall, **2:**79
Göring, Hermann, **3:294**
Gorky, Maxim, **1:**254
Gornick, Vivian, *Fierce Attachments,* **1:**279
Gorra, Michael, **1:**88
Gossamer Years, The (Michitsuna), **2:**189, 290, **297–299**
Gossen, Gary H., *Telling Maya Tales,* **3:**167
Go Tell It on the Mountain (Baldwin), **1:**167, 261
Gotlieb, Howard, **2:**101
Gottesmann, Christoph, **2:**282
Gougeon, Len, **2:**141
Gowon, Yakubu, **1:**214, 215, 216
Goyens, Tom, *Beer and Revolution,* **3:**5
Goyette, Gabriele, **1:10**
Graburn, Nelson, **3:**140
Grace Abounding to the Chief of Sinners (Bunyan), **2:**26
Graden, Dale, **3:**8
Graham, Elspeth, **1:**231
Graham, John, **1:**98
Grammy Award, for Obama's (Barack) audio adaptations, **1:**80
Granado, Alberto, **2:**220
Grandmothers, Mothers, and Daughters (Krause), **3:**305–307
Grand Prix Littéraire d'Afrique Noir, for *Riwan ou le chemin de sable* (Bugul), **1:**64
Grant, Duncan, **2:**268
Graphic autobiographies
    Barefoot Gen (Nakazawa), **1:**293–295
    Fun Home (Bechdel), **1:**139–141
    Persepolis (Satrapi), **1:**155–157
Grasmere (England), Dove Cottage in, **2:**300, *301*
Grasmere Journals (Wordsworth), **2:16, 300–302**
Grass Is Singing, The (Lessing), **1:**169

Graulich, Melody, **2:**91, 92
Graves, Phyllis, **1:**311
Graves, Robert, **2:**248
    Goodbye to All That, **1:**329
Gray, Doris H., *Muslim Women on the Move,* **3:**48
Gray, Francine du Plessix, **2:**102
Gray, Rockwell, **1:**247
Gray, Thomas, **2:**146
Greasley, Philip, **3:**213
Great Awakening, **1:**179, **2:**197
Great Boer War, The (Conan Doyle), **2:**241
Great Britain. *See* Britain
Great Depression
    African Americans during, **3:**99
    in Appalachia, **3:**96
    in Britain, **3:**53
    end of, **3:**161
    global impact of, **3:**212
    in Harlem, **1:**84
    in Idaho, **3:**93, 94
    Jews during, **3:**118
    Native Americans during, **1:**69
    New Deal in, **3:**161 (*See also* Federal Writers' Project)
    oral histories of, **3:**86, 161–163, *162*
    start of, **3:**161, 212
    unemployment in, **3:**161, 212
Great Exodus (1879), **1:**50
Great Famine (Ireland), **3:**315
Great Famine of 1932–1933 (Ukraine), **3:**19
Great Gatsby, The (Fitzgerald), **1:**47
Great Lakes Review, **3:**213
Great Leap Forward, **3:**287, 299, 300
"Great Men" project, of Nevins (Allan), **3:**161, 173, 179, 181, 186
Great Migration, **1:**50, 52, 84, 273, **3:**99
Great Plains Quarterly, **2:**164
Great Proletarian Cultural Revolution. *See* Cultural Revolution
Great Reforms (Russia), **1:**193
Great Society, **3:**254
"Great Wall of China, The" (Kafka), **2:**120

Great War, The (television series), **3:**234, 236
Greece, ancient
    letter writing in, **2:**94
    slavery in, **2:**96
Green, Anna, **3:**175
Green, John, **2:**276
Green, Maia, **3:**142
Green, Roland, **3:**203
Greenberg, Jack, **1:**38
Greenberg, Martin, **2:**121
Greenberger, Evelyn B., **2:**141
Greene, Graham, **2:**130, 136, 152
    A Sort of Life, **1:**47
Greene, Janet Wells, **3:**97
Greenfield, Sidney, *Entrepreneurs in Cultural Context,* **3:**121
Greenwell, Regina, **3:**254
Greer, Germaine, **3:**37
Gregory, Horace, **2:**121
Gregory, Lady, **2:**126, 128
Grele, Ronald J., **3:**45, 51, 52, 174
Grewal, Inderpal, **1:**88–89
Grey, Jane, **2:**99
Grice, Helena, **1:**160
Griffith, Andy, **2:**295
Griffith, Elisabeth, **1:**13–14
Griffith, Julia, *The Liberty Bell,* **1:**142
Griffith, Kenneth, *Ireland's Unfinished Revolution,* **3:**27–30
Grillo, Evelio, *Black Cuban, Black American,* **1:**296
Grimes, Tom, *Mentor,* **1:**164
Grimes, William, **1:**209
Grimké, Angelina, **2:**31
Grimké, Angelina Weld, **2:**31
Grimké, Charlotte Forten
    "At the Home of Frederick Douglass," **2:**29
    The Extraordinary Work of Ordinary Writing (Sinor) compared to, **2:**163
    Higginson (Thomas Wentworth) and, **2:**29, 238
    The Journals of Charlotte Forten Grimké, **2:**29–31
    "Life in the Sea Islands," **2:**31
Grimké, Francis, **2:**31

Grimké, Sarah, **2:**31
Grindle, Merilee S., **3:**303
Griswold, Rufus W., **2:**41
Grob-Fitzgibbon, Benjamin, *The Irish Experience during the Second World War,* **3:**315–316
Gronniosaw, James Albert Ukawsaw, **1:**81, **2:**44
Grose, John Henry, *Voyage to the East Indies,* **2:**229
Gross, Robert, **1:**19
Grossman, Michele, **3:**335, 336
Grossmith brothers, *The Diary of a Nobody,* **2:**174
Grotius, Hugo, **2:**177
Group, The (McCarthy), **1:**258
Group Areas Act of 1950 (South Africa), **1:**24
Growing Up Jewish in America (Frommer and Frommer), **3:118–120**
Grundtvig, N. F. S., **2:**166
Gruppi di Azione Patriottica (GAP), **3:**265
Gruwell, Erin, *The Freedom Writers Diary,* **2:**338, 339, 340
Gu, Ming Dong, **2:**172
Guajardo, Paul, **1:**16
Guardian (newspaper), **1:**330, **2:**133, 154, **3:**243
Guardian of the Word, The (Laye), **1:**129
Guatemala
    Civil War of, **1:**99, **3:**164, 165–166
    human rights abuses in, **1:**99, 100, **3:**164–166
    indigenous populations of, massacres of, **1:**99, **3:**164
    indigenous populations of, oral histories of, **3:**164–166
    Perera (Victor) on life in, **1:**99–101
"Guatemala: Always La Violencia" (Perera), **1:**99
Guatemalan Civil War (1960–1996), **1:**99, **3:**164, 165–166
Guatemala: Never Again! (Archdiocese of Guatemala), **1:**99
Guattari, Félix, **2:**122
Guavas, **1:**109

Gubar, Susan, **2:**237
Gubarev, Vladimir, *Sarcophagus,* **3:**282, 284
Guerilla Days in Ireland (Barry), **3:**27
Guérin, Daniel, *No Gods, No Masters,* **3:**3
Guérin, Eugénie de, **2:**306
Guevara, Antonio, *Golden Book of the Emperor Marcus Aurelius,* **1:**218
Guevara, Ernesto "Che," **2:**221
    Che: A Graphic Biography (Buhle and Rodriguez) on, **3:**330
    Motorcycle Diaries, **1:**223, **2:220–222**
Guggenheim, Peggy, **2:**152
Guglielmo, Jennifer, *Living the Revolution,* **3:**5
Guiler, Hugh Parker, **2:**123
Guilt, in *Country of My Skull* (Krog), **3:**243
Guinea
    French colonial rule of, **1:**128, 129, 130
    independence of (1958), **1:**130
    Laye (Camara) on life in, **1:**128–130, *129*
Guisson, Lorraine, *Image du monde,* **1:**105
Guiteras-Holmes, Calixta, *Perils of the Soul,* **3:**167
Gulag Archipelago, The (Solzhenitsyn), **1:**201, **3:**17
Gulag system, oral histories of, **3:**17–19, *18*
Gulag Voices (Gheith and Jolluck), **3:17–19**, 331
Gulf War (1991), **2:**275, 278–280, *279*
Gulliford, Andrew, **3:**77
Gundy, Jeff, **1:**109
Gunning, Sarah Ogan, **3:**159
Gurewitsch, Brana
    Holocaust Oral History Manual, **3:**35
    Mothers, Sisters, Resisters, **3:34–36**
Gusdorf, George, **1:**246, 248
Gustavson, Andrea, **3:**162–163, 213
Guy, Josephine M., **2:**10
Guy Domville (James), **2:**114
Guylforde, John, **2:**228

SUBJECT INDEX

Guylforde, Richarde, *The Pylgrymage of Sir Richarde Guylforde*, **2:**226–228
Gyn/Ecology (Daly), **2:**3, 5

H

Ha, Quan Manh, **1:**307
Habit of Being, The (O'Connor), **2:129–132**
Habits of Change (Rogers), **3:308–310**
Habits of mind, Darwin (Charles) on, **1:**65–67
Habyarimana, Juvénal, **3:**257
Hachicho, Mohamad Ali, **2:**227, 228
Hachiya, Michihiko, *Hiroshima Diary*, **1:**293
Hackett, Albert, **2:**253
Haddad, Malek, *La Dernière impression*, **2:**262
Hadot, Pierre, **1:**221
Hagiographies
    The Autobiography of Malcolm X (Malcolm X) as, **1:**186, 188
    and *The Book of Margery Kempe* (Kempe), **1:**189, 190, 191
Hagood, Taylor, **1:**8
Hagopian, Patrick, **3:**201, 209, 211, 277
Haizlip, Shirlee, *The Sweeter the Juice*, **1:**73
Hakakian, Roya, *Journey to the Land of No*, **1:**155
Hakluyt, Richard, **2:**199
    Divers Voyages Touching the Discoverie of America, **2:**229
    The Principle Navigations, Voiages, Traffiques and Discoveries of the English Nation, **2:**229
Hakluyt Society, **2:**198, 199
Halas, John, **2:118**
Hale, Sondra, **3:**48–49, 191
Halevy, Irving, **3:**154–155
Haley, Alex, **1:**262
    "Black History, Oral History, and Genealogy," **3:**186
    "My Furthest-Back Person— 'The African,'" **1:261–263**
    Roots, **1:**18, 78, 261–263
    in writing of *The Autobiography of Malcolm X*, **1:**78, 186, 187, **3:**44

Halkett, Anne, *The Memoirs of Lady Anne Halkett*, **1:**230, **315–317**
Halkett, James, **1:**315
Hall, Betty Jean, **3:**339
Hall, Joan Wylie, **2:**153
Hall, Peter, **3:**59
Halperin, John, **2:**322
Halpern, Frida, **1:**76
Halsband, Robert, **2:**36
Hamdani, Abu Firas al-, **2:**52
Hamilton, J. Angus, *The Siege of Mafeking*, **2:**241
Hamilton, Paula, **3:**188
Hamilton, Robert A., **3:**294
Hamilton, William, **2:196**
Hamlet (Shakespeare), **1:**277
Hammon, Britton, **2:**44
Hammon, Jupiter, **2:**44
Hampton, Henry
    The Black Chronicle, **3:**44
    in *Eyes on the Prize* (television series), **2:**34
    Voices of Freedom, **3:44–46**
Hamsun, Knut, **2:**120
Handbook of Oral History, The (Humphries), **3:**313
Handley, George B., **1:**223–224
Han dynasty, Confucianism in, **3:**124
Hansberry, Lorraine, **1:274**
    A Raisin in the Sun, **1:**273, 274, 275
    The Sign in Sidney Brustein's Window, **1:**274
    To Be Young, Gifted and Black, **1:273–275**
Hansen, Arthur A., **3:**80–81, 197
    Japanese American World War II Evacuation Oral History Project, **3:**215
    Voices Long Silent, **3:**195
Han Yong Un, **1:**322
Hao Ping, **3:**289
Happiest Refugee, The (Do), **1:**337
Happy Foreigner, The (Bagnold), **2:**259
Haralson, Eric, **2:**115
Harbach, Patricia, **3:**326
Harbord, Gordon, **2:**249
Hardack, Richard, **1:**281

Hard-Earned Lives (Cornwell), **3:**170
Harder Journey, The (Tuqan), **1:**226
Hardships and Happy Times (Russell), **3:**93
Hard Times: An Oral History of the Great Depression (Terkel), **3:161–163**, 179, 199, 212, 279, 343
Hardy, Thomas, **2:**136–137, 180, 181, 321
Harem Years (Shaarawi), **1:**225–226
Harlan, Louis R., **1:**52
Harlan County (Kentucky)
    oral histories of coal miners in, **3:**96–98, 157
    oral histories of working class in, **3:**157–159
Harlan County, USA (documentary), **3:**98
Harlan Miners Speak (Dreiser), **3:**96
Harlem, in Great Depression, **1:**84
"Harlem" (Hughes), **1:**275
Harlem: Negro Metropolis (McKay), **1:**85
Harlem Renaissance
    autobiographies of participants in, **1:**3
    vs. Chicago Renaissance, **1:**273
    Du Bois (W. E. B.) in, **1:**3
    gay subculture of, **1:**84
    Hurston (Zora Neale) in, **1:**9
    McKay (Claude) in, **1:**84–86
    origins of, **1:**84
Harling, Sean, **3:**28
Harman, Claire, **2:**313–314
Harney, Mary, **3:**315
Harper, Frances Ellen Watkins, *Iola Leroy*, **1:**143
Harper, Helen, **1:**162, **2:**276
Harries, Meirion, *Soldiers of the Sun*, **3:**215
Harries, Susie, *Soldiers of the Sun*, **3:**215
Harrington, Ann, **3:**309
Harris, Frank, **2:**261
Harris, Lillian Craig, **3:**126
Harrison, Thomas, **2:**235
Harrold, Charles, **2:**76
Hart, Frederick, **3:200**
Hart-Davis, Rupert, **2:**247, 248

Hartle, Ann, **1:**202

Harvard Book Review, **1:**48, 280

Harvard Iranian Oral History Project (HIOHP), **3:**218–220

Harvey, Clodagh Brennan, *Contemporary Irish Traditional Narrative,* **3:**315

Harvey, P., **3:**249

Harwood, Ronald, **1:**6

Haskins, Jim, *Rosa Parks: My Story,* **1:37–39**

Hassan, Kenja, **3:**12

Hastings, Selina, **2:**185

Hatch, Ozias M., **3:**263

Hatcher, Richard, **3:**45

Hate crimes, against gay men and lesbians, **1:**139

Hathaway, Donny, **1:**274

Hatherell, William, **2:**260

Hattin, Battle of (1187), **1:**286

Hatzfeld, Jean
 The Antelope's Strategy, **3:**258
 Life Laid Bare, **3:**258, 259
 Machete Season, **1:**312, **3:257–260**

Hauptman, L. M., **3:**326

Hausa people, **1:**214

Haushofer, Karl, **1:**32

Haviland, John B., **3:**169

Hawaii. *See* Pearl Harbor

Hawkesworth, E. C., **3:**135, 136, 137

Hawthorne, Julian, **2:**224

Hawthorne, Nathaniel
 The Blithedale Romance, **2:**225
 The Centenary Edition of the Works of Nathaniel Hawthorne, **2:**223
 Emerson (Ralph Waldo) and, **2:**139, 223
 The House of the Seven Gables, **2:**223–224
 James (Henry) and, **2:**113, 114, 115
 lost notebook of, **2:**224, 225
 The Love Letters of Nathaniel Hawthorne, **2:**225
 The Marble Faun, **2:**224, 225
 Notebooks and Letters, **2:**113, **223–225**
 Robinson (Henry Crabb) compared to, **2:**75
 The Scarlet Letter, **2:**223–224

Hawthorne, Sophia Peabody, **2:**223, 224, 225

Haxton, Frederick Gerald, **2:**183

Hay, John M., **3:**262
 Abraham Lincoln: A History, **3:**261–262
 Abraham Lincoln: Complete Works, **3:**262
 Letters of John Hay, **3:**263
 Lincoln and the Civil War Diaries and Letters of John Hay, **3:**262–263

Haydon, Benjamin, **2:**146

Hayes, Thomas, **1:**216

Hayls, John, **2:**73

Haymarket Riot (1886), **3:**4

Haynes, Katherine, **3:**344

Hays, Mary, **2:**109, 110

Hays, Megan, **3:**136–137

Hays, Rusel Everett, **3:**185

Hayslip, Le Ly, **1:336**
 When Heaven and Earth Changed Places, **1:**170–171, **335–337**
 Woman of Peace, **1:**335

Haywood, Harry, *Black Bolshevik,* **1:**4

Hazlitt, William, **2:**146

H.D. (Hilda Doolittle), **2:**123

Heading South, Looking North (Dorfman), **1:**75

Head of the Class (Morris), **3:20–22**

Head Start program, **3:**254

Healey, Mark, **3:**74

Health-care industry
 British, oral histories of, **3:**170–172
 South African, oral histories of, **3:**272–274

Health problems. *See also specific types*
 of Bauby (Jean-Dominique), **1:**6–8
 of Mansfield (Katherine), **2:**133, 134
 of Styron (William), **1:**204–205

Healy, George Peter Alexander, **2:**70

Heartland (film), **2:**91

Heart of Darkness (Conrad), **2:**192–193, 194

Heaven and Earth (film), **1:**335, *336*

Hecker, Earl, **3:**232

Heflin, Ruth J., **3:**112

Hegel, Georg Wilhelm Friedrich, **2:**166

Heian period (Japan)
 Michitsuna No Haha on life in, **2:**297–299
 Murasaki Shikibu on life in, **2:**290–292
 Nijo (Lady) on life in, **2:**60, 61
 Sarashina (Lady) on life in, **2:**189–191

Heilman, Anna, **3:**35

Heinemann Award, for *Akenfield* (Blythe), **3:**59

Heisenberg, Werner, **3:**239

Helfand, Judy, **1:**336

Helgeson, Jeffrey, **3:**255–256

Hélias, Pierre Jakez, *The Horse of Pride,* **3:**61

Heline, Oscar, **3:**162

Heller, Walter, **3:**254

Hellman, Lillian, **1:**260

Helms, Jessie, **2:**5

Helsinger, Elizabeth K., **1:**264, 265, 266

Helstern, Linda Lizut, **3:**12

Hemenway, Robert, **1:**9

Hemingway, Ernest
 A Farewell to Arms, **2:**259
 The Fifth Column, **2:**102
 For Whom the Bell Tolls, **2:**101
 Gellhorn's (Martha) marriage to, **2:**101, 102
 Notebooks (Williams) on, **2:**152
 The Sun Also Rises, **2:**259
 Wolff (Tobias) influenced by, **1:**47

Hemlow, Joyce, **2:**314

Henderson, John, **2:**96

Henderson, Thelton, **3:**20

Hendricks, Cecilia Hennel, **2:**91

Henige, David, **2:**203

Hennepin, Louis, *A New Discovery of a Vast Country in America,* **2:**205

Henrietta Maria (queen of England), **1:**229

Henry, Milton, **3:**248

Henry, Mona, **3:**316

Henry the Navigator, **2:**198

Henry VII (king of England), **2:**226, 228

Henry VIII (king of England), **2:**72, 97, 226

Hensher, Philip, **2:**153

Hentges, Frank, **3:**162

Hentges, Rome, **3:**162

Henze, Hans Werner, **3:**7

Hepburn, James, **2:**138

Hepburn, Katharine, **2:**261

Here I Stand (Robeson), **1:**37

Here's to You, Jesus (Poniatowska), **3:**32

Heresy, Teresa of Ávila and, **1:**211, 212

Here Too, Domitila (Barrios de Chungara), **3:**322

Herman, David, **2:**128

Hermione, Countess of Ranfurly, **2:**235

Herndon, Angelo, **1:**85

Herndon's Informants (Wilson and Davis), **3:**264

Herodotus, **3:**186

Herr, Michael, *Dispatches,* **1:**259, **3:**209

Herrera, Spencer, **1:**17

Herron, L. E., **1:**52

Hershatter, Gail, **1:**340

Herzen, Alexander, **1:**270, **2:**120

Hess, Rudolph, **1:**32, **3:**294

Hester, Elizabeth, **2:**130–131

H-Ethnic (journal), **3:**8

Hevener, John W., *Which Side Are You On?,* **3:**96

Hewitt, David, **2:**311

Hewitt, Martin, **2:**66, 67

Heyerdahl, Marian, **1:339**

Heylin, Peter, **2:**99

Heyns, Michiel, **3:**243

Heywood, Christopher, **2:**242

Heywood, Thomas, **2:**162

H. G. Wells in Love (Wells), **1:**252, 253, 254

Hibakusha literature, **1:**293

Hibberd, Dominic, **2:**248, 249

Hibbert, Christopher, **2:**210

Hickey, Jim, **3:**316

Hickey, Margaret, *Irish Days,* **3:315–317**

Higa, Tomiko, *The Girl with the White Flag,* **1:**153

Higgins, Marguerite, **2:**278

Higginson, Thomas Wentworth
 Army Life in a Black Regiment, **2:238–240**
 Grimké (Charlotte Forten) and, **2:**29, 238

Hijuelos, Oscar, *Thoughts without Cigarettes,* **1:**75

Hikmet, Nazim, **2:**51

Hilda Lessways (Bennett), **2:**138

Hill, Joan, **3:**68

Hill, W. Nick, **3:**7, 8

"Hillbilly" culture, **3:**86

Hill Country Teacher (Manning), **3:77–79**

Hillenbrand, Carole, **1:**286, 287

Hillers, Marta, **2:**281

Hillesum, Etty
 An Interrupted Life, **2:22–25**
 The Letters and Diaries of Etty Hillesum, **2:**253

Him, Chanrithy, *When Broken Glass Floats,* **1:**306

Hinds, Hilary, **2:**27

Hind Swaraj (Gandhi), **1:**289

Hinduism, **1:**242, 244

Hindus, Maurice, **1:**271

Hinnant, Charles, **2:**329–330

Hinton, Deane, **3:**206

Hinton, James, **2:**267

Hintz, Carrie, **2:**326

HIOHP. *See* Harvard Iranian Oral History Project

Hipp, Daniel, **2:**249

Hirohito (emperor of Japan), **3:**215

Hiroshima (Japan), U.S. nuclear bombing of, **1:**293–294, **3:**239

Hiroshima Diary (Hachiya), **1:**293

Hiroshima: The Autobiography of Barefoot Gen (Nakazawa), **1:**293, 295

Hirsch, Jerrold, **3:**22, 192

Hirsch, Julia, **3:**306

Hirsi Ali, Ayaan, **1:**208
 Infidel, **1:**207–210
 Nomad, **1:**209

Hispanic-American Entrepreneur, The (Owsley), **3:121–123**

Hispanic American Historical Review (journal), **2:**7, **3:**122, 303, 323

Hispanic and Latino Americans
 as entrepreneurs, oral histories of, **3:**121–123
 Medina (Pablo) on experience of, **1:**296–298
 Santiago (Esmeralda) on experience of, **1:**108–110
 in South, **3:**123
 women, oral histories of, **3:**131–133

Historia Augusta, **1:**220

Historian (journal), **2:**231

Historia Romana (Cassius Dio), **1:**220

Historical Clarifications Commission, UN, **3:**166

Historical Journal of Film, Radio and Television, **3:**234

Historie de ma vie (Amrouche). *See My Life Story* (Amrouche)

History, field of. *See also* Oral histories
 Popular Memory Group's critique of, **3:**176–178
 role of oral histories in, **3:**281

History (journal), **2:**206, **3:**145

History and Theory (journal), **1:**26

History in Africa (journal), **1:**25

History of Alta California, The (Osio et al.), **3:**115

History of Education Quarterly, **3:**307

History of Everyday Life in Twentieth Century Scotland, A (Abrams), **3:**173, 175

History of Indies (Las Casas), **2:**201

History of Mary Prince, The (Prince), **1:**111, 113, **3:23–26**

History of the German Resistance (Hoffmann), **3:**245

History of Woman Suffrage (Stanton et al.), **1:**12

History Today (journal), **2:**200, **3:**246, 267

History Workshop Journal, **3:**54, 146, 173, 176, 209, 277

Hitchcott, Nicki, **1:**64

Hitchens, Christopher
 on Guevara (Ernesto "Che"), **2:**222
 on *Infidel* (Hirsi Ali), **1:**209
 Letters to a Young Contrarian, **2:**150
 on Orwell (George), **2:**117, 118, 119

Hitler, Adolf, **1:**31. *See also* Holocaust; Nazi Germany
    Chilean support for, **1:**75
    fall of Berlin and, **2:**281
    Final Solution of, **1:**318
    Mein Kampf, **1:**30–32
    Nella Last's War (Last) on, **2:**265
    Rabe's (John) letter on Nanking Massacre to, **2:**19, 21
    rise to power, **3:**14
    Speer's (Albert) relationship with, **2:**54, 55, 56
    Stein (Gertrude) on, **1:**332
    suicide of, **2:**281
Hitti, Philip K., **1:**287
HIV. *See* AIDS
Hoak, Dale, **2:**98, 99
Hobart, Mary, **2:**331
Hobbs, Nancy, **1:**38
Hobsbawm, Eric J., **2:**18
Hoby, Margaret, **2:**62
Hochstadt, Steve, *Exodus to Shanghai,* **3:**14–16
Hodgson, Dorothy L., **1:**115–116
Hoess, Rudolph, *My Soul,* **2:**54
Ho Feng-Shan, **3:**14
Hoffaman, Abraham, *Vision or Villainy,* **3:**102
Hoffe, Esther, **2:**122
Hoffman, Abbie, **1:**205
Hoffman, Michael J., **1:**333
Hoffman, Nancy, *Woman's "True" Profession,* **3:**77
Hoffmann, Peter, *History of the German Resistance,* **3:**245
Hofstadter, Richard, **1:**134
Hogarth Press, **2:**268
Hoggart, Richard
    The Uses of Literacy, **1:**16
    The Worst of Times, **3:**53
Holcomb, Gary Edward, **1:**85
Holden, Philip, **1:**290, 291
Holland. *See* Netherlands
Holland, Tom, **2:**145
Hollander, Tom, **2:**10
Holler, Clyde, **3:**112
Holmes, Amy J., **2:**244
Holmes, Henry Bry, **2:**245, 246

Holmes, Oliver Wendell, Jr., **1:**134
Holmes, Richard, *The World at War,* **3:**234–236, *235*
Holmes, Stephen, **1:**209
Holocaust
    denial of, **3:**50
    goal of, **3:**50
    Jewish immigration to escape, **1:**75, 76, **3:**14–16
    memorials to, **1:**319, **3:**51
    Nuremberg Laws in, **2:**253, **3:**14
    origins of, **3:**14, 34, 50
    rape in, **2:**283
    targets of, **3:**36, 50
    women survivors of, **3:**34–36
Holocaust autobiographies
    by Frank (Anne), **2:**253–255
    by Hillesum (Etty), **2:**22–24, 253
    by Klemperer (Victor), **2:**303–305
    by Nazis, **2:**54–56
    rise of, **1:**318
    by Wiesel (Elie), **1:**318–320
Holocaust concentration camps
    Auschwitz, **1:**318–320, **2:**22, **3:**35, 51
    Bergen-Belsen, **2:**253, **3:**51
    Buchenwald, **3:**51
    Mauthausen, **3:**51
    Westerbork, **2:**22–24, 253
Holocaust oral histories
    of American survivors and witnesses, **3:**50–52
    of Jewish refugees in China, **3:**14–16
    rise of, **3:**15, 34, 50
    of women survivors, **3:**34–36
    in *The World at War* (Holmes), **3:**235
Holocaust Oral History Manual (Gurewitsch and Eliach), **3:**35
Holoch, Adele, **2:**13
Holroyd, Michael, **2:**269
Holtby, Winifred, **1:**330, 331
    South Riding, **1:**331
Holton, Woody, **2:**90
Holy Club, **2:**195, 197
Holy Land, Guylforde's (Richarde) pilgrimage to, **2:**226–228

Homans, Margaret, **2:**211
Home Elsewhere, A (Stepto), **1:**80
Home Front, The (Satterfield), **3:**202
Homeland Security Department, U.S., **3:**245
Homes, A. M., **1:**48
Homestead Act of 1862 (U.S.), **2:**163, 165
Homesteading
    oral histories of, **3:**93–95
    Ray (Annie) on experience of, **2:**163–164
    Stewart (Elinore Pruitt) on experience of, **2:**91–93, *92*
Home to Harlem (McKay), **1:**84, 86
Homoeroticism
    in James's (Henry) novels, **2:**115
    in Marcus Aurelius's letters, **1:**220
    in *Red Azalea* (Min), **1:**160
Homosexuality
    of Bechdel (Alison), **1:**139, 140
    in Britain, legal ban on, **2:**9, 183, **3:**70
    in Britain, oral histories of, **3:**70–72
    Byron (George Gordon Noel) and, **2:**144
    Chinese persecution of, **1:**158
    in *Fun Home* (Bechdel), **1:**139–141
    gay rights movement, **3:**70, 72, 83–84
    in Harlem Renaissance, **1:**84
    in *Hunger of Memory* (Rodriguez), **1:**17
    James (Henry) and, **2:**115
    in *A Long Way from Home* (McKay), **1:**85
    of Lorde (Audre), **1:**39, **2:**3, 5
    of Maugham (W. Somerset), **2:**183, 185
    of McKay (Claude), **1:**84
    of Sassoon (Siegfried), **2:**247, 248
    in U.S., oral histories of, **3:**83–85
    U.S. attitudes toward, evolution of, **1:**139
    in U.S. military, **1:**139
    of Wilde (Oscar), **2:**9–10
    of Williams (Tennessee), **2:**152

Hong, Christina, **1:**294
Hood River Issei, The (Tamura), **3:**80–82
Hooke, Robert, *The Diary of Robert Hooke,* **2:**72
hooks, bell, **1:**250
    Ain't I a Woman, **1:**250
    Bone Black, **1:**249–251
    Wounds of Passion, **1:**250, 251
Hooligan: A History of Respectable Fears (Pearson), **3:**312
Hooligans or Rebels? (Humphries), **3:**144, 311–314
Hooper, Charles, **1:**24
Hooper, Finley, **2:**96
Hooper, Sheila, **1:**24
Hooten, Elizabeth, **2:**26
Hope against Hope (Mandlestam), **1:**271
Hopi, in land dispute with Navajo, oral histories of, **3:**10–12
Hopkins, Anthony, **2:**71
Hopkins, Gerard Manley, **2:**147
Hopkinson, Amanda, **2:**221
Hopkinson, Francis, **2:**316
Hopkinson, Mrs. Thomas, **2:**316, 317
Horacek, Parson, **2:**149
Horn, Eva, **1:**32
Horn Book Magazine, **1:**162
Horniman, Annie, **2:**128
Horowitz, David, **3:**165
Horse of Pride, The (Hélias), **3:**61
Hortensius (Cicero), **1:**196, 198
Horwitz, Tony, **1:**280
Hosbawm, Eric, **3:**186
Hoskins, Katherine, **2:**115
Hospicio é Deus (Lopes Cançado), **2:**6
Hosseini, Khaled, *The Kite Runner,* **1:**40
Houlbrook, Matt, **3:**72
House Arrest (film), **1:**6, 7
Households, isolated vs. collective, Stanton (Elizabeth Cady) on, **1:**14
House Made of Dawn (Momaday), **1:**54
House of Confucius, The (Kong). *See In the Mansion of Confucius' Descendants* (Kong)

House of Representatives, U.S., gag rule on slavery in, **2:**70
House of Si Abd Allah, The (Munson), **3:**47
House of the Seven Gables, The (Hawthorne), **2:**223–224
House on Mango Street, The (Cisneros), **1:**108
House Un-American Activities Committee (HUAC), **2:**152
Housewife, 49 (television show), **2:**265
Houston, James D., *Farewell to Manzanar,* **1:**299–301
Houston, Jeanne Wakatsuki, **1:**300
    Beyond Manzanar, **1:**299
    Farewell to Manzanar, **1:**299–301, 309
    The Legend of Fire Horse Woman, **1:**299
Houston Chronicle (newspaper), **2:**85
Hoveyda, Abbas, **3:**218
Hoveyda, Fereydoun, *Fall of the Shah,* **3:**218
Howard, Maureen, **2:**48
Howard, Neil, **1:**244
Howard-Stepney, Marged, **1:**127
Howe, Barbara, **3:**68
Howe, Florence, *With Wings,* **1:**8
Howe, Lawrence, **1:**146, 147, 148
Howells, William Dean, **1:**146, **2:**239–240, **3:**261
Hower, Edward, **1:**23
How I Grew (McCarthy), **1:**258
Howkins, Alun, **3:**64–65
How the Garcia Girls Lost Their Accents (Alvarez), **1:**108
Hron, Madelaine, **3:**259
HUAC. *See* House Un-American Activities Committee
Huang Dinghui, **3:**148
Hubbell, J. L., **3:**290, 291
Hudson, Derek, **2:**77
Hudson, Hosea
    Black Worker in the Deep South, **1:**3
    The Narrative of Hosea Hudson, **1:**3–4
Hudson Review (journal), **1:**165, 168, **2:**115
Hughes, Barbara, **2:**159

Hughes, Langston
    The Big Sea, **1:**84, 122
    "Harlem," **1:**275
    I Wonder as I Wander, **1:**37
    Mulatto, **1:**72
Hughes, Ted, **2:**47, 48, 49
Human body. *See* Body
Humanism
    Cereta (Laura) in, **2:**160, 161
    Kierkegaard's (Søren) critique of, **2:**166, 167
Human rights
    "Letter from the Birmingham Jail" (King) as argument for, **2:**32
    universal, development of concept, **2:**316
Human rights abuses. *See also* Genocide
    in Cambodia, **1:**306
    in China, **1:**158, 161
    in Guatemala, **1:**99, 100, **3:**164–166
    in Iran, **1:**155
    in Iraq, **2:**275
    in Nazi Germany (*See* Holocaust)
    in Nigeria, **1:**214, 215, 216
    in Sierra Leone, **1:**312
    in South Africa, **3:**242
    in Ukraine, **3:**19
    in Vietnam, **1:**171, 172
Hume, David, **2:**328
Humor
    in *Angela's Ashes* (McCourt), **1:**119
    in *The Autobiography of Ben Franklin* (Franklin), **1:**181
    in *Confessions of Lady Nijo* (Nijo), **2:**60
    in *The Diary of Anne Frank* (Frank), **2:**253–254, 255
    in *Journals of Ralph Waldo Emerson* (Emerson), **2:**141
    in "Letter to Her Daughter from the New White House" (Adams), **2:**87
    in *Life on the Mississippi* (Twain), **1:**147
    in *Praeterita* (Ruskin), **1:**265
    in *Prison Writings* (Peltier), **1:**97

in *Selected Letters of Martha Gellhorn* (Gellhorn), **2:**102

in *Up from Slavery* (Washington), **1:**51–52

in *A Woman in Berlin* (anonymous), **2:**282

Humphrey, Carol Sue, **2:**318

Humphries, Stephen

The Handbook of Oral History, **3:**313

Hooligans or Rebels?, **3:**144, 311–314

on *The World at War* (Holmes), **3:**235

Hunger of Memory (Rodriguez), **1:**15–17, 47

Hunsaker, Steven V., **1:**100

Hunt, Evelyn, **3:**269

Hunt, Leigh, **2:**143, 144, 146

Hunt, Richard, **3:**277

Hunt, Swanee, *This Was Not Our War,* **3:**268

Huntington, Countess of, **2:**44, 46

Huntsman, Jeffrey, **1:**56

Hurst, Fannie, **1:**10

Imitation of Life, **1:**72

Hurston, Zora Neale

Angelou (Maya) inspired by, **1:**18

Dust Tracks on a Road, **1:**9–11, 18, 122

Mules and Men, **1:**9

Polk County, **1:**10

Seraph on the Suwanee, **1:**9

Tell My Horse, **1:**9, 11

Their Eyes Were Watching God, **1:**11

in tradition of Prince (Mary), **3:**24

Hurvitz, Yair, **2:**50

Husain, Adnan, **1:**287–288

Husayn, Taha. *See* Hussein, Taha

Hussain, Soofia, **3:**81

Hussein, Saddam, **2:**275, 276, 278, 279

Hussein, Taha, *An Egyptian Childhood,* **1:**135–138

Hutchinson, Mary, **2:**300

Hutchisson, James M., **2:**42

Hutu people, **3:**257–259, *258*

Huxley, Elspeth, **2:**12

Huxley, Thomas, **1:**67

Huynh, Jade Ngoc Quang, *South Wind Changing,* **1:**171

Hyde-Lees, Georgie, **2:**126

Hypocrisy

in American Revolution, **2:**44, 45

in European culture, **1:**90

in slavery, **1:**34, 144, **2:**44, 45, 46

I

I, Rigoberta Menchú (Menchú), **3:**164–166

Californio Voices (Savage) vs., **3:**114

Child of the Dark (de Jesus) vs., **2:**8

Doña María's Story (James) vs., **3:**73–74

Let Me Speak! (Viezzer and Barrios de Chungara) vs., **3:**322

Rites: A Guatemalan Boyhood (Perera) vs., **1:**99

Women's Words (Gluck and Patai) on, **3:**191

IAD. *See* Institute for Aboriginal Development

I Am Rosa Parks (Parks), **1:**38

Ibn Asakir, **1:**287

Ibrahim, Christy Thompson, **1:**8

I Can Almost See the Lights of Home (Portelli), **3:**265–266

Ichijō (emperor of Japan), **2:**290, 291, 292

Ida (Stein), **1:**332

Idaho, oral histories of life in, **3:**93–95, *94*

Idealization

of Africa, by Laye (Camara), **1:**130

of childhood, by Laye (Camara), **1:**128

of colonial America, by Crèvecoeur (Michel-Guillaume Saint-Jean de), **2:**213–215

Identity. *See also* Ethnic identity; Multicultural and multiracial identities; National identity; *specific groups*

divided nature of, Rousseau (Jean-Jacques) on, **1:**200–202

language in, role of, **1:**15–17, **3:**108, 109

postcolonial, **1:**87–89

Identity formation

in *Angela's Ashes* (McCourt), **1:**121

in *Dust Tracks on a Road* (Hurston), **1:**11

of Irish immigrants, **1:**121

in *Journal, 1955–1962* (Feraoun), **2:**262–263

in *The Journals of Charlotte Forten Grimké* (Grimké), **2:**31

in *Praeterita* (Ruskin), **1:**265

in *Wars I Have Seen* (Stein), **1:**333–334

Identity politics

Columbus's (Christopher) legacy and, **2:**203

cultural studies and, **1:**15

disability studies and, **1:**8

Rodriguez's (Richard) critique of, **1:**15–16

IEDs. *See* Improvised explosive devices

If This Is a Man (Levi), **1:**318

"If We Must Die" (McKay), **1:**84

Igbo people, **1:**214, 215

Ignatius of Loyola (saint), **1:**211

"I Have a Dream" (King), **1:**79, **2:**32

I Know Why the Caged Bird Sings (Angelou), **1:**18–20, 249

Ilagiinniq (Tulugarjuk and Christopher), **3:**138

Ill-Fated People, An (Vambe), **3:**251–253

Illinois, Lincoln's (Abraham) life and career in, **3:**261, 263. *See also* Chicago

Illness. *See* Health problems

Illustrated Times of London, **1:**112

Imad al-Din al-Katib al-Isfahani, *The Syrian Thunderbolt,* **1:**286

Image du monde (Guisson), **1:**105

Images and Conversations (Preciado Martin), **3:**121

Imitation of Life (Hurst), **1:**72

Imlay, Gilbert, **2:**111

Immigrant Women in the Land of Dollars (Ewen), **3:**305

Immigration
- to Australia, from Vietnam, **1:**337
- to Chile, from Germany, **1:**75, 77
- to France, by Bashkirtseff (Marie), **2:**306–308
- from Ireland, **1:**119
- to Ireland, by Mahomet (Dean), **2:**229
- Jewish (*See* Jewish immigration)

Immigration, to U.S.
- by Agosín (Marjorie), **1:**75
- by Ahmedi (Farah), **1:**40, 41
- by Cheng Yu-hsiu, **1:**152
- Cuban, **1:**296–298
- by Hayslip (Le Ly), **1:**335
- Japanese, **1:**309, **3:**80–82, 127–129, 195
- Jewish, **3:**14, 118, 120
- Latin American, **1:**108–110, **3:**121
- by Medina (Pablo), **1:**296, 297
- by Min (Anchee), **1:**158
- by Nabokov (Vladimir), **1:**270
- by Nguyen (Kien), **1:**170, 171
- oral histories of, **3:**80–82, 305–307
- by Santiago (Esmeralda), **1:**108–110
- by Siv (Sichan), **1:**306, 307
- Southeast Asian, **1:**170, 171, 306–307, 337
- by Suleri (Sara), **1:**87
- after Vietnam War, **1:**170, 171, 337

Immigration Act of 1924 (U.S.), **3:**80, 127, 195

Immigration Act of 1982, Amerasian (U.S.), **1:**170

Immigration and Nationality Act of 1952 (U.S.), **3:**127

Immigration Reform and Control Act of 1986 (U.S.), **3:**121

Impeachment, of Johnson (Andrew), **1:**5

Imprisonment
- of Fox (George), **2:**26
- of Gandhi (Mohandas), **1:**242
- of Ghazzawi ('Izzat), **2:**50
- of Khomeini (Ruhollah), **3:**218, 219
- of Kong Demao, **3:**124
- of Mandela (Nelson), **1:**24, 27–29, **3:**242
- of Nehru (Jawaharlal), **1:**289, 290, 291
- of Ngũgĩ wa Thiong'o, **2:**12–14, *13*
- of Peltier (Leonard), **1:**96–98
- of Polo (Marco), **1:**105
- in Soviet Gulag system, oral histories of, **3:**17–19
- of Soyinka (Wole), **1:**214–216
- of Speer (Albert), **2:**54–56
- of Wilde (Oscar), **2:**9–10

Improvised explosive devices (IEDs), **3:**233

Inada, Lawson Fusao, *Only What We Could Carry,* **3:**80

In All the West No Place Like This (Kincaid and Dahlgren), **3:**93

Incarceration. *See* Imprisonment

Incest, Nin's (Anaïs) experience of, **2:**124

Incident at Oglala (documentary), **1:**96

Incidents in the Life of a Slave Girl (Jacobs), **1:142–145**
- autobiographies inspired by, **1:**18
- *A Diary from Dixie* (Chesnut) vs., **2:**250
- Equiano's (Olaudah) influence on, **1:**83
- *The Journals of Charlotte Forten Grimké* (Grimké) vs., **2:**29
- *Narrative of the Life of Frederick Douglass* (Douglass) vs., **1:**34, 35, 142, 143

In Country (Mason), **1:**335

In Custody (Desai), **1:**87

Independent (newspaper), **2:**239, 269, 276, **3:**316

Indexicality, **2:**267

India
- British partition of (1947), **1:**87, 244
- food of, in Britain, **2:**230, 231
- Gama's (Vasco da) first voyage to, **2:**198–200
- under Mogul Empire, **2:**229
- nationalism in, **1:**289–290

India, British colonial rule of
- Chaudhuri (Nirad C.) on life under, **3:**253
- East India Company in, **2:**229
- end of (1947), **1:**87, 244
- establishment of, **2:**229, 328
- Gandhi (Mohandas) in movement against, **1:**242–244, 289–290
- legacy of, **1:**87–89
- Mahomet (Dean) on culture of, **2:**229–231
- Nehru (Jawaharlal) in movement against, **1:**289–291

Indiana Magazine of History, **3:**109

Indian nationalism, **1:**289–290

Indian Removal Act of 1830 (U.S.), **1:**302, **3:**107

Indian Reorganization Act of 1934 (U.S.), **3:**107

Indian Territory, **3:**325

Indian Trader (Blue), **3:**290, 291

Indigenous people. *See also specific countries and groups*
- Columbus's (Christopher) encounters with, **2:**201, 202, *202*
- Gama's (Vasco da) encounters with, **2:**199

Individual actions, in identity, Rousseau (Jean-Jacques) on, **1:**200, 201

Individuals
- authors as, Lejeune (Philippe) on value of, **1:**239
- in Romantic era, focus on, **2:**16
- "self-made," **1:**180

Indochina, French colonial rule of, **3:**279

Indochinese Refugees (Scott), **1:**335

Indoctrination, in Cultural Revolution, **1:**159, 161, 162

Indonesia, Obama (Barack) in, **1:**78

Industrialization
- in Argentina, **3:**73
- and international labor movement, **3:**157
- in Soviet Union, **3:**17
- of U.S., Thoreau (Henry David) on, **1:**233

Industrialization, in Britain
- of agriculture, **3:**59, 63

in concepts of progress, **2:**146
economic inequality in, **2:**300
social inequality in, **2:**16
Industrial Revolution, Second
Adams (Henry) on, **1:**132, 134
Twain (Mark) and, **1:**146
Industrial Workers of the World (IWW), **3:**329
establishment of, **3:**328
oral histories of, **3:**328–330
working conditions improved by, **3:**93
Infidel (Hirsi Ali), **1:207–210**
Influenza pandemic of 1918, **1:**258
Ingle, H. Larry, **2:**26, 28
Inheritance law, English, women in, **2:**62–63, 64
In Her Own Words (Morantz), **3:**170
In Light of India (Paz), **1:**222–223
Inman, Henry, **2:336**
In My Country (film), **3:**242
Innocence, loss of
in *The Dark Child* (Laye), **1:**129
in *Incidents in the Life of a Slave Girl* (Jacobs), **1:**144
Innocents Abroad, The (Twain), **1:**146
Innovations, in autobiographical writing
of Cavendish (Margaret), **1:**230, 231
of Conroy (Frank), **1:**165
of Hussein (Taha), **1:**135–136
of Kingston (Maxine Hong), **1:**173
of Pepys (Samuel), **2:**72
of Rousseau (Jean-Jacques), **1:**200–202
of Stein (Gertrude), **1:**332, 333, 334
In Pharaoh's Army (Wolff), **1:**47
In Search of Lost Time (Proust), **1:**265, 270
In Search of Our Roots (Gates), **1:**263
Inside the Third Reich (Speer), **2:**54
In Sierra Leone (Jackson), **1:**312
Institute for Aboriginal Development (IAD), **3:**334, 336
Insurgencies
in Iraq War, **3:**231, 232, 233

in Salvadoran Civil War, **3:**205, 206, 207
Insurrection Act of 1796 (Britain), **2:**159
Intellectual development, in *The Autobiography of Giambattista Vico* (Vico), **1:**183–185
Intellectual Memoirs (McCarthy), **1:**258
Intercultural adoption, Kim (Elizabeth) on, **1:**102–104
Interesting Narrative of the Life of Olaudah Equiano, The (Equiano), **1:34, 81–83,** 142, **3:**23
Interior, U.S. Department of, **3:**11
Interior Castle (Teresa of Ávila), **1:**212
International Affairs (journal), **1:**25, 291
International Court of Justice, **1:**306
International Jew, The (Ford), **1:**30, 32
International Journal of African Historical Studies, **3:**142, 252
International Journal of Middle East Studies, **3:**220
International Law Commission, UN, **2:**56
International Migration Review (journal), **3:**81, 225
International Review (journal), **2:**70
International Review of Social Research (journal), **3:**320
International Women's Conference, **3:**322
International Women's Year Tribunal, **3:**322
International Workingmen's Association, **3:**3
Internment. See Japanese American internment
Interpreter of Maladies (Lahiri), **1:**87
Interpreting the Self (Reynolds), **1:**136, 137, 286, 287
Interracial adoption, Kim (Elizabeth) on, **1:**102–104
Interracial relationships
in Appalachia, **3:**92
in Korean War, **1:**102
McBride (James) on, **1:**72–74
U.S. attitudes toward, **1:**72–74
in U.S. postwar occupation of Japan, **3:**127–129

U.S. Supreme Court on, **1:**72, 78
Vietnamese attitudes toward, **1:**170, 171
in Vietnam War, **1:**170
Interrupted Life, An (Hillesum), **2:22–25**
Intertexts (journal), **3:**116
"Interviewing Women" (Oakley), **3:**190
Interviews. See Oral histories
In the Cities of the South (Seabrook), **3:**54
In the Combat Zone (Marshall), **3:**221, 279
In the Garden of North American Martyrs (Wolff), **1:**47
In the Mansion of Confucius' Descendants (Kong and Ke), **3:124–126,** 299
In the Presence of Absence (Darwish), **1:255–257**
Intifada, first, **1:**225, **2:**50–52
Into the Jet Age (Wooldridge), **3:**203
Introspection, Ruskin's (John) fear of, **1:**265, 266
Inuits, oral histories of, **3:**138–140, *139*
Inuktitut language, **3:**138, 139–140
Invention of Loneliness, The (Auster), **1:**279
Investigation of Dogmatic Theology (Tolstoy), **1:**194
Invisible Cities (Calvino), **1:**105
Invisible Soldier, The (Motley), **3:**212
Invisible Thread, The (Uchida), **1:309–311**
Iola Leroy (Harper), **1:**143
Iowa, labor movement in, **3:**153
Iran
coup of 1953 in, **3:**218
in Iran–Iraq War, **1:**155, 157
Islam in, **1:**155, 156
oral histories of political history of, **3:**218–220
Revolution of 1979 in, **1:**155, 157, **3:**218, 220
Satrapi (Marjane) on life in, **1:**155–157
uprising of 1963 in, **3:**218, 219
White Revolution in, **3:**218
women's rights in, **3:**218

Iranian Studies (journal), **3:**219

Iran–Iraq War (1980–1988), **1:**155, 157

Iraq. *See also* Iraq War
    in Gulf War, **2:**275, 278–280
    in Iran–Iraq War, **1:**155, 157

IraqGirl: Diary of a Teenage Girl in Iraq, **2:**275

Iraq Veterans against the War, **3:**232

Iraq War (2003–2011), **2:**276
    Al-Windawi (Thura) on experience of, **2:**275–276
    embedded journalists in, **2:**278, 280
    vs. Salvadoran Civil War, **3:**207
    U.S. veterans of, oral histories of, **3:**231–233, *232*

Ireland
    Catholicism in, **1:**119–120
    Civil War in, **3:**27, 315
    Easter Uprising in, **3:**27, 315
    English conquest of, **3:**315
    famine in, **3:**27, 315
    gender roles in, **2:**157
    independence movement in, **3:**27–29
    independence of (1922), **1:**119, **3:**315
    Leadbeater (Mary) on life in, **2:**157–159
    Mahomet's (Dean) move to, **2:**229
    McCourt (Frank) on life in, **1:**119–121
    nationalism in, **1:**119, **2:**127, 128, **3:**315
    oral histories of, **3:**27–29, 315–317
    oral traditions of, **1:**121
    poverty in, **1:**119–121
    Quakerism in, **2:**157–159
    Rebellion of 1798 in, **2:**157, *158*, 159
    War of Independence in, **3:**27–29, 315
    Yeats (William Butler) on life in, **2:**126–128

Ireland's Unfinished Revolution (Griffith and O'Grady), **3:27–30**

Irele, Abiola, **1:**130

Irish Americans, McCourt (Frank) on experience of, **1:**119–121

Irish autobiographical writing
    by Leadbeater (Mary), **2:**157–159
    rise in popularity of, **1:**119, 120
    tradition of, **1:**119, 121
    by Yeats (William Butler), **2:**126–128

Irish Civil War (1922–1923), **3:**27, 315

Irish Days (Hickey), **3:315–317**

Irish Experience during the Second World War, The (Grob-Fitzgibbon), **3:**315–316

Irish identity, **1:**121

Irish nationalism, **1:**119, **2:**127, 128, **3:**315

Irish National Theatre Society, **2:**128

Irish oral histories
    on life in twentieth century, **3:**315–317
    on War of Independence, **3:**27–29

Irish Rebellion (1798), **2:**157, *158*, 159

Irish Republican Brotherhood, **3:**27

Irish University Review (journal), **1:**121

Irish Voice (newspaper), **3:**29

Irish War of Independence (1919–1921), **3:**27–29, 315

Irizarry, Estelle, **2:**203

Irvine, Weldon, **1:**274

Isabella of Castille, **2:**201

Isani, Mukhtar Ali, **2:**45

Isay, David, **3:**174

Isca, Valerio, **3:**5

Isham, Ralph Hayward, **2:**330

Isherwood, Christopher, *The World in the Evening*, **2:**152

Islam. *See also* Muslim *entries*
    fundamentalist, **1:**156, 208
    Hirsi Ali's (Ayaan) critique of, **1:**207–209
    in Iran, **1:**155, 156
    Malcolm X's conversion to, **1:**186–188
    violence against women in, **1:**207–209

Islamic education, in Egypt, **1:**135

Isocrates, *To Nicocles*, **2:**94

Isolation
    of households, Stanton (Elizabeth Cady) on, **1:**14
    personal, Hawthorne (Nathaniel) on, **2:**223, 224

Israel
    establishment of (1948), **1:**225, 255, **2:**104, **3:**118
    Palestinian territories occupied by, **1:**225, **2:**50, *51*

Israeli–Palestinian conflict, **1:**225, 255, 257, **2:**50–52

Issei, **3:**80–82

Italian Americans, relocation during World War II, oral histories of, **3:**224–226

Italian autobiographical writing
    by Cereta (Laura), **2:**160–162
    by Polo (Marco), **1:**105–107
    by Vico (Giambattista), **1:**183–185

Italian oral histories
    on Fosse Ardeatine massacre, **3:**265–267
    on working class, **3:**157–159

Italian Quattrocento, **2:**160

Italy. *See also* Italian autobiographical writing
    education of women in, **2:**160–161
    Fosse Ardeatine massacre in, **3:**265–267
    labor movement in, **3:**157–159, *158*
    Montagu's (Mary Wortley) move to, **2:**35
    Nazi occupation of, **3:**265–267
    Renaissance, women in, **2:**160–162
    working class in, **3:**157–159

It Happened in Brooklyn (Frommer and Frommer), **3:**118

It Happened to Nancy (Sparks), **2:**294

Iverson, Peter, **3:**291

Iwakoshi, Miyo, **3:**82

I Will Bear Witness (Klemperer), **2:303–305**

I Will Marry When I Want (Ngũgĩ), **2:**12

I Wonder as I Wander (Hughes), **1:**37

IWW. *See* Industrial Workers of the World

Izumi Shikibu, **2:**189, 190, 290

J

Jabra, Jabra Ibrahim, *The First Well*, **1**:136

Jacinthe Noir (Amrouche), **1**:93

Jack, Peter Monro, **2**:149

Jacka, Tamara, **3**:301

Jackson, Andrew, **1**:302, **2**:335

Jackson, Anna, **2**:134, 135

Jackson, Ernest, **2**:263

Jackson, Jamie Smith, **2:295**

Jackson, Michael, *In Sierra Leone*, **1**:312

Jackson, Molly, **3**:157

Jackson, Samuel L., **3**:242

Jackson, Timothy P., **2**:24

Jackson-Schebetta, Lisa, **2**:102

JACL. *See* Japanese American Citizens League

Jacobs, Harriet A., *Incidents in the Life of a Slave Girl*, **1:142–145**, *143*

    autobiographies inspired by, **1**:18

    A Diary from Dixie (Chesnut) vs., **2**:250

    Equiano's (Olaudah) influence on, **1**:83

    The Journals of Charlotte Forten Grimké (Grimké) vs., **2**:29

    Narrative of the Life of Frederick Douglass (Douglass) vs., **1**:34, 35, 142, 143

Jacobsen, Jens Peter, **2**:149

Jacob's Room (Woolf), **2**:138

Jaffer, Zubeida, **3**:243

Jamaica

    English colonial rule of, **1**:111

    McKay's (Claude) youth in, **1**:84, 85

    slavery in, **1**:111

Jamaican autobiographical writing

    by McKay (Claude), **1**:84–86

    by Seacole (Mary), **1**:111–113

James, Alice, **2**:113

James, Daniel, *Doña María's Story*, **3:73–76**

James, Henry, **2:114**

    Adams (Henry) influenced by, **1**:132–133

    The Bostonians, **2**:113

    The Complete Notebooks of Henry James, **2:113–116**

    Confidence, **2**:114

    Daisy Miller, **1**:133, **2**:114

    Gellhorn (Martha) on, **2**:101

    Guy Domville, **2**:114

    on *Journal des Goncourt* (Goncourt and Goncourt), **2**:82–83

    Kemble's (Fanny) friendship with, **2**:335, 336

    The Notebooks of Henry James, **2**:113, 114, 115

    The Portrait of a Lady, **1**:133, **2**:113

    Roderick Hudson, **2**:114

    The Spoils of Poynton, **2**:115

    Wells's (H. G.) letters to, **1**:252, 253

    The Wings of the Dove, **2**:113, 115

James, William, **1**:197, **2**:113

James I (king of England), **1**:316, **2**:62

James II (king of England), **1**:315

Jameson, Anna, **2**:335

Jamison, Kay Redfield, *An Unquiet Mind*, **1**:204

Japan. *See also* Japanese autobiographical writing

    Buddhism in (*See* Buddhism)

    China invaded by (1931), **3**:215

    Chinese relations with, **1**:340, **3**:149

    gender roles in, **2**:60–61

    Heian period in (*See* Heian period)

    hibakusha literature of, **1**:293

    immigration to U.S. from, **1**:309, **3**:80–82, 127–129, 195

    Kamakura period in, **2**:59–61

    Korea under rule of, **1**:322–324

    marriage in, **2**:297–299

    Mongol invasions of, **2**:59

    in Nanking Massacre, **1**:340, **2**:19–21

    Nara period in, **2**:189

    nationalism in, **3**:234

    in Russo–Japanese War, **1**:322, **3**:234

    in Sino–Japanese Wars, **1**:322, 339, 340, **3**:234

    in World War II, oral histories of, **3**:127–129, 215–217 (*See also* World War II)

Japan at War (Cook and Cook), **3:215–217**

Japanese, Nazis & Jews (Kranzler), **3**:15

Japanese American(s)

    autobiographical tradition of, **1**:299, 309

    first-generation, oral histories of, **3**:80–82

    Houston (Jeanne Wakatsuki) on experience of, **1**:299–301

    internment of (*See* Japanese American internment)

    Japanese war brides, oral histories of, **3**:127–129, *128*

    racism against, **1**:309, **3**:81, 82, 127, 195

    Uchida (Yoshiko) on experience of, **1**:309–311

Japanese American Citizens League (JACL), **3**:197

Japanese American internment, **1:310, 3**:196

    establishment of policy, **1**:299, 311, **3**:104, 195

    Houston (Jeanne Wakatsuki) on experience of, **1**:299–301

    Italian American relocation and, **3**:224

    at Manzanar, **1**:299–301, **3**:102–104, 197, *225*

    oral histories of, **3**:80–81, 102–104, 195–197

    reparations for, **3**:195, 197

    Uchida (Yoshiko) on experience of, **1**:309–311

Japanese American Oral History Project, **3**:80, 102, 195

Japanese American World War II Evacuation Oral History Project (Hansen), **3**:215

Japanese autobiographical writing. *See also specific works and writers*

    by Michitsuna No Haha, **2**:297–299

    by Murasaki Shikibu, **2**:290–292

    by Nakazawa (Keiji), **1**:293–295

    by Nijo (Lady), **2**:59–61

    by Sarashina (Lady), **2**:189–191

    by women, tradition of, **2**:59, 60

Japanese War Brides in America (Crawford et al.), **3:**127–130
Japan-Russia Treaty of Peace, **3:**234
Jarrell, Randall, **1:**205
Jaspers, Karl, **2:**167
Jawhariyyeh, Wasif, **2:**104
Jay's Journal (Sparks), **2:**294
Jayyusi, Salma Khadra, **1:**225, 227
Jazz
    and *Stop-Time* (Conroy), **1:**165, 166
    Terkel's (Louis "Studs") writing style compared to, **3:**214
Jefferson, Alexander, **3:**249
Jefferson, Lucy, **2:**316
Jefferson, Martha, **2:**316–318
Jefferson, Mary, **2:**316
Jefferson, Thomas, **2:**317
    Autobiography, 1743–1790, **1:**179, **2:**69
    on coal in Appalachia, **3:**86
    Crèvecoeur (Michel-Guillaume Saint-Jean de) and, **2:**213, 215
    The Family Letters of Thomas Jefferson, **2:**317
    Letters from Jefferson to His Daughter, **2:**38, 316–319
    Notes on the State of Virginia, **2:**45, 215
    on Wheatley's (Phillis) poetry, **2:**45
Jeffrey, Francis, **2:**35, 36, 73
Jelinek, Estelle, **1:**246
Jelmek, Estelle C., **1:**14
Jemima Condict (Condict), **2:**78–80
Jemison, Mary, **1:**326
Jenner, W. J. F., **3:**299
Jennings, Humphrey, **2:**235
Jeon, Miseli, **1:**103, 104
Jerome, **2:**94
Jerusalem, **2:**227
    under British Mandate, 'Amr (Sāmī) on, **2:**104, 105, *105*
    Guylforde's (Richarde) pilgrimage to, **2:**226–228
    secular education in, **2:**106
Jessee, Erin, **3:**180
Jesus, Carolina Maria de. *See* De Jesus, Carolina Maria

Jew(s)
    anarchism among, **3:**3
    in Chile, **1:**75–77
    in Guatemala, **1:**99–100
    in interracial relationships, **1:**72–74
    prejudice against (*See* Anti-Semitism)
    The Protocols of the Elder of Zion on conspiracy of, **1:**32
    in World War II (*See* Holocaust)
Jewel of the Desert (Taylor), **3:**80
Jewish American Committee, **3:**118
Jewish autobiographical writing. *See also specific works and writers*
    by Agosín (Marjorie), **1:**75–77
    by D'Israeli (Isaac), **2:**177, 179
    by Frank (Anne), **2:**253–255
    by Hillesum (Etty), **2:**22–24
    by Kafka (Franz), **2:**120–122
    by Klemperer (Victor), **2:**303–305
    by Perera (Victor), **1:**99–101
    by Stein (Gertrude), **1:**332, 333
    by Wiesel (Elie), **1:**318–320
Jewish Community of North Minneapolis, The (Lewin), **3:**50
Jewish identity
    of Jewish Americans, **3:**119
    of Jewish refugees, **1:**75–77
Jewish immigration
    to China, **3:**14–16
    to Latin America, **1:**75, 76, *76*
    to Palestine, **2:**105, **3:**14
    to U.S., **3:**14, 118, 120
Jewish oral histories. *See also* Holocaust oral histories
    of anarchists, **3:**3
    of U.S. life, **3:**118–120
Jewish Social Studies (journal), **1:**31
Jeyifo, Biodun, **1:**215, 216
Jiang, Ji-li
    Magical Monkey King, **1:**163
    Red Scarf Girl, **1:**153, 154, 159, **161–163**
Jiang Quing, **1:**158
Jiang Zemin, **1:**158
Jim Crow laws. *See* Racial segregation

Job Corps, **3:**254
Johansen, Bruce, **1:**97
John, Augustus Edwin, **2:**127
John II (king of Portugal), **2:**198
John of the Cross (saint), **1:**211
Johnson, Andrew, **1:**5
Johnson, Arvid, **3:**94
Johnson, Charles, **1:**10
Johnson, David, **2:**219, **3:**143
Johnson, E. D. H., **2:**300
Johnson, James Weldon, *Along This Way,* **1:**13, 84, 122
Johnson, Josephine, **2:**152
Johnson, Kendall, **1:**54, **2:**115
Johnson, Lyndon Baines, **3:**254–256, *255*
Johnson, Martin, **3:**261, 264
Johnson, Pamela Hansford, **1:**127
Johnson, Penny, **1:**226
Johnson, Richard, *Making History,* **3:**176, 177
Johnson, Robert David, **3:**254
Johnson, Samuel
    on *Evelina* (Burney), **2:**313
    letters of, **2:**217
    Life of Samuel Johnson (Boswell) on, **2:**177, 195, 309, 328, 329–330
    on *Turkish Embassy Letters* (Montagu), **2:**37
Johnson, Tom, **3:**200, 338
Johnsrud, Harold, **1:**258
Jolluck, Katherine R., *Gulag Voices,* **3:**17–19, 331
Jolote, Juan Pérez, **3:**167–169
Jones, Bob, **3:**5
Jones, Catherine, **2:**311
Jones, Edward P., **1:**122
Jones, John Paul, **1:**180
Jones, J. William, **2:**38, 39
Jones, Lu Ann, **3:**135–136, 137
Jones, Roderick, **2:**261
Jörgensen, Beth Ellen, **3:**31, 32
Josephson, Paul, **3:**285
Journal(s). *See also specific works and writers*
    Lejeune (Philippe) on study of, **2:**174–175

rise in popularity of, in England, **2:**177

of ships' captains, Spanish law on, **2:**201

as source for biographies, **2:**177, 178

Journal, 1955–1962 (Feraoun), **2:262–264**

Journal and Remarks 1832–1835 (Darwin), **1:**65

Journal des Goncourt (Goncourt and Goncourt), **2:81–83**

Journal for Early Modern Cultural Studies, **2:**199

Journal for the Scientific Study of Religion, **3:**41

Journalism

African Americans in, **3:**199–200

Gellhorn's (Martha) career in, **2:**101–102

on hooliganism in Britain, **3:**312

literary, in Enlightenment England, **2:**328

Moore's (Molly) career in, **2:**278–280

Orwell's (George) work in, **2:**117

Journal of Acquired Immune Deficiency Syndromes, **3:**274

Journal of Adolescent & Adult Literacy, **1:**41, 162, **2:**276

Journal of American Ethnic History, **3:**5, 81, 306, 320

Journal of American Folklore, **3:**88, 91, 109

Journal of American History

on *And Justice for All* (Tateishi), **3:**197

on *Bloods* (Terry), **3:**201

on *Brokenburn* (Stone), **2:**246

on *Children of Los Alamos* (Mason), **3:**240

on *The Death of Luigi Trastulli* (Portelli), **3:**159

on *Freedom Flyers* (Moye), **3:**249

on *Habits of Change* (Rogers), **3:**309

on *Head of the Class* (Morris), **3:**22

on *Hill Country Teacher* (Manning), **3:**77

on *The Hispanic-American Entrepreneur* (Owsley), **3:**122

on *The Hood River Issei* (Tamura), **3:**80

on *Launching the War on Poverty* (Gillette), **3:**254

on *A Midwife's Tale* (Ulrich), **2:**333

on *Our Appalachia* (Shackelford and Weinberg), **3:**87

on *Peacework* (Adams), **3:**269

on *A Shared Authority* (Frisch), **3:**181

on *Solidarity Forever* (Bird et al.), **3:**329

on *They Say in Harlan County* (Portelli), **3:**98

on *"We Have Just Begun to Not Fight"* (Frazer and O'Sullivan), **3:**229

Journal of American Studies, **3:**5, 163, 213

Journal of an Ordinary Grief (Darwish), **1:**255

Journal of Appalachian Studies, **3:**68

Journal of Arabic and Islamic Studies, **1:**255

Journal of a Residence in America (Kemble), **2:**335, 336

Journal of a Residence on a Georgian Plantation (Kemble), **2:**335, 336, 337

Journal of Asian American Studies, **3:**84, 85

Journal of Asian and African Studies, **3:**148

Journal of Asian Studies, **3:**148, 280, 281

Journal of a Tour into the Interior (Barnard), **2:**217, 218

Journal of a Tour to the Hebrides, The (Boswell), **2:**328

Journal of a Voyage to North-America (Charlevoix), **2:**205

Journal of Black Studies, **1:**5, 188

Journal of Canadian Studies, **3:**181

Journal of Commonwealth Literature, **1:**88

Journal of Conflict Studies, **3:**207

Journal of Contemporary History, **3:**35

Journal of English Studies, **1:**251

Journal of Family History, **2:**91, **3:**126

Journal of Folklore Research Reviews, **3:**12, 326

Journal of General Education, **3:**345

Journal of George Fox (Fox), **2:26–28**

Journal of Ideology, **3:**291

Journal of Japanese Studies, **2:**60, **3:**216

Journal of John Woolman, The (Woolman), **2:**213

Journal of Jules Renard, The (Renard), **2:**183

Journal of Katherine Mansfield (Mansfield), **2:133–135**

Journal of Literary Studies, **1:**29

Journal of Madam Knight, The (Knight), **2:**78

Journal of Magellan's Voyage (Pigafetta), **2:**201

Journal of Marie Bashkirtseff, The (Bashkirtseff), **2:306–308**

Journal of Military History, **3:**116, 216

Journal of Modern African Studies, **1:**26

Journal of Modern History, **3:**19

Journal of Modern Literature, **1:**17, **2:**122, 269

Journal of Narrative Theory, **1:**121

Journal of Negro History, **1:**11, **2:**45

Journal of New Zealand Literature, **2:**134

Journal of Pan African Studies, **1:**244

Journal of Sir Walter Scott, The (Scott), **2:**67, **309–311**

Journal of Social and Clinical Psychology, **1:**205

Journal of Social Archaeology, **3:**116

Journal of Social History, **3:**75, 145, 311

Journal of Southeast Asian American Education and Advancement, **1:**307

Journal of Southern History, **3:**78, 91, 96, 261

Journal of the American Oriental Society, **1:**287

Journal of the First Voyage of Vasco da Gama, A (Author Unknown), **2:198–200**, 201

Journal of the First Voyage to America (Columbus), **2:201–204**, 205

Journal of the History of Medicine and Applied Science, **3:**272

Journal of the History of Sexuality, **3:**84

Journal of the Midwest Modern Language Association, **3:**329

Journal of the Plague Year (Defoe), **2:**174

SUBJECT INDEX

Journal of the Royal Anthropological Institute, **3:**142

Journal of Women's History, **3:**136

Journals of Arnold Bennett, The (Bennett), **2:**136–138

Journals of Charlotte Forten Grimké, The (Grimké), **2:**29–31

Journals of John Wesley (Wesley), **2:**195–197

Journals of Jonathan Carver and Related Documents, The (Carver), **2:**205–208

Journals of Ralph Waldo Emerson (Emerson), **2:**139–142

Journals of Søren Kierkegaard (Kierkegaard), **2:**166–169

Journey of Tai-me, The (Momaday), **1:**54

Journey's End (Sherriff), **1:**329

Journey to the Land of No (Hakakian), **1:**155

Jouvenel, Bertrand de, **2:**102

Joyce, James
  Conroy (Frank) influenced by, **1:**164
  Evelyn's (John) influence on, **2:**67
  Finnegans Wake, **1:**185
  Goethe's (Johann Wolfgang von) influence on, **1:**276
  Literary Fund and, **2:**207
  Portrait of the Artist as a Young Man, **1:**276, **2:**126
  Thomas (Dylan) influenced by, **1:**125
  Ulysses, **1:**146, **2:**67, 180
  Vico's (Giambattista) influence on, **1:**185
  Woolf's (Virginia) critique of, **2:**180

Joye, Harlon, *Living Atlanta,* **3:**44

Juan Pérez Jolote (Pozas). *See Juan the Chamula* (Pozas)

Juan the Chamula (Pozas), **3:**167–169

Jubilee (Alexander), **1:**262

Judaism. *See* Jew(s)

Judas Kiss, The (play), **2:**10

Judgment at Nuremberg (film), **3:**295

Judicial system, U.S. *See also* Supreme Court
  racism of, in Peltier's (Leonard) trial, **1:**96

Judy Lopez Memorial Award for Children's Literature, for *Red Scarf Girl* (Jiang), **1:**161

Julian (Roman emperor), **1:**220

Julian of Eclanum, **1:**198

Julian of Norwich, **1:**189
  Showings, **1:**211

Jung, Carl, **1:**252, **3:**111

Junod, Violaine, **1:**25

Justice Department, U.S., **3:**224

K

Kabyle culture, preservation of, **1:**93–95

Kadi, Joanna, **1:**227

Kafka, Franz, **2:**121
  Amerika, **2:**120
  The Blue Octavo Notebooks, **2:**122
  The Castle, **2:**120
  The Diaries of Franz Kafka, 2:120–122
  "The Great Wall of China," **2:**120
  The Trial, **2:**120, 121–122

Kagan, Richard C., **1:**172

Kagero Diary, The (Michitsuna). *See Gossamer Years, The* (Michitsuna)

Kahf, Mohja, *The Girl in the Tangerine Scarf,* **1:**41–42

Kahn, Ava, **3:**51–52

Kahn-Levitt, Laurie, **2:**331

Kakutani, Michiko, **1:**79, 120, **3:**183, 184, 185, 201

Kalvelage, Lisa Schmidt, **3:**269

Kamakura period (Japan), Nijo (Lady) on life in, **2:**59–61

Kameyama (Japanese emperor), **2:**59

Kana writing, **2:**290, 292

Kandinsky, Wassily, **1:**272

Kane, Cheikh Hamidou, *L'Aventure ambiguë,* **1:**61

Kanon, Joseph, **2:**282

KANU. *See* Kenya African National Union

Kaori Hayashi, Katie, *Japanese War Brides in America,* **3:**127–130

Kaplan, Morris, **3:**72

Kappus, Franz Xaver, **2:**149–150

Kapungu, Leonard T., *The United Nations and Economic Sanctions against Rhodesia,* **3:**251

Karkabi, Barbara, **2:**85

Karlsen, Carol F., **2:**333

Karr, Mary, **1:**40, 251, 259–260

Karush, Matthew, **3:**74, 75

Kashiwahara, Ken, **3:**280

Kashmir, dispute over, **1:**87

Katherine Mansfield Notebooks, The (Mansfield), **2:**133, 134

Katovsky, Bill, *Embedded,* **3:**276

Katz, Kimberly, **2:**104, 105, 106

Kaunda, Kenneth, *Zambia Must Be Free,* **1:**290

Kazan, Elia, **2:**152

Kazin, Alfred, **1:**320, **2:**47

Kearney, Michael, **3:**303

Kearns, Judith, **1:**316

Kearns, Kevin C.
  Dublin Pub Life and Lore, **3:**315, 317
  Dublin Voices, **3:**315

Keats, George, **2:**147

Keats, John, **2:**147
  The Letters of John Keats, 2:146–148
  Life, Letters, and Literary Remains, **2:**146
  Selected Letters, **2:**146

Keckley, Elizabeth Hobbes, *Behind the Scenes,* **1:**52

Keenan, Edward N., **3:**219

Keene, Donald, **2:**191

Kehagia, Angie, **2:**124–125

Kéita, Aoua, *Femme d'Afrique,* **1:**64

Keitel, Wilhelm, **2:**54

Ke Lan, *In the Mansion of Confucius' Descendants,* **3:**124–126, 299

Keller, Bill, **1:**28, 29

Keller, Helen, **1:**44
  Midstream, **1:**44
  "My Life," **1:**43
  The Story of My Life, **1:**43–46
  The World I Live In, **1:**44, 45

Kellerman, Stewart, **1:**100

Kelley, James E., Jr., **2:**203
Kelly, Debra, **2:**263–264
Kelly, Éamon, **3:**315
Kelly, Orrin, **3:**162
Kelly, Sheldon, **1:**307
Kemble, Charles, **2:**335
Kemble, Fanny, **2:336**
    Journal of a Residence in America, **2:**335, 336
    Journal of a Residence on a Georgian Plantation, **2:**335, 336, 337
    "An Old Woman's Gossip," **2:**335
    Records of a Girlhood, **2:335–337**
    A Year of Consolation, **2:**336
Kemp, Lysander, **3:**167, 168
Kempe, Margery, *The Book of Margery Kempe,* **1:189–192**, 211, **2:**226
Kendall-Smith, Malcolm, **3:**229
Kennedy, John F., **2:**32, **3:**254
Kennedy, Randall, *Blacks at Harvard,* **3:**21
Kentucky
    coal mining in, oral histories of, **3:**86–87, 96–98, *97,* 157
    Coe Ridge community in, oral histories of, **3:**90–92
    school desegregation in, **1:**249
    working class in, oral histories of, **3:**157–159
Kenya
    borders of, establishment of, **1:**114
    British colonial rule of, **2:**12, **3:**141–143
    independence of (1963), **2:**12, **3:**141
    Mau Mau rebellion in, **2:**12
    Meru people of, oral histories of, **3:**141–143, *142*
    Ngũgĩ wa Thiong'o on life in, **2:**12–14
    Obama's (Barack) visits to, **1:**78, 79
Kenya African National Union (KANU), **2:**12
Kenyatta, Jomu, **2:**12
Keppel-Jones, Arthur, **3:**252
Keppler, Joseph, **1:147**
Kermode, Frank, **1:**268, 269
Kerouac, Jack, *On the Road,* **1:**234
Kerr, Walter, **2:**154

Kertész, Imre, **1:**318
Kesselman, Wendy, **2:**253
Kessler, Lauren, *Stubborn Twig,* **3:**80
Keynes, John Maynard, **2:**180
Keyser, Katherine, **1:**258
KGB, Stasi modeled on, **3:**245
Khalid, Robina Josephine, **2:**5
Khalifat movement, **1:**244
Khan, Shahnaz, **1:**88
Khashan, 'Abd al-Karim, **2:**52
Khmer Rouge, **1:**306–308
Khomeini, Ruhollah, **1:**155, **3:**218, 219
Khrushchev, Nikita, **3:**331, 333
Kidder, Annemarie S., **2:**149
Kiehr, Kathy, **3:**187
Kierkegaard, Søren, *Journals of Søren Kierkegaard,* **2:166–169**, *167*
Kihn, W. Langdon, **1:**55
Kikumura, Akemi, **1:**300
Kilani, Sami, *Three Minus One,* **2:**52
Kilinc, Ibrahim, **3:**219
Killam, Douglas, **2:**14
Kilvert, Francis, **2:**287, 288
Kim, Eleana J., *Adopted Territory,* **1:**102–103
Kim, Elizabeth, *Ten Thousand Sorrows,* **1:102–104,** *103*
Kim, Richard E., *Lost Names,* **1:**102
Kim Gu. *See* Kim Ku
Kim Ku, *Paekpom Ilchi,* **1:322–324,** *323*
Kimura, Saeko, **2:**61
Kincaid, Jamaica, **1:**111
Kincaid, Simone Carbonneau, *In All the West No Place Like This,* **3:**93
Kindersley, Jemima, *Letters from the Island of Teneriffe,* **2:**229
King, Adele, **1:**128, 130
King, Clarence, **1:**132
King, Florence, **2:**331
King, Martin Luther, Jr., **2:33**
    assassination of, **1:**20
    Gandhi's (Mohandas) influence on, **1:**242
    "I Have a Dream," **1:**79, **2:**32
    "Letter from the Birmingham Jail," **2:32–34**

    vs. Malcolm X, approaches of, **1:**186
    national holiday celebrating, **1:**37, **2:**33
    in SCLC, **1:**20, **2:**32, 34
    Voices of Freedom (Hampton and Fayer) on, **3:**44
King, Mary Elizabeth, **2:**52
King, Peter, **2:**24
King, R. W., **2:**76–77
King Lear (Shakespeare), **2:**147
King Philip's War (1675–1676), **1:**325–328, *326*
Kingsley, Mary, *Travels in West Africa,* **2:**335
Kingston, Maxine Hong
    China Men, **1:**173
    Tripmaster Monkey, **1:**173
    The Woman Warrior, **1:**75, 100, **173–176**
Kinnell, Galway, **2:**150
Kinsington (London), **2:**321
Kiowa Tribe, Momaday (N. Scott) on history of, **1:**54–56
Kipling, Rudyard, **1:**88, **2:**192
Kirkus Reviews (magazine)
    on *Bone Black* (hooks), **1:**250
    on *Golden Bones* (Siv), **1:**307
    on *Growing Up Jewish in America* (Frommer and Frommer), **3:**119
    on *Machete Season* (Hatzfeld), **3:**259
    on *Spandau* (Speer), **2:**56
    on *Strange Ground* (Maurer), **3:**277
    on *The Strength Not to Fight* (Tollefson), **3:**222
    on *Tears before the Rain* (Engelmann), **3:**280
    on *The Unwanted* (Nguyen), **1:**172
Kirsch, Jonathan, **2:**279, **3:**45
Kitab al-I'tibar (Usamah). *See Arab-Syrian Gentleman and Warrior in the Period of the Crusades, An* (Usamah)
Kite Runner, The (Hosseini), **1:**40
Ki Tsurayuki, **2:**191
Klæstrup, Peter, **2:167**
Klaus, Ida, **3:**155
Klee, Paul, **2:**120

SUBJECT INDEX

Kleege, Georgina, **1:**45
Klein, Josephine, *Samples from English Culture,* **3:**144
Klemperer, Eva, **2:**303, 305
Klemperer, Victor
  Curriculum Vitae, **2:**304, 305
  I Will Bear Witness, **2:303–305**
  The Lesser Evil, **2:**304
  Lingua Tertii Imperii (LTI), **2:**304, 305
Klinkhammer, Stephen, **3:**209
Klotter, James C., **3:**88
Kluckhohn, Clyde, **3:**290
Klum, Heidi, **3:**345
K'Meyer, Tracy E., **3:**192, 309
Knight, Sarah Kemble, *The Journal of Madam Knight,* **2:**78
Knight, William Angus, **2:**300
Kniss, Lloy, **3:**229
"Knole Diary" (Clifford), **2:**62, 64
Knoll, Kristina R., **1:**41
Ko, Dorothy, **3:**147
Koch, Grace, **3:**335, 336
Koch, John T., **3:**29
Koegel, John, **3:**133
Kohbieter, Gérard, **3:**15
Kohn, Alfred, **3:**15
Kohn, Hans, **1:**291
Kohn, Rita T.
  Always a People, **3:107–109,** 325
  Long Journey Home, **3:**107, 325–327
Koker, David, *At the Edge of the Abyss,* **2:**253
Kong Decheng, **3:**124
Kong Demao, *In the Mansion of Confucius' Descendants,* **3:124–126,** 299
Konile, Notrose Nobomvu, **3:**242
Konner, Melvin, **3:**37
Konrad Wallenrod (Mickiewicz), **2:**192
Koppedrayer, Kay, **1:**244
Kopple, Barbara, **3:**98
Korea
  division of (1945), **1:**322
  independence movement in, **1:**322–324
  interracial children in, **1:**102

Japanese imperialist rule of, **1:**322–324
  Kim Ku on life in, **1:**322–324
Korea Herald (newspaper), **1:**103
Korean Americans, Kim (Elizabeth) on experience of, **1:**102–104
Korean Provisional Government (KPG), **1:**322–324
Korean War (1950–1953), **1:**102, **3:**199
Korg, Jacob, **1:**126, **2:**322
Kornbluh, Joyce L, *Rocking the Boat,* **3:**337
Kostopulos-Cooperman, Celeste, **1:**77
Kotkin, Stephen, **3:**341
Kotze, Annemare, **1:**198
Kovic, Ron, *Born on the Fourth of July,* **1:**335, **3:**209
Kovner, Sarah, *Occupying Power,* **3:**128
Kozol, Jonathon, *Letters to a Young Teacher,* **2:**150
KPG. *See* Korean Provisional Government
Kramer, Jane, **1:**175
Kramer, Samuel, **2:**94
Kramer, Stanley, **3:**295
Kramskoy, Nicholas, **1:194**
Kranzler, David, *Japanese, Nazis & Jews,* **3:**15
Krapf, Ludwig, **1:**115
Krause, Corinne Azen, *Grandmothers, Mothers, and Daughters,* **3:305–307**
Kreider, Robert, *Sourcebook,* **3:**227
Kresh, Joseph, **2:**121
Kristof, Nicholas, **1:**209
Krog, Antjie
  Begging to Be Black, **3:**242
  A Change of Tongue, **3:**242
  Country of My Skull, **3:242–244**
  There Was This Goat, **3:**242
Kropotkin, Peter, **2:**120
Krowl, Michelle, **2:**273
Krupat, Arnold, *For Those Who Come After,* **1:**71
Kruse, Horst, **1:**146, 147
Kublai Khan, **1:**105, 106, 107
Kuhn, Clifford, *Living Atlanta,* **3:**44
Kukis, Mark, **3:**212

Ku Klux Klan, **1:**186–187
Kumashiro, Kevin, *Restoried Selves,* **3:**83
!Kung people, oral histories of, **3:**37–38
Kunin, Aaron, **2:**64
Künstler, Mort, **2:**273
Künstler-Roman, **1:**276
Kushner, Tony, **3:**235
Kusmer, Kenneth, **3:**87–88
Kuwait, in Gulf War (1991), **2:**278–280
Kwong, Luke S. K., **3:**301
Kyalanova, Irina, **1:**314
Kyoto (Japan), **2:**59, 61, 189, 290, 297, *298*

L

Labor, forced
  in China, **1:**158
  in Soviet Union (*See* Gulag system)
Labor arbitration, oral histories of, **3:**153–155
Labor History (journal), **3:**341
Labor movement, oral histories of
  arbitration in, **3:**153–155
  in Argentina, **3:**73–75
  in Bolivia, **3:**322–324
  in Idaho, **3:**93
  in Iowa, **3:**153
  in Italy, **3:**157–159, *158*
  by IWW members, **3:**328–330
  in Kentucky, **3:**96–98, 157–159
  in Michigan, **3:**99, 101
  tradition of, **3:**153, 157
Labor Party (Argentina), **3:**73
Labor strikes
  by coal miners, **3:**96–98
  by IWW, **3:**328
Labor Studies Journal, **3:**68
Labour (journal), **3:**338
Labour History (journal), **3:**177, 313
Labour History Review (journal), **3:**64, 341
Labour Party (Britain), **2:**16
Lacan, Jacques, **1:**267, **3:**188
Ladies' Home Journal, **1:**43

Ladjevardi, Habib
- *Memoirs of Fatemeh Pakravan*, **3:**218–220
- *Memoirs of Prince Hamid Kadjar*, **3:**219
- *Memoirs of Shapour Bakhtiar*, **3:**220

Lady Murasaki Shu (Murasaki), **2:**291
LaFarge, Oliver, **3:**318
Laffont, Robert, **2:**338
La Forte, Robert S., *Remembering Pearl Harbor*, **3:**202
Lagos de Moreno (Mexico), land redistribution movement in, **3:**302–303
Lahiri, Jhumpa, *Interpreter of Maladies*, **1:**87
Lahontan, Baron de, *New Voyages to North-America*, **2:**205
Lakota Sioux
- Black Elk on life as, **3:**110–113
- Brave Bird (Mary) on life as, **1:**21–23, *22*

Lakota Woman (Brave Bird), **1:21–23**
Lalla Aicha (princess of Morocco), **3:**49
Lamb, Caroline, **2:**143, 145
- *Glenarvon*, **2:**145

Lamb, Charles, **2:**75
Lamb, Mary Ellen, **2:**64
Lame Deer, **1:**23
Lamentation of a Sinner (Parr), **2:**97
Lamott, Anne, *Bird by Bird*, **1:**280
Lampert, Jo, **3:**336
Lampkins, Robert, **3:**87
Lampman, Robert, **3:**255
La Navidad, **2:**203
Lancashire (England), **3:**64
Lancaster, Burt, **3:**295
Land
- of Australian Aborigines, **1:**149, **3:**334–335
- British, inheritance by women, **2:**62–63, 64
- of Maasai people, **1:**114
- Mexican, redistribution of, **3:**302–304
- of Native Americans, **1:**302, **3:**10–12, 110

- U.S., restrictions on immigrant ownership of, **3:**195
- of VaShawasha people, **3:**251

Landlord's Friend, The (Leadbeater), **2:**157
Land Ordinance of 1785 (U.S.), **2:**163
Land redistribution movement, in Mexico, **3:**302–304
Lane, Charles, **1:**235
Lane, James B., **3:**161
Langbauer, Laurie, **2:**209, 211
Langer, Lawrence, **2:**24
Langford, Rachel, **2:**174
Langhamer, Claire, **3:**146
Language(s)
- acquisition of, by Keller (Helen), **1:**44
- in identity, **1:**15–17, **3:**108, 109
- power of, Momaday (N. Scott) on, **1:**55
- in U.S. education, **1:**15, 16

Language of Blood, The (Trenka), **1:**102
La Niña (ship), **2:**203
Lanzmann, Claude, **3:**50, 52
La Pinta (ship), **2:**203
Larcius Macedo, **2:**96
Larg, D. G., **2:**77
Larner, John, **1:**107
Larson, Charles R., **1:**129
Larson, Ronald, *Camp and Community*, **3:**102, 103–104
Larson, Wendy, **3:**148
La Salle, Robert de, **1:**146–147
Las Casas, Bartolomé de
- *History of Indies*, **2:**201
- *Journal of the First Voyage to America* (Columbus) assembled by, **2:**201–203, 205
- *A Short Account of the Destruction of the Indies*, **2:**201

Lassner, Phyllis, **2:**269
Last, Clifford, **2:**265, 266
Last, Nella
- Mitchison (Naomi) compared to, **2:**235
- *Nella Last's Peace*, **2:**265
- *Nella Last's War*, **2:**265–267

Last, William, **2:**265

Last Confessions of Marie Bashkirtseff, The (Bashkirtseff), **2:**306
Last Diary of Tsaritsa Alexandra, The (Alexandra), **2:84–86**
Last Essays (Conrad), **2:**193, 194
Last Maasai Warrior, The (Meikuaya and Ntirkana), **1:**114
Last Man, The (Shelley), **2:**145
Last of the Mohicans (Cooper), **1:**56
"Late Benjamin Franklin, The" (Twain), **1:**181–182
Latimer, Hugh, **2:**97
Latin America. *See also specific countries*
- Agosín (Marjorie) on experience of Jews in, **1:**75–77
- autobiographical tradition of, **1:**222–223
- culture of, in U.S. culture, **1:**109
- Guevara's (Ernesto "Che") journey through, **2:**220–222
- immigration to U.S. from, **1:**108–110, **3:**121
- Perera (Victor) on experience of Jews in, **1:**99–100
- poverty in, **2:**220–221
- right-wing dictators in, rise of, **3:**185
- testimonios of (*See* Testimonios)

Latin American Perspectives (journal), **3:**323
Latino Americans. *See* Hispanic and Latino Americans
Lau, Peter, **3:**22
Launching the War on Poverty (Gillette), **3:254–256**
La Viers, Henry, **3:**87
Lavrin, Asunción, **3:**323
Law and Literature (journal), **1:**314
Lawlor, Bruce, **3:**210
Law of Flight (Guatemala), **1:**101
Lawrence, D. H., **2:**123, 136, 152, 207, 213
Lawtoo, Nidesh, **1:**16–17
Lay Bare the Heart (Farmer), **3:**44
Laye, Camara
- *The Dark Child*, **1:**128–131
- *A Dream of Africa*, **1:**129
- *The Guardian of the Word*, **1:**129
- *The Radiance of the King*, **1:**128

Lazraq, Zhor, **3:**48
Leadbeater, Betsy, **2:**157–158
Leadbeater, Lydia, **2:**158
Leadbeater, Mary
    The Annals of Ballitore, **2:157–159**
    Cottage Dialogues among the Irish Peasantry, **2:**157
    The Cottage Diaries, **2:**157
    The Landlord's Friend, **2:**157
    Tales for Cottagers, **2:**157
Leadbeater, William, **2:**157
Leading the Way (Santoli), **3:**210
League of Nations, **3:**257
League of Nations Union, **1:**329
Lears, Jackson, **1:**134
Leaves from the Journal of Our Life in the Highlands (Victoria), **2:209–212**
"Leaves of Memory" (Unaipon), **1:**149
Lebovitz, Hal, **1:**247
Lecar, Mike, **3:**119
Ledoux, Charles Alexandre Picard, **2:**184
Ledy, Cheik, **1:28**
Lee, Chong-Sik, **1:**323
Lee, Ellen, *Once They Hear My Name,* **1:**102
Lee, Felicia R., **1:**74
Lee, Hannah, **3:**16
Lee, Hermione, **2:**133, 134
Lee, Jennie, **2:**235
Lee, Joan Faung Jean, *Oral Histories of First to Fourth Generation Americans,* **3:**83
Lee, Jongsoo, **1:**322
Lee, Leo Ou-Fan, **2:**172
Lee, Margaret Juhae, **1:**103
Lee, Mary, **2:**38
Lee, Maryat, **2:**129, 131
Lee, Mary Custis, **2:**40
Lee, Richard, **3:**37
Lee, Robert E., **2:39**
    Buck (Lucy) and, **2:**273
    "Letter to His Son," **2:38–40**
Lee, Susan Savage, **2:**153
Lee Kuan Yew, *The Singapore Story,* **1:**290

Leepson, Marc, **3:**211
Leeson, David, **3:**29
Lefevre, Mike, **3:**345
Left Handed, *Left Handed, Son of Old Man Hat,* **3:318–321**
Left Handed, Son of Old Man Hat (Left Handed and Dyk), **3:318–321**
Legacy (journal), **2:**29
Legend of Fire Horse Woman, The (Houston), **1:**299
Legislation. *See specific laws*
Legvold, Robert, **3:**246, 332
LeHeew, Justin, **3:**232
Lehmann-Haupt, Christopher, **1:**48
Leibniz, Gottfried Wilhelm, **1:**183
Leigh, Augusta, **2:**143
Leighton, Frederic, **2:**335
Leighton, Roland, **1:**329, 330
Leipzig war crimes trials (1921), **3:**293
Leiris, Michel, **1:**247
Lejeune, Philippe
    The Autobiographical Pact, **1:239–241**
    Autobiography in France, **1:**239, **2:**174
    Me Too, **2:**174
    On Diary, **2:**174, 175
    "Practice of the Private Journal," **2:174–176**
Lenape. *See* Delaware Indians
L'Enfant, Pierre, **2:**87
Lenin, Vladimir, **1:**270, **3:**331
Lenta, Margaret, **2:**218
Lenz, Peter, **1:**121
Leonard, Karen, **3:**81
Leon Montiel, Livia, **3:**131
Leopold II (king of Belgium), **2:**192
Leppmann, Wolfgang, **2:**149
Lesbians. *See* Homosexuality
Lesinska, Zofia, **1:**333
Lesser Evil, The (Klemperer), **2:**304
Lessing, Doris, **1:168**
    The Grass Is Singing, **1:**169
    Memoirs of a Survivor, **1:**167
    Under My Skin, **1:167–169**
    Walking in the Shade, **1:**167
Le Sueur, James, **2:**263, 264

Let Me Speak! (Viezzer and Barrios de Chungara), **3:**74, 114–115, **322–324**
Let My People Go (Luthuli), **1:24–26**
Let One Hundred Flowers Bloom (Feng), **1:**161
Letter(s), writing of. *See also specific works and writers*
    in Britain, art of, **2:**146, 217
    consideration of audience in, **2:**217
    early history of, **2:**94
    in France, **2:**217
    manuals on, **2:**217
    in U.S., as social convention, **2:**223
"Letter from the Birmingham Jail" (King), **2:32–34**
Letters and Diaries of Etty Hillesum, The (Hillesum), **2:**253
Letters and Journals of Fanny Burney (Burney), **2:312–315**
Letters and Journals of Lord Byron (Byron), **2:143–145**, 309
Letters between Two (Lu and Xu), **2:170–173**
Letters from an American Farmer (Crèvecoeur), **2:213–216**
Letters from Jefferson to His Daughter (Jefferson), **2:**38, **316–319**
Letters from the Island of Teneriffe (Kindersley), **2:**229
Letters Home (Plath), **2:47–49**
Letters of Arnold Bennett (Bennett), **2:**138
Letters of a Woman Homesteader (Stewart), **2:91–93**
Letters of John Hay (Hay), **3:**263
Letters of John Keats, The (Keats), **2:146–148**
Letters of Lady Anne Barnard to Henry Dundas, The (Barnard), **2:217–219**
Letters of Mrs. Adams (Adams), **2:**87, 89
Letters of Rainer Maria Rilke (Rilke), **2:**150
Letters of Sidney and Beatrice Webb, The (Webb and Webb), **2:**172
Letters of the Younger Pliny, The (Pliny), **2:94–96**

Letters on an Elk Hunt (Stewart), **2:**91

Letters on God and Letters to a Young Woman (Rilke), **2:**149

Letters to a Young Contrarian (Hitchens), **2:**150

Letters to a Young Gymnast (Comaneci), **2:**150

Letters to a Young Novelist (Vargas Llosa), **2:**150

Letters to a Young Poet (Rilke), **2:**149–151

Letters to a Young Teacher (Kozol), **2:**150

Letters Underway (Ghazzawi), **2:**50–53

Letters Written during a Short Residence in Sweden, Norway, and Denmark (Wollstonecraft), **2:**111

"Letter to Her Daughter" (Montagu), **2:**35–37

"Letter to Her Daughter from the New White House" (Adams), **2:**87–90

"Letter to His Daughter" (Jefferson), **2:**38

"Letter to His Son" (Lee), **2:**38–40

"Letter to Maria Clemm" (Poe), **2:**41–43

"Letter to the Reverend Samson Occom" (Wheatley), **2:**44–46

Let the People Decide (Moye), **3:**249

Lettsom, John Coakley, **2:**207

Leung, Laifong, *Morning Sun,* **3:**301

Levi, Primo
    If This Is a Man, **1:**318
    suicide of, **1:**204, 205

Levin, Meyer, **2:**253

Levin, Susan M., **2:**301

Levine, Robert, **2:**7–8

Levine, Steven, **1:**339, **3:**288

Lévi-Strauss, Claude, *Tristes Tropiques,* **3:**37

Levy, Eric P., **1:**121

Lewalski, Barbara, **2:**64

Lewin, Recha, **3:**50

Lewin, Rhoda
    The Jewish Community of North Minneapolis, **3:**50
    Witnesses to the Holocaust, **3:**50–52

Lewis, Jane, **2:**18

Lewis, Oscar
    Children of Sanchez, **3:**31
    Pedro Martinez, **3:**31

Lewis, R. W. B., **1:**235

Lewy, Guenter, **3:**42

Ley, Robert, **3:**293–294

Ley de Fuga (Guatemala), **1:**101

Liberalism, in Russia, rise of, **1:**193

Liberator (newspaper), **1:**33, 35, **2:**29, 31, 45

Liberty Bell, The (Chapman and Griffith), **1:**142

Libowitz, Richard, **1:**320

Library Journal
    on *Exiled Memories* (Medina), **1:**297
    on *Mothers, Sisters, Resisters* (Gurewitsch), **3:**35
    on *Prison Writings* (Peltier), **1:**97
    on *Solidarity Forever* (Bird et al.), **3:**329
    on *Ten Thousand Sorrows* (Kim), **1:**103
    on *Voices from the Whirlwind* (Feng), **3:**288
    on *A Woman at War* (Moore), **2:**279
    on *A Woman Soldier's Own Story* (Xie), **1:**339
    on *The Woman Warrior* (Kingston), **1:**175

Lieberman, Thorney, **3:**66

Liédet, Loyset, **1:286**

Lie Down in Darkness (Styron), **1:**204, 206

Life (magazine), **1:**304, **3:**61

Life, Letters, and Literary Remains (Keats), **2:**146

Life, The (Teresa of Ávila), **1:**211–213

Life and Times of Frederick Douglass (Douglass), **1:**34

Life for Africa, A (Mitchison), **2:**237

"Life in the Sea Islands" (Grimké), **2:**31

Life Laid Bare (Hatzfeld), **3:**258, 259

Life Lived Like a Story (Cruikshank), **3:**320

Life of Samuel Johnson (Boswell), **2:**177, 195, 309, 328, 329–330

Life on the Mississippi (Twain), **1:**146–148

Life under a Cloud (Winkler), **3:**239

Life-writing movement, of Aborigines, **3:**334

Lifton, Betty Jean, *Twice Born,* **1:**102

"Ligeia" (Poe), **3:**38

Light, Kenneth
    Coal Hollow, **3:**66–69
    Valley of Shadows and Dreams, **3:**67

Light, Melanie
    Coal Hollow, **3:**66–69
    Valley of Shadows and Dreams, **3:**67

Light, Steve, **1:**251

Likud party (Israel), **1:**225, **2:**52

Lincoln, Abraham, **3:**262
    and African American soldiers, **2:**240
    assassination of, **2:**246, **3:**261
    election of, **2:**38, 250
    Emancipation Proclamation of, **1:**50, **3:**261
    Homestead Act under, **2:**164
    oral history of life of, **3:**261–264
    views on slavery, **2:**38

Lincoln, Kenneth, **1:**54

Lincoln, Mary Todd, **1:**52, **3:**261, 263, 264

Lincoln, Robert Todd, **3:**261, 262, 263

Lincoln and the Civil War Diaries and Letters of John Hay (Hay), **3:**262–263

Lincoln Prize, for *Abraham Lincoln: A Life* (Burlingame), **3:**264

Linderman, Frank, *Pretty-Shield,* **1:**70

Lindstrom, Naomi, **1:**76

Lingua Tertii Imperii (LTI) (Klemperer), **2:**304, 305

Linguistic autobiographies, *Hunger of Memory* (Rodriguez) as, **1:**17

Linneaus, Carl, **2:**300

Linton, Sherri LaVie, **1:10**

Lin Yutang, **1:**338

Lionnet, Françoise, **1:**11

Lipsitz, George, **3:**191

LIS Organization, **1:**7

Liszt, Franz, **1:**272

Literacy
    in Britain, rise of, **2:**136, 146, 320
    in Middle Ages, **1:**189
    in *Narrative of the Life of Frederick Douglass* (Douglass), **1:**35
    and slave narratives, **1:**35

Literary autobiographies. *See also specific works and writers*
    Lejeune (Philippe) on study of, **2:**174
    religious struggle in, **2:**26
    self as topic in, **1:**167

Literary criticism
    Bennett's (Arnold) career in, **2:**136
    disability studies in, **1:**8
    as form of autobiography, **1:**247
    French theories in, **1:**239
    by Hawthorne (Nathaniel), **2:**223–224
    Hussein's (Taha) career in, **1:**135
    by Maugham (W. Somerset), **2:**183
    poststructuralism in, **1:**267
    structuralism in, **1:**239, 267
    by Woolf (Virginia), **2:**137, 138, 180

Literary Fund, **2:**207

Literary references
    in *De Profundis* (Wilde), **2:**9
    in *Fun Home* (Bechdel), **1:**140, 141
    in *Walden* (Thoreau), **1:**235

Literary Remains of Edward VI, The (Edward VI), **2:97–100**

Literary Review (journal), **1:**256

Literary theory, Barthes's (Roland) work in, **1:**267

Literature and Medicine (journal), **1:**7, 8

Lithuania, Jewish immigration to China from, **3:**16

Little Big Horn, Battle of (1876), **3:**110

Litz, Alyce, **1:**40

Liu Xiaobo, **3:**301

Lives of Others, The (film), **3:**245

Living Atlanta (Kuhn et al.), **3:**44

Living by Fiction (Dillard), **1:**279

Living My Life (Goldman), **3:**3

Living the Revolution (Guglielmo), **3:**5

Living through the Soviet System (Bertaux et al.), **3:**331

Lloréns Torres, Luis, **1:**108

Lloyd, Constance, **2:**9

Lloyd's Evening Post, **2:**196

Lobato, Mirta Zaida, **3:**74, 75

Locke, Alain, **1:**84, 85

Locke, John, **2:**140

Locked-in syndrome, **1:**6–8

Lockhart, John Gibson, **2:**143, 144
    Memoirs of the Life of Sir Walter Scott, **2:**309, 310

Lockhart, Sophia Scott, **2:**309

Loftis, John, **1:**316

Logan, Andy, **3:**295

Log-book of the Coiners (Gide), **2:**180, 182

Logging industry, in Idaho, **3:**93

Loisel, Clary, **3:**33

Lomax, Alan, **1:**9

Lomax, Dana Teen, **2:**150

Lombardi, Irma, **3:**329

Lomov, Nikolai, **3:**235

London (England)
    Boswell's (James) move to, **2:**328
    Great Fire of, **2:**73
    Kinsington district in, **2:321**
    literary journalism in, **2:**328

London and the Life of Literature in Late Victorian England (Gissing), **2:320–323**

London Journal (Boswell), **2:328–330**

London Review of Books, **2:**14

London School of Economics and Political Science, **2:**16, 172

Long, Huey, **1:**5

Long, Janet Nakamarra, **3:**107, 335

Long, Judith, **2:**92

Long, Lisa, **2:**29, 31

Longfellow, Henry Wadsworth, **2:**223

Long Journey Home (Brown and Kohn), **3:**107, **325–327**

Long Journey Home (documentary), **3:**325

Long March, **1:**338

Long Walk to Freedom, The (Mandela), **1:25, 27–29**, 96, 290

Long Way from Home, A (McKay), **1:84–86**

Long Way Gone, A (Beah), **1:312–314**

Looking Cloud, Arlo, **1:**98

Look up for Yes (Tavalaro), **1:**6

Lopes Cançado, Maura, *Hospicio é Deus*, **2:**6

Lopez, Barry, *Arctic Dreams*, **1:**279

Lorde, Audre, **2:**4
    The Black Unicorn, **2:**4
    A Burst of Light, **2:**3
    The Cancer Journals, **2:3–5**
    hooks (bell) compared to, **1:**249, 251
    Hurston's (Zora Neale) influence on, **1:**9
    in tradition of Prince (Mary), **3:**24
    Zami, **1:**9, 37, 39, 249, **2:**5

Lorifo, Marie, **1:**128

Lori-Parks, Suzan, **1:**273

Lort, Michael, **2:**313

Los Alamos (New Mexico), oral histories of, **3:**239–241

Los Angeles (California)
    gay Asian Americans in, **3:**83–85
    water resources for, **3:**102, 103

Los Angeles Times (newspaper)
    on *Barefoot Gen* (Nakazawa), **1:**294
    on *Diaries, 1931–1949* (Orwell), **2:**118
    on *A Diary without Dates* (Bagnold), **2:**260
    on *Farewell to Manzanar* (Houston and Houston), **1:**299, 300
    on *The Long Walk to Freedom* (Mandela), **1:**29
    on *The Strength Not to Fight* (Tollefson), **3:**222
    on *Voices of Freedom* (Hampton and Fayer), **3:**45
    on *When Heaven and Earth Changed Places* (Hayslip), **1:**336
    on *When I Was Puerto Rican* (Santiago), **1:**109
    on *A Woman at War* (Moore), **2:**279
    on *Zlata's Diary* (Filipovic), **2:**339

Lost-Found Nation of Islam. *See* Black Muslims

Lost generation, **1:**329

Lost Names (Kim), **1:**102

Lost Years (Vu), **1:**170

Lotte in Weimar (Mann), **1:**277

Louisiana
    during Civil War, Stone (Kate) on life in, **2:**244–246, *245*
    Hispanic American entrepreneurs in, oral histories of, **3:**121–123
    U.S. purchase of, **2:**69

Louis XVI (king of France), **2:**213

Love Carried Me Home (Miller), **3:**35

Lovejoy, David, **2:**27

Love Letters of Dorothy Osborne to Sir William Temple, The (Osborne), **2:324–327**

Love Letters of Dylan Thomas, The (Thomas), **1:**127

Love Letters of Nathaniel Hawthorne, The (Hawthorne), **2:**225

Lovesey, Oliver, **1:**88, 215, 216

Loving v. Virginia, **1:**72, 78

Lowell, Amy, **2:**190, 292

Lowell, James Russell, **1:**235

Lowell, Robert, **2:**129

Lowenthal, Cynthia, **2:**36, 37

"Low-intensity" conflicts, **3:**207

Loyalty
    in Japanese American internment, **3:**196
    to monarchy, Slingsby (Henry) on, **2:**256–258

Lozano, Connie, **3:**103

LSD, **2:**295

Lucas, E. V., **2:**10

Lucassen, Jan, **3:**75

Lucky Child, A (Buergenthal), **1:**312

Lugo, Catherine, **3:**88

Luis, Keridwen, **3:**38

Luis, William, **3:**8

Lukas, Christopher, *Blue Genes*, **1:**204–205

Lu Lihua, **3:**148

Luna, Rachael, **3:**78

Luongo, Katherine, **3:**143

Lupus, **2:**129

Luscombe, Belinda, **1:**312, 314

Luthuli, Albert, **1:**24
    Let My People Go, **1:24–26**
    "Our Struggles for Progress," **1:**25
    "We Don't Want Crumbs," **1:**25

Lu Xiuyuan, **3:**288

Lu Xun, *Letters between Two*, **2:170–173,** *171*

Ly, Monirith, **1:**307

Lydgate, John, **1:190**

Lydston, Stub, **3:**103

Lyell, Charles, *Principles of Geology*, **1:**65

Lynch, Claire, **3:**316–317

Lynchings, **1:**18, 50

Lynd, Alice, *Rank and File*, **3:**179

Lynd, Staughton, *Rank and File*, **3:**179

Lynn, Kenneth, **2:**251

Lyon, Isabel Van Kleek, **1:**148

M

Maalouf, Amin, **1:**286

Maasai (Beckwith and Saitoti), **1:**114

Maasai people, Saitoti (Tepilit Ole) on experience of, **1:**114–116, *115*

Maathai, Wangari, *Unbound*, **1:**114

Macaulay, Thomas Babington, **2:**144, 314, 329

MacCarthy, Desmond, **2:**268

MacCarthy, Molly, **2:**268

MacDonald, John, **3:**139

MacDonald, Ramsay, **2:**17

MacEoin, Uinseann, *Survivors*, **3:**27, 315

Machete Season (Hatzfeld), **1:**312, **3:257–260**

MacKenzie, Jeanne, **2:**16, 17

MacKenzie, Norman, **2:**16, 17, 172

MacLane, Mary, **2:**306

MacLennan, Birdie, **1:**280

Macqueen, James, **3:**25

Macy, John, **1:**43

Maddocks, Melvin, **3:**61

Maddy-Weitzman, Bruce, **3:**49

Madero, Francisco, **3:**167

Madge, Charles, **2:**235

Madison, James, **2:**316

Madison, R. D., **2:**240

Madmen and Specialists (Soyinka), **1:**214

Madsen, Kim, **3:**174–175

Mafeking, siege of (1899–1900), **2:**241–243

Magan, Hirsi, **1:**207

Magellan, Ferdinand, **2:**201

Magical Monkey King (Jiang), **1:**163

Mahomet, Dean, *The Travels of Dean Mahomet*, **2:229–232**

Mahoney, Dennis F., **1:**277, 278

Mai, Angelo, **1:**220

Maid's Daughter, The (Romero), **1:**108

Maier, Joseph, **3:**295

Mail and Guardian (newspaper), **3:**243

Mailer, Norman, **1:**165

Maitland, Sarah, **1:**280

Makin, Bathsua, *An Essay to Revive the Antient Education of Gentlewomen*, **2:**35

Making History (Johnson et al.), **3:**176, 177

Making of a Gay Asian Community, The (Wat), **3:83–85**

Making of Modern London, The (television series), **3:**313

Makley, Charlene, **3:**288–289

Malan, Daniel François, **1:**27

Malan, Rian, *My Traitor's Heart*, **3:**242

Malcolmson, Patricia, **2:**265

Malcolmson, Robert, **2:**265

Malcolm X, *The Autobiography of Malcolm X*, **1:**78, **186–188,** *187*, **3:**44

Malik ibn al-Rayb, **1:**255

Malingre, Rose, **2:**83

Malinke people, **1:**128, 130

Mallon, Thomas, **1:**7

Malone, Edmond, **2:**330

Malthus, Thomas, *Essay on the Principles of Population*, **1:**65

Malti-Douglas, Fedwa, **1:**92, 137, 227

Mammeri, Mouloud, **2:**262

Man (journal), **3:**168

Manalansan, Martin F., IV, **3:**83, 84, 85

Manar, Al- (journal), **1:**135

Manchester (England), oral histories of working-class youth in, **3:**311–313, *312*

Manchu dynasty, **1:**152, 153

Manchurian Incident (1931), **3:**215

Mandel, Barrett John, **1:**187, 246, 247

Mandel, Naomi, **1:**320

Mandela, Nelson, **1:28**
 AIDS epidemic and, **3:**272, *273*
 Conversations with Myself, **1:**27–28
 imprisonment of, **1:**24, 27–29, **3:**242
 The Long Walk to Freedom, **1:**25, **27–29**, 96, 290
Mandela, Winnie, **1:**28, 29
Mandeville, John, *The Travels of Sir John Mandeville,* **2:**198, 227
Man Died, The (Soyinka), **1:214–217**, **2:**12, 14
Mandlestam, Nadezhda, *Hope against Hope,* **1:**271
Man from the North, A (Bennett), **2:**136
Manga (Japanese comics), **1:**293
Manhattan Project, oral histories of, **3:**239–240
Manichaeans, **1:**196
Manji, Irshad, *The Trouble with Islam Today,* **1:**207
Mann, Abby, **3:**295
Mann, Thomas, *Lotte in Weimar,* **1:**277
Manning, Bradley, **3:**229
Manning, Diane, *Hill Country Teacher,* **3:77–79**
"Man of Constant Sorrow" (song), **3:**159
Man of the Serengeti (documentary), **1:**114
Mansart Builds a School (Du Bois), **1:**5
Mansfield, Katherine, **2:134**
 Bashkirtseff's (Marie) influence on, **2:**306
 Journal of Katherine Mansfield, **2:133–135**
 The Katherine Mansfield Notebooks, **2:**133, 134
 Partridge (Frances) compared to, **2:**269
 Scrapbook of Katherine Mansfield, **2:**134
 A Writer's Diary (Woolf) on, **2:**180
Mansfield decision (1789, Britain), **1:**81, 83, **3:**23
Mantel, Hilary, **1:**169
Manter, Lisa, **1:**191
Manuel I (king of Portugal), **2:**198, 199

Manwaring, Max G.
 El Salvador at War, **3:205–208**
 Small Wars & Insurgencies, **3:**206
 Uncomfortable Wars, **3:**207
 Uncomfortable Wars Revisited, **3:**207
Manzanar (Wehrey), **3:**102
Manzanar internment camp (California), **1:**299–301, **3:**102–104, 197, *225*
Manzano, Juan Francisco, *The Autobiography of a Slave,* **3:**7
Mao Zedong, **1:**158, **3:**288. *See also* Cultural Revolution
 death of, **3:**299
 in Long March, **1:**338
 Lu Xun and, **2:**170
 rise to power, **3:**287
Mapes, Elizabeth A., **2:**254
Mara, Michael, **2:**61
Marble Faun, The (Hawthorne), **2:**224, 225
Marcello, Ronald E., *Remembering Pearl Harbor,* **3:**202
Marchand, Leslie A., **2:**144
Marchesi, Ilaria, **2:**96
March 1 Movement (Korea), **1:**324
March on Washington (1963), **1:**20
Marcus, Eric, *The Struggle for Gay and Lesbian Equal Rights,* **3:**83
Marcus, Jane, **2:**17
Marcus Aurelius, *The Meditations of the Emperor Marcus Aurelius Antoninus,* **1:218–221**, *219*
Marek, Kurt, **2:**282
Margaret (princess), **2:**152
Marie, Adrien, **2:**82
Marijuana, **2:**295
Maritime literature, tradition of, **3:**183
Mark, Thomas, **2:**126
Mark Twain Project, **1:**148
Marquette, Jacques, **1:**146–147
Marrant, John, **1:**81
Marriage
 arranged, in China, **1:**153, 154, 338, 339, **2:**170
 arranged, in Montenegro, **3:**136, 137
 in eighteenth century, limitations of, **2:**35, 36

 forced, **1:**209
 in Heian period of Japan, **2:**297–299
 interracial (*See* Interracial relationships)
 Osborne's (Dorothy) ideas about, **2:**324–325
 Pepys's (Samuel) depiction of, accuracy of, **2:**73
 same-sex, **1:**139
 of women teachers in U.S., ban on, **3:**78, 79
Marse Chan (Page), **2:**250
Marsh, Dawn, **3:**326
Marshall, Dick, **1:**98
Marshall, Jack, *From Baghdad to Brooklyn,* **3:**120
Marshall, Joanna, **1:**109
Marshall, Kathryn, *In the Combat Zone,* **3:**221, 279
Martin, Isabella, **2:**250, 251
Martin, Keavy, *Stories in a New Skin,* **3:**138
Martin, Ramela, *Out of Darkness,* **3:**40
Martin, Tera, **1:**174
Martineau, Harriet, **2:**29, 335
Martone, Michael, **1:**48
Martyn, Edward, **2:**128
Marwick, Arthur, **3:**234
Marxism
 in Cultural Revolution, **1:**161
 of Guevara (Ernesto "Che"), **2:**220
Mary Chesnut's Civil War (Chesnut), **2:**250, 251, 271
Mary I (queen of England), **2:**98, 99
Mary II (queen of England), **2:**324, *325*
Maryland, interracial marriage in, **1:**72
Masculine writing style, vs. feminine writing style, **1:**250
Masculinity, in *Journal of George Fox* (Fox), **2:**27
Masking, African American tradition of, **1:**144
Masks, Chinese ghost, **1:**174
Mason, Bobbie Ann, *In Country,* **1:**335
Mason, Katrina, *Children of Los Alamos,* **3:239–241**
Mason, Keith, **2:**206

Mason, Mary, **1:**246

Mason, Terry, **3:**344

Massacre in Mexico (Poniatowska), **3:**31–33

Massey, Mary Elizabeth, **2:**246

Mass Observation Project, **2:**235, 236, 237, 265, 266, 267

Masson, David, **2:**310–311

Masson, Madeleine, **2:**218

Mast, Robert, *Detroit Lives,* **3:**99

Mastectomies, **2:**3

Masumoto, David Mas, *Country Voices,* **3:**224

Matagari (Ngũgĩ), **2:**14

Mather, Cotton, **1:**326, 328

Mather, Increase, **1:**325, 326

    A Brief History of the War with the Indians in New England, **1:**325

Matrilineal culture, of Navajo, **3:**318

Matsumoto, Valerie, *Farming the Home Place,* **3:**80

Mattachine Society, **3:**83

Matthews, William, **2:**65

Matthiessen, F. O., **1:**235, **2:**113, 114, 115

Maturation, Conroy (Frank) on experience of, **1:**164

Maugham, Robin, **2:**185

Maugham, W. Somerset, **2:184**

    Bennett (Arnold) compared to, **2:**136

    The Razor's Edge, **2:**185

    The Summing Up, **2:**183

    A Writer's Notebook, **2:**183–185

Mau Mau rebellion, **2:**12

Maunsell, Jerome, **2:**122

Maupassant, Guy de, **2:**113, 183, 306

Maurer, Harry

    Not Working, **3:**277

    Sex: An Oral History, **3:**276, 277

    Strange Ground, **3:**275–278

    Webs of Power, **3:**277

Mauriac, François, **1:**318, **2:**130

Maus (Spiegelman), **1:**139, 141, 156, 293

Mauthausen concentration camp, **3:**51

Mawer, William, **1:**67

"Mawtini" (Tuqan), **1:**227

Mayans, **3:**166, 167

Mayer, Henry, **3:**45

May Fourth (New Culture) Movement (China), **1:**338, **3:**126, 147–149, *148*

Mayo, John, **3:**87

M'Baye, Mariétou. *See* Bugul, Ken

Mbeki, Thabo, **1:**29, **3:**272, 274

McBride, James, *The Color of Water,* **1:72–74,** *73*

McBride, Ruth, **1:**72–74

McCabe, Dabney, **2:**39

McCann, Justin, **1:**191

McCarthy, Cormac, *Blood Meridian,* **1:**304

McCarthy, Justin, **3:**42

McCarthy, Kevin, **1:**259

McCarthy, Mary, **1:259**

    Cast a Cold Eye, **1:**258

    The Group, **1:**258

    How I Grew, **1:**258

    Intellectual Memoirs, **1:**258

    Memories of a Catholic Girlhood, **1:**258–260

McCloy, John, **3:**234

McColloch, Mark, **3:**329

McCombs, Edward, **3:**291

McCourt, Angela, **1:**120

McCourt, Frank

    Angela's Ashes, **1:119–121**

    A Couple of Blaguards, **1:**119

    Teacher Man, **1:**119

    'Tis, **1:**119

McCourt, Malachy, **1:**119

McCulloch, Mark, **3:**247

McDonald, Cornelia Peake, *A Diary with Reminiscences of the War and Refugee Life in the Shenandoah Valley,* **2:**271

McDonald, F. W., **2:**196

McDonough, A. R., **2:**336

McDougall, Bonnie S., **2:**171, 172

McElroy, John Harmon, **2:**214, 215

McGill, Robert, **2:**131

McKay, Claude, **1:85**

    Banjo, **1:**86

    Harlem: Negro Metropolis, **1:**85

    Home to Harlem, **1:**84, 86

    "If We Must Die," **1:**84

    A Long Way from Home, **1:**84–86

McKay, Nellie, **1:**10, 11

McKee, Guian A., **3:**254, 256

McKelvey, Tara, **3:**233

McKenzie, Barbara, **1:**260

McKinney, Gordon B., **3:**92

McLean, Norman, *A River Runs through It,* **1:**281

McLeod, Calum, *China Remembers,* **3:**301

McLynn, Frank, **1:**220

McNeil, Linda, **3:**78

McNeill, Laurie, **2:**175

McPherson, Dolly, **1:**20

McPherson, Robert S., **3:**12

    Navajo Land, Navajo Culture, **3:**10

Mead, Margaret, **1:**9

Meatless Days (Suleri), **1:87–89**

Meatpacking industry, in Argentina, **3:**73–75

Medeiros-Lichem, María Teresa, **3:**32

Media coverage. *See* Journalism; War correspondents

Mediation, vs. arbitration, **3:**155

Medical conditions. *See* Health problems; *specific conditions*

Medicine

    British, oral histories of, **3:**170–172

    midwifery in, **2:**331–333, *332*

    technological advances in, **3:**170

Medieval era. *See* Middle Ages

Medina, Pablo

    Exiled Memories, **1:**296–298

    Pork Rind and Cuban Songs, **1:**296

Meditations of the Emperor Marcus Aurelius Antoninus, The (Marcus Aurelius), **1:218–221**

Medwick, Cathleen, **1:**212

Mee, Jon, **2:**146, 147

Meikuaya, Wilson, *The Last Maasai Warrior,* **1:**114

Meinecke, Friedrich, **1:**185

Mein Kampf (Hitler), **1:30–32**

Melancholy, in *Confessions of Lady Nijo* (Nijo), **2:**60

Melhuish, Mary, **3:**311

Melman, Billie, **1**:91
MELUS (journal), **1**:17, 71, 109, 175
Melville, Herman, **1**:277, **2**:215, 223, 224
   Moby Dick, **2**:224
Memmott, Carol, **1**:172
Memoir. *See also specific works and writers*
   vs. autobiography, **1**:248, 279
   construction of, to appeal to audience, **1**:164
Memoir (Godwin), **2**:109
Memoir Club, **2**:182
Memoirs (Fanshawe), **1**:229–230, 315, 316, 317
Memoirs (Neruda), **1**:222–224
Memoirs (Scott), **2**:309
Memoirs (Williams), **2**:152, 153
Memoirs and Letters of Sara Coleridge (Coleridge), **2**:16
Memoirs of a Fox-Hunting Man (Sassoon), **1**:329, **2**:247
Memoirs of an Arabian Princess from Zanzibar (Ruete), **1**:90–92
Memoirs of a Spacewoman (Mitchison), **2**:237
Memoirs of a Survivor (Lessing), **1**:167
Memoirs of Dr. Burney, The (Burney), **2**:312, 313
Memoirs of Fatemeh Pakravan (Ladjevardi), **3**:218–220
Memoirs of Lady Anne Halkett, The (Halkett), **1**:230, **315–317**
Memoirs of Naim Bey, The (Andonian), **3**:40
Memoirs of Prince Hamid Kadjar (Ladjevardi), **3**:219
Memoirs of Shapour Bakhtiar (Ladjevardi), **3**:220
Memoirs of the Life of Sir Walter Scott (Lockhart), **2**:309, 310
Memoirs of the Princess Daschkaw (Dashkova), **2**:306
Memorial de isla negra (Neruda), **1**:223
Memories of a Catholic Girlhood (McCarthy), **1**:258–260
Memory(ies)
   of Christmas, Thomas (Dylan) on, **1**:125–126
   enigmatic nature of, Suleri (Sara) on, **1**:87, 88
   fluid nature of, Agosín (Marjorie) on, **1**:75–76
   in locked-in syndrome, Bauby (Jean-Dominique) on, **1**:6–7
   in oral history field, **3**:176–178, 186
   of survivors of Armenian genocide, reliability of, **3**:42
   and time, Conroy (Frank) on, **1**:164, 165, 166
   and time, Nabokov (Vladimir) on, **1**:271, 272
   of witnesses, Portelli (Alessandro) on, **3**:265, 266
Memory and Narrative (Olney), **1**:246, 248
Memory for Forgetfulness (Darwish), **1**:255, 257, **2**:50
Memory Studies (journal), **3**:98
Menchú, Rigoberta, *I, Rigoberta Menchú,* **3**:164–166, *165*
   Californio Voices (Savage) vs., **3**:114
   Child of the Dark (de Jesus) vs., **2**:8
   Doña María's Story (James) vs., **3**:73–74
   Let Me Speak! (Viezzer and Barrios de Chungara) vs., **3**:322
   Rites: A Guatemalan Boyhood (Perera) vs., **1**:99
   Women's Words (Gluck and Patai) on, **3**:191
Mencken, H. L., **2**:137
Mendibil, Claude, **1**:6, 7
Meng Jixin, *The First Household under Heaven,* **3**:125
Mennonites, **3**:223, 227
Mental freedom, in locked-in syndrome, **1**:6–7
Mental illness
   of Ruskin (John), **1**:264
   Styron (William) on struggle with, **1**:204–205
Mentor (Grimes), **1**:164
Merchant, G. W., **1**:67
Mercier, Laurie, **3**:81
Meredith, George, **2**:320
Merlo, Frank, **2**:153
Mernissi, Fatima, *Dreams of Trespass,* **1**:226, 227
Mersky, Peter, **3**:203
Meru people, oral histories of, **3**:141–143, *142*
Meschia, Karen, **2**:237
Mesopotamia, letter writing in, **2**:94
Messerschmidt, J. W., **2**:282
Metacomet, **1**:325
Metaphors of Self (Olney), **1**:246
Meth, Rose, **3**:35
Methodism, **2**:195–196
Me Too (Lejeune), **2**:174
Mexican Americans
   Rodriguez (Richard) on experience of, **1**:15–17
   women, oral histories of, **3**:131–134, *132*
Mexican-American War (1846–1848), **1**:304
Mexican Indians, oral histories of, **3**:167–169
Mexican oral histories
   on agrarian reform movement, **3**:302–304
   of indigenous people, **3**:167–169
   on Tlatelolco massacre of 1968, **3**:31–33
Mexican Revolution (1910–1920), **3**:167, 302
Mexico
   agrarian reform movement in, **3**:302–304
   California as colony of, **3**:114
   constitution of, **3**:302
   indigenous people of, **3**:167–169, 304
   Revolution of 1910–1920 in, **3**:167, 302
   Tlatelolco massacre of 1968 in, **3**:31–33
Meyer, Melissa, *The Politics of AIDS Denialism,* **3**:272
Meyers, Gladys Peterson, **3**:78
MFS Modern Fiction Studies (journal), **1**:85
Mhudi (Plaatje), **2**:241, 243
Michaels, Walter Benn, *The Trouble with Diversity,* **1**:16

Michelet, Jules, **1:**267
Michelet par lui-même (Barthes), **1:**267
Michigan. *See* Detroit
Michigan Equal Accommodations Act of 1938, **3:**99
Michigan Historical Review (journal), **2:**207, **3:**100
Michilimackinac, Fort, **2:**205–207, *206*
Michi's Memories (Tamura), **3:**127
Michitsuna No Haha, *The Gossamer Years,* **2:**189, 290, **297–299**
Mickiewicz, Adam
    Forefathers' Eve, **2:**192
    Konrad Wallenrod, **2:**192
Middle Ages
    Christianity in, **1:**189
    Confessions (Augustine) in, **1:**198
    Kempe (Margery) on life in, **1:**189–191
    literacy in, **1:**189
    pilgrimages in, **1:190,** 191, **2:**226
Middle class, English
    expansion of, **2:**177
    Last (Nella) on life of, **2:**265
    Pepys (Samuel) on life of, **2:**72
    Victoria and, **2:**209, 211
    Woodforde (James) on life of, **2:**287–288
Middle East Journal, **1:**209, **3:**49, 219
Middle East Report, **1:**209
Middle East Studies Association Bulletin, **3:**48, 220
Middle Passage, **1:**82, 83
Midgley, Peter, **2:**242
Midnight's Children (Rushdie), **1:**87
Midstream (Keller), **1:**44
Midwest Book Review, **3:**263
Midwifery, **2:**331–333, *332*
Midwife's Tale, A (Ulrich), **2:331–334**
Midwives of the Future (Ware), **3:**308
Mieder, Wolfgang, **2:**305
Mielke, Erich, **3:246**
Migration, of African Americans within U.S., **1:**50, 52, 84, 273. *See also* Immigration
Mihailovic, Draza, **3:**135
Milani, Abbas, *The Persian Sphinx,* **3:**218, 219
Milani, Farzaneh, **1:**209

Milburn, Clara, **2:**235
    Mrs. Milburn's Diary, **2:**265
Mildmay, Grace, **1:**229
Miles, Jack, **2:**339
Miles, Nelson, **1:**303
Milich, Zorka, *A Stranger's Supper,* **3:135–137**
Military, Australian, in World War I, **3:**177
Military, Chinese, women in, **1:**338–340
Military, Colombian, **3:**183–185
Military, U.S. *See also* Veterans; *specific wars*
    African Americans in, **2:**238–240, **3:**199–201, 248–250
    desegregation of, **3:**199, 248, 249
    draft in, **3:**221–223
    homosexuality in, **1:**139
    Japanese Americans in, **3:**196
    Japanese war brides and, **3:**127–129, *128*
    journalists embedded with, **2:**278–280
    Korean American children of, **1:**102
    racism in, **3:**44, 199–201, 248–250
    slaves as soldiers in, **2:**238–240
    Styron (William) in, **1:**206
    Vietnamese American children of, **1:**170
    Wolff (Tobias) in, **1:**47
Military Review (journal), **3:**233
Militia groups, in Scotland, **2:**309
Mill, James, **2:**177
Mill, John Stuart, *Autobiography,* **2:**16
Millay, Edna St. Vincent, **1:**258
Miller, Anita, **2:**138
Miller, Donald E., *Survivors,* **3:40–43,** 50
Miller, Henry, **2:**123, 124
    Tropic of Cancer, **2:**123
Miller, Jack, **3:**329
Miller, Joy E., *Love Carried Me Home,* **3:**35
Miller, June, **2:**124
Miller, Lorna Touryan, *Survivors,* **3:40–43,** 50

Miller, Michele, **3:**233
Miller, William Lee, **2:**71
Millett, Kate, **3:**37
Mill Hunk Herald (magazine), **3:**342
Milligan, Don, **3:**71–72
Million Little Pieces, A (Frey), **1:**313, **2:**296
Milosz, Czeslaw, **1:**255
Milton, John, **2:**140, 146
Min, Anchee
    Becoming Madame Mao, **1:**159
    Pearl of China, **1:**159
    Red Azalea, **1:158–160**
Minamoto no Rinshi, **2:**290, 292
Minamoto no Yoritomo, **2:**61
Minear, Richard, **1:**295
Mine of Her Own, A (Zanjani), **3:**337
Mining. *See also* Coal mining
    in Bolivia, oral histories of, **3:**322–324
    prohibitions on women in, **3:**337
    in Ukraine, oral histories of, **3:**340–342
Mining Cultures (Murphy), **3:**337
Minneapolis Star Tribune (newspaper), **1:**172
Minnesota History (journal), **3:**51
Minorities Research Group, **3:**70
Minority groups. *See* Assimilation; *specific groups*
Minority Report to the Commission of the Poor Law (Webb), **2:**16
Minus, Ed, **2:**269
Miracle Worker, The (teleplay), **1:**44, 45
Miranda, Deborah A., **3:**116
Mirollo, James V., **1:**213
Mirow, Kurt Rudolf, *Webs of Power,* **3:**277
Mirra, Carl, *Soldiers and Citizens,* **3:**231–232
Mirsky, Jonathan, **3:**280, 288
Miscellanies (D'Israeli), **2:**177
Misery memoirs, *Angela's Ashes* (McCourt) as, **1:**120–121
Missing Pages (Terry), **3:**199–200
Missionary work
    in colonial California, **3:**114–116
    in Great Awakening, **2:**197
    of Wesley (John), **2:**195–196

Mississippi Quarterly, **1:**35, 38, **2:**42
Mississippi River, Twain (Mark) on, **1:**146–147
Mississippi Valley Historical Review (journal), **2:**92
Missouri Compromise (1820), **1:**33
Miss Ravenel's Conversion (De Forest), **2:**240
Mistral, Gabriela, **1:**222, 223
Mitchell, Stephen, **2:**149
Mitchell, Virginia R., **3:**307
Mitchison, Clemency, **2:**235, 236
Mitchison, Naomi, *Among You Taking Notes,* **2:**235–237, 236
Mitford, John, **2:**143
Mitford, Mary Russell, *Our Village,* **3:**59
Mitson, Betty E., *Voices Long Silent,* **3:**195
Mittler, Barbara, **3:**148
Miyata Waichirō, **2:**191
MK. *See* Umkhonto we Sizwe
Mkhize, Sibongiseni, **1:**26
Mlambo, Eshmael, *Rhodesia,* **3:**251
MLN (journal), **3:**8
Moby Dick (Melville), **2:**224
Mock autobiographies, *Stop-Time* (Conroy) as, **1:**164, 165
Modern Asia Studies (journal), **2:**198, 200
Modern Drama (journal), **2:**102
Modern Fiction Studies (journal), **3:**74, 243
Modernism
    Bagnold (Enid) in, **2:**261
    Bennett (Arnold) in, **2:**136, 138
    Brittain (Vera) in, **1:**330
    Lu Xun in, **2:**172
    Nin (Anaïs) in, **2:**123
    origins and rise of, **2:**180
    Stein (Gertrude) in, **1:**332, 333, 334
    vs. traditionalism, Woolf (Virginia) on, **2:**138
    Woolf (Virginia) in, **2:**180
Modernization
    in Iran, rise of, **3:**218
    in Russia, rise of, **1:**193
    in U.S., Thoreau's (Henry David) critique of, **1:**233

Modern Judaism (journal), **1:**320
Modern Language Journal, **3:**301
Modern Motherhood (Davis), **3:**145
Modern Painters (Ruskin), **1:**264
Modern Philology (journal), **1:**247, 248, 264
Modern schools, **3:**5
Modisane, Bloke, **3:**251
Modkad, Jessica, **1:**209
Mogul Empire, **2:**229, *230*
Mohammed Reza Pahlavi (shah of Iran), **1:**155, **3:**218, *219*
    The Shah's Story, **3:**218
Mohammed V (sultan of Morocco), **3:**47, 49
Mohegan tribe, **1:**56, **2:**44, 46
Mohr, Nicholasa, **1:**108
Moi, Daniel arap, **2:**12, 14
Moira, Fran, **2:**4
Momaday, Al, **1:**54, 55
Momaday, N. Scott
    House Made of Dawn, **1:**54
    The Journey of Tai-me, **1:**54
    The Names: A Memoir, **1:**54
    The Way to Rainy Mountain, **1:**54–57, 55
Moment of Conquest, The (Fadiman), **3:**141
Moments of Being (Woolf), **1:**249, **2:**182
Momoh, Joseph, **1:**312
Monaghan, Patricia, **1:**97
Monarchy. *See* British monarchy
Monasticism
    Teresa of Ávila on, **1:**211–213
    in U.S., oral histories of, **3:**308–310
Mondor, Colleen, **3:**249
Money. *See* Finances
Möngke Khan, **1:**107
Mongol Empire, **1:**105–107, **2:**59
Monroe, Ed, **1:**335
Montagu, Edward Wortley, **2:**35
Montagu, Mary Wortley, **2:**36
    audience of letters of, **2:**217
    "Letter to Her Daughter," **2:**35–37
    Ruete (Emily) compared to, **1:**90
    Turkish Embassy Letters, **2:**35, 37

Montaigne, Michel de, **2:**62, 256, 257
    Essais, **2:**72
Monteiro, Anthony, **1:**5
Montejo, Esteban, *Biography of a Runaway Slave,* **3:**7–9
Montell, William Lynwood
    Always a People, **3:**107–109, 325
    From Memory to History, **3:**90
    The Saga of Coe Ridge, **3:**90–92
Montenegro, oral histories of women of, **3:**135–137, *136*
Montgomery, James A., **1:**287
Montgomery bus boycott (1955), **1:**20, 37, 38, 39, **2:**32, **3:**44, 45
Monthly Review (journal), **1:**82
Montoya, Maria, **3:**133
Mont-Saint-Michel and Chartres (Adams), **1:**132
Moody, Anne, *Coming of Age in Mississippi,* **1:**37
Moon, Elaine Latzman, *Untold Tales, Unsung Heroes,* **3:**99–101
Moon, in Japanese poetry, **2:**191
Mooney, Christopher Gerald, **1:**150
Moonshine
    in Appalachia, **3:**90, 91
    in Idaho, **3:**95
Moore, Dorothy, **2:**333
Moore, Elijah, **2:**333
Moore, G. E., **2:**268
Moore, Gerald, **1:**128, 129
Moore, James, **1:**67
Moore, Kofoworola Aina, **1:**64
Moore, Marat, *Women in the Mines,* **3:**157, 328, **337–339**
Moore, Molly, *A Woman at War,* **2:**278–280
Moore, Thomas, **2:**143, 144
Moorehead, Caroline, **2:**101, 102
Moorhead-Rosenberg, Florence, **1:**77
Moosa, Matti, **1:**137
Moral Economy of AIDS in South Africa, The (Nattrass), **3:**272
Morality
    Conrad's (Joseph) concern with, **2:**192, 193
    Neruda (Pablo) on poetry and, **1:**223

Morantz, Regina, *In Her Own Words*, **3:**170

Mora-Torres, Gregorio, **3:**114, 115, 116

Moravians, **2:**196, 197

More Leaves from the Journal of Our Life in the Highlands (Victoria), **2:**209

Morello, Ruth, **2:**95, 96

Moreno Franglinal, Manuel, *The Sugarmill*, **3:**7

Morgan, Sarah, *The Civil War Diary of Sarah Morgan*, **2:**271

Morgan, Ted, **2:**56

Morgan, Winifred, **1:**35

Morgenthau, Henry, Jr., **3:**293

Morgenthau Plan, **3:**293

Morley, Christopher, **2:**330

Morley, Edith, **2:**77

Mormino, Gary R., **3:**191

Morning Sun (Leung), **3:**301

Moroccan Soul, The (Segalla), **3:**48

Morocco, oral histories of women in independence movement of, **3:**47–49, 48

Morris, Gabrielle, *Head of the Class*, **3:**20–22

Morris, Ivan, **2:**190

Morris, John N., **1:**247

Morris, Margaret Hill, **2:**80

Morrison, Toni, *The Bluest Eye*, **1:**19, 175

Morse, Richard M., **2:**7

Mort, John, **3:**100

Mortensen, Peter, **2:**163, 164, 165

Mortimer, Mildred, **1:**62

Mortimer, Raymond, **2:**268

Mosaic (journal), **1:**110, **3:**320

Mosby, John Singleton, *War Reminiscences*, **2:**250

Moss, William W., **3:**125–126, 213

Mossadegh, Mohammad, **3:**218, 219

Mostow, Joshua, **2:**292

Mother and Son (Seabrook), **3:**55

Mother-daughter relationships
   in *A Mountainous Journey* (Tuqan), **1:**226, 227
   in Plath's (Sylvia) writings, **2:**47–49
   in *Ten Thousand Sorrows* (Kim), **1:**102–104

Motherhood
   Jacobs (Harriet A.) on, **1:**142
   Stanton (Elizabeth Cady) on, **1:**13

Mothers, Sisters, Resisters (Gurewitsch), **3:34–36**

Motley, Mary Penick, *The Invisible Soldier*, **3:**212

Motoori Norinaga, **2:**190

Motorcycle Diaries (Guevara), **1:**223, **2:220–222**

Motsa, Zodwa, **1:**29

Mouffe, Barbara S., **2:**224

Moujahide, Ghalia, **3:**48

Moulton, Seth, **3:**231

Mountain, Carolyn, **3:**122, 123

Mountainous Journey, A (Tuqan), **1:225–228**

Mount Holyoke College, **1:**109

Mount Kenya, oral histories of Meru people of, **3:**141–143

Mount Vesuvius, eruption of, **2:**94, 95

Mourão, Manuela, **2:**199, 200

Movies. *See* Film adaptations; *specific movies*

Moving Out (Spence), **2:**163

Moya, Jose C., **3:**75

Moye, J. Todd
   Freedom Flyers, **3:**99, **248–250**
   Let the People Decide, **3:**249

Mpolweni, Nosisi, *There Was This Goat*, **3:**242

Mrs. Milburn's Diary (Milburn), **2:**265

Mrs. Miniver (film), **2:**265

Ms. magazine, **1:**11

Mudimbe-Boyi, Elisabeth, **1:**64

Muecke, Stephen, **1:**151

Muhammad, Elijah, **1:**186, 188

Muhlen, Norbert, **2:**56

Muhlenfeld, Elisabeth, **2:**250, 251

Mu'in al-Din Unur, **1:**285

Muir, John (naturalist), **1:**234

Muir, John (Vietnam veteran), **3:**209

Mujahidin, **3:**233

Mulan (legendary figure), **1:**152, 153, 340

Mulatto (Hughes), **1:**72

Mulattos
   Jewish–black, **1:**74
   as "tragic," in literary tradition, **1:**72

Mules and Men (Hurston), **1:**9

Mulford, Jeremy, **2:**266

Mullan, Fitzhugh, **3:**274

Muller, Bobby, **3:**232, 233

Muller, James, **3:**273

Mullin, Janet E., **2:**289

Mullins, Emer, **3:**29

Multicultural and multiracial identities
   Kim (Elizabeth) on, **1:**102–103
   Kingston (Maxine Hong) on, **1:**173–175
   McBride (James) on, **1:**72–74
   Nguyen (Kien) on, **1:**170
   Obama (Barack) on, **1:**78–80
   Santiago (Esmeralda) on, **1:**108–110
   Suleri (Sara) on, **1:**87–88
   "tragic mulatto" tradition and, **1:**72

Multicultural Autobiography (Payne), **1:**247–248

Multicultural families
   Kim (Elizabeth) on, **1:**102–103
   McBride (James) on, **1:**72–74
   Obama (Barack) on, **1:**78–80
   Suleri (Sara) on, **1:**87–88

Multiculturalism
   academic debate over, **1:**16
   and Columbus's (Christopher) legacy, **2:**203

Multicultural literary studies, *The Story of My Life* (Ahmedi) in, **1:**40–42

Multiracial individuals, racism against
   in Korea, **1:**102
   in Vietnam, **1:**170, 171

Multiracial literature, rise of, **1:**73–74

Munck, Ronnie, **3:**29

Munif, Abdelrahman, *East of the Mediterranean*, **2:**50

Munns, Jessica, **2:**67

Munson, Henry, Jr., *The House of Si Abd Allah*, **3:**47

Murao, Helen, **3:**197

Murasaki Shikibu, **2:190**
   The Diary of Lady Murasaki, **2:**59, **290–293**
   Lady Murasaki Shu, **2:**291
   Michitsuna No Haha in family of, **2:**297
   The Tale of Genji, **2:**59, 60, 189, 190, 290–292, *291*
Murder in Amsterdam (Buruma), **1:**209
Murdock, Kenneth B., **2:**113, 114, 115
Murphy, Caryle, **2:**278
Murphy, Mary, **2:**17
   Mining Cultures, **3:**337
Murray, Albert, *The Omni-Americans,* **1:**124
Murray, John, **2:**143
Murry, John Middleton, **2:**133, 134, 135
Museum of North Idaho, **3:**93, 95
Music
   Conroy (Frank) on, **1:**166
   folk music revival of 1960s, **3:**96
   in Japanese American internment camps, **3:**104
   of labor movement, **3:**329
   of Mexican American women, **3:**131–133
   of working class, **3:**157, 159
Muslim(s)
   African American, **1:**186–188
   in conflict with Christians, after Crusades, **2:**226
   in conflict with Hindus, in India, **1:**244
   of India, **1:**244, **2:**230
   Malinke people as, **1:**128
   racial profiling of, in U.S., **3:**195, 197
   slavery in countries of, **1:**90, 92
Muslim autobiographical writing. *See also specific works and writers*
   by Ahmedi (Farah), **1:**40–42
   by Hirsi Ali (Ayaan), **1:**207–209
   by Laye (Camara), **1:**128–130
   by Malcolm X, **1:**186–188
   by Usāmah ibn Munqidh, **1:**285–288
Muslim women
   Ahmedi (Farah) on experience of, **1:**40–42

   circumcision of, **1:**207
   vs. European women, roles of, **1:**90
   Hirsi Ali (Ayaan) on mistreatment of, **1:**207–209
   Ruete (Emily) on rights and roles of, **1:**90–92
   Western biases in narratives depicting, **1:**40, 41
   Western misconceptions about, **1:**90, 91
Muslim Women on the Move (Gray), **3:**48
My Apprenticeship (Webb), **2:**17
My Bondage and My Freedom (Douglass), **1:**34
My Brother Ibrahim (Tuqan), **1:**227
My Confessions (Chamberlain), **1:**304
Myers, Brian, **1:**103
Myers, Constance, **3:**87
Myerson, Joel, **2:**224, 225
My Forty Year Fight for Korea (Yim), **1:**323
"My Furthest-Back Person— 'The African'" (Haley), **1:261–263**
My Life (Das), **1:**87
"My Life" (Keller), **1:**43
My Life and Work (Ford), **1:**30
My Life Story (Amrouche), **1:93–95**
My Life Story (Unaipon), **1:149–151**
Myrdal, Jan, *Report from a Chinese Village,* **3:**299
My Revolutionary Years (Cheng), **1:152–154**
My Soul (Hoess), **2:**54
My Soul Is My Own (Etter-Lewis), **3:**21
Mystery and Manners (O'Connor), **2:**131
Mysticism
   of Kempe (Margery), **1:**189–191
   of Teresa of Ávila, **1:**211–213
Myth and Materiality in a Woman's World (Abrams), **3:**175
Myth of Sisyphus, The (Camus), **1:**204
Mythology
   of Aborigines, **1:**149
   of Kiowas, **1:**54–56
   of Navajo, **3:**320

Myths and Legends of the Australian Aboriginals (Unaipon), **1:**149
My Traitor's Heart (Malan), **3:**242

N

NAACP. *See* National Association for the Advancement of Colored People
Nablus (West Bank), **1:**225, *226*
Nabokov, Vladimir, **1:271**
   Speak, Memory, **1:**249, 270
   Speak, Memory: An Autobiography Revisited, **1:270–272**
Nadeau, Remi, *The Water Seekers,* **3:**102
Nafisi, Azar, *Reading Lolita in Tehran,* **1:**155, 157, 209
NAFTA. *See* North American Free Trade Agreement
Nagai, Takashi
   The Bells of Nagasaki, **1:**293
   We of Nagasaki, **1:**293
Nagasaki (Japan), U.S. nuclear bombing of, **3:**239
Nagel, Paul C., **2:**71
Naghibi, Nima, **1:**157
Naipaul, V. S., **1:**88
Najder, Zdzisław, **2:**192
Nakazawa, Keiji, **1:294**
   Barefoot Gen, **1:293–295**
   Hiroshima, **1:**293, 295
Nam (Baker), **3:**199, 209, 210, 221, 231
Names, of slaves, **1:**52
Names, The: A Memoir (Momaday), **1:**54
Nanking (Nanjing) Massacre (1937)
   Rabe's (John) account of, **2:**19–21
   Sino–Japanese relations after, **1:**340
Napangardi, Georgina, **3:**107, 335
Napoleon (Scott), **2:**310
Napoléon Bonaparte, **1:**276, **2:**217
Napoleonic wars, **1:**276
Napoleon III, **2:**82
Narain, Mona, **2:**231
Nara period (Japan), **2:**189
Narrative (Brown), **1:**50
Narrative (journal), **1:**164, 165

Narrative of Hosea Hudson, The (Hudson), **1:**3–4

Narrative of Sojourner Truth (Truth), **1:**37

Narrative of the Life and Travels of Mrs. Nancy Prince (Prince), **3:**24

Narrative of the Life of Frederick Douglass (Douglass), **1:**33–36

    Eighty Years and More (Stanton) vs., **1:**12

    Equiano's (Olaudah) influence on, **1:**82–83

    Incidents in the Life of a Slave Girl (Jacobs) vs., **1:**34, 35, 142, 143

    Up from Slavery (Washington) vs., **1:**50

Narrative point of view (perspective)

    in *The Autobiography of Giambattista Vico* (Vico), **1:**184

    in *Bone Black* (hooks), **1:**249, 250, 251

    in *A Cross and a Star* (Agosín), **1:**76

    in *The Woman Warrior* (Kingston), **1:**173

    in *The Writing Life* (Dillard), **1:**280, 281

Narrative voice

    of *Angela's Ashes* (McCourt), **1:**120

    of *The Autobiography of Malcolm X* (Malcolm X), **1:**187

    of *Bone Black* (hooks), **1:**250

    of *The Color of Water* (McBride), **1:**73

    of *A Cross and a Star* (Agosín), **1:**76

    of *The Education of Henry Adams* (Adams), **1:**133

    of *An Egyptian Childhood* (Hussein), **1:**136

    of *Go Ask Alice* (anonymous), **2:**295

    of *I Know Why the Caged Bird Sings* (Angelou), **1:**18, 19

    of *Lakota Woman* (Brave Bird), **1:**23

    of *My Revolutionary Years* (Cheng), **1:**153

    of *Nella Last's War* (Last), **2:**266

    of *Paekpom Ilchi* (Kim), **1:**323

    of *Red Scarf Girl* (Jiang), **1:**161, 162

    of *Ten Thousand Sorrows* (Kim), **1:**103

    of *When Heaven and Earth Changed Places* (Hayslip), **1:**336

    of *The Woman Warrior* (Kingston), **1:**173

    of *The Writing Life* (Dillard), **1:**281

Nasar, Sylvia, **2:**18

Nash, Charles Elventon, *The History of Augusta*, **2:**331, 333

Nash, Christine, **3:**61

Nash, John, **3:**61

Nash, Philip Tajitsu, **3:**197

Nassiri, Nematollah, **3:**219

Nation (magazine), **1:**100, 103, 258, **2:**92, 102

Nation, Michael, **3:**211

National Academy of Arbitrators, **3:**153

National American Women's Suffrage Association (NAWSA), **1:**12, 13

National Anti-Slavery Standard (newspaper), **1:**144

National Association for the Advancement of Colored People (NAACP)

    on anti-lynching legislation, **1:**18

    in civil rights movement, **3:**44

    Du Bois (W. E. B.) in, **1:**4

    establishment of, **3:**44

    in military desegregation, **3:**248

National Book Award, for *Roots* (Haley), **1:**261

National Book Critics Circle Award

    for *Voices from Chernobyl* (Alexievich), **3:**282

    for *The Woman Warrior* (Kingston), **1:**173

National Geographic, **1:**114

National Health Service (Britain), **3:**170

National identity

    Danish, **2:**166

    Portuguese, **2:**199–200

Nationalism

    Armenian, **3:**40

    black, **1:**4, 78, 79

    British, **2:**219

    Chinese, **2:**170

    German, **1:**30–32, 329, **2:**120, **3:**234

    Indian, **1:**289–290

    Irish, **1:**119, **2:**127, 128, **3:**315

    Japanese, **3:**234

    Moroccan, **3:**47–49

    Palestinian, **1:**225, 227

    Puerto Rican, **1:**108

Nationalist Party (China), **1:**338

Nationalization

    in Cuba, **1:**296

    in Iran, **3:**218

National Liberation Front (FLN) (Algeria), **2:**262

National Party (South Africa), **1:**24, 27, **3:**242

National Republican Alliance (ARENA), **3:**205

National Savings Movement (Britain), **3:**145

National security, U.S.

    East German Stasi and, **3:**245

    racism and, **3:**195, 197

National Socialist German Workers' Party, **1:**30. See also Nazi Germany

National Velvet (Bagnold), **2:**259, 260, 261

National War Labor Board, The (Conner), **3:**153–154

National War Labor Board (NWLB), U.S., **3:**153–154

National Woman Suffrage Association, **1:**12

Nation of Islam. See Black Muslims

Nation of Women, A (Fur), **3:**326

Native American(s)

    in AIM (See American Indian Movement)

    Carver's (Jonathan) encounters with, **2:**205, 206, 207

    civil rights of, **1:**21, **3:**291, 292

    Columbus's (Christopher) encounters with, **2:**202

    conversion to Christianity, **1:**56, **2:**46, **3:**114, 115

    cultural transmission by, **3:**107–109, 325–326

    education of, at boarding schools, **3:**109, 318

SUBJECT INDEX

Native American(s), *continued*
  forced removal of, **1:**302, **3:**290, *291*, 318, 325, 327
  in King Philip's War, **1:**325–328, *326*
  oral traditions of, **1:**21, 54, 55, 96, 302, 304, **3:**138
  in Pan-Indian movement, **1:**54
  racism against, **1:**96
  religion of, **3:**110–112
  U.S. treaties with, **1:**69, **3:**107, 110, 290, 327
  U.S. wars with, **1:**302–304, **3:**110
Native American autobiographical writing. *See also specific works and writers*
  by Brave Bird (Mary), **1:**21–23
  by Chona (Maria), **1:**69–71
  in collective narratives vs. autobiographies, **1:**54
  by Geronimo, **1:**302–304
  by Momaday (N. Scott), **1:**54–56
  non–Native writers' collaboration in, **1:**21, 23, 56, 69–70
  by Peltier (Leonard), **1:**96–98
  rise of, **1:**54
  tradition of, **1:**54, 56, **3:**110, 318, 320
Native American identity
  language in, **3:**108, 109
  search for, **1:**22, 55, 56
Native American oral histories
  from Alta California, **3:**114–116, *115*
  of Black Elk, **3:**110–113
  of Delaware Indians, **3:**107–109
  of Inuits, **3:**138–140
  of Left Handed, **3:**318–320
  of Navajo, **3:**10–12, 290–292, 318–320
  from Owens Valley (California), **3:**102, 103
  of Woodland Indians, **3:**107–109
Native American renaissance, **1:**54
Native American reservations
  Brave Bird (Mary) on life on, **1:**21
  Chona (Maria) on life on, **1:**69
  economic disparities in, **3:**290
  establishment of system of, **1:**69, 302, **3:**318

Geronimo on life on, **1:**302
Navajo, **3:**10–12, 290–291, 318
Navajo–Hope land dispute in, **3:**10–12
Peltier (Leonard) on life on, **1:**96
social change in, **3:**290
water resources of, **1:**69, **3:**11
Native Land Act of 1913 (South Africa), **2:**241
Native Life in South Africa (Plaatje), **2:**241, 242, 243
Native Son (Wright), **1:**122, 123, 273
NATO, demonstrations against, **3:**157, 158
Nattrass, Nicoli, *The Moral Economy of AIDS in South Africa,* **3:**272
Natural History (journal), **3:**38
Naturalistic diction, in *Notebooks and Letters* (Hawthorne), **2:**224
Natural philosophy, **2:**300
Natural selection, **1:**65
Natural Theology (Paley), **1:**65
Natural world
  British writing on, golden age of, **2:**300
  Dillard's (Annie) essays on, **1:**279
  Neruda's (Pablo) love of, **1:**223–224
  Thoreau (Henry David) on, **1:**233–236
  in transcendental fiction, **1:**281
  Wordsworth's (Dorothy) descriptions of, **2:**300–302
"Nature" (Emerson), **2:**141
Nature's Pictures Drawn by Fancy's Pencil to the Life (Cavendish), **1:**229, 231
Naudowessee tribe, **2:**206
Navajivan (journal), **1:**242
Navajo, **3:319**
  in land dispute with Hopi, oral histories of, **3:**10–12
  Left Handed on life of, oral history of, **3:**318–320
  "Long Walk" of, **3:**290, *291*
  matrilineal culture of, **3:**318
  origins of, **3:**318
  witch purge of 1878 among, oral histories of, **3:**290–292
Navajo as Seen by the Franciscans, The (Bahr), **3:**290

Navajo-Hopi Land Dispute, The (Brugge), **3:**10
Navajo-Hopi Settlement Act of 1974 (U.S.), **3:**10
Navajo Land, Navajo Culture (McPherson), **3:**10
Navajo language, **3:**11, 12
Navajos, The (Underhill), **3:**290
Navajo Times (newspaper), **3:**12
"Navajo Witch Purge of 1878, The" (Brugge), **3:**290
Naval Aviation News, **3:**203
Navarrete, Martín Fernández de, **2:**201
Navy, Colombian, **3:**183–185
Navy, U.S., in World War II, oral histories of, **3:**202–204, *203*
NAWSA. *See* National American Women's Suffrage Association
Naylor, James, **2:**26
Naylor, Phillip, **2:**263
Nazi Germany. *See also* Holocaust
  autobiographies written after end of, **2:**54
  bombardment of Britain by, **2:**265, 269, 270
  Chilean support for, **1:**75
  establishment of, **3:**14
  extent of conquest by, **3:**14
  fall of, **2:**281–282
  Fosse Ardeatine massacre by, **3:**265–267
  France occupied by, **1:**332–334
  Italy occupied by, **3:**265–267
  Klemperer (Victor) on rise of, **2:**303–305
  Nanking Massacre and, **2:**19, 20, 21
  Netherlands occupied by, **2:**22–24, 253–255
  Speer's (Albert) role in, **2:**54–56
  war crimes of, **1:**77, **2:**54–56, **3:**293–295
Nazi Seizure of Power, The (Allen), **3:**245
NCR Book Award, for *Wild Swans* (Chang), **1:**159
Neal, R. S., **3:**178
Ned, Annie, **3:**320
Nedjma (Yacine), **2:**262

Neeson, Liam, **2:***10*
Negative capability, **2:**146, 147
Négritude movement, **1:**61, 128
Negro in the American Rebellion, The (Brown), **2:**238
Nehru, Jawaharlal, **1:290**
   An Autobiography, with Musings on Recent Events in India, **1:289–292**
   The Discovery of India, **1:**290, 291
   Whither India?, **1:**290
Neihardt, John G., *Black Elk Speaks,* **1:**21, 56, 302, **3:110–113,** 318
Neilson, William Allan, **1:**44–45
Nella Last's Peace (Last), **2:**265
Nella Last's War (Last), **2:265–267**
Nelson, Edward, **3:**51
Nelson, Truman, **1:**4
Nemiroff, Robert, **1:**273, 274, 275
Neoliberalism, in Argentina, rise of, **3:**74
Neoplatonism, of Augustine, **1:**196, 197
Neruda, Pablo
   Canto general, **1:**223
   Memoirs, **1:222–224**
   Memorial de isla negra, **1:**223
Nesbitt, Gussie, **3:**45
Netherlands
   colonialism of, Barnard's (Anne) critique of, **2:**218
   Hillesum (Etty) on life in, **2:**22–24
   Hirsi Ali (Ayaan) on life in, **1:**207–209
   Nazi occupation of, **2:**22–24, 253–255
Neubauer, Carol, **1:**18
Never in Anger (Briggsoth), **3:**138
Nevins, Allan
   on *The Diary of John Quincy Adams* (Adams), **2:**70
   "Great Men" project of, **3:**161, 173, 179, 181, 186
   influence on oral history field, **3:**37, 173
New Age (journal), **1:**25
New Burlington (Baskin), **3:**86
New Challenge (journal), **1:**85
New Criterion (journal), **2:**73, 185, 337

New Culture Movement. *See* May Fourth Movement
New Deal, **3:**161. *See also* Federal Writers' Project
New Discovery of a Vast Country in America, A (Hennepin), **2:**205
Newell, Esther Pollack, **3:**269
New England Quarterly, **2:**114
New German Critique (journal), **1:**32
New Grub Street (Gissing), **2:**320, 321, 322
New Harmony (utopian community), **1:**14
Newman, Andrew, *On Records,* **3:**326
Newman, John Henry, *Apologia Pro Vita Sua,* **1:**65
New Mexico
   Bosque Redondo Reservation in, **3:**10, 290, *291*
   oral histories of development of atom bomb in, **3:**239–241
New Negro movement, **1:**84. *See also* Harlem Renaissance
New Orleans (Louisiana), oral histories of Hispanic American entrepreneurs in, **3:**121–123, *122*
New Republic (magazine), **1:**4, 258, **2:**150, 340, **3:**61
New Science (Vico), **1:**183, 184, 185
New Statesman (journal), **3:**59
New Statesman & Society (journal), **2:**221
Newsweek (magazine), **1:**19
New Voyages to North-America (Lahontan), **2:**205
New War Diary (Xie), **1:**339–340
New West Indian Guide (journal), **3:**7, 8
New Woman, **2:**259
New World, Columbus's (Christopher) discovery of, **2:**201–203
New York (state), interracial marriage in, **1:**72
New York City. *See also* Harlem Renaissance
   African American migration to, **1:**84
   City College in, **1:**249, 251
   in Great Depression, **1:**84
   Hansberry (Lorraine) on life in, **1:**273

   Jews living in, **3:**118, 119, *119,* 120
New York Daily Tribune (newspaper), **1:**142
New Yorker (magazine), **1:**258, 270, 300
New York Intellectuals, **1:**258
New York Post (newspaper), **3:**165
New York Review of Books, **1:**7, 79, **3:**60, 165, 280, 288
New York Times (newspaper)
   on *The Abandoned Baobab* (Bugul), **1:**62–63
   on *Along This Way* (Johnson), **1:**84
   on *Angela's Ashes* (McCourt), **1:**120
   on *Bloods* (Terry), **3:**201
   on *Bone Black* (hooks), **1:**250
   on *The Color of Water* (McBride), **1:**73, 74
   on *Diaries of Beatrice Webb* (Webb), **2:**17
   on *The Diaries of Franz Kafka* (Kafka), **2:**121
   on *A Diary from Dixie* (Chesnut), **2:**251
   on *The Diary of Anne Frank* (Frank), **2:**253
   on *The Diary of John Quincy Adams* (Adams), **2:**70
   on *The Diary of Samuel Pepys* (Pepys), **2:**73
   on *Dreams from My Father* (Obama), **1:**79
   on *Everything We Had* (Santoli), **3:**211
   on *Geronimo* (Geronimo and Barrett), **1:**304
   on *Hard Times* (Terkel), **3:**162
   on *Hunger of Memory* (Rodriguez), **1:**16
   on *Infidel* (Hirsi Ali), **1:**209
   on *Letters to a Young Poet* (Rilke), **2:**149
   on Levi's (Primo) suicide, **1:**204, 205
   on *London and the Life* (Gissing), **2:**322
   on *The Long Walk to Freedom* (Mandela), **1:**28, 29
   on *Mein Kampf* (Hitler), **1:**32

New York Times (newspaper), **continued**
- on *Memoirs* (Neruda), **1:**223
- on *Memories of a Catholic Girlhood* (McCarthy), **1:**259
- on *Motorcycle Diaries* (Guevara), **2:**220
- "My Furthest-Back Person— 'The African'" (Haley) in, **1:**261
- on *Our Appalachia* (Shackelford and Weinberg), **3:**87
- on *Persepolis* (Satrapi), **1:**156–157
- on *Red Azalea* (Min), **1:**158
- on *Rites: A Guatemalan Boyhood* (Perera), **1:**100
- on *Roots* (Haley), **1:**262
- on *Rosa Parks: My Story* (Parks and Haskins), **1:**38
- on *Selected Letters of Martha Gellhorn* (Gellhorn), **2:**102
- on *Shoah* (film), **3:**52
- on *Speak, Memory* (Nabokov), **1:**271
- on *The Story of a Shipwrecked Sailor* (García Márquez), **3:**183
- on *This Boy's Life* (Wolff), **1:**48
- on *Up from Slavery* (Washington), **1:**52
- on *When Heaven and Earth Changed Places* (Hayslip), **1:**336
- on *Witnesses to Nuremberg* (Stave et al.), **3:**294
- on *A Woman in Berlin* (anonymous), **2:**282
- on *The Woman Warrior* (Kingston), **1:**175
- on *Working* (Terkel), **3:**344
- on *The Writing Life* (Dillard), **1:**280

New York Times Book Review
- on *Chinese Lives* (Zhang and Sang), **3:**301
- on *Darkness Visible* (Styron), **1:**205
- on *A Diary without Dates* (Bagnold), **2:**260
- on *Dust Tracks on a Road* (Hurston), **1:**10–11
- on *Farewell to Manzanar* (Houston and Houston), **1:**300
- on *Fun Home* (Bechdel), **1:**141
- on *The Good Man of Nanking* (Rabe), **2:**20
- on "*The Good War*" (Terkel), **3:**213
- on *The Habit of Being* (O'Connor), **2:**131
- on *The Journals of Charlotte Forten Grimké* (Grimké), **2:**30
- on *Letters Home* (Plath), **2:**48
- on *A Midwife's Tale* (Ulrich), **2:**333
- on *The Travels of Dean Mahomet* (Mahomet), **2:**231
- on *Voices of Freedom* (Hampton and Fayer), **3:**45
- on *What Was Asked of Us* (Wood), **3:**233
- on *A Writer's Diary* (Woolf), **2:**181
- on *Zlata's Diary* (Filipovic), **2:**339

New York Times Magazine, **1:**99
New Zealand, Mansfield (Katherine) on life in, **2:**133–135
Next Year in Cuba (Pérez Firmat), **1:**296
Ng, Wendy, **3:**81
Ngarrindjeri people, **1:**149, 151
Ngor, Haing, *Survival in the Killing Fields,* **1:**306
Ngũgĩ wa Mirii, **2:**12
Ngũgĩ wa Thiong'o
- *Barrel of a Pen,* **2:**12
- *Decolonising the Mind,* **2:**13
- *Detained: A Writer's Prison Diary,* **1:**215, **2:**12–15
- *Devil on the Cross,* **2:**12, 13
- *I Will Marry When I Want,* **2:**12
- *Matagari,* **2:**14
- *Petals of Blood,* **2:**12

Nguyen, Kien, *The Unwanted,* **1:**170–172
Nguyen, Nathalie Huynh Chau, **1:**172
Nguyen, Viet Thanh, **1:**336–337
Nguyen Thi Thu Lam, *Fallen Leaves,* **1:**335
Nicene Creed, **1:**196
Nicholas II (tsar of Russia), **1:**270, **2:**84, 85
Nichols, John Gough, **1:**316, **2:**97, 99
Nichols, Julie, **2:**164
Nichols, Madaline W., **2:**7
Nichols, Martha, **1:**251
Nichols-Ledermann, Deborah, **3:**325, 326
Nicholson-Preuss, Mari, **3:**246

Nicolay, Helen, **3:**263
Nicolay, Helena, **3:**263
Nicolay, John G., **3:262**
- *Abraham Lincoln: A History,* **3:**261–262
- *Abraham Lincoln: Complete Works,* **3:**262
- in *An Oral History of Abraham Lincoln* (Burlingame), **3:**261–264

Nicolay, John Jacob, **3:**263
Nies, Judith, **3:**292
Nietzsche, Friedrich
- Andreas-Salomé (Lou) and, **2:**151
- *Ecce Homo,* **1:**183
- Vico (Giambattista) compared to, **1:**183, 184–185

Nigeria
- Civil War of, **1:**214–216
- Equiano (Olaudah) in, **1:**81–83
- independence of (1960), **1:**214
- postcolonial governments of, **1:**214–216
- Soyinka (Wole) on life in, **1:**214–216

Nigerian Civil War (1967–1970), **1:**214–216
Night (Wiesel), **1:318–321**
Night Comes to the Cumberlands (Caudill), **3:**66
Nightingale, Florence, **1:**111, 112, 113
Nijo, Lady, *Confessions of Lady Nijo,* **2:59–61**
Nikki genre, **2:**191
Nilsen, Alleen Pace, **2:**294, 295
Nin, Anaïs, **2:**124
- Bashkirtseff's (Marie) influence on, **2:**306
- *The Diary of Anaïs Nin,* **2:123–125**
- *The Extraordinary Work of Ordinary Writing* (Sinor) compared to, **2:**163

Nineteen Eighty-Four (Orwell), **2:**117, 118, 255
Nineteenth Amendment, **1:**13
Nineteenth Century (journal), **2:**307
Ninety-Four Years of a Floating Life (Su), **1:**338

Nisa: The Life and Words of a !Kung Woman (Shostak), **3**:37–39
Nisei Daughter (Sone), **1**:299, 309
Nisei Soldiers Break Their Silence (Tamura), **3**:80
Nixon, Richard, **1**:21, **2**:294, **3**:279
Nkrumah, Kwame, **1**:4
    Ghana, **1**:290, **2**:12, 13
Nobel prizes
    to Buck (Pearl S.), **1**:159
    to García Márquez (Gabriel), **3**:183
    to King (Martin Luther, Jr.), **2**:32
    to Lessing (Doris), **1**:168
    to Luthuli (Albert), **1**:25
    to Maathai (Wangari), **1**:114
    to Mandela (Nelson), **1**:29
    to Menchú (Rigoberta), **3**:164, 165, 166
    to Mistral (Gabriela), **1**:222
    to Neruda (Pablo), **1**:222
    to Soyinka (Wole), **1**:214
    to Wiesel (Elie), **1**:320
Noche de Tlatelolco, La (Poniatowska). See *Massacre in Mexico* (Poniatowska)
Noël Coward Diaries, The (Coward), **2**:152
No Future without Forgiveness (Tutu), **3**:244
No Gods, No Masters (Guérin), **3**:3
Nolan, Janet, **3**:269
Nomad (Hirsi Ali), **1**:209
Nominalism, **1**:239
Nomura, Mary, **3**:104
Nonchronological order
    in *The Dark Child* (Laye), **1**:129
    in *Stop-Time* (Conroy), **1**:164, 165
Nonfiction essays, tradition of, **1**:279
No-No Boy (Okada), **1**:309
Nonviolent movements
    in India, Gandhi (Mohandas) in, **1**:242–244, 289–290
    in South Africa, against apartheid, **1**:24–26
    in U.S., King (Martin Luther, Jr.) in, **2**:32–34
Noonan, Lucille Brody, **3**:119
Norma Rae (film), **3**:98

Norrell, Robert J., **1**:38, 52
Norris, Bruce, *Clybourne Park,* **1**:273
Norris, Leslie, **1**:126
Norris, Randall, *Women of Coal,* **3**:337
North, James W., **2**:333
North, U.S.
    abolitionism in, **1**:33
    in Civil War (See American Civil War)
    Great Migration to, **1**:50, 52, 84, 273, **3**:99
    racial segregation in, **3**:250
    racism in, **1**:122
North American Free Trade Agreement (NAFTA), **3**:304
North American Review (journal), **1**:132, 134, 148, 202, **2**:89, 336
North Carolina, oral histories of coal mining in, **3**:86–87
Northern Expedition, **1**:338
Northern Ireland
    conflict over, **3**:27
    establishment of, **1**:119
North Fork of the Coeur d'Alene River (Russell), **3**:93
North Korea, establishment of (1945), **1**:322
Northside Chronicle, **3**:342
Northup, Solomon, *Twelve Years a Slave,* **1**:50
North Vietnam, establishment of (1954), **1**:335, **3**:279. See also Vietnam War
Norton, M. D. Herter, **2**:149
Norton, W. W., **2**:150
Nostalgia
    for Christmas, Thomas (Dylan) on, **1**:125, 126
    for English rural landscapes, **3**:63
    of Ukrainian miners, **3**:340, 341
Notarianni, Philip, **3**:225
Notebooks (Williams), **2**:152–154
Notebooks and *Letters* (Hawthorne), **2**:113, 223–225
Notebooks of Henry James, The (James), **2**:113, 114, 115
Notes of a Native Son (Baldwin), **1**:79–80

Notes on the State of Virginia (Jefferson), **2**:45, 215
Not Working (Maurer), **3**:277
Novel(s). See also Fiction
    collective, **3**:282, 285
    of manners, **2**:312
Ntirkana, Jackson, *The Last Maasai Warrior,* **1**:114
Nuclear disaster, Chernobyl, **3**:282–285
Nuclear weapons
    movement against, **3**:239, 268, 269
    Pakistani, **1**:87
    U.S. development of, oral histories of, **3**:239–241
    U.S. use of, in World War II, **1**:293–294
Nunavut (Canada), oral histories of Inuits in, **3**:138–140, *139*
Nungarrayi, Molly, **3**:336
Nungarrayi, Rosie, **3**:335
Nuns, American, oral histories of, **3**:308–310
Nuremberg Interviews, The (Goldensohn), **3**:293
Nuremberg Laws of 1935 (Germany), **2**:253, **3**:14
Nuremberg Rallies, **1**:31
Nuremberg trials (1945–1946), **3**:294
    critics of, **2**:56
    oral histories of, **3**:293–295
    outcome of, **2**:56
    Speer (Albert) in, **2**:54, 56
Nursing
    in Crimean War, **1**:111–113
    in World War I, **1**:329, 330, **2**:259–261, *260*
NWLB. See National War Labor Board
NWSA Journal, **3**:338

O

OAH Magazine of History, **3**:101
Oakley, Ann
    "Interviewing Women," **3**:190
    The Sociology of Housework, **3**:144

Obama, Barack, **1:**79
    The Audacity of Hope, **1:**78, 80
    Dreams from My Father, **1:78–80**
    King's (Martin Luther, Jr.) influence on, **2:**33
Obama, Barack, Sr., **1:**78, 79, 80
Obama, Sasha, **1:**79
Obermeyer, Brice, *Delaware Tribe in a Cherokee Nation,* **3:**326
O'Brien, Glen, **3:**316
O'Brien, Tim, **3:**201
    Going after Cacciato, **1:**335
O Brother Where Art Thou (film), **3:**159
Observer (newspaper), **1:**80, **2:**153, **3:**235, 236
O'Casey, Sean, **1:**119, **3:**27
    The Silver Tassie, **1:**329
Ocasio-Melendez, Marcial, **3:**122
Occom, Samson
    "A Short Narrative of My Life," **1:**56
    Wheatley's (Phillis) letter to, **2:**44–46
Occupying Power (Kovner), **3:**128
"Occupy" movement, **3:**328
O'Connor, Flannery, **2:**130
    "A Good Man Is Hard to Find," **2:**130
    The Habit of Being, **2:129–132**
    Mystery and Manners, **2:**131
O'Connor, Frank, **1:**119
O'Connor, K. C., **3:**19, 332
October Revolution (1917), **1:**270
O'Donnell, James, **1:**197, 198
O'Faolain, Sean, **1:**119
O'Faolin, Nuala, **1:**119
O'Farrell, Brigid, *Rocking the Boat,* **3:**337
Ofer, Dalia, **3:**35
Offences Against the Person Act of 1861 (Britain), **3:**70
Off Our Backs (magazine), **1:**336, **2:**4
Oglala Sioux. *See* Lakota Sioux
O'Grady, Sean, **3:**316
O'Grady, Timothy, *Ireland's Unfinished Revolution,* **3:27–30**
Ogun (deity), **1:**216
O'Hara, Daniel, **2:**128

O'Hara, John, **2:**137
Ohio History (journal), **3:**326
Ohitika Woman (Brave Bird), **1:**21, 23
Oil industry, in Iran, **3:**218
Okada, John, *No-No Boy,* **1:**309
Okigbo, Christopher, **1:**214
Okihiro, Gary Y., **3:**197
Oklahoma, forced relocation of Delaware Indians to, **3:**325
Okubo, Miné, *Citizen 13660,* **1:**299
"Old Times on the Mississippi" (Twain), **1:**146
Old Wives' Tale, The (Bennett), **2:**136
"Old Woman's Gossip, An" (Kemble), **2:**335
Oliphant, Margaret, **2:**210
    Autobiography, **2:**335
Olive Schreiner Prize, for *Country of My Skull* (Krog), **3:**243
Olivier, Gerrit, **3:**243
Olivieri, Giovanni, **2:**160
Olney, James
    Autobiography: Essays Theoretical and Critical, **1:246–248,** 247
    Memory and Narrative, **1:**246, 248
    Metaphors of Self, **1:**246
    Tell Me Africa, **1:**246
Olschki, Leonardo, **1:**105, 107
Olson, Ray, **3:**229
Olympica, Nazaria, **2:**160, 161
Olympics, **1:**158, **3:**32
O'Malley, Andrew, **1:**157
O'Malley, Ernie, *The Singing Flame,* **3:**27
Ombudsman, origin of term, **3:**154
Omni-Americans, The (Murray), **1:**124
Omori, Annie Shepley, **2:**190, 290, 292
O'Nan, Stewart, **3:**211
"On Being Brought from Africa to America" (Wheatley), **2:**46
Once They Hear My Name (Lee et al.), **1:**102
Ondaatje, Michael, *Running in the Family,* **1:**88
On Diary (Lejeune), **2:**174, 175
One Day in the Life of Ivan Denisovich (Solzhenitsyn), **3:**17
O'Neill, Eugene, **2:**152

O'Neill, Kevin, **2:**159
O'Neill, Michael, **3:**55
Only What We Could Carry (Inada), **3:**80
Ono Kazuko, **3:**149
On Records (Newman), **3:**326
On the Origin of Species (Darwin), **1:**65
"On the Pulse of the Morning" (Angelou), **1:**20
On the Road (Kerouac), **1:**234
Opequon, Battle of (1862), **2:**272
Operas, Chinese, **1:**159
Operation Bootstrap, **1:**108
Operation Desert Storm. *See* Gulf War
Operation Pedro Pan, **1:**298
Opium, Marcus Aurelius and, **1:**221
Oppenheimer, Gerald M.
    AIDS Doctors, **3:**272, 273, 274
    Shattered Dreams?, **3:272–274**
Oppenheimer, J. Robert, **3:**240, *240,* 241
Oppenheimer, Peter, **3:**240
Oppenheimer, Toni, **3:**240
Opper, Frederick, **3:**4
Oppression
    communist, in China, **1:**338
    of indigenous people of Guatemala, **3:**164–166
    political, in East Germany, **3:**245–246
    racial, Angelou (Maya) on, **1:**18
Oral American Historians Magazine, **3:**21
Oral contraceptives, **3:**170, *171*
Oral histories. *See also* specific works and writers
    Abrams (Lynn) on theory of, **3:**173–175
    audio vs. print recording of, **3:**65
    class differences in collection of, **3:**177
    definitions of, **3:**97, 158, 285
    economic disparities in collection of, **3:**190
    evaluation of reliability of, **3:**281
    four forms of, **3:**174
    Frisch (Michael) on shared authority in, **3:**179–181, 190

guidelines for collecting, **3:**187–188, 313

internationalization of, **3:**129

motivations for collecting, **3:**135

origins and development of field, **3:**37, 157, 173, 179–181, 186

Popular Memory Group on need for, **3:**176–178

Portelli (Alessandro) in field of, **3:**159, 173, 267

as primary sources in field of history, **3:**281

recognition of value of, **3:**20, 64, 90, 173, 186

as social change agent, **3:**86, 186, 187

subjectivity in, **3:**162, 173, 186

technological advances in, **3:**181

Thompson (Paul) on value of, **3:**186–189, 209

of women, feminist approach to, **3:**190–192

Oral Histories of First to Fourth Generation Americans (Lee), **3:**83

Oral History (journal)

"ANZAC Memories" (Thomson) in, **3:**177, 178

on *Daring Hearts* (Brighton Ourstory), **3:**72

on *The Death of Luigi Trastulli* (Portelli), **3:**159

on *Ireland's Unfinished Revolution* (Griffith and O'Grady), **3:**29

"popular memory" issue of, **3:**177, 178

on *The Voice of the Past* (Thompson), **3:**188

on *Women's Words* (Gluck and Patai), **3:**192

on *Working-Class Childhood* (Seabrook), **3:**54

on *The World at War* (Holmes), **3:**235

Oral History, Health and Welfare (Bornat et al.), **3:170–172**

"Oral History and the Digital Revolution" (Frisch), **3:**181

Oral History Association Book Award, for *The Order Has Been Carried Out* (Portelli), **3:**265, 267

Oral History of Abraham Lincoln, An (Burlingame), **3:261–264**

Oral History of Tribal Warfare, An (Fadiman), **3:**141

Oral History Project: The Early Days of Labor Arbitration (Dash), **3:**153

Oral History Reader, The (Perks and Thomson), **3:**173, 178, 179, 181

Oral History Review (journal)

on *Always a People* (Kohn and Montell), **3:**109

on *And Justice for All* (Tateishi), **3:**197

on *Children of Los Alamos* (Mason), **3:**240

on *Chinese Lives* (Zhang and Sang), **3:**301

on *Coal Hollow* (Light and Light), **3:**67

on *The Death of Luigi Trastulli* (Portelli), **3:**159

on *El Salvador at War* (Manwaring and Prisk), **3:**207

on *Everything We Had* (Santoli), **3:**210, 211

on *The Firm* (Bruce), **3:**246

on *The First Agraristas* (Craig), **3:**303

on *"The Good War"* (Terkel), **3:**213

on *Habits of Change* (Rogers), **3:**309

on *The Hispanic-American Entrepreneur* (Owsley), **3:**122

on *In the Mansion of Confucius' Descendants* (Kong and Ke), **3:**125

on *Japan at War* (Cook and Cook), **3:**216

on *Japanese War Brides in America* (Crawford et al.), **3:**128, 129

on *Long Journey Home* (Brown and Kohn), **3:**326

on *Oral History Theory* (Abrams), **3:**174

on *The Order Has Been Carried Out* (Portelli), **3:**266

on *Peacework* (Adams), **3:**269

on *A Shared Authority* (Frisch), **3:**179, 180, 181

on *Shattered Dreams?* (Oppenheimer and Bayer), **3:**273

on *The Strength Not to Fight* (Tollefson), **3:**223

on *Survivors* (Miller and Miller), **3:**41

on *Swiftwater People* (Russell), **3:**95

on *They Say in Harlan County* (Portelli), **3:**97

Thomson (Alistair) in, **3:**135

on *The Voice of the Past* (Thompson), **3:**188

on *Voices from this Long Brown Land* (Wehrey), **3:**103

on *Witnesses to Nuremberg* (Stave et al.), **3:**294

on *Witnesses to the Holocaust* (Lewin), **3:**51

on *Women in the Mines* (Moore), **3:**339

on *Women's Words* (Gluck and Patai), **3:**191

Oral History Society, **3:**65, 170, 172

Oral History Society (journal), **3:**5

Oral History Theory (Abrams), **3:173–175**, **179**, **181**, **285**

Oral traditions

African, **1:**64, **2:**242

African American, **1:**262

Irish, **1:**121

Kabyle, **1:**93

Native American, **1:**21, 54, 55, 96, 302, 304, **3:**138

VaShawasha, **3:**251, 252

Welsh, **1:**125

Oratorical autobiography, *Eighty Years and More* (Stanton) as, **1:**14

Ordeal of Mansart, The (Du Bois), **1:**5

Order Has Been Carried Out, The (Portelli), **3:**158, **265–267**

Oregon, Japanese immigrants in, **3:**80–82, *81*

Oregon Historical Quarterly, **3:**82

Oregon Trail, The (Parkman), **1:**234

Oregon Treaty (1846), **2:**69

Organisation de l'Armee Secrete, **2:**262

Organization of American Historians: Magazine of History, **3:**277

Oriental Observer (periodical), **1:**277

Origin and Development of Psychoanalysis, The (Freud), **2:**175

SUBJECT INDEX

Origin myths. *See* Creation stories
Orlando (Woolf), **1:**173, **2:**64, 181
Orleck, Annelise, *Storming Caesars Palace,* **3:**254
Orphans
    of influenza pandemic, **1:**258
    Kim (Elizabeth) as, **1:**102
    Korean, **1:**102
    McCarthy (Mary) as, **1:**259
Orthodox Jews, **3:**16
Orwell, George
    Animal Farm, **2:**117, *118*
    on *An Autobiography* (Gandhi), **1:**244
    Burmese Days, **2:**119
    Complete Works of George Orwell, **2:**117, 118
    Conroy (Frank) influenced by, **1:**164
    Diaries, 1931–1949, **2:117–119**
    Nineteen Eighty-Four, **2:**117, 118, 255
    The Road to Wigan Pier, **2:**117, **3:**66
Osamu, Tezuka, *Atom Boy,* **1:**293
Osborne, Dorothy, *The Love Letters of Dorothy Osborne to Sir William Temple,* **2:324–327**
Osio, Antonio María, *The History of Alta California,* **3:**115
Oslo Accords (1993), **2:**50, 52
Osorio, Arana, **1:**99
Osterud, Nancy Gray, **3:**135–136, 137
O'Sullivan, John, *"We Have Just Begun to Not Fight",* **3:227–230**
Osur, Alan M., **3:**249
Ota, Shelley, *Upon Their Shoulders,* **1:**309
Otero Silva, Miguel, **1:**222
O'Toole, Sean, **2:**115
Ottoman Empire
    in Armenian genocide, **3:**40–42
    in Crimean War, **1:**113
    Jewish immigration to China from, **3:**16
    Young Turk Revolution in, **2:**106
Ottway, Sheila, **1:**316–317
Ou, Li, **2:**147

Our Appalachia (Shackelford and Weinberg), **3:**66, **86–89**
Our Nig (Wilson), **1:**142
Our Partnership (Webb), **2:**17, 172
OurStory Scotland, **3:**70
"Our Struggles for Progress" (Luthuli), **1:**25
Our Village (Mitford), **3:**59
Outlook (journal), **1:**50, 51, **3:**119
Out of Darkness (Martin), **3:**40
"Outpost of Progress, An" (Conrad), **2:**192, 194
Outsider literature, *The Cancer Journals* (Lorde) as, **2:**3
Overboe, James, **1:**8
Overland Monthly and Out West Magazine, **2:**127
Owen, Robert Dale, **1:**14
Owen, Wilfred
    "Disabled," **1:**8
    Sassoon (Siegfried) and, **2:**247, 248
Owens Valley, The (Wehrey), **3:**102
Owens Valley (California), oral histories of, **3:**102–104, *103*
Owsley, Beatrice Rodriguez, *The Hispanic-American Entrepreneur,* **3:121–123**
Oxford University, **2:**287
Ozersky, Josh, **1:**188
Oziewicz, Stanley, **3:**301

P

PAC. *See* Pan African Congress
Pace, Michael, **3:**326
Pacheco, José Emilio, **3:**31, 32
Pacific Coast Philology (journal), **1:**93
Pacific Historical Review (journal), **3:**148, 225
Pacific Review (journal), **3:**126
Pacifism. *See also* Conscientious objectors
    of Brittain (Vera), **1:**329–331, **2:**269
    of Kingston (Maxine Hong), **1:**175
    of Partridge (Frances), **2:**268–269

Pacifist's War, A (Partridge), **2:268–270**
Pack, Sam, **3:**320
Packer, George, **2:**322
Pacte autobiographique, Le (Lejeune). *See Autobiographical Pact, The* (Lejeune)
Paderni, Paola, **3:**149
Padilla, Herberto, *Self-Portrait of the Other,* **1:**296
Padilla, Tanalis, **3:**303
Paekpom Ilchi (Kim), **1:322–324**
Page, Thomas Nelson, *Marse Chan,* **2:**250
Pahlavi, Ashraf, *Faces in a Mirror,* **3:**218
Paige, Leroy "Satchel," **1:**247
Paine, Albert Bigelow, **1:**148
Painter, Nell Irvin, **1:**3–4
Paintings, by Bashkirtseff (Marie), **2:**306, *307,* 308
Paiute tribe, **3:**102, 103
Pakistan
    Ahmedi's (Farah) escape from Afghanistan to, **1:**40, 41
    establishment of (1947), **1:**87, 244
    legacy of colonialism in, **1:**87–89
    Suleri (Sara) on life in, **1:**87–89
    U.S. relations with, **1:**87
Pakravan, Fatemeh, *Memoirs of Fatemeh Pakravan,* **3:**218–220
Pakravan, Hassan, **3:**218–220
Pakravan, Saïdeh, **3:**218
Palestine, under British Mandate
    'Amr (Sāmī) on life in, **2:**104–106
    Jewish immigration to, **2:**105, **3:**14
Palestine Broadcasting Service (PBS), **1:**227
Palestine-Israel Journal of Politics, Economics, and Culture, **2:**50
Palestine Liberation Organization (PLO), **2:**50
Palestinian autobiographical writing. *See also specific works and writers*
    by 'Amr (Sāmī), **2:**104–106
    by Darwish (Mahmoud), **1:**255–257
    by Ghazzawi ('Izzat), **2:**50–52
    tradition of, **1:**225–226, **2:**50, 104
    by Tuqan (Fadwa), **1:**225–227

Palestinian–Israeli conflict. *See* Israeli–Palestinian conflict
Palestinian nationalism, **1:**225, 227
Palestinian Notebooks (Bisisu), **2:**50
Palestinian Policeman (Courtney), **2:**104
Palestinian statehood, calls for, **2:**50, 52
Palestinian territories, Israeli occupation of, **1:**225, **2:**50, *51*
Paley, William, *Natural Theology,* **1:**65
Pall Mall Gazette (newspaper), **2:**83
Palmer, Michele, *Witnesses to Nuremberg,* **3:293–295**
Pan African Congress (PAC), **1:**25
Pan-Indian movement, **1:**54
Papago culture, Chona (Maria) on life in, **1:**69, 69–71
Paquet, Sandra, "The Enigma of Arrival," **1:**112–113
Paradise of the Blind (Duong), **1:**335
Paradox, in *In the Presence of Absence* (Darwish), **1:**255, 256
Paranoia, in East Germany, **3:**245
Paretskaya, Anna, **3:**332
Paris (France)
American expatriates in, **2:**101
Gellhorn (Martha) in, **2:**101
nineteenth-century, Goncourts (Jules and Edmond de) on life in, **2:**81–83
Wright's (Richard) move to, **1:**124
Paris, Treaty of (1783), **2:**69
Paris Commune of 1871, **3:**3
Paris France (Stein), **1:**332
Park, Eugene, **1:**324
Parker, Dorothy, **1:**258, **2:**133, 134
Parker, John, **2:**205, 206, 207
Parkins, Ilya, **1:**331
Parkman, Francis, **1:**146
The Oregon Trail, **1:**234
Parks, Rosa, **1:38, 3:45**
and civil rights movement in Detroit, **3:**101
I Am Rosa Parks, **1:**38
Quiet Strength, **1:**38
Rosa Parks: My Story, **1:**19, **37–39**

Parliament, British
in English Civil War (*See* English Civil War)
on women miners, **3:**337
Parliament, European, **3:**292
Parr, Joy, **3:**181
Parr, Katherine, **2:**97, 99
Lamentation of a Sinner, **2:**97
Parrington, Vernon, **2:**213
Parry, David, **1:**183, 184–185
Parry, Edward Abbott, **2:**324, 325
Parsons, Daniel, **2:**256, 257–258
Parsons, Neil, **2:**241
Partido Independiente de Color (PIC), **3:**8
Partido Revolucionario Institucional, **3:**303
Partisan Review (journal), **1:**258, 272
Partridge, Frances, *A Pacifist's War,* **2:268–270,** *269*
Partridge, Ralph, **2:**268, 269
Pascal, Blaise, *Pensées,* **1:**218
Pascal, Roy, **1:**246
Passerini, Luisa, **3:**74, 159, 173
"Passing"
as black, **1:**74
as white, **1:**72
Pass Laws Act of 1952 (South Africa), **1:**24, 25
Patai, Daphne, *Women's Words,* **3:190–192**
Pater, Walter, **1:**264, **2:**183, 184
The Child in the House, **1:**276
Patmore, Coventry, **2:**147
Paton, Alan, *Cry, the Beloved Country,* **1:**27
Patriarchy
Italian Renaissance, **2:**160
in Montenegro, **3:**135, 136, 137
Palestinian, Tuqan's (Fadwa) critique of, **1:**226, 227
Patriotism. *See also* Nationalism
British, of Barnard (Anne), **2:**217, 218, 219
Patterson, David, **2:**24
Paul, Moses, **2:**46
Paula (Allende), **1:**222
Payn, Graham, **2:**152

Payne, Ethel, **3:**199–200
Payne, James Robert, *Multicultural Autobiography,* **1:**247–248
Paz, Octavio, **3:**32
In Light of India, **1:**222–223
PBS. *See* Palestine Broadcasting Service
Peabody Western Coal Company, **3:**11
Peace activists, women, oral histories of, **3:**268–271
Peace Like a River (Enger), **1:**281
Peacework (Adams), **3:268–271**
Peacocks Fly to the Southeast, The, **1:**338
Peake, Cyrus H., *Chinese Missionaries Oral History Collection,* **3:**299
Pearce, Jenny, *Promised Land,* **3:**205–206
Pearl Harbor, Japanese bombing of, **1:**299, 300, 309, **3:**195, 202, 212, 215, 234
Pearlman, Elihu, **2:**73
Pearl of China (Min), **1:**159
Pearse, Patrick, **3:**27
Pearson, Geoffrey, *Hooligan,* **3:**312
Pechonick, Paula Martin, **3:**326
Peckard, Peter, **1:**83
Pedersen, David, **3:**207
Pedro Martinez (Lewis), **3:**31
Pedro Pan, Operation, **1:**298
Peer pressure, *Go Ask Alice* (anonymous) on, **2:**295
Pekar, Harvey
American Splendor, **1:**139, **3:**330
Students for a Democratic Society, **3:**330
Studs Turkel's Working, **3:**330
Pelagius, **1:**196, 198
Peled-Elhanan, Nurit, **2:**50–51
Peltier, Leonard, *Prison Writings,* **1:96–98,** *97*
PEN/Faulkner Award, for *The Barracks Thief* (Wolff), **1:**47
Penn, William, **2:**26, **3:**327
Pennsylvania
Ukraine compared to, **3:**340, 342
women immigrants in, oral histories of, **3:**305–307
Pennsylvania History (journal), **2:**79, **3:**191, 306

Pensées (Pascal), **1:**218
Pepys, Samuel, **2:73**
  Boswell (James) compared to, **2:**328
  The Diary of Samuel Pepys, **2:72–74**, 174, 309, 328
  Evelyn (John) compared to, **2:**65, 66, 72
  on *A True Relation of My Birth, Breeding, and Life* (Cavendish), **1:**230
Percy, Walker, **2:**129
Peregrinationes in Montem Zion (Breidenbach), **2:**227
Perera, Victor
  The Cross and the Pear Tree, **1:**99
  "Guatemala: Always La Violencia," **1:**99
  Rites: A Guatemalan Boyhood, **1:75, 99–101**
  Unfinished Conquest, **1:**99
Perestroika, **3:**17, 331
Perestroika from Below (documentary), **3:**340
Pérez Firmat, Gustavo, *Next Year in Cuba*, **1:**296
Pérez Rosales, Vicente, *Recuerdos del pasado*, **1:**222
Perils of the Soul (Guiteras-Holmes), **3:**167
Perissinotto, Giorgio, **3:**116
Perkins, Charlie, **1:**149
Perks, Robert
  Oral History, Health and Welfare, **3:170–172**
  The Oral History Reader, **3:**173, 178, 179, 181
Perlman, Itzhak, **1:**272
Perloff, Marjorie, **2:**150
Pernicone, Nunzio, *Carlo Tresca*, **3:**5
Perón, Eva, **3:**73, *74*, 75
Perón, Juan, **2:**220, **3:**73, 75
Peronism, **3:**73–75
Perrucci, Robert, **3:**207
Perry, Lorry, **2:**175
Perry, Yaakov, **1:**17
Persecution, of Jews. *See* Holocaust
Persepolis (Satrapi), **1:**139, 141, **155–157**, *156*, 293

Persia
  Lessing (Doris) on life in, **1:**167
  Polo's (Marco) travels in, **1:**106, 107
Persian Gulf War (1991). *See* Gulf War
Persian Sphinx, The (Milani), **3:**218, 219
Persona, Wells (H. G.) on, **1:**252
Personal finances. *See* Finances
Personalist Forum (journal), **1:**183
Personality and Individual Differences (journal), **2:**124
Perspective. *See* Narrative point of view
Petals of Blood (Ngũgĩ), **2:**12
Peters, H. F., **2:**150
Peterson, Andrea, **1:**331
Petilianus, **1:**196
Peyser, Seymour, **3:**293–294
Phaler, Karl, **3:**209
Pham Thanh Cong, **1:336**
Pham Van Xinh, **3:**281
Phelps, Elizabeth Porter, **2:**332
Philadelphia Inquirer (newspaper), **3:**222
Philadelphia Jewish Voice (journal), **3:**16
Philippi, Bernardo, **1:**77
Phillips, Bruce "Utah," **3:**329
Phillips, Richard, **2:**35
Phillips, Wendell, **1:**33
Phillpotts, Eden, **2:**137
Philosophical autobiographies
  The Autobiography of Giambattista Vico (Vico) as, **1:**183–185
  Confessions (Rousseau) as, **1:**200–202
  Journals of Søren Kierkegaard (Kierkegaard) as, **2:**166–168
  Meditations (Marcus Aurelius) as, **1:**218–221
  tradition of, **1:**183–184
Philosophy, natural, **2:**300
Philosophy and Social Criticism (journal), **2:**168
Philosophy East and West (journal), **3:**148
Photography
  in *Coal Hollow* (Light and Light), **3:**66, 67

  in *Long Journey Home* (Brown and Kohn), **3:**326
  in oral history field, **3:**181
  in *Solidarity Forever* (Bird et al.), **3:**329
Phylon (journal), **2:**33
PIC. *See* Partido Independiente de Color
Picasso, Pablo, **1:**332
Picture of Dorian Gray, The (Wilde), **2:**9
Pierce, Franklin, **2:**223
Piercy, Marge, **2:**4
Pif Magazine, **1:**297
Pigafetta, Antonio, *Journal of Magellan's Voyage*, **2:**201
Pignalosa, Giovanni, **3:**159
Pilgrimages
  of Guylforde (Richarde), **2:**226–228
  in Middle Ages, **1:190**, 191, **2:**226
  tradition of narratives of, **2:**198–199, 226
Pilgrim at Tinker Creek (Dillard), **1:**279
Pillow Book, The (Sei), **2:**59, 189, 190, 290
Pine, Frank Woodworth, **1:**181
Pine Ridge Reservation (South Dakota)
  AIM occupation of Wounded Knee at, **1:**21, 22–23, 96
  Peltier (Leonard) in shootout at, **1:**96
Pini, Robert, **1:**115
Pinochet, Augusto, **1:**75, 77, 222, **3:**185
Piper, Jane, **3:**276, 277
Pipino, Francesco, **1:**107
Pitt, William, the Elder, **2:**328
Pitt, William, the Younger, **2:**217
Pitt-Rivers, Julian, **3:**168, 169
Pittsburgh (Pennsylvania)
  Ukraine compared to, **3:**340, 342
  women immigrants in, oral histories of, **3:**305–307
Pittsburgh Courier (newspaper), **3:**248
Pittsfield Free Press, **3:**263
Plaatje, Solomon Tshekisho
  The Boer War Diary of Sol Plaatje, **2:241–243**

Mhudi, **2:**241, 243
Native Life in South Africa, **2:**241, 242, 243
Places of Origin (Edwards and Siebentritt), **3:**205
Plagiarism. *See also* Authorship
    Carver (Jonathan) accused of, **2:**205, 206, 207
    Cereta (Laura) accused of, **2:**160
    by Mahomet (Dean), **2:**229
Plain, Gill, **2:**237
Plassey, Battle of (1757), **2:**229
Plath, Aurelia Schober, **2:**47–49
Plath, Sylvia, **2:**48
    Ariel, **2:**47
    The Bell Jar, **2:**47
    Letters Home, **2:**47–49
    The Unabridged Journals of Sylvia Plath, **2:**49
Plath, Warren, **2:**47
Plato, *Seventh Letter,* **2:**94
Plessy v. Ferguson, **1:**37, 50, 122
Pliny the Elder, **2:**94, 96
Pliny the Younger, *The Letters of the Younger Pliny,* **2:**94–96, 95
PLO. *See* Palestine Liberation Organization
Plöckinger, Othmar, **1:**32
Plotinus, *Enneads,* **1:**196
Plum, Fred, **1:**6
Plumstead, A. W., **2:**215
Plunka, Gene A., **2:**255
PMLA (journal), **1:**147, **2:**63
Poddar, Prem, **3:**143
Poe, Edgar Allan, **2:**42
    Collected Letters, **2:**41
    "Letter to Maria Clemm," **2:**41–43
    "Ligeia," **3:**38
Poe, Neilson, **2:**41–42
Poe, Virginia Clemm, **2:**41–43
Poems on Various Subjects (Wheatley), **2:**44
Poetic style
    of *Black Boy* (Wright), **1:**123
    of *Child of the Dark* (de Jesus), **2:**6, 7

    of *A Cross and a Star* (Agosín), **1:**76
    of *The Dark Child* (Laye), **1:**128, 129
    of *The Journals of Charlotte Forten Grimké* (Grimké), **2:**30
    of *Memoirs* (Neruda), **1:**223
    of *A Mountainous Journey* (Tuqan), **1:**227
    of *Narrative of the Life of Frederick Douglass* (Douglass), **1:**35
    of *The Way to Rainy Mountain* (Momaday), **1:**55
    of *The Writing Life* (Dillard), **1:**280
Poetique (journal), **2:**174
Poetry. *See also specific poets*
    in *Confessions of Lady Nijo* (Nijo), **2:**59, 60
    Japanese *waka,* **2:**189, 191, 292
    in *Letters Underway* (Ghazzawi), **2:**51–52
    in medieval Arab education, **1:**287
    on racism, effects of, **1:**50
    Romantic, **2:**143, 146
    social role of, Neruda (Pablo) on, **1:**222, 223
    in *Ten Thousand Sorrows* (Kim), **1:**103
    in *When I Was Puerto Rican* (Santiago), **1:**108
Point of view. *See* Narrative point of view
Pokagon, Simon, *Queen of the Woods,* **3:**110
Poland
    Jewish immigration to China from, **3:**16
    Russian occupation of, **2:**192
Police, East German. *See* Stasi
Polish American Studies (journal), **3:**307
Polish autobiographical writing, by Conrad (Joseph), **2:**192–194
Politeness, in letter writing, **2:**217
Political activism
    of Douglass (Frederick), **1:**34, 35
    of Kingston (Maxine Hong), **1:**175
    of Soyinka (Wole), **1:**214

Political autobiography, *Dreams from My Father* (Obama) as, **1:**78–80
Political development
    of Guevara (Ernesto "Che"), **2:**220–222
    of Lu Xun, **2:**170–172
Political parties. *See specific parties*
Politics and Irish Life (Fitzpatrick), **3:**27
Politics of AIDS Denialism, The (Fourie and Meyer), **3:**272
Polk County (Hurston), **1:**10
Pollard, Edward, **2:**39
Pollin, Burton R., **2:**41, 42
Pollitt, Katha, **2:**124
Polner, Murray, **3:**16
Polo, Marco, *The Travels of Marco Polo,* **1:**105–107, 106, **2:**198, 201
Pol Pot, **1:**306
Pommelier, Alfred, **3:**344
Pompeii, destruction of, **2:**94, 95
Poniatowska, Elena, **3:**32
    Here's to You, Jesus, **3:**32
    Massacre in Mexico, **3:**31–33
Poole, Elijah. *See* Muhammad, Elijah
Pooley, William V., **2:**92
Poor Bear, Myrtle, **1:**97
Poore, Charles, **1:**259
Poor Man's Son, The (Feraoun), **2:**262, 263, 264
Poor Richard's Almanac (Franklin), **2:**88
Pope, Alexander, **2:**146, 217, 328
Popkin, Jeremy D., **2:**174, 175
Popular culture
    Boswell (James) in, **2:**328
    Byron (George Gordon Noel) in, **2:**145
    Darwin (Charles) in, **1:**67
    Guevara (Ernesto "Che") in, **2:**221
Popular Memory Group, "Popular Memory: Theory, Politics, Method," **3:**176–178
"Popular Memory: Theory, Politics, Method" (Popular Memory Group), **3:**176–178
Popular Movements and Political Change in Mexico (Craig), **3:**302
Pork Rind and Cuban Songs (Medina), **1:**296
Porte, Joel, **2:**140

Portelli, Alessandro
    The Battle of Valle Giula, **3:**97, 157
    The Death of Luigi Trastulli, **3:**96, **157–160**
    in field of oral history, **3:**159, 173
    I Can Almost See the Lights of Home, **3:**265–266
    The Order Has Been Carried Out, **3:**158, **265–267**
    They Say in Harlan County, **3:**87, **96–98,** 158
Porter, Jay, *Fighting Words,* **1:**97
Porter, Katherine Anne, **2:**152
Porter, Tracey, *Treasures in the Dust,* **1:**161
Porterfield, Amanda, **3:**112
Portrait of a Lady, The (James), **1:**133, **2:**113
Portrait of the Artist as a Young Man (Joyce), **1:**276, **2:**126
Portraits in Steel (Frisch), **3:**181
Port Royal Experiment, **2:**29–31
Portugal
    colonial power of, origins of, **2:**198
    Gama's (Vasco da) exploration for, **2:**198–200
    national identity of, **2:**199–200
Portuguese Studies (journal), **2:**200
Positions Asia Critique (journal), **1:**336
Positions: East Asia Cultures Critique (journal), **2:**292
Posner, Jerome B., **1:**6
Possession (Byatt), **2:**77
Postcolonial identity, **1:**87–89
Postcolonialism
    in *Meatless Days* (Suleri), **1:**87–89
    Orwell (George) in, **2:**119
Postcolonial studies
    The Boer War Diary of Sol Plaatje (Plaatje) in, **2:**243
    The Letters of Lady Anne Barnard to Henry Dundas (Barnard) in, **2:**218–219
    Memoirs of an Arabian Princess from Zanzibar (Ruete) in, **1:**90–91
    My Life Story (Amrouche) in, **1:**94
    The Unwanted (Nguyen) in, **1:**172
    The Wonderful Adventures of Mrs. Seacole (Seacole) in, **1:**112

Postman, Neil, **3:**119
Postmodern, origins of term, **1:**167
Postmodern autobiography
    Dreams from My Father (Obama) as, **1:**79
    Meatless Days (Suleri) as, **1:**87–89
    Under My Skin (Lessing) as, **1:**167–169
    The Woman Warrior (Kingston) as, **1:**173, 174
Postmodernism
    Kierkegaard's (Søren) influence on, **2:**167
    origins and rise of, **1:**167
    self in, **1:**167
    truth in, **1:**168
Poststructuralism, **1:**267
Potawatomi tribe, **3:**110
Potter, Hillary, **3:**122
Potter, Martha Beatrice. *See* Webb, Beatrice
Potter, Tiffany, **1:**327–328
Pottle, Frederick, **2:**328
Pound, Ezra, **2:**126
Poverty
    difficulty of defining, **3:**255
    primary, **3:**53
Poverty, in Britain
    in English villages, **3:**59
    McCourt (Frank) on, **1:**119–121
    in Victorian era, **2:**16
    among working class, **3:**53
Poverty, in Latin America
    in Brazil, de Jesus (Carolina Maria) on, **2:**6–8
    in Guatemala, Menchú (Rigoberta) on, **3:**164–165
    Guevara (Ernesto "Che") on, **2:**220–221
Poverty, in U.S.
    among coal miners, **3:**66, 67
    war on, oral histories of, **3:**254–256
    Wright (Richard) on, **1:**122
Powell, Enoch, **3:**186
Powell, Malea, **3:**109
Powers, Lyall H., **2:**113, 115
Powers, William, **3:**111–112

Powwows, **3:108**
Pozas, Ricardo, *Juan the Chamula,* **3:167–169**
Pozzetta, George, **3:**225
"Practice of the Private Journal" (Lejeune), **2:174–176**
Praeterita (Ruskin), **1:264–266**
Pragmatism, of Washington (Booker T.), **1:**51, 52
Prague (Czechoslovakia), Kafka (Franz) on life in, **2:**120–122
Prague Spring (1968), **3:**33
Pran, Dith, *Children's of Cambodia's Killing Fields,* **1:**306
Pratt, Mary Louise, **3:**166
Pratt, Richard Henry, **3:**109
Preciado Martin, Patricia
    Beloved Land, **3:**131
    Images and Conversations, **3:**121
    Songs My Mother Sang to Me, **3:131–134,** 302
Preece, Harold, **1:**10
Prejudice. *See also* Anti-Semitism; Racism
    against homosexuality, **1:**139
Prelude, The (Wordsworth), **1:**201, 264, **2:**302
Prendergast, Christopher, **1:**268–269
Prescott, Orville, **1:**271
Presidential elections, U.S.
    of 1860, **3:**261
    of 1992, **3:**221
Presidential oral histories
    of Johnson (Lyndon Baines), **3:**254–256
    of Lincoln (Abraham), **3:**261–264
    tradition of, **3:**254
Presidential Studies Quarterly, **2:**33, **3:**263
Presidios, of California, **3:**114–116
Press coverage. *See* Journalism; War correspondents
Prester John's Letter on the Wonders of India, **1:**105
Pretty-Shield (Linderman), **1:**70
Pride, cultural, of Woodland Indians, **3:**108, 109
Priestley, J. B., **2:**137
Primary poverty, **3:**53

"Primitive" mind, theories of, **3**:37
Primm, Alex T., **3**:326
Prince, Mary, *The History of Mary Prince*, **1**:111, 113, **3**:23–26
Prince, Nancy, *Narrative of the Life and Travels of Mrs. Nancy Prince*, **3**:24
Principle Navigations, Voiages, Traffiques and Discoveries of the English Nation, The (Hakluyt), **2**:229
Principles of Geology (Lyell), **1**:65
Pringle, Thomas, **3**:23, 24–25
Printz, Mike, **3**:225
Prisk, Court, *El Salvador at War*, **3**:205–208
Prison. *See* Imprisonment
Prison narratives, Arabic tradition of, **2**:50. *See also specific works*
Prison Writings (Peltier), **1**:96–98
Pritchard, William, **1**:168
Pritchett, V. S., **3**:60
Privacy
    of diaries, as defining characteristic, **2**:174
    under East German Stasi, **3**:245
    James's (Henry) concern with, **2**:114, 115
    of Kierkegaard (Søren), violation of, **2**:166, 167
    in *Letters between Two* (Lu and Xu), **2**:171
    Maugham's (W. Somerset) concern with, **2**:183, 185
Private Journal of Aaron Burr, The (Burr), **2**:88
Private Mary Chesnut, The (Chesnut), **2**:250
Prix Européen de l'Essai Charles Veillon, Le, for *The Dark Child* (Laye), **1**:128
Prix Goncourt, establishment of, **2**:82
Profiling, racial, **3**:195, 197
Progoff, Ira, **2**:123
Progress
    industrialization in Keats's (John) concept of, **2**:146
    national, Emerson (Ralph Waldo) on, **2**:139, 140
Prohibition, in Idaho, **3**:95

Prohibition of Mixed Marriages Act of 1949 (South Africa), **1**:27
Project Gen, **1**:294
Proletarian Cultural Revolution. *See* Cultural Revolution
Promised Land (Pearce), **3**:205–206
Propaganda
    British, in World War II, **2**:270
    in Cultural Revolution of China, **1**:158, 159, *162*
    Orwell (George) on, **2**:117, 118
    Soviet, in World War II, **2**:282
    in Vietnam, **1**:171
Proposition 209 (California), **3**:20
Prose, Francine, **2**:231, 339, 340
Protection of State Information Bill (South Africa), **1**:29
Protestantism. *See also specific types*
    origins of, **1**:211
    rise of, in England, **2**:97–99
Protestant Reformation, **1**:211, **2**:72, 166
Protocols of the Elder of Zion, The, **1**:32
Proust, Marcel
    In Search of Lost Time, **1**:265, 270
    and *Speak, Memory* (Nabokov), **1**:272
Prouty, Olive Higgins, **2**:47
Psalms, book of, **1**:196, 198
Pseudonyms
    Bugul (Ken) as, **1**:61, 62
    Twain (Mark) as, **1**:146, 147
Psychoanalysis
    Nin's (Anaïs) experience with, **2**:123
    and rise of diaries, **2**:120
Public Historian (journal), **3**:68, 97
Publishers Weekly
    on *Barefoot Gen* (Nakazawa), **1**:294
    on *Bone Black* (hooks), **1**:250
    on *Carrier Warfare in the Pacific* (Wooldridge), **3**:203
    on *Growing Up Jewish in America* (Frommer and Frommer), **3**:119
    on *In the Cities of the South* (Seabrook), **3**:54

    on *Red Scarf Girl* (Jiang), **1**:161, 162
    on *A Stranger's Supper* (Milich), **3**:136
    on *A Woman at War* (Moore), **2**:279
    on *Zlata's Diary* (Filipovic), **2**:339
Puck (magazine), **3**:4
Puerto Rico
    Santiago (Esmeralda) on life in, **1**:108–110
    Spanish colonial rule of, **1**:108
    as U.S. territory, **1**:108
Pulitzer Prize
    for *Angela's Ashes* (McCourt), **1**:120
    for *The Confessions of Nat Turner* (Styron), **1**:204
    for *The Education of Henry Adams* (Adams), **1**:132, 134
    for "The Good War" (Terkel), **3**:161, 212, 234, 279, 343
    for *House Made of Dawn* (Momaday), **1**:54
    for *Maus* (Spiegelman), **1**:293
    for *A Midwife's Tale* (Ulrich), **2**:331
    for *Pilgrim at Tinker Creek* (Dillard), **1**:279
    for *Roots* (Haley), **1**:261
Puritanism
    in Britain, **2**:72, 74
    in U.S., **1**:325–327
Purves, Bill, **3**:16
Pushkin, Aleksandr, **2**:143
Pylgrymage of Sir Richarde Guylforde, The (Guylforde), **2**:226–228
Pynson, Richard, **2**:227

Q

Qa'ida, al-, **2**:275
Qasim, Samih al-, **1**:225
Qawuqji, Fawzi al-, **2**:104
Qing dynasty (China), **3**:147
Qiu Jin, **1**:152
Quade, Penelope, **1**:253
Quadriplegia, **1**:6–8

SUBJECT INDEX

Quakerism
    conscientious objection in, **3**:223, 227
    of Fox (George), **2**:26–28
    of Leadbeater (Mary), **2**:157–159
    origins of, **2**:26–28, 157
    persecution of, **2**:26–28
    women's role in, **2**:28, 157
Quan, Adan, **2**:221
Quarterly Journal of Speech, **2**:33
Quarterly Review, **2**:309, 314
Queen of the Woods (Pokagon), **3**:110
Queer studies
    Daring Hearts (Brighton Ourstory) in, **3**:70
    Fun Home (Bechdel) in, **1**:141
    Hunger of Memory (Rodriguez) in, **1**:17
    A Long Way from Home (McKay) in, **1**:85
Querelle de femmes, **2**:160
Quiche tribe, **3**:164, 165
Quiet Strength (Parks), **1**:38
Quigley, Kathy, **3**:309
Quinn, Arthur Hobson, **2**:42
Quintilian, **2**:95
Quintus, **2**:94
Quinzaine litteraire (journal), **1**:267
Quite Early One Morning (Thomas), **1**:125
Quit India movement, **1**:291
Qur'an, Hussein's (Taha) study of, **1**:135, 136

R

Rabe, John, *The Good Man of Nanking,* **2**:19–21, *20*
Rabelais, Kevin, **1**:48
Rabin, Yitzhak, **2**:50
Rabinowitz, Dorothy, **1**:300
Race
    development of concept of, **2**:200
    in education, Rodriguez (Richard) on, **1**:15–16
    sociology of, Du Bois (W. E. B.) on, **1**:5

Race relations, in U.S.
    Du Bois (W. E. B.) on, **1**:3–5
    Hurston (Zora Neale) on, **1**:9
    in military, in Vietnam War era, **3**:199–201
    in Reconstruction era, **1**:50–52
    Washington (Booker T.) on, **1**:50–52
Race riots
    in Chicago, **3**:45
    in Detroit, **3**:99, 100, *100,* 101
Racial consciousness, Du Bois (W. E. B.) in advancement of, **1**:4
Racial equality
    Communist Party on, **1**:84
    Washington (Booker T.) on, **1**:50, 51
Racial identity. *See* African American identity; Multicultural and multiracial identities
Racial oppression, Angelou (Maya) on, **1**:18
Racial profiling, of Arab and Muslim Americans, **3**:195, 197
Racial purity
    in Korea, **1**:102
    in Vietnam, **1**:170
Racial quotas, in U.S. higher education, **3**:20
Racial segregation, in South Africa. *See* Apartheid
Racial segregation, in U.S.
    de jure vs. *de facto,* **3**:20
    in Detroit, oral histories of, **3**:99–100
    in higher education, **3**:20
    hooks (bell) on end of, **1**:249
    institutionalization of, **1**:37, 50, 122, **3**:44
    in military, end of, **3**:199, 248, 249
    in North vs. South, **3**:250
    Parks (Rosa) on experience of, **1**:37–39
    in schools, end of, **1**:122, 249, **3**:44
    Supreme Court on, **1**:37, 50, 122, 249, **3**:44
    Wright (Richard) on experience of, **1**:122–124, *123*

Racial tropes, in *Dreams from My Father* (Obama), **1**:80
Racism
    in Australia, against Aborigines, **1**:149
    in Britain, **2**:230
    in Chile, against Jews, **1**:75–77
    in Korea, against multiracial individuals, **1**:102
    in South Africa, under apartheid, **1**:24–26, 27–29
    in Vietnam, against multiracial individuals, **1**:170, 171
Racism, in U.S.
    Angelou (Maya) on experience of, **1**:18–19
    Du Bois (W. E. B.) on pervasiveness of, **1**:3–5
    gradualist approach to, King (Martin Luther, Jr.) on, **2**:32–33
    Hansberry (Lorraine) on experience of, **1**:273
    in higher education, oral histories of, **3**:20–22
    hooks (bell) on experience of, **1**:249–250
    against Italian Americans, **3**:224–226
    against Japanese Americans, **1**:309, **3**:81, 82, 127, 195
    against Korean Americans, **1**:103
    Malcolm X on experience of, **1**:186–187
    in military, **3**:44, 199–201, 248–250
    in national security policy, **3**:195, 197
    against Native Americans, **1**:96
    in North vs. South, **1**:122
    Parks (Rosa) on experience of, **1**:37–39
    in Peltier's (Leonard) trial, **1**:96
    in Reconstruction era, **1**:50
    against Vietnamese Americans, **1**:171
    Wright (Richard) on experience of, **1**:122–124
Radar, development of, **3**:202
Radcliffe College, **1**:43
Radhakrishnan, S., **1**:244

Radiance of the King, The (Laye), **1:**128
Radicalism, in U.S., history of, **3:**328–329
Radin, Paul, *Crashing Thunder,* **3:**318
Radio broadcasts, of Thomas (Dylan), **1:**125, 126
Raftery, Judith, **3:**307
Rahv, Philip, **1:**260
Railroads, U.S.
    expansion of, **1:**233
    racial segregation in, **3:**250
Rainbow, Edward, **2:**63
Raines, Edgar F., Jr., **3:**229
Raisin in the Sun, A (Hansberry), **1:**273, 274, 275
Rak, Julie, **1:**248, **2:**174, 175
Raleigh, Donald J.
    Russia's Sputnik Generation, **3:**331, 332, 333
    Soviet Baby Boomers, **3:331–333**
Ramey, Delphia, **3:**87
Ramose, Mogobe B., **3:**253
Ramsdell, Lea, **1:**17
Ramsey, Roger, **1:**165
Ramsland, John, **1:**150
Ranching, in U.S. West, **2:**91–93
Rancour-Laferriere, Daniel, **1:**195
Randolph, A. Philip, **3:**248
Rank, Otto, **2:**123
Rank and File: Histories of Working Class Organizers (Lynd and Lynd), **3:**179
Raoul, Valerie, **1:**7, **2:**307
Rape
    in *I Know Why the Caged Bird Sings* (Angelou), **1:**18, 19
    in *A Woman in Berlin* (anonymous), **2:**281–282
    in World War II, **2:**281–283
Raphael, Jody, **2:**282
Rappaport, Helen, **2:**210
Rasputin, Grigori, **2:**85, 86
Ratele, Kopano, *There Was This Goat,* **3:**242
Rationalism
    Cartesian, **1:**183, 184
    Kierkegaard's (Søren) critique of, **2:**166, 167
Rauff, Walter, **1:**77

Rauwerda, A. M., **3:**25
Ravel, Maurice, **2:**137
Ravenstein, Ernest, **2:**199
Rawick, George P., *The American Slave,* **1:**35
Rawlings, Claude, **1:**166
Ray, Annie, **2:**163–165
Ray, Charles, **2:**163, 164
Ray, Sangeeta, **1:**88
Raynaud, Claudine, **1:**9, 11
Rayson, Ann, **1:**300–301
Razor's Edge, The (Maugham), **2:**185
Read, Florence, **1:**4
Read, J., *Speaking Our Minds,* **3:**170
Reading Lolita in Tehran (Nafisi), **1:**155, 157, 209
Reagan, Ronald, **1:**37, 311, **2:**32–33
Realism
    in American literature, rise of, **2:**240
    in depictions of war, **2:**240
Recession, agricultural, in Britain, **3:**59, 61
Reconstruction era, **1:**50–52, **2:**238, 252
Records of a Girlhood (Kemble), **2:335–337**
Recuerdos del pasado (Pérez Rosales), **1:**222
Red Air Fighter, The (Richthofen), **1:**30
Red Azalea (Min), **1:158–160**
Red Buffalo (journal), **3:**162, 179
Redford, Rachel, **1:**80
Red Guards (China), **1:**158, 161, **3:**287, 288, 289
Red Lantern, The (opera), **1:**159
Redman, Ben Ray, **1:**333
Red Man's Religion (Underhill), **1:**70
Red Mirror, The (Wen), **3:**287
Redmond, Lucille, **2:**159, **3:**316
Red Power movement, **1:**21
Red Scarf Girl (Jiang), **1:**153, 154, 159, **161–163**
Reed, Matt, **1:**272
Reel, A. Frank, **3:**294
Reese, Florence, **3:**98
Reeves, Amber, **1:**254
Reeves, Ambrose, **1:**25

Reformation. *See* Protestant Reformation
Refugees
    Jewish, **1:**75–77, **3:**14–16
    Southeast Asian, **1:**306–307, 337
Regard, Frédéric, **1:**240
Regents of the University of California v. Bakke, **3:**20
Region (journal), **3:**332
Reich-Ranicki, Marcel, **2:**304
Reidy, Joseph, **3:**200–201
Reitell, Elizabeth, **1:**127
Relief of Mafeking, The (Young), **2:**241
Religion. *See also specific religions*
    in abolitionist movement, **1:**142
    in conscientious objection, **3:**221, 223, 227, 228
    theological certainty in, Robinson (Henry Crabb) on, **2:**76
    tradition of autobiographies of, **1:**193, 211
    women's roles in, Stanton (Elizabeth Cady) on, **1:**12
Religious faith
    Darwin's (Charles) loss of, **1:**65–67
    struggles with, in literary autobiographies, **2:**26
    Wiesel's (Elie) loss of, **1:**319–320
Religious Life in a New Millennium (Schneiders), **3:**308
Relocation law (Public Law 93–531), **3:**11
Remembering Pearl Harbor (La Forte and Marcello), **3:**202
Remembrance
    Clifford (Anne) on, **2:**62, 63
    Wiesel (Elie) on, **1:**318
"Remembrance of Things Pakistani" (Gates), **1:**88
Rementer, James A., **3:**325, 326
Remini, Robert V., **2:**71
Renaissance
    English monarchy in, **2:**97–99
    origins of autobiography in, **1:**239
    rise of diaries in, **2:**120
    women's role in, **2:**160–162
Renard, Jules, *The Journal of Jules Renard,* **2:**183

Reparations
  for Japanese American internment, **3:**195, 197
  for World War I, **1:**30
Reporter (journal), **1:**320
Report from a Chinese Village (Myrdal), **3:**299
Report of the Departmental Committee on Homosexual Offences and Prostitution (1957), **3:**70
Rerhaye, Narjis, *Femmes et Politique,* **3:**47
Research in African Literatures (journal), **1:**215, **2:**14, 263, **3:**253
Reservations. *See* Native American reservations
"Resistance to Civil Government" (Thoreau), **1:**242
Rest for Travelers (Bioy Casares), **1:**223
Restoration (England), **2:**65, 72, 73
Restoration and 18th Century Theatre Research (journal), **2:**337
Restored Selves (Kumashiro), **3:**83
Retractions (Augustine), **1:**196, 198
Return to Nisa (Shostak), **3:**38
Reuss, Richard A., **3:**91
Revelli, Nuto, *The World of the Defeated,* **3:**61
Reverdy, Pierre, **1:**223
Reveries of the Solitary Walker (Rousseau), **1:**200
Reveries over Childhood and Youth (Yeats), **2:**126, 127
Review of Contemporary Fiction (journal), **1:**256
Review of English Studies (journal), **2:**77
Review of Religious Research (journal), **3:**309
Reviews in American History (journal), **3:**4, 87, 116
Revolutionary Democratic Front (FDR), **3:**205
Revolutionary United Front (RUF), **1:**312
Revolutionary War, American. *See* American Revolutionary War
Revoyr, Nina, *Southland,* **1:**309
Reynolds, Dwight F., *Interpreting the Self,* **1:**136, 137, 286, 287
Reynolds, Harriet, **2:**224

Reynolds, J., *Speaking Our Minds,* **3:**170
Reynolds, John Hamilton, **2:**146
Reynolds, William James, **2:**224
Rhee, Syngman, **1:**323, 324
Rhetoric, of Augustine, **1:**198
Rhetoric of English India, The (Suleri), **1:**87–88
Rhetoric Review (journal), **2:**30
Rhodes, Cecil, **1:**218, **3:**251
Rhodes, James, **1:**297
Rhodes, Richard, **3:**162, 241
Rhodesia
  British colonial rule of, **1:**167, **3:**251–253
  Lessing (Doris) on life in, **1:**167
Rhodesia (Mlambo), **3:**251
Rhys, Jean, **1:**111
Ribière, Mireille, **1:**269
Rice, Howard C., **2:**215
Rice, Judith A., **3:**261, 263
Rice, Julian, **1:**23
Rice bars, **3:**83, 84
Rich, Adrienne, **2:**3
Rich, Elizabeth, **1:**98
Richard III (king of England), **2:**228
Richards, Cynthia D., **2:**111
Richardson, Bob, **1:**279–280
Richardson, Dorothy, **2:**123
Richardson, Jonathan, **2:36**
Richardson, Karl Spence, **2:**163
Richardson, Robert D., **2:**141
Richardson, Samuel, **2:**328
  Clarissa, **2:**301
Richardson, Sue, **2:**271
Richlin, Amy, **1:**220
Richthofen, Manfred von, *The Red Air Fighter,* **1:**30
Rick, Dorothy, **3:**5
Rickard, W., **3:**273
Ricosti, Neide, **2:**8
Rida, Rashid, **1:**136
Ridley, Glynis, **2:**67
Rieff, Davic, **2:**340
Riegle, Rosalie, *Doing Time for Peace,* **3:**229
Riesco, Laura, **1:**76

Rife, Flora, **3:**87
Rigaur, Gerd, **2:304**
Rightist movements, Hitler's (Adolf) influence on, **1:**30, 32
Right-wing dictators, Latin American, rise of, **3:**185
Rigney, Anne, **2:**311
Rilke, Rainer Maria, **2:150**
  An Interrupted Life (Hillesum) on, **2:**22
  Letters of Rainer Maria Rilke, **2:**150
  Letters on God and Letters to a Young Woman, **2:**149
  Letters to a Young Poet, **2:149–151**
  Notebooks (Williams) on, **2:**152
Rilke, Ruth, **2:**149
Rime of the Ancient Mariner, The (Coleridge), **3:**183
Rinehart, Melissa, *Contested Territories,* **3:**326
Ringelheim, Joan, **3:**35–36
Ripley, George, **1:**235
Ripley, Sophia, **1:**235
Ritchie, Donald
  on *Between Management and Labor* (Friedman), **3:**155
  Doing Oral History, **3:**186, 294, 345
  on *Head of the Class* (Morris), **3:**21
  on *Witnesses to Nuremberg* (Stave et al.), **3:**294
Rites: A Guatemalan Boyhood (Perera), **1:**75, **99–101**
Ritter, Evelyn J., **3:**107
Rittner, Carol, *Different Voices,* **3:**34
Ritts, Morton, **3:**120
Ritualism, Chinese, **3:**124, 125
Rivas, Gladys C., **3:**207
Rive, Richard, *Writing Black,* **1:**25
Rivera, José, **2:**220
Riverbend
  Baghdad Burning, **2:**275
  Baghdad Burning II, **2:**275
River Runs through It, A (McLean), **1:**281
Rivers, W. H. R., **2:**248
Riwan ou le chemin de sable (Bugul), **1:**61, 64

Roach, John, **3**:250

Road to Wigan Pier, The (Orwell), **2**:117, **3**:66

Robbins, Amy Catherine, **1**:254

Roberts, Adam, **2**:33

Roberts, David, **1**:302, 304

Roberts, Elizabeth
    in *Oral History, Health and Welfare* (Bornat et al.), **3**:171
    in origins of oral history, **3**:64
    A Woman's Place, **3**:144, 145, 146
    Women and Families, **3**:144–146

Roberts, Nesta, **3**:54

Roberts, Rosemary, **3**:124, 125

Roberts, Sasha, **2**:325

Robeson, Paul, **1**:273
    Here I Stand, **1**:37

Robideau, Bob, **1**:96

Robin, Diana, **2**:160

Robinson, A. M. Lewin, **2**:217

Robinson, Amy, **1**:113

Robinson, Henry Crabb, *Diary, Reminiscences and Correspondence of Henry Crabb Robinson*, **2**:75–77

Robinson, Jo Ann Gibson, **1**:37

Robinson, Jo Ann O., **3**:223

Robinson Crusoe (Defoe), **3**:183

Robles, Emmanuel, **2**:262, 263

Rock Burst (Russell), **3**:93, 95

Rocking the Boat (O'Farrell and Kornbluh), **3**:337

Rocky Mountain Review (journal), **2**:153

Roderick Hudson (James), **2**:114

Rodier, Katharine, **2**:31

Rodin, Auguste, **2**:149

Rodina, Nina Ivanovna, **3**:18

Rodríguez, Andrés, **2**:146, 147

Rodriguez, Richard, *Hunger of Memory*, **1**:15–17, 47

Rodriguez, Spain, *Che: A Graphic Biography*, **3**:330

Roessel, Monty, **3**:291

Roett, Riordan, *Dialogue and Armed Conflict*, **3**:205

Rogers, Byron, **2**:102

Rogers, Carole Garibaldi, *Habits of Change*, **3**:308–310

Rogers, Katharine, **2**:37

Rogers, Robert, **2**:205, 207

Rogers, Seth, **2**:31

Rogovin, Milton, **3**:181

Rohlmann, Monika, **3**:140

Rohrbach, Augusta, **2**:252

Rohter, Larry, **2**:220

Rojas Pinilla, Gustavo, **3**:183, 184, 185

Roland Barthes (Barthes), **1**:249, 267–269

Roldán, María, **3**:73–75

Rolle, Andrew, **3**:225

Rollins, Edwin, **1**:39

Roman autobiographical writing
    by Augustine, **1**:196–198
    by Marcus Aurelius, **1**:218–221
    by Pliny the Younger, **2**:94–96

Roman Empire, under Marcus Aurelius, **1**:218–221

Romanov dynasty (Russia), **2**:84–86

Romanticism
    Byron (George Gordon Noel) in, **2**:143
    D'Israeli's (Isaac) influence on, **2**:179
    egotism in, **2**:177, 179
    German, **2**:76
    Keats (John) in, **2**:146
    surge of autobiographies in era of, **2**:16, 177

Romantic relationships
    in *An Interrupted Life* (Hillesum), **2**:22, 24
    of Wells (H. G.), **1**:252, 253, 254

Romantic Review (journal), **2**:175

Rome, ancient
    under Marcus Aurelius, **1**:218–221
    Pliny the Younger on history of, **2**:94–96
    slavery in, **2**:96

Rome (Italy), Fosse Ardeatine massacre in, **3**:265–267

Romero, Mary, *The Maid's Daughter*, **1**:108

Rooke, Tetz, **1**:255, 256, 257

Roosevelt, Eleanor, **2**:101, 103, 254, **3**:248

Roosevelt, Franklin D.
    African American votes for, **3**:44
    Great Depression and, **3**:161, 212
    Italian American relocation under, **3**:224–226
    Japanese American internment under, **1**:299, 309, 311, **3**:104, 195
    labor arbitration under, **3**:153
    Manhattan Project under, **3**:239
    on Morgenthau Plan, **3**:293
    racism in military under, **3**:44, 248

Roosevelt, Kermit, **2**:220

Roosevelt, Theodore
    Geronimo and, **1**:302, 304
    in Japan-Russia Treaty of Peace, **3**:234
    Through the Brazilian Wilderness, **2**:220

Roots (Haley), **1**:18, 78, 261–263

Roque Ramirez, Horatio, **3**:85

Rosa Parks: My Story (Parks and Haskins), **1**:19, 37–39

Roscoe, Adrian, **3**:252–253

Rose, Ellen Cronon, **1**:169

Rose, Jacqueline, **2**:49

Rose, Mary Beth, **1**:231

Rose, Michael E., **3**:145

Roseberry, William, **3**:324

Rose Hill (Wolcott), **3**:86

Roseman, Mark, **3**:35

Rosen, Edgar, **2**:17

Rosenbaum, Arthur L., *Chinese Missionaries Oral History Collection*, **3**:299

Rosenfeld, Maya, **2**:52

Rosengarten, Theodore, *All God's Dangers*, **3**:73, 179

Rosenthal, Anton, **3**:329

Rosenwald, Lawrence Alan, **2**:140, 141

Rosianus Geminus, **2**:96

Rosie the Riveter Revisited (Gluck), **3**:224

Ross, David, **3**:209, 210

Ross, Ellen, **3**:145

Ross, James, *Caught in a Tornado*, **3**:287

Ross, Robert, **2**:9, 10

Ross, Sarah Gwyneth, **2**:160

SUBJECT INDEX

Roth, John, *Different Voices,* **3:**34
Rothchild, Sylvia, *Voices of the Holocaust,* **3:**50
Rotkirch, Anna, *Living through the Soviet System,* **3:**331
Roughing It (Twain), **1:**146
Rouse, David, **3:**155
Rousseau, Jean-Jacques, **1:201**
    Boswell (James) and, **2:**329
    Confessions, **1:**193, 197, **200–203,** 276
    Dialogues, **1:**200
    Laye (Camara) compared to, on childhood, **1:**128
    Olney (James) on, **1:**248
    Reveries of the Solitary Walker, **1:**200
    U.S. anarchists influenced by, **3:**3
Rowe, John Carlos, **1:**133, 134
Rowlandson, Mary, *The Sovereignty and Goodness of God,* **1:**81, **325–328,** **3:**24
Rowlatt Acts of 1919 (Britain), **1:**242, 289
Rowley, Hazel, **1:**124
Rowley, Susan, *Uqalurait,* **3:**107, **138–140**
Rowntree, Seebohm, **3:**53
Roy, Arundhati, *The God of Small Things,* **1:**87
Royal Literary Fund, **2:**207
Royal Society, **2:**65
RPF. *See* Rwandan Patriotic Front
Ruark, Robert, **2:**12
Ruch, Barbara, **2:**61
Rudnytsky, P., **1:**247
Ruete, Emily, *Memoirs of an Arabian Princess from Zanzibar,* **1:90–92**
Ruete, Rudolph Heinrich, **1:**90
RUF. *See* Revolutionary United Front
Ruiz, Vicki L., **3:**303
Rule and Exercises of Holy Living and Dying (Taylor), **2:**195
"Rule of taste," **2:**189
Rumor of War, A (Caputo), **3:**209
Running in the Family (Ondaatje), **1:**88
Rupert, Harry Cramer, **2:**93
Ruppin, Arthur, *Arthur Ruppin,* **2:**104

Rural England
    depopulation of, **3:**59
    oral histories of life in, **3:**59–61, 63–65
Rural Ireland, oral histories of life in, **3:**315–317, *316*
Rural women, tradition of oral histories of, **3:**135–136
Rush, Benjamin, *Autobiography of Benjamin Rush,* **1:**179–180
Rush, Norman, **1:**63
Rushdie, Salman
    fatwa against, **1:**155
    on *Infidel* (Hirsi Ali), **1:**207
    Midnight's Children, **1:**87
    Shame, **1:**87
    Suleri (Sue) and, **1:**88
Rusk, Dean, **3:**279
Ruskin, John, **1:**265
    Fors Clavigera, **1:**264
    Modern Painters, **1:**264
    Praeterita, **1:264–266**
    Unto This Last, **1:**242
    The Works of John Ruskin, **1:**265
Ruskin, John James, **1:**264
Ruskin, Margaret (Cock), **1:**264
Russell, Bert
    Calked Boots and Other Northwest Writings, **3:**93
    Hardships and Happy Times, **3:**93
    North Fork of the Coeur d'Alene River, **3:**93
    Rock Burst, **3:**93, 95
    The Sawdust Dream, **3:**93
    Swiftwater People, **3:93–95**
Russell, George, **2:**126, 128
Russell, Marie, **3:**93, 95
Russia. *See also* Soviet Union
    Alexandra Feodorovna on life in, **2:**84–86
    autobiographical tradition of, **1:**270
    Bolshevik Revolution in, **2:**84, **3:**331
    censorship in, **1:**193, 194
    communism in, establishment of, **1:**270
    February Revolution in, **2:**84

    Great Reforms in, **1:**193
    Jewish immigration to China from, **3:**16
    liberalism in, rise of, **1:**193
    Maugham's (W. Somerset) travels in, **2:**183, 184
    Nabokov (Vladimir) on life in, **1:**270–272
    October Revolution in, **1:**270
    Poland occupied by, **2:**192
    Revolution of 1917 in, **1:**270
    Romanov dynasty in, end of, **2:**84–86
    in Russo–Japanese War, **1:**322
    Tolstoy (Leo) on life in, **1:**193–195
Russian Americans, Nabokov (Vladimir) as, **1:**270–272
Russian Orthodox Church, **1:**193, 194
Russian Review (journal), **3:**285, 333
Russian Revolution (1917), **1:**270
Russian Thought (journal), **1:**194
Russia's Sputnik Generation (Raleigh), **3:**331, 332, 333
Russo–Japanese War (1904–1905), **1:**322, **3:**234
Rustichiello of Pisa, **1:**105, **2:**201
Rustin, Bayard, **1:**20
Rutherford, R. B., **1:**220
Rwanda, Belgian colonial rule of, **3:**257
Rwandan genocide
    oral histories of, **1:**312, **3:**257–259
    war crimes trials after, **3:**293, 294
Rwandan Patriotic Front (RPF), **3:**257
Rwililiza, Innocent, **3:**257, 259
Ryan, Allan A., Jr., **3:**294
Ryan, Hugh, **1:**168
Ryerson, Richard Alan, **2:**90

S

Saadawi, Nawal El, *A Daughter of Isis,* **1:**226
Sabbagh, Suha, **1:**94
SABC. *See* South African Broadcasting Corporation
Sabor, Peter, **2:**314
Sachs, Nelly, *Eli,* **2:**255

Sackville, Margaret, **2:**64
Sackville-West, Vita, **2:**62, 64, 181
SACP. *See* South African Communist Party
Sad Earth, Sweet Heaven (Buck), **2:**271, 273
Sadler, Thomas, **2:**75, 77
Saemann, Karyn, **2:**276
Safeir, Gwendolen, *American Leaders in Nursing,* **3:**170
Safer, Morley, **3:**279
Safundi (journal), **3:**243
Saga of Coe Ridge, The (Montell), **3:90–92**
Sago mine disaster of 2006 (West Virginia), **3:**66, 67
Saigon, fall of, **3:**209, 279, *280*
Saints. *See also specific saints*
  lives of (*See* Hagiographies)
  relics of, **2:**226
Saint-Simon, Duc de, **2:**174
Saitoti, Tepilit Ole
  Maasai, **1:**114
  The Worlds of a Maasai Warrior, **1:114–116**
Sajdi, Dana, **1:**287
Sakakini, Khalil al-, *The Diary of Khalil al-Sakakini,* **2:**104, 106
Saladin, **1:**285–286, *286*
Salama, Gwen, **3:**45
Salamini, Heather Fowler, **3:**303
Salazar, Claudia, **3:**191
Sale, Roger, **1:**165
Salemi, Esmail, **3:**218
Saliba, Sue, *Watching Seagulls,* **1:**161
Salisbury, Richard, **3:**207
Salles, Walter, **2:**220
Salm, Arthur, **3:**67
Salmagundi (journal), **1:**247
Salme, Sayyida. *See* Ruete, Emily
Salomé (Wilde), **2:**183
Salter, Andrea, **2:**267
Salter, John R., Jr., **3:**329
Salter, Michael, **3:**294
Salt Lake Tribune (newspaper), **1:**38
Salvadoran Civil War, oral histories of, **3:**205–208, *206*
Same-sex marriage, **1:**139

Samkange, Stanlake, **3:**251
Samples from English Culture (Klein), **3:**144
Sampson, Anthony, **1:**27
Samway, Patrick H., **3:**45–46
Sánchez, Rosaura, **3:**114, 116
  Telling Identities, **3:**115, 121–122
Sancho, Ignatius, **1:**81, **2:**44
Sand, Georges, **2:**82
Sanders, Mark, **1:**314, **3:**243
Sanders, Robert, *Brothers,* **3:**199
Sanders, Valerie, **2:**336
San Diego Union-Tribune (newspaper), **3:**67
Sandos, James A., **3:**116
Sands, Kathleen M., **1:**70, 71
Sandul, Paul, **3:**188
Sang Ye
  China Candid, **3:**299–300
  Chinese Lives, **3:**288, **299–301**
Sansibar Blues (Buch), **1:**92
Sansom, George, **2:**189
Santa Fe, USS, **3:**203
Santa María (ship), **2:**203
Santiago, Esmeralda
  Almost a Woman, **1:**108, 109
  The Turkish Lover, **1:**108
  When I Was Puerto Rican, **1:108–110**
Santoli, Al
  Everything We Had, **3:**199, 201, **209–211,** 231, 275, 279
  Leading the Way, **3:**210
  To Bear Any Burden, **3:**210
Santoni, Pedro, **3:**116
Santrouschitz, Hermine, **2:**253
Sao Paulo (Brazil), de Jesus (Carolina Maria) on favelas of, **2:**6–8
Sapia, Yvonne, **1:**109
Sarajevo (Bosnia), Bosnian War in, **2:**338–340
Sarashina, Lady
  As I Crossed a Bridge of Dreams, **2:189–191,** 290–291
  Michitsuna No Haha as aunt of, **2:**297
Sarashina Diary. See As I Crossed a Bridge of Dreams

Sarcasm, in *The Education of Henry Adams* (Adams), **1:**132, 133
Sarcophagus (Gubarev), **3:**282, 284
Sargent, John Singer, **2:**114
Saro-Wiwa, Ken, **1:**214
  Sozaboy, **1:**312
Sarra, Edith, **2:**191, 299
Sarraute, Nathalie, *Enfance,* **1:**268
Sartre, Jean-Paul, **1:**124, 318, **2:**152, 167
Sasha and Emma (Avrich), **3:**3
Sassoon, Siegfried, **2:**247
  on *A Country Parson* (Woodforde), **2:**287, 289
  Diaries, 1915–1918, **2:247–249**
  Memoirs of a Fox-Hunting Man, **1:**329, **2:**247
  Orwell (George) compared to, **2:**117
  Sherston's Progress, **2:**247
Satire, in "Letter to the Reverend Samson Occom" (Wheatley), **2:**44, 45
Satirist, The (newspaper), **1:**277
Satrapi, Marjane
  Chicken with Plums, **1:**155–156
  Embroideries, **1:**155
  Persepolis, **1:**139, 141, **155–157,** *156,* 293
Sattelmeyer, Robert, **1:**235
Satterfield, Archie, *The Home Front,* **3:**202
Saturday Evening Post (magazine), **2:**250
Saturday Review (magazine), **1:**271, **2:**185, **3:**318
Saturday Review of Literature (magazine), **1:**333
Saturday Review/World (magazine), **1:**300
Satyagraha, **1:**242
Saudi Arabia, in Gulf War, **2:**278, 279
Saunders, Anna, **3:**247
Saunders, Keith B., **1:**149
Saunders, Loraine, **2:**118–119
Saussure, Ferdinand de, **1:**267
Savage, Priscilla, **3:**64
Savage, Thomas, *Californio Voices,* **3:114–117,** 121

SAVAK, **3:**219
Savicheva, Tanya, **2:**277
Savin, Ada, **1:**100
Savoye, Jeffrey A., **2:**41
Sawdust Dream, The (Russell), **3:**93
Saxton, Marsha, *With Wings,* **1:**8
Sayigh, Mai, *The Siege,* **1:**226
Sayre, Robert, **2:**207
Scalp hunters, **1:**304
Scammell, G. V., **2:**198, 200
Scandinavia, Wollstonecraft's (Mary) travels in, **2:**111
Scaphandre et le papillon, Le (Bauby). See *Diving Bell and the Butterfly, The* (Bauby)
Scarlet Letter, The (Hawthorne), **2:**223–224
Scar literature, *Voices from the Whirlwind* (Feng) as, **3:**287
Schaefer, Paul, **1:**77
Schapera, Isaac, **2:**242
Scharnhorst, Gary, **1:**235
Schayegh, Cyrus, **3:**220
Schiller, Friedrich, **1:**277
Schimpf, Albrecht, **3:**235
Schmelz, Peter J., **3:**333
Schmidt, Matthias, **2:**54
Schmidt, Rob, **3:**68
Schmitz, John Eric, *Enemies among Us,* **3:**224
Schnabel, Julian, **1:**6
Schneider, Karen, **2:**269
Schneiders, Sandra Marie, *Religious Life in a New Millennium,* **3:**308
Schoeneman, Katherine A., **1:**205
Schoeneman, Thomas J., **1:**205
Schonbrun, Eva, **3:**35
School Library Journal, **1:**311, **3:**45, 225
Schoolma'am, The (Donovan), **3:**77
Schools. See Education
Schopenhauer, Arthur, **1:**193, 194
  The World as Will and Representation, **1:**193
Schrager, Samuel, **3:**329
Schreiber, Harry, **3:**21
Schubnell, Matthias, **1:**56
Schulkind, Jeanne, **2:**182
Schulman, Nicole, *Wobblies!,* **3:**330

Schuth, Katarina, **3:**309
Schwanitz, Wolfgang, **1:**209
Schwartz, Matthew, **2:**96
Schwarz-Bart, Simone, *Ti Jean L'Horizon,* **1:**64
Schwarzkopf, Norman, **2:**279
Scibetta, Barbara, *War Brides of World War II,* **3:**127
Science, Darwin (Charles) on success in, **1:**65–67
Science and Engineering Ethics (journal), **2:**168
Science fiction
  by Cavendish (Margaret), **1:**231
  feminist, **2:**237
SCLC. See Southern Christian Leadership Conference
Scotland. See also Scottish autobiographical writing
  in Enlightenment, contributions of, **2:**328
  in establishment of Great Britain, **2:**328
  militia groups in, **2:**309
  oral histories of life in, **3:**173, 175
  Victoria's visits to Highlands of, **2:**209–211
  during World War II, Mitchison (Naomi) on life in, **2:**235–237
Scott, David, **2:**258
Scott, Joanna C., *Indochinese Refugees,* **1:**335
Scott, Margaret, **2:**133, 134
Scott, Rebecca, **3:**68
Scott, Shaunna L., *Two Sides to Everything,* **3:**96
Scott, Walter, **2:**310
  "Auld Robin Gray" (Barnard) and, **2:**217
  The Bride of Lammermoor, **2:**209
  The Journal of Sir Walter Scott, **2:**67, **309–311**
  Kemble's (Fanny) friendship with, **2:**335
  Memoirs, **2:**309
  Napoleon, **2:**310
  Shadows on My Heart (Buck) on, **2:**271
  Waverly, **2:**309

Scottish autobiographical writing
  by Boswell (James), **2:**328–330
  by Mitchison (Naomi), **2:**235–237
  by Scott (Walter), **2:**309–311
Scottish Geographical Magazine, **2:**198
Scottish Historical Review (journal), **2:**236, 288–289, **3:**146
Scott-Moncrieff, G., **2:**329
Scrapbook of Katherine Mansfield (Mansfield), **2:**134
Scribner, Charles, **2:**101
Scribner, Doris, **3:**282, 285
Scribner's Monthly, **2:**114
Scrots, Guillaume, **2:98**
Sculptura (Evelyn), **2:**65
Seabrook, Jeremy
  In the Cities of the South, **3:**54
  Mother and Son, **3:**55
  Unemployment, **3:**54
  The Unprivileged, **3:**55
  Working-Class Childhood, **3:53–55**
Seacole, Mary, *The Wonderful Adventures of Mrs. Seacole in Many Lands,* **1:111–113,** *112*
Seaman, Donna, **1:**104, **2:**339
Season of Anomy (Soyinka), **1:**214
Seaver, Paul S., **2:**74
Secession, Lee's (Robert E.) views on, **2:**38, 39
Sechehaye, Marguerite, *The Autobiography of a Schizophrenic Girl,* **1:**164
Second Common Reader (Woolf), **2:**289
Secundinus, **1:**196
Sedgwick, Ellery, **2:**91
See, Lisa, **1:**159
Seeger v. United States, **3:**223
Seelig, Sharon, **1:**317
Seelig, Sharon Cadman, **2:**64
Segalla, Spencer D., *The Moroccan Soul,* **3:**48
Segregation. See Racial segregation; Sexual segregation
Seidensticker, Edward, **2:**297, 298, 299
Seidler, Ned M., **1:**66

Sei Shōnagon
- *The Diary of Lady Murasaki* (Murasaki) on, **2:**290, 291
- Michitsuna No Haha in family of, **2:**297
- *The Pillow Book,* **2:**59, 189, 190, 290

Seitz, James, **1:**268
Selected Autobiographies by Women Writers (Xie), **1:**340
Selected Letters (Keats), **2:**146
Selected Letters of Martha Gellhorn (Gellhorn), **2:101–103**
Selective Service, U.S., **3:**221, 227, 229
Self. *See also* Identity
- Hurston's (Zora Neale) views on, **1:**9, 10
- in identity, Rousseau (Jean-Jacques) on, **1:**200–202
- importance in society, and rise of autobiographies, **1:**246
- Lessing (Doris) on nature of, **1:**167, 168
- Native American vs. Western conceptions of, **1:**56
- in postmodernism, **1:**167

Self-actualization, in *Ten Thousand Sorrows* (Kim), **1:**103
Self-doubt, of Hawthorne (Nathaniel), **2:**223–224
Self-education, Franklin (Benjamin) on, **1:**179, 180
Self-elegy, of Darwish (Mahmoud), **1:**255–257
Self-Help (Smiles), **2:**310
Self-help books, *The Autobiography of Ben Franklin* (Franklin) as precursor to, **1:**182
Self-knowledge, Styron's (William) struggle for, **1:**204
"Self-made" individuals, Franklin (Benjamin) and, **1:**180
"Self-Made Men" (Douglass), **1:**180
Self-Portrait of the Other (Padilla), **1:**296
"Self-Reliance" (Emerson), **1:**180
Selkirk, Andrew, **3:**183
Sellin, Eric, **1:**128, **2:**263
Selochan, Viberto, **3:**207
Selznick, Irene Mayer, **2:**261
Seme, Pixley ka Isaka, **2:**241

Semiology, **1:**267
Sending My Heart Back across the Years (Wong), **1:**56
Seneca, **2:**94, 96
Seneca Falls Convention (1848), **1:**12
Senegal
- Bugul (Ken) on life in, **1:**61–64
- French colonial rule of, **1:**61
- independence of (1960), **1:**61

Senesh, Hannah, **2:**22
Senghor, Léopold-Sédar, **1:**61, 128
Senkaku/Diaoyu (islands), **1:**340
Senkewicz, Robert M.
- *The History of Alta California,* **3:**115
- *Testimonios,* **3:**116

Senna, Danzy, *Caucasia,* **1:**72, 74
Sentimental Education (Flaubert), **1:**128
"Separate but equal" doctrine
- end of, **3:**44
- establishment of, **1:**37, 50

Sephardic Jews
- in Guatemala, **1:**99–100
- immigration to U.S., **3:**118, 120

September 11, 2001, terrorist attacks
- East German Stasi and, **3:**245
- Hirsi Ali (Ayaan) on aftermath of, **1:**207
- national security after, **3:**195, 197, 245
- racial profiling after, **3:**195, 197
- *The Story of My Life* (Ahmedi) after, **1:**40
- U.S.-led invasion of Iraq after, **2:**275

Septicus Clarus, **2:**95
Seraph on the Suwanee (Hurston), **1:**9
Serbs, in Bosnian War, **2:**338
Serengeti National Park, **1:**114
Serious Proposal to the Ladies, A (Astell), **2:**35
Serrano, Jorge, **1:**99
Sestigers, **3:**242
Seton, William, **2:**213
Set This House on Fire (Styron), **1:**206
Seutonius Tranquillus, **2:**94
Seventh Letter (Plato), **2:**94

Seven Years' War (1754–1763), **1:**276, **2:**205, 328
Sévigné, Madame de, **2:**35
Sewanee Review (journal), **1:**165, **2:**76, 153, 269
Seward, Anna, **2:**217
Sex: An Oral History (Maurer), **3:**276, 277
Sexual activity
- adolescent, *Go Ask Alice* (anonymous) on, **2:**294
- in *The Diary of Anaïs Nin* (Nin), **2:**123
- in Japan, in Kamakura period, **2:**60–61
- in *Nisa* (Shostak), **3:**37, 38

Sexual discrimination
- in China, **3:**148
- in coal mining, **3:**337, 339

Sexuality, of African American women
- Angelou (Maya) on, **1:**18
- hooks (bell) on, **1:**250
- Jacobs (Harriet A.) on, **1:**143–144

Sexual orientation. *See* Homosexuality
Sexual segregation, among Meru people, **3:**143
Sexual violence, in Guatemala, **1:**100. *See also* Rape
Sforza, Ascanio Maria, **2:**160, 161
Sganga, Cristina, *El Salvador,* **3:**206
Shaarawi, Huda, **1:**136
- *Harem Years,* **1:**225–226

Shackelford, Laurel, *Our Appalachia,* **3:**66, **86–89**
Shackleton, Abraham, **2:**157
Shackleton, Elizabeth, **2:**157
Shackleton, Richard, **2:**157
Shadows on My Heart (Buck), **2:38, 271–274**
Shaffer, Deborah, *Solidarity Forever,* **3:328–330**
Shah, Saira, *The Storyteller's Daughter,* **1:**40
Shah's Story, The (Mohammed Reza), **3:**218
Shaka (Zulu leader), **1:**25
Shake Hands with the Devil (Dallaire), **3:**258

SUBJECT INDEX

Shakespeare, William
    Hamlet, **1:**277
    Journal of Katherine Mansfield (Mansfield) on, **2:**133
    Journals of Ralph Waldo Emerson (Emerson) on, **2:**140
    Kemble's (Fanny) performances of, **2:**337
    King Lear, **2:**147
    The Letters of John Keats (Keats) on, **2:**146
    pilgrimage narratives used by, **2:**226
    Two Gentlemen of Verona, **2:**226, 228
Shame (Rushdie), **1:**87
Shamuyarira, Nathan, **3:**251
Shanghai (China), oral histories of Jewish refugees in, **3:**14–16, *15*
Shapin, Steven, **3:**240
Shapiro, Judith, **3:**301
Shapiro, Karin, **3:**272
Shapiro, Stephen A., **1:**277–278
Shared Authority, A (Frisch), **3:**173, **179–182,** 190, 192
Sharma, Govind, **2:**14
Sharp, Granville, **1:**83
Shattered Dreams? (Oppenheimer and Bayer), **3:**272–274
Shaw, George Bernard, **1:**84, **2:**16, 17, 128
Shaw, Nate, **3:**73
Shawqi, Ahmad, *al-Shawqiyyat,* **1:**135–136
Shawqiyyat, al- (Shawqi), **1:**135–136
Sheard, S., **3:**171
Shelley, Mary, *The Last Man,* **2:**145
Shelley, Percy Bysshe, **2:**143, 145, 146, 154
Shell shock, **2:**247, 248
Shepard, Alex, **3:**175
Shepard, Matthew, **1:**139
Sheridan, Dorothy, **2:**236
Sheridan, Richard Brinsley, **1:**34, **2:**217
Sherman, Beatrice, **1:**10–11
Sherman, L. A., *Bengali Girls Don't,* **1:**312
Sherman, William T., **3:**290
Sherriff, R. C., *Journey's End,* **1:**329

Sherry, Norman, **2:**194
Sherston's Progress (Sassoon), **2:**247
Sherwin-White, A. N., **2:**95
Shi, Shumei, **2:**172
Shields, Brooke, *Down Came the Rain,* **1:**204
Shinoda, Paul, **3:**196
Shipler, David, **1:**336
Shirane, Haruo, **2:**59
Shirinian, Lorne, **3:**42
Shizuo, Tanisuga, **3:**216
Shoah (film), **3:**50, 52
Shockley, Evelyn, **1:**250
Shoemaker, Adam, *Black Words, White Page,* **1:**150, 151
Shona people, **3:**251, *252*
Shopes, Linda, **3:**98, 181
Short, John, **2:**167
Short, William, **2:**213
Short Account of the Destruction of the Indies, A (Las Casas), **2:**201
"Short Narrative of My Life, A" (Occom), **1:**56
Shōshi (empress of Japan), **2:**290, 291, 292
Shostak, Marjorie
    Nisa, **3:**37–39
    Return to Nisa, **3:**38
Showings (Julian of Norwich), **1:**211
Shrader, Charles R., **3:**210
Shrier, Helene, **3:**119, 120
Shriver, Robert Sargent, Jr., **3:**254, 256
Shua, María, *The Book of Memories,* **1:**75
Shukert, Elfreida, *War Brides of World War II,* **3:**127
Shumaker, Wayne, **1:**246
Shuman, Amy, **3:**159
Shupe, Kevin, **1:**304
Shuttle in the Crypt, A (Soyinka), **1:**214
Sidney, Angela, **3:**320
Siebentritt, Gretta Tovar, *Places of Origin,* **3:**205
Siege, The (Sayigh), **1:**226
Siegelbaum, Lewis H., *Workers of the Donbass Speak,* **3:**157, **340–342**
Siege of Mafeking, The (Hamilton), **2:**241

Siemens, **2:**19
Sierra Eye (magazine), **1:**313
Sierra Leone
    Beah (Ishmael) on life in, **1:**312–314
    civil war of, **1:**312–314
Siglo XX (Bolivia), **3:**322
Siglo XX Housewives Committee, **3:**322
Sign in Sidney Brustein's Window, The (Hansberry), **1:**274
Sign language, Warlpiri, **3:**335–336
Signs (journal), **1:**88
Silver Tassie, The (O'Casey), **1:**329
Silvester, Christopher, **2:**276
Sim, Lorraine, **2:**269
Simmons, Allan H., **2:**194
Simms, Laura, **1:**314
Simone, Nina, **1:**274
Simplicity, Thoreau's (Henry David) advocacy of, **1:**233, 234
Simpson, Carol Chung, **3:**127
Simpson, Wallis, **2:**235
Sin, struggle with
    Augustine on, **1:**196–198
    Kempe (Margery) on, **1:**189, 190
Sindall, Rob, *Street Violence in the Nineteenth Century,* **3:**312
Singapore, Neruda (Pablo) in, **1:**224
Singapore Story, The (Lee), **1:**290
Singh, Ajay, **1:**299, 300
Singh, Amar, **2:**231
Singh, Amardeep, **2:**231
Singh, Nikky-Guninder Kaur, **2:**185
Singing Flame, The (O'Malley), **3:**27
Singing for Power (Underhill), **1:**70
Singletary, Otis A., **2:**245
Sino–Japanese War, First (1894–1895), **1:**322, 340, **3:**234
Sino–Japanese War, Second (1937–1945), **1:**339, 340
Sino-Judaic Institute, **3:**16
Sinor, Jennifer, *The Extraordinary Work of Ordinary Writing,* **2:163–165**
Sioux. *See* Lakota Sioux
Sisterhood, in oral history field, **3:**190
Sithole, Jabulani, **1:**26
Sithole, Ndabaningi, **3:**251

Siv, Sichan, *Golden Bones,* **1**:306–308, *307*
Skenazy, Paul, **1**:174
Skin color, hooks (bell) on meanings of, **1**:250
Skinner, B. F., **1**:234
Skinner, John, **1**:190, 191
Skousen, Mark, **1**:182
Slade, Carole, **1**:213
Slantchev, Brantislav, **2**:299
Slave(s)
    as Civil War soldiers, **2**:238–240
    education of, in preparation for emancipation, **2**:29–31, *30*
    former, oral histories of, **3**:23–25
    genealogy of, **1**:261–263
    Jacobs (Harriet A.) on families of, **1**:142–143
    naming of, **1**:52
    rebellions by, **2**:238
    runaway, oral histories of, **3**:7–9
    separation of families of, **1**:261, 262
Slave narratives. *See also specific works and writers*
    authorship of, **1**:82–83
    Behind the Scenes (Keckley) as, **1**:52
    A Diary from Dixie (Chesnut) compared to, **2**:250
    Incidents in the Life of a Slave Girl (Jacobs) as, **1**:18, 34, 35, 142–145
    The Interesting Narrative of the Life of Olaudah Equiano (Equiano) as, **1**:34, 81–83, 142
    The Journals of Charlotte Forten Grimké (Grimké) vs., **2**:29
    modern autobiographies inspired by, **1**:18, 37
    Narrative (Brown) as, **1**:50
    Narrative of the Life of Frederick Douglass (Douglass) as, **1**:33–35
    Twelve Years a Slave (Northup) as, **1**:50
    Up from Slavery (Washington) as, **1**:50–52
    WPA collection of, **1**:35
Slave owners
    effects of slavery on, Douglass (Frederick) on, **1**:34
    naming of slaves by, Washington (Booker T.) on, **1**:52
    power of, Jacobs (Harriet A.) on, **1**:142
Slavery. *See also* Abolitionist movement
    Adams (John Quincy) on debate over, **2**:69, 70, 71
    in ancient Greece and Rome, **2**:96
    Arab vs. Western institution of, **1**:90, 92
    in Bermuda, oral histories of, **3**:23–25
    British abolition of, **1**:81, **3**:23
    Chesnut (Mary Boykin Miller) on, **2**:251
    Christianity and, **1**:34, 144, **2**:44, 46
    as Civil War issue, **1**:50, **2**:38, 250
    in Cuba, oral histories of, **3**:7–9
    Cuban abolition of, **3**:7
    Douglass's (Frederick) critique of, **1**:33–35
    Equiano's (Olaudah) critique of, **1**:81–83
    Jacobs's (Harriet A.) critique of, **1**:142–145
    in Jamaica, **1**:111
    Kemble's (Fanny) critique of, **2**:335
    Lincoln's (Abraham) views on, **2**:38
    Ruete (Emily) on, **1**:90, 92
    Stone (Kate) on, **2**:245
    U.S. abolition of, **1**:50
    Wheatley's (Phillis) critique of, **2**:44–46
Slave trade
    British abolition of, **1**:34, 111, **3**:23
    British debate over, **1**:81
    Equiano's (Olaudah) critique of, **1**:81–83
    increase in access to records of, **1**:263
    U.S. abolition of, **1**:33
Slavic Review (journal), **3**:332
Slavonic and East European Studies (journal), **3**:135
Sleeper, Jim, **3**:119
Slingsby, Henry
    The Diary of Sir Henry Slingsby, **2**:256–258
    "A Father's Legacy," **2**:256, 257, 258
Slouching towards Bethlehem (Didion), **1**:88
Small, Ian, **2**:9, 10
Small, Meredith, **3**:38
Small Talk (Mitchison), **2**:235
Small War (1895–1898), **3**:7. *See also* Spanish–American War
Small Wars & Insurgencies (Manwaring), **3**:206
Smiles, Samuel, **1**:65
    Self-Help, **2**:310
Smith, Abigail Adams, **2**:87–90
Smith, Adam, **2**:328
    Wealth of Nations, **2**:200
Smith, Angela K., **2**:18, 261
Smith, Betty, **2**:251
Smith, Bruce, **3**:177–178
Smith, Charlotte, **2**:300
Smith, Clark, *Brothers,* **3**:199
Smith, David Lee, **3**:108
Smith, Donald, **2**:236
Smith, Ethel Day, **3**:338
Smith, Gail K., **2**:331
Smith, Gayle, **3**:210
Smith, Geoffrey, **3**:229
Smith, Graham, **3**:171
Smith, Heather, **3**:123
Smith, John (captain), **1**:218
Smith, Joseph, **2**:178
Smith, Kitty, **3**:320
Smith, Mary F., *Baba of Karo,* **3**:141
Smith, Nadia Clare, **2**:308
Smith, Sidonie, **1**:246
Smith, Stevie, **2**:235
Smith, Thomas, **3**:345
Smith, W. Ramsay, **1**:149
Smith College, **2**:47
Smollett, Tobias, **2**:37, 328
Smyth, Frank, *Dialogue and Armed Conflict,* **3**:205
Snodgrass, Mary Ellen, **1**:301
Snow, C. B., **1**:149

SUBJECT INDEX

Snow, Edward, **2:**150, 151
Snow, William, **2:**39
Sobukwe, Robert, **1:**25
Social change
  in Appalachia, **3:**86
  in English villages, **3:**59–61, 63–64
  in English working class, **3:**53, 144
  on Native American reservations, **3:**290
  oral histories as agent for, **3:**86, 186, 187
Social class divisions. *See also* Middle class; Working class
  in Brazil, **2:**6, 7
  in Britain, **1:**252–253, **2:**259
  in China, **1:**338, **3:**299
  in collection of oral histories, **3:**177
  in India, **1:**244, 289
  in Ireland, **1:**119–120
  in U.S., **3:**328
Social construction, of "able-bodied," **1:**8
Social equality
  in Britain, in Victorian era, **1:**252, **2:**16
  in U.S., affirmative action and, **1:**15, 16
Social History (journal), **3:**149, 176, 178
Socialism
  in field of history, **3:**176, 177
  in India, Nehru's (Jawaharlal) advocacy of, **1:**289, 290, 291
  in labor movement, **3:**157
  in *The Voice of the Past* (Thompson), **3:**186, 188
  during World War II, Mitchison (Naomi) on, **2:**235
Socialist market economy, of China, **1:**158
Social mobility, in Britain, **1:**252–253
Social reform
  in Brazil, **2:**6
  in Britain, **1:**264, 329, **2:**16
Social Studies of Science (journal), **3:**240
Social welfare, in Britain, oral histories of, **3:**170–172

Society
  poetry in, Neruda (Pablo) on, **1:**222, 223
  self in, and rise of autobiographies, **1:**246
Society of Friends. *See* Quakerism
Society of United Irishmen, **2:**159
Sociological Theory (journal), **3:**332
Sociology
  of race, Du Bois (W. E. B.) on, **1:**5
  Webb's (Beatrice) career in, **2:**16, 17
Sociology of Housework, The (Oakley), **3:**144
Soetoro, Lolo, **1:**78
Soldiers and Citizens (Mirra), **3:**231–232
Soldiers of the Sun (Harries and Harries), **3:**215
Solidarity and Survival (Stromquist), **3:**153
Solidarity Forever (Bird et al.), **3:328–330**
"Solidarity Forever" (song), **3:**329
Soliloquies (Augustine), **1:**196
Solimena, Francesco, **1:184**
Sollors, Werner, *Blacks at Harvard,* **3:**21
Solomon, Charles, **1:**294
Solomon, Martha, **1:**14
Solotaroff-Enzer, Sandra, **2:**254
Solzhenitsyn, Aleksandr
  The Gulag Archipelago, **1:**201, **3:**17
  One Day in the Life of Ivan Denisovich, **3:**17
Somalia
  Hirsi Ali (Ayaan) on life in, **1:**207–209
  interpretation of Islam in, **1:**207
  women in, treatment of, **1:**207
Somali Salvation Democratic Front, **1:**207
Some Memories of the Life of Job (Bluett), **3:**141
"Some Observations on Diaries, Self-Biography, and Self-Characters" (D'Israeli), **2:177–179**
Somerson, Wendy, **1:**160
Sommer, Barbara, **3:**109
Somoza Debayle, Anastasio, **3:**185

Sone, Monica, *Nisei Daughter,* **1:**299, 309
Song Flung Up to Heaven, A (Angelou), **1:**18
Songs My Mother Sang to Me (Preciado Martin), **3:131–134,** 302
Son of Old Man Hat (Left Handed and Dyk). *See Left Handed, Son of Old Man Hat* (Left Handed and Dyk)
Son of the Forest, A (Apess), **1:**56, **3:**318
Sontag, Susan, **2:**122
Sophie's Choice (Styron), **1:**204, 206, **3:**36
Sorghaghtani Beki, **1:**107
Sorin, Gerald, **3:**5
Sorrel, Lorraine, **2:**4
Sorrows of Young Werther, The (Goethe), **1:**276, 277, 339, **2:**166
Sort of Life, A (Greene), **1:**47
Soul, Augustine on, **1:**196
Souls of Black Folk, The (Du Bois), **1:**4, 51
Sourcebook (Kreider), **3:**227
South, U.S.
  abolitionism in, **1:**33
  Angelou (Maya) on life in, **1:**18–20
  in Civil War (*See* American Civil War)
  Great Migration out of, **1:**50, 52, 84, 273, **3:**99
  Latino Americans in, **3:**123
  lynchings in, **1:**18, 50
  racial segregation in, vs. North, **3:**250
  racism in, vs. North, **1:**122
  Reconstruction era in, **1:**50–52, **2:**238, 252
  slavery in economy of, **1:**33
  Wright (Richard) on life in, **1:**122–124
South Africa. *See also* South African autobiographical writing
  AIDS in, **1:**29, **3:**272–274
  Anglo–Boer War in, **2:**241–243
  apartheid in (*See* Apartheid)
  British colonial rule of, Barnard (Anne) on life under, **2:**217–219
  British colonial rule of, establishment of, **2:**241–243

freedom of expression in, **1:**29
Truth and Reconciliation Commission of, **3:**242–244
unification of (1910), **2:**241, 242

South African autobiographical writing. *See also specific works and writers*
by Lessing (Doris), **1:**167–169
by Luthuli (Albert), **1:**24–26
by Mandela (Nelson), **1:**27–29
by Plaatje (Solomon Tshekisho), **2:**241–243

South African Broadcasting Corporation (SABC), **3:**242

South African Communist Party (SACP), **1:**27

South African Native National Congress, **2:**241

South African oral histories
on AIDS epidemic, **3:**272–274
on Truth and Reconciliation Commission, **3:**242–244

South African War. *See* Anglo–Boer War

South Africa's "Black" Market (Fadiman), **3:**142

South Carolina, during Civil War, Chesnut (Mary Boykin Miller) on, **2:**250–252

South Central Review (journal), **2:**255

South Dakota. *See* Pine Ridge Reservation; Wounded Knee

Southeast Asia. *See also specific countries*
immigration to U.S. from, **1:**170, 171, 306
refugees from, **1:**306–307, 337

Southeast Review of Asian Studies (journal), **1:**307

Southern Christian Leadership Conference (SCLC)
Angelou (Maya) in, **1:**18, 20
establishment of, **1:**20
King (Martin Luther, Jr.) in, **1:**20, **2:**32, 34

Southern Command, U.S., **3:**205, 207

Southern Horrors (Wells), **1:**50

Southern Literary Journal, **2:**131

Southern Literary Messenger (magazine), **2:**41

Southern Manifesto (1956), **1:**249

Southern Workman (journal), **1:**52
Southey, Robert, **2:**66–67, 196
South Korea
establishment of (1945), **1:**322
Kim Ku on life in, **1:**322–324

Southland (Revoyr), **1:**309
South Riding (Holtby), **1:**331
South Vietnam. *See also* Vietnam War
establishment of (1954), **1:**335, **3:**279
fall of, oral histories of, **3:**279–281
U.S. military involvement in, origins of, **3:**279

Southwestern American Literature (journal), **3:**12

Southwestern Historical Quarterly, **2:**245, **3:**255

South Wind Changing (Huynh), **1:**171

Sovereignty and Goodness of God, The (Rowlandson), **1:**81, **325–328,** **3:**24

Soviet Baby Boomers (Raleigh), **3:331–333**

Soviet Union. *See also* Russia
Afghan war with, **1:**40, **3:**233
baby boomers of, oral histories of, **3:**331–333
Berlin occupied by, **2:**281–282
Chernobyl nuclear disaster in, **3:**282–285
collapse of, **3:**282, 331, 333, 340
Du Bois (W. E. B.) and, **1:**3, 4
establishment of, **3:**331
glasnost in, **3:**282, 331, 333
Gulag system in, oral histories of, **3:**17–19
industrialization in, **3:**17
KGB of, Stasi modeled on, **3:**245
McKay's (Claude) reception in, **1:**84, 85
perestroika in, **3:**17, 331

Sowden, Benjamin, **2:**37
Soyinka, Wole, **1:**215
Madmen and Specialists, **1:**214
The Man Died, **1:214–217,** **2:**12, 14
Season of Anomy, **1:**214
A Shuttle in the Crypt, **1:**214

Sozaboy (Saro-Wiwa), **1:**312
Spacks, Patricia Meyer, **2:**35

Spain
California as colony of, **3:**114
colonial power of, origins of, **2:**201, 202
Columbus's (Christopher) exploration for, **2:**201–203
in Cuban War of Independence, **3:**7
Morocco as protectorate of, **3:**47
Puerto Rico as colony of, **1:**108
in Ten Years' War, **3:**7
Teresa of Ávila in, **1:**211–213

Spandau (Speer), **2:54–56**
Spandau prison (Berlin), **2:**54–56, 55
Spanish–American War (1898), **1:**108, 332, **3:**7
Spanish Civil War (1936–1939)
Gellhorn's (Martha) reporting on, **2:**101–103
Guevara (Ernesto "Che") influenced by, **2:**220
Neruda's (Pablo) experience in, **1:**222

Spanish Inquisition, **1:**211
Spanish language
in identity, **1:**15–17
in Puerto Rico, **1:**109
in U.S. education, **1:**15, 16, 17

Spared Angola (Suárez), **1:**296
Sparks, Beatrice
Annie's Baby, **2:**294
as author of *Go Ask Alice* (anonymous), **2:**294–296
It Happened to Nancy, **2:**294
Jay's Journal, **2:**294

Spartacus (magazine), **3:**70
Speak, Memory (Nabokov), **1:**249, 270
Speak, Memory: An Autobiography Revisited (Nabokov), **1:270–272**
Speak for England (Bragg), **3:**144
Speaking Our Minds (Read and Reynolds), **3:**170
Spear, Thomas, **3:**143
Spectator (magazine), **2:**102, 231, 328, **3:**59, 235
Spector, Scott, **2:**122
Speer, Albert
Inside the Third Reich, **2:**54
Spandau, **2:54–56**
in *The World at War* (Holmes), **3:**235

SUBJECT INDEX

Spence, Polly, *Moving Out,* **2:**163
Spencer, Terence, **2:**228
Spender, Stephen, **2:236**
Spengemann, William, **1:**246
Spenser, Edmund, **2:**62, 146
Spiegelman, Art
    Maus, **1:**139, 141, 156, 293
    Nakazawa's (Keiji) influence on, **1:**293, 294
Spielberg, Steven, **2:**71
Spier, Julius, **2:**22
Spion Kop, Battle of (1900), **2:242**
Spiritual fulfillment, Wells (H. G.) on, **1:**252
Spiritual suffering, Peltier (Leonard) on, **1:**96, 97
Spitzack, Carole J., "Body Talk," **3:**190
Spivak, Gayatri Chakravorty, **1:**87
Spoils of Poynton, The (James), **2:**115
Spokesman Review (newspaper), **3:**95
Spratt, Margaret, **3:**306–307
Sprinkler, Michael, **1:**246, 247
Stacey, Judith, **3:**191
Staël, Madame de, **2:**75–76
Staempfle, Bernhard, **1:**32
Stalin, Joseph, **3:**332
    Gulag system under, **3:**17, 18, 19
    Khrushchev (Nikita) on, **3:**333
    oral histories about life under, **3:**340, 341
    rise to power, **3:**331
Stalingrad, Battle of (1942–1943), **2:**281
Stallings, Selona, **1:**205
Stallworthy, John, **2:**248
Stalp, Marybeth, **3:**309
Stanford University, **1:**15, *16*
Stanton, Elizabeth Cady, **1:13**
    Eighty Years and More, **1:12–14**
    History of Woman Suffrage, **1:**12
    The Woman's Bible, **1:**12, 13
Stanton, Harriot, **1:**13
Stanton, Henry, **1:**13
Stanton, Theodore, **1:**13
Staples, Suzanne Fisher, **1:**41
Starfield, Jane, **2:**242
Stark, Arthur, **3:**155
Starr, Louis M., **3:**186, 188

Starr, Roger, **3:**61
Stasi, oral histories of, **3:**245–247
Staten, Henry, **1:**16–17
Staub, Michael E., **1:**71
Stavanger International Prize for Freedom of Expression, for *Letters Underway* (Ghazzawi), **2:**50
Stave, Bruce M., *Witnesses to Nuremberg,* **3:293–295**
St. Clair, David, **2:**6
Steel Shavings (magazine), **3:**161
Steelworkers Trilogy, **3:**153
Steer, George, **2:**101
Steffen-Fluhr, Nancy, **1:**253
Stein, Daniel, **1:**78
Stein, Emmanuel, **3:**154
Stein, Gertrude
    The Autobiography of Alice B. Toklas, **1:**332, 334
    Brewsie and Willie, **1:**333
    Everybody's Autobiography, **1:**332
    Ida, **1:**332
    Paris France, **1:**332
    Wars I Have Seen, **1:332–334**
    Wright's (Richard) friendship with, **1:**124
Steinhoff, Johannes, *Voices from the Third Reich,* **3:**215
Stelzig, Eugene, **2:**77
Stengel, Richard, **1:**28
Stephens, Gregory, **1:**109
Stepto, Robert B.
    From Behind the Veil, **1:**35
    A Home Elsewhere, **1:**80
Stereotypes
    of Appalachian culture, **3:**68, 86, 96
    of Chinese Americans, **1:**173, 174
    of Chinese women, **1:**173, **3:**147
    of Japanese war brides, **3:**128
    of Japan in World War II, **3:**215
    of Mexican Americans, **3:**131, 133
Sterling, Bruce, **2:**145
Sterne, Laurence, **2:**328
Stevens, Ayako, **3:**128
Stevens, Elizabeth Zofchak, **3:**338
Stevenson, Adlai, **2:**101
Stevenson, Brenda, **2:**29, 30, 31

Stevenson, Robert Louis, **2:**73
Stewart, Clyde, **2:**91
Stewart, Elinore Pruitt
    Letters of a Woman Homesteader, **2:91–93**
    Letters on an Elk Hunt, **2:**91
Stewart, Gary, *Black Man's Grave,* **1:**312
Stewart, Henry C., **1:**8
Stewart, Jon, **1:**312
Stewart, Randall, **2:**225
Stille, Alexander, **3:**159
Still Ready (film), **3:**48
Stizia, Lorraine, **3:**192
St. John, J. Hector. *See* Crèvecoeur, Michel-Guillaume Saint-Jean de
St. Louis Globe-Democrat (newspaper), **1:**147
St. Louis Post Dispatch (newspaper), **1:**85, 299
Stock, Brian, **1:**198
Stock market, U.S., 1929 crash of, **3:**161, 212
Stock Reduction Act (U.S.), **3:**318
"Stoïcien, Le" (Frederick the Great), **1:**218
Stoicism, **1:**218–221
Stoll, David, **3:**164, 165, 166
Stone, Albert E., **2:**213, 214
Stone, Harlan Fiske, **2:**56
Stone, Kate, *Brokenburn,* **2:244–246**
Stone, Norman, **2:**85
Stone, Oliver, **1:**335, *336*
Stone, William, **2:**244, 246
Stoppard, Tom, *Arcadia,* **2:**145
Stop-Time (Conroy), **1:164–166**, 270
Stories in a New Skin (Martin), **3:**138
Storming Caesars Palace (Orleck), **3:**254
StoryCorps, **3:**174, 345
Story of a Shipwrecked Sailor, The (García Márquez), **3:183–185**
Story of My Life, The: An Afghan Girl on the Other Side of the Sky (Ahmedi), **1:40–42**
Story of My Life, The: Helen Keller (Keller), **1:43–46**
Story of My Life and Work, The (Washington), **1:**37
Storyteller's Daughter, The (Shah), **1:**40

SUBJECT INDEX

Storytelling traditions
   German, **1:**30
   Irish, **3:**315
   Native American, **1:**21, 22, 55, 302, 304, **3:**320
Stowe, Harriet Beecher, **2:**143
   Uncle Tom's Cabin, **1:**33, 144
Strachey, Alix, **2:**268
Strachey, James, **2:**268
Strachey, Julia, **2:**268
Strachey, Lionel, **1:**90, 91
Strachey, Lytton, **2:**268
Strange Ground (Maurer), **3:275–278**
Stranger's Supper, A (Milich), **3:135–137**
Strata (journal), **3:**174
Stream-of-consciousness
   A Diary without Dates (Bagnold) compared to, **2:**260
   Life on the Mississippi (Twain) as precursor to, **1:**146
   in *The Man Died* (Soyinka), **1:**216
   in *Memoirs* (Neruda), **1:**223
   in *The Woman Warrior* (Kingston), **1:**174
Street, Brian, **2:**237
Streetcar Named Desire, A (film), **2:**152
Streetcar Named Desire, A (Williams), **2:**152
Street Violence in the Nineteenth Century (Sindall), **3:**312
Strength Not to Fight, The (Tollefson), **3:221–223**, 227, 276
Strickland, Susanna, **3:**23, 24, 25
Strikes. *See* Labor strikes
Strindberg, August, **2:**120
Strobel, Larry, *When the Mill Whistle Blew,* **3:**93
Stromquist, Shelton, *Solidarity and Survival,* **3:**153
Strong, Pauline, **3:**320
Strottman, Theresa, **3:**240
Strozier, Charles B., **3:**263–264
Structuralism, **1:**239, 267
Struggle for Gay and Lesbian Equal Rights, The (Marcus), **3:**83
Struggle for the Land (Churchill), **3:**10
Strychacz, Thomas, **1:**166

Stuart, John T., **3:**261
Stubborn Twig (Kessler), **3:**80
Stuck Rubber Baby (Cruse), **1:**139
Students
   in Cultural Revolution, **1:**161
   deferments for, in Vietnam War, **3:**221
   in movements of 1968, **3:**31–33
Students for a Democratic Society (Buhle et al.), **3:**330
Studies in American Indian Literatures (journal), **1:**23, 70, **3:**109
Studies in English Literature (journal), **2:**231
Studies in the Novel (journal), **1:**313, 314
Studs Turkel Program, The (radio show), **3:**161
Studs Turkel's Working (Buhle and Pekar), **3:**330
Study of the Negro Problem, The (Du Bois), **1:**50
Sturgis, Caroline, **2:**139
Sturgis, Howard, **2:**115
Sturrock, John, **1:**67
Styron, William, **1:205**
   The Confessions of Nat Turner, **1:**204, 206
   Darkness Visible, **1:204–206**
   Lie Down in Darkness, **1:**204, 206
   Set This House on Fire, **1:**206
   Sophie's Choice, **1:**204, 206, **3:**36
   on *Stop-Time* (Conroy), **1:**165
Suárez, Virgil, *Spared Angola,* **1:**296
Subjectivity, in oral histories, **3:**162, 173, 186
Submission, in Islam, Hirsi Ali (Ayaan) on, **1:**208
Submission, Part 1 (film), **1:**207, 208
Suenaga, Shizuko, *Japanese War Brides in America,* **3:127–130**
Suffolk (England), oral histories of village life in, **3:**59–61, 63–65
Suffrage. *See* Voting rights
Sugarmill, The (Moreno Franglinal), **3:**7
Sugawara no Michizane, **2:**189
Sugawara no Takasue, daughter of. *See* Sarashina, Lady
Sugiman, Pamela, **3:**178

Suicide
   of Hitler (Adolf), **2:**281
   of Levi (Primo), **1:**204, 205
   of Plath (Sylvia), **2:**47
   Styron's (William) battle with, **1:**204–205
   of Woolf (Virginia), **2:**268
   Xie Bingying's idealization of, **1:**339
Sukhu, Gopal, **3:**288
Suleri, Sara
   Boys Will Be Boys, **1:**88
   Meatless Days, **1:87–89**
   The Rhetoric of English India, **1:**87–88
Sullivan, Anne, **1:**43–46
Sullivan, Walter, **1:**165
Sully, Thomas, **2:317**
Sumerians, letter writing by, **2:**94
Summerfield, Penny, **2:**237, **3:**336
Summers, Carol, **3:**253
Summerskill, Edith, **2:**235
Summing Up, The (Maugham), **2:**183
Sumner, Fort. *See* Bosque Redondo Reservation
Sun Also Rises, The (Hemingway), **2:**259
Sun Dance ceremony, **1:**23, 96, 97
Sunday Times (newspaper), **2:**85
Sunrise Tomorrow (Mitchison), **2:**237
Sun Yat-sen, **1:**338, **2:**170
Suppression of Communism Act of 1950 (South Africa), **1:**27
Supreme Court, U.S.
   Amistad case in, **2:**70, 71
   on conscientious objectors, **3:**223
   on interracial marriage, **1:**72, 78
   on labor arbitration, **3:**153
   on racial quotas in higher education, **3:**20
   on racial segregation, **1:**37, 50, 122, 249, **3:**44
   on slavery, **2:**38
Survival, literature of
   The Story of a Shipwrecked Sailor (García Márquez) as, **3:**183–185
   They Say in Harlan County (Portelli) as, **3:**96–97
   The Unwanted (Nguyen) as, **1:**170

SUBJECT INDEX

Survival in the Killing Fields (Ngor), **1:**306
Surviving the Slaughter (Umutesi), **3:**258
Survivors: An Oral History of the Armenian Genocide (Miller and Miller), **3:40–43,** 50
Survivors: The Story of Ireland's Struggle (MacEoin), **3:**27, 315
Suter, Thomas, **2:**271
Sutherland, John, **2:**311
Sutherland, Sibyl, **3:**78
Sutton, Roger, **1:**162
Sutzkever, Abraham, **1:**255
Su Xuelin, *Ninety-Four Years of a Floating Life,* **1:**338
Suyeoshi, Amy, **3:**84
Suzuki, Mihoko, **2:**64
Sweeney, Joseph, **3:**29
Sweet and Sour Milk (Farah), **1:**207
Sweeter the Juice, The (Haizlip), **1:**73
Swiftwater People (Russell), **3:93–95**
Swinburne, Algernon Charles, **2:**82, 147
Swinnerton, Frank, **2:**138
Symmachus, **2:**94–95
Symons, Julian, **2:**42–43
"Sympathy" (Dunbar), **1:**50
Symposium (journal), **1:**183
Synethesia, **1:**272
Synge, John Millington, **2:**126, 128
Syria, Greater, Usāmah ibn Munqidh on history of, **1:**285–286
Syrian Thunderbolt, The (Imad al-Din), **1:**286
Syrkin, Marie, **2:**22–23, 24
Szadziuk, Maria, **1:**110

T

Taccola, Mariano, **2:161**
Tacitus, Cornelius, **2:**94, **3:**186
Taggart, Cynthia, **3:**95
Taine, Hippolyte, **2:**82
Taino people, **2:**202
Tait's Edinburgh Magazine, **2:**178
Takaki, Shintaro, **3:**82
Takasue's daughter. *See* Sarashina, Lady

Takeshita, Ben, **3:**196
Takooshian, Harold, **3:**41
Talcott, Samuel, **1:**325
Tale of Genji, The (Murasaki), **2:**59, 60, 189, 190, 290–292, *291*
Tales for Cottagers (Leadbeater), **2:**157
Taliban, rise of, **1:**40
Talking to Myself (Terkel), **3:**214
Tallichet, Suzanne E., **3:**338–339
Talmadge, Herman, **1:**5
Talmage, Thomas de Witt, **1:**150
Tamai Kōsuke, **2:**189, 190–191
Tamari, Salim, **2:**104, 105, 106
Tamura, Keiki, *Michi's Memories,* **3:**127
Tamura, Linda
    The Hood River Issei, **3:80–82**
    Nisei Soldiers Break Their Silence, **3:**80
Tan, Amy, **1:**159
Tanzania
    establishment of borders of, **1:**114
    Ruete (Emily) on life in, **1:**90–92
    Saitoti (Tepilit Ole) on life in, **1:**114–116
Taplin, George, **1:**149, 150
Tappes, Shelton, **3:**101
Tarhan, Mehmet, **3:**229
Tatars, **3:**17, 19
Tateishi, John, *And Justice for All,* **3:195–198,** 224
Tateishi, Yuri, **3:**197
Tavalaro, Julia, *Look up for Yes,* **1:**6
Taylor, Barbara, **2:**111
Taylor, Charles G., **1:**312
Taylor, Craig, **3:**59, 60, 61
Taylor, Elizabeth, **2:**261
Taylor, Ethel Barol, **3:**269, 270–271
Taylor, Jeremy, *Rule and Exercises of Holy Living and Dying,* **2:**195
Taylor, Paul F., *Bloody Harlan,* **3:**96
Taylor, Phyllis, **3:**119
Taylor, Richard, *Destruction and Reconstruction,* **2:**250
Taylor, Sandra, *Jewel of the Desert,* **3:**80
Taylor, Steven J., *Acts of Conscience,* **3:**227
Taylor, Telford, **3:**212
Taylor, Vic, **3:**103

Tchaikovsky, Pyotr Ilyich, **2:**143
Tcheng, Soumay. *See* Cheng Yu-hsiu
Teacher Man (McCourt), **1:**119
Teachers, U.S., oral histories of, **3:**77–79
Teachers College Record (periodical), **3:**77
Teaching a Stone to Talk (Dillard), **1:**279
Tears before the Rain (Engelmann), **3:**210, 265, **279–281**
Tebutt, Melanie, **3:**178
Technological advances
    Adams (Henry) on, **1:**132–134
    in agriculture, in England, **3:**59, 63
    Emerson (Ralph Waldo) on, **2:**139
    in medicine, **3:**170
    in oral history field, **3:**181
    Thoreau (Henry David) on, **1:**233
    in World War I, **2:**180
Technological Revolution, **1:**134
Teel, Witcher, **3:**78
Teenagers. *See* Adolescents
Telegraph (newspaper), **1:**7–8, **2:**153, 261
Telegraph, invention of, **1:**233
Television adaptations. *See also specific programs*
    of *Go Ask Alice* (anonymous), **2:**294, *295*
    of *Nella Last's War* (Last), **2:**265, 266
    of *Testament of Experience* (Brittain), **1:**330
    of *Working* (Terkel), **3:**343
Telling Identities (Sánchez), **3:**115, 121–122
Telling Maya Tales (Gossen), **3:**167
Tell Me Africa (Olney), **1:**246
Tell My Horse (Hurston), **1:**9, 11
Temple, Mary "Minny," **2:**113
Temple, William, **2:**324–327
Ten Africans (collected stories), **1:**64
"Tenir un journal" (Lejeune). *See* "Practice of the Private Journal" (Lejeune)
Tennyson, Alfred, **1:**264, **2:**140, 271, 335
Ten Thousand Sorrows (Kim), **1:102–104**

Ten Years of Madness (Feng), **3:**287
Ten Years' War (1868–1878), **3:**7
Teorey, Matthew, **1:**311
Teresa of Ávila, **1:**212
    Interior Castle, **1:**212
    The Life, **1:**211–213
    The Way of Perfection, **1:**212
Terkel, Louis "Studs," **3:**213, *344*
    on *AIDS Doctors* (Oppenheimer and Bayer), **3:**274
    American Dreams, **3:**300
    Chinese Lives (Zhang and Sang) inspired by, **3:**299, 300
    Division Street, **3:**161, 299, 343
    "The Good War", **3:**161, 199, 202, **212–214,** 234, 343
    Hard Times, **3:161–163,** 179, 199, 212, 279, 343
    in origins and rise of oral history, **3:**173, 179, 279, 345
    Talking to Myself, **3:**214
    Touch and Go, **3:**214
    Working, **3:**161, 300, **343–345**
Terni (Italy), oral histories of working class in, **3:**157–159
Terrorism. *See* September 11 terrorist attacks
Terry, Ellen, **2:**335
Terry, Wallace, *Missing Pages,* **3:**199–200. *See also Bloods* (Terry)
Tertullian, **2:**94
Testament of Experience (Brittain), **1:**330
Testament of Friendship (Brittain), **1:**330, 331
Testament of Youth (Brittain), **1:329–331, 2:**247–248, 259, 269, **3:**176
Testimonios. *See also specific works*
    definition of, **3:**7, 322
    origins of, **3:**7
    tradition of, **3:**73–74, 114–115, 164, 322
Testimonios: Early California Through the Eyes of Women (Senkewicz and Beebe), **3:**116
Testimony Films, **3:**313
Tet Offensive (1968), **3:**275
Texas, oral histories of teachers in, **3:**77–79, *78*

Texas Studies in Literature and Language (journal), **1:**213, 316
Textual Cultures (journal), **2:**252
Textual Practice (journal), **2:**182
Thackeray, William, **2:**335
    Vanity Fair, **2:**312
Thames Television, **3:**234
Theater, Hansberry's (Lorraine) writing for, **1:**273–275
Theatre History Studies (journal), **2:**153
Their Eyes Were Watching God (Hurston), **1:**11
Thelen, David, **3:**181
Themistius (orator), **1:**218, 220
Theobald, Paul, **3:**78
Theoharis, Jeanne, **3:**101
Theological Studies (journal), **3:**309
Theology. *See* Religion
Thérèse Raquin (Zola), **1:**6
There Was This Goat (Krog et al.), **3:**242
These Are Our Lives (Federal Writers' Project), **3:**86
They Say in Harlan County (Portelli), **3:**87, **96–98,** 158
Thirteenth Amendment, **1:**50
This Boy's Life (Wolff), **1:47–49**
This Was Not Our War (Hunt), **3:**268
Thomas, Caitlin, **1:**127
Thomas, David, **2:**247, 248
Thomas, Dylan
    A Child's Christmas in Wales, **1:125–127**
    Eighteen Poems, **1:**125
    The Love Letters of Dylan Thomas, **1:**127
    Quite Early One Morning, **1:**125
Thomas, John Peter (Piri), *Down These Mean Streets,* **1:**109
Thompson, Dorothy, **2:**278
Thompson, Paul
    on *Akenfield* (Blythe), **3:**59–61
    on *The Death of Luigi Trastulli* (Portelli), **3:**159
    The Edwardians, **3:**176, 186, 311
    Hooligans or Rebels? (Humphries) influenced by, **3:**311–312
    on *In the Mansion of Confucius' Descendants* (Kong and Ke), **3:**126

    Living through the Soviet System, **3:**331
    Oral History, Health and Welfare, **3:170–172**
    on *The Saga of Coe Ridge* (Montell), **3:**92
    Vietnam War literature influenced by, **3:**209
    The Voice of the Past, **3:**59–61, 92, **186–189,** 209, 311–312
Thompson, Stephen, **3:**126
Thompson, Thea, *Edwardian Childhoods,* **3:**312
Thomson, Alistair
    "ANZAC Memories," **3:**177, 178
    on internationalization of oral history, **3:**129
    The Oral History Reader, **3:**173, 178, 179, 181
    on origins of oral history, **3:**135
    on Portelli (Alessandro), **3:**267
    on *The Voice of the Past* (Thompson), **3:**188
    on *Women's Words* (Gluck and Patai), **3:**192
Thomson, David, **3:**65
Thorberg, Raymond, **2:**115
Thoreau, Henry David, **1:**234
    conscientious objectors influenced by, **3:**228
    Dillard (Annie) influenced by, **1:**279
    Emerson (Ralph Waldo) and, **1:**233, **2:**139, 140
    Gandhi (Mohandas) influenced by, **1:**242
    Hawthorne (Nathaniel) and, **2:**223
    James (Henry) compared to, **2:**115
    "Resistance to Civil Government," **1:**242
    Walden, **1:233–236, 2:**140, 215
    A Week on the Concord and Merrimack Rivers, **1:**233, 234, 235, **2:**140
Thoreau, John, **1:**233
Thornbrough, Emma Lou, **3:**91
Thornhill, James, **2:325**
Thornton, Alice, *Autobiography,* **1:**230
Thornton, Margaret Bradham, **2:**153, 154

SUBJECT INDEX

Thornton, Michael, **2:**261
Thorpe, Charles, **3:**240
Those Devils in Baggy Pants (Carter), **3:**212
Thoughts and Sentiments on the Evil and Wicked Traffic of the Slavery and Commerce of the Human Species (Cugoana), **1:**81
Thoughts without Cigarettes (Hijuelos), **1:**75
Thrasher, Max, **1:**50
Thrasher, Sesali Storm, **3:**233
Three-Inch Golden Lotus, The (Feng), **3:**289
Three Minus One (Kilani), **2:**52
Threepenny Review (journal), **1:**168
Through the Brazilian Wilderness (Roosevelt), **2:**220
Thura's Diary (Al-Windawi), **2:**275–277
Tieck, Ludwig, *Franz Sternbalds Wanderungen,* **1:**276
Tiefenbrun, Susan, **2:**33
Tighe, C., **1:**216
Ti Jean L'Horizon (Schwarz-Bart), **1:**64
Tiller, Emma, **3:**162
Tilley, M. P., **2:**228
Tilton, Theodore, **2:**239
Time (magazine)
  on *Bloods* (Terry), **3:**201
  on *I, Rigoberta Menchú* (Menchú), **3:**165
  on *A Long Way Gone* (Beah), **1:**312, 313, 314
  on *Red Azalea* (Min), **1:**159
  Terry (Wallace) at, **3:**199
Time, and memory
  Conroy (Frank) on, **1:**164, 165, 166
  Nabokov (Vladimir) on, **1:**271, 272
Times Higher Education (magazine), **3:**247
Times Literary Supplement
  on *Akenfield* (Blythe), **3:**59, 61
  on *A Country Parson* (Woodforde), **2:**288
  on *The Dark Child* (Laye), **1:**129
  on *De Profundis* (Wilde), **2:**10
  on *Diaries, 1915–1918* (Sassoon), **2:**248
  on *An Experiment in Autobiography* (Wells), **1:**253
  on *The Journals of Jonathan Carver and Related Documents* (Carver), **2:**206
  on *Testament of Youth* (Brittain), **1:**330
  on *Working-Class Childhood* (Seabrook), **3:**54
  on *The Worlds of a Maasai Warrior* (Saitoti), **1:**115
  on *The Writing Life* (Dillard), **1:**280
Times of London (newspaper), **1:**32, 141, 191, **2:**75, 275
Timmons, Stuart, *Gay L.A.,* **3:**83–84
Tin mining, in Bolivia, oral histories of, **3:**322–324
Tippett, Mehetable, **2:**213
'Tis (McCourt), **1:**119
Tishler, Jennifer, **3:**285
Titcomb, Caldwell, *Blacks at Harvard,* **3:**21
Tito, **3:**135
Titon, Jeff, **3:**88
Tlatelolco massacre of 1968 (Mexico), **3:**31–33
To Bear Any Burden (Santoli), **3:**210
To Be Young, Gifted and Black (Hansberry), **1:**273–275
Tocqueville, Alexis de, **2:**214
Todd, Janet, **2:**109, 110, 111
"To His Excellency General Washington" (Wheatley), **2:**44
Tohono O'odham culture, Chona (Maria) on life in, **1:**69–71
Tóibín, Colm, **1:**79–80
Toilet paper, prisoners writing on, **1:**214, **2:**12, 13, 54
Toki, Tanaka, **3:**216
Toklas, Alice B., **1:**332, 333, 334
Tollefson, James W., *The Strength Not to Fight,* **3:**221–223, 227, 276
Tolstoy, Leo, **1:**194
  Anna Karenina, **1:**193
  A Confession, **1:**193–195, 270
  conscientious objectors influenced by, **3:**228
  Gandhi (Mohandas) influenced by, **1:**242
  Investigation of Dogmatic Theology, **1:**194
  Kafka (Franz) influenced by, **2:**120
  Rilke (Rainer Maria) and, **2:**151
  Translation and Harmony of the Four Gospels, **1:**193–194
  What I Believe, **1:**194, 195
Tolstoy, Sonya, **1:**195
Tolui Khan, **1:**107
Tomalin, Claire, **2:**73
Tomasini, Giacomo Filippo, **2:**160, 161
Tomberlin, Joseph, **1:**38
Tomko, Steve, **3:**87
Tommaso da Milano, **2:**160
Tomorrow (magazine), **1:**10
Tompkins, Sally, **2:**273
Tone, Theobald Wolfe, **2:**159
Tonghak religion, Kim Ku influenced by, **1:**322, 323, 324
To Nicocles (Isocrates), **2:**94
Tonna, Charlotte, **2:**335
Tonomura, Hitomi, **2:**61
Too Long Been Silent (Axford), **3:**196
Top Girls (Churchill), **2:60**
Torkington, Richard, **2:**227
Totah, Khalil, **2:**106
To the Edge of the Sky (Gao), **1:**159
To the Lighthouse (Woolf), **1:**146
Touch and Go (Terkel), **3:**214
Toulouse, Teresa A., **1:**328
Touré, Sékou, **1:**130
Towazugatari (Nijo). See *Confessions of Lady Nijo* (Nijo)
Townsend, Francis G., **1:**265
Townsend, Sue, **2:**338
Trade, between West and East
  expansion of, **1:**90, 105
  Gama's (Vasco da) exploration and, **2:**198–200
Trade routes, in colonial U.S., **2:**205
Tragic Life (Bai), **1:**338
"Tragic mulatto" tradition, **1:**72
Trail of Broken Tears Caravan (1972), **1:**21
Trajan (Roman emperor), **2:**94
Tramp Abroad, A (Twain), **1:**146

Transcendental fiction, **1**:281
Transcendentalism
    Dillard (Annie) influenced by, **1**:279
    Emerson (Ralph Waldo) in, **2**:140
    James's (Henry) views on, **2**:113
    Thoreau (Henry David) in, **1**:233–236
    utopian societies inspired by, **1**:235
Transforming State-Society Relations in Mexico (Craig), **3**:302
Transition (journal), **1**:88
Translation and Harmony of the Four Gospels (Tolstoy), **1**:193–194
Transnational autobiography, *Dreams from My Father* (Obama) as, **1**:79
Trask, Michael, **1**:260
Trastulli, Luigi, **3**:157, 158
Trauma, autobiographies of
    by Africans, **1**:313–314
    definition of, **1**:102
    Ten Thousand Sorrows (Kim) as, **1**:102
    The Unwanted (Nguyen) as, **1**:170–171, 172
Traveling Heavy (Behar), **1**:297
Travel narratives. *See also specific works and writers*
    The Autobiography of Ben Franklin (Franklin) as, **1**:179
    borrowing from other sources in, **2**:227, 229
    Life on the Mississippi (Twain) as, **1**:146–147
    A Long Way from Home (McKay) as, **1**:84–86
    Memoirs of an Arabian Princess from Zanzibar (Ruete) as, **1**:90–92
    Motorcycle Diaries (Guevara) as, **2**:220–221
    The Pylgrymage of Sir Richarde Guylforde (Guylforde) as, **2**:226–228
    rise in popularity of, **1**:90, **2**:229
    The Travels of Dean Mahomet (Mahomet) as, **2**:229–231
    The Travels of Marco Polo (Polo) as, **1**:105–107
    Western biases in, **1**:90
    The Wonderful Adventures of Mrs. Seacole (Seacole) as, **1**:111
Travels in West Africa (Kingsley), **2**:335
Travels of Dean Mahomet, The (Mahomet), **2:229–232**
Travels of Marco Polo, The (Polo), **1:105–107**, *106*, **2**:198, 201
Travels of Sir John Mandeville, The (Mandeville), **2**:198, 227
Travels through the Interior Parts of North America (Carver), **2**:205
TRC. *See* Truth and Reconciliation Commission
Treadwell, James, **2**:179
Treason
    Slingsby (Henry) convicted of, **2**:257, 258
    in Treason Trials of South Africa, **1**:24
Treasonable Growth, A (Blythe), **3**:61
Treasures in the Dust (Porter), **1**:161
Treaties. *See specific treaties*
Treister, Kenneth, **3**:51
Trelawney, Edward John, **2**:143, 154
Trembling of the Veil, The (Yeats), **2**:126, 127
Trench warfare, in World War I, **2**:247
Trenka, Jane Jeong, *The Language of Blood*, **1**:102
Trent, Council of, **1**:211
Trevelyan, G. O., **2**:143
Trial, The (Kafka), **2**:120, 121–122
Trials
    of anarchists, **3**:4
    Nuremberg, **2**:54, 56, **3**:293–295
    of Peltier (Leonard), **1**:96
    Treason, of South Africa, **1**:24
    of Wilde (Oscar), **2**:9, 183, 185
Tribune Books, **2**:338
Tricknor, William D., **2**:224
Trickster stories
    African, **2**:3
    Chinese, **1**:163
Trill, Suzanne L., **1**:316, 317
Trilling, Lionel, **1**:123
Trilogy Principle, **1**:248
Trimmer, Sarah, **2**:300
Triple Alliance (1668), **2**:324
Tripmaster Monkey (Kingston), **1**:173
Trippa, Elchide, **3**:158
Tristes Tropiques (Lévi-Strauss), **3**:37
Troide, Lars, **2**:314
Trollope, Anthony, **2**:101, 320
Trollope, Frances, *Domestic Manners of the Americans*, **2**:223
Tropes, racial, in *Dreams from My Father* (Obama), **1**:80
Tropic of Cancer (Miller), **2**:123
Trotsky, Leon, **1**:84, **2**:172
Trouble I've Seen, The (Gellhorn), **2**:101
Troubles, The (Ireland), **3**:27, 29
Trouble with Diversity, The (Michaels), **1**:16
Trouble with Islam Today, The (Manji), **1**:207
True Relation of My Birth, Breeding, and Life, A (Cavendish), **1:229–232**
Truman, Harry, **3**:199, 248, 249, 293
Trumpener, Katie, **2**:305
Truth
    authors' pact regarding, Lejeune (Philippe) on, **1**:239–240, **2**:174
    of *Biography of a Runaway Slave* (Barnet and Montejo), **3**:8
    of *Bloods* (Terry), **3**:199, 201
    in Cartesian rationalism, **1**:183
    of *Dust Tracks on a Road* (Hurston), **1**:9–11
    of *Everything We Had* (Santoli), **3**:211
    of *Go Ask Alice* (anonymous), **2**:294, 295
    of *The Good Man of Nanking* (Rabe), **2**:19, 20–21
    of *The History of Mary Prince* (Prince), **3**:25
    of *I, Rigoberta Menchú* (Menchú), **3**:164, 165–166
    of *The Journal of Marie Bashkirtseff* (Bashkirtseff), **2**:307
    of *Journal of the First Voyage to America* (Columbus), **2**:203
    Lessing (Doris) on nature of, **1**:167
    of *Letters of a Woman Homesteader* (Stewart), **2**:92
    of *A Long Way from Home* (McKay), **1**:85

SUBJECT INDEX

Truth, *continued*
 of *A Long Way Gone* (Beah), **1:**313
 in *Memories of a Catholic Girlhood* (McCarthy), **1:**259–260
 of *A Million Little Pieces* (Frey), **2:**296
 of *Night* (Wiesel), **1:**319, 320
 in postmodernism, **1:**168
 of *Roots* (Haley), **1:**262
 of *Spandau* (Speer), **2:**54–55
 of *Survivors* (Miller and Miller), **3:**42
 of *Ten Thousand Sorrows* (Kim), **1:**103
 of *The Travels of Marco Polo* (Polo), **1:**107
 of *A True Relation of My Birth, Breeding, and Life* (Cavendish), **1:**230
 of *The Unwanted* (Nguyen), **1:**172
 of *A Woman in Berlin* (anonymous), **2:**281, 282
 of *The Woman Warrior* (Kingston), **1:**175
 of *Zlata's Diary* (Filipovic), **2:**340
Truth, Sojourner, *Narrative of Sojourner Truth*, **1:**37
Truth and Fiction Relating to My Life (Goethe), **1:276–278**
Truth and Reconciliation Commission (TRC), oral histories of, **3:**242–244
Try to Remember (Gomez), **1:**108
Tso, Mae, **3:**11
Tsuchino (Forrester), **3:**127–128
Tsukamoto, Mary, **3:**197
Tuberculosis
 Bashkirtseff's (Marie) struggle with, **2:**306, 307, 308
 Mansfield's (Katherine) struggle with, **2:**133
Tubman, Harriet, **2:**29
Tuchman, Barbara, **3:**186
Tuhami (Crapanzano), **3:**47
Tulsa Studies in Women's Literature (journal), **2:**111, 124
Tulugarjuk, Leo, *Ilagiinniq*, **3:**138
Tunisia, Amrouche (Fadhma Aïth Mansour) in, **1:**93, 94

Tuqan, Fadwa
 The Harder Journey, **1:**226
 A Mountainous Journey, **1:225–228**
 My Brother Ibrahim, **1:**227
Tuqan, Ibrahim, **1:**226, 227
Turgenev, Ivan, **2:**183
Turkey
 Armenian genocide denied by, **3:**40, 42
 in Crimean War, **1:**113
Turkish Embassy Letters (Montagu), **2:**35, 37
Turkish Lover, The (Santiago), **1:**108
Turner, D. R., **3:**255
Turner, Frederick W., III, **1:**304
Turner, J. M. W., **2:**143
Turner, Nat, **1:**206, **2:**238
Tuskegee Airmen, oral histories of, **3:**248–250
Tuskegee Airmen, The (film), **3:249**
Tuskegee Airmen, The (Francis), **3:**212
Tuskegee Institute, **1:**50, 51, *51*, 52
Tute, James, **2:**205
Tutsi people, **3:**257–259
Tutu, Desmond
 No Future without Forgiveness, **3:**244
 on Peltier's (Leonard) imprisonment, **1:**96
 in Truth and Reconciliation Commission, **3:**243, 244
Twain, Henry, **1:**147
Twain, Mark, **1:**147
 Adventures of Huckleberry Finn, **1:**146, 147–148
 The Innocents Abroad, **1:**146
 "The Late Benjamin Franklin," **1:**181–182
 Life on the Mississippi, **1:146–148**
 "Old Times on the Mississippi," **1:**146
 in realist movement, **2:**240
 Roughing It, **1:**146
 A Tramp Abroad, **1:**146
Twelve Years a Slave (Northup), **1:**50
Twentieth-Century Literary Criticism (journal), **2:**24
Twentieth Century Literature (journal), **2:**134

27 Wagons Full of Cotton (Williams), **2:**152
Twice Born (Lifton), **1:**102
Twichell, Joseph, **1:**147
Two Gentlemen of Verona (Shakespeare), **2:**226, 228
Two Sides to Everything (Scott), **3:**96
Two Years before the Mast (Dana), **1:**234
Ty, Eleanor, **2:**111
Tyminski, Dan, **3:**159
Tyndale, William, **2:**97
Typhus, in German concentration camps, **2:**253
Tzotzil language, **3:**167

U

UAW. *See* United Automobile Workers
Ubico, Jorge, **1:**99, 101
UC. *See* University of California
Uchida, Yoshiko, **1:**300
 Desert Exile, **1:**309
 The Invisible Thread, **1:309–311**
UDI. *See* Unilateral Declaration of Independence
Ukraine
 Bashkirtseff's (Marie) emigration to France from, **2:**306–308
 Chernobyl nuclear disaster in, **3:**282–285
 Great Famine of 1932–1933 in, **3:**19
 independence of (1991), **3:**340
 miners in, oral histories of, **3:**340–342, *341*
Ulin, David, **2:**118
Ulrich, Laurel Thatcher
 Good Wives, **2:**331–332
 A Midwife's Tale, **2:331–334**
Ulysses (Joyce), **1:**146, **2:**67, 180
Umara al-Hakami al-Yamani, **1:**286
Umkhonto we Sizwe (MK), **1:**27
Umutesi, Marie Béatrice, *Surviving the Slaughter*, **3:**258
UMW. *See* United Mine Workers
UMWA. *See* United Mine Workers of America
UN. *See* United Nations

Unabridged Journals of Sylvia Plath, The (Plath), **2:**49
Unaipon (ballet), **1:**149
Unaipon, David, **1:150**
　"Leaves of Memory," **1:**149
　My Life Story, **1:149–151**
　Myths and Legends of the Australian Aboriginals, **1:**149
Unaipon, James, **1:**149, 151
Una Storia Segreta (DiStasi), **3:**224
Unbound (Maathai), **1:**114
Uncertain Travelers (Agosín), **1:**75
UnCivil Liberties (Fox), **3:**226
Uncle Tom's Cabin (Stowe), **1:**33, 144
Uncomfortable Wars (Manwaring), **3:**207
Uncomfortable Wars Revisited (Manwaring and Fishel), **3:**207
Underhill, Evelyn, **1:**191
Underhill, Ruth
　The Autobiography of a Papago Woman, **3:**318
　Chona, **1:69–71**
　The Navajos, **3:**290
　Red Man's Religion, **1:**70
　Singing for Power, **1:**70
Under My Skin (Lessing), **1:167–169**
Undertones of War (Blunden), **1:**329
Underwood, Thomas, *Blacks at Harvard,* **3:**21
Unemployment (Seabrook), **3:**54
Unemployment, during Great Depression, **3:**161, 212
UNESCO, **3:**334
Unfinished Conquest (Perera), **1:**99
Ung, Loung, *First They Killed My Father,* **1:**306
Unger, Harlow Giles, **2:**71
Ungo, Guillermo M., **3:**205
UNICEF, **1:**312, 314, **2:**338
Uniformitarianism, **1:**65
Unilateral Declaration of Independence (UDI), **3:**251
Union Maids (film), **3:**179
Union of Automobile Workers, **3:**99
Unions. *See* Labor movement
Unitarian movement, in England, **2:**76
United Automobile Workers (UAW), **3:**153

United Kingdom. *See* Britain
United Mine Workers (UMW), **3:**98
United Mine Workers of America (UMWA), **3:**337, 339
United Nations (UN)
　First International Children's Parliament at, **1:**314
　Historical Clarifications Commission of, **3:**166
　International Law Commission of, **2:**56
　in International Women's Year Tribunal, **3:**322
　on Iraqi invasion of Kuwait, **2:**278
　on Rwandan genocide, **3:**257, 258
　Siv (Sichan) as U.S. ambassador to, **1:**306, *307*
　on workers' rights, **3:**157
United Nations and Economic Sanctions against Rhodesia, The (Kapungu), **3:**251
United Nations Children's Fund (UNICEF), **1:**312, 314, **2:**338
United Nations Educational, Scientific and Cultural Organization (UNESCO), **3:**334
United Negro College Fund, **1:**273, 274
United States. *See also* American *entries*
　anarchism in, **3:**3–5
　censorship in, **1:**20, **2:**123
　Cheng Yu-hsiu in, **1:**152
　coal mining in, **3:**66–69, 86, 87, 96–98, 157
　colonial era of (*See* United States, colonial)
　containment policy of, **3:**205
　economy of (*See* Economy)
　education in (*See* Education)
　expansion of (*See* Westward expansion)
　flu pandemic of 1918 in, **1:**258
　gender roles in, eighteenth-century, **2:**316
　gender roles in, twentieth-century, **2:**47
　in Guatemalan Civil War, **3:**166
　homosexuality in, attitudes toward, **1:**139
　immigration to (*See* Immigration)

　industrialization of, **1:**233
　interracial adoption in, **1:**102–104
　interracial relationships in, attitudes toward, **1:**72–74
　labor movement in (*See* Labor movement)
　Latin American culture in, **1:**109
　letter writing in, **2:**223
　midwifery in, **2:**331–333
　minorities in (*See* Assimilation; Civil rights; *specific groups*)
　national progress of, Emerson (Ralph Waldo) on, **2:**139, 140
　Native American treaties with, **1:**69, **3:**107, 110, 290, 327
　nuclear weapons of, **1:**293–294, **3:**239–241
　Pakistani relations with, **1:**87
　poverty in, **1:**122, **3:**66, 67, 254–256
　presidential election of 1860 in, **3:**261
　presidential election of 1992 in, **3:**221
　Puerto Rico as territory of, **1:**108
　Puritanism in, **1:**325–327
　Reconstruction in, **1:**50–52, **2:**238
　Saitoti's (Tepilit Ole) education in, **1:**114, 115
　in Salvadoran Civil War, **3:**205–207
　slavery in (*See* Slavery)
　on Vietnamese human rights violations, **1:**171, 172
　Vietnamese relations with, **1:**335
　wars of (*See* Military; *specific wars*)
　women of (*See* American women)
United States, colonial
　Afro-Atlantic writers in, **2:**44
　in Alta California, **3:**114–116
　Condict (Jemima) on life in, **2:**78–80
　Crèvecoeur (Michel-Guillaume Saint-Jean de) on life in, **2:**213–215
　French and Indian War in, **2:**205, 213
　Great Awakening in, **1:**179, **2:**197
　idealization of, **2:**213–215
　King Philip's War in, **1:**325–328

SUBJECT INDEX

United States, colonial, *continued*
    Rowlandson (Mary) on life in, **1:**325–328
    Wesley's (John) mission to, **2:**195, 196
    women's autobiographical writing in, **2:**78–79
University of California (UC), Mark Twain Project of, **1:**148
University of California at Berkeley, **3:**21
    African Americans at, oral histories of, **3:**20–22
    student movements of 1968 at, **3:**33
University of Iowa Writers' Workshop, **1:**164, 165
University of London, **2:**77
University of Nairobi, **2:**12, 13
University of Pennsylvania, **2:**275, 276
University of Toronto Quarterly, **3:**140
Unknown Internment, The (Fox), **3:**215, **224–226**
Unlawful Organizations Act of 1960 (South Africa), **1:**25
Unprivileged, The (Seabrook), **3:**55
Unquiet Mind, An (Jamison), **1:**204
Untold Tales, Unsung Heroes (Moon), **3:99–101**
Unto This Last (Ruskin), **1:**242
Unwanted, The (Nguyen), **1:170–172**
Unwinding Threads (Bruner), **1:**94
Up (documentary series), **3:**53
Upcott, William, **2:**65
Updike, John, **3:**59–60
Up from Slavery (Washington), **1:**3, 15, **50–53**
Upon Their Shoulders (Ota), **1:**309
"Up-river Book" (Conrad), **2:**194
Up the Swiftwater (Crowell and Asleson), **3:**93
Uqalurait (Bennett and Rowley), **3:**107, **138–140**
Urban Anthropology (journal), **3:**122
Urban II (pope), **1:**285
Urchin, The (Bedoukian), **3:**40
Urey, Harold, **3:**239
Urogi (witchcraft), among Meru people, **3:**141–143

Urrea, José de, **1:**304
Urrutia, Matilde, **1:**222, 223
Ury, Marian, **2:**60, 292
Usāmah ibn Munqidh, *An Arab-Syrian Gentleman and Warrior in the Period of the Crusades,* **1:285–288**
USA Today (newspaper), **1:**172
U.S. Catholic Historian (journal), **3:**309
Uses of Literacy, The (Hoggart), **1:**16
Utopian societies, **1:**14, 235
Utopian Studies (journal), **2:**255

V

Vaarzon-Morel, Petronella, *Warlpiri Women's Voices,* **3:**107, **334–336**
VAD. *See* Voluntary Aid Detachment
Valerius (bishop), **1:**196
Valéry, Paul, **2:**150
Vallejo, César, **1:**224
Valley of Shadows and Dreams (Light and Light), **3:**67
Vambe, Lawrence Chinyani
    From Rhodesia to Zimbabwe, **3:**251
    An Ill-Fated People, **3:**251–253
Van Brunt, H. L., **3:**87
Vance, Kevin, **2:**40
Van Derlinder, Jean, **3:**291
Van der Veen, Jon, **3:**181
Van Donzel, Emeri, **1:**91, 92
Van Horssen, Jessica, **3:**181
Vanity Fair (magazine), **1:**204, 205, **2:**118
Vanity Fair (Thackeray), **2:**312
Van Orman, Richard A., **3:**91
Van Vechten, Carl, **1:**84
Van Vorst, Mrs. John, **1:**154
Vanzan, Anna, **3:**219
Vargas Llosa, Mario
    A Fish in the Water, **1:**168
    Letters to a Young Novelist, **2:**150
VaShawasha people, oral histories of, **3:**251–253
Vasquez, Jose "Pepe," **3:**122
Vasvári, Louise, **1:**76–77
Vatican Council, Second (Vatican II), **3:**308, 309

Vaughan, Benjamin, **1:**180
Vega, Ed, **1:**108
Vega, Jaime, **2:**222
Vega-González, Susana, **1:**251
Veganism, of Gandhi (Mohandas), **1:**243
Velasco, Luis Alejandro, **3:**183–185
Velho, Álvaro, **2:**198
Velikova, Rumiana, **1:**5
Venice, Republic of, **2:**198
Veracity. *See* Truth
Verene, Donald P., **1:**183
Verisimilitude. *See* Truth
Versailles, Treaty of (1919)
    Chinese disappointment with, **1:**338, **3:**126, 147, 149
    Germany after, **1:**30, **3:**234
Vesey, Denmark, **2:**238
Vesuvius, Mount, eruption of, **2:**94, 95
Veterans, oral histories of
    by African Americans, **3:**199–201, 248–250
    from Iraq War, **3:**231–233, *232*
    from Vietnam War, **3:**199–201, 209–211, 275–277
    from World War II, **3:**202–204, 248–250
Veterans History Project, **3:**128
Vettini, Amanda, **3:**171–172
Viareggio Book Prize, for *The Order Has Been Carried Out* (Portelli), **3:**265
Vico, Giambattista, **1:**184
    The Autobiography of Giambattista Vico, **1:183–185**
    Dell'antichissima sapienza italica, **1:**183
    New Science, **1:**183, 184, 185
Victoria (queen of Great Britain), **2:**210
    expansion of empire under, **2:**16
    Leaves from the Journal of Our Life in the Highlands, **2:209–212**
    More Leaves from the Journal of Our Life in the Highlands, **2:**209
    Seacole (Mary) and, **1:**112
Victorian era (1837–1901)
    autobiographies in, traits of, **1:**65, 67

biographies in, approach to, **2:**143
end of, **1:**329–330
expansion of empire in, **2:**16
Gissing (George) on culture of, **2:**320–322
literary marketplace of, **2:**320–322
social inequality in, **1:**252, **2:**16
social mobility in, barriers to, **1:**252
social reform at end of, **1:**329, **2:**16
women in, Webb (Beatrice) on, **2:**16–18
working-class youth in, **3:**311–312
Victorian Literature and Culture (journal), **2:**210
Victorian Studies (journal), **2:**17, 322, 337, **3:**313
Victory at Sea (television show), **3:**234
Vidal, Gore, **2:**152, 153
Videla, Jorge Rafael, **3:**185
Vien, Joseph Marie, **1:219**
Vietnam
    French rule of, **1:**335, **3:**279
    history of occupations of, **1:**335
    partition of (1954), **1:**335
    postwar social conditions in, **1:**170–172
    racism against multiracial individuals in, **1:**170, 171
    reunification of (1975), **1:**170, 171
    U.S. relations with, **1:**335
    in Vietnam War, oral histories of, **3:**279–281
Vietnamese American(s)
    autobiographical tradition of, **1:**170–171
    Hayslip (Le Ly) on experience of, **1:**335–337
    Nguyen (Kien) on experience of, **1:**170–172
    racism against, **1:**171
Vietnam Veterans Memorial, **3:200,** 223
Vietnam Veterans Memorial Fund, **3:**223
Vietnam War, **1:171, 3:210**
    antiwar movement against, **3:**221, 222, *269,* 275, 277
    conscientious objectors in, **3:**221–223
    and drug use, rise of, **2:**294
    escalation under Johnson (Lyndon Baines), **3:**254, 256
    fall of Saigon in, **3:**209
    fall of South Vietnam in, **3:**279–281
    Hayslip (Le Ly) on life during, **1:**335–337
    literature on consequences of, **1:**335
    media coverage of, **2:**280, **3:**199
    mistakes made in, **3:**275–276
    Nguyen (Kien) on life after, **1:**170–172
    refugees from, **1:**306, 337
    start of, **1:**335, **3:**275, 279
    Tet Offensive in, **3:**275
    U.S. entry into, **1:**335, **3:**209, 275
    U.S. withdrawal from, **3:**275, 279
Vietnam War oral histories
    by African American veterans, **3:**199–201
    by American civilians, **3:**275–277, *276*
    by American veterans, **3:**199–201, 275–277
    by conscientious objectors, **3:**221–223
    on fall of South Vietnam, **3:**279–281
    by Vietnamese civilians and veterans, **3:**279–281
View in Winter, The (Blythe), **3:**60
Viezzer, Moema, *Let Me Speak!,* **3:**74, 114–115, **322–324**
Vigne, Thea, **3:**311
Villa, Pancho, **3:**167, 302
Village Voice (newspaper), **1:**119, 313
Vindication of the Rights of Women, A (Wollstonecraft), **2:**314
Violence
    in British gangs, **3:**311–313
    domestic (*See* Domestic violence)
    in Guatemala, Perera (Victor) on, **1:**99–100
    in Israeli–Palestinian conflict, Ghazzawi ('Izzat) on, **2:**50–51
    sexual, in Guatemala, **1:**100 (*See also* Rape)
    against women, in Islam, **1:**207–209
Violence against Women (journal), **2:**282
Violent Adventure (Wesley), **1:**48
Virginia
    in Civil War, **2:**38
    coal mining in, oral histories of, **3:**86–87
    interracial marriage in, **1:**72
Virginia Magazine of History and Biography, **2:**38
Virginia Quarterly Review, **2:**137
Vision or Villainy (Hoffaman), **3:**102
Visions, divine, of Teresa of Ávila, **1:**211, 212
VISTA. *See* Volunteers in Service to America
Visual elements, in *The Way to Rainy Mountain* (Momaday), **1:**54, 55, *55*
Vitier, Cintio, **2:**220
Vizgalova, Irina, **3:**332
Voice. *See* Narrative voice
Voice of the Past, The (Thompson), **3:186–189**
    on *Akenfield* (Blythe), **3:**59–61
    Hooligans or Rebels? (Humphries) influenced by, **3:**311–312
    on *The Saga of Coe Ridge* (Montell), **3:**92
    Vietnam War literature influenced by, **3:**209
Voice of Witness (Eggers and Vollen), **3:**161
Voices from Chernobyl (Alexievich), **3:265, 282–286**
Voices from the Grave (film), **3:**29
Voices from the Third Reich (Steinhoff), **3:**215
Voices from the Whirlwind (Feng), **3:287–289,** 301
Voices from this Long Brown Land (Wehrey), **3:102–104**
Voices Long Silent (Hansen and Mitson), **3:**195
Voices of Freedom (Hampton and Fayer), **3:44–46**
Voices of Resistance (Baker), **3:47–49**

SUBJECT INDEX

Voices of the Holocaust (Rothchild), **3:**50
Vollen, Lola, *Voice of Witness,* **3:**161
Voltaire, **2:**37, 329
Voluntary Aid Detachment (VAD), **1:**329, **2:**259–261
Volunteers in Service to America (VISTA), **3:**254
Vo Nguyen Giap, **3:**279
Voss, Barbara L., **3:**116
Voter registration drives, **1:**20
Voting rights
　　for African Americans, **1:**50, **2:**238
　　for women, **1:**12, 13, 14
Voting Rights Act of 1965 (U.S.), **1:**20
Voyage and Travels of Sir John Mandeville, The, **1:**105
Voyages: The Trans-Atlantic Slave Trade Database, **1:**263
Voyage to the East Indies (Grose), **2:**229
V-2 rockets, **2:**270
Vu, Tran Tri, *Lost Years,* **1:**170
Vuic, Kara Dixon, **3:**277

W

Wada, Ernest, **3:**85
Wagenknecht, Edward, **2:**137
Waggoner, Hyatt, **2:**225
Waheenee (Wilson), **1:**69–70
Wainwright, Loudon, **3:**213
Waiting for Snow in Havana (Eire), **1:**296–297
Waka (Japanese poems), **2:**189, 191, 292
Wakatsuki, George Ko, **1:**300, 301
Wakatsuki, Riku, **1:**301
Wakefield, Priscilla, **2:**300
Wakeman, Stephen H., **2:**224
Walden (Thoreau), **1:233–236,** **2:**140, 215
Waldron, Philip, **2:**134
Waldsteicher, David, **2:**45
Wales, Thomas (Dylan) on life in, **1:**125–126
Walker, Alice
　　Angelou's (Maya) influence on, **1:**18–19
　　The Color Purple, **1:**18, 175

on Hurston (Zora Neale), **1:**11
The Way Forward Is with a Broken Heart, **1:**18–19
Walker, Pierre, **1:**20
Walker, Reuben, **1:**149
Walker, Robert, **2:66**
Walking in the Shade (Lessing), **1:**167
Walking Purchase of 1737, **3:**327
Walkowitz, Daniel J., *Workers of the Donbass Speak,* **3:**157, **340–342**
Wall, Irwin, **2:**263
Wallace, Alfred Russel, **1:**67
Wallace, John R., **2:**191
Waller, P. J., **3:**313
Wallington, Nehemiah, **2:**74
Walls, Jeanette, **1:**251
Walls, Laura Dassow, **1:**236
Wall Street Journal, **2:**20, **3:**164
Walmsley, Jan, *Oral History, Health and Welfare,* **3:170–172**
Walpole, Horace, **2:**97, 146, 195, 196
Walpole, Hugh, **2:**115
Walton, Edith, **2:**260
Walton, John, *Western Times and Water Wars,* **3:**102
Walton, Martin, **3:**28
Wang, Jing M., **1:**340
Wang Zheng, *Women in the Chinese Enlightenment,* **3:147–149**
Wansink, Hans, **1:**207
War(s). *See also specific wars*
　　childhood during, memoirs of, **1:**312–314
　　"low-intensity," **3:**207
　　realism in depictions of, **2:**240
War brides, Japanese, **3:**127–129, *128*
War Brides of World War II (Shukert and Scibetta), **3:**127
War correspondents
　　Chapelle (Dickey) as, **2:**280
　　Gellhorn (Martha) as, **2:**101–103
　　in Gulf War, **2:**278–280
　　in Iraq War, **2:**278, 280
　　in Vietnam War, **2:**280, **3:**199
War crimes
　　in Sierra Leone civil war, **1:**312
　　in World War II, **1:**77, **2:**54–56, **3:**293–295

Ward, Fumiko, **3:**128
Ward, Hiley, **2:**279
War Department, U.S., **3:**248
Wardle, Ralph M., **2:**109, 111
Ware, Ann Patrick, *Midwives of the Future,* **3:**308
Warhol, Robyn, **1:**141
Warlpiri people, oral histories of, **3:**334–336
Warlpiri sign language, **3:**335–336
Warlpiri Women's Voices (Vaarzon-Morel), **3:**107, **334–336**
Warner, Edith, **3:**241
Warner, Fara, **2:**20
War of 1812, **1:**233, **2:**69
War on drugs, U.S., **2:**294
War on poverty, U.S., **3:**254–256
War Reminiscences (Mosby), **2:**250
Warrior, Robert Allen, **1:**56
Wars I Have Seen (Stein), **1:332–334**
War Walks (television series), **3:**236
Washington, Booker T.
　　and Du Bois (W. E. B.), debate between, **1:**186
　　The Story of My Life and Work, **1:**37
　　Up from Slavery, **1:**3, 15, **50–53**
Washington, D.C.
　　Adams (Abigail) on life in, **2:**87–90
　　establishment of, **2:**87
Washington, George, **2:**44, 87
Washington Post (newspaper), **1:**16, **2:**56, 278, 331
Washington Post Book World, **3:**213
Washington Times (newspaper), **2:**40
Wasserman, George, **1:**269
Waswo, Richard, **2:**309–310
Wat, Eric, *The Making of a Gay Asian Community,* **3:83–85**
Watching Seagulls (Saliba), **1:**161
Watergate scandal, **3:**279
Waterloo, Battle of (1815), **2:**312
Water Margins (Chinese novel), **1:**338
Water resources
　　in Australia, **3:**334
　　in California, **3:**102, 103
　　on Native American reservations, **1:**69, **3:**11

444　　THE LITERATURE OF AUTOBIOGRAPHICAL NARRATIVE ✦ VOLUME 2 ✦ DIARIES AND LETTERS

Waters, Chris, **3**:72
Waters, Ethel, **1**:10
Water Seekers, The (Nadeau), **3**:102
Watkins, Gloria Jean. *See* hooks, bell
Watson, James, **3**:37
Watson, Nora, **3**:343
Watson, Reginald, **1**:74
Wattenberg, Miriam, **2**:253
Watts, William, **1**:196
Waverly (Scott), **2**:309
Way Forward Is with a Broken Heart, The (Walker), **1**:18–19
Wayne, John, **1**:100
Way of Perfection, The (Teresa of Ávila), **1**:212
Way to Rainy Mountain, The (Momaday), **1**:54–57, *55*
Wealth
    in Ireland, **1**:119–120
    of Native Americans, **3**:290
Wealth of Nations (Smith), **2**:200
Weapons of mass destruction (WMD), in Iraq, **2**:275
Webb, Beatrice
    Diaries of Beatrice Webb, **2**:16–18
    The Letters of Sidney and Beatrice Webb, **2**:172
    Minority Report to the Commission of the Poor Law, **2**:16
    My Apprenticeship, **2**:17
    Our Partnership, **2**:17, 172
Webb, Richard Davis, **2**:157–158
Webb, Sidney, **2**:16, 17, 172
Webs of Power (Maurer and Mirow), **3**:277
Webster, Daniel, **2**:75
Webster, Robert, **2**:195
Wedderburn, Alexander, **1**:265
"We Don't Want Crumbs" (Luthuli), **1**:25
Weekly Anglo-African, **1**:144
Week on the Concord and Merrimack Rivers, A (Thoreau), **1**:233, 234, 235, **2**:140
Weglyn, Michi, *Years of Infamy*, **3**:212
"We Have Just Begun to Not Fight" (Frazer and O'Sullivan), **3**:227–230
Wehrey, Jane
    Manzanar, **3**:102

The Owens Valley, **3**:102
Voices from this Long Brown Land, **3**:102–104
Weil, Simone, **2**:22, 24
Weinberg, Bill, *Our Appalachia*, **3**:66, **86–89**
Weinberg, Sidney J., **3**:163
Weinberg, Sydney Stahl, *The World of Our Mothers*, **3**:305
Weiner, Marli, **2**:273
Weise, Robert, **3**:96, 97
Weisiger, Marsha L., *Dreaming of Sheep in Navajo Country*, **3**:10
Weiss, Brad, **3**:142–143
Weiss, Cora, **3**:269
Weiss, Gillian, **3**:334
Wei Tao-Ming, **1**:152, 154
Wei Tao-Ming, Madame. *See* Cheng Yu-hsiu
Weitzman, Lenore J., **3**:35
Welcher, Jeanne K., **2**:67
Weld, Theodore, *American Slavery as It Is*, **1**:33, 142
Wellcome Trust, **3**:170
Wellesley, Arthur, **2**:217
Wells, G. P., **1**:252, 254
Wells, H. G., **1**:253
    Bennett (Arnold) compared to, **2**:136
    on *A Diary without Dates* (Bagnold), **2**:260
    An Experiment in Autobiography, **1**:252–254
    Gellhorn (Martha) and, **2**:101
    H. G. Wells in Love, **1**:252, 253, 254
    letters of, **1**:252, 253
    London and the Life (Gissing) on, **2**:320
    Woolf (Virginia) on novels of, **2**:138
    A Writer's Notebook (Maugham) on, **2**:183
Wells, Ida B., *Southern Horrors*, **1**:50
Wells, Sarah, **1**:253
Welsh, Michael, **3**:240
Welsh autobiographical writing, by Thomas (Dylan), **1**:125–127
Welsh v. United States, **3**:223

Wen, Chihua, *The Red Mirror*, **3**:287
We of Nagasaki (Nagai), **1**:293
Werfel, Franz, **2**:120
Werner, Craig, **1**:247–248
Werner, Marta L., **1**:45–46
Wesley, Charles, **2**:195
Wesley, John, *Journals of John Wesley*, **2**:195–197, *196*
Wesley, Marilyn, *Violent Adventure*, **1**:48
West, E. Bernard, *Living Atlanta*, **3**:44
West, Geoffrey, **1**:253
West, Kanye, **1**:312
West, Russell, **2**:174
West, U.S., Carver's (Jonathan) exploration of, **2**:205–207. *See also* Westward expansion
West Bank, **2**:51
    Darwish (Mahmoud) in, **1**:255
    Israeli occupation of, **1**:225
    Tuqan (Fadwa) on life in, **1**:225
Westerbork concentration camp, **2**:22–24, *23*, 253
Western Folklore (journal), **2**:92
Western Historical Quarterly, **2**:163, **3**:12, 133, 225
Western Humanities Review (journal), **1**:56
Western Times and Water Wars (Walton), **3**:102
Westfall, Joseph, **2**:168
Westfall, Suzanne, **2**:99
West Indies
    Columbus's (Christopher) voyage to, **2**:201–203, *202*
    slavery in, **3**:23–25
Westoff, Clara, **2**:151
West Virginia
    coal mining in, **3**:66–69, *67*, *91*
    colonial era in, **3**:66
    statehood for, **3**:66
Westward expansion, U.S.
    Adams (John Quincy) on history of, **2**:69
    Black Elk on experience of, **3**:110
    Chona (Maria) on experience of, **1**:69
    Emerson (Ralph Waldo) on potential of, **2**:139

Westward expansion, U.S., *continued*
   Geronimo on experience of, **1**:302–304
   Ray (Annie) on experience of, **2**:163–164
   Stewart (Elinore Pruitt) on experience of, **2**:91–93, *92*
   Thoreau's (Henry David) critique of, **1**:233

Wey, William, **2**:226

Weyer, Edward Moffat, *The Eskimo*, **3**:138

Wharton, Edith, **2**:113

"What, to the Slave, Is the Fourth of July?" (Douglass), **1**:79

What I Believe (Tolstoy), **1**:194, 195

What's a Woman Doing Here? (Chapelle), **2**:280

What Was Asked of Us (Wood), **3:231–233**, 276

Wheatley, Phillis, **2**:45
   Equiano (Olaudah) compared to, **1**:81, **2**:44
   "Letter to the Reverend Samson Occom," **2:44–46**
   "On Being Brought from Africa to America," **2**:46
   Poems on Various Subjects, **2**:44
   Prince (Mary) compared to, **3**:23
   "To His Excellency General Washington," **2**:44

Wheatley, Susanna, **2**:44, 46

Wheelock, Eleazar, **2**:46

Whelan-Stewart, Wendy, **2**:49

When Bodies Remember (Fassin), **3**:272

When Broken Glass Floats (Him), **1**:306

When Heaven and Earth Changed Places (Hayslip), **1**:170–171, **335–337**

When I Was Puerto Rican (Santiago), **1:108–110**

When the Mill Whistle Blew (Strobel), **3**:93

When We Began, There Were Witchmen (Fadiman), **3:141–143**

Which Side Are You On? (Hevener), **3**:96

Whitaker, Katie, **1**:229

White, E. B., **1**:234, 235

White, Gilbert, **2**:300

White, Jerry, **3**:54

White, Mike, **2**:255

White, Raymond O., **3**:107, 108

White, Thomas Willis, **2**:41

White audience
   of *Dust Tracks on a Road* (Hurston), **1**:9, 11
   of *Incidents in the Life of a Slave Girl* (Jacobs), **1**:142, 143
   of "Letter from the Birmingham Jail" (King), **2**:33
   of *Up from Slavery* (Washington), **1**:50–52

White colleges, African Americans at, **3**:20–22

Whitefield, George, **2**:46, 197

White Revolution (Iran), **3**:218

Whitesinger, Pauline, **3**:11

Whither India? (Nehru), **1**:290

Whitley, Glenna, **3**:201, 211

Whitlock, Gillian, **1**:40, **3**:25

Whitman, Walt, **1**:173, 234, 265

Whitsitt, Novian, **1**:144

Whittier, John Greenleaf, **2**:29

Wickert, Erwin, **2**:19

Widder, Keith, **2**:207

Wiesel, Elie, **1:319**
   Dawn, **1**:319
   Day, **1**:319
   Night, **1:318–321**

Wiggins, Sarah Woodfolk, **2**:246

WikiLeaks, **3**:229

Wilburn, Oleson, **3**:92

Wilde, Oscar
   The Ballad of Reading Gaol, **2**:9
   De Profundis, **2:9–11**
   indecency trial of, **2**:9, 183, 185
   Maugham (W. Somerset) influenced by, **2**:183, 184, 185
   on *Memoirs of an Arabian Princess from Zanzibar* (Ruete), **1**:91
   The Picture of Dorian Gray, **2**:9
   Salomé, **2**:183

Wilde-Menozzi, Wallis, **2**:255

Wild Swans (Chang), **1**:158–159

Wilenski, R. H., **1**:265

Wilford, Hugh, **3**:5

Wilhelm Meister's Apprenticeship (Goethe), **1**:30

Wilkins, William Henry, **2**:217

Wilkinson, Edmund L., **3**:248–249

Wilkinson, James, **1**:202

Wilkinson, Jane, **2**:14

Will. *See* Divine will; Free will

Will, Herman, **3**:228

Willenson, Kim, *The Bad War*, **3**:275

William and Mary Quarterly, **1**:134

William of Orange, **2**:324, *325*

Williams, Ben Ames, **2**:250

Williams, Bill, **3**:186

Williams, David, **2**:207

Williams, Gweno, **1**:230, 231

Williams, Lynne, **3**:175

Williams, Ronald, **1**:96

Williams, Rowan, **1**:212

Williams, Tennessee, **2**:153
   Camino Real, **2**:154
   The Glass Menagerie, **2**:152
   Memoirs, **2**:152, 153
   Notebooks, **2:152–154**
   A Streetcar Named Desire, **2**:152
   27 Wagons Full of Cotton, **2**:152

Willis, Lord, **2:236**

Willison, George, **2:329**

Wills, Garry, **1**:197, 198

WILPF. *See* Women's International League for Peace and Freedom

Wilsey, Sean, **1**:141

Wilson, August, **1**:273

Wilson, Bee, **2**:289

Wilson, Douglas L., *Herndon's Informants*, **3**:264

Wilson, Edmund, **2**:246

Wilson, Gilbert L., *Waheenee*, **1**:69–70

Wilson, Harriet E., *Our Nig*, **1**:142

Wilson, Jean Moorcroft, **2**:249

Wilson, Kathleen, **1**:159

Wilson, Sonia, **2**:81, 307

Wilson, Woodrow, **3**:29, 153

Winder, Robert, **3**:59, 61

Windham, William, **2**:217

Winfrey, Oprah, **2**:296

Wing, Sandra Koa, **2**:265, 267

Wings of the Dove, The (James), **2:**113, 115

Winkler, Allan, *Life under a Cloud,* **3:**239

Winkler, Michael, **2:**151

Winn, Mathew, **3:**233

Winter, Naomi, **2:**27

Winter Soldier (Iraq Veterans against the War), **3:**232

Winterthur Portfolio (journal), **3:**320

Wirzba, Norman, **3:**67–68

Wisconsin Magazine of History, **3:**329

Wise, Christopher, **1:**23

Wise, R. Todd, **1:**23

Wister, Sally, **2:**78–79

Witchcraft
    among Meru, **3:**141–143
    among Navajo, **3:**290–291

Witch Purge of 1878, The (Blue), **3:**290–292

With Wings (Saxton and Howe), **1:**8

Witke, Roxanne, **3:**147

Witnesses, memory of, **3:**265, 266

Witnesses to Nuremberg (Stave et al.), **3:**293–295

Witnesses to the Holocaust (Lewin), **3:**50–52

WMD. *See* Weapons of mass destruction

Wobblies, **3:**93, 328–330

Wobblies, The (documentary), **3:**328

Wobblies!: A Graphic History (Buhle and Schulman), **3:**330

Woerner, Fred F., **3:**205

Wolcott, Reed, *Rose Hill,* **3:**86

Wolf, Benjamin, **3:**155

Wolfe, Charles, **3:**159

Wolff, Tobias
    Back in the World, **1:**47
    The Barracks Thief, **1:**47
    In Pharaoh's Army, **1:**47
    In the Garden of North American Martyrs, **1:**47
    This Boy's Life, **1:**47–49

Wolford, John B., **3:**266

Wolfson, Susan, **2:**147

Wollett, Jan, **3:**280

Wollstonecraft, Mary
    The Collected Letters of Mary Wollstonecraft, **2:**109–112
    on *The Interesting Narrative of the Life of Olaudah Equiano* (Equiano), **1:**82
    Letters Written during a Short Residence in Sweden, Norway, and Denmark, **2:**111
    A Vindication of the Rights of Women, **2:**314

Wolpert, Stanley, **1:**290

Woman (periodical), **2:**136

Woman at War, A (Moore), **2:**278–280

Woman in Berlin, A (anonymous), **2:**281–283

Woman of Peace (Hayslip), **1:**335

Woman Prisoner, The (Ghazzawi), **2:**50

Woman's Bible, The (Stanton), **1:**12, 13

Woman Soldier's Own Story, A (Xie), **1:**338–340

Woman's Place, A (Roberts), **3:**144, 145, 146

Woman's "True" Profession (Hoffman), **3:**77

Woman's World (magazine), **1:**91

Woman Warrior, The (Kingston), **1:**75, 100, **173–176**

Women. *See also* specific countries, ethnicities, and religions
    in abolitionist movement, **1:**142
    education of (*See* Education)
    oral histories of, feminist approach to, **3:**190–192, *191*
    religious roles of, Stanton (Elizabeth Cady) on, **1:**12
    Renaissance, **2:**160–162
    social roles of (*See* Gender roles)

Women Activists (Garland), **3:**268

Women and Families (Roberts), **3:**144–146

Women and the Holocaust (Fuchs), **3:**35

Women in the Chinese Enlightenment (Wang), **3:**147–149

Women in the Mines (Moore), **3:**157, 328, **337–339**

Women of Algiers in Their Apartment (Djebar), **1:**207

Women of Coal (Norris and Cyprès), **3:**337

Women religious, oral histories of, **3:**308–310

Women's International Congress, **3:**268

Women's International League for Peace and Freedom (WILPF), **3:**268, 269, 270

Women's Peace Oral History Project, **3:**268–270

Women's Review of Books (journal)
    on *Bone Black* (hooks), **1:**251
    on *A Mountainous Journey* (Tuqan), **1:**226
    on *My Life Story* (Amrouche), **1:**94
    on *Songs My Mother Sang to Me* (Preciado Martin), **3:**133
    on *Under My Skin* (Lessing), **1:**169
    on *Voices of Resistance* (Baker), **3:**48
    on *A Woman Soldier's Own Story* (Xie), **1:**340
    on *Women in the Mines* (Moore), **3:**338

Women's rights movement. *See also* Feminism
    in Britain, **1:**329, 331, **2:**109
    in China, **1:**338
    in France, **2:**306
    in Iran, **3:**218
    in U.S., **1:**12–14, **2:**47

Women's studies, *Letters of a Woman Homesteader* (Stewart) in, **2:**91

Women's Studies Quarterly, **1:**141

Women Strike for Peace (WSP), **3:**268

Women's Voluntary Service, **2:**265

Women's Words (Gluck and Patai), **3:**190–192

Women's Writing (journal), **2:**325

Wonderful Adventures of Mrs. Seacole in Many Lands, The (Seacole), **1:**111–113

Wong, Alan, **3:**181

Wong, Hertha D., **1:**71
    Sending My Heart Back across the Years, **1:**56

Wong, Sharon, **1:**175

Wood, Frances, **1:**107

Wood, Gordon S., **1:**181

Wood, John, **3:**25

Wood, Trish, *What Was Asked of Us,* **3:**231–233, 276

Woodforde, Anna Maria, **2:**289

Woodforde, James, *A Country Parson,* **2:287–289**

Woodland Indians, oral histories of, **3:**107–109, *108*

Woodley, Arthur E., Jr., **3:**200

Woodson, Dorothy C., **1:**25

Woodward, Comer Vann, **2:**250, 251

Woodworth-Nay, Laura, **3:**12

Wooldridge, E. T.
  Carrier Warfare in the Pacific, **3:202–204**
  Into the Jet Age, **3:**203

Woolf, Leonard, **2:**180, 181, 182, 235, 268

Woolf, Virginia, **2:**181
  on Bennett's (Arnold) novels, **2:**137, 138
  in Bloomsbury group, **2:**180, 268
  Clifford (Anne) as inspiration for, **2:**64
  on *A Country Parson* (Woodforde), **2:**287, 288, 289
  Diaries of Beatrice Webb (Webb) on, **2:**16
  on *The Diary of John Evelyn* (Evelyn), **2:**66, 67
  The Diary of Virginia Woolf, **2:**133, 163, 180–182
  Hogarth Press of, **2:**268
  Jacob's Room, **2:**138
  Kingston (Maxine Hong) influenced by, **1:**173
  Moments of Being, **1:**249, **2:**182
  Nin (Anaïs) compared to, **2:**123
  Orlando, **1:**173, **2:**64, 181
  on Osborne (Dorothy), **2:**324, 325
  A Pacifist's War (Partridge) on, **2:**268
  Second Common Reader, **2:**289
  suicide of, **2:**268
  on *Testament of Youth* (Brittain), **1:**330
  To the Lighthouse, **1:**146
  A Writer's Diary, **2:180–182**

Woolman, John, *The Journal of John Woolman,* **2:**213

Worde, Wynken de, **1:**189, 191

Wordsworth, Christopher, **2:**301

Wordsworth, Dorothy
  Grasmere Journals, **2:**16, **300–302**
  Osborne (Dorothy) compared to, **2:**324

Wordsworth, William
  Byron (George Gordon Noel) compared to, **2:**143
  Grasmere Journals (Wordsworth) and, **2:**300–302
  Journals of Ralph Waldo Emerson (Emerson) on, **2:**141
  Keats (John) and, **2:**146
  The Prelude, **1:**201, 264, **2:**302
  Robinson (Henry Crabb) and, **2:**75

Workers of the Donbass Speak (Siegelbaum and Walkowitz), **3:**157, **340–342**

Workforce, English women's entry into, **2:**266, **3:**145

Work in America report, **3:**343

Working (Terkel), **3:**161, 300, **343–345**

Working class
  in Bolivia, oral histories of women in, **3:**322–324
  in Italy and Kentucky, oral histories of, **3:**157–159
  in Ukraine, oral histories of, **3:**340–342

Working class, in Britain
  education of, **3:**311–313
  social change in, **3:**53, 144
  in Victorian era, **2:**16
  women in, oral histories of, **3:**144–146
  youth in, oral histories of, **3:**53–54, 311–313

Working-Class Childhood (Seabrook), **3:53–55**

Works of John Ruskin, The (Ruskin), **1:**265

Works Progress Administration (WPA), **1:**35, **3:**99

World Affairs (journal), **1:**32

World as Will and Representation, The (Schopenhauer), **1:**193

World at War, The (Holmes), **3:234–236**

World at War, The (television series), **3:**234, 236

World I Live In, The (Keller), **1:**44, 45

World in the Evening, The (Isherwood), **2:**152

World Literature Today (journal), **1:**76, 128, 137, 247, **2:**191

World of Our Mothers, The (Weinberg), **3:**305

World of the Defeated, The (Revelli), **3:**61

Worlds of a Maasai Warrior, The (Saitoti), **1:114–116**

Worlds of Color (Du Bois), **1:**5

World Today (journal), **2:**33

World War I
  Australian military in, **3:**177
  Bagnold's (Enid) service in, **2:**259–261
  conscientious objectors in, **3:**223
  in England, Brittain (Vera) on life during, **1:**329–331, **3:**176
  Germany after defeat in, **1:**30, **3:**234
  Japanese nationalism after, **3:**234
  lost generation of, **1:**329
  Mansfield's (Katherine) writing during, **2:**133
  in modernism, rise of, **2:**180
  nursing in, **1:**329, 330, **2:**259–261, *260*
  Sassoon's (Siegfried) service in, **2:**247–249
  Stein (Gertrude) on experience of, **1:**332
  technological advances in, **2:**180
  war crimes trials after, **3:**293
  women's experience of, **1:**329–331, **2:**259

World War II. *See also* Holocaust; Japanese American internment; Nazi Germany
  autobiographies after, rise of interest in, **1:**239
  China during, **1:**152, 153, **3:**14–16
  conscientious objectors in, **2:**268–269, **3:**223, 227–229
  and *Dust Tracks on a Road* (Hurston), changes to, **1:**9
  end of, **2:**281, **3:**239

England during, Last (Nella) on life in, **2:**265–267

England during, Partridge (Frances) on life in, **2:**268–269

in France, Stein (Gertrude) on experience of, **1:**332–334

Gellhorn's (Martha) reporting on, **2:**101–103

German bombardment of Britain in, **2:**265, 269, 270

German occupation of France in, **1:**332–334

in Germany, Klemperer (Victor) on experience of, **2:**303–305

Iran in, **3:**218

Italian American relocation in, **3:**224–226

Italy in, Nazi occupation of, **3:**265–267

Japanese bombing of Pearl Harbor in, **1:**299, 300, 309, **3:**195, 202, 212, 215, 234

Japanese names for, **3:**215

Korea after, division of, **1:**322

Nuremberg trials after, **2:**54, 56, **3:**293–295

oral histories of (See World War II oral histories)

Palestine during, **2:**104

propaganda in, **2:**117, 118, 270, *282*

rape in, **2:**281–283

Scotland during, Mitchison (Naomi) on life in, **2:**235–237

Soviet occupation of Berlin in, **2:**281–282

start of, **3:**215, 234

U.S. entry into, **1:**299, 309, **3:**161, 202, 212, 234

U.S. liberation of France in, **1:**332, 333

U.S. naval aviation in, **3:**202–204

U.S. occupation of Japan after, **3:**127–129

U.S. use of nuclear weapons in, **1:**293–294, **3:**239

war crimes in, **1:**77, **2:**54–56, **3:**293–295

women's autobiographical writing during, **2:**235, 237

World War II oral histories. *See also* Holocaust oral histories

international, **3:**234–236

Italian, **3:**265–267

Japanese, **3:**127–129, 215–217

World War II oral histories, U.S.

by conscientious objectors, **3:**227–230

by Italian Americans, **3:**224–226

by Japanese Americans, **3:**80–81, 102–104, 195–197

by naval veterans, **3:**202–204

by ordinary people, **3:**212–214

by Tuskegee Airmen, **3:**248–250

by war brides, **3:**127–129

Worst of Times, The (Hoggart), **3:**53

Wotton, Edward, **2:**256

Wounded, literature of the, *Voices from the Whirlwind* (Feng) as, **3:**287

Wounded Knee (South Dakota)

AIM occupation of (1973), **1:**21, 22–23, 96

massacre at (1890), **3:**110, 111

Wounds of Passion (hooks), **1:**250, 251

WPA. *See* Works Progress Administration

Wren, Christopher, **2:**65

Wretched of the Earth, The (Fanon), **1:**207, **2:**263

Wright, Esmond, **1:**182

Wright, John Michael, **1:316**

Wright, Richard

Black Boy, **1:122–124**

A Father's Law, **1:**124

Native Son, **1:**122, 123, 273

Writer's Chronicle (journal), **1:**167–168

Writer's Diary, A (Woolf), **2:180–182**

Writer's Notebook, A (Maugham), **2:183–185**

Writing

Dillard (Annie) on vocation of, **1:**279–281

Gissing's (George) struggle to earn living with, **2:**320, 321

Mansfield (Katherine) on process of, **2:**133

Poe's (Edgar Allan) struggle to earn living with, **2:**41

Woolf (Virginia) on process of, **2:**180–182

Writing Black (Rive), **1:**25

Writing Life, The (Dillard), **1:168, 279–281**

Wrong Turn (film), **3:**68

Wroth, Mary, **2:**62

WSP. *See* Women Strike for Peace

Wudunn, Sheryl, **2:**20–21

Wunyabari, Maloba, **3:**142

Wurts, Jay, **1:**335

Wyman, Leland, **3:**320

Wynn, Antony, **3:**220

Wyoming, homesteaders in, **2:**91–93, *92*

X

X, Malcolm. *See* Malcolm X

Xavier, Silvia, **2:**30

Xie Bingying

Girl Rebel, **1:**338

New War Diary, **1:**339–340

Selected Autobiographies by Women Writers, **1:**340

A Woman Soldier's Own Story, **1:338–340**

Xu Guangping, *Letters between Two,* **2:170–173**

Xu Xin, **2:**20

Y

Yablonski, Jock, **3:**98

Yacine, Kateb, **1:**95

Nedjma, **2:**262

Yaddo artists' colony, **2:**129

Yale Law Journal, **3:**197

Yale Review (periodical), **2:**193

Yale University, **1:**251

Yamamoto, Tak, **3:**84

Yardley, Jonathan, **3:**213

Yasgur, Batya, *Behind the Burqa,* **1:**40

Yasutomi, Shigeyoshi, **3:**129

Ye, Weili, **1:**339, **3:**149

Yearbook of English Studies, **2:**322

Year of Consolation, A (Kemble), **2:**336

Years of Infamy (Weglyn), **3:**212
Yeats, Elizabeth, **2:**126
Yeats, William Butler, **2:**127
    The Autobiography of William Butler Yeats, **2:**127–128
    The Collected Works of W. B. Yeats, **2:**126, 128
    The Death of Synge, **2:**126, 127
    Estrangement, **2:126–128**
    Reveries over Childhood and Youth, **2:**126, 127
    The Trembling of the Veil, **2:**126, 127
Yellin, Jean Fagan, **1:**144, 145
Yen Mah, Adeline, *Falling Leaves,* **1:**159
Yglesias, José, **1:**223
Yiddish language, *Night* (Wiesel) in, **1:**318
Yim, Louise, *My Forty Year Fight for Korea,* **1:**323
Yoda, Tomiko, **2:**292
Yoruba people, **1:**214, 216
Yoselevska, Rivka, **3:**235
You May Well Ask (Mitchison), **2:**235
Young, Andrew, **3:**45
Young, Filson, *The Relief of Mafeking,* **2:**241
Young, Jennifer Rene, **2:**45
Young, John Wesley, **2:**305
Young, Marilyn, **3:**280, 281

Young Palestinian's Diary, A ('Amr), **2:104–106**
Young Turk Revolution (1908), **2:**106
Young Turks, **3:**40
Youth. *See* Adolescents; Children
Yurechko, John, **2:**279
Yurovsky, Yakov, **2:**84

Z

Zahn, Gordon, **3:**228
Zaleski, Jeff, **1:**294
Zambia Must Be Free (Kaunda), **1:**290
Zami (Lorde), **1:**9, 37, 39, 249, **2:**5
Zane, Paolo, **2:**161
Zanjani, Sally Springmeyer, *A Mine of Her Own,* **3:**337
Zanzibar, Ruete (Emily) on life in, **1:**90–92
Zapata, Emiliano, **3:**302, 303, 304
Zapatistas, **3:**304
Zen Buddhism, **2:**59, 61
Zerbini, Euricledes, **2:**6
Zeuske, Michael, **3:**7, 8, 9
Zhang Kijian, *China Remembers,* **3:**301
Zhang Xinxin, *Chinese Lives,* **3:288, 299–301**
Zhang Ya-Jie, **1:**175
Zhu Su'e, **3:**148
Ziegler, Philip, **2:**266, **3:**235

Zimbabwe
    British colonial rule of, **1:**167, **3:**251–253
    VaShawasha people of, oral histories of, **3:**251–253
Zimmerman, Lee, **1:**205–206
Zinzendorf, Nikolaus Ludwig von, **2:**197
Zionism, Palestinian views on, **2:**104, 105, 106
Zlata's Diary (Filipovic), **2:275, 338–340**
Zola, Émile
    Bashkirtseff (Marie) influenced by, **2:**306
    The Complete Notebooks of Henry James (James) on, **2:**113
    Journal des Goncourt (Goncourt and Goncourt) and, **2:**82, 83
    Thérèse Raquin, **1:**6
Zong (slave ship), **1:**83
Zora Neale Hurston: Jump at the Sun (documentary), **1:**18
Zorzi, Rosella Mamoli, **2:**115
Zoya, *Zoya's Story,* **1:**40
Zoya's Story (Zoya), **1:**40
Zuma, Jacob, **1:**29
Zunes, Stephen, **1:**25–26
Zunigha, Curtis, **3:**108
Zwick, Edward, **1:**312
Zylska, Ruchel. *See* McBride, Ruth

Author Index

The author index includes author names represented in *The Literature of Autobiographical Narrative*. Numbers in **Bold** indicate volume, with page numbers following after colons.

A

Abrams, Lynn, **3**: 173
Adams, Abigail, **2**: 87
Adams, Henry, **1**: 132
Adams, John Quincy, **2**: 69
Adams, Judith Porter, **3**: 268
Agosín, Marjorie, **1**: 75
Ahmedi, Farah, **1**: 40
Alexievich, Svetlana, **3**: 282
Al-Windawi, Thura, **2**: 275
Amr, Sāmī, **2**: 104
Amrouche, Fadhma Aïth Mansour, **1**: 93
Angelou, Maya, **1**: 18
Augustine, **1**: 196
Aurelius, Marcus, **1**: 218
Avrich, Paul, **3**: 3

B

Bagnold, Enid, **2**: 259
Baker, Alison, **3**: 47
Barnard, Anne, **2**: 217
Barnet, Miguel, **3**: 7
Barrett, S. M., **1**: 302
Barrios de Chungara, Domitila, **3**: 322
Barthes, Roland, **1**: 267
Bashkirtseff, Marie, **2**: 306
Bauby, Jean-Dominique, **1**: 6
Bayer, Ronald, **3**: 272
Beah, Ishmael, **1**: 312
Bechdel, Alison, **1**: 139
Benally, Malcolm D., **3**: 10
Bennett, Arnold, **2**: 136
Bennett, John, **3**: 138
Bird, Stewart, **3**: 328
Black Elk, **3**: 110
Blue, Martha, **3**: 290
Blythe, Ronald, **3**: 59
Bornat, Joanna, **3**: 170
Boswell, James, **2**: 328
Brighton Ourstory, **3**: 70
Brittain, Vera, **1**: 329
Brown, James W., **3**: 325
Bruce, Gary, **3**: 245
Buck, Lucy, **2**: 271
Bugul, Ken, **1**: 61
Burlingame, Michael, **3**: 261
Burney, Fanny, **2**: 312
Byron, George Gordon Noel, **2**: 143

C

Carver, Jonathan, **2**: 205
Cavendish, Margaret, **1**: 229
Cereta, Laura, **2**: 160
Cheng Yu-hsiu, **1**: 152
Chesnut, Mary Boykin Miller, **2**: 250
Chona, Maria, **1**: 69
Clifford, Anne, **2**: 62
Columbus, Christopher, **2**: 201
Condict, Jemima, **2**: 78
Conrad, Joseph, **2**: 192
Conroy, Frank, **1**: 164
Cook, Haruko Taya, **3**: 215
Cook, Theodore F., **3**: 215
Craig, Ann L., **3**: 302
Crawford, Miki Ward, **3**: 127
Crévecoeur, Michel-Guillaume Saint-Jean de, **2**: 213

D

Darwin, Charles, **1**: 65
Darwish, Mahmoud, **1**: 255
De Jesus, Carolina Maria, **2**: 6
Dillard, Annie, **1**: 279
D'Israeli, Isaac, **2**: 177
Dog, Mary Crow, **1**: 21
Douglass, Frederick, **1**: 33
Du Bois, W. E. B., **1**: 3
Dyk, Walter, **3**: 318

E

Edward VI, **2**: 97
Emerson, Ralph Waldo, **2**: 139
Engelmann, Larry, **3**: 279
Equiano, Olaudah, **1**: 81
Evans, George Ewart, **3**: 63
Evelyn, John, **2**: 65

F

Fadiman, Jeffrey A., **3**: 141
Fayer, Steve, **3**: 44
Feng Jicai, **3**: 287

AUTHOR INDEX

Feodorovna, Alexandra, **2**: 84
Feraoun, Mouloud, **2**: 262
Filipovic, Zlata, **2**: 338
Fox, George, **2**: 26
Fox, Stephen, **3**: 224
Frank, Anne, **2**: 253
Frank, Leslie, **3**: 293
Franklin, Benjamin, **1**: 179
Frazer, Heather T., **3**: 227
Friedman, Clara, **3**: 153
Frisch, Michael, **3**: 179
Frommer, Harvey, **3**: 118
Frommer, Myrna Katz, **3**: 118

G

Gandhi, Mohandas, **1**: 242
García Márquez, Gabriel, **3**: 183
Gellhorn, Martha, **2**: 101
Georgakas, Dan, **3**: 328
Geronimo, **1**: 302
Ghazzawi, 'Izzat, **2**: 50
Gheith, Jehanne M., **3**: 17
Gillette, Michael L., **3**: 254
Gissing, George, **2**: 320
Gluck, Sherna Berger, **3**: 190
Goethe, Johann Wolfgang von, **1**: 276
Goncourt, Edmond de, **2**: 81
Goncourt, Jules de, **2**: 81
Griffith, Kenneth, **3**: 27
Grimké, Charlotte Forten, **2**: 29
Guevara, Ernesto "Che," **2**: 220
Gurewitsch, Brana, **3**: 34
Guylforde, Richarde, **2**: 226

H

Haley, Alex, **1**: 261
Halkett, Lady Anne, **1**: 315
Hampton, Henry, **3**: 44
Hansberry, Lorraine, **1**: 273
Haskins, Jim, **1**: 37
Hatzfeld, Jean, **3**: 257
Hawthorne, Nathaniel, **2**: 223
Hayashi, Katie Kaori, **3**: 127

Hayslip, Le Ly, **1**: 335
Hickey, Margaret, **3**: 315
Higginson, Thomas Wentworth, **2**: 238
Hillesum, Etty, **2**: 22
Hirsi Ali, Ayaan, **1**: 207
Hitler, Adolf, **1**: 30
Hochstadt, Steve, **3**: 14
Holmes, Richard, **3**: 234
hooks, bell, **1**: 249
Houston, James D., **1**: 299
Houston, Jeanne Wakatsuki, **1**: 299
Humphries, Stephen, **3**: 311
Hurston, Zora Neale, **1**: 9
Hussein, Taha, **1**: 135

J

Jacobs, Harriet A., **1**: 142
James, Daniel, **3**: 73
James, Henry, **2**: 113
Jefferson, Thomas, **2**: 316
Jiang, Ji-li, **1**: 161
Jolluck, Katherine R., **3**: 17

K

Kafka, Franz, **2**: 120
Keats, John, **2**: 146
Ke Lan, **3**: 124
Keller, Helen, **1**: 43
Kemble, Fanny, **2**: 335
Kempe, Margery, **1**: 189
Kierkegaard, Søren, **2**: 166
Kim, Elizabeth, **1**: 102
Kim Ku, **1**: 322
King, Martin Luther, Jr., **2**: 32
Kingston, Maxine Hong, **1**: 173
Klemperer, Victor, **2**: 303
Kohn, Rita, **3**: 107, 325
Kong Demao, **3**: 124
Krause, Corinne Azen, **3**: 305
Krog, Antjie, **3**: 242

L

Ladjevardi, Habib, **3**: 218
Last, Nella, **2**: 265
Laye, Camara, **1**: 128
Leadbeater, Mary, **2**: 157
Lee, Robert E., **2**: 38
Left Handed, **3**: 318
Lejeune, Philippe, **1**: 239, **2**: 174
Lessing, Doris, **1**: 167
Lewin, Rhoda, **3**: 50
Light, Kenneth, **3**: 66
Light, Melanie, **3**: 66
Lorde, Audre, **2**: 3
Luthuli, Albert, **1**: 24
Lu Xun, **2**: 170

M

Mahomet, Dean, **2**: 05
Malcolm X, **1**: 186
Mandela, Nelson, **1**: 27
Manning, Diane, **3**: 77
Mansfield, Katherine, **2**: 133
Manwaring, Max G., **3**: 205
Martin, Patricia Preciado, **3**: 131
Mason, Katrina, **3**: 239
Maugham, W. Somerset, **2**: 183
Maurer, Harry, **3**: 275
McBride, James, **1**: 72
McCarthy, Mary, **1**: 258
McCourt, Frank, **1**: 119
McKay, Claude, **1**: 84
Medina, Pablo, **1**: 296
Menchú, Rigoberta, **3**: 164
Michitsuna No Haha, **2**: 297
Milich, Zorka, **3**: 135
Miller, Donald E., **3**: 40
Miller, Lorna Touryan, **3**: 40
Min, Anchee, **1**: 158
Mitchison, Naomi, **2**: 235
Momaday, N. Scott, **1**: 54
Montagu, Lady Mary Wortley, **2**: 35
Montejo, Esteban, **3**: 7

AUTHOR INDEX

Montell, William Lynwood, **3**: 90, 107
Moon, Elaine Latzman, **3**: 99
Moore, Marat, **3**: 337
Moore, Molly, **2**: 278
Morris, Gabrielle, **3**: 20
Moye, J. Todd, **3**: 248

N

Nabokov, Vladimir, **1**: 270
Nakazawa, Keiji, **1**: 293
Neihardt, John G., **3**: 110
Nehru, Jawaharlal, **1**: 289
Neruda, Pablo, **1**: 222
Nguyen, Kien, **1**: 170
Nijo, Lady, **2**: 59
Nin, Anaïs, **2**: 123

O

Obama, Barack, **1**: 78
O'Conner, Flannery, **2**: 129
O'Grady, Timothy, **3**: 27
Olney, James, **1**: 246
Oppenheimer, Gerald M., **3**: 272
Orwell, George, **2**: 117
Osborne, Dorothy, **2**: 324
O'Sullivan, John, **3**: 227
Owsley, Beatrice Rodriguez, **3**: 121

P

Palmer, Michele, **3**: 293
Patai, Daphne, **3**: 190
Parks, Rosa, **1**: 37
Partridge, Frances, **2**: 268
Peltier, Leonard, **1**: 96
Pepys, Samuel, **2**: 72
Perera, Victor, **1**: 99
Perks, Robert, **3**: 170
Plaatje, Solomon Tshekisho, **2**: 241
Plath, Sylvia, **2**: 47
Pliny the Younger, **2**: 94
Poe, Edgar Allan, **2**: 41

Polo, Marco, **1**: 105
Poniatowska, Elena, **3**: 31
Popular Memory Group, **3**: 176
Portelli, Alessandro, **3**: 96, 157, 265
Pozas, Ricardo, **3**: 167
Prince, Mary, **3**: 23
Prisk, Court, **3**: 205

R

Rabe, John, **2**: 19
Raleigh, Donald J., **3**: 331
Rilke, Rainer Maria, **2**: 149
Roberts, Elizabeth, **3**: 144
Robinson, Henry Crabb, **2**: 75
Rodriguez, Richard, **1**: 15
Rogers, Carole Garibaldi, **3**: 308
Rousseau, Jean-Jacques, **1**: 200
Rowlandson, Mary, **1**: 325
Rowley, Susan, **3**: 138
Ruete, Emily, **1**: 90
Ruskin, John, **1**: 264
Russell, Bert, **3**: 93

S

Saitoti, Tepilit Ole, **1**: 114
Sang Ye, **3**: 299
Santiago, Esmeralda, **1**: 108
Santoli, Al, **3**: 209
Sarashina, Lady, **2**: 189
Sassoon, Siegfried, **2**: 247
Satrapi, Marjane, **1**: 155
Savage, Thomas, **3**: 114
Scott, Sir Walter, **2**: 309
Seabrook, Jeremy, **3**: 5301
Seacole, Mary, **1**: 111
Shackelford, Laurel, **3**: 86
Shaffer, Deborah, **3**: 328
Shikibu, Lady Murasaki, **2**: 290
Shostak, Marjorie, **3**: 37
Siegelbaum, Lewis H., **3**: 340
Sinor, Jennifer, **2**: 163
Siv, Sichan, **1**: 306
Slingsby, Sir Henry, **2**: 256

Soyinka, Wole, **1**: 214
Speer, Albert, **2**: 54
Stanton, Elizabeth Cady, **1**: 12
Stave, Bruce M., **3**: 293
Stein, Gertrude, **1**: 332
Stewart, Elinore Pruitt, **2**: 91
Stone, Kate, **2**: 244
Styron, William, **1**: 204
Suenaga, Shizuko, **3**: 127
Suleri, Sara, **1**: 87

T

Tamura, Linda, **3**: 80
Tateishi, John, **3**: 195
Teresa of Ávila, **1**: 211
Terkel, Louis "Studs," **3**: 161, 212, 343
Terry, Wallace, **3**: 199
Thiong'o, Ngũgĩ wa, **2**: 12
Thomas, Dylan, **1**: 125
Thompson, Paul, **3**: 170, 186
Thoreau, Henry David, **1**: 233
Tollefson, James W., **3**: 221
Tolstoy, Leo, **1**: 193
Tuqan, Fadwa, **1**: 225
Twain, Mark, **1**: 146

U

Uchida, Yoshiko, **1**: 309
Ulrich, Laurel Thatcher, **2**: 331
Unaipon, David, **1**: 149
Underhill, Ruth, **1**: 69
Usāmah ibn Munqidh, **1**: 285

V

Vaarzon-Morel, Petronella, **3**: 334
Vambe, Lawrence Chinyani, **3**: 251
Vico, Giambattista, **1**: 183
Victoria, Queen, **2**: 209
Viezzer, Moema, **3**: 322

AUTHOR INDEX

W

Walkowitz, Daniel J., **3**: 340
Walmsley, Jan, **3**: 170
Wang Zheng, **3**: 147
Washington, Booker T., **1**: 50
Wat, Eric, **3**: 83
Webb, Beatrice, **2**: 16
Wehrey, Jane, **3**: 102
Weinberg, Bill, **3**: 86
Wells, H. G., **1**: 252
Wesley, John, **2**: 195
Wheatley, Phillis, **2**: 44
Wiesel, Elie, **1**: 318
Wilde, Oscar, **2**: 9
Williams, Tennessee, **2**: 152
Wolff, Tobias, **1**: 47
Wollstonecraft, Mary, **2**: 109
Wood, Trish, **3**: 231
Woodforde, James, **2**: 287
Wooldridge, E. T., **3**: 202
Woolf, Virginia, **2**: 180
Wordsworth, Dorothy, **2**: 300
Wright, Richard, **1**: 122
Wurts, Jay, **1**: 335

X

Xie Bingying, **1**: 338
Xu Guangping, **2**: 170

Y

Yeats, William Butler, **2**: 126

Z

Zhang Xinxin, **3**: 299

Title Index

The title index includes works that are represented in *The Literature of Autobiographical Narrative*. Bolded numbers refer to volumes, with page numbers following colons.

A

Abandoned Baobab, The: The Autobiography of a Senegalese Woman [Ken Bugul], **1**: 61

Akenfield: Portrait of an English Village [Ronald Blythe], **3**: 59

Always a People: Oral Histories of Contemporary Woodland Indians [Rita Kohn and William Lynwood Montell], **3**: 107

Among You Taking Notes: The Wartime Diary of Naomi Mitchison, 1939–1945 [Naomi Mitchison], **2**: 235

Anarchist Voices: An Oral History of Anarchism in America [Paul Avrich], **3**: 3

And Justice for All: An Oral History of the Japanese American Detention Camps [John Tateishi], **3**: 195

Angela's Ashes [Frank McCourt], **1**: 119

Annals of Ballitore, The [Mary Leadbeater], **2**: 157

Arab-Syrian Gentleman and Warrior in the Period of the Crusades, An: Memoirs of Usāmah ibn Munqidh [Usāmah ibn Munqidh], **1**: 285

Army Life in a Black Regiment [Thomas Wentworth Higginson], **2**: 238

As I Crossed a Bridge of Dreams [Lady Sarashina], **2**: 189

Ask the Fellows Who Cut the Hay [George Ewart Evans], **3**: 63

Autobiographical Pact, The [Philippe Lejeune], **1**: 239

Autobiography, An, or The Story of My Experiments with Truth [Mohandas Gandhi], **1**: 242

Autobiography, An, with Musings on Recent Events in India [Jawaharlal Nehru], **1**: 289

Autobiography: Essays Theoretical and Critical [James Olney], **1**: 246

Autobiography of Ben Franklin, The [Benjamin Franklin], **1**: 179

Autobiography of Charles Darwin, The [Charles Darwin], **1**: 65

Autobiography of Giambattista Vico, The [Giambattista Vico], **1**: 183

Autobiography of Malcolm X, The [Malcolm X], **1**: 186

Autobiography of W. E. B. Du Bois, The: A Soliloquy on Viewing My Life from the Last Decade of Its First Century [W. E. B. Du Bois], **1**: 3

B

Barefoot Gen: A Cartoon Story of Hiroshima [Keiji Nakazawa], **1**: 293

Between Management and Labor: Oral Histories of Arbitration [Clara Friedman], **3**: 153

Biography of a Runaway Slave [Miguel Barnet and Esteban Montejo], **3**: 7

Bitter Water: Diné Oral Histories of the Navajo-Hopi Land Dispute [Malcolm D. Benally], **3**: 10

Black Boy [Richard Wright], **1**: 122

Black Elk Speaks: Being the Life Story of a Holy Man of the Oglala Sioux [Black Elk and John G. Neihardt], **3**: 110

Bloods: An Oral History of the Vietnam War by Black Veterans [Wallace Terry], **3**: 199

Boer War Diary of Sol Plaatje, The: An African at Mafeking [Solomon Tshekisho Plaatje], **2**: 241

Bone Black: Memories of Girlhood [bell hooks], **1**: 249

Book of Margery Kempe, The [Margery Kempe], **1**: 189

Brokenburn: The Journal of Kate Stone, 1861–1868 [Kate Stone], **2**: 244

C

Californio Voices: The Oral Memoirs of José María Amador and Lorenzo Asisara [Thomas Savage], **3**: 114

Cancer Journals, The [Audre Lorde], **2**: 3

Carrier Warfare in the Pacific: An Oral History Collection [E. T. Wooldridge], **3**: 202

Child of the Dark: The Diary of Carolina Maria de Jesus [Carolina Maria de Jesus], **2**: 6

Children of Los Alamos: An Oral History of the Town Where the Atomic Bomb Began [Katrina Mason], **3**: 239

455

TITLE INDEX

Child's Christmas in Wales, A [Dylan Thomas], **1**: 125

Chinese Lives: An Oral History of Contemporary China [Zhang Xinxin and Sang Ye], **3**: 299

Chona: The Autobiography of a Papago Woman [Maria Chona and Ruth Underhill], **1**: 69

Coal Hollow: Photographs and Oral Histories [Kenneth Light and Melanie Light], **3**: 66

Collected Letters of a Renaissance Feminist [Laura Cereta], **2**: 160

Collected Letters of Mary Wollstonecraft, The [Mary Wollstonecraft], **2**: 109

Color of Water, The: A Black Man's Tribute to His White Mother [James McBride], **1**: 72

Complete Notebooks of Henry James, The [Henry James], **2**: 113

Confession, A [Leo Tolstoy], **1**: 193

Confessions [Augustine], **1**: 196

Confessions [Jean-Jacques Rousseau], **1**: 200

Confessions of Lady Nijo [Lady Nijo], **2**: 59

Congo Diary, The [Joseph Conrad], **2**: 192

Country of My Skull: Guilt, Sorrow, and the Limits of Forgiveness in the New South Africa [Antjie Krog], **3**: 242

Country Parson, A: James Woodforde's Diary, 1759–1802 [James Woodforde], **2**: 287

Cross and a Star, A: Memoirs of a Jewish Girl in Chile [Marjorie Agosín], **1**: 75

D

Daring Hearts: Lesbian and Gay Lives of the 50s and 60s Brighton [Brighton Ourstory], **3**: 70

Dark Child, The: The Autobiography of an African Boy [Camara Laye], **1**: 128

Darkness Visible [William Styron], **1**: 204

Death of Luigi Trastulli and Other Stories, The [Alessandro Portelli], **3**: 157

De Profundis [Oscar Wilde], **2**: 9

Detained: A Writer's Prison Diary [Ngũgĩ wa Thiong'o], **2**: 12

Diaries, 1915–1918 [Siegfried Sassoon], **2**: 247

Diaries, 1931–1949 [George Orwell], **2**: 117

Diaries of Beatrice Webb [Beatrice Webb], **2**: 16

Diaries of Franz Kafka, The [Franz Kafka], **2**: 120

Diaries of Lady Anne Clifford, The [Lady Anne Clifford], **2**: 62

Diary, Reminiscences and Correspondence of Henry Crabb Robinson, Barrister-at-Law [Henry Crabb Robinson], **2**: 75

Diary from Dixie, A [Mary Boykin Miller Chesnut], **2**: 250

Diary of Anaïs Nin, The [Anaïs Nin], **2**: 123

Diary of Anne Frank, The [Anne Frank], **2**: 253

Diary of John Evelyn, The [John Evelyn], **2**: 65

Diary of John Quincy Adams, The [John Quincy Adams], **2**: 69

Diary of Lady Murasaki, The [Lady Murasaki Shikibu], **2**: 290

Diary of Samuel Pepys, The [Samuel Pepys], **2**: 72

Diary of Sir Henry Slingsby, The [Sir Henry Slingsby], **2**: 256

Diary without Dates, A [Enid Bagnold], **2**: 259

Diving Bell and the Butterfly, The [Jean-Dominique Bauby], **1**: 6

Doña María's Story: Life History, Memory and Political Identity [Daniel James], **3**: 73

Dreams from My Father: A Story of Race and Inheritance [Barack Obama], **1**: 78

Dust Tracks on a Road [Zora Neale Hurston], **1**: 9

E

Education of Henry Adams, The [Henry Adams], **1**: 132

Egyptian Childhood, An [Taha Hussein], **1**: 135

Eighty Years and More, Reminiscences 1815–1897 [Elizabeth Cady Stanton], **1**: 12

El Salvador at War: An Oral History of Conflict from the 1979 Insurrection to the Present [Max G. Manwaring and Court Prisk], **3**: 205

Estrangement, Being Some Fifty Extracts from a Diary Kept in 1909 [William Butler Yeats], **2**: 126

Everything We Had [Al Santoli], **3**: 209

Exiled Memories: A Cuban Childhood [Pablo Medina], **1**: 296

Exodus to Shanghai: Stories of Escape from the Third Reich [Steve Hochstadt], **3**: 14

Experiment in Autobiography, An [H. G. Wells], **1**: 252

Extraordinary Work of Ordinary Writing, The: Annie Ray's Diary [Jennifer Sinor], **2**: 163

F

Farewell to Manzanar [Jeanne Wakatsuki Houston and James D. Houston], **1**: 299

Firm: The Inside Story of the Stasi, The [Gary Bruce], **3**: 245

First Agraristas, The: An Oral History of a Mexican Agrarian Reform Movement [Ann L. Craig], **3**: 302

Freedom Flyers: The Tuskegee Airmen of World War II [J. Todd Moye], **3**: 248

Fun Home: A Family Tragicomic [Alison Bechdel], **1**: 139

G

Geronimo: His Own Story [Geronimo and S. M. Barrett], **1**: 302

Go Ask Alice [Anonymous], **2**: 294

Golden Bones: An Extraordinary Journey from Hell in Cambodia to a New Life in America [Sichan Siv], **1**: 306

Good Man of Nanking, The: The Diaries of John Rabe [John Rabe], **2**: 19

"Good War, The": An Oral History of World War II [Louis "Studs" Terkel], **3**: 212

Gossamer Years, The [Michitsuna No Haha], **2**: 297

Grandmothers, Mothers, and Daughters: Oral Histories of Three Generations of Ethnic American Women [Corinne Azen Krause], **3**: 305

Grasmere Journals [Dorothy Wordsworth], **2**: 300

Growing Up Jewish in America [Myrna Katz Frommer and Harvey Frommer], **3**: 118

Gulag Voices: Oral Histories of Soviet Incarceration and Exile [Jehanne M. Gheith and Katherine R. Jolluck], **3**: 17

H

Habit of Being, The: Letters of Flannery O'Connor [Flannery O'Conner], **2**: 129

Habits of Change: An Oral History of American Nuns [Carole Garibaldi Rogers], **3**: 308

Hard Times: An Oral History of the Great Depression [Louis "Studs" Terkel], **3**: 161

Head of the Class: An Oral History of African American Achievement in Higher Education and Beyond [Gabrielle Morris], **3**: 20

Hill Country Teacher: Oral Histories from the One-Room School and Beyond [Diane Manning], **3**: 77

Hispanic-American Entrepreneur, The: An Oral History of the American Dream [Beatrice Rodriguez Owsley], **3**: 121

History of Mary Prince, a West Indian Slave, Related by Herself, The [Mary Prince], **3**: 23

Hood River Issei, The: An Oral History of Japanese Settlers in Oregon's Hood River Valley [Linda Tamura], **3**: 80

Hooligans or Rebels?: An Oral History of Working-Class Childhood and Youth, 1889–1939 [Stephen Humphries], **3**: 311

Hunger of Memory: The Education of Richard Rodriguez [Richard Rodriguez], **1**: 15

I

I, Rigoberta Menchú: An Indian Woman in Guatemala [Rigoberta Menchú], **3**: 164

I Know Why the Caged Bird Sings [Maya Angelou], **1**: 18

Ill-Fated People, An: Zimbabwe before and after Rhodes [Lawrence Chinyani Vambe], **3**: 251

Incidents in the Life of a Slave Girl, Written by Herself [Harriet A. Jacobs], **1**: 142

Infidel [Ayaan Hirsi Ali], **1**: 207

Interesting Narrative of the Life of Olaudah Equiano, The, or Gustavus Vassa, the African, Written by Himself [Olaudah Equiano], **1**: 81

Interrupted Life, An: The Diaries of Etty Hillesum [Etty Hillesum], **2**: 22

In the Mansion of Confucius' Descendants: An Oral History [Kong Demao and Ke Lan], **3**: 124

In the Presence of Absence [Mahmoud Darwish], **1**: 255

Invisible Thread, The [Yoshiko Uchida], **1**: 309

Ireland's Unfinished Revolution: An Oral History [Kenneth Griffith and Timothy O'Grady], **3**: 27

Irish Days: Oral Histories of the Twentieth Century [Margaret Hickey], **3**: 315

I Will Bear Witness: A Diary of the Nazi Years, 1933–1945 [Victor Klemperer], **2**: 303

J

Japan at War: An Oral History [Haruko Taya Cook and Theodore F. Cook], **3**: 215

Japanese War Brides in America: An Oral History [Miki Ward Crawford, Katie Kaori Hayashi, and Shizuko Suenaga], **3**: 127

Jemima Condict: Her Book, Being a Transcript of the Diary of an Essex County Maid during the Revolutionary War [Jemima Condict], **2**: 78

Journal, 1955–1962: Reflections on the French-Algerian War [Mouloud Feraoun], **2**: 262

Journal des Goncourt: Mémoires de la vie littéraire [Jules de Goncourt and Edmond de Goncourt], **2**: 81

Journal of George Fox [George Fox], **2**: 26

Journal of Katherine Mansfield [Katherine Mansfield], **2**: 133

Journal of Marie Bashkirtseff, The [Marie Bashkirtseff], **2**: 306

Journal of Sir Walter Scott, The [Sir Walter Scott], **2**: 309

Journal of the First Voyage of Vasco da Gama, 1497–1499, A [Author Unknown], **2**: 201

Journal of the First Voyage to America [Christopher Columbus], **2**: 201

Journals of Arnold Bennett, 1896–1928, The [Arnold Bennett], **2**: 136

Journals of Charlotte Forten Grimké, The [Charlotte Forten Grimké], **2**: 29

Journals of John Wesley [John Wesley], **2**: 195

Journals of Jonathan Carver and Related Documents, 1766–1770, The [Jonathan Carver], **2**: 205

Journals of Ralph Waldo Emerson [Ralph Waldo Emerson], **2**: 139

Journals of Søren Kierkegaard [Søren Kierkegaard], **2**: 166

Juan the Chamula: An Ethnological Re-creation of the Life of a Mexican Indian [Ricardo Pozas], **3**: 167

L

Lakota Woman [Mary Crow Dog], **1**: 21

Last Diary of Tsaritsa Alexandra, The [Alexandra Feodorovna], **2**: 84

Launching the War on Poverty: An Oral History [Michael L. Gillette], **3**: 254

Leaves from the Journal of Our Life in the Highlands, from 1848 to 1861 [Queen Victoria], **2**: 209

Left Handed, Son of Old Man Hat: A Navajo Autobiography [Left Handed and Walter Dyk], **3**: 318

Let Me Speak!: Testimony of Domitila, a Woman of the Bolivian Mines [Moema Viezzer and Domitila Barrios de Chungara], **3**: 322

Let My People Go [Albert Luthuli], **1**: 24

"Letter from the Birmingham Jail" [Martin Luther King Jr.], **2**: 32

Letters and Journals of Fanny Burney [Fanny Burney], **2**: 312

TITLE INDEX

Letters and Journals of Lord Byron, with Notices of His Life [George Gordon Noel Byron], **2**: 143

Letters between Two [Lu Xun and Xu Guangping], **2**: 170

Letters from an American Farmer [Michel-Guillaume Saint-Jean de Crévecoeur], **2**: 213

Letters from Jefferson to His Daughter [Thomas Jefferson], **2**: 316

Letters Home [Sylvia Plath], **2**: 47

Letters of a Woman Homesteader [Elinore Pruitt Stewart], **2**: 91

Letters of John Keats, 1814–1821, The [John Keats], **2**: 146

Letters of Lady Anne Barnard to Henry Dundas, from Cape and Elsewhere, The [Anne Barnard], **2**: 217

Letters of the Younger Pliny, The [Pliny the Younger], **2**: 94

Letters to a Young Poet [Rainer Maria Rilke], **2**: 149

Letters Underway ['Izzat Ghazzawi], **2**: 50

"Letter to Her Daughter" [Lady Mary Wortley Montagu], **2**: 35

"Letter to Her Daughter from the New White House" [Abigail Adams], **2**: 87

"Letter to His Son" [Robert E. Lee], **2**: 38

"Letter to Maria Clemm" [Edgar Allan Poe], **2**: 41

"Letter to the Reverend Samson Occom" [Phillis Wheatley], **2**: 44

Life, The [Teresa of Ávila], **1**: 211

Life on the Mississippi [Mark Twain], **1**: 146

Literary Remains of Edward VI, The [Edward VI], **2**: 97

London and the Life of Literature in Late Victorian England: The Diary of George Gissing, Novelist [George Gissing], **2**: 320

London Journal, 1762–1763 [James Boswell], **2**: 328

Long Journey Home: Oral Histories of Contemporary Delaware Indians [James W. Brown and Rita T. Kohn], **3**: 325

Long Walk to Freedom, The [Nelson Mandela], **1**: 27

Long Way from Home, A [Claude McKay], **1**: 84

Long Way Gone, A: Memoirs of a Boy Soldier [Ishmael Beah], **1**: 312

Love Letters of Dorothy Osborne to Sir Wiliam Temple, 1652–54, The [Dorothy Osborne], **2**: 324

M

Machete Season: The Killers in Rwanda Speak [Jean Hatzfeld], **3**: 257

Making of a Gay Asian Community, The: An Oral History of Pre-AIDS Los Angeles [Eric Wat], **3**: 83

Man Died, The: Prison Notes of Wole Soyinka [Wole Soyinka], **1**: 214

Massacre in Mexico [Elena Poniatowska], **3**: 31

Meatless Days [Sara Suleri], **1**: 87

Meditations of the Emperor Marcus Aurelius Antoninus, The [Marcus Aurelius], **1**: 218

Mein Kampf [Adolf Hitler], **1**: 30

Memoirs [Pablo Neruda], **1**: 222

Memoirs of an Arabian Princess from Zanzibar [Emily Ruete], **1**: 90

Memoirs of Fatemeh Pakravan [Habib Ladjevardi], **3**: 218

Memoirs of Lady Anne Halkett, The [Lady Anne Halkett], **1**: 315

Memories of a Catholic Girlhood [Mary McCarthy], **1**: 258

Midwife's Tale, A: The Life of Martha Ballard, Based on Her Diary, 1785–1812 [Laurel Thatcher Ulrich], **2**: 331

Mothers, Sisters, Resisters: Oral Histories of Women Who Survived the Holocaust [Brana Gurewitsch], **3**: 34

Motorcycle Diaries [Ernesto "Che" Guevara], **2**: 220

Mountainous Journey, A: A Poet's Autobiography [Fadwa Tuqan], **1**: 225

"My Furthest-Back Person—'The African'" [Alex Haley], **1**: 261

My Life Story [Fadhma Aïth Mansour Amrouche], **1**: 93

My Life Story [David Unaipon], **1**: 149

My Revolutionary Years: The Autobiography of Madame Wei Tao-Ming [Cheng Yu-hsiu], **1**: 152

N

Narrative of the Life of Frederick Douglass [Frederick Douglass], **1**: 33

Nella Last's War: The Second World War Diaries of Housewife, 49 [Nella Last], **2**: 265

Night [Elie Wiesel], **1**: 318

Nisa: The Life and Words of a !Kung Woman [Marjorie Shostak], **3**: 37

Notebooks [Tennessee Williams], **2**: 152

Notebooks and *Letters* [Nathaniel Hawthorne], **2**: 223

O

Oral History, Health and Welfare [Joanna Bornat, Robert Perks, Paul Thompson, and Jan Walmsley], **3**: 170

Oral History of Abraham Lincoln, An: John G. Nicolay's Interviews and Essays [Michael Burlingame], **3**: 261

Oral History Theory [Lynn Abrams], **3**: 173

Order Has Been Carried Out, The: History, Memory, and Meaning of a Nazi Massacre in Rome [Alessandro Portelli], **3**: 265

Our Appalachia [Laurel Shackelford and Bill Weinberg], **3**: 86

P

Pacifist's War, A: Diaries 1939–1945 [Frances Partridge], **2**: 268

Paekpom Ilchi: The Autobiography of Kim Ku [Kim Ku], **1**: 322

Peacework: Oral Histories of Women Peace Activists [Judith Porter Adams], **3**: 268

Persepolis [Marjane Satrapi], **1**: 155

"Popular Memory: Theory, Politics, Method" [Popular Memory Group], **3**: 176

"Practice of the Private Journal" [Philippe Lejeune], **2**: 174

Praeterita [John Ruskin], **1**: 264

Prison Writings: My Life Is My Sun Dance [Leonard Peltier], **1**: 96

Pylgrymage of Sir Richarde Guylforde, The [Richarde Guylforde], **2**: 226

TITLE INDEX

R

Records of a Girlhood [Fanny Kemble], **2**: 335

Red Azalea [Anchee Min], **1**: 158

Red Scarf Girl: A Memoir of the Cultural Revolution [Ji-li Jiang], **1**: 161

Rites: A Guatemalan Boyhood [Victor Perera], **1**: 99

Roland Barthes [Roland Barthes], **1**: 267

Rosa Parks: My Story [Rosa Parks and Jim Haskins], **1**: 37

S

Saga of Coe Ridge, The: A Study in Oral History [William Lynwood Montell], **3**: 90

Selected Letters of Martha Gellhorn [Martha Gellhorn], **2**: 101

Shadows on My Heart: The Civil War Diary of Lucy Rebecca Buck of Virginia [Lucy Buck], **2**: 271

Shared Authority, A: Essays on the Craft and Meaning of Oral and Public History [Michael Frisch], **3**: 179

Shattered Dreams?: An Oral History of the South African AIDS Epidemic [Gerald M. Oppenheimer and Ronald Bayer], **3**: 272

Solidarity Forever: An Oral History of the IWW [Stewart Bird, Dan Georgakas, and Deborah Shaffer], **3**: 328

"*Some Observations on Diaries, Self-Biography, and Self-Characters*" [Isaac D'Israeli], **2**: 177

Songs My Mother Sang to Me: An Oral History of Mexican American Women [Patricia Preciado Martin], **3**: 131

Sovereignty and Goodness of God, The [Mary Rowlandson], **1**: 325

Soviet Baby Boomers: An Oral History of Russia's Cold War Generation [Donald J. Raleigh], **3**: 331

Spandau: The Secret Diaries [Albert Speer], **2**: 54

Speak, Memory: An Autobiography Revisited [Vladimir Nabokov], **1**: 270

Stop-Time [Frank Conroy], **1**: 164

Story of a Shipwrecked Sailor, The [Gabriel García Márquez], **3**: 183

Story of My Life, The: An Afghan Girl on the Other Side of the Sky [Farah Ahmedi], **1**: 40

Story of My Life, The: Helen Keller [Helen Keller], **1**: 43

Strange Ground: Americans in Vietnam 1945–1975: An Oral History [Harry Maurer], **3**: 275

Stranger's Supper, A: An Oral History of Centenarian Women in Montenegro [Zorka Milich], **3**: 135

Strength Not to Fight, The: An Oral History of Conscientious Objectors of the Vietnam War [James W. Tollefson], **3**: 221

Survivors: An Oral History of the Armenian Genocide [Donald E. Miller and Lorna Touryan Miller], **3**: 40

Swiftwater People: Lives of Old Timers on the Upper St. Joe & St. Maries Rivers [Bert Russell], **3**: 93

T

Tears before the Rain: An Oral History of the Fall of South Vietnam [Larry Engelmann], **3**: 279

Ten Thousand Sorrows: The Extraordinary Journey of a Korean War Orphan [Elizabeth Kim], **1**: 102

Testament of Youth [Vera Brittain], **1**: 329

They Say in Harlan County: An Oral History [Alessandro Portelli] **3**: 96

This Boy's Life [Tobias Wolff], **1**: 47

Thura's Diary: A Young Girl's Life in War-Torn Baghdad [Thura Al-Windawi], **2**: 275

To Be Young, Gifted and Black: An Informal Autobiography of Lorraine Hansberry [Lorraine Hansberry], **1**: 273

Travels of Dean Mahomet, a Native of Patna in Bengal, through Several Parts of India, While in the Service of the Honourable the East India Company Written by Himself, in a Series of Letters to a Friend, The [Dean Mahomet], **2**: 229

Travels of Marco Polo, The [Marco Polo], **1**: 105

True Relation of My Birth, Breeding, and Life, A [Margaret Cavendish], **1**: 229

Truth and Fiction Relating to My Life [Johann Wolfgang von Goethe], **1**: 276

U

Under My Skin: Volume One of My Autobiography, to 1949 [Doris Lessing], **1**: 167

Unknown Internment, The: An Oral History of the Relocation of Italian Americans during World War II [Stephen Fox], **3**: 224

Untold Tales, Unsung Heroes: An Oral History of Detroit's African-American Community, 1918–1967 [Elaine Latzman Moon], **3**: 99

Unwanted, The [Kien Nguyen], **1**: 170

Up from Slavery [Booker T. Washington], **1**: 50

Uqalurait: An Oral History of Nunavut [John Bennett and Susan Rowley], **3**: 138

V

Voice of the Past, The: Oral History [Paul Thompson], **3**: 186

Voices from Chernobyl: The Oral History of a Nuclear Disaster [Svetlana Alexievich], **3**: 282

Voices from the Whirlwind: An Oral History of the Chinese Cultural Revolution [Feng Jicai], **3**: 287

Voices from this Long Brown Land: Oral Recollections of Owens Valley Lives and Manzanar Pasts [Jane Wehrey], **3**: 102

Voices of Freedom: An Oral History of the Civil Rights Movement from the 1950s through the 1980s [Henry Hampton and Steve Fayer], **3**: 44

Voices of Resistance: Oral Histories of Moroccan Women [Allison Baker], **3**: 47

TITLE INDEX

W

Walden; or, Life in the Woods [Henry David Thoreau], **1**: 233

Warlpiri Women's Voices: Our Lives, Our History [Petronella Vaarzon-Morel], **3**: 334

Wars I Have Seen [Gertrude Stein], **1**: 332

Way to Rainy Mountain, The [N. Scott Momaday], **1**: 54

"We Have Just Begun to Not Fight": An Oral History of Conscientious Objectors in Civilian Public Service during World War II [Heather T. Frazer and John O'Sullivan], **3**: 227

What Was Asked of Us: An Oral History of the Iraq War by the Soldiers Who Fought It [Trish Wood], **3**: 231

When Heaven and Earth Changed Places: A Vietnamese Woman's Journey from War to Peace [Le Ly Hayslip and Jay Wurts], **1**: 335

When I Was Puerto Rican [Esmeralda Santiago], **1**: 108

When We Began, There Were Witchmen: An Oral History from Mount Kenya [Jeffrey A. Fadiman], **3**: 141

Witch Purge of 1878, The: Oral and Documentary History in the Early Navajo Reservation Years [Martha Blue], **3**: 290

Witnesses to Nuremberg: An Oral History of American Participants at the War Crimes Trials [Bruce M. Stave, Michele Palmer, and Leslie Frank], **3**: 293

Witnesses to the Holocaust: An Oral History [Rhoda Lewin], **3**: 50

Woman at War, A [Molly Moore], **2**: 278

Woman in Berlin, A: Eight Weeks in the Conquered City: A Diary [Anonymous], **2**: 281

Woman Soldier's Own Story, A [Xie Bingying], **1**: 338

Woman Warrior, The: Memoirs of a Girlhood among Ghosts [Maxine Hong Kingston], **1**: 173

Women and Families: An Oral History, 1940–1970 [Elizabeth Roberts], **3**: 144

Women in the Chinese Enlightenment: Oral and Textual Histories [Wang Zheng], **3**: 14703

Women in the Mines: Stories of Life and Work [Marat Moore], **3**: 337

Women's Words [Sherna Berger Gluck and Daphne Patai], **3**: 190

Wonderful Adventures of Mrs. Seacole in Many Lands, The [Mary Seacole], **1**: 111

Workers of the Donbass Speak: Survival and Identity in the New Ukraine, 1989–1992 [Lewis H. Siegelbaum and Daniel J. Walkowitz], **3**: 340

Working: People Talk about What They Do All Day and How They Feel about What They Do [Louis "Studs" Terkel], **3**: 343

Working-Class Childhood: An Oral History [Jeremy Seabrook], **3**: 5301

World at War, The [Richard Holmes], **3**: 234

Worlds of a Maasai Warrior, The: An Autobiography [Tepilit Ole Saitoti], **1**: 114

Writer's Diary, A [Virginia Woolf], **2**: 180

Writer's Notebook, A [W. Somerset Maugham], **2**: 183

Writing Life, The [Annie Dillard], **1**: 279

Y

Young Palestinian's Diary, 1941–1945, A: The Life of Sāmī 'Amr [Sāmī 'Amr], **2**: 104

Z

Zlata's Diary: A Child's Life in Sarajevo [Zlata Filipovic], **2**: 338